BASIC CONTRACT LAW

Eighth Edition

By

Lon L. Fuller
Late Carter Professor of General Jurisprudence,
Harvard University

Melvin Aron Eisenberg
Koret Professor of Law,
University of California at Berkeley

AMERICAN CASEBOOK SERIES®

THOMSON

™

WEST

Mat #40334111

COPYRIGHT © 1946 LON L. FULLER
COPYRIGHT © 1947, 1964, 1972, 1981, 1990, 1996 WEST PUBLISHING CO.
© West, a Thomson business, 2001
© 2006 Thomson/West
      610 Opperman Drive
      P.O. Box 64526
      St. Paul, MN 55164–0526
      1–800–328–9352

Printed in the United States of America

ISBN–13: 978–0–314–15901–4
ISBN–10: 0–314–15901–0

TEXT IS PRINTED ON 10% POST CONSUMER RECYCLED PAPER

Acknowledgments

In any book of this kind it is impossible to acknowledge all those whose influence has made itself felt. Lon Fuller's work and thought continues to permeate this book. Special thanks are due to Shawn Bayern and Joel Willard, who performed exceptionally valuable work as research assistants, and to Steve Vercelloni for his skill and diligence in helping to prepare the manuscript for publication. I am also indebted to Bob Berring for important suggestions, and to the authors and publishers who generously gave me permission to reprint excerpts from their works.

*

Acknowledgments

Summary of Contents

	Page
ACKNOWLEDGMENTS	iii
TABLE OF CASES	xxix
TABLE OF UNIFORM COMMERCIAL CODE CITATIONS	xxxix
TABLE OF UNIFORM CONSUMER CREDIT CODE CITATIONS	xliii
TABLE OF CITATIONS TO THE RESTATEMENT OF CONTRACTS	xlv

PART I. WHAT PROMISES SHOULD THE LAW ENFORCE?— THE DOCTRINE OF CONSIDERATION

Chapter 1. Donative Promises, Form, and Reliance — **6**
1. Simple Donative Promises — 6
2. The Element of Form — 13
3. The Element of Reliance — 23

Chapter 2. The Bargain Principle and Its Limits — **47**
1. The Bargain Principle — 47
2. Unconscionability — 63
3. The Problem of Mutuality — 86
4. Performance of a Legal Duty as Consideration; Modification and Waiver of Contractual Duties — 107

Chapter 3. Past Consideration — **151**

Chapter 4. The Limits of Contract — **163**

PART II. REMEDIES FOR BREACH OF CONTRACT

Chapter 5. An Introduction to Contract Damages — **190**

Chapter 6. The Expectation Measure — **217**
1. Damages for Breach of a Contract to Perform Services — 217
2. Damages for Breach of a Contract for the Sale of Goods — 241
3. Mitigation; Contracts for Employment — 266
4. Foreseeability — 279
5. Certainty — 292
6. Damages for Mental Distress — 302
7. Liquidated Damages — 308

Chapter 7. Specific Performance — **324**

Chapter 8. The Reliance and Restitution Measures — **341**
1. Reliance Damages in a Bargain Context — 341
2. The Restitution Measure — 348

Page

PART III.   ASSENT

Chapter 9.   An Introduction to Interpretation ---------------- **368**
1.   Subjective and Objective Elements in the Principles of Interpretation in Contract Law -- 368
2.   Problems of Interpreting Purposive Language -------------------- 397
3.   The Role of Usage, Course of Dealing, and Course of Performance in Interpretation --- 406

Chapter 10.   The Mechanics of a Bargain (I)—Offer and Revocation --- **413**
1.   What Constitutes an Offer -------------------------------------- 413
2.   Termination of the Offeree's Power of Acceptance: Lapse, Rejection, and Counter–Offer -- 424
3.   Termination of the Offeree's Power of Acceptance: Revocation -------- 438

Chapter 11.   The Mechanics of a Bargain (II)—Transacting at a Distance --- **456**

Chapter 12.   The Mechanics of a Bargain (III)—Modes of Acceptance --- **461**
1.   Acceptance by Act --- 462
2.   Subjective Acceptance --- 471
3.   Acceptance by Conduct --- 475
4.   The Effect of Using a Subcontractor's Bid --------------------- 478
5.   The Effect of Failing to Notify an Offeree That His Acceptance is Too Late --- 488
6.   Silence as Acceptance --- 491
7.   Acceptance by Electronic Agent -------------------------------- 501

Chapter 13.   Implied–in–Law and Implied–in–Fact Contracts; Unilateral Contracts Revisited -------------------------- **504**

Chapter 14.   Preliminary Negotiations, Indefiniteness, and the Duty to Bargain in Good Faith --------------------------- **536**

Chapter 15.   The Parol Evidence Rule and the Interpretation of Written Contracts --- **584**
1.   The Parol Evidence Rule --------------------------------------- 584
2.   The Interpretation of Written Contracts ----------------------- 608
3.   Trade Usage, Course of Performance and Course of Dealing as Part of a Written Contract ------------------------------------- 626

PART IV.   FORM CONTRACTS IN COMMERCIAL AND CONSUMER CONTEXTS

Chapter 16.   Contract Formation in a Form–Contract Setting ---- **641**
1.   Battle of the Forms: The Basic Issues ------------------------- 641
2.   "Rolling Contracts" --- 664

Chapter 17.   Interpretation and Unconscionability in a Form–Contract Setting --- **692**

Page

PART V. MISTAKE AND UNEXPECTED CIRCUMSTANCES

Chapter 18. Mistake **714**
1. Unilateral Mistakes (Mechanical Errors) 715
2. Mistakes in Transcription; Reformation 728
3. Mutual Mistakes (Shared Mistaken Assumptions) 732
4. Nondisclosure 750

Chapter 19. The Effect of Unexpected Circumstances **765**

PART VI. PROBLEMS INVOLVING PERSONS OTHER THAN THE PARTIES TO THE ORIGINAL CONTRACT

Chapter 20. Third–Party Beneficiaries **812**

Chapter 21. Assignment and Negotiation **853**
1. Introduction 853
2. Assignability of Rights and Delegability of Duties 860
3. Financing Through the Assignment of Claims 874
4. Defenses of the Obligor Against the Assignee in a Commercial Context 878
5. Negotiation; Defenses in the Consumer Context 879

PART VII. PROBLEMS OF PERFORMANCE

Chapter 22. The Obligation to Perform in Good Faith **886**

Chapter 23. The Doctrine of Substantial Performance **915**
1. The General Principle 915
2. Contracts for the Sale of Goods 923

Chapter 24. Express Conditions **934**
1. Introduction 934
2. The Distinctions Between the Operation of a Promise and the Operation of a Condition 935
3. Conditions Precedent and Conditions Subsequent 942
4. Problems of Interpretation in Distinguishing Between Conditions and Promises 945
5. Conditions of Cooperation; Prevention; The Implication of a Promise From an Express Condition 950
6. Conditions of Satisfaction 954
7. Conditions of Payment 962
8. Excuse 965

Chapter 25. Breach and Response **975**
1. The Order of Performance 977
2. Ability to Perform 979
3. Material Breach: Failure of Performance by One Party as an Excuse for Nonperformance by the Other 982

Chapter 26. Anticipatory Breach, Prospective Inability to Perform, and Adequate Assurance of Performance **997**
1. Anticipatory Breach 997
2. Prospective Inability to Perform and Adequate Assurance of Performance 1016

                                                                  Page
Appendix A.   The Statute of Frauds ------------------------------ **1031**
1.   Introduction -- 1032
2.   The Text of the Original Statute ------------------------------ 1032
3.   The Purpose of the Statute ----------------------------------- 1034
4.   How it Was Decided What Kinds of Contracts Should be Required to
      be in Writing --- 1035
5.   American Variations on the English Theme ---------------------- 1037
6.   Judicial Interpretations of the Various Subsections of the Statute of
      Frauds—Introduction -- 1038
7.   Contracts for the Sale of an Interest in Land (Section 4(4)) ------ 1038
8.   Contracts for the Sale of Goods ------------------------------- 1039
9.   Some Other Formal Requirements in the Uniform Commercial Code 1044
10. Agreements Not to be Performed Within One Year From the Making
      Thereof (Section 4(5)) -------------------------------------- 1045
11. The Suretyship Section (Section 4(2))—Generally --------------- 1048
12. The Suretyship Section Continued—"The Main Purpose Rule" ------ 1049
13. The Suretyship Section Continued—Miscellaneous Problems -------- 1050
14. Promises Made by Executors and Administrators (Section 4(1)) ----- 1051
15. Contracts Upon Consideration of Marriage (Section 4(3)) --------- 1052
16. What Kind of Writing Will Satisfy the Statute ----------------- 1053
17. Electronic Contracting and the Statute of Frauds -------------- 1057
18. The Effect of Part Performance of, or Reliance Upon, an Oral
      Contract Within the Statute—Introduction ------------------- 1060
19. The Restitution of Benefits Conferred Under the Oral Agreement ---- 1060
20. Reimbursement for Reliance on the Oral Contract --------------- 1061
21. The Right to the "Value of the Bargain" Where There Has Been
      Part Performance of, or Reliance Upon, the Oral Contract --------- 1064
22. The Effect of Non–Compliance—Legal Consequences of the Unen-
      forceable Agreement --------------------------------------- 1067
23. Oral Rescission --- 1069
24. Oral Modifications -- 1070
25. The Interaction of the Statute of Frauds With the Parol Evidence
      Rule -- 1072
26. The Interaction of the Statute of Frauds With the Remedy of
      Reformation --- 1073
27. Pleading and Procedural Problems in Connection With the Statute --- 1074
28. A Glance Backward and Ahead --------------------------------- 1074

**Appendix B.   A Note on the History of Contract in the Common
      Law** -- **1077**

Appendix C.   Incidents of the Seal ----------------------------- **1085**

Appendix D.   History of the Assignability of Choses in Action ----- **1087**

INDEX --- 1093

Table of Contents

                                                     Page

ACKNOWLEDGMENTS iii
TABLE OF CASES xxix
TABLE OF UNIFORM COMMERCIAL CODE CITATIONS xxxix
TABLE OF UNIFORM CONSUMER CREDIT CODE CITATIONS xliii
TABLE OF CITATIONS TO THE RESTATEMENT OF CONTRACTS xlv

INTRODUCTION

J. Rawls, A Theory of Justice 1
Thomas M. Scanlon, Promises and Practices 2
Gardner, Observations on the Course in Contracts 4

PART I. WHAT PROMISES SHOULD THE LAW ENFORCE?— THE DOCTRINE OF CONSIDERATION

Chapter 1. Donative Promises, Form, and Reliance **6**
1. Simple Donative Promises 6
   Dougherty v. Salt 6
   Restatement, Second, Contracts §§ 1, 17, 71, 79 7
   Note on the Restatement of Contracts 7
   Note on the Concept of Consideration 8
   Note on Gifts 9
   Note on Donative Promises 10
   Note on Conditional Donative Promises 12
2. The Element of Form 13
   Von Mehren, Civil–Law Analogues to Consideration: An Exercise in Comparative Analysis 13
   Note on the Channeling Function of Contract–Law Rules ... 14
   Schnell v. Nell 14
   Statutes Applicable in Schnell v. Nell 16
   Note on Nominal Consideration 17
   Note on Consideration and the Seal 18
   Note on Form 21
3. The Element of Reliance 23
   Kirksey v. Kirksey 24
   Restatement, Second, Contracts § 90 25
   Note on Estoppel in Pais and Promissory Estoppel 25
   Problem 28
   Feinberg v. Pfeiffer Co. 29
   Hayes v. Plantations Steel Co. 34
   Note on Contract Remedies and Consideration 35
   Goldstick v. ICM Realty 39
   D & G Stout, Inc. v. Bacardi Imports, Inc. 40
   Note on the Bacardi Case 45
   Walters v. Marathon Oil Co. 45
   Note on Reliance in Commercial Contexts 46

Page

Chapter 2. The Bargain Principle and Its Limits ----------------------- **47**

1. The Bargain Principle --- 47
    Westlake v. Adams --- 47
    Hamer v. Sidway --- 47
    Note on the Statute of Frauds --- 49
    Davies v. Martel Laboratory Services, Inc. ---------------------------------- 49
    Hancock Bank & Trust Co. v. Shell Oil Co. ----------------------------------- 50
    Restatement, Second, Contracts §§ 71, 72, 79 -------------------------------- 51
    Batsakis v. Demotsis -- 51
    B. Sweet–Escott, Greece—A Political and Economic Survey 1939–1953 ----------- 54
    Further Note on Consideration and Remedies ---------------------------------- 54
    Restatement, Second, Contracts §§ 175, 176 ---------------------------------- 55
    Restatement, Second, Contracts § 176, Illustration 16 ----------------------- 55
    Unidroit Principles of International Commercial Contracts Art. 3.9 ----------- 55
    Note on Unidroit -- 55
    Principles of European Contract Law § 4.108 --------------------------------- 56
    Note on the Principles of European Contract Law ----------------------------- 56
    Chouinard v. Chouinard -- 56
    Post v. Jones --- 57
    Eisenberg, The Bargain Principle and Its Limits ----------------------------- 58
    New York Gen. Bus. Law § 396–r -- 60
    Note on People v. Two Wheel Corp. --- 62
2. Unconscionability --- 63
    Williams v. Walker–Thomas Furniture Co. ------------------------------------- 63
    Note on Williams v. Walker–Thomas --- 67
    *Skilton & Helstad, Protection of the Installment Buyer of Goods Under the
        Uniform Commercial Code* -- 68
    Note on Pricing by Low–Income Market Retailers ------------------------------ 69
    *Joseph B. Cahill, Here's the Pitch: How Kirby Persuades Uncertain Consum-
        ers to Buy $1,500 Vacuum* --- 70
    Restatement Contracts, Second § 208 --- 72
    UCC § 2–302 --- 72
    Uniform Consumer Credit Code §§ 1.301, 5.108 -------------------------------- 72
    Federal Trade Commission Regulations—Door–To–Door Sales --------------------- 72
    Note on the Uniform Commercial Code --- 72
    Pittsley v. Houser -- 74
    Note on the Comments to the UCC --- 75
    Unidroit Principles of International Commercial Contracts Art. 3.10 ---------- 75
    Principles of European Contract Law §§ 4.109, 4.110 ------------------------- 75
    Commission of the European Communities, Council Directive 93/13/EEC --------- 76
    Maxwell v. Fidelity Financial Services, Inc. -------------------------------- 76
    Note on Classical and Modern Contract Law ----------------------------------- 83
3. The Problem of Mutuality -- 86
    Introductory Note --- 86
    Scott v. Moragues Lumber Co. -- 88
    Note on Scott v. Moragues --- 89
    Wickham & Burton Coal Co. v. Farmers' Lumber Co. ---------------------------- 91
    Miami Coca–Cola Bottling Co. v. Orange Crush Co. ---------------------------- 94
    Corbin, The Effect of Options on Consideration ------------------------------ 95
    Williston on Contracts § 103b --- 95
    Restatement, Second, Contracts § 77 --- 96
    Note on Illusory Promises --- 96
    Lindner v. Mid–Continent Petroleum Corp. ------------------------------------ 98
    Gurfein v. Werbelovsky -- 99
    Mattei v. Hopper -- 99
    Helle v. Landmark, Inc. --- 100
    Harris v. Time, Inc. -- 100
    Wood v. Lucy, Lady Duff–Gordon -- 101

Page

3. The Problem of Mutuality—Continued
UCC § 2–306 -- 103
Note on Requirements and Output Contracts --------------------------- 103
Grouse v. Group Health Plan, Inc. ----------------------------------- 104
Note on Grouse --- 106
White v. Roche Biomedical Laboratories, Inc. ----------------------- 106
4. Performance of a Legal Duty as Consideration; Modification and
Waiver of Contractual Duties ------------------------------------ 107
Slattery v. Wells Fargo Armored Service Corp. -------------------- 107
Pollock, Principles of Contract ------------------------------------- 108
Shadwell v. Shadwell --- 109
Restatement, Second, Contracts § 73 ----------------------------- 109
N.Y. Penal Law §§ 200.30, 200.35 --------------------------------- 109
Denney v. Reppert --- 110
Lingenfelder v. Wainwright Brewery Co. ----------------------- 111
Foakes v. Beer --- 114
Note on the Legal–Duty Rule --------------------------------------- 116
Austin Instrument, Inc. v. Loral Corp. ----------------------------- 117
Austin Instrument, Inc. v. Loral Corp. ----------------------------- 120
Further Note on the Legal–Duty Rule ----------------------------- 123
Note on Contract Practice --- 125
Schwartzreich v. Bauman–Basch, Inc. ---------------------------- 126
Restatement, First, Contracts § 406, Illustration 1 -------------- 126
Restatement, Second, Contracts § 73 ----------------------------- 127
McMahon Food Corp. v. Burger Dairy Co. ------------------------ 127
UCC §§ 3–103(a)(4), 3–104, 3–311 -------------------------------- 135
Restatement, Second, Contracts §§ 279, 281 --------------------- 135
Note on the Legal Effect of the "Executory Accord" ------------- 135
Restatement, Second, Contracts § 89 ----------------------------- 138
Angel v. Murray -- 138
Watkins & Son v. Carrig --- 141
Sugarhouse Finance Co. v. Anderson ------------------------------ 142
UCC § 2–209 -- 143
CISG Art. 29 -- 143
Note on the CISG --- 143
Clark v. West --- 144
Restatement, Second, Contracts § 84 ----------------------------- 148
Restatement, Second, Contracts § 84, Illustrations 3, 4, 6 ----- 148
Nassau Trust Co. v. Montrose Concrete Products Corp. --------- 149
UCC §§ 1–107, 2–209 -- 149
BMC Industries, Inc. v. Barth Industries, Inc. ------------------- 149

Chapter 3. Past Consideration ---------------------------------- **151**
Restatement, Second, Contracts §§ 82, 83 ----------------------- 151
Bankruptcy Code, 11 U.S.C. § 524 --------------------------------- 151
Three Situations in Which a Promise to Discharge an Unenforceable Obligation is
Binding --- 151
Mills v. Wyman --- 152
Background Note on Mills v. Wyman -------------------------------- 155
Webb v. McGowin --- 156
Webb v. McGowin --- 159
Harrington v. Taylor --- 159
Restatement, Second, Contracts § 86 ----------------------------- 160
Restatement, Second, Contracts § 86, Illustrations 1, 2, 6, 10, 12, 13 -------------- 160
American Law Institute, 42d Annual Proceedings ---------------- 160
Note on Past Consideration -- 161

Chapter 4. The Limits of Contract ------------------------------ **163**
Balfour v. Balfour -- 163
In re the Marriage of Witten --- 164
T.F. v. B.L. -- 173

Page

Note on Who is a Parent --- 182
R.R. v. M.H. -- 183
Note on Surrogate–Parenting Legislation --------------------------------- 185
42 U.S. Code § 274e. Prohibition of Organ Purchases --------------------- 185
Radin, Market–Inalienability -- 186

PART II.   REMEDIES FOR BREACH OF CONTRACT

Chapter 5.   An Introduction to Contract Damages --------------- 190
Restatement, Second, Contracts § 344 ------------------------------------ 190
Hawkins v. McGee -- 190
McGee v. United States Fidelity & Guar. Co. ----------------------------- 193
McQuaid v. Michou --- 194
Background Note on Hawkins v. McGee ------------------------------------ 195
Van Zee v. Witzke --- 197
Sullivan v. O'Connor -- 198
Unidroit Principles of International Commercial Contracts Art. 7.4.2 ----- 200
Cooter & Eisenberg, Damages for Breach of Contract --------------------- 200
United States Naval Institute v. Charter Communications, Inc. ----------- 203
Coppola Enterprises, Inc. v. Alfone ------------------------------------- 207
Laurin v. DeCarolis Construction Co. ------------------------------------ 208
Note on the Theory of Efficient Breach ---------------------------------- 209
Greer Properties, Inc. v. LaSalle National Bank ------------------------- 214
Note on Punitive Damages -- 215

Chapter 6.   The Expectation Measure --------------------------- 217
1.   Damages for Breach of a Contract to Perform Services --------------- 217
    (a) Breach by the Person Who Has Contracted to Perform Services 217
        Louise Caroline Nursing Home, Inc. v. Dix Construction Co. --------- 218
        Hawkins v. McGee -- 219
        Peevyhouse v. Garland Coal & Mining Co. ---------------------- 220
        Note --- 227
        Restatement, Second, of Contracts § 348(2) -------------------- 227
        Note on Additional Facts in Peevyhouse ------------------------ 227
        Note on Oklahoma Mining Lands Reclamation Act ---------------- 228
        Schneberger v. Apache Corp. ----------------------------------- 228
        H.P. Droher & Sons v. Toushin --------------------------------- 231
        Eastern Steamship Lines, Inc. v. United States ---------------- 231
        City School District of the City of Elmira v. McLane Construction Co. ----- 232
        Fox v. Webb --- 233
        Grossman Holdings Ltd. v. Hourihan --------------------------- 233
        Advanced, Inc. v. Wilks --------------------------------------- 234
        Note on Ruxley Electronics and Construction Ltd. v. Forsyth ---- 235
    (b) Breach by a Person Who Has Contracted to Have Services
        Performed --- 237
        Aiello Construction, Inc. v. Nationwide Tractor Trailer Training and
            Placement Corp. --- 237
        Note on Formulas for Measuring Damages for Breach by a Person Who
            Has Contracted to Have Services Performed ----------------- 239
        Restatement, Second, Contracts -------------------------------- 239
        Wired Music, Inc. v. Clark ------------------------------------ 240
        Vitex Mfg. Corp. v. Caribtex Corp. ---------------------------- 240
2.   Damages for Breach of a Contract for the Sale of Goods ------------- 241
    (a) Breach by the Seller -- 241
        Note on Damages for the Seller's Breach of a Contract for the Sale of
            Goods -- 241
        UCC §§ 2–711(1), 2–712, 2–713, 2–714, 2–715(1), 2–723, 2–724 ---- 242
        CISG Arts. 45, 49, 50, 74, 75, 76 ----------------------------- 242
        Continental Sand & Gravel, Inc. v. K & K Sand & Gravel, Inc. --- 242
        Manouchehri v. Heim --- 243
        Egerer v. CSR West, LLC --------------------------------------- 243
        Panhandle Agri–Service, Inc. v. Becker ------------------------ 246
        J. White & R. Summers, Uniform Commercial Code --------------- 246

Page

2. Damages for Breach of a Contract for the Sale of Goods—Continued
   Note on the Availability of Market–Price Damages to a Buyer Who Has
   Covered --- 247
   Delchi Carrier SpA v. Rotorex Corp. ------------------------------- 248
   (b) Breach by the Buyer -- 253
   UCC §§ 2–501(1), 2–703, 2–704(1), 2–706, 2–708, 2–709, 2–710, 2–723,
   2–724 --- 253
   CISG Arts. 61, 62, 64, 74, 75, 76 --------------------------------- 253
   KGM Harvesting Co. v. Fresh Network ------------------------------ 253
   Neri v. Retail Marine Corp. --------------------------------------- 260
   Teradyne, Inc. v. Teledyne Industries, Inc. ----------------------- 264
   Childres & Burgess, Seller's Remedies: The Primacy of UCC 2–708(2) --- 264
   R.E. Davis Chemical Corp. v. Diasonics, Inc. ---------------------- 264
   Lazenby Garages Ltd. v. Wright ----------------------------------- 265
3. Mitigation; Contracts for Employment ----------------------------- 266
   Rockingham County v. Luten Bridge Co. ---------------------------- 266
   Madsen v. Murrey & Sons Co. -------------------------------------- 269
   In re Kellett Aircraft Corp. -------------------------------------- 269
   Bank One, Texas N.A. v. Taylor ----------------------------------- 270
   S.J. Groves & Sons Co. v. Warner Co. ----------------------------- 270
   Restatement, Second, Contracts § 350 ----------------------------- 271
   UCC §§ 2–704(2), 2–715(2) -- 271
   CISG Art. 77-- 271
   Unidroit Principles of International Commercial Contracts Arts. 7.4.7, 7.4.8 271
   Principles of European Contract Law Arts. 9.504, 9.505------------ 272
   Shirley MacLaine Parker v. Twentieth Century–Fox Film Corp. ------ 272
   Punkar v. King Plastic Corp. ------------------------------------- 275
   Mr. Eddie, Inc. v. Ginsberg -------------------------------------- 275
   Southern Keswick, Inc. v. Whetherholt --------------------------- 276
   Note on Damages for Loss of the Opportunity to Practice One's Profession ----- 276
4. Foreseeability -- 279
   Hadley v. Baxendale-- 279
   Background Note on Hadley v. Baxendale --------------------------- 282
   Victoria Laundry (Windsor) Ltd. v. Newman Indus. Ltd. ----------- 283
   Koufos v. C. Czarnikow, Ltd. [The Heron II] --------------------- 285
   Hector Martinez and Co. v. Southern Pacific Transp. Co. --------- 287
   Note on the Scope of Hadley v. Baxendale ------------------------ 288
   Restatement, Second, Contracts § 351 --------------------------- 289
   UCC §§ 2–713, 2–715(2) --- 289
   Panhandle Agri–Service, Inc. v. Becker ------------------------- 289
   CISG Art. 74-- 290
   Unidroit Principles of International Commercial Contracts Art. 7.4.4 ---------- 290
   Principles of European Contract Law Art. 9.503 ----------------- 290
   Note—Limitations on Contract Damages --------------------------- 290
   Note on Causation -- 290
   Independent Mechanical Contractors, Inc. v. Gordon T. Burke & Sons--------- 291
   S.J. Groves & Sons Co. v. Warner Co. --------------------------- 291
5. Certainty -- 292
   Kenford Co. v. Erie County------------------------------------- 292
   Note on Kenford -- 294
   Ashland Management Inc. v. Janien ----------------------------- 295
   Note on the New–Business Rule ---------------------------------- 296
   Rombola v. Cosindas-- 297
   Contemporary Mission, Inc. v. Famous Music Corp. -------------- 298
   UCC § 1–106(1) --- 298
   Restatement, Second, Contracts § 352 -------------------------- 298
   Unidroit Principles of International Commercial Contracts Art. 7.4.3 ---------- 299
   Note on Uncertainty --- 299
   Mears v. Nationwide Mutual Ins. Co. --------------------------- 302
6. Damages for Mental Distress ---------------------------------- 302
   Hawkins v. McGee -- 302

Page

6. Damages for Mental Distress—Continued
   Sullivan v. O'Connor -- 302
   Valentine v. General American Credit, Inc. ------------------------------- 302
   Lane v. KinderCare Learning Centers, Inc. ------------------------------ 305
   Restatement, Second, Contracts § 353 ------------------------------------- 306
   Unidroit Principles of International Commercial Contracts Art. 7.4.2 --------- 307
   Jarvis v. Swan Tours, Ltd. -- 307
   Jackson v. Horizon Holidays, Ltd. -- 308
   Deitsch v. Music Co. -- 308
   Restatement, Second, Contracts § 355 ------------------------------------- 308
7. Liquidated Damages --- 308
   Wasserman's Inc. v. Middletown -- 308
   Lee Oldsmobile, Inc. v. Kaiden -- 315
   Hutchison v. Tompkins -- 316
   UCC § 2–718(1) --- 317
   Restatement, Second, Contracts § 356 ------------------------------------- 318
   Unidroit Principles of International Commercial Contracts Art. 7.4.13 -------- 318
   Principles of European Contract Law Art. 9.509 --------------------------- 318
   Note on Liquidated Damages --- 318
   Note on Provisions that Limit Damages ----------------------------------- 322

Chapter 7. Specific Performance --- **324**
Introductory Note --- 324
London Bucket Co. v. Stewart --- 326
Restatement, Second, Contracts §§ 359, 360 --------------------------------- 327
Unidroit Principles of International Commercial Contracts Arts. 7.2.1, 7.2.2, 7.2.3 327
Principles of European Contract Law Arts. 9.101, 9.102, 9.103 -------------- 328
Walgreen Co. v. Sara Creek Property Co. --------------------------------------- 328
Stokes v. Moore --- 333
Van Wagner Advertising Corp. v. S & M Enterprises ---------------------- 333
UCC §§ 2–709, 2–716 --- 334
CISG Arts. 46, 62 -- 334
Note on the Traditional Rule Concerning Specific Performance of Contracts for the Sale of Goods --- 334
Laclede Gas Co. v. Amoco Oil Co. --- 335
Weathersby v. Gore -- 337
Note on Specific Performance of Contracts for the Sale of Land and Employment Contracts -- 338

Chapter 8. The Reliance and Restitution Measures ------------ **341**
1. Reliance Damages in a Bargain Context ------------------------------------- 341
   Security Stove & Mfg. Co. v. American Rys. Express Co. ----------------- 341
   Anglia Television Ltd. v. Reed --- 345
   Beefy Trail, Inc. v. Beefy King Int'l, Inc. ----------------------------------- 345
   L. Albert & Son v. Armstrong Rubber Co. --------------------------------- 346
   C.C.C. Films (London) v. Impact Quadrant Films Ltd. ------------------ 346
   Sullivan v. O'Connor -- 347
   D & G Stout, Inc. v. Bacardi Imports, Inc. -------------------------------- 347
   Walters v. Marathon Oil Co. -- 347
   Westside Galvanizing Services, Inc. v. Georgia–Pacific Corp. ----------- 347
2. The Restitution Measure --- 348
   (a) Restitutionary Damages for Breach of Contract ------------------------ 348
       Osteen v. Johnson -- 348
       Restatement, Second, Contracts §§ 344, 345, 370, 371 ---------------- 350
       Restatement, Second, Contracts § 370, Illustrations 2, 5 ------------ 350
       United States v. Algernon Blair, Inc. ------------------------------------- 351
       Oliver v. Campbell --- 353
       1 G. Palmer, The Law of Restitution -------------------------------------- 353
       Note on Restitutionary and Reliance Damages -------------------------- 354
       Note on Expectation as a Cap on Reliance Damages ------------------- 354
   (b) Restitution in Favor of a Plaintiff in Default ------------------------ 355
       Kutzin v. Pirnie --- 355
       United States ex rel. Palmer Construction, Inc. v. Cal State Electric, Inc. 362

Page

2. The Restitution Measure—Continued

R.J. Berke & Co. v. Griffin, Inc. 363
Vines v. Orchard Hills, Inc. 363
Nelson v. Hazel 364
UCC § 2–718(2), (3) 365

PART III. ASSENT

Chapter 9. An Introduction to Interpretation 368

1. Subjective and Objective Elements in the Principles of Interpretation in Contract Law 368
Introductory Note 368
Restatement, [First,] Contracts § 227 369
Lucy v. Zehmer 370
Keller v. Holderman 374
Raffles v. Wichelhaus 374
Simpson, Contracts for Cotton to Arrive: The Case of the Two Ships Peerless 375
Frigaliment Importing Co. v. B.N.S. Intern. Sales Corp. 376
Oswald v. Allen 380
Falck v. Williams 380
Colfax Envelope Corp. v. Local No. 458–3M 381
Embry v. Hargadine, McKittrick Dry Goods Co. 381
Restatement, Second, Contracts §§ 20, 201 384
CISG Art. 8 384
Unidroit Principles of International Commercial Contracts Arts. 4.1, 4.2, 4.3 384
Principles of European Contract Law Arts. 5.101, 5.102 384
MCC–Marble Ceramic Center, Inc. v. Ceramica Nuova d'Agostino 385
Mayol v. Weiner Companies, Ltd. 389
Note on Objective and Subjective Elements in Interpretation 393
Berke Moore Co. v. Phoenix Bridge Co. 396
Note on "Intention" as a Test of Legal Consequences 396

2. Problems of Interpreting Purposive Language 397
Williams, Language and the Law—Part IV 397
Fish, Normal Circumstances, Literal Language, Direct Speech Acts, the Ordinary, the Everyday, the Obvious, What Goes Without Saying, and Other Special Cases 398
Haines v. New York 399
Restatement, Second, Contracts § 204 402
Unidroit Principles of International Commercial Contracts Art. 4.8 402
Spaulding v. Morse 402
Lawson v. Martin Timber Co. 404
Lieber, Legal and Political Hermeneutics 405

3. The Role of Usage, Course of Dealing, and Course of Performance in Interpretation 406
Foxco Industries, Ltd. v. Fabric World, Inc. 406
Restatement, Second, Contracts § 221, Illustration 2 409
Restatement, Second, Contracts § 222 409
Restatement, Second, Contracts § 222, Illustrations 1–3 409
Hurst v. W.J. Lake & Co. 409
Restatement, Second, Contracts § 220 410
Flower City Painting Contractors, Inc. v. Gumina 411
UCC §§ 1–201(3), (11), 1–205, 2–208 412
Restatement, Second, Contracts §§ 219–223 412
CISG Art. 9 412
Unidroit Principles of International Commercial Contracts Art. 1.9 412
Principles of European Contract Law Art. 1.105 412
J. White & R. Summers, Uniform Commercial Code 412

Page

Chapter 10. The Mechanics of a Bargain (I)—Offer and Revocation 413

1. What Constitutes an Offer 413
   Restatement, Second, Contracts § 24 413
   CISG Art. 14(1) 413
   Unidroit Principles of International Commercial Contracts Art. 2.1.2 414
   Principles of European Contract Law § 2.201(1) 414
   Lonergan v. Scolnick 414
   Regent Lighting Corp. v. CMT Corp. 416
   Lefkowitz v. Great Minneapolis Surplus Store 417
   Ford Motor Credit Co. v. Russell 419
   Donovan v. RRL Corp. 420
   Fisher v. Bell 421
   Restatement, Second, Contracts § 26 422
   CISG Article 14(2) 422
   Principles of European Contract Law Art. 2.201(2), (3) 422
   Uniform Deceptive Trade Practices Act 422
   Federal Trade Commission Regulations—Retail Food Store Advertising and Marketing Practices 422
   UCC § 2–328 422
   Hoffman v. Horton 422
   Note on Auctions 423
   Note on Offer and Acceptance 424
2. Termination of the Offeree's Power of Acceptance: Lapse, Rejection, and Counter–Offer 424
   Akers v. J.B. Sedberry, Inc. 424
   Restatement, Second, Contracts §§ 38, 41 428
   CISG Art. 17 428
   Unidroit Principles of International Commercial Contracts Arts. 2.1.5, 2.1.7 428
   Principles of European Contract Law Arts. 2.203, 2.206 428
   Note on the Effect of the Rejection of an Offer 429
   Ardente v. Horan 430
   Rhode Island Dep't of Transportation v. Providence & Worcester R.R. 433
   Restatement, Second, Contracts § 39 434
   Restatement, Second, Contracts § 39, Illustrations 1–3 434
   Price v. Oklahoma College of Osteopathic Medicine and Surgery 434
   Restatement, Second, Contracts § 59 435
   CISG Art. 19 435
   Unidroit Principles of International Commercial Contracts Art. 2.1.11 435
   Principles of European Contract Law Art. 2.208 435
   Note on the Mirror–Image Rule 435
   Livingstone v. Evans 436
   Culton v. Gilchrist 436
   Restatement, Second, Contracts § 37 436
   Note on the Effect of the Offeror's Death or Incapacity Before Acceptance 436
3. Termination of the Offeree's Power of Acceptance: Revocation 438
   Dickinson v. Dodds 438
   Restatement, Second, Contracts §§ 42, 43 441
   CISG Art. 16 441
   Unidroit Principles of International Commercial Contracts Art. 2.1.4 441
   Principles of European Contract Law Art. 2.202 441
   Note on Contract Practice 441
   Note on What Constitutes Receipt of a Written Acceptance 441
   Restatement, Second, Contracts § 45 442
   Ragosta v. Wilder 442
   Note on Offers for Unilateral Contracts 446
   Drennan v. Star Paving Co. 448
   Pavel Enterprises, Inc. v. A.S. Johnson Co. 452
   UCC § 2–205 453
   Dodge, Teaching the CISG in Contracts 453
   Preload Technology, Inc. v. A.B. & J. Construction Co., Inc. 454
   Allen M. Campbell Co. v. Virginia Metal Industries, Inc. 454

Page

3. Termination of the Offeree's Power of Acceptance: Revocation—
   Continued
   Restatement, Second, Contracts § 87(2) 454
   Note on Restatement Second § 87(2) 455

Chapter 11. The Mechanics of a Bargain (II)—Transacting at a Distance 456
Introductory Note 456
Restatement, Second, Contracts §§ 30, 49, 60, 63–68 458
UCC § 2–206(1) 458
CISG Arts. 15, 16, 18(2), 20, 22, 23, 24 458
Unidroit Principles of International Commercial Contracts Arts. 2.1.3, 2.1.6(2),
   2.1.7, 2.1.8, 2.1.10 458
Principles of European Contract Law Arts. 2.205(1), 2.206 458
Dodge, Teaching the CISG in Contracts 458
Note on Electronic Commerce 459
Note on the Concept of "Record" 460

Chapter 12. The Mechanics of a Bargain (III)—Modes of Acceptance 461
Note on the Consequences of Utilizing the Wrong Mode of Acceptance 461
Restatement, Second, Contracts § 32 462
UCC § 2–206(1) 462

1. Acceptance by Act 462
   Klockner v. Green 462
   De Cicco v. Schweizer 465
   Simmons v. United States 465
   Stephens v. Memphis 466
   Carlill v. Carbolic Smoke Ball Co. 466
   A.W.B. Simpson, Quackery and Contract Law: The Case of the Carbolic
      Smoke Ball 468
   Bishop v. Eaton 469
   Restatement, Second, Contracts § 54 471
   UCC § 2–206(2) 471

2. Subjective Acceptance 471
   International Filter Co. v. Conroe Gin, Ice & Light Co. 471
   Restatement, Second, Contracts § 56, Illustration 2 474

3. Acceptance by Conduct 475
   Polaroid Corp. v. Rollins Environmental Services (NJ), Inc. 475

4. The Effect of Using a Subcontractor's Bid 478
   Holman Erection Co. v. Orville E. Madsen & Sons, Inc. 478
   Note on Southern California Acoustics Co. v. C.V. Holder, Inc. 485
   Williams v. Favret 485
   Electrical Construction & Maintenance Co. v. Maeda Pacific Corp. 486
   Industrial Electric–Seattle, Inc. v. Bosko 487
   Loranger Const. Corp. v. E.F. Hauserman Company 487
   Pavel Enterprises, Inc. v. A.S. Johnson Co. 487

5. The Effect of Failing to Notify an Offeree That His Acceptance is
   Too Late 488
   Phillips v. Moor 488
   Note on the Risk of Loss 490
   Restatement, Second, Contracts §§ 69, 70 490
   CISG Art. 21 490
   Unidroit Principles of International Commercial Contracts Art. 2.1.9 490
   Principles of European Contract Law Art. 2.207 490

6. Silence as Acceptance 491
   Vogt v. Madden 491
   Restatement, Second, Contracts § 69 494
   CISG Art. 18(1), (3) 494
   Unidroit Principles of International Commercial Contracts Art. 2.1.6(3) 494
   Principles of European Contract Law Art. 2.204(2) 495

Page

6. Silence as Acceptance—Continued
   Laurel Race Courses v. Regal Const. Co. --- 495
   Cole–McIntyre–Norfleet Co. v. Holloway --------------------------------------- 495
   Kukuska v. Home Mut. Hail–Tornado Ins. Co. ------------------------------- 498
   Hobbs v. Massasoit Whip Co. --- 498
   Louisville Tin & Stove Co. v. Lay --- 499
   Austin v. Burge --- 499
   39 U.S.C. § 3009 [Mailing of Unordered Merchandise] ----------------------- 500
   Note on Negative–Option Plans --- 500
   *Note on the Significance of Unjust Enrichment and Loss Through Reliance
     in Cases Where Silence is Treated as Acceptance* ---------------------------- 500
7. Acceptance by Electronic Agent -- 501

**Chapter 13. Implied–in–Law and Implied–in–Fact Contracts;
     Unilateral Contracts Revisited** -- **504**
Nursing Care Services, Inc. v. Dobos --- 504
Sceva v. True -- 506
Note on Terminology --- 507
Note on Implied–in–Fact and Implied–in–Law Contracts ----------------------- 508
Mary Jane Morrison, I Imply What You Infer Unless You Are a Court ------ 510
Day v. Caton -- 511
Note on Day v. Caton -- 513
Bastian v. Gafford -- 514
Hill v. Waxberg -- 515
Ramsey v. Ellis --- 515
Paffhausen v. Balano --- 516
Wagenseller v. Scottsdale Memorial Hospital -- 516
Note on Employment at Will -- 530
Pine River State Bank v. Mettille -- 531
Note on Modification of Employee Handbooks --------------------------------------- 531
Note on the Effect of Disclaimers in Employee Handbooks --------------------- 533
Pettit, Modern Unilateral Contracts --- 534

**Chapter 14. Preliminary Negotiations, Indefiniteness, and the
     Duty to Bargain in Good Faith** -- **536**
Academy Chicago Publishers v. Cheever -- 537
*Peter Kurth, Book Review of Anita Miller, Uncollecting Cheever, the Family of
     John Cheever v. Academy Chicago Publisher* --------------------------------- 540
Ridgway v. Wharton --- 541
Berg Agency v. Sleepworld–Willingboro, Inc. --------------------------------------- 541
Rego v. Decker --- 541
AROK Construction Co. v. Indian Construction Services --------------------- 542
Saliba–Kringlen Corp. v. Allen Engineering Co. -------------------------------- 542
Crook v. Mortenson–Neal --- 543
Restatement, Second, Contracts §§ 33, 34 --- 544
UCC §§ 2–204, 2–305, 2–308, 2–309, 2–310 --------------------------------------- 544
CISG Arts. 14(1), 31, 33, 55, 57, 58 --- 544
*Unidroit Principles of International Commercial Contracts Arts. 2.1.2, 2.1.13,
     2.1.14, 5.1.7, 5.1.8, 6.1.1, 6.6.6* --- 544
Principles of European Contract Law §§ 2.201(1), 6.104, 6.109, 7.01, 7.102 --------- 545
Note on Gap–Fillers -- 545
Hawkland, Sales Contract Terms Under the UCC ----------------------------- 545
Joseph Martin, Jr., Delicatessen, Inc. v. Schumacher --------------------------- 546
Moolenaar v. Co–Build Companies Inc. -- 547
Channel Home Centers v. Grossman --- 548
*A/S Apothekernes Laboratorium for Specialpraeparater v. I.M.C. Chemical Group,
     Inc.* -- 556
Unidroit Principles of International Commercial Contracts Art. 2.1.15 -------------- 556
Principles of European Contract Law Art. 2.301 ------------------------------------ 556
Teachers Insurance and Annuity Association of America v. Tribune Co. ---------- 557

Page

Venture Associates Corp. v. Zenith Data Systems Corp. 570
Kansas Municipal Gas Agency v. Vesta Energy Co. 571
Hoffman v. Red Owl Stores, Inc. 573
Comment, Once More Into the Breach: Promissory Estoppel and Traditional
    Contract Doctrine 580
Gruen Industries, Inc. v. Biller 581
Neiss v. Ehlers 582
Racine & Laramie, Ltd. v. California Dept. of Parks & Recreation 583

Chapter 15. The Parol Evidence Rule and the Interpretation of Written Contracts **584**

1. The Parol Evidence Rule 584
    Mitchill v. Lath 584
    Von Mehren, Civil Law Analogues to Consideration: An Exercise in Compar-
        ative Analysis 589
    James Bradley Thayer, A Preliminary Treatise on Evidence 590
    Calamari & Perillo, A Plea for a Uniform Parol Evidence Rule and Princi-
        ples of Interpretation 590
    Restatement, First, Contracts §§ 228, 237, 239, 240 592
    Restatement, Second, Contracts §§ 209, 210, 213, 214, 215, 216 593
    Braucher, Interpretation and Legal Effect in the Second Restatement of
        Contracts 593
    Hatley v. Stafford 593
    Interform Co. v. Mitchell Constr. Co. 594
    Murray, The Parol Evidence Process and Standardized Agreements Under
        the Restatement, Second, Contracts 594
    CISG Art. 8(3) 595
    Dodge, Teaching the CISG in Contracts 595
    Unidroit Principles of International Law Art. 4.3 595
    Masterson v. Sine 595
    UCC § 2–202 599
    Interform v. Mitchell Constr. Co. 599
    Hunt Foods and Industries, Inc. v. Doliner 599
    Alaska Northern Development, Inc. v. Alyeska Pipeline Service Co. 601
    Note on Merger Clauses 602
    ARB (American Research Bureau), Inc. v. E–Systems, Inc. 602
    Seibel v. Layne & Bowler, Inc. 603
    Unidroit Principles of International Commercial Contracts Art. 2.1.17 604
    Note on the Fraud Exception to the Parol Evidence Rule 604
    Note on the Condition–to–Legal–Effectiveness Exception to the Parol Evi-
        dence Rule 606
    UCC § 2–209(2), (4), (5) 607
    Unidroit Principles of International Commercial Contracts Art. 2.1.18 607
    Principles of European Contract Law Art. 2.106 607
    Note on No–Oral–Modification Clauses 607

2. The Interpretation of Written Contracts 608
    Steuart v. McChesney 608
    Mellon Bank, N.A. v. Aetna Business Credit, Inc. 614
    Amoco Production Co. v. Western Slope Gas Co. 614
    Pacific Gas & Electric Co. v. G.W. Thomas Drayage & Rigging Co. 615
    Garden State Plaza Corp. v. S.S. Kresge Co. 618
    Trident Center v. Connecticut General Life Ins. Co. 619
    Fish, The Law Wishes to Have a Formal Existence 621
    Holmes, The Theory of Legal Interpretation 622
    Williston on Contracts 622
    Restatement, [First,] Contracts § 231 623
    Corbin on Contracts 623
    Restatement, Second, Contracts § 212 623
    Berg v. Hudesman 623

Page

2. The Interpretation of Written Contracts—Continued
   Note—Is the Interpretation of Written Contracts a Question for the Judge or for the Jury? 625
3. Trade Usage, Course of Performance and Course of Dealing as Part of a Written Contract 626
   Nanakuli Paving and Rock Co. v. Shell Oil Co. 626
   C-Thru Container Corp. v. Midland Mfg. Co. 636
   Note on the Plain–Meaning Rule and the Parol Evidence Rule 637

PART IV.   FORM CONTRACTS IN COMMERCIAL AND CONSUMER CONTEXTS

Chapter 16.   Contract Formation in a Form–Contract Setting 641
1. Battle of the Forms: The Basic Issues 641
   Note on the Battle of the Forms 641
   UCC §§ 2–204(1), 2–204, 2–207 642
   ABA Task Force Report on Article 2 642
   Note on What Constitutes an Acceptance Under UCC § 2–207 643
   Columbia Hyundai, Inc. v. Carll Hyundai, Inc. 644
   CISG Art. 19 644
   Unidroit Principles of International Commercial Contracts Arts. 2.1.12, 2.1.22 645
   Principles of European Contract Law Art. 2.209 645
   Gardner Zemke Co. v. Dunham Bush, Inc. 645
   Note on Gardner Zemke 653
   Note on the Meaning of "Materially Alter" Under UCC § 2–207(2)(b) 653
   Note on the "Expressly Made Conditional" Clause 655
   Note on the Effect of Confirmations With Additional Terms 656
   Diamond Fruit Growers, Inc. v. Krack Corp. 657
   C. Itoh & Co. (America), Inc. v. Jordan International Co. 661
   Transwestern Pipeline Co. v. Monsanto Co. 662
   JOM, Inc. v. Adell Plastics, Inc. 663
2. "Rolling Contracts" 664
   ProCD, Inc. v. Zeidenberg 664
   Note 669
   Hill v. Gateway 2000 670
   M.A. Mortenson, Co. v. Timberline Software Corp. 672
   Klocek v. Gateway, Inc. 672
   Chateau des Charmes Wines Ltd. v. Sabate USA Inc. 672
   Arizona Cartridge Remanufacturers' Ass'n. v. Lexmark Int'l Inc. 675
   Specht v. Netscape Communications Corp. 676
   Register.com, Inc. v. Verio, Inc. 686

Chapter 17.   Interpretation and Unconscionability in a Form–Contract Setting 692
Sardo v. Fidelity & Deposit Co. 692
Llewellyn, The Common Law Tradition: Deciding Appeals 694
Weaver v. American Oil Co. 696
Restatement, Second, Contracts § 211 699
Unidroit Principles of International Commercial Contracts Arts. 2.1.19, 2.1.22 699
Principles of European Contract Law Art. 4.110 699
Darner Motor Sales v. Universal Underwriters 699
Gordinier v. Aetna Casualty & Surety Co. 711
Farm Bureau Mutual Insurance Co. v. Sandbulte 712

Page

PART V. MISTAKE AND UNEXPECTED CIRCUMSTANCES

Chapter 18. Mistake ---- **714**
1. Unilateral Mistakes (Mechanical Errors) ---- 715
    Donovan v. RRL Corp. ---- 715
    Speckel v. Perkins ---- 725
    The Nolan Ryan Baseball Card Case ---- 726
    Restatement, Second, Contracts §§ 153, 154 ---- 727
    Note on Unilateral Mistake ---- 728
2. Mistakes in Transcription; Reformation ---- 728
    Travelers Ins. Co. v. Bailey ---- 728
    Restatement, Second, of Contracts § 155 ---- 731
    Chimart Associates v. Paul ---- 731
3. Mutual Mistakes (Shared Mistaken Assumptions) ---- 732
    Wittgenstein, Philosophical Investigations ---- 733
    Sherwood v. Walker ---- 733
    Nester v. Michigan Land & Iron Co. ---- 739
    Griffith v. Brymer ---- 739
    Wood v. Boynton ---- 740
    Firestone & Parson, Inc. v. Union League of Philadelphia ---- 742
    Everett v. Estate of Sumstad ---- 742
    Restatement, Second, Contracts §§ 151, 152, 154 ---- 743
    Unidroit Principles of International Commercial Contracts Arts. 3.4, 3.5, 3.18 ---- 743
    Principles of European Contract Law Art. 4.103 ---- 743
    Lenawee County Board of Health v. Messerly ---- 743
    Beachcomber Coins, Inc. v. Boskett ---- 749
    UCC §§ 2–312, 2–313, 2–314, 2–315 ---- 749
4. Nondisclosure ---- 750
    Melvin A. Eisenberg, Disclosure in Contract Law ---- 750
    Hill v. Jones ---- 757
    Weintraub v. Krobatsch ---- 762
    Restatement, Second, Contracts §§ 159, 161 ---- 762
    Restatement, Second, Contracts § 161, Illustrations 7, 10, 11 ---- 762
    Restatement, Second, Torts § 551, Illustrations 6, 8 ---- 763
    United States v. Dial ---- 763

Chapter 19. The Effect of Unexpected Circumstances ---- **765**
Introductory Note ---- 765
Taylor v. Caldwell ---- 765
Tacit Assumptions—Continued ---- 768
Ocean Tramp Tankers Corp. v. V/O Sovfracht ---- 769
Mineral Park Land Co. v. Howard ---- 770
United States v. Wegematic Corp. ---- 771
Dills v. Town of Enfield ---- 773
Transatlantic Financing Corp. v. United States ---- 774
American Trading & Production Corp. v. Shell Int'l Marine Ltd. ---- 778
Restatement, Second, Contracts § 261 ---- 779
Joskow, Commercial Impossibility, the Uranium Market and the Westinghouse Case ---- 779
Mishara Constr. Co. v. Transit–Mixed Concrete Corp. ---- 780
UCC §§ 1–103, 2–509, 2–510, 2–613, 2–614, 2–615, 2–616 ---- 781
Restatement, Second, Contracts §§ 261–272 ---- 781
CISG Arts. 66–69 ---- 781
Unidroit Principles of International Commercial Contracts Arts. 6.2.1, 6.2.2, 6.2.3, 7.1.7 ---- 782
Principles of European Contract Law Arts. 4.102, 6.111, 8.108 ---- 782
ABA Task Force Report on Article 2 ---- 782
J. White & R. Summers, Uniform Commercial Code § 3.10 ---- 782
American Institute of Architects, General Conditions of the Contract for Construction ---- 782
Albre Marble & Tile Co. v. John Bowen Co. ---- 783
Note on the Equitable Apportionment of Losses Following Impossibility ---- 785

Page

Missouri Public Service Co. v. Peabody Coal Co. ---- 786
Georgia Power Co. v. Cimarron Coal Corp. ---- 793
Note on the Effect of Significantly Increased Costs Under UCC § 2–615 ---- 794
Alamance County Board of Education v. Bobby Murray Chevrolet, Inc. ---- 795
Selland Pontiac–GMC, Inc. v. King ---- 800
Note on Contracts to Sell Crops ---- 801
Wickliffe Farms, Inc. v. Owensboro Grain Co. ---- 801
Krell v. Henry ---- 802
Wladis, Common Law and Uncommon Events: The Development of the Doctrine of Impossibility of Performance in English Contract Law ---- 805
Lloyd v. Murphy ---- 806
Alfred Marks Realty Co. v. Hotel Hermitage Co. ---- 806
La Cumbre Golf & Country Club v. Santa Barbara Hotel Co. ---- 806
Chase Precast Corp. v. John J. Paonessa Co. ---- 807
Power Engineering & Manufacturing, Ltd. v. Krug International ---- 808

PART VI. PROBLEMS INVOLVING PERSONS OTHER THAN THE PARTIES TO THE ORIGINAL CONTRACT

Chapter 20. Third–Party Beneficiaries ---- **812**
Preliminary Analysis of the Problem of This Chapter ---- 812
Restatement, Second, of Contracts § 302, Illustrations 16–19 ---- 814
Lawrence v. Fox ---- 814
Note on Lawrence v. Fox ---- 818
Seaver v. Ransom ---- 819
Restatement, First, Contracts § 133 ---- 823
Restatement, Second, Contracts §§ 302, 304, 315 ---- 823
Eisenberg, Third–Party Beneficiaries ---- 823
Hale v. Groce ---- 826
Scarpitti v. Weborg ---- 831
UCC § 2–318 ---- 835
Restatement, Second, Contracts § 313 ---- 835
Martinez v. Socoma Companies, Inc. ---- 835
Zigas v. Superior Court ---- 844
H.B. Deal & Co. v. Head ---- 846
H.R. Moch Co. v. Rensselaer Water Co. ---- 846
Ogden v. Earl R. Howarth & Sons, Inc. ---- 847
Doyle v. South Pittsburgh Water Co. ---- 847
La Mourea v. Rhude ---- 848
Copeland v. Beard ---- 848
Note on the Power of the Contracting Parties to Vary the Promisor's Duty to the Beneficiary ---- 851
Restatement, Second, Contracts §§ 309, 311 ---- 851
Rouse v. United States ---- 851

Chapter 21. Assignment and Negotiation ---- **853**
1. Introduction ---- 853
Note on the Economic Significance of the Assignment of Claims ---- 853
Clapp v. Orix Credit Alliance, Inc. ---- 854
UCC Article 9, § 9–406(a) ---- 857
Pre–2000 UCC Article 9, § 9–318(3) ---- 857
Ertel v. Radio Corporation of America ---- 858
Note on What Formalities are Necessary to Make an Effective Assignment ---- 858
Speelman v. Pascal ---- 859
2. Assignability of Rights and Delegability of Duties ---- 860
Evening News Ass'n v. Peterson ---- 860
Restatement, Second, Contracts § 317 ---- 865
UCC § 2–210(2), (4) ---- 865
Kendall v. Ernest Pestana, Inc. ---- 865

Page

2. Assignability of Rights and Delegability of Duties—Continued
    Restatement, Second, Contracts § 322 866
    Restatement, Second, Contracts § 322, Illustrations 1, 2 866
    UCC Article 9, § 9–306(d) 866
    Pre–2000 UCC Article 9, § 9–318(4) 866
    Macke Co. v. Pizza of Gaithersburg, Inc. 866
    British Waggon Co. v. Lea & Co. 869
    Bashir v. Moayedi 869
    Restatement, Second, Contracts § 318 870
    Restatement, Second, Contracts § 318, Illustrations 1–3, 5–7 870
    Contemporary Mission, Inc. v. Famous Music Corp. 870
    UCC § 2–210(1) 871
    Sally Beauty Co. v. Nexxus Products Co. 871
    Baxter Healthcare Corporation v. O.R. Concepts, Inc. 872
    Restatement, Second, Contracts § 328 873
    Note on the Right of the Obligee Under a Contract to Demand Performance From an Assignee of the Contract 873
3. Financing Through the Assignment of Claims 874
    Background Note on Financing Through the Assignment of Claims 874
    Note on UCC Article 9 and the Law of Assignments 875
    Note on Priority Between Competing Assignees of the Same Claim 876
4. Defenses of the Obligor Against the Assignee in a Commercial Context 878
    UCC Article 9, §§ 9–404, 9–405 878
    Pre–2000 UCC Article 9, § 318(1) 878
    United California Bank v. Eastern Mountain Sports, Inc. 878
    Bank of Kansas v. Hutchinson Health Services, Inc. 878
5. Negotiation; Defenses in the Consumer Context 879
    Note on the Distinction Between Negotiable and Non–Negotiable Claims 879
    National Commission on Consumer Finance, Report—Consumer Credit in the United States 881
    Federal Trade Commission Regulations—Preservation of Consumers' Claims and Defenses 884
    UCC §§ 1–201(19), 3–104, 3–106, 3–201, 3–302, 3–305 884
    UCC Article 9, §§ 9–403, 9–404 884
    Pre–2000 UCC Article 9, § 9–318 884

PART VII. PROBLEMS OF PERFORMANCE

Chapter 22.   The Obligation to Perform in Good Faith **886**
Patterson v. Meyerhofer 886
Iron Trade Products Co. v. Wilkoff Co. 888
Restatement, Second, Contracts § 237, Illustrations 6, 7 890
Kirke La Shelle Co. v. Paul Armstrong Co. 890
Restatement, Second, Contracts § 205 890
Pre–2001 UCC Article 1 (in Force in Most States), §§ 1–201(19), 1–203 890
UCC § 2–103(1)(b) 890
2001 Version of Article 1, § 1–201(20) 890
Note on the UCC Definitions of Good Faith 890
CISG Art. 7(1) 891
Unidroit Principles of International Commercial Contracts Art. 1.7 891
Principles of European Contract Law Art. 1.201 891
Note on the Duty to Perform in Good Faith Under the UCC and Restatement Second 891
E. Allan Farnsworth, Good Faith in Contract Performance, in Good Faith and Fault in Contract Law 892
Southwest Savings and Loan Ass'n v. SunAmp Systems 893
Best v. United States National Bank 894
Hilton Hotels v. Butch Lewis Productions, Inc. 899
Bloor v. Falstaff Brewing Corp. 900

	Page
Wood v. Lucy, Lady Duff–Gordon	905
UCC § 2–306	905
Market Street Associates v. Frey	905
Wagenseller v. Scottsdale Memorial Hospital	914

Chapter 23.   The Doctrine of Substantial Performance **915**

1. The General Principle | 915
   Jacob & Youngs v. Kent | 915
   R. Danzig, The Capability Problem in Contract Law | 918
   Bruner v. Hines | 918
   Goetz & Scott, The Mitigation Principle: Toward a General Theory of Contractual Obligation | 918
   Jardine Estates, Inc. v. Donna Brook Corp. | 919
   Vincenzi v. Cerro | 919
   Kreyer v. Driscoll | 919
   O.W. Grun Roofing & Constr. Co. v. Cope | 922
2. Contracts for the Sale of Goods | 923
   UCC §§ 2–508, 2–601, 2–608, 2–612 | 923
   CISG Arts. 35(1), 37, 45, 46, 48, 49 | 923
   J. White & R. Summers, Uniform Commercial Code | 923
   Note on the Perfect–Tender Rule and the UCC | 924
   Ramirez v. Autosport | 926
   Comments of Grant Gilmore, in ALI–ABA, Advanced ALI–ABA Course of Study on Banking and Secured Transactions under the Uniform Commercial Code | 926
   T.W. Oil, Inc. v. Consolidated Edison Co. | 927
   Zabriskie Chevrolet v. Smith | 932
   Midwest Mobile Diagnostic Imaging, L.L.C. v. Dynamics Corporation of America | 932
   Note on Cure | 932

Chapter 24.   Express Conditions **934**

1. Introduction | 934
   Note on the Difference Between Promises and Conditions | 934
2. The Distinctions Between the Operation of a Promise and the Operation of a Condition | 935
   Oppenheimer & Co. v. Oppenheimer, Appel, Dixon & Co. | 935
   Merritt Hill Vineyards, Inc. v. Windy Heights Vineyard, Inc. | 940
3. Conditions Precedent and Conditions Subsequent | 942
   Note on the Distinction Between Conditions Precedent and Conditions Subsequent | 942
   Federal Rules of Civil Procedure, Rule 9(c) | 945
4. Problems of Interpretation in Distinguishing Between Conditions and Promises | 945
   Howard v. Federal Crop Insurance Corp. | 945
   Harmon Cable Communications v. Scope Cable Television | 948
   Restatement, Second, Contracts § 227 | 949
5. Conditions of Cooperation; Prevention; The Implication of a Promise From an Express Condition | 950
   Vanadium Corp. v. Fidelity & Deposit Co. | 950
   Winslow v. Mell | 953
   Lach v. Cahill | 953
   Note on Implied Conditions of Notice | 954
6. Conditions of Satisfaction | 954
   Introductory Note | 954
   McCartney v. Badovinac | 955
   Morin Building Products Co. v. Baystone Construction, Inc. | 955

Page

6. Conditions of Satisfaction—Continued
Mattei v. Hopper -- 959
Forman v. Benson --- 959
Fursmidt v. Hotel Abbey Holding Corp. ---------------------- 960
E. Allan Farnsworth, Contracts ----------------------------- 961
Restatement, Second, Contracts § 227, Illustrations 5–8 ----------- 961
7. Conditions of Payment -- 962
Koch v. Construction Technology, Inc. --------------------- 962
Note on Pay–When–Paid Provisions --------------------------- 965
8. Excuse -- 965
Aetna Casualty and Surety Co. v. Murphy ------------------ 965
Restatement, Second, Contracts § 229 ---------------------- 970
Restatement, Second, Contracts § 229, Illustrations 1, 2 --------- 970
Burne v. Franklin Life Ins. Co. ---------------------------- 971
Great American Ins. Co. v. C.G. Tate Construction Co. ----------- 972
Restatement, Second, Contracts § 230 ---------------------- 973
Restatement, Second, Contracts § 230, Illustrations 1, 2 --------- 973
Restatement, Second, Contracts § 271 ---------------------- 973
Restatement, Second, Contracts § 271, Illustrations 1, 2 --------- 973
Royal–Globe Insurance Co. v. Craven ---------------------- 974
Clark v. West --- 974
Restatement, Second, Contracts § 84 ---------------------- 974
Vanadium Corp. v. Fidelity & Deposit Co. ----------------- 974

Chapter 25. Breach and Response ---------------------------- 975
Introductory Note on the Mutual Dependency of Performances and the Order of Performance --- 975
1. The Order of Performance ----------------------------------- 977
Restatement, Second, Contracts §§ 233, 234 --------------- 977
Restatement, Second, Contracts § 234, Illustrations 1–5, 9 ------ 977
UCC §§ 2–507, 2–511 -- 978
CISG Art. 58 --- 978
Unidroit Principles of International Commercial Contracts Arts. 6.1.4, 7.1.3 --- 978
Principles of European Contract Law Arts. 7.104, 9.201 ---------- 978
Note on Concurrent Conditions ----------------------------- 978
2. Ability to Perform --- 979
Ilemar Corp. v. Krochmal ---------------------------------- 979
Kanavos v. Hancock Bank & Trust Co. -------------------- 979
3. Material Breach: Failure of Performance by One Party as an Excuse for Nonperformance by the Other ------------- 982
Restatement, Second, Contracts § 237 -------------------- 982
K & G Constr. Co. v. Harris ------------------------------ 983
E. Allan Farnsworth, Contracts ----------------------------- 987
Walker & Co. v. Harrison ---------------------------------- 988
Zulla Steel, Inc. v. A & M Gregos, Inc. ------------------ 991
Restatement, Second, Contracts §§ 241, 242 ------------- 992
CISG Arts. 25, 49 -- 992
Unidroit Principles of International Commercial Contracts Arts. 7.3.1, 7.3.5, 7.3.6 --- 992
Principles of European Contract Law Arts. 9.301, 9.302, 9.305, 9.307–309 ----- 992
Note on the Doctrines of Material Breach and Substantial Performance -------- 992
Note on the Concept of Cure Under Restatement Second ----------- 994
Unidroit Principles of International Commercial Contracts Art. 7.1.4 ---------- 995
Principles of European Contract Law Art. 8.104 ----------------- 995
Stanley Gudyka Sales, Inc. v. Lacy Forest Products Co. ----------- 995

Page

Chapter 26. Anticipatory Breach, Prospective Inability to Perform, and Adequate Assurance of Performance ----------------- **997**

1. Anticipatory Breach --- 997
   Hochster v. De la Tour-- 997
   Daniels v. Newton-- 1001
   Williston, Repudiation of Contracts ----------------------------------- 1002
   Equitable Trust Co. v. Western Pac. Ry.-------------------------------- 1002
   Ballantine, Anticipatory Breach and the Enforcement of Contractual Duties -- 1003
   Wholesale Sand & Gravel, Inc. v. Decker------------------------------- 1003
   Unique Systems, Inc. v. Zotos International, Inc. --------------------- 1005
   Thermo Electron Corp. v. Schiavone Construction Co. ------------------ 1005
   Record Club of America, Inc. v. United Artists Records, Inc. --------- 1006
   Taylor v. Johnston --- 1006
   United States v. Seacoast Gas Co.------------------------------------- 1006
   Note on Remedies for the Breach of a Contract in Which All the Duties on One Side Have Been Performed -- 1007
   Restatement, Second, Contracts §§ 250, 253, 256 ---------------------- 1008
   UCC §§ 2–610, 2–611, 2–708(1), 2–713, 2–723------------------------- 1008
   CISG Art. 72--- 1009
   Unidroit Principles of International Commercial Contracts Art. 7.3.3 -- 1009
   Oloffson v. Coomer-- 1009
   Trinidad Bean and Elevator Co. v. Frosh --------------------------- 1012
   Hess Energy, Inc. v. Lightning Oil Co. ---------------------------- 1014
   Note on the Measure of Damages for Anticipatory Breach------------- 1015
2. Prospective Inability to Perform and Adequate Assurance of Performance --- 1016
   UCC §§ 2–609, 2–702(1), 2–705(1)-------------------------------- 1016
   Restatement, Second, Contracts § 251 -------------------------- 1016
   CISG Art. 71 -- 1016
   Unidroit Principles of International Commercial Contracts Art. 7.3.4 -- 1016
   Principles of European Contract Law Art. 8.105 ----------------- 1017
   Pittsburgh–Des Moines Steel Co. v. Brookhaven Manor Water Co. -- 1017
   J. White & R. Summers, Uniform Commercial Code § 6–2 --------- 1022
   BAII Banking Corp. v. UPG, Inc. ------------------------------- 1022
   Norcon Power Partners v. Niagara Mohawk Power Corp.----------- 1023
   Note on Affirmative Recovery Under UCC § 2–609 --------------- 1029

Appendix A. The Statute of Frauds------------------------------**1031**
1. Introduction--- 1032
2. The Text of the Original Statute ------------------------------ 1032
3. The Purpose of the Statute------------------------------------ 1034
4. How it Was Decided What Kinds of Contracts Should be Required to be in Writing--- 1035
5. American Variations on the English Theme --------------------- 1037
6. Judicial Interpretations of the Various Subsections of the Statute of Frauds—Introduction ------------------------------------- 1038
7. Contracts for the Sale of an Interest in Land (Section 4(4))---- 1038
8. Contracts for the Sale of Goods------------------------------- 1039
9. Some Other Formal Requirements in the Uniform Commercial Code 1044
10. Agreements Not to be Performed Within One Year From the Making Thereof (Section 4(5))---------------------------------- 1045
11. The Suretyship Section (Section 4(2))—Generally------------- 1048
12. The Suretyship Section Continued—"The Main Purpose Rule" ------- 1049
13. The Suretyship Section Continued—Miscellaneous Problems --------- 1050
14. Promises Made by Executors and Administrators (Section 4(1))------- 1051
15. Contracts Upon Consideration of Marriage (Section 4(3)) -------- 1052
16. What Kind of Writing Will Satisfy the Statute------------------- 1053
17. Electronic Contracting and the Statute of Frauds -------------- 1057

Page

18. The Effect of Part Performance of, or Reliance Upon, an Oral Contract Within the Statute—Introduction ----------------------------- 1060
19. The Restitution of Benefits Conferred Under the Oral Agreement ---- 1060
20. Reimbursement for Reliance on the Oral Contract----------------------- 1061
21. The Right to the "Value of the Bargain" Where There Has Been Part Performance of, or Reliance Upon, the Oral Contract ----------- 1064
22. The Effect of Non–Compliance—Legal Consequences of the Unenforceable Agreement--- 1067
23. Oral Rescission --- 1069
24. Oral Modifications --- 1070
25. The Interaction of the Statute of Frauds With the Parol Evidence Rule-- 1072
26. The Interaction of the Statute of Frauds With the Remedy of Reformation --- 1073
27. Pleading and Procedural Problems in Connection With the Statute--- 1074
28. A Glance Backward and Ahead -- 1074

Appendix B. A Note on the History of Contract in the Common Law---**1077**

Appendix C. Incidents of the Seal--**1085**

Appendix D. History of the Assignability of Choses in Action-----**1087**

INDEX--- 1093

*

Table of Cases

The principal cases are in bold type. Cases cited or discussed in the text are roman type. References are to pages. Cases cited in principal cases and within other quoted materials are not included.

Abney v. Baptist Medical Centers, 597 So.2d 682 (Ala.1992), 533

Academy Chicago Publishers v. Cheever, 144 Ill.2d 24, 161 Ill.Dec. 335, 578 N.E.2d 981 (Ill.1991), **537**

Aceros Prefabricados, S.A. v. TradeArbed, Inc., 282 F.3d 92 (2nd Cir.2002), 654, 655, 656

Adams v. Lindsell, 1 Barn. & Ald. 681 (K.B. 1818), 456

Advanced, Inc. v. Wilks, 711 P.2d 524 (Alaska 1985), 234

Aetna Cas. and Sur. Co. v. Murphy, 206 Conn. 409, 538 A.2d 219 (Conn.1988), **965**

Aiello Const., Inc. v. Nationwide Tractor Trailer Training and Placement Corp., 122 R.I. 861, 413 A.2d 85 (R.I.1980), **237, 239**

Akers v. J. B. Sedberry, Inc., 39 Tenn.App. 633, 286 S.W.2d 617 (Tenn.Ct.App.1955), **424**

Alamance County Bd. of Educ. v. Bobby Murray Chevrolet, Inc., 121 N.C.App. 222, 465 S.E.2d 306 (N.C.App.1996), **795**

Alaska Northern Development, Inc. v. Alyeska Pipeline Service Co., 666 P.2d 33 (Alaska 1983), 601

Albre Marble & Tile Co. v. John Bowen Co., 338 Mass. 394, 155 N.E.2d 437 (Mass. 1959), **783**

Alfred Marks Realty Co. v. Hotel Hermitage Co., 170 A.D. 484, 156 N.Y.S. 179 (N.Y.A.D. 2 Dept.1915), 806

Algernon Blair, Inc., United States v., 479 F.2d 638 (4th Cir.1973), **351, 354**

Allen v. Harris, 1 Lord Raymond 122 (1701), 136

Allen M. Campbell Co., General Contractors, Inc. v. Virginia Metal Industries, Inc., 708 F.2d 930 (4th Cir.1983), 454

Aller v. Aller, 40 N.J.L. 446 (1878), 20

Aluminum Co. of America (ALCOA) v. Essex Group, Inc., 499 F.Supp. 53 (W.D.Pa.1980), 794, 795

American Trading & Production Corp. v. Shell Intern. Marine Limited, 453 F.2d 939 (2nd Cir.1972), 778

Amoco Production Co. v. Western Slope Gas Co., 754 F.2d 303 (10th Cir.1985), 614

Angel v. Murray, 113 R.I. 482, 322 A.2d 630 (R.I.1974), **138**

Anglia Television Ltd. v. Reed, 3 All E.R. 690 (C.A.1971), 345

ARB (American Research Bureau), Inc. v. E–Systems, Inc., 663 F.2d 189, 214 U.S.App. D.C. 12 (D.C.Cir.1980), 602

Ardente v. Horan, 117 R.I. 254, 366 A.2d 162 (R.I.1976), **430**

Arizona Cartridge Remanufacturers Ass'n, Inc. v. Lexmark Intern., Inc., 421 F.3d 981 (9th Cir.2005), 675

AROK Const. Co. v. Indian Const. Services, 174 Ariz. 291, 848 P.2d 870 (Ariz.App. Div. 1 1993), 542

A/S Apothekernes Laboratorium for Special-praeparater v. I.M.C. Chemical Group, Inc., 873 F.2d 155 (7th Cir.1989), 556

Ashland Management Inc. v. Janien, 604 N.Y.S.2d 912, 624 N.E.2d 1007 (N.Y.1993), 295

Asmus v. Pacific Bell, 96 Cal.Rptr.2d 179, 999 P.2d 71 (Cal.2000), 531

Austin v. Burge, 156 Mo.App. 286, 137 S.W. 618 (Mo.App.1911), 499

Austin Instrument, Inc. v. Loral Corp., 324 N.Y.S.2d 22, 272 N.E.2d 533 (N.Y. 1971), **120**

Austin Instrument, Inc. v. Loral Corp., 35 A.D.2d 387, 316 N.Y.S.2d 528 (N.Y.A.D. 1 Dept.1970), 107, 117, **117**

Australia, Commonwealth of v. Verwayen, 170 C.L.R. 394 (H.C.A.1990), 28

A.Z. v. B.Z., 431 Mass. 150, 725 N.E.2d 1051 (Mass.2000), 164

BAII Banking Corp. v. UPG, Inc., 985 F.2d 685 (2nd Cir.1993), 1022

Balfour v. Balfour, 2 K.B. 571 (1919), 163

Baltic Shipping Company v. Dillon, 67 ALJR 228 (1993), 308

Bank of Kansas v. Hutchinson Health Services, Inc., 13 Kan.App.2d 421, 773 P.2d 660 (Kan.App.1989), 878

Bank One, Texas, N.A. v. Taylor, 970 F.2d 16 (5th Cir.1992), 270

Bashir v. Moayedi, 627 A.2d 997 (D.C.1993), 869

Bastian v. Gafford, 98 Idaho 324, 563 P.2d 48 (Idaho 1977), **514**

Batsakis v. Demotsis, 226 S.W.2d 673 (Tex. Civ.App.-El Paso 1949), **51,** 55

Baxter Healthcare Corp. v. O.R. Concepts, Inc., 69 F.3d 785 (7th Cir.1995), 872

Beach Boys Equipment Co., Inc., People v., 273 A.D.2d 850, 709 N.Y.S.2d 729 (N.Y.A.D. 4 Dept.2000), 63

Beachcomber Coins, Inc. v. Boskett, 166 N.J.Super. 442, 400 A.2d 78 (N.J.Super.A.D.1979), 749

Beefy Trail, Inc. v. Beefy King Intern., Inc., 267 So.2d 853 (Fla.App. 4 Dist.1972), 345

Berg v. Hudesman, 115 Wash.2d 657, 801 P.2d 222 (Wash.1990), 623

Berg Agency v. Sleepworld–Willingboro, Inc., 136 N.J.Super. 369, 346 A.2d 419 (N.J.Super.A.D.1975), 541

Berke Moore Co. v. Phoenix Bridge Co., 98 N.H. 261, 98 A.2d 150 (N.H.1953), 396

Best v. United States Nat. Bank of Oregon, 303 Or. 557, 739 P.2d 554 (Or.1987), **894**

Bishop v. Eaton, 161 Mass. 496, 37 N.E. 665 (Mass.1894), **469,** 954

Bloor v. Falstaff Brewing Corp., 601 F.2d 609 (2nd Cir.1979), **900**

BMC Industries, Inc. v. Barth Industries, Inc., 160 F.3d 1322 (11th Cir.1998), 149

Board of Control of Eastern Michigan University v. Burgess, 45 Mich.App. 183, 206 N.W.2d 256 (Mich.App.1973), 18

Brinkibon v. Stahag Stahl und Stahlwarenhandels GmbH, [1982] All E.R. 293 (H.L.), 459

British Waggon Co. v. Lea & Co., [1880] 5 Q.B.D. 149, p. 869

Brown v. KMR Services Ltd., 4 All E.R. 598 (C.A.1995), 289

Bruner v. Hines, 295 Ala. 111, 324 So.2d 265 (Ala.1975), 918

Bunge Corp. v. Miller, 381 F.Supp. 176 (W.D.Tenn.1974), 801

Bunge Corp. v. Recker, 519 F.2d 449 (8th Cir. 1975), 801

Burne v. Franklin Life Ins. Co., 451 Pa. 218, 301 A.2d 799 (Pa.1973), 971

Byrne v. Auckland Irish Society Inc., [1979] 1 N.Z.L.R. 351, p. 308

Caldwell v. Cline, 109 W.Va. 553, 156 S.E. 55 (W.Va.1930), 457

Cal State Elec., Inc., United States ex rel. Palmer Const., Inc. v., 940 F.2d 1260 (9th Cir.1991), 362

Campbell v. Hostetter Farms, Inc., 251 Pa.Super. 232, 380 A.2d 463 (Pa.Super.1977), 801

Carlill v. Carbolic Smoke Ball Co., [1893] 1 Q.B. 256 (C.A.1892), **466**

Carr v. Maine Cent. R. R., 78 N.H. 502, 102 A. 532 (N.H.1917), 25

Case v. Barber, Th. Raymond 450 (1681), 136

C.C.C. Films (London) v. Impact Quadrant Films, [1985] 1 Q.B. 16, p. 346

Channel Home Centers v. Grossman, 795 F.2d 291 (3rd Cir.1986), **548**

Chaplin v. Hicks, [1911] 2 K.B. 786, p. 299, 300

Chase Precast Corp. v. John J. Paonessa Co., Inc., 409 Mass. 371, 566 N.E.2d 603 (Mass. 1991), 807

Chateau des Charmes Wines Ltd. v. Sabate USA Inc., 328 F.3d 528 (9th Cir. 2003), **672**

Chimart Associates v. Paul, 498 N.Y.S.2d 344, 489 N.E.2d 231 (N.Y.1986), 731

Chouinard v. Chouinard, 568 F.2d 430 (5th Cir.1978), 56

C. Itoh & Co. (America) Inc. v. Jordan Intern. Co., 552 F.2d 1228 (7th Cir.1977), 661

City of (see name of city)

City School Dist. of City of Elmira v. McLane Const. Co., Inc., 85 A.D.2d 749, 445 N.Y.S.2d 258 (N.Y.A.D. 3 Dept.1981), 232

Clapp v. Orix Credit Alliance, Inc., 192 Or.App. 320, 84 P.3d 833 (Or.App.2004), **854**

Clark v. West, 193 N.Y. 349, 86 N.E. 1 (N.Y. 1908), **144,** 974

Cochran v. Taylor, 273 N.Y. 172, 7 N.E.2d 89 (N.Y.1937), 19

Cole–McIntyre–Norfleet Co. v. Holloway, 141 Tenn. 679, 214 S.W. 817 (Tenn.1919), **495**

Colfax Envelope Corp. v. Local No. 458–3M, 20 F.3d 750 (7th Cir.1994), 381

Colley v. Bi-State, Inc., 21 Wash.App. 769, 586 P.2d 908 (Wash.App. Div. 3 1978), 801

Columbia Hyundai, Inc. v. Carll Hyundai, Inc., 326 S.C. 78, 484 S.E.2d 468 (S.C.1997), 644

Colvig v. RKO General, Inc., 232 Cal.App.2d 56, 42 Cal.Rptr. 473 (Cal.App. 1 Dist.1965), 278

Commonwealth of (see name of commonwealth)

Community College of Beaver County v. Community College, Soc. of the Faculty, 473 Pa. 576, 375 A.2d 1267 (Pa.1977), 625

Comunale v. Traders & General Ins. Co., 50 Cal.2d 654, 328 P.2d 198 (Cal.1958), 215

Contemporary Mission, Inc. v. Famous Music Corp., 557 F.2d 918 (2nd Cir.1977), 298, 870

Continental Sand & Gravel, Inc. v. K & K Sand & Gravel, Inc., 755 F.2d 87 (7th Cir.1985), 242

Copeland v. Beard, 217 Ala. 216, 115 So. 389 (Ala.1928), **848**

Coppola Enterprises, Inc. v. Alfone, 531 So.2d 334 (Fla.1988), **207**

C.R. Anthony Co. v. Loretto Mall Partners, 112 N.M. 504, 817 P.2d 238 (N.M.1991), 625

Creusot–Loire Intern., Inc. v. Coppus Engineering Corp., 585 F.Supp. 45 (S.D.N.Y. 1983), 1029

Crook v. Mortenson–Neal, 727 P.2d 297 (Alaska 1986), 543

C–Thru Container Corp. v. Midland Mfg. Co., 533 N.W.2d 542 (Iowa 1995), 636

Culton v. Gilchrist, 92 Iowa 718, 61 N.W. 384 (Iowa 1894), 436

Dadourian Export Corp. v. United States, 291 F.2d 178 (2nd Cir.1961), 380

Dame, People v., 289 A.D.2d 997, 734 N.Y.S.2d 789 (N.Y.A.D. 4 Dept.2001), 63

Danann Realty Corp. v. Harris, 184 N.Y.S.2d 599, 157 N.E.2d 597 (N.Y.1959), 605

Daniels v. Newton, 114 Mass. 530 (Mass.1874), 1001

Darner Motor Sales, Inc. v. Universal Underwriters Ins. Co., 140 Ariz. 383, 682 P.2d 388 (Ariz.1984), **699,** 711

Davies v. Martel Laboratory Services, Inc., 189 Ill.App.3d 694, 136 Ill.Dec. 951, 545 N.E.2d 475 (Ill.App. 1 Dist.1989), 49

Davis v. Davis, 842 S.W.2d 588 (Tenn.1992), 166

Day v. Caton, 119 Mass. 513 (Mass.1876), **511,** 513

De Cicco v. Schweizer, 221 N.Y. 431, 117 N.E. 807 (N.Y.1917), 465

Deitsch v. Music Co., 6 Ohio Misc.2d 6, 453 N.E.2d 1302 (Ohio Mun.1983), 308

Delchi Carrier SpA v. Rotorex Corp., 71 F.3d 1024 (2nd Cir.1995), **248**

Demasse v. ITT Corp., 194 Ariz. 500, 984 P.2d 1138 (Ariz.1999), 532

Denney v. Reppert, 432 S.W.2d 647 (Ky.1968), 110

D & G Stout, Inc. v. Bacardi Imports, Inc., 923 F.2d 566 (7th Cir.1991), **40,** 45, 46, 347

Dial, United States v., 757 F.2d 163 (7th Cir. 1985), 763

Diamond Fruit Growers, Inc. v. Krack Corp., 794 F.2d 1440 (9th Cir.1986), **657**

Dickinson v. Dodds, 2 Ch.Div. 463 (1876), **438**

Dills v. Town of Enfield, 210 Conn. 705, 557 A.2d 517 (Conn.1989), 773

Doering Equipment Co. v. John Deere Co., 61 Mass.App.Ct. 850, 815 N.E.2d 234 (Mass. App.Ct.2004), 355

Donovan v. RRL Corp., 109 Cal.Rptr.2d 807, 27 P.3d 702 (Cal.2001), 420, **715,** 727

Dorton v. Collins & Aikman Corp., 453 F.2d 1161 (6th Cir.1972), 653, 655

Dougherty v. Salt, 227 N.Y. 200, 125 N.E. 94 (N.Y.1919), **6,** 9, 37

Doyle v. South Pittsburgh Water Co., 414 Pa. 199, 199 A.2d 875 (Pa.1964), 847

Drennan v. Star Paving Co., 51 Cal.2d 409, 333 P.2d 757 (Cal.1958), **448**

Eagle Ins. Co. v. Albright, 3 Wash.App. 256, 474 P.2d 920 (Wash.App. Div. 2 1970), 624

Eastern Air Lines, Inc. v. Gulf Oil Corp., 415 F.Supp. 429 (S.D.Fla.1975), 794

Eastern S. S. Lines v. United States, 125 Ct.Cl. 422, 112 F.Supp. 167 (Ct.Cl.1953), 231

Egerer v. CSR West, LLC, 116 Wash.App. 645, 67 P.3d 1128 (Wash.App. Div. 1 2003), **243**

Electrical Const. & Maintenance Co., Inc. v. Maeda Pacific Corp., 764 F.2d 619 (9th Cir. 1985), 486

Elisa B. v. Superior Court, 33 Cal.Rptr.3d 46, 117 P.3d 660 (Cal.2005), 182

Embry v. Hargadine, McKittrick Dry Goods Co., 127 Mo.App. 383, 105 S.W. 777 (Mo.App.1907), **381**

Entores Ld. v. Miles Far East Corp., [1985] 2 Q.B. 327, p. 459

Equitable Trust Co. of New York v. Western Pac. Ry. Co., 244 F. 485 (S.D.N.Y.1917), 1002

Ertel v. Radio Corp. of America, 261 Ind. 573, 307 N.E.2d 471 (Ind.1974), 858

Evening News Ass'n v. Peterson, 477 F.Supp. 77 (D.D.C.1979), **860**

Everett, City of v. Sumstad's Estate, 95 Wash.2d 853, 631 P.2d 366 (Wash.1981), 742

Fairbanks, Morse & Co. v. Consolidated Fisheries Co., 190 F.2d 817 (3rd Cir.1951), 73

Falck v. Williams, [1900] Appeal Cases 176, p. 380

Falconer v. Mazess, 403 Pa. 165, 168 A.2d 558 (Pa.1961), 457

Farm Bureau Mut. Ins. Co. v. Sandbulte, 302 N.W.2d 104 (Iowa 1981), 712

Feinberg v. Pfeiffer Co., 322 S.W.2d 163 (Mo.App.1959), **29**

Fera v. Village Plaza, Inc., 396 Mich. 639, 242 N.W.2d 372 (Mich.1976), 296

Firestone & Parson, Inc. v. Union League of Philadelphia, 672 F.Supp. 819 (E.D.Pa. 1987), 742

Fisher v. Bell, 1 Q.B. 394 (1960), 421

Flower City Painting Contractors, Inc. v. Gumina Const. Co., 591 F.2d 162 (2nd Cir. 1979), 411

Foakes v. Beer, 9 App.Cas. 605 (H.L.1884), 107, **114,** 116, 136

Foley v. Interactive Data Corp., 254 Cal.Rptr. 211, 765 P.2d 373 (Cal.1988), 215

Foltz v. First Trust & Savings Bank of Pasadena, 86 Cal.App.2d 59, 194 P.2d 135 (Cal. App. 2 Dist.1948), 22

Ford v. Beach, 11 Q.B. 852 (1848), 136

Ford Motor Credit Co. v. Russell, 519 N.W.2d 460 (Minn.App.1994), 419

Forman v. Benson, 112 Ill.App.3d 1070, 68 Ill.Dec. 629, 446 N.E.2d 535 (Ill.App. 2 Dist. 1983), 959

Fox v. Webb, 268 Ala. 111, 105 So.2d 75 (Ala. 1958), 233

Foxco Industries, Ltd. v. Fabric World, Inc., 595 F.2d 976 (5th Cir.1979), **406**

Frigaliment Importing Co. v. B.N.S. Intern. Sales Corp., 190 F.Supp. 116 (S.D.N.Y.1960), **376,** 380

Fursmidt v. Hotel Abbey Holding Corp., 10 A.D.2d 447, 200 N.Y.S.2d 256 (N.Y.A.D. 1 Dept.1960), 960

Garden State Plaza Corp. v. S. S. Kresge Co., 78 N.J.Super. 485, 189 A.2d 448 (N.J.Super.A.D.1963), 618

Gardner Zemke Co. v. Dunham Bush, Inc., 115 N.M. 260, 850 P.2d 319 (N.M.1993), **645,** 653, 655

General Time Corp. v. Eye Encounter, Inc., 50 N.C.App. 467, 274 S.E.2d 391 (N.C.App. 1981), 459

Georgia Power Co. v. Cimarron Coal Corp., 526 F.2d 101 (6th Cir.1975), 793

Glass Service Co., Inc. v. State Farm Mut. Auto. Ins. Co., 530 N.W.2d 867 (Minn.App. 1995), 424

Global Octanes Texas, L.P. v. BP Exploration & Oil Inc., 154 F.3d 518 (5th Cir.1998), 322

Goldstick v. ICM Realty, 788 F.2d 456 (7th Cir.1986), 39

Goodisson v. Nunn, 4 Term R. 761 (1792), 976

Gordinier v. Aetna Cas. & Sur. Co., 154 Ariz. 266, 742 P.2d 277 (Ariz.1987), 711

Great American Ins. Co. v. C. G. Tate Const. Co., 303 N.C. 387, 279 S.E.2d 769 (N.C. 1981), 972

Greer Properties, Inc. v. LaSalle Nat. Bank, 874 F.2d 457 (7th Cir.1989), 214

Greguhn v. Mutual of Omaha Ins. Co., 23 Utah 2d 214, 461 P.2d 285 (Utah 1969), 1008

Griffith v. Brymer, 19 T.L.R. 434 (K.B.1903), **739**

Griswold v. Haven, 25 N.Y. 595 (N.Y.1862), 26

Grossman Holdings Ltd. v. Hourihan, 414 So.2d 1037 (Fla.1982), 233

Grouse v. Group Health Plan, Inc., 306 N.W.2d 114 (Minn.1981), **104,** 106

Groves v. John Wunder Co., 205 Minn. 163, 286 N.W. 235 (Minn.1939), 231

Gruen Industries, Inc. v. Biller, 608 F.2d 274 (7th Cir.1979), 581

Gurfein v. Werbelovsky, 97 Conn. 703, 118 A. 32 (Conn.1922), 99

Haddle v. Garrison, 525 U.S. 121, 119 S.Ct. 489, 142 L.Ed.2d 502 (1998), 530

Hadley v. Baxendale, 9 Exch. 341 (1854), 210, **279,** 282, 283, 284, 286, 287, 288, 290

Haines v. City of New York, 396 N.Y.S.2d 155, 364 N.E.2d 820 (N.Y.1977), **399**

Hale v. Groce, 304 Or. 281, 744 P.2d 1289 (Or.1987), **826**

Hamer v. Sidway, 124 N.Y. 538, 27 N.E. 256 (N.Y.1891), **47,** 49

Hancock Bank & Trust Co. v. Shell Oil Co., 365 Mass. 629, 309 N.E.2d 482 (Mass. 1974), **50**

Harmon Cable Communications of Nebraska Ltd. Partnership v. Scope Cable Television, Inc., 237 Neb. 871, 468 N.W.2d 350 (Neb. 1991), 948

Harrington v. Taylor, 225 N.C. 690, 36 S.E.2d 227 (N.C.1945), 159

Harris v. Time, Inc., 191 Cal.App.3d 449, 237 Cal.Rptr. 584 (Cal.App. 1 Dist.1987), 100

Hartford–Connecticut Trust Co. v. Divine, 97 Conn. 193, 116 A. 239 (Conn.1922), 21

Hatley v. Stafford, 284 Or. 523, 588 P.2d 603 (Or.1978), 593

Hawkins v. McGee, 84 N.H. 114, 146 A. 641 (N.H.1929), **190,** 193, 194, 195, 219, 302

Hayes v. Plantations Steel Co., 438 A.2d 1091 (R.I.1982), 34

H. B. Deal & Co. v. Head, 221 Ark. 47, 251 S.W.2d 1017 (Ark.1952), 846

Hector Martinez and Co. v. Southern Pac. Transp. Co., 606 F.2d 106 (5th Cir.1979), 287

Helle v. Landmark, Inc., 15 Ohio App.3d 1, 472 N.E.2d 765 (Ohio App. 6 Dist.1984), 100

Herbert Clayton & Jack Waller, Ltd. v. Oliver, 1930 App.Cas. 209 (H.L.), 277

Hess Energy, Inc. v. Lightning Oil Co. Ltd., 338 F.3d 357 (4th Cir.2003), 1014, 1015

Hill v. Gateway 2000, Inc., 105 F.3d 1147 (7th Cir.1997), 670

Hill v. Jones, 151 Ariz. 81, 725 P.2d 1115 (Ariz.App. Div. 1 1986), **757**

Hill v. Waxberg, 16 Alaska 477, 237 F.2d 936 (9th Cir.1956), 515

Hilton Hotels Corp. v. Butch Lewis Productions, Inc., 107 Nev. 226, 808 P.2d 919 (Nev.1991), 899

Hobbs v. Massasoit Whip Co., 158 Mass. 194, 33 N.E. 495 (Mass.1893), 498

Hochster v. De la Tour, 2 Ellis & Bl. 678 (Q.B.1853), **997,** 1001

Hoffman v. Horton, 212 Va. 565, 186 S.E.2d 79 (Va.1972), 422

Hoffman v. Red Owl Stores, Inc., 26 Wis.2d 683, 133 N.W.2d 267 (Wis.1965), **573**

Holman Erection Co. v. Orville E. Madsen & Sons, Inc., 330 N.W.2d 693 (Minn.1983), **478,** 485

Horning Co., Inc. v. Falconer Glass Industries, Inc., 730 F.Supp. 962 (S.D.Ind.1990), 655

Hotchkiss v. National City Bank of New York, 200 F. 287 (S.D.N.Y.1911), 394

Howard v. Federal Crop Ins. Corp., 540 F.2d 695 (4th Cir.1976), **945**

H.P. Droher and Sons v. Toushin, 250 Minn. 490, 85 N.W.2d 273 (Minn.1957), 231

H.R. Moch Co. v. Rensselaer Water Co., 247 N.Y. 160, 159 N.E. 896 (N.Y.1928), 846, 847

Hunt Foods & Industries, Inc. v. Doliner, 26 A.D.2d 41, 270 N.Y.S.2d 937 (N.Y.A.D. 1 Dept.1966), **599**

Hurst v. W.J. Lake & Co., 141 Or. 306, 16 P.2d 627 (Or.1932), 409

Hutchison v. Tompkins, 259 So.2d 129 (Fla. 1972), 316, 322

Hyman v. Cohen, 73 So.2d 393 (Fla.1954), 316

Ilemar Corp. v. Krochmal, 405 N.Y.S.2d 444, 376 N.E.2d 917 (N.Y.1978), 979

Independent Mechanical Contractors, Inc. v. Gordon T. Burke & Sons, Inc., 138 N.H. 110, 635 A.2d 487 (N.H.1993), 291

Industrial Electric–Seattle, Inc. v. Bosko, 67 Wash.2d 783, 410 P.2d 10 (Wash.1966), 487

In re (see name of party)

Interform Co. v. Mitchell, 575 F.2d 1270 (9th Cir.1978), 594, 599

International Filter Co. v. Conroe Gin, Ice & Light Co., 277 S.W. 631 (Tex.Com. App.1925), **471**

International Financial Services, Inc. v. Franz, 534 N.W.2d 261 (Minn.1995), 323

Iowa Elec. Light and Power Co. v. Atlas Corp., 467 F.Supp. 129 (N.D.Iowa 1978), 794

Iron Trade Products Co. v. Wilkoff Co., 272 Pa. 172, 116 A. 150 (Pa.1922), **888**

Jackson v. Horizon Holidays Ltd., [1975] 1 W.L.R. 1468 (1974), 308

Jacob & Youngs v. Kent, 230 N.Y. 239, 129 N.E. 889 (N.Y.1921), **915,** 918

James T. Taylor & Son, Inc. v. Arlington Independent School Dist., 160 Tex. 617, 335 S.W.2d 371 (Tex.1960), 728

Jarboe v. Landmark Community Newspapers of Indiana, Inc., 644 N.E.2d 118 (Ind.1994), 45

Jardine Estates, Inc. v. Donna Brook Corp., 42 N.J.Super. 332, 126 A.2d 372 (N.J.Super.A.D.1956), 919

Jarvis v. Swan Tours, Ltd., [1972] W.L.R. 954, pp. 307, 308

JOM, Inc. v. Adell Plastics, Inc., 193 F.3d 47 (1st Cir.1999), 663

Joseph Martin, Jr., Delicatessen, Inc. v. Schumacher, 436 N.Y.S.2d 247, 417 N.E.2d 541 (N.Y.1981), 546

Kanavos v. Hancock Bank & Trust Co., 395 Mass. 199, 479 N.E.2d 168 (Mass.1985), **979**

Kansas Mun. Gas Agency v. Vesta Energy Co., Inc., 843 F.Supp. 1401 (D.Kan.1994), 571

Kass v. Kass, 673 N.Y.S.2d 350, 696 N.E.2d 174 (N.Y.1998), 166

Keller v. Holderman, 11 Mich. 248 (Mich. 1863), 374

Kellett Aircraft Corp., In re, 186 F.2d 197 (3rd Cir.1950), 269

Kelly v. Marx, 44 Mass.App.Ct. 825, 694 N.E.2d 869 (Mass.App.Ct.1998), 322

Kendall v. Ernest Pestana, Inc., 220 Cal.Rptr. 818, 709 P.2d 837 (Cal.1985), 865

Kenford Co., Inc. v. Erie County, 502 N.Y.S.2d 131, 493 N.E.2d 234 (N.Y.1986), **292,** 294, 295, 299, 301

K & G Const. Co. v. Harris, 223 Md. 305, 164 A.2d 451 (Md.1960), **983**

KGM Harvesting Co. v. Fresh Network, 42 Cal.Rptr.2d 286 (Cal.App. 6 Dist.1995), **253**

Kingston v. Preston, 2 Douglas 689 (1773), 976

Kirke La Shelle Co. v. Paul Armstrong Co., 263 N.Y. 79, 188 N.E. 163 (N.Y.1933), 890

Kirksey v. Kirksey, 8 Ala. 131 (Ala.1845), **24,** 25, 26

Klocek v. Gateway, Inc., 104 F.Supp.2d 1332 (D.Kan.2000), 672

Klockner v. Green, 54 N.J. 230, 254 A.2d 782 (N.J.1969), **462**

Klose v. Sequoia Union High School Dist., 118 Cal.App.2d 636, 258 P.2d 515 (Cal.App. 1 Dist.1953), 485

Koch v. Construction Technology, Inc., 924 S.W.2d 68 (Tenn.1996), **962,** 965

Koehring Co. v. Glowacki, 77 Wis.2d 497, 253 N.W.2d 64 (Wis.1977), 643

Koufos v. C. Czarnikow, Ltd. [The Heron II], [1969] A.C. 350 (H.L.1967), 285

Krauss v. Greenbarg, 137 F.2d 569 (3rd Cir. 1943), 290

Krell v. Henry, 2 K.B. 740 (C.A.1903), **802**

Kreyer v. Driscoll, 39 Wis.2d 540, 159 N.W.2d 680 (Wis.1968), **919**

Kukuska v. Home Mut. Hail–Tornado Ins. Co., 204 Wis. 166, 235 N.W. 403 (Wis.1931), 498, 500

Kutzin v. Pirnie, 124 N.J. 500, 591 A.2d 932 (N.J.1991), **355**

Lach v. Cahill, 138 Conn. 418, 85 A.2d 481 (Conn.1951), 953

Laclede Gas Co. v. Amoco Oil Co., 522 F.2d 33 (8th Cir.1975), **335**

La Cumbre Golf and Country Club v. Santa Barbara Hotel Co., 205 Cal. 422, 271 P. 476 (Cal.1928), 806

Ladd v. General Ins. Co., 236 Or. 260, 387 P.2d 572 (Or.1963), 137

L. Albert & Son v. Armstrong Rubber Co., 178 F.2d 182 (2nd Cir.1949), 346, 355

La Mourea v. Rhude, 209 Minn. 53, 295 N.W. 304 (Minn.1940), 848

Lane v. KinderCare Learning Centers, Inc., 231 Mich.App. 689, 588 N.W.2d 715 (Mich. App.1998), 305

Langel v. Betz, 250 N.Y. 159, 164 N.E. 890 (N.Y.1928), 874

Laurel Race Course, Inc. v. Regal Const. Co., Inc., 274 Md. 142, 333 A.2d 319 (Md.1975), 495

Laurin v. DeCarolis Const. Co., Inc., 372 Mass. 688, 363 N.E.2d 675 (Mass.1977), 208

Lawrence v. Fox, 20 N.Y. 268 (N.Y.1859), **814,** 818

Lawson v. Martin Timber Co., 238 La. 467, 115 So.2d 821 (La.1959), 404

Lazenby Garages v. Wright, 2 All E.R. 770 (C.A.1976), 265

Lee Oldsmobile, Inc. v. Kaiden, 32 Md.App. 556, 363 A.2d 270 (Md.App.1976), 315

Lefkowitz v. Great Minneapolis Surplus Store, Inc., 251 Minn. 188, 86 N.W.2d 689 (Minn.1957), **417**

Lenawee County Bd. of Health v. Messerly, 417 Mich. 17, 331 N.W.2d 203 (Mich. 1982), **743**

Linder v. Commissioner, 68 T.C. 792 (U.S.Tax Ct.1977), 20

Lindner v. Mid–Continent Petroleum Corp., 221 Ark. 241, 252 S.W.2d 631 (Ark.1952), 98

Lingenfelder v. Wainwright Brewing Co., 103 Mo. 578, 15 S.W. 844 (Mo.1891), 107, **111,** 116

Livingstone v. Evans, [1925] 4 D.L.R. 769, p. 436

Lloyd v. Murphy, 25 Cal.2d 48, 153 P.2d 47 (Cal.1944), 806

Lobosco V. New York Telephone Company/NYNEX, 727 N.Y.S.2d 383, 751 N.E.2d 462 (N.Y.2001), 533

London Bucket Co. v. Stewart, 314 Ky. 832, 237 S.W.2d 509 (Ky.1951), **326**

Lonergan v. Scolnick, 129 Cal.App.2d 179, 276 P.2d 8 (Cal.App. 4 Dist.1954), **414**

Long Island R. Co. v. Northville Industries Corp., 393 N.Y.S.2d 925, 362 N.E.2d 558 (N.Y.1977), 1008

Loranger Const. Corp. v. E. F. Hauserman Co., 376 Mass. 757, 384 N.E.2d 176 (Mass.1978), 487

Lord's & Lady's Enterprises, Inc. v. John Paul Mitchell Systems, 46 Mass.App.Ct. 262, 705 N.E.2d 302 (Mass.App.Ct.1999), 355

Louise Caroline Nursing Home, Inc. v. Dix Const. Corp., 362 Mass. 306, 285 N.E.2d 904 (Mass.1972), **218**

Louisville Tin & Stove Co. v. Lay, 251 Ky. 584, 65 S.W.2d 1002 (Ky.1933), 499

Lucy v. Zehmer, 196 Va. 493, 84 S.E.2d 516 (Va.1954), **370**

Lynn v. Bruce, 2 Henry Blackstone 317 (1794), 136

Macke Co. v. Pizza of Gaithersburg, Inc., 259 Md. 479, 270 A.2d 645 (Md.1970), **866**

Madsen v. Murrey & Sons Co., Inc., 743 P.2d 1212 (Utah 1987), 269

M.A. Mortenson Co., Inc. v. Timberline Software Corp., 140 Wash.2d 568, 998 P.2d 305 (Wash.2000), 672

Manouchehri v. Heim, 123 N.M. 439, 941 P.2d 978 (N.M.App.1997), 243

Market Street Associates Ltd. Partnership v. Frey, 941 F.2d 588 (7th Cir.1991), **905**

Marriage of (see name of party)

Martinez v. Socoma Companies, Inc., 113 Cal.Rptr. 585, 521 P.2d 841 (Cal.1974), **835**

Masterson v. Sine, 68 Cal.2d 222, 65 Cal. Rptr. 545, 436 P.2d 561 (Cal.1968), **595**

Mattei v. Hopper, 51 Cal.2d 119, 330 P.2d 625 (Cal.1958), 99, 959

Maxon Corp. v. Tyler Pipe Industries, Inc., 497 N.E.2d 570 (Ind.App. 2 Dist.1986), 655

Maxton Builders, Inc. v. Lo Galbo, 509 N.Y.S.2d 507, 502 N.E.2d 184 (N.Y.1986), 940

Maxwell v. Fidelity Financial Services, Inc., 184 Ariz. 82, 907 P.2d 51 (Ariz.1995), **76**

Mayol v. Weiner Companies, Ltd., 98 Ill. App.3d 985, 54 Ill.Dec. 533, 425 N.E.2d 45 (Ill.App. 4 Dist.1981), **389**

McCartney v. Badovinac, 62 Colo. 76, 160 P. 190 (Colo.1916), 955

MCC–Marble Ceramic Center, Inc., v. Ceramica Nuova d'Agostino, S.p.A., 144 F.3d 1384 (11th Cir.1998), **385**

McDonald v. Mobil Coal Producing, Inc., 820 P.2d 986 (Wyo.1991), 534

McGee v. United States Fidelity & Guaranty Co., 53 F.2d 953 (1st Cir.1931), 193

McMahon Food Corp. v. Burger Dairy Co., 103 F.3d 1307 (7th Cir.1996), **127**

McQuaid v. Michou, 85 N.H. 299, 157 A. 881 (N.H.1932), 194

Mears v. Nationwide Mut. Ins. Co., 91 F.3d 1118 (8th Cir.1996), 302

Mellon Bank, N.A. v. Aetna Business Credit, Inc., 619 F.2d 1001 (3rd Cir.1980), 614

Merritt Hill Vineyards Inc. v. Windy Heights Vineyard, Inc., 472 N.Y.S.2d 592, 460 N.E.2d 1077 (N.Y.1984), **940**

Meyers v. Selznick Co., 373 F.2d 218 (2nd Cir.1966), 625

Miami Coca–Cola Bottling Co. v. Orange Crush Co., 296 F. 693 (5th Cir.1924), 94

Midwest Mobile Diagnostic Imaging, L.L.C. v. Dynamics Corp. of America, 965 F.Supp. 1003 (W.D.Mich.1997), 932

Miller v. Byrne, 916 P.2d 566 (Colo.App.1995), 216

Mills v. Wyman, 20 Mass. 207 (Mass.1825), **152,** 155

Mineral Park Land Co. v. Howard, 172 Cal. 289, 156 P. 458 (Cal.1916), 770

Minor v. Minor, 184 Cal.App.2d 118, 7 Cal. Rptr. 455 (Cal.App. 1 Dist.1960), 1007, 1008

Mishara Const. Co., Inc. v. Transit–Mixed Concrete Corp., 365 Mass. 122, 310 N.E.2d 363 (Mass.1974), 780

Missouri Public Service Co. v. Peabody Coal Co., 583 S.W.2d 721 (Mo.App. W.D. 1979), **786**

Mitchill v. Lath, 247 N.Y. 377, 160 N.E. 646 (N.Y.1928), **584**

Moolenaar v. Co–Build Companies, Inc., 354 F.Supp. 980 (D.Virgin Islands 1973), 547

Moorgate Mercantile Co. Ltd. v. Twitchings, [1976] Q.B. 225 (C.A.1975), 28

Morin Bldg. Products Co., Inc. v. Baystone Const., Inc., 717 F.2d 413 (7th Cir. 1983), **955**

Mr. Eddie, Inc. v. Ginsberg, 430 S.W.2d 5 (Tex.Civ.App.-Eastland 1968), 275

Nanakuli Paving and Rock Co. v. Shell Oil Co., Inc., 664 F.2d 772 (9th Cir.1981), **626**

Nassau Trust Co. v. Montrose Concrete Products Corp., 451 N.Y.S.2d 663, 436 N.E.2d 1265 (N.Y.1982), 149

Neeld v. American Hockey League, 439 F.Supp. 459 (W.D.N.Y.1977), 279

Neiss v. Ehlers, 135 Or.App. 218, 899 P.2d 700 (Or.App.1995), 582

Nelson v. Hazel, 91 Idaho 850, 433 P.2d 120 (Idaho 1967), 364

Neri v. Retail Marine Corp., 334 N.Y.S.2d 165, 285 N.E.2d 311 (N.Y.1972), **260**

Nester v. Michigan Land & Iron Co., 69 Mich. 290, 37 N.W. 278 (Mich.1888), 739

Nicholson v. United Pacific Ins. Co., 219 Mont. 32, 710 P.2d 1342 (Mont.1985), 215

Nicosia v. Wakefern Food Corp., 136 N.J. 401, 643 A.2d 554 (N.J.1994), 534

Nolan Ryan Baseball Card Case, 726

Norcon Power Partners, L.P. v. Niagara Mohawk Power Corp., 682 N.Y.S.2d 664, 705 N.E.2d 656 (N.Y.1998), **1023**

Norrington v. Wright, 115 U.S. 188, 6 S.Ct. 12, 29 L.Ed. 366 (1885), 924

Norse Petroleum A/S v. LVO Intern., Inc., 389 A.2d 771 (Del.Super.1978), 459

Nursing Care Services, Inc. v. Dobos, 380 So.2d 516 (Fla.App. 4 Dist.1980), **504**

Ocean Tramp Tankers Corp. v. V/O Sovfracht (The Eugenia), 2 Q.B. 226 (1963), 769

Ogden, Town of v. Earl R. Howarth & Sons, Inc., 58 Misc.2d 213, 294 N.Y.S.2d 430 (N.Y.Sup.1968), 847

Okazaki v. Collett, 2001 WL 1243362 (Utah App.2001), 137

Oliver v. Campbell, 43 Cal.2d 298, 273 P.2d 15 (Cal.1954), 353

Oloffson v. Coomer, 11 Ill.App.3d 918, 296 N.E.2d 871 (Ill.App. 3 Dist.1973), **1009,** 1012, 1015

Oppenheimer & Co., Inc. v. Oppenheim, Appel, Dixon & Co., 636 N.Y.S.2d 734, 660 N.E.2d 415 (N.Y.1995), **935**

Ortez v. Bargas, 29 Haw. 548 (Hawai'i Terr. 1927), 21

Osteen v. Johnson, 473 P.2d 184 (Colo.App. 1970), **348**

Oswald v. Allen, 417 F.2d 43 (2nd Cir.1969), 380

O. W. Grun Roofing & Const. Co. v. Cope, 529 S.W.2d 258 (Tex.Civ.App.-San Antonio 1975), 922

Pacific Gas & Elec. Co. v. G. W. Thomas Drayage & Rigging Co., 69 Cal.2d 33, 69

Cal.Rptr. 561, 442 P.2d 641 (Cal.1968), **615, 620**

Paffhausen v. Balano, 708 A.2d 269 (Me.1998), 516

Palmer Const., Inc., United States ex rel. v. Cal State Elec., Inc., 940 F.2d 1260 (9th Cir. 1991), 362

Panhandle Agri–Service, Inc. v. Becker, 231 Kan. 291, 644 P.2d 413 (Kan.1982), 246, 289

Parker v. Twentieth Century–Fox Film Corp., 89 Cal.Rptr. 737, 474 P.2d 689 (Cal. 1970), **272**

Patterson v. Meyerhofer, 204 N.Y. 96, 97 N.E. 472 (N.Y.1912), **886**

Paul v. Lankenau Hosp., 524 Pa. 90, 569 A.2d 346 (Pa.1990), 106

Pavel Enterprises, Inc. v. A.S. Johnson Co., Inc., 342 Md. 143, 674 A.2d 521 (Md.1996), 452, 487

Paymaster Oil Mill Co. v. Mitchell, 319 So.2d 652 (Miss.1975), 801

Peevyhouse v. Garland Coal & Min. Co., 382 P.2d 109 (Okla.1962), **220,** 227, 231, 234

Pembroke v. Caudill, 160 Fla. 948, 37 So.2d 538 (Fla.1948), 316

People v. _____ (see opposing party)

Perma Research & Development Co. v. Singer Co., 402 F.Supp. 881 (S.D.N.Y.1975), 295

Petropoulos v. Lubienski, 220 Md. 293, 152 A.2d 801 (Md.1959), 239

Phillips v. Moor, 71 Me. 78 (Me.1880), **488**

Pine River State Bank v. Mettille, 333 N.W.2d 622 (Minn.1983), 531

Pittsburgh–Des Moines Steel Co. v. Brookhaven Manor Water Co., 532 F.2d 572 (7th Cir.1976), **1017**

Pittsley v. Houser, 125 Idaho 820, 875 P.2d 232 (Idaho App.1994), 74

Polaroid Corp. v. Rollins Environmental Services (NJ), Inc., 416 Mass. 684, 624 N.E.2d 959 (Mass.1993), **475**

Post v. Jones, 60 U.S. 150, 19 How. 150, 15 L.Ed. 618 (1856), 57

Power Engineering & Mfg., Ltd. v. Krug Intern., 501 N.W.2d 490 (Iowa 1993), 808

Preload Technology, Inc. v. A.B. & J. Const. Co., Inc., 696 F.2d 1080 (5th Cir.1983), 454

Price v. Oklahoma College of Osteopathic Medicine and Surgery, 733 P.2d 1357 (Okla. App. Div. 4 1986), 434

Printing Center of Texas, Inc. v. Supermind Pub. Co., Inc., 669 S.W.2d 779 (Tex.App.-Hous. (14 Dist.) 1984), 925

ProCD, Inc. v. Zeidenberg, 86 F.3d 1447 (7th Cir.1996), **664,** 669

Punkar v. King Plastic Corp., 290 So.2d 505 (Fla.App. 2 Dist.1974), 275

Quinn v. Straus Broadcasting Group, Inc., 309 F.Supp. 1208 (S.D.N.Y.1970), 277

Racine & Laramie, Ltd. v. California Department of Parks & Recreation, 14 Cal.Rptr.2d 335 (Cal.App. 4 Dist.1992), 583

Raffles v. Wichelhaus (The Peerless Case), 2 Hurl. & C. 906 (1864), **374,** 375, 380, 395

Ragosta v. Wilder, 156 Vt. 390, 592 A.2d 367 (Vt.1991), **442,** 446, 448

Ramirez v. Autosport, 88 N.J. 277, 440 A.2d 1345 (N.J.1982), 926

Ramsey v. Ellis, 168 Wis.2d 779, 484 N.W.2d 331 (Wis.1992), 515

Randolph v. Castle, 190 Ky. 776, 228 S.W. 418 (Ky.1921), 354

Rassa v. Rollins Protective Services Co., 30 F.Supp.2d 538 (D.Md.1998), 322

Record Club of America, Inc. v. United Artists Records, Inc., 890 F.2d 1264 (2nd Cir.1989), 1006

R.E. Davis Chemical Corp. v. Diasonics, Inc., 826 F.2d 678 (7th Cir.1987), 264

Redgrave v. Boston Symphony Orchestra, Inc., 855 F.2d 888 (1st Cir.1988), 276, 277

Regent Lighting Corp. v. CMT Corp., 1997 WL 441297 (M.D.N.C.1997), 416

Register.com, Inc. v. Verio, Inc., 356 F.3d 393 (2nd Cir.2004), **686**

Rego v. Decker, 482 P.2d 834 (Alaska 1971), 541

Rhode Island Dept. of Transp. v. Providence and Worcester R. Co., 674 A.2d 1239 (R.I. 1996), 433

Rice v. Community Health Ass'n, 203 F.3d 283 (4th Cir.2000), 277

Ricketts v. Scothorn, 57 Neb. 51, 77 N.W. 365 (Neb.1898), 25, 27

Ridgway v. Wharton, 6 Clark's H.L. Cases 238 (1856), 541

R. J. Berke & Co., Inc. v. J. P. Griffin, Inc., 116 N.H. 760, 367 A.2d 583 (N.H.1976), 363

Rockingham County v. Luten Bridge Co., 35 F.2d 301 (4th Cir.1929), **266**

Rombola v. Cosindas, 351 Mass. 382, 220 N.E.2d 919 (Mass.1966), 297

Rouse v. United States, 215 F.2d 872, 94 U.S.App.D.C. 386 (D.C.Cir.1954), **851**

Royal–Globe Ins. Co. v. Craven, 411 Mass. 629, 585 N.E.2d 315 (Mass.1992), 974

R.R. v. M.H., 426 Mass. 501, 689 N.E.2d 790 (Mass.1998), 183

Ruxley Electronics & Construction Ltd. v. Forsyth, 3 All E.R. 268 (H.L.1995), 235

Sabo v. Delman, 164 N.Y.S.2d 714, 143 N.E.2d 906 (N.Y.1957), 604, 605

Safeco Ins. Co. of America v. City of White House, Tenn., 36 F.3d 540 (6th Cir.1994), 90

Saliba–Kringlen Corp. v. Allen Engineering Co., 15 Cal.App.3d 95, 92 Cal.Rptr. 799 (Cal.App. 2 Dist.1971), 542

Sally Beauty Co., Inc. v. Nexxus Products Co., Inc., 801 F.2d 1001 (7th Cir.1986), 871

Sanchez v. Life Care Centers of America, Inc., 855 P.2d 1256 (Wyo.1993), 534

Sardo v. Fidelity & Deposit Co. of Md., 134 A. 774 (N.J.Err. & App.1926), **692**

Scarpitti v. Weborg, 530 Pa. 366, 609 A.2d 147 (Pa.1992), **831**

Sceva v. True, 53 N.H. 627 (N.H.1873), 506

Schneberger v. Apache Corp., 890 P.2d 847 (Okla.1994), 228

Schnell v. Nell, 17 Ind. 29 (Ind.1861), **14,** 16, 17, 18

Schultz & Lindsay Const. Co. v. State, 83 N.M. 534, 494 P.2d 612 (N.M.1972), 626

Schwartzreich v. Bauman–Basch, 231 N.Y. 196, 131 N.E. 887 (N.Y.1921), 126

Scott v. Moragues Lumber Co., 202 Ala. 312, 80 So. 394 (Ala.1918), **88,** 89, 90

Seacoast Gas Co., United States v., 204 F.2d 709 (5th Cir.1953), 1006

Seaver v. Ransom, 224 N.Y. 233, 120 N.E. 639 (N.Y.1918), **819**

Security Stove & Mfg. Co. v. American Ry. Express Co., 227 Mo.App. 175, 51 S.W.2d 572 (Mo.App.1932), **341**

Seibel v. Layne & Bowler, Inc., 56 Or.App. 387, 641 P.2d 668 (Or.App.1982), 603

Selland Pontiac–GMC, Inc. v. King, 384 N.W.2d 490 (Minn.App.1986), 800

Semelhago v. Paramadevan, 136 D.L.R. (4th) 1 (1996), 339

Shadwell v. Shadwell, 30 L.J.C.P. 145 (1860), p. 109

Shea–S&M Ball v. Massman–Kiewit–Early, 606 F.2d 1245, 196 U.S.App.D.C. 338 (D.C.Cir. 1979), 271

Sherwood v. Walker, 66 Mich. 568, 33 N.W. 919 (Mich.1887), **733,** 739

Simmons v. United States, 308 F.2d 160 (4th Cir.1962), 465

S. J. Groves & Sons Co. v. Warner Co., 576 F.2d 524 (3rd Cir.1978), 270, 291

Slade's Case, 4 Coke 92b., 509

Slattery v. Wells Fargo Armored Service Corp., 366 So.2d 157 (Fla.App. 3 Dist. 1979), **107**

Smart v. Huckins, 82 N.H. 342, 134 A. 520 (N.H.1926), 396

Smith v. Beloit Corp., 40 Wis.2d 550, 162 N.W.2d 585 (Wis.1968), 276

Smith v. Tinley, 100 N.M. 663, 674 P.2d 1123 (N.M.1984), 626

Southern California Acoustics Co. v. C. V. Holder, Inc., 71 Cal.2d 719, 79 Cal.Rptr. 319, 456 P.2d 975 (Cal.1969), 485

Southern Illinois Riverboat Casino Cruises, Inc. v. Triangle Insulation and Sheet Metal Co., 302 F.3d 667 (7th Cir.2002), 654

Southern Keswick, Inc. v. Whetherholt, 293 So.2d 109 (Fla.App. 2 Dist.1974), 276

Southwest Sav. and Loan Ass'n v. SunAmp Systems, Inc., 172 Ariz. 553, 838 P.2d 1314 (Ariz.App. Div. 1 1992), 893

Sparks v. Gustafson, 750 P.2d 338 (Alaska 1988), 513

Spaulding v. Morse, 322 Mass. 149, 76 N.E.2d 137 (Mass.1947), **402**

Specht v. Netscape Communications Corp., 306 F.3d 17 (2nd Cir.2002), **676**

Speckel v. Perkins, 364 N.W.2d 890 (Minn.App. 1985), 725

Speelman v. Pascal, 222 N.Y.S.2d 324, 178 N.E.2d 723 (N.Y.1961), 859

Stanley Gudyka Sales Co., Inc. v. Lacy Forest Products Co., 915 F.2d 273 (7th Cir.1990), 995

State v. _____ (see opposing party)

Stephens v. City of Memphis, 565 S.W.2d 213 (Tenn.Ct.App.1977), 466

Step–Saver Data Systems, Inc. v. Wyse Technology, 939 F.2d 91 (3rd Cir.1991), 655

Steuart v. McChesney, 498 Pa. 45, 444 A.2d 659 (Pa.1982), **608,** 637

Stokes v. Moore, 262 Ala. 59, 77 So.2d 331 (Ala.1955), 333

Strangborough and Warner's Case, 4 Leon. 3 (1589), p. 86

Suffolk Sports Center, Inc. v. Belli Const. Corp., 212 A.D.2d 241, 628 N.Y.S.2d 952 (N.Y.A.D. 2 Dept.1995), 216

Sugarhouse Finance Co. v. Anderson, 610 P.2d 1369 (Utah 1980), 142

Sullivan v. O'Connor, 363 Mass. 579, 296 N.E.2d 183 (Mass.1973), 198, 302, 347

Swanson v. Liquid Air Corp., 118 Wash.2d 512, 826 P.2d 664 (Wash.1992), 534

Swift & Co. v. Smigel, 115 N.J.Super. 391, 279 A.2d 895 (N.J.Super.A.D.1971), 437, 438

Tayloe v. Merchants' Fire Ins. Co., 50 U.S. 390, 9 How. 390, 13 L.Ed. 187 (1850), 457

Taylor v. Caldwell, 3 Best & S. 826 (Q.B. 1863), **765,** 768

Taylor v. Johnston, 123 Cal.Rptr. 641, 539 P.2d 425 (Cal.1975), 1006

Teachers Ins. and Annuity Ass'n of America v. Tribune Co., 670 F.Supp. 491 (S.D.N.Y.1987), **557**

Teradyne, Inc. v. Teledyne Industries, Inc., 676 F.2d 865 (1st Cir.1982), 264

T.F. v. B.L., 442 Mass. 522, 813 N.E.2d 1244 (Mass.2004), **173,** 182

Thermo Electron Corp. v. Schiavone Const. Co., 958 F.2d 1158 (1st Cir.1992), 1005

Times–Mirror Co. v. Superior Court in and for Los Angeles County, 3 Cal.2d 309, 44 P.2d 547 (Cal.1935), 27, 28

Tolland Enterprises v. Scan–Code, Inc., 239 Conn. 326, 684 A.2d 1150 (Conn.1996), 137

Town of (see name of town)

Transatlantic Financing Corp. v. United States, 363 F.2d 312, 124 U.S.App.D.C. 183 (D.C.Cir.1966), **774**

Transwestern Pipeline Co. v. Monsanto Co., 53 Cal.Rptr.2d 887 (Cal.App. 2 Dist.1996), 662

Travelers Indem. Co. v. Maho Mach. Tool Corp., 952 F.2d 26 (2nd Cir.1991), 271

Travelers Ins. Co. v. Bailey, 124 Vt. 114, 197 A.2d 813 (Vt.1964), **728**

Trident Center v. Connecticut General Life Ins. Co., 847 F.2d 564 (9th Cir.1988), 619, 621

Trinidad Bean and Elevator Co. v. Frosh, 1 Neb.App. 281, 494 N.W.2d 347 (Neb.App. 1992), 1012, 1015

T.W. Oil, Inc. v. Consolidated Edison Co. of New York, Inc., 457 N.Y.S.2d 458, 443 N.E.2d 932 (N.Y.1982), **927**

Two Wheel Corp., People v., 530 N.Y.S.2d 46, 525 N.E.2d 692 (N.Y.1988), 62

Union Carbide Corp. v. Oscar Mayer Foods Corp., 947 F.2d 1333 (7th Cir.1991), 655

Unique Systems, Inc. v. Zotos Intern., Inc., 622 F.2d 373 (8th Cir.1980), 1005

United California Bank v. Eastern Mountain Sports, Inc., 546 F.Supp. 945 (D.Mass. 1982), 878

United & Globe Rubber Mfg. Cos. v. Conard, 78 A. 203 (N.J.Err. & App.1910), 20

United States v. _____ (see opposing party)

United States ex rel. v. _____ (see opposing party and relator)

United States Naval Institute v. Charter Communications, Inc., 936 F.2d 692 (2nd Cir.1991), **203**

Universal Builders Corp. v. United Methodist Convalescent Homes of Connecticut, Inc., 7 Conn.App. 318, 508 A.2d 819 (Conn.App. 1986), 1029

Valentine v. General American Credit, Inc., 420 Mich. 256, 362 N.W.2d 628 (Mich. 1984), **302**

Vanadium Corp. of America v. Fidelity & Deposit Co. of Md., 159 F.2d 105 (2nd Cir.1947), **950, 974**

Van Gulik v. Resource Development Council for Alaska, Inc., 695 P.2d 1071 (Alaska 1985), 300

Van Steenhouse v. Jacor Broadcasting of Colorado, Inc., 958 P.2d 464 (Colo.1998), 279

Van Wagner Advertising Corp. v. S & M Enterprises, 501 N.Y.S.2d 628, 492 N.E.2d 756 (N.Y.1986), 333

Van Zee v. Witzke, 445 N.W.2d 34 (S.D.1989), 197

Venture Associates Corp. v. Zenith Data Systems Corp., 96 F.3d 275 (7th Cir.1996), 570

Victoria Laundry (Windsor) Ltd. v. Newman Indus. Ltd., [1949] 2 K.B. 528, pp. 283, 286, 288

Vincenzi v. Cerro, 186 Conn. 612, 442 A.2d 1352 (Conn.1982), 919

Vines v. Orchard Hills, Inc., 181 Conn. 501, 435 A.2d 1022 (Conn.1980), 363

Vitex Mfg. Corp. v. Caribtex Corp., 377 F.2d 795 (3rd Cir.1967), 240

Vogt v. Madden, 110 Idaho 6, 713 P.2d 442 (Idaho App.1985), **491**

Vorvis v. Insurance Corp. of British Columbia, 58 D.L.R. (4th) 193 (1989), 308

Wagenseller v. Scottsdale Memorial Hosp., 147 Ariz. 370, 710 P.2d 1025 (Ariz. 1985), 106, **516,** 530, 914

Walgreen Co. v. Sara Creek Property Co., B.V., 966 F.2d 273 (7th Cir.1992), **328**

Walker & Co. v. Harrison, 347 Mich. 630, 81 N.W.2d 352 (Mich.1957), **988**

Walters v. Marathon Oil Co., 642 F.2d 1098 (7th Cir.1981), 45, 46, 347

Warfield v. Baltimore Gas and Elec. Co., 307 Md. 142, 512 A.2d 1044 (Md.1986), 21

Wasserman's Inc. v. Township of Middletown, 137 N.J. 238, 645 A.2d 100 (N.J. 1994), **308**

Watkins v. Paul, 95 Idaho 499, 511 P.2d 781 (Idaho 1973), 339

Watkins & Son v. Carrig, 91 N.H. 459, 21 A.2d 591 (N.H.1941), 141

Weathersby v. Gore, 556 F.2d 1247 (5th Cir. 1977), 337

Weaver v. American Oil Co., 257 Ind. 458, 276 N.E.2d 144 (Ind.1971), **696**

Webb v. McGowin, 232 Ala. 374, 168 So. 199 (Ala.1936), **159**

Webb v. McGowin, 27 Ala.App. 82, 168 So. 196 (Ala.App.1935), **156**

Wegematic Corp., United States v., 360 F.2d 674 (2nd Cir.1966), **771**

Weintraub v. Krobatsch, 64 N.J. 445, 317 A.2d 68 (N.J.1974), 762

Weisbrod v. Weisbrod, 27 Cal.App.2d 712, 81 P.2d 633 (Cal.App. 4 Dist.1938), 22

Wells v. Holiday Inns, Inc., 522 F.Supp. 1023 (W.D.Mo.1981), 424

West–Fair Elec. Contractors v. Aetna Cas. & Sur. Co., 638 N.Y.S.2d 394, 661 N.E.2d 967 (N.Y.1995), 965

Westlake v. Adams, 5 C.B. (N.S.) 248 (1858), 47

Westmount Country Club v. Kameny, 82 N.J.Super. 200, 197 A.2d 379 (N.J.Super.A.D.1964), 311

Westside Galvanizing Services, Inc. v. Georgia–Pacific Corp., 921 F.2d 735 (8th Cir.1990), 347

White v. Roche Biomedical Laboratories, Inc., 807 F.Supp. 1212 (D.S.C.1992), 106

Whitehead v. Villapiano, 16 N.J.Super. 415, 84 A.2d 731 (N.J.Super.A.D.1951), 20

Wholesale Sand & Gravel, Inc. v. Decker, 630 A.2d 710 (Me.1993), **1003**

Wickham & Burton Coal Co. v. Farmers' Lumber Co., 189 Iowa 1183, 179 N.W. 417 (Iowa 1920), **91**

Wickliffe Farms, Inc. v. Owensboro Grain Co., 684 S.W.2d 17 (Ky.App.1984), 801

Wilder v. Cody Country Chamber of Commerce, 933 P.2d 1098 (Wyo.1997), 277

Williams v. Favret, 161 F.2d 822 (5th Cir. 1947), 485

Williams v. Walker–Thomas Furniture Co., 350 F.2d 445, 121 U.S.App.D.C. 315 (D.C.Cir.1965), **63,** 67

Winslow v. Mell, 48 Wash.2d 581, 295 P.2d 319 (Wash.1956), 953

Winston v. Mediafare Entertainment Corp., 777 F.2d 78 (2nd Cir.1985), 560

Wired Music, Inc. v. Clark, 26 Ill.App.2d 413, 168 N.E.2d 736 (Ill.App. 2 Dist.1960), 240

Witten, In re Marriage of, 672 N.W.2d 768 (Iowa 2003), **164**

Woburn Nat. Bank v. Woods, 77 N.H. 172, 89 A. 491 (N.H.1914), 393

Wood v. Boynton, 64 Wis. 265, 25 N.W. 42 (Wis.1885), 740

Wood v. Lucy, Lady Duff–Gordon, 222 N.Y. 88, 118 N.E. 214 (N.Y.1917), **101,** 298, 905

W. R. Clarke Corp. v. Safeco Ins. Co., 64 Cal. Rptr.2d 578, 938 P.2d 372 (Cal.1997), 965

Wroth v. Tyler, [1974] Ch. 80, p. 288

Zabriskie Chevrolet, Inc. v. Smith, 99 N.J.Super. 441, 240 A.2d 195 (N.J.Super.L.1968), 932

Zigas v. Superior Court, 120 Cal.App.3d 827, 174 Cal.Rptr. 806 (Cal.App. 1 Dist.1981), 844

Zirk v. Nohr, 21 A.2d 766 (N.J.Err. & App. 1941), 20

Zulla Steel, Inc. v. A & M Gregos, Inc., 174 N.J.Super. 124, 415 A.2d 1183 (N.J.Super.A.D.1980), 991

Table of Uniform Commercial Code Citations

UNIFORM COMMERCIAL CODE

Sec.	This Work Page
Art. 1	73
Art. 1	149
Art. 1	890
Art. 1	891
1–103	73
1–103	781
1–106	257
1–106(1)	298
1–107	149
1–201	663
1–201(3)	412
1–201(11)	412
1–201(19)	884
1–201(19)	890
1–201(19)	925
1–201(20)	890
1–201(20)	891
1–201(27)	442
1–201(b)(20)	73
1–203	890
1–203	891
1–203	892
1–203	925
1–205	412
1–301	73
1–306	149
Art. 2	72
Art. 2	73
Art. 2	143
Art. 2	247
Art. 2	317
Art. 2	653
Art. 2	874
Art. 2	890
Art. 2	891
Art. 2	932
Art. 2	933
Art. 2	1015
Art. 2	1016
2–102	72
2–103(1)(b)	890
2–103(1)(b)	925
2–103(2)	925
2–105(1)	72
2–201	890
2–202	599
2–202	603
2–202	636
2–202(a)	408
2–202, Comment 1	599
2–203	20
2–203	21
2–204	544
2–204	642

UNIFORM COMMERCIAL CODE

Sec.	This Work Page
2–204	672
2–204(1)	642
2–205	22
2–205	453
2–206(1)	458
2–206(1)	461
2–206(1)	462
2–206(2)	471
2–207	435
2–207	642
2–207	643
2–207	653
2–207	655
2–207	656
2–207(1)	640
2–207(1)	653
2–207(1)	655
2–207(1)	662
2–207(1)	663
2–207(2)	662
2–207(2)(a)	653
2–207(2)(a)	657
2–207(2)(b)	653
2–207(2)(b)	654
2–207(2)(b)	655
2–207(2)(b)	657
2–207(2)(c)	653
2–207(2)(c)	657
2–207(3)	662
2–207(3)	663
2–207(3)	664
2–207, Comment	654
2–207, Comment	655
2–208	412
2–209	143
2–209	149
2–209	608
2–209(1)	608
2–209(2)	607
2–209(2)	608
2–209(4)	149
2–209(4)	607
2–209(4)	608
2–209(5)	607
2–209(5)	608
2–210	872
2–210(1)	871
2–210(2)	865
2–210(4)	865
2–302	51
2–302	66
2–302	72
2–302	76
2–302	603

UNIFORM COMMERCIAL CODE

Sec.	This Work Page
2–305	544
2–306	103
2–306	905
2–306(1)	103
2–308	544
2–309	544
2–310	544
2–310(2)	874
2–311(1)	891
2–312	749
2–313	749
2–314	749
2–315	749
2–316	603
2–318	835
2–328	422
2–328(2)	422
2–501(1)	253
2–507	978
2–508	923
2–508	925
2–508	932
2–508	933
2–508(1)	925
2–508(2)	925
2–508(2)	932
2–509	490
2–509	781
2–509(3)	490
2–510	781
2–511	978
2–601	923
2–601	924
2–601	925
2–608	923
2–608	924
2–609	1016
2–609	1023
2–609	1026
2–609	1029
2–609(4)	1029
2–610	1008
2–611	1008
2–612	923
2–612	925
2–612(2)	925
2–612(3)	925
2–613	781
2–614	781
2–614(1)	776
2–615	781
2–615	782
2–615	794
2–615	800
2–615	801
2–615	808
2–615, Comment 6	786
2–616	781
2–702(1)	1016
2–703	253
2–704(1)	253
2–704(2)	271
2–705(1)	1016
2–706	253
2–708	253
2–708	1016

UNIFORM COMMERCIAL CODE

Sec.	This Work Page
2–708(1)	1008
2–708(1)(b)	1016
2–708(2)	264
2–709	253
2–709	334
2–710	253
2–711	255
2–711(1)	242
2–712	242
2–713	242
2–713	289
2–713	1008
2–713(1)(a)	247
2–713(1)(b)	1015
2–713, Comment 4	1015
2–714	242
2–715(1)	242
2–715(2)	271
2–715(2)	289
2–716	334
2–716(1)	338
2–718	317
2–718(1)	317
2–718(2)	365
2–718(3)	365
2–719	322
2–719(1)(a)	323
2–719(2)	323
2–719(c)	81
2–719, Comment 1	334
2–723	242
2–723	253
2–723	1008
2–724	242
2–724	253
Art. 3	73
Art. 3	879
3–103(4)	135
3–104	135
3–104	884
3–106	884
3–201	884
3–302	884
3–305	884
3–311	135
Art. 4	879
Art. 5	879
Art. 5	891
Art. 8	879
Art. 9	73
Art. 9	857
Art. 9	858
Art. 9	859
Art. 9	866
Art. 9	875
Art. 9	876
Art. 9	877
Art. 9	878
Art. 9	884
9–109(a)	875
9–109(d)	876
9–306(d)	866
9–318	884
9–318(1)	878
9–318(3)	857
9–318(4)	866

UNIFORM COMMERCIAL CODE

Sec.	This Work Page
9–403	884
9–404	878
9–404	884
9–404(a)	878

UNIFORM COMMERCIAL CODE

Sec.	This Work Page
9–404(a)(2)	878
9–405	878
9–406(a)	857

*

Table of Uniform Consumer Credit Code Citations

UNIFORM CONSUMER CREDIT CODE		UNIFORM CONSUMER CREDIT CODE	
	This Work		This Work
Sec.	Page	Sec.	Page
1.301	72	5.108	72

*

Table of Citations to the Restatement of Contracts

Principal citations only.

RESTATEMENT 1ST CONTRACTS

Sec.	This Work Page
133	823
227	369
228	592
231	623
237	592
239	592
240	592
406	126

RESTATEMENT 2ND CONTRACTS

Sec.	This Work Page
1	7
17	7
20	384
24	413
26	422
30	458
32	462
33	544
34	544
37	436
38	428
39	434
41	428
42	441
43	441
45	442
49	458
54	471
56	474
59	435
60	458
63—68	458
69	490
69	494
70	490
71	7
71	51
72	51
73	109
73	127
77	96
79	7
79	51
82	151
83	151

RESTATEMENT 2ND CONTRACTS

Sec.	This Work Page
84	148
84	974
86	160
87(2)	454
89	138
90	25
151	743
152	743
153	727
154	727
154	743
155	731
159	762
161	762
175	55
176	55
201	384
204	402
205	890
208	72
209	593
210	593
211	699
212	623
213	593
214	593
215	593
216	593
219—223	412
220	410
221	409
222	409
227	949
227	961
229	970
230	973
233	977
234	977
237	890
237	982
241	992
242	992
250	1008
251	1016
253	1008
256	1008
261	779
261—272	781
271	973

RESTATEMENT 2ND CONTRACTS

Sec.	This Work Page
279	135
281	135
302	814
302	823
304	823
309	851
311	851
313	835
315	823
317	865
318	870
322	866
328	873
344	190

RESTATEMENT 2ND CONTRACTS

Sec.	This Work Page
344	350
345	350
347	239
348(2)	227
350	271
351	289
352	298
353	306
355	308
356	318
359	327
360	327
370	350
371	350

BASIC
CONTRACT LAW

Eighth Edition

*

INTRODUCTION

The law of contracts is, broadly speaking, the law of voluntary obligations; that is, the law of obligations that arise because of an express or implied commitment—in particular, a promise. (In contrast, the law of torts, broadly speaking, involves obligations that are imposed upon persons without regard to any commitment they have made.) A promise may be defined as an expression of an intention to act or refrain from acting in a specified way, so made as to justify the person to whom the expression is addressed in understanding that a commitment has been made to that person. Restatement, First, of Contracts § 2(1). A person who makes a promise is called a *promisor*. A person to whom a promise is made is called a *promisee*.

Because contract law normally does not get off the ground unless there is a promise, or at least a promissory matrix, it is useful to begin the study of contract law with a brief treatment of the moral, as opposed to the legal, obligation that a promise imposes. Although it is widely accepted in social life that there is a moral obligation to keep a promise, there has been a continuing debate over how to justify that obligation. The next two selections are important parts of that debate.

J. RAWLS, A THEORY OF JUSTICE
342–47 (1971).

... [T]he principle of fairness.... holds that a person is under an obligation to do his part as specified by the rules of an institution whenever he has voluntarily accepted the benefits of the scheme or has taken advantage of the opportunities it offers to advance his interests, provided that this institution is just or fair....

... Now the principle of fidelity [to one's promise] is but a special case of the principle of fairness applied to the social practice of promising....

... [B]y making a promise one invokes a social practice and accepts the benefits that it makes possible. What are these benefits and how does the practice work? To answer this question, let us assume that the standard reason for making promises is to set up and to stabilize small-scale schemes of cooperation, or a particular pattern of transactions. The role of promises is analogous to that which Hobbes attributed to the sovereign. Just as the sovereign maintains and stabilizes the system of social cooperation by publicly maintaining an effective schedule of penalties, so men in the absence of coercive arrangements establish and stabilize their private ventures by giving one another their word. Such ventures are often hard to initiate and to maintain. This is especially evident ... in those instances where one person is to perform before the other. For this person may believe that the second party

1

will not do his part, and therefore the scheme never gets going. It is subject to [this kind of instability] ... even though the person to perform later would in fact carry through. Now in these situations there may be no way of assuring the party who is to perform first except by giving him a promise, that is, by putting oneself under an obligation to carry through later. Only in this way can the scheme be made secure so that both can gain from the benefits of their cooperation. The practice of promising exists for precisely this purpose; and so while we normally think of moral requirements as bonds laid upon us, they are sometimes deliberately self-imposed for our advantage. Thus promising is an act done with the public intention of deliberately incurring an obligation the existence of which in the circumstances will further one's ends. We want this obligation to exist and to be known to exist, and we want others to know that we recognize this tie and intend to abide by it. Having, then, availed ourselves of the practice for this reason, we are under an obligation to do as we promised by the principle of fairness.

————

THOMAS M. SCANLON, PROMISES AND PRACTICES

19 Philosophy & Public Affairs 199 (1990).*

Consider the following example, which I will call the case of the Guilty Secret. Suppose that you are visiting for a [fifteen-week] term at a university where you know almost no one, and at a party shortly after your arrival you are surprised to encounter Harold, whom you have not seen for years. Long ago, when you were young together, Harold did something that at the time he regarded as perfectly all right but that he now recalls with shame and embarrassment. It was not really that bad (you would not be violating any duty to others by failing to tell them about it), but Harold has come to be extremely sensitive about the incident. So, when the two of you are having a brief conversation apart from the rest of the party, he brings the matter up. "Remember that awful night in Chicago?" he asks. "I'll never forget it. The thought of how I behaved that night has haunted me ever since. It would be terribly embarrassing for me if anyone here were to learn of it. I know it seems as if I'm excessively concerned with this, but will you promise not to mention it to anyone while you are here?" Suppose that you do promise and Harold, looking much relieved, moves off in the direction of the bar. I assume that as a result of this encounter you now have two moral reasons not to tell the amusing story of that night in Chicago: you would be gratuitously injuring Harold, and you would be violating the obligation to him that you have just incurred. The question is how to account for this [second] obligation ... It seems that Harold does not rely on the expectation you have created by taking or forgoing any action, because there is nothing he could do to shield himself from the embarrassment that would result from your telling the story. He can't leave town, and I am assuming that murder and bribery are ruled out. He's not that kind of guy. So there are no options that he is passing up as the days of your visit go by. There may have already been reliance of [some] kind.... If you had not promised so readily, Harold might have gotten down on his knees to plead with you or shown you pictures of his wife and children, whose happy lives, he believes, could be reduced to shambles by your loose lips. But, given that you promised to remain silent, he did not do these things. Even if there was reliance of this kind, however, it does not seem sufficiently important to be the basis of your obligation.

What is important is the value of assurance itself. It may seem that if you were to tell the Chicago story on the last night of your visit (having promised on the first night that you would not), your overall course of action would leave Harold better off than if you had told the story without having promised not to. After all, the promise gave him fifteen weeks of peace of mind. But this is to assume that the value of assurance is purely experiential, that it can be reduced to the values of freedom from worry, increased ability to sleep at night, and so on. I would maintain, however, that this assumption is false. What people in Harold's position, and many other positions, reasonably want is not mere freedom from worry; they also want certain things to happen (or, as in Harold's case, to not happen). They want to be given assurances, and they care about whether these assurances are genuine. One reason for caring is that they may rely on these assurances in deciding what to do. This is not, however, the only reason, as Harold's case demonstrates. Given the reasons which potential promisees have for wanting assurance, potential promisors have reason to want to be able to provide it. From the point of view of both potential promisees and potential promisors, then, it is reasonable to want a principle of fidelity that requires performance.... Such a principle can be stated as follows.

Principle F: If (1) A voluntarily and intentionally leads B to expect that A will do x (unless B consents to A's not doing x); (2) A knows that B wants to be assured of this; (3) A acts with the aim of providing this assurance, and has good reason to believe that he or she has done so; (4) B knows that A has the beliefs and intentions just described; (5) A intends for B to know this, and knows that B does know it; and (6) B knows that A has this knowledge and intent; then, in the absence of some special justification. A must do x unless B consents to x's not being done.

The fact that potential B's have reason to insist on such a duty of fidelity is in my view sufficient to establish it as a duty unless it would be reasonable for potential A's to reject such a principle. Would the duty described impose an unreasonable burden on those who create expectations in others? They could of course avoid bearing any burden at all simply by refraining from intentional creation of any expectations about their future conduct. This would be quite limiting if it meant that we could never tell people what we intend to do without being bound to seek their permission before changing course. But Principle F would not have this effect, since it applies only when A knows that B wants assurance, and when A has acted with the aim of supplying this assurance and has reason to believe that he or she has done so, and when this and other features of the situation are mutual knowledge. No one could reasonably object to a principle imposing, in such cases, at least a duty to warn at the time the expectation is created—to say, "This is my present intention, but of course I may change my mind," or to make this clear in some other way if it is not already clear in the context. Since the burden of such a duty to warn is so slight, one can hardly complain if failure to fulfill it leaves one open to the more stringent duty to perform or seek permission to substitute. But this is just the duty stated by Principle F, since the conditions of that principle specify that no such warning has been given and, indeed, that quite the opposite has occurred, since A has refrained from providing such a warning in situations in which he or she knows that the difference between an expectation qualified by that warning and one without that qualification is important to B.

When the conditions of Principle F are fulfilled, it would be wrong, in the absence of special justification, for the first party not to perform. In addition, the second party has a "right to rely" on this performance: that is, the second party has grounds for insisting that the first party fulfill the expectation he or she has created. . . .

Saying "I promise to . . ." normally binds one to do the thing promised, but it does not bind unconditionally or absolutely. It does not bind unconditionally because the binding force of promising depends on the conditions under which the promise is made: a promise may not bind if it was obtained by coercion or through deceit. It does not bind absolutely because, while a promise binds one against reconsidering one's intention simply on grounds of one's own convenience, it does not bind one to do the thing promised whatever the cost to oneself and others.

GARDNER, OBSERVATIONS ON THE COURSE IN CONTRACTS, 1934. "The ethical problems involved in the law of contracts result as I see them from four elementary ideas:

"(1) *The Tort Idea,* i.e. that one ought to pay for the injuries he does to another. As applied to promises this means that one ought to pay for losses which others suffer in reliance on his promises.

"(2) *The Bargain Idea,* i.e. that one who gets anything of value by promising to pay an agreed price for it ought to pay the seller the price he agreed.

"(3) *The Promissory Idea,* i.e. that promises are binding in their own nature and ought to be kept in all cases.

"(4) *The Quasi–Contractual Idea,* i.e. that one who receives anything of value from another ought to pay for it unless it came to him as a voluntary gift.

"These ideas, which at first seem trite and wholly harmonious, are in fact profoundly in conflict. The first and fourth proceed from the premise that justice is to be known after the event, and that it is the business of the court to correct whatever consequences of voluntary intercourse between men may be found to have turned out unjustly. The second and third proceed from the premise that justice is to be known before the event in transactions voluntarily entered into, and that it is the parties' business to settle the justice and injustice of their voluntary transactions at the start. The conflict between these two standpoints is perennial; it can be traced throughout the history of the law of contracts and noted in nearly every debatable contact question; there is no reason to think that it can ever be gotten rid of or to suppose that the present compromises of the issue will be any more permanent than the other compromises that have gone before."

Part I

WHAT PROMISES SHOULD THE LAW ENFORCE?—THE DOCTRINE OF CONSIDERATION

The first great question of contract law is, what promises should and does the law enforce? This question is subsumed under the heading of *consideration,* and it is the question that will be addressed in Part I of this Book.

Part I consists of four Chapters. Chapter 1 primarily concerns the enforceability of donative promises, that is, promises to make a gift. Chapter 2 concerns bargain promises. Chapter 3 concerns promises to pay for a benefit that was previously conferred by the promisee upon the promisor. Chapter 4 concerns the limits of contract as a technique for social ordering.

Chapter 1

DONATIVE PROMISES, FORM, AND RELIANCE

SECTION 1. SIMPLE DONATIVE PROMISES

Section 1 begins with *simple donative promises*, that is, promises that are made for affective reasons (such as love, friendship, or the like); that are not cast in a form to which modern contract law gives special significance; and that have not been demonstrably relied upon. Section 2 considers donative promises that are cast in a special form. Section 3 considers the effect of reliance.

DOUGHERTY v. SALT

New York Court of Appeals, 1919.
227 N.Y. 200, 125 N.E. 94.

CARDOZO, J. The plaintiff, a boy of eight years, received from his aunt, the defendant's testatrix, a promissory note for $3,000 payable at her death or before. Use was made of a printed form, which contains the words "value received." How the note came to be given, was explained by the boy's guardian, who was a witness for his ward. The aunt was visiting her nephew. "When she saw Charley coming in, she said 'Isn't he a nice boy?' I answered her, yes, that he is getting along very nice, and getting along nice in school, and I showed where he had progressed in school, having good reports, and so forth, and she told me that she was going to take care of that child, that she loved him very much. I said, 'I know you do, Tillie, but your taking care of the child will be done probably like your brother and sister done, take it out in talk.' She said: 'I don't intend to take it out in talk, I would like to take care of him now.' I said, 'Well, that is up to you.' She said, 'Why can't I make out a note to him?' I said, 'You can, if you wish to.' She said, 'Would that be right?' And I said, 'I do not know, but I guess it would; I do not know why it would not.' And she said, 'Well, will you make out a note for me?' I said, 'Yes, if you wish me to,' and she said, 'Well, I wish you would.'" A blank was then produced, filled out, and signed. The aunt handed the note to her nephew

6

with these words, "You have always done for me, and I have signed this note for you. Now, do not lose it. Some day it will be valuable."

The trial judge submitted to the jury the question whether there was any consideration for the promised payment. Afterwards, he set aside the verdict in favor of the plaintiff, and dismissed the complaint. The Appellate Division, by a divided court, reversed the judgment of dismissal, and reinstated the verdict on the ground that the note was sufficient evidence of consideration.

We reach a different conclusion. The inference of consideration to be drawn from the form of the note has been so overcome and rebutted as to leave no question for a jury. This is not a case where witnesses summoned by the defendant and friendly to the defendant's cause, supply the testimony in disproof of value (Strickland v. Henry, 175 N.Y. 372). This is a case where the testimony in disproof of value comes from the plaintiff's own witness, speaking at the plaintiff's instance. The transaction thus revealed admits of one interpretation, and one only. The note was the voluntary and unenforceable promise of an executory gift (Harris v. Clark, 3 N.Y. 93; Holmes v. Roper, 141 N.Y. 64, 66). This child of eight was not a creditor, nor dealt with as one. The aunt was not paying a debt. She was conferring a bounty (Fink v. Cox, 18 Johns. 145). The promise was neither offered nor accepted with any other purpose. "Nothing is consideration that is not regarded as such by both parties" (Philpot v. Gruninger, 14 Wall. 570, 577; Fire Ins. Ass'n. v. Wickham, 141 U.S. 564, 579; Wisconsin & M. Ry. Co. v. Powers, 191 U.S. 379, 386; DeCicco v. Schweizer, 221 N.Y. 431, 438). A note so given is not made for "value received," however its maker may have labeled it. The formula of the printed blank becomes, in the light of the conceded facts, a mere erroneous conclusion, which cannot overcome the inconsistent conclusion of the law (Blanshan v. Russell, 32 App.Div. 103; affd., on opinion below, 161 N.Y. 629; Kramer v. Kramer, 181 N.Y. 477; Bruyn v. Russell, 52 Hun, 17). The plaintiff, through his own witness, has explained the genesis of the promise, and consideration has been disproved (Neg.Instr.Law, sec. 54; Consol.Laws, chap. 43).

We hold, therefore, that the verdict of the jury was contrary to law, and that the trial judge was right in setting it aside. . . .

Hiscock, Ch. J., Chase, Collin, Hogan, Crane and Andrews, JJ., concur.

Judgment accordingly.

––––––––

RESTATEMENT, SECOND, CONTRACTS §§ 1, 17, 71, 79

[See Selected Source Materials Supplement*]

––––––––

NOTE ON THE RESTATEMENT OF CONTRACTS

The American Law Institute (ALI) is an organization composed of lawyers, judges, and legal academics. The ALI's objective is to promote the

---

* References in this casebook to "Selected Source Materials Supplement" are to S. Bur- ton & M. Eisenberg, Contract Law: Selected Source Materials (West Publishing Co.).

clarification and simplification of the law and its better adaptation to social needs. It has sought to achieve this objective in part by preparing "Restatements" of various branches of the common law, including Contracts.

The theory of the Restatements has changed somewhat over time. The introduction to the Restatement [First] of Contracts stated that "The function of the Institute is to state clearly and precisely in the light of the [courts'] decisions the principles and rules of the common law." The present theory is that the ALI "should feel obliged in [its] deliberations to give weight to all of the considerations that the courts, under a proper view of the judicial function, deem it right to weigh in theirs." Wechsler, The Course of the Restatements, 55 A.B.A.J. 147, 156 (1969).

The first Restatement of Contracts (hereafter cited as Restatement First) was published by the ALI in 1932. The Reporter was Samuel Williston of the Harvard Law School. Williston was one of the leaders of a school of thought that is now called classical contract law. This school treated contract law as a set of axioms that were deemed to be self-evident, together with a set of subsidiary rules that were purportedly deduced from the axioms. Among the axioms of classical contract law were that bargains constituted consideration, that bargains were formed by offer and acceptance, and that the remedy for breach of an enforceable promise was expectation damages.

Many of the original Restatements were eventually superseded by revised versions. Restatement, Second, of Contracts (hereafter cited as Restatement Second) was published in 1981. The Reporter for the first portion of Restatement Second was Robert Braucher, then of Harvard Law School. On Professor Braucher's appointment to the bench, he was succeeded as Reporter by Professor Allan Farnsworth of Columbia.

Arthur Corbin of the Yale Law School was, until his death, Consultant to the Restatement Second. From the 1920s through the 1960s, Williston and Corbin were the two giants of contract law. Each authored famous multi-volume treatises on contracts that are still in use. Williston was a leader of the classical school of contract law. Corbin was instrumental in laying the foundation for modern contract law. To a significant extent, the differences in approach between Williston and Corbin are paralleled by differences in approach between Restatement First and Restatement Second. Restatement First had much that is admirable, and Restatement Second marks a considerable advance over Restatement First. However, both the theory of the Restatements and other factors often work to prevent a Restatement from setting out the best possible rule in any given area. The Restatements of Contracts are not exceptions.

———

NOTE ON THE CONCEPT OF CONSIDERATION

The term *consideration* may be conceived in two very different ways, one broad and one narrow.

Under the *broad* conception, consideration is simply a collective term for the whole set of elements that make promises legally enforceable. Bargain is one such element. As will be seen in subsequent Chapters, there are others, such as reliance.

Under the *narrow* conception of consideration, consideration is equated with the single element of bargain. This narrow conception, often referred to as the "bargain theory of consideration," was adopted in Restatement First and continued in Restatement Second. In Restatement Second, this conception is embodied in section 71(1): "To constitute consideration, a performance or a return promise must be bargained for."

The bargain theory of consideration can produce two kinds of distortion in contract law. The first kind of distortion concerns terminology. As will be seen in succeeding Chapters, a number of elements other than bargain should and do make a promise legally enforceable. Restatement Second recognizes these elements, but only in sections that are grouped in a Topic called "Contracts [Enforceable] Without Consideration." The result is that under the terminology of Restatement Second, a promise needs consideration to be enforceable unless it does not need consideration to be enforceable.

The second distortion produced by the bargain theory of consideration is substantive. If consideration means the whole set of elements that make promises legally enforceable, the meaning of the term will be continually adjusted as it becomes socially desirable to add new elements or drop old ones. In contrast, the bargain theory of consideration suggests a closed system, in which all nonbargain promises are presumptively unenforceable. If taken seriously, such an approach tends to stifle the growth of the law.

The bargain theory of consideration is certainly not mandated by contract doctrine. On the contrary, the theory cannot account for many elements of enforceability, such as reliance, except by relegating these elements to the purgatory of "Contracts [Enforceable] Without Consideration." Nor is the theory mandated by judicial decisions. A number of courts use the term "consideration" as equivalent to bargain, but many other courts use the term in its broader sense to embrace nonbargain elements, such as reliance, that make a promise enforceable.

––––––

NOTE ON GIFTS

The common law distinguishes between a gift and a promise to make a gift. As *Dougherty v. Salt* illustrates, a promise to make a gift is not enforceable as such. (As will be shown later in this Chapter, such a promise may be enforceable if other elements, such as reliance, are present.) In contrast, a completed gift is recognized by the law as a valid and binding legal transaction, which cannot be reversed by the donor, in the absence of fraud or the like. Thus if A promises to give B $1000 as a gift, A's promise is unenforceable, absent reliance or some other special element. However, if A keeps her promise and gives B the $1000, A cannot recover the money; it belongs to B.

The classical way to make a gift is to deliver possession of the gift to the donee. However, that is not the only way. Normally, a person who owns personal property can make a gift of that property, even without delivering possession, by executing a signed writing in which the donor and the donee are identified, the subject matter of the gift is described, the nature of the interest given is specified, and the donor manifests an intention to make the gift by means of the instrument. (Such a writing is known as a *deed of gift* or an *inter vivos document of transfer*.) This rule is exemplified by two illustrations to Section 32.2 of the Restatement, Second, of the Law of Property (Donative Transfers) (1990).

> Illustration 3. O, by an inter vivos donative document of transfer, transfers the ownership of his watch to his son S. O continues to wear the watch after such transfer. S can demand possession of the watch at any time but does not. O dies. S requests the watch from the personal representatives of O's estate. S is entitled to the watch.

> Illustration 4. O, by an inter vivos donative document of transfer, transfers his stock in the X Company to his daughter D. The stock certificate is retained by O. After such transfer and before the stock certificate has been delivered to D or transferred to D's name on the books of the corporation, a dividend is declared. The dividend is made payable to O and received by O. D is entitled to the amount of the dividend check.

(Notice that the technique of using a deed of gift will not work where the donor wants to make a gift of services, or to make a gift of personal property that she does not presently own, or to make only a future rather than a present gift.)

There is at least one other way to make what is in effect a gift. A person may declare herself *trustee* of property she owns, for the benefit of another. Under the law of trusts, a person who makes such a declaration continues to hold *legal title* to the property, but *beneficial ownership* (that is, the right to enjoy the benefits of the property) vests in the beneficiary of the trust.

————

NOTE ON DONATIVE PROMISES

1. Why does a person make a donative promise? Why does she not simply wait until the time when she expects to perform, and make the gift then, rather than committing herself in advance to make the gift?*

One possibility is that the promisor believes that she has better and worse instincts at different times; that her present intention to make the gift reflects his better instincts; and that if she does not commit himself to making the gift now, her worse instincts may keep her from actually making the gift later.

Another possibility is that the promisor hopes to derive satisfaction not only from the promisee's happiness and gratitude at the time the gift is actually made, but from the promisee's happiness and gratitude between the time the promise is made and the time the gift is made.

Still a third possibility is that the promisor wants to maximize the promisee's wealth or satisfaction. Making a promise before making the actual gift may create more wealth or satisfaction than making the gift without having made a promise. This is because if the promise is made before the gift is given, the promisee may be able to make plans on the basis of the promise

---

* In this casebook, unless the context indicates otherwise, feminine pronouns will be used to refer to promisors, and masculine pronouns will be used to refer to promisees.

that will enhance the value of the gift. For example, suppose Aunt intends to pay for Niece's college education, and Niece would not be able to afford college if Aunt did not pay. If Aunt keeps her intention to herself, Niece may plan her high school education to prepare herself for the job market rather than for college. If instead Aunt promises Niece a college education, Niece can take a curriculum in high school that prepares her for college. If she does, college will be more valuable to her than it would have been if she had not prepared for it. This is an example of a more general phenomenon. Promisees may frequently take action in reliance on a promise that is intended to enhance the value of the promise. This is even more obvious in a commercial setting than in a donative setting. For example, suppose a music group agrees with a promoter that it will play a concert in two months. The promoter can then take actions in reliance on the promise, such as advertising the concert, that will increase gate receipts from the concert and therefore increase the value of the music group's promise. Reliance that increases the value of a promise is sometimes referred to as *beneficial reliance*.

2. Donative promises may seem to comprise an exceptionally small segment of contract law. In fact, however, the treatment of donative promises is fundamental to contract doctrine, particularly consideration. Under classical contract law, the basic fault line in consideration ran at the boundary between bargain promises and gratuitous promises, because under the bargain theory of consideration every promise that was not a bargain promise was viewed as a gratuitous promise. "Gratuitous" was therefore virtually synonymous with "unenforceable," so that in a sense the main enterprise of consideration in classical contract law doctrine was to separate out enforceable promises from donative promises.

The legal treatment of donative promises also carries heavy social freight. The concept that bargain promises are legally enforceable, while donative promises are not, implicates fundamental questions of social value. The enforceability of donative promises also bears directly on one of the deepest social questions of contract law: whether contract law should be based on (i) the deontological objective of ensuring that promisors keep their promises, because it is morally right that promises are kept; or (ii) more particular, utilitarian objectives, such as compensating injured promisees and increasing social wealth.

In Consideration and Form, 41 Colum. L. Rev. 799 (1941), Lon Fuller posited various substantive and "formal" bases—we might now say "process" bases—for enforcing promises. The two process bases were the provision of evidentiary safeguards that ensured that a promise had actually been made, and cautionary safeguards that prevented inconsiderate action by the promisor.

Simple donative promises fall short on both process bases. First, they raise serious problems of proof: Because of the nature of such promises, a false claim by A that B made such a promise may be found credible by a jury despite the absence of corroborating evidence. Second, simple donative promises raise serious problems of deliberativeness, because characteristically a donative promisor is emotionally involved with the promisee, and therefore may tend to look mainly to the promisee's interests rather than her own.

The substantive and process bases for enforcing, or not enforcing, any given kind of promise are interrelated. The stronger the substantive interest in enforcing a given kind of promise, the more the law can tolerate process concerns. Certainly there are some substantive reasons for enforcing simple donative promises. For example, a failure to keep a donative promise causes an injury to the promisee, in the form of disappointment. Moreover, gifts probably tend to move assets from persons with more wealth to persons with less. Furthermore, the enforcement of donative promises might increase the rate of beneficial reliance.

However, the strength of these substantive bases for enforcing simple donative promises is open to question. For example, although a non-relying donative promisee may suffer disappointment if the promise is broken, that injury seems relatively slight. Similarly, the social-welfare effects of making simple donative promises enforceable are indeterminate: Certainly, it is possible that more gifting would occur if simple donative promises were enforceable, because unwilling donative promisors would be forced to keep their promises. However, it is also possible that making simple donative promises enforceable would result in less gifting: Many donative promisors make gifts only because they have earlier promised to do so, and many prospective donative promisors might refrain from promising in the first place if the promise was legally enforceable.

Moreover, just as a donative promisor has moral obligations, so too does a donative promisee. Suppose that a promisor lacks an objectively satisfactory excuse for not keeping a promise, but nevertheless does not want to perform. Perhaps the promisor has an excuse that he believes is satisfactory, although reasonable persons would not agree. Perhaps the promisor has simply changed his mind. Under the morality of *duty*, the promisor is obliged to keep his promise. Accordingly, in the world of commercial contracts, if the promisor has a duty to keep his promise, it is normally proper for the promisee to enforce the promise. In the world of gift, however, matters are not so straightforward. It may be wrong for a donative promisor to break a donative promise, but also wrong for the promisee to insist on performance, because under the morality of *aspiration*, where a donative promise is made for affective reasons, such as love or friendship, a donative promisee is often morally obliged to release a repenting promisor.

An article by Andrew Kull, Reconsidering Gratuitous Promises, 21 J. Legal Stud. 39 (1992), is instructive in this regard. Kull argues that simple donative promises should be enforceable. However, Kull also concludes that if, say, Uncle has made a donative promise to Nephew and later changes his mind, it might well be "unthinkable" for Nephew to sue Uncle. But if suit is unthinkable, how can enforceability be desirable? The principle that simple donative promises are unenforceable prevents the unthinkable from occurring, by capturing, as an enforceability regime would not, the promisee's moral obligation to release a repenting promisor from a simple, affective donative promise.

NOTE ON CONDITIONAL DONATIVE PROMISES

Bargain promises often are made in a conditional form. For example, A may say to B, "If you mow my lawn, I will pay you $20." Donative promises may also be made in conditional form. For example, C may say to D, "If you select a car costing no more than $15,000, I will buy it for you as a graduation present.'' What's the difference between a conditional bargain promise and a conditional donative promise? In the case of a bargain, the parties view performance of the condition as the *price* of the promise. In the case of a gift, the parties view performance of the condition as the necessary *means* to make the gift, not as the price of the gift. Thus in the first example, B's act of mowing A's lawn is viewed by A and B as the price that B must pay to get $20 from A. (And, of course $20 is viewed by A and B as the price that A must pay to get B to mow her lawn.) In contrast, in the second example, D's act of selecting a car is not viewed by C and D as a price D pays to get the gift, but as a mechanical requisite for making the gift.

How do we know whether performance of a condition in a conditional promise is a bargained-for price or simply the necessary means make the gift? We make a judgement based on all the circumstances and on our knowledge of how people normally act. All this was well put by Williston, who used a now-famous example:

> It is of course ... possible to make a gratuitous conditional promise.... [A]ny event may be named in a promise as fixing the moment, on the happening of which a promisor (not as an exchange for the happening but as a mere coincidence in time) will perform a promise intended and understood to be gratuitous. The same thing, therefore, stated as the condition of a promise may or may not be consideration, according as a reasonable man would or would not understand that the performance of the condition was requested as the price or exchange for the promise. If a benevolent man says to a tramp, "if you go around the corner to the clothing shop there, you may purchase an overcoat on my credit," no reasonable person would understand that the short walk was requested as the consideration for the promise, but that in the event of the tramp going to the shop the promisor would make him a gift. Yet the walk to the shop is in its nature capable of being consideration. It is a legal detriment to the tramp to take the walk, and the only reason why the walk is not consideration is because on a reasonable interpretation, it must be held that the walk was not requested as the price of the promise, but was merely a condition of a gratuitous promise.

Williston on Contracts § 112 (3d ed. 1957).

———

SECTION 2. THE ELEMENT OF FORM

———

VON MEHREN, CIVIL–LAW ANALOGUES TO CONSIDERATION: AN EXERCISE IN COMPARATIVE ANALYSIS, 72 Harv.L.Rev. 1009, 1016–1017 (1959). "In French, German, and common–law thinking four general, interrelated concerns lead the systems to treat a given transaction type as unenforceable. There is a concern for evidentiary security, a desire to protect both the individual citizen and the courts against manufactured evidence and difficulties resulting from insufficiencies in the available proof. The individual must be safeguarded against his own rashness and the importuning of others. The enforceable obligation needs to be marked off or signalized so as to ensure an awareness on the individual's part that his action may have legal significance and to simplify the administration of justice. Finally, there is unwillingness to enforce transaction types considered suspect or of marginal value. To facilitate exposition, these four concerns will be referred to as evidentiary, cautionary, channeling, and deterrent policies.''

NOTE ON THE CHANNELING FUNCTION
OF CONTRACT–LAW RULES

The channeling function referred to by von Mehren depends on the assumption that actors will know contract law, so that rules of contract law can in fact provide incentives and disincentives to engage in given kinds of behavior. However, experience suggests that most nonlawyers don't know contract law.

Whether actors are likely to know any given rule of contract law will depend in part on whether the rule is one that is probably relevant only to actors who regularly negotiate contracts, or is relevant even to actors who don't regularly negotiate contracts. However, even actors who regularly negotiate contracts are likely to know the relevant rules of contract law only if they are tutored by lawyers on those rules, or get into court on a repeated basis, or are normally counseled when they make contracts. In most cases, none of these conditions will prevail. For example, even lawyers who regularly draft contracts for a certain client are unlikely to tutor the client on contract law, except to the extent that a given contract raises minefield issues. This is especially true where the client is an organization and decisionmaking power over contracts is dispersed over a large number of different persons in the organization.

Whether it is likely that actors will know any given rule of contract law therefore must be determined on a rule-by-rule basis. There are some areas where it *is* likely that actors will either know the law in advance or will be counseled on the law when they make a contract. In such cases, contract law does provide incentives and disincentives. In other cases, it doesn't.

SCHNELL v. NELL

Supreme Court of Indiana, 1861.
17 Ind. 29, 79 Am.Dec. 453.

Perkins, J. Action by J.B. Nell against Zacharias Schnell, upon the following instrument:

"This agreement, entered into this 13th day of February, 1856, between Zach. Schnell, of Indianapolis, Marion county, State of Indiana, as party of the first part, and J.B. Nell, of the same place, Wendelin Lorenz, of Stilesville, Hendricks county, State of Indiana, and Donata Lorenz, of Frickinger, Grand Duchy of Baden, Germany, as parties of the second part witnesseth: The said Zacharias Schnell agrees as follows:

Whereas his wife, Theresa Schnell, now deceased, has made a last will and testament in which, among other provisions, it was ordained that every one of the above-named second parties, should receive the sum of $200; and whereas the said provisions of the will must remain a nullity, for the reason that no property, real or personal, was in the possession of the said Theresa Schnell, deceased, in her own name, at the time of her death, and all property held by Zacharias and Theresa Schnell jointly, therefore reverts to her husband; and whereas the said Theresa Schnell has also been a dutiful and loving wife to the said Zach. Schnell, and has materially aided him in the acquisition of all property, real and personal, now possessed by him; for, and in consideration of all this and the love and respect he bears to his wife; and, furthermore, in consideration of one cent, received by him of the second parties, he, the said Zach. Schnell, agrees to pay the above named sums of money to the parties of the second part, to wit: $200 to the said J.B. Nell; $200 to the said Wendelin Lorenz; and $200 to the said Donata Lorenz, in the following installments, viz., $200 in one year from the date of these presents; $200 in two years; and $200 in three years; to be divided between the parties in equal portions of $66⅔ each year, or as they may agree, till each one has received his full sum of $200. And the said parties of the second part, for, and in consideration of this, agree to pay the above-named sum of money (one cent), and to deliver up to said Schnell, and abstain from collecting any real or supposed claims upon him or his estate, arising from the said last will and testament of the said Theresa Schnell, deceased. In witness whereof, the said parties have, on this 13th day of February, 1856, set hereunto their hands and seals. Zacharias Schnell. [Seal.] J.B. Nell. [Seal.] Wen. Lorenz. [Seal.]''

The complaint contained no averment of a consideration for the instrument, outside of those expressed in it; and did not aver that the one cent agreed to be paid, had been paid or tendered.

A demurrer to the complaint was overruled.

The defendant answered, that the instrument sued on was given for no consideration whatever.

He further answered, that it was given for no consideration, because his said wife, Theresa, at the time she made the will mentioned, and at the time of her death, owned neither separately, nor jointly with her husband, or anyone else (except so far as the law gave her an interest in her husband's property), any property, real or personal, etc. . . .

The court sustained a demurrer to these answers, evidently on the ground that they were regarded as contradicting the instrument sued on, which particularly set out the considerations upon which it was executed. But the instrument is latently ambiguous on this point. See Ind.Dig., p. 110.

The case turned below, and must turn here, upon the question whether the instrument sued on does express a consideration sufficient to give it legal obligation, as against Zacharias Schnell. It specifies three distinct considerations for his promise to pay $600:

(1) A promise, on the part of the plaintiffs, to pay him one cent.

(2) The love and affection he bore his deceased wife, and the fact that she had done her part, as his wife, in the acquisition of the property.

(3) The fact that she had expressed her desire, in the form of an inoperative will, that the persons named therein should have the sums of money specified.

The consideration of one cent will not support the promise of Schnell. It is true, that as a general proposition, inadequacy of consideration will not vitiate an agreement. Baker v. Roberts, 14 Ind. 552. But this doctrine does not apply to a mere exchange of sums of money of coin, whose value is exactly fixed, but to the exchange of something of, in itself, indeterminate value, for money, or, perhaps, for some other thing of indeterminate value. In this case had the one cent mentioned been some particular one cent, a family piece, or ancient, remarkable coin, possessing an indeterminate value, extrinsic from its simple value, a different view might be taken. As it is, the mere promise to pay six hundred dollars for one cent, even had the portion of that cent due from the plaintiff been tendered, is an unconscionable contract, void, at first blush, upon its face, if it be regarded as an earnest one. Hardesty v. Smith, 3 Ind. 39. The consideration of one cent is, plainly, in this case, merely nominal, and intended to be so. As the will and testament of Schnell's wife imposed no legal obligation upon him to discharge her bequests out of his property, and as she had none of her own, his promise to discharge them was not legally binding upon him, on that ground. A moral consideration, only, will not support a promise. Ind.Dig., p. 13. And for the same reason, a valid consideration for his promise cannot be found in the fact of a compromise of a disputed claim; for where such claim is legally groundless, a promise upon a compromise of it, or of a suit upon it, is not legally binding. Spahr v. Hollingshead, 8 Blackf. 415. There was no mistake of law or fact in this case, as the agreement admits the will inoperative and void. The promise was simply one to make a gift. The past services of his wife, and the love and affection he had borne her, are objectionable as legal considerations for Schnell's promise, on two grounds: (1) They are past considerations. Ind.Dig., p. 13. (2) The fact that Schnell loved his wife and that she had been industrious, constituted no consideration for his promise to pay J.B. Nell, and the Lorenzes, a sum of money. Whether, if his wife, in her lifetime had made a bargain with Schnell, that, in consideration of his promising to pay, after her death, to the persons named, a sum of money, she would be industrious, and worthy of his affection, such a promise would have been valid and consistent with public policy, we need not decide. Nor is the fact that Schnell now venerates the memory of his deceased wife a legal consideration for a promise to pay any third person money.

The instrument sued on, interpreted in the light of the facts alleged in the second paragraph of the answer, will not support an action. The demurrer to the answer should have been overruled. See Stevenson v. Druley, 4 Ind. 519.

Judgment reversed.

STATUTES APPLICABLE IN SCHNELL v. NELL. A statute in Indiana, which was in effect when *Schnell v. Nell* was decided, provided as follows: "A failure or want of consideration, in whole or in part, may be pleaded in any action, set–off or counter–claim upon or arising out of any specialty,* bond or deed, except instruments negotiable by the law merchant and negotiated before falling due." 2 Ind.Rev.Stats. 44–45 (1852). Another statute provided, "There shall be no difference in evidence between sealed and unsealed writings; and every writing not sealed, shall have the same force and effect that it would have if sealed. A writing under seal, except conveyances of real estate, or any interest therein, may therefore be changed, or altogether discharged, by a writing not under seal. An agreement in writing, without a seal, for the compromise or settlement of a debt, is as obligatory as if a seal were affixed." Id. § 492.

––––––––

NOTE ON NOMINAL CONSIDERATION

The problem in *Schnell v. Nell* concerns what is now known as nominal consideration. Essentially, the term *nominal consideration* plays off the bargain theory of consideration. A bargain is a *substantive* transaction, consisting of an exchange in which each party views what he gives up as the price of what he gets. A transaction is said to involve nominal consideration when it has the *form* of a bargain, but not the substance of a bargain, because it is clear that the promisor did not view what she got as the price of her promise. So, for example, it is clear that in *Schnell v. Nell* the promisor, Schnell, did not view one cent as the price of his promise to pay $600. (It is possible that the promisees in *Schnell v. Nell* agreed to do other things, such as not bringing suit against Mrs. Schnell's estate, and that Schnell viewed these other things as the price of his promise. Even if that were the case, however, it remains true that Schnell did not view the one cent as the price of his promise.)

A basic axiom of the classical school was the bargain theory of consideration—that to constitute consideration a promise or performance must be bargained for. Ironically, however, as the bargain theory of consideration was actually elaborated by the classical school, it could be satisfied even though no bargain had been made. Both Holmes and Restatement First took the view that the *form* of a bargain would suffice to make a promise enforceable.

Holmes expressed his view in two well-known aphorisms:

Consideration is as much a form as a seal.

and

[I]t is the essence of a consideration, that, by the terms of the agreement, it is given and accepted as the motive or inducement of the promise. Conversely, the promise must be made and accepted as the conventional motive or inducement for furnishing the consideration. The root of the whole matter is the relation of reciprocal conventional inducement, each for the other, between consideration and promise.

By the term "reciprocal inducement," Holmes meant bargain. By the term "conventional," Holmes apparently meant a formal expression whose meaning and significance is artificially determined, like a bidding convention in the game of bridge. Thus, in Holmes's view, if the parties deliberately

––––––––

* A "specialty" is a contract under seal.
(Footnote by ed.)

adopted the convention—that is, the form—of a bargain, the law would enforce their promises as though they had made an *actual* bargain.

Illustration 1 to Restatement First § 84 reflected the same idea:

> A wishes to make a binding promise to his son B to convey to B Blackacre, which is worth $5000. Being advised that a gratuitous promise is not binding, A writes to B an offer to sell Blackacre for $1. B accepts. B's promise to pay $1 is sufficient consideration.

Restatement Second has retained the bargain definition of consideration. In two Illustrations, however, Restatement Second has reversed the position of Restatement First on nominal consideration, and adopted a test that requires a bargain in fact rather than in form:

> 4. A desires to make a binding promise to give $1000 to his son B. Being advised that a gratuitous promise is not binding, A writes out and signs a false recital that B has sold him a car for $1000 and a promise to pay that amount. There is no consideration for A's promise.

> 5. A desires to make a binding promise to give $1000 to his son B. Being advised that a gratuitous promise is not binding, A offers to buy from B for $1000 a book worth less than $1. B accepts the offer knowing that the purchase of the book is a mere pretense. There is no consideration for A's promise to pay $1000.

Although Restatement Second rejects the concept of nominal consideration as a general principle, it does provide that nominal consideration makes a promise enforceable in two specific areas—options and guaranties. (An option is an offer accompanied by an enforceable promise to hold the offer open.) The cases in this area are not entirely consistent. The majority rule under the cases is that a *recital* of nominal consideration does not make an option binding. On the other hand, many of the cases hold that even the most negligible consideration will make an option enforceable if it is *paid*. See, e.g., Board of Control v. Burgess, 45 Mich.App. 183, 206 N.W.2d 256 (1973) ($1 nominal consideration not paid; option unenforceable; it would have been enforceable if the $1 had been paid). The reason for this distinction is not clear. If the consideration is really nominal, it is no less a form just because it is paid. Perhaps actual payment of nominal consideration is viewed as a better form than the mere recital of a bargain, because a physical transfer of money may have more psychological impact than a mere recital.

NOTE ON CONSIDERATION AND THE SEAL

The opinion in *Schnell v. Nell* tells us that Schnell's contract ended as follows: "In witness whereof, the said parties have . . . set hereunto their hands and seals. Zacharias Schnell. [Seal.] J.B. Nell. [Seal.] Wen. Lorenz. [Seal.]" Prior to modern statutory reforms, a promise under seal occupied a special status in contract law, differing from an unsealed promise in a number of respects. The most important difference was that a promise under seal was enforceable even though it was donative.[1]

---

1. It should be noted, however, that if we view the legal system as a whole—so as to include not only the remedies available through the courts of the common law, but

This rule was sometimes expressed by the statement that a seal "imports" or "raises a presumption of" consideration. Under developed English law, the presumption was not rebuttable. 3 W. Holdsworth, A History of English Law 419B20 (3d Ed. 1923). Probably the same held true in most American states prior to modern statutory developments, although some jurisdictions may have treated the presumption as rebuttable. See Cochran v. Taylor, 273 N.Y. 172, 7 N.E.2d 89 (1937); Note, The Status of the Common–Law Seal in Florida, 1 U.Fla.L.Rev. 385, 391–93 (1948).[2]

Originally, a seal consisted of a bit of wax placed at the end of a document and bearing the impression of an individual's signet ring. In early times, a signet ring was a ring incised with a symbol that was intimately identified with the ring's owner, such as the owner's coat of arms or initials. Normally the wax would be heated, dripped onto the paper, and then impressed with the signet. In its origin, therefore, the seal was a "natural formality"—that is, a promissory form that is popularly understood to carry legal significance—involving a writing, a ritual of hot wax, and a physical object, the signet ring, that personified its owner—elements that ensured both deliberation and proof. However, "in the United States the courts have not required either wax or impression. Impressions directly on the paper [usually made with a metal form] were recognized early and are still common for notarial and corporate seals, and gummed paper wafers have been widely used. In the absence of statute decisions have divided on the effectiveness of the written or printed word 'seal,' the printed initials 'L.S.' (locus sigilli, meaning place of the seal), a scrawl made with a pen (often called a 'scroll') and a recital of sealing. Most states in which the seal is still recognized now have statutes giving effect to one or more such devices." Restatement Second § 96, comment *a*. With this development, the seal not only ceased to be a natural formality but became an empty device whose legal consequences were not widely understood.

About two-thirds of the states have now adopted statutory provisions depriving the seal of its binding effect. These provisions fall into four basic categories:

1. *Statutory provisions that allow a lack of consideration to be pleaded as a defense in suits based on sealed instruments.* The first of the

also those available exclusively through courts of equity—the seal was not a complete substitute for consideration. A sealed promise for which no consideration was paid would not normally be specifically enforced by a court of equity. (Restatement First § 366.) The maxim quoted was that "equity will not aid a volunteer." Equity insisted on some "valuable" consideration, something more than a mere seal or a nominal consideration, before it would grant the remedy of specific performance. The chief practical consequence of this rule may be summarized as follows: The seal sufficed to make a promise enforceable through a suit for damages or to recover a specific sum of money promised; it did not suffice to make a promise (to convey land, for example) specifically enforceable by a judicial order commanding that the promise be performed.

The equity rule that a seal does not make a promise specifically enforceable was not, how-ever, applied to an option, that is, to an offer combined with a promise not to revoke the offer during a stated period of time. Thus, if Seller gave Buyer an option to buy Blackacre at any time during ten days for $100,000 and the option was stated to be irrevocable and was under seal, Buyer could secure specific performance even though Seller repudiated the option before Buyer's acceptance or exercise of the option. Although Buyer was a "volunteer" in the sense that he paid nothing for the option, the contract resulting from the exercise of the option was for a valuable consideration (Blackacre for $100,000) and was enforced in spite of the fact that but for the seal on Seller's offer, it would have been subject to revocation by him.

2. For other respects in which sealed contracts were afforded special treatment, see Appendix C.

two Indiana statutes quoted in the Note on Statutes Applicable in Schnell v. Nell, supra, is an example of such a statute.

2. *Statutory provisions that abolish the distinction between sealed and unsealed instruments.* The second Indiana statute quoted in that Note is an example of this type of statute. See also, e.g. Cal.Civ.Code § 1629. On their face, provisions of this type could be interpreted to mean either that sealed instruments should be treated as if they were unsealed, or the other way around. The former reading is almost certainly the one intended, given the historical context. This type of provision is often accompanied by a related statute which provides that a written instrument, sealed or unsealed, shall be presumptive of or shall import consideration. See, e.g., Cal.Civ.Code § 1614; Iowa Code Ann. § 537A.2. The presumption raised under this type of statute is almost certainly rebuttable.

3. *Statutory provisions that abolish the use of a seal in contracts.* See, e.g., Iowa Code Ann. § 537A.1. This type of provision is often accompanied by the type of statute described in paragraph 1, supra.

4. *Statutory provisions that limit the seal's effect.* Statutes in this category frequently provide that the seal shall be only presumptive evidence of consideration. See, e.g., N.J.Rev.Stat. § 2A:82B3. As with the common law rule, a question can be raised whether the statutory presumption is rebuttable or conclusive. It hardly seems likely that conclusive effect was intended, because if the presumption were conclusive the statute would make no change in the common law, and would therefore be unnecessary. See Note, Contracts Without Consideration; the Seal and the Uniform Obligations Act, 3 U.Chi.L.Rev. 312, 314 (1936).[3]

In about one-third of the states there is no statute or decision depriving the seal of its binding effect. Restatement Second Ch. 4, Topic 3 (Introductory Note). Few if any of these states have statutes that explicitly validate the common-law rule, but most do have statutory provisions that recognize in some way a distinction between sealed and unsealed instruments. For example, Mass.Gen.Laws Ann. ch. 4, § 9A provides that "In any written instrument, a recital that such instrument is sealed by or bears the seal of the person signing the same or is given under the hand and seal of the person signing the same, or that such instrument is intended to take effect as a sealed instrument, shall be sufficient to give such instrument the legal effect of a sealed instrument without the addition of any seal of wax, paper or other substance or any semblance of a seal by scroll, impression or otherwise...."(Caveat: Section 2–203 of the Uniform Commercial Code, which

---

3. In Aller v. Aller, 40 N.J.L. 446 (1878), the New Jersey court held that a statute which provided "that in every action upon a sealed instrument ... the seal thereof shall be only presumptive evidence of a sufficient consideration, which may be rebutted, as if such instrument was not sealed," did not change the common law rule that a *donative* promise under seal was enforceable. "[The statute] does not reach the case of a voluntary agreement, where there was no consideration, and none intended by the parties." Id. at 452. In 1900, the New Jersey statute was amended in a manner that may seem to negate the holding of Aller v. Aller. Nevertheless, the result reached in *Aller* was reaffirmed in a 1941 decision of the New Jersey Court of Errors and Appeals, Zirk v. Nohr, 127 N.J.L. 217, 21 A.2d 766. See also United & Globe Rubber Mfg. Cos. v. Conard, 80 N.J.L. 286, 78 A. 203 (Ct.Err. & App. 1910). In Joseph Linder v. Commissioner, 68 T.C. 792 (1977), the United States Tax Court took the position that a modern New Jersey court would not follow the interpretation of the New Jersey statute given in Zirk v. Nohr. Cf. Whitehead v. Villapiano, 16 N.J.Super. 415, 84 A.2d 731 (1951).

governs contracts for the sale of goods in almost every state, provides that "The affixing of a seal to a writing evidencing a contract for sale or an offer to buy or sell goods does not constitute the writing a sealed instrument and the law with respect to sealed instruments does not apply to such a contract or offer." Under section 2–203, a statutory provision, such as that in Massachusetts, that recognizes or gives effect to the seal will usually be inapplicable to contracts for the sale of goods.) In some states, there is some legislative recognition of a distinction between sealed and unsealed contracts, but it is less direct than in a state like Massachusetts, and instead consists of different periods of limitations for the two types of contract. See, e.g., Me.Rev.Stat.Ann. tit. 14, § 751.

It is conceivable that in the absence of the kind of explicit statutory validation found in Massachusetts, a modern court would not regard itself as bound by the common-law rule governing enforceability. See Hartford–Connecticut Trust Co. v. Divine, 97 Conn. 193, 116 A. 239 (1922); cf. Ortez v. Bargas, 29 Hawaii 548 (1927) (instrument is sealed only if it bears actual wax seal, and even if sealed, it may be attacked for lack of consideration). But see Warfield v. Baltimore Gas & Electric Co., 307 Md. 142, 512 A.2d 1044 (1986) (longer statute of limitations applied to a contract that included the printed term "(SEAL)." Alternatively, a modern court could reinterpret the common law rule to mean only that a seal creates a rebuttable presumption of consideration.

––––––

NOTE ON FORM

In general, the history of the seal can be summarized in terms of two movements: (1) A gradual "liberalization" of the requirement (from impressed wax, to an attached paper wafer, to a "scroll" in ink, to the printed word "Seal"). (2) A gradual but widespread elimination of the various special legal effects of the seal. There is a close interrelation between these two movements. A sealed promise deserves special treatment (enforcement without consideration, longer statute of limitations, etc.) only to the extent that the seal is socially recognized as special, in particular, to the extent that the seal is a natural formality. Where the requirements for what constitutes a seal have been relaxed to the point of social meaninglessness, there is no longer any justification for giving a sealed promise a special effect.

However, the consequence of the widespread elimination of the special treatment of sealed promises is that in most states there is no longer available any legal device that can be employed with the certainty that it will bind a promisor to a donative promise. Accordingly, the question arises whether the legislature should adopt, or the courts should recognize, some substitute formality that would have this effect.

Many legislatures have adopted statutes which provide that a written instrument is presumptive evidence of a consideration. See, e.g., Cal.Civ.Code § 1614. Presumably, the presumption under these statutes is rebuttable, but even so these statutes can have a substantive effect, because it may sometimes be difficult to rebut the inference, particularly where the promisor has died and suit is brought against his legal representative.[4]

One or two legislatures have gone further, and made all written promises legally enforceable. Thus a Mississippi statute provides that "[a]ny instrument of writing made and delivered by a private person without a seal . . . shall be operative according to the intent of the maker, as expressed in the writing, in the same manner and [to as] full extent as if the seal of the maker were thereto affixed." Miss.Code Ann. § 75–19–3.

Other statutes provide that a writing imports (constitutes) consideration in specifically defined cases. For example, Mo.Ann.Stat. § 431.020 provides that "All instruments of writing made and signed by any person or his agent, whereby he shall promise to pay to any other, or his order, or unto bearer, any sum of money or property therein mentioned, shall import a consideration, and be due and payable as therein specified." Similarly, a series of New York statutes, enacted on the recommendation of the New York Law Revision Commission and now collected in N.Y. General Obligations Law §§ 5–1101 to 5–1115, 15–303, dispenses with consideration for certain types of promises—for example, promises to discharge a contract—if the promises are made in writing and signed. See Braucher, The Commission and The Law of Contracts, 40 Corn.L.Q. 696, 698–703 (1955). The Uniform Commercial Code contains a number of comparable provisions, including § 2–205 on firm offers.

Now that the seal no longer operates to make a promise enforceable, the question arises, should the law recognize some new formality to play the role once played by the seal? An obvious candidate for this role is nominal consideration—that is, the *form* of a bargain—because it can be safely assumed that parties who falsely cast a nonbargain promise as a bargain do so for the express purpose of making the promise legally enforceable. A rule that nominal consideration makes a promise enforceable would have obvious benefits, but would also involve some costs. As a practical matter, such a rule would be primarily employed to render donative promises enforceable. Both morally and legally, however, an obligation created by a donative promise should normally be excused either by acts of the promisee amounting to ingratitude, or by personal circumstances of the promisor that render it improvident to keep the promise. If Uncle promises to give Nephew $20,000 in two years, and Nephew later wrecks Uncle's living room in an angry rage, Uncle should not remain obliged. The same result should ordinarily follow if Uncle suffers a serious financial setback and is barely able to take care of the needs of his immediate family, or if Uncle's wealth remains constant but his personal obligations significantly increase in an unexpected manner, as through illness or the birth of children.

Form alone cannot meet these problems. Thus the French and German Civil Codes, while providing special formalities that enable a donative promise to be made legally enforceable, also provide extensive treatment of improvidence and ingratitude as defenses. For example, under article 519(1) of the German Civil Code, a promisor may refuse to perform an otherwise-enforceable donative promise "insofar as, having regard to his other obligations, he is not in a position to fulfill the promise without endangering his own reason-

---

4. California has a statute of this type, but the scope of the California statute has been narrowed by cases holding that the term "written instrument," as used in the statute, means a formal document, and does not include an ordinary letter. See Weisbrod v. Weisbrod, 27 Cal.App.2d 712, 81 P.2d 633 (1938); Foltz v. First Trust & Sav. Bank, 86 Cal.App.2d 59, 194 P.2d 135 (1948).

able maintenance or the fulfillment of obligations imposed upon him by law to furnish maintenance to others." Under article 530(1), a donative promise may be revoked "if the donee, by any serious misconduct towards the donor or a close relative of the donor shows himself guilty of gross ingratitude." Similarly, under articles 960–966 of the French Civil Code, a donative promise made by a person with no living descendants is normally revoked by operation of law upon the birth of a child. Under articles 953 and 955, a donative promise can be revoked on the ground of ingratitude that involves serious cruelty, wrongs, or injuries.

As these rules suggest, the common law could not appropriately make donative promises enforceable solely on the basis of form unless the courts were also prepared to develop and administer a body of rules dealing with the problems of improvidence and ingratitude. Certainly such an enterprise is possible. It may be questioned, however, whether the benefits would be worth the costs. An inquiry into changed personal circumstances involves the measurement of wealth, lifestyle, dependents' needs, and even personal utilities. An inquiry into ingratitude involves the measurement of a maelstrom, because many or most donative promises arise in an intimate context in which emotions, motives, and cues are invariably complex and highly interrelated. Perhaps the civil-law style of adjudication is suited to wrestling with these kinds of inquiries, but they have held little appeal for common-law courts, which traditionally have been oriented toward inquiry into acts rather than into personal characteristics. Given these problems, the nonrecognition of a formality for making donative promises enforceable is understandable, if not preferable.

SECTION 3. THE ELEMENT OF RELIANCE

The cases in Sections 1 and 2 illustrate that the *moral* obligation to keep a promise is not a sufficient ground for concluding that there is a *legal* obligation to keep a promise. The moral obligation to keep a promise is a strong starting-point for concluding that there should be a legal obligation to keep a promise, because the courts should take moral norms into account in making law. It is not, however, conclusive, because in making legal rules a lawmaker must also consider social policy and experiential concerns, such as problems of proof.

More generally, that private conduct violates a moral norm does not alone justify the use of collective (governmental) resources to legally sanction the conduct. In some cases, like cutting in line, the injury caused by violation of a moral norm is not significant enough to justify a legal sanction. In other cases, like the failure to support aged parents who cannot support themselves, legal enforceability of a moral norm would intrude too far, without sufficient justification, into intimate areas better governed by social norms. In still other cases, legal enforceability of a moral norm would raise difficult problems of administrability. Thus as stated by Thomas Scanlon, "The fact that some action is morally required is not, in general, a sufficient justification for legal intervention to force people to do it; and the rationale for the law of contracts does not seem to be ... an instance of the legal enforcement of morality."

The issue then is, what additional moral or policy elements, beyond the moral obligation to keep a promise, should make a given type of promise enforceable. This Section explores one such element: a significant injury to the promise; in particular, a cost that the promisee incurs in reliance on the promise.

KIRKSEY v. KIRKSEY

Supreme Court of Alabama, 1845.
8 Ala. 131.

Assumpsit by defendant, against the plaintiff in error.

The plaintiff was the wife of defendant's brother, but had for some time been a widow, and had several children. In 1840, the plaintiff resided on public land, under a contract of lease, she had held over, and was comfortably settled, and would have attempted to secure the land she lived on. The defendant resided in Talladega county, some sixty or seventy miles off. On the 10th October, 1840, he wrote to her the following letter:

"Dear Sister Antillico,—Much to my mortification, I heard that brother Henry was dead, and one of his children. I know that your situation is one of grief and difficulty. You had a bad chance before, but a great deal worse now. I should like to come and see you, but cannot with convenience at present ... I do not know whether you have a preference on the place you live on or not. If you had, I would advise you to obtain your preference, and sell the land and quit the country, as I understand it is very unhealthy, and I know society is very bad. If you will come down and see me, I will let you have a place to raise your family, and I have more open land than I can tend; and on the account of your situation, and that of your family, I feel like I want you and the children to do well."

Within a month or two after the receipt of this letter, the plaintiff abandoned her possession, without disposing of it, and removed with her family, to the residence of the defendant, who put her in comfortable houses, and gave her land to cultivate for two years, at the end of which time he notified her to remove, and put her in a house, not comfortable, in the woods, which he afterwards required her to leave.

A verdict being found for the plaintiff, for $200, the above facts were agreed, and if they will sustain the action, the judgment is to be affirmed, otherwise it is to be reversed.

ORMOND, J. The inclination of my mind is that the loss and inconvenience which the plaintiff sustained in breaking up and moving to the defendant's a distance of sixty miles is a sufficient consideration to support the promise to furnish her with a house and land to cultivate until she could raise her family. My brothers, however, think that the promise on the part of the defendant was a mere gratuity, and that an action will not lie for its breach.

The judgment of the court below must therefore be reversed, pursuant to the agreement of the parties.

————

RESTATEMENT, SECOND, CONTRACTS § 90

[See Selected Source Materials Supplement]

————

NOTE ON ESTOPPEL IN PAIS AND PROMISSORY ESTOPPEL

1. *The law prior to 1932.* From the middle of the nineteenth century until the first part of the twentieth century, contract law was dominated by a school of thought now known as classical contract law. One of the axioms of classical contract law was that only a bargain is consideration. Kirksey v. Kirksey reflects that axiom. Even during the classical era, however, courts often found a way around that axiom where a donative promise had been relied upon. For example, in Carr v. Maine Central R.R. Co., 78 N.H. 502, 102 A. 532 (1917), Railway had received a freight overcharge from Shipper, but could not make a rebate of the overcharge without the consent of the Interstate Commerce Commission. Railway promised Shipper that if he would make out the necessary papers, it would send them to the ICC and procure the consent. Shipper made out the papers and delivered them to Railway, but Railway neglected to send them within the time allowed by the ICC's rules. The court sustained Shipper's action against Railway on the ground of negligence, saying that no consideration was necessary since the action was in tort.

In Ricketts, Executor v. Scothorn, 57 Neb. 51, 77 N.W. 365 (1898), a comparable result was reached through a different path. Testator was distressed because his granddaughter had to work in a store. To enable her to give up her job, he delivered to her a promissory note for $2,000, saying "I have fixed out something that you have not got to work any more." In reliance on the note, the granddaughter quit work. Testator died without either paying or repudiating the note. The granddaughter brought suit on the note against the executor, and the court held for the granddaughter. The Court side-stepped the issue of whether reliance constituted consideration by concluding that reliance "estopped" (prevented) the executor from *pleading* a lack of consideration.

2. *Estoppel in pais.* The approach taken in *Ricketts* drew by analogy on a well-established doctrine known as *equitable estoppel* or *estoppel in pais.* Under this doctrine, if A has made a statement of fact to B, and B has foreseeably relied upon the statement, A is prevented—"estopped"—from denying the truth of the statement. The mechanics of estoppel in pais are as follows:

> (i) A files a complaint against B. In his complaint, A alleges the existence of facts X, Y, and Z. If X, Y, and Z are true, they give rise to a legally recognized claim against B, such as a tort. Therefore, if A can prove that X, Y, and Z are true, A wins.

(ii) At the trial, A attempts to prove X and Y by direct evidence. He attempts to prove Z only by showing that B herself had said that Z was true, and A had relied on B's statement.

(iii) B then seeks to introduce evidence to show that Z is not true, even though she had told A that it was.

(iv) A objects to the evidence, and shows that he had taken some action in foreseeable reliance on B's assertion that Z was true.

(v) The court holds that B is estopped (prevented) from introducing evidence to show that Z is untrue.

(vi) Z now is taken as "proved" for purposes of A's case, and therefore A now has established all the allegations necessary to make out his case. A has established X and Y by direct evidence. He has established Z by establishing *B's assertion* that Z is true, and then estopping B from contradicting her own earlier assertion.

For example, in Griswold v. Haven, 25 N.Y. 595 (1862), Wright was a member of a partnership engaged in operating a warehouse, and had signed storage receipts for grain purportedly received by the warehouse from Ford, and purportedly stored in the warehouse on Ford's behalf. The grain receipts entitled the holder of the receipts to take delivery, upon request, of the grain described in the receipts. In fact, however, Ford had not stored any grain in the partnership's warehouse.

Wright then introduced Ford to the plaintiff. Wright told the plaintiff that Ford wished to borrow money from the plaintiff; that the loan would be secured by grain that Ford had stored in the partnership's warehouse; and that the grain was in good order and all right. In reliance on Wright's statements, the plaintiff lent money to Ford, taking an assignment of the grain receipts as security.

Later, Ford apparently defaulted on the loan, and the plaintiff demanded the grain from the partnership. The partnership refused to deliver the grain described in the grain receipts—not surprisingly, since there was no such grain—and the plaintiff then sued the partnership for conversion of the grain. Conversion is a tort based on interference with another's property. Essentially, the plaintiff alleged that the partnership held grain to which he was entitled by virtue of his possession of the grain receipts; that it had refused to deliver this grain; and that this refusal to deliver his grain was an interference with his property that constituted conversion. In its defense, the partnership sought to introduce evidence that it had not received the grain from Ford described in the grain receipts, and therefore could not be guilty of converting the grain. Held, the partnership was estopped from introducing evidence that it had not received any grain from Ford. Since (1) if the partnership had the grain it was obliged to deliver the grain to the plaintiff; (2) the partnership had not done so; and (3) the partnership was estopped to deny that it had the grain, the case was decided as if the partnership did have the grain, and the partnership was held liable for converting the nonexistent grain.

3. *Promissory estoppel.* In 1932, the result in cases like Kirksey v. Kirksey was overthrown by a now-famous provision of Restatement First, Section 90. As adopted in Restatement First, Section 90 provided as follows:

A promise which the promisor should reasonably expect to induce action or forbearance of a definite and substantial character on the part of the promisee and which does induce such action or forbearance is binding if injustice can be avoided only by enforcement of the promise.

The doctrine of Section 90 is often referred to as "promissory estoppel." Partly this nomenclature reflects cases like *Ricketts*, which held that because A had relied on B's promise, B was estopped to *plead* lack of consideration. The nomenclature also reflects a substantive element: the doctrine of Section 90 and the doctrine of estoppel in pais both turn on the core idea of reliance. This nomenclature is fairly well established, and there is no particular harm in using it. However, it should be borne in mind that there are two important substantive differences between the doctrine of promissory estoppel and the doctrine of estoppel in pais. First, promissory estoppel is based on a promise, while estoppel in pais is based on a statement of fact. Second, the mechanics of estoppel in pais are not used in promissory estoppel cases. Under the mechanics of estoppel in pais, a defendant is prevented from denying something. (In *Ricketts*, the defendant was prevented from denying that there was consideration.) Under the mechanics of promissory estoppel, where a plaintiff has relied upon a defendant's promise in a way that makes the promise enforceable, the defendant is not estopped to deny lack of consideration. Instead, reliance is treated either as consideration itself or as a substitute for consideration. The promisor can only deny that there *was* reliance, or that the other elements of the principle of promissory estoppel are satisfied.

4. *The Reliance principle.* Both estoppel in pais and promissory estoppel are best understood as particular instances of a broader concept: When one person, A, uses words or actions that he knows or should know would induce another, B, to reasonably believe that A is committed to take a certain course of action, and A knows or should know that B will incur costs if A doesn't take action, A should take steps to ensure that if he doesn't take the action, B will not suffer a loss. See T.M. Scanlon, Promises and Practices, 19 Phil. & Pub. Affairs 199 (1990). This broader concept has not received formal recognition in the law to the same extent as promissory estoppel and estoppel in pais, but it is reflected in some important cases.

For example, in Times–Mirror Co. v. The Superior Court, 3 Cal.2d 309, 44 P.2d 547 (1935), the City of Los Angeles planned a civic center, which would include public buildings and park areas. It was contemplated that this project would ultimately embrace an area within which the Times–Mirror newspaper plant was located. Without acquiring the Times–Mirror property, the city began work on its project. After the first buildings were completed, there was a movement that the City should secure title to the Times–Mirror property in order to complete the project as it was originally planned, and the matter became an issue in local politics. At this juncture, Times–Mirror communicated with the City Council and stated that the expansion of its newspaper business compelled it to enlarge its plant, but that it hesitated to make expenditures on its present property because "a good deal of talk" was "floating around" that the property would ultimately be taken by the City. Negotiations between City officials and Times–Mirror were begun, but the parties were unable to agree on a price. The City then instituted a proceeding, under the power of eminent domain, to secure the Times–Mirror property. After the proceeding was begun, Times–Mirror purchased other land, and built a new plant on that land, on which it spent $4,500,000. Thereupon the City, apparently fearing that the valuation of the old Times–Mirror property in the eminent-domain proceeding would be higher than had been anticipated, applied to the Superior Court for a discontinuance of the proceeding. The Superior Court granted this application. On appeal, the California Supreme Court held that the City was estopped by its conduct from abandoning the eminent-domain proceeding, and directed the Superior Court to reopen the suit.

Times–Mirror did not involve estoppel in pais, because bringing the eminent-domain proceeding was not a representation of fact. The case also did not involve promissory estoppel, because bringing the proceeding was not a promise. Instead, the case involved a course of conduct by the City that the Times–Mirror relied upon. The case suggests, therefore, that there is a broad principle of protecting reliance that transcends—or, more accurately under-lies—estoppel in pais and promissory estoppel. Those two doctrines are important expressions of that broad principle, but they do not exhaust the principle. This point has been explicitly recognized by two leading judges, one English and one Australian. In Moorgate Mercantile Co. Ltd. v. Twitchings, [1976] Q.B. 225, 241–42, Lord Denning stated:

> Estoppel is. . . . a principle of justice and of equity. It comes to this: when a man, by his words or conduct, has led another to believe in a particular state of affairs, he will not be allowed to go back on it when it would be unjust for him to do so.

Similarly, in Commonwealth of Australia v. Verwayen, 170 C.L.R. 394 (High Court of Appeals 1990) Chief Justice Mason stated:

> . . . [T]he consistent trend in the modern decisions points inexorably towards the emergence of one overarching doctrine of estoppel rather than a series of independent rules. . . .

> . . . [I]t should be accepted that there is but one doctrine of estoppel, which provides that a court of common law or equity may do what is required, but not more, to prevent a person who has relied upon an assumption as to a present, past or future state of affairs (including a legal state of affairs), which assumption the party estoppel has induced him to hold, from suffering detriment in reliance upon the assumption as a result of the denial of its corrections.

PROBLEM

An uncle writes to his nephew: "My friend Green is in town and tells me that you have been talking to him about buying his grocery store. I hope you go ahead with this deal. He has a good location, and I've always wanted to see you in business for yourself. I'm pretty sure you will want to buy the store when you learn the news I have for you. I have just deposited $50,000 in the First National Bank in your name. You are free to draw on this to finance the deal with Green and set yourself up in business." The nephew received this letter the next day, and immediately entered into a contract with Green to buy the store for $40,000. A few hours after the contract was signed, the uncle was killed in a traffic accident. No money was ever deposited by him in the nephew's name. It appears that he had intended to arrange the transfer of funds shortly after mailing the letter, but had absent-mindedly neglected to do so. The uncle's executor refuses to recognize any claim in favor of the nephew. Can the nephew base an action against the executor on (1) deceit, (2) estoppel in pais, (3) a promise made enforceable by unbargained-for reliance, (4) a promise supported by bargained-for consideration?

FEINBERG v. PFEIFFER CO.

Missouri Court of Appeals, 1959.
322 S.W.2d 163.

DOERNER, COMMISSIONER. This is a suit brought in the Circuit Court of the City of St. Louis by plaintiff, a former employee of the defendant corporation, on an alleged contract whereby defendant agreed to pay plaintiff the sum of $200 per month for life upon her retirement. A jury being waived, the case was tried by the court alone. Judgment below was for plaintiff for $5,100, the amount of the pension claimed to be due as of the date of the trial, together with interest thereon, and defendant duly appealed.

The parties are in substantial agreement on the essential facts. Plaintiff began working for the defendant, a manufacturer of pharmaceuticals, in 1910, when she was but 17 years of age. By 1947 she had attained the position of bookkeeper, office manager, and assistant treasurer of the defendant, and owned 70 shares of its stock out of a total of 6,503 shares issued and outstanding. Twenty shares had been given to her by the defendant or its then president, she had purchased 20, and the remaining 30 she had acquired by a stock split or stock dividend. Over the years she received substantial dividends on the stock she owned, as did all of the other stockholders. Also, in addition to her salary, plaintiff from 1937 to 1949, inclusive, received each year a bonus varying in amount from $300 in the beginning to $2,000 in the later years.

On December 27, 1947, the annual meeting of the defendant's Board of Directors was held at the Company's offices in St. Louis, presided over by Max Lippman, its then president and largest individual stockholder. The other directors present were George L. Marcus, Sidney Harris, Sol Flammer, and Walter Weinstock, who, with Max Lippman, owned 5,007 of the 6,503 shares then issued and outstanding. At that meeting the Board of Directors adopted the following resolution, which because it is the crux of the case, we quote in full:

"The Chairman thereupon pointed out that the Assistant Treasurer, Mrs. Anna Sacks Feinberg, has given the corporation many years of long and faithful service. Not only has she served the corporation devotedly, but with exceptional ability and skill. The President pointed out that although all of the officers and directors sincerely hoped and desired that Mrs. Feinberg would continue in her present position for as long as she felt able, nevertheless, in view of the length of service which she has contributed provision should be made to afford her retirement privileges and benefits which should become a firm obligation of the corporation to be available to her whenever she should see fit to retire from active duty, however many years in the future such retirement may become effective. It was, accordingly, proposed that Mrs. Feinberg's salary which is presently $350.00 per month, be increased to $400.00 per month, and that Mrs. Feinberg would be given the privilege of retiring from active duty at any time she may elect to see fit so to do upon a retirement pay of $200.00 per month for life, with the distinct understanding that the retirement plan is merely being adopted at the present time in order to afford Mrs. Feinberg security for the future and in the hope that her active services will continue with the corporation for many years to come. After due discussion and consideration, and upon motion duly made and seconded, it was—

> "Resolved, that the salary of Anna Sacks Feinberg be increased from $350.00 to $400.00 per month and that she be afforded the privilege of retiring from active duty in the corporation at any time she may elect to see fit so to do upon retirement pay of $200.00 per month, for the remainder of her life."

At the request of Mr. Lippman his sons-in-law, Messrs. Harris and Flammer, called upon the plaintiff at her apartment on the same day to advise her of the passage of the resolution. Plaintiff testified on cross-examination that she had no prior information that such a pension plan was contemplated, that it came as a surprise to her, and that she would have continued in her employment whether or not such a resolution had been adopted. It is clear from the evidence that there was no contract, oral or written, as to plaintiff's length of employment, and that she was free to quit, and the defendant to discharge her, at any time.

Plaintiff did continue to work for the defendant through June 30, 1949, on which date she retired. In accordance with the foregoing resolution, the defendant began paying her the sum of $200 on the first of each month. Mr. Lippman died on November 18, 1949, and was succeeded as president of the company by his widow. Because of an illness, she retired from that office and was succeeded in October, 1953, by her son-in-law, Sidney M. Harris. Mr. Harris testified that while Mrs. Lippman had been president she signed the monthly pension check paid plaintiff, but fussed about doing so, and considered the payments as gifts. After his election, he stated, a new accounting firm employed by the defendant questioned the validity of the payments to plaintiff on several occasions, and in the Spring of 1956, upon its recommendation, he consulted the Company's then attorney, Mr. Ralph Kalish. Harris testified that both Ernst and Ernst, the accounting firm, and Kalish told him there was no need of giving plaintiff the money. He also stated that he had concurred in the view that the payments to plaintiff were mere gratuities rather than amounts due under a contractual obligation, and that following his discussion with the Company's attorney plaintiff was sent a check for $100 on April 1, 1956. Plaintiff declined to accept the reduced amount, and this action followed. Additional facts will be referred to later in this opinion.

Appellant's first assignment of error relates to the admission in evidence of plaintiff's testimony over its objection, that at the time of trial she was sixty-five and a half years old, and that she was no longer able to engage in gainful employment because of the removal of a cancer and the performance of a colocholecystostomy operation on November 25, 1957. Its complaint is not so much that such evidence was irrelevant and immaterial, as it is that the trial court erroneously made it one basis for its decision in favor of plaintiff. As defendant concedes, the error (if it was error) in the admission of such evidence would not be a ground for reversal, since, this being a jury-waived case, we are constrained by the statutes to review it upon both the law and the evidence, Sec. 510.310 RSMo 1949, V.A.M.S., and to render such judgment as the court below ought to have given. Section 512.160, Minor v. Lillard, Mo., 289 S.W.2d 1; Thumm v. Lohr, Mo.App., 306 S.W.2d 604. We consider only such evidence as is admissible, and need not pass upon questions of error in the admission and exclusion of evidence. Hussey v. Robison, Mo., 285 S.W.2d 603. However, in fairness to the trial court it should be stated that while he briefly referred to the state of plaintiff's health as of the time of the trial in his amended findings of fact, it is obvious from his amended grounds for decision and judgment that it was not, as will be seen, the basis for his decision.

Appellant's next complaint is that there was insufficient evidence to support the court's findings that plaintiff would not have quit defendant's employ had she not known and relied upon the promise of defendant to pay her $200 a month for life, and the finding that, from her voluntary retirement until April 1, 1956, plaintiff relied upon the continued receipt of the pension installments. The trial court so found, and, in our opinion, justifiably so. Plaintiff testified, and was corroborated by Harris, defendant's witness, that knowledge of the passage of the resolution was communicated to her on December 27, 1947, the very day it was adopted. She was told at that time by Harris and Flammer, she stated, that she could take the pension as of that day, if she wished. She testified further that she continued to work for another year and a half, through June 30, 1949; that at that time her health was good and she could have continued to work, but that after working for almost forty years she thought she would take a rest. Her testimony continued:

"Q. Now, what was the reason—I'm sorry. Did you then quit the employment of the company after you—after this year and a half? A. Yes.

"Q. What was the reason that you left? A. Well, I thought almost forty years, it was a long time and I thought I would take a little rest.

"Q. Yes. A. And with the pension and what earnings my husband had, we figured we could get along.

"Q. Did you rely upon this pension? A. We certainly did.

"Q. Being paid? A. Very much so. We relied upon it because I was positive that I was going to get it as long as I lived.

"Q. Would you have left the employment of the company at that time had it not been for this pension? A. No.

"Mr. Allen: Just a minute, I object to that as calling for a conclusion and conjecture on the part of this witness.

"The Court: It will be overruled.

"Q. (Mr. Agatstein continuing): Go ahead, now. The question is whether you would have quit the employment of the company at that time had you not relied upon this pension plan? A. No, I wouldn't.

"Q. You would not have. Did you ever seek employment while this pension was being paid to you—A. (interrupting): No.

"Q. Wait a minute, at any time prior—at any other place? A. No, sir.

"Q. Were you able to hold any other employment during that time? A. Yes, I think so.

"Q. Was your health good? A. My health was good."

It is obvious from the foregoing that there was ample evidence to support the findings of fact made by the court below.

We come, then, to the basic issue in the case. While otherwise defined in defendant's third and fourth assignments of error, it is thus succinctly stated in the argument in its brief: " ... whether plaintiff has proved that she has a right to recover from defendant based upon a legally binding contractual obligation to pay her $200 per month for life."

It is defendant's contention, in essence, that the resolution adopted by its Board of Directors was a mere promise to make a gift, and that no contract resulted either thereby, or when plaintiff retired, because there was no consideration given or paid by the plaintiff. It urges that a promise to make a gift is not binding unless supported by a legal consideration; that the only apparent consideration for the adoption of the foregoing resolution was the "many years of long and faithful service" expressed therein; and that past services are not a valid consideration for a promise. Defendant argues further that there is nothing in the resolution which made its effectiveness conditional upon plaintiff's continued employment, that she was not under contract to work for any length of time but was free to quit whenever she wished, and that she had no contractual right to her position and could have been discharged at any time.

Plaintiff concedes that a promise based upon past services would be without consideration, but contends that there were two other elements which supplied the required element: First, the continuation by plaintiff in the employ of the defendant for the period from December 27, 1947, the date when the resolution was adopted, until the date of her retirement on June 30, 1949. And, second, her change of position, i.e., her retirement, and the abandonment by her of her opportunity to continue in gainful employment, made in reliance on defendant's promise to pay her $200 per month for life.

We must agree with the defendant that the evidence does not support the first of these contentions. There is no language in the resolution predicating plaintiff's right to a pension upon her continued employment. She was not required to work for the defendant for any period of time as a condition to gaining such retirement benefits. She was told that she could quit the day upon which the resolution was adopted, as she herself testified, and it is clear from her own testimony that she made no promise or agreement to continue in the employ of the defendant in return for its promise to pay her a pension. Hence there was lacking that mutuality of obligation which is essential to the validity of a contract....

But as to the second of these contentions we must agree with plaintiff....

Section 90 of the Restatement, Law of Contracts states that: "A promise which the promisor should reasonably expect to induce action or forbearance of a definite and substantial character on the part of the promisee and which does induce such action or forbearance is binding if injustice can be avoided only by enforcement of the promise." This doctrine has been described as that of "promissory estoppel," as distinguished from that of equitable estoppel or estoppel in pais, the reason for the differentiation being stated as follows:

"It is generally true that one who has led another to act in reasonable reliance on his representations of fact cannot afterwards in litigation between the two deny the truth of the representations, and some courts have sought to apply this principle to the formation of contracts, where, relying on a gratuitous promise, the promisee has suffered detriment. It is to be noticed, however, that such a case does not come within the ordinary definition of estoppel. If there is any representation of an existing fact, it is only that the promisor at the time of making the promise intends to fulfill it. As to such intention there is usually no misrepresentation and if there is, it is not that which has injured the promisee. In other words, he relies on a promise and not on a misstatement of fact; and the term 'promissory' estoppel or something equivalent should be used to make the distinction." Williston on Contracts, Rev.Ed., Sec. 139, Vol. 1.

In speaking of this doctrine, Judge Learned Hand said in Porter v. Commissioner of Internal Revenue, 2 Cir., 60 F.2d 673, 675, that " ... 'promissory estoppel' is now a recognized species of consideration."

As pointed out by our Supreme Court in In re Jamison's Estate, Mo., 202 S.W.2d 879, 887, it is stated in the Missouri Annotations to the Restatement under Section 90 that:

" 'There is a variance between the doctrine underlying this section and the theoretical justifications that have been advanced for the Missouri decisions.' "

That variance, as the authors of the Annotations point out, is that:

"This § 90, when applied with § 85, means that the promise described is a contract without any consideration. In Missouri the same practical result is reached without in theory abandoning the doctrine of consideration. In Missouri three theories have been advanced as ground for the decisions (1) *Theory of act for promise.* The induced 'action or forbearance' is the consideration for the promise.... (2) *Theory of promissory estoppel.* The induced 'action or forbearance' works an estoppel against the promisor.... (3) *Theory of bilateral contract.* When the induced 'action or forbearance' is begun, a promise to complete is implied, and we have an enforceable bilateral contract, the implied promise to complete being the consideration for the original promise." (Citing cases.)

Was there such an act on the part of plaintiff, in reliance upon the promise contained in the resolution, as will estop the defendant, and therefore create an enforceable contract under the doctrine of promissory estoppel? We think there was. One of the illustrations cited under Section 90 of the Restatement is: "2. A promises B to pay him an annuity during B's life. B thereupon resigns a profitable employment, as A expected that he might. B receives the annuity for some years, in the meantime becoming disqualified from again obtaining good employment. A's promise is binding." This illustration is objected to by defendant as not being applicable to the case at hand. The reason advanced by it is that in the illustration B became "disqualified" from obtaining other employment *before* A discontinued the payments, whereas in this case the plaintiff did not discover that she had cancer and thereby became unemployable until *after* the defendant had discontinued the payments of $200 per month. We think the distinction is immaterial. The only reason for the reference in the illustration to the disqualification of A is in connection with that part of Section 90 regarding the prevention of injustice. The injustice would occur regardless of when the disability occurred. Would defendant contend that the contract would be enforceable if the plaintiff's illness had been discovered on March 31, 1956, the day before it discontinued the payment of the $200 a month, but not if it occurred on April 2nd, the day after? Furthermore, there are more ways to become disqualified for work, or unemployable, than as the result of illness. At the time she retired plaintiff was 57 years of age. At the time the payments were discontinued she was over 63 years of age. It is a matter of common knowledge that it is virtually impossible for a woman of that age to find satisfactory employment, much less a position comparable to that which plaintiff enjoyed at the time of her retirement.

The fact of the matter is that plaintiff's subsequent illness was not the "action or forbearance" which was induced by the promise contained in the resolution. As the trial court correctly decided, such action on plaintiff's part was her retirement from a lucrative position in reliance upon defendant's promise to pay her an annuity or pension. In a very similar case, Ricketts v. Scothorn, 57 Neb. 51, 77 N.W. 365, 367, 42 L.R.A. 794, the Supreme Court of Nebraska said:

> "... Having intentionally influenced the plaintiff to alter her position for the worse on the faith of the note being paid when due, it would be grossly inequitable to permit the maker, or his executor, to resist payment on the ground that the promise was given without consideration."

The Commissioner therefore recommends, for the reasons stated, that the judgment be affirmed.

PER CURIAM.

The foregoing opinion by DOERNER, C., is adopted as the opinion of the court. The judgment is, accordingly, affirmed.

WOLFE, P.J., and ANDERSON and RUDDY, JJ., concur.

HAYES v. PLANTATIONS STEEL CO., 438 A.2d 1091 (R.I.1982). Plantations Steel Co. was founded by Hugo R. Mainelli, Sr., and Alexander A. Dimartino. Hayes was employed by Plantations from 1947 to 1972. In January 1972, Hayes announced his intention to retire in July, because he had worked continuously for fifty–one years. Hayes was then sixty–five, and was Plantation's general manager, a position of considerable responsibility. About a week before his actual retirement, Hayes spoke with Hugo R. Mainelli, Jr., an officer and a shareholder of Plantations. Mainelli, Jr. said that the company "would take care" of Hayes, although there was no mention of a sum of money or a percentage of salary that Hayes would receive. Mainelli, Jr.'s father, Hugo R. Mainelli, Sr., authorized the first payment "as a token of appreciation for the many years of [Hayes's] service." It was implied that payments would continue on an annual basis, and it was Mainelli, Jr.'s personal intention that the payments would continue for as long as he was around. Four annual payments of $5,000 each were made.

After Hayes's retirement, he visited Plantations each year to say hello and renew old acquaintances. During the course of his visits, Hayes would thank Mainelli, Jr. for the previous check, and ask how long the checks would continue, so that he could plan an orderly retirement. In 1976, the DiMartinos assumed full control of Plantations as a result of a dispute between the two founding families. After 1976, the payments to Hayes were discontinued. A succession of several poor business years and the takeover by the DiMartino family contributed to the decision to stop the payments. Hayes brought suit. Held, for Plantations.

"[T]he important distinction between *Feinberg* and the case before us is that in *Feinberg* the employer's decision definitely shaped the thinking of the plaintiff. In this case the promise did not. It is not reasonable to infer from the facts that Hugo R. Mainelli, Jr., expected retirement to result from his conversation with Hayes. Hayes had given notice of his intention seven months previously. Here there was thus no inducement to retire which would satisfy the demands of § 90 of the Restatement. Nor can it be said that Hayes's refraining from other employment was 'action or forbearance of a definite and substantial character.' The underlying assumption of Hayes's initial decision to retire was that upon leaving the defendant's employ, he would no longer work. It is impossible to say that he changed his position any more so because of what Mainelli had told him in light of his own initial decision. These circumstances do not lead to a conclusion that injustice can be avoided only by enforcement of Plantations's promise. Hayes received $20,000 over the course of four years. He inquired each year about whether he could expect a check for the following year. Obviously, there was no absolute certainty on his part that the pension would continue. Furthermore, in the face of his uncertainty, the mere fact that payment for several years did occur is insufficient by itself to meet the requirements of reliance under the doctrine of promissory estoppel."

NOTE ON CONTRACT REMEDIES AND CONSIDERATION

The essential question considered in Part I of this casebook, under the heading "Consideration," is what promises should and does the law enforce? On both a theoretical and a practical level, this question is inseparable from the issue, *to what extent* shall a particular kind of promise be enforced?

When issues of remedy are examined in detail (as they will be in Part II), they present a great number of complexities and policy choices. At this point it is useful to examine some of these issues in a broad way.

Injury. One way to address the issue of damages for breach of an enforceable promise is to ask what injury the promisee has suffered. In a contract setting, the term "injury" to a promisee can have several different meanings. One meaning is that the promisee is worse off than he would have been if the promise had not been made. Another meaning is that the promisee is worse off than he would have been if the promise had been performed. The interests of a promisee that are invaded by these two different types of injuries are known as the *reliance interest* and the *expectation interest,* respectively.

These two distinct meanings of injury correspond to two distinct purposes of damages for breach of contract. Reliance damages have the purpose of restoring a promisee back to the position that he would have been in if the promise had not been made. If this purpose is perfectly achieved, a potential promisee is equally well off whether there is (i) no promise, or (ii) promise, breach, and payment of damages. Expectation damages have the purpose of placing a promisee forward to the position that he would have been in if the promise had been performed. If this purpose is perfectly achieved, the promisee is equally well off whether there is (i) promise and performance, or (ii) promise, breach, and payment of damages.*

Compensation. In our legal system, compensation is measured in money. In contract law, compensation is the sum of money that is sufficient to make the victim of an injury equally well off with the money and the injury as he would have been without the money and the injury. In this sense, compensatory damages are the money equivalent of the injury. The idea of a money equivalent to injury can be clarified with help from economic theory. Economists measure the well-being of individuals by the amount of satisfaction they enjoy, and measure the well-being of firms by their profits. Compensation for an injury is "perfect" if it enables the victim to enjoy the same level of satisfaction (if an individual) or profits (if a firm) as would have prevailed without the injury. Computing compensatory damages involves comparing the victim's uninjured state with the injured state, in order to determine how much money is needed to make up the difference.

Because there are two different conceptions of the uninjured state in a contract setting, there are also two different conceptions of compensation. Protection of the reliance interest requires an award such that the injured promisee will achieve the level of satisfaction (if an individual) or profits (if a firm) that would have been achieved if the promise had never been made. Under the reliance conception of compensation, therefore, compensation is the amount required to put the injured promisee in a state just as good as if the promise had not been made.

In contrast, protection of the expectation interest requires an award such that the injured party will achieve the level of satisfaction or profits that would have been achieved if the promise had been performed. Under the expectation conception of compensation, therefore, compensation is the amount required to make the promisee indifferent between performance and damages. (Expectation damages are not compensatory in the normal sense of that term, because they make the promisee better off than he was before he encountered the promisor. However, such damages are commonly described as compensatory, and that usage will be followed here.)

Reliance damages. Let us focus here on the reliance conception. What compensation is necessary to put a relying promisee in a state just as good as he would have been in if the promise had not been made? When a promise is made, the promisee may rely upon it by incurring various financial and nonfinancial costs that cannot be fully recouped if the promise is broken. Broadly speaking, these costs fall into two classes—out-of-pocket costs and opportunity costs.

---

* To keep matters simple, other interests and remedies will not be considered in this Note. For the same reason, this Note will not consider remedies other than damages.

Out-of-pocket-costs. Out-of-pocket costs are the net costs incurred by a promisee in reliance on the promise prior to breach, less the value produced by those costs that can be realized after breach. To illustrate, assume that Aunt promises Niece that she will reimburse Niece for the cost of a $12,000 car. Niece purchases a car for $12,000 cash on January 5, and immediately tells Aunt about the purchase. Aunt immediately states that she will not keep her promise. Niece's out-of-pocket costs are the difference between her outlay of $12,000 and the resale value of the car on January 5.

Opportunity costs. Engaging in an activity often entails forgoing an opportunity to do something else. *Opportunity costs* are the surplus that the promisee would have enjoyed if he had taken the opportunity that the promise led him to forgo. More specifically, if as a result of a breach the injured party must purchase a substitute performance, the opportunity cost equals the difference between the price of the substitute performance and the best alternative contract price that was available to the party at the time of contracting. To illustrate, assume that at a time when Niece is about to buy a certain inexpensive make of car, Aunt promises Niece that if she purchases a certain more expensive make, Aunt will pay the full price. Niece begins shopping for the more expensive make of car, but before she makes the purchase, Aunt revokes her promise. Meanwhile, the less expensive make has gone up in price from $12,000 to $13,000. If Niece then purchases that make of car, she has suffered an opportunity cost of $1,000, because the promise led her to forgo buying that make when it cost $1,000 less.

With this background, let us return to the best measure of damages for breach of a relied-upon donative promise. *Dougherty v. Salt* teaches that a simple unrelied-upon donative promise is normally unenforceable. Section 90 of the Restatement teaches that reliance may make a donative promise enforceable. But to what *extent* should a relied-upon promise be enforceable? Or, to put it differently, what injury to a relying donative promisee should the law compensate? Since a relied-upon donative promise is enforced because, and only because, it has been relied upon, in the normal case the promise should be enforced to the extent of the reliance, that is, by a reliance (rather than an expectation) measure of damages. For reasons of policy or administrability, however, in at least some cases it might be desirable to employ an expectation measure as a surrogate for reliance. Indeed, when Restatement First was being debated on the floor of the ALI, Williston, the Reporter, went much further, and took the position that the expectation measure should be used in all Section 90 cases:

> MR. WILLISTON: ... Johnny says, "I want to buy a Buick car." Uncle says, "Well, I will give you $1000." ... [Uncle] knows that that $1000 is going to be relied on by the nephew for the purchase of a car....

> [MR.] PRICKETT: May I ask the Reporter if in the example he gave of Johnny and the car, his uncle's promise would be enforceable when Johnny buys the car?

> MR. WILLISTON: I should say so, because the promise was made as a direct reply to Johnny's expression of a desire for a car....

> MR. PRICKETT: Suppose Johnny pays no money down.

MR. WILLISTON: If he has got the car and is liable for the price he gets the $1000 under this Section. . . .

MR. PRICKETT: My idea is this: If he gets the car and pays no money down, if the car is taken away from him, has he suffered any substantial injury?

MR. WILLISTON: Oh, I think he has, as long as he is liable for the price. . . .

[MR.] TUNSTALL: . . . Suppose the car had been a Ford instead of a Buick, costing $600.

. . . Johnny says, "I want to buy a Ford" and . . . not being familiar with the market price of a Ford, the uncle says, "I will give you $1000." Now, is the uncle obligated for the $1000 or for the price of the Ford?

MR. WILLISTON: I think he might be bound for the $1000.

MR. COUDERT: . . . Please let me see if I understand it rightly. Would you say, Mr. Reporter, in your case of Johnny and the uncle, the uncle promising the $1000 and Johnny buying the car—say, he goes out and buys the car for $500—that uncle would be liable for $1000 or would he be liable for $500?

MR. WILLISTON: If Johnny had done what he was expected to do, or is acting within the limits of his uncle's expectation, I think the uncle would be liable for $1000; but not otherwise . . .

In Restatement Second, Section 90 was revised to explicitly negate Williston's view. This was accomplished by adding a new sentence to Section 90: "The remedy granted for breach may be limited as justice requires." The express purpose of this sentence is to permit the use of a reliance measure of damages in Section 90 cases.

This revision, while salutary, leaves open the following questions: (1) On what basis is it to be determined when "justice requires" the use of a reliance rather than an expectation measure? (2) Precisely how are reliance damages to be measured in a donative-promise context?

As applied to strictly financial interests, these questions often are relatively straightforward. If Aunt promises to give Niece $500 for opera tickets during the 2006 season, and retracts her promise after Niece has purchased and used $250 worth of tickets, it seems clear that Aunt's liability should ordinarily be $250, not $500.

Issues involving nonfinancial interests, however, tend to present greater difficulty. For example, suppose Aunt promises to give Niece $20,000 for the purchase of a new car, to be paid in one year. Aunt retracts her promise, but only after Niece has purchased the car and driven it for six months. At the point of retraction, Niece's financial loss is the difference between $20,000 and the car's resale value. Should Aunt's liability be limited to that difference, or should she also be liable for the entire $20,000 because of the deprivation Niece would experience if she must now switch back to subways after having become accustomed to driving?

Similar problems may arise in connection with opportunity costs. Suppose, for example, Uncle promises to reimburse Nephew for his expenses, up to $7,000, for a four-week vacation in New York City. Nephew purchases a round-trip plane ticket for $600 and goes to New York. After he is there for a week, and has spent another $1,500 on hotels, meals, and entertainment, Uncle calls and says, "I'm not giving you any more money than you've already spent. Come back now, or pay for the rest of your vacation yourself." Nephew's financial loss at that point is only $2,100. But suppose that Nephew is entitled to only one four-week vacation each year, and except for Uncle's promise of a full four weeks in New York, Nephew would have gone backpacking with friends, who have now set off without him. On these facts, Nephew has incurred a nonfinancial opportunity cost equal to the difference between the value he places on the vacation that he got and the value he places on the vacation that he lost out on. Assuming this opportunity cost was reasonably foreseeable, should Uncle be liable for this cost as well? If so, how should it be measured? One answer is that the best way to approximate this kind of cost may be to use the value of the promise that caused the promisee to forgo the opportunity. To put this differently, in cases where reliance damages are difficult to establish but obviously significant, the expectation measure may be used as a surrogate for reliance damages.

The treatment of a promisee's benefits may also raise problems in determining reliance damages. If the benefits are financial, the amount of the benefits should normally be deducted from the recovery. For example, suppose Aunt makes a donative promise to buy, on Nephew's behalf, a $10,000 fire insurance policy covering Nephew's goods. Nephew accordingly forbears from insuring the goods himself. Aunt does not buy the policy, and the goods are destroyed by fire. If the goods had been insured, the premium would have been $200. Nephew's damages against Aunt should be $9800, his net proceeds if he had insured the goods himself.

The issue is more difficult when nonfinancial benefits are involved. For example, suppose that in the vacation case, Uncle does not retract until after Nephew has been in New York for four weeks and has spent $7,000. In an action by Nephew to recover the $7,000, is Uncle entitled to an offset for the value of the enjoyment that Nephew derived from the trip? For these purposes, the value of a benefit to the promisee would ordinarily be the amount he would have been willing to pay for the benefit out of his own pocket. This amount will be very difficult to determine. Usually, it would be less than the cost of the benefit. Often, it would be considerably less, because a gift often consists of a luxury that the donee would not have purchased if he had been given an amount equal to the price of the gift, instead of the gift itself. The difficulty of determining the amount that the promisee would have paid for such a benefit, coupled with the likelihood that in many cases the amount would be relatively small, suggests that nonfinancial or intangible benefits should often—perhaps ordinarily—be disregarded in determining a donative promisee's recovery.

———

GOLDSTICK v. ICM REALTY, 788 F.2d 456 (7th Cir.1986). "As a matter of strict logic one might suppose that the plaintiffs, even if they succeeded in establishing a promissory estoppel, would not necessarily be able to recover the value of the promise.... It would seem they would have to show their actual damages: what they gave up ... in reliance on [the] promise...."

"This approach treats promissory estoppel as a tort doctrine for purposes of damages, though it is conventionally classified as a contract doctrine.... Some cases do award just the tort measure of damages in promissory estoppel cases, rather than giving the plaintiff the value of the promise, which he would be entitled to in a breach of contract action.... In Gerson Electric Construction Co. v. Honeywell, Inc., 117 Ill.App.3d 309, 312–13, 72 Ill.Dec. 851, 853, 453 N.E.2d 726, 728 (1983), however, the Illinois Appellate Court held that a plaintiff in a promissory estoppel case could recover damages for the profits he would have made had the defendant kept his promise—provided such an award was necessary to do justice to the plaintiff.

"There is much to be said for using the value of the promise as the measure of damages, simply on grounds of simplicity.... In addition, an expectation measure of damages will frequently cover opportunity costs (which are real, but not out-of-pocket, costs), that the reliance measure would miss...."

D & G STOUT, INC. v. BACARDI IMPORTS, INC.

United States Court of Appeals, Seventh Circuit, 1991.
923 F.2d 566.

Before CUDAHY, POSNER and FLAUM, CIRCUIT JUDGES.

CUDAHY, CIRCUIT JUDGE.

D & G Stout, Inc., operating at all relevant times under the name General Liquors, Inc. (General), was distributing liquor in the turbulent Indiana liquor market in 1987. When two of its major suppliers jumped ship in early 1987, General faced a critical dilemma: sell out at the best possible price or continue operating on a smaller scale. It began negotiating with another Indiana distributor on the terms of a possible sale. Bacardi Imports, Inc. (Bacardi), was still one of General's remaining major suppliers. Knowing that negotiations were ongoing for General's sale, Bacardi promised that General would continue to act as Bacardi's distributor for Northern Indiana. Based on this representation, General turned down the negotiated selling price it was offered. One week later, Bacardi withdrew its account. Realizing it could no longer continue to operate, General went back to the negotiating table, this time settling for an amount $550,000 below the first offer. The question is whether General can recover the price differential from Bacardi on a theory of promissory estoppel. The district court believed that as a matter of law it could not, and entered summary judgment for defendant Bacardi. We disagree, and so we remand for trial.

I.

General was (and D & G Stout, Inc., is) an Indiana corporation with its main place of business in South Bend. Bacardi is a corporation organized in New York and doing business primarily in Miami, Florida. General served at Bacardi's will as its wholesale distributor in Northern Indiana for over 35 years. During the 1980s, liquor suppliers in Indiana undertook an extensive effort to consolidate their distribution, the effect of which was to reduce the number of distributors in the state from approximately twenty in 1980 to only two in 1990.

General weathered the storm until April 1987, when two of its major suppliers withdrew their lines, taking with them the basis of more than fifty percent of General's gross sales. By June, General recognized that it must choose between selling out and scaling back operations in order to stay in business. Despite the recent setbacks, General calculated that remaining operational was possible as long as it held on to its continuing two major suppliers, Bacardi and Hiram Walker.

About this time (and probably in connection with the same forces concentrating distribution) Bacardi lost its distributor in Indianapolis and southern Indiana. Bacardi decided to convene a meeting on July 9, 1987, of applicants for the open distributorship. General's president, David Stout, attended the meetings as an observer, with no designs on the new opening. Stout did intend to seek assurances from Bacardi about its commitment to General in Northern Indiana. While in Indianapolis, Stout was approached by National Wine & Spirits Company (National), which expressed an interest in buying General. Stout agreed to begin negotiations the following weekend. Stout also received the assurances from Bacardi he sought: after listening to Stout's concerns and hearing about his contemplated sale of General, Bacardi emphatically avowed that it had no intention of taking its line to another distributor in Northern Indiana. This promise was open-ended—no one discussed how long the continuing relationship might last.

During the ensuing two weeks, General carried on negotiations with National to reach a price for the purchase of General's assets. Bacardi kept in close contact with General to find out whether it would indeed sell. The negotiations yielded a final figure for Stout to consider. On July 22 and again on July 23—with negotiations concluded and only the final decision remaining—Stout again sought assurances from Bacardi. The supplier unequivocally reconfirmed its commitment to stay with General, and Stout replied that, as a result, he was going to turn down National's offer and would continue operating. Later on the 23rd, Stout rejected National's offer. That same afternoon, Bacardi decided to withdraw its line from General.

General learned of Bacardi's decision on July 30. The news spread quickly through the industry, and by August 3, Hiram Walker had also pulled its line, expressing a belief that General could not continue without Bacardi on board. By this time, sales personnel were abandoning General for jobs with the two surviving distributors in Indiana (one of which was National). General quickly sought out National to sell its assets, but National's offer was now substantially reduced. The ensuing agreement, executed on August 14 and closed on August 28, included a purchase price $550,000 lower than the one National offered in mid-July. Stout's successor company brought suit under the diversity jurisdiction against Bacardi, claiming that the supplier was liable by reason of promissory estoppel for this decline in the purchase price. Judge Miller entered summary judgment for Bacardi, holding that the promises plaintiff alleged were not the type upon which one may rely under Indiana law. Plaintiff appeals.

II.

We have generally stated General's version of the facts, many of which are undisputed. On appeal, Bacardi does not argue the facts and is apparently willing to rest on Judge Miller's legal analysis. Both parties also agree with Judge Miller that Indiana law governs this case and we do not question this conclusion. Before us then is the legal question whether the plaintiff has alleged any injury which Indiana's law of promissory estoppel redresses.

Indiana has adopted the Restatement's theory of promissory estoppel:

> A promise which the promisor should reasonably expect to induce action or forbearance on the part of the promisee or a third person and which does induce such action or forbearance is binding if injustice can be avoided only by the enforcement of the promise. The remedy for breach may be limited as justice requires.

Restatement (Second) of Contracts § 90(1) (1981); *Eby v. York–Division, Borg–Warner,* 455 N.E.2d 623, 627 (Ind.App.1983); *Pepsi–Cola General Bottlers, Inc. v. Woods,* 440 N.E.2d 696, 698 (Ind.App.1982). The district judge dismissed the complaint on the ground that Bacardi's alleged promise was not one on which it should reasonably have expected General to rely.

The district court first noted that the relationship between General and Bacardi had always been terminable at will. Because Bacardi's promises that it would continue to use General as its distributor contained no language indicating that they would be good for any specific period,[1] the court reasoned that the relationship remained terminable at will. It then concluded that the promise was not legally enforceable, and thus was not one on which General reasonably might rely. We agree with each of these conclusions but the last. Notwithstanding the continuation of an at-will relationship between Bacardi and General, the promises given between July 9 and July 23 were not without legal effect.

In Indiana, as in many states, an aspiring employee cannot sue for lost wages on an unfulfilled promise of at-will employment. *Pepsi–Cola,* 440 N.E.2d 696; *accord Ewing v. Board of Trustees of Pulaski Memorial Hosp.,* 486 N.E.2d 1094, 1098 (Ind.App.1985) (employment contract for indefinite tenure is unenforceable for future employment). Because the employer could have terminated the employee without cause at any time after the employment began, the promise of a job brings no expectation of any determinable period of employment or corresponding amount of wages. The promise is therefore unenforceable under either a contract or a promissory estoppel theory in an action for lost wages. Nevertheless, lost wages are not the only source of damages flowing from a broken promise of employment, enforceable or not. Indiana courts acknowledge certain damages as recoverable when the employer breaks a promise of employment, even if the employment is to be terminable at will. For example, in *Eby v. York–Division, Borg–Warner,* 455 N.E.2d at 627, a plaintiff who gave up a job and moved from Indiana to Florida on a promise of employment sued for recovery of preparation and moving expenses incurred on the basis of the promise. The Indiana appellate court reversed the lower court's summary judgment for the defendant employer, holding that the plaintiff employee had stated a cause of action for promissory estoppel. The court found that the defendant could have expected the plaintiff and his wife to move in reliance on the promise of employment

---

1. Given the context of the promise, we see a plausible argument that the promise was one for a term, namely that Bacardi would stay on at least until the rush toward consolidation passed. But the district judge found differently, and we need not question his factual conclusion in light of our legal analysis.

and therefore might be liable for reneging. *See also Pepsi–Cola,* 440 N.E.2d 696; *accord Lorson v. Falcon Coach,* 214 Kan. 670, 522 P.2d 449 (1974).

Our review of Indiana law thus leaves us a simple if somewhat crude question: are the damages plaintiff seeks here more like lost future wages or like moving expenses? We can better answer the question if we determine why Indiana draws this distinction. Unlike lost wages, moving expenses represent out-of-pocket losses; they involve a loss of something already possessed. It would be plausible, although not very sophisticated, to distinguish between the loss of something yet to be received and the loss of something already in hand. But this is not precisely where Indiana draws the distinction, nor where we would draw it if it were our choice to make. *Eby* itself involved not only moving expenses, but wages lost at plaintiff's old job during the few days plaintiff was preparing to move. 455 N.E.2d at 625. Those wages were not out-of-pocket losses: plaintiff had no more received those wages than he had received wages from his promised employment.

In fact, the line Indiana draws is between expectation damages and reliance damages. In future wages, the employee has only an expectation of income, the recovery of which promissory estoppel will not support in an at-will employment setting. In wages forgone in order to prepare to move, as in moving expenses themselves, the employee gave up a presently determinate sum for the purpose of relocating. Both moving expenses and forgone wages were the hopeful employee's costs of positioning himself for his new job; moving expenses happen to be out-of-pocket losses, while forgone wages are opportunity costs. Both are reliance costs, not expectancy damages.

Thus, the question has become whether the loss incurred from the price drop was attributable to lost expectations of future profit or resulted from an opportunity forgone in reliance on the promise. At first blush, the injury might seem more like the loss of future wages. Bacardi was a major supplier whose business was extremely valuable to General. While the loss of this "asset" might cause a decline in General's market value as measured by the loss of future income from the sale of Bacardi's products, this loss is not actionable on a promissory estoppel theory. Those damages would presumably be measured by the present value of General's anticipated profit from the sale of Bacardi's products, and Indiana will not grant relief based on promissory estoppel to compensate an aggrieved party for such expectancy damages. Lost future income expected from an at-will relationship, whether from wages or from profits, is not recoverable on a theory of promissory estoppel, and neither is the present value of such losses.

But the fact is that recovery of lost profits is not a question before us. Bacardi's account was never an "asset" that National could acquire by purchasing General. As counsel for the defendant candidly but carefully explained, National never assumed that it would retain the Bacardi account by buying General; in fact, National assumed the opposite. Bacardi's major competitor in the rum distilling business distributed through National, and the two top distillers in a given category of liquor would not choose the same distributor. Both before and after Bacardi decided to withdraw its products, all National wanted from General were its assets other than the Bacardi account. But Bacardi's repudiation of its promise ostensibly affected the price of General's business so drastically because, as everyone in the industry understood, General's option to stay in business independently was destroyed by Bacardi's withdrawal of its account. Thus, through its repudiation, Bacardi destroyed General's negotiating leverage since General no longer had the alternative of continuing as an independent concern. Presumably, after Bacardi's withdrawal General's only alternative to selling to National was to liquidate. Thus, Bacardi's repudiation turned General's discussions with National from negotiations to buy a going concern into a liquidation sale. Instead of bargaining from strength, knowing it could reject a junk-value offer and carry on its business, General was left with one choice: sell at any price.

Under these facts, General had a reliance interest in Bacardi's promise. General was in lively negotiations with National, and it repeatedly informed Bacardi of this fact. A price was agreed upon, and based on that figure, Stout had to decide whether to close his doors or continue operating. General had a business opportunity that all parties knew would be devalued once Bacardi announced its intention to go elsewhere. The extent of that devaluation represents a reliance injury, rather than an injury to General's expectation of future profit. The injury is analogous to the cost of moving expenses incurred as a result of promised employment in *Eby* and *Pepsi–Cola*.

Nor were these promises merely meaningless restatements of an understood at-will relationship. With its current business opportunity, General stood at a crossroads. Circumstances foreshadowed a costly demise for the company, but it was able to negotiate an alternative. Far from confirming the obvious, Bacardi wrote its assurances on a clean slate with full knowledge that General was just as likely to reject the offered relationship as embrace it. That this was the situation is indicated most clearly by Bacardi's repeated calls to check on Stout's impending decision. Bacardi reassured Stout of its commitment in full knowledge that he planned to reject National's offer and with the reasonable expectation that an immediate pull out would severely undermine General's asking price. Like the plaintiffs in *Eby* who moved based on the promise of a job, General incurred a cost in rejecting the deal that was non-recoverable once Bacardi's later decision became known.

There may always exist the potential for a quandary in a promissory estoppel action based on a promise of at-will employment. When could Bacardi terminate the relationship with General without fear of liability for reliance costs, once it made the assurances in question? Obviously we do not hold that General and Bacardi had formed a new, permanent employment relationship. How long an employee can rely on the employer's promise is not a matter we can decide here. The issue is one of reasonable reliance, and to the extent that there might be questions, they should be for trial.

III.

We have, of course, reviewed this case in the posture of summary judgment. General's allegations still must be proven at trial. However, under Indiana law, we think that Bacardi's promise was of a sort on which General might rely, with the possibility of damages for breach. For that reason the judgment of the district court is

REVERSED AND REMANDED.

NOTE ON THE BACARDI CASE

In Jarboe v. Landmark Community Newspapers of Indiana, Inc., 644 N.E.2d 118 (Ind.1994), the Indiana Supreme Court approved the Seventh Circuit's interpretation of Indiana law in *Bacardi*. The court made clear that in cases involving the discharge of an at-will employee who had a justified claim based on reliance, the employee's remedy would be limited to reliance damages and would not include restoration of employment.

————

WALTERS v. MARATHON OIL CO., 642 F.2d 1098 (7th Cir.1981). Marathon Oil was engaged in the business of distributing petroleum products. Mr. and Mrs. Walters contacted Marathon in late December 1978 about the possibility of locating a combination food store and service station on a vacant service station site in Indianapolis. Based upon promises made by, and continuing negotiations with, Marathon representatives, the Walters purchased the service station in February 1979, and continued to make improvements upon it. The negotiations and paperwork proceeded normally, and the Walters delivered to Marathon an agreement signed by them. After the agreement was received, but before it was accepted, Marathon placed a moratorium on considering new applications for dealerships, and refused to sign the agreement. The Walters brought suit.

The trial court held for the Walters, on the theory of promissory estoppel. It found that the Walters lost anticipated profits of six cents per gallon for the 370,000 gallons they were to receive under their allocation for the first year's gasoline sales, totaling $22,200, and awarded this amount in damages. On appeal, Marathon argued that since the Walters succeeded at trial solely on a promissory estoppel theory, loss of profits was not a proper measure of damages. Instead, damages should have been based on the amount of the Walters' reliance, measured by the difference between their expenditures on the site and its present value. Using this measure of damages, the Walters would receive no recovery, because the present value of the site as improved was slightly more than the amount the Walters had expended. The Court of Appeals rejected this argument.

"[I]n reliance upon appellant's promise to supply gasoline supplies to them, appellees purchased the station, and invested their funds and their time. It is unreasonable to assume that they did not anticipate a return of profits from this investment of time and funds, but, in reliance upon appellant's promise, they had foregone the opportunity to make the investment elsewhere. As indicated, the record reflects that had appellant performed according to its promise, appellees would have received the anticipated net profit of $22,200.00. The findings of the trial court in this regard were fully supported by the evidence. . . .

"Since promissory estoppel is an equitable matter, the trial court has broad power in its choice of a remedy. . . ."

————

NOTE ON RELIANCE IN COMMERCIAL CONTEXTS

As originally conceived in Restatement First, the principle of reliance in general, and Section 90 in particular, seemed to be primarily directed to donative promises. However, as evidenced by D & G Stout, Inc. v. Bacardi Imports, Inc., and Walters v. Marathon Oil Co., since the adoption of Section 90 the courts have steadily increased the ambit of the reliance principle, and applied it in a wide variety of commercial contexts where for one reason or another the bargain principle was not sufficient to make a promise enforceable or to redress a perceived injury. Many other cases invoking the reliance principle in commercial contexts will be examined in succeeding Chapters.

Chapter 2

THE BARGAIN PRINCIPLE
AND ITS LIMITS

This Chapter introduces the major type of consideration, that is, the bargain. (Indeed, recall that under the terminology used by the Restatement and many courts, the terms "bargain" and "consideration" are almost equivalent.) The first several cases in Section 1 implicitly or explicitly set out *the bargain principle*, under which bargains are not only enforced, but enforced according to their terms. These cases also suggest, again explicitly or implicitly, some of the reasons that lie behind the bargain principle. Section 2 explores the limits placed on the bargain principle by the principle of unconscionability. Sections 3 and 4 explore two further, more technical limits on the bargain principle: the doctrine of mutuality and the legal-duty rule.

SECTION 1. THE BARGAIN PRINCIPLE

WESTLAKE v. ADAMS, C.P., 5 C.B. (N.S.) 248, 265 (1858). Byles, J., said: "It is an elementary principle, that the law will not enter into an inquiry as to the adequacy of the consideration.... The jury have, I think, made an end of the question [of consideration]; for they have found (as well they might) that the defendant received what he bargained for, and all that he bargained for."

HAMER v. SIDWAY

Court of Appeals of New York, 1891.
124 N.Y. 538, 27 N.E. 256.

Appeal from an order of the general term of the supreme court in the fourth judicial department, reversing a judgment entered on the decision of the court at special term in the county clerk's office of Chemung county on the 1st day of October, 1889. The plaintiff presented a claim to the executor of

William E. Story, Sr., for $5,000 and interest from the 6th day of February, 1875. She acquired it through several mesne assignments from William E. Story, 2d. The claim being rejected by the executor, this action was brought. It appears that William E. Story, Sr., was the uncle of William E. Story, 2d; that at the celebration of the golden wedding of Samuel Story and wife, father and mother of William E. Story, Sr., on the 20th day of March, 1869, in the presence of the family and invited guests, he promised his nephew that if he would refrain from drinking, using tobacco, swearing, and playing cards or billiards for money until he became 21 years of age, he would pay him the sum of $5,000. The nephew assented thereto, and fully performed the conditions inducing the promise. When the nephew arrived at the age of 21 years, and on the 31st day of January, 1875, he wrote to his uncle, informing him that he had performed his part of the agreement, and had thereby become entitled to the sum of $5,000.

The uncle received the letter, and a few days later, and on the 6th day of February, he wrote and mailed to his nephew the following letter: "Buffalo, Feb. 6, 1875, W.E. Story, Jr.—Dear Nephew: Your letter of the 31st ult. came to hand all right, saying that you had lived up to the promise made to me several years ago. I have no doubt but you have, for which you shall have five thousand dollars, as I promised you. I had the money in the bank the day you was twenty-one years old that I intend for you, and you shall have the money certain. Now Willie, I do not intend to interfere with this money in any way till I think you are capable of taking care of it, and the sooner that time comes the better it will please me. I would hate very much to have you start out in some adventure that you thought all right and lose this money in one year. The first five thousand dollars that I got together cost me a heap of hard work. . . . This money you have earned much easier than I did, besides, acquiring good habits at the same time, and you are quite welcome to the money. Hope you will make good use of it. I was ten long years getting this together after I was your age. . . . Truly yours, W.E. Story. P.S. You can consider this money on interest."

The nephew received the letter, and thereafter consented that the money should remain with his uncle in accordance with the terms and conditions of the letter. The uncle died on the 29th day of January, 1887, without having paid over to his nephew any portion of the said $5,000 and interest.

PARKER, J. . . . The defendant contends that the contract was without consideration to support it, and therefore invalid. He asserts that the promisee, by refraining from the use of liquor and tobacco, was not harmed, but benefited; that that which he did was best for him to do, independently of his uncle's promise,—and insists that it follows that, unless the promisor was benefited, the contract was without consideration,—a contention which, if well founded, would seem to leave open for controversy in many cases whether that which the promisee did or omitted to do was in fact of such benefit to him as to leave no consideration to support the enforcement of the promisor's agreement. Such a rule could not be tolerated, and is without foundation in the law. The Exchequer Chamber in 1875 defined "consideration" as follows: "A valuable consideration, in the sense of the law, may consist either in some right, interest, profit, or benefit accruing to the one party, or some forbearance, detriment, loss, or responsibility given, suffered, or undertaken by the other." Courts "will not ask whether the thing which forms the consideration does in fact benefit the promisee or a third party, or is of any substantial value to any one. It is enough that something is promised, done, forborne, or suffered by the party to whom the promise is made as consideration for the promise made to him." Anson.Cont. 63. "In general a waiver of any legal right at the request of another party is a sufficient consideration for a promise." Pars.Cont. *444. "Any damage, or suspension, or forbearance of a right will be sufficient to sustain a promise." 2 Kent.Comm. (12th Ed.) *465. Pollock in his work on Contracts (page 166), after citing the definition given by the Exchequer Chamber, already quoted, says: "The second branch of this judicial description is really the most important one. 'Consideration' means not so much that one party is profiting as that the other abandons some legal right in the present, or limits his legal freedom of action in the future, as an inducement for the promise of the first."

Now, applying this rule to the facts before us, the promisee used tobacco, occasionally drank liquor, and he had a legal right to do so. That right he abandoned for a period of years upon the strength of the promise of the testator that for such forbearance he would give him $5,000. We need not speculate on the effort which may have been required to give up the use of those stimulants. It is sufficient that he restricted his lawful freedom of action within certain prescribed limits upon the faith of his uncle's agreement, and now, having fully performed the conditions imposed, it is of no moment whether such performance actually proved a benefit to the promisor, and the court will not inquire into it; but, were it a proper subject of inquiry, we see nothing in this record that would permit a determination that the uncle was not benefited in a legal sense. Few cases have been found which may be said to be precisely in point, but such as have been, support the position we have taken. . . .

Order appealed from reversed, and judgment of the special term affirmed.*

––––––

NOTE ON THE STATUTE OF FRAUDS

William E. Story's original promise was not in writing. Did that affect the issue whether it was legally enforceable? The question, what promises must be in writing to be enforceable (or at least, to be enforceable in full), is addressed by a group of rules known as the Statute of Frauds. This casebook is designed so that Statute of Frauds problems are to be considered continuously, in the context of cases involving oral promises, rather than in one batch. To that end, an extended Note on the Statute of Frauds is set forth at Appendix A. You should study Appendix A generally at this point. Thereafter, whenever a case involves an oral promise you should turn to the relevant sections of Appendix A to consider the impact of the Statute of Frauds on that case.

––––––

DAVIES v. MARTEL LABORATORY SERVICES, INC., 189 Ill. App.3d 694, 136 Ill.Dec. 951, 545 N.E.2d 475 (1989). Davies alleged that at a

––––––

* For historical background to both the definition of consideration and the approach to the issue of consideration employed in Hamer v. Sidway, see Appendix B. (Footnote by ed.)

time when she was an at-will employee of Martel, Martel offered her a contract of employment under which (1) she would be made a Vice–President, earning $40,000 per year, if she would obtain an MBA degree, and (2) if she accepted the offer, she would immediately be designated a permanent employee, and also appointed a member of Martel's President's Council. Martel also promised to contribute one-half of Davies's expenses incurred in obtaining her MBA. Davies accepted the offer. One week later, Davies attended her first meeting as a member of the President's Council, and in the fall she enrolled in the Northwestern University MBA program. A year later, Martel terminated Davies' employment without cause. Martel argued that Davies failed to allege sufficient consideration for its promise, because her pursuit of a MBA degree was a benefit to her, not a disadvantage or detriment. The trial court agreed, and granted Martel summary judgment. Reversed.

The words "benefit" and "detriment" in contract cases involving consideration have technical meanings. "Detriment" as used in determining the sufficiency of consideration to support a contract means " 'legal detriment as distinguished from detriment in fact. It means giving up something which immediately prior thereto the promisee was privileged to retain, or doing or refraining from doing something which he was then privileged not to do, or not to refrain from doing.' "(Hamilton Bancshares, Inc. v. Leroy (1985), 131 Ill.App.3d 907, 913, quoting 1 Williston, Contracts sec. 102A at 380–82 (3d ed. 1957).) For example, a promise to give up smoking may be a benefit to the promisee's health, but a promise to give up smoking is also a legal detriment and sufficient consideration to support a contract.... In the present case, Davies did not have to obtain a MBA degree and expend her own time and money in doing so in order to continue as an at-will employee of Martel's; she could have continued to perform oil analyses and mapping work rather than enter the ivied walls of Northwestern. Nor does it appear that Davies was obligated to serve as a member on Martel's President's Council and to assume additional duties and responsibilities. In other words, Davies was privileged to refrain from serving on Martel's Council and from pursuing a MBA degree. By giving up her privilege to refrain from so acting, Davies clearly could be said to have suffered a legal detriment, which would constitute sufficient consideration to support the alleged oral contract between the parties. Based on the foregoing ... we find that Davies' amended complaint sufficiently alleged consideration in support of the contract at issue.

HANCOCK BANK & TRUST CO. v. SHELL OIL CO.

Supreme Judicial Court of Massachusetts, 1974.
365 Mass. 629, 309 N.E.2d 482.

Before QUIRICO, BRAUCHER, KAPLAN and WILKINS, JJ.

RESCRIPT.

The plaintiff bank argues exceptions to a Superior Court judge's findings and rulings in an action of summary process. The defendant Shell Oil Company (Shell) occupied premises in Taunton under a written lease. The lease, executed on May 15, 1962, for a term of fifteen years commencing on August 1, 1962, with options to extend the term, contained a provision that "Shell may terminate this lease at any time by giving Lessor at least ninety (90) days' notice." The lease further provided for a fixed monthly rental, obligated Shell to make certain minor repairs, and required Shell to reimburse the lessor "for any amount by which the general taxes on the premises allocable to any full year of the term of this lease exceed ... [$525]." The bank acquired the premises, subject to the lease agreement, at a public auction following foreclosure proceedings against the lessor. The bank asserts that a lease for fifteen years, with options in the lessee to extend the term for an additional fifteen years, which permits the lessee to terminate the lease on ninety days' notice, is "so lacking in mutuality as to be void as against public policy." The bank cites no authority for such a conclusion. Once it appears that there was consideration to support a contract, and in the absence of statute (see, e.g., G.L. c. 106, § 2–302; G.L. c. 255B, § 20; G.L. c. 255D, § 29, subsection C),* courts have traditionally declined to relieve a party from the terms of a contract merely because he made what he regards as a bad or uneven bargain. See Shaw v. Appleton, 161 Mass. 313, 315, 37 N.E. 372 (1894); Manson v. Flanagan, 233 Mass. 150, 153, 123 N.E. 614 (1919); Eliopoulos v. Makros, 322 Mass. 485, 488, 77 N.E.2d 777 (1948); Graphic Arts Finishers, Inc. v. Boston Redevelopment Authy., 357 Mass. 40, 43, 255 N.E.2d 793 (1970). See also Williston, Contracts (3d ed.) § 115 (1957); Corbin, Contracts, § 127 (1963). On this record it is not clear that the original lessor made a bad bargain. In any event, there is no basis for treating the lease as void on public policy grounds. There was consideration to support the lessor's obligations under the lease....

Exceptions overruled.

RESTATEMENT, SECOND, CONTRACTS §§ 71, 72, 79

[See Selected Source Materials Supplement]

BATSAKIS v. DEMOTSIS

Court of Civil Appeals of Texas, 1949.
226 S.W.2d 673.

McGILL, JUSTICE. This is an appeal from a judgment of the 57th judicial District Court of Bexar County. Appellant was plaintiff and appellee was defendant in the trial court. The parties will be so designated.

---

* G.L. c. 106, § 2–302 is UCC § 2–302. The two other cited provisions are part of comprehensive statutes dealing with certain kinds of retail installment-sales contracts. G.L. c. 255B, § 20, which relates to retail installment motor-vehicle sales contracts, renders unenforceable agreements in such contracts providing for confession of judgments, assignment of wages, or authorization of the seller to unlawfully enter the buyer's premises. G.L. c. 255D, § 29, Subsection C, provides that agreements which violate the Massachusetts Retail Installment Sales and Services Act may be declared void in a civil action brought by the buyer. (Footnote by ed.)

Plaintiff sued defendant to recover $2,000 with interest at the rate of 8% per annum from April 2, 1942, alleged to be due on the following instrument, being a translation from the original, which is written in the Greek language:

"Peiraeus

April 2, 1942

"Mr. George Batsakis

Konstantinou Diadohou # 7

Peiraeus

"Mr. Batsakis:

"I state by my present (letter) that I received today from you the amount of two thousand dollars ($2,000.00) of United States of America money, which I borrowed from you for the support of my family during these difficult days and because it is impossible for me to transfer dollars of my own from America.

"The above amount I accept with the expressed promise that I will return to you again in American dollars either at the end of the present war or even before in the event that you might be able to find a way to collect them (dollars) from my representative in America to whom I shall write and give him an order relative to this. You understand until the final execution (payment) to the above amount an eight per cent interest will be added and paid together with the principal.

"I thank you and I remain yours with respects.

"The recipient,

(Signed) Eugenia The. Demotsis."

Trial to the court without the intervention of a jury resulted in a judgment in favor of plaintiff for $750.00 principal, and interest at the rate of 8% per annum from April 2, 1942 to the date of judgment, totaling $1163.83, with interest thereon at the rate of 8% per annum until paid. Plaintiff has perfected his appeal.

The court sustained certain special exceptions of plaintiff to defendant's first amended original answer on which the case was tried, and struck therefrom paragraphs II, III and V. Defendant excepted to such action of the court, but has not cross-assigned error here. The answer, stripped of such paragraphs, consisted of a general denial contained in paragraph I thereof, and of Paragraph IV, which is as follows:

"IV. That under the circumstances alleged in Paragraph II of this answer, the consideration upon which said written instrument sued upon by plaintiff herein is founded, is wanting and has failed to the extent of $1975.00, and defendant pleads specially under the verification hereinafter made the want and failure of consideration stated, and now tenders, as defendant has heretofore tendered to plaintiff, $25.00 as the value of the loan of money received by defendant from plaintiff, together with interest thereon.

"Further, in connection with this plea of want and failure of consideration defendant alleges that she at no time received from plaintiff himself or from anyone for plaintiff any money or thing of value other than, as hereinbefore alleged, the original loan of 500,000 drachmae. That at the time of the loan by plaintiff to defendant of said 500,000 drachmae the value of 500,000 drachmae in the Kingdom of Greece in dollars of money of the United States of America, was $25.00, and also at said time the value of 500,000 drachmae of Greek money in the United States of America in dollars was $25.00 of money of the United States of America. The plea of want and failure of consideration is verified by defendant as follows."

The allegations in paragraph II which were stricken, referred to in paragraph IV, were that the instrument sued on was signed and delivered in the Kingdom of Greece on or about April 2, 1942, at which time both plaintiff and defendant were residents of and residing in the Kingdom of Greece, and

> *"Plaintiff* (emphasis ours) avers that on or about April 2, 1942 she owned money and property and had credit in the United States of America, but was then and there in the Kingdom of Greece in straitened financial circumstances due to the conditions produced by World War II and could not make use of her money and property and credit existing in the United States of America. That in the circumstances the plaintiff agreed to and did lend to defendant the sum of 500,000 drachmae, which at that time, on or about April 2, 1942, had the value of $25.00 in money of the United States of America. That the said plaintiff knowing defendant's financial distress and desire to return to the United States of America, exacted of her the written instrument plaintiff sues upon, which was a promise by her to pay to him the sum of $2,000.00 of United States of America money."

Plaintiff specially excepted to paragraph IV because the allegations thereof were insufficient to allege either want of consideration or failure of consideration, in that it affirmatively appears therefrom that defendant received what was agreed to be delivered to her, and that plaintiff breached no agreement. The court overruled this exception, and such action is assigned as error. Error is also assigned because of the court's failure to enter judgment for the whole unpaid balance of the principal of the instrument with interest as therein provided.

Defendant testified that she did receive 500,000 drachmas from plaintiff. It is not clear whether she received all the 500,000 drachmas or only a portion of them before she signed the instrument in question. Her testimony clearly shows that the understanding of the parties was that plaintiff would give her the 500,000 drachmas if she would sign the instrument. She testified:

> "Q.... who suggested the figure of $2,000.00?

> "A. That was how he asked me from the beginning. He said he will give me five hundred thousand drachmas provided I signed that I would pay him $2,000.00 American money."

The transaction amounted to a sale by plaintiff of the 500,000 drachmas in consideration of the execution of the instrument sued on, by defendant. It is not contended that the drachmas had no value. Indeed, the judgment indicates that the trial court placed a value of $750.00 on them or on the other consideration which plaintiff gave defendant for the instrument if he believed plaintiff's testimony. Therefore the plea of want of consideration was unavailing. A plea of want of consideration amounts to a contention that the instrument never became a valid obligation in the first place....

Mere inadequacy of consideration will not void a contract. 10 Tex.Jur., Contracts, Sec. 89, p. 150; Chastain v. Texas Christian Missionary Society, Tex.Civ.App., 78 S.W.2d 728, loc. cit. 731(3), Wr. Ref.

Nor was the plea of failure of consideration availing. Defendant got exactly what she contracted for according to her own testimony. The court should have rendered judgment in favor of plaintiff against defendant for the principal sum of $2,000.00 evidenced by the instrument sued on, with interest as therein provided. We construe the provision relating to interest as providing for interest at the rate of 8% per annum. The judgment is reformed so as to award appellant a recovery against appellee of $2,000.00 with interest thereon at the rate of 8% per annum from April 2, 1942. Such judgment will bear interest at the rate of 8% per annum until paid on $2,000.00 thereof and on the balance interest at the rate of 6% per annum. As so reformed, the judgment is affirmed.

Reformed and affirmed.

B. SWEET–ESCOTT, GREECE—A POLITICAL AND ECONOMIC SURVEY 1939–1953, 93–96 (1954). "It has been said that Greece suffered more heavily during the war than any other Allied country except Soviet Russia. From 1941 to 1944 the country was visited by famine, destruction, and inflation. Greece normally requires to import some 600,000 tons of grain a year. Most of this comes by sea. As soon as the Axis occupied Greece the usual sea routes ceased to be available—except those from the Black Sea and the Adriatic. And in any case there were few ships on which the Axis could lay their hands for feeding the country. Moreover, the only other main line of communication, the railway to Belgrade and Sofia, was fully occupied in supplying the Axis armies of occupation. Even if the Axis had been determined to maintain the existing standard of nutrition in Greece, it would have been a difficult task. As things were, the standard fell disastrously. It is estimated that the average daily diet in 1941, the worst of the three war winters, fell to 900 calories per person, and that it never exceeded 1,400 calories during the occupation. As the daily diet of a healthy man should be in the region of 3,000 calories, it is hardly surprising that Greece fell a prey to famine, especially in the towns. At one period in the winter of 1941–2 people were dying daily in the streets of Athens by the score. It will probably never be known how many perished of malnutrition and the diseases occasioned thereby, but the figure may well run into hundreds of thousands...."

FURTHER NOTE ON CONSIDERATION AND REMEDIES

It has already been pointed out that the question, what promises should the law enforce, is inseparable from the issue, *to what extent* should a particular type of promise be enforced? This is not a problem when the three basic damage measures—expectation, reliance, and restitution—produce identical results. For example, suppose that Plumber P, whose normal rate is $60 an hour, agrees to perform a repair for Homeowner H, and spends one hour on the job. H fails to pay. P's expectation damages are $60, the value of H's promised performance. P's reliance damages are also probably $60, because the plumbing business being what it is, in accepting H's job, P probably gave up an opportunity to use his time doing plumbing repairs for someone else. Restitution damages may also be deemed to be $60, because H has received $60 worth of plumbing services.

Often, however, the three damage measures will differ. In *Batsakis v. Demotsis*, the defendant argued in effect that the value of what she had received was much less than the value of what she had promised. She was willing to pay the value of what she had received—that is, restitution damages. What the defendant resisted was payment of the value of what she had promised—that is, expectation damages. Conversely, the plaintiff rejected restitution damages and insisted on expectation damages. In short, both parties admitted that the contract was enforceable to some extent; the question was, to what extent. In a very real way, therefore, when the court said that adequacy of consideration will not be reviewed, it was making a damages rule, namely, that when a bargain has been made the normal remedy for breach is expectation damages, and it is no defense that the value of one promised performance exceeded the value of the other.

———

RESTATEMENT, SECOND, CONTRACTS §§ 175, 176

[See Selected Source Materials Supplement]

———

RESTATEMENT, SECOND, CONTRACTS § 176, ILLUSTRATION

16: A, a municipal water company seeking to induce B, a developer outside the city limits, to make a contract for water at rates greatly in excess of those similarly situated, threatens to refuse to supply to B unless B makes the contract. B, having no reasonable alternative, makes the contract. Because the threat amounts to a use for illegitimate ends of A's power not to supply water, the contract is voidable by B. . . .

———

UNIDROIT PRINCIPLES OF INTERNATIONAL COMMERCIAL CONTRACTS ART. 3.9

[See Selected Source Materials Supplement]

———

NOTE ON UNIDROIT

In 1971, the governing council of the International Institute for the Unification of Private Law determined to include a codification of the law of contracts in its program. A Working Group consisting of academics, judges, and civil servants was created in 1980. The members of the Working Group were of different nationalities, but sat in their personal capacities, not to express the views of their governments. The ultimate result was the Unidroit Principles of International Commercial Contracts, which was finalized in 1994. The goal of the Unidroit Principles is to set forth general rules for international commercial contracts. The Principles are intended to enunciate communal principles and rules of existing legal systems, and to select the solutions that are best adapted to the special requirements of international commercial contracts. In preparing the Principles, particular attention was paid to recent codifications of contract and commercial law, including the UCC, the Restatement Second of Contracts, the Netherlands Civil Code, the 1985 Foreign Economic Contract law of the People's Republic of China, the Draft New Civil Code of Quebec, and the Convention for the International Sale of Goods.

The Unidroit Principles are not intended for adoption by any country, and are not legally binding. Instead, they are a sort of international Restatement of Contract Law.

PRINCIPLES OF EUROPEAN CONTRACT LAW § 4.108

NOTE ON THE PRINCIPLES OF EUROPEAN CONTRACT LAW

The Principles of European Contract Law are the product of the Commission on European Contract Law, a body of lawyers, drawn from all the member States of the European Union under the chairmanship of Professor Ole Lando. The Principles are a response to a perceived need for a European Union-wide infrastructure of contract law. They are intended to reflect the common core of solutions to problems of contract law. In preparing the Principles, the Commission drew on a wide range of legal materials from both within and outside Europe, including the Uniform Commercial Code and the Restatements of Contracts and of Restitution. Some of the provisions in the Principles reflect suggestions and ideas that have not yet materialized in the law of the European Union States. See Introduction, Principles of European Contract Law, parts I and II (1999).

CHOUINARD v. CHOUINARD, 568 F.2d 430 (5th Cir.1978). Arc Corporation was owned by Fred Chouinard; Fred's father, Al Chouinard; and Fred's twin brother, Ed Chouinard. Fred was the president and apparently ran the business. Over the years, the parties were in dispute concerning the precise nature of the ownership interests of Ed and Al. At one point, Ed concluded that he and Al each owned 37½ percent of Arc, and that the value of each of their interests was close to $500,000. These conclusions were not shared by Fred. In 1974, Arc got into substantial financial difficulties, due in part to a bad decision by Fred, and badly needed new financing. Fred was able to obtain a financing commitment from the Heller Company, a commercial lender, but when Heller learned that Ed and Al each claimed a stock–ownership interest, Heller made it clear that it would not make a loan until the stock–ownership dispute was settled. Fred's attorney drafted a proposed instrument under which all parties would agree that Heller could make the loan, but no one would acknowledge anyone else's ownership claim. This proposal was apparently never "put on the table," because the attorney for Ed and Al informed Fred's counsel that this was a good occasion to settle the ownership issue. Fred's counsel labeled that approach as "blackmail," but Fred realized that the Heller loan was essential. Accordingly, he agreed to pay Ed and Al $95,000 each, mostly in the form of promissory notes, in exchange for releases by Ed and Al of all their claims to ownership in Arc. Fred then closed the loan with Heller, and Arc obtained the needed funds. Subsequently, Fred brought suit to set the promissory notes aside. Held, for Ed and Al.

"While there is ample evidence of economic necessity and financial peril, neither the 'threat of considerable financial loss' nor 'impending bankruptcy' establish economic duress. Such economic stress must be attributable to the party against whom duress is alleged. 'Mere hard bargaining positions, if lawful, and the press of financial circumstances, not caused by the [party against whom the contract is sought to be voided], will not be deemed duress.' Business Incentives Co. v. Sony Corp. of America, 397 F.Supp. 63, 69 (S.D.N.Y.1975).

"The only possible claim of duress is that Ed and Al, recognizing the weakened state of the company, seized that opportunity to settle the long-standing dispute regarding stock-ownership. Because duress may not be implied merely from the making of a hard bargain, the question becomes whether the conduct of Ed and Al was wrongful. The law in Georgia and other jurisdictions makes clear that it was not, for the two men were merely asserting a legal right, *i.e.,* their right to a certain share of the stock in the company. *See* Causey v. Matson, 215 Ga. 306, 110 S.E.2d 356 (1959); Williams v. Ruben, 216 Ga. 431, 117 S.E.2d 456 (1960). Fred admitted that Ed and Al were stockholders in the company, and the long-standing dispute was over the percentage of the company each owned. Thus, while there is no doubt that Fred was between the proverbial rock and a hard place, it is clear that his own actions put him there and that Ed and Al merely took advantage of the situation to insist upon settlement of the intrafamilial stock squabble....

"We conclude, therefore, that there is simply no duress shown on this record, for one crucial element is missing: a wrongful act by the defendants to create and take advantage of an untenable situation. Ed and Al had nothing to do with the financial quagmire in which Fred found himself, and we cannot find duress simply because they refused to throw him a rope free of any 'strings.' "

————

POST v. JONES, 60 U.S. (19 How.) 150, 15 L.Ed. 618 (1856). The whaling vessel Richmond, with a nearly full cargo of whale oil, was inextricably run aground in a deserted area 5,000 miles from the nearest port of safety. Several days later, the whaling vessels Elizabeth Frith, Panama, and Junior came into the vicinity. These vessels did not have full cargoes, but the Richmond had more whale oil than the three vessels could all take. At the instance of the Junior's captain, the Richmond's captain agreed to hold an auction for its oil. The Frith's captain bid $1 per barrel for as much as he needed, and the captains of the Panama and the Junior bid 75¢ per barrel.

The three vessels took enough of the Richmond's oil to complete their cargoes, and returned to port with the oil and the Richmond's crew. The Richmond's owners then brought this action to recover part of the value of the oil taken by the Frith and the Panama, on the theory that while these vessels were entitled to salvage (a maritime concept under which one who saves property is entitled to a reward) for the oil they took, they were not entitled to keep the oil at the auction price. Held, for the owners of the Richmond.

"The contrivance of an auction sale, under such circumstances, where the master of the Richmond was hopeless, helpless, and passive—where there was no market, no money, no competition—where one party had absolute power, and the other no choice but submission where the vendor must take what is offered or get nothing—is a transaction which has no characteristic of a valid contract. It has been contended by the claimants that it would be a great hardship to treat this sale as a nullity, and thus compel them to assume the character of Salvors, because they were not bound to save this property, especially at so great a distance from any port of safety, and in a place where they could have completed their cargo in a short time from their own catchings, and where salvage would be no compensation for the loss of this opportunity. The force of these arguments is fully appreciated, but we think they are not fully sustained by the facts of the case. Whales may have been plenty around their vessels on the 6th and 7th of August, but, judging of the future from the past, the anticipation of filling up their cargo in the few days of the season in which it would be safe to remain, was very uncertain, and barely probable. The whales were retreating towards the North Pole, where they could not be pursued, and, though seen in numbers on one day, they would disappear on the next; and, even when seen in greatest numbers, their capture was uncertain. By this transaction, the vessels were enabled to proceed at once on their home voyage; and the certainty of a liberal salvage allowance for the property rescued will be ample compensation for the possible chance of greater profits, by refusing their assistance in saving their neighbor's property.

"It has been contended, also, that the sale was justifiable and valid, because it was better for the interests of all concerned to accept what was offered, than suffer a total loss. But this argument proves too much, as it would justify every sale to a salvor. Courts of admiralty will enforce contracts made for salvage service and salvage compensation, where the salvor has not taken advantage of his power to make an unreasonable bargain; but they will not tolerate the doctrine that a salvor can take the advantage of his situation, and avail himself of the calamities of others to drive a bargain; nor will they permit the performance of a public duty to be turned into a traffic of profit."

EISENBERG, THE BARGAIN PRINCIPLE AND ITS LIMITS

95 Harvard Law Review 741 (1982).

Suppose that *A* makes a bargain with *B* at a time when, through no fault of *B*, *A* is in a state of necessity that effectively compels him to enter into a bargain on any terms he can get—a condition that I shall refer to as distress. . . . [Take the following example:]

The Desperate Traveler. T, a symphony musician, has been driving through the desert on a recreational trip, when he suddenly hits a rock jutting out from the sand. *T*'s vehicle is disabled and his ankle is fractured. He has no radio and little water, and will die if he is not soon rescued. The next day, *G,* a university geologist who is returning to Tucson from an inspection of desert rock formations, adventitiously passes within sight of the accident and drives over to investigate. *T* explains the situation and asks *G* to take him back to Tucson, which is sixty miles away. *G* replies that he will help only if *T* promises to pay him two-thirds of his wealth or $100,000, whichever is more. *T* agrees, but after they return to Tucson he refuses to keep his promise, and *G* brings an action to enforce it.

Under traditional contract doctrines, *T*'s promise would be enforceable to its full extent. He has made a bargain, and none of the orthodox contract defenses apply. The defense of duress might seem apposite, but traditionally that defense has required not only that the promisor was in distress, but that he was put in distress by a wrongful act or threat of the promisee. *G* did not put *T* in distress, and because the common law imposes no duty on strangers to rescue persons in distress even when life is at stake, *G*'s threat of refusing aid would probably not constitute a wrongful act within the meaning of this rule.

It seems clear, however, that [*T*'s promise, extracted through *G*'s distress,] should not be enforced to its full extent. Neither fairness nor efficiency, the two major props of the bargain principle, supports its application in such a case. In terms of fairness, our society posits, as part of its moral order, some degree of concern for others. In *The Desperate Traveler, G* has acted wrongly in treating *T* as simply an economic object.

The efficiency argument also fails. When a commodity is sold under perfect competition, the doctrine of distress would usually have no application, even to contracts for necessities. A sale at a perfectly competitive price would normally not be regarded as exploitive, because the price is generated by a mechanism that is conventionally regarded as fair, and normally equals the seller's opportunity cost and approximates the seller's marginal cost. Furthermore, traditional economic analysis suggests that such a price normally allocates supply to its highest-valued uses and encourages the appropriate amount of investment in productive capacity. *G,* however, is not a perfect competitor, but a monopolist. Full enforcement of promises like that made by *T* is not required to move rescue services to their highest-valued uses, and would have no measurable effect on the allocation of resources to rescue-capacity, since the rescue is adventitious, there are no other bidders for the rescue services at the time of the rescue, and prior to the accident there was no market on which the victim could have purchased a contingent contract to rescue. Indeed, there is an argument that full enforcement would be inefficient. If it were known that persons in distress could be required to pay the price demanded for adventitious rescue, however high, people either might be reluctant to engage in activity in which rescue is sometimes necessary or might spend on precautions an aggregate amount exceeding the cost of adventitious rescue.

. . . [O]ther mature legal systems . . . allow the courts to review bargains made under distress for fairness of terms. For example, section 138(2) of the

German Civil Code provides that a transaction is void "when a person [exploits] the distressed situation, inexperience, lack of judgmental ability, or grave weakness of will of another to obtain the grant or promise of pecuniary advantages ... which are obviously disproportionate to the performance given in return." French law is in accord. At home, it is well established in admiralty law that a contract for salvage services—that is, a contract to rescue a vessel or its cargo—is reviewable for fairness of terms if entered into while the promisor is in distress.... [as evidenced] in *Post v. Jones*....

This ... leaves open how to measure the promisee's recovery in such cases. Financial cost is one possibility. Such a solution, however, would often fail to recognize adequately the benefit conferred upon the promisor. Furthermore, a financial-cost rule might not provide a sufficient incentive to act. In *The Desperate Traveler,* for example, *G*'s financial cost is close to zero. Assuming *G* is under no legal duty to rescue *T,* he would have no economic incentive to perform the rescue if his recovery were limited to financial cost. The need for an economic incentive in such cases should not be overemphasized; most individuals in *G*'s position would be likely to rescue *T* whether they had an economic incentive to do so or not. Nevertheless, an economic incentive would probably be helpful at the margin. Admiralty again suggests a solution. Although it will not enforce unfair rescue contracts, it does provide ample compensation for rescuers under the principle of salvage. Recovery under this principle is viewed both as a reward and as an inducement. Accordingly, in measuring recovery the courts take into account the degree of danger to the rescued property; the value of the rescued property; the risk incurred by the salvors; their promptness, skill, and energy; the value of the property the salvor employed; the degree of danger to that property; and the salvor's time and labor. In more general terms, the recovery in distress cases involving an adventitious rescuer should not only compensate the promisee for all costs, tangible and intangible, but should also include a generous bonus to provide a clear incentive for action and compensation for the benefit conferred. Recovery measured in this way admits of no great precision, but that is not fatal in situations in which, by hypothesis, planning is not important. The viability of this approach is evidenced by the fact that it has stood the test of time in an area in which distress and adventitious rescue are common occurrences.

NEW YORK GEN. BUS. LAW § 396–r

§ 396–r. Price gouging

1. Legislative findings and declaration. The legislature hereby finds that during periods of abnormal disruption of the market caused by strikes, power failures, severe shortages or other extraordinary adverse circumstances, some parties within the chain of distribution of consumer goods have taken unfair advantage of consumers by charging grossly excessive prices for essential consumer goods and services....

In order to prevent any party within the chain of distribution of consumer goods from taking unfair advantage of consumers during abnormal disruptions of the market, the legislature declares that the public interest requires that such conduct be prohibited and made subject to civil penalties.

2. During any abnormal disruption of the market for consumer goods and services vital and necessary for the health, safety and welfare of consumers, no party within the chain of distribution of such consumer goods or services or both shall sell or offer to sell any such consumer goods or services or both for an amount which represents an unconscionably excessive price. For purposes of this section, the phrase "abnormal disruption of the market" shall mean any change in the market, whether actual or imminently threatened, resulting from stress of weather, convulsion of nature, failure or shortage of electric power or other source of energy, strike, civil disorder, war, military action, national or local emergency, or other cause of an abnormal disruption of the market which results in the declaration of a state of emergency by the governor. For the purposes of this section, the term consumer goods and services shall mean those used, bought or rendered primarily for personal family or household purposes. This prohibition shall apply to all parties within the chain of distribution, including any manufacturer, supplier, wholesaler, distributor or retail seller of consumer goods or services or both sold by one party to another when the product sold was located in the state prior to the sale. Consumer goods and services shall also include any repairs made by any party within the chain of distribution of consumer goods on an emergency basis as a result of such abnormal disruption of the market.

Whether a price is unconscionably excessive is a question of law for the court.

(a) The court's determination that a violation of this section has occurred shall be based on any of the following factors: (i) that the amount of the excess in price is unconscionably extreme; or (ii) that there was an exercise of unfair leverage or unconscionable means; or (iii) a combination of both factors in subparagraphs (i) and (ii) of this paragraph.

(b) In any proceeding commenced pursuant to subdivision four of this section, prima facie proof that a violation of this section has occurred shall include evidence that

(i) the amount charged represents a gross disparity between the price of the goods or services were the subject of the transaction of their value measured by the price at which such consumer goods or services were sold or offered for sale by the defendant in the usual course of business immediately prior to the onset of the abnormal disruption of the market or

(ii) the amount charged grossly exceeded the price at which the same or similar goods or services were readily obtainable by other consumers in the trade area. A defendant may rebut a prima facie case with evidence that additional costs not within the control of the defendant were imposed on the defendant for the goods or services.

4. Where a violation of this section is alleged to have occurred, the attorney general may apply in the name of the People of the State of New York to the supreme court of the State of New York within the judicial district in which such violations are alleged to have occurred, on notice of five days, for an order enjoining or restraining commission or continuance of the alleged unlawful acts. In any such proceeding, the court shall impose a civil penalty in

an amount not to exceed ten thousand dollars and, where appropriate, order restitution to aggrieved consumers.

————

NOTE ON PEOPLE v. TWO WHEEL CORP.

In People v. Two Wheel Corp., 71 N.Y.2d 693, 530 N.Y.S.2d 46, 525 N.E.2d 692 (1988), the Attorney General of New York charged that Two Wheel Corporation had violated N.Y.Gen.Bus.Law § 396–r by selling approximately 100 power generators at inflated prices—ranging from 4% to 67% over base price—in anticipation of and during a hurricane that left much of Long Island without electrical power for around ten days. The trial court ordered Two Wheel to pay a civil penalty of $5,000, to make restitution to 13 consumers who had submitted affidavits, and to establish a $20,000 restitution fund for other consumers who had purchased generators from Two Wheel during the relevant period at prices exceeding the base prices. Affirmed.

"Respondents [Two Wheel] ... contend that the prices charged were not unconscionably excessive. They note that, for some of the sales during the period, the sales price exceeded the base price by less than 5%; for others the differential fell between 5 and 15%. In fact, in the vast majority of the sales, the prices were inflated by less than 30%. In only five sales, according to the Attorney–General's figures, did the disparity reach as high as 60%. Even if some of the prices can be considered unconscionably excessive, they claim, others are clearly not, and they should not be required to make restitution to all consumers who were charged more than the base price.

"To support their argument, respondents point to General Business Law § 396–r(3), which provides in essence that evidence of a 'gross disparity' between the sales price at the time of the market disruption and the price charged before the disruption is prima facie proof of price gouging. From this provision and case law applying the unconscionability standard of the Uniform Commercial Code (UCC 2–302), respondents argue that the Legislature intended the price-gouging statute to apply only to extremely large price increases and that, accordingly, the majority of their sales did not offend the price-gouging prohibition.

"Respondents' argument places undue emphasis on the 'gross disparity' language of [§ 396–r(3)], treating it as a definition of price gouging. But the provision is procedural rather than definitional; it simply establishes a means of providing presumptive evidence that the merchant has engaged in price gouging. A showing of a gross disparity in prices, coupled with proof that the disparity is not attributable to supplier costs, raises a presumption that the merchant used the leverage provided by the market disruption to extract a higher price. The use of such leverage is what defines price gouging, not some arbitrarily drawn line of excessiveness.

"Furthermore, the term 'unconscionably excessive' does not limit the statute's prohibition to 'extremely large price increases', as respondents would have it. The doctrine of unconscionability, as developed in the common law of contracts and in the application of UCC 2–302, has both substantive and procedural aspects.... Respondents' argument focuses solely on the substantive aspect, which considers whether one or more contract terms are unreasonably favorable to one party.... The procedural aspect, on the other hand, looks to the contract formation process, with emphasis on such factors as inequality of bargaining power, the use of deceptive or high-pressure sales techniques, and confusing or hidden language in the written agreement (State of New York v. Wolowitz, 96 A.D.2d 47, 67, 468 N.Y.S.2d 131; see, Williams v. Walker–Thomas Furniture Co., D.C.Cir., 350 F.2d 445, 449). Thus, a price may be unconscionably excessive because, substantively, the amount of the excess is unconscionably extreme, or because, procedurally, the excess was obtained through unconscionable means, or because of a combination of both factors....

"Here, the Attorney–General's prima facie case established, at least presumptively, that respondents' price increases were attributable solely to their use of the bargaining advantage created by the natural disaster—that is, through means that are 'unconscionable according to the mores and business practices of the time and place' ... because General Business Law § 396–r defines the mores governing this business setting and excises the use of such advantage from the repertoire of legitimate business practices. Furthermore, in this case, where the sales occurred over a relatively short period of time and were associated with a single market disruption, the presumption that the excess was unconscionably obtained, though established through proof of gross disparities, extends as well to the sales marked by lesser increases. The evidence, including the deposition testimony of two of respondents' employees, makes the inference inescapable that all of the price increases were tainted by respondents' use of the superior bargaining position attributable to the power outage."

See also People v. Beach Boys Equip. Co., 273 A.D.2d 850, 851, 709 N.Y.S.2d 729 (App.Div.2000) (trial court required restitution from a business that charged $1,200 for generators following an ice storm, when other retailers were charging less than $600. The appellate court upheld the award of restitution, and announced that even a small increase in price may be unconscionably excessive under General Business Law § 396–r if "the excess was obtained through unconscionable means," which was the case here.); People v. Dame, 289 A.D.2d 997, 734 N.Y.S.2d 789 (App.Div.2001) (roofers who charged excessive prices when a storm was pending were ordered to pay restitution and penalties).

SECTION 2. UNCONSCIONABILITY

WILLIAMS v. WALKER–THOMAS FURNITURE CO.

United States Court of Appeals, District of Columbia Circuit, 1965.
121 U.S.App.D.C. 315, 350 F.2d 445.

J. Skelly Wright, Circuit Judge. Appellee, Walker–Thomas Furniture Company, operates a retail furniture store in the District of Columbia. During the period from 1957 to 1962 each appellant in these cases purchased a number of household items from Walker–Thomas, for which payment was to be made in installments. The terms of each purchase were contained in a printed form contract which set forth the value of the purchased item and purported to lease the item to appellant for a stipulated monthly rent payment. The contract then provided, in substance, that title would remain in Walker–Thomas until the total of all the monthly payments made equaled the stated value of the item, at which time appellants could take title. In the event of a default in the payment of any monthly installment, Walker–Thomas could repossess the item.

The contract further provided that "the amount of each periodical installment payment to be made by [purchaser] to the Company under this present lease shall be inclusive of and not in addition to the amount of each installment payment to be made by [purchaser] under such prior leases, bills or accounts; *and all payments now and hereafter made by [purchaser] shall be credited pro rata on all outstanding leases, bills and accounts* due the Company by [purchaser] at the time each such payment is made." (Emphasis added.) The effect of this rather obscure provision was to keep a balance due on every item purchased until the balance due on all items, whenever purchased, was liquidated. As a result, the debt incurred at the time of purchase of each item was secured by the right to repossess all the items previously purchased by the same purchaser, and each new item purchased automatically became subject to a security interest arising out of the previous dealings.

On May 12, 1962, appellant Thorne purchased an item described as a Daveno, three tables, and two lamps, having total stated value of $391.10. Shortly thereafter, he defaulted on his monthly payments and appellee sought to replevy all the items purchased since the first transaction in 1958. Similarly, on April 17, 1962, appellant Williams bought a stereo set of stated value of $514.95.[1] She too defaulted shortly thereafter, and appellee sought to replevy all the items purchased since December, 1957. The Court of General Sessions granted judgment for appellee. The District of Columbia Court of Appeals affirmed, and we granted appellants' motion for leave to appeal to this court.

Appellants' principal contention, rejected by both the trial and the appellate courts below, is that these contracts, or at least some of them, are unconscionable and, hence, not enforceable. In its opinion in Williams v. Walker–Thomas Furniture Company, 198 A.2d 914, 916 (1964), the District of Columbia Court of Appeals explained its rejection of this contention as follows:

> "Appellant's second argument presents a more serious question. The record reveals that prior to the last purchase appellant had reduced the balance in her account to $164. The last purchase, a stereo set, raised the balance due to $678. Significantly, at the time of this and the preceding purchases, appellee was aware of appellant's financial position. The reverse side of the stereo contract listed the name of appellant's social worker and her $218 monthly stipend from the government. Nevertheless, with full knowledge that appellant had to feed, clothe and support both herself and seven children on this amount, appellee sold her a $514 stereo set.

1. At the time of this purchase her account showed a balance of $164 still owing from her prior purchases. The total of all the purchases made over the years in question came to $1,800. The total payments amounted to $1,400.

"We cannot condemn too strongly appellee's conduct. It raises serious questions of sharp practice and irresponsible business dealings. A review of the legislation in the District of Columbia affecting retail sales and the pertinent decisions of the highest court in this jurisdiction disclose, however, no ground upon which this court can declare the contracts in question contrary to public policy. We note that were the Maryland Retail Installment Sales Act, Art. 83 §§ 128–153, or its equivalent, in force in the District of Columbia, we could grant appellant appropriate relief. We think Congress should consider corrective legislation to protect the public from such exploitive contracts as were utilized in the case at bar."

We do not agree that the court lacked the power to refuse enforcement to contracts found to be unconscionable. In other jurisdictions, it has been held as a matter of common law that unconscionable contracts are not enforceable.[2] While no decision of this court so holding has been found, the notion that an unconscionable bargain should not be given full enforcement is by no means novel. In Scott v. United States, 79 U.S. (12 Wall.) 443, 445, 20 L.Ed. 438 (1870), the Supreme Court stated:

" ... If a contract be unreasonable and unconscionable, but not void for fraud, a court of law will give to the party who sues for its breach damages, not according to its letter, but only such as he is equitably entitled to...."[3]

Since we have never adopted or rejected such a rule, the question here presented is actually one of first impression.

Congress has recently enacted the Uniform Commercial Code, which specifically provides that the court may refuse to enforce a contract which it finds to be unconscionable at the time it was made. 28 D.C.Code § 2–302 (Supp. IV 1965). The enactment of this section, which occurred subsequent to the contracts here in suit, does not mean that the common law of the District of Columbia was otherwise at the time of enactment, nor does it preclude the court from adopting a similar rule in the exercise of its powers to develop the common law for the District of Columbia. In fact, in view of the absence of prior authority on the point, we consider the congressional adoption of § 2–302 persuasive authority for following the rationale of the cases from which the section is explicitly derived.[4] Accordingly, we hold that where the element of unconscionability is present at the time a contract is made, the contract should not be enforced.

Unconscionability has generally been recognized to include an absence of meaningful choice on the part of one of the parties together with contract

2. Campbell Soup Co. v. Wentz, 3 Cir., 172 F.2d 80 (1948); Indianapolis Morris Plan Corporation v. Sparks, 132 Ind.App. 145, 172 N.E.2d 899 (1961); Henningsen v. Bloomfield Motors, Inc., 32 N.J. 358, 161 A.2d 69, 84–96, 75 A.L.R.2d 1 (1960). Cf. 1 Corbin, Contracts § 128 (1963).

3. See Luing v. Peterson, 143 Minn. 6, 172 N.W. 692 (1919); Greer v. Tweed, N.Y.C.P., 13 Abb.Pr., N.S., 427 (1872); Schnell v. Nell, 17 Ind. 29 (1861); and see generally the discussion of the English authorities in Hume v. United States, 132 U.S. 406, 10 S.Ct. 134, 33 L.Ed. 393 (1889).

4. See Comment, § 2–302, Uniform Commercial Code (1962). Compare Note, 45 Va. L.Rev. 583, 590 (1959), where it is predicted that the rule of § 2–302 will be followed by analogy in cases which involve contracts not specifically covered by the section. Cf. 1 State of New York Law Revision Commission, Report and Record of Hearings on the Uniform Commercial Code 108–110 (1954) (remarks of Professor Llewellyn).

terms which are unreasonably favorable to the other party.[5] Whether a meaningful choice is present in a particular case can only be determined by consideration of all the circumstances surrounding the transaction. In many cases the meaningfulness of the choice is negated by a gross inequality of bargaining power.[6] The manner in which the contract was entered is also relevant to this consideration. Did each party to the contract, considering his obvious education or lack of it, have a reasonable opportunity to understand the terms of the contract, or were the important terms hidden in a maze of fine print and minimized by deceptive sales practices? Ordinarily, one who signs an agreement without full knowledge of its terms might be held to assume the risk that he has entered a one-sided bargain.[7] But when a party of little bargaining power, and hence little real choice, signs a commercially unreasonable contract with little or no knowledge of its terms, it is hardly likely that his consent, or even an objective manifestation of his consent, was ever given to all the terms. In such a case the usual rule that the terms of the agreement are not to be questioned[8] should be abandoned and the court should consider whether the terms of the contract are so unfair that enforcement should be withheld.[9]

In determining reasonableness or fairness, the primary concern must be with the terms of the contract considered in light of the circumstances existing when the contract was made. The test is not simple, nor can it be mechanically applied. The terms are to be considered "in the light of the general commercial background and the commercial needs of the particular trade or case."[10] Corbin suggests the test as being whether the terms are "so extreme as to appear unconscionable according to the mores and business practices of the time and place." 1 Corbin, op. cit. supra Note 2.[11] We think

5. See Henningsen v. Bloomfield Motors, Inc., supra Note 2; Campbell Soup Co. v. Wentz, supra Note 2.

6. See Henningsen v. Bloomfield Motors, Inc., supra Note 2, 161 A.2d at 86, and authorities there cited. Inquiry into the relative bargaining power of the two parties is not an inquiry wholly divorced from the general question of unconscionability, since a one-sided bargain is itself evidence of the inequality of the bargaining parties. This fact was vaguely recognized in the common law doctrine of intrinsic fraud, that is, fraud which can be presumed from the grossly unfair nature of the terms of the contract. See the oft-quoted statement of Lord Hardwicke in Earl of Chesterfield v. Janssen, 28 Eng.Rep. 82, 100 (1751):

" . . . [Fraud] may be apparent from the intrinsic nature and subject of the bargain itself; such as no man in his senses and not under delusion would make. . . ."

And cf. Hume v. United States, supra Note 3, 132 U.S. at 413, 10 S.Ct. at 137, where the Court characterized the English cases as "cases in which one party took advantage of the other's ignorance of arithmetic to impose upon him, and the fraud was apparent from the face of the contracts." See also Greer v. Tweed, supra Note 3.

7. See Restatement, Contracts § 70 (1932); Note, 63 Harv.L.Rev. 494 (1950). See also Daley v. People's Building, Loan & Savings Ass'n,

178 Mass. 13, 59 N.E. 452, 453 (1901), in which Mr. Justice Holmes, while sitting on the Supreme Judicial Court of Massachusetts, made this observation:

" . . . Courts are less and less disposed to interfere with parties making such contracts as they choose, so long as they interfere with no one's welfare but their own. . . . It will be understood that we are speaking of parties standing in an equal position where neither has any oppressive advantage or power. . . ."

8. This rule has never been without exception. In cases involving merely the transfer of unequal amounts of the same commodity, the courts have held the bargain unenforceable for the reason that "in such a case, it is clear, that the law cannot indulge in the presumption of equivalence between the consideration and the promise." 1 Williston, Contracts § 115 (3d ed. 1957).

9. See the general discussion of "Boiler-Plate Agreements" in Llewellyn, The Common Law Tradition 362–371 (1960).

10. Comment, Uniform Commercial Code [§ 2–302].

11. See Henningsen v. Bloomfield Motors, Inc., supra Note 2; Mandel v. Liebman, 303 N.Y. 88, 100 N.E.2d 149 (1951). The traditional test as stated in Greer v. Tweed, supra Note 3, 13 Abb.Pr., N.S., at 429, is "such as no man in this formulation correctly states the test to be applied in those cases where no meaningful choice was exercised upon entering the contract.

Because the trial court and the appellate court did not feel that enforcement could be refused, no findings were made on the possible unconscionability of the contracts in these cases. Since the record is not sufficient for our deciding the issue as a matter of law, the cases must be remanded to the trial court for further proceedings.

So ordered.

DANAHER, CIRCUIT JUDGE (dissenting):

The District of Columbia Court of Appeals obviously was as unhappy about the situation here presented as any of us can possibly be. Its opinion in the *Williams* case, quoted in the majority text, concludes: "We think Congress should consider corrective legislation to protect the public from such exploitive contracts as were utilized in the case at bar."

My view is thus summed up by an able court which made no finding that there had actually been sharp practice. Rather the appellant seems to have known precisely where she stood.

There are many aspects of public policy here involved. What is a luxury to some may seem an outright necessity to others. Is public oversight to be required of the expenditures of relief funds? A washing machine, e.g., in the hands of a relief client might become a fruitful source of income. Many relief clients may well need credit, and certain business establishments will take long chances on the sale of items, expecting their pricing policies will afford a degree of protection commensurate with the risk. Perhaps a remedy when necessary will be found within the provisions of the "Loan Shark" law, D.C.Code § § 26–601 et seq. (1961).

I mention such matters only to emphasize the desirability of a cautious approach to any such problem, particularly since the law for so long has allowed parties such great latitude in making their own contracts. I dare say there must annually be thousands upon thousands of installment credit transactions in this jurisdiction, and one can only speculate as to the effect the decision in these cases will have.

I join the District of Columbia Court of Appeals in its disposition of the issues.

———

NOTE ON WILLIAMS v. WALKER–THOMAS

A number of states have adopted statutes that prohibit the type of provision that was at issue in Williams v. Walker–Thomas. After the decision in that case, the District of Columbia adopted such a statute, D.C. Code § 28–3805(a):

> If debts arising from two or more consumer credit sales other than sales pursuant to a revolving charge account ... are secured by cross-

his senses and not under delusion would make
on the one hand, and as no honest or fair man
would accept, on the other."

collateral, or consolidated into one debt payable on a single schedule of payments, and the debt is secured by security interests taken with respect to one or more of the sales, payments received by the seller after the taking of the cross-collateral or the consolidation are deemed, for the purpose of determining the amount of the debt secured by the various security interests, to have been first applied to the payment of the debts arising from the sales first made. To the extent debts are paid according to this section, security interests in items of property terminate as the debts originally incurred with respect to each item are paid.

SKILTON & HELSTAD, PROTECTION OF THE INSTALLMENT BUYER OF GOODS UNDER THE UNIFORM COMMERCIAL CODE, 65 Mich.L.Rev. 1465, 1476–81. "It appeared that from 1957 to 1962 Ora Lee Williams had made sixteen separate purchases of furniture and household appliances from the store, all on installment credit, and in each case had signed fine print bailment–lease contracts which provided for monthly rental payments and reserved title in the store until payment was made in full. Most of these purchases were made when a representative of the store came to her home. . . .

" . . . The seller maintained that it still had title to everything because, under the pro rata clause, a balance remained due on each item, despite Ora's payments of over $1,000. The store's records showed that of a combined total claim of $444 as of December 26, 1962, Ora still owed 25 cents on item 1, purchased December 23, 1957 (price $45.65); 3 cents on item 2, purchased December 31, 1957 (price $13.21); $2.34 on item 3, purchased August 12, 1958 (price $127.40); and similarly for subsequent purchases, with balances of $.96, $1.70, $2.86, $1.08, $7.21, $1.53, $2.38, $5.66, $10.32, and $1.61. The only claims which were significant in relation to the purchase price were for the last three purchases: an item for $254.95, on which a balance of $65.98 was claimed; the $514.95 stereo, on which a balance of $327.89 was claimed; and an item for $15.45, on which a balance of $12.60 was claimed. . . .

"Was there anything inherently wrong about what the seller did in Williams? Forget for the nonce that he was dealing with an impoverished buyer who asserted that she did not understand the pro rata plan and would not have bought the stereo had she known that the seller would continue to tie up all of her previous purchases. Is there any difference between this case and a case in which, to induce a loan or a credit sale, a person agrees to give the creditor a security interest in most of his personal property which he owns outright? Or in which he gives his creditor a security interest in all such property to secure the balance of a consolidated indebtedness? Is it simply the indirectness of what was done that raises questions? . . .

"The appellants in *Williams* . . . argued that to allow the store to utilize the pro-rata clause to enforce its claim upon so much of appellants' household goods would, in effect, subvert the policy of the statutes of the District of Columbia exempting household goods from attachment. Of course, the statutes on their face do not prevent creditors from taking security interests in such goods and then seizing them on default, but the point nevertheless has merit: if our exemption statutes are to accomplish their patent purpose of protecting debtors from complete impoverishment as a result of creditor action, their provisions should be correlated with statutory provisions restricting the use of such property as security in certain kinds of transactions...."

NOTE ON PRICING BY LOW–INCOME MARKET RETAILERS

There have been very few systematic studies of retail pricing in low-income neighborhoods. Some years ago, however, the Federal Trade Commission (FTC) did a study comparing the prices charged by low-income and general-market appliance and household-furnishings retailers in the District of Columbia in 1966. U.S. Federal Trade Commission, Economic Report on Installment Credit and Retail Sales Practices of District of Columbia Retailers (1968). One factor that stood out was the very significant disparity between the prices charged by low-income and general-market retailers. The prices charged by the former were often twice the price charged by the latter for identical brand-name products. The FTC commented:

> The general conclusion that emerges ... is that the low-income market is a very expensive place to buy durable goods. On television sets (most of which are the popular 19–inch black and white portables) the general market retailer price is about $130. In the low-income market a customer can pay up to $250 for similar sets. Other comparisons include a dryer selling for $149.95 from a general market retailer and for $299.95 from a low-income market retailer; and a vacuum cleaner selling for $59.95 in the general market and $79.95 in the low-income market.

In addition to comparing the pricing practices of low-income and general–market retailers, the FTC Study also compared their relative profitability. The data, although limited and perhaps not completely reliable, indicated that the total expenses of low-income market retailers in proportion to selling prices were not that different from the total expenses of general market retailers in proportion to selling prices, although the make-up of the expenses differed considerably. The FTC commented:

> ... A major reason for low-income market retailers' higher personnel expense is believed to be their use of outside salesmen who canvass house-to-house or follow up requests for home demonstrations and often make collections of installment payments at the home of the customer. Several of the low-income market retailers ... pay their outside salesmen-collectors commissions on both sales and collections. Other reasons for higher personnel costs of low-income market retailers could be that they have more sales personnel and pay higher rates of compensation compared to small-volume general market retailers; and since they finance all or a larger proportion of their own installment contracts, they require most employees to keep records of small payments on installment credit accounts.

> Another issue was the relative profitability of low-income and general market retailers. The most important index of business profitability is net profit after taxes as a percentage of the owner's equity or investment. Judged on this index (and again, on the basis of limited and perhaps unreliable data), the low-income market retailers were less profitable than the general market retailers....

Low-income market retailers reported an average rate of return after taxes on net worth of 10.1 percent. Rates of return on net worth varied considerably among general market retailers. Appliance, radio, and television retailers reported the highest rate of return after taxes, 20.3 percent of net worth. Next in order were furniture and home-furnishings retailers with 17.6 percent, and department stores with 13 percent return on net worth.

Data on profits reported above are limited and to some extent inconclusive. It does not appear, however, that low-income market retailers made profits which were substantially higher on the average than general market retailers. The high prices charged by low-income market retailers must have been accompanied in many instances by substantially higher costs arising from the method of doing business. Some of these costs probably arose from greater losses on credit sales. To some extent, costs may have been higher because of smaller volume and generally more costly and less efficient store operation.

JOSEPH B. CAHILL, HERE'S THE PITCH: HOW KIRBY PERSUADES UNCERTAIN CONSUMERS TO BUY $1,500 VACUUM

The Wall Street Journal, October 4, 1999

In the world of home appliances, Kirby Co. likes to consider its product the Porsche of vacuum cleaners.

The sweeper features a die-cast aluminum base and handle and wooden brushrollers, rather than the plastic parts found in competitors' models. Its motor is so powerful that it can suck up a bucket of dirt dumped on a thick shag rug, leaving barely a speck behind. Assorted attachments convert it into a leaf blower and even a spray painter.

With a price tag of around $1,500, it also costs more than four times what other top-of-the-line vacuum cleaners do. "Why does a Porsche cost more than a Chevy?" asks Ralph Schey, chief executive officer of Kirby parent Scott Fetzer Co., a unit of Berkshire Hathaway Inc., which is controlled by billionaire Warren Buffett.

It's worth noting that luxury-car dealers don't make house calls in trailer parks. But Kirby dealers do. After 64 years, the Kirby (there is only one model, updated periodically) continues to be marketed exclusively door-to-door-often to people who can ill afford a $1,500 gadget but succumb to the sales pitch nonetheless. That has led consumer-protection agencies to question the company's tactics. In March of last year, 68–year-old Henrietta Taylor and her husband, Dennis, 79, answered a knock on the door of their mobile home in Fort Meade, Fla., to find two Kirby salesmen standing on the stoop.

The Taylors didn't need a vacuum cleaner; their old Electrolux was working fine. But the salesmen persisted with an hour-and-a-half demonstration that included dumping dirt on the carpet to show off the Kirby's cleaning power. "They were the pushiest people I ever saw," Mrs. Taylor says.

The Taylors agreed to buy the machine for $1,749. That far exceeded the value of their only carpet, a 12–foot by 18–foot living-room rug. It also exceeded their monthly income of $1,100 in Social Security. To finance the purchase, the salesmen arranged for a loan—with a 21.19% annual interest rate—that brought the total in payments to $2,553.06. . . .

The Taylors are hardly alone in their experience with the Kirby sales force. One class-action suit has been filed against Kirby over the sales practices of some of its distributors. And of 22 state consumer-protection agencies queried, 15 have received a total of more than 600 complaints in recent years about Kirby distributors and their sales techniques. Most handle the complaints on an individual basis. . . .

. . . Kirby says it isn't responsible for the behavior of its independent sales force. They are self-employed distributors, and Kirby prides itself on giving them the opportunity to build their own businesses.

Of course, many Kirby customers say they couldn't be happier with their purchases. "I've noticed a difference in my carpet," says Melinda Nielsen, 31, of Fremont, Neb. "The carpet feels softer and fluffier." She also has praise for the Kirby salesmen who recently sold her the machine for $1,440, saying they "were very relaxed and didn't push me at all." . . .

The Kirby complaints often involve older customers who lack the will to stand up to grueling sales pitches. One evening in May 1996, Stephen and Wilma Tucker were sitting down to dinner when three Kirby salesmen showed up at their Springfield, Vt., home and spent five hours, despite protests from the 60–year-old Mr. Tucker that he was disabled, unemployed and incapable of buying so expensive a vacuum cleaner. One salesman even helped himself to some fried chicken, the Tuckers say. Finally, "more or less just to get them out of there, we agreed to it," Mr. Tucker says.

. . . Ms. [Thorhild] Christopher, who died in December 1996 at age 76, lived alone in a mobile home in Hernando, Fla., scraping by on about $1,000 a month in Social Security payments and money from her late husband's U.S. Coast Guard pension. When she died, she owned two Kirby vacuum cleaners, the last one sold to her in September 1995 by a Kirby distributor in Spring Hill, Fla.

Ms. Christopher's niece, Gail Bosworth, says her aunt was suffering from Alzheimer's disease by the time she paid $1,747.94 for the second Kirby. . . .

About 70% of Kirbys are financed through distributors, with 20%-plus interest rates driving the total cost well above $2,000. . . .

To Kirby's advantage, in-home sales pitches don't allow the consumer much room for comparison shopping. In appliance stores, customers can weigh the price of Eurekas against Bissells, or try out the $350 Hoover that Consumer Reports last year ranked first in quality, ahead of No. 2–ranked Kirby. But in their own living rooms, people submitting to Kirby sales pitches face pressure to make a decision on the spot. . . .

————

RESTATEMENT CONTRACTS, SECOND § 208

[See Selected Source Materials Supplement]

UCC § 2–302

[See Selected Source Materials Supplement]

UNIFORM CONSUMER CREDIT CODE §§ 1.301, 5.108

[See Selected Source Materials Supplement]

FEDERAL TRADE COMMISSION REGULATIONS— DOOR–TO–DOOR SALES

[See Selected Source Materials Supplement]

NOTE ON THE UNIFORM COMMERCIAL CODE

The National Conference of Commissioners on Uniform State Laws (NCCUSL) consists of commissioners appointed by each state. NCCUSL recommends legislation to the states on subjects in which uniformity of law among the states is thought to be desirable. Among its successful projects was the Uniform Sales Act, drafted by Professor Williston.

In 1940, the idea of a Uniform Commercial Code was proposed to NCCUSL, to take the place of numerous disparate statutes, including the Uniform Sales Act, which had direct bearing on commercial transactions. Thereafter the UCC became a joint project of NCCUSL and the American Law Institute (ALI), with Karl N. Llewellyn of Columbia Law School, and later of the University of Chicago Law School, as the Chief Reporter. The UCC was adopted by NCCUSL and the ALI in 1952, and comprehensively revised in 1956; further amendments were promulgated thereafter. It has now been enacted in forty-nine states and the District of Columbia. (Louisiana, whose law is based on a civil code, has not adopted the UCC as such. However, it has adopted most Articles of the UCC other than Article 2 ("Sales") and it has incorporated many of the concepts of Article 2 into its Civil Code.)

Many provisions of the UCC are of major interest in the study of contract law, and will be referred to in this book. Most of these provisions are in Article 2. The direct applicability of that Article is set out in UCC § 2–102, which provides that "Unless the context otherwise requires, this Article applies to transactions in goods...." UCC § 2–105(1) defines "goods" to mean "all things (including specially manufactured goods) which are movable at the time of identification to the contract for sale other than the money in which the price is to be paid, investment securities ... and things in action." Other UCC provisions of interest in the study of contract law are contained in Article 1 ("General Provisions") and Article 9 ("Secured Transactions"). Articles 1 and 2, and selected portions of Articles 3 and 9, are set forth in the Selected Source Materials Supplement.

Within recent years, NCCUSL and the ALI have approved revised versions of, or significant amendments to, four articles of the UCC that bear on contract law—Articles 1, 2, 3, and 9. However, it is important to distinguish between the approval of revisions or amendments to the UCC by NCCUSL and the ALI, and the enactment of those revisions or amendments by the states. Like the UCC itself, revisions and amendments of the UCC that are approved by NCCUSL and the ALI become law only if and to the extent they are enacted by state legislatures. The revised versions of Article 3 and 9 have been widely enacted. In contrast, as of early 2006, the revised version of Article 1, which was approved by NCCUSL and the ALI in 2001, has been enacted by only sixteen states. Furthermore, none of those states adopted the choice-of-law provisions in section 1–301 of the revised Article, and only about half of those states adopted the definition of good faith in new section 1–201(b)(20). Substantial amendments to Article 2, which were approved by NCCUSL and the ALI in 2003, have so far not been enacted by any state, and because of strong opposition might never be enacted. Accordingly, the UCC Articles that are both relevant to contract law and enacted in all or most states are the pre–2001 version of Article 1 (General Provisions); the unamended version of Article 2 (Sales); revised Article 3 (Commercial Paper); and revised Article 9 (Secured Transactions).

In considering the UCC provisions referred to in this book, it should be borne in mind that even where a UCC provision is not directly applicable to a transaction—for example, where the provision is in Article 2 and the transaction involves services—the *principle* embodied in the provision may be applicable, so that the provision may serve as a source of law. "[P]rovisions of the Uniform Commercial Code which do not conflict with statute or settled case law are entitled to as much respect and weight as courts have been inclined to give the various Restatements. It, like the Restatements, has the stamp of approval of a large body of American Scholarship." Fairbanks, Morse & Co. v. Consolidated Fisheries Co., 190 F.2d 817, 822 n. 9 (3d Cir.1951). See generally Murray, The Spreading Analogy of Article 2 of the Uniform Commercial Code, 39 Fordham L.Rev. 447 (1971). For general discussion of the use of statutes as a source of law, see Landis, Statutes and the Sources of Law, *in* Harvard Legal Essays 213 (R. Pound ed. 1934); Pound, Sources and Forms of Law, pt. III, 22 Notre Dame Law. 1, 36–45 (1946).

Conversely, the UCC itself rests on the foundation of general law. Section 1–103 of the UCC, entitled "Supplementary General Principles of Law Applicable," provides that "Unless displaced by the particular provisions of this Act, the principles of law and equity, including the law merchant and the law relative to capacity to contract, principal and agent, estoppel, fraud, misrepresentation, duress, coercion, mistake, bankruptcy, or other validating or invalidating cause shall supplement its provisions." As stated in PEB Study Group, Uniform Commercial Code Article 2—Preliminary Report 22–23 (1990), Section 1–103 gives rise to two questions:

... (1) Does the UCC displace the common law in a particular area: and, if not, (2) What common law principle should the court choose? A broader interpretive question is whether § 1–103 provides sufficient flexibility and guidance for the courts to develop principles within the framework of the UCC, without having to find and integrate other "principles of law and equity."

For example, Article 2 uses but does not define the term "offer." See § 2–206(1) & § 2–207(1). Arguably, under § 1–103 these Sections do not displace the common law definition. Is a court bound willy nilly by whatever concept of offer is applicable in the state or may the court develop a definition which is consistent with the formation policies found in Article 2, Part 2? This is an important question for which there is no clear answer.

———

PITTSLEY v. HOUSER, 125 Idaho 820, 875 P.2d 232 (App.1994). This was a contract for the purchase and installation of residential carpeting. On the issue whether the contract was governed by the UCC, the court said, "although there is little dispute that carpets are 'goods,' the transaction in this case also involved installation, a service. Such hybrid transactions, involving both goods and services, raise difficult questions about the applicability of the UCC. Two lines of authority have emerged to deal with such situations.

"The first line of authority, and the majority position, utilizes the 'predominant factor' test. The Ninth Circuit, applying the Idaho Uniform Commercial Code to the subject transaction, restated the predominant factor test as:

> The test for inclusion or exclusion is not whether they are mixed, but, granting that they are mixed, whether their predominant factor, their thrust, their purpose, reasonably stated, is the rendition of service, with goods incidentally involved (e.g., contract with artist for painting) or is a transaction of sale, with labor incidentally involved (e.g., installation of a water heater in a bathroom)....

"This test essentially involves consideration of the contract in its entirety, applying the UCC to the entire contract or not at all.

"The second line of authority ... allows the contract to be severed into different parts, applying the UCC to the goods involved in the contract, but not to the nongoods involved, including ... services as well as other nongoods assets and property. Thus, an action focusing on defects or problems with the goods themselves would be covered by the UCC, while a suit based on the service provided or some other nongoods aspect would not be covered by the UCC....

"We believe the predominant factor test is the more prudent rule. Severing contracts into various parts, attempting to label each as goods or nongoods and applying different law to each separate part clearly contravenes the UCC's declared purpose 'to simplify, clarify and modernize the law governing commercial transactions.' ... As the Supreme Court of Tennessee suggested in Hudson v. Town & Country True Value Hardware, Inc., 666 S.W.2d 51 (Tenn.1984), such a rule would, in many contexts, present 'difficult and in some instances insurmountable problems of proof in segregating assets and determining their respective values at the time of the original contract and at the time of resale, in order to apply two different measures of damages.' *Id.* at 54.

"Applying the predominant factor test to the case before us, we conclude that the UCC was applicable to the subject transaction. The record indicates that the contract between the parties called for '165 yds Masterpiece #2122—Installed' for a price of $4319.50. There was an additional charge for removing the existing carpet. The record indicates that Hilton paid the installers $700 for the work done in laying Pittsley's carpet. It appears that Pittsley entered into this contract for the purpose of obtaining carpet of a certain quality and color. It does not appear that the installation, either who would provide it or the nature of the work, was a factor in inducing Pittsley to choose Hilton as the carpet supplier. On these facts, we conclude that the sale of the carpet was the predominant factor in the contract, with the installation being merely incidental to the purchase."

NOTE ON THE COMMENTS TO THE UCC

Each section of the UCC is accompanied by an Official Comment. A Comment may simply state the background of the relevant Section, or explain the way in which the Section is related to other sections. Often, however, the Comment plays a substantive role, by explaining the intention of the Section, putting a gloss on the language of the Section, providing examples of how the Section operates, or in other ways. The courts normally give deference to the Comments, but the exact legal status of the Comments is not completely clear. It has been said that "In the great majority of cases, courts cite the Comments to support the application or purpose described in them. In some cases, however, courts specifically reject the Comments as authority for their propositions." Note, The Jurisprudence and Judicial Treatment of the Comments to the Uniform Commercial Code, 75 Cornell L.Rev. 962, 975 (1990).

UNIDROIT PRINCIPLES OF INTERNATIONAL COMMERCIAL CONTRACTS ART. 3.10

[See Selected Source Materials Supplement]

PRINCIPLES OF EUROPEAN CONTRACT LAW §§ 4.109, 4.110

[See Selected Source Materials Supplement]

COMMISSION OF THE EUROPEAN COMMUNITIES, COUNCIL DIRECTIVE 93/13/EEC

[See Selected Source Materials Supplement]

MAXWELL v. FIDELITY FINANCIAL SERVICES, INC.

Supreme Court of Arizona, En Banc, 1995.
184 Ariz. 82, 907 P.2d 51.

FELDMAN, Chief Justice.

Elizabeth Maxwell petitions us to review a court of appeals opinion affirming a trial court ruling that the doctrine of novation barred Maxwell's claim that a contract was unconscionable and therefore unenforceable. See Maxwell v. Fidelity Fin. Servs., Inc., 179 Ariz. 544, 880 P.2d 1090 (Ct.App. 1993). We granted review . . .

FACTS AND PROCEDURAL HISTORY

The facts, taken in the light most favorable to Maxwell, against whom summary judgment was granted, are that in December 1984, Elizabeth Maxwell and her then husband, Charles, were approached by Steve Lasica, a door-to-door salesman representing the now defunct National Solar Corporation (National). Lasica sold the Maxwells a solar home water heater for a total purchase price of $6,512. Although National was responsible for installation, the unit was never installed properly, never functioned properly, and was eventually declared a hazard, condemned, and ordered disconnected by the City of Phoenix. Thus, although the unit may have been intrinsically worthless, the question of unconscionability is determined as of the time the contract was made. A.R.S. § 47–2302. [U.C.C. § 2–302].

Financing for the purchase was accomplished through a loan to the Maxwells from Fidelity Financial Services, Inc. (Fidelity). The sale price was financed for a ten-year period at 19.5 percent interest, making the total cost nearly $15,000.

At the time of the transaction, Elizabeth Maxwell earned approximately $400 per month working part-time as a hotel maid and her husband earned approximately $1,800 per month working for the local paper. At Fidelity's request, an appraisal was made of the Maxwells' South Phoenix home, where they had resided for the preceding twelve years. The appraisal showed that the Maxwells lived in a modest neighborhood, that their 1,539 square foot home was in need of a significant amount of general repair and maintenance, and that its market value was approximately $40,000.

In connection with the financing transaction, Elizabeth Maxwell signed numerous documents, including a loan contract, a deed of trust, a truth-in-lending disclosure form, and a promissory note and security agreement. The effect of these documents was not only to secure the deferred purchase price with a lien on the merchandise sold, but also to place a lien on Maxwell's house as additional security for payment on the water heater contract. The forms and their terms were unambiguous and clearly indicated that Maxwell was placing a lien on her house. Included in the consumer credit contract between Maxwell and Fidelity was a clause expressly stating that Fidelity was subject to all claims by and defenses that Maxwell could assert against National.

Despite the fact that the water heater was never installed or working properly, Maxwell made payments on it for approximately three and one-half years, reducing the deferred purchase balance to $5,733. In 1988, Maxwell approached Fidelity to borrow an additional $800 for purposes unrelated to the original loan. In making this second loan, Fidelity required Maxwell to again sign a bundle of documents essentially identical to those she signed in 1984. Instead of simply adding $800 to Maxwell's outstanding balance on the 1984 contract, Fidelity created a new contract that included the unpaid balance of $5,733 on the 1984 loan, a term life insurance charge of $313, as well as the new $800 loan. In all, Maxwell financed the sum of $6,976 with this second loan. The terms of this latest loan also included interest at 19.5 interest and payments for a period of six years, making Maxwell's new payments, including interest, total nearly $12,000. The combined amount Maxwell would pay under the two contracts for a non-functioning water heater and the additional $800 loan thus totals approximately $17,000, or nearly one-half the value of her home.

Maxwell continued to make payments until 1990, when she brought this declaratory judgment action seeking, *inter alia*, a declaration that the 1984 contract was unenforceable on the grounds that it was unconscionable.

Following discovery, Fidelity moved for summary judgment asserting, among other things, that the statute of limitations had run on Maxwell's claim of unconscionability and, if not, that the 1988 contract worked a novation, thereby barring any action by Maxwell on the 1984 contract. Maxwell filed a memorandum in opposition to this motion and pointed to sworn testimony in her deposition, which Fidelity submitted with its motion, as raising genuine issues of material fact.

In a brief order, the trial court granted Fidelity's motion on the theory of novation. . . .

The court of appeals affirmed [partly on procedural grounds]. . . .

On review from summary judgment, the appellate court views the record in a light most favorable to the party opposing summary judgment (Maxwell) and will affirm only if no genuine issue of material fact exists. We therefore review this record to determine whether it could support a finding that Maxwell's claim of unconscionability was barred by the 1988 loan.

PRELIMINARY ISSUES

Before discussing the merits of Maxwell's petition, we must address. . . . [the issue, must Maxwell show an agency relationship between Fidelity and National to defeat Fidelity's motion for summary judgment]. . . .

The court of appeals found that Maxwell failed to establish an agency relationship between National and Fidelity. The court reasoned that, absent such a relationship, Maxwell could not defeat Fidelity's motion for summary judgment on grounds of novation. We fail to see the relationship between establishing agency and defeating a claim of novation or pursuing a claim of unconscionability in this case. Fidelity stands in the shoes of National by virtue of both federal law and the terms of the contract to which it is a party. The 1984 and 1988 consumer credit contracts between Maxwell and Fidelity clearly state, in bold face, capital letters:

> ANY HOLDER OF THIS CONSUMER CREDIT CONTRACT IS SUBJECT TO ALL CLAIMS AND DEFENSES WHICH THE DEBTOR COULD ASSERT AGAINST THE SELLER OF GOODS OR SERVICES OBTAINED WITH THE PROCEEDS HEREOF.

Thus, Maxwell need not establish an agency relationship between National and Fidelity to maintain a claim against Fidelity for unconscionability or to overcome Fidelity's claim of novation....

DISCUSSION

A. Unconscionability ...

2. The Test for Unconscionability

The court of appeals found the 1984 contract valid because Maxwell "failed to raise a material issue of fact that the agreement evidenced by [the contract documents] was beyond her reasonable expectations or was unconscionable." It is not clear why the court of appeals applied the test of "reasonable expectations" as this test is more correctly associated with contracts of adhesion, not claims of unconscionability, and the issue of adhesion contracts was neither before the trial court nor briefed or argued on appeal. This court previously has noted the rule that "reasonable expectations" and unconscionability are two distinct grounds for invalidating or limiting the enforcement of a contract and has stated that "even if [the contract provisions are] consistent with the reasonable expectations of the party" they are unenforceable if they are oppressive or unconscionable. Broemmer v. Abortion Serv. of Phoenix, 173 Ariz. 148, 151, 840 P.2d 1013, 1016 (1992) (quoting Graham v. Scissor–Tail, Inc., 28 Cal.3d 807, 171 Cal. Rptr. 604, 611–12, 623 P.2d 165, 172–73 (1981)).

3. The History of Unconscionability ...

... Although U.C.C. § 2–302 recognized and codified the amorphous equitable doctrine [of unconscionability], it did little to provide a set of rules for analyzing claims of unconscionability. Also lacking in the statutory recognition of unconscionability is a definition of that term. Courts and respected commentators alike have grappled with defining and applying unconscionability under the Code since its adoption. To this day, both groups remain divided on the proper method for doing so, though they share some common ground on defining such a test.

Within this common area, the elements of unconscionability can be ascertained to fulfill the Code's obvious intent of protecting against unconscionable contracts while not unnecessarily denying parties the benefit of their bargain. Although no litmus test exists, the cases do provide a reasonable, workable analysis.

4. Divisions of Unconscionability under the U.C.C.

This court previously has acknowledged that the unconscionability principle involves an assessment by the court of whether, in the light of the general commercial background and the commercial needs of the particular trade or case, the clauses involved are so one-sided as to be unconscionable under the circumstances existing at the time of the making of the contract.... The principle is one of the prevention of oppression and unfair surprise ... not of disturbance of allocation of risks because of superior bargaining power.

Seekings v. Jimmy GMC of Tucson, Inc., 130 Ariz. 596, 602, 638 P.2d 210, 216 (1981) (citations omitted). This somewhat circular articulation of the principle, however, is not readily applicable to the infinite variety of cases that may involve the doctrine of unconscionability.

The framework upon which the vast majority of courts construct their analysis consists of the well recognized division of unconscionability into substantive and procedural parts. See, e.g., James J. White & Robert S. Summers, 1 Uniform Commercial Code 204, N. 8 and cases cited therein; John D. Calamari & Joseph M. Perillo, Contracts 406 (3d ed. 1987). Professor Dobbs provides the following explanation of the difference between these two types:

> Procedural or process unconscionability is concerned with "unfair surprise," fine print clauses, mistakes or ignorance of important facts or other things that mean bargaining did not proceed as it should. Substantive unconscionability is an unjust or "one-sided" contract. Substantive unconscionability is important in two ways. First, substantive unconscionability sometimes seems sufficient in itself to avoid a term in the contract. Second, substantive unconscionability sometimes helps confirm or provide evidence of procedural unconscionability.

Dobbs, supra at 706 (footnote omitted). This dichotomy evolved from a distinction made by the late Professor Leff in his oft-cited article Unconscionability and The Code—The Emperor's New Clause, 115 U.Pa.L.Rev. 485, 487 (1967). In his article, Professor Leff distinguished between "bargaining naughtiness" (procedural unconscionability) and overly harsh terms (substantive unconscionability). Id.

Over the years, courts have refined the two divisions of unconscionability and identified several factors that are indicative of each. Procedural unconscionability was well-explained in Johnson v. Mobil Oil Corp.:

> Under the procedural rubric come those factors bearing upon ... the real and voluntary meeting of the minds of the contracting party: age, education, intelligence, business acumen and experience, relative bargaining power, who drafted the contract, whether the terms were explained to the weaker party, whether alterations in the printed terms were possible, whether there were alternative sources of supply for the goods in question.

415 F.Supp. 264, 268 (E.D.Mich.1976) (internal quotations omitted). As Professors White and Summers have noted, procedural unconscionability bears a strong resemblance to its "common-law cousins" of fraud and duress. White & Summers, supra at 204.

Substantive unconscionability concerns the actual terms of the contract and examines the relative fairness of the obligations assumed. Resource Management Co. v. Weston Ranch & Livestock Co., 706 P.2d 1028, 1041 (Utah 1985). Indicative of substantive unconscionability are contract terms so one-sided as to oppress or unfairly surprise an innocent party, an overall imbalance in the obligations and rights imposed by the bargain, and significant cost-price disparity. Id. (citations and internal quotations omitted).

We believe these authorities provide useful illustrations of both divisions of unconscionability under the U.C.C., although we do not restrict applicability of the doctrine to the factors outlined.

5. Application

The point of agreement by courts on the substantive-procedural elements also marks a point of departure in analyzing claims of unconscionability. See generally White & Summers, supra at 218–20. Many courts, perhaps a majority, have held that there must be some quantum of *both* procedural and substantive unconscionability to establish a claim, and take a balancing approach in applying them. Id. at 219. See also 2 William D. Hawkland, Uniform Commercial Code Series § 2–302:05 (1984) and cases cited therein. Other courts have held that it is sufficient if *either* is shown. See, e.g., Gillman v. Chase Manhattan Bank, N.A., 73 N.Y.2d 1, 537 N.Y.S.2d 787, 794, 534 N.E.2d 824, 829 (1988) ("While determinations of unconscionability are ordinarily based on the court's conclusion that both the procedural and substantive components are present ... , there have been exceptional cases where a provision of the contract is so outrageous as to warrant holding it unenforceable on the ground of substantive unconscionability alone.") (citing State v. Wolowitz, 96 A.D.2d 47, 468 N.Y.S.2d 131 (1983)). In addition to the numerous courts holding that either procedural or substantive unconscionability is sufficient,[12] the leading commentators in this field have also endorsed this position. See White & Summers, supra at 220 (advocating the sufficiency of excessive price alone).

The cases that require a showing of both procedural and substantive unconscionability appear to be rather fact-specific, based more on the historical reluctance of courts to disturb contracts than on valid doctrinal underpinning.

In some cases substantive unconscionability is found because the contract price is grossly excessive (or sometimes grossly inadequate). Most of these cases present additional elements such as actual misrepresentations, gross mistreatment of people who are already disadvantaged, or a subject matter such as premarital settlements that calls for intense state scrutiny by judges. In some of them, the substantive unconscionabil-

12. See, e.g., Resource Management Co. v. Weston Ranch & Livestock Co., 706 P.2d 1028, 1043 (Utah 1985) ("Gross disparity in terms, absent evidence of procedural unconscionability, can support a finding of unconscionability."); American Home Improvement, Inc. v. MacIver, 105 N.H. 435, 201 A.2d 886, 889 (1964) (relying explicitly on U.C.S. § 2–302 and finding unconscionable, based on price-value disparity, a contract requiring payment of $1,609 for goods and services valued at "far less"); World Enter., Inc. v. Midcoast Aviation Serv., Inc., 713 S.W.2d 606, 610 (Mo.App.1986) ("Unconscionability is defined as either procedural or substantive."); Frank's Maintenance & Eng'g, Inc. v. C.A. Roberts Co., 86 Ill.App.3d 980, 42 Ill.Dec. 25, 31–32, 408 N.E.2d 403, 409–10 (1980) ("Unconscionability can be either procedural or substantive or a combination of both.") (emphasis added). Cf. Schroeder v. Fageol Motors, Inc., 86 Wash.2d 256, 544 P.2d 20, 23 (1975) (en banc) (recognizing that cases fall within the two classifications of procedural and substantive unconscionability). Indeed, it has long been recognized that gross disparity in terms may satisfy the standard for unconscionability by itself. See Marks v. Gates, 154 F. 481, 483 (9th Cir.1907) (inadequacy of consideration sufficient ground for withholding specific performance if it is so gross as to render the contract unconscionable).

ity really seems to be evidentiary only, that is, as confirming the conclusion that the process of bargaining was itself defective.

Dobbs, supra at 707 (footnote omitted) (emphasis added); see also Calamari & Perillo, supra at 406 ("[C]ontracts involving grossly unequal exchanges almost always involve some impropriety in the negotiating process or disability of a party."); White & Summers, supra at 218 ("Almost all of [the cases finding substantively unconscionable terms] exhibit creditor behavior that may be regarded as both procedurally and substantively unconscionable.").

Additional evidence that the dual requirement position is more coincidental than doctrinal is found within the very text of the statute on unconscionability, which explicitly refers to "the contract *or any clause* of the contract." A.R.S. § 47–2302 (emphasis added). Conspicuously absent from the statutory language is any reference to procedural aspects. That the U.C.C. contemplated substantive unconscionability alone to be sufficient is the most plausible reading of the language in § 47–2302, given that the Code itself provides for *per se* unconscionability if there exists, without more, a substantive term in the contract limiting consequential damages for injury to the person in cases involving consumer goods. See A.R.S. § 47–2719(c) [U.C.C. § 2–719 (c)]. It is wholly inconsistent to assert that unconscionability under § 47–2302 requires some procedural irregularity when unconscionability under § 47–2719 clearly does not.

Therefore, we conclude that under A.R.S. § 47–2302, a claim of unconscionability can be established with a showing of substantive unconscionability alone, especially in cases involving either price-cost disparity or limitation of remedies. If only procedural irregularities are present, it may be more appropriate to analyze the claims under the doctrines of fraud, misrepresentation, duress, and mistake, although such irregularities can make a case of procedural unconscionability. See Resource Management Co., 706 P.2d at 1043.

However, we leave for another day the questions involving the remedy for procedural unconscionability alone. We conclude further that this case presents a question of at least substantive unconscionability to be decided by the trial court. From the face of it, we certainly cannot conclude that the contract as a whole is not unconscionable, given the $6,500 price of a water heater for a modest residence, payable at 19.5 percent interest, for a total time-payment price of $14,860.43. These facts present at least a question of grossly-excessive price, constituting substantive unconscionability. See Dobbs, supra at 707; White & Summers, supra at § 4–5 and cases cited therein. This contract is made even more harsh by its security terms, which, in the event of non-payment, permit Fidelity not only to repossess the water heater but foreclose on Maxwell's home. The apparent injustice and oppression in these security provisions not only may constitute substantive unconscionability but also may provide evidence of procedural unconscionability. See Dobbs, supra at 706–07 (citing Williams v. Walker–Thomas Furniture Co., 350 F.2d 445 (D.C.Cir. 1965)).

Under the U.C.C. as enacted in A.R.S. § 47–2302, the court may "refuse enforcement of the contract altogether." Dobbs, supra at 705; Restatement § 208. The present factual record, before the statutorily required evidentiary hearing, certainly contains some evidence that the entire 1984 contract, including sale price, security provisions, and remedies, is unenforceable. We therefore turn to the effect of the doctrine of novation in such a situation.

B. Novation

1. Can the Doctrine of Novation Preclude an Action to Void a Pre-existing Contract on Grounds of Unconscionability?

The thrust of Maxwell's argument on this issue is that the trial court erred in finding her claim of unconscionability barred by the doctrine of novation. Maxwell argues that a finding of unconscionability with respect to the 1984 contract would have prevented the formation of a valid agreement through the 1988 contract. We agree. "Novation may be defined as the substitution by mutual agreement of ... a new debt or obligation for an existing one which is thereby extinguished." Western Coach Corp. v. Roscoe, 133 Ariz. 147, 152, 650 P.2d 449, 454 (1982) (citations and internal quotations omitted). In this case, therefore, a valid novation requires a previously enforceable debt, the agreement of all parties to a new contract, the extinguishment of the old debt, and the validity of the new one. See Dunbar v. Steiert, 31 Ariz. 403, 404, 253 P. 1113, 1113 (1927); United Sec. Corp. v. Anderson Aviation Sales Co., 23 Ariz.App. 273, 275, 532 P.2d 545, 547 (1975). The effect of a novation is to discharge the original debt. See Restatement § 280 cmt. b. . . .

2. How Valid Must the Prior Obligation Be to Support a Novation?

... If the debt created by the 1984 contract was unconscionable when entered into, then it was unenforceable; therefore Maxwell had no obligation, and there is nothing to novate or substitute for. Because the doctrine of unconscionability forbids using courts as instruments of oppression, under such circumstances the *original* contract obligation would be a nullity. Fidelity cannot revive a dead branch by grafting it onto a living tree. It is not clear, moreover, how simply reciting the terms of the 1984 contract, in a new and substantially identical instrument and under substantially identical circumstances four years later, provides any help to Fidelity.

If anything, Fidelity's argument for novation raises substantial questions about the unconscionability of the 1988 contract, as that contract is nearly identical to the 1984 contract. By the terms of the 1988 contract, the outstanding $5,700 principle balance due on the water heater after Maxwell had already made forty-two payments on the 1984 contract was "bundled" with the unrelated $800 cash loan and a term life insurance policy. The 1988 loan amount, totaling $6,976.92, was financed again at 19.5 percent interest and stretched for another six years, with another $5,000 of precomputed interest added, for a total deferred price of $11,887.20. This amount, when added to what Maxwell had already paid, made the total deferred purchase price of the inoperable water heater and the $800 cash loan more than $17,000. Our unconscionability analysis of the 1984 contract applies a *fortiori* to the 1988 contract. If the 1984 contract was substantively unconscionable, the resulting unenforceability could not be avoided by redrafting the documents with essentially identical provisions under a new date. By preparing a new set of almost identical papers in 1988, Fidelity could not transmogrify the water heater deal made in 1984. Finally, it is necessary to point out that the 1988 contract was not a compromise and settlement of a claim. Fidelity presented no evidence and made no allegation that Maxwell intended to settle a claim of unconscionability or that she even presented a claim when she executed the 1988 contract. Accordingly, we hold that if found to be unconscionable, Maxwell's contracts with Fidelity are invalid for purposes of novation. . . .

CONCLUSION

. . . [W]e vacate the court of appeals' opinion, reverse the trial court's judgment, and remand to the trial court for proceedings consistent with this opinion and A.R.S. § 47–2302.

MOELLER, V.C.J., and CORCORAN and ZLAKET, JJ., concur.

[The opinion of Judge MARTONE, concurring in the judgment, is omitted.]

————

NOTE ON CLASSICAL AND MODERN CONTRACT LAW

From the middle of the nineteenth century until the first part of the twentieth century, contract law was dominated by a school of thought, now known as classical contract law, which found its central inspiration in Christopher Columbus Langdell, Oliver Wendell Holmes, and Samuel Williston, and its central expression in Restatement First. Beginning in the middle of the twentieth century, modern contract law began to oust classical contract law. Today, classical contract law survives largely in the form of backdrop rules that have been heavily eroded but not entirely superceded. The movement from classical to modern contract law has occurred in a variety of dimensions.

1. *The nature of contract-law reasoning.* To begin with, there has been a shift in the nature of contract-law reasoning. Reasoning in common law areas, like contracts, may be substantive or formal. The premise of *substantive* legal reasoning is that the validity of a doctrine turns in part on normative considerations, that is, on the congruence of the doctrine with morals, policy, and experience. In contrast, the premise of *formal* legal reasoning is that law consists of doctrines that are autonomous from policy, morality, and experience—that doctrines are valid without regard to whether they are normatively justified.

Formal legal reasoning may be axiomatic, deductive, or both. *Axiomatic* legal reasoning takes as a premise that fundamental doctrines can be established on the ground that they are self-evident. In the strictest versions of axiomatic theories, such as classical contract law, no room is allowed for justifying doctrinal propositions on the basis of moral and policy propositions. So, for example, Langdell, speaking to the question whether an acceptance by mail was effective on dispatch or on receipt, said:

> The acceptance . . . must be communicated to the original offeror, and until such communication the contract is not made. It has been claimed that the purposes of substantial justice, and the interests of contracting parties as understood by themselves, will be best served by holding that the contract is complete the moment the letter of acceptance is mailed; and cases have been put to show that the contrary view would produce not only unjust by absurd results. The true answer to this argument is that it is irrelevant.

Deductive legal reasoning is based on the idea that many or most doctrines can be established solely by deduction from other, more fundamental doctrines that are taken as the major premises of syllogisms. As Holmes observed, disparagingly, axiomatic theories may easily be coupled with deductive theories: "I sometimes tell students that the law schools pursue and inspirational combined with a logical method, that is, the postulates are taken for granted upon authority without inquiry into their worth, and then logic is used as the only tool to develop the results."

Classical contract law was based on just such a coupling. It conceived contract law as a small set of core doctrines—axioms—that were justified on the ground that they were self-evident, and as a larger set of doctrines that were justified largely on the ground that they could be deduced from the core axioms. For example, it was an axiom of classical contract law that only bargain promises had consideration—that is, were enforceable (although exceptions were recognized for certain kinds of promises, such as those under seal, that were considered to be enforceable on strictly precedential, rather than principled, grounds).

In contrast to the formal reasoning of classical contract law, modern contract-law reasoning seeks to justify doctrines on the basis of policy, morality, and experience. Doctrines have an important role to play even in substantive legal reasoning, because of the social value that underlies doctrinal stability, but that value must always be weighed against the value of normative justification.

In general, the algorithm that describes modern contract-law reasoning is this: (1) If the rule that is stated in applicable precedents is the normatively best rule—that is, the rule that is best justified by morality, policy, and experience—the rule should and will be followed by the courts. (2) Even if the rule stated in applicable precedents is not the normatively best rule, the rule stated in applicable precedents normally should and will be followed by the courts if it is substantially congruent with the normatively best rule, although it falls somewhat short of the best rule. Small differences between the best possible rule and a reasonably good rule are likely to be highly debatable, difficult to perceive, or both. Therefore, if the courts failed to follow a doctrinal rule just because the rule was modestly less desirable than a competing alternative, it would be difficult to put reliance on doctrine. To put this differently, at least over the short term, the value of making minor improvements in legal rules is normally outweighed by the value of doctrinal stability. (3) If the rule stated in applicable precedents is not even substantially congruent with the normatively best rule, the courts should not and normally will not consistently apply and extend the stated rule. The value of major substantive improvements in legal rules normally outweighs the value of doctrinal stability. Accordingly, in the modern period many of the most firmly rooted doctrines of classical contract law have been either radically transformed, significantly modified, or wholly uprooted, because the courts have come to perceive these doctrines as lacking normative justification. This is true, for example of the classical-contract-law rule that only bargain promises are enforceable.

2. *The deep structure of contract-law rules.* A second aspect of the movement from classical to modern contract law concerns the deep structure of contract-law rules. Legal rules can be ranged along various spectra. Four

such spectra, which are particularly salient in contract law, will be discussed in the balance of this Note.

a. *Objectivity/subjectivity.* One of these spectra runs from objectivity to subjectivity. A contract-law doctrine lies at the objective end of this spectrum if its application depends on a directly observable state of the world, and lies at the subjective end if its application depends on a mental state. For example, the classical-law rule that nominal consideration made a promise enforceable was objective, because it asked only whether there was the objective form of a bargain. In contrast, the modern rule that nominal consideration does not make a promise enforceable allows the courts to inquire whether the parties were actually (subjectively) bargaining for the consideration that is recited in their contract.

b. *Standardization/individualization.* A second spectrum runs from standardization to individualization. A contract-law doctrine lies at this standardized end of this spectrum if its application depends on an abstract variable that is unrelated to the intentions of the parties or the particular circumstances of the transaction. A contract-law doctrine lies at the individualized end of this spectrum if its application depends on situation-specific variables that are related to intentions and circumstances. For example, application of the classical doctrine that adequacy of consideration will not be reviewed depends on a single variable—the presence of a bargain—that is deliberately designed to screen out all information concerning intentions and circumstances. In contrast, application of the modern doctrine of unconscionability depends on a number of situation-specific variables that are wholly concerned with that sort of information.

c. *Static/dynamic.* A third spectrum runs from the static to the dynamic. A contract-law doctrine lies at the static end of this spectrum if its application turns entirely on what occurred at the moment in time when a contract was formed. A contract-law doctrine lies at the dynamic end if its application turns in significant part on a moving stream of events that precedes, follows, or constitutes the formation of a contract. For example, the bargain theory of consideration is static, because its application wholly depends on what occurs at the moment in time when the bargain was made. In contrast, the reliance principle is dynamic, because its application turns on events after the promise is made. Similarly, the classical legal-duty rule (see Section 4, infra) was static, because all rights and duties were frozen at the moment of contract-formation. In contrast, a regime under which modifications are enforceable is dynamic, because it takes account of importance of voluntary reciprocity after contract-formation.

d. *Binary/multifaceted.* A forth spectrum runs from the binary to the multi-faceted. Contract law doctrines are *binary* if they organize the experience within their scope into two categories. Contract law doctrines are *multifaceted* if they organize the experience within their scope into several categories, including one or more intermediate categories. For example, recall that Williston argued that when it came to damages, the only choice in contract law was the binary choice between no damages and expectation damages. In contrast, modern contract law provides a multi-faceted menu of no damages, expectation damages, reliance damages, and restitutionary damages.

Classical contract law was a rigid rather than a supple instrument. It gave an overriding priority to objective, standardized, static, and binary rules, which were often responsive to neither the actual objectives of the parties, the actual facts and circumstances of the parties' transaction, nor the dynamic character of contracts. In contrast, modern contact law pervasively (although not completely) consists of principles that are individualized, dynamic, multi-faceted, and, in appropriate cases, subjective. Many of the Chapters in this book illustrate the movement from classical to modern contract law along one or more of these dimensions.

————

The remaining Sections of this Chapter are devoted to limits on the bargain principle that for the most part are nominally conceived as *part* of the bargain principle, rather than as reflecting the concept of unconscionability. In fact, however, many of these limits essentially seem to be surrogates for unconscionability, which were developed before the law courts openly accepted the principle of unconscionability. As you read these Sections, you should therefore consider to what extent the limits on the bargain principle set out in each Section are (1) a corollary of the bargain principle, (2) a policy limit on the bargain principle, or (3) a surrogate for the principle of unconscionability. More specifically, the next two Sections will address the following questions: whether and when a bargain must involve "mutuality" to constitute consideration (Section 3); and whether and when a bargain to perform an act that the promisor is already legally obliged to perform will constitute consideration (Section 4).

————

SECTION 3. THE PROBLEM OF MUTUALITY

————

INTRODUCTORY NOTE

For several centuries no suit for breach of an unsealed executory agreement was possible in England. One had generally a suit (in *debt* or *detinue*) for the price of a performance that had been rendered, or a suit (in *covenant*) for breach of a promise under seal. However, one generally could not sue for breach of an unsealed contract that had not been performed on one side. When, toward the end of the sixteenth century, this state of affairs was finally changed, the reform was accomplished with surprising ease. No cumbersome fiction was used to cover the courts' departure from precedent; there was no forcing of the reform into some inappropriate framework furnished by previous law. In the most cited of the cases signaling this development, the report observes simply that "a promise against a promise will maintain an action upon the case." (Strangborough and Warner's Case, 1589, 4 Leon. 3)

The rationalizations and fictions came about three centuries later. During the last part of the nineteenth century and the first part of the twentieth, legal thinking went through a period characterized by an intense interest in the "logical" or internal symmetry of the law. In the common law, "consideration" had by that time acquired a more or less fixed definition, as a detriment incurred by the promisee or a benefit received by the promisor. The question was therefore raised, how can this definition be applied to an executory (that is, not-yet performed) exchange of a promise for a promise? The attempts to answer this question resulted in a considerable body of literature.

The first attempt to answer the question, that of Langdell, was rather quickly rejected. Langdell suggested that if A promises to pay $10 for B's horse, and B promises to sell the horse for $10, the consideration for B's promise lies in the fact that A incurred a detriment in binding himself to pay B. It was soon pointed out that this argument moves in a circle, since it presupposes the binding effect of A's promise, a question as much in issue as the binding effect of B's. After the failure of Langdell's theory to win approval, the explanations diverged along two lines. It was argued either that the detriment is furnished by the making of the promise, considered as a fact without regard to its legal effect (Ames), or that consideration in bilateral contracts rests on "a distinct principle" (Williston). So inconclusive did this whole discussion seem to Sir Frederick Pollock that he was moved to declare: "What logical justification is there for holding mutual promises good consideration for each other? None, it is submitted." (1912, 28 L.Q.Rev. 101) In another place he treats the fact that an exchange of promises results in an enforceable contract as "one of the secret paradoxes of the Common Law." (1914, 30 L.Q.Rev. 129.)

Certainly the fault must lie with legal theory if it is incapable of "explaining" so commonplace a phenomenon as the binding effect of mutual promises. A proper explanation would run, not in terms of definitions or abstract juristic conceptions, but in terms of the policies that underlie the requirement of consideration: *Bargains* serve social-welfare purposes because they create wealth through trade, and because they facilitate private economic planning by allowing actors to allocate risks, and to coordinate economic activity through the acquisition of control over inputs and outputs. *Enforcing bargain promises* furthers the welfare purposes that such promises serve.

Even after it became accepted that bargain promises were enforceable as such—that is, although not under seal and not performed on one side—classical contract law had trouble with certain classes of bargain promises. One of these problems was reflected in the concept of mutuality. In hundreds of American cases, it has been asserted as a general rule of contract law that both parties must be bound or neither is bound. This notion has usually been called "the principle of mutuality."

This principle obviously needs more qualification than it usually receives in judicial opinions.

First, the principle has no application to a unilateral contract. In a *bilateral* contract, the parties exchange a promise for a promise. (For example, Seller agrees to sell Buyer a used car for $2,000, delivery in three days, and Buyer agrees to pay $2,000 on delivery.) In a *unilateral* contract, the parties exchange a promise for an act. (For example, A promises to pay B $50 for mowing A's lawn, and makes clear that only B's act of mowing the lawn, not B's promise to do so, will suffice.) In a unilateral contract, the party who exchanges an act for promise may never be bound, because he is not bound to do anything before he chooses to do the act, and he may not be bound to do anything after he does the act. Thus suppose, in the last example, that B mows the lawn. B was not bound to mow the lawn before he mowed it, and is not bound to A in any way after he mowed it. Nevertheless, A is bound to B.

Second, the principle of mutuality is not applied to bargains in which both parties have made real promises but one party is not legally bound by his promise. For example, suppose A fraudulently induces B to agree to buy Blackacre. Although B is not legally bound, he can enforce the contract, notwithstanding the doctrine of mutuality. The same result follows in many other kinds of cases, such as those in which one but not both parties has a defense under the Statute of Frauds or a defense of incapacity.

(WARNING: In certain equity cases involving the right to specific performance it has been held that this remedy will not be granted to a plaintiff unless the defendant might also have obtained specific performance. This concept, which is described as a requirement of "mutuality of remedy," in contrast to the less stringent requirement of "mutuality of obligation," has been applied only in equity cases. The rule is of doubtful standing today, and is mentioned here only to avoid conveying a misleading impression.)

Williston took the view that cases holding that the various types of cases in which a plaintiff may enforce a contract, even though he cannot be sued on the contract (because, for example, he did not sign the memorandum required by the Statute of Frauds), constitute "an exception to the general principles of consideration." 4th ed., at § 7:13. He argued that if the right to bring suit in these cases (for example, the right of a defrauded party, a minor, or a non-signing party) was spelled out in words in the contract itself, the promise would be held to be "illusory" and therefore insufficient as consideration for the promise of the other party.

Whether these cases are exceptions to the requirement of consideration depends, of course, upon the view taken of the policies that define the requirement. In any event, the existence of these cases shows that under some circumstances a promise by the plaintiff that is not itself binding on him can nevertheless act as consideration for the promise of the defendant, and demonstrates again that the alleged principle of "mutuality" requires a good deal of qualification.

SCOTT v. MORAGUES LUMBER CO.

Supreme Court of Alabama, 1918.
202 Ala. 312, 80 So. 394.

Suit by the Moragues Lumber Company, a corporation, against J.M. Scott, for damages for breach of an agreement of charter party. Judgment for plaintiff, and defendant appeals. Affirmed.

Count 2 of the complaint as amended is as follows:

"The plaintiff claims of the defendant $13,000 as damages from breach of an agreement entered into between the plaintiff and the defendant on the 27th day of June, 1917, consisting of an offer by the defendant that, subject to his buying a certain American vessel, 15 years old, which he was then figuring on and which was of about 1,050 tons and then due in Chile, he would charter said vessel to the plaintiff for the transportation of a cargo of lumber from any port in the Gulf of Mexico to Montevideo or Buenos Aires, for the freight of $65 per thousand feet of lumber, freight to be prepaid, free of discount and of insurance, and the vessel to be furnished to the plaintiff within a reasonable time after its purchase by the defendant, which said offer was accepted by the plaintiff, and the plaintiff avers that although the defendant purchased said vessel, and although the plaintiff was at all times ready, willing, and able to comply with all the provisions of said contract on its part, the defendant without notifying the plaintiff of said purchase, and before said vessel was delivered to him, chartered said vessel to a third person, and thereby rendered himself unable to comply with the said contract." . . .

SAYRE, J. . . . It is said, in the first place, that the alleged contract between the parties was conditioned upon the will of appellant, defendant, and was therefore void for want of consideration or mutuality of obligation. A valid contract may be conditioned upon the happening of an event, even though the event may depend upon the will of the party, who afterwards seeks to avoid its obligation. This principle is illustrated in McIntyre Lumber Co. v. Jackson Lumber Co., 165 Ala. 268, 51 So. 767, 138 Am.St.Rep. 66. Appellant was not bound to purchase the vessel; but, when he did, the offer—or the contract, if the offer had been accepted—thereafter remained as if this condition had never been stipulated, its mutuality or other necessary incidents of obligation depending upon its other provisions and the action of the parties thereunder. Davis v. Williams, 121 Ala. 542, 25 So. 704; 3 Page on Contracts, § 1358. See, also, Jones v. Lanier, 198 Ala. 363, 73 So. 535. . . .

The effect of appellee's acceptance, if communicated while the offer was yet open, was to convert it into a binding contract. 6 R.C.L. p. 605, § 27. In substance, it is alleged in the complaint that appellant's offer was accepted; that appellant purchased the vessel; that appellee was able, ready, and willing to perform the contract on its part; but that appellant disabled himself, or failed and refused to perform on his part. From the order in which the facts are alleged it is to be inferred that appellee accepted appellant's offer before the latter purchased the vessel, and there is no ground of demurrer questioning the sufficiency of the complaint to that effect. Thereupon the offer was converted into a binding contract to be performed, if not otherwise stipulated, within a reasonable time; the promise on either hand constituting the consideration of the promise on the other. Appellant's purchase of the vessel was a condition precedent to the existence of a binding contract, it is true; but that was alleged, as it was necessary that it should be. 13 C.J. p. 724, § 847, citing McCormick v. Badham, 191 Ala. 339, 67 So. 609; Long v. Addix, 184 Ala. 236, 63 So. 982; Flouss v. Eureka Co., 80 Ala. 30. And so with respect to appellee's acceptance of the offer. It was necessary that appellee communicate its acceptance to appellant. 1 Page, § 43. But this communication was a part of the acceptance and was covered by the general allegation of acceptance. . . .

Affirmed.

––––––

NOTE ON SCOTT v. MORAGUES

Up to now, the materials in this casebook have chiefly concerned promises, which constitute one basic building-block of contracts. There is another basic building block of contracts—conditions. What is a condition? In everyday language, the term has various meanings, including "state" and "state of events." Thus we say, "under favorable conditions the tree will prosper," or "the patient's condition is good," or "the human condition is tragic." Similarly, in contract law the term *express condition* normally refers to an explicit provision in a contract which provides either that: (1) A party to the contract does not come under a duty to perform unless and until some designated state of events occurs or fails to occur; or (2) If some designated state of events occurs or fails to occur, the duty of a party to perform is suspended or terminated.

The state of events that the condition concerns may lie outside the control of either party—as where Corporation A agrees to merge with Corporation B on condition that the Commissioner of Internal Revenue rules that the merger will be tax-free. Or the state of events may lie partly or wholly within the control of one of the parties—as in Scott v. Moragues Lumber Co., supra, where it was a condition to the obligation of both parties under the contract that Scott would have purchased a certain vessel. Similarly, the condition may qualify the obligations of *both* parties, as in the two examples just considered, or it may qualify only the obligation of only one party, as where A agrees to sell her house to B, and B agrees to purchase the house on condition that a termite-inspection report shows no infestation.

The opinion in Scott v. Moragues states that Scott's "purchase of the vessel was a condition precedent to the existence of a binding contract." Under standard contracts principles, however, a contract was *formed* even before Scott purchased the vessel, although each party's obligation to *perform* under the contract was subject to the condition that the purchase was made. This issue is well-analyzed in Safeco Ins. Co. of America v. City of White House, 36 F.3d 540 (6th Cir.1994). In that case, the City of White House, Tennessee, solicited bids from contractors to build a wastewater-treatment facility. The bid specifications stated that: (1) The project was partly funded by the Environmental Protection Agency (the EPA). (2) The EPA required contractors working on projects it funded to make an effort to ensure that small, minority, and women's businesses were employed. (3) EPA approval of the contractor's compliance with EPA's requirements was required. (4) The low bidder was required to forward to the City, no later than ten days after the bids were opened, documents reflecting the low bidder's compliance with the EPA's equal-opportunity policy.

Eatherly submitted the lowest bid on the project. The City accepted the bid on March 19, 1987, and Eatherly and the City executed an agreement on April 16. Safeco, a surety company, guaranteed Eatherly's performance. A dispute then arose whether Eatherly had complied with the equal-opportunity provisions in the bid specifications. At that point, Eatherly withdrew its bid, claiming that no contract had been formed because compliance with those provisions was a condition to the formation of a contract. The City sued Safeco on the ground that Eatherly was in breach. The court held that a contract had been formed when the agreement was made:

> ... Safeco maintains that EPA approval was a condition precedent to the existence of a contract, and the nonoccurrence of that condition (EPA never approved Eatherly for work on the project) prevented the formation of a contract....

... It is apparent that the City was requiring bidders to make their bids (offers) subject to the EPA's minority business enterprise requirements. This was clearly understood by Eatherly; in its bid Eatherly agreed "to perform all WORK ... in strict accordance with the CONTRACT DOCUMENTS." Thus, the condition of satisfying the EPA of compliance with its requirements was incorporated into the bid itself, and when the City accepted the bid, subject to EPA approval, a binding contract was formed. As Professor Corbin states, "An acceptance may be unconditional even though the acceptor makes a conditional promise." 1 Arthur L. Corbin, Corbin on Contracts § 3.29 at 464 (rev. ed.1993).

> To accept, the offeree must assent unconditionally to the offer as made, but the fact that the offeree makes a conditional promise is not sufficient to show that his acceptance is conditional. The offer itself may either expressly or by implication propose that the offeree make a conditional promise as his part of the exchange. By assenting to such a proposal the offeree makes a conditional promise, but his acceptance is unconditional.

Restatement (Second) of Contracts § 59 cmt. b at 146 (1979) ...

Since Eatherly's bid included the condition of EPA approval and was accepted by the City, both parties became bound in accordance with their mutual assent. The City accepted Eatherly's offer *unconditionally*, and thus this is a classic case of an unconditional acceptance of a conditional promise. A contract was formed when the City accepted Eatherly's offer on Eatherly's terms—one of those terms rendered the contract subject to EPA approval.

————

WICKHAM & BURTON COAL CO.
v. FARMERS' LUMBER CO.

Supreme Court of Iowa, 1920.
189 Iowa 1183, 179 N.W. 417, 14 A.L.R. 1293.

Appeal from District Court, Webster County; R.M. Wright, Judge. Counterclaim asserting that damages were due from plaintiff because of a contract made between plaintiff and defendant. A demurrer to the counterclaim was overruled; hence this appeal. Reversed.

SALINGER, J. The counterclaim alleges that about August 18, 1916, defendant, through an agent, entered into an oral agreement, "whereby plaintiff agreed to furnish and to deliver to defendant orders given them" for carload shipments of coal from defendant f.o.b. mines, "to be shipped to defendant at such railroad yard stations as defendant might direct, at the price of $1.50 a ton on all orders up to September 1, 1916, and $1.65 a ton on all orders from then to April 1, 1917." It is further alleged that "said coal ordered would be and consist" of what was known as plaintiff's Paradise 6 lump, 6 3 egg, or 3 2 nut coal. It is next alleged that defendant has for several years last past been engaged in owning and operating what is commonly known as a line of lumber yards, located at different railroad station points tributary to Ft. Dodge, where defendant has its principal place of business; that at these several lumber yards, among other merchandise and commodities, the defendant handles coal in carload lots, with purpose of selling the same at retail to its patrons.

Then comes an allegation that the agent made oral agreement "that plaintiff would furnish unto defendant coal in carload lots, that defendant would want to purchase from plaintiff" on stated terms, with character of the coal described, and that the oral contract was confirmed by the letter Exhibit 1. It is of date August 21, 1916, and recites that plaintiff is in receipt of a letter from their agent—

"asking us to name you a price [repeating the price and coal description found in the counterclaim]. Although this is a very low price, our agent, Mr. Spalding, has recommended that we quote you this price, and we hereby confirm it. Any orders received between now and September 1st are to be shipped at $1.50. We would like to have a letter from you accepting these prices, and if this is satisfactory will consider same as a contract."

On August 26, 1916, the defendant responded:

"We have your favor of the 21st accepting our order for coal for shipment to March 31, 1917."

The basis of the counterclaim, so far as damages are concerned, is the allegation that a stated amount of coal had to be purchased by defendant in the open market at a greater than the contract price, and that therefore there is due the defendant from the plaintiff the sum of $3,090.

The demurrer asserts that the alleged contract is "void for failure of mutuality and certainty;" is void because there is no consideration between the parties; because it appears affirmatively that the offer was simply an offer on part of plaintiff, which might be accepted by giving an order until such time as it was actually withdrawn or expired by limitation, each order and acceptance of a carload lot constituting a separate and distinct contract; and void because the agreement could not be enforced by the plaintiff on any certain or specified amount of tonnage, or for the payment of any specified tonnage.

The demurrer makes, in effect, three assertions: (a) That the arrangement between the parties is void for uncertainty; (b) that it lacks consideration; (c) that it lacks mutuality of obligation. We have given the argument and the citations on the first two propositions full consideration. But we conclude these first two are of no importance if mutuality is wanting....

... [T]he asserted lack of consideration is bottomed on the claim that mutuality is lacking. Appellant does not deny that a promise may be a consideration for a promise. Its position is that this is so only of an enforceable promise. That is the law. If, from lack of mutuality, the promise is not binding, it cannot form a consideration.... Campbell v. Lambert, 36 La.Ann. 35, 51 Am.Rep. 1. In the last-named case it is said that, while a promise may be a good consideration for another promise, this is not so "unless there is an absolute mutuality of engagement, so that each party has the right at once to hold the other to a positive agreement"—citing 1 Parsons on Contracts, 448....

The question of first importance, then, is whether there is a lack of mutuality. In the last analysis the counterclaim is based on the allegation that plaintiff undertook to furnish defendant such described coal "as defendant would want to purchase from plaintiff." The defendant never "accepted." Indeed, it is its position that it gave orders, and that plaintiff did the accepting. But concede, for argument's sake, that defendant did accept. What was the acceptance? At the utmost, it was a consent that plaintiff might ship it such coal as defendant "would want to purchase from plaintiff." What obligation did this fasten upon defendant? It did not bind itself to buy all it could sell. It did not bind itself to buy of plaintiff only. It merely "agreed" to buy what it pleased. It may have been ascertainable how much it would need to buy of some one. But there was no undertaking to buy that much, or, indeed, any specified amount of coal of plaintiff. . . .

The "contract" on part of appellee is to buy if it pleased, when it pleased, to buy if it thought it advantageous, to buy much, little, or not at all, as it thought best.

A contract of sale is mutual where it contains an agreement to sell on the one side, and an agreement to purchase on the other. But it is not mutual where there is an obligation to sell, but no obligation to purchase, or an obligation to purchase, but no obligation to sell. 13 Corpus Juris, 339. . . .

Where one party agrees to cut for the other hay "not to exceed 200 tons," there is lack of mutuality, because the offerant was not bound to deliver any particular quantity of hay, and could cut as little as he pleased. Houston R. Co. v. Mitchell, 38 Tex. 85. So where a defendant who binds himself to receive and pay for all the ties plaintiff could produce and ship at a stated price between stated dates. As to this it was held mutuality was lacking, because there was no enforceable duty to deliver any ties. Hazelhurst v. Supply Co. (C.C.) 166 F. 191. And so of an offer to receive and transport railroad iron, not to exceed a stated number of tons, during specified periods, and at a specified rate per ton. As to this it was held that, though plaintiff answered, assenting to the proposal, there was still no contract, because there was no agreement on his part that he would deliver any iron for transportation. Railroad v. Dane, 43 N.Y. 240; Hoffmann v. Maffioli, 104 Wis. 630, 80 N.W. 1032, 47 L.R.A. 427. An agreement to purchase all that the manufacturer desires to sell at a specified price is void. 13 C.J. at 340. . . .

A contract to sell personal property is void for want of mutuality if the quantity to be delivered is conditioned entirely on the will, wish, or want of the buyer. 13 Corpus Juris, 339; Cold Blast Co. v. Bolt Co., 114 F. 77, 52 C.C.A. 25, 57 L.R.A. 696. So of an agreement to supply all pig iron wanted by defendants in their business between stated dates, at specified prices, even though the other party promised to purchase such iron. The argument advanced is that the buyer did not engage "to want any quantity whatever," nor even agree to continue in their business. Bailey v. Austrian, 19 Minn. 535 (Gil. 465). It is said in Hickey v. O'Brien, 123 Mich. 611, 82 N.W. 241, 49 L.R.A. 594, 81 Am.St.Rep. 227, that in National Furnace Co. v. Manufacturing Co., 110 Ill. 427, the case of Bailey v. Austrian is distinguished by pointing out that in the *Bailey* Case stress is laid on the word "want"; while in the Illinois case the plaintiff agreed to sell to defendant all the iron "needed" in its business during the three ensuing years at $22.35 a ton, and the defendant agreed to take its year's supply at that price. We are unable to find any substantial difference between an "agreement" to buy what one might "want" and what one might "need". Be that as it may, in the case at bar the language was, "would want to purchase." And the *Austrian* Case is well supported in authority. . . .

Three cars of coal were shipped and received. Upon this appellee urges that thereby the so-called contract was completed and made mutual. Part performance was ineffectual in Hoffmann v. Maffioli, 104 Wis. 630, 80 N.W. 1032, 47 L.R.A. 427, to found a case as for breach of contract on refusal to ship more. . . .

If there never was a contract to ship anything, that is still the situation when a contract to ship what has not yet been shipped is asserted as the basis of an action. As said in Cold Blast Co. v. Bolt Co., 114 F. 80, 52 C.C.A. 25, 57 L.R.A. 696, even though there had been some shipments, there was still no consideration and no mutuality in the contract as to any articles which defendant had not ordered, or which plaintiff had not delivered, and therefore the refusal of plaintiff to honor the orders of defendants was no breach of any valid contract, and formed no legal cause of action whereon to base a counterclaim. It was further said:

"As to all undelivered articles, that defect still inheres in the agreement. The plaintiff is not bound to deliver, nor the defendant to take and pay for, any articles that have not been delivered [that is to say, so much as has not been performed still rests upon an agreement which is not enforceable, and for the refusal to honor which there can be no recovery]. . . . The defendant never agreed to order or to pay for any quantity of these undelivered articles. If it had refused to order and take them, no action could have been maintained for its failure, because no court could have determined what amount it was required to take." . . .

Defendant alleges further that, by reason of the conduct of plaintiff in furnishing defendant two carloads at $1.50 per ton under the contract terms, plaintiff is now estopped from claiming there was no binding contract between the parties for furnishing coal to defendant under the contract contended for by defendant. But the claimed estoppel is no broader than the claimed breach of a contract which is no contract.

Cases relied on by appellee do not, on careful consideration, militate with what we have declared. All that Keller v. Ybarru, 3 Cal. 147, holds is that, when one party offers to sell as much as the other wishes, there is a contract after the other declares what quantity he will take. . . .

The demurrer should have been sustained.

Reversed.

MIAMI COCA–COLA BOTTLING CO. v. ORANGE CRUSH CO., 296 Fed. 693 (5th Cir.1924). Under a "license agreement" the manufacturer of "Orange Crush" concentrate gave the licensee the exclusive right to manufacture the soft drink "Orange Crush" in a certain territory, and agreed to supply concentrate for the licensee's operations in mixing and bottling the drink and to do certain advertising. The licensee, on the other hand, agreed to manufacture the drink and to distribute it under the trademark of the manufacturer. The licensee also agreed to purchase a specified quantity of concentrate, and to promote the sale of the drink in the territory granted to it. The license granted was perpetual, with a proviso that the licensee might at any time cancel the contract. The agreement was carried out on both sides for about a year, when the manufacturer gave notice of cancellation. The licensee brought a suit in equity to enjoin cancellation of the contract. An order dismissing the plaintiff's suit was affirmed: " . . . [T]he contract was void for lack of mutuality. It may be conceded that the [manufacturer] is liable to the [licensee] for damages for the period during which the contract was performed; but for such damages the [licensee] has an adequate remedy at law. So far, however, as the contract remains executory, it is not binding, since it can be terminated at the will of one of the parties to it. The consideration was a promise for a promise. But the [licensee] did not promise to do anything, and could at any time cancel the contract."

CORBIN, THE EFFECT OF OPTIONS ON CONSIDERATION, 34 Yale L.J. 571, 574 (1925). "[T]he chief feature of contract law is that by an expression of his will to–day the promisor limits his freedom of voluntary choice in the future. Society controls his future action by affording the stimulus described as *compulsion*. With this element absent we are no longer dealing with what is called contract or with contract law. To fall within this field therefore, a promise must in its terms express a willingness to effect this limitation on freedom of choice. Thus, if A asks B to promise some future performance and B makes no answer, B has made no promise. This is true, even though when the future time arrives B may then be willing to perform as requested and may actually so perform. If, under these circumstances, A thinks that B has made a promise, he is under an illusion. The same is true if instead of making no answer B had replied, 'I predict that when the time comes I shall be willing to do what you ask.' A prediction of future willingness is not an expression of present willingness and is not a promise. To see a promise in it is to be under an illusion. We reach the same result if B's reply to A is, 'I promise to do as you ask if I please to do so when the time arrives.' In form this is a conditional promise, but the condition is the pleasure or future will of the promisor himself. The words used do not purport to effect any limitation upon the promisor's future freedom of choice. They do not lead the promisee to have an expectation of performance because of a present expression of will. He may hope that a future willingness will exist; but he has no more reasonable basis for such a hope than if B had merely made a prediction or had said nothing at all. As a promise, B's words are mere illusion. Such an illusory promise is neither enforceable against the one making it, nor is it operative as a consideration for a return promise."

WILLISTON ON CONTRACTS § 103B (Rev. ed. 1937). In this section the author refers to the cases holding that an illusory promise will not serve as consideration to support a return promise. He asserts, however, that this result cannot be explained on the ground that the illusory promise is not in fact bargained for, or is not the requested exchange for the real promise. "[That illusory promises] are frequently . . . so requested with intent to make a bargain cannot be successfully disputed. A contractor or seller is often so eager to obtain work, or a sale, that he will gladly subject himself to an absolute promise in return for one which leaves performance optional with the other party. This is most commonly illustrated in agreements to buy or sell goods where the quantity is fixed by the wishes of one of the parties."

———

RESTATEMENT, SECOND, CONTRACTS § 77

[See Selected Source Materials Supplement]

———

NOTE ON ILLUSORY PROMISES

A promise is a commitment to take some future action. By virtue of a promise, therefore, the promisor shrinks the boundaries of her realm of choice. Whatever that realm was before she made the promise, it is slightly smaller after she made the promise, because some action that she was morally free to choose before the promise is no longer an action that she is morally free to choose. The illusory-promise rule is applicable to commercial transactions in which one party, A, makes a real promise, while the other party, B, uses an expression that seems to be a real promise—a commitment—but is not, because it does not shrink the boundaries of B's realm of choice. Under the illusory-promise rule, A is not bound in such a case, despite the fact that *she* made a real promise, on the theory that there was no consideration for her promise. As stated in Restatement Second Section 77, "A promise or apparent promise is not consideration if by its terms the promisor or purported promisor reserves a choice of alternative performances unless ... each of the alternative performances would have been consideration if it alone had been bargained for...."

The Illustrations to Section 77 exemplify the illusory-promise rule as follows:

> 1.   A offers to deliver to B at $2 a bushel as many bushels of wheat, not exceeding 5,000, as B may choose to order within the next 30 days. B accepts, agreeing to buy at that price as much as he shall order from A within that time. B's acceptance involves no promise by him, and is not consideration....

> 2.   A promises B to act as B's agent for three years from a future date on certain terms; B agrees that A may so act, but reserves the power to terminate the agreement at any time. B's agreement is not consideration, since it involves no promise by him.

Illustrations 1 and 2 are classic examples of recurring types of cases in which the illusory-promise rule is applied. In one recurring case, exemplified in Illustration 1, B does not shrink the boundaries of his realm of choice because he only agrees to do whatever he may choose to do. In a second recurring case, exemplified in Illustration 2, B does not shrink the boundaries of his realm of choice because he reserves the right to chose to terminate his apparent commitment at any time.

However, while it is true that if one party to a bargain makes only an illusory promise, the parties have not made a bilateral contract, it is not true that they have not made a bargain. On the contrary: normally in such cases a bargain *has* been made. It is true that in illusory-promise cases there is no *bilateral* contract, because only one party has shrunk the boundaries of her realm of choice. The fallacy of the illusory-promise rule is that it treats transactions involving illusory promises as if they were failed bilateral contracts, intended to involve a promise for a promise. In fact, however, properly understood these transactions typically do not involve failed bilateral contracts. Instead, they involve successful *unilateral* contracts designed to increase the probability of exchange.

Call the person who makes the real promise in an illusory-promise transaction, A, and call the person who makes the illusory promise, B. In illusory-promise cases, like Illustrations 1 and 2 to Restatement Second Section 77, the promisor, A, does not make a promise to B for nothing, as a gift. She makes it to advance her own interests, by increasing the probability of exchange.

Choosing to exchange with one trading partner rather than another is not cost-free. In Illustration 1 to Restatement Second Section 77, A must believe that B is unlikely to trade with her unless A agrees to allow B the choice of ordering as many bushels as he wants to at the stated price during the stated time. In Illustration 2, A must believe that B would be unlikely to retain her as his agent unless she agreed that B could terminate the arrangement at any time. In each Illustration, A presumably makes her promise because she believes that B's incentives to exchange with A, rather than with others, would be insufficient unless the promise is made. In effect, there is a disparity of information and incentives between A and B. A has confidence in the attractiveness of her performance, which she believes that B does not share. A therefore makes a promise to B that is intended to change B's incentives to exchange with A, so as to increase the probability of exchange. A does this by making a commitment that she believes will induce B to give A a *chance* to show that her performance is attractive, either by sampling A's commodities or perhaps simply by giving more serious consideration to purchasing A's commodities than he otherwise would be likely to do.

The value of a chance to increase the probability of exchange is widely evidenced: book clubs give free books for the opportunity to sell future books; developers give free vacations for the opportunity to present a sales pitch; retailers offer free prizes in promotional contests to induce customers to shop; direct sellers pay substantial amounts for mailing lists. Correspondingly, if, in an illusory-promise transaction, B responds to A's inducement by giving A a chance to increase the probability of exchange, the act of giving A the chance concludes a unilateral contract by giving A something of value in a bargained exchange for A's promise.

This proposition can be illustrated by the following hypothetical:

A, a third-year law student whose grades are only fair but whose confidence is great, interviews the well-known Washington litigation firm, F, G & H. After the interview, which A feels went very well, she writes to F, G & H as follows:

Dear F, G & H:

I very much enjoyed meeting you at my recent interview. I know my grades are below the level F, G & H usually requires. However, I also know they are not a fair indicator of my skills, particularly in litigation. (As you may recall, I did exceptionally well in several moot court settings.) I am sure that if you gave me a chance you would be more than pleased with my work. In order to induce you to give me a chance I make the following offer: I will work for you for one year at $60,000 (one-half of your normal starting salary), beginning September 1. You may discharge me at any time, without notice, no questions asked.

Sincerely yours,

A

F, G & H concurs, and A begins work. After three months, however, A leaves for another job, over the firm's objection. F, G & H brings suit against A for breach of contract.

Under the illusory-promise rule, A would not be bound to her promise. Clearly, however, A has made a bargain. If F, G & H had paid $500 for A's promise, that promise would clearly be enforceable. The act of giving A a chance to prove herself may be worth much more to A (and may cost F, G & H much more) than $500. A has received exactly what she bargained for, and should be bound by her promise.

In short, the illusory-promise rule is not so much wrong as irrelevant. Recall that under this rule, as formulated in Restatement Second, "[a] promise or apparent promise is not consideration if by its terms the promisor or purported promisor reserves a choice of alternative performances unless ... each of the alternative performances would have been consideration if it alone had been bargained for...." That is true, but beside the point. B's "promise or apparent promise" may not conclude a bargain, but B's act of giving A a bargained-for chance does conclude a bargain.

The illusory-promise rule is a creature of classical contract law. Although the rule is still on the books, it is being effectively whittled away under modern contract law, as illustrated by the remaining cases in this Section.

———

LINDNER v. MID–CONTINENT PETROLEUM CORP., 221 Ark. 241, 252 S.W.2d 631 (1952). Lindner leased a filling station to Mid–Continent for three years, with an option in Mid–Continent to renew for two more years. Mid–Continent had the right to terminate the lease at any time, on ten days' notice. Following an attempt by Lindner to cancel the lease, Mid–Continent brought suit to regain possession. Lindner defended on the ground that the lease lacked mutuality. Held, for Mid–Continent. "[T]he requirement of mutuality does not mean that the promisor's obligation must be exactly coextensive with that of the promisee. It is enough that the duty unconditionally undertaken by each party be regarded by the law as a sufficient consideration for the other's promise.... In this view it will be seen that Mid–Continent's option to cancel the lease upon ten days' notice to Mrs. Lindner is not fatal to the validity of the contract. This is not an option by which the lessee may terminate the lease at pleasure and without notice; at the very least the lessee bound itself to pay rent for ten days."

————

GURFEIN v. WERBELOVSKY, 97 Conn. 703, 118 A. 32 (1922). A contract for the sale of five cases of plate glass "to be shipped within 3 months from date" stated that the buyer should "have the option to cancel the above order before shipment." During the three months, the buyer repeatedly requested performance, and finally brought suit against the seller for breach of contract. The seller argued that by virtue of the cancellation clause, the buyer's promise was illusory, and therefore the seller's promise lacked consideration. The court held that there was consideration for the seller's promise, because the seller could have bound the buyer by shipping the glass before the buyer had a chance to cancel the order. The seller had "one clear opportunity to enforce the entire contract" by shipping as soon as he received the order. "This is all that is necessary to constitute a legal consideration and to bring the contract into existence. If the defendant voluntarily limited his absolute opportunity of enforcing the contract to the shortest possible time, the contract may have been improvident, but it was not void for want of consideration."

————

MATTEI v. HOPPER, 51 Cal.2d 119, 330 P.2d 625 (1958). Plaintiff was a real-estate developer. He was planning to construct a shopping center on a tract adjacent to defendant's land, and wanted to acquire the defendant's land in connection with the development of the shopping center. For several months, a real-estate agent attempted to negotiate a purchase of defendant's land under terms agreeable to both parties. After several of plaintiff's proposals had been rejected by defendant because of the inadequacy of the price that the plaintiff offered, defendant submitted an offer of $57,000, which the plaintiff accepted.

The parties' written agreement was evidenced on a form of deposit receipt supplied by the real-estate agent. Under its terms, plaintiff was required to deposit $1,000 with the real-estate agent, and was given 120 days to "examine the title and consummate the purchase." At the expiration of that period, the balance of the price was "due and payable upon tender of a good and sufficient deed of the property sold." The concluding paragraph of the deposit receipt provided: "Subject to Coldwell Banker & Company [a real-estate broker] obtaining leases satisfactory to the purchaser." Plaintiff wanted this clause, and the 120–day period, to make sure that he could arrange satisfactory leases of the shopping-center buildings prior to the time at which he was finally committed to pay the balance of the purchase price and take title to defendant's land.

Thereafter, defendant's attorney notified plaintiff that defendant would not sell her land under the terms contained in the deposit receipt. Subsequently, defendant was informed that satisfactory leases had been obtained and that plaintiff offered to pay the balance of the purchase price. Defendant failed to tender the deed as provided in the deposit receipt. Plaintiff sued for damages, and defendant argued that the plaintiff's promise was illusory. Held, for plaintiff.

"While contracts making the duty of performance of one of the parties conditional upon his satisfaction would seem to give him wide latitude in avoiding any obligation and thus present serious consideration problems, such 'satisfaction' clauses have been given effect. They have been divided into two primary categories and have been accorded different treatment on that basis. First, in those contracts where the condition calls for satisfaction as to commercial value or quality, operative fitness, or mechanical utility, dissatisfaction cannot be claimed arbitrarily, unreasonably, or capriciously ... and the standard of a reasonable person is used in determining whether satisfaction has been received.... Of the cited cases, two have expressly rejected the arguments that such clauses either rendered the contracts illusory ... or deprived the promises of their mutuality of obligation....

"[The] multiplicity of factors which must be considered in evaluating a lease shows that this case more appropriately falls within the second line of authorities dealing with 'satisfaction' clauses, being those involving fancy, taste, or judgment. Where the question is one of judgment, the promisor's determination that he is not satisfied, when made in good faith, has been held to be a defense to an action on the contract.... Although these decisions do not expressly discuss the issues of mutuality of obligation or illusory promises, they necessarily imply that the promisor's duty to exercise his judgment in good faith is an adequate consideration to support the contract...."

———

HELLE v. LANDMARK, INC., 15 Ohio App.3d 1, 472 N.E.2d 765 (1984). " 'The modern decisional tendency is against lending the aid of courts to defeat contracts on technical grounds of want of mutuality.' Texas Gas Utilities Co. v. Barrett (Tex.1970), 460 S.W.2d 409, 412. As a contract defense, the mutuality doctrine has become a faltering rampart to which a litigant retreats at his own peril."

———

HARRIS v. TIME, INC., 191 Cal.App.3d 449, 237 Cal.Rptr. 584 (1987). Joshua Gnaizda received a letter from Time, Inc. The front of the envelope contained a small see–through window, which revealed part of the enclosed letter. The part of the letter that could be seen through the window contained a picture of a calculator watch under the following statement: "Joshua A. Gnaizda, I'll give you this versatile new calculator watch free just for opening this envelope before Feb. 15, 1985." However, the see–through window did not reveal the full text of the letter. Printed in the letter below the picture of the calculator watch, and not viewable through the see–through window, were the following additional words: "And mailing this certificate today!" The certificate required Joshua to purchase a subscription to *Fortune* magazine to receive the calculator watch.

Joshua demanded the calculator watch without purchasing a subscription to *Fortune*. Time refused. Joshua then brought a class action for $15 million. Time argued there was no contract because the mere act of opening the envelope was valueless, and therefore did not constitute adequate consideration. The court rejected this argument.

" ... It is basic modern contract law that, with certain exceptions not applicable here (such as illegality or preexisting legal duty), *any* bargained-for act or forbearance will constitute adequate consideration for a unilateral contract.... Courts will not require equivalence in the values exchanged or otherwise question the adequacy of the consideration.... If a performance is bargained for, there is no further requirement of benefit to the promisor or detriment to the promisee....

"Moreover, the act at issue here—the opening of the envelope, with consequent exposure to Time's sales pitch—may have been relatively insignificant to the plaintiffs, but it was of great value to Time. At a time when our homes are bombarded daily by direct mail advertisements and solicitations, the name of the game for the advertiser or solicitor is to *get the recipient to open the envelope*. Some advertisers, like Time in the present case, will resort to ruse or trick to achieve this goal. From Time's perspective, the opening of the envelope was 'valuable consideration' in every sense of that phrase."

(The court nevertheless dismissed the action on the grounds that (i) members of the class other than Joshua had not given Time notice of performance, and (ii) Joshua fell within the legal maxim "de minimis non curat lex"—the law disregards trifles—embodied in Cal.Civil Code § 3533.)

————

WOOD v. LUCY, LADY DUFF–GORDON

Court of Appeals of New York, 1917.
222 N.Y. 88, 118 N.E. 214.

CARDOZO, J. The defendant styles herself "a creator of fashions." Her favor helps a sale. Manufacturers of dresses, millinery, and like articles are glad to pay for a certificate of her approval. The things which she designs, fabrics, parasols, and what not, have a new value in the public mind when issued in her name. She employed the plaintiff to help her to turn this vogue into money. He was to have the exclusive right, subject always to her approval, to place her indorsements on the designs of others. He was also to have the exclusive right to place her own designs on sale, or to license others to market them. In return she was to have one-half of "all profits and revenues" derived from any contracts he might make. The exclusive right was to last at least one year from April 1, 1915, and thereafter from year to year unless terminated by notice of 90 days. The plaintiff says that he kept the contract on his part, and that the defendant broke it. She placed her indorsement on fabrics, dresses, and millinery without his knowledge and withheld profits. He sues her for the damages, and the case comes here on demurrer.

The agreement of employment is signed by both parties. It has a wealth of recitals. The defendant insists, however, that it lacks the elements of a contract. She says that the plaintiff does not bind himself to anything. It is true that he does not promise in so many words that he will use reasonable efforts to place the defendant's indorsements and market her designs. We think, however, that such a promise is fairly to be implied. The law has outgrown its primitive stage of formalism when the precise word was the sovereign talisman, and every slip was fatal. It takes a broader view to-day. A promise may be lacking, and yet the whole writing may be "instinct with an obligation," imperfectly expressed (Scott, J., in McCall Co. v. Wright, 133 App.Div. 62, 117 N.Y.S. 775; Moran v. Standard Oil Co., 211 N.Y. 187, 198, 105 N.E. 217). If that is so, there is a contract.

The implication of a promise here finds support in many circumstances. The defendant gave an exclusive privilege. She was to have no right for at least a year to place her own indorsements or market her own designs except through the agency of the plaintiff. The acceptance of the exclusive agency was an assumption of its duties. Phoenix Hermetic Co. v. Filtrine Mfg. Co., 164 App.Div. 424, 150 N.Y.S. 193; W.G. Taylor Co. v. Bannerman, 120 Wis. 189, 97 N.W. 918; Mueller v. Mineral Spring Co., 88 Mich. 390, 50 N.W. 319. We are not to suppose that one party was to be placed at the mercy of the other. Hearn v. Stevens & Bro., 111 App.Div. 101, 106, 97 N.Y.S. 566; Russell v. Allerton, 108 N.Y. 288, 15 N.E. 391. Many other terms of the agreement point the same way. We are told at the outset by way of recital that:

> "The said Otis F. Wood possesses a business organization adapted to the placing of such indorsements as the said Lucy, Lady Duff–Gordon, has approved."

The implication is that the plaintiff's business organization will be used for the purpose for which it is adapted. But the terms of the defendant's compensation are even more significant. Her sole compensation for the grant of an exclusive agency is to be one-half of all the profits resulting from the plaintiff's efforts. Unless he gave his efforts, she could never get anything. Without an implied promise, the transaction cannot have such business "efficacy, as both parties must have intended that at all events it should have." Bowen, L.J., in the Moorcock, 14 P.D. 64, 68. But the contract does not stop there. The plaintiff goes on to promise that he will account monthly for all moneys received by him, and that he will take out all such patents and copyrights and trade-marks as may in his judgment be necessary to protect the rights and articles affected by the agreement. It is true, of course, as the Appellate Division has said, that if he was under no duty to try to market designs or to place certificates of indorsement, his promise to account for profits or take out copyrights would be valueless. But in determining the intention of the parties the promise *has* a value. It helps to enforce the conclusion that the plaintiff *had* some duties. His promise to pay the defendant one-half of the profits and revenues resulting from the exclusive agency and to render accounts monthly was a promise to use reasonable efforts to bring profits and revenues into existence. For this conclusion the authorities are ample.

The judgment of the Appellate Division should be reversed, and the order of the Special Term affirmed, with costs in the Appellate Division and in this court.

CUDDEBACK, McLAUGHLIN, and ANDREWS, JJ., concur. HISCOCK, C.J., and CHASE and CRANE, JJ., dissent.

Judgment reversed, etc.

————

UCC § 2–306

[See Selected Source Materials Supplement]

———

NOTE ON REQUIREMENTS AND OUTPUT CONTRACTS

Many agreements for the sale of commodities take the form of requirements or output contracts. In a *requirements* contract (1) a seller promises to supply all of the buyer's requirements of a defined commodity at a stated price (or at a price determined under a stated formula) over a designated period of time, and (2) the buyer promises to purchase all of his requirements of the commodity during that time from the seller at the stated price. In an *output* contract (1) a buyer promises to buy all of a seller's output of a given commodity at a stated price (or at a price determined under a stated formula) over a given period of time, and (2) the seller promises to sell all of her output of the commodity during that time to the buyer at the stated price.

In the era of classical contract law, the courts often refused to enforce requirements contracts in cases where the buyer could choose to have no requirements—because, for example, the buyer had no established business, or was a middleman, or required the commodity only in a part of his operations that he could easily abandon.

However, even in cases where the buyer may choose to have no requirements, by making the agreement the seller reveals that in her view, the value of the chance that the buyer will have requirements exceeds the cost to the seller of making her commitment. Furthermore, even when the buyer may choose to have no requirements, requirements contracts are classical bargains. The seller clearly shrinks her realm of choice. So does the buyer. Before the buyer enters into such a contract, he is morally free to purchase the commodity from anyone he chooses. After the buyer enters into such a contract, if he requires the commodity during the contract period he is morally obliged to purchase the commodity from the seller at the contract price. Because both parties have made real promises—have shrunk their realms of choice—and each has exchanged its promise as the price of the other's, courts that refused to enforce requirements contracts because the buyer might have no requirements violated the bargain principle.

UCC § 2–306(1) now provides that "A term which measures the quantity by the output of the seller or the requirements of the buyer means such actual output or requirements as may occur in good faith, except that no quantity unreasonably disproportionate to any stated estimate or in the absence of a stated estimate to any normal or otherwise comparable prior output or requirements may be tendered or demanded." The Official Comment adds that "Under this article, a contract for output or requirements ... [does not] lack mutuality of obligation since, under this section, the party who will determine quantity is required to operate his plant or conduct his business in good faith and according to commercial standards of fair dealing in the trade so that his output or requirements will approximate a reasonably foreseeable figure." Although UCC § 2–306(1) applies only to the sale of goods, most requirements and output contracts fall into that category. In any event, a modern court would almost certainly hold that all requirements and output contracts have consideration.

———

GROUSE v. GROUP HEALTH PLAN, INC.

Supreme Court of Minnesota, 1981.
306 N.W.2d 114.

Considered and decided by the court en banc without oral argument.

OTIS, JUSTICE.

Plaintiff John Grouse appeals from a judgment in favor of Group Health Plan, Inc., in this action for damages resulting from repudiation of an employment offer. The narrow issue raised is whether the trial court erred by concluding that Grouse's complaint fails to state a claim upon which relief can be granted. In our view, the doctrine of promissory estoppel entitles Grouse to recover and we, therefore, reverse and remand for a new trial on the issue of damages.

The facts relevant to this appeal are essentially undisputed. Grouse, a 1974 graduate of the University of Minnesota School of Pharmacy, was employed in 1975 as a retail pharmacist at Richter Drug in Minneapolis. He worked approximately 41 hours per week earning $7 per hour. Grouse desired employment in a hospital or clinical setting, however, because of the work environment and the increased compensation and benefits. In the summer of 1975 he was advised by the Health Sciences Placement office at the University that Group Health was seeking a pharmacist.

Grouse called Group Health and was told to come in and fill out an application. He did so in September and was, at that time, interviewed by Cyrus Elliott, Group Health's Chief Pharmacist. Approximately 2 weeks later Elliott contacted Grouse and asked him to come in for an interview with Donald Shoberg, Group Health's General Manager. Shoberg explained company policies and procedures as well as salary and benefits. Following this meeting Grouse again spoke with Elliott who told him to be patient, that it was necessary to interview recent graduates before making an offer.

On December 4, 1975, Elliott telephoned Grouse at Richter Drug and offered him a position as a pharmacist at Group Health's St. Louis Park Clinic. Grouse accepted but informed Elliott that 2 week's notice to Richter Drug would be necessary. That afternoon Grouse received an offer from a Veteran's Administration Hospital in Virginia which he declined because of Group Health's offer. Elliott called back to confirm that Grouse had resigned.

Sometime in the next few days Elliott mentioned to Shoberg that he had hired, or was thinking of hiring, Grouse. Shoberg told him that company hiring requirements included a favorable written reference, a background check, and approval of the general manager. Elliott contacted two faculty members at the School of Pharmacy who declined to give references. He also contacted an internship employer and several pharmacies where Grouse had done relief work. Their responses were that they had not had enough exposure to Grouse's work to form a judgment as to his capabilities. Elliott did not contact Richter because Grouse's application requested that he not be contacted. Because Elliott was unable to supply a favorable reference for Grouse, Shoberg hired another person to fill the position.

On December 15, 1975 Grouse called Group Health and reported that he was free to begin work. Elliott informed Grouse that someone else had been hired. Grouse complained to the director of Group Health who apologized but took no other action. Grouse experienced difficulty regaining full time employment and suffered wage loss as a result. He commenced this suit to recover damages; the trial judge found that he had not stated an actionable claim.

In our view the principle of contract law applicable here is promissory estoppel. Its effect is to imply a contract in law where none exists in fact. *Del Hayes & Sons, Inc. v. Mitchell,* 304 Minn. 275, 230 N.W.2d 588 (1975). On these facts no contract exists because due to the bilateral power of termination neither party is committed to performance and the promises are, therefore, illusory. The elements of promissory estoppel are stated in *Restatement of Contracts* § 90 (1932):

> A promise which the promisor should reasonably expect to induce action or forbearance * * * on the part of the promisee and which does induce such action or forbearance is binding if injustice can be avoided only by enforcement of the promise.

Group Health knew that to accept its offer Grouse would have to resign his employment at Richter Drug. Grouse promptly gave notice to Richter Drug and informed Group Health that he had done so when specifically asked by Elliott. Under these circumstances it would be unjust not to hold Group Health to its promise.

The parties focus their arguments on whether an employment contract which is terminable at will can give rise to an action for damages if anticipatorily repudiated. Compare *Skagerberg v. Blandin Paper Co.,* 197 Minn. 291, 266 N.W. 872 (1936); *Degen v. Investors Diversified Services, Inc.,* 260 Minn. 424, 110 N.W.2d 863 (1961); and *Bussard v. College of St. Thomas, Inc.,* 294 Minn. 215, 200 N.W.2d 155 (1972) with *Hackett v. Foodmaker, Inc.,* 69 Mich.App. 591, 245 N.W.2d 140 (1976). Group Health contends that recognition of a cause of action on these facts would result in the anomalous rule that an employee who is told not to report to work the day before he is scheduled to begin has a remedy while an employee who is discharged after the first day does not. We cannot agree since under appropriate circumstances we believe section 90 would apply even after employment has begun.

When a promise is enforced pursuant to section 90 "[t]he remedy granted for breach may be limited as justice requires." Relief may be limited to damages measured by the promisee's reliance.

The conclusion we reach does not imply that an employer will be liable whenever he discharges an employee whose term of employment is at will. What we do hold is that under the facts of this case the appellant had a right to assume he would be given a good faith opportunity to perform his duties to the satisfaction of respondent once he was on the job. He was not only denied that opportunity but resigned the position he already held in reliance on the firm offer which respondent tendered him. Since, as respondent points out, the prospective employment might have been terminated at any time, the measure of damages is not so much what he would have earned from respondent as what he lost in quitting the job he held and in declining at least one other offer of employment elsewhere.

Reversed and remanded for a new trial on the issue of damages.

_____

NOTE ON GROUSE

Grouse needs to be read against the background of the at-will rule that governs employment contracts. Under this rule, an employer can discharge an employee at will at any time without cause. (Correspondingly, the employee is free to leave at any time without cause.) Moreover, any employment contract in which a fixed duration is neither explicit nor clearly implied is deemed to be at will. Although the at-will rule is often presented as an interpretative rule, in fact it is essentially based on judicial concepts—correct or incorrect—of sound policy.

The at-will rule has come under increasing pressure in recent years, and is now subject to major exceptions. The at-will rule and its exceptions are discussed in Wagenseller v. Scottsdale Memorial Hospital, Chapter 13, infra, and the Note that follows that case.

_____

WHITE v. ROCHE BIOMEDICAL LABORATORIES, INC., 807 F.Supp. 1212 (D.S.C.1992), affirmed, 998 F.2d 1011 (4th Cir.1993). In a case with facts similar to those of *Grouse,* the court held for the employer:

> Plaintiff relies on the decision of the Minnesota Supreme Court in Grouse v. Group Health Plan, 306 N.W.2d 114 (Minn.1981), a case with facts similar to this case, in arguing that an employee may base a promissory estoppel claim on a promise of at-will employment. . . .

> Other courts have also held that promissory estoppel may be applicable under these circumstances. *See, e.g.,* Humphreys v. Bellaire Corp., 966 F.2d 1037, 1042 (6th Cir.1992) ("we conclude that reliance on a promise of permanent employment might be considered reasonable" for purposes of promissory estoppel). . . .

> However, numerous courts have reached a contrary result under these or similar circumstances. . . .

See also Paul v. Lankenau Hospital, 524 Pa. 90, 569 A.2d 346 (1990) ("The doctrine of equitable estoppel is not an exception to the employment at-will doctrine. An employee may be discharged with or without cause, and [Pennsylvania] law does not prohibit firing an employee for relying on an employer's promise.")

_____

SECTION 4. PERFORMANCE OF A LEGAL DUTY AS CONSIDERATION; MODIFICATION AND WAIVER OF CONTRACTUAL DUTIES

Just as classical contract law excluded illusory promises from the operation of the bargain principle, so too it excluded promises to perform an act that the promisor was already obliged to do. Under the legal-duty rule, such a promise is not consideration, so that a bargain in which one party only promises to perform an act that he is already obliged to perform is unenforceable. That rule is the subject of this Section.

This Section begins with a series of cases that together illustrate the various facets of the legal-duty rule. Slattery v. Wells Fargo Armored Service Corp. concerns a promise to perform an act that the promisor is already obliged to perform under general law or that is within the scope of an official's authority. Lingenfelder v. Wainwright Brewery Co. concerns a promise to perform an act that the promisor is already obliged to perform under a contract. Foakes v. Beer concerns a common variation of the legal-duty rule, in which the promisor agrees to pay less than she was legally obliged to pay, in exchange for a release from her full obligation. Austin v. Loral explicitly concerns the problem that is implicit in the earlier cases: whether and when a threat to not perform a contract can constitute duress. The remaining cases in this Section show how the legal-duty rule has been substantially eroded under modern contract law.

SLATTERY v. WELLS FARGO ARMORED SERVICE CORP.

District Court of Appeal of Florida, Third District, 1979.
366 So.2d 157.

Before PEARSON, HENDRY and BARKDULL, JJ.

PER CURIAM.

Appellant/plaintiff, a licensed polygraph operator, appeals from an "order granting summary judgment and summary final judgment" rendered in favor of appellee/defendant Wells Fargo Armored Service Corp., in an action wherein appellant claimed and was denied the following reward offered by appellee:

"$25,000 REWARD"

"Wells Fargo Armored Service Corporation of Florida announces a reward of up to $25,000 for information leading to the arrest and conviction of the person or persons participating in the shooting of a Wells Fargo agent, the subsequent robbery which occurred on Saturday, February 22, 1975 at Miami, Florida, and the recovery of valuables lost as a result of this occurrence."

"Information should be directed to Wells Fargo Armored Service Corporation of Florida, P. O. Box 011028, Miami, Florida 33101, Telephone Number (305) 324–4900. The person or persons to whom the reward or any part thereof should be paid will be determined by the Board of Directors of Wells Fargo Armored Service Corporation of Florida.''

Appellant contends that he was entitled to the reward by virtue of his questioning of the perpetrator of the crime during a polygraph examination on an unrelated matter. Such questioning, which occurred on two separate days, eventually resulted in a statement by the perpetrator that he had shot and killed the Wells Fargo guard, which ultimately led to his conviction and sentence for the crime. Appellant argues that, but for his expertise in interrogation and the operation of a polygraph, the authorities would not have linked the perpetrator to the crime. Thus, appellant contends, he is entitled to the reward offered by appellee.

The trial judge, rejecting appellant's argument, entered summary final judgment in favor of appellee. . . .

After carefully reviewing the record on appeal, it is our opinion that summary judgment was proper. . . .

. . . [W]hile appellant was an independent contractor, during the polygraph interrogation he was employed by either the office of the State Attorney or the Dade County Public Safety Department and was paid for his services on an hourly rate. Further, while so employed, appellant was under a duty to provide his employers with any and all information ascertained by him through interrogation which might be of aid to the State Attorney or Public Safety Department in their capacity as law enforcement agencies. . . .

. . . [A]ppellant was under a pre-existing duty to furnish his employers with all useful information revealed to him through interrogation of the perpetrator. Thus, when appellant "accepted" the offer of reward by furnishing information to the authorities, he was doing no more than he was already bound to do as part of his employment. The performance of a existing duty does not amount to the consideration necessary to support a contract. Brinson v. Herlong, 121 Fla. 505, 164 So. 137 (1935); 7 Fla.Jur. Contracts § 48.

. . . [A]s a corollary to the above and as a matter of public policy, it is our opinion that to allow appellant to recover a reward for the furnishing of information to the authorities, when he was under a duty to furnish such information as part of his employment, would be tantamount to undermining the integrity and the efforts of those involved in law enforcement. See Davis v. Mathews, 361 F.2d 899 (4th Cir. 1966); Chester v. State, 176 So.2d 104 (Fla. 1st DCA 1965); 67 Am.Jur.2d, Reward § 15; American Law Institute, Restatement of the Law of Contracts 2d (Tentative Draft) § 76A.

Affirmed.

––––––––

POLLOCK, PRINCIPLES OF CONTRACT 196 (9th ed. 1921). " . . . [N]either the promise to do a thing nor the actual doing of it will be a good consideration if it is a thing which the party is already bound to do either by the general law or by a subsisting contract with the other party. It seems obvious that an express promise by A. to B. to do something which B. can already call on him to do can in contemplation of law produce no fresh advantage to B. or detriment to A.''

————

SHADWELL v. SHADWELL, 30 L.J.C.P. 145 (1860). Byles, J., said in this case: ''The reason why the doing what a man is already bound to do is no consideration, is not only because such a consideration is in judgment of law of no value, but because a man can hardly be allowed to say that the prior legal obligation was not his determining motive.''

————

RESTATEMENT, SECOND, CONTRACTS § 73

[See Selected Source Materials Supplement]

————

N.Y. PENAL LAW §§ 200.30, 200.35

§ 200.30 Giving Unlawful Gratuities

A person is guilty of giving unlawful gratuities when he knowingly confers, or offers or agrees to confer, any benefit upon a public servant for having engaged in official conduct which he was required or authorized to perform, and for which he was not entitled to any special or additional compensation.

Giving unlawful gratuities is a class A misdemeanor.

§ 200.35 Receiving Unlawful Gratuities

A public servant is guilty of receiving unlawful gratuities when he solicits, accepts or agrees to accept any benefit for having engaged in official conduct which he was required or authorized to perform, and for which he was not entitled to any special or additional compensation.

Receiving unlawful gratuities is a class A misdemeanor. . . .

[Prior Practice Commentary]

The need for § § 200.30 and 200.35 is apparent. ''Tipping'' a public servant undermines the integrity of governmental administration. The giver of unlawful gratuities to a public servant puts all citizens who have dealings with such venal official under pressure to ''tip,'' or risk his disfavor. In United States v. Irwin, C.A.N.Y.1965, 354 F.2d 192 (C.A.N.Y. 1965), certiorari denied 383 U.S. 967, 86 S.Ct. 1272, 16 L.Ed.2d 308 (1966), the court, in discussing Title 18 U.S.C.A. § 201(f), made this observation: ''It is apparent from the language of the subsection that what Congress had in mind was to prohibit an individual, dealing with a Government employee in the course of his official duties, from giving the employee additional compensation or a tip or gratuity for or because of an official act already done or about to be done. The awarding of gifts thus related to an employee's official acts is an evil in itself, even though the donor does not corruptly intend to influence the employee's official acts, because it tends subtly or otherwise, to bring about preferential treatment by Government officials or employees, consciously or unconsciously, for those who give gifts as distinguished from those who do not. The preference may concern nothing more than fixing the time for a hearing or giving unusually prompt consideration to the application of a donor while earlier applications of nondonors are made to wait, even though there is no evidence that the donor sought the particular preference. Moreover, the behavior prohibited by § 201(f) embraces those cases in which all of the essential elements of the bribery offense (corrupt giving) stated in § 201(b) are present except for the element of specific intent to influence an official act or induce a public official to do or omit to do an act in violation of his lawful duty. The iniquity of the procuring of public officials, be it intentional or unintentional, is so fatally destructive to good government that a statute designed to remove the temptation for a public official to give preferment to one member of the public over another, by prohibiting all gifts 'for or because of any official act,' is a reasonable and proper means of insuring the integrity, fairness and impartiality of the administration of the law."

––––––––

DENNEY v. REPPERT, 432 S.W.2d 647 (Ky.Ct.App.1968). Three armed men robbed the first State Bank of Eubank of more than $30,000. The Bank was a member of the Kentucky Bankers Association, which advertised a reward of $500 for the arrest and conviction of each bank robber, a total reward of $1,500. The three robbers were arrested. Many persons claimed the reward, including Murrell Denney, Joyce Buis, Rebecca McCollum, and Jewell Snyder, who were employees of the bank; Garret Godby and Johnny Simms, who were state policemen; and Tilford Reppert, who was a deputy sheriff. The Bankers Association asked the court to adjudge who was entitled to receive or share in the reward. Held, the only person entitled to the award was Reppert, the deputy sheriff.

"At the time of the robbery [Denney, Buis, McCollum, and Snyder] ... were employees of [the Bank]. They were under duty to protect and conserve the resources and moneys of the bank, and safeguard every interest of the institution furnishing them employment. Each of these employees exhibited great courage, and cool bravery, in a time of stress and danger. The community and the county have recompensed them in commendation, admiration and high praise, and the world looks on them as heroes. But in making known the robbery and assisting in acquainting the public and the officers with details of the crime and with identification of the robbers, they performed a duty to the bank and the public, for which they cannot claim a reward....

"State Policemen Garret Godby [and] Johnny Simms ... made the arrest of the bank robbers and captured the stolen money. All participated in the prosecution. At the time of the arrest, it was the duty of the state policemen to apprehend the criminals. Under the law they cannot claim or share in the reward and they are interposing no claim to it.

"This leaves ... Tilford Reppert the sole eligible claimant. The record shows that at the time of the arrest he was a deputy sheriff in Rockcastle County, but the arrest and recovery of the stolen money took place in Pulaski

County. He was out of his jurisdiction, and was thus under no legal duty to make the arrest, and is thus eligible to claim and receive the reward."

———

LINGENFELDER v. WAINWRIGHT BREWERY CO.

Supreme Court of Missouri, 1891.
103 Mo. 578, 15 S.W. 844.

GANTT, P.J. This was an action by Phillip J. Lingenfelder and Leo Rassieur, executors of Edmund Jungenfeld against the Wainwright Brewery Company upon a contract for services as an architect....

The controversy in the court below finally turned upon the single question whether or not, upon the facts found by the referee and the evidence returned by him, the deceased was entitled to commissions on the cost of the refrigerator plant. In considering the subject it should be borne in mind that Jungenfeld's contract with the brewery company was made on or about the 16th of June, 1883; that under and by it he undertook to design the buildings, and superintend their erection to completion; that the superintending or placing of machinery in the building was no part of his contract, and that the claim for commissions on the cost of the refrigerator plant is based solely on a subsequent promise, the facts of which are thus found and stated by the referee:

"[The refrigerator plant] was ordered not only without Mr. Jungenfeld's assistance, but against his wishes. He was in no way connected with its erection. Plaintiff's claim as to this item rests on a distinct ground, as to which I make the following finding of facts:

"Mr. Jungenfeld was president of the Empire Refrigerating Company, and was largely interested therein. The De la Vergne Ice–Machine Company was a competitor in business. Against Mr. Jungenfeld's wishes, Mr. Wainwright awarded the contract for the refrigerating plant to the De la Vergne Company. The brewery was at the time in process of erection, and most of the plans were made. When Mr. Jungenfeld heard that the contract was awarded he took away his plans, called off his superintendent on the ground, and notified Mr. Wainwright that he would have nothing more to do with the brewery. The defendant was in great haste to have its new brewery completed for divers reasons. It would be hard to find an architect to fill Mr. Jungenfeld's place, and the making of new plans and arrangements when another architect was found would involve much loss of time. Under these circumstances, Mr. Wainwright promised to give Mr. Jungenfeld five per cent on the cost of the De la Vergne ice machine if he would resume work. Mr. Jungenfeld accepted, and fulfilled the duties of superintending architect till the completion of the brewery.

"It is not clear to me how plaintiffs can bring their claim for this extra compensation on special agreement under their petition, which asks for the *quantum meruit* of Mr. Jungenfeld's labor; but I pass all questions of pleading, and treat the claim as properly before me, since it is desirable that this report should present findings as to the merits of all branches of the case.

"What was the consideration for defendant's promise to pay five per cent on the cost of the refrigerating plant, in addition to the regular charges?

"Plaintiffs submit two theories accounting for the consideration: (1) It is claimed that the transaction was the compromise of a doubtful claim. I do not find that Mr. Jungenfeld claimed that defendant had broken the contract, or intended to do so. I infer that Mr. Jungenfeld had confidently expected to get for his 'Empire Company' the contract for putting the refrigerating plant into the Wainwright brewery. When the De la Vergne machine was selected, he felt disappointed, aggrieved, angry; but I can find in the whole record no evidence that he ever claimed that any of his legal rights had been violated. With this understanding of the evidence, I find no basis for upholding defendant's promise to pay commission on this refrigerating plant as the compromise of any doubtful claim.

"(2) Plaintiffs also contend that the original contract between the parties was abrogated; that a new contract was entered into between the parties, differing from the old only in the fact that defendant was to pay a sum over and above the compensation agreed on in the discarded, original contract. The services to be performed (and thereafter actually performed) by Jungenfeld would, in this view, constitute a sufficient consideration. Such a principle has been recognized in a number of cases: Munroe v. Perkins, 9 Pick. 305; Holmes v. Doan, 9 Cush. 135; Lattimore v. Harsen, 14 Johns. 330; Peck v. Requa, 13 Gray 408. Without discussing the legal doctrine involved, (of the accuracy of which I may say, however, I am not convinced), I do not think the case in hand warrants its application. I find in the evidence no substitution of one contract for another. As I understand the facts, and as I accordingly formally find, defendant promised Mr. Jungenfeld a bonus to resume work, and complete the original contract under the original terms. This case seems to me analogous to that of seamen who, when hired for a voyage, under threats of desertion in a foreign port receive promises of additional compensation. It has been uniformly held they could not recover. I accordingly submit that in my view defendant's promise to pay Mr. Jungenfeld five per cent on the cost of the refrigerating plant was without consideration, and recommend that the claim be not allowed."

The referee's finding of fact is based on the testimony of Adolphus Busch, Philip Stock, Ellis Wainwright, and is amply borne out by the testimony. Upon this state of facts the referee was of opinion that the promise to pay the 5 per cent commissions on the cost of the refrigerator plant was void, and the claim should be rejected; whereas, the learned circuit judge was of opinion that the promise was good in law, and that the commission should be allowed; and this question of law is the sole matter presented by this record. . . .

Was there any consideration for the promise of Wainwright to pay Jungenfeld the 5 per cent on the refrigerator plant? If there was not, plaintiffs cannot recover the $3,449.75, the amount of that commission. The report of the referee and the evidence upon which it is based alike show that Jungenfeld's claim to this extra compensation is based upon Wainwright's promise to pay him this sum to induce him, Jungenfeld, to complete his original contract under its original terms. It is urged upon us by respondents that this was a new contract. New in what? Jungenfeld was bound by his contract to design and supervise this building. Under the new promise he was not to do any more or anything different. What benefit was to accrue to Wainwright? He was to receive the same service from Jungenfeld under the new, that Jungenfeld was bound to render under the original, contract. What loss, trouble, or inconvenience could result to Jungenfeld that he had not already assumed? No amount of metaphysical reasoning can change the plain fact that Jungenfeld took advantage of Wainwright's necessities, and extorted the promise of 5 per cent on the refrigerator plant as the condition of his complying with his contract already entered into. Nor was there even the flimsy pretext that Wainwright had violated any of the conditions of the contract on his part. Jungenfeld himself put it upon the simple proposition that "if he, an architect, put up the brewery, and another company put up the refrigerating machinery, it would be a detriment to the Empire Refrigerating Company," of which Jungenfeld was president. To permit plaintiff to recover under such circumstances would be to offer a premium upon bad faith, and invite men to violate their most sacred contracts that they may profit by their own wrong. "That a promise to pay a man for doing that which he is already under contract to do is without consideration" is conceded by respondents. The rule has been so long imbedded in the common law and decisions of the highest courts of the various states that nothing but the most cogent reasons ought to shake it. [Citation of cases omitted.] But "it is carrying coals to New Castle" to add authorities on a proposition so universally accepted, and so inherently just and right in itself.

The learned counsel for respondents do not controvert the general proposition. Their contention is, and the circuit court agreed with them, that when Jungenfeld declined to go further on his contract, that defendant then had the right to sue for damages, and, not having elected to sue Jungenfeld, but having acceded to his demand for the additional compensation, defendant cannot now be heard to say his promise is without consideration. While it is true Jungenfeld became liable in damages for the obvious breach of his contract we do not think it follows that defendant is estopped from showing its promise was made without consideration.

It is true that as eminent a jurist as Judge Cooley, in Goebel v. Linn, 47 Mich. 489, 11 N.W. 284, held that an ice company which had agreed to furnish a brewery with all the ice they might need for their business from November 8, 1879, until January 1, 1881, at $1.75 per ton, and afterwards, in May, 1880, declined to deliver any more ice unless the brewery would give it $3 per ton, could recover on a promissory note given for the increased price. Profound as is our respect for the distinguished judge who delivered that opinion, we are still of the opinion that his decision is not in accord with the almost universally accepted doctrine, and is not convincing, and certainly so much of the opinion as held that the payment by a debtor of a part of his debt then due would constitute a defense to a suit for the remainder is not the law of this state, nor, do we think, of any other where the common law prevails.

The case of Bishop v. Busse, 69 Ill. 403, is readily distinguishable from the case at bar. The price of brick increased very considerably, and the owner changed the plan of the building, so as to require nearly double the number. Owing to the increased price and change in the plans the contractor notified the party for whom he was building that he could not complete the house at the original prices, and thereupon a new arrangement was made and it is expressly upheld by the court on the ground that the change in the buildings was such a modification as necessitated a new contract.

Nothing we have said is intended as denying parties the right to modify their contracts, or make new contracts, upon new or different considerations, and binding themselves thereby. What we hold is that, when a party merely does what he has already obligated himself to do, he cannot demand an additional compensation therefor, and although by taking advantage of the necessities of his adversary he obtains a promise for more, the law will regard it as *nudum pactum,* and will not lend its process to aid in the wrong. So holding, we reverse the judgment of the circuit court of St. Louis to the extent that it allows the plaintiffs below (respondents here) the sum of $3,449.75, the amount of commission at 5 per cent on the refrigerator plant, and at the request of both sides we proceed to enter the judgment here which, in our opinion, the circuit court of St. Louis should have entered, and accordingly it is adjudged that the report of the referee be in all things approved, and that defendant have and recover of plaintiffs, as executors of Edmund Jungenfeld, the sum of $1,492.17, so found by the referee, with interest from March 9, 1887. All the judges of this division concur.

FOAKES v. BEER

In the House of Lords, 1884.
[1884]   9 App.Cas. 605.

[Dr. Foakes owed Julia Beer, £2090.19s. on a judgment. The parties entered into an agreement which, as interpreted by the Court of Appeal, provided that if Dr. Foakes would pay Mrs. Beer £500 at once, and the remainder of the principal in certain installments, Mrs. Beer would forgive the interest on the debt. This is a suit for the interest brought by Mrs. Beer against Dr. Foakes, alleging that if any agreement to forgive the interest was in fact entered, it was without consideration, since the consideration consisted only in Dr. Foakes' doing what he was already bound to do in paying the principal of the debt. Decision in the Court of Appeal went for Mrs. Beer.]

W.H. HOLL Q.C. for the appellant:—Apart from the doctrine of Cumber v. Wane [that £5 cannot be satisfaction of £15] there is no reason in sense or law why the agreement should not be valid, and the creditor prevented from enforcing his judgment if the agreement is performed. It may be much more advantageous to the creditor to obtain immediate payment of part of his debt than to wait to enforce payment, or perhaps by pressing his debtor to force him into bankruptcy with the result of only a small dividend. Moreover if a composition is accepted friends, who would not otherwise do so, may be willing to come forward to assist the debtor. And if the creditor thinks that the acceptance of part is for his benefit who is to say it is not? ... It is every day practice for tradesmen to take less in satisfaction of a larger sum, and give discount, where there is neither custom nor right to take credit.... It has often been held that a sheet of paper or a stick of sealing wax is a sufficient consideration.... Here the agreement is not to take less than the debt, but to give time for payment of the whole without interest. Mankind have never acted on the doctrine of Cumber v. Wane, but the contrary; nay few are aware of it. By overruling it the House will only declare the universal practice to be good law as well as good sense.

[EARL OF SELBORNE, L.C. Whatever may be the ultimate decision of this appeal the House is much indebted to Mr. Holl for his exceedingly able argument.]

BOMPAS Q.C. (Gaskell with him) for the respondent: . . . There is a strong current of authority that what the law implies as a duty is no consideration. Therefore where a debt is due part payment is no reason for giving up the residue. The doctrine is too well settled to be now overthrown. . . . It is contrary to public policy to make the performance of a legal duty a good consideration. . . .

EARL OF SELBORNE L.C.: . . . [T]he question remains, whether the agreement is capable of being legally enforced. Not being under seal, it cannot be legally enforced against the respondent, unless she received consideration for it from the appellant, or unless, though without consideration, it operates by way of accord and satisfaction, so as to extinguish the claim for interest. What is the consideration? On the face of the agreement none is expressed, except a present payment of £500, on account and in part of the larger debt then due and payable by law under the judgment. The appellant did not contract to pay the future instalments of £150 each, at the time therein mentioned; much less did he give any new security, in the shape of negotiable paper, or in any other form. The promise de futuro was only that of the respondent, that if the half-yearly payments of £150 each were regularly paid, she would "take no proceedings whatever on the judgment." . . .

The question, therefore, is nakedly raised by this appeal, whether your Lordships are now prepared, not only to overrule, as contrary to law, the doctrine stated by Sir Edward Coke to have been laid down by all the judges of the Common Pleas in Pinnel's Case [that payment of a lesser sum on the day cannot be a satisfaction of a greater sum] . . . but to treat a prospective agreement, not under seal, for satisfaction of a debt, by a series of payments on account to a total amount less than the whole debt, as binding in law, provided those payments are regularly made. . . . The doctrine itself, as laid down by Sir Edward Coke, may have been criticised, as questionable in principle, by some persons whose opinions are entitled to respect, but it has never been judicially overruled; on the contrary I think it has always, since the sixteenth century, been accepted as law. If so, I cannot think that your Lordships would do right, if you were now to reverse, as erroneous, a judgment of the Court of Appeal, proceeding upon a doctrine which has been accepted as part of the law of England for 280 years. . . .

. . . It might be (and indeed I think it would be) an improvement in our law, if a release or acquittance of the whole debt, on payment of any sum which the creditor might be content to receive by way of accord and satisfaction (though less than the whole), were held to be, generally, binding, though not under seal; nor should I be unwilling to see equal force given to a prospective agreement, like the present, in writing though not under seal; but I think it impossible, without refinements which practically alter the sense of the word, to treat such a release or acquittance as supported by any new consideration. . . .

My conclusion is, that the order appealed from should be affirmed, and the appeal dismissed, with costs, and I so move your Lordships.

LORD BLACKBURN. . . .

What principally weighs with me in thinking that Lord Coke made a mistake of fact is my conviction that all men of business, whether merchants or tradesmen, do every day recognise and act on the ground that prompt payment of a part of their demand may be more beneficial to them than it would be to insist on their rights and enforce payment of the whole. Even where the debtor is perfectly solvent, and sure to pay at last, this often is so. Where the credit of the debtor is doubtful it must be more so. I had persuaded myself that there was no such long-continued action on this dictum as to render it improper in this House to reconsider the question. I had written my reasons for so thinking; but as they were not satisfactory to the other noble and learned Lords who heard the case, I do not now repeat them nor persist in them.

I assent to the judgment proposed, though it is not that which I had originally thought proper. . . .

LORD FITZGERALD. . . . I concur . . . that it would have been wiser and better if the resolution in Pinnel's Case had never been come to. . . . [but we] find the law to have been accepted as stated for a great length of time, and I apprehend that it is not now within our province to overturn it. . . .

NOTE ON THE LEGAL–DUTY RULE

Under the legal-duty rule, as embodied in Restatement Second § 73, performance of a preexisting legal duty is not consideration. Insofar as the preexisting duty is imposed by contract, rather than by law, the cases to which the rule is applicable tend to fall into two basic patterns.

Pattern I is exemplified by Lingenfelder v. Wainwright. This pattern can be illustrated as follows. Conrad Change is under a contractual duty to render Performance P to Cecily Holdfast in exchange for $10,000. Change and Holdfast then agree that Change will render performance P, but Holdfast will pay Change $12,000. Change renders performance P, but Holdfast pays only $10,000. Change then sues Holdfast under the second agreement for the additional $2,000 that Holdfast had promised. Holdfast defends on the ground that the second agreement is unenforceable under the legal-duty rule.

Pattern II is exemplified by Foakes v. Beer. This pattern can be illustrated as follows. Change owes Holdfast $10,000 for a past-due debt under a contract. Change and Holdfast then agree that if Change pays $8,000, Holdfast will accept that amount in full satisfaction of the debt. Change pays $8,000. Holdfast then sues under the original contract for $2,000, the remainder of the original debt. Change raises the second agreement as a defense. Holdfast responds that the second agreement is unenforceable under the legal-duty rule, so that Change's defense fails.

As a matter of either doctrine or policy, there is no reason to distinguish between these two patterns. As a practical matter, however, the difference in the way cases arise under the two patterns may lead to special issues. For example, in a variation of Pattern I, Holdfast may actually pay $12,000, and later sue to recover the additional $2,000. If Holdfast was under no improper pressure from Change at the time she made the $12,000 payment, she cannot invoke the legal-duty rule as a defense to Change's suit. The legal-duty rule makes a *promise* unenforceable, but in the variation, Change is not trying to enforce Holdfast's promise. Rather, Holdfast is trying to undo a completed transaction—to get back money she has paid. The legal-duty rule is not applicable. An analogy would be a case in which Holdfast makes a donative promise to give Change $2,000. Change could not sue Holdfast to enforce the promise, but if Holdfast actually *pays* the $2,000, Holdfast cannot sue to get the money back.

Suppose, however, that Holdfast paid the additional $2,000 only because Change had put Holdfast under improper pressure at the time she made the payment? That issue is the subject of Austin v. Loral, infra.

The immediately following materials consist of a 3–2 decision by the New York Appellate Division in Austin v. Loral, and a 4–3 reversal of that decision. The Appellate Division decision is included, despite the fact that it was reversed, because taken together the two decisions illustrate (1) The potential difficulty of determining when pressure is unfairly applied by a party to a contract. (2) More generally, how a given set of facts can be cast in two entirely different and indeed opposed ways, not only by lawyers, but by courts.

AUSTIN INSTRUMENT, INC. v. LORAL CORP.

New York Supreme Court, Appellate Division, 1970.
35 A.D.2d 387, 316 N.Y.S.2d 528.

Eager, J. P.

Following a trial before Honorable Thomas A. Aurelio, Special Referee, the plaintiff (Austin) was awarded judgment for the full amount of the balance owing under subcontracts with defendant (Loral), including agreed upon price increases, for the manufacture and delivery of precision gear parts and assemblies used in connection with a quantity of radar dopplers which Loral had agreed to furnish for Navy use under contracts with the United States Government. Tried at the same time as Austin's action was an action brought by Loral against Austin to recover damages for alleged economic duress in the extorting of price increases for the gear parts and assemblies covered by a first subcontract. The Referee concluded that Loral had failed to establish its alleged cause of action against Austin and dismissed Loral's complaint.

Agreeing fully with the conclusions of the Referee, we affirm the judgment for the plaintiff Austin. . . .

In December of 1965, Loral had placed with Austin firm orders for the purchase of gear parts and assemblies needed for the Navy radar sets (this forming the "first subcontract" between the parties). After Austin had entered upon the performance of that subcontract, Loral was awarded an additional contract by the government for radar equipment and Austin sought to supply Loral with the machine parts to be used by Loral in performing this newly procured contract. Austin about this time demanded retroactive price increases on the items agreed to be furnished by it under the first subcontract and also demanded that it be given the right to furnish all of the similar machine parts and assemblies which Loral needed in performing the additional Navy contract. Negotiations between the parties continued during which Loral was considering the bids submitted by Austin and others for the parts needed under the second Navy contract. Austin claimed that it was losing a substantial sum on the existing job; that it could not afford this; and that the prices being paid to it were only a fraction of what it was entitled to. Parenthetically, we may note that it is well known that in this time of continual rising of material and manufacturing costs, renegotiation of contract prices does sometimes occur in business and commercial dealings. As a matter of fact, these parties were talking and negotiating for a period of some three to four weeks concerning the performance by Austin under the first subcontract, the awarding to it of price increases covering such subcontract, and its demand that it be awarded a second subcontract to cover all the similar gears and assemblies required by Loral to fill the second Navy contract.

The talks between the parties continued until about the middle of July, 1966, and then, according to Loral's contentions, Austin actually stopped all work under the first subcontract and refused to proceed thereunder unless Loral met Austin's demands for the price increases and awarded to it a second subcontract for the additional items. As a matter of fact, however, Loral in July, 1966, did receive deliveries of machine parts covered by the first subcontract. On July 18, the vacation period of two weeks started in Austin's plant and this would normally result in a general slowdown of work and deliveries, and Loral was so advised. Although there is sufficient evidence to support a finding that Loral was then told that deliveries would be stopped, the situation was still fluid in the sense that Austin could be prevailed upon to resume normal deliveries following the vacation period.

On July 22, 1966, following the considerable negotiations between the parties and the alleged stopping of work by Austin, Loral wrote a self-serving letter to Austin noting that the latter had stopped work on the items, that Loral feared "drastic consequences" if it defaulted under the Navy contract, and that it was left "no choice or alternative but to meet your conditions". Then, some two weeks later (on August 4, 1966), Loral issued revised purchase orders binding it to the price increases for the items covered by the first subcontract and also issued to Austin purchase orders covering the items needed by Loral to fill the second Navy contract. The delivery of these purchase orders was accompanied by another self-serving letter dated August 4. These letters of July 22 and August 4 indicate that the defendant was deliberately acting with the intent of attempting to lay the basis for an alleged cause of action for economic duress and we conclude that it was voluntarily doing so.

Loral's claim of duress, based on the foregoing facts, rests upon its contention, as alleged in its complaint, that it was "obliged to yield and capitulate" to Austin's demands because of fear of "liability for breach, default, reprocurement damages, liquidated damages and other possible legal consequences" which would result from a failure of Loral to meet the delivery requirements under the first Navy contract. As a matter of fact, however, Loral was at no time under any immediate urgency or government pressure for deliveries under the Navy contract. There had not been any default under such contract nor had Loral received any warning or notice from the government of dissatisfaction. Loral did not find it necessary to contact the government or seek any extension from it. Certainly, its "self-imposed, undisclosed, and subjective fears do not constitute an act of duress by the defendant cognizable in law." (Joseph F. Egan, Inc. v. City of New York, 17 N.Y. 2d 90, 98.)

Furthermore, as indicative of the fact that Loral was under no immediate pressure, it is significant that, following the negotiations between Loral and Austin and their agreement as to the price increases, Loral extended until September, 1966, the time for delivery of all but one of the remaining 23 items covered by the first subcontract. Upon a consideration of all the circumstances, we find that Loral was acting calmly and with considerable deliberation rather than because of an immediate urgency due to fear of governmental reprisals.

Under the circumstances, Austin's threat to break the first subcontract by a work stoppage does not constitute the basis for a recovery on the theory of actionable duress. "[A] threat to break a contract does not in itself constitute duress. Before the coercive effect of the threatened action can be inferred, there must be evidence of some probable consequences of it to person or property for which the remedy afforded by the courts is inadequate." (Hartsville Mill v. United States, 271 U.S. 43, 49, citing cases. See, also, Doyle v. Rector, etc., Trinity Church, 133 N.Y. 372, 377; Clasen v. Doherty, 242 App. Div. 502; Halperin v. Wolosoff, 282 App. Div. 876, mot. for lv. to app. den. 306 N.Y. 983.)

Accordingly, as the Special Referee put it, "a party who enters into a new agreement modifying one already existing may not disavow the new agreement for economic duress asserted to have been exercised through threat of a breach of the original agreement, without establishing that his normal legal remedy for the breach would be inadequate or ineffectual in the situation in which he finds himself and that no other means of immediate relief is available to him...."

Austin was a responsible manufacturer and it was not established that its claims for retroactive price increases were made other than in good faith. If Loral really believed that Austin would run the risk of a suit for breach of contract, the proper course for Loral to have followed was to procure from others the items still deliverable by Austin under the first subcontract and thereby lay the basis for a suit for breach of that contract. If the items were so procurable, then there was no necessity to submit to Austin's price demands. But as the Referee found, "Loral's proof does not satisfactorily establish that with reasonable effort it could not have obtained the items in question from other sources in time to meet its commitment to the Navy under the first contract. All Loral did was to make a few telephone calls to other possible sources of supply. As the trier of the facts, I find that Loral's effort to obtain the items elsewhere was neither reasonable nor commensurate with the urgency and gravity of the situation with which Loral asserts it was confronted, and, therefore, wholly insufficient to support a finding that the items were not obtainable elsewhere. Without such finding obviously there is no basis for a finding of duress."

In the final analysis, however, the conclusion that Loral acted deliberately and voluntarily, without being under immediate pressure of incurring severe business reverses, precludes a recovery on the theory of economic duress. As Williston puts it, to make out a cause of action in economic duress, "1. The party alleging economic duress must show that he has been the victim of a wrongful or unlawful act or threat, and 2. Such act or threat must be one which deprives the victim of his unfettered will." (13 Williston, Contracts [3d ed.], § 1617, p. 704.)

The key element in every case is the state of mind of the person alleged to be threatened. Of course, the existence of a choice between two alternatives does not necessarily disprove the existence of duress. The question is always one of degree and to be determined on the basis of whether there was such severe impairment of bargaining power that it may be found that the victim was precluded from exercising free will and judgment in the transaction. (See Restatement, Contracts, § 492 [1932]; Boss v. Hutchinson, 182 App. Div. 88; Hellenic Lines Ltd. v. Louis Dreyfus Corp., 372 F. 2d 753; Commonwealth Edison Co. v. Allis–Chalmers Mfg. Co., 245 F. Supp. 889.) But, here, as the Special Referee put it, the conclusion "becomes inescapable that Loral weighed all the considerations and determined as a matter of business judgment to continue with Austin and acted voluntarily." ...

... The judgment in favor of the plaintiffs should be affirmed, with costs.

[The dissenting opinion of Steuer, J., is omitted]

Markewich and McNally, JJ., concur with Eager, J. P.; Steuer, J., dissents in opinion in which Nunez, J., concurs....

AUSTIN INSTRUMENT, INC. v. LORAL CORP.

Court of Appeals of New York, 1971.
29 N.Y.2d 124, 324 N.Y.S.2d 22, 272 N.E.2d 533.

FULD, CHIEF JUDGE.

The defendant, Loral Corporation, seeks to recover payment for goods delivered under a contract which it had with the plaintiff Austin Instrument, Inc., on the ground that the evidence establishes, as a matter of law, that it was forced to agree to an increase in price on the items in question under circumstances amounting to economic duress.

In July of 1965, Loral was awarded a $6,000,000 contract by the Navy for the production of radar sets. The contract contained a schedule of deliveries, a liquidated damages clause applying to late deliveries and a cancellation clause in case of default by Loral. The latter thereupon solicited bids for some 40 precision gear components needed to produce the radar sets, and awarded Austin a subcontract to supply 23 such parts. That party commenced delivery in early 1966.

In May, 1966, Loral was awarded a second Navy contract for the production of more radar sets and again went about soliciting bids. Austin bid on all 40 gear components but, on July 15, a representative from Loral informed Austin's president, Mr. Krauss, that his company would be awarded the subcontract only for those items on which it was low bidder. The Austin officer refused to accept an order for less than all 40 of the gear parts and on the next day he told Loral that Austin would cease deliveries of the parts due under the existing subcontract unless Loral consented to substantial increases in the prices provided for by that agreement—both retroactively for parts already delivered and prospectively on those not yet shipped—and placed with Austin the order for all 40 parts needed under Loral's second Navy contract. Shortly thereafter, Austin did, indeed, stop delivery. After contacting 10 manufacturers of precision gears and finding none who could produce the parts in time to meet its commitments to the Navy,[13] Loral acceded to Austin's demands; in a letter dated July 22, Loral wrote to Austin that "We have feverishly surveyed other sources of supply and find that because of the prevailing military exigencies, were they to start from scratch as would have to be the case, they could not even remotely begin to deliver on time to meet the delivery requirements established by the Government. * * * Accordingly, we are left with no choice or alternative but to meet your conditions."

Loral thereupon consented to the price increases insisted upon by Austin under the first subcontract and the latter was awarded a second subcontract making it the supplier of all 40 gear parts for Loral's second contract with the Navy.[14] Although Austin was granted until September to resume deliveries, Loral did, in fact, receive parts in August and was able to produce the radar sets in time to meet its commitments to the Navy on both contracts. After Austin's last delivery under the second subcontract in July, 1967, Loral notified it of its intention to seek recovery of the price increases. . . .

The applicable law is clear and, indeed, is not disputed by the parties. A contract is voidable on the ground of duress when it is established that the party making the claim was forced to agree to it by means of a wrongful threat precluding the exercise of his free will. (See Allstate Med. Labs., Inc. v. Blaivas, 20 N.Y.2d 654, 282 N.Y.S.2d 268, 229 N.E.2d 50; Kazaras v. Manufacturers Trust Co., 4 N.Y.2d 930, 175 N.Y.S.2d 172, 151 N.E.2d 356; Adams v. Irving Nat. Bank, 116 N.Y. 606, 611, 23 N.E. 7, 9; see, also, 13 Williston, Contracts [3d ed., 1970], § 1603, p. 658.) The existence of economic duress or business compulsion is demonstrated by proof that "immediate possession of needful goods is threatened" (Mercury Mach. Importing Corp. v. City of New York, 3 N.Y.2d 418, 425, 165 N.Y.S.2d 517, 520, 144 N.E.2d 400) or, more particularly, in cases such as the one before us, by proof that one party to a contract has threatened to breach the agreement by withholding goods unless the other party agrees to some further demand. (See, e.g., Du Pont de Nemours & Co. v. J.I. Hass Co., 303 N.Y. 785, 103 N.E.2d 896; Gallagher Switchboard Corp. v. Heckler Elec. Co., 36 Misc.2d 225, 232 N.Y.S.2d 590; see, also, 13 Williston, Contracts [3d ed., 1970], § 1617, p. 705.) However, a mere threat by one party to breach the contract by not delivering the required items, though wrongful, does not in itself constitute economic duress. It must also appear that the threatened party could not obtain the goods from another source of supply and that the ordinary remedy of an action for breach of contract would not be adequate.

We find without any support in the record the conclusion reached by the courts below that Loral failed to establish that it was the victim of economic duress. On the contrary, the evidence makes out a classic case, as a matter of law, of such duress.

13. The best reply Loral received was from a vendor who stated he could commence deliveries sometime in October.

14. Loral makes no claim in this action on the second subcontract.

It is manifest that Austin's threat—to stop deliveries unless the prices were increased—deprived Loral of its free will. As bearing on this, Loral's relationship with the Government is most significant. As mentioned above, its contract called for staggered monthly deliveries of the radar sets, with clauses calling for liquidated damages and possible cancellation on default. Because of its production schedule, Loral was, in July, 1966, concerned with meeting its delivery requirements in September, October and November, and it was for the sets to be delivered in those months that the withheld gears were needed. Loral had to plan ahead, and the substantial liquidated damages for which it would be liable, plus the threat of default, were genuine possibilities. Moreover, Loral did a substantial portion of its business with the Government, and it feared that a failure to deliver as agreed upon would jeopardize its chances for future contracts. These genuine concerns do not merit the label " 'self-imposed, undisclosed and subjective' "which the Appellate Division majority placed upon them. It was perfectly reasonable for Loral, or any other party similarly placed, to consider itself in an emergency, duress situation.

Austin, however, claims that the fact that Loral extended its time to resume deliveries until September negates its alleged dire need for the parts. A Loral official testified on this point that Austin's president told him he could deliver some parts in August and that the extension of deliveries was a formality. In any event, the parts necessary for production of the radar sets to be delivered in September were delivered to Loral on September 1, and the parts needed for the October schedule were delivered in late August and early September. Even so, Loral had to "work * * * around the clock" to meet its commitments. Considering that the best offer Loral received from the other vendors it contacted was commencement of delivery sometime in October, which, as the record shows, would have made it late in its deliveries to the Navy in both September and October, Loral's claim that it had no choice but to accede to Austin's demands is conclusively demonstrated.

We find unconvincing Austin's contention that Loral, in order to meet its burden, should have contacted the Government and asked for an extension of its delivery dates so as to enable it to purchase the parts from another vendor. Aside from the consideration that Loral was anxious to perform well in the Government's eyes, it could not be sure when it would obtain enough parts from a substitute vendor to meet its commitments. The only promise which it received from the companies it contacted was for *commencement* of deliveries, not full supply, and, with vendor delay common in this field, it would have been nearly impossible to know the length of the extension it should request. It must be remembered that Loral was producing a needed item of military hardware. Moreover, there is authority for Loral's position that nonperformance by a subcontractor is not an excuse for default in the main contract. (See, e.g., McBride & Wachtel, Government Contracts, § 35.10, [11].) In light of all this, Loral's claim should not be held insufficiently supported because it did not request an extension from the Government.

Loral, as indicated above, also had the burden of demonstrating that it could not obtain the parts elsewhere within a reasonable time, and there can be no doubt that it met this burden. The 10 manufacturers whom Loral contacted comprised its entire list of "approved vendors" for precision gears, and none was able to commence delivery soon enough.[15] As Loral was

---

15. Loral, as do many manufacturers, maintains a list of "approved vendors," that is, vendors whose products, facilities, techniques and performance have been inspected and found satisfactory.

producing a highly sophisticated item of military machinery requiring parts made to the strictest engineering standards, it would be unreasonable to hold that Loral should have gone to other vendors, with whom it was either unfamiliar or dissatisfied, to procure the needed parts. As Justice Steuer noted in his dissent, Loral "contacted all the manufacturers whom it believed capable of making these parts" (35 A.D.2d at p. 393, 316 N.Y.S.2d at p. 534), and this was all the law requires.

It is hardly necessary to add that Loral's normal legal remedy of accepting Austin's breach of the contract and then suing for damages would have been inadequate under the circumstances, as Loral would still have had to obtain the gears elsewhere with all the concomitant consequences mentioned above. In other words, Loral actually had no choice, when the prices were raised by Austin, except to take the gears at the "coerced" prices and then sue to get the excess back.

Austin's final argument is that Loral, even if it did enter into the contract under duress, lost any rights it had to a refund of money by waiting until July, 1967, long after the termination date of the contract, to disaffirm it. It is true that one who would recover moneys allegedly paid under duress must act promptly to make his claim known. (See Oregon Pacific R.R. Co. v. Forrest, 128 N.Y. 83, 93, 28 N.E. 137, 139; Port Chester Elec. Constr. Corp. v. Hastings Terraces, 284 App.Div. 966, 967, 134 N.Y.S.2d 656, 658.) In this case, Loral delayed making its demand for a refund until three days after Austin's last delivery on the second subcontract. Loral's reason—for waiting until that time—is that it feared another stoppage of deliveries which would again put it in an untenable situation. Considering Austin's conduct in the past, this was perfectly reasonable, as the possibility of an application by Austin of further business compulsion still existed until all of the parts were delivered.

In sum, the record before us demonstrates that Loral agreed to the price increases in consequence of the economic duress employed by Austin. Accordingly, the matter should be remanded to the trial court for a computation of its damages.

The order appealed from should be modified, with costs, by reversing so much thereof as affirms the dismissal of defendant Loral Corporation's claim and, except as so modified, affirmed.

[The dissenting opinion of Bergan, J., is omitted.]

Burke, Scileppi and Gibson, JJ., concur with Fuld, C.J.

Bergan, J., dissents and votes to affirm in a separate opinion in which Breitel and Jasen, JJ., concur.

Ordered accordingly.

FURTHER NOTE ON THE LEGAL–DUTY RULE

The area of consideration manifests the shift from classical to modern contract law in a number of ways. For example, the classical rule that as a matter of principle only bargains had consideration—that is, were enforceable—was objective and standardized, particularly when coupled with the rule that the use of the bargain *form* sufficed. In contrast, the modern rules that a promise is enforceable where a party has relied on it, or where the promise is to pay for a past benefit that gives rise to a moral obligation to make compensation (see Chapter 3), are individualized, because they depend on the facts and circumstances of each case. The modern rules concerning the enforceability of such promises are also dynamic. The application of the bargain principle turns on a single moment in time. In contrast, the reliance principle, for example, ties a promise to a course of action that occurs after the promise is made.

However, the most striking movement from static to dynamic rules in the area of consideration involves the legal-duty rule. In an elegant article, Aivazian, Trebilock, and Penny argue that a regime under which modifications are enforceable would be based on static considerations, while the legal-duty rule (or more precisely, a rule under which modifications are presumptively unenforceable) reflects dynamic considerations:

> The nature of the apparent analytical paradox presented by contract modifications can be stated briefly.... If [most modification situations occur in a context in which one party seeks to exploit bargaining power he has obtained during the course of the relationship] ... then it might be argued that the law should attempt to discourage extortionary, coercive, opportunistic or monopolistic behaviour by refusing to enforce most modifications, perhaps by means of a presumption of invalidity.... On the other hand, especially in commercial contexts where most litigated modification cases seem to arise, it might be argued that parties would typically not enter into modifications unless they both felt better off as a result relative to the position that would or might have been obtained without a modification. Hence, the law should respect the parties' assessment of what course of action best advances their joint welfare and enforce modifications, that is, apply a presumption of validity.
>
> ... The paradox described above is the product of a tension between two competing sets of efficiency considerations, which in some cases require difficult trade-offs.... Static efficiency considerations will generally require that contract modifications be enforced on the grounds that the immediate contracting parties perceive mutual gains from recontracting that cannot, at the time modification is proposed, be realized as fully by any alternative strategy. On the other hand, dynamic efficiency considerations focus on the long-run incentives for contracting parties at large.... In the modification context, these dynamic efficiency considerations adopt an ex ante perspective, rather than the ex post perspective implicit in the static efficiency considerations. Adopting the former perspective, rules that impose no constraints on recontracting may increase the over-all costs of contracting by creating incentives for opportunistic behavior in cases where "holdup" possibilities arise during contract performance.... Thus, what is in the best interests of two particular contracting parties ex post contract formation when a modification is proposed and what is in the interests ex ante of contracting parties generally in terms of legally ordained incentives and constraints that minimize the over-all costs of contracting may lead to divergent policy perspectives.

Varouj A. Aivazian, et al., The Law of Contract Modifications: The Uncertain Quest for a Bench Mark of Enforceability, 22 Osgoode Hall L.J. 173, 174–75 (1984).

In fact, however, the matter is the other way around. It is often the case that B accedes to A's request for a modification out of either reciprocity or the hope of reciprocity. For example, B may agree to a modification that favors A for the purpose of reciprocating for past modifications, of either the same or other contracts, that favored B. Or, B may agree to a modification that favors A because he believes his agreement will increase the probability that A will consent to future modifications in B's favor when B is in A's position, under either the same or other contracts. Thus modifications that appear to be one-sided if examined in isolation will often be reciprocal when account is taken of the dynamic ebb and flow of the contractual stream in which the modification is located.

Accordingly, it is the legal-duty rule that is based on a static view of contract, while a regime under which modifications are enforceable is based upon and furthers a dynamic view of contract. The legal-duty rule conceives contracts as static transactions whose terms are fully determined at the moment of contract formation. In contrast, an enforceability regime conceives contracts as evolving processes. The legal-duty rule conceives modifications as individual events that occur in isolation. In contrast, an enforceability regime recognizes that there is often an ongoing stream of reciprocity between contracting parties, which may be manifested in modifications. The legal-duty rule ignores the values of ongoing dynamic cooperation and accommodation between both parties. In contrast, an enforceability regime takes account of those values. Accordingly, the legal-duty rule inhibits both the dynamic evolution of contracts and dynamic reciprocity between contracting parties, while an enforceability regime encourages both the dynamic evolution of contracts as circumstances unfold, and dynamic reciprocity between contracting parties. An enforceability regime also makes the contracting process more efficient, because it allows parties to enter into contracts without negotiating every possible contingency on a static, ex ante basis,, knowing that if misapprehensions or changed circumstances do occur, they can be dealt with by dynamic modifications, ex post.

NOTE ON CONTRACT PRACTICE

In 1988, Professor Russell Weintraub sent a questionnaire to the general counsels of 182 corporations of various sizes, asking for their views on certain contracts issues. Weintraub, A Survey of Contract Practice and Policy, [1992] Wisc. L. Rev. 1. The survey, which had a response rate of 46%, produced a great deal of extremely valuable information and analysis.

One of the questions in the survey was as follows: "If, because of a shift in market prices, one of your suppliers or customers requested a modification of the contracted-for price, would your company always insist on compliance with the contract?" Virtually all of the respondents (95%) said that their companies would not always insist on compliance with the contract. A follow-up question asked those respondents to list the factors deemed relevant in deciding whether a request for a modification would be granted. In response, 80% of the respondents listed whether relations with the company making the request has been long and satisfactory, and 76% listed whether the request was reasonable under trade practice.

A parallel question asked, "How frequently has your company asked relief from or modification of its contractual obligations?" Only 17% of the respondents said that their companies never made such requests. In contrast, 22% said that their companies made such requests an average of one to five times a year, and 18% said that their companies made such requests an average of over five times a year. In most cases, the respondents reported, the problem was amicably worked out by either a modification of the contract in question or adjustments in future contracts.

———

SCHWARTZREICH v. BAUMAN–BASCH, INC., 231 N.Y. 196, 131 N.E. 887 (1921). The plaintiff entered into a written agreement with the defendant for a year's employment as a designer of coats and wraps at $90 a week. About a month before his services were to begin, the plaintiff received an offer of a higher salary from another firm. A conversation then took place between the defendant and the plaintiff, which was rather differently recollected by the two parties afterward. According to the defendant, the plaintiff threatened to quit at a time when the defendant had to get his sample line out on the road and could not secure another designer. According to the plaintiff, he merely discussed the offer with the defendant and sought his advice as a friend. In any event, the result of the conversation was that a new typewritten contract was drafted, word for word the same as the first contract except that the salary was stated to be $100. The parties then tore their signatures off the old contract. The jury rendered a verdict for the plaintiff under an instruction that "the test question is whether by word or by act, either prior to or at the time of signing the $100 contract, these parties mutually agreed that the old contract from that instant should be null and void." It was held that judgment should be rendered for the plaintiff on this verdict.

———

RESTATEMENT, FIRST, CONTRACTS § 406, ILLUSTRATION 1: "A contracts to build a house for B for which B contracts to pay $25,000. A does a portion of the work, but finding that he will lose more money by completing the contract than by giving up at once makes B an offer to rescind. B accepts. Both parties are discharged. B is under no duty to pay A for what he has done." Comment *a*: "Where ... there is a bilateral contract, and each party is still subject to some duty thereunder, the agreement of each party to surrender his rights under the contract affords sufficient consideration to the other for his corresponding agreement.... Adequacy of consideration is immaterial.... Therefore, since each party surrenders something which he might have retained, the agreement to rescind is effectual."

———

RESTATEMENT, SECOND, CONTRACTS § 73, Comment d: *"Contractual duty to third person.* The rule that performance of legal duty is not consideration for a promise has often been applied in cases involving a contractual duty owed to a person other than the promisor. In such cases, however, there is less likelihood of economic coercion or other unfair pressure than there is if the duty is owed to the promisee. In some cases consideration can be found in the fact that the promisee gives up his right to propose to the third person the rescission or modification of the contractual duty. But the tendency of the law has been simply to hold that performance of contractual duty can be consideration if the duty is not owed to the promisor. Relief may still be given to the promisor in appropriate cases under the rules governing duress and other invalidating causes. . . .

————

McMAHON FOOD CORP. v. BURGER DAIRY CO.

United States Court of Appeals, Seventh Circuit, 1996.
103 F.3d 1307.

Before CUDAHY, COFFEY, and FLAUM, Circuit Judges.

COFFEY, Circuit Judge. Burger Dairy Company ("Burger") and McMahon Food Corporation ("MFC") were involved in a contract dispute over milk products that Burger sold to MFC, as well as credits for empty milk cases that MFC returned. MFC brought a declaratory judgment action against Burger, asserting that it effected an accord and satisfaction of its debt by tendering two checks with attached vouchers, one marked "payment in full through 6/6/92," the other marked, "paid in full thru 8/8/92," to Burger. Burger countersued, seeking $58,518.41 from MFC. The trial court denied MFC relief, ruling that the accord which the first check purported to satisfy was obtained by deceit, while the second check was a unilateral action by MFC, on which the parties reached no accord. The court awarded Burger the full amount claimed. . . . We are of the opinion that the trial court's findings of fact are not clearly erroneous. Therefore, we affirm.

I. BACKGROUND

Burger Dairy Company, an Indiana vendor of dairy products, regularly sold milk products to McMahon Food Corporation, a Chicago distributor of dairy products, from October, 1991, until August 15, 1992. MFC generally placed several orders each week. Burger's product manager entered the orders onto a "load ticket," which the loading crew relied upon when shipping a truckload of plastic milk cases[2] for the respective order. If there was a discrepancy between the amount MFC ordered and the amount Burger was able to ship, the load ticket reflected that discrepancy, including the exact number of milk cases. Burger used the load tickets to itemize the charges in its invoices for MFC. In addition, to make sure that MFC returned Burger's plastic milk cases, Burger charged MFC a $1.00 deposit for each milk case delivered to MFC, and gave an equal credit for each case returned. Burger prepared and mailed a weekly invoice for MFC.

---

2. "Milk cases"—essentially open-topped plastic boxes—are widely used throughout the dairy industry to ship cartons of milk. Each case holds several cartons (half gallons, pints, etc.).

In addition to buying dairy products, MFC had a side-business selling used plastic milk cases to Burger. MFC had acquired a large stockpile of these cases from various suppliers, including Burger. Burger agreed that when MFC returned a truckload of cases to its plant, it could add some of its "stockpiled" cases to the shipment, and Burger would credit MFC $1.00/case. Frank McMahon, MFC's vice-president, claimed that Burger did not give MFC sufficient credit for extra cases MFC returned. For this reason, when he paid Burger's invoices, McMahon deducted from his check the amount of credit he thought MFC was entitled to.

In contrast, Burger's general manager, Richard L. Bylsma, asserted that not only was MFC always late in its payments, but more frequently than not Burger had difficulty collecting. Bylsma also stated his belief that when Frank McMahon remitted payment, he made unauthorized deductions for dairy products shipped and delivered which he claimed not to have received. In addition, Bylsma maintained that MFC was short-changing Burger, by consistently claiming credits for returning full truckloads of empty cases, while the count which Burger's loading-dock personnel made reflected only partial truckloads of returned cases: Burger did not give MFC the credit McMahon demanded, Bylsma asserted, because Burger never received the number of cases MFC claimed to have returned. These disputes over the unauthorized deductions for milk cases became a major source of friction between the two companies throughout the period of their business relationship. Burger's records indicated that by mid-February of 1992, MFC was in arrears $58,518.41 ("the February debt"). About half of this total was for unauthorized credits for returned milk-cases.

Bylsma, on behalf of Burger, met with Frank McMahon on February 27, 1992, to discuss MFC's account with Burger, including the February debt. The parties dispute the results of that meeting. Both parties agree that they examined the invoices in question, and ultimately agreed that Burger would no longer charge MFC a deposit for milk cases—according to Bylsma, in exchange for MFC's agreement to pay the invoices as they became due. Bylsma testified that he and McMahon did not otherwise resolve the amounts past due, nor did they agree upon the amount of credit due for the empty milk cases allegedly returned.

Bylsma further claimed that he never agreed to excuse MFC from making payment in full for the past due accounts. Instead, he claims he made clear during their conversation, when he and McMahon were unable to reach an agreement, that they would simply table further discussion of the February debt at that time. Upon returning to Burger's plant and checking the records, Bylsma satisfied himself that the company had been giving MFC proper credit for the cases returned. Bylsma left Burger's employment shortly thereafter, without further communication with McMahon and MFC about the February debt. Burger's records reflect that after the February 27th meeting, it continued to bill MFC for the full $58,518.41 it claimed was in arrears at the time Bylsma and McMahon met. McMahon, in contrast, testified that he believed he had probably paid for some of the amount in arrears with a lump-sum check; that he had never received one of the shipments for which Burger billed him; and that MFC had returned a sufficient number of additional empty milk cases to make up for the amount which Burger claimed was due in February. Nonetheless, McMahon conceded that Bylsma told him he would have to return to Burger's headquarters and check the record there before he could straighten out the old charges and credits.

After the February meeting, MFC made full payments for three weeks of current purchases (nothing was done to pay off the February debt), but then made no further payments until May 13, 1992, when it remitted a $100,000 check to Burger with an accompanying voucher stating "on account detail to follow." Burger's records, however, reflected that the $100,000 covered less than half the debt that MFC had amassed by that time, including the $58,518.41 February debt which was the subject of McMahon's meeting with Bylsma.

II.   The June 17th Check

A.   Background

Larry Carter, who replaced Bylsma as Burger's general sales manager about the first of May, 1992, met with McMahon on June 17, 1992, to review MFC's account. McMahon asserts that at the beginning of the meeting he told Carter that if they could agree on the amount that MFC owed, he would pay it on the spot. According to Carter's notes, made contemporaneously during the June 17th meeting, McMahon assured Carter that he had settled the February debt with Bylsma. Carter's notes included both a reminder to himself to call Bylsma to confirm McMahon's assertion, and a statement that McMahon "want[ed] a new statement of account reflecting these events."[3] Accordingly, Carter and McMahon went through only the invoices dated February 15 through June 6, 1992. They determined that MFC still owed a balance of $51,812.98. McMahon promptly made out a check to Burger for that amount. He attached a voucher to the check on which was typed, "payment in full thru 6/6/92 . . . $51,812.98." Below the typed language McMahon added a handwritten note stating, "Clear statement of account thru 6/6/92 to follow," followed by his signature. Burger never sent McMahon the "statement of account." McMahon also asked Carter to sign the voucher as a condition of receiving the check, which Carter did without protest. At the end of his notes, Carter wrote, "current to 6-6-92."

After returning to Burger, Carter contacted Bylsma, who told Carter that he had never reached an agreement with McMahon about the February debt. Thereafter, sometime before the end of June, Carter called McMahon and told him that it was Burger's position that the February debt had not been settled. When McMahon replied that he refused to pay the February debt, and continued to insist that he had settled it with Bylsma, Carter held McMahon's June 17th check throughout the summer of 1992.

On September 24, Edward J. Geoghan, Burger's accounting manager and comptroller of Burger's parent company, negotiated the June 17th check. Before doing so, and without consulting with Carter, Geoghan crossed out MFC's restrictive endorsement "payment in full" and "full statement of account to follow" from the voucher, and added the notation "without prejudice," followed by his own signature. Geoghan later testified that he struck out the language on the voucher because he knew it was insufficient to

---

3. The district court, interpreting Carter and McMahon's testimony, concluded that "these events" referred to the June 17th agreement with Carter and the alleged agreement with Bylsma regarding the February debt. The notation meant that Burger was to supply MFC with a new statement reflecting the two agreements, and showing that MFC's account was no longer in arrears.

make MFC's account current. The next day, Geoghan wrote to McMahon, informing him that the check had been cashed, the restrictive endorsement stricken, and that MFC still owed Burger over $64,000.

On January 14, 1993, MFC filed suit against Burger, asking the federal district court to issue a declaratory judgment that it had reached an accord and satisfaction relieving it of any debt to Burger. Burger countersued, seeking the money which it claimed MFC still owed. With the consent of the parties, the case was tried before a magistrate judge without a jury. The trial court found MFC in arrears and awarded Burger damages in the amount of $58,518.41, plus interest and costs. This appeal followed.

B. Analysis ...

Initially, MFC argues that Burger's negotiation of the check which McMahon tendered to Carter at their June 17th meeting constituted an accord and satisfaction. An accord and satisfaction is a contractual method of discharging a debt: the "accord" is the agreement between the parties, while the "satisfaction" is the execution of the agreement. *Fremarek v. John Hancock Mutual Life Ins. Co.,* 272 Ill.App.3d 1067, 209 Ill.Dec. 423, 427, 651 N.E.2d 601, 605 (1995). The parties accept that Illinois law, including Illinois' enactment of the Uniform Commercial Code, governs the case at bar.

Shortly before this dispute arose, Illinois adopted a revised version of Article Three of the Uniform Commercial Code, including a new section specifically addressing the creation of an accord and satisfaction by use of a negotiable instrument.... Section 3–311 provides:

> (a) If a person against whom a claim is asserted proves that (i) that person in good faith tendered an instrument to the claimant as full satisfaction of the claim, (ii) the amount of the claim was unliquidated or subject to a bona fide dispute, and (iii) the claimant obtained payment of the instrument, the following subsections apply.

> (b) Unless subsection (c) applies, the claim is discharged if the person against whom the claim is asserted proves that the instrument or an accompanying written communication contained a conspicuous statement to the effect that the instrument was tendered as full satisfaction of the claim.

> (c) Subject to subsection (d), a claim is not discharged under subsection (b) if either of the following applies:

>> (1) The claimant, if an organization, proves that (i) within a reasonable time before the tender, the claimant sent a conspicuous statement to the person against whom the claim is asserted that communications concerning disputed debts, including an instrument tendered as full satisfaction of a debt, are to be sent to a designated person, office, or place, and (ii) the instrument or accompanying communication was not received by that designated person, office, or place.

>> (2) The claimant, whether or not an organization, proves that within 90 days after payment of the instrument, the claimant tendered repayment of the amount of the instrument to the person against whom the claim is asserted. This paragraph does not apply if

the claimant is an organization that sent a statement complying with paragraph (1)(i).

(d) A claim is discharged if the person against whom the claim is asserted proves that within a reasonable time before collection of the instrument was initiated, the claimant or an agent of the claimant having direct responsibility with respect to the disputed obligation knew that the instrument was tendered in full satisfaction of the claim.

... The purpose of § 3–311 is to encourage "informal dispute resolution by full satisfaction checks." UCC § 3–311, comment 3. Its drafters intended to codify the common law of accord and satisfaction "with some minor variations to reflect modern business conditions." *Id.*

In the case at bar, Burger does not dispute that the voucher attached to MFC's June 17th check contained a conspicuous notation that it was tendered as full satisfaction of MFC's entire debt, thus satisfying the prerequisites of § 3–311(b) (*supra*) for discharging the claim. Neither did Burger follow the procedures which § 3–311(c) (*supra*) establishes to keep a claim from being discharged: it neither instructed MFC to send any full satisfaction checks to a specific person or office, nor sought to repay MFC after it deposited the check.... 311(c)(1)-(2). Furthermore, Geoghan's attempt to cash MFC's check without jeopardizing Burger's claim against MFC was improper under the UCC Assuming there was an accord, Geoghan's bid to prevent a satisfaction by accepting the check but scratching out the restrictive endorsement and adding the words "without prejudice" before he cashed the check was to no avail, for under the revised version of the UCC, words of protest cannot change the legal effect of an accord and satisfaction. [UCC §] 1–207(2). Accordingly, MFC argues, because the voucher clearly stated that the instrument was a full satisfaction check, and because Geoghan clearly understood that the check was tendered in full satisfaction of MFC's claim before he deposited it, Burger's acceptance and negotiation of the check completed the accord and satisfaction.

We disagree. Initially, under the plain language of the statute, in order to establish an accord and satisfaction, MFC bore the burden of establishing that it met the criteria of § 3–311(a) before the other subsections establishing the discharge of a claim come into play.... To meet the criteria of § 3–311(a) under Illinois law, "a party must ordinarily prove that he or she acted in good faith *in tendering* an instrument as full satisfaction of a claim[.]" *Fremarek,* 209 Ill.Dec. at 427, 651 N.E.2d at 605 (emphasis added). Thus, Illinois courts interpreting § 3–311 follow the common law of accord and satisfaction in holding that "there must be an honest dispute between the parties as to the amount due *at the time payment was tendered.*" A.F.P. *Enterprises, Inc. v. Crescent Pork, Inc.,* 243 Ill.App.3d 905, 183 Ill.Dec. 356, 360, 611 N.E.2d 619, 623 (1993) (emphasis added). Consequently, under Illinois law, there can be no accord and satisfaction unless there was an "honest dispute" between MFC and Burger at the time McMahon tendered the $51,812.98 check to Carter on June 17th. No such "honest dispute" existed.

The trial court found that McMahon deliberately misled Carter, who had but recently been appointed to his position of general manager and did not know the specifics of his predecessor's dealings with MFC. McMahon did so, according to the court, by assuring Carter from the outset of their June 17th meeting that he had settled with Bylsma, the former general manager, all accounts prior to mid-February, 1992. The court found that McMahon was acting dishonestly and taking advantage of Carter at the time he tendered payment, and therefore MFC failed to meet the good faith requirement of § 3–311(a).[4] A trial court's conclusion that a party failed to act in good faith is a finding of fact which we reverse only for clear error. *Covey v. Commercial Nat'l Bank of Peoria,* 960 F.2d 657, 662 (7th Cir.1992); *Winters v. Dallman,* 238 F.2d 912, 914 (7th Cir.1956). We find no such error in the case before us. . . .

. . . Because we are convinced that the trial court did not clearly err in finding that McMahon demonstrated a lack of good faith, MFC has failed to present facts sufficient to convince us that it complied with the requirements for an accord and satisfaction under the UCC.

III. THE AUGUST 18TH CHECK

A. *Background*

Despite the conflict which arose when McMahon refused to pay the February debt, MFC continued to purchase milk from Burger through August 15, 1992. On August 18th, MFC sent two checks to Burger. The first check paid off three invoices dated July 4th, 11th, and 18th, while the second check covered invoices from July 25th, August 1st, and August 8th. A voucher accompanying each check listed the invoices being paid, and the deductions which MFC was making. The voucher accompanying the second of the two checks dated August 18, 1992, bore a list reflecting that MFC was paying off three specified invoices, and also deducting $1,758.46 for milk cases for which MFC believed it should receive credit. Typed in capital letters at the bottom of this list was the notation, "PAID IN FULL THRU 8/8/92." Burger immediately deposited both checks without further inquiry, as well as a check the following week for an August 15 invoice whose accompanying voucher also included a line stating, "PAYMENT IN FULL THRU 8/15/92." Denise Blough, Burger's assistant controller, testified that she received and deposited the two checks without noticing the "payment in full" language on the attached voucher. She added that it was her habit to examine the checks themselves, but that she ignored the memos or vouchers accompanying payments.

B. *Analysis* . . .

. . . [B]efore a full satisfaction check can create an accord and satisfaction, the party who offers or presents the check must make it clear that the cashing of the check is intended to act as a settlement of all outstanding claims between the parties. [UCC §] 3–311(b). We are convinced that MFC's actions in tendering the August 18th check were not sufficiently clear to make Burger aware that the check was meant to settle all MFC's outstanding claims. First, it is significant that MFC actually tendered not one but two checks dated August 18th. Both were in payment for invoices billed after McMahon made Carter aware of the fact that he would not pay the February debt; each check included a deduction for empty milk cases for which MFC believed it was entitled to receive credit. Only one of the two checks, however, bore the notation "paid in full." In addition, the restrictive language, although typed

---

4. Article Three of the Uniform Commercial Code defines "good faith" as "honesty in fact and the observance of reasonable commer- cial standards of fair dealing." 810 ILCS 5/3–103(4).

in capital letters, was simply the last of several lines of information inscribed on the voucher accompanying the check, reflecting the items included for payment.

As noted above, an accord and satisfaction is a "contractual method of discharging a debt," *Fremarek,* 209 Ill.Dec. at 427, 651 N.E.2d at 605, and like any contract the intentions of the parties must be viewed objectively. Viewing the record as a whole, it is objectively reasonable to conclude that MFC intended the August 18th check to be full payment only for those invoices to which the accompanying voucher made reference. The parties' long history of disputes over credits for empty milk cases makes this conclusion seem even more likely. Otherwise, it is difficult to understand why MFC would not have applied the "paid in full" notation to both of the checks it issued on August 18th, instead of just one. Thus, since the "paid in full" language on the August 18th check was at best ambiguous, its tender cannot serve as full satisfaction of Burger's claim against MFC.

Second, even if the "paid in full" language were clear, we refuse to impute to Burger knowledge that MFC intended the August 18th check as full satisfaction of its claim. MFC never contested the statement of Denise Blough, the Burger official who deposited the August checks, that she simply did not notice the "paid in full" language on the voucher accompanying the August 18th check. Though hardly dispositive, this is probative of the fact that the "paid in full" language was not sufficiently conspicuous. *See* 810 ILCS 5/1–201(10) (a statement is conspicuous if "it is so written that a reasonable person against whom it is to operate ought to have noticed it"). Moreover, MFC never refuted Blough's deposition testimony that she would not have understood the significance of the notation unless Carter had told her. Instead, MFC argued that if Carter had exercised due diligence regarding the dispute over MFC's account, he would have informed Blough of the problem and told her to be on the lookout for precisely the sort of check which MFC tendered.

The problem with this argument is that the drafters of § 3–311 have anticipated and rejected it. Where a person who processes a company's checks has no responsibility with respect to an accord and satisfaction, it makes no difference whether that person "did or did not see [a] statement that [a] check was tendered as full satisfaction of the claim;" the person's knowledge "is not imputed to the organization" for which she works. [UCC §] 3–311, comment 7. Failure to instruct the person who processes the organization's checks to look for full satisfaction statements falls short of constituting a lack of due diligence on the part of the creditor. *Id.* (citing UCC § 1–207(27))....

Thus, based on the record before us, we cannot impute knowledge of the August 18th full payment check to Carter—who, as the person with direct responsibility for the dispute with MFC, would have realized that the check was tendered as full satisfaction of Burger's claim. [UCC §] 3–311(d) and comment 7. The Uniform Commercial Code, in effect, delineates when knowledge of a full satisfaction tender may be imputed to a claimant. *See* UCC § § 3–311, comments 3, 7; 1–201(25), 1–201(27). Thus, the statute accommodates modern business practices in receiving and processing checks, ... while the cumulative result of its provisions is to preserve the common law rule that a debtor cannot unilaterally create an accord and satisfaction. *Shea, Rogal & Assoc. v. Leslie Volkswagen, Inc.,* 216 Ill.App.3d 66, 159 Ill.Dec. 540, 543–44,

576 N.E.2d 209, 212–13 (1991). Because MFC failed to establish a sufficient foundation from which to impute knowledge of the full satisfaction tender to Burger, we hold that Burger's depositing of the August 18th check failed to create an accord and satisfaction as defined by UCC § 3–311.

Finally, despite MFC's assertion to the contrary, we cannot agree that just because the conflict over the February debt was out in the open by the end of June, MFC acted in good faith when it tendered the August 18th check as full satisfaction of its outstanding debt to Burger. ... [T]he existence of a good faith dispute between the parties is a prerequisite to an accord and satisfaction under [UCC §] 3–311(a). There was no such underlying good faith dispute because, as noted above, McMahon misled Carter about having settled MFC's February debt. That McMahon later made a statement to Carter that he wouldn't pay the February debt is not, of itself, sufficient to create a good faith dispute within the meaning of the statute:

> The debtor's mere refusal to pay the full claim does not make it a disputed claim. Where the refusal is arbitrary and the debtor knows it has no just basis, the payment of less than the full amount claimed does not operate as an accord and satisfaction even though it is tendered and received as such.

Gerald R. Turner & Assoc. v. Moriarty, 25 F.3d 1356, 1360 (7th Cir.1993). Thus, it is not enough for MFC to demonstrate that it openly refused to pay the February debt: MFC must also show that it had a just basis for refusing to pay. Under the *Turner* rationale, the trial court's findings concerning MFC's lack of good faith at the June 17th meeting between Carter and McMahon carry over into our analysis of MFC's later actions. As stated above, the trial court concluded that MFC proffered no credible reasons for believing it did not have to pay the February debt. Because after review we are convinced that this finding was not clearly erroneous, supra, we conclude that MFC has failed to carry its burden of establishing that there was a just basis for its dispute with Burger. Since MFC had no more basis for its refusal to pay the February debt in August than it had in June, there was no good faith dispute between the parties within the meaning of UCC § 3–311, and the August 18th check cannot operate as an accord and satisfaction.

CONCLUSION

The trial court did not clearly err in concluding that MFC's first tender marked "paid in full" did not effect a satisfaction, because the accord which it purported to satisfy was reached only as a result of MFC's bad faith and deception.... Neither did the second tender satisfy MFC's debt to Burger, because MFC failed to make it sufficiently clear that depositing the check would settle all outstanding disputes between the parties. The district court's determination that neither tender was a full satisfaction check within the meaning of UCC § 3–311, and MFC was not entitled to declaratory relief, was proper.

AFFIRMED.

UCC §§ 3–103(a)(4), 3–104, 3–311

[See Selected Source Materials Supplement]

————

RESTATEMENT, SECOND, CONTRACTS §§ 279, 281

[See Selected Source Materials Supplement]

————

NOTE ON THE LEGAL EFFECT OF
THE "EXECUTORY ACCORD"

Assume that A and B have a contract that requires B to render performance P to A. A and B then enter into an agreement under which A agrees to accept some other performance, Q, as full satisfaction of B's obligation under the original contract. Such an agreement is known as an *accord*. For example, suppose B owes A $1,000 under a contract. B promises to give her car to A in settlement of the debt, and A agrees to accept the car in settlement of the debt. This new agreement is an accord, and until the accord is performed, it is an *executory* (unperformed) accord.

If in the new agreement B simply agrees to do less than what she was already obliged to do—if, for example, B agrees to pay $900 in satisfaction of her $1000 obligation—we have a legal-duty-rule problem. Often, however, both parties agree to do something that they were not obliged to do. Thus in the above example, B promises to give A her car, which she was not obliged to do, and A promises to accept the car instead of $1000, which he was not obliged to do.

If an accord is performed—that is, if B tenders the performance she promised to render under the accord, and A accepts the performance—there is said to be a *satisfaction* of the accord. If there is consideration for an accord, as there is in the example, the satisfaction of the accord discharges both the accord and the original contractual duty. Thus in the example, if B tenders her car to A, and A accepts it, the accord is discharged and so is B's original duty to pay A $1,000.

Suppose, however, that A breaches the accord by refusing B's tender. If B agrees to render a performance that she was not obliged to render, so that there is no problem of consideration, then even before satisfaction occurs, an accord should be a fully enforceable modification of the original contract. After all, if both parties to a contract agree to do something *different* from what they were obliged to do, the parties have made a bargain, and a bargain is consideration. For purely historical reasons, however, the traditional rule was that an executory accord is unenforceable.

The precise meaning of that rule, and its underlying rationale, constitute one of the major mysteries of the common law. Various justifications have been advanced for it. It is said that there is in the common law another rule (itself unexplained) which says that a "cause of action" cannot be "suspended". (Ford v. Beach, 1848, 11 Q.B. 852.) The executory accord, it is assumed, attempts to "suspend" the claim. Since the executory accord cannot be used as a bar, it must follow that the executory accord is without any legal effect, and from this it follows that neither party may sue on it. Lynn v. Bruce, 2 Henry Blackstone 317 (1794). Furthermore, adds the court in Lynn v. Bruce, if one were to uphold the executory accord, this would permit the substitution of one cause of action for another, which might go on forever, whereas it is to the interest of the commonwealth that there should be "an end of litigation." The brittle logic of this argument, which relentlessly assumes in turn every proposition required for the conclusion, has perhaps never been equaled in the history of the common law.

Other courts have been less concerned to justify the traditional rule, and more inclined to explain how it happened to come into being. It has been suggested that the rule that an executory accord is unenforceable is merely a vestigial survival of the old rule according to which no wholly executory informal contract was enforceable. Case v. Barber, Th. Raymond 450 (1681). It has been suggested that the rule took its origin in cases where the executory accord was without consideration because an attempt was made to discharge an undisputed claim by the payment of a sum of money less than that due, so that even the executed accord would have been invalid under the principle of Foakes v. Beer. Finally, in Allen v. Harris, (1701, 1 Lord Raymond 122) the court said, with an air of resignation, " . . . [U]pon [an] accord no remedy lies. And the books are so numerous that an accord ought to be executed [if it is to be enforceable] that it is now impossible to overthrow all the books. But if it had been a new point, it might be worthy of consideration."

In short, the traditional legal rule, that an executory accord is unenforceable, is inconsistent with the bargain principle, basically inexplicable, and wrong. As a result, although in theory the traditional rule is still the law, in modern times the rule has been hedged with a number of exceptions and distinctions, so that in practice the bite of the rule has been severely reduced.

Substituted contract. One major exception applies if a new agreement is deemed to be a *substituted contract,* rather than an accord. If a new agreement is deemed to be a substituted contract, the original contract is immediately discharged—that is, the new agreement is treated as a complete substitute for the old one, which is deemed to no longer exist. An action can then be brought only on the new agreement, not on the old one. This rule is reflected in Illustration 1 to Restatement Second § 279:

> A is under a duty to deliver a tractor to B on July 1. On June 1, A offers to deliver a bulldozer to B on July 1 if B will accept his promise in satisfaction of A's duty to deliver the tractor, and B accepts. The contract is a substituted contract. A's duty to deliver the tractor is discharged. If A does not deliver the bulldozer, B can enforce the duty to deliver it but not the original duty to deliver the tractor. . . .

Unfortunately, the test for determining whether a new agreement is a substituted contract, rather than an accord, is vague. The matter is said to be a question of the parties' intent, but that characterization of the issue is more fictitious than real. In practice, the courts are likely to find that an accord is a substituted contract if the duty under the original contract was disputed, unliquidated, had not matured, and involved a performance other than the payment of money. Correspondingly, the courts are likely to find that an accord is not a substituted contract if the duty under the original contract was undisputed, liquidated, had matured, and involved the payment of money. Restatement Second § 281, comment e.

For example, suppose B agrees that she will perform agricultural services for A in March, and A agrees to pay B, in cattle, on June 3. On June 1, the parties disagree over what payment is due. B claims that A is obliged to deliver three cows. A claims that his obligation is to deliver one cow. A and B then agree that A will deliver two sheep instead of one or more cows, and that B will accept the two sheep as full payment of A's obligation. The accord is likely to be treated as a substituted contract, because the original duty was not to pay money, was disputed, was unliquidated, and had not matured.

Now suppose, in contrast, that A originally agreed to pay $900 for B's services, and A does not dispute B's claim. On July 5, the parties agree that A will deliver two sheep instead of paying $900. This agreement is not likely to be treated as a substituted contract, because the duty under the original contract was to pay money, the duty was not in dispute, and B's claim was liquidated and had matured.

Other modern rules. Even where agreement is an executory accord rather than a substituted contract, so that the original contract is not discharged, under modern law the accord nevertheless has several significant effects:

1. *Performance.* If an accord involving a different performance by B is executed (performed)—that is, if there is both an accord and a satisfaction—B has a complete defense against A under the original contract.

2. *Suspension of old contract.* Under the modern rule, an executory accord operates to suspend A's rights under the original contract during the period in which B is supposed to perform the accord.

3. *Suit by A under the accord.* If B fails to tender performance under the executory accord, A can sue B under either the old contract or the accord.

4. *Other effects.* Restatement Second § 281 Comment c states a rule that almost wholly undercuts the traditional law concerning accord and satisfaction. According to the Comment, if the obligee (or creditor) breaches an accord, the obligor (or debtor) can sue for specific performance to enforce the accord, and can even sue for damages. Similarly, Farnsworth states that, "[T]he term *executory accord* is sometimes used to underscore the point that the accord itself does not discharge the duty. It also reflects an historical anachronism, now generally rejected, under which an unperformed accord was not a defense to an action on the underlying duty." E. Allan Farnsworth, Farnsworth on Contracts § 4.24, n.10 (4th ed. 2004). The modern cases agree. For example, Ladd v. General Ins. Co., 387 P.2d 572, 575 (Or. 1963), states that "[I]f the creditor breached the accord, [although] the debtor's original duty would not be discharged, the debtor would acquire a right of action for damages for the breach of the accord or, if practicable, the alternative remedy of specific enforcement." See also Okazaki v. Collett, 2001 Utah App. LEXIS 166 (Utah Ct. App. 2001) (citing and applying the Restatement rule); Tolland Enters. v. Scan–Code, 684 A.2d 1150, 1153 (Conn. 1996); Peters v. Wallach, 321 N.E.2d 806, 810 (Mass. 1975) ("Although an unexecuted accord does not operate as an accord and satisfaction, discharging the original claim, it is nonetheless enforceable as a contract. Such an agreement may be specifically

enforced, and may be set up as an equitable defense in an action on the original claim."). As a result, it appears that in many or most jurisdictions the traditional rule concerning accord and satisfaction has been substantially or almost completely eroded.

RESTATEMENT, SECOND, CONTRACTS § 89

[See Selected Source Materials Supplement]

ANGEL v. MURRAY

Supreme Court of Rhode Island, 1974.
113 R.I. 482, 322 A.2d 630.

ROBERTS, C.J. This is a civil action brought by Alfred L. Angel and others against John E. Murray, Jr., Director of Finance of the City of Newport, the city of Newport, and James L. Maher, alleging that Maher had illegally been paid the sum of $20,000 by the Director of Finance and praying that the defendant Maher be ordered to repay the city such sum. The case was heard by a justice of the Superior Court, sitting without a jury, who entered a judgment ordering Maher to repay the sum of $20,000 to the city of Newport. Maher is now before this court prosecuting an appeal.

The record discloses that Maher has provided the city of Newport with a refuse-collection service under a series of five-year contracts beginning in 1946. On March 12, 1964, Maher and the city entered into another such contract for a period of five years commencing on July 1, 1964, and terminating on June 30, 1969. The contract provided, among other things, that Maher would receive $137,000 per year in return for collecting and removing all combustible and noncombustible waste materials generated within the city.

In June of 1967 Maher requested an additional $10,000 per year from the city council because there had been a substantial increase in the cost of collection due to an unexpected and unanticipated increase of 400 new dwelling units. Maher's testimony, which is uncontradicted, indicates the 1964 contract had been predicated on the fact that since 1946 there had been an average increase of 20 to 25 new dwelling units per year. After a public meeting of the city council where Maher explained in detail the reasons for his request and was questioned by members of the city council, the city council agreed to pay him an additional $10,000 for the year ending on June 30, 1968. Maher made a similar request again in June of 1968 for the same reasons, and the city council again agreed to pay an additional $10,000 for the year ending on June 30, 1969.

The trial justice found that each such $10,000 payment was made in violation of law. . . . [H]e found that Maher was not entitled to extra compensation because the original contract already required him to collect all refuse generated within the city and, therefore, included the 400 additional units. The trial justice further found that these 400 additional units were within the contemplation of the parties when they entered into the contract. It appears that he based this portion of the decision upon the rule that Maher had a preexisting duty to collect the refuse generated by the 400 additional units, and thus there was no consideration for the two additional payments. . . .

A.

As previously stated, the city council made two $10,000 payments. The first was made in June of 1967 for the year beginning on July 1, 1967, and ending on June 30, 1968. Thus, by the time this action was commenced in October of 1968, the modification was completely executed. That is, the money had been paid by the city council, and Maher had collected all of the refuse. Since consideration is only a test of the enforceability of executory promises, the presence or absence of consideration for the first payment is unimportant because the city council's agreement to make the first payment was fully executed at the time of the commencement of this action. . . . However, since both payments were made under similar circumstances, our decision regarding the second payment (Part B, infra) is fully applicable to the first payment.

B.

It is generally held that a modification of a contract is itself a contract, which is unenforceable unless supported by consideration. . . .

The primary purpose of the preexisting duty rule is to prevent what has been referred to as the "hold-up game." See 1A Corbin . . . § 171. A classic example of the "hold-up game" is found in Alaska Packers' Ass'n v. Domenico, 117 F. 99 (9th Cir.1902). There 21 seamen entered into a written contract with Domenico to sail from San Francisco to Pyramid Harbor, Alaska. They were to work as sailors and fishermen out of Pyramid Harbor during the fishing season of 1900. The contract specified that each man would be paid $50 plus two cents for each red salmon he caught. Subsequent to their arrival at Pyramid Harbor, the men stopped work and demanded an additional $50. They threatened to return to San Francisco if Domenico did not agree to their demand. Since it was impossible for Domenico to find other men, he agreed to pay the men an additional $50. After they returned to San Francisco, Domenico refused to pay the men an additional $50. The court found that the subsequent agreement to pay the men an additional $50 was not supported by consideration because the men had a preexisting duty to work on the ship under the original contract, and thus the subsequent agreement was unenforceable.

Another example of the "hold-up game" is found in the area of construction contracts. Frequently, a contractor will refuse to complete work under an unprofitable contract unless he is awarded additional compensation. The courts have generally held that a subsequent agreement to award additional compensation is unenforceable if the contractor is only performing work which would have been required of him under the original contract. See, e.g., Lingenfelder v. Wainwright Brewing Co., 103 Mo. 578, 15 S.W. 844 (1891), which is a leading case in this area. . . .

These examples clearly illustrate that the courts will not enforce an agreement that has been procured by coercion or duress and will hold the parties to their original contract regardless of whether it is profitable or unprofitable. However, the courts have been reluctant to apply the preexisting duty rule when a party to a contract encounters unanticipated difficulties and the other party, not influenced by coercion or duress, voluntarily agrees to pay additional compensation for work already required to be performed under the contract. For example, the courts have found that the original contract was rescinded, Linz v. Schuck, 106 Md. 220, 67 A. 286 (1907); abandoned, Connelly v. Devoe, 37 Conn. 570 (1871), or waived, Michaud v. McGregor, 61 Minn. 198, 63 N.W. 479 (1895).

Although the preexisting duty rule has served a useful purpose insofar as it deters parties from using coercion and duress to obtain additional compensation, it has been widely criticized as a general rule of law. . . .

The modern trend appears to recognize the necessity that courts should enforce agreements modifying contracts when unexpected or unanticipated difficulties arise during the course of the performance of a contract, even though there is no consideration for the modification, as long as the parties agree voluntarily.

Under the Uniform Commercial Code, § 2–209(1), which has been adopted by 49 states, "[a]n agreement modifying a contract [for the sale of goods] needs no consideration to be binding." See G.L.1956 (1969 Reenactment) § 6A–2–209(1). Although at first blush this section appears to validate modifications obtained by coercion and duress, the comments to this section indicate that a modification under this section must meet the test of good faith imposed by the Code, and a modification obtained by extortion without a legitimate commercial reason is unenforceable.

The modern trend away from a rigid application of the preexisting duty rule is reflected by [§ 89(a)] of the American Law Institute's Restatement, Second, Law of Contracts. . . .

We believe that [§ 89(a)] is the proper rule of law and find it applicable to the facts of this case.[16] It not only prohibits modifications obtained by coercion, duress, or extortion but also fulfills society's expectation that agreements entered into voluntarily will be enforced by the courts.[17] See generally

---

16. The fact that these additional payments were made by a municipal corporation rather than a private individual does not, in our opinion, affect the outcome of this case. . . .

17. The drafters of [§ 89(a)] of the Restatement Second of the Law of Contracts use the following illustrations in comment (b) as examples of how this rule is applied to certain transactions:

"1. By a written contract A agrees to excavate a cellar for B for a stated price. Solid rock is unexpectedly encountered and A so notifies B. A and B then orally agree that A will remove the rock at a unit price which is reasonable but that used in computing the original price, and A completes the job. B is bound to pay the increased amount.

"2. A contracts with B to supply for $300 a laundry chute for a building B has contracted to build for the government for $150,000. Later A discovers that he made an error as to the type of material to be used and should have bid $1,200. A offers to supply the chute for $1,000, eliminating overhead and profit. After ascer-

taining that other suppliers would charge more, B agrees. The new agreement is binding.

"3. A is employed by B as a designer of coats at $90 a week for a year beginning November 1 under a written contract executed September 1. A is offered $115 a week by another employer and so informs B. A and B then agree that A will be paid $100 a week and in October execute a new written contract to that effect, simultaneously tearing up the prior contract. The new contract is binding.

"4. A contracts to manufacture and sell to B 2,000 steel roofs for corn cribs at $60. Before A begins manufacture a threat of a nationwide steel strike raises the cost of steel about $10 per roof, and A and B agree orally to increase the price to $70 per roof. A thereafter manufactures and delivers 1,700 of the roofs, and B pays for 1,500 of them at the increased price without protest, increasing the selling price of the corn cribs by $10. The new agreement is binding.

"5. A contracts to manufacture and sell to B 100,000 castings for lawn mowers at 50 cents each. After partial delivery and after B has

Horwitz, The Historical Foundations of Modern Contract Law, 87 Harv.L.Rev. 917 (1974). Section [89(a)], of course, does not compel a modification of an unprofitable or unfair contract; it only enforces a modification if the parties voluntarily agree and if (1) the promise modifying the original contract was made before the contract was fully performed on either side, (2) the underlying circumstances which prompted the modification were unanticipated by the parties, and (3) the modification is fair and equitable.

The evidence, which is uncontradicted, reveals that in June of 1968 Maher requested the city council to pay him an additional $10,000 for the year beginning on July 1, 1968, and ending on June 30, 1969. This request was made at a public meeting of the city council, where Maher explained in detail his reasons for making the request. Thereafter, the city council voted to authorize the Mayor to sign an amendment to the [1964] contract which provided that Maher would receive an additional $10,000 per year for the duration of the contract. Under such circumstances we have no doubt that the city voluntarily agreed to modify the 1964 contract.

Having determined the voluntariness of this agreement, we turn our attention to the three criteria delineated above. First, the modification was made in June of 1968 at a time when the five-year contract which was made in 1964 had not been fully performed by either party. Second, although the 1964 contract provided that Maher collect all refuse generated within the city, it appears this contract was premised on Maher's past experience that the number of refuse-generating units would increase at a rate of 20 to 25 per year. Furthermore, the evidence is uncontradicted that the 1967–1968 increase of 400 units "went beyond any previous expectation." Clearly, the circumstances which prompted the city council to modify the 1964 contract were unanticipated. Third, although the evidence does not indicate what proportion of the total this increase comprised, the evidence does indicate that it was a "substantial" increase. In light of this, we cannot say that the council's agreement to pay Maher the $10,000 increase was not fair and equitable in the circumstances.

The judgment appealed from is reversed, and the cause is remanded to the Superior Court for entry of judgment for the defendants.

———

WATKINS & SON v. CARRIG, 91 N.H. 459, 21 A.2d 591 (1941). "In common understanding there is, importantly, a wide divergence between a bare promise and a promise in adjustment of a contractual promise already outstanding. A promise with no supporting consideration would upset well and long–established human interrelations if the law did not treat it as a vain thing. But parties to a valid contract generally understand that it is subject to any mutual action they may take in its performance. Changes to meet changes in circumstances and conditions should be valid if the law is to carry out its

contracted to sell a substantial number of lawn mowers at a fixed price, A notifies B that increased metal costs require that the price be increased to 75 cents. Substitute castings are available at 55 cents, but only after several months delay. B protests but is forced to agree to the new price to keep its plant in operation. The modification is not binding."

function and service by rules conformable with reasonable practices and understandings in matters of business and commerce."

———

SUGARHOUSE FINANCE CO. v. ANDERSON, 610 P.2d 1369 (Utah 1980). In December 1976, Sugarhouse recovered a judgment against Anderson for $2,423.86, plus interest, costs, and attorneys' fees, on account of an unpaid promissory note. Anderson failed to satisfy the judgment, and in January 1979 Sugarhouse served Anderson with an order in supplemental proceedings to collect the judgment. Two days after receiving this order, Anderson met with Petty, Sugarhouse's president, to discuss an alternative to full payment of the judgment. Anderson informed Petty of the existence of numerous outstanding obligations against him, including medical expenses incurred pursuant to treatment for injuries sustained in an automobile accident in 1978. He asserted that he was contemplating bankruptcy, which would result in Sugarhouse's judgment being discharged. The parties finally settled on a figure of $2,200 in full satisfaction of Sugarhouse's claim. Anderson agreed to borrow money from a third party to enable him to pay the $2,200. Anderson then gave Petty a check for this amount, but asked him not to negotiate the check immediately because there was some uncertainty as to the sufficiency of funds in Anderson's account to cover the check. Two days later, Anderson called to inform Sugarhouse that there were sufficient funds in the account to cover the check. Sugarhouse responded that it did not intend on going through with the settlement, and returned the check. Thereafter, Anderson filed a motion asking the court to order Sugarhouse to comply with the terms of the settlement. Held, for Anderson.

"... Where ... the underlying claim is liquidated and certain as to amount, separate consideration must be found to support [an] accord; otherwise, the obligor binds himself to do nothing he was not already obligated to do, and the obligee's promise to accept a substitute performance is unenforceable. The original obligation in the present case being of a definite and undisputed amount, the question presented is whether or not separate consideration was given to support the accord reached by the parties....

"It is to be noted that, in the present case, plaintiff held a judgment which had been outstanding for more than two years. Pursuant to the parties' conversation of January 31, 1979, defendant agreed that, for a release of the judgment upon payment of a lesser agreed amount, he would negotiate a loan with a third party to enable him to pay off the substitute obligation immediately. A check was given for the agreed amount at the conclusion of that conversation, and authorization to cash it followed two days later. In effect, defendant had agreed to transfer the debt, represented by plaintiff's judgment to a third party, thereby immediately satisfying the obligation owed to plaintiff. This was something defendant had no legal obligation to do; by law, plaintiff could only move by levy of execution against property already owned by the defendant—plaintiff could not legally require defendant to incur additional obligations to satisfy the judgment. By so doing, defendant deliberately incurred the detriment of surrendering his right to limit plaintiff's ability to obtain satisfaction of the underlying judgment, and bestowed upon plaintiff the benefit of immediate payment by means of the incurrence of additional indebtedness. We hold such action to constitute sufficient consideration to support the accord negotiated by the parties.

"We note, in addition, that this jurisdiction recognizes the doctrine of promissory estoppel, whereby an individual who has made a promise which the individual should reasonably expect to induce action or forbearance on the part of the promisee or a third person and which does induce such action or forbearance is estopped to deny or repudiate the promise should the promisee or some third party suffer detriment thereby. We note that, in the present case, defendant agreed to incur additional indebtedness pursuant to the terms of the accord, in reliance on plaintiff's promise to accept immediate payment of a lesser amount in full satisfaction of the underlying obligation. As such, plaintiff should now be estopped to deny or reject the promise made."

UCC § 2–209

[See Selected Source Materials Supplement]

CISG ART. 29

[See Selected Source Materials Supplement]

NOTE ON THE CISG

In 1969, the United Nations Commission on International Trade Law (UNCITRAL) appointed a working group to prepare a new draft of an international convention (treaty) on the sale of goods. The United States was an active participant in the working group. The ultimate result was the Convention for the International Sale of Goods (the CISG), which was adopted in 1980, and came into force in 1988 when it had been ratified by the requisite ten countries. The CISG is binding only in those countries that have ratified it. As of 2000, the CISG had been ratified by fifty-three countries, including the United States, Canada, China, France, Germany, and Mexico.

Although in form the CISG is an international treaty, in substance it is a code, much like Article 2 of the UCC. Article 2 governs contracts for the sale of goods between a seller and a buyer in the United States. The CISG governs contracts for the sale of goods (with certain exclusions, such as consumer goods) between a seller and a buyer who have their places of business in different countries, both of which have ratified the CISG. Accordingly, if, for example, a seller with its place of business in the United States enters into a contract for the sale of goods to a buyer with its place of business in France, then unless the parties otherwise provide, the contract is governed by the provisions of the CISG.

Like the UCC, the CISG does not govern the issue whether a contract is substantively valid; that is, it does not govern matters such as fraud, capacity, duress, mistake, legality, or the like. However, the CISG does govern whether a contract satisfies requisite formal requirements, such as whether a contract is required to be in writing, and also governs such matters as whether a contract was formed and whether a contract is sufficiently definite to be enforceable.

CLARK v. WEST

Court of Appeals of New York, 1908.
193 N.Y. 349, 86 N.E. 1.

On February 12, 1900, the plaintiff and defendant entered into a written contract, under which the former was to write and prepare for publication for the latter a series of law books, the compensation for which was provided in the contract. After the plaintiff had completed a three-volume work known as "Clark & Marshall on Corporations," the parties disagreed. The plaintiff claimed that the defendant had broken the contract by causing the book to be copyrighted in the name of a corporation which was not a party to the contract, and he brought this action to recover what he claims to be due him, for an accounting and other relief. The defendant demurred to the complaint on the ground that it did not state facts sufficient to constitute a cause of action. The Special Term overruled the demurrer, but upon appeal to the Appellate Division that decision was reversed, and the demurrer sustained. [125 App.Div. 654, 110 N.Y.S. 110.]

Those portions of the contract which are germane to the present stage of the controversy are as follows: The plaintiff agreed to write a series of books relating to specified legal subjects. The manuscript furnished by him was to be satisfactory to the defendant. The plaintiff was not to write or edit anything that would interfere with the sale of books to be written by him under the contract, and he was not to write any other books unless requested so to do by the defendant, in which latter event he was to be paid $3,000 a year. The contract contained a clause which provided that "the first party (the plaintiff) agrees to totally abstain from the use of intoxicating liquors during the continuance of this contract, and the payment to him in accordance with the terms of this contract of any money in excess of $2 per page is dependent on the faithful performance of this as well as the other conditions of this contract. . . ." In a later paragraph it further recited that, "in consideration of the above promises of the first party (the plaintiff), the second party (the defendant) agrees to pay to the first party $2 per page, . . . on each book prepared by the first party under this contract and accepted by the second party, and if said first party abstains from the use of intoxicating liquor and otherwise fulfills his agreements as hereinbefore set forth, he shall be paid an additional $4 per page in manner hereinbefore stated." This was followed by a specification of the method and times of payment. . . .

The plaintiff in his complaint alleges completion of the work on Corporations and publication thereof by the defendant, the sale of many copies thereof from which the defendant received large net receipts, the number of pages it contained (3,469), for which he had been paid at the rate of $2 per page, amounting to $6,938, and that defendant has refused to pay him any sum over and above that amount, or any sum in excess of $2 per page. Full performance of the agreement on plaintiff's part is alleged, except that he "did not totally abstain from the use of intoxicating liquor during the continuance of said contract; but such use by the plaintiff was not excessive and did not prevent or interfere with the due and full performance by the plaintiff of all the other stipulations in said contract." The complaint further alleges a waiver on the part of the defendant of the plaintiff's stipulation to totally abstain from the use of intoxicating liquors, as follows: "(12) That defendant waived plaintiff's breach of the stipulation to totally abstain from the use of intoxicating liquors during the continuance of said contract; that long prior to the completion of said manuscript on Corporations, and its delivery to and acceptance by the defendant, the defendant had full knowledge and well knew of plaintiff's said use of intoxicating liquor during the continuance of said contract, but nevertheless acquiesced in and failed to object thereto, and did not terminate the contract on account thereof; that with full knowledge of said breach by the plaintiff defendant continued to exact and require of the plaintiff performance of all the other stipulations and conditions of said contract, and treated the same as still in force, and continued to receive, and did receive, installments of manuscript under said contract, and continued to make and did make payments to plaintiff by way of advancements, and finally accepted and published said manuscript as aforesaid; that at no time during the performance of said contract by the plaintiff did the defendant notify or intimate to the plaintiff that defendant would insist upon strict compliance with said stipulation to totally abstain from the use of intoxicating liquor, or that defendant intended to take advantage of plaintiff's said breach, and on account and by reason thereof refuse to pay plaintiff the royalty stipulated in said contract; that, on the contrary, and with full knowledge of plaintiff's said use of intoxicating liquors, defendant repeatedly avowed and represented to the plaintiff that he was entitled to and would receive said royalty payment, and plaintiff believed and relied on said representation, and in reliance thereon continued in the performance of said contract until the time of the breach thereof by the defendant, as hereinafter specifically alleged, and at all times during the writing of said treatise on Corporations, and after as well as before publication thereof, as aforesaid, it was mutually understood, agreed, and intended by the parties hereto that, notwithstanding plaintiff's said use of intoxicating liquors, he was nevertheless entitled to receive and would receive said royalty as the same accrued under said contract." The defendant's breach of the contract is then alleged, which is claimed to consist in his having taken out a copyright upon the plaintiff's work on Corporations in the name of a publishing company which had no relation to the contract, and the relief asked for is that the defendant be compelled to account, and that the copyright be transferred to the plaintiff, or that he recover its value.

The appeal is by permission of the Appellate Division, and the following questions have been certified to us: (1) Does the complaint herein state facts sufficient to constitute a cause of action? (2) Under the terms of the contract alleged in the complaint, is the plaintiff's total abstinence from the use of intoxicating liquors a condition precedent which can be waived so as to render defendant liable upon the contract notwithstanding plaintiff's use of intoxicating liquors? (3) Does the complaint herein allege facts constituting a valid and effective waiver of plaintiff's nonperformance of such condition precedent?

WERNER, J. . . . . Briefly stated, the defendant's position is that the stipulation as to plaintiff's total abstinence is the consideration for the payment of the difference between $2 and $6 per page, and therefore could not be waived except by a new agreement to that effect based upon a good consideration; that the so-called waiver alleged by the plaintiff is not a waiver, but a modification of the contract in respect of its consideration. The plaintiff, on the other hand, argues that the stipulation for his total abstinence was merely a condition precedent, intended to work a forfeiture of the additional compensation in case of a breach, and that it could be waived without any formal agreement to that effect based upon a new consideration.

The subject-matter of the contract was the writing of books by the plaintiff for the defendant. The duration of the contract was the time necessary to complete them all. The work was to be done to the satisfaction of the defendant, and the plaintiff was not to write any other books except those covered by the contract unless requested so to do by the defendant, in which latter event he was to be paid for that particular work by the year. The compensation for the work specified in the contract was to be $6 per page, unless the plaintiff failed to totally abstain from the use of intoxicating liquors during the continuance of the contract, in which event he was to receive only $2 per page. That is the obvious import of the contract construed in the light of the purpose for which it was made, and in accordance with the ordinary meaning of plain language. It is not a contract to write books in order that the plaintiff shall keep sober, but a contract containing a stipulation that he shall keep sober so that he may write satisfactory books. When we view the contract from this standpoint, it will readily be perceived that the particular stipulation is not the consideration for the contract, but simply one of its conditions which fits in with those relating to time and method of delivery of manuscript, revision of proof, citation of cases, assignment of copyrights, keeping track of new cases and citations for new editions, and other details which might be waived by the defendant, if he saw fit to do so. This is made clear, it seems to us, by the provision that, "in consideration of the above promises," the defendant agrees to pay the plaintiff $2 per page on each book prepared by him, and if he "abstains from the use of intoxicating liquor and otherwise fulfills his agreements as hereinbefore set forth, he shall be paid an additional $4 per page in manner hereinbefore stated." The compensation of $2 per page, not to exceed $250 per month, was an advance or partial payment of the whole price of $6 per page, and the payment of the two-thirds, which was to be withheld pending the performance of the contract, was simply made contingent upon the plaintiff's total abstention from the use of intoxicants during the life of the contract. . . .

It is obvious that the parties thought that the plaintiff's normal work was worth $6 per page. That was the sum to be paid for the work done by the plaintiff, and not for total abstinence. If the plaintiff did not keep to the condition as to total abstinence, he was to lose part of that sum. . . . This, we think, is the fair interpretation of the contract, and it follows that the stipulation as to the plaintiff's total abstinence was nothing more nor less than a condition precedent. If that conclusion is well founded, there can be no escape from the corollary that this condition could be waived; and, if it was waived, the defendant is clearly not in a position to insist upon the forfeiture which his waiver was intended to annihilate. The forfeiture must stand or fall with the condition. If the latter was waived, the former is no longer a part of the contract. Defendant still has the right to counterclaim for any damages which he may have sustained in consequence of the plaintiff's breach, but he cannot insist upon strict performance. Dunn v. Steubing, 120 N.Y. 232, 24 N.E. 315; Parke v. Franco–American Trading Co., 120 N.Y. 51, 56, 23 N.E. 996; Brady v. Cassidy, 145 N.Y. 171, 39 N.E. 814.

This whole discussion is predicated, of course, upon the theory of an express waiver. We assume that no waiver could be implied from the defendant's mere acceptance of the books and his payment of the sum of $2 per page without objection. It was the defendant's duty to pay that amount in any event after acceptance of the work. The plaintiff must stand upon his allegation of an express waiver, and if he fails to establish that he cannot maintain his action.

The theory upon which the defendant's attitude seems to be based is that, even if he has represented to the plaintiff that he would not insist upon the condition that the latter should observe total abstinence from intoxicants, he can still refuse to pay the full contract price for his work. The inequity of this position becomes apparent when we consider that this contract was to run for a period of years, during a large portion of which the plaintiff was to be entitled only to the advance payment of $2 per page; the balance being contingent, among other things, upon publication of the books and returns from sales. Upon this theory the defendant might have waived the condition while the first book was in process of production, and yet, when the whole work was completed, he would still be in a position to insist upon the forfeiture because there had not been strict performance. Such a situation is possible in a case where the subject of the waiver is the very consideration of a contract (Organ v. Stewart, 60 N.Y. 413, 420), but not where the waiver relates to something that can be waived. In the case at bar, as we have seen, the waiver is not of the consideration or subject-matter, but of an incident to the method of performance. The consideration remains the same. The defendant has had the work he bargained for, and it is alleged that he has waived one of the conditions as to the manner in which it was to have been done. He might have insisted upon literal performance, and then he could have stood upon the letter of his contract. If, however, he has waived that incidental condition, he has created a situation to which the doctrine of waiver very precisely applies.

The cases which present the most familiar phases of the doctrine of waiver are those which have arisen out of litigation over insurance policies where the defendants have claimed a forfeiture because of the breach of some condition in the contract (Insurance Co. v. Norton, 96 U.S. 234, 24 L.Ed. 689; Titus v. Glens Falls Ins. Co., 81 N.Y. 410; Kiernan v. Dutchess Co. Mut. Insurance Co., 150 N.Y. 190, 44 N.E. 698), but it is a doctrine of general application which is confined to no particular class of cases. A "waiver" has been defined to be the intentional relinquishment of a known right. It is voluntary and implies an election to dispense with something of value, or forego some advantage which the party waiving it might at its option have demanded or insisted upon (Herman on Estoppel & Res Adjudicata, vol. 2, p. 954; Cowenhoven v. Ball, 118 N.Y. 234, 23 N.E. 470), and this definition is supported by many cases in this and other states. In the recent case of Draper v. Oswego Co. Fire R. Ass'n, 190 N.Y. 12, 16, 82 N.E. 755, Chief Judge Cullen, in speaking for the court upon this subject, said: "While that doctrine and the doctrine of equitable estoppel are often confused in insurance litigation, there is a clear distinction between the two. A 'waiver' is the voluntary abandonment or relinquishment by a party of some right or advantage. As said by my

Brother Vann in the Kiernan Case, 150 N.Y. 190, 44 N.E. 698: 'The law of waiver seems to be a technical doctrine, introduced and applied by the court for the purpose of defeating forfeitures.... While the principle may not be easily classified, it is well established that, if the words and acts of the insurer reasonably justify the conclusion that with full knowledge of all the facts it intended to abandon or not to insist upon the particular defense afterwards relied upon, a verdict or finding to that effect establishes a waiver, which, if it once exists, can never be revoked.' The doctrine of equitable estoppel, or estoppel in pais, is that a party may be precluded by his acts and conduct from asserting a right to the detriment of another party who, entitled to rely on such conduct, has acted upon it.... As already said, the doctrine of waiver is to relieve against forfeiture. It requires no consideration for a waiver, nor any prejudice or injury to the other party." To the same effect, see Knarston v. Manhattan Life Ins. Co., 140 Cal. 57, 73 P. 740.

It remains to be determined whether the plaintiff has alleged facts which, if proven, will be sufficient to establish his claim of an express waiver by the defendant of the plaintiff's breach of the condition to observe total abstinence. In the 12th paragraph of the complaint, the plaintiff alleges facts and circumstances which we think, if established, would prove defendant's waiver of plaintiff's performance of that contract stipulation....

The three questions certified should be answered in the affirmative, the order of the Appellate Division reversed, the interlocutory judgment of the Special Term affirmed, with costs in both courts, and the defendant be permitted to answer the complaint within 20 days upon payment of costs.

———

RESTATEMENT, SECOND, CONTRACTS § 84

[See Selected Source Materials Supplement]

———

RESTATEMENT, SECOND, CONTRACTS § 84, ILLUSTRATIONS 3, 4, 6

3.   A employs B to build a house, promising to pay therefor $10,000 on the production of a certificate from A's architect, C, stating that the work has been satisfactorily completed. B builds the house but the work is defective in certain trivial particulars. C refuses to give B a certificate. A says to B, "My architect rightfully refuses to give you a certificate but the defects are not serious; I will pay you the full price which I promised." A is bound to do so, and has no power to restore the requirement of the condition.

4.   A, an insurance company, insures B's house for $5000 against loss by fire. The insurance policy provides that it shall be payable only if B gives written notification of any loss within thirty days after its occurrence. An insured loss occurs and B gives only oral notification thereof within thirty days. A tells him, either before or after the lapse of thirty days from the loss, that this notification is sufficient. A cannot thereafter rely upon B's failure to give written notification as an excuse for failure to pay for the loss....

6. In Illustration 4, A can restore the requirement of the condition by notifying B of his intention to do so if there still remains a reasonable time for the occurrence of the condition before the expiration of the thirty-day period, unless such action would be unjust in view of a material change of position by B in reliance on A's waiver. If a reasonable time does not remain, A cannot restore the requirement of the condition by extending the time.

NASSAU TRUST CO. v. MONTROSE CONCRETE PRODUCTS CORP., 56 N.Y.2d 175, 451 N.Y.S.2d 663, 436 N.E.2d 1265 (1982), reargument denied 57 N.Y.2d 674, 454 N.Y.S.2d 1032, 439 N.E.2d 1247 (1982). "Modification ... requires consideration.... [In contrast, waiver does not rest] upon consideration or agreement. A modification, because it is an agreement based upon consideration, is binding according to its terms and may only be withdrawn by agreement.... A waiver, to the extent that it has been executed, cannot be expunged or recalled ... but, not being a binding agreement, can, to the extent that it is executory, be withdrawn, provided the party whose performance has been waived is given notice of withdrawal and a reasonable time after notice within which to perform...."

UCC §§ 1–107,* 2–209

[See Selected Source Materials Supplement]

BMC INDUSTRIES, INC. v. BARTH INDUSTRIES, INC., 160 F.3d 1322 (11th Cir.1998), certiorari denied, 526 U.S. 1132, 119 S.Ct. 1807, 143 L.Ed.2d 1010, (1999). "As an initial matter, we must determine whether, under the UCC, waiver must be accompanied by detrimental reliance.... [C]ourts disagree on whether the UCC retains this requirement. We conclude, however, that the UCC does not require consideration or detrimental reliance for waiver of a contract term.

"Our conclusion follows from the plain language of subsections [2–209(4)] and (5). While subsection (4) states that an attempted modification that fails may still constitute a waiver, subsection (5) provides that the waiver may be retracted unless the non-waiving party relies on the waiver. Consequently, the statute recognizes that waivers may exist in the absence of detrimental reliance—these are the retractable waivers referred to in subsection (5). Only this interpretation renders meaning to subsection (5), because reading subsec-

---

* In 2003, the National Commissioners on Uniform State Laws and the American Law Institute promulgated a revised version of Article 1. The revised version has not been widely adopted by state legislatures. Therefore, the cross-reference in the text is to the pre–2003 version of Article 1. In the revised version, the counterpart to pre–2003 section 1–107 is section 1–306:

Waiver or Renunciation of Claim or Right After Breach

A claim or right arising out of an alleged breach may be discharged in whole or in part without consideration by agreement of the aggrieved party in an authenticated record.

(Footnote by ed.)

tion (4) to require detrimental reliance for all waivers means that waivers would never be retractable. See Wisconsin Knife Works v. National Metal Crafters, 781 F.2d 1280, 1291 (7th Cir.1986) (Easterbrook, J., dissenting) (noting that reading a detrimental reliance requirement into the UCC would eliminate the distinction between subsections (4) and (5)). Subsection (5) would therefore be meaningless.

"Although [some] courts have held that waiver requires reliance under the UCC, those courts have ignored the UCC's plain language. The leading case espousing this view of waiver is Wisconsin Knife Works v. National Metal Crafters, 781 F.2d 1280 (7th Cir.1986) ... in which a panel of the Seventh Circuit addressed a contract that included a term prohibiting oral modifications, and considered whether an attempted oral modification could instead constitute a waiver. Writing for the majority, Judge Posner concluded that the UCC's subsection (2), which gives effect to 'no oral modification' provisions, would become superfluous if contract terms could be waived without detrimental reliance. Judge Posner reasoned that if attempted oral modifications that were unenforceable because of subsection (2) were nevertheless enforced as waivers under subsection (4), then subsection (2) is 'very nearly a dead letter.' Id. at 1286. According to Judge Posner, there must be some difference between modification and waiver in order for both subsections (2) and (4) to have meaning. This difference is waiver's detrimental reliance requirement.

"Judge Posner, however, ignores a fundamental difference between modifications and waivers: while a party that has agreed to a contract modification cannot cancel the modification without giving consideration for the cancellation, a party may unilaterally retract its waiver of a contract term provided it gives reasonable notice. The fact that waivers may unilaterally be retracted provides the difference between subsections (2) and (4) that allows both to have meaning. We therefore conclude that waiver under the UCC does not require detrimental reliance."

Chapter 3

PAST CONSIDERATION

Chapter 3 considers the enforceability of promises that are, for the most part, motivated by a moral obligation that preexists the promise. Such a promise is a special case of donative promise, in the sense that it is not bargained for. It differs from a simple donative promise, because a simple donative promise the promise may *give rise* to a moral obligation, but it is not *based* on a preexisting moral obligation.

RESTATEMENT, SECOND, CONTRACTS §§ 82, 83

[See Selected Source Materials Supplement]

BANKRUPTCY CODE, 11 U.S.C. § 524

[See Selected Source Materials Supplement]

THREE SITUATIONS IN WHICH A PROMISE TO DISCHARGE AN UNENFORCEABLE OBLIGATION IS BINDING

Forming the core of any discussion of the doctrine of "past consideration" are three cases in which a promise to pay based on a past event, rather than a present bargain, was traditionally enforceable. These cases are: (1) A promise to pay a debt barred by the statute of limitations. (2) A promise by an adult to pay a debt incurred when the adult was under legal age (so that the contract was not enforceable against her). (3) A promise to pay a debt that has been discharged in bankruptcy. (The practical significance of the bankruptcy case has been limited by § 524 of the Bankruptcy Code, which creates a number of hurdles that must be jumped to make such a promise enforceable, but the doctrinal significance of this case is likely to persist.)

In all three of these cases, the discussion in the traditional commentaries was not concerned with anticipating the result, which is fairly clear, but in

151

reconciling the result with the requirement of the bargain theory of consideration. There were two competing lines of explanation.

The first explanation was that in all of these cases there exists from the beginning a moral obligation to make compensation for a benefit conferred, which supports and serves as consideration for the later promise. Though the law will not enforce the promise of an infant, or the obligation of a debtor whose debt has been barred by the statute or discharged in bankruptcy, the infant or debtor in these cases ought in morality to pay his obligation unless there exists some meritorious defense against it, such as fraud or the like. When the debtor recognizes this moral obligation by making a new promise to pay, he becomes liable.

The competing—and less satisfactory—explanation for these cases ran along the following lines: In all these situations the creditor really has, prior to the new promise by the debtor, not merely a *moral* claim, but a *legal* claim. This legal claim is, for the time being, unenforceable, since the debtor may assert the defense of infancy, the statute of limitations, or the discharge in bankruptcy. When the new promise is made, the effect is not to create a legal right in the creditor where none existed before (for that would require consideration), but rather to remove from the hands of the debtor a defense against the assertion of a legal right that already exists. This explanation was expressed in a variety of ways. For example, it was said that in the case of the infant's contract, the original contract is not "void," but "voidable," and that when the infant, after coming of age, promises to perform it, he "affirms" the contract, and gives up his power to avoid it. Then in the case of the debt barred by the statute of limitations and the discharged bankrupt, it was said that the new promise of the debtor "waives" the defense of the statute or the discharge, and that a "waiver" does not require consideration.

This general mode of analysis raises at least two questions: (1) If a "legal" obligation can "exist" even though the debtor has a completely effective defense to it, what is the difference between such an obligation and an obligation that is merely "moral"? (2) The analysis assumes that consideration is required to create a legal obligation, but is not required to make effective the debtor's surrender of a defense to an existing obligation. What justification is there for this distinction?

The significant question, addressed by the materials in the remainder of this Chapter, is whether these core cases stand by themselves or are instances of a more general principle.

———

MILLS v. WYMAN

Supreme Judicial Court of Massachusetts, 1825.
3 Pick. [20 Mass.] 207.

This was an action of assumpsit brought to recover a compensation for the board, nursing, & c., of Levi Wyman, son of the defendant, from the 5th to the 20th of February, 1821. The plaintiff then lived at Hartford, in Connecticut; the defendant, at Shrewsbury, in this county. Levi Wyman, at the time when the services were rendered, was about 25 years of age, and had long ceased to be a member of his father's family. He was on his return from a voyage at sea, and being suddenly taken sick at Hartford, and being poor and in distress, was relieved by the plaintiff in the manner and to the extent above stated. On the 24th of February, after all the expenses had been incurred, the defendant wrote a letter to the plaintiff, promising to pay him such expenses. There was no consideration for this promise, except what grew out of the relation which subsisted between Levi Wyman and the defendant, and Howe, J., before whom the cause was tried in the court of common pleas, thinking this not sufficient to support the action, directed a nonsuit. To this direction the plaintiff filed exceptions.

PARKER, C.J. General rules of law established for the protection and security of honest and fair-minded men, who may inconsiderately make promises without any equivalent, will sometimes screen men of a different character from engagements which they are bound in *foro conscientiae* to perform. This is a defect inherent in all human systems of legislation. The rule that a mere verbal promise, without any consideration, cannot be enforced by action, is universal in its application, and cannot be departed from to suit particular cases in which a refusal to perform such a promise may be disgraceful.

The promise declared on in this case appears to have been made without any legal consideration. The kindness and services towards the sick son of the defendant were not bestowed at his request. The son was in no respect under the care of the defendant. He was twenty-five years old, and had long left his father's family. On his return from a foreign country, he fell sick among strangers, and the plaintiff acted the part of the good Samaritan, giving him shelter and comfort until he died. The defendant, his father, on being informed of this event, influenced by a transient feeling of gratitude, promises in writing to pay the plaintiff for the expenses he had incurred. But he has determined to break this promise, and is willing to have his case appear on record as a strong example of particular injustice sometimes necessarily resulting from the operation of general rules.

It is said a moral obligation is a sufficient consideration to support an express promise; and some authorities lay down the rule thus broadly; but upon examination of the cases we are satisfied that the universality of the rule cannot be supported, and that there must have been some preexisting obligation, which has become inoperative by positive law, to form a basis for an effective promise. The cases of debts barred by the statute of limitations, of debts incurred by infants, of debts of bankrupts, are generally put for illustration of the rule. Express promises founded on such preexisting equitable obligations may be enforced; there is a good consideration for them; they merely remove an impediment created by law to the recovery of debts honestly due, but which public policy protects the debtors from being compelled to pay. In all these cases there was originally a quid pro quo; and according to the principles of natural justice the party receiving ought to pay; but the legislature has said he shall not be coerced; then comes the promise to pay the debt that is barred, the promise of the man to pay the debt of the infant, of the discharged bankrupt to restore to his creditor what by the law he had lost. In all these cases there is a moral obligation founded upon an antecedent valuable consideration. These promises therefore have a sound legal basis. They are not promises to pay something for nothing; not naked pacts; but the voluntary revival or creation of obligation which before existed in natural law, but which had been dispensed with, not for the benefit of the party obliged solely, but principally for the public convenience. If moral obligation, in its fullest sense, is a good substratum for an express promise, it is not easy to perceive why it is not equally good to support an implied promise. What a man ought to do, generally he ought to be made to do, whether he promise or refuse. But the law of society has left most of such obligations to the interior forum, as the tribunal of conscience has been aptly called. Is there not a moral obligation upon every son who has become affluent by means of the education and advantages bestowed upon him by his father, to relieve that father from pecuniary embarrassment, to promote his comfort and happiness, and even to share with him his riches, if thereby he will be made happy? And yet such a son may, with impunity, leave such a father in any degree of penury above that which will expose the community in which he dwells, to the danger of being obliged to preserve him from absolute want. Is not a wealthy father under strong moral obligation to advance the interest of an obedient, well disposed son, to furnish him with the means of acquiring and maintaining a becoming rank in life, to rescue him from the horrors of debt incurred by misfortune? Yet the law will uphold him in any degree of parsimony, short of that which would reduce his son to the necessity of seeking public charity.

Without doubt there are great interests of society which justify withholding the coercive arm of the law from these duties of imperfect obligation, as they are called; imperfect, not because they are less binding upon the conscience than those which are called perfect, but because the wisdom of the social law does not impose sanctions upon them.

A deliberate promise, in writing, made freely and without any mistake, one which may lead the party to whom it is made into contracts and expenses, cannot be broken without a violation of moral duty. But if there was nothing paid or promised for it, the law, perhaps wisely, leaves the execution of it to the conscience of him who makes it. It is only when the party making the promise gains something, or he to whom it is made loses something, that the law gives the promise validity. And in the case of the promise of the adult to pay the debt of the infant, of the debtor discharged by the statute of limitations or bankruptcy, the principle is preserved by looking back to the origin of the transaction, where an equivalent is to be found. An exact equivalent is not required by the law; for there being a consideration, the parties are left to estimate its value: though here the courts of equity will step in to relieve from gross inadequacy between the consideration and the promise.

These principles are deduced from the general current of decided cases upon the subject as well as from the known maxims of the common law. The general position, that moral obligation is a sufficient consideration for an express promise, is to be limited in its application, to cases where at some time or other a good or valuable consideration has existed.

A legal obligation is always a sufficient consideration to support either an express or an implied promise; such as an infant's debt for necessaries, or a father's promise to pay for the support and education of his minor children. But when the child shall have attained to manhood, and shall have become his own agent in the world's business, the debts he incurs, whatever may be their nature, create no obligation upon the father; and it seems to follow, that his promise founded upon such a debt has no legally binding force.

The cases of instruments under seal and certain mercantile contracts, in which considerations need not be proved, do not contradict the principles above suggested. The first import a consideration in themselves, and the second belong to a branch of the mercantile law, which has found it necessary to disregard the point of consideration in respect to instruments negotiable in their nature and essential to the interests of commerce.

Instead of citing a multiplicity of cases to support the positions I have taken, I will only refer to a very able review of all the cases in the note in 3 Bos. & P. 249. The opinions of the judges had been variant for a long course of years upon this subject, but there seems to be no case in which it was nakedly decided, that a promise to pay the debt of a son of full age, not living with his father, though the debt were incurred by sickness which ended in the death of the son, without a previous request by the father proved or presumed, could be enforced by action.

It has been attempted to show a legal obligation on the part of the defendant by virtue of our statute, which compels lineal kindred in the ascending or descending line to support such of their poor relations as are likely to become chargeable to the town where they have their settlement. But it is a sufficient answer to this position, that such legal obligation does not exist except in the very cases provided for in the statute, and never until the party charged has been adjudged to be of sufficient ability thereto. We do not know from the report any of the facts which are necessary to create such an obligation. Whether the deceased had a legal settlement in this common-wealth at the time of his death, whether he was likely to become chargeable had he lived, whether the defendant was of sufficient ability, are essential facts to be adjudicated by the court to which is given jurisdiction on this subject. The legal liability does not arise until these facts have all been ascertained by judgment, after hearing the party intended to be charged.

For the foregoing reasons we are all of opinion that the nonsuit directed by the court of common pleas was right, and that judgment be entered thereon for costs for the defendant.

BACKGROUND NOTE ON MILLS v. WYMAN

Based on an analysis of original judicial and historical records, Professor Geoffrey Watson reports that Levi Wyman's "illness was a protracted one: by all accounts it lasted at least two weeks. Daniel Mills, the Good Samaritan who housed and cared for Levi Wyman, arranged for two men to guard Levi for four days and nights while Levi 'was in his derang'd state.' Levi was so sick that 'he leaped out of a chamber window to the imminent hazard of his life, and to the very great alarm of the family and the boarders.' ... Mills also hired John Lee Comstock, a prominent Hartfort physician, to care for Wyman. Comstock found Levi 'in a state of indisposition' and, for some time 'in a state of delirium' that required two or three persons 'to prevent him from injuring himself.' [Mills's] expenses amounted to about twenty-two dollars—a considerable sum in those days—and included six dollars for fourteen days' board and lodging, three dollars for "Room pine and Candles," one dollar for a gallon of "Spirits," six dollars in expenses for the two men hired to restrain

Levi, and six dollars for Dr. Comstock's fee." Wilson, In the Tribunal of Conscience: Mills v. Wyman Reconsidered, 71 Tul. L. Rev. 1749 (1997). (This article contains a wealth of other information about the facts and background of the case, including facts that suggest that Levi might actually have survived his illness and died much later.)

WEBB v. McGOWIN

Court of Appeals of Alabama, 1935.
27 Ala.App. 82, 168 So. 196.

Action by Joe Webb against N. Floyd McGowin and Joseph F. McGowin, as executors of the estate of J. Greeley McGowin, deceased. From a judgment of nonsuit, plaintiff appeals.

Reversed and remanded. . . .

BRICKEN, PRESIDING JUDGE. This action is in assumpsit. The complaint as originally filed was amended. The demurrers to the complaint as amended were sustained, and because of this adverse ruling by the court the plaintiff took a nonsuit, and the assignment of errors on this appeal are predicated upon said action or ruling of the court.

A fair statement of the case presenting the questions for decision is set out in appellant's brief, which we adopt.

"On the 3d day of August, 1925, appellant while in the employ of the W.T. Smith Lumber Company, a corporation, and acting within the scope of his employment, was engaged in clearing the upper floor of mill No. 2 of the company. While so engaged he was in the act of dropping a pine block from the upper floor of the mill to the ground below; this being the usual and ordinary way of clearing the floor, and it being the duty of the plaintiff in the course of his employment to so drop it. The block weighed about 75 pounds.

"As appellant was in the act of dropping the block to the ground below, he was on the edge of the upper floor of the mill. As he started to turn the block loose so that it would drop to the ground, he saw J. Greeley McGowin, testator of the defendants, on the ground below and directly under where the block would have fallen had appellant turned it loose. Had he turned it loose it would have struck McGowin with such force as to have caused him serious bodily harm or death. Appellant could have remained safely on the upper floor of the mill by turning the block loose and allowing it to drop, but had he done this the block would have fallen on McGowin and caused him serious injuries or death. The only safe and reasonable way to prevent this was for appellant to hold to the block and divert its direction in falling from the place where McGowin was standing and the only safe way to divert it so as to prevent its coming into contact with McGowin was for appellant to fall with it to the ground below. Appellant did this, and by holding to the block and falling with it to the ground below, he diverted the course of its fall in such way that McGowin was not injured. In thus preventing the injuries to McGowin appellant himself received serious bodily injuries, resulting in his right leg being broken, the heel of his right foot torn off and his right arm broken. He was badly crippled for life and rendered unable to do physical or mental labor.

"On September 1, 1925, in consideration of appellant having prevented him from sustaining death or serious bodily harm and in consideration of the injuries appellant had received, McGowin agreed with him to care for and maintain him for the remainder of appellant's life at the rate of $15 every two weeks from the time he sustained his injuries to and during the remainder of appellant's life; it being agreed that McGowin would pay this sum to appellant for his maintenance. Under the agreement McGowin paid or caused to be paid to appellant the sum so agreed on up until McGowin's death on January 1, 1934. After his death the payments were continued to and including January 27, 1934, at which time they were discontinued. Thereupon plaintiff brought suit to recover the unpaid installments accruing up to the time of the bringing of the suit. . . ."

The action was for the unpaid installments accruing after January 27, 1934, to the time of the suit.

The principal grounds of demurrer to the original and amended complaint are: (1) It states no cause of action; (2) its averments show the contract was without consideration; (3) it fails to allege that McGowin had, at or before the services were rendered, agreed to pay appellant for them; (4) the contract declared on is void under the statute of frauds.

The averments of the complaint show that appellant saved McGowin from death or grievous bodily harm. This was a material benefit to him of infinitely more value than any financial aid he could have received. Receiving this benefit, McGowin became morally bound to compensate appellant for the services rendered. Recognizing his moral obligation, he expressly agreed to pay appellant as alleged in the complaint and complied with this agreement up to the time of his death; a period of more than 8 years.

Had McGowin been accidentally poisoned and a physician, without his knowledge or request, had administered an antidote, thus saving his life, a subsequent promise by McGowin to pay the physician would have been valid. Likewise, McGowin's agreement as disclosed by the complaint to compensate appellant for saving him from death or grievous bodily injury is valid and enforceable.

Where the promisee cares for, improves, and preserves the property of the promisor, though done without his request, it is sufficient consideration for the promisor's subsequent agreement to pay for the service, because of the material benefit received. . . . Edson v. Poppe, 24 S.D. 466, 124 N.W. 441, 26 L.R.A. (N.S.) 534.

In Boothe v. Fitzpatrick, 36 Vt. 681, the court held that a promise by defendant to pay for the past keeping of a bull which had escaped from defendant's premises and been cared for by plaintiff was valid, although there was no previous request, because the subsequent promise obviated that objection; it being equivalent to a previous request. On the same principle, had the promisee saved the promisor's life or his body from grievous harm, his subsequent promise to pay for the services rendered would have been valid. Such service would have been far more material than caring for his bull. Any holding that saving a man from death or grievous bodily harm is not a material benefit sufficient to uphold a subsequent promise to pay for the service, necessarily rests on the assumption that saving life and preservation of the body from harm have only a sentimental value. The converse of this is true. Life and preservation of the body have material, pecuniary values, measurable in dollars and cents. Because of this, physicians practice their profession charging for services rendered in saving life and curing the body of its ills, and surgeons perform operations. The same is true as to the law of negligence authorizing the assessment of damages in personal injury cases based upon the extent of the injuries, earnings, and life expectancies of those injured.

In the business of life insurance, the value of a man's life is measured in dollars and cents according to his expectancy, the soundness of his body, and his ability to pay premiums. The same is true as to health and accident insurance.

It follows that if, as alleged in the complaint, appellant saved J. Greeley McGowin from death or grievous bodily harm, and McGowin subsequently agreed to pay him for the service rendered, it became a valid and enforceable contract.

It is well settled that a moral obligation is a sufficient consideration to support a subsequent promise to pay where the promisor has received a material benefit, although there was no original duty or liability resting on the promisor. [Extensive citation of cases omitted.]

The case at bar is clearly distinguishable from that class of cases where the consideration is a mere moral obligation or conscientious duty unconnected with receipt by promisor of benefits of a material or pecuniary nature. . . . Here the promisor received a material benefit constituting a valid consideration for his promise.

Some authorities hold that, for a moral obligation to support a subsequent promise to pay, there must have existed a prior legal or equitable obligation, which for some reason had become unenforceable, but for which the promisor was still morally bound. This rule, however, is subject to qualification in those cases where the promisor, having received a material benefit from the promisee, is morally bound to compensate him for the services rendered and in consideration of this obligation promises to pay. In such cases the subsequent promise to pay is an affirmance or ratification of the services rendered carrying with it the presumption that a previous request for the service was made. . . .

Under the decisions above cited, McGowin's express promise to pay appellant for the services rendered was an affirmance or ratification of what appellant had done raising the presumption that the services had been rendered at McGowin's request.

The averments of the complaint show that in saving McGowin from death or grievous bodily harm, appellant was crippled for life. This was part of the consideration of the contract declared on. McGowin was benefited. Appellant was injured. Benefit to the promisor or injury to the promisee is a sufficient legal consideration for the promisor's agreement to pay. . . .

Under the averments of the complaint the services rendered by appellant were not gratuitous. The agreement of McGowin to pay and the acceptance of payment by appellant conclusively shows the contrary.

The contract declared on was not void under the statute of frauds (Code 1923, § 8034).

From what has been said, we are of the opinion that the court below erred in the ruling complained of; that is to say, in sustaining the demurrer, and for this error the case is reversed and remanded.

Reversed and remanded.

SAMFORD, JUDGE (concurring). The questions involved in this case are not free from doubt, and perhaps the strict letter of the rule, as stated by judges, though not always in accord, would bar a recovery by plaintiff, but following the principle announced by Chief Justice Marshall in Hoffman v. Porter, Fed.Cas. No. 6,577, 2 Brock. 156, 159, where he says, "I do not think that law ought to be separated from justice, where it is at most doubtful," I concur in the conclusions reached by the court.

WEBB v. McGOWIN

Supreme Court of Alabama, 1936.
232 Ala. 374, 168 So. 199.

Certiorari to Court of Appeals.

Petition of N. Floyd McGowin and Joseph F. McGowin, as executors of the estate of J. Greeley McGowin, deceased, for certiorari to the Court of Appeals to review and revise the judgment and decision of that court in Joe Webb v. McGowin, et al. Ex'rs, 168 So. 196. . . .

FOSTER, JUSTICE. . . .

The opinion of the Court of Appeals here under consideration recognizes and applies the distinction between a supposed moral obligation of the promisor, based upon some refined sense of ethical duty, without material benefit to him, and one in which such a benefit did in fact occur. We agree with that court that if the benefit be material and substantial, and was to the person of the promisor rather than to his estate, it is within the class of material benefits which he has the privilege of recognizing and compensating either by an executed payment or an executory promise to pay. The cases are cited in that opinion. The reason is emphasized when the compensation is not only for the benefits which the promisor received, but also for the injuries either to the property or person of the promisee by reason of the service rendered.

Writ denied.

ANDERSON, C.J., and GARDNER and BOULDIN, JJ., concur.*

HARRINGTON v. TAYLOR, 225 N.C. 690, 36 S.E.2d 227 (1945). According to the complaint, defendant assaulted his wife and she took refuge in plaintiff's house. The next day defendant went there and assaulted his wife again. She knocked him down with an axe and was about to decapitate him. Plaintiff caught the axe, "and the blow intended for defendant fell upon her hand, mutilating it badly, but saving defendant's life. Subsequently defendant orally promised to pay the plaintiff her damages; but after paying a small sum, failed to pay anything more."

---

* In The Capability Problem in Contract Law (2d ed. 2004), Richard Danzig and Geoffrey R. Watson report that after the decisions by Alabama's Court of Appeals and Supreme Court, upholding Webb's complaint against a demurrer, the case was settled for $900. There was some indication that the McGowin family also gave Webb the use of a home and several acres of land. Danzig and Watson further report that J. Greeley McGowin was the President of W.T. Smith Lumber Co. Id. at 159, 178–79.

A judgment below, sustaining the defendant's demurrer, was affirmed. "The Court is of the opinion that however much the defendant should be impelled by common gratitude to alleviate the plaintiff's misfortune, a humanitarian act of this kind, voluntarily performed, is not such consideration as would entitle her to recover at law."

RESTATEMENT, SECOND, CONTRACTS § 86

[See Selected Source Materials Supplement]

RESTATEMENT, SECOND, CONTRACTS § 86, ILLUSTRATIONS 1, 2, 6, 10, 12, 13

1.   A gives emergency care to B's adult son while the son is sick and without funds far from home. B subsequently promises to reimburse A for his expenses. The promise is not binding under this Section.

2.   A lends money to B, who later dies. B's widow promises to pay the debt. The promise is not binding under this Section. . . .

6.   A finds B's escaped bull and feeds and cares for it. B's subsequent promise to pay reasonable compensation to A is binding. . . .

10.   A digs a well on B's land in performance of a bargain with B's tenant C. C is unable to pay as agreed, and B promises to pay A the reasonable value of the well. The promise is binding. . . .

12.   A, a married woman of sixty, has rendered household services without compensation over a period of years for B, a man of eighty living alone and having no close relatives. B has a net worth of three million dollars and has often assured A that she will be well paid for her services, whose reasonable value is not in excess of $6,000. B executes and delivers to A a written promise to pay A $25,000 "to be taken from my estate." The promise is binding.

13.   The facts being otherwise as stated in Illustration 12, B's promise is made orally and is to leave A his entire estate. A cannot recover more than the reasonable value of her services.

AMERICAN LAW INSTITUTE, 42D ANNUAL PROCEEDINGS 273–74 (1965) (comments of Professor Robert Braucher, the Reporter for the Restatement, Second, of Contracts).

"Section [86] is a new provision. . . .

". . . [W]ith the help of the Advisers we went into the cases where past consideration has been upheld, and it has been a traditional thing to say: Well, there is an orthodox view that past consideration does not make a promise binding; and then there is a scattering of cases which represents a minority view which holds that some kinds of past considerations—or sometimes it is called moral considerations—do make a promise binding.

"Actually, when you go through the cases in which this problem has been raised, it seemed to us that you discover that there is a principle, and so we have tried to capture the principle, although I think it is more of a principle than it is a rule.

"If you look at section [86], it bristles with non-specific concepts; in particular, the qualification that the promise is binding to the extent necessary to prevent injustice would be entirely at large if we did not add subsection (2) which refers to the concept of unjust enrichment.

"I think in the light of the comment the principle takes on meaning, and I think there is not a division here between a majority view and a minority view. One of the famous cases on this subject is the great case of Webb v. McGowin, which is summarily stated . . . as illustration 7.

"Now, that's in Alabama. The cases in Alabama were, I suppose, as firm as the cases anywhere in rejecting the notion of past consideration or moral obligation as consideration; and yet when this case came along the case was decided for the plaintiff, as described in this illustration, and I would suppose that, given those facts and that situation, this would be likely to happen in most courts. What you have, really, is a line of distinction between essentially gratuitous transactions and cases which are on the borderline of quasi-contracts, where promise removes the difficulty which otherwise would bar quasi-contractual relief.

"We strained quite a lot to phrase this as precisely as we could. I think you cannot make it more precise—certainly not very much more precise—than we have it in the black letter here, without getting into something that you are not all able to sustain. If you look through the cases, the cases are a wide variety of miscellany, but we think there is a principle. . . ."

NOTE ON PAST CONSIDERATION

Suppose that A confers a benefit on B without B's prior request. The resulting relationship will then fall into one of three categories:

I. B is legally obliged to compensate A under the law of unjust enrichment, as where A has paid B money by mistake.

II. B is morally but not legally obliged to compensate A, as where A has suffered a loss in rescuing B.

III. B is neither legally nor morally obliged to compensate A, as where A has given B a wedding gift.

If a case falls into Category I, a later promise by B to compensate A does not create a new liability (although if the value of the benefit is unclear, the promise may bear on the extent of A's recovery). If a case falls into Category III, a later promise to compensate A is essentially a donative promise, and also should be unenforceable.

Difficult problems arise, however, where B makes a later promise to compensate A in a case that falls into Category II. Traditionally this kind of promise was characterized as based on "past" or "moral" consideration. The general position of classical contract law, grounded on the bargain theory of consideration, was that promises based on past benefits were unenforceable, with limited exceptions.

This position had little to recommend it. By hypothesis, *A* has conferred a benefit on *B,* and *B* is morally obliged to make compensation. Presumably, therefore, the case is in Category II, rather than Category I, only because it is deemed desirable to protect persons against liability for benefits that they might have declined to accept and pay for if given the choice, and because of the severe difficulty in many such cases of measuring the value of the benefit to *B.* A later promise to make compensation invariably removes the first obstacle and normally removes the second. Such a promise should therefore be enforceable—or, perhaps more precisely, should render the promisor liable to make compensation.

Fortunately, Restatement Second has dramatically broken away from classical contract law in this area and has adopted a sweeping new principle in section 86. In its emphasis on benefit conferred, this section represents a significant reform; but in its limitation on enforceability, the section has moved too far from its roots in moral principles. To distinguish between those benefits that will and those that will not support a subsequent promise, section 86(2)(a) adopts the test whether "the promisor has ... been unjustly enriched." But if the promisor has been unjustly enriched in a legal sense, the law of unjust enrichment normally permits recovery even without the subsequent promise; and whether the promisor is unjustly enriched in any other sense must turn on concepts of morality. Indeed, even a requirement of unjust enrichment in a moral sense seems too narrow. For example, if *A's* life or property is rescued by *B,* who later makes a promise of compensation, it cannot be said that *A* is unjustly enriched. What is unjust about needing and receiving rescue? The question should simply be whether, at the time he made his promise, *A* may be morally obliged, by reason of a past benefit conferred, to make some compensation to *B.* The courts should decide this question, like the question of unconscionability, directly rather than covertly.

———

Chapter 4

THE LIMITS OF CONTRACT

The term "contract" is ambiguous. The Restatement defines a contract as any legally enforceable promise. Under this definition, a relied-upon donative promise is a contract. For some purposes that is a useful definition, but in everyday life the term "contract" usually means an agreement—especially a legally enforceable agreement. The Chapters succeeding this one will deal for the most part with contracts consisting of commercial bargains, in which legal enforceability is pretty clearly appropriate. In contrast, the cases and materials in this Chapter concern situations in which contract—used in the sense of a legally enforceable bargain—may or may not be an appropriate means of social ordering.

BALFOUR v. BALFOUR, 2 K.B. 571, 578 (1919) (opinion of Atkin, L.J.). "[I]t is necessary to remember that there are agreements between parties which do not result in contracts within the meaning of that term in our law. The ordinary example is where two parties agree to take a walk together, or where there is an offer and an acceptance of hospitality. Nobody would suggest in ordinary circumstances that those agreements result in what we know as a contract, and one of the most usual forms of agreement which does not constitute a contract appears to me to be the arrangements which are made between husband and wife. It is quite common, and it is the natural and inevitable result of the relationship of husband and wife, that the two spouses should make arrangements between themselves.... To my mind those agreements, or many of them, do not result in contracts at all, and they do not result in contracts even though there may be what as between other parties would constitute consideration for the agreement. The consideration, as we know, may consist either in some right, interest, profit or benefit accruing to one party, or some forbearance, detriment, loss or responsibility given, suffered or undertaken by the other. That is a well–known definition, and it constantly happens, I think, that such arrangements made between husband and wife are arrangements in which there are mutual promises, or in which there is consideration in form within the definition that I have mentioned. Nevertheless they are not contracts, and they are not contracts because the parties did not intend that they should be attended by legal consequences.... in respect of these promises each house is a domain into

163

which the king's writ does not seek to run, and to which his officers do not seek to be admitted."

IN RE THE MARRIAGE OF WITTEN

Supreme Court of Iowa, 2003.
672 N.W.2d 768.

TERNUS, Justice.

The primary issue raised on appeal of the district court's decree in this dissolution action is whether the court properly determined the rights of Arthur (known as Trip) and Tamera Witten with respect to the parties' frozen human embryos stored at a medical facility. While we agree with Tamera that the informed consent signed by the parties at the request of the medical facility does not control the current dispute between the donors over the use or disposition of the embryos, we reject Tamera's request that she be allowed to use the embryos over Trip's objection. Therefore, we affirm the trial court's order that neither party may use or dispose of the embryos without the consent of the other party. . . .

I. BACKGROUND FACTS AND PROCEEDINGS.

The appellee, Arthur (Trip) Witten, and the appellant, Tamera Witten, had been married for approximately seven and one-half years when Trip sought to have their marriage dissolved in April 2002. One of the contested issues at trial was control of the parties' frozen embryos. During the parties' marriage they had tried to become parents through the process of in vitro fertilization. Because Tamera was unable to conceive children naturally, they had eggs taken from Tamera artificially fertilized with Trip's sperm. Tamera then underwent several unsuccessful embryo transfers in an attempt to become pregnant. At the time of trial seventeen fertilized eggs remained in storage at the University of Nebraska Medical Center (UNMC).[1]

Prior to commencing the process for in vitro fertilization, the parties signed informed consent documents prepared by the medical center. These documents included an "Embryo Storage Agreement," which was signed by Tamera and Trip as well as by a representative of UNMC. It provided in part:

> Release of Embryos. The Client Depositors [Trip and Tamera] understand and agree that containers of embryos stored pursuant to this agreement will be used for transfer, release or disposition only with the signed approval of both Client Depositors. UNMC will release the containers of embryos only to a licensed physician recipient of written authorization of the Client Depositors.

The agreement had one exception to the joint-approval requirement that governed the disposition of the embryos upon the death of one or both of the

---

1. No medical testimony was introduced at trial with respect to the cell stage of the parties' fertilized eggs. Therefore, while some cases refer to fertilized eggs in the early stages of division as "pre-zygotes" or "preembryos," we use the term "embryo" in discussing the present appeal, since that is the terminology used in the Wittens' contract with UNMC. This term is used interchangeably with the term "fertilized egg." [Ed.: Compare A.Z. v. B.Z., 431 Mass. 150, 752 N.E.2d 1051 (2000), where the court said "We use the term 'preembryo' to refer to the four-to-eight cell stage of a developing fertilized egg." *Id*. at footnote 1.]

client depositors. Another provision of the contract provided for termination of UNMC's responsibility to store the embryos upon several contingencies: (1) the client depositors' written authorization to release the embryos or to destroy them; (2) the death of the client depositors; (3) the failure of the client depositors to pay the annual storage fee; or (4) the expiration of ten years from the date of the agreement.

At trial, Tamera asked that she be awarded "custody" of the embryos. She wanted to have the embryos implanted in her or a surrogate mother in an effort to bear a genetically linked child. She testified that upon a successful pregnancy she would afford Trip the opportunity to exercise parental rights or to have his rights terminated. She adamantly opposed any destruction of the embryos, and was also unwilling to donate the eggs to another couple.

Trip testified at the trial that while he did not want the embryos destroyed, he did not want Tamera to use them. He would not oppose donating the embryos for use by another couple. Trip asked the court to enter a permanent injunction prohibiting either party from transferring, releasing, or utilizing the embryos without the written consent of both parties.

The district court decided the dispute should be governed by the "embryo storage agreement" between the parties and UNMC, which required both parties' consent to any use or disposition of the embryos. Enforcing this agreement, the trial court enjoined both parties "from transferring, releasing or in any other way using or disposing of the embryos ... without the written and signed approval and authorization" of the other party.

Tamera has appealed the trial court's order, challenging only the court's resolution of the parties' dispute over the fertilized eggs. She claims the storage agreement is silent with respect to disposition or use of the embryos upon the parties' dissolution because there is no provision specifically addressing that contingency. Therefore, she argues, the court should have applied the "best interests [of the child]" test of Iowa Code chapter 598 (2001) and, pursuant to that analysis, awarded custody of the embryos to her. She makes the alternative argument that she is entitled to the fertilized eggs due to her fundamental right to bear children. Finally, Tamera claims it would violate the public policy of this state if Trip were allowed to back out of his agreement to have children. She claims such an agreement is evidenced by his participation in the in vitro fertilization procedure....

III. DISPOSITION OF EMBRYOS.

A. *Scope of storage agreement.* We first consider Tamera's contention that the storage agreement does not address the situation at hand. As noted earlier, the agreement had a specific provision governing control of the embryos if one or both parties died, but did not explicitly deal with the possibility of divorce. Nonetheless, we think the present predicament falls within the general provision governing "release of embryos," in which the parties agreed that the embryos would not be transferred, released, or discarded without "the signed approval" of both Tamera and Trip. This provision is certainly broad enough to encompass the decision-making protocol when the parties are unmarried as well as when they are married.

The only question, then, is whether such agreements are enforceable when one of the parties later changes his or her mind with respect to the proper disposition of the embryos. In reviewing the scarce case law from other jurisdictions on this point, we have found differing views of how the parties' rights should be determined. There is, however, abundant literature that has scrutinized the approaches taken to date. Some writers have suggested refinements of the analytical framework employed by the courts thus far; some have proposed an entirely new model of analysis. From these various sources, we have identified three primary approaches to resolving disputes over the disposition of frozen embryos, which we have identified as (1) the contractual approach, (2) the contemporaneous mutual consent model, and (3) the balancing test.

Tamera's argument that her right to bear children should override the parties' prior agreement as well as Trip's current opposition to her use of the embryos resembles the balancing test. As for Tamera's alternative argument, we have found no authority supporting a "best interests" analysis in determining the disposition of frozen embryos. Nonetheless, we will first consider whether chapter 598 requires application of that analysis under the circumstances presented by this case. Then, we will discuss and consider the three approaches suggested by decisions from other jurisdictions and the literature on this subject.

B. *"Best interests" test.* [The court began by considering the effect of an Iowa statute, § 598.41. This statute set forth various standards governing the award of child custody in a marital-dissolution case, including a requirement that any custody award reflect "the best interest of the child." The court held that the best-interest standard was not applicable to the issue at hand. "First, we note the purposes of the 'best interest' standard set forth in that statute are to 'assure the child the opportunity for the maximum continuing physical and emotional contact with both parents' and to 'encourage parents to share the rights and responsibilities of raising the child.' Iowa Code § 598.41(1)(*a*). The principles developed under this statute are simply not suited to the resolution of disputes over the control of frozen embryos. Such disputes do not involve maximizing physical and emotional contact between both parents and the child; they involve the more fundamental decision of whether the parties will be parents at all. Moreover, it would be premature to consider which parent can most effectively raise the child when the "child" is still frozen in a storage facility. The principles of section 598.41 do not fit because what is really at issue here is not the custody of children as that concept is generally viewed and analyzed in dissolution cases. Rather, the issue here is who will have decision-making authority with respect to the fertilized eggs."
. . .

C. *Enforcement of storage agreement.* We now consider the appropriateness of the trial court's decision to allow Tamera and Trip's agreement with the medical center to control the current dispute between them. As we noted above, there are three methods of analysis that have been suggested to resolve disputes over frozen embryos. We will discuss them separately.

1. *Contractual approach.* The currently prevailing view—expressed in three states—is that contracts entered into at the time of in vitro fertilization are enforceable so long as they do not violate public policy. *See* [*Kass v. Kass,* 91 N.Y.2d 554, 673 N.Y.S.2d 350, 696 N.E.2d 174, 179 (1998)] (stating agreements between donors "regarding disposition of pre-zygotes should generally be presumed valid and binding"); [*Davis v. Davis,* 842 S.W.2d 588 (Tenn. 1992)], 842 S.W.2d at 597 (holding agreement regarding disposition of

embryos "should be considered binding"); *In re Litowitz,* 146 Wash.2d 514, 48 P.3d 261, 271 (2002) (enforcing parties' contract providing for disposition of preembryos after five years of storage).[2] The New York Court of Appeals expressed the following rationale for this contractual approach:

> [It is] particularly important that courts seek to honor the parties' expressions of choice, made before disputes erupt, with the parties' overall direction always uppermost in the analysis. Knowing that advance agreements will be enforced underscores the seriousness and integrity of the consent process. Advance agreements as to disposition would have little purpose if they were enforceable only in the event the parties continued to agree. To the extent possible, it should be the progenitors—not the State and not the courts—who by their prior directive make this deeply personal life choice.

Kass, 673 N.Y.S.2d 350, 696 N.E.2d at 180.

This approach has been criticized, however, because it "insufficiently protects the individual and societal interests at stake":

> First, decisions about the disposition of frozen embryos implicate rights central to individual identity. On matters of such fundamental personal importance, individuals are entitled to make decisions consistent with their contemporaneous wishes, values, and beliefs. Second, requiring couples to make binding decisions about the future use of their frozen embryos ignores the difficulty of predicting one's future response to life-altering events such as parenthood. Third, conditioning the provision of infertility treatment on the execution of binding disposition agreements is coercive and calls into question the authenticity of the couple's original choice. Finally, treating couples' decisions about the future use of their frozen embryos as binding contracts undermines important values about families, reproduction, and the strength of genetic ties.

[Carl H. Coleman, *Procreative Liberty and Contemporaneous Choice: An Inalienable Rights Approach to Frozen Embryo Disputes,*] 84 Minn. L.Rev. at 88–89. Another legal writer has echoed these concerns:

> Binding a couple to a prior disposition agreement has its roots in contract law. The primary advantage of treating the disposition of preembryos as a contract dispute is that it binds individuals to previous obligations, even if their priorities or values change. This advantage, while maximizing the efficiency of commercial transactions, is ill-suited to govern the disposition of human tissue with the potential to develop into

---

2. Application of the contractual approach in *Kass* resulted in enforcement of the parties' agreement that the fertilized eggs would be donated for research should the parties be "unable to make a decision regarding the disposition of [the] stored, frozen pre-zygotes." 696 N.E.2d at 176–77, 181. In *Litowitz,* the court permitted execution of the parties' previous agreement that the preembryos would be "disposed of" after five years. 48 P.3d at 271. The resolution of the divorcing couple's dispute was more complex in *Davis* because the parties did not have a contract addressing the disposition of any unused preembryos. 842 S.W.2d at 590. Noting that a "prior agreement concerning disposition should be carried out," the court concluded in the absence of such an agreement, "the relative interests of the parties in using or not using the preembryos must be weighed." *Id.* at 604. The court awarded the preembryos to the husband, concluding his interest in not becoming a parent outweighed his former wife's interest in donating the preembryos to another couple for implantation. *Id.* The court noted the issue might be closer if the wife had wanted to use the preembryos herself; but in view of the fact she had "a reasonable possibility of achieving parenthood by means other than use of the preembryos in question," she would not have prevailed even under those circumstances. *Id.*

a child. The potential of the embryo requires that couples be allowed to make contemporaneous decisions about the fate of the embryo that reflect their current values.

Christina C. Lawrence, Note, *Procreative Liberty and the Preembryo Problem: Developing a Medical and Legal Framework to Settle the Disposition of Frozen Embryos,* 52 Case W. Res. L.Rev. 721, 729 (2002) [hereinafter "Lawrence Note"]; *accord J.B. v. M.B.,* 170 N.J. 9, 783 A.2d 707, 718–19 (2001). In response to such concerns, one commentator has suggested an alternative model requiring contemporaneous mutual consent. We now examine that approach.

2. *Contemporaneous mutual consent.* The contractual approach and the contemporaneous mutual consent model share an underlying premise: "decisions about the disposition of frozen embryos belong to the couple that created the embryo, with each partner entitled to an equal say in how the embryos should be disposed." Coleman, 84 Minn. L.Rev. at 81. Departing from this common starting point, the alternative framework asserts the important question is "at what time does the partners' consent matter?" *Id.* at 91. Proponents of the mutual-consent approach suggest that, with respect to "decisions about intensely emotional matters, where people act more on the basis of feeling and instinct than rational deliberation," it may "be impossible to make a knowing and intelligent decision to relinquish a right in advance of the time the right is to be exercised." *Id.* at 98; *see also* Sara D. Petersen, Comment, *Dealing With Cryopreserved Embryos Upon Divorce: A Contractual Approach Aimed at Preserving Party Expectations,* 50 UCLA L.Rev. 1065, 1090 & n. 156 (2003) (stating "surveys of couples that have stored frozen embryos suggest that they may be prone to changing their minds while their embryos remain frozen" and citing a study that found " '[o]f the 41 couples that had recorded both a pre-treatment and post-treatment decision about embryo disposition, only 12(29%) kept the same disposition choice' "(citation omitted)). One's erroneous prediction of how she or he will feel about the matter at some point in the future can have grave repercussions. "Like decisions about marriage or relinquishing a child for adoption, decisions about the use of one's reproductive capacity have lifelong consequences for a person's identity and sense of self":

> When chosen voluntarily, becoming a parent can be an important act of self-definition. Compelled parenthood, by contrast, imposes an unwanted identity on the individual, forcing her to redefine herself, her place in the world, and the legacy she will leave after she dies. For some people, the mandatory destruction of an embryo can have equally profound consequences, particularly for those who believe that embryos are persons. If forced destruction is experienced as the loss of a child, it can lead to life-altering feelings of mourning, guilt, and regret.

Coleman, 84 Minn. L.Rev. at 96–97. To accommodate these concerns, advocates of the mutual-consent model propose "no embryo should be used by either partner, donated to another patient, used in research, or destroyed without the [contemporaneous] mutual consent of the couple that created the embryo." *Id.* at 110. Under this alternate framework,

> advance instructions would not be treated as binding contracts. If either partner has a change of mind about disposition decisions made in advance, that person's current objection would take precedence over the

prior consent. If one of the partners rescinds an advance disposition decision and the other does not, the mutual consent principle would not be satisfied and the previously agreed-upon disposition decision could not be carried out. . . .

> When the couple is unable to agree to any disposition decision, the most appropriate solution is to keep the embryos where they are—in frozen storage. Unlike the other possible disposition decisions—use by one partner, donation to another patient, donation to research, or destruction—keeping the embryos frozen is not final and irrevocable. By preserving the status quo, it makes it possible for the partners to reach an agreement at a later time.

Id. at 110–12; *see also id.* at 89 (suggesting "the embryo would remain in frozen storage until the parties reach a new agreement, the embryo is no longer viable, or storage facilities are no longer available"); *accord* Lawrence Note, 52 Case W. Res. L.Rev. at 742. Although this model precludes one party's use of the embryos to have children over the objection of the other party, the outcome under the contractual approach and the balancing test would generally be the same. *See A.Z. v. B.Z.*, 431 Mass. 150, 725 N.E.2d 1051, 1057–58 (2000) ("As a matter of public policy, . . . forced procreation is not an area amenable to judicial enforcement."); *J.B.*, 783 A.2d at 717 (evaluating relative interests of parties in disposition of embryos, concluding husband should not be able to use embryos over wife's objection); *Davis*, 842 S.W.2d at 604 ("Ordinarily, the party wishing to avoid procreation should prevail."); Susan B. Apel, *Disposition of Frozen Embryos: Are Contracts the Solution?,* Vermont Bar Journal, March 2001, at 31 ("Some argue that the party seeking to avoid procreation should prevail, and indeed, this appears to be the one harmonizing rationale of the four reported cases.") [hereinafter "Apel"].

    3. *Balancing test.* The New Jersey Supreme Court appears to have adopted an analysis regarding the disposition of frozen human embryos that incorporates the idea of contemporaneous decision-making, but not that of mutual consent. In *J.B.,* the New Jersey court rejected the *Kass* and *Davis* contractual approach, noting public policy concerns in "[e]nforcement of a contract that would allow the implantation of preembryos at some future date in a case where one party has reconsidered his or her earlier acquiescence." 783 A.2d at 718. The court stated:

> We believe that the better rule, and the one we adopt, is to enforce agreements entered into at the time in vitro fertilization is begun, *subject to the right of either party to change his or her mind about disposition up to the point of use or destruction of any stored preembryos.*

Id. at 719 (emphasis added). The court based its decision on "[t]he public policy concerns that underlie limitations on contracts involving family relationships." *Id.; see also A.Z.,* 725 N.E.2d at 1057–58 (refusing, in light of the same public policy concerns, to enforce an agreement that allowed the wife, upon the parties' separation, to use the couple's preembryos for implantation).

    The New Jersey court did not, however, adopt the requirement for mutual consent as a prerequisite for any use or disposition of the preembryos. Rather, that court stated that "if there is a disagreement between the parties as to disposition . . . , the interests of both parties must be evaluated" by the court. *J.B.,* 783 A.2d at 719. This balancing test was also the default analysis employed by the Tennessee Supreme Court in *Davis* where the parties had not executed a written agreement. *See Davis,* 842 S.W.2d at 604 (holding in the absence of a prior agreement concerning disposition, "the relative interests of the parties in using or not using the preembryos must be weighed" by the court).

The obvious problem with the balancing test model is its internal inconsistency. *See generally* Lawrence Note, 52 Case W. Res. L.Rev. at 738 (suggesting "[t]he premise of the balancing test . . . is flawed"). Public policy concerns similar to those that prompt courts to refrain from enforcement of contracts addressing reproductive choice demand even more strongly that we not substitute the courts as decision makers in this highly emotional and personal area. Nonetheless, that is exactly what happens under the decisional framework based on the balancing test because the court must weigh the relative interests of the parties in deciding the disposition of embryos when the parties cannot agree. *See J.B.,* 783 A.2d at 719.

D. *Discussion.* With these alternative approaches in mind, we turn to the present case. . . .

[A]re prior agreements regarding the future disposition of embryos enforceable when one of the donors is no longer comfortable with his or her prior decision? We first note our agreement with other courts considering such matters that the partners who created the embryos have the primary, and equal, decision-making authority with respect to the use or disposition of their embryos. We think, however, that it would be against the public policy of this state to enforce a prior agreement between the parties in this highly personal area of reproductive choice when one of the parties has changed his or her mind concerning the disposition or use of the embryos.

Our statutes and case law evidence an understanding that decisions involving marital and family relationships are emotional and subject to change. For example, Iowa law imposes a seventy-two hour waiting period after the birth of a child before the biological parents can release parental rights. *See* Iowa Code § 600A.4(2)(*g*). In addition, although this court has not abolished claims for breach of promise to marry,[3] only recovery of monetary damages is permitted; the court will not force a party to actually consummate the marriage. *See* Herbert F. Goodrich, *Iowa Decisions on Breach of Marriage Promise,* 4 Iowa L. Bull. 166, 177 (1918). It has also long been recognized in this state that agreements for the purpose of bringing about a dissolution of marriage are contrary to public policy and therefore void. *Barngrover v. Pettigrew,* 128 Iowa 533, 535, 104 N.W. 904, 904 (1905) . . . .

This court has also expressed a general reluctance to become involved in intimate questions inherent in personal relationships. *See Miller v. Miller,* 78 Iowa 177, 179–80, 42 N.W. 641, 641 (1889). In *Miller,* we refused to enforce a contract between husband and wife that required, in part, each "to behave respectfully, and fairly treat the other." *Id.* at 180, 42 N.W. at 641. We explained our refusal on the following grounds:

---

3. This court has not had a breach-of-contract-to-marry case before it in over fifty years. *See Bearbower v. Merry,* 266 N.W.2d 128, 132 (Iowa 1978) (citing *Benson v. Williams,* 239 Iowa 742, 32 N.W.2d 813 (1948)).

[J]udicial inquiry into matters of that character, between husband and wife, would be fraught with irreparable mischief, and forbidden by sound considerations of public policy.

It is the genius of our laws, as well as of our civilization, that matters pertaining so directly and exclusively to the home, and its value as such, and which are so generally susceptible of regulation and control by those influences which surround it, are not to become matters of public concern or inquiry.

Id. at 182, 42 N.W. at 642; *accord Heacock v. Heacock,* 108 Iowa 540, 542, 79 N.W. 353, 354 (1899) ("Husband and wife cannot contract with each other to secure the performance of their marital rights and duties."). Certainly reproductive decisions are likewise not proper matters of judicial inquiry and enforcement.

We have considered and rejected the arguments of some commentators that embryo disposition agreements are analogous to antenuptial agreements and divorce stipulations, which courts generally enforce. *See* Apel, Vermont Bar Journal at 31. Whether embryos are viewed as having life or simply as having the potential for life, this characteristic or potential renders embryos fundamentally distinct from the chattels, real estate, and money that are the subjects of antenuptial agreements. Divorce stipulations are also distinguishable. While such agreements may address custody issues, they are contemporaneous with the implementation of the stipulation, an attribute noticeably lacking in disposition agreements.

In addition to decisional and statutory authority supporting a public policy against judicial enforcement of personal decisions concerning marriage, family, and reproduction, our statutes also anticipate the effect of a couple's dissolution on their prior decisions. For example, Iowa Code section 633.271 provides that if a testator is divorced after making a will, "all provisions in the will in favor of the testator's spouse" are automatically revoked. Similarly, Iowa Code section 633.3107 revokes all provisions in a revocable trust in favor of the settlor's spouse upon divorce or dissolution of the marriage. Similar considerations make enforcement of contracts between partners involving such personal decisions as the use and disposition of their combined genetic material equally problematic. As noted by one commentator, embryos are originally created as "a mutual undertaking by [a] couple to have children together." Coleman, 84 Minn. L.Rev. at 83. Agreements made in that context are not always consistent with the parties' wishes once the mutual undertaking has ended.

We think judicial decisions and statutes in Iowa reflect respect for the right of individuals to make family and reproductive decisions based on their current views and values. They also reveal awareness that such decisions are highly emotional in nature and subject to a later change of heart. For this reason, we think judicial enforcement of an agreement *between a couple* regarding their future family and reproductive choices would be against the public policy of this state.

Our decision should not be construed, however, to mean that disposition agreements *between donors and fertility clinics* have no validity at all. We recognize a disposition or storage agreement serves an important purpose in defining and governing the relationship between the couple and the medical facility, ensuring that all parties understand their respective rights and obligations. *See A.Z.,* 725 N.E.2d at 1057 n. 22 ("We also recognize that agreements among donors and IVF clinics are essential to clinic operations."). In fact, it is this relationship, between the couple on the one side and the medical facility on the other, that dispositional contracts are intended to address. *See generally* Ellen A. Waldman, *Disputing Over Embryos: Of Contracts and Consents,* 32 Ariz. St. L.J. 897, 918 (2000) (noting "courts and most scholarly authorities would transform documents designed to record the transmission of medical information from clinic to couple, and the couple's acceptance of medical treatment, into a binding agreement between the couple itself"). Within this context, the medical facility and the donors should be able to rely on the terms of the parties' contract. *See A.Z.,* 725 N.E.2d at 1057 n. 22 (noting court's decision not to enforce agreement between partners is not an "impediment to the enforcement of such contracts by the clinics or by the donors against the clinics"); *J.B.,* 783 A.2d at 719.

In view of these competing needs, we reject the contractual approach and hold that agreements entered into at the time in vitro fertilization is commenced are enforceable and binding on the parties, "subject to the right of either party to change his or her mind about disposition up to the point of use or destruction of any stored embryo." *J.B.,* 783 A.2d at 719. This decisional model encourages prior agreements that can guide the actions of all parties, unless a later objection to any dispositional provision is asserted. It also recognizes that, *absent a change of heart by one of the partners,* an agreement governing disposition of embryos does not violate public policy. Only when one person makes known the agreement no longer reflects his or her current values or wishes is public policy implicated. Upon this occurrence, allowing either party to withdraw his or her agreement to a disposition that person no longer accepts acknowledges the public policy concerns inherent in enforcing prior decisions of a fundamentally personal nature. In fairness to the medical facility that is a party to the agreement, however, any change of intention must be communicated in writing to all parties in order to reopen the disposition issues covered by the agreement. *Id.*

That brings us, then, to the dilemma presented when one or both partners change their minds and the parties cannot reach a mutual decision on disposition. We have already explained the grave public policy concerns we have with the balancing test, which simply substitutes the court as decision maker. A better principle to apply, we think, is the requirement of contemporaneous mutual consent. Under that model, no transfer, release, disposition, or use of the embryos can occur without the signed authorization of both donors. If a stalemate results, the status quo would be maintained. The practical effect will be that the embryos are stored indefinitely unless both parties can agree to destroy the fertilized eggs. Thus, any expense associated with maintaining the status quo should logically be borne by the person opposing destruction. *See* Coleman, 84 Minn. L.Rev. at 112 ("The right to insist on the continued storage of the embryos should be dependent on a willingness to pay the associated costs.").

Turning to the present case, we find a situation in which one party no longer concurs in the parties' prior agreement with respect to the disposition of their frozen embryos, but the parties have been unable to reach a new agreement that is mutually satisfactory. Based on this fact, under the principles we have set forth today, we hold there can be no use or disposition of the

Wittens' embryos unless Trip and Tamera reach an agreement.[4] Until then, the party or parties who oppose destruction shall be responsible for any storage fees. Therefore, we affirm the trial court's ruling enjoining both parties from transferring, releasing, or utilizing the embryos without the other's written consent. . . .

. . . DISPOSITION.

We affirm the trial court's decree [concerning the disposition of the embryos]. . . .

T.F. v. B.L.

Supreme Judicial Court of Massachusetts, 2004.
442 Mass. 522, 813 N.E.2d 1244.

Present: MARSHALL, C.J., GREANEY, IRELAND, SPINA, COWIN, SOSMAN, & CORDY, JJ.

COWIN, J.

The plaintiff, T.F., and the defendant, B.L., are two women who lived together from 1996 to 2000. During this time, the plaintiff became pregnant through artificial insemination, and in July, 2000, after the couple had separated, she gave birth to a child. In January, 2001, the plaintiff filed a complaint in the Probate and Family Court Department. Based on theories of promissory estoppel and breach of an oral contract, she requested that the defendant be ordered to pay child support under the child support guidelines. See G.L. c. 119, § 28 (*d*). The judge found that there was an agreement "to create a child," which the defendant had breached. However, the judge did not issue an order of support. Instead, she reported the matter to the Appeals Court pursuant to G.L. c. 215, § 13, see *Gray v. Commissioner of Revenue,* 422 Mass. 666, 667, 665 N.E.2d 17 (1996), for a determination whether "parenthood by contract is the law of Massachusetts." If this question were answered in the affirmative, she opined, "then [the defendant] is a parent." We granted the plaintiff's application for direct appellate review. We conclude that while the plaintiff has established the existence of an implied agreement, "parenthood by contract" is not the law of Massachusetts and the agreement is unenforceable as against public policy. Therefore, this defendant has no obligation of child support and the Probate and Family Court cannot create such an obligation pursuant to its equity jurisdiction.

BACKGROUND

We summarize the facts found by the Probate and Family Court judge, which findings were warranted by the evidence. The plaintiff and defendant met in 1995, and began living together in the fall of 1996. On May 30, 1999, the couple held a "commitment ceremony." Subsequently, they pooled their money and nominated each other as beneficiaries of their respective life insurance policies and retirement plans. The plaintiff had long wanted to have a child, and communicated her feelings to the defendant on several occasions.

---

4. We do not mean to imply that UNMC's obligation to store the embryos extends beyond the ten-year period provided in the parties' contract.

The first such conversation occurred as early as six months into the relationship. The defendant, who had grown up in an abusive household, doubted her own fitness to be a parent. She also had experienced psychological problems in the past, and was undergoing treatment for a recurrence of depression in the spring and summer of 1999. The defendant continued her resistance to having a child until one day in June or July of 1999, when she telephoned the plaintiff at work and told her that she had changed her mind. The plaintiff suggested they talk more about it that evening.

The couple did discuss the matter further (the 1999 conversation). They covered such topics as whether they would rather have a boy or a girl, the defendant's reasons for her change of heart, whether the defendant's brother would be a suitable sperm donor, baptism and schooling, and the division of labor between the couple, should they have a child. As a result of the 1999 conversation, the plaintiff scheduled an appointment with her doctor to discuss pregnancy. The plaintiff went to that appointment alone, but subsequently both parties attended appointments with a second doctor at a facility specializing in reproduction and fertility procedures (clinic). This doctor performed tests that disclosed that the plaintiff had a condition that would make pregnancy difficult and would require delivery by Caesarian section. The parties discussed whether the defendant could be the birth mother instead, but a degenerative disc in her back would have made pregnancy even more difficult for her. After rejecting other options such as adoption or a foster child, the parties decided to proceed with the plaintiff's artificial insemination.

On August 6, 1999, the clinic presented the couple with a document entitled "Consent Form: Therapeutic Donor Sperm Insemination."[2] The parties worked together to select an anonymous donor. The couple used joint funds for insemination and prenatal care expenses. The defendant's actions during this period were at least in part an effort to preserve her relationship with the plaintiff, which she believed would have suffered had she attempted to prevent the plaintiff from having a child. The defendant told her sister and a friend that, from the time of the 1999 conversation, she "went along" with having a baby because she got "tired of the arguments" and "didn't want to take [the plaintiff's] dream away."

After one unsuccessful insemination, the parties discussed how many more such procedures they could afford, and agreed to go forward with a further attempt. In December, 1999, the plaintiff became pregnant as the result of the second insemination.

The parties' relationship deteriorated in the following months, and the defendant moved out of their apartment in May, 2000. Prior to leaving, the defendant expressed her regrets about being a "separated parent," said she desired to adopt the child, and "promised financial support and promised to talk later about the details since she wanted to just focus on the break-up of the relationship at that time." On July 1, 2000, the plaintiff went into premature labor and gave birth to a boy.

2. The consent form, among other things, memorialized the parties' agreement to hold the clinic and its personnel harmless for the support of any child born as the result of procedures performed there. Both the plaintiff and defendant signed the form in the space labeled "Recipient."

We recite the facts following the conception and birth of the child as they may be relevant to the parties' contractual intent. See *Martino v. First Nat'l Bank,* 361 Mass. 325, 332, 280 N.E.2d 174 (1972), quoting *Pittsfield & N.A.R. Corp. v. Boston & A. R. Co.,* 260 Mass. 390, 398, 157 N.E. 611 (1927) ("There is no surer way to find out what parties meant, than to see what they have done"). The defendant visited the mother and child in the hospital several times, participated in selecting his name, and promised to provide support and to change her work hours to help raise him. During one of these visits, the defendant gave the plaintiff $800. On July 26, 2000, the defendant sent pictures of herself with the child, via the Internet, to friends accompanied by the message: "I hope you all enjoy the pics of my wonderful, beautiful boy." In October, 2000, the parties argued for over an hour about support for the child, who, as the result of his premature birth, required a great deal of medical attention. The plaintiff had been parenting the child and working full time, and wanted financial assistance from the defendant. The defendant "acknowledged that she was not paying child support because she was angry at [the plaintiff]." Later that month, the defendant sent a letter to the plaintiff, declaring that she desired no further contact with the plaintiff or the child.

The judge found that there was no written agreement between the parties regarding having a child together, that the defendant is not biologically related to the child, and that she has never lived with him. The judge found further that the defendant's name does not appear on the birth certificate, that she did not adopt the child, and that she has made no financial contributions for the benefit of the child, except the payment of $800 to the plaintiff shortly after the baby was born.*

Analyzing the facts, the judge concluded that there was no evidence of an explicit oral promise by the defendant, except to "explore the possibility of having a child." However, the judge concluded that this promise, because of

---

* Other facts found by the trial judge were included in an Appendix to the dissenting opinion in this case. Among these other facts were the following:

"65. In May, 2000 [the defendant] moved out of the apartment, and the parties divided their joint money. By that time they were no longer speaking to each other. . . .

"75. [The defendant] visited the baby two more times at the [hospital]. There were discussions between the parties about finances ([the defendant] gave [the plaintiff] $800) and about [the plaintiff's] discomfort with [the defendant's] having introduced [her friend] into the visits. [The friend], formerly a good friend of [the plaintiff], had become [the defendant's] new partner. . . .

"79. [The defendant] continued until as late as August, 2000 to reiterate her wish to support the child. . . .

"81. In the argument, [the defendant] offered to take the child if he were such a burden to [the plaintiff]. [The plaintiff] responded that she was not asking to be relieved of the child but only wanted financial assistance.

"82. [The defendant] acknowledged that she was not paying child support because she was angry at [the plaintiff] about the arguments they were having.

"83. [The plaintiff] testified that she received a letter (the original of which has been lost). The copy of the letter (offered over objection and taken *de bene*) is undated and unsigned, and, although it bears a postmark which indicates that it was mailed on October 31, it shows no legible year. The letter is addressed to [the plaintiff's first name] and it refers to [the child's first name]. It relates the reasoning of the writer who has decided not to have any further relationship with [the child] 'for the well-being of my son.'

"84. The Court finds that the letter was written by [the defendant] in late October, 2000. In the letter, [the defendant] expresses her intention to have no further interaction with the child. It asserts that [the defendant's] motivation is to protect [the child] by her withdrawal from his life. She asserts her love for the boy. She ends by requesting that [the plaintiff] stop contacting her at all."

(Footnote by ed.)

the defendant's subsequent behavior and failure to "stop or slow down" the plaintiff's pregnancy, "grew naturally and actively into the creation of a child," and thus the creation of a binding contract between the parties. The defendant breached this contract, the judge continued, by refusing to perform the obligations of parenthood (i.e., to provide child support).

ANALYSIS

The plaintiff's argument for imposing a child support obligation on the defendant is essentially two pronged. First, she claims that the defendant entered into an enforceable implied contract with her to coparent a child, or at least that she impliedly promised to support the child, and is now estopped from denying that support. The defendant's refusal to pay child support, the argument goes, is therefore a breach of contract. Second, the plaintiff asserts that an order of child support in the present situation would be consistent with oft-expressed legislative policies as manifested in related statutes, and that the "broad and flexible" equity powers of the Probate and Family Court can and should be invoked to implement said polices. We discuss these arguments in turn.

a. "Parenthood by contract."

The plaintiff does not contend that there was any express written agreement between the parties,[3] but rather that the defendant's initial statement, in the summer of 1999, that she wished to discuss having a child, followed by her course of conduct, reflect an implied contract to create a child. In the absence of an express agreement, an implied contract may be inferred from (1) the conduct of the parties and (2) the relationship of the parties. See *W.A. Snow Iron Works, Inc. v. Chadwick,* 227 Mass. 382, 390, 116 N.E. 801 (1917); *LiDonni, Inc. v. Hart,* 355 Mass. 580, 583, 246 N.E.2d 446 (1969). See also *Grant v. Carlisle,* 328 Mass. 25, 29, 101 N.E.2d 376 (1951). An implied contract requires proof that there was a benefit to the defendant, that the plaintiff expected the defendant to pay for that benefit, and that the defendant expected, or a reasonable person should have expected, that he or she would have to pay for that benefit.[4] *LiDonni, Inc. v. Hart, supra* at 583, 246 N.E.2d 446. When the defendant was, or should have been, aware of the plaintiff's expectations in this regard, the defendant's failure to object can create a contract. E.g., *Therrien v. LeBlanc,* 282 Mass. 328, 331, 185 N.E. 15 (1933); *Maynard v. Fabyan,* 267 Mass. 312, 315, 166 N.E. 629 (1929). The defendant's subjective intent is irrelevant when she knows or has reason to know that her objective actions manifest the existence of an agreement. See Restatement (Second) of Contracts § 19 (1981).

In this case, the evidence warranted the judge's finding that there was an agreement by the defendant to undertake the responsibilities of a parent in consideration of the plaintiff's conceiving and bearing a child. Although the defendant claims that the plaintiff should not have relied on her passive

---

3. The clinic "consent form" is not a written contract between the plaintiff and the defendant, for its primary purposes were to explain the risks of the insemination procedure and to define the couple's legal relationship as a unit with the clinic. See *A.Z. v. B.Z.,* 431 Mass. 150, 158, 725 N.E.2d 1051 (2000). That form does not state, nor does the record show, that the parties intended it to act as, or be a part of, any binding agreement between them. See *id.*

4. We do not address the issue of consideration but assume, without deciding, that there was consideration for this contract.

silence, the judge reasonably concluded that the circumstances and relations of the parties, as stated in her findings, told a different story. The parties cohabited for several years as a couple, pooling all their financial resources. After the 1999 conversation, the plaintiff agreed to conceive and give birth to a child. Following this agreement, the defendant not only did not object, but actively participated in medical decisions and procedures, and in discussions about the child's future and the finances related to the conception and raising of the child. Furthermore, the judge found that the defendant intentionally manifested an outward desire to have a child in order to maintain her relationship with the plaintiff. A finding of an implied contract based on these facts, while not compelled, was certainly permissible.

The conclusion does not end our analysis; the question remains whether the court can enforce this contract. Contracts between unmarried cohabitants regarding property, finance, and other matters are normally enforceable. See *Wilcox v. Trautz,* 427 Mass. 326, 332, 693 N.E.2d 141 (1998). Such contracts may concern the welfare and support of children, provided they do not contravene the best interests of the child. *Id.* at 334 n. 7, 693 N.E.2d 141. See *E.N.O. v. L.M.M.,* 429 Mass. 824, 831, 711 N.E.2d 886, cert. denied, 528 U.S. 1005, 120 S.Ct. 500, 145 L.Ed.2d 386 (1999). Contracts between unmarried same-sex couples concerning the welfare and support of a child stand on the same footing as any other agreement between unmarried cohabitants. See *id.* at 831 n. 9, 711 N.E.2d 886. However, when a contract violates or conflicts with public policy, we treat it as void and will not enforce it. *A.Z. v. B.Z.,* 431 Mass. 150, 160, 725 N.E.2d 1051 (2000), and cases cited....

In *A.Z. v. B.Z., supra* at 159–160, 725 N.E.2d 1051, we refused to enforce an agreement that compelled a party "to become a parent against his or her will." In that case, the plaintiff successfully prevented his estranged wife from using his own sperm (which had been frozen and stored by an in vitro fertilization clinic) to create a child. *Id.* at 150–153, 725 N.E.2d 1051. "[F]orced procreation," we concluded, "is not an area amenable to judicial enforcement." *Id.* at 160, 725 N.E.2d 1051. The present case is factually distinguishable in that the defendant's contribution to the conception and birth of the child arose from contractual intent rather than from her genetic material. However, important concerns underlying that decision also apply here.

We determine public policy by looking "to the expressions of the Legislature and to those of this court." *Id.* at 160–161, 725 N.E.2d 1051, citing *Capazzoli v. Holzwasser,* 397 Mass. 158, 160, 490 N.E.2d 420 (1986). In the *A.Z.* case we noted that, by statute, a contract to enter into a marital relationship is not enforceable. *Id.* at 161, 725 N.E.2d 1051, citing G.L. c. 207, § 47A. We also discussed earlier cases that had "indicated a reluctance to enforce prior agreements that bind individuals to future family relationships." *Id.,* citing *R.R. v. M.H.,* 426 Mass. 501, 510, 689 N.E.2d 790 (1998) (agreement by which surrogate mother agreed to give up child at birth was unenforceable unless agreement contained, inter alia, "reasonable" waiting period consistent with waiting period in adoption surrender); *Capazzoli v. Holzwasser, supra* at 160–161, 490 N.E.2d 420 (contract requiring individual to abandon marriage unenforceable). See *A.R. v. C.R.,* 411 Mass. 570, 574–575, 583 N.E.2d 840 (1992) (where plaintiff was not biological father of two children, he could not be equitably estopped from denying paternity based on representations he made to their mother). We concluded that in order to protect the "freedom of personal choice in matters of marriage and family life," *A.Z. v. B.Z., supra* at 162, 725 N.E.2d 1051, quoting *Moore v. East Cleveland,* 431 U.S. 494, 499, 97 S.Ct. 1932, 52 L.Ed.2d 531 (1977), "prior agreements to enter into familial relationships (marriage or parenthood) should not be enforced against individuals who subsequently reconsider their decisions." *A.Z. v. B.Z., supra.*

The principles expressed by this court in *A.Z. v. B.Z., supra,* are applicable, and of like force, in the present case. The decision to become, or not to become, a parent is a personal right of "such delicate and intimate character that direct enforcement ... by any process of the court should never be attempted." *Id.,* quoting *Kenyon v. Chicopee,* 320 Mass. 528, 534, 70 N.E.2d 241 (1946). "Parenthood by contract" is not the law in Massachusetts, and to the extent the plaintiff and the defendant entered into an agreement, express or implied, to coparent a child, that agreement is unenforceable.[8]

The dissent acknowledges that the agreement to create a child was unenforceable, but insists that this agreement "includes" an enforceable promise to pay child support. *Post* at 535, 813 N.E.2d at 1255. Our authority to enforce the lawful portion of an otherwise illegal contract depends on whether that portion is severable from the larger agreement. *Bishop v. Palmer,* 146 Mass. 469, 474, 16 N.E. 299 (1888) ("If the bad part of the consideration is not severable from the good, the whole promise fails"). In the present case, the appropriate inquiry is whether there was a specific identifiable agreement to support the child contained within the implied contract to create and parent the child, and, if so, whether that agreement is severable from the implied contract. The Probate and Family Court judge suggested that an agreement to become a parent inherently involves four promises: (1) that the "parties will continue to love the child," (2) "support each other," (3) "provide child care," and (4) "provide financial support for the child." Nothing in the record gives substance or meaning to any specific promise to provide child support separate and apart from the implied agreement to create a child; support was, as the judge stated, one of the inherent consequences of parenthood. Furthermore, where a portion of a contract is separably enforceable, that portion would ordinarily confer delineated benefits and obligations on both sides. E.g., *Carrig v. Gilbert–Varker Corp.,* 314 Mass. 351, 357–358, 50 N.E.2d 59 (1943). But here, nothing in the record shows a distinct consideration in return for child support apart from the core, unenforceable promise to coparent. Therefore, any implied promise that the defendant made respecting child support is inextricably linked to her unenforceable promise to coparent the child, and is similarly unenforceable.

[The majority also concluded as follows: (1) The defendant did not have a statutory obligation to support the child, because she was not a "parent" within the meaning of the Massachusetts statute that governed child support. (2) The defendant was not a "de facto" parent, because she had no relationship with the child. (3) In the absence of a statutory duty, equity did not provide a remedy against the defendant. (4) The best-interests-of-the-child standard did not apply to this case because that standard applies only to classes of persons who have a legal obligation to a child.]

---

8. Concluding, as we do, that there was an implied contract to create a child but that it was unenforceable, we need not address the plaintiff's promissory estoppel argument. The same public policy considerations apply to this alternative theory of recovery.

In response to the Probate and Family Court judge's report of the matter, we conclude that "parenthood by contract" is not the law in Massachusetts. This case is remanded to the Probate and Family Court for further proceedings consistent with this opinion.

So ordered.

GREANEY, J. (concurring in part and dissenting in part, with whom Marshall, C.J., and Ireland, J., join).

An obligation to support a child can be created by express or implied agreement (as the court recognizes because the proposition is indisputable) or by conduct showing that the party to be charged has affirmatively committed to the obligation (equally indisputable). Based on the strong findings of the judge in the Probate and Family Court, there is an enforceable obligation to pay support here.

a.   I agree that parenthood by contract is not the law in Massachusetts, for the reason, if no other, that parenthood is a status conferred by law and not one that can be conferred by a private agreement to which the child is not (and cannot be) a party. See *R.R. v. M.H.*, 426 Mass. 501, 512, 689 N.E.2d 790 (1998). Both the Legislature and this court have stated many times, and in many contexts, that the Probate and Family Court has full authority to review any agreement within its purview that implicates a child's best interests. Parenthood by contract could oust, or at least weaken, the established power of the court to protect the child's best interests. . . .

b.   The inquiry, however, does not end here. The judge, who heard testimony from eight witnesses and examined numerous exhibits during three days of trial, made careful findings and concluded that: "The decision to create this child was even more conscious and deliberate than the decision that is made by some couples who are both biological parents and conceive a child by direct sexual intercourse. That was the agreement: to create a child. First the parties explored the ways to accomplish that agreement and then they went forward together to accomplish it." The defendant cannot be held to be a parent by contract, but her agreement with the plaintiff includes a promise to support the child that she and the plaintiff agreed to create (by way of artificial insemination) and to parent together. That promise to support is well established by the judge's findings and should not be facilely cast aside as the court does. . . . A person cannot participate, in the way the defendant did, in bringing a child into the world, and then walk away from a support obligation.

The plaintiff ultimately seeks an order of child support. The Legislature has long recognized the importance of child support for all children. It has expressed, in unmistakable terms, that "dependent children shall be maintained, as completely as possible, from the resources of their parents" and not by the taxpayers, and that support determinations should be made in "the best interests of the child." G.L. c. 119A, § 1. . . . With respect to children born out of wedlock, the Legislature has declared that "[c]hildren born to parents who are not married to each other shall be entitled to the same rights and protections of the law as all other children." G.L. c. 209C, § 1. . . . The Legislature has in many ways "affirmatively supported the assistive reproductive technologies" that enable couples to conceive children in the absence of sexual intercourse. . . . In G.L. c. 46, § 4B, the Legislature made clear that the parentage of children born as a result of artificial insemination does not depend on biology but may be determined on the basis of consent. See *R.R. v. M.H., supra* at 510, 689 N.E.2d 790 (§ 4B "concern[s] the status of a child born to a fertile mother whose husband, presumably infertile, consented to her artificial insemination with the sperm of another man so that the couple could have a child biologically related to the mother"). We have stated that "[r]epeatedly, forcefully, and unequivocally, the Legislature has expressed its will that all children be 'entitled to the same rights and protections of the law' regardless of the accidents of their birth." . . . The Legislature has yet to contemplate the situation here.

The plaintiff's resort to the equity jurisdiction of the Probate and Family Court is entirely appropriate. That our statutes offer the plaintiff no remedy, because the defendant is not a legal parent, does not preclude an order of child support. Cf. *E.N.O.* v. *L.M.M., supra* at 828 & n. 4, 711 N.E.2d 886 (visitation). The Legislature has declared that the Probate and Family Court "shall have original and concurrent jurisdiction with the supreme judicial court and the superior court department of all cases and matters of equity cognizable under the general principles of equity jurisprudence and, with reference thereto, shall be courts of general equity jurisdiction." G.L. c. 215, § 6. This grant of equitable power is plenary and "extends to actions necessary to afford any relief in the best interests of a person under [the court's] jurisdiction." *Matter of Moe,* 385 Mass. 555, 561, 432 N.E.2d 712 (1982). . . . This authority extends as well to the specific enforcement of agreements, including, as here, one to support a child. See *Ross v. Ross,* 371 Mass. 439, 439–440, 358 N.E.2d 437 (1976) (separation agreement); *Suga v. Maum,* 29 Mass.App.Ct. 733, 736, 565 N.E.2d 793 (1991) (agreement to convey land); *Ross v. Friedman,* 22 Mass.App.Ct. 513, 515–516, 495 N.E.2d 321 (1986) (agreement to sell shares of stock).[1] . . . The Legislature, thus, has conferred on the Probate and Family Court broad equitable authority (including the power to compel specific performance) that, although not unbounded, extends to deciding many specific and complex child-related issues that have not been foreseen by statute. . . .

The existence of an agreement to support on the part of the defendant, buttressed by society's interests (as expressed through our statutes and our case law) and the best interests of the child standard, requires relief here.[3]

---

1. The court's power to compel compliance with an agreement is not limited to circumstances where performance is promised in return for traditional consideration but includes those where the party held liable is bound by another's reasonable reliance on the promise. We do not use the term "promissory estoppel," but have treated the principles of estoppel as sufficient to create a contract. See *Cataldo Ambulance Serv., Inc. v. Chelsea,* 426 Mass. 383, 386 & n. 6, 688 N.E.2d 959 (1998); *Loranger Constr. Corp. v. E.F. Hauserman Co.,* 376 Mass. 757, 760, 384 N.E.2d 176 (1978). The prerequisites for a successful claim based on a theory of promissory estoppel are met in this case: (1) promises to parent and support a child that (2) the defendant should reasonably have known would cause the plaintiff to proceed with their joint plan for her to become pregnant by means of artificial insemination (3) which the plaintiff did (4) justifiably relying

on the defendant's affirmative conduct and promises, leaving the plaintiff in circumstances such that (5) injustice (to the plaintiff and to the child) can be avoided only by enforcement of the promise to support.

3. My analysis would be no different were the defendant an unmarried male partner who purposefully put himself in the position of a parent, by taking affirmative steps that resulted in the birth of a child whom he considered, for a time, to be his son, but subsequently attempted to disavow all of his parental responsibilities when his relationship with the child's mother deteriorated. This case is not about establishing parental rights of same-sex couples. It is about the defendant's taking financial responsibility for a child whom she had promised, by words and deeds, to support. When two adults decide together to create a child by way of artificial insemination, and agree together to assume financial responsibili-

See *A.R. v. C.R.*, 411 Mass. 570, 575–576, 583 N.E.2d 840 (1992). This conclusion finds support in decisions of courts in other jurisdictions involving facts of a similar nature. See Chambers *vs.* Chambers, No. CN 00–09493 (Del.Fam.Ct. Feb. 5, 2002); *L.S.K. v. H.A.N.*, 2002 PA Super 390, 813 A.2d 872, 878–879 (2002). See also *In re Marriage of Buzzanca*, 61 Cal.App.4th 1410, 1412, 72 Cal.Rptr.2d 280 (1998). But see *State ex rel. D.R.M.* and *Wood*, 109 Wash.App. 182, 189, 195, 34 P.3d 887 (2001) (that mother's former same-sex partner not obligated to pay child support because not parent under Uniform Parentage Act).

The conclusion is also in accord with those principles of the American Law Institute's (ALI) Principles of the Law of Family Dissolution, which, insofar as this case is concerned, recommend imposing a parental support obligation on a "person who may be not the child's parent under [S]tate law, but whose prior course of affirmative conduct equitably estops that person from denying a parental support obligation to the child." ALI Principles of the Law of Family Dissolution: Analysis and Recommendations § 3.03 & comment c (2002).[4] Section 3.03(1)(c) allows imposition of an order of support when a child is conceived "pursuant to an agreement between the person [to be charged] and the child's parent that they would share responsibility for raising the child and each would be a parent to the child." Where the conception of a child is achieved through artificial insemination, comment c suggests that, in the case of married or unmarried couples that execute a procreation agreement, the man "is to be treated as the father for purposes of child support." *Id.* at 417, 34 P.3d 887. In the case of same-sex couples that "wish to have children together [by way of] a sperm donation or a surrogate mother," a support obligation may be imposed on a party "who is not a parent but who has made a [§ 3.03(1)(c)] agreement with the child's parent."[5] *Id.*

ty for that child, and their decision and subsequent conduct leads to the birth of a child, that child is no less entitled to the financial support of both adults than had the adults been married, or had the child been conceived through sexual intercourse and thus was biologically linked to both adults.

4. Section 3.03(1) of the American Law Institute's (ALI) Principles of the Law of Family Dissolution: Analysis and Recommendations (2002) provides that a support obligation may arise when:

"(a) there was an explicit or implicit agreement or undertaking by the person to assume a parental support obligation to the child;

"(b) the child was born during the marriage or cohabitation of the person and the child's parent; or

"(c) the child was conceived pursuant to an agreement between the person and the child's parent that they would share responsibility for raising the child and each would be a parent to the child."

In determining whether a support obligation is justified, § 3.03(2) of the ALI Principles directs that a judge should consider:

"(a) whether the person and the child act toward each other as parent and child and, if so, the duration and strength of that behavior;

"(b) whether the parental undertaking of the person supplanted the child's opportunity to develop a relationship with an absent parent and to look to that parent for support;

"(c) whether the child otherwise has two parents who owe the child a duty of support and are able and available to provide support; and

"(d) any other facts that may relate to the equity of imposing a parental support duty on the person."

5. Nowhere in the ALI Principles does it state the requirement that this agreement need be in writing. Moreover, comment b of § 2.03, setting forth definitions for purposes of determining custodial responsibilities for children, makes clear that "[a] formal, written agreement is not required to create a parent-by-estoppel status." Principles of the Law of Family Dissolution: Analysis and Recommendations, *supra* at § 2.03 comment b, at 114 (allowing, however, that "the absence of for-

In summary: even though we do not recognize parenthood by contract, an agreement between the parties has been proved, which includes a promise of support, and the Probate and Family Court, acting under G.L. c. 215, § 6, has jurisdiction to hear the case and specifically to enforce that promise. That the defendant may regret her words and conduct, and view the remedy as harsh, is of no consequence. Equity does not relieve from difficult agreements simply because they are regretted. The child may have been abandoned by the defendant, but he should not be abandoned by the court. . . .

————

NOTE ON WHO IS A PARENT

In T.F. v. B.L., the majority concluded that the defendant was not a parent of the child within the meaning of the Massachusetts child-support statute. The California Supreme Court reached a different result, on analogous although perhaps distinguishable facts, in Elisa B. v. Superior Court, 37 Cal.4th 108, 117 P.3d 660, 33 Cal.Rptr.3d 46 (2005), under the Uniform Parentage Act (UPA).

In this case, Elisa B. and Emily B. were living together as partners. By joint agreement, Emily became pregnant through artificial insemination, and gave birth to twins. Elisa supported the household financially, and Elisa and her family publicly and privately treated the twins as Elisa's children. Subsequently, Elisa and Emily separated, and Emily sued for child support for the twins. Held, for Emily:

[T]he UPA provides that the parentage of a child does not depend upon " 'the marital status of the parents' ". . .

The UPA contains separate provisions defining who is a "mother" and who is a "father." Section 7610 provides that "[t]he parent and child relationship may be established . . . : [¶] (a) Between a child and the natural mother . . . by proof of her having given birth to the child, or under this part." Subdivision (b) of section 7610 states that the parental relationship "[b]etween a child and the natural father . . . may be established under this part."

Section 7611 provides several circumstances in which "[a] man is presumed to be the natural father of a child," including . . . if "[h]e receives the child into his home and openly holds out the child as his natural child" (§ 7611, subd. (d)).

Although . . . the UPA contains separate provisions defining who is a mother and who is a father, it expressly provides that in determining the existence of a mother and child relationship, "[i]nsofar as practicable, the provisions of this part applicable to the father and child relationship apply." (§ 7650.) . . .

malities may also affect the factfinder's determination of whether an agreement was made"). The proviso in § 7.04(1), cited by the defendant, that "[a]n agreement is not enforceable if it is not set forth in a writing signed by both parties," is not determinative in this case.

Id. at 960. The entire text of chapter 7, as well as its accompanying comments and illustrations, demonstrates that § 7.04 contemplates premarital, marital, and separation agreements, and not agreements purporting to assume responsibility for parenting a child.

We perceive no reason why both parents of a child cannot be women. That result now is possible under the current version of the domestic partnership statutes, which took effect this year. (§ 297 et seq.) Two women "who have chosen to share one another's lives in an intimate and committed relationship of mutual caring" and have a common residence (§ 297) can file with the Secretary of State a "Declaration of Domestic Partnership" (§ 298). Section 297.5, subdivision (d) provides, in pertinent part: "The rights and obligations of registered domestic partners with respect to a child of either of them shall be the same as those of spouses."

. . .

Subdivision (d) of [UPA] section 7611 states that a man is presumed to be the natural father of a child if "[h]e receives the child into his home and openly holds out the child as his natural child." The Court of Appeal in *In re Karen C.* (2002) 101 Cal.App.4th 932, 938, 124 Cal.Rptr.2d 677, held that subdivision (d) of section 7611 "should apply equally to women."

Applying section 7611, the court concluded that Elisa had received the twins into her home and held them out as her natural children, and therefore was a mother of the twins and liable for child support.

————

R.R. v. M.H., 426 Mass. 501, 689 N.E.2d 790 (1998). "On a report by a judge in the Probate and Family Court, we are concerned with the validity of a surrogacy parenting agreement between the plaintiff (father) and the defendant (mother). Both the mother and the father are married but not to each other. A child was conceived through artificial insemination of the mother with the father's sperm, after the mother and father had executed the surrogate parenting agreement [under which the father agreed to pay the surrogate mother $10,000, and the surrogate mother agreed] that the father would have custody of the child. [The mother actively sought to become a surrogate and entered into the surrogacy agreement voluntarily, advised by counsel, not under duress, and fully informed.] During the sixth month of her pregnancy and after she had received funds from the father pursuant to the surrogacy agreement, the mother changed her mind and decided that she wanted to keep the child.

"The father thereupon brought this action and obtained a preliminary order awarding him temporary custody of the child. . . .

". . . Policies underlying our adoption legislation suggest that a surrogate parenting agreement should be given no effect if the mother's agreement was obtained prior to a reasonable time after the child's birth or if her agreement was induced by the payment of money. Adoption legislation is, of course, not applicable to child custody, but it does provide us with some guidance. Although the agreement makes no reference to adoption and does not concern the termination of parental rights or the adoption of the child by the father's wife, the normal expectation in the case of a surrogacy agreement seems to be that the father's wife will adopt the child with the consent of the mother (and the father). Under G.L. c. 210, § 2, adoption requires the written consent of the father and the mother but, in these circumstances, not the mother's husband. Any such consent, written, witnessed, and notarized, is not to be executed "sooner than the fourth calendar day after the date of birth of the child to be adopted." *Id.* That statutory standard should be interpreted as providing that no mother may effectively agree to surrender her child for adoption earlier than the fourth day after its birth, by which time she better knows the strength of her bond with her child. Although a consent to surrender custody has less permanency than a consent to adoption, the legislative judgment that a mother should have time after a child's birth to reflect on her wishes concerning the child weighs heavily in our consideration whether to give effect to a prenatal custody agreement. No private agreement concerning adoption or custody can be conclusive in any event because a judge, passing on custody of a child, must decide what is in the best interests of the child. . . .

" . . . . [We conclude that the] mother's purported consent to custody in the agreement is ineffective because no such consent should be recognized unless given on or after the fourth day following the child's birth. In reaching this conclusion, we apply to consent to custody the same principle which underlies the statutory restriction on when a mother's consent to adoption may be effectively given. Moreover, the payment of money to influence the mother's custody decision makes the agreement as to custody void. Eliminating any financial reward to a surrogate mother is the only way to assure that no economic pressure will cause a woman, who may well be a member of an economically vulnerable class, to act as a surrogate. It is true that a surrogate enters into the agreement before she becomes pregnant and thus is not presented with the desperation that a poor unwed pregnant woman may confront. However, compensated surrogacy arrangements raise the concern that, under financial pressure, a woman will permit her body to be used and her child to be given away. . . .

"We recognize that there is nothing inherently unlawful in an arrangement by which an informed woman agrees to attempt to conceive artificially and give birth to a child whose father would be the husband of an infertile wife. We suspect that many such arrangements are made and carried out without disagreement.

"If no compensation is paid beyond pregnancy-related expenses and if the mother is not bound by her consent to the father's custody of the child unless she consents after a suitable period has passed following the child's birth, the objections we have identified in this opinion to the enforceability of a surrogate's consent to custody would be overcome. Other conditions might be important in deciding the enforceability of a surrogacy agreement, such as a requirement that (a) the mother's husband give his informed consent to the agreement in advance; (b) the mother be an adult and have had at least one successful pregnancy; (c) the mother, her husband, and the intended parents have been evaluated for the soundness of their judgment and for their capacity to carry out the agreement; (d) the father's wife be incapable of bearing a child without endangering her health; (e) the intended parents be suitable persons to assume custody of the child; and (f) all parties have the advice of counsel. The mother and father may not, however, make a binding best-interests-of-the-child determination by private agreement. Any custody agreement is subject to a judicial determination of custody based on the best interests of the child.

"The conditions that we describe are not likely to be satisfactory to an intended father because, following the birth of the child, the mother can refuse to consent to the father's custody even though the father has incurred substantial pregnancy-related expenses. A surrogacy agreement judicially approved before conception may be a better procedure, as is permitted by statutes in Virginia and New Hampshire."

————

NOTE ON SURROGATE–PARENTING LEGISLATION

As of the time this casebook is written, seventeen states have adopted statutes concerning surrogacy. These statutes vary widely. For example, the District of Columbia, Indiana, Michigan, New York, and North Dakota either forbid surrogacy contracts or make such contracts void and unenforceable. See D.C. Code § 16–402; Indiana Code § 31–20–1–1; Mich. Comp. Laws § 722.855; N.Y. Dom. Rel. Law § 122; N.D. Cent. Code § 14–18–05. Arkansas allows surrogacy contracts. See Ark. Code § 9–10–201. Washington allows uncompensated surrogacy contracts. See Wash. Rev. Code §§ 26.26.210–260. New Mexico allows uncompensated surrogacy contracts and payment of the surrogate's medical and similar expenses. See N.M. Stat. §§ 32A–5–34(B), (F). Nebraska renders paid surrogacy contracts unenforceable, but says nothing about unpaid surrogacy. Neb. Rev. Stat. § 25–21,200. Nevada and Virginia allow unpaid surrogacy contracts but only where the prospective parents are married couples. See Nev. Rev. Stat. § 126.045; Va. Code § 20–158.

————

42 U.S. CODE § 274e. PROHIBITION OF ORGAN PURCHASES

(a) *Prohibition*. It shall be unlawful for any person to knowingly acquire, receive, or otherwise transfer any human organ for valuable consideration for use in human transplantation if the transfer affects interstate commerce.

(b) *Penalties*. Any person who violates subsection (a) of this section shall be fined not more than $50,000 or imprisoned not more than five years, or both.

(c) *Definitions*. For purposes of subsection (a) of this section:

(1) The term "human organ" means the human (including fetal) kidney, liver, heart, lung, pancreas, bone marrow, cornea, eye, bone, and skin or any subpart thereof and any other human organ (or any subpart thereof, including that derived from a fetus) specified by the Secretary of Health and Human Services by regulation.

(2) The term "valuable consideration" does not include the reasonable payments associated with the removal, transportation, implantation, processing, preservation, quality control, and storage of a human organ or the expenses of travel, housing, and lost wages incurred by the donor of a human organ in connection with the donation of the organ. . . .

————

RADIN, MARKET–INALIENABILITY

100 Harvard L.Rev. 1849 (1987).*

Since the declaration of "unalienable rights" of persons at the founding of our republic, inalienability has had a central place in our legal and moral culture. Yet there is no one sharp meaning for the term "inalienable." Sometimes inalienable means nontransferable; sometimes only nonsalable.... In this Article I explore nonsalability, a species of inalienability I call market-inalienability. Something that is market-inalienable is not to be sold, which in our economic system means it is not to be traded in the market.

Controversy over what may be bought and sold—blood or babies— pervades our news.... About fifteen years ago, for example, Richard Titmuss advocated in his book, *The Gift Relationship,* that human blood should not be allocated through the market; others disagreed. More recently, Elisabeth Landes and Richard Posner suggested the possibility of a thriving market in infants, yet most people continue to believe that infants should not be allocated through the market....

In [one] important set of meanings, inalienability is ascribed to an entitlement, right, or attribute that cannot be voluntarily transferred from one holder to another. Inalienability in these uses may mean nongiveable, nonsalable, or completely nontransferable. If something is nontransferable, the holder cannot designate a successor holder. Nongiveability and nonsalability are subsets of nontransferability. If something is inalienable by gift, it might be transferred by sale; if it is inalienable by sale, it might be transferred by gift. This nonsalability is what I refer to as market-inalienability. In precluding sales but not gifts, market-inalienability places some things outside the marketplace but not outside the realm of social intercourse.

Market-inalienability negates a central element of traditional property rights, which are conceived of as fully alienable. But market-inalienability differs from the nontransferability that characterizes many nontraditional property rights—entitlements of the regulatory and welfare state—that are both nongiveable and nonsalable. [Examples are entitlements to social security and welfare benefits.] Market-inalienability also differs from the inalienability of other things, like voting rights, that seem to be moral or political duties related to a community's normative life; they are subject to broader inalienabilities that preclude loss as well as transfer. Unlike the inalienabilities attaching to welfare entitlements or political duties, market-inalienability does not render something inseparable from the person, but rather specifies that market trading may not be used as a social mechanism of separation. Finally, market-inalienability differs from the inalienability of things, like heroin, that are made nontransferable in order to implement a prohibition, because it does not signify that something is social anathema. Indeed, preclusion of sales often coexists with encouragement of gifts. For example, the market-inalienability of human organs does not preclude—and, indeed, may seek to foster—transfer from one individual to another by gift....

Market-inalienability often expresses an aspiration for noncommodification. By making something nonsalable we proclaim that it should not be

---

* This article now forms the basis of a book, Margaret Jane Radin, Contested Commodities (1996). (Footnote by ed.)

conceived of or treated as a commodity. When something is noncommodifiable, market trading is a disallowed form of social organization and allocation. We place that thing beyond supply and demand pricing, brokerage and arbitrage, advertising and marketing, stockpiling, speculation, and valuation in terms of the opportunity cost of production.

Market-inalienability poses for us more than the binary choice of whether something should be wholly inside or outside the market, completely commodified or completely noncommodified. Some things are completely commodified—deemed suitable for trade in a laissez-faire market. Others are completely noncommodified—removed from the market altogether. But many things can be described as incompletely commodified—neither fully commodified nor fully removed from the market. Thus, we may decide that some things should be market-inalienable only to a degree, or only in some aspects.

To appreciate the need to develop a satisfactory analysis of market-inalienability, consider the deeply contested issues of commodification that confront us. Infants and children, fetal gestational services, blood, human organs, sexual services, and services of college athletes are some salient things whose commodification is contested. Our division over whether to place a monetary equivalent on a spouse's professional degree or homemaker services in a divorce; or on various kinds of injuries in tort actions, such as loss of consortium, is another form of contest over commodification. Monetization—commodification—of clean air and water is likewise deeply contested. Moreover, debates about some kinds of regulation can be seen as contested incomplete commodification, with the contest being over whether to allow full commodification (a laissez-faire market regime) or something less. If we see the debates this way, residential rent control, minimum wage requirements, and other forms of price regulation, as well as residential habitability requirements, safety regulation, and other forms of product-quality regulation all become contests over the issue of commodification.

How are we to determine the extent to which something ought to be noncommodified, so that we can determine to what extent market-inalienability is justified? Because the question asks about the appropriate relationship of particular things to the market, normative theories about the appropriate social role of the market should be helpful in trying to answer it. We can think of such theories as ordered on a continuum stretching from universal noncommodification (nothing in markets) to universal commodification (everything in markets). On this continuum, Karl Marx's theory can symbolize the theoretical pole of universal noncommodification, and Richard Posner's can be seen as close to the opposite theoretical pole. . . .

Universal commodification undermines personal identity by conceiving of personal attributes, relationships, and philosophical and moral commitments as monetizable and alienable from the self. A better view of personhood should understand many kinds of particulars—one's politics, work, religion, family, love, sexuality, friendships, altruism, experiences, wisdom, moral commitments, character, and personal attributes—as integral to the self. To understand any of these as monetizable or completely detachable from the person—to think, for example, that the value of one person's moral commitments is commensurate or fungible with those of another, or that the "same" person remains when her moral commitments are subtracted—is to do violence to our deepest understanding of what it is to be human. . . .

---

*

Part II

REMEDIES FOR BREACH
OF CONTRACT

―――――

Part II concerns remedies for breach of contract, chiefly in the bargain context.

An introductory Chapter, Chapter 5, explores three themes: (1) The nature and theory of the most characteristic remedy for breach of contract, expectation damages. (2) The question whether contract remedies should be based on the innocent party's loss, or may also take into account the wrongdoer's gain through breach. (3) In that connection, the theory of efficient breach.

Chapter 6 considers the remedy of expectation damages in more detail.

Chapter 7 concerns the remedy of specific performance, under which a breaching party is ordered to perform the contract, rather than only to pay damages for breach.

Finally, Chapter 8 explores the use of the reliance and restitution measures in a bargain context (as opposed to the use of the reliance measure in a donative context, which was explored in Chapter 1).

Chapter 5

AN INTRODUCTION TO CONTRACT DAMAGES

RESTATEMENT, SECOND, CONTRACTS § 344

[See Selected Source Materials Supplement]

HAWKINS v. McGEE

Supreme Court of New Hampshire, 1929.
84 N.H. 114, 146 A. 641.

Assumpsit, against a surgeon for breach of an alleged warranty of the success of an operation. Trial by jury and verdict for the plaintiff. The writ also contained a count in negligence upon which a nonsuit was ordered, without exception.

[The defendant moved to have the verdict set aside on several grounds, one of them being that the damages awarded were excessive. The trial court ordered that the verdict be set aside unless the plaintiff would remit all damages in excess of $500. On the plaintiff's refusal to consent to a reduction, the trial court set the verdict aside as being "excessive and against the weight of the evidence." The plaintiff excepted to this ruling of the trial court; his exception and numerous exceptions taken by the defendant were transferred to the Supreme Court.]

BRANCH, J. 1. The operation in question consisted in the removal of a considerable quantity of scar tissue from the palm of the plaintiff's right hand and the grafting of skin taken from the plaintiff's chest in place thereof. The scar tissue was the result of a severe burn caused by contact with an electric wire, which the plaintiff received about nine years before the time of the transactions here involved. There was evidence to the effect that before the operation was performed the plaintiff and his father went to the defendant's office, and that the defendant in answer to the question, "How long will the boy be in the hospital?" replied, "Three or four days, ... not over four; then the boy can go home and it will be just a few days when he will go back to work with a perfect hand." Clearly this and other testimony to the same effect would not justify a finding that the doctor contracted to complete the hospital treatment in three or four days or that the plaintiff would be able to go back

190

to work within a few days thereafter. The above statements could only be construed as expressions of opinion or predictions as to the probable duration of the treatment and plaintiff's resulting disability, and the fact that these estimates were exceeded would impose no contractual liability upon the defendant. The only substantial basis for the plaintiff's claim is the testimony that the defendant also said before the operation was decided upon, "I will guarantee to make the hand a hundred per cent perfect hand" or "a hundred per cent good hand." The plaintiff was present when these words were alleged to have been spoken, and, if they are to be taken at their face value, it seems obvious that proof of their utterance would establish the giving of a warranty in accordance with his contention.

The defendant argues, however, that, even if these words were uttered by him, no reasonable man would understand that they were used with the intention of entering into any "contractual relation whatever," and that they could reasonably be understood only "as his expression in strong language that he believed and expected that as a result of the operation he would give the plaintiff a very good hand." It may be conceded, as the defendant contends, that, before the question of the making of a contract should be submitted to a jury, there is a preliminary question of law for the trial court to pass upon, i.e. "whether the words could possibly have the meaning imputed to them by the party who founds his case upon a certain interpretation," but it cannot be held that the trial court decided this question erroneously in the present case. It is unnecessary to determine at this time whether the argument of the defendant, based upon "common knowledge of the uncertainty which attends all surgical operations," and the improbability that a surgeon would ever contract to make a damaged part of the human body "one hundred per cent perfect," would, in the absence of countervailing considerations, be regarded as conclusive, for there were other factors in the present case which tended to support the contention of the plaintiff. There was evidence that the defendant repeatedly solicited from the plaintiff's father the opportunity to perform this operation, and the theory was advanced by plaintiff's counsel in cross-examination of defendant that he sought an opportunity to "experiment on skin grafting," in which he had had little previous experience. If the jury accepted this part of plaintiff's contention, there would be a reasonable basis for the further conclusion that, if defendant spoke the words attributed to him, he did so with the intention that they should be accepted at their face value, as an inducement for the granting of consent to the operation by the plaintiff and his father, and there was ample evidence that they were so accepted by them. The question of the making of the alleged contract was properly submitted to the jury.

2. The substance of the charge to the jury on the question of damages appears in the following quotation: "If you find the plaintiff entitled to anything, he is entitled to recover for what pain and suffering he has been made to endure and for what injury he has sustained over and above what injury he had before." To this instruction the defendant seasonably excepted. By it, the jury was permitted to consider two elements of damage, (1) pain and suffering due to the operation, and (2) positive ill effects of the operation upon the plaintiff's hand. Authority for any specific rule of damages in cases of this kind seems to be lacking, but, when tested by general principle and by analogy, it appears that the foregoing instruction was erroneous.

"By 'damages,' as that term is used in the law of contracts, is intended compensation for a breach, measured in the terms of the contract." Davis v. New England Cotton Yarn Co., 77 N.H. 403, 404, 92 A. 732, 733. The purpose of the law is "to put the plaintiff in as good a position as he would have been in had the defendant kept his contract." 3 Williston Cont. § 1338; Hardie–Tynes Mfg. Co. v. Easton Cotton Oil Co., 150 N.C. 150, 63 S.E. 676, 134 Am.St.Rep. 899. The measure of recovery "is based upon what the defendant should have given the plaintiff, not what the plaintiff has given the defendant or otherwise expended." 3 Williston Cont. § 1341. "The only losses that can be said fairly to come within the terms of a contract are such as the parties must have had in mind when the contract was made, or such as they either knew or ought to have known would probably result from a failure to comply with its terms." Davis v. New England Cotton Yarn Co., 77 N.H. 403, 404, 92 A. 732, 733, Hurd v. Dunsmore, 63 N.H. 171.

The present case is closely analogous to one in which a machine is built for a certain purpose and warranted to do certain work. In such cases, the usual rule of damages for breach of warranty in the sale of chattels is applied and it is held that the measure of damages is the difference between the value of the machine if it had corresponded with the warranty and its actual value, together with such incidental losses as the parties knew or ought to have known would probably result from a failure to comply with its terms....

We therefore conclude that the true measure of the plaintiff's damage in the present case is the difference between the value to him of a perfect hand or a good hand, such as the jury found the defendant promised him, and the value of his hand in its present condition, including any incidental consequences fairly within the contemplation of the parties when they made their contract. 1 Sutherland, Damages (4th Ed.) § 92. Damages not thus limited, although naturally resulting, are not to be given.

The extent of the plaintiff's suffering does not measure this difference in value. The pain necessarily incident to a serious surgical operation was a part of the contribution which the plaintiff was willing to make to his joint undertaking with the defendant to produce a good hand. It was a legal detriment suffered by him which constituted a part of the consideration given by him for the contract. It represented a part of the price which he was willing to pay for a good hand, but it furnished no test of the value of a good hand or the difference between the value of the hand which the defendant promised and the one which resulted from the operation.

It was also erroneous and misleading to submit to the jury as a separate element of damage any change for the worse in the condition of the plaintiff's hand resulting from the operation, although this error was probably more prejudicial to the plaintiff than to the defendant. Any such ill effect of the operation would be included under the true rule of damages set forth above, but damages might properly be assessed for the defendant's failure to improve the condition of the hand, even if there were no evidence that its condition was made worse as a result of the operation.

It must be assumed that the trial court, in setting aside the verdict, undertook to apply the same rule of damages which he had previously given to the jury, and, since this rule was erroneous, it is unnecessary for us to consider whether there was any evidence to justify his finding that all damages awarded by the jury above $500 were excessive.

3. Defendant's requests for instructions were loosely drawn, and were properly denied. A considerable number of issues of fact were raised by the evidence, and it would have been extremely misleading to instruct the jury in accordance with defendant's request No. 2, that "The only issue on which you have to pass is whether or not there was a special contract between the plaintiff and the defendant to produce a perfect hand." Equally inaccurate was defendant's request No. 5, which reads as follows: "You would have to find, in order to hold the defendant liable in this case, that Dr. McGee and the plaintiff both understood that the doctor was guaranteeing a perfect result from this operation." If the defendant said that he would guarantee a perfect result, and the plaintiff relied upon that promise, any mental reservations which he may have had are immaterial. The standard by which his conduct is to be judged is not internal, but external.... Defendant's request number 7 was as follows: "If you should get so far as to find that there was a special contract guaranteeing a perfect result, you would still have to find for the defendant unless you further found that a further operation would not correct the disability claimed by the plaintiff." In view of the testimony that the defendant had refused to perform a further operation, it would clearly have been erroneous to give this instruction. The evidence would have justified a verdict for an amount sufficient to cover the cost of such an operation, even if the theory underlying this request were correct....

New trial.

MARBLE, J., did not sit: the others concurred.

———

McGEE v. UNITED STATES FIDELITY & GUAR. CO., 53 F.2d 953 (1st Cir.1931). Dr. McGee carried insurance against liability for "malpractice, error or mistake." Counsel for the insurance company participated in the trial of Hawkins v. McGee. When a motion was made for a nonsuit on the negligence count, the insurance company notified Dr. McGee that it disclaimed any liability based on a guarantee of the results of the operation, but counsel for the company continued to assist Dr. McGee's lawyer. Hawkins' action was for $10,000, and the jury verdict was for $3,000. After the Supreme Court of New Hampshire ordered a new trial, Dr. McGee gave notice to the insurance company of his intention to settle, and settled with Hawkins for $1,400.

After settling with Hawkins, Dr. McGee sued the insurance company in the federal court for $1,400 and his expenses, mostly attorney's fees, a total of $4,248.48. Judgment for the insurance company was affirmed because the policy did not cover Dr. McGee's liability under his contract with Hawkins.

The report of this case reveals the following additional facts concerning Hawkins v. McGee itself: (1) The plaintiff had alleged that by reason of the operation he had been laid up in the hospital for three months, and that before the operation his hand had been "a practical, useful hand," but that as a result of the operation the motion of his hand had become so restricted that the hand was useless to him. (2) The nonsuit on the negligence count in Hawkins v. McGee resulted from the granting of defendant's motion for a directed verdict on that count. (3) The trial-court verdict was on the second trial of the case—in the first trial, the jury had been unable to agree on a verdict. (4) Apparently Hawkins' principal grievance was that the new tissue filled his hand with a "matted" and "unsightly growth"—presumably hair.

———

McQUAID v. MICHOU, 85 N.H. 299, 157 A. 881 (1932). This case, like Hawkins v. McGee, was an action for breach of a contract to cure. In reviewing a jury verdict for plaintiff, the New Hampshire court elaborated several of the points in *Hawkins:*

... The defendant excepted to evidence, the charge, and the denial of requested instructions, in relation to damages. The exceptions may be considered together as presenting generally the issue how far the ill effects, both physical and pecuniary, sustained by the plaintiff from the treatment are an element of damage.

The rule of damages in such cases as this is expounded in Hawkins v. McGee, 84 N.H. 114, 146 A. 641. It gives as compensation only the difference between the values of the condition promised and the actual condition, including incidental consequences fairly subject to contemplation by the parties when the contract is made. As the case holds, a plaintiff's suffering incident to treatment does not enter into this difference of value nor is it a separate incidental consequence to be given allowance. It is a part of the price the plaintiff is ready to pay for the agreed result. He may not have a return in damages of the price and also receive what was to be obtained for the price.

The actual condition may include suffering as an attendant feature of it, and hence such suffering may be shown. The suffering of an uncured condition is a factor in the estimate of its value. But unless relevant to show such suffering, suffering incident to the treatment would appear to be without bearing in the computation of damages.

It is claimed here, however, that the suffering incident to the treatment was greater than that contracted for, and that as a term of the contract the defendant agreed that it would be confined within certain limits. There was evidence that the treatment was to consist of five injections to be given a week apart and that at the end of the period, according to the defendant's promise, the cure would be accomplished. And there was evidence that the effect of the injections was so serious that the plaintiff could take only three of them. . . .

It therefore might be found that the plaintiff paid a higher price for the cure than was agreed. Ordinarily, if to obtain a promised result one is obliged to pay more than the agreed price, the excess payment may be recovered as well as the loss in not obtaining the result. If the result is obtained, the overpayment is still recoverable.

It does not follow, however, that the plaintiff may have recovery on account of this excess of suffering as a special item of damage. Her condition due to the treatment would reflect and show such suffering, as practically a part of it, and enhance the difference between it and a condition of cure. . . .

Conceding that suffering incident to treatment and beyond the terms of the contract and suffering as a part of the actual condition following the treatment may not be in all respects the same, yet distinctions and separation between them cannot be practically made. To value the former as an item by itself, and to include the latter in the estimate of value of the actual condition, would here and ordinarily, if not in all cases, probably lead to arbitrary and excessive totals. The suffering here which was incident to treatment was the outcome of treatment. The plaintiff does not complain of the pain of administering the injections, but of the distress that followed. This distress led into her actual condition. The suffering as a whole is incapable of division into the suggested grouping for the purpose of any satisfactory and reasonable division of allowance. The parts are so connected that the suffering of condition is essentially a continuance of the suffering of treatment with the boundary line too difficult to be fairly ascertained. If allocation is in theory called for, its inexpediency is too great to undertake to carry the theory into play.

The plaintiff claims a loss of earnings and expense as a result of the suffering which she alleges it was agreed she should not sustain. This pecuniary loss would not enter into the difference between the actual and promised conditions. But it might be found to be an incidental loss which the parties, if they thought about it, might expect would be incurred if the terms of the contract limiting suffering were not fulfilled, and for which allowance should thereupon be made....

BACKGROUND NOTE ON HAWKINS v. McGEE

The following background facts concerning Hawkins v. McGee (based on interviews and correspondence with the Hawkins family and a local lawyer) are reported in Roberts, Hawkins Case: A Hair–Raising Experience, Harvard Law School Record, March 17, 1978, at 1, 7, 13.

... George Hawkins was born in January, 1904—the second of Rose Wilkinson and Charles Augustus Hawkins' six children....

One morning in 1915, 11–year–old George burned his right hand while preparing breakfast for his father on the family's wood-burning stove. At the time, George was trying to turn on the kitchen light to illuminate the stove, but an electrical storm the night before had damaged the wiring so that George received a severe shock. One of George's younger brothers, Howard Hawkins, now an insurance agent in Berlin, described George's initial scar as a "small pencil-size scar" which was between his thumb and index finger and did not substantially affect his use of the hand. Nevertheless, Charles Hawkins took his son George to skin specialists in Montreal after the accident; but there the doctors advised the Hawkinses against doing anything to restore the hand.

During this period, the family physician, Edward McGee, while treating one of George's younger brothers for pneumonia, also became aware of George's scarred hand. Later, in 1919, after returning from several years of medical service in Europe during World War I, McGee requested George and his parents to let him operate on the hand in order to restore it to "perfect" condition.

According to Dorothy St. Hilaire, George's younger sister, McGee claimed to have done a number of similar skin grafts on soldiers in Germany during the war, although he later admitted that he had really only observed such operations.

St. Hilaire recollects that McGee, in persuading George to undergo the surgery, emphasized the social problems which his scarred hand might create. McGee encouraged the Hawkinses to allow him to operate on the hand for three years, until finally George agreed shortly after his 18th birthday. . . .

McGee operated on George's hand in the St. Louis Hospital in Berlin in March of 1922. The skin graft operation was supposed to be quick, simple, and effective, and to require only a few days of hospitalization. Instead, St. Hilaire recalls that her brother bled very badly for several days. . . .

. . . George was, in the words of his brother Howard, "in the throes of death" for quite a while after the operation because of his extensive bleeding and the ensuing infection. Moreover, the post-operation scar covered his thumb and two fingers and was densely covered with hair. Howard Hawkins remembers that George's hand was partially closed up and continued to bleed periodically throughout his life. . . .

The jury only awarded the Hawkinses $3,000 for damages, and the final settlement was for $1,400 and lawyers fees. St. Hilaire believes the jurors, while at heart solidly behind the Hawkinses' cause, were afraid to return heavier damages against McGee because he was one of the more prominent physicians in the area. Charles Hawkins took the $1,400 and his injured son back to Montreal to see if any subsequent operations would alleviate George's deformity, but the doctors there said that the grafted skin was so tough that nothing more could be done. . . .

Hawkins' crippled hand affected his employment and outlook throughout his lifetime. After the operation, George Hawkins never returned to high school, even though, in Howard's opinion, "George was very bright, learned quickly, and had a pleasing personality." He was encouraged by his parents to finish school, but would not because, in his siblings' view, he was embarrassed by his hand.

George also gave up tennis and riflery after the operation, although previously he had won several medals as a marksman for the State Home Guard. Because of his hand, George was unable to perform any heavy manual labor or learn to type. He worked for many years in the printing division of the Brown Company, a pulp and paper manufacturer in Berlin, and later in a tire store. . . .

. . . According to his family members, George was always very sensitive about his hand and suffered lifelong emotional distress. His parents also grieved until their deaths because of the tragic and unnecessary crippling of their son's hand.

The Hawkins family was unaware of the widespread study of Hawkins v. McGee in law schools until, in 1964, Howard and Edith Hawkins' daughter Gail encountered the case early in her contracts course at Boston University Law School. Moreover, the Hawkins family did not know about the case's use in "The Paper Chase" contracts class scene until Edith Hawkins happened to see the 1972 movie during its first run.

Howard Hawkins, however, believes that George was somewhat aware of the case's importance before his 1958 death. Howard states: "I think he became aware of the importance of his case through a lawyer friend, an O. (Ovide) J. Coulombe. I think it gave him a sense of importance, in that this was bringing the facts out in the public eye, but this was only temporary, as he really lived with this incapacity all his life, and he did suffer mentally as well as physically."

————

VAN ZEE v. WITZKE, 445 N.W.2d 34 (S.D.1989). In 1982, Van Zee began attending a school to learn to be a court reporter school. As a child, Van Zee had suffered a trauma to her right third finger. The trauma created a deformity in the finger, which caused the finger to lock up when Van Zee extended it to type. In August 1984, Van Zee consulted Dr. Witzke, a reconstructive and plastic surgeon, about performing surgery on the finger. Dr. Witzke examined and x-rayed the finger. He found metallic sutures in the flexor tendons, and he diagnosed a hyperextension of the first joint. Three months later, Van Zee again consulted Dr. Witzke, and Dr. Witzke agreed to operate on her finger. Seven days later, Van Zee's finger had developed an acute infection. Dr. Witzke treated and monitored the infection, and encouraged Van Zee to see a physical therapist. Van Zee began physical therapy, but quit because the therapist fractured her finger. Thereafter, her finger slowly deteriorated and got stiffer. Dr. Witzke last saw Van Zee in October 1985. By this time her finger was stiff, had a slight deformity of the distal tip, and was not very useful. Van Zee sued, alleging breach of an express agreement to correct the deformity in her finger, and negligence. The trial court granted summary judgment in favor of Dr. Witzke. Van Zee appealed only from the summary judgment on her breach-of-contract claim. Affirmed:

"... Dr. Witzke's office notes indicated that he discussed all of the risks, alternatives and imponderables of surgery with Van Zee. During his deposition he explained that this included an increased risk of infection and delayed healing due to previous scarring, and the possibility of a useless or lost finger. According to Van Zee, Dr. Witzke, 'never said there were any risks.' Dr. Witzke testified that he told Van Zee during her initial consultation that he would only consider doing the surgery if she felt that the functional disability was so great that she could not continue court reporting school. Van Zee testified that she delayed having surgery after the initial consultation in order to arrange financing for the operation. Van Zee's mother ... was opposed to the operation and wanted Van Zee to obtain a guarantee from the doctor that the finger would be all right. Van Zee herself testified that she told her mother that no doctor would do that. Nevertheless, Van Zee stated that she did ask Dr. Witzke for a guarantee. According to Van Zee, Dr. Witzke, 'took my hand and he looked at it and he said I can tell you right now no matter what it won't be any worse than it is right now,'and assured her that, 'there would be no problem at all.' According to Dr. Witzke, he told her, '[t]here are no absolute guarantees.'

"Viewing the claimed statements as detailed by Van Zee in a light most favorable to her, we agree that they fail the clear proof of an express contract upon which to ground liability. Van Zee's sole proof of any express agreement by Dr. Witzke to heal her finger is limited to the statement made by him in response to her request for a guarantee....

"We ... find Dr. Witzke's statement that Van Zee's finger would not be worse off after surgery insufficient as a matter of law to constitute an express contract to heal the finger. The statement falls into the category of statements constituting mere therapeutic reassurances of a good result."

SULLIVAN v. O'CONNOR, 363 Mass. 579, 296 N.E.2d 183 (1973). "It has been suggested on occasion that agreements between patients and physicians by which the physician undertakes to effect a cure or to bring about a given result should be declared unenforceable on grounds of public policy. See Guilmet v. Campbell, 385 Mich. 57, 76 (dissenting opinion). But there are many decisions recognizing and enforcing such contracts, see Annotation, 43 A.L.R.3d 1221, 1225, 1229–1233, and the law of Massachusetts has treated them as valid, although we have had no decision meeting head on the contention that they should be denied legal sanction....

"It is not hard to see why the courts should be unenthusiastic or skeptical about the contract theory. Considering the uncertainties of medical science and the variations in the physical and psychological conditions of individual patients, doctors can seldom in good faith promise specific results. Therefore it is unlikely that physicians of even average integrity will in fact make such promises. Statements of opinion by the physician with some optimistic coloring are a different thing, and may indeed have therapeutic value. But patients may transform such statements into firm promises in their own minds, especially when they have been disappointed in the event, and testify in that sense to sympathetic juries.[1] If actions for breach of promise can be readily maintained, doctors, so it is said, will be frightened into practicing 'defensive medicine.' On the other hand, if these actions were outlawed, leaving only the possibility of suits for malpractice, there is fear that the public might be exposed to the enticements of charlatans, and confidence in the profession might ultimately be shaken. See Miller, The Contractual Liability of Physicians and Surgeons, 1953 Wash.L.Q. 413, 416–423. The law has taken the middle of the road position of allowing actions based on alleged contract, but insisting on clear proof. Instructions to the jury may well stress this requirement and point to tests of truth, such as the complexity or difficulty of an operation as bearing on the probability that a given result was promised. See annotation, 43 A.L.R.3d 1225, 1225–1227.

"If an action on the basis of contract is allowed, we have next the question of the measure of damages to be applied where liability is found. Some cases [such as Hawkins v. McGee] have taken the simple view that the promise by the physician is to be treated like an ordinary commercial promise, and accordingly that the successful plaintiff is entitled to a standard measure of recovery for breach of contract—'compensatory' ('expectancy') damages, an

---

1. Judicial skepticism about whether a promise was in fact made derives also from the possibility that the truth has been tortured to give the plaintiff the advantage of the longer period of limitations sometimes available for actions on contract as distinguished from those in tort or for malpractice. See Lillich, The Malpractice Statute of Limitations in New York and Other Jurisdictions, 47 Cornell L.Q. 339; annotation, 80 A.L.R.2d 368.

amount intended to put the plaintiff in the position he would be in if the contract had been performed, or, presumably, at the plaintiff's election, 'restitution' damages, an amount corresponding to any benefit conferred by the plaintiff upon the defendant in the performance of the contract disrupted by the defendant's breach. . . .

"Other cases, including a number in New York, without distinctly repudiating the *Hawkins* type of analysis, have indicated that a different and generally more lenient measure of damages is to be applied in patient-physician actions based on breach of alleged special agreements to effect a cure, attain a stated result, or employ a given medical method. This measure is expressed in somewhat variant ways, but the substance is that the plaintiff is to recover any expenditures made by him and for other detriment (usually not specifically described in the opinions) following proximately and foreseeably upon the defendant's failure to carry out his promise. . . . This, be it noted, is not a 'restitution' measure, for it is not limited to restoration of the benefit conferred on the defendant (the fee paid) but includes other expenditures, for example, amounts paid for medicine and nurses; so also it would seem according to its logic to take in damages for any worsening of the plaintiff's condition due to the breach. Nor is it an 'expectancy' measure, for it does not appear to contemplate recovery of the whole difference in value between the condition as promised and the condition actually resulting from the treatment. Rather the tendency of the formulation is to put the plaintiff back in the position he occupied just before the parties entered upon the agreement, to compensate him for the detriments he suffered in reliance upon the agreement. This kind of intermediate pattern of recovery for breach of contract is discussed in the suggestive article by Fuller and Perdue, The Reliance Interest in Contract Damages, 46 Yale L.J. 52, 373, where the authors show that, although not attaining the currency of the standard measures, a 'reliance' measure has for special reasons been applied by the courts in a variety of settings, including noncommercial settings. See 46 Yale L.J. at 396–401.[2]

"For breach of the patient-physician agreements under consideration, a recovery limited to restitution seems plainly too meager, if the agreements are to be enforced at all. On the other hand, an expectancy recovery may well be excessive. . . .

"There is much to be said, then, for applying a reliance measure to the present facts, and we have only to add that our cases are not unreceptive to the use of that formula in special situations. . . .

"The question of recovery on a reliance basis for pain and suffering or mental distress requires further attention. . . . Suffering or distress resulting from the breach going beyond that which was envisaged by the treatment as agreed, should be compensable on the same ground as the worsening of the patient's conditions because of the breach. Indeed it can be argued that the very suffering or distress 'contracted for'—that which would have been incurred if the treatment achieved the promised result—should also be compensable on the theory underlying the New York cases. For that suffering is 'wasted' if the treatment fails. Otherwise stated, compensation for this

---

2. Some of the exceptional situations mentioned where reliance may be preferred to expectancy are those in which the latter measure would be hard to apply or would impose too great a burden; performance was interfered with by external circumstances; the contract was indefinite. See 46 Yale L.J. at 373–386; 394–396.

waste is arguably required in order to complete the restoration of the status quo ante.''

———

UNIDROIT PRINCIPLES OF INTERNATIONAL COMMERCIAL CONTRACTS ART. 7.4.2

[See Selected Source Materials Supplement]

———

COOTER & EISENBERG, DAMAGES FOR BREACH OF CONTRACT

73 Calif.L.Rev. 1434 (1985)*

We now consider whether reliance or expectation damages should be preferred on breach of a bargain contract. In examining this question, we turn from problems of definition to problems of fairness and policy.

Fairness seems to require that a person who breaches a contract should pay compensation to the victim of breach for the injury he suffers as a result. But the meanings of the terms ''compensation'' and ''injury'' are fundamentally ambiguous. Under a reliance conception, the uninjured state is the condition the victim would have been in if he had not made the contract with the breaching party. Under an expectation conception, the uninjured state is the condition the victim would have been in if the breaching party had performed the contract. Which conception should govern is far from obvious.

In many cases, the issue of selecting between reliance and expectation damages is not significant, because the two measures will yield virtually identical damages. In particular ... in a competitive market reliance damages normally will equal expectation damages [because the contract price promised by the wrongdoer will equal the forgone price at which the injured party could have contracted with a third party]. While it is true that few markets satisfy all the conditions of perfect competition, many come close enough so that the difference between expectation and reliance damages would be insignificant.

Often, however, the two measures may diverge significantly. This may occur, for example, in imperfectly competitive markets whose conditions differ materially from those of perfectly competitive markets.... The question of choice between competing conceptions of injury and compensation then becomes material. Traditionally, courts and commentators were united in holding that the expectation conception of injury governed in such cases. In fact, prior to the 1930's the reliance principle operated in only a covert manner. However, with the promulgation in 1932 of section 90 of the Restatement of Contracts, and the publication in 1934 of Fuller and Perdue's landmark article *The Reliance Interest in Contract Damages,* the reliance principle began to undergo a process of steady and impressive growth. Until the last ten years or so, this growth served to expand liability in contract. Recently, however, some commentators have taken the position that the reliance

---

* The text is somewhat reorganized from the original. (Footnote by ed.)

principle should be used to reduce liability, by substituting the reliance conception for the expectation conception in the law of damages.

The reasons for this position are complex. Partly it is an attack on the very institution of contract: liability based on reliance may be conceptualized as liability in tort. It also results, however, from the apparent lack of a clear rationale for expectation damages. The reliance conception of injury reflects the basic intuition that if somebody is worse off than he was before, he has been hurt. The expectation conception reflects a much more subtle intuition, and indeed it is plausible to argue that the mere defeat of an expectation is not a very serious injury.

The question remains what measure of damages should be used in cases where expectation and reliance may materially diverge. We begin our analysis of that question with the concept of efficient contract terms.

Economists often distinguish between efficiency and distribution. For present purposes, efficiency concerns the amount of value created by a contract, and distribution concerns the division of that value between the parties. Economists say that a contract is efficient if its terms maximize the value that can be created by the contemplated exchange. Put differently, if a contract is inefficient, revising the inefficient terms can increase the value it creates.

The distinction between distribution and efficiency parallels a distinction between the price and nonprice terms of a contract. Adjusting *nonprice* terms often makes it possible to control a contract's efficiency. For example, suppose that a contract to make and sell a boat includes a term that imposes very high liquidated damages if Seller breaches. There are many types of precaution Seller can take to decrease the probability of breach, such as ordering materials well in advance, hiring extra workers to protect against someone's quitting or falling ill, and reserving dry-dock facilities needed in the final stages of construction. If the very high liquidated-damages term is enforceable, it may cause Seller to take excessive precaution, in the sense that the cost of the precaution to Seller is greater than the value to Buyer of the increased probability that Seller will perform. In that case, the liquidated damages term is inefficient. If, however, the term is modified by reducing the liquidated damages, the saving to Seller from taking less precaution would exceed the cost to Buyer of exposure to additional risk of nonperformance. This would result in a net increase in the value created by the contract.

The *price* term of a contract controls the distribution of the value that the contract creates. Revision of an inefficient nonprice term can produce an increase in value, and this increase can be distributed between the parties by adjusting the price term so that each party is better off. Thus in the boat case, an increase in value from adjusting the liquidated-damages provision, initially enjoyed by Seller, could be split with Buyer by lowering the price of the boat. The revised contract, containing lower liquidated damages and a lower price, would make both parties better off. Put differently, the original contract stipulates damages in the event of Seller's breach, thus creating a right in Buyer. If Seller is willing to pay more for a modification of this right than the price Buyer would demand, efficiency requires that the contract be modified. In this respect, the exchange of legal rights is no different than the exchange of ordinary commodities.

Under ideal conditions—that is, where negotiation and drafting are cost-free—self-interest compels a rational buyer and seller to create an efficient contract, so that the process of bargaining leads to the maximization of the value a contract creates. In practice, however, there are many obstacles to creating efficient contracts. For example, it is costly to write contract terms. Instead of including explicit terms covering all contingencies, therefore, most contracts leave many issues to be resolved by the courts in case an irreconcilable dispute should arise. Specifically, many contracts leave out terms covering damages for breach, and the courts, in effect, must fill in the contract with legal damages rules.

The damage rules that the courts apply to fill in contracts should be both fair and efficient. Contracts negotiated under ideal conditions will be efficient, and enforcing the terms of such contracts will usually be regarded as fair. Thus we take as a theorem that a damage rule is both fair and efficient if it corresponds to the terms that rational parties situated like the contracting parties would have reached when bargaining under ideal conditions.

The question then is, why might rational parties, who address the issue, choose an expectation measure over a reliance measure? One reason is administrative: it is usually easier to establish in court the value of performance than the extent of reliance. The very fact of reliance is often difficult to prove, as in cases where the reliance consists of passive inaction (such as failure to pursue alternatives) rather than a positive change of position. Even if the fact of reliance can be proved, reliance damages may be difficult to measure. In a noncompetitive market, for example, reliance damages would normally be calculated by the [victim's opportunity cost], which requires determining the forgone price. Often, however, the forgone price is very hard to determine, as where the buyer breaches and the commodity is so unusual that there is no way to establish exactly what the next-best alternative buyer would have paid. In contrast, expectation damages are based on the contract price, which is known, rather than the forgone price, which is speculative. This administrative consideration has implications for both fairness and efficiency. In terms of fairness, the difficulty of proving reliance damages might, paradoxically, result in a failure to protect the reliance interest unless an expectation measure is chosen. In terms of efficiency, a damage measure that was difficult to prove, and therefore unreliable, would undercut the goal of facilitating private planning.

An intimately related set of considerations has to do with the incentive effects of the expectation and reliance measures. Most contracts are made with the expectation of mutual gain. . . . The total gain to both parties—the surplus from exchange—is the value created by the contract. The terms of a contract have incentive effects upon behavior that influence how much value the contract will create. Accordingly, one index to whether a damage rule would have been agreed to by rational parties situated like the contracting parties, and bargaining under ideal conditions, is whether the rule provides incentives for efficient behavior. . . .

We begin with the incentive effects of damage measures on the decision whether to perform, that is, on the rate of breach. A contract involves a promise by at least one party, and it is always possible that events will induce a promisor to refuse to perform, either because performance has become unprofitable or because an alternative performance has become more profitable. If a promisor were liable only for the promisee's reliance damages, the value of the promisor's performance to the promisee would not enter into a purely self-interested calculation by the promisor whether to perform. In contrast, expectation damages place on the promisor the promisee's loss of his share of the contract's value in the event of breach, and thereby sweep that loss into the promisor's calculus of self-interest.

The effect of expectation damages on the promisor's calculations can be stated in terms of externalities. Economists say that an externality exists when one person imposes a cost upon another without paying for it. Incentives for performance are efficient if they compel a promisor to balance the cost to him of performing against the losses to himself and to others that will result if he does not perform. If the promisor does not perform, the promisee loses his share of the value of the contract. If the promisor is liable for that loss, he internalizes not only his own loss but the losses to the promisee that result from his failure to perform. In contrast, if the promisor is liable only for reliance damages, he will not internalize the full value of performance to the promisee. Thus expectation damages create efficient incentives for the promisor's performance, while reliance damages do not, unless they are identical to expectation damages.

By directly affecting the probability that the promisor will perform, the expectation measure has an indirect effect upon the promisee's behavior, which can be stated in terms of planning. Knowing that expectation damages give the promisor strong incentives to perform, the promisee will be more confident that his reliance on the promisor will not expose him to undue risk. The promisee can therefore plan more effectively, because once a contract is made he can order his affairs with the confidence that he will realize its value, whether by performance or damages. In contrast, under a regime of reliance damages, a promisee could plan only on the basis that if breach occurs the law will put him back to where he was when he started. Since planning is by nature forward-looking, this backward-looking nature of reliance damages would be a shaky foundation for ordering complex affairs. Furthermore, it is in the promisor's interest that the promisee be able to plan reliably, because the ability to do so will make the promisee willing to pay a higher price for the promise.

These ideas can also be expressed in institutional terms. The purpose of the social institution of bargain is to create joint value through exchange. In recognition of the desirability of creating value in this manner, the legal institution of contract supports the social institution of the bargain with official sanctions. It is rational to design the legal sanctions so that the joint value from exchange is maximized. This goal is achieved by protecting the expectation interest.

UNITED STATES NAVAL INSTITUTE v. CHARTER COMMUNICATIONS, INC.

United States Court of Appeals, Second Circuit, 1991.
936 F.2d 692.

Before KEARSE, WINTER and ALTIMARI, CIRCUIT JUDGES.

KEARSE, CIRCUIT JUDGE:

This case returns to us following our remand in *United States Naval Institute v. Charter Communications, Inc.*, 875 F.2d 1044 (2d Cir.1989) ("*Na-*

val I''), to the United States District Court for the Southern District of New York, Pierre N. Leval, *Judge,* for the fashioning of relief in favor of plaintiff United States Naval Institute ("Naval") against defendant Charter Communications, Inc., and Berkley Publishing Group (collectively "Berkley"), for breach of an agreement with respect to the publication of the paperback edition of *The Hunt For Red October* ("*Red October*" or the "Book"). On remand, the district court awarded Naval $35,380.50 in damages, $7,760.12 as profits wrongfully received by Berkley, and $15,319.27 as prejudgment interest on the damages awarded, plus costs. Naval appeals from so much of the judgment as failed to award a greater amount as profits, denied prejudgment interest on the profits awarded, and refused to award attorney's fees under the Copyright Act of 1976, 17 U.S.C. § 101 *et seq.* (1988) (the "Copyright Act" or the "Act"). Berkley cross-appeals from the judgment as a whole and from such parts of it as awarded moneys to Naval. For the reasons below, we reverse the award of profits; we affirm the award of damages, the award of prejudgment interest, and the denial of attorney's fees.

I. Background

The events leading to this action are fully set forth in *Naval I,* 875 F.2d at 1045–47, and will be summarized here only briefly. Naval, as the assignee of the author's copyright in *Red October,* entered into a licensing agreement with Berkley in September 1984 (the "Agreement"), granting Berkley the exclusive license to publish a paperback edition of the Book "not sooner than October 1985." Berkley shipped its paperback edition to retail outlets early, placing those outlets in position to sell the paperback prior to October 1985. As a result, retail sales of the paperback began on September 15, 1985, and early sales were sufficiently substantial that the Book was near the top of paperback bestseller lists before the end of September 1985.

Naval commenced the present action when it learned of Berkley's plans for early shipment, and it unsuccessfully sought a preliminary injunction. After trial, the district judge dismissed the complaint. He ruled that Berkley had not breached the Agreement because it was entitled, in accordance with industry custom, to ship prior to the agreed publication date. On appeal, we reversed. Though we upheld the district court's finding that the Agreement did not prohibit the early shipments themselves, we concluded that if the "not sooner than October 1985" term of the Agreement had any meaning whatever, it meant at least that Berkley was not allowed to cause such voluminous paperback retail sales prior to that date, and that Berkley had therefore breached the Agreement. *Naval I,* 875 F.2d at 1049–51. Accordingly, we remanded for entry of a judgment awarding Naval appropriate relief.

On the remand, Naval asserted that it was entitled to recovery for copyright infringement, and it sought judgment awarding it all of Berkley's profits from pre-October 1985 sales of the Book; it estimated those profits at $724,300. It also requested prejudgment interest, costs, and attorney's fees. Berkley, on the other hand, challenged Naval's right to any recovery at all, contending, *inter alia,* that Berkley could not be held liable for copyright infringement since the Agreement had made it the exclusive licensee of the paperback edition copyright as of September 14, 1984; it argued that Naval therefore had at most a claim for breach-of-contract but that Berkley could not be held liable on that basis because Naval had disavowed its pursuit of a contract claim. Berkley also argued that the profits attributed to it by Naval were inflated, and it opposed any award of prejudgment interest or attorney's fees.

In a Memorandum and Order dated July 17, 1990, 1990 WL 104027 ("July 17 Order"), the district judge rejected Berkley's claim that "its premature publication of the paperback edition constituted only a contract violation and not an infringement of Naval's copyright." *Id.* at 8. He found that Naval's copyright was infringed by the early publication because, though "the *extent* of the breach was a relatively trivial matter of two weeks of sales, the *term* breached was crucial to the scope of the license, as it governed when the license would take effect." *Id.* (emphasis in original). He concluded that Naval was entitled to recover damages for copyright infringement, comprising actual damages suffered by Naval plus Berkley's profits "attributable to the infringement," 17 U.S.C. § 504(b).

The court calculated Naval's "actual damages from Berkley's wrongful pre-October 'publication'" as the profits Naval would have earned from hardcover sales in September 1985 if the competing paperback edition had not then been offered for sale. July 17 Order at 8. Noting the downward trend of hardcover sales of the Book from March through August 1985, the court found that there was no reason to infer that Naval's September 1985 sales would have exceeded its August 1985 sales. The court calculated Naval's lost sales as the difference between the actual hardcover sales for those two months, and awarded Naval $35,380.50 as actual damages.

The district judge held that Berkley's profits "attributable to the infringement" were only those profits that resulted from "sales to customers who would not have bought the paperback but for the fact it became available in September." July 17 Order at 10. He found that most of the September paperback sales were made to buyers who would not have bought a hardcover edition in September, and therefore only those September sales that displaced hardcover sales were attributable to the infringement. Berkley's profit on the displacing copies totaled $7,760.12, and the court awarded that amount to Naval.

The court awarded Naval prejudgment interest (totaling $15,319.27) on the $35,380.50 awarded as actual damages but denied such interest on the award of Berkley's profits. It also denied Naval's request for attorney's fees.

Judgment was entered accordingly, and these appeals followed.

II. DISCUSSION . . .

A. *Naval's Claim of Copyright Infringement* . . .

The Agreement between Naval and Berkley, headed "Agreement made this 14th day of September 1984," granted Berkley, in & 1, "the exclusive right to publish and reproduce, distribute and sell English-language paperback editions" of the Book in the United States and certain other areas. Paragraph 2 of the Agreement stated that "[t]he term of this license will begin on the date written above"; it stated that the term of the license would continue until at least five years after the date of Berkley's "first publication" of the Book. Paragraph 4 provided that Berkley was to publish the paperback edition "not sooner than October 1985."

These provisions contradict the district court's finding that Berkley's publication date "governed when the license would take effect." Paragraph 2 provided that the license took effect on "the date written above"; since September 14, 1984, was the only date mentioned in the Agreement prior to & 3, the license term began on that date. Further, & 2's distinct references to (a) "the date written above" to define the start of the license term, and (b) Berkley's "first publication" date to anchor the continuation of the license term reveal that the parties deliberately did not define the start of the term by Berkley's first publication date. Thus, according to the express provisions of the Agreement, Berkley became the owner of the right to publish the paperback edition of the book in September 1984 and remained the owner of that right for at least five years after its first publication of that edition in 1985. Its publication of that edition in 1985 therefore could not constitute copyright infringement. . . .

B.   Contract Damages

Our ruling that Naval is not entitled to recover under the Copyright Act does not, as Berkley would have it, require the entry of judgment in favor of Berkley. Though Berkley argues that Naval had abandoned its contract claim for money damages prior to trial, we thereafter ruled in *Naval I* that Naval was entitled to recover for breach of contract. . . . Our ruling in *Naval I* that Naval was entitled to recover for breach of the Agreement is the law of the case. . . .

As Naval has renounced any effort at rescission and has accepted Berkley's payments of substantial copyright royalties for paperback sales under the Agreement, plainly the relief to which Naval is entitled on its meritorious breach-of-contract claim is money damages.

The damages awarded by the district court on remand had two components: (1) Naval's lost profits resulting from Berkley's early publication of the paperback edition of the Book, and (2) Berkley's profits attributable to its assumed infringement. For the reasons discussed above, the latter component of the award cannot stand. The former component, however, may properly measure damages under a breach-of-contract theory.

Since the purpose of damages for breach of contract is to compensate the injured party for the loss caused by the breach, 5 *Corbin On Contracts* '1002, at 31 (1964), those damages are generally measured by the plaintiff's actual loss, *see, e.g., Restatement (Second) of Contracts* § 347 (1981). While on occasion the defendant's profits are used as the measure of damages, *see, e.g., Cincinnati Siemens–Lungren Gas Illuminating Co. v. Western Siemens–Lungren Co.,* 152 U.S. 200, 204–07, 14 S.Ct. 523, 525–26, 38 L.Ed. 411 (1894); *Murphy v. Lischitz,* 183 Misc. 575, 577, 49 N.Y.S.2d 439, 441 (Sup.Ct.N.Y. County 1944), *aff'd mem.,* 268 A.D. 1027, 52 N.Y.S.2d 943 (1st Dep't), *aff'd mem.,* 294 N.Y. 892, 63 N.E.2d 26 (1945), this generally occurs when those profits tend to define the plaintiff's loss, for an award of the defendant's profits where they greatly exceed the plaintiff's loss and there has been no tortious conduct on the part of the defendant would tend to be punitive, and punitive awards are not part of the law of contract damages. *See generally Restatement (Second) of Contracts* § 356 comment *a* ("The central objective behind the system of contract remedies is compensatory, not punitive."); *id.* comment *b* (agreement attempting to fix damages in amount vastly greater than what approximates actual loss would be unenforceable as imposing a penalty); *id.* § 355 (punitive damages not recoverable for breach of contract unless conduct constituting the breach is also a tort for which such damages are recoverable).

Here, the district court found that Berkley's alleged $724,300 profits did not define Naval's loss because many persons who bought the paperback in September 1985 would not have bought the book in hardcover but would merely have waited until the paperback edition became available. This finding is not clearly erroneous. . . .

[The court then held that Naval had proved with sufficient certainty the damages of $33,380.50 awarded by the trial court as the profits Naval would have earned on hardcover sales in September 1985 if the paperback edition had not then been offered for sale.]

CONCLUSION

. . . For the foregoing reasons, we reverse so much of the judgment as granted Naval $7,760.12 as an award of Berkley's profits. In all other respects, the judgment is affirmed.

No costs.

————

COPPOLA ENTERPRISES, INC. v. ALFONE

Supreme Court of Florida, 1988.
531 So.2d 334.

KOGAN, Justice. . . .

On April 18, 1978, Helen Alfone contracted with Coppola Enterprises, Inc. (Coppola) to purchase a residential lot and single family home to be constructed by Coppola (Unit 53). The purchase price of Unit 53 was $105,690.00. Alfone placed a $10,568.00 deposit on the property.

Closing was projected for "Winter 1978–79" but did not take place until late summer 1980 due to construction delays. The contract provided that the closing was to occur after ten days written notice from the seller to the purchaser.

Upon receipt of the letter informing her of the tentative date set for closing, Alfone immediately sought financing to purchase the property. However, when she was unable to acquire the necessary financing within the time required, Alfone's attorney requested additional time within which to pay the balance due on the property. Taking the position that time was of the essence, Coppola refused Alfone's request and subsequently resold the property for $170,000.00.

The trial court found that Coppola failed to exercise good faith by refusing Alfone a reasonable time to close and by terminating the contract. Final judgment was entered for Alfone, and she was awarded "benefit of bargain" damages of $64,310.00 together with prejudgment interest of $43,295.38. The Fourth District Court of Appeal affirmed the judgment and damages award, holding the "award of damages to a contractual vendee [includes] the profit made by the vendor on the sale of the property to a subsequent purchaser even though there is no proof of fraud or bad faith." 506 So.2d at 1181.

The district court was correct to award damages to Alfone equal to the profit made by Coppola on the subsequent sale.[2] Under this Court's opinion in *Gassner v. Lockett,* 101 So.2d 33, 34 (Fla.1958), "where a vendor is unable to perform a prior contract for the sale of the lands because of a subsequent sale of the same land, he should be held, to the extent of any profit in the subsequent sale, to be a trustee for the prior vendee and accountable to such vendee for any profit." In *Gassner* the seller, who was old and extremely forgetful, conveyed certain property to the buyer. Some months later he conveyed the same property to a subsequent purchaser. This Court concluded the record showed the transaction was not made in bad faith, but nevertheless the seller should not be permitted to profit from his mistake, even though it was made in good faith. The Court awarded, among other things, damages to the buyer that included any profit the seller may have made as a result of the second sale.

The *Gassner* rationale also applies here. Coppola was obligated to sell Unit 53 to Alfone under their contract. The provisions of the contract making time of the essence were waived because construction delays postponed the closing for more than a year and a half past the "Winter 1978–1979" date originally set for closing. Under these circumstances Alfone was entitled to a reasonable time in which to acquire the funds to pay the balance due on the property. Once Coppola breached its contract with Alfone and was unable to perform due to the sale of Unit 53 to a subsequent purchaser, Alfone was entitled to damages equal to Coppola's profits from the sale.

We need not address whether Coppola's decision to sell Unit 53 to a subsequent purchaser involved bad faith. Resolution of that issue is not dispositive here. As in *Gassner* the buyer is entitled to these damages whether the sale to the subsequent purchaser involved bad faith or was merely the result of a good-faith mistake. A seller will not be permitted to profit from his breach of a contract with a buyer, even absent proof of fraud or bad faith, when the breach is followed by a sale of the land to a subsequent purchaser. . . .

It is so ordered.

EHRLICH, C.J., and OVERTON, McDONALD, SHAW and GRIMES, JJ., concur.

BARKETT, J., did not participate in this case.

———

LAURIN v. DeCAROLIS CONSTRUCTION CO., 372 Mass. 688, 363 N.E.2d 675 (1977). In March 1971, the Laurins agreed to purchase a home that DeCarolis was then constructing. The home was situated on a well-wooded lot. Prior to the closing, the Laurins found that after the contract had been signed, DeCarolis had bulldozed many of the trees on the property. The Laurins ordered DeCarolis to desist, but DeCarolis continued to bulldoze trees

---

2. The award should also include a return to Alfone of her initial deposit on Unit 53. (Footnote relocated by ed.)

and also removed gravel and loam worth $6,480. The Laurins paid the purchase price of $26,900 at the closing, and then sued DeCarolis for the value of the trees, gravel, and loam that DeCarolis had removed.

The case was tried by a master, who concluded that the Laurins were the "equitable owners" of the property from and after the signing of the agreement, so that DeCarolis had unlawfully converted the trees, gravel, and loam. In other words, the master reasoned that the Laurins were entitled to disgorgement under a property theory. The Massachusetts Supreme Judicial Court rejected this reasoning, on the ground that under Massachusetts law, "the rights of the purchaser of real property prior to closing are contract rights rather than property rights." Accordingly, the Court concluded, "[this] case must be decided, not as [an] action for injury to or conversion of property, but as a claim for a deliberate and willful breach of contract...."

This left the contract theory. The problem was that taking the trees, gravel, and loam had not diminished the value of the property. Therefore, although DeCarolis had made a gain from breach, the Laurins had not suffered a loss. Nevertheless, the Court held that the Laurins were entitled to disgorgement, because DeCarolis should not be allowed to retain its gains from a willful breach of contract:

> ... Particularly where the defendant's breach is deliberate and willful, we think damages limited to diminution in value of the premises may sometimes be seriously inadequate. "Cutting a few trees on a timber tract, or taking a few hundred tons of coal from a mine, might not diminish the market value of the tract, or of the mine, and yet the value of the wood or coal, severed from the soil, might be considerable. The wrongdoer would, in the cases instanced, be held to pay the value of the wood and coal, and he could not shield himself by showing that the property from which it was taken was, as a whole, worth as much as it was before." *Worrall v. Munn*, 53 N.Y. 185, 190 (1873). This reasoning does not depend for its soundness on the holding of a property interest, as distinguished from a contractual interest, by the plaintiffs. Nor is it punitive; it merely deprives the defendant of a profit wrongfully made, a profit which the plaintiff was entitled to make....

NOTE ON THE THEORY OF EFFICIENT BREACH

A well-known theory in the law-and-economics of contract is the theory of efficient breach. This theory holds that breach of contract is efficient, and therefore desirable, if the promisor's gain from breach, after payment of expectation damages, will exceed the promisee's loss from breach. Probably the best-known exposition of the theory of efficient breach is that given by Richard Posner in his book, *Economic Analysis of Law*. This exposition has changed somewhat over the six editions of that book. Here is the core of the exposition in the first edition:

> ... [I]n some cases a party [to a contract] would be tempted to breach the contract simply because his profit from breach would exceed his expected profit from completion of the contract. If his profit from breach would also exceed the expected profit to the other party from

completion of the contract, and if damages are limited to loss of expected profit, there will be an incentive to commit a breach. There should be.

Although the theory of efficient breach is typically presented in very generalized terms, in fact the theory can only be properly understood and evaluated in the context of paradigm cases to which it might meaningfully be applied. The most salient paradigm for present purposes is one that might be called the Overbidder Paradigm. In this Paradigm, a seller who has contracted to sell a commodity to a buyer breaches the contract in order to sell the commodity to a third party who comes along later and offers a higher price.

The Resale Paradigm is the poster child of the theory of efficient breach. Proponents of the theory, including Posner, typically include an illustration that exemplifies this Paradigm as part of their argument for the theory. Here is the centerpiece illustration of the theory of efficient breach in the first edition of Posner's *Economic Analysis of Law*:

> ... I sign a contract to deliver 100,000 custom-ground widgets at $.10 apiece to A, for use in his boiler factory. After I have delivered 10,000, B comes to me, explains that he desperately needs 25,000 custom-ground widgets at once since otherwise he will be forced to close his pianola factory at great cost, and offers me $.15 apiece for 25,000 widgets. I sell him the widgets and as a result do not complete timely delivery to A, who sustains $1000 in damages from my breach. Having obtained an additional profit of $1250 on the sale to B, I am better off even after reimbursing A for his loss. Society is also better off. Since B was willing to pay me $.15 per widget, it must mean that each widget was worth at least $.15 to him. But it was worth only $.14 to A—$.10, what he paid, plus $.04 ($1000 divided by 25,000), his expected profit. Thus the breach resulted in a transfer of the 26,000 widgets from a lower valued to a higher valued use.

There are two major criteria under which the theory of efficient breach needs to be evaluated. One is whether the predicates of the theory are correct; the other is whether if the predicates of the theory are correct the theory is justified on the ground that it promotes efficiency. The theory could be valid only if it satisfies both criteria.

Predicates. The theory of efficient breach rests on two basic predicates, both of which feature in Posner's illustration. The first predicate is that the expectation measure makes the promisee indifferent between performance and damages. This predicate is incorrect because expectation damages do not have that effect. For example, expectation damages are based on objective rather than subjective value; the recovery of a buyer's lost profits under the expectation measure is often cut off by the principle of Hadley v. Baxendale, the certainty rule, or both (see Chapter 6, infra); expectation damages do not include legal fees and other costs of litigation; and prejudgment interest for breach of contract is often not awarded, and when awarded is almost invariably less than the time value of the gains that the promisee would have made from performance.

The second predicate of the theory of efficient breach is that at the time of the perform-or-breach decision, the promisor knows the value that the promisee places on the commodity. In the context of the Overbidder Paradigm, this predicate is incorrect because the seller will seldom know what value the buyer puts on a contracted-for commodity. At least in the case of differentiated commodities (which is the only case in which the theory of efficient breach is relevant), at the time of contract formation a buyer will rarely if ever tell a seller what profits he expects to make from a contract, because a seller could use that information to lever up the price. Even if the buyer did disclose that information, the seller would normally have no way of knowing what profits the buyer expected to make at the time of the perform-or-breach decision, because between the time of contract-formation and the time of that decision, markets may have shifted, or the buyer may have increased his potential profits through investment in beneficial reliance such as advertising or the purchase of complimentary commodities.

Efficiency. Even assuming, counterfactually, that the predicates of the theory of efficient breach were correct, the encouragement of breach in the Overbidder Paradigm would decrease rather than promote efficiency. The efficiency justification of the theory is that if a seller's gain on sale to an overbidder exceeds the buyer's loss, breach is an instrument for transferring a commodity to a higher-valued use. However, in a world without transaction costs, commodities will always flow to higher-valued uses, so that if the overbidder values the commodity more than the buyer, he will end up with the commodity even under a performance regime. Commodities will also normally flow to higher-valued uses in a world *with* transaction costs. If a third party values the commodity more than the buyer, and knows the buyer's identity, he will purchase from the buyer either an assignment of the contract or the commodity itself. If the third party does not know the buyer's identity, a rational seller will either negotiate with the buyer to be released from the contract, so that she can sell to the overbidder, or will sell the overbidder's identity to the buyer, or the buyer's identity to the overbidder. Posner more or less admitted that if an overbidder values the contracted-for commodity more than the buyer, the overbidder will end up with the commodity even if the seller is not allowed to breach, and fell back on an argument that the transaction costs of moving a commodity to an overbidder will be less in an efficient-breach regime than in a performance regime. However, it is impossible to establish that the transaction costs of moving commodities to higher-valued uses would be less under an efficient-breach regime than under a performance regime. Indeed, given the cost of litigation, the transaction costs of such movements would almost certainly be greater in an efficient-breach regime.

In short, in the context of the Overbidder Paradigm there is no convincing efficiency justification for the theory of efficient breach. Moreover, if the theory was widely followed, it would lead to inefficiency, by remaking the parties' contract, reducing the rewards for planning and investing, and weakening the contracting system.

Remaking Contracts. The efficiency of a contract rule can normally be measured by asking whether it is the rule that well-informed contracting parties would normally agree upon if bargaining were cost-free. There is an easy way to determine whether the theory of efficient breach corresponds to what contracting parties in the Overbidder Paradigm would normally agree upon. Suppose a seller and a buyer have negotiated a contract under which the seller agrees to sell a differentiated commodity to buyer—say, a home to live in, or a used machine that the buyer will employ as a factor of production. As the parties are about to sign a written contract, the seller says, "In all honesty, I should tell you that although I have no present intention to breach this contract, neither do I have a present intention to perform. If a better offer comes along, I will take it and pay you expectation damages. In fact, I will begin actively looking for a better offer right after we sign this contract. Let's insert a provision that recognizes that I will do just that."

What would be the buyer's likely response? Under the theory of efficient breach, the buyer would say, "Of course, I expect no more." Experience strongly suggests, however, that in real life most buyers would be surprised if not shocked by such a statement, and would either walk away; insist on an explicit contractual provision stating that the seller has a present intent to perform and that any profit on breach and resale will go to buyer; or demand a payment, in the form of a reduced price, for the seller's right to resell. Buyers will react this way because normally one of the very points of a bargain promise is to convince the promisee that the promisor has an intent to perform.

Moreover, at the time a contract for the sale of a differentiated commodity is made, the buyer and the seller know that an overbid might later be forthcoming. Because the buyer and the seller know this, the buyer will need to pay the seller an implicit premium for taking the risk of forgoing an overbid. The amount of this premium will be the expected value of an overbid, based on a rough probability-weighted average of potential overbid prices. To put this differently, if the seller is economically rational, her price will include a premium paid by the buyer to ensure that the seller will take the contracted-for commodity off the market–a premium equal to the reduction in price that the buyer would demand for giving the seller a right to resell to an overbidder. Allowing the seller to obtain and retain the amount of this premium takes from the buyer an amount that he has bought and paid for, and inefficiently remakes the parties contract.

Reducing the rewards for planning and investing. The theory of efficient breach also inefficiently reduces the rewards for planning and investing. Where the buyer's damages are based on the difference between contract price and market price, under the theory of efficient breach the seller will gain from breach only if the price paid by the overbidder exceeds the market price. There are two basic reasons why an overbidder may pay more than market price.

First, market price is an inexact, midpoint construct based on extrapolations from comparable transactions, and the overbidder may be willing to pay a price above the artificial midpoint. In that case the theory has no positive efficiency implication: there is no reason to believe that the overbidder values the commodity more highly than the buyer, because the buyer may also have been willing to pay a price above the constructed market price.

Second, the overbidder may have a special strategic need for the commodity that leads him to place a higher value on the commodity than anyone else, and the constructed market price is almost certain to be less than that value. However, if the third party had a special strategic need for the commodity when he made his overbid, he probably had a prospect of the strategic need when the original contract was made. The question then arises, why didn't the overbidder make a contract with the seller at that time? The answer to this question is likely to involve issues of foresight and investment. For example, it may often be that the commodity takes time to produce, and the buyer foresaw a future need for the commodity and was willing to invest in a contract for production of the commodity, at a time when the overbidder lacked the foresight, was unwilling to make the investment, or both. Or, it may be that the commodity essentially consists of productive capacity, and the buyer foresaw a future need for that capacity, and was willing to invest in a contract to lock up that capacity, at a time when the overbidder lacked the foresight, was unwilling to make the investment, or both.

In either type of case, the overbidder may be willing to pay more than the constructed market price because the supply or productive capacity that he needs has now become highly constrained. However, providing the seller with an incentive to sell the commodity to the overbidder in either type of case would deny the buyer the benefit of his foresight and investment. Efficient incentives should be just the other way around. The law should reward the ant, not the grasshopper. It is the buyer who has earned the opportunity to acquire the commodity, by having foresight and investing when the third party was either not smart enough or willing enough to do so. Accordingly, in such cases too, the theory of efficient breach would have efficiency costs, because it would reduce the rewards for planning and investing.

Weakening the contracting system. There is a third way the theory of efficient breach, if widely followed, would reduce efficiency. The theory of efficient breach is based on a static and short-run approach to the issue of breach, because it addresses only the efficiency of performing or breaching an individual contract. In contrast, a dynamic, long-run approach to the issue of breach addresses the efficiency of the contracting system as a whole. From that perspective, the theory of efficient breach is inefficient because if widely followed, it would diminish the efficiency of that system.

The efficiency of the contracting system does not rest, as the theory of efficient breach implies, solely on legal remedies. Rather, the efficiency of the contracting system rests on a tripod whose legs are legal remedies, reputational constraints, and the internalization of social norms, in particular, the moral norm of promise-keeping. These three legs are mutually supportive. Legal rules rest in significant part on social norms, reputational effects rest principally on social norms, and moral norms are reinforced by legal rules and supported by reputational effects.

All three of these legs are necessary to ensure the reliability of the contracting system. Legal rules are not alone sufficient, because dispute-settlement under law is expensive and chancy. The moral norm of promise-keeping is not alone sufficient, because not all actors fully internalize moral norms and there are limits on the power of norms. Reputational effects are not alone sufficient, because reputations are fully effective only if third parties have reliable knowledge concerning a promisor's history of breach, and this kind of information is hard to come by, both because many breaches do not become widely known and because many promisors will often claim that they had a valid excuse for not performing.

Because all three legs are necessary to support the efficiency of the contracting system, anything that weakens one leg seriously threatens the efficiency of the system. The theory of efficient breach, if widely adopted, would do precisely that, because the effect of the theory is to remove the moral force of promising in a bargain context. The moral meaning of making a promise is to commit yourself to take a given action in the future even if, when the action is due to be taken, all things considered you do not wish to take it. The theory of efficient breach turns this upside down. Under that theory, if you don't wish to take a promised action when it is due, because all things considered you believe that the cost to you of taking the action would exceed the gain to the promise, you not only needn't, but shouldn't keep the promise. As Posner states, if the seller's gain from breach will exceed the buyer's loss, then "if damages are limited to loss of expected profit, there will be an incentive to commit breach. *There should be.*"

Given the dilution or elimination of the moral force of promises under the theory of efficient breach, that theory, if widely adopted, would decrease the efficiency of the contracting system in three ways. (1) It would increase the need to resort to litigation, which is very expensive, as opposed to achieving performance of contracts through the internalization of the moral norm of promise-keeping, which is very inexpensive. (2) It would lead contracting parties to make greater use of costly noncontractual measures to ensure performance, such as self-enforcing deposits. (3) It would diminish the force of reputational constraints, because reputational constraints rest in part on a moral basis.

To summarize, in the context of the Overbidder Paradigm the theory of efficient breach is inefficient in three major respects. First, the theory would inefficiently remake the parties' contract by converting a contract under which the seller agrees to provide a commodity, and to not search for or sell to an overbidder, into a contract that allows and indeed encourages sellers to both search for and sell to overbidders. Second, the theory would reduce the rewards for planning and investing, by encouraging sellers to transfer commodities away from buyers who have planned and invested, to overbidders who have done neither. Third, the theory would reduce the efficiency of the contracting system by seriously weakening one of the three legs upon which that efficiency rests.

———

GREER PROPERTIES, INC. v. LaSALLE NATIONAL BANK, 874 F.2d 457 (7th Cir. 1989). In February 1987, the Sellers contracted to sell a parcel of real estate to Searle Chemicals for approximately $1,100,000. Searle had the right to terminate the contract if the soil was contaminated by environmental waste. The deal fell through because an environmental consulting firm that Searle hired reported that the site was contaminated, and that a clean-up would cost more than $500,000.

The Sellers then contracted to sell the property to Greer for $1,250,000. Under this contract the Sellers were required to remove the environmental contamination at their own expense, but were allowed to terminate the contract if the cost of the clean-up became economically impracticable. The Sellers then retained a soil consultant, who estimated the cost of the clean-up at $100,000—$200,000. At that point, the Sellers went back to Searle and entered into a new round of negotiations. A purchase price of $1,455,000 was proposed in these negotiations and embodied in a draft contract prepared by Searle. The Sellers then terminated the contract with Greer, purportedly under the clean-up provision.

Greer brought an action for specific performance and damages. The district court held for Sellers, on the ground that upon receipt of the soil consultant's study, Sellers had broad discretion to terminate the contract under the clean-up provision. The Seventh Circuit reversed, on the ground that by making the contract with Searle, Sellers had given up their right to look for a better price:

> Under Illinois law, "every contract implies good faith and fair dealing between the parties to it." ... This implied obligation of good faith and fair dealing in the performance of contracts acts as a limit on the discretion possessed by the parties.... With this limitation on the discretion of the Sellers in mind, their decision to terminate the contract must be analyzed to determine if they acted in good faith. If the Sellers terminated the contract to obtain a better price from Searle, their action would have been in bad faith. *When the Sellers entered the contract with Greer and Greer agreed to pay them a specific price for the property, the Sellers gave up their opportunity to shop around for a better price.* By using the termination clause to recapture that opportunity, the Sellers would have acted in bad faith. (Emphasis added.)

NOTE ON PUNITIVE DAMAGES

It is often said that punitive damages are normally unavailable for breach of contract. Thus Restatement Second § 355 states that "Punitive damages are not recoverable for a breach of contract unless the conduct constituting the breach is also a tort for which punitive damages are recoverable."

Under § 355, punitive damages are available if the conduct constituting the breach is independently a tort. Some of the "torts" in question look suspiciously like breaches of contract. For example, under Illustration 3 to Section 355:

> A, a telephone company, contracts with B to render uninterrupted service. A, tortiously as well as in breach of contract, fails to maintain service at night and B is unable to telephone a doctor for his sick child. B's right to recover punitive damages is governed by Restatement, Second, Torts § 908.

Punitive damages may be available for a breach of the duty of good faith, on the theory that a breach of good faith is tortious. It is now well accepted that there is a duty to perform contractual duties in good faith. Accordingly, this exception, if rigorously followed, could have a very wide ambit. In practice, however, the exception has been relatively limited. Its most significant application has been in suits by insureds against their insurance companies for failure to settle or defend in good faith. See Comunale v. Traders & General Insurance Co., 50 Cal.2d 654, 328 P.2d 198 (1958). Some cases have also applied the exception in cases involving a breach of an employment contract by an employer, and in certain other limited contexts, see, e.g., Nicholson v. United Pacific Insurance Co., 219 Mont. 32, 710 P.2d 1342 (1985). However, in Foley v. Interactive Data Corp., 47 Cal.3d 654, 254 Cal.Rptr. 211, 765 P.2d 373 (1988), the California Supreme Court held that punitive damages were not available for breach of the duty of good faith by an employer.

Many jurisdictions have adopted tests that are more expansive than that of Section 355. For example, in Suffolk Sports Center, Inc. v. Belli Construction Corp., 212 A.D.2d 241, 628 N.Y.S.2d 952 (1995), a landlord had barricaded the entrances to the tenant's leased sports facilities during a dispute concerning the lease. In approving punitive damages against the landlord, the court said that punitive damages were available where the breach evinces a " 'high degree of moral turpitude' or is 'actuated by evil and reprehensible motives,' and demonstrates 'such wanton dishonesty as to imply a criminal indifference to civil obligations.' " In Miller v. Byrne, 916 P.2d 566 (Colo.App. 1995), the court said that "Punitive damages are available ... when a plaintiff is able to prove beyond a reasonable doubt that the defendant engage in 'willful and wanton' misconduct. Willful and wanton conduct means conduct purposefully committed which the actor must have realized is dangerous, done heedlessly and recklessly, without regard to consequences, or of the rights and safety of others, particularly of the plaintiff."

In practice, punitive damages for breach of contract are not that uncommon. Marc Galanter analyzes data concerning contract litigation in his article, Contract in Court; Or Almost Everything You May or May Not Want to Know about Contract Litigation, 2001 Wis. L. Rev. 577. Among Galanter's sources is a Bureau of Justice Statistics study of contract litigation in 1992 in the seventy-five largest counties in the United States, which account for about one-third of the population. That study, Galanter reports, found that 12% of all winning plaintiffs in jury-tried contracts cases were awarded punitive damages (as compared to only 4% of winning plaintiffs in jury-tried tort cases). Even in judge-tried contracts cases, which outnumbered jury-tried cases by two to one, winning plaintiffs in contracts cases were awarded punitive damages 3.6% of the time.

Chapter 6

THE EXPECTATION MEASURE

Chapter 6 considers the basic principle of expectation damages, that is, the principle that upon breach of a bargain contract the injured party should be put in the position she would have been in if the contract had been performed. When that very general principle is applied to concrete, recurring kinds of cases, like breach of contracts for the sale of goods, much more specific rules are applied. The first few Sections of Chapter 6 examine some of these rules—specifically, the rules that apply to breach of a contract for services by the person who contracted to perform the services (Section 1(a)); breach of a contract for services by the person who contracted to have the services performed (Section 1(b)); breach of a contract for the sale of goods by the seller (Section 2(a)); breach of a contract for the sale of goods by the buyer (Section 2(b)); and breach of an employment contract by the employer (Section 3). The remaining the materials in Chapter 6 concern limits that the law sets on the principle of expectation damages. These include the innocent party's duty to mitigate (minimize) damages, the requirement that the damages that were incurred were reasonably foreseeable at the time of breach, and the certainty with which damages must be established. The last Section of Chapter 6 concerns the test for the enforceability of "liquidated damages" provisions, that is, contractual provisions in which the parties themselves set the damages for breach.

SECTION 1. DAMAGES FOR BREACH OF A CONTRACT TO PERFORM SERVICES

(a) Breach by the Person Who Has Contracted to Perform Services

LOUISE CAROLINE NURSING HOME, INC. v. DIX CONSTRUCTION CO.

Supreme Judicial Court of Massachusetts, 1972.
362 Mass. 306, 285 N.E.2d 904.

Before TAURO, C.J., and REARDON, QUIRICO, BRAUCHER and HENNESSEY, JJ.

QUIRICO, JUSTICE.

This is an action of contract in which Louise Caroline Nursing Home, Inc. (Nursing Home) seeks damages from Dix Construction Corp. (Dix) for breach of a contract to build a nursing home. . . .

The case was referred to an auditor for hearing pursuant to a stipulation of the parties that his findings of fact would be final. After hearing the parties, the auditor filed a report in which he found generally: (1) that the Nursing Home had fulfilled all of its contractual obligations to Dix; (2) that Dix had committed a breach of its contractual obligations to the Nursing Home by failing, without justification, to complete the contract within the time agreed. . . . However, he further found that the Nursing Home "suffered no compensable damages as a result of the breach by Dix . . . in that the cost to complete the nursing home . . . was within the contract price . . . less what had been paid to Dix. . . ." . . .

. . . Two of the Nursing Home's objections relate to the measure of the damages applied by the auditor in reaching his conclusion that it suffered no "compensable damages." The rule of damages applied by the auditor was that if the cost of completing the contract by the use of a substitute contractor is within the contract price, less what had already been paid on the contract, no "compensable damages" have occurred. The Nursing Home argues that the proper rule of damages would entitle it to the difference between the value of the building as left by Dix and the value it would have had if the contract had been fully performed. Under this rule the Nursing Home contends that it was entitled to the "benefits of its bargain," meaning that if the fair market value of the completed building would have exceeded the contractual cost of construction, recovery should be allowed for this lost extra value. It bases this argument primarily upon our statement in Province Sec. Corp. v. Maryland Cas. Co., 269 Mass. 75, 94, 168 N.E. 252, 257, that "[i]t is a settled rule that the measure of damages where a contractor has failed to perform a contract for the construction of a building for business uses is the difference between the value of the building as left by the contractor and its value had it been finished according to contract. In other words the question is how much less was the building worth than it would have been worth if the contract had been fully performed. Powell v. Howard, 109 Mass. 192. White v. McLaren, 151 Mass. 553, 24 N.E. 911. Norcross Brothers Co. v. Vose, 199 Mass. 81, 95, 96, 85 N.E. 468. Pelatowski v. Black, 213 Mass. 428, 100 N.E. 831." This statement was probably not necessary to the court's decision in the *Province Sec. Corp.* case and, in any event, must be read in light of the cases cited by the court in support of it. All of these cases involved failure of performance in the sense of defective performance, as contrasted with abandonment of performance. In one of the cases, Pelatowski v. Black, 213 Mass. 428, 431, 100 N.E. 831, 832, the court expressly distinguished "cases where a contractor has abandoned his work while yet unfinished."

The fundamental rule of damages applied in all contract cases was stated by this court in Ficara v. Belleau, 331 Mass. 80, 82, 117 N.E.2d 287, 289, in the following language: "It is not the policy of our law to award damages which would put a plaintiff in a better position than if the defendant had carried out his contract. . . . 'The fundamental principle upon which the rule of damages is based is compensation. . . . Compensation is the value of the performance of the contract, that is, what the plaintiff would have made had the contract been performed.' F.A. Bartlett Tree Expert Co. v. Hartney, 308 Mass. 407, 412, 32 N.E.2d 237, 240. . . . The plaintiff is entitled to be made whole and no more."

Consonant with this principle we have held that in assessing damages for failure to complete a construction contract, "[t]he measure of the plaintiffs' damages (at least in the absence of other elements of damage, as, for example, for delay in construction, which the master has not found here) can be only in the amount of the reasonable cost of completing the contract and repairing the defendant's defective performance less such part of the contract price as has not been paid." Di Mare v. Capaldi, 336 Mass. 497, 502, 146 N.E.2d 517, 521. This principle was recently reiterated in Providence Washington Ins. Co. v. Beck, 356 Mass. 739, 255 N.E.2d 600. In the face of this principle the Nursing Home's arguments attempting to demonstrate the amount of alleged "benefits of its bargain" lost are to no avail. In any event, it should be noted that any such "benefits of its bargain" as would derive from obtaining a building worth much more than the actual costs of construction are preserved if the building can be completed at a total cost which is still within the contract price, less any amount which has already been paid on the contract. The auditor was correct in applying the "cost of completion" measure of damages which excluded any separate recovery for lost "benefits of its bargain."

The Nursing Home additionally contends that even under the rule of damages applied by the auditor they were entitled, in the words of the *DiMare* case, *supra,* to recover "other elements of damage, as, for example, for delay in construction." 336 Mass. at 502, 146 N.E.2d at 521. The short answer to this contention is the auditor's express statement, in his summary of the evidence, that "[t]here was no specific evidence as to the costs of delay, if any." . . .

. . . For the foregoing reasons the Nursing Home's exceptions to the denial of its motion to recommit the auditor's report and to the granting of Reliance's motion for entry of judgment in accordance with the auditor's report must be overruled.

Exceptions overruled.

––––––

HAWKINS v. McGEE

Chapter 5, supra

––––––

PEEVYHOUSE v. GARLAND COAL & MINING CO.

Supreme Court of Oklahoma, 1962.
382 P.2d 109, cert. denied, 375 U.S. 906, 84 S.Ct. 196, 11 L.Ed.2d 145 (1963).

JACKSON, J. In the trial court, plaintiffs Willie and Lucille Peevyhouse sued the defendant, Garland Coal and Mining Company, for damages for breach of contract. Judgment was for plaintiffs in an amount considerably less than was sued for. Plaintiffs appeal and defendant cross-appeals.

In the briefs on appeal, the parties present their argument and contentions under several propositions; however, they all stem from the basic question of whether the trial court properly instructed the jury on the measure of damages.

Briefly stated, the facts are as follows: plaintiffs owned a farm containing coal deposits, and in November, 1954, leased the premises to defendant for a period of five years for coal mining purposes. A "strip-mining" operation was contemplated in which the coal would be taken from pits on the surface of the ground, instead of from underground mine shafts. In addition to the usual covenants found in a coal mining lease, defendant specifically agreed to perform certain restorative and remedial work at the end of the lease period. It is unnecessary to set out the details of the work to be done, other than to say that it would involve the moving of many thousands of cubic yards of dirt, at a cost estimated by expert witnesses at about $29,000.00. However, plaintiffs sued for only $25,000.00.

During the trial, it was stipulated that all covenants and agreements in the lease contract had been fully carried out by both parties, except the remedial work mentioned above; defendant conceded that this work had not been done.

Plaintiffs introduced expert testimony as to the amount and nature of the work to be done, and its estimated cost. Over plaintiffs' objections, defendant thereafter introduced expert testimony as to the "diminution in value" of plaintiffs' farm resulting from the failure of defendant to render performance as agreed in the contract—that is, the difference between the present value of the farm, and what its value would have been if defendant had done what it agreed to do.

At the conclusion of the trial, the court instructed the jury that it must return a verdict for plaintiffs, and left the amount of damages for jury determination. On the measure of damages, the court instructed the jury that it might consider the cost of performance of the work defendant agreed to do, "together with all of the evidence offered on behalf of either party".

It thus appears that the jury was at liberty to consider the "diminution in value" of plaintiffs' farm as well as the cost of "repair work" in determining the amount of damages.

It returned a verdict for plaintiffs for $5000.00—only a fraction of the "cost of performance", *but more than the total value of the farm even after the remedial work is done.*

On appeal, the issue is sharply drawn. Plaintiffs contend that the true measure of damages in this case is what it will cost plaintiffs to obtain performance of the work that was not done because of defendant's default.

Defendant argues that the measure of damages is the cost of performance "limited, however, to the total difference in the market value before and after the work was performed".

It appears that this precise question has not heretofore been presented to this court. In Ardizonne v. Archer, 72 Okl. 70, 178 P. 263, this court held that the measure of damages for breach of a contract to drill an oil well was the reasonable cost of drilling the well, but here a slightly different factual situation exists. The drilling of an oil well will yield valuable geological information, even if no oil or gas is found, and of course if the well is a producer, the value of the premises increases. In the case before us, it is argued by defendant with some force that the performance of the remedial work defendant agreed to do will add at the most only a few hundred dollars to the value of plaintiffs' farm, and that the damages should be limited to that amount because that is all plaintiffs have lost.

Plaintiffs rely on Groves v. John Wunder Co., 205 Minn. 163, 286 N.W. 235, 123 A.L.R. 502. In that case, the Minnesota court, in a substantially similar situation, adopted the "cost of performance" rule as opposed to the "value" rule. The result was to authorize a jury to give plaintiff damages in the amount of $60,000, where the real estate concerned would have been worth only $12,160, even if the work contracted for had been done.

It may be observed that Groves v. John Wunder Co., supra, is the only case which has come to our attention in which the cost of performance rule has been followed under circumstances where the cost of performance greatly exceeded the diminution in value resulting from the breach of contract. Incidentally, it appears that this case was decided by a plurality rather than a majority of the members of the court.

Defendant relies principally upon Sandy Valley & E.R. Co., v. Hughes, 175 Ky. 320, 194 S.W. 344; Bigham v. Wabash–Pittsburg Terminal Ry. Co., 223 Pa. 106, 72 A. 318; and Sweeney v. Lewis Const. Co., 66 Wash. 490, 119 P. 1108. These were all cases in which, under similar circumstances, the appellate courts followed the "value" rule instead of the "cost of performance" rule. Plaintiff points out that in the earliest of these cases (Bigham) the court cites as authority on the measure of damages an earlier Pennsylvania *tort* case, and that the other two cases follow the first, with no explanation as to why a measure of damages ordinarily followed in cases sounding in tort should be used in contract cases. Nevertheless, it is of some significance that three out of four appellate courts have followed the diminution in value rule under circumstances where, as here, the cost of performance greatly exceeds the diminution in value.

The explanation may be found in the fact that the situations presented are artificial ones. It is highly unlikely that the ordinary property owner would agree to pay $29,000 (or its equivalent) for the construction of "improvements" upon his property that would increase its value only about ($300) three hundred dollars. The result is that we are called upon to apply principles of law theoretically based upon reason and reality to a situation which is basically unreasonable and unrealistic.

In Groves v. John Wunder Co., supra, in arriving at its conclusions, the Minnesota court apparently considered the contract involved to be analogous to a building and construction contract, and cited authority for the proposition that the cost of performance or completion of the building as contracted is ordinarily the measure of damages in actions for damages for the breach of such a contract.

In an annotation following the Minnesota case beginning at 123 A.L.R. 515, the annotator places the three cases relied on by defendant (Sandy Valley, Bigham and Sweeney) under the classification of cases involving "grading and excavation contracts".

We do not think either analogy is strictly applicable to the case now before us. The primary purpose of the lease contract between plaintiffs and defendant was neither "building and construction" nor "grading and excavation". It was merely to accomplish the economical recovery and marketing of coal from the premises, to the profit of all parties. The special provisions of the lease contract pertaining to remedial work were incidental to the main object involved.

Even in the case of contracts that are unquestionably building and construction contracts, the authorities are not in agreement as to the factors to be considered in determining whether the cost of performance rule or the value rule should be applied. The American Law Institute's Restatement of the Law, Contracts, Volume 1, Sections 346(1)(a)(i) and (ii) submits the proposition that the cost of performance is the proper measure of damages "if this is possible and does not involve *unreasonable economic waste*"; and that the diminution in value caused by the breach is the proper measure "if construction and completion in accordance with the contract would involve *unreasonable economic waste*". (Emphasis supplied.) In an explanatory comment immediately following the text, the Restatement makes it clear that the "economic waste" referred to consists of the destruction of a substantially completed building or other structure. Of course no such destruction is involved in the case now before us.

On the other hand, in McCormick, Damages, Section 168, it is said with regard to building and construction contracts that " . . . in cases where the defect is one that can be repaired or cured without *undue expense* "the cost of performance is the proper measure of damages, but where" . . . the defect in material or construction is one that cannot be remedied without *an expenditure for reconstruction disproportionate to the end to be attained* "(emphasis supplied) the value rule should be followed. The same idea was expressed in Jacob & Youngs, Inc. v. Kent, 230 N.Y. 239, 129 N.E. 889, 23 A.L.R. 1429, as follows:

"The owner is entitled to the money which will permit him to complete, unless the cost of completion is grossly and unfairly out of proportion to the good to be attained. When that is true, the measure is the difference in value."

It thus appears that the prime consideration in the Restatement was "economic waste"; and that the prime consideration in McCormick, Damages, and in Jacob & Youngs, Inc. v. Kent, supra, was the relationship between the expense involved and the "end to be attained"—in other words, the "relative economic benefit".

In view of the unrealistic fact situation in the instant case, and certain Oklahoma statutes to be hereinafter noted, we are of the opinion that the "relative economic benefit" is a proper consideration here. This is in accord with the recent case of Mann v. Clowser, 190 Va. 887, 59 S.E.2d 78, where, in applying the cost rule, the Virginia court specifically noted that " ... the defects are remediable from a practical standpoint and the costs *are not grossly disproportionate to the results to be obtained"* (Emphasis supplied).

23 O.S.1961 §§ 96 and 97 provide as follows:

"§ 96.... Notwithstanding the provisions of this chapter, no person can recover a greater amount in damages for the breach of an obligation, than he would have gained by the full performance thereof on both sides....

"§ 97.... Damages must, in all cases, be reasonable, and where an obligation of any kind appears to create a right to unconscionable and grossly oppressive damages, contrary to substantial justice no more than reasonable damages can be recovered."

Although it is true that the above sections of the statute are applied most often in tort cases, they are by their own terms, and the decisions of this court, also applicable in actions for damages for breach of contract. It would seem that they are peculiarly applicable here where, under the "cost of performance" rule, plaintiffs might recover an amount about nine times the total value of their farm. Such would seem to be "unconscionable and grossly oppressive damages, contrary to substantial justice" within the meaning of the statute. Also, it can hardly be denied that if plaintiffs here are permitted to recover under the "cost of performance" rule, they will receive a greater benefit from the breach than could be gained from full performance, contrary to the provisions of Sec. 96.

An analogy may be drawn between the cited sections, and the provisions of 15 O.S.1961 §§ 214 and 215. These sections tend to render void any provisions of a contract which attempt to fix the amount of stipulated damages to be paid in case of a breach, except where it is impracticable or extremely difficult to determine the actual damages. This results in spite of the agreement of the parties, and the obvious and well known rationale is that insofar as they exceed the actual damages suffered, the stipulated damages amount to a penalty or forfeiture which the law does not favor.

23 O.S.1961 §§ 96 and 97 have the same effect in the case now before us. *In spite of the agreement of the parties,* these sections limit the damages recoverable to a reasonable amount not "contrary to substantial justice"; they prevent plaintiffs from recovering a "greater amount in damages for the breach of an obligation" than they would have "gained by the full performance thereof".

We therefore hold that where, in a coal mining lease, lessee agrees to perform certain remedial work on the premises concerned at the end of the lease period, and thereafter the contract is fully performed by both parties except that the remedial work is not done, the measure of damages in an action by lessor against lessee for damages for breach of contract is ordinarily the reasonable cost of performance of the work; however, where the contract provision breached was merely incidental to the main purpose in view, and where the economic benefit which would result to lessor by full performance of the work is grossly disproportionate to the cost of performance, the damages which lessor may recover are limited to the diminution in value resulting to the premises because of the non-performance.

We believe the above holding is in conformity with the intention of the Legislature as expressed in the statutes mentioned, and in harmony with the better-reasoned cases from the other jurisdictions where analogous fact situations have been considered. It should be noted that the rule as stated does not interfere with the property owner's right to "do what he will with his own" (Chamberlain v. Parker, 45 N.Y. 569), or his right, if he chooses, to contract for "improvements" which will actually have the effect of reducing his property's value. Where such result is in fact contemplated by the parties, and is a main or principal purpose of those contracting, it would seem that the measure of damages for breach would ordinarily be the cost of performance.

The above holding disposes of all of the arguments raised by the parties on appeal.

Under the most liberal view of the evidence herein, the diminution in value resulting to the premises because of nonperformance of the remedial work was $300.00. After a careful search of the record, we have found no evidence of a higher figure, and plaintiffs do not argue in their briefs that a greater diminution in value was sustained. It thus appears that the judgment was clearly excessive, and that the amount for which judgment should have been rendered is definitely and satisfactorily shown by the record.

We are asked by each party to modify the judgment in accordance with the respective theories advanced, and it is conceded that we have authority to do so. 12 O.S.1961 § 952; Busboom v. Smith, 199 Okl. 688, 191 P.2d 198; Stumpf v. Stumpf, 173 Okl. 1, 46 P.2d 315.

We are of the opinion that the judgment of the trial court for plaintiffs should be, and it is hereby, modified and reduced to the sum of $300.00, and as so modified it is affirmed.

WELCH, DAVISON, HALLEY, and JOHNSON, JJ., concur.

WILLIAMS, C.J., BLACKBIRD, V.C.J., and IRWIN and BERRY, JJ., dissent.

IRWIN, JUSTICE (dissenting).

By the specific provisions in the coal mining lease under consideration, the defendant agreed as follows:

> "... 7b Lessee agrees to make fills in the pits dug on said premises on the property line in such manner that fences can be placed thereon and access had to opposite sides of the pits.

> "[7]c Lessee agrees to smooth off the top of the spoil banks on the above premises.

> "7d Lessee agrees to leave the creek crossing the above premises in such a condition that it will not interfere with the crossings to be made in pits as set out in 7b.

> . . .

> "7f Lessee further agrees to leave no shale or dirt on the high wall of said pits...."

Following the expiration of the lease, plaintiffs made demand upon defendant that it carry out the provisions of the contract and to perform those covenants contained therein.

Defendant admits that it failed to perform its obligations that it agreed and contracted to perform under the lease contract and there is nothing in the record which indicates that defendant could not perform its obligations. Therefore, in my opinion defendant's breach of the contract was wilful and not in good faith.

Although the contract speaks for itself, there were several negotiations between the plaintiffs and defendant before the contract was executed. Defendant admitted in the trial of the action, that plaintiffs insisted that the above provisions be included in the contract and that they would not agree to the coal mining lease unless the above provisions were included.

In consideration for the lease contract, plaintiffs were to receive a certain amount as royalty for the coal produced and marketed and in addition thereto their land was to be restored as provided in the contract.

Defendant received as consideration for the contract, its proportionate share of the coal produced and marketed and in addition thereto, the *right to use* plaintiffs' land in the furtherance of its mining operations.

The cost for performing the contract in question could have been reasonably approximated when the contract was negotiated and executed and there are no conditions now existing which could not have been reasonably anticipated by the parties. Therefore, defendant had knowledge, when it prevailed upon the plaintiffs to execute the lease, that the cost of performance might be disproportionate to the value or benefits received by plaintiff for the performance.

Defendant has received its benefits under the contract and now urges, in substance, that plaintiffs' measure of damages for its failure to perform should be the economic value of performance to the plaintiffs and not the cost of performance.

If a peculiar set of facts should exist where the above rule should be applied as the proper measure of damages, (and in my judgment those facts do not exist in the instant case) before such rule should be applied, consideration should be given to the benefits received or contracted for by the party who asserts the application of the rule.

Defendant did not have the right to mine plaintiffs' coal or to use plaintiffs' property for its mining operations without the consent of plaintiffs. Defendant had knowledge of the benefits that it would receive under the contract and the approximate cost of performing the contract. With this knowledge, it must be presumed that defendant thought that it would be to its economic advantage to enter into the contract with plaintiffs and that it would reap benefits from the contract, or it would have not entered into the contract.

Therefore, if the value of the performance of a contract should be considered in determining the measure of damages for breach of a contract, the value of the benefits received under the contract by a party who breaches a contract should also be considered. However, in my judgment, to give consideration to either in the instant action, completely rescinds and holds for naught the solemnity of the contract before us and makes an entirely new contract for the parties. . . .

In Great Western Oil & Gas Company v. Mitchell, Okl., 326 P.2d 794, we held:

"The law will not make a better contract for parties than they themselves have seen fit to enter into, or alter it for the benefit of one party and to the detriment of the others; the judicial function of a court of law is to enforce a contract as it is written."

I am mindful of Title 23 O.S.1961 § 96, which provides that no person can recover a greater amount in damages for the breach of an obligation than he could have gained by the full performance thereof on both sides, except in cases not applicable herein. However, in my judgment, the above statutory provision is not applicable here.

In my judgment, we should follow the case of Groves v. John Wunder Company, 205 Minn. 163, 286 N.W. 235, 123 A.L.R. 502, which defendant agrees "that the fact situation is apparently similar to the one in the case at bar", and where the Supreme Court of Minnesota held:

"The owner's or employer's damages for such a breach (i.e. breach hypothesized in 2d syllabus) are to be measured, not in respect to the value of the land to be improved, but by the reasonable cost of doing that which the contractor promised to do and which he left undone."

The hypothesized breach referred to states that where the contractor's breach of a contract is wilful, that is in bad faith, he is not entitled to any benefit of the equitable doctrine of substantial performance.

In the instant action defendant has made no attempt to even substantially perform. The contract in question is not immoral, is not tainted with fraud, and was not entered into through mistake or accident and is not contrary to public policy. It is clear and unambiguous and the parties understood the terms thereof, and the approximate cost of fulfilling the obligations could have been approximately ascertained. There are no conditions existing now which could not have been reasonably anticipated when the contract was negotiated and executed. The defendant could have performed the contract if it desired. It has accepted and reaped the benefits of its contract and now urges that plaintiffs' benefits under the contract be denied. If plaintiffs' benefits are denied, such benefits would inure to the direct benefit of the defendant.

Therefore, in my opinion, the plaintiffs were entitled to specific performance of the contract and since defendant has failed to perform, the proper measure of damages should be the cost of performance. Any other measure of damage would be holding for naught the express provisions of the contract; would be taking from the plaintiffs the benefits of the contract and placing those benefits in defendant which has failed to perform its obligations; would be granting benefits to defendant without a resulting obligation; and would be completely rescinding the solemn obligation of the contract for the benefit of the defendant to the detriment of the plaintiffs by making an entirely new contract for the parties.

I therefore respectfully dissent to the opinion promulgated by a majority of my associates.

NOTE

In a petition for rehearing, plaintiffs argued that the trial court had wrongfully excluded evidence they presented to show that the diminution in the value of their farm was greater than $300 because the farm consisted not merely of the 60 acres covered by the coal-mining lease, but other lands as well. The court held, 5–4, that the evidence was properly excluded because the complaint related only to the 60 acres covered by the lease and the case had been tried and argued by plaintiffs on a cost-of-performance rather than a diminished-value theory.

RESTATEMENT, SECOND, OF CONTRACTS § 348(2)

[See Selected Source Materials Supplement]

NOTE ON ADDITIONAL FACTS IN PEEVYHOUSE

1. The following excerpt from defendant's brief in *Peevyhouse* (as brought out by Professor Richard Danzig in unpublished materials) proposes an explanation why Garland, the defendant-appellee, did not perform the remedial work:

> A review of the testimony of the witness, G.B. Cumpton, will indicate that the defendant, at time of execution of the contract, had [a] good faith intention of complying with all of the terms; but, after partial performance, it became apparent that the amount of coal under the leased property was limited; and the operations were not extended far enough toward the southeastward to permit economic compliance with the terms of the lease requiring remedial work.

> Attention of the court is specifically invited to the following excerpt from the testimony of Mr. Cumpton: . . .

>> "Q. Now then, you were asked also by Mr. McConnell if when you executed this lease you intended to comply with the provisions for installing a fence. And I will ask you if you had been able economically to mine further coal toward the southeast, would you have been able to establish that fence on the spoil bank?

>> "A. Yes, we could have.

>> "Q. Having stopped when you ran out of coal down in here, can you now establish that fence line without putting in a very useless and expensive fill?

>> "A. No. . . ."

> From all the testimony of Mr. Cumpton and the engineer, Curry, it is obvious that the Appellee, at the inception of the contract, intended to comply with the terms; but, after it became economically impossible to complete performance of mining operations across the entire tract of

land, construction of dikes for erection of fences became impracticable. Appellee went as far with performance of the remedial work as could reasonably be expected under the circumstances, without futile expenditure of money which would accomplish no constructive purpose.

It is respectfully submitted that Appellee did not willfully, or in bad faith, enter into a contract which it did not intend to perform.

2.   In Peevyhouse v. Garland Coal & Mining Co. Revisited: The Ballad of Willie and Lucille, 89 Nw.U.L.Rev. 1341 (1995), Professor Judith Maute reports that the Peevyhouses were reluctant to allow mining on their land, while Garland needed immediate access to the land to divert a creek from a neighboring piece of land that it was already mining. Thus the Peevyhouses seem to have had a relatively strong bargaining position. What they negotiated for was Garland's promise to do the restorative work on their land. The standard strip-mining lease used in the area did not contain provisions for restorative work. Instead, lessors typically received an up-front per-acre payment to compensate them for the damage that would be done to their land in the course of the mining. This amount would usually equal the total value of the land before mining began. The Peevyhouses were aware of this standard provision, and they had seen the damage done to their neighbors' land over the years. The Peevyhouses gave up the standard advance payment for surface damage, which in their case would have been $3,000, in return for Garland's promise to do certain restorative work on their land.

Maute questions Garland's claim that because the coal on the Peevyhouse's land was less accessible than Garland expected, the promised restoration was much more costly to implement than Garland had anticipated.

NOTE ON OKLAHOMA MINING LANDS RECLAMATION ACT

In 1967, Oklahoma adopted a statute entitled the Open Cut Land Reclamation Act, which was replaced in 1971 by the Mining Lands Reclamation Act. That Act declares it to be the policy of Oklahoma "to provide for the reclamation ... of land subjected to surface disturbance by mining and thereby to preserve natural resources, to encourage the productive use of such lands after mining, ... to protect the natural beauty and aesthetic values in the affected areas of this state, and to protect and promote the health, safety and general welfare of the people of this state." Under the Act, it is unlawful to engage in any mining operations without first obtaining a permit to do so. Each application for a permit must be accompanied by a plan of reclamation that meets the requirements of the Act, which include grading the banks of pits and depressions in a manner that gives due consideration to the natural topography of the land, and grading overburden ridges and peaks to a rolling topography traversable by equipment customarily employed in the use to which the land will be put after reclamation. Each application for a permit must be accompanied by a bond for the faithful performance of the Act's requirements.

SCHNEBERGER v. APACHE CORP., 890 P.2d 847 (Okl.1994). In June 1982, Apache corporation began drilling an oil and gas well on a property owned by Fred and Zola Schneberger. In 1984, the Schnebergers sued Apache on the ground that in drilling and operating that well and another well located on nearby property, Apache had polluted the Schneberger property with harmful substances. In 1986, the parties made an agreement that settled the 1984 action. In 1989, the Schnebergers filed a new complaint against Apache, alleging that Apache had breached the 1986 settlement agreement by failing to achieve the reduced level of water contaminants that the settlement agreement specified. The Schnebergers sought to measure damages by the cost of achieving the reduced level of contamination. Apache argued that the proper measure of damages was the diminution in value of the Schneberger property. Held, for Apache.

Apache relies on *Peevyhouse* for the proposition that the correct measure of damages for breach of the settlement agreement is the loss in value of the plaintiff's property. Plaintiffs estimate that it will cost approximately $1.3 million to complete remediation to the standards set forth in the agreement, while Apache estimates that the loss in market value of the property to be $5,175.00. Therefore, Apache contends that under the rule established in *Peevyhouse*, plaintiffs' recovery should be limited to the diminution in value since remediation costs are grossly disproportionate to the loss in value of the land.

Contrarily, plaintiffs argue that recent statutory enactments and federal case law reflect a change in Oklahoma policy regarding protecting the environment from pollution caused by oil and gas drilling operations. Plaintiffs cite the enactment of statutes designed to protect the environment from pollution including:

52 O.S. [Oklahoma Statutes] 1965, §§ 309–320, providing for the use of the state police power to regulate and remediate oil and gas wells which are causing pollution of waters or land;

82 O.S.1972, § 1020.15 (Oklahoma Groundwater Law), prohibiting pollution of fresh groundwater;

82 O.S.1968, §§ 931 et seq. (Oklahoma Pollution Control Coordinating Act), creating the Department of Pollution Control and delegating the power to prevent and abate pollution; 52 O.S.1982, §§ 318.2–318.9 (Surface Damage Act), providing that a mineral owner or lessee negotiate with the surface owner for the payment of damages which may be caused by oil and gas drilling operations.

52 O.S.1982, §§ 318.2–318.9 (Surface Damage Act), providing that a mineral owner or lessee negotiate with the surface owner for the payment of damages which may be caused by oil and gas drilling operations.

Plaintiffs urge that the policy change reflected in these statutes clearly indicates that the diminution in value rule established in *Peevyhouse* is outdated and contend that the cost of remediation is the proper measure of damages for pollution caused by oil and gas drilling operations....

... [T]he state of Oklahoma is committed to protecting the environment and preserving the state's natural resources. This is all the more evident given the passage of the Surface Damage Act, 52 O.S.Supp.1982, § 318.2 et seq., which states Oklahoma's policy regarding damage to land caused by oil and gas drilling operations. However, the intent of the Act was never to tip the scale in favor of one interest over the other, but rather, provide a balance between these two competing interests....

Prior to the Surface Damage Act, the holder of an oil and gas lease had almost an unrestricted right to go on the leased land and prospect for oil. The only basis for recovery of damages was proof of wanton or negligent destruction of the land or use of lands not reasonably necessary for oil and gas exploration. Wilcox Oil Co. v. Lawson, 341 P.2d 591, 594 (Okla.1959). The measure of damages for negligent destruction of land or crops was the difference between the value of such land before the injury and the value after the injury. Id. at 595.

The Surface Damage Act changed the standard of liability for damages to the surface estate, requiring the holder of an oil and gas lease to negotiate with the surface owner, prior to beginning operations, for the payment of damages which may be caused by the drilling. 52 O.S.1991, § 318.5. As noted above this change in liability reflected a legislative effort to balance the interests of the two resource owners and expressed a change in policy toward promoting environmental conservation. Davis Oil Co., 766 P.2d at 1351.

However, even under the Surface Damage Act, we have determined that the measure of damage to the surface estate to be the diminution in the value of the land caused by the drilling operations....

The Surface Damage Act accurately reflects Oklahoma policy concerning conservation of the state's natural resources and balancing the interests of oil and gas operators with those of surface estate owners. Under this Act, we have consistently determined that diminution in value is the proper measure for permanent damages....

Our earlier decisions were grounded on a statutory basis for holding to diminution in value as a proper measure of damage as well. The current statute, 23 Okla.Stat.1991, § 97 (titled "Damages must be reasonable") provides as follows:

> Damages must, in all cases, be reasonable, and where an obligation of any kind appears to create a right to unconscionable and grossly oppressive damages, contrary to substantial justice, no more than reasonable damages can be recovered.

In *Peevyhouse*, for example, this court noted that the above statute was most often cited in tort cases, but recognized that the statute, by its own terms, was applicable in breach of contract actions. The statutory language closely resembles the reasoning this court has employed in adhering to the diminution in value rule in breach of contract actions.

In the present action, plaintiffs argue that Apache's attempt to abate the pollution on plaintiffs' property and its subsequent inability to reach the standards required by the agreement constitute defective or unfinished performance. Plaintiffs' estimated costs of remediation are $1.3 million dollars. The estimated diminution in value of plaintiffs' land is estimated at $5,175.00. Certainly, in a breach of contract action, the "cost to complete" must be given consideration as a measure of damages. However, where the cost is grossly disproportionate to the cost of reclamation as in *Peevyhouse,* a review of recent case law suggests that courts are adhering to the diminution in value award. . . .

H.P. DROHER & SONS v. TOUSHIN, 250 Minn. 490, 85 N.W.2d 273 (1957). This case was decided by the Minnesota court, which also decided Groves v. John Wunder Co., discussed in *Peevyhouse.* Droher agreed to build a house for the Toushins for an adjusted price of just under $44,000. When the house was completed, a steel post in the basement, which supported a beam on which the floor joists rested, was too low. As a result, the level of the floor, and of other parts of the house, sagged noticeably. To correct this defect it would have been necessary to jack up the beam. If that were done the plaster would crack and parts of the house would need to be rebuilt, so that the cost of repair would exceed $20,000. The diminution in the value of the house resulting from the defect was apparently much less than $20,000. Held, the diminished-value rule should be applied:

> . . . [The decision in Groves v. John Wunder Co.] was by a divided court, three members of the court concurring in the opinion, two dissenting, and two taking no part. The majority opinion is based, at least in part, on the fact that the breach of the contract was wilful and in bad faith. . . .
>
> It would seem that the better rule and the one followed by a majority of the courts is that, where there is a substantial good-faith effort to perform the contract but there are defects of such a nature that the contract has not been performed according to its terms, which defects can be remedied without the destruction of a substantial part of the building, the owner is entitled to recover the cost of making the work conform to the contract but, where it appears that the cost of remedying the defects is grossly disproportionate to the benefits to be derived therefrom, the owner is entitled to recover the difference between the value of the property as it would have been if the contract had been performed according to its terms and the value in its condition as constructed. Cases such as we have here, where the evidence establishes a substantial good-faith performance, are to be distinguished from those where there has been a wilful failure to perform at all, such as we had in Groves v. John Wunder Co. . . .

EASTERN STEAMSHIP LINES, INC. v. UNITED STATES, 125 Ct.Cl. 422, 112 F.Supp. 167 (1953). The United States Government chartered the steamship *Acadia* as a troop transport during World War II. The charter provided:

> Clause 7. . . . Before redelivery, the Charterer [that is, the Government], at its own expense, and on its time, shall restore the Vessel to at least as good condition and class as upon delivery, ordinary wear and tear excepted, and do all work and make all repairs necessary to satisfy any outstanding classification or steamboat inspection requirements necessary to place her in such condition and class. . . . [provided] that at the

Charterer's option, redelivery of the Vessel to the Owner may be made prior to satisfying such requirements or prior to completion of such repairs or work, in which event the Charterer shall pay to the Owner the amount reasonably expended to place the Vessel in such class and condition. . . .

After the war, the owner sued the government for $4,000,000, which the owner claimed to be due under Clause 7 of the charter as the estimated cost of restoring the *Acadia* to its pre-war condition. The Government claimed that it was not bound to pay more than $2,000,000, the estimated value of the ship after restoration, and that it was not bound to pay anything until the ship was restored. The court rejected the owner's claim:

> [We will assume, based on the evidence] that after some $4,000,000 had been spent in restoring the ship, it would be worth $2,000,000. . . .
>
> . . . According to the plaintiff's interpretation [of the charter] the Government has now become obligated to pay it $4,000,000. Candor compels the plaintiff to say that it will not feel obliged to spend the $4,000,000 when it gets it, to restore the *Acadia*. Common sense and reality tell us that it will not so spend the money, since after the expenditures it would have only a $2,000,000 ship. The result would be that the Government would pay out $2,000,000 more than the plaintiff had lost by the Government's chartering and use of its ship. The extra $2,000,000 would not be a subsidy to get ships built or sailing. The *Acadia* would still rust at anchor. We decline to . . . produce such a result.
>
> . . . We think that neither party anticipated what actually happened, *viz.* that the market for old ships on the one hand, and the market for labor and materials, on the other, would be such as to make the restoration of old ships a useless and wasteful expenditure of public funds. . . .
>
> The plaintiff has urged that, regardless of the waste of public money that would be entailed by compelling the Government to pay $4,000,000 when the plaintiff's loss is $2,000,000 the weight of authority is that what is "nominated in the bond" will be compelled, regardless of economic waste. We think that is not the law. . . .
>
> . . . The case will be assigned to a commissioner of this court for trial upon the question of the value of the *Acadia*.

CITY SCHOOL DISTRICT OF THE CITY OF ELMIRA v. McLANE CONSTRUCTION CO., 85 A.D.2d 749, 445 N.Y.S.2d 258 (1981). In 1976, the Elmira school district contracted with McLane Construction Company for the construction of a swimming-pool building, which was to feature a roof consisting of natural-wood decking supported by laminated-wood beams. The appearance of the beams was central to the aesthetics of the architectural scheme, which contrasted the natural beauty of the beams with the relatively stark unfinished concrete that comprised the balance of the structure. Even the effectiveness of the indirect lighting system employed in the building depended on the beams. As the building was to be a showplace, and the site of large regional swimming competitions, the design was intentionally dramatic. It was contemplated that the beams, properly treated, would be essentially maintenance-free. However, Weyerhauser Company, which supplied the beams, and was aware of the plans and specifications, used a method of treating the beams that it knew would result in staining and discoloration, and the beams became permanently discolored.

The school district recovered a verdict of $357,000 against Weyerhauser, based on the cost of replacing the beams. On appeal, Weyerhauser argued that damages should have been limited to $3,000, the difference between the value of the structure as built and its value if the beams had been as agreed-upon. Held, for the school district.

"[W]here the contractor's performance has been incomplete or defective, the usual measure of damages is the reasonable cost of replacement or completion (*American Std. v. Schectman,* 80 A.D.2d 318, 321, 439 N.Y.S.2d 529). That rule does not apply if the contractor performs in good faith but defects nevertheless exist and remedying them could entail economic waste. Then, diminution in value becomes the proper measure of damages. A classic illustration of when the general rule is abandoned in favor of this exception is *Jacob & Youngs v. Kent,* 230 N.Y. 239, 129 N.E. 889, where the contractor did not use the brand of pipe specified in the contract, but other brands of like quality. Inasmuch as the cost of replacing the pipe was grievously out of proportion to any damages actually suffered by the house owner, the proper award was the nominal difference in value of the house with and without the specified brand of pipe.

"But Weyerhaeuser does not come within this exception, for here the defect, in relation to the entire project, was not of inappreciable importance. One of the school district's principal objectives was to have an aesthetically prepossessing structure, and that goal has by all accounts been frustrated. Moreover, as the facts already recited indicate, Weyerhaeuser's conduct cannot be said to be innocent oversight or inattention...."

———

FOX v. WEBB, 268 Ala. 111, 105 So.2d 75 (1958). "[I]t may be observed further that a distinction exists between a contract to construct a dwelling for the owner who plans to live therein and a contract to construct a commercial structure where the aesthetic taste of the owner is not so deeply involved. It seems to us that when the owner contracts to have a dwelling constructed he wants a particular structure, not just any structure that could be built for the same price. We, therefore, think that the trial court was correct in awarding damages equal to the amount required to reconstruct the dwelling so as to make it conform to the specifications, rather than adopting the difference in loan value on the dwelling as the measure of damages, as contended by appellant."

———

GROSSMAN HOLDINGS LTD. v. HOURIHAN, 414 So.2d 1037 (Fla. 1982). In October 1978, the Hourihans contracted with Grossman Holdings to purchase a house to be built in a planned development. Prior to entering into the contract, the Hourihans had examined a model and office drawings of the proposed house. Both the model and the office drawings showed the house with a southeast exposure, and the contract stated that Grossman would construct the house "substantially the same" as the model or the plans and specifications at the seller's office. In December, a new drawing went on display in the Grossman office. The new drawing showed the Hourihan's soon-to-be-built house facing in the opposite direction from the southeast exposure that the Hourihans wanted and expected.

The Hourihans brought this discrepancy to the attention of Grossman's employees and remonstrated against construction of a mirror image of the house they had contracted for. In spite of the Hourihans' objections, the contractors refused to change their plans and began constructing the house depicted in the December drawings. The Hourihans then sued for breach of contract. The trial court found that Grossman had breached its contract, but refused to award damages, on the grounds that (i) cost-of-completion damages would be economically wasteful and out of proportion to the good to be attained, under the rule of Restatement First § 346(a)(ii) (referred to in *Peevyhouse*) and (ii) diminished-value damages were improper because the value of the house had increased substantially since the date of the contract. The intermediate court of appeals reversed, on the ground that the unreasonable-economic-waste doctrine does not apply to residential construction. The Florida Supreme Court held that the trial court was correct in applying that doctrine:

> ... We disagree with the [appeal] court's conclusion that the rule as enunciated in subsection 346(1)(a)(ii) is applicable only to commercial buildings....
>
> ... The record supports the trial court's finding that reconstructing the house would result in economic waste, and we will not disturb this finding.

However, the court held, the fact that the house had appreciated in value after the date of delivery was not a bar to diminution in-value damages:

> Damages for breach of contract should be measured as of the date of the breach. Fluctuations in value after the breach do not affect the nonbreaching party's recovery. Here it may be possible to demonstrate a difference in value as of the date of delivery between the house the Hourihans contracted for and the house that Grossman built. If such difference exists, the Hourihans should have the opportunity to prove it on remand and recover that amount as damages.

———

ADVANCED, INC. v. WILKS, 711 P.2d 524 (Alaska 1985). "An owner's recovery is not necessarily limited to diminution in value whenever that figure is less than the cost of repair. It is true that in a case where the cost of repair exceeds the damages under the value formula, an award under the cost of repair measure may place the owner in a better economic position than if the contract had been fully performed, since he could pocket the award and then sell the defective structure. On the other hand, it is possible that the owner will use the damage award for its intended purpose and turn the structure into the one originally envisioned. He may do this for a number of reasons, including personal esthetics or a hope for increased value in the future. If he does this his economic position will equal the one he would have been in had the contractor fully performed. The fact finder is the one in the best position to determine whether the owner will actually complete performance, or whether he is only interested in obtaining the best immediate economic position he can. In some cases, such as where the property is held solely for investment, the court may conclude as a matter of law that the damage award can not exceed the diminution in value. Where, however, the property has special significance to the owner and repair seems likely, the cost of repair may be appropriate even if it exceeds the diminution in value."

NOTE ON RUXLEY ELECTRONICS AND CONSTRUCTION LTD. v. FORSYTH

In Ruxley Electronics and Construction Ltd. v. Forsyth [1996] 1 A.C. 344, [1995] 3 All E.R. 268 (H.L.1995), Ruxley contracted to build a swimming pool for Forsyth for £ 70,000. The maximum depth of the pool was to be 7' 6". After the work had been completed, Forsyth discovered that the maximum depth was only 6' 9", and at the point where swimmers would dive into the pool the depth was only 6'. Forsyth refused to pay the balance of the price, £39,072. Ruxley sued for that amount, and Forsyth counterclaimed for breach of contract.

The trial judge made the following findings of fact: (1) The pool as constructed was safe for diving; a depth of 6' is adequate, even for a beginner. According to an official handbook, the minimum safe depth is 5'. (2) Because the pool was safe for diving, the shortfall in depth did not decrease the value of the pool. (3) The only way of increasing the depth of the pool was to demolish the existing pool altogether, and start again, at a cost of £21,560. (4) Forsyth had no intention of building a new pool.

The trial judge concluded that to spend £21,560 on a new pool would be unreasonable since the cost would be wholly disproportionate to the advantage, if any, of having a pool 7' 6" deep. Therefore, if Forsyth was awarded cost-of-completion damages he would end up with both a pool that was substantially complete in accordance with the contract and a windfall profit of £21,560. The trial court did, however, award damages to Forsyth for the loss of pleasure and amenity that he had suffered by reason of the lack not being able to dive 7' 6" in deep, as opposed to 6' deep. The trial court said:

> In the course of his written submissions Mr. Forsyth reminded me that "This is not a matter of commerce to be nicely measured in money. Swimming pools are not necessities, they are for fun. Due to [the contractor's] default I have lost some fun." I think that where a contract is for the provision of a pleasurable amenity, such as a swimming pool, it is entirely proper to award a general sum for the loss of amenity. I accept that there has been a loss of amenity brought about by the shortfall in depth and I award damages for loss of that amenity in the sum of £2,500.

The House of Lords affirmed the trial judge's verdict. Lord Mustill stated:

> ... It is a common feature of small building works performed on residential property that the cost of the work is not fully reflected by an increase in the market value of the house, and that comparatively minor deviations from specification or sound workmanship may have no direct

financial effect at all. Yet the householder must surely be entitled to say that he chose to obtain from the builder a promise to produce a particular result because he wanted to make his house more comfortable, more convenient and more conformable to his own particular tastes; not because he had in mind that the work might increase the amount which he would receive if, contrary to expectation, he thought it expedient in the future to exchange his home for cash. To say that in order to escape unscathed the builder has only to show that to the mind of the average onlooker, or the average potential buyer, the results which he has produced seem just as good as those which he had promised would make a part of the promise illusory and unbalance the bargain....

In my opinion there would indeed be something wrong if ... [cost-of-completion damages and diminished-value damages] were the only available measures of recovery ... Having taken on the job the contractor is morally as well as legally obliged to give the employer what he stipulated to obtain, and this obligation ought not to be devalued.... There are not two alternative measures of damage, at opposite poles, but only one: namely the loss truly suffered by the promisee. In some cases the loss cannot be fairly measured except by reference to the full cost of repairing the deficiency in performance. In others, and in particular those where the contract is designed to fulfil a purely commercial purpose, the loss will very often consist only of the monetary detriment brought about by the breach of contract. But these remedies are not exhaustive, for the law must cater for those occasions where the value of the promise to the promisee exceeds the financial enhancement of his position which full performance will secure. This excess, often referred to in the literature as the "consumer surplus" ... is usually incapable of precise valuation in terms of money, exactly because it represents a personal, subjective and non-monetary gain. Nevertheless, where it exists the law should recognise it and compensate the promisee if the misperformance takes it away.... [T]he test of reasonableness plays a central part in determining the basis of recovery, and will indeed be decisive in a case such as the present when the cost of [completion] would be wholly disproportionate to the non-monetary loss suffered by the employer. But it would be equally unreasonable to deny all recovery for such a loss. The amount may be small, and since it cannot be quantified directly there may be room for difference of opinion about what it should be. But in several fields the judges are well accustomed to putting figures to intangibles, and I see no reason why the imprecision of the exercise should be a barrier, if that is what fairness demands.*

---

* One of my students, Lewis Stiller, commented on *Ruxley* as follows: "In my opinion [the] trial judge must not have been a swimmer. A 7'6" pool is clearly superior for swimming and diving to a 6' pool." (Footnote by ed.)

(b) Breach by a Person Who Has Contracted to Have Services Performed

AIELLO CONSTRUCTION, INC. v. NATIONWIDE TRACTOR TRAILER TRAINING AND PLACEMENT CORP.

Supreme Court of Rhode Island, 1980.
122 R.I. 861, 413 A.2d 85.

Opinion

WEISBERGER, JUSTICE.

This case comes before us on appeal from a judgment of the Superior Court which awarded damages to the plaintiffs for a breach of contract allegedly committed by the defendant when it failed to make certain installment payments required by the contract. The case was tried by a justice sitting without the intervention of a jury. The facts as found in his decision are as follows.

The plaintiffs, Aiello Construction, Inc., and Smithfield Peat Co., Inc., as joint venturers, entered into a written contract with defendant in March of 1973. The contract required plaintiffs to haul fill and perform grading work in order to bring a large area owned by defendant to an approximately level condition. The contract further provided that plaintiffs would remove ledge on a portion of the premises, grade eight inches of bank run gravel over the entire yard, grade two inches of crushed run gravel over the entire yard, and finally apply penetration and seal coats of oil topped by application of peastone. The surface was then to be rolled. The defendant was in the trucking business and also engaged in the training and instruction of tractor-trailer operators. The yard area was to be used in the operation of this training enterprise.

In payment for the work to be performed and the material to be furnished, defendant agreed to pay $33,000 in five monthly installments of $6,600 each. The installments were to become due on April 15, May 15, June 15, July 15, and August 15, all during the year 1973. The contract provided that any amount not paid would bear a service charge of 1½ percent per month.

The plaintiffs began work in late March 1973 and continued the work until on or about May 10, 1973, at which time all of the preliminary work had been done save applying and grading the two inches of crushed run gravel, which was a prerequisite to the performance of the oiling. The plaintiffs then stopped work to allow the ground to settle. Meanwhile, defendant paid the monthly installment that was due on April 15. Thereafter, defendant did not pay the May installment, although over a period from June to August of 1973 it did make partial payments which, when added to the April installment, aggregated $10,500. No further payments were made, and the president of the defendant company indicated that funds were not available to make the payments that were due. As a result of the failure to make payments, plaintiffs did not resume work. The plaintiffs brought the instant action for breach of contract. . . .

The trial justice found as a fact that defendant was in breach of the contract and that this breach relieved plaintiffs of the obligation to perform any further work under the contract. . . . The trial justice awarded damages for the breach of contract by calculating the costs which plaintiffs had incurred in the performance of the work up to the time they withdrew from the project as a result of the breach. He found that the costs amounted to

$21,500. To this sum he added $3,000 which he determined from the testimony to be the profit which plaintiffs would have made had the contract been completely performed by both parties. From the sum of $24,500 the trial justice deducted the payments made by defendant in the amount of $10,500. He ordered judgment to enter for plaintiffs in the amount of $14,000 together with interest at the rate of 8 percent per annum from the time of filing of the complaint to the date of judgment.... Thus judgment was entered for the plaintiffs for $16,800. This appeal ensued....

The defendant argues that the trial justice did not correctly assess damages. He cites in support of his argument *George v. George F. Berkander, Inc.*, 92 R.I. 426, 169 A.2d 370 (1961). In that case the rule of damages for breach of contract was stated to be such "as will serve to put the injured party as close as is reasonably possible to the position he would have been in had the contract been fully performed." *Id.* at 430, 169 A.2d at 372. It is precisely this rule that the trial justice attempted to apply. Although the measure of damages may be variously stated under the principle of our holding in *Berkander,* certain alternatives are well set forth in Restatement *Contracts* § 346(2) as follows:

> "For a breach by one who has promised to pay for construction, if it is a partial breach the builder can get judgment for the instalment due, with interest; and if it is a total breach he can get judgment, with interest so far as permitted by the rules stated in § 337, for either

> "(a) the entire contract price ... less installments already paid and the cost of completion that the builder can reasonably save by not completing the work; or

> "(b) the amount of his expenditure in part [pe]rformance of the contract, subject to the limitations stated in § 333."[1]

The general rules set forth in the Restatement are further elucidated by the commentary. A portion of the comment on subsection (2) of Restatement § 346 reads as follows:

> "*h.* Another common form of stating the measure of recovery is as follows: Damages, measured by the builder's actual expenditure to date of breach less the value of materials on hand, plus the profit that he can prove with reasonable certainty would have been realized from full performance. * * * The builder has a right to his expenditures as well as his profits, because payment of the full price would have reimbursed those expenditures in full and given him his profit in addition * * *."

An examination of the record in this case discloses that the trial justice scrupulously followed this method of assessment of damages, that his findings of fact were amply supported by the evidence, and that he did not overlook or misconceive the evidence in arriving at his conclusion.... [A] court must

---

1. Restatement *Contracts* § 333 (1932) reads in part as follows:

"(a) Such expenditures are not recoverable in excess of the full contract price promised by the defendant.

"(b) Expenditures in preparation are not recoverable unless they can fairly be regarded as part of the cost of performance in estimating profit and loss.

"(c) Instalments of the contract price already received and the value of materials on hand that would have been consumed in completion must be deducted.

"(d) If full performance would have resulted in a net loss to the plaintiff, the amount of this loss must be deducted, the burden of proof being on the defendant."

select the most appropriate remedy depending upon the factual posture of the case and the election of remedy by the plaintiff. The remedy selected by the trial justice in this case was appropriately relevant to the factual posture and the remedy sought by plaintiffs. Therefore, the trial justice cannot be faulted for his assessment of damages either in regard to the law or to the facts. . . .

For the reasons stated, the defendant's appeal is denied and dismissed, the judgment of the Superior Court is affirmed, and the case is remitted to the Superior Court.

DORIS, J., did not participate.

————

NOTE ON FORMULAS FOR MEASURING DAMAGES FOR BREACH BY A PERSON WHO HAS CONTRACTED TO HAVE SERVICES PERFORMED

Call a person who agrees to perform services a Contractor, and call the person for whom the services are to be performed the Owner. The trial court in *Aiello* measured the Contractor's damages for breach by the Owner under the following formula: (i) expenditures incurred prior to breach, plus (ii) lost profits, offset by (iii) the amount paid by the Owner prior to the breach. As the Rhode Island Supreme Court pointed out, this formula is reflected in Comment h to Restatement First § 346.

The Supreme Court also pointed out that a different (and algebraically equivalent) formula is reflected in the black letter of § 346: (i) contract price, less (ii) the cost of completion that the builder saved by not completing the work, offset by (iii) the amount paid by the Owner prior to the breach.

Although the two formulas are algebraically equivalent, the second formula is the one that is usually employed. Under the first formula, the court must determine lost profits. Since profits equal contract price minus costs (by definition), to apply the first formula the court must calculate (i) all the costs the Contractor incurred prior to breach and (ii) all the costs remaining to be incurred at that point. In contrast, to apply the second formula the court need only calculate the costs remaining to be incurred at the time of breach.

For a demonstration that the two measures are equivalent, see Petropoulos v. Lubienski, 220 Md. 293, 152 A.2d 801, 804–05 (1959).

Although § 346 and Comment h are in terms limited to construction contracts, the formulas they embody are generally applicable to the breach of any contract for the performance of services.

————

RESTATEMENT, SECOND, CONTRACTS § 347, Illustrations 6, 7: "6. A contracts to build a house for B for $100,000. When it is partly built, B repudiates the contract and A stops work. A would have to spend $60,000 more to finish the house. The $60,000 cost avoided by A as a result of not having to finish the house is subtracted from the $100,000 price lost in determining A's damages. A has a right to $40,000 in damages from B, less any progress payments that he has already received.

"7. The facts being otherwise as stated in Illustration 6, A has bought materials that are left over and that he can use for other purposes, saving him $5,000. The $5,000 cost avoided is subtracted in determining A's damages, resulting in damages of only $35,000 rather than $40,000."

WIRED MUSIC, INC. v. CLARK, 26 Ill.App.2d 413, 168 N.E.2d 736 (1960). Wired Music distributed recorded music to various locations, through direct wires rented from the telephone company. Clark executed a contract with Wired Music providing for three years of service at $24.30 per month. The contract provided that there could be no assignment without Wired Music's written consent.

After seventeen months, Clark moved his business and discontinued the service. The tenant who rented the space formerly occupied by Clark requested the right to take an assignment of Clark's contract, but Wired Music refused. Thereafter, the new tenant entered into a new contract for Wired Music's service at the same location and at a higher monthly charge. Wired Music sued Clark for its lost profits, based on the contract price to Clark minus Wired Music's costs for renting the telephone wires. Clark argued that Wired Music failed to show damages, because under the contract with the new tenant, Wired Music would realize more revenue from Clark's former location than it would have received from Clark. The trial court entered judgment for Wired Music in an amount that reflected the contract price for nineteen months minus the wire charges that Wired Music had to pay to the telephone company. Affirmed.

"[T]he evidence is uncontradicted that plaintiff could supply any number of additional customers without incurring further expenses except for wire rental. If defendant's contention were adopted by this court, it would have the effect of denying to the plaintiff the benefit of his bargain. This case is not at all like the situation where a plaintiff has one house to rent or one car to sell or a fixed quantity of personal property or real estate. Here, plaintiff has so far as the evidence shows, an unlimited supply of music, limited in its distributions only by the number of contracts which plaintiff can secure."

VITEX MFG. CORP. v. CARIBTEX CORP., 377 F.2d 795 (3d Cir. 1967). Vitex agreed to shower-proof 125,000 yards of material for Caribtex at a price of 26 cents per yard. No goods were forthcoming from Caribtex, and Vitex sued for breach of contract. Vitex alleged that its gross revenues for processing the material would have been $31,250 and that its variable costs would have been $10,136, leaving its damages at $21,114. The trial court so found. On appeal, Caribtex argued that the trial court erred by failing to include Vitex's overhead expenses in Vitex's costs, which would have reduced Vitex's lost profits and, therefore, its damages. Affirmed.

"Although there is authority to the contrary, we feel that the better view is that normally, in a claim for lost profits, overhead ... should not be considered as part of the seller's costs. A number of cases hold that since overhead expenses are not affected by the performance of the particular contract, there should be no need to deduct them in computing lost profits. . . . The theory of these cases is that the seller is entitled to recover losses incurred and gains prevented in excess of savings made possible, Restatement, Contracts § 329 (made part of the law of the Virgin Islands, 1 V.I.C. § 4); since overhead is fixed and nonperformance of the contract produced no overhead cost savings, no deduction from profits should result.

"The soundness of the rule is exemplified by this case. Before negotiations began between Vitex and Caribtex, Vitex had reached a lull in business activity and had closed its plant. . . . When this opportunity arose to process Caribtex's wool, the only additional expenses Vitex would incur would be those of re-opening its plant and the direct costs of processing, such as labor, chemicals and fuel oil. Overhead would have remained the same whether or not Vitex and Caribtex entered their contract and whether or not Vitex actually processed Caribtex's goods. Since this overhead remained constant, in no way attributable-to or affected-by the Caribtex contract, it would be improper to consider it as a cost of Vitex's performance to be deducted from the gross proceeds of the Caribtex contract. . . .

". . . [E]ven were we to recognize the allocation of overhead as proper, we should uphold the tacit award of overhead expense to Vitex as a 'loss incurred.' . . . [A]s the number of transactions over which overhead can be spread becomes smaller, each transaction must bear a greater portion or [allocable] share of the fixed overhead cost. Suppose a company has fixed overhead of $10,000 and engages in five similar transactions; then the receipts of each transaction would bear $2000 of overhead expense. If the company is now forced to spread this $10,000 over only four transactions, then the overhead expense per transaction will rise to $2500, significantly reducing the profitability of the four remaining transactions. Thus, where the contract is between businessmen familiar with commercial practices, as here, the breaching party should reasonably foresee that his breach will not only cause a loss of 'clear' profit, but also a loss in that the profitability of other transactions will be reduced. . . . Therefore, this loss is within the contemplation of 'losses caused and gains prevented,' and overhead should be considered to be a compensable item of damage."

SECTION 2. DAMAGES FOR BREACH
OF A CONTRACT FOR THE SALE
OF GOODS

(a) Breach by the Seller

NOTE ON DAMAGES FOR THE SELLER'S BREACH
OF A CONTRACT FOR THE SALE OF GOODS

The remedies for breach of a contract for the sale of goods are governed by the Uniform Commercial Code. A buyer's remedies for breach by the seller fall into two broad categories—specific relief (in which the buyer is awarded the actual goods) and damages. Specific relief will be covered in Chapter 7, infra.

The buyer's damage remedies, in turn, fall into several subcategories. One subcategory consists of the buyer's remedies when the seller fails to deliver or the buyer properly rejects the goods or rightfully revokes his acceptance (UCC §§ 2–712, 2–713). A second subcategory consists of the buyer's remedies when the buyer has accepted the goods, and cannot or does not want to rightfully revoke his acceptance, but the goods are defective (UCC § 2–714). Typically, such an action is for breach of warranty.

––––––

UCC §§ 2–711(1), 2–712, 2–713, 2–714, 2–715(1), 2–723, 2–724

[See Selected Source Materials Supplement]

––––––

CISG ARTS. 45, 49, 50, 74, 75, 76

[See Selected Source Materials Supplement]

––––––

CONTINENTAL SAND & GRAVEL, INC. v. K & K SAND & GRAVEL, INC., 755 F.2d 87 (7th Cir.1985). Defendant sold buyer certain mobile equipment (front-loaders, cranes, and so forth) for $50,000, and made various express warranties concerning the equipment. The warranties were breached, and plaintiff sued for damages. The trial court awarded $104,206.75, the cost of repairs to bring the equipment up to the warranted condition. Affirmed.

"Defendants argue that, since the clear bargain of the parties was to sell and purchase the mobile equipment for $50,000, the plaintiff is only entitled to receive an amount of damages that represents the diminution in value from the purchase price as the result of the breach of warranty. In other words, defendants contend that the maximum amount of recoverable damages is the difference between the fair market value of the equipment as accepted, which they define as $50,000, and the fair market value of the equipment in the defective condition. Under this method of computing damages, Continental would be entitled to recover no more than the $50,000 purchase price, and as little as nothing, depending on the court's assessment of the value of the equipment in the defective condition. . . .

"The court below rejected this argument, and instead applied section 2–714(2) of the Illinois Uniform Commercial Code, . . . which provides that damages generally should represent the difference between the value of the goods at the time of acceptance and the value they would have had if they had been as warranted. The court stated that under this section the cost of repair is the proper standard. This was the correct approach under Illinois law, as well as under the general commercial law. . . . As the district court noted, it is not unusual for damages in a breach of warranty case to exceed the purchase price of the goods. . . . This result is logical, since to limit recoverable damages by the purchase price, as defendants suggest, would clearly deprive the purchaser of the benefit of its bargain in cases in which the value of the goods as warranted exceeds that price. Thus we find that the district court properly computed the damages recoverable for the defendants' breach of the warranties."

MANOUCHEHRI v. HEIM, 123 N.M. 439, 941 P.2d 978 (N.M. Ct. App. 1997). "Although [U.C.C. §] 2–714(2) sets the measure of direct damages for breach of warranty as the difference between the value of the goods as warranted and the value of the goods as accepted, often that difference can be approximated by the cost to repair the goods so that they conform to the warranty. For example, if it costs $200 to fix [a] machine so that it performed as [warranted,] then one could assume that the unrepaired machine (the 'goods accepted') was worth $200 less than the repaired machine (the goods 'as warranted'). Thus, the cost of repair is commonly awarded as the direct damages."

EGERER v. CSR WEST, LLC

Court of Appeals of Washington, 2003.
116 Wash.App. 645, 67 P.3d 1128.

BECKER, C.J.

Appellant CSR West breached a contract to supply fill for land development. Issues on appeal include the calculation of damages based on "hypothetical cover".... We affirm in all respects.

According to unchallenged findings of fact entered after a bench trial, Robert Egerer owned a 10 acre parcel of land in Skagit County that he planned to develop into commercial property. The property required a considerable amount of fill to make it suitable for development.

Egerer first purchased fill material in 1995, when he contracted at the rate of $1.10 per cubic yard to have Wilder Construction haul to his property some material being excavated from the shoulders of Interstate 5 as a part of a highway improvement project. In its suitability to serve as structural fill, the shoulder material resembled a gravel known as "pit run", but it was cheaper than pit run because it contained asphalt grindings.

Beyond what Wilder Construction could supply, Egerer needed roughly 17,000 cubic yards of fill material. In May 1997, Egerer learned that CSR West had contracted with the Washington State Department of Transportation to excavate material from the shoulder areas of Interstate 5 near Lake Samish. He met with John Grisham, CSR's sales manager, and they reached an agreement to have CSR transport "all" the shoulder excavations from the project to Egerer's site at the rate of $.50 per cubic yard.

CSR brought fill material to Egerer's property on only two nights: July 9 and 10, 1997. Shortly thereafter, the Department of Transportation issued a change order that allowed CSR to use the excavated shoulder material in the reconstruction of the shoulder area. It was more profitable for CSR to supply the material for the State's use than to fulfill its contract with Egerer. CSR excavated a total of 16,750 cubic yards of material during its work on the shoulder project in 1997, and supplied virtually all of it to the Department of Transportation.

Egerer did not purchase replacement fill at the time of the breach in July 1997. Asked about this at trial, he explained that it would have been too expensive, and he also did not think there was time to find replacement fill and get it onto his property before the end of the summer. Egerer said that his window of opportunity to place fill on the property was June through September, before the weather became too wet. In January and February 1998, he obtained price quotes for pit run ranging from $8.25 per cubic yard to $9.00 per cubic yard. These prices exceeded Egerer's budget, and he did not contract for replacement fill at that time either.

In the summer of 1999, Egerer learned of an unexpected landslide at a gravel pit not far from his property. The company agreed to sell Egerer the unwanted slide material at a cost of $6.39 per cubic yard, including the cost of hauling and spreading.

Egerer filed suit in November 2000, alleging that CSR breached its contract by failing to deliver all the excavated shoulder material in the summer of 1997. After a bench trial, the court found breach. The court then turned to the Uniform Commercial Code to determine the measure of damages. CSR raises several legal issues with respect to the award of damages. . . .

Where a seller fails to make delivery of goods sold to a buyer, the buyer has two alternative remedies under the Uniform Commercial Code. One is the remedy of "cover": the buyer may purchase substitute goods and recover as damages the difference between the cost of this cover and the contract price, provided the buyer covers in good faith and without unreasonable delay. U.C.C. § 2–712.* The other, a complete alternative, is damages for non-delivery, also known as "hypothetical cover"[1]: the buyer may recover as damages from the seller "the difference between the market price at the time when the buyer learned of the breach and the contract price".** U.C.C. § 2–713. This measure applies only when and to the extent that the buyer does not cover. Uniform Commercial Code Comment 5, § 2–713. "The general baseline adopted in this section uses as a yardstick the market in which the buyer would have obtained cover had he sought that relief." U.C.C. Comment 1, § 2–713. "The market or current price to be used in comparison with the contract price under this section is the price for goods of the same kind and in the same branch of trade." U.C.C. Comment 2, § 2–713.

The court determined that Egerer was limited to damages for non-delivery under section 2–713: "Mr. Egerer is limited to damages reflecting the difference between CSR contract price and the price he could have obtained replacement material for at the time of the breach in 1997. See U.C.C. § 2–713(1) and Comment 3." The court found that Egerer could have obtained

---

* For simplicity, citations to the UCC have been inserted in place of citations to the counterpart sections of the Washington UCC. (Footnote by ed.)

1. *Allied Canners & Packers, Inc. v. Victor Packing Co.*, 162 Cal.App.3d 905, 911–12, 209 Cal.Rptr. 60, 61 (1984).

** The more conventional name for the damages that the court refers to as "hypothetical cover" is "market-price damages." (Footnote by ed.)

replacement material at the time of the breach for a cost of $8.25 per cubic yard—a price quoted to Egerer in early 1998. The court calculated his damages for the non-delivery of fill to be $129,812.50, which was the difference between the market price of $8.25 per cubic yard and the contract price of $.50 per cubic yard.

CSR accepts the trial court's decision to apply the remedy furnished by section 2–713, but contends the court erred by calculating damages based on a market price of $8.25 per cubic yard for pit run. CSR argues that $8.25 was not "the price for goods of the same kind" (as U.C.C. Comment 2 calls for) because pit run is a product superior to shoulder excavations containing asphalt grindings. CSR further argues that $8.25 was not "the market price at the time when the buyer learned of the breach" (as section 2–713 calls for) because the breach was in July 1997 and the $8.25 price was as of six months later—in January, 1998. CSR takes the position that the trial court should instead have used the $1.10 per cubic yard price reflected in Egerer's 1995 contract with Wilder Construction, because that was the only evidence in the record of a price for shoulder excavations. Use of the much higher price for pit run resulted in a windfall for Egerer, according to CSR.

The trial court expressly relied on Comment 3 to U.C.C. 2–713 in determining that $8.25 per cubic yard was the price for which Egerer could have obtained replacement material at the time of the breach. That comment states in part, "When the current market price under this section is difficult to prove the section on determination and proof of market price is available to permit a showing of a comparable market price or, where no market price is available, evidence of spot sale prices is proper." U.C.C. Comment 3, § 2–713. The section on determination and proof of market price provides,

> If evidence of a price prevailing at the times or places described in this Article is not readily available the price prevailing within any reasonable time before or after the time described or at any other place which in commercial judgment or under usage of trade would serve as a reasonable substitute for the one described may be used, making any proper allowance for the cost of transporting the goods to or from such other place.

U.C.C. § 2–723(2).

A court is granted a "reasonable leeway" in measuring market price under section 2–723. *Sprague v. Sumitomo Forestry Co., Ltd.,* 104 Wash.2d 751, 760, 709 P.2d 1200 (1985). Contrary to CSR's argument, a trial court may use a market price for goods different in quality from those for which the buyer contracted. That possibility is encompassed in the reference to "price . . . which in commercial judgment or under usage of trade would serve as a reasonable substitute for the one described". And section 2–723 expressly permits looking to a price "prevailing within any reasonable time before or after the time described."

We conclude the trial court did not misapply the law in concluding that the January 1998 price for pit run was the relevant market price. The court found the 1998 quotes for replacement material and hauling "were reasonable and customary", and noted that CSR "did not offer evidence that suitable replacement material was available at a lower price at the time of breach." There was testimony that shoulder excavation material, though cheap when available, is rarely available. John Grisham, CSR's sales manager, acknowledged that it would have been difficult for Egerer to locate an alternative supplier of shoulder excavations in 1997 because "quantities like that are few and far between". Grisham said he was unaware of any other pit in the area that would have had similar material available at a price anywhere near $.50 per cubic yard in the summer of 1997. Egerer's eventual purchase in 1999 was possible only because of the landslide that unexpectedly deposited unwanted fill material in a local gravel pit. If Egerer had covered at the time of the breach, higher-priced pit run would have been a reasonable substitute for the shoulder excavations. . . .

Affirmed.

WE CONCUR: SCHINDLER, COX, JJ.

————

PANHANDLE AGRI–SERVICE, INC. v. BECKER, 231 Kan. 291, 644 P.2d 413 (1982). "Failure of the buyer to utilize the remedy of cover when such is reasonably available will preclude recovery of consequential damages, such as loss of profits. . . . However, [UCC §] 2–712, which provides for cover, i.e., the buyer's procurement of substitute goods, states:

> '(3) Failure of the buyer to effect cover within this section does not bar him from any other remedy.'

"Therefore, cover is not a mandatory remedy for the buyer. The buyer is free to choose between cover and damages for nondelivery."

————

J. WHITE & R. SUMMERS, UNIFORM COMMERCIAL CODE 220–21 (5th ed. 2000). "We come now to the problem of a buyer who has covered but who seeks to ignore 2–712 and sue for a larger contract-market differential under 2–713. On first reading, it seems that he can disregard 2–712; section 2–711 tells buyers that they can 'cover' or they can recover damages for nondelivery under 2–713. Commenting on the relationship between 2–712 and 2–713, Judge Peters has argued that an aggrieved buyer who purchases goods 'in substitution' may disregard 2–712 and seek recovery under the contract-market differential of 2–713. However, this interpretation allows a buyer to learn of a breach on September 2 when the market is at $25,000, wait until September 15 to cover, when the market is at $23,000, and then sue under 2–713 for the higher damages of contract-market differential, all contrary to the general principle of 1–106 (in as good a position as if the other party had performed and no more). Moreover comment 5 to 2–713 indicates that a buyer who has covered may not use 2–713:

> The present section provides a remedy which is *completely alternative* to cover under the preceding section and applies only *when and to the extent that the buyer has not covered.*

If the Code's goal is to put the buyer in the same position as though there had been no breach, and if 2–712 will accomplish that goal but 2–713 will do so only by coincidence, why not force the covering buyer to use 2–712? There is no room for punitive damages here. . . . Notwithstanding Judge Peters' arguments concerning the statutory history ... both the message of Comment 5 to 2–713 and the policy of the Code properly deny the covering buyer any use of 2–713.... Of course, whether purchases following seller's breach are cover purchases may be a disputed question of fact. If the facts at trial show cover, 2–712 applies. If the facts do not show cover, 2–713 applies."

NOTE ON THE AVAILABILITY OF MARKET–PRICE DAMAGES TO A BUYER WHO HAS COVERED

In 2003, the National Conference of Commissioners on State Laws and the American Law Institute, who are jointly responsible for promulgating and amending the Uniform Commercial Code, adopted a number of amendments to the official version of Article 2. Amended section 2–713 (1)(a) ("Buyer's Damages for Nondelivery of Repudiation") provides as follows:

> ... Subject to Section 2–723, if the seller wrongfully fails to deliver or repudiates or the buyer rightfully rejects or justifiably revokes acceptance ... the measure of damages in the case of wrongful failure to deliver by the seller or rightful rejection or justifiable revocation of acceptance by the buyer is the difference between the market price at the time of tender under the contract and the contract price together with any incidental or consequential damages under Section 2–715, but less expenses saved in consequence of the seller's breach....

Comment 7 states:

> A buyer that has covered under Section 2–712 may not recover the contract price market price difference under this section, but instead must base the damages on those provided in Section 2–712. To award an additional amount because the buyer could show the market price was higher than the contract price would put the buyer in a better position than performance would have. Of course, the seller would bear the burden of proving that cover had the economic effect of limiting the buyer's actual loss to an amount less than the contract price-market difference.

> An apparent cover, which does not in fact replace the goods contracted for, should not foreclose the use of the contract price-market price measure of damages. If the breaching seller cannot prove that the new purchase is in fact a replacement for the one not delivered under the contract, the "cover" purchase should not foreclose the buyer's recovery under 2–713 of the market contract difference.

For various reasons, the amended version of Article 2 has not been widely adopted by state legislatures, so that at least for the time being, in most states the question whether a buyer who covers can nevertheless sue for market-price damage is still governed by the pre–2003 version of Article 2.

DELCHI CARRIER SpA v. ROTOREX CORP.

United States Court of Appeals, Second Circuit, 1995.
71 F.3d 1024.

WINTER, Circuit Judge:

Rotorex Corporation, a New York corporation, appeals from a judgment of $1,785,772.44 in damages for lost profits and other consequential damages awarded to Delchi Carrier SpA following a bench trial before Judge Munson. The basis for the award was Rotorex's delivery of nonconforming compressors to Delchi, an Italian manufacturer of air conditioners. Delchi cross-appeals from the denial of certain incidental and consequential damages. We affirm the award of damages; we reverse in part on Delchi's cross-appeal and remand for further proceedings.

BACKGROUND

In January 1988, Rotorex agreed to sell 10,800 compressors to Delchi for use in Delchi's "Ariele" line of portable room air conditioners. The air conditioners were scheduled to go on sale in the spring and summer of 1988. Prior to executing the contract, Rotorex sent Delchi a sample compressor and accompanying written performance specifications. The compressors were scheduled to be delivered in three shipments before May 15, 1988. Rotorex sent the first shipment by sea on March 26. Delchi paid for this shipment, which arrived at its Italian factory on April 20, by letter of credit. Rotorex sent a second shipment of compressors on or about May 9. Delchi also remitted payment for this shipment by letter of credit. While the second shipment was en route, Delchi discovered that the first lot of compressors did not conform to the sample model and accompanying specifications. On May 13, after a Rotorex representative visited the Delchi factory in Italy, Delchi informed Rotorex that 93 percent of the compressors were rejected in quality control checks because they had lower cooling capacity and consumed more power than the sample model and specifications. After several unsuccessful attempts to cure the defects in the compressors, Delchi asked Rotorex to supply new compressors conforming to the original sample and specifications. Rotorex refused, claiming that the performance specifications were "inadvertently communicated" to Delchi.

In a faxed letter dated May 23, 1988, Delchi cancelled the contract. Although it was able to expedite a previously planned order of suitable compressors from Sanyo, another supplier, Delchi was unable to obtain in a timely fashion substitute compressors from other sources and thus suffered a loss in its sales volume of Arieles during the 1988 selling season. Delchi filed the instant action under the United Nations Convention on Contracts for the International Sale of Goods ("CISG" or "the Convention") for breach of contract and failure to deliver conforming goods. On January 10, 1991, Judge Cholakis granted Delchi's motion for partial summary judgment, holding Rotorex liable for breach of contract.

After three years of discovery and a bench trial on the issue of damages, Judge Munson, to whom the case had been transferred, held Rotorex liable to Delchi for $1,248,331.87. This amount included consequential damages for: (i) lost profits resulting from a diminished sales level of Ariele units, (ii) expenses that Delchi incurred in attempting to remedy the nonconformity of the compressors, (iii) the cost of expediting shipment of previously ordered Sanyo compressors after Delchi rejected the Rotorex compressors, and (iv) costs of handling and storing the rejected compressors. The district court also awarded prejudgment interest under CISG art. 78.

The court denied Delchi's claim for damages based on other expenses, including: (i) shipping, customs, and incidentals relating to the two shipments of Rotorex compressors; (ii) the cost of obsolete insulation and tubing that Delchi purchased only for use with Rotorex compressors; (iii) the cost of obsolete tooling purchased only for production of units with Rotorex compressors; and (iv) labor costs for four days when Delchi's production line was idle because it had no compressors to install in the air conditioning units. The court denied an award for these items on the ground that it would lead to a double recovery because "those costs are accounted for in Delchi's recovery on its lost profits claim." It also denied an award for the cost of modification of electrical panels for use with substitute Sanyo compressors on the ground that the cost was not attributable to the breach. Finally, the court denied recovery on Delchi's claim of 4000 additional lost sales in Italy.

On appeal, Rotorex argues that it did not breach the agreement, that Delchi is not entitled to lost profits because it maintained inventory levels in excess of the maximum number of possible lost sales, that the calculation of the number of lost sales was improper, and that the district court improperly excluded fixed costs and depreciation from the manufacturing cost in calculating lost profits. Delchi cross-appeals, claiming that it is entitled to the additional out-of-pocket expenses and the lost profits on additional sales denied by Judge Munson.

DISCUSSION

The district court held, and the parties agree, that the instant matter is governed by the CISG, reprinted at 15 U.S.C.A. Appendix (West Supp.1995), a self-executing agreement between the United States and other signatories, including Italy.[2] Because there is virtually no caselaw under the Convention, we look to its language and to "the general principles" upon which it is based. See CISG art. 7(2). The Convention directs that its interpretation be informed by its "international character and ... the need to promote uniformity in its application and the observance of good faith in international trade." See CISG art. 7(1); see generally John Honnold, Uniform Law for International Sales Under the 1980 United Nations Convention 60–62 (2d ed. 1991) (addressing principles for interpretation of CISG). Caselaw interpreting analogous provisions of Article 2 of the Uniform Commercial Code ("UCC"), may also inform a court where the language of the relevant CISG provisions tracks that of the UCC. However, UCC caselaw "is not per se applicable." Orbisphere Corp. v. United States, 726 F.Supp. 1344, 1355 (Ct.Int'l Trade 1989).

We first address the liability issue. We review a grant of summary judgment de novo. Burgos v. Hopkins, 14 F.3d 787, 789 (2d Cir.1994).

---

2. Generally, the CISG governs sales contracts between parties from different signatory countries. However, the Convention makes clear that the parties may by contract choose to be bound by a source of law other than the CISG, such as the Uniform Commercial Code. See CISG art. 6 ("The parties may exclude the application of this Convention or ... derogate from or vary the effect of any of its provisions.") If, as here, the agreement is silent as to choice of law, the Convention applies if both parties are located in signatory nations. See CISG art. 1.

Summary judgment is appropriate if "there is no genuine issue as to any material fact" regarding Rotorex's liability for breach of contract. See Fed. R.Civ.P. 56(c).

Under the CISG, "[t]he seller must deliver goods which are of the quantity, quality and description required by the contract," and "the goods do not conform with the contract unless they . . . [p]ossess the qualities of goods which the seller has held out to the buyer as a sample or model." CISG art. 35. The CISG further states that "[t]he seller is liable in accordance with the contract and this Convention for any lack of conformity." CISG art. 36.

Judge Cholakis held that "there is no question that [Rotorex's] compressors did not conform to the terms of the contract between the parties" and noted that "[t]here are ample admissions [by Rotorex] to that effect." We agree. The agreement between Delchi and Rotorex was based upon a sample compressor supplied by Rotorex and upon written specifications regarding cooling capacity and power consumption. After the problems were discovered, Rotorex's engineering representative, Ernest Gamache, admitted in a May 13, 1988 letter that the specification sheet was "in error" and that the compressors would actually generate less cooling power and consume more energy than the specifications indicated. Gamache also testified in a deposition that at least some of the compressors were nonconforming. The president of Rotorex, John McFee, conceded in a May 17, 1988 letter to Delchi that the compressors supplied were less efficient than the sample and did not meet the specifications provided by Rotorex. Finally, in its answer to Delchi's complaint, Rotorex admitted "that some of the compressors . . . did not conform to the nominal performance information." There was thus no genuine issue of material fact regarding liability, and summary judgment was proper. See Perma Research & Dev. Co. v. Singer Co., 410 F.2d 572, 577–78 (2d Cir.1969) (affirming grant of summary judgment based upon admissions and deposition testimony by nonmoving party).

Under the CISG, if the breach is "fundamental" the buyer may either require delivery of substitute goods, CISG art. 46, or declare the contract void, CISG art. 49, and seek damages. With regard to what kind of breach is fundamental, Article 25 provides:

> A breach of contract committed by one of the parties is fundamental if it results in such detriment to the other party as substantially to deprive him of what he is entitled to expect under the contract, unless the party in breach did not foresee and a reasonable person of the same kind in the same circumstances would not have foreseen such a result.

CISG art. 25. In granting summary judgment, the district court held that "[t]here appears to be no question that [Delchi] did not substantially receive that which [it] was entitled to expect" and that "any reasonable person could foresee that shipping non-conforming goods to a buyer would result in the buyer not receiving that which he expected and was entitled to receive." Because the cooling power and energy consumption of an air conditioner compressor are important determinants of the product's value, the district court's conclusion that Rotorex was liable for a fundamental breach of contract under the Convention was proper.

We turn now to the district court's award of damages following the bench trial. A reviewing court must defer to the trial judge's findings of fact unless they are clearly erroneous. Anderson v. City of Bessemer, 470 U.S. 564, 575,

105 S.Ct. 1504, 1512, 84 L.Ed.2d 518 (1985); Allied Chem. Int'l Corp. v. Companhia de Navegacao Lloyd Brasileiro, 775 F.2d 476, 481 (2d Cir.1985), cert. denied, 475 U.S. 1099, 106 S.Ct. 1502, 89 L.Ed.2d 903 (1986). However, we review questions of law, including "the measure of damages upon which the factual computation is based," de novo. Wolff & Munier, Inc. v. Whiting–Turner Contracting Co., 946 F.2d 1003, 1009 (2d Cir.1991) (internal quotation marks and citation omitted); see also Travellers Int'l, A.G. v. Trans World Airlines, 41 F.3d 1570, 1574–75 (2d Cir.1994).

The CISG provides:

> Damages for breach of contract by one party consist of a sum equal to the loss, including loss of profit, suffered by the other party as a consequence of the breach. Such damages may not exceed the loss which the party in breach foresaw or ought to have foreseen at the time of the conclusion of the contract, in the light of the facts and matters of which he then knew or ought to have known, as a possible consequence of the breach of contract.

CISG art. 74. This provision is "designed to place the aggrieved party in as good a position as if the other party had properly performed the contract." Honnold, supra, at 503.

Rotorex contends, in the alternative, that the district court improperly awarded lost profits for unfilled orders from Delchi affiliates in Europe and from sales agents within Italy. We disagree. The CISG requires that damages be limited by the familiar principle of foreseeability established in Hadley v. Baxendale, 156 Eng.Rep. 145 (1854). CISG art. 74. However, it was objectively foreseeable that Delchi would take orders for Ariele sales based on the number of compressors it had ordered and expected to have ready for the season. The district court was entitled to rely upon the documents and testimony regarding these lost sales and was well within its authority in deciding which orders were proven with sufficient certainty.

Rotorex also challenges the district court's exclusion of fixed costs and depreciation from the manufacturing cost used to calculate lost profits. The trial judge calculated lost profits by subtracting the 478,783 lire "manufacturing cost"—the total variable cost—of an Ariele unit from the 654,644 lire average sale price. The CISG does not explicitly state whether only variable expenses, or both fixed and variable expenses, should be subtracted from sales revenue in calculating lost profits. However, courts generally do not include fixed costs in the calculation of lost profits. See Indu Craft, Inc. v. Bank of Baroda, 47 F.3d 490, 495 (2d Cir.1995) (only when the breach ends an ongoing business should fixed costs be subtracted along with variable costs); Adams v. Lindblad Travel, Inc., 730 F.2d 89, 92–93 (2d Cir.1984) (fixed costs should not be included in lost profits equation when the plaintiff is an ongoing business whose fixed costs are not affected by the breach). This is, of course, because the fixed costs would have been encountered whether or not the breach occurred. In the absence of a specific provision in the CISG for calculating lost profits, the district court was correct to use the standard formula employed by most American courts and to deduct only variable costs from sales revenue to arrive at a figure for lost profits.

In its cross-appeal, Delchi challenges the district court's denial of various consequential and incidental damages, including reimbursement for: (i) shipping, customs, and incidentals relating to the first and second shipments—

rejected and returned—of Rotorex compressors; (ii) obsolete insulation materials and tubing purchased for use only with Rotorex compressors; (iii) obsolete tooling purchased exclusively for production of units with Rotorex compressors; and (iv) labor costs for the period of May 16–19, 1988, when the Delchi production line was idle due to a lack of compressors to install in Ariele air conditioning units. The district court denied damages for these items on the ground that they "are accounted for in Delchi's recovery on its lost profits claim," and, therefore, an award would constitute a double recovery for Delchi. We disagree.

The Convention provides that a contract plaintiff may collect damages to compensate for the full loss. This includes, but is not limited to, lost profits, subject only to the familiar limitation that the breaching party must have foreseen, or should have foreseen, the loss as a probable consequence. CISG art. 74; see Hadley v. Baxendale, supra.

An award for lost profits will not compensate Delchi for the expenses in question. Delchi's lost profits are determined by calculating the hypothetical revenues to be derived from unmade sales less the hypothetical variable costs that would have been, but were not, incurred. This figure, however, does not compensate for costs actually incurred that led to no sales. Thus, to award damages for costs actually incurred in no way creates a double recovery and instead furthers the purpose of giving the injured party damages "equal to the loss." CISG art. 74.

The only remaining inquiries, therefore, are whether the expenses were reasonably foreseeable and legitimate incidental or consequential damages. The expenses incurred by Delchi for shipping, customs, and related matters for the two returned shipments of Rotorex compressors, including storage expenses for the second shipment at Genoa, were clearly foreseeable and recoverable incidental expenses. These are up-front expenses that had to be paid to get the goods to the manufacturing plant for inspection and were thus incurred largely before the nonconformities were detected. To deny reimbursement to Delchi for these incidental damages would effectively cut into the lost profits award. The same is true of unreimbursed tooling expenses and the cost of the useless insulation and tubing materials. These are legitimate consequential damages that in no way duplicate lost profits damages.

The labor expense incurred as a result of the production line shutdown of May 16–19, 1988 is also a reasonably foreseeable result of delivering nonconforming compressors for installation in air conditioners. However, Rotorex argues that the labor costs in question were fixed costs that would have been incurred whether or not there was a breach. The district court labeled the labor costs "fixed costs, but did not explore whether Delchi would have paid these wages regardless of how much it produced. Variable costs are generally those costs that "fluctuate with a firms' output," and typically include labor (but not management) costs. Northeastern Tel. Co. v. AT & T, 651 F.2d 76, 86 (2d Cir.1981). Whether Delchi's labor costs during this four-day period are variable or fixed costs is in large measure a fact question that we cannot answer because we lack factual findings by the district court. We therefore remand to the district court on this issue.

The district court also denied an award for the modification of electrical panels for use with substitute Sanyo compressors. It denied damages on the ground that Delchi failed to show that the modifications were not part of the regular cost of production of units with Sanyo compressors and were therefore attributable to Rotorex's breach. This appears to have been a credibility determination that was within the court's authority to make. We therefore affirm on the ground that this finding is not clearly erroneous.

Finally, Delchi cross-appeals from the denial of its claimed 4000 additional lost sales in Italy. The district court held that Delchi did not prove these orders with sufficient certainty. The trial court was in the best position to evaluate the testimony of the Italian sales agents who stated that they would have ordered more Arieles if they had been available. It found the agents' claims to be too speculative, and this conclusion is not clearly erroneous.

CONCLUSION

We affirm the award of damages. We reverse in part the denial of incidental and consequential damages. We remand for further proceedings in accord with this opinion.

(b) Breach by the Buyer

UCC §§ 2–501(1), 2–703, 2–704(1), 2–706, 2–708, 2–709, 2–710, 2–723, 2–724

[See Selected Source Materials Supplement]

CISG ARTS. 61, 62, 64, 74, 75, 76

[See Selected Source Materials Supplement]

KGM HARVESTING CO. v. FRESH NETWORK

California Court of Appeal, Sixth Appellate District, 1995.
36 Cal.App.4th 376, 42 Cal.Rptr.2d 286.

COTTLE, P. J.

California lettuce grower and distributor KGM Harvesting Company (hereafter seller) had a contract to deliver 14 loads of lettuce each week to Ohio lettuce broker Fresh Network (hereafter buyer). When the price of lettuce rose dramatically in May and June 1991, seller refused to deliver the required quantity of lettuce to buyer. Buyer then purchased lettuce on the open market in order to fulfill its contractual obligations to third parties. After a trial, the jury awarded buyer damages in an amount equal to the difference between the contract price and the price buyer was forced to pay for substitute lettuce on the open market. On appeal, seller argues that the damage award is excessive. We disagree and shall affirm the judgment....

FACTS

In July 1989 buyer and seller entered into an agreement for the sale and purchase of lettuce. Over the years, the terms of the agreement were modified. By May 1991 the terms were that seller would sell to buyer 14 loads of lettuce each week and that buyer would pay seller 9 cents a pound for the lettuce. (A load of lettuce consists of 40 bins, each of which weighs 1,000 to 1,200 pounds. Assuming an average bin weight of 1,100 pounds, 1 load would equal 44,000 pounds, and the 14 loads called for in the contract would weigh 616,000 pounds. At 9 cents per pound, the cost would approximate $55,440 per week.) Buyer sold all of the lettuce it received from seller to a lettuce broker named Castellini Company who in turn sold it to Club Chef, a company that chops and shreds lettuce for the fast food industry (specifically, Burger King, Taco Bell, and Pizza Hut). Castellini Company bought lettuce from buyer on a "cost plus" basis, meaning it would pay buyer its actual cost plus a small commission. Club Chef, in turn, bought lettuce from Castellini Company on a cost plus basis.

Seller had numerous lettuce customers other than buyer, including seller's subsidiaries Coronet East and West. Coronet East supplied all the lettuce for the McDonald's fast food chain. In May and June 1991, when the price of lettuce went up dramatically, seller refused to supply buyer with lettuce at the contract price of 9 cents per pound. Instead, it sold the lettuce to others at a profit of between $800,000 and $1.1 million. Buyer, angry at seller's breach, refused to pay seller for lettuce it had already received. Buyer then went out on the open market and purchased lettuce to satisfy its obligations to Castellini Company. Castellini covered all of buyer's extra expense except for $70,000. Castellini in turn passed on its extra costs to Club Chef which passed on at least part of its additional costs to its fast food customers.

In July 1991 buyer and seller each filed complaints [with the Department of Agriculture] under the Perishable Agricultural Commodities Act (PACA). Seller sought the balance due on its outstanding invoices ($233,000), while buyer sought damages for the difference between what it was forced to spend to buy replacement lettuce and the contract price of nine cents a pound (approximately $700,000).

Subsequently, seller filed suit [in court] for the balance due on its invoices, and buyer cross-complained for the additional cost it incurred to obtain substitute lettuce after seller's breach. At trial, the parties stipulated that seller was entitled to a directed verdict on its complaint for $233,000, the amount owing on the invoices. Accordingly, only the cross-complaint went to the jury, whose task was to determine whether buyer was entitled to damages from seller for the cost of obtaining substitute lettuce and, if so, in what amount. The jury determined that seller breached the contract, that its performance was not excused, and that buyer was entitled to $655,960.22, which represented the difference between the contract price of nine cents a pound and what it cost buyer to cover by purchasing lettuce in substitution in May and June 1991. It also determined that such an award would not result in a windfall to buyer and that buyer was obligated to the Castellini Company for the additional costs. The court subtracted from buyer's award of $655,960.22 the $233,000 buyer owed to seller on its invoices, leaving a net award in favor of buyer in the amount of $422,960.22. The court also awarded buyer prejudgment interest commencing 30 days before trial. . . .

DISCUSSION ...

A. *Seller's Appeal*

Section 2711 of the California Uniform Commercial Code [U.C.C. 2–711][3] provides a buyer with several alternative remedies for a seller's breach of contract. The buyer can " 'cover' by making in good faith and without unreasonable delay any reasonable purchase of ... goods in substitution for those due from the seller." (§ 2712, subd. (1).) In that case, the buyer "may recover from the seller as damages the difference between the cost of cover and the contract price...." (§ 2712, subd. (2).) If the buyer is unable to cover or chooses not to cover, the measure of damages is the difference between the market price and the contract price. (§ 2713.) Under either alternative, the buyer may also recover incidental and consequential damages. (§§ 2711, 2715.) In addition, in certain cases the buyer may secure specific performance or replevin "where the goods are unique" (§ 2716) or may recover goods identified to a contract (§ 2502).

In the instant case, buyer "covered" as defined in section 2712 in order to fulfill its own contractual obligations to the Castellini Company. Accordingly, it was awarded the damages called for in cover cases—the difference between the contract price and the cover price. (§ 2712.)

In appeals from judgments rendered pursuant to section 2712, the dispute typically centers on whether the buyer acted in "good faith," whether the "goods in substitution" differed substantially from the contracted for goods, whether the buyer unreasonably delayed in purchasing substitute goods in the mistaken belief that the price would go down, or whether the buyer paid too much for the substitute goods. (See generally, 1 White & Summers, Uniform Commercial Code (3d ed. 1988) Buyer's Remedies, Cover, § 6–3, pp. 284–292 [hereafter White & Summers], and cases cited therein.)

In this case, however, none of these typical issues is in dispute. Seller does *not* contend that buyer paid too much for the substitute lettuce or that buyer was guilty of "unreasonable delay" or a lack of "good faith" in its attempt to obtain substitute lettuce. Nor does seller contend that the lettuce purchased was of a higher quality or grade and therefore not a reasonable substitute.

Instead, seller takes issue with section 2712 itself, contending that despite the unequivocal language of section 2712, a buyer who covers should not necessarily recover the difference between the cover price and the contract price. Seller points out that because of buyer's "cost plus" contract with Castellini Company, buyer was eventually able to pass on the extra expenses (except for $70,000) occasioned by seller's breach and buyer's consequent purchase of substitute lettuce on the open market. It urges this court under these circumstances not to allow buyer to obtain a "windfall."[4]

---

3. Unless otherwise specified, all further statutory references are to the California Uniform Commercial Code....

4. In answering special interrogatories, the jury found (1) that if buyer were awarded the difference between the contract price and the cost of cover, it would not result in a windfall to buyer, and (2) that buyer had an obligation to pay Castellini Company for the amount Castellini Company paid buyer to acquire the substitute lettuce. On appeal, seller contends that these findings were not supported by substantial evidence. As we shall explain, however, these findings were not necessary to justify the section 2712 award. Accordingly, we need not reach the issue whether the evidence supports the jury's findings on these two special interrogatories.

The basic premise of contract law is to effectuate the expectations of the parties to the agreement, to give them the "benefit of the bargain" they struck when they entered into the agreement. In its basic premise, contract law therefore differs significantly from tort law. As the California Supreme Court explained in Foley v. Interactive Data Corp. (1988) 47 Cal.3d 654 [254 Cal.Rptr. 211, 765 P.2d 373], "... contract actions are created to enforce the intentions of the parties to the agreement [while] tort law is primarily designed to vindicate 'social policy.' " (Id. at p. 683, citing Prosser, Law of Torts (4th ed. 1971) p. 613.)

" 'The basic object of damages is compensation, and in the law of contracts the theory is that the party injured by breach should receive as nearly as possible the equivalent of the benefits of performance. [Citations.]' " (Lisec v. United Airlines, Inc. (1992) 10 Cal.App.4th 1500, 1503 [11 Cal. Rptr.2d 689].) A compensation system that gives the aggrieved party the benefit of the bargain, and no more, furthers the goal of "predictability about the cost of contractual relationships ... in our commercial system." (Foley v. Interactive Data Corp., supra, 47 Cal.3d at p. 683; Putz & Klippen, Commercial Bad Faith: Attorney Fees—Not Tort Liability—Is the Remedy for "Stonewalling" (1987) 21 U.S.F. L.Rev. 419, 432.)

With these rules in mind, we examine the contract at issue in this case to ascertain the reasonable expectations of the parties. The contract recited that its purpose was "to supply [buyer] with a consistent quality raw product at a fair price to [seller], which also allows [buyer] profitability for his finished product." Seller promised to supply the designated quantity even if the price of lettuce went up ("We agree to supply said product and amount at stated price regardless of the market price or conditions") and buyer promised to purchase the designated quantity even if the price went down ("[Buyer] agrees to purchase said product and amounts at stated price regardless of the market price or conditions, provided quality requirements are met"). The possibility that the price of lettuce would fluctuate was consequently foreseeable to both parties.

Although the contract does not recite this fact, seller was aware of buyer's contract with the Castellini Company and with the Castellini Company's contract with Club Chef. This knowledge was admitted at trial and can be inferred from the fact that seller shipped the contracted for 14 loads of lettuce directly to Club Chef each week. Thus, seller was well aware that if it failed to provide buyer with the required 14 loads of lettuce, buyer would have to obtain replacement lettuce elsewhere or would itself be in breach of contract. This was within the contemplation of the parties when they entered into their agreement.

As noted earlier, the object of contract damages is to give the aggrieved party " 'as nearly as possible the equivalent of the benefits of performance.' " (Lisec v. United Airlines, Inc., supra, 10 Cal.App.4th at p. 1503; see also § 1106 ["The remedies provided by this code shall be liberally administered to the end that the aggrieved party may be put in as good a position as if the other party had fully performed. . . ."].) In the instant case, buyer contracted for 14 loads of lettuce each week at 9 cents per pound. When seller breached its contract to provide that lettuce, buyer went out on the open market and purchased substitute lettuce to fulfill its contractual obligations to third parties. However, purchasing replacement lettuce to continue its business did not place buyer "in as good a position as if the other party had fully performed." This was because buyer paid more than 9 cents per pound for the replacement lettuce. Only by reimbursing buyer for the additional costs above 9 cents a pound could buyer truly receive the benefit of the bargain. This is the measure of damages set forth in section 2712.

As White and Summers point out, "Since 2–712 measures buyer's damages by the difference between his actual cover purchase and the contract price, the formula will often put buyer in the identical economic position that performance would have." (White & Summers, supra, Buyer's Remedies, Cover, 6–3, p. 285.) Therefore, "[i]n the typical case a timely 'cover' purchase by an aggrieved buyer will preclude any 2–715 [incidental and consequential] damages." (Ibid.) "Not only does the damage formula in 2–712 come close to putting the aggrieved buyer in the same economic position as actual performance would have," White and Summers conclude, "but it also enables him to achieve his prime objective, namely that of acquiring his needed goods." (Id. at p. 292.)

In this case, the damage formula of section 2712 put buyer in the identical position performance would have: it gave buyer the contracted for 14 loads of lettuce with which to carry on its business at the contracted for price of 9 cents per pound. Despite the obvious applicability and appropriateness of section 2712, seller argues in this appeal that the contract-cover differential of section 2712 is inappropriate in cases, as here, where the aggrieved buyer is ultimately able to pass on its additional costs to other parties. Seller contends that Section 1106's remedial injunction to put the aggrieved party "in as good a position as if the other party had fully performed" demands that all subsequent events impacting on buyer's ultimate profit or loss be taken into consideration (specifically, that buyer passed on all but $70,000 of its loss to Castellini Company, which passed on all of its loss to Club Chef, which passed on most of its loss to its fast food customers).[5] . . .

. . . [In Allied Canners & Packers, Inc. v. Victor Packing Co., [162 Cal.App.3d 905 (1984),] the court held that [California Uniform Commercial Code § 1106 (U.C.C. § 1–106)] acts as a limitation on the amount of damages otherwise recoverable under section 2713. Before discussing the *Allied Canners* case, however, a few observations on the differences between the contract-cover differential of section 2712 and the contract-market differential of section 2713 are called for.

As noted earlier, section 2712 "will often put buyer in the identical economic position that performance would have." (White & Summers, supra, Buyer's Remedies, Cover, § 6–3, p. 285.) In contrast, the contract-market differential of section 2713 "bears no necessary relation to the change in the buyer's economic status that the breach causes. It is possible that this differential might yield the buyer a handsome sum even though the breach actually saved him money in the long run (as for example when a middleman buyer's resale markets dry up after the breach). It is also quite possible that the buyer's lost profit from resale or consumption would be greater than the contract-market difference." (Id., § 6–4, at p. 294.)

---

5. Seller, not surprisingly, does not focus on postbreach events impacting on seller's ultimate profit or loss. As noted earlier, seller made a profit of between $800,000 and $1.1 million for selling the lettuce at the higher market price rather than the lower 9 cent per pound contract price.

White and Summers argue that the drafters of section 2713 could not have intended to put the buyer in the same position as performance since "[p]erformance would have given the buyer certain goods for consumption or resale" (White & Summers, supra, Buyer's Remedies, Cover, § 6–4, at p. 294) which would have resulted in "either a net economic gain for the buyer or a net economic loss." (Ibid.) The best explanation of section 2713, they suggest, is that it is a "statutory liquidated damage clause, a breach inhibitor the payout of which need bear no close relation to the plaintiff's actual loss." (White & Summers, supra, at p. 295....) In discussing the "problem of a buyer who has covered but who seeks to ignore 2–712 and sue for a larger contract-market differential under 2–713," the authors suggest: "If the Code's goal is to put the buyer in the same position as though there had been no breach, and if 2–712 will accomplish that goal but 2–713 will do so only by coincidence, why not force the covering buyer to use 2–712?" (White & Summers, supra, at p. 304.)....

With these prefatory comments in mind, we look to the *Allied Canners* case. In *Allied Canners*, [a] raisin supplier (Victor Packing Company) ... breached [a] contract to sell raisins in 1976. The buyer, Allied Canners, had contracts to resell the raisins it bought from Victor to two Japanese companies for its cost plus 4 percent. Such a resale would have resulted in a profit of $4,462.50 to Allied. When Victor breached the contract, Allied sued for the difference between the market price and the contract price as authorized by section 2713. As the market price of raisins had soared due to the disastrous 1976 rains, the market-contract price formula would have yielded damages of approximately $150,000. Allied did not purchase substitute raisins and did not make any deliveries under its resale contracts to the Japanese buyers. One of the Japanese buyers simply released Allied from its contract because of the general unavailability of raisins. The other buyer did not release Allied, but it did not sue Allied either. By the time Allied's case against Victor went to trial, the statute of limitations on the Japanese buyer's claim had run.

Under these circumstances, the court held that the policy of section 1106 (that the aggrieved party be put in as good a position as if the other party had performed) required that the award of damages to Allied be limited to its actual loss. It noted that for this limitation to apply, three conditions must be met: (1) "the seller knew that the buyer had a resale contract"; (2) "the buyer has not been able to show that it will be liable in damages to the buyer on its forward contract";[6] and (3) "there has been no finding of bad faith on the part of the seller...." (Allied Canners & Packers, Inc. v. Victor Packing Co., supra, 162 Cal.App.3d at p. 915.)

The result in *Allied Canners* seems to have derived in large part from the court's finding that Victor had not acted in bad faith in breaching the contract....[7]

6. The court apparently never considered anything other than whether the Japanese buyers would sue Allied Canners. For example, it did not consider whether the breach adversely affected Allied Canners's goodwill with its Japanese customers. Should the court not have also considered Allied Canners's potential loss of future contracts?

7. In view of Allied Canners' three-part test, we assume the results would have been

different here if the court had found Victor was "a deliberately breaching seller." Perhaps in that case, the court would not have focused on what the aggrieved buyer ultimately would have received on resale but might have focused on what benefits the seller reaped from breaching. In Allied Canners, the price of raisins went up from 30 cents a pound to 87 cents a pound. If seller had not breached, it would have had to go out on the market and buy raisins for Allied

We believe that this focus on the good or bad faith of the breaching party is inappropriate in a commercial sales case. As our California Supreme Court recently explained, courts should not differentiate between good and bad motives for breaching a contract in assessing the measure of the nonbreaching party's damages. (Applied Equipment Corp. v. Litton Saudi Arabia Ltd. (1994) 7 Cal.4th 503, 513–515 [28 Cal.Rptr.2d 475, 869 P.2d 454].) Such a focus is inconsistent with the policy "to encourage contractual relations and commercial activity by enabling parties to estimate in advance the financial risks of their enterprise." (Id. at p. 515.) " 'Courts traditionally have awarded damages for breach of contract to compensate the aggrieved party rather than to punish the breaching party.' [Citations.]" (Foley v. Interactive Data Corp., supra, 47 Cal.3d at p. 683.)

The *Allied Canners* opinion has been sharply criticized in numerous law review articles and in at least one sister-state opinion. In Tongish v. Thomas (1992) 251 Kan. 728 [840 P.2d 471], the Kansas Supreme Court rejected the Allied Canners approach and instead applied the "majority view [which] would award market damages even though in excess of plaintiff's loss." (Id. at p. 475.) Relying on an article by Professors Simon and Novack, Limiting the Buyer's Market Damages to Lost Profits: A Challenge to the Enforceability of Market Contracts (1979) 92 Harv. L.Rev. 1395, the *Tongish* court explained that use of the market price/contract price damage scheme of section 2713 " 'encourages a more efficient market and discourages the breach of contracts.' " (Tongish v. Thomas, supra, 840 P.2d at p. 476.) . . . .

In addition numerous New York courts have chosen not to limit a buyer's damages to actual losses. (See, e.g., Fertico Belgium v. Phosphate Chem. Export (1987) 70 N.Y.2d 76 [517 N.Y.S.2d 465, 510 N.E.2d 334]; Apex Oil Co. v. Vanguard Oil & Service Co. Inc. (2d Cir.1985) 760 F.2d 417; G.A. Thompson & Co. v. Wendell J. Miller, etc. (S.D.N.Y.1978) 457 F.Supp. 996.)

As the foregoing discussion makes clear, we have serious reservations about whether the result in *Allied Canners*, with its emphasis on the good faith of the breaching party, is appropriate in an action seeking damages under section 2713. We have no reservations, however, in not extending the *Allied Canners* rationale to a section 2712 case. . . . [T]he cover-contract differential puts a buyer who covers in the exact same position as performance would have done. This is the precisely what is called for in section 1106. In this respect, the cover/contract differential of section 2712 is very different than the market/contract differential of section 2713, which "need bear no close relation to the plaintiff's actual loss." (White & Summers, supra, Buyer's Remedies, Cover, at p. 295.)

In summary, we hold that where a buyer " 'cover[s]' by making in good faith and without unreasonable delay any reasonable purchase of . . . goods in substitution for those due from the seller, . . . [that buyer] may recover from the seller as damages the difference between the cost of cover and the contract price. . . ." (§ 2712.) This gives the buyer the benefit of its bargain.

---

at considerably more than it was contracted to sell them for to Allied. By breaching, it avoided a loss that might have been more in the $150,000 range (market-contract differential) than the $4,000 range (Allied's lost profits). Thus, the court prevented a windfall to Allied at the cost of providing a windfall to Victor. Such a result is curious if the intent of contract damages is to effectuate the expectations of the parties to the contract. Here, the parties clearly contemplated when they entered into their fixed price agreement that the price of raisins would fluctuate and that sometimes buyer would receive a price better than the market price and that other times it would have to pay more than the market price.

What the buyer chooses to do with that bargain is not relevant to the determination of damages under section 2712. . . .

[The court went on to hold that the buyer should have received prejudgment interest beginning July or August 1991, the time at which the buyer filed its original complaint with the Department of Agriculture, under the Perishable Agricultural Commodities Act, rather than beginning thirty days before trial, as awarded by the trial judge.]

DISPOSITION

The order of the trial court awarding prejudgment interest from 30 days before trial is reversed and the cause is remanded. The trial court is directed to enter a new order awarding buyer prejudgment interest from August 1, 1991. In all other respects, the judgment is affirmed. Costs on appeal to buyer.

Premo, J., and Elia, J., concurred.

NERI v. RETAIL MARINE CORP.

Court of Appeals of New York, 1972.
30 N.Y.2d 393, 334 N.Y.S.2d 165, 285 N.E.2d 311.

GIBSON, JUDGE. The appeal concerns the right of a retail dealer to recover loss of profits and incidental damages upon the buyer's repudiation of a contract governed by the Uniform Commercial Code. This is, indeed, the correct measure of damage in an appropriate case and to this extent the code (§ 2–708, subsection [2]) effected a substantial change from prior law, whereby damages were ordinarily limited to "the difference between the contract price and the market or current price".[8] Upon the record before us, the courts below erred in declining to give effect to the new statute and so the order appealed from must be reversed.

The plaintiffs contracted to purchase from defendant a new boat of a specified model for the price of $12,587.40, against which they made a deposit of $40. They shortly increased the deposit to $4,250 in consideration of the defendant dealer's agreement to arrange with the manufacturer for immediate delivery on the basis of "a firm sale", instead of the delivery within approximately four to six weeks originally specified. Some six days after the date of the contract plaintiffs' lawyer sent to defendant a letter rescinding the sales contract for the reason that plaintiff Neri was about to undergo hospitalization and surgery, in consequence of which, according to the letter, it would be "impossible for Mr. Neri to make any payments". The boat had already been ordered from the manufacturer and was delivered to defendant at or before the time the attorney's letter was received. Defendant declined to refund plaintiffs' deposit and this action to recover it was commenced. Defendant counterclaimed, alleging plaintiffs' breach of the contract and defendant's resultant damage in the amount of $4,250, for which sum defendant demanded judgment. Upon motion, defendant had summary judgment on the issue of liability tendered by its counterclaim; and Special Term

---

8. Personal Property Law, Consol.Laws, c. 41, §145, repealed by Uniform Commercial Code, § 10–102 (L.1962, ch. 553, eff. Sept. 27, 1964); Lenobel, Inc. v. Senif, 252 App.Div. 533, 300 N.Y.S. 226.

directed an assessment of damages, upon which it would be determined whether plaintiffs were entitled to the return of any portion of their down payment.

Upon the trial so directed, it was shown that the boat ordered and received by defendant in accordance with plaintiffs' contract of purchase was sold some four months later to another buyer for the same price as that negotiated with plaintiffs. From this proof the plaintiffs argue that defendant's loss on its contract was recouped, while defendant argues that but for plaintiffs' default, it would have sold two boats and have earned two profits instead of one. Defendant proved, without contradiction, that its profit on the sale under the contract in suit would have been $2,579 and that during the period the boat remained unsold incidental expenses aggregating $674 for storage, upkeep, finance charges and insurance were incurred. Additionally, defendant proved and sought to recover attorneys' fees of $1,250.

The trial court found "untenable" defendant's claim for loss of profit, inasmuch as the boat was later sold for the same price that plaintiffs had contracted to pay; found, too, that defendant had failed to prove any incidental damages; further found "that the terms of section 2–718, subsection 2(b), of the Uniform Commercial Code are applicable and same make adequate and fair provision to place the sellers in as good a position as performance would have done" and, in accordance with paragraph (b) of subsection (2) thus relied upon, awarded defendant $500 upon its counterclaim and directed that plaintiffs recover the balance of their deposit, amounting to $3,750. The ensuing judgment was affirmed, without opinion, at the Appellate Division, 37 A.D.2d 917, 326 N.Y.S.2d 984, and defendant's appeal to this court was taken by our leave.

The issue is governed in the first instance by section 2–718 of the Uniform Commercial Code which provides, among other things, that the buyer, despite his breach, may have restitution of the amount by which his payment exceeds: (a) reasonable liquidated damages stipulated by the contract or (b) absent such stipulation, 20% of the value of the buyer's total performance or $500, whichever is smaller (§ 2–718, subsection [2], pars. [a], [b]). As above noted, the trial court awarded defendant an offset in the amount of $500 under paragraph (b) and directed restitution to plaintiffs of the balance. Section 2–718, however, establishes, in paragraph (a) of subsection (3), an alternative right of offset in favor of the seller, as follows: "(3) The buyer's right to restitution under subsection (2) is subject to offset to the extent that the seller establishes (a) a right to recover damages under the provisions of this Article other than subsection (1)".

Among "the provisions of this Article other than subsection (1)" are those to be found in section 2–708, which the courts below did not apply. Subsection (1) of that section provides that "the measure of damages for non-acceptance or repudiation by the buyer is the difference between the market price at the time and place for tender and the unpaid contract price together with any incidental damages provided in this Article (Section 2–710), but less expenses saved in consequence of the buyer's breach." However, this provision is made expressly subject to subsection (2), providing: "(2) If the measure of damages provided in subsection (1) is inadequate to put the seller in as good a position as performance would have done then the measure of damages is the profit (including reasonable overhead) which the seller would have made from full performance by the buyer, together with any incidental damages provided in this Article (Section 2–710), due allowance for costs reasonably incurred and due credit for payments or proceeds of resale."

The provision of the code upon which the decision at Trial Term rested (§ 2–718, subsection [2], par. [b]) does not differ greatly from the corresponding provisions of the prior statute (Personal Property Law, § 145–a, subd. 1, par. [b]), except as the new act includes the alternative remedy of a lump sum award of $500. Neither does the present reference (in § 2–718, subsection [3], par. [a]) to the recovery of damages pursuant to other provisions of the article differ from a like reference in the prior statute (Personal Property Law, § 145–a, subd. 2, par. [a]) to an alternative measure of damages under section 145 of that act; but section 145 made no provision for recovery of lost profits as does section 2–708 (subsection [2]) of the code. The new statute is thus innovative and significant and its analysis is necessary to the determination of the issues here presented.

Prior to the code, the New York cases "applied the 'profit' test, contract price less cost of manufacture, only in cases where the seller [was] a manufacturer or an agent for a manufacturer" (1955 Report of N.Y.Law Rev.Comm., vol. 1, p. 693). Its extension to retail sales was "designed to eliminate the unfair and economically wasteful results arising under the older law when fixed price articles were involved. This section permits the recovery of lost profits in all appropriate cases, which would include all standard priced goods." (Official Comment 2, McKinney's Cons.Laws of N.Y., Book 62½, Part 1, p. 605, under Uniform Commercial Code, § 2–708.) Additionally, and "[i]n all cases the seller may recover incidental damages" (id., Comment 3). The buyer's right to restitution was established at Special Term upon the motion for summary judgment, as was the seller's right to proper offsets, in each case pursuant to section 2–718; and, as the parties concede, the only question before us, following the assessment of damages at Special Term, is that as to the proper measure of damage to be applied. The conclusion is clear from the record—indeed with mathematical certainty—that "the measure of damages provided in subsection (1) is inadequate to put the seller in as good a position as performance would have done" (Uniform Commercial Code, § 2–708, subsection [2]) and hence—again under subsection (2)—that the seller is entitled to its "profit (including reasonable overhead) ... together with any incidental damages ..., due allowance for costs reasonably incurred and due credit for payments or proceeds of resale."

It is evident, first, that this retail seller is entitled to its profit and, second, that the last sentence of subsection (2), as hereinbefore quoted, referring to "due credit for payments or proceeds of resale" is inapplicable to this retail sales contract.[9] Closely parallel to the factual situation now before

9. The concluding clause, "due credit for payments or proceeds of resale", is intended to refer to "the privilege of the seller to realize junk value when it is manifestly useless to complete the operation of manufacture" (Supp. No. 1 to the 1952 Official Draft of Text and Comments of the Uniform Commercial Code, as Amended by the Act of the American Law Institute of the National Conference of Commissioners on Uniform Laws [1954], p. 14). The commentators who have considered the language have uniformly concluded that "the reference is to a resale as scrap under ... Section 2–704" (1956 Report of N.Y.Law Rev. Comm., p. 397; 1955 Report of N.Y.Law Rev. Comm., vol. 1, p. 761; New York Annotations, McKinney's Cons.Laws of N.Y., Book 62½, Part 1, p. 606, under Uniform Commercial Code, § 2–708; 1 Willier and Hart, Bender's Uniform Commercial Code Service, § 2–708, pp. 1–180—1–181). Another writer, reaching the same conclusion, after detailing the history of the clause, says that " 'proceeds of resale' pre-us is that hypothesized by Dean Hawkland as illustrative of the operation of the rules: "Thus, if a private party agrees to sell his automobile to a buyer for $2,000, a breach by the buyer would cause the seller no loss (except incidental damages, i.e., expense of a new sale) if the seller was able to sell the automobile to another buyer for $2000. But the situation is different with dealers having an unlimited supply of standard-priced goods. Thus, if an automobile dealer agrees to sell a car to a buyer at the standard price of $2000, a breach by the buyer injures the dealer, even though he is able to sell the automobile to another for $2000. If the dealer has an inexhaustible supply of cars, the resale to replace the breaching buyer costs the dealer a sale, because, had the breaching buyer performed, the dealer would have made two sales instead of one. The buyer's breach, in such a case, depletes the dealer's sales to the extent of one, and the measure of damages should be the dealer's profit on one sale. Section 2–708 recognizes this, and it rejects the rule developed under the Uniform Sales Act by many courts that the profit cannot be recovered in this case." (Hawkland, Sales and Bulk Sales [1958 ed.], pp. 153–154; and see Comment, 31 Fordham L.Rev. 749, 755–756.)

The record which in this case establishes defendant's entitlement to damages in the amount of its prospective profit, at the same time confirms defendant's cognate right to "any incidental damages provided in this Article (Section 2–710)"[10] (Uniform Commercial Code, § 2–708, subsection [2]). From the language employed it is too clear to require discussion that the seller's right to recover loss of profits is not exclusive and that he may recoup his "incidental" expenses as well (Proctor & Gamble Distr. Co. v. Lawrence Amer. Field Warehousing Corp., 16 N.Y.2d 344, 354, 266 N.Y.S.2d 785, 792, 213 N.E.2d 873, 878). Although the trial court's denial of incidental damages in the uncontroverted amount of $674 was made in the context of its erroneous conclusion that paragraph (b) of subsection (2) of section 2–718 was applicable and was "adequate . . . to place the sellers in as good a position as performance would have done", the denial seems not to have rested entirely on the court's mistaken application of the law, as there was an explicit finding "that defendant completely failed to show that it suffered any incidental damages." We find no basis for the court's conclusion with respect to a deficiency of proof inasmuch as the proper items of the $674 expenses (being for storage, upkeep, finance charges and insurance for the period between the date performance was due and the time of the resale) were proven without objection and were in no way controverted, impeached or otherwise challenged, at the trial or on appeal. Thus the court's finding of a failure of proof cannot be supported upon the record and, therefore, and contrary to plaintiffs' contention, the affirmance at the Appellate Division was ineffective to save it.

The trial court correctly denied defendant's claim for recovery of attorney's fees incurred by it in this action. Attorney's fees incurred in an action such as this are not in the nature of the protective expenses contemplated by the statute (Uniform Commercial Code, § 1–106, subd. [1]; § 2–710; § 2–708,

---

viously meant the resale value of the goods in finished form; now it means the resale value of the components on hand at the time plaintiff learns of breach" (Harris, Seller's Damages, 18 Stanf.L.Rev. 66,104).

10. Incidental damages to an aggrieved seller include any commercially reasonable charges, expenses or commissions incurred in stopping delivery, in the transportation, care and custody of goods after the buyer's breach, in connection with return or resale of the goods or otherwise resulting from the breach (Uniform Commercial Code, § 2–710).

subsection [2]) and by our reference to "legal expense" in Procter & Gamble Distr. Co. v. Lawrence Amer. Field Warehousing Corp. (16 N.Y.2d 344, 354–355, 266 N.Y.S.2d 785, 792–793, 213 N.E.2d 873, 878–879, supra), upon which defendant's reliance is in this respect misplaced.

It follows that plaintiffs are entitled to restitution of the sum of $4,250 paid by them on account of the contract price less an offset to defendant in the amount of $3,253 on account of its lost profit of $2,579 and its incidental damages of $674.

The order of the Appellate Division should be modified, with costs in all courts, in accordance with this opinion, and, as so modified, affirmed.

FULD, C.J., and BURKE, SCILEPPI, BERGAN, BREITEL, and JASEN, JJ., concur.

Ordered accordingly.

————

TERADYNE, INC. v. TELEDYNE INDUSTRIES, INC., 676 F.2d 865 (1st Cir.1982). "A literal reading of the last sentence of § 2–708(2) providing for 'due credit for payments or proceeds of resale'—would indicate that Teradyne recovers nothing because the proceeds of the resale exceeded the price set in the Teledyne–Teradyne contract. However, in light of the statutory history of the subsection, it is universally agreed that in a case where after the buyer's default a seller resells the goods, the proceeds of the resale are not to be credited to the buyer if the seller is a lost volume seller—that is, one who had there been no breach by the buyer, could and would have had the benefit of both the original contract and the resale contract."

————

CHILDRES & BURGESS, SELLER'S REMEDIES: THE PRIMACY OF UCC 2–708(2), 48 N.Y.U.L.Rev. 833, 881–82 (1973). ". . . [The lost-profit rule of 2–708(2)] has a strange and confusing contextual situation: besides being buried . . . it is hedged in on all sides. It seems to be (though it is not) unavailable if one resells, unavailable unless the price action fails, and not to be used unless 2–708(1) for unannounced reasons fails to produce enough damages.

"Yet the lost-profit rule of 2–708(2) is no rule of last resort for the few cases that fail to fit the specific rules. It is the dominant damages rule or principle. It must, if the UCC system is to make any sense at all, apply to all cases of reasonably unfinished goods and all cases in which the seller's customers, during the contract period, are fewer than can be supplied at the prevailing price, save in the cases where the seller can force the buyer to pay the price. We think it probable that in the American economy of today and the foreseeable future, the overwhelming proportion of sales contracts should produce the 2–708(2) situation if repudiated by the buyer."

————

R.E. DAVIS CHEMICAL CORP. v. DIASONICS, INC., 826 F.2d 678 (7th Cir.1987). ". . . [W]e disagree with the definition of 'lost volume seller' adopted by other courts. Courts awarding lost profits to a lost volume seller have focused on whether the seller had the capacity to supply the breached units in addition to what it actually sold. In reality, however, the relevant questions include, not only whether the seller could have produced the breached units in addition to its actual volume, but also whether it would have been profitable for the seller to produce both units. Goetz & Scott, Measuring Sellers' Damages: The Lost–Profits Puzzle, 31 Stan.L.Rev. 323, 332–33, 346–47 (1979). As one commentator has noted, under the economic law of diminishing returns or increasing marginal costs[,] ... as a seller's volume increases, then a point will inevitably be reached where the cost of selling each additional item diminishes the incremental return to the seller and eventually makes it entirely unprofitable to conclude the next sale.

... Thus, under some conditions, awarding a lost volume seller its presumed lost profit will result in overcompensating the seller, and 2–708(2) would not take effect because the damage formula provided in 2–708(1) does place the seller in as good a position as if the buyer had performed. Therefore, on remand, Diasonics must establish, not only that it had the capacity to produce the breached unit in addition to the unit resold, but also that it would have been profitable for it to have produced and sold both. Diasonics carries the burden of establishing these facts because the burden of proof is generally on the party claiming injury to establish the amount of its damages; especially in a case such as this, the plaintiff has easiest access to the relevant data."

LAZENBY GARAGES LTD. v. WRIGHT, [1976] 2 All E.R. 770, [1976] 1 W.L.R. 459 (Ct.App. Eng. 1976) (Lord Denning M.R.) "Mr. Wright works on the land. On February 19, 1974 he went to the showrooms of motor dealers called Lazenby Garages Ltd. He saw some secondhand cars there. He agreed to buy a BMW 2002. He signed a contract to pay £1,670 for it. It was to be delivered to him on March 1, 1974. He went back home to his wife and told her about it. She persuaded him not to buy it. So next day he went back to the garage and said he would not have it after all. They kept it there offering it for re-sale. Two months later on April 23, 1974 they re-sold it for £1,770, that is, for £100 more than Mr. Wright was going to pay.

"Notwithstanding this advantageous re-sale, the garage sued Mr. Wright for damages. They produced evidence that they had themselves bought the car secondhand on 14th February 1974, that is five days before Mr. Wright had come in and agreed to buy it. They said that they had bought it for £1,325. He had agreed to buy it from them for £1,670. So they had lost £345 and they claimed that sum as damages.

"In answer Mr. Wright said: 'You haven't lost anything; you've sold it for a higher price.' The garage people said that they were dealers in secondhand cars; that they had had a number of cars of this sort of age and type, BMW 2002s; and that they had lost the sale of another car. They said that, if Mr. Wright had taken this car, they would have been able to sell one of those other cars to the purchaser. So they had sold one car less and were entitled to profit accordingly....

"... Now there is an appeal to this court. The cases show that if there are a number of new cars, all exactly of the same kind, available for sale, and the dealers can prove that they sold one car less than they otherwise would have done, they would be entitled to damages amounting to their loss of profit on the one car. . . .

"But it is entirely different in the case of a secondhand car. Each secondhand car is different from the next, even though it is the same make. The sales manager of the garage admitted in evidence that some secondhand cars, of the same make, even of the same year, may sell better than others of the same year. Some may sell quickly, others sluggishly. You simply cannot tell why. But they are all different.

"In the circumstances the cases about new cars do not apply. . . ."

SECTION 3. MITIGATION; CONTRACTS FOR EMPLOYMENT

ROCKINGHAM COUNTY v. LUTEN BRIDGE CO.

Circuit Court of Appeals, Fourth Circuit, 1929.
35 F.2d 301.

PARKER, CIRCUIT JUDGE. This was an action at law instituted in the court below by the Luten Bridge Company, as plaintiff, to recover of Rockingham county, North Carolina, an amount alleged to be due under a contract for the construction of a bridge. The county admits the execution and breach of the contract, but contends that notice of cancellation was given the bridge company before the erection of the bridge was commenced, and that it is liable only for the damages which the company would have sustained, if it had abandoned construction at that time. The judge below . . . excluded evidence offered by the county in support of its contentions as to notice of cancellation and damages, and instructed a verdict for plaintiff for the full amount of its claim. From judgment on this verdict the county has appealed.

The facts out of which the case arises, as shown by the affidavits and offers of proof appearing in the record, are as follows: On January 7, 1924, the board of commissioners of Rockingham county voted to award to plaintiff a contract for the construction of the bridge in controversy. Three of the five commissioners favored the awarding of the contract and two opposed it. Much feeling was engendered over the matter, with the result that on February 11, 1924, W.K. Pruitt, one of the commissioners who had voted in the affirmative, sent his resignation to the clerk of the superior court of the county. The clerk received this resignation on the same day, and immediately accepted same and noted his acceptance thereon. Later in the day, Pruitt called him over the telephone and stated that he wished to withdraw the resignation, and later sent him written notice to the same effect. The clerk, however, paid no attention to the attempted withdrawal, and proceeded on the next day to appoint one W.W. Hampton as a member of the board to succeed him.

After his resignation, Pruitt attended no further meetings of the board, and did nothing further as a commissioner of the county. Likewise Pratt and McCollum, the other two members of the board who had voted with him in favor of the contract, attended no further meetings. Hampton, on the other hand, took the oath of office immediately upon his appointment and entered upon the discharge of the duties of a commissioner. He met regularly with the two remaining members of the board, Martin and Barber. . . .

At one of these meetings, a regularly advertised called meeting held on February 21st, a resolution was unanimously adopted declaring that the contract for the building of the bridge was not legal and valid, and directing the clerk of the board to notify plaintiff that it refused to recognize same as a valid contract, and that plaintiff should proceed no further thereunder. This resolution also rescinded action of the board theretofore taken looking to the construction of a hard-surfaced road, in which the bridge was to be a mere connecting link. The clerk duly sent a certified copy of this resolution to plaintiff.

At the regular monthly meeting of the board on March 3d, a resolution was passed directing that plaintiff be notified that any work done on the bridge would be done by it at its own risk and hazard, that the board was of the opinion that the contract for the construction of the bridge was not valid and legal, and that, even if the board were mistaken as to this, it did not desire to construct the bridge, and would contest payment for same if constructed. A copy of this resolution was also sent to plaintiff. . . .

At the time of the passage of the first resolution, very little work toward the construction of the bridge had been done, it being estimated that the total cost of labor done and material on the ground was around $1,900; but, notwithstanding the repudiation of the contract by the county, the bridge company continued with the work of construction.

On November 24, 1924, plaintiff instituted this action against Rockingham county. . . .

As the county now admits the execution and validity of the contract, and the breach on its part, the ultimate question in the case is one as to the measure of plaintiff's recovery, and the exceptions must be considered with this in mind. Upon these exceptions, [the question arises]. . . . whether plaintiff, if the notices are to be deemed action by the county, can recover under the contract for work done after they were received, or is limited to the recovery of damages for breach of contract as of that date. . . .

Coming, then, to . . . the measure of plaintiff's recovery—we do not think that, after the county had given notice, while the contract was still executory, that it did not desire the bridge built and would not pay for it, plaintiff could proceed to build it and recover the contract price. It is true that the county had no right to rescind the contract, and the notice given plaintiff amounted to a breach on its part; but, after plaintiff had received notice of the breach, it was its duty to do nothing to increase the damages flowing therefrom. If A enters into a binding contract to build a house for B, B, of course, has no right to rescind the contract without A's consent. But if, before the house is built, he decides that he does not want it, and notifies A to that effect, A has no right to proceed with the building and thus pile up damages. His remedy is to treat the contract as broken when he receives the notice, and sue for the recovery of such damages as he may have sustained from the breach, including any profit which he would have realized upon performance, as well as any other losses which may have resulted to him. In the case at bar, the county decided not to build the road of which the bridge was to be a part, and did not build it. The bridge, built in the midst of the forest, is of no value to the county because of this change of circumstances. When, therefore, the county gave notice to the plaintiff that it would not proceed with the project, plaintiff should have desisted from further work. It had no right thus to pile up damages by proceeding with the erection of a useless bridge.

The contrary view was expressed by Lord Cockburn in Frost v. Knight, L.R. 7 Ex. 111, but, as pointed out by Prof. Williston (Williston on Contracts, vol. 3, p. 2347), it is not in harmony with the decisions in this country. The American rule and the reasons supporting it are well stated by Prof. Williston as follows:

> "There is a line of cases running back to 1845 which holds that, after an absolute repudiation or refusal to perform by one party to a contract, the other party cannot continue to perform and recover damages based on full performance. This rule is only a particular application of the general rule of damages that a plaintiff cannot hold a defendant liable for damages which need not have been incurred; or, as it is often stated, the plaintiff must, so far as he can without loss to himself, mitigate the damages caused by the defendant's wrongful act. The application of this rule to the matter in question is obvious. If a man engages to have work done, and afterwards repudiates his contract before the work has been begun or when it has been only partially done, it is inflicting damage on the defendant without benefit to the plaintiff to allow the latter to insist on proceeding with the contract. The work may be useless to the defendant, and yet he would be forced to pay the full contract price. On the other hand, the plaintiff is interested only in the profit he will make out of the contract. If he receives this it is equally advantageous for him to use his time otherwise."

The leading case on the subject in this country is the New York case of Clark v. Marsiglia, 1 Denio (N.Y.) 317, 43 Am.Dec. 670. In that case defendant had employed plaintiff to paint certain pictures for him, but countermanded the order before the work was finished. Plaintiff, however, went on and completed the work and sued for the contract price. In reversing a judgment for plaintiff, the court said:

> "The plaintiff was allowed to recover as though there had been no countermand of the order; and in this the court erred. The defendant, by requiring the plaintiff to stop work upon the paintings, violated his contract, and thereby incurred a liability to pay such damages as the plaintiff should sustain. Such damages would include a recompense for the labor done and materials used, and such further sum in damages as might, upon legal principles, be assessed for the breach of the contract; but the plaintiff had no right, by obstinately persisting in the work, to make the penalty upon the defendant greater than it would otherwise have been." . . .

. . . It follows that there was error in directing a verdict for plaintiff for the full amount of its claim. The measure of plaintiff's damage, upon its appearing that notice was duly given not to build the bridge, is an amount sufficient to compensate plaintiff for labor and materials expended and expense incurred in the part performance of the contract, prior to its repudiation, plus the profit which would have been realized if it had been carried out in accordance with its terms. . . .

... The judgment below will accordingly be reversed, and the case remanded for a new trial.

Reversed.

———

MADSEN v. MURREY & SONS CO., 743 P.2d 1212 (Utah 1987). Seller was in the business of manufacturing and selling pool tables. Buyer agreed to acquire 100 pool tables, to which it planned to add special electronic lighting-and-sound effects. To accommodate the electrical components that the buyer planned to install, Seller was to customize its pool tables by adding various holes, notches, and routings. Buyer encountered problems in developing the special effects, and notified seller that he would be unable to take delivery of the pool tables. Seller then dismantled the 100 pool tables that it had customized, used part of the salvageable materials to manufacture other pool tables, and used the balance as firewood. Seller claimed that selling the tables, rather than dismantling them, would have damaged its reputation for quality, and that the special holes, notches, and routings weakened the structure of the pool tables and would have exposed Seller to potential liability if the tables were sold on the market. However, Buyer's expert testified that the customizing would not have adversely affected the quality or marketability of the 100 pool tables, and that the tables could have been sold at full value or at a discounted price.

In an opinion affirmed by the Utah Supreme Court, the trial court concluded that seller had a duty to mitigate its damages and had failed to do so, because dismantling the tables for salvage and firewood, rather than attempting to sell or market the tables at full value or a discounted price, was not commercially reasonable.

———

IN RE KELLETT AIRCRAFT CORP., 186 F.2d 197 (3d Cir.1950). Amerform entered into a contract with Kellett under which Kellett undertook to fabricate 5,000 shower cabinets at $13.18 each, plus $3,331 for tooling costs. As Kellett knew, the cabinets were needed by Amerform to fulfill a government order calling for deliveries in July, August, and September, 1946. On September 16, 1946, Kellett stated in writing its inability to perform. Amerform immediately approached four or five companies located in various Pennsylvania and New Jersey cities in an effort to procure the cabinets as soon as possible. Cutler, which had previously made identical cabinets for Amerform, and already had the necessary dies and tools, offered to perform at a price of $18 per cabinet. Production was to be scheduled in accordance with the immediate availability of materials, and a night shift was to be added to accelerate production. Several days after the Cutler offer, still another company, Luscombe, proposed to make the cabinets at the price formerly agreed by Kellett, $13.18, plus an additional $500 for tooling. Luscombe, however, informed Amerform that it had to look to Kellett to fabricate the tools and dies, and promised to begin delivery of the cabinets four weeks after the tools and dies were to be delivered. Amerform awarded the contract to Cutler. The district court held that by contracting with Cutler rather than Luscombe, Kellett had failed to properly mitigate damages. Reversed.

"Whether or not the buyer's obligation to mitigate damages has been discharged depends on the reasonableness of its conduct. In this connection, reasonable conduct is to be determined from all the facts and circumstances of each case, and must be judged in the light of one viewing the situation at the time the problem was presented. Where a choice has been required between two reasonable courses, the person whose wrong forced the choice can not complain that one rather than the other was chosen. The rule of mitigation of damages may not be invoked by a contract breaker as a basis for hypercritical examination of the conduct of the injured party, or merely for the purpose of showing that the injured person might have taken steps which seemed wiser or would have been more advantageous to the defaulter. One is not obligated to exalt the interests of the defaulter to his own probable detriment....

". . . The claimant acted promptly and diligently. In all the circumstances, we consider it the exercise of prudent business judgment and in no way unreasonable conduct for Amerform to have awarded the contract at somewhat increased cost to one whose performance had on previous occasions proved satisfactory, who had at hand proper and adequate tools for the job, and who promised to get on with it at once."

BANK ONE, TEXAS N.A. v. TAYLOR, 970 F.2d 16 (5th Cir.1992). MBank had wrongfully frozen bank accounts of Taylor. As a result, Taylor was unable to continue her participation in certain oil-drilling ventures, and sued MBank for damages. MBank maintained that the loss of the drilling prospects could easily have been avoided if Taylor had used her own assets, including her personal jewelry, geophysical data, and cash, to either pay for or finance the drilling prospects during the wrongful freeze on her bank accounts. Held, for Taylor:

> Although an injured party is required to use reasonable diligence to minimize his losses, he is not required to "make unreasonable personal outlays of money," . . . or to "sacrifice a substantial right of his own." . . . Rather, an injured party is required to incur "only slight expense and reasonable effort" in mitigating his damages.... One who claims a failure to mitigate damages has the burden to prove not only lack of diligence on the part of injured party, but also the amount by which damages were increased by such failure to mitigate.

S.J. GROVES & SONS CO. v. WARNER CO., 576 F.2d 524 (3d Cir.1978). As part of a highway improvement program, Pennsylvania undertook the erection of the Girard Point Bridge in southwest Philadelphia. Groves was awarded a subcontract for the placement of the bridge's concrete decks and parapets, and contracted with Warner for the delivery of ready-mixed concrete for use at the Girard Point site. Subsequently, Groves sued Warner, claiming extensive losses due largely to Warner's failure to deliver adequate supplies at scheduled times. The trial court found that as of a certain date during the contract, Groves had no reasonable expectation that Warner's performance would improve to totally satisfactory levels. The court concluded that Groves could not recover damages for defective performance after that date, because Groves should have mitigated by employing another firm, Trap Rock, as a supplemental supplier. Reversed.

"... Engaging Trap Rock as an additional source of supply was a course of action open to Warner as well as Groves. Indeed, on other commercial work Warner *had* used Trap Rock as a supplemental supplier.... Such an arrangement by Warner would have had the distinct advantage of having one subcontractor directly answerable to Groves for proper delivery, timing and quality.

"Where both the plaintiff and the defendant have had equal opportunity to reduce the damages by the same act and it is equally reasonable to expect the defendant to minimize damages, the defendant is in no position to contend that the plaintiff failed to mitigate. Nor will the award be reduced on account of damages the defendant could have avoided as easily as the plaintiff.... The duty to mitigate damages is not applicable where the party whose duty it is primarily to perform a contract has equal opportunity for performance and equal knowledge of the consequences of nonperformance...."

Accord: Travelers Indemnity Co. v. Maho Machine Tool Corp., 952 F.2d 26 (2d Cir.1991); Shea–S & M Ball v. Massman–Kiewit–Early, 606 F.2d 1245 (D.C.Cir.1979).

RESTATEMENT, SECOND, CONTRACTS § 350

[See Selected Source Materials Supplement]

UCC §§ 2–704(2), 2–715(2)

[See Selected Source Materials Supplement]

CISG ART. 77

[See Selected Source Materials Supplement]

UNIDROIT PRINCIPLES OF INTERNATIONAL COMMERCIAL CONTRACTS ARTS. 7.4.7, 7.4.8

[See Selected Source Materials Supplement]

PRINCIPLES OF EUROPEAN CONTRACT LAW ARTS. 9.504, 9.505

[See Selected Source Materials Supplement]

———

SHIRLEY MacLAINE PARKER v. TWENTIETH CENTURY–FOX FILM CORP.

California Supreme Court, 1970.
3 Cal.3d 176, 89 Cal.Rptr. 737, 474 P.2d 689.

BURKE, J. Defendant Twentieth Century–Fox Film Corporation appeals from a summary judgment granting to plaintiff the recovery of agreed compensation under a written contract for her services as an actress in a motion picture. As will appear, we have concluded that the trial court correctly ruled in plaintiff's favor and that the judgment should be affirmed.

Plaintiff is well known as an actress, and in the contract between plaintiff and defendant is sometimes referred to as the "Artist." Under the contract, dated August 6, 1965, plaintiff was to play the female lead in defendant's contemplated production of a motion picture entitled "Bloomer Girl."[*] The contract provided that defendant would pay plaintiff a minimum "guaranteed compensation" of $53,571.42 per week for 14 weeks commencing May 23, 1966, for a total of $750,000. Prior to May 1966 defendant decided not to produce the picture and by a letter dated April 4, 1966, it notified plaintiff of that decision and that it would not "comply with our obligations to you under" the written contract.

By the same letter and with the professed purpose "to avoid any damage to you," defendant instead offered to employ plaintiff as the leading actress in another film tentatively entitled "Big Country, Big Man" (hereinafter, "Big Country"). The compensation offered was identical, as were 31 of the 34 numbered provisions or articles of the original contract.[11] Unlike "Bloomer Girl," however, which was to have been a musical production, "Big Country"

---

[*] Victor Goldberg reports that *Bloomer Girl* was an adaptation of a stage musical written by Harold Arlen and Yip Harburg, which ran for 654 performances on Broadway in the mid–1940's. Harburg's son summarized the play's plot and political themes as follows:

> *Bloomer Girl* concerns the political activities of Amelia (renamed Dolly) Bloomer and the effect they have on a pre-Civil War family of her brother-in-law, hoopskirt king Horace Applegate, and his feminist daughter, Evalina. Evalina is the youngest and only remaining unmarried Applegate daughter; her older sisters are all married to company salesmen, and as *Bloomer Girl* begins, Horace is trying to unify business and family by encouraging his chief Southern salesman, Jefferson Calhoun, to court Evalina. On the eve of the Civil War, *Bloomer Girl* centers around Evalina's tutelage of Jeff in matters of gender and racial equality. Evalina, Dolly, and the other feminists of Cicero Falls not

only campaign against Applegate's hoopskirts and sexism but also stage their own version of Uncle Tom's Cabin and conceal a runaway slave—Jeff's own manservant, Pompey. It was, said Yip, a show about "the indivisibility of human freedom."

> *Bloomer Girl* interweaves the issues of black and female equality and war and peace with the vicissitudes of courtship and pre-Civil War politics.... [I]t was at no point an escapist entertainment....

Goldberg, "Bloomer Girl Revisited or how to Frame an Unmade Picture," 1998 *Wisconsin Law Review* 1051 (1998) (quoting Harold Meyerson and Ernie Harburg, *Who Put the Rainbow in* The Wizard of Oz? *Yip Harburg, Lyricist* (1993). (Footnote by ed.)

11. Among the identical provisions was the following found in the last paragraph of Article 2 of the original contract: "We [defendant] shall not be obligated to utilize your [plain-was a dramatic "western type" movie. "Bloomer Girl" was to have been filmed in California; "Big Country" was to be produced in Australia. Also, certain terms in the proffered contract varied from those of the original.[12] Plaintiff was given one week within which to accept; she did not and the offer lapsed. Plaintiff then commenced this action seeking recovery of the agreed guaranteed compensation.

The complaint sets forth two causes of action. The first is for money due under the contract; the second, based upon the same allegations as the first, is for damages resulting from defendant's breach of contract. Defendant in its answer admits the existence and validity of the contract, that plaintiff complied with all the conditions, covenants and promises and stood ready to complete the performance, and that defendant breached and "anticipatorily repudiated" the contract. It denies, however, that any money is due to plaintiff either under the contract or as a result of its breach, and pleads as an affirmative defense to both causes of action plaintiff's allegedly deliberate failure to mitigate damages, asserting that she unreasonably refused to accept its offer of the leading role in "Big Country."

Plaintiff moved for summary judgment under Code of Civil Procedure section 437c, the motion was granted, and summary judgment for $750,000 plus interest was entered in plaintiff's favor. This appeal by defendant followed.

The familiar rules are that the matter to be determined by the trial court on a motion for summary judgment is whether facts have been presented which give rise to a triable factual issue. The court may not pass upon the issue itself. Summary judgment is proper only if the affidavits or declarations in support of the moving party would be sufficient to sustain a judgment in his favor and his opponent does not by affidavit show facts sufficient to present a triable issue of fact....

The general rule is that the measure of recovery by a wrongfully discharged employee is the amount of salary agreed upon for the period of

---

tiff's] services in or in connection with the Photoplay hereunder, our sole obligation, subject to the terms and conditions of this Agreement, being to pay you the guaranteed compensation herein provided for."

12. Article 29 of the original contract specified that plaintiff approved the director already chosen for "Bloomer Girl" and that in case he failed to act as director plaintiff was to have approval rights of any substitute director. Article 31 provided that plaintiff was to have the right of approval of the "Bloomer Girl" dance director, and Article 32 gave her the right of approval of the screenplay.

Defendant's letter of April 4 to plaintiff, which contained both defendant's notice of breach of the "Bloomer Girl" contract and offer of the lead in "Big Country," eliminated or impaired each of those rights. It read in part as follows: "The terms and conditions of our offer of employment are identical to those set forth in the 'Bloomer Girl' Agreement, Articles 1 through 34 and Exhibit A to the Agreement, except as follows:

"1. Article 31 of said Agreement will not be included in any contract of employment re-

garding 'Big Country, Big Man' as it is not a musical and it thus will not need a dance director.

"2. In the 'Bloomer Girl' agreement, in Articles 29 and 32, you were given certain director and screenplay approvals and you had preapproved certain matters. Since there simply is insufficient time to negotiate with you regarding your choice of director and regarding the screenplay and since you already expressed an interest in performing the role in 'Big Country, Big Man,' we must exclude from our offer of employment in 'Big Country, Big Man' any approval rights as are contained in said Articles 29 and 32; however, we shall consult with you respecting the director to be selected to direct the photoplay and will further consult with you with respect to the screenplay and any revisions or changes therein, provided, however, that if we fail to agree ... the decision of ... [defendant] with respect to the selection of a director and to revisions and changes in the said screenplay shall be binding upon the parties to said agreement."

service, less the amount which the employer affirmatively proves the employee has earned or with reasonable effort might have earned from other employment.... However, before projected earnings from other employment opportunities not sought or accepted by the discharged employee can be applied in mitigation, the employer must show that the other employment was comparable, or substantially similar, to that of which the employee has been deprived; the employee's rejection of or failure to seek other available employment of a different or inferior kind may not be resorted to in order to mitigate damages. (Gonzales v. Internat. Assn. of Machinists (1963) 213 Cal.App.2d 817, 822–824 [29 Cal.Rptr. 190]; Harris v. Nat. Union etc. Cooks, Stewards (1953) 116 Cal.App.2d 759, 761 [254 P.2d 673].... de la Falaise v. Gaumont–British Picture Corp., 39 Cal.App.2d 46 [103 P.2d 447 (1940)]....

In the present case defendant has raised no issue of *reasonableness of efforts* by plaintiffs to obtain other employment; the sole issue is whether plaintiff's refusal of defendant's substitute offer of "Big Country" may be used in mitigation. Nor, if the "Big Country" offer was of employment different or inferior when compared with the original "Bloomer Girl" employment, is there an issue as to whether or not plaintiff acted reasonably in refusing the substitute offer. Despite defendant's arguments to the contrary, no case cited or which our research has discovered holds or suggests that reasonableness is an element of a wrongfully discharged employee's option to reject, or fail to seek, different or inferior employment lest the possible earnings therefrom be charged against him in mitigation of damages.[13]

Applying the foregoing rules to the record in the present case, with all intendments in favor of the party opposing the summary judgment motion— here, defendant—it is clear that the trial court correctly ruled that plaintiff's failure to accept defendant's tendered substitute employment could not be applied in mitigation of damages because the offer of the "Big Country" lead was of employment both different and inferior, and that no factual dispute was presented on that issue. The mere circumstance that "Bloomer Girl" was to be a musical review calling upon plaintiff's talents as a dancer as well as an actress, and was to be produced in the City of Los Angeles, whereas "Big Country" was a straight dramatic role in a "Western Type" story taking place in an opal mine in Australia, demonstrates the difference in kind between the

---

13. Instead, in each case the reasonableness referred to was that of the *efforts* of the employee to obtain other employment that was not different or inferior; his right to reject the latter was declared as an unqualified rule of law. Thus Gonzales v. Internat. Assn. of Machinists, supra, 213 Cal.App.2d 817, 823–824, holds that the trial court correctly instructed the jury that plaintiff union member, a machinist, was required to make "such *efforts* as the average [member of his union] desiring employment would make at that particular time and place" (italics added); but, further, that the court *properly rejected* defendant's offer of proof of the availability of other kinds of employment at the same or higher pay than plaintiff usually received and all outside the jurisdiction of his union, as plaintiff could not be required to accept different employment or a non-union job.

In Harris v. Nat. Union etc. Cooks, Stewards, supra, 116 Cal.App.2d 759, 761, the issues were stated to be, inter alia, whether comparable employment was open to each plaintiff employee, and if so whether each plaintiff made a *reasonable effort* to secure such employment. It was held that the trial court *properly sustained an objection to an offer to prove a custom of accepting a job in a lower rank* when work in the higher rank was not available, as "The duty of mitigation of damages ... does not require the plaintiff 'to seek or to accept other employment of a different or inferior kind.' " (P. 764[5].)

See also: Lewis v. Protective Security Life Ins. Co. (1962) 208 Cal.App.2d 582, 584 [25 Cal.Rptr. 213]: "*honest effort* to find similar employment...." (Italics added.) ...

de la Falaise v. Gaumont–British Picture Corp., supra, 39 Cal.App.2d 461, 469: "reasonable effort."

two employments; the female lead as a dramatic actress in a western style motion picture can by no stretch of imagination be considered the equivalent of or substantially similar to the lead in a song-and-dance production.

Additionally, the substitute "Big Country" offer proposed to eliminate or impair the director and screenplay approvals accorded to plaintiff under the original "Bloomer Girl" contract (see fn. 2, ante), and thus constituted an offer of inferior employment. No expertise or judicial notice is required in order to hold that the deprivation or infringement of an employee's rights held under an original employment contract converts the available "other employment" relied upon by the employer to mitigate damages, into inferior employment which the employee need not seek or accept. (See Gonzales v. Internat. Assn. of Machinists, supra, 213 Cal.App.2d 817, 823–824; and fn. 5. . . .)

Statements found in affidavits submitted by defendant in opposition to plaintiff's summary judgment motion, to the effect that the "Big Country" offer was not of employment different from or inferior to that under the "Bloomer Girl" contract, merely repeat the allegations of defendant's answer to the complaint in this action, constitute only conclusionary assertions with respect to undisputed facts, and do not give rise to a triable factual issue so as to defeat the motion for summary judgment. . . .

In view of the determination that defendant failed to present any facts showing the existence of a factual issue with respect to its sole defense—plaintiff's rejection of its substitute employment offer in mitigation of damages—we need not consider plaintiff's further contention that for various reasons, including the provisions of the original contract set forth in footnote 1, ante, plaintiff was excused from attempting to mitigate damages.

The judgment is affirmed.

McCOMB, J., PETERS, J., TOBRINER, J., KAUS, J.,* and ROTH, J.,** concurred.

[The dissenting opinion of Sullivan, Acting C.J., is omitted.]

MOSK, J., did not participate.

———

PUNKAR v. KING PLASTIC CORP., 290 So.2d 505 (Fla.App.1974). "A wrongfully discharged employee is not necessarily obligated to mitigate damages by accepting alternative employment at a distance from his home. . . . Our research discloses that a majority of jurisdictions have confined the search required to the immediate community or neighborhood. 44 A.L.R.3d 629. We believe this to be the better view."

———

MR. EDDIE, INC. v. GINSBERG, 430 S.W.2d 5 (Tex.Civ.App.1968). Ginsberg was wrongfully dismissed by defendant early in the term of a three-year employment contract. Immediately after the dismissal Ginsberg took another job, which he held for thirty-four weeks, earning $13,760. After Ginsberg left that job, he spent $1,340 unsuccessfully seeking further employ-

* Assigned by the Acting Chairman of the Judicial Council.

** Assigned by the Acting Chairman of the Judicial Council.

ment. Held, Ginsberg was entitled to recover his remaining salary under his contract with defendant, minus the $13,760 earned on the other job, but plus the $1,340 he unsuccessfully expended in looking for further employment. As to the $1,340 expense, the court said, "the rule in such cases is ... as follows: 'The expenses for which a recovery may be had include necessary and reasonable disbursements made in an effort to avoid or mitigate the injurious consequences of the defendant's wrong.... if such expenses are the result of a prudent attempt to minimize damages they are recoverable even though the result is an aggravation of the damages rather than a mitigation.' "

SOUTHERN KESWICK, INC. v. WHETHERHOLT, 293 So.2d 109 (Fla.App.1974). This was an action for breach of an employment contract. The jury was instructed, "[It is] the general rule that employment of different or inferior nature cannot be used in reduction of damages." Reversed. "While we would agree that a wrongfully discharged employee is not obliged to *seek* employment of a different or inferior nature, if he in fact *obtains* such employment within the contract period his earnings should be used in mitigation of damages. The foregoing charge was therefore clearly wrong...." (Emphasis added.)

NOTE ON DAMAGES FOR LOSS OF THE OPPORTUNITY TO PRACTICE ONE'S PROFESSION

1. For many employees, one of the injuries that results from an employer's breach of contract is injury to the employee's reputation. According to Dobbs, "Most commonly, general loss of reputation claims resulting from contract breach are denied." 3 D. Dobbs, Law of Remedies 486 (2d ed. 1993). For example, in Smith v. Beloit Corp., 40 Wis.2d 550, 162 N.W.2d 585 (1968), the court said:

> What then is the measure of damages? The trial court listed a number of factors which he held the jury was entitled to consider in fixing damages. They included the humiliation sustained by a proud man, permanent injury to professional reputation and additional living expenses occasioned by his new employment. These elements of damages aside from being quite speculative in nature, appear to us to fall outside the pale as being outside the reasonable contemplation of the parties and without basis in the record here established.

However, courts have allowed employees and others whose reputation was impaired by a breach of contract to recover specific losses that resulted from the injury to the plaintiff's reputation. For example, in Redgrave v. Boston Symphony Orchestra, Inc., 855 F.2d 888 (1st Cir.1988), cert. denied 488 U.S. 1043, 109 S.Ct. 869, 102 L.Ed.2d 993 (1989), in March 1982 the Boston Symphony Orchestra (BSO) engaged Vanessa Redgrave to narrate Stravinsky's *Oedipus Rex* in a series of concerts in Boston and New York. Following announcement of the engagement, the BSO received calls from its subscribers and from community members protesting the engagement because of Redgrave's political support for the Palestine Liberation Organization and her views regarding the state of Israel. In April 1982, the BSO cancelled its contract with Redgrave and its performances of *Oedipus Rex*.

Redgrave brought suit on various grounds. One of her claims was that as a result of the BSO's cancellation, a significant number of movie and theater offers that she would ordinarily have received in 1982 and thereafter were in fact not offered to her. The BSO characterized this claim as one for damage to Redgrave's reputation, and argued that Massachusetts law did not permit a plaintiff to recover consequential damages for harm to reputation in a breach-of-contract action. The Court of Appeals held that Redgrave was entitled to recover those losses if she could establish them:

> The claim advanced by Redgrave is significantly different ... from a general claim of damage to reputation. Redgrave is not claiming that her general reputation as a professional actress has been tarnished by the BSO's cancellation. Rather, she claims that a number of specific movie and theater performances that would have been offered to her in the usual course of events were not offered to her as a result of the BSO's cancellation. . . .

> ... [W]e hold that, as a matter of Massachusetts contract law, a plaintiff may receive consequential damages if the plaintiff proves with sufficient evidence that a breach of contract proximately caused the loss of identifiable professional opportunities. This type of claim is sufficiently different from a nonspecific allegation of damage to reputation that it appropriately falls outside the general rule that reputation damages are not an acceptable form of contract damage.

The court went on to conclude, however, that Redgrave had only proved that she had lost one fee of $12,000 as a result of the BSO cancellation.

Other courts have followed *Redgrave* in holding that although damages will be granted for loss of specific and identifiable job opportunities as a result of a breach of an employment contract, damages for lost reputation, as such, will not be granted, on the ground that such damages could not have reasonably been contemplated by the parties, are too speculative, or both. See e.g., Rice v. Community Health Ass'n, 203 F.3d 283 (4th Cir.2000); Wilder v. Cody Country Chamber of Commerce, 933 P.2d 1098 (Wyo.1997). It's not easy to understand this reasoning, because the injury to an employee's reputation if she is fired in breach of contract would usually be reasonably foreseeable, and whether the damages are too uncertain should be decided on a case-by-case basis, as is usually done under modern contract law.

2. Another, distinct type of injury caused by the improper discharge of an employee is the loss of the opportunity to practice the employee's profession. The English courts have permitted actors to recover damages for this type of injury. See Herbert Clayton & Jack Waller, Ltd. v. Oliver, 1930 App.Cas. 209, 220 (H.L.); Note, Recovery in Contract for Damage to Reputation: Redgrave v. Boston Symphony Orchestra, Inc., 63 St. John's L.Rev. 110, 119–20 (1988).

The English approach has not always been accepted in the United States. For example, in Quinn v. Straus Broadcasting Group, Inc., 309 F.Supp. 1208, 1210 (S.D.N.Y.1970), the plaintiff was employed under contract as a "staff announcer" for one year at a salary of $50,000. Plaintiff alleged that the employer wrongfully discharged him after four months, and claimed $500,000 damages for loss of the opportunity to appear before the public. The court denied damages for this claim. However, in Colvig v. RKO General, Inc., 232 Cal.App.2d 56, 69, 42 Cal.Rptr. 473, 481 (1965), the California District Court of Appeals reached the opposite conclusion on strikingly similar facts. Plaintiff claimed that he had been terminated from employment by defendant as a staff announcer, and that the defendant employer had been ordered by an arbitrator to restore plaintiff to his position, but that the defendant had refused to do so. As a result, plaintiff claimed, he had been damaged in his profession by not being able to be and remain known to the public as a radio announcer. The court said:

> As a general rule an employer does not have the duty to provide work for his employee but may utilize his employee's services, when and how he chooses, so long as he pays the employee the agreed-upon salary. An exception to this rule exists where the employee's reputation will suffer if he is not allowed to practice his profession. The rationale of this exception is that the parties are deemed to have contracted on the assumption that the employee was to be given opportunities for the exercise of his abilities during a reasonable portion of the period covered by the contract.

> ... In the Restatement Second of Agency, section 433, we find this statement: "If the agent's compensation is not dependent upon the amount of work done, as where he is to receive a fixed salary, a promise by the principal to furnish him with work is inferred from a promise to employ only if it is found that the anticipated benefit to the agent from doing the work is a material part of the advantage to be received by him from the employment. This anticipated benefit may be the acquisition of skill or reputation by the employee or the acquisition of subsidiary pecuniary advantages, as in the case of the employment of public performers whose reputation will be enhanced by their appearance or diminished by their failure to appear...."

> With respect to cases in other jurisdictions, we find an application of the foregoing principles in several cases. In some of these, the facts involved situations in which the employee was assigned lesser duties than those specified in the employment contract (*Clayton & Waller Ltd. v. Oliver* (England 1930) A.C. 209 (an actor who had been hired to perform a lead role was assigned to a secondary role); *Mair v. Southern Minnesota Broadcasting Co.,* 226 Minn. 13 [32 N.W.2d 177, 4 A.L.R.2d 273] (a radio station manager, although permitted to retain his title and salary, was divested of most of his managerial duties)); in others, the employee was assigned no duties at all (*McLaughlin v. Union–Leader Corporation,* 99 N.H. 492 [116 A.2d 489] (advertising manager was put on an indefinite leave of absence with pay); *Sigmon v. Goldstone,* 116 App.Div. 490 [101 N.Y.S. 984] (clothes design-cutter, although paid a salary, was prevented from working at his job)). In *Sigmon,* the court, in affirming the right of the employee to recover for breach of the contract of employment, made the following statement: "The contract between plaintiff and defendants was that he should serve in the capacity of designer and cutter and foreman of defendants' manufacturing establishment at a salary comparatively large. In order thereafter to command this salary or a higher one, plaintiff must continue to be skillful and to enjoy a reputation for skill. It was one of the implied covenants of plaintiff's contract that he should be permitted to labor in the manner specified."

Similarly, in Van Steenhouse v. Jacor Broadcasting of Colorado, Inc., 958 P.2d 464 (Colo.1998), in 1991, Van Steenhouse, a radio personality and practicing psychologist, signed a three-year agreement with Jacor to be a radio talk-show host with KOA, a station owned by Jacor. In October 1993, Jacor acquired the rights to broadcast the Rush Limbaugh show, and in January 1994, Jacor started broadcasting Rush Limbaugh in place of Van Steenhouse. Although Jacor paid Van Steenhouse's salary until the expiration of the contract in August 1994, Van Steenhouse did not work as a radio talk-show host for a period of approximately eight months. The Colorado Supreme Court upheld an award of damages to Van Steenhouse based on her lost opportunity to work under the contract. See also Neeld v. American Hockey League, 439 F.Supp. 459 (W.D.N.Y.1977).

SECTION 4. FORESEEABILITY

HADLEY v. BAXENDALE
In the Court of Exchequer, 1854.
9 Exch. 341.

... At the trial before Crompton, J., at the last Gloucester Assizes, it appeared that the plaintiffs carried on an extensive business as millers at Gloucester; and that, on the 11th of May, their mill was stopped by a breakage of the crank shaft by which the mill was worked. The steam-engine was manufactured by Messrs. Joyce & Co., the engineers, at Greenwich, and it became necessary to send the shaft as a pattern for a new one to Greenwich. The fracture was discovered on the 12th, and on the 13th the plaintiffs sent one of their servants to the office of the defendants, who are the well-known carriers trading under the name of Pickford & Co., for the purpose of having the shaft carried to Greenwich. The plaintiffs' servant told the clerk that the mill was stopped, and that the shaft must be sent immediately; and in answer to the inquiry when the shaft would be taken, the answer was, that if it was sent up by twelve o'clock any day, it would be delivered at Greenwich on the following day. On the following day the shaft was taken by the defendants before noon, for the purpose of being conveyed to Greenwich, and the sum of £2, 4s. was paid for its carriage for the whole distance; at the same time the defendants' clerk was told that a special entry, if required, should be made to hasten its delivery. The delivery of the shaft at Greenwich was delayed by some neglect; and the consequence was, that the plaintiffs did not receive the new shaft for several days after they would otherwise have done and the working of their mill was thereby delayed, and they thereby lost the profits they would otherwise have received.*

On the part of the defendants, it was objected that these damages were too remote, and that the defendants were not liable with respect to them. The

---

* In The Capability Problem in Contract Law (2d ed. 2004), Richard Danzig and Geoffrey R. Watson set out the following statement from the Assize Report in August 8, 1853, edition of The Times of London: "[I]nstead of being forwarded by wagon immediately, [the crankshaft] was kept for several days in London, and was at length forwarded by water on the 20th, along with many tons of iron goods which had been consigned to the same parties." Id. at 59 n. 5.

learned Judge left the case generally to the jury, who found a verdict with £25 damages beyond the amount paid into Court.**

WHATELEY, in last Michaelmas Term, obtained a rule nisi for a new trial, on the ground of misdirection.

KEATING and DOWDESWELL (Feb. 1) showed cause. The plaintiffs are entitled to the amount awarded by the jury as damages. These damages are not too remote, for they are not only the natural and necessary consequence of the defendants' default, but they are the only loss which the plaintiffs have actually sustained. The principle upon which damages are assessed is founded upon that of rendering compensation to the injured party....

[PARKE, B. The sensible rule appears to be that which has been laid down in France, and which is declared in their code—Code Civil, liv, iii, tit. iii. ss. 1149, 1150, 1151, and which is thus translated in Sedgwick [on Damages, p. 67]: "The damages due to the creditor consist in general of the loss that he has sustained, and the profit which he has been prevented from acquiring, subject to the modifications hereinafter contained. The debtor is only liable for the damages foreseen, or which might have been foreseen, at the time of the execution of the contract, when it is not owing to his fraud that the agreement has been violated. Even in the case of non-performance of the contract, resulting from the fraud of the debtor, the damages only comprise so much of the loss sustained by the creditor, and so much of the profit which he has been prevented from acquiring, as directly and immediately results from the non-performance of the contract."] If that rule is to be adopted, there was ample evidence in the present case of the defendants' knowledge of such a state of things as would necessarily result in the damage the plaintiffs suffered through the defendants' default....

[... MARTIN, B. Take the case of the non-delivery by a carrier of a delicate piece of machinery, whereby the whole of an extensive mill is thrown out of work for a considerable time; if the carrier is to be liable for the loss in that case, he might incur damages to the extent of 10,000*l*....] These extreme cases, and the difficulty which consequently exists in the estimation of the true amount of damages, supports the view for which the plaintiffs contend, that the question is properly for the decision of a jury, and therefore that this matter could not properly have been withdrawn from their consideration....

WHATELEY, WILLES, and PHIPSON, in support of the rule (Feb. 2). It has been contended, on the part of the plaintiffs, that the damages found by the jury are a matter fit for their consideration; but still the question remains, in what way ought the jury to have been directed? It has been also urged, that, in awarding damages, the law gives compensation to the injured individual. But it is clear that complete compensation is not to be awarded; for instance, the non-payment of a bill of exchange might lead to the utter ruin of the holder, and yet such damage could not be considered as necessarily resulting from the breach of contract, so as to entitle the party aggrieved to recover in respect of it. Take the case of the breach of a contract to supply a rick-cloth, whereby and in consequence of bad weather the hay, being unprotected, is spoiled, that damage would not be recoverable. Many similar cases might be added.... Sedgwick says [p. 28], "In regard to the quantum of damages, instead of adhering to the term compensation, it would be far more accurate to say, in the language of Domat, which we have cited above, 'that the object is to discriminate between that portion of the loss which must be borne by the offending party and that which must be borne by the sufferer.' The law in fact

** According to the report of the case, the amount which the defendant had paid into court was £25. See 9 Exch.Rep. at 343. (Footnote by ed.)

aims not at the satisfaction but at a division of the loss." . . . This therefore is a question of law, and the jury ought to have been told that these damages were too remote; and that, in the absence of the proof of any other damage, the plaintiffs were entitled to nominal damages only. . . .

The judgment of the Court was now delivered by Alderson, B.

We think that there ought to be a new trial in this case; but, in so doing, we deem it to be expedient and necessary to state explicitly the rule which the Judge, at the next trial, ought, in our opinion, to direct the jury to be governed by when they estimate the damages.

It is, indeed, of the last importance that we should do this; for, if the jury are left without any definite rule to guide them, it will, in such cases as these, manifestly lead to the greatest injustice. The Courts have done this on several occasions; and, in Blake v. Midland Railway Company, 18 Q.B. 93, the Court granted a new trial on this very ground, that the rule had not been definitely laid down to the jury by the learned Judge at Nisi Prius.

"There are certain established rules," this Court says, in Alder v. Keighley, 15 M. & W. 117, "according to which the jury ought to find." And the Court, in that case, adds: "and here there is a clear rule, that the amount which would have been received if the contract had been kept, is the measure of damages if the contract is broken."

Now we think the proper rule in such a case as the present is this:— Where two parties have made a contract which one of them has broken, the damages which the other party ought to receive in respect of such breach of contract should be such as may fairly and reasonably be considered either arising naturally, i.e., according to the usual course of things, from such breach of contract itself, or such as may reasonably be supposed to have been in the contemplation of both parties, at the time they made the contract, as the probable result of the breach of it. Now, if the special circumstances under which the contract was actually made were communicated by the plaintiffs to the defendants, and thus known to both parties, the damages resulting from the breach of such a contract, which they would reasonably contemplate, would be the amount of injury which would ordinarily follow from a breach of contract under these special circumstances so known and communicated. But, on the other hand, if these special circumstances were wholly unknown to the party breaking the contract, he, at the most, could only be supposed to have had in his contemplation the amount of injury which would arise generally, and in the great multitude of cases not affected by any special circumstances, from such a breach of contract. For, had the special circumstances been known, the parties might have specially provided for the breach of contract by special terms as to the damages in that case; and of this advantage it would be very unjust to deprive them. Now the above principles are those by which we think the jury ought to be guided in estimating the damages arising out of any breach of contract. It is said, that other cases such as breaches of contract in the non-payment of money, or in the not making a good title to land, are to be treated as exceptions from this, and as governed by a conventional rule. But as, in such cases, both parties must be supposed to be cognizant of that well-known rule, these cases may, we think, be more properly classed under the rule above enunciated as to cases under known special circumstances, because there both parties may reasonably be presumed to contemplate the estimation of the amount of damages according to the conventional rule. Now, in the present case, if we are to apply the principles above laid down, we find that the only circumstances here communicated by the plaintiffs to the defendants at the time the contract was made, were, that the article to be carried was the broken shaft of a mill, and that the plaintiffs were the millers of that mill. But how do these circumstances [show] reasonably that the profits of the mill must be stopped by an unreasonable delay in the delivery of the broken shaft by the carrier to the third person? Suppose the plaintiffs had another shaft in their possession put up or putting up at the time, and that they only wished to send back the broken shaft to the engineer who made it; it is clear that this would be quite consistent with the above circumstances, and yet the unreasonable delay in the delivery would have no effect upon the intermediate profits of the mill. Or, again, suppose that, at the time of the delivery to the carrier, the machinery of the mill had been in other respects defective, then, also, the same results would follow. Here it is true that the shaft was actually sent back to serve as a model for a new one, and that the want of a new one was the only cause of the stoppage of the mill, and that the loss of profits really arose from not sending down the new shaft in proper time, and that this arose from the delay in delivering the broken one to serve as a model. But it is obvious that, in the great multitude of cases of millers sending off broken shafts to third persons by a carrier under ordinary circumstances, such consequences would not, in all probability, have occurred; and these special circumstances were here never communicated by the plaintiffs to the defendants. It follows, therefore, that the loss of profits here cannot reasonably be considered such a consequence of the breach of contract as could have been fairly and reasonably contemplated by both the parties when they made this contract. For such loss would neither have flowed naturally from the breach of this contract in the great multitude of such cases occurring under ordinary circumstances, nor were the special circumstances, which, perhaps, would have made it a reasonable and natural consequence of such breach of contract, communicated to or known by the defendants. The Judge ought, therefore, to have told the jury, that, upon the facts then before them, they ought not to take the loss of profits into consideration at all in estimating the damages. There must therefore be a new trial in this case.

Rule absolute.

BACKGROUND NOTE ON HADLEY v. BAXENDALE

Who was Hadley? Who was Baxendale? And what caused the delay? These and other questions concerning the players and the play are extensively addressed in Danzig, Hadley v. Baxendale: A Study in the Industrialization of the Law, 4 J.Leg.Stud. 249 (1975). A brief extract follows:

In Gloucester, England, on Thursday, May 12, 1853, the engine shaft at City Flour Mills broke, preventing the further milling of corn. On May 13, the mill proprietors, Joseph and Jonah Hadley, dispatched an employee to Pickford and Co., "common carriers," to inquire as to the fastest means of conveying the shaft to W. Joyce and Co., Greenwich, where it would serve as a model for the crafting of a new shaft.... The shaft was delivered to Pickfords on Saturday, May 14, but it did not, in fact, reach W. Joyce and Co. until the 21st, because at the last stage of the voyage

the shaft was shipped with a consignment of iron bound for Joyce and Co. by canal rather than by rail.... When Pickfords refused to make good these losses, the Hadleys brought suit ... naming Joseph Baxendale, the London-based managing director of Pickford's, as the defendant. (Baxendale was personally liable for the failings of his unincorporated business.)
...

Id. at 251.

In the same article, Professor Danzig contends that the decision in Hadley v. Baxendale was essentially a product of historical circumstances, particularly the peculiar state of industry, law, and the judicial system in England in the mid–1850's. This contention, however, is hard to reconcile with the fact that the principle adopted in Hadley v. Baxendale also appears in the great French treatise by Pothier, *Traité des obligations,* first published in 1761:

> For instance, suppose I sell a person a horse which I am obliged to deliver in a certain time, and I cannot deliver it accordingly: if in the meantime horses have increased in price, whatever the purchaser is obliged to pay more than he would have given for mine, in order to procure another of the like quality, is a damage for which I am obliged to indemnify him, because it is a damage ... which only relates to the thing that was the object of the contract, and which I might have foreseen; the price of horses like that of all other things being subject to variation. But if this purchaser was a canon, who for want of having the horse that I had engaged to deliver to him, and not having been enabled to get another, was prevented from arriving at the place of his benefice in time to be entitled to his revenue, I should not be liable for the loss which he sustained thereby, although it was occasioned by the non-performance of my obligation; for this is a damage which is foreign to the obligation, which was not contemplated at the time of the contract, and to which it cannot be supposed that I had any intention to submit....

(1 R. Pothier, supra, § 159, as translated by W. Evans in an English edition first published in 1806.) In view of the differences between mid–1700's France and mid–1800's England, it seems highly unlikely that a principle that appears in both times and places is essentially a product of the peculiar state of industry, law, and the judicial system in either time or place. See Simpson, The Horwitz Thesis and the History of Contracts, 46 U.Chi.L.Rev. 533, 591 (1979).

―――――

VICTORIA LAUNDRY (WINDSOR) LTD. v. NEWMAN INDUS. LTD., Court of Appeal, [1949] 2 K.B. 528. Plaintiffs did business as launderers and dyers at Windsor. They wanted to expand their business, and to that end they needed a boiler of much greater capacity than the one they possessed, whose capacity was 1,500–1,600 lbs. evaporation per hour. In January 1946, they saw an advertisement by defendants for two "vertical Cochran boilers of 8,000 lb. per hour capacity heavy steaming," and began negotiating for the purchase of one of these. By April 26, they had concluded a contract for purchase of the boiler at a price of £ 2,150, loaded free on transport at Harpenden, where it was then installed in the defendants' premises. The defendants knew the plaintiffs were launderers and dyers and wanted the boiler for use in their business. Also, during the negotiations the plaintiffs expressed their intention to put the boiler into use in the shortest possible time.

Arrangements were made between the parties to take delivery at Harpenden on June 5, and the plaintiffs on that date sent a truck to Harpenden, but it was then learned that four days earlier the boiler had been damaged by the carelessness of a third person who had been employed by the defendants to dismantle the boiler. Plaintiffs refused to take delivery unless the damage was made good, and ultimately defendants agreed to arrange for the necessary repairs. Plaintiffs did not receive delivery of the boiler until November 8, 1946. They then brought suit for breach of contract, claiming lost profits during the period from June 5 to November 8, 1946. Evidence showed that if the boiler had been punctually delivered, during the twenty weeks between June 5 and November 8 plaintiffs could have taken on a very large number of new customers in the course of their laundry business (since the demand for laundry services at that time was insatiable), and would have accepted highly lucrative dyeing contracts for the Ministry of Supply. In the complaint, the loss of profits under the first of these heads was quantified at £ 16 a week, and under the second at £ 262 a week. The trial judge held that damages for lost profits were not recoverable, under the principle of Hadley v. Baxendale. The court of appeal, in an opinion by Asquith, L.J., reversed:

> What propositions applicable to the present case emerge from the authorities as a whole ... ? We think they include the following:
>
> (1) It is well settled that the governing purpose of damages is to put the party whose rights have been violated in the same position, so far as money can do so, as if his rights had been observed.... This purpose, if relentlessly pursued, would provide him with a complete indemnity for all loss de facto resulting from a particular breach, however improbable, however unpredictable. This, in contract at least, is recognized as too harsh a rule. Hence,
>
> (2) In cases of breach of contract the aggrieved party is only entitled to recover such part of the loss actually resulting as was at the time of the contract reasonably foreseeable as liable to result from the breach.
>
> (3) What was at that time reasonably so foreseeable depends on the knowledge then possessed by the parties or, at all events, by the party who later commits the breach.
>
> (4) For this purpose, knowledge "possessed" is of two kinds; one imputed, the other actual. Everyone, as a reasonable person, is taken to know the "ordinary course of things" and consequently what loss is liable to result from a breach of contract in that ordinary course. This is the subject matter of the "first rule" in Hadley v. Baxendale. But to this knowledge, which a contract-breaker is assumed to possess whether he actually possesses it or not, there may have to be added in a particular case knowledge which he actually possesses, of special circumstances outside the "ordinary course of things," of such a kind that a breach in those special circumstances would be liable to cause more loss. Such a case attracts the operation of the "second rule" so as to make additional loss also recoverable.

(5) In order to make the contract-breaker liable under either rule it is not necessary that he should actually have asked himself what loss is liable to result from a breach. As has often been pointed out, parties at the time of contracting contemplate not the breach of the contract, but its performance. It suffices that, if he had considered the question, he would as a reasonable man have concluded that the loss in question was liable to result.

(6) Nor, finally, to make a particular loss recoverable, need it be proved that upon a given state of knowledge the defendant could, as a reasonable man, foresee that a breach must necessarily result in that loss. It is enough if he could foresee it was likely so to result. It is indeed enough, to borrow from the language of Lord du Parcq ... if the loss (or some factor without which it would not have occurred) is a "serious possibility" or a "real danger." For short, we have used the word "liable" to result. Possibly the colloquialism "on the cards" indicates the shade of meaning with some approach to accuracy....

If these, indeed, are the principles applicable, what is [their effect]? ... (We shall speak henceforward not of loss of profit, but of "loss of business.") No commercial concern commonly purchases for the purposes of its business a very large and expensive structure like this—a boiler 19 feet high and costing over 2,000*l.*—with any other motive, and no supplier, let alone an engineering company, which has promised delivery of such an article by a particular date, with knowledge that it was to be put into use immediately on delivery, can reasonably contend that it could not foresee that loss of business (in the sense indicated above) would be liable to result to the purchaser from a long delay in the delivery thereof.... [The defendant company] knew they were supplying the boiler to a company carrying on the business of laundrymen and dyers, for use in that business. The obvious use of a boiler, in such a business, is surely to boil water for the purpose of washing or dyeing.... If the purpose then be to wash or dye, why does the company want to wash or dye, unless for purposes of business advantage, in which term we, for the purposes of the rest of this judgment, include maintenance or increase of profit, or reduction of loss?

... [As to the particularly lucrative dyeing contracts for the Minister of Supply, we] agree that in order that the plaintiffs should recover specifically and as such the profits expected on these contracts, the defendants would have had to know, at the time of their agreement with the plaintiffs, of the prospect and terms of such contracts. We also agree that they did not in fact know these things. It does not, however, follow that the plaintiffs are precluded from recovering some general (and perhaps conjectural) sum for loss of business in respect of dyeing contracts to be reasonably expected, any more than in respect of laundering contracts to be reasonably expected....

————

KOUFOS v. C. CZARNIKOW, LTD. [THE HERON II], [1969] A.C. 350 (H.L.1967). The facts in this case were stated by Lord Reid as follows:

By charter party of Oct. 15, 1960, the respondents chartered the appellant's vessel, Heron II, to proceed to Constanza, there to load a cargo of three thousand tons of sugar; and to carry it to Basrah, or, in the charterers' option, to Jeddah. The vessel left Constanza on Nov. 1. The option was not exercised and the vessel arrived at Basrah on Dec. 2. The umpire has found that "a reasonably accurate prediction of the length of the voyage was twenty days". But the vessel had in breach of contract made deviations which caused a delay of nine days.

It was the intention of the respondent charterers to sell the sugar "promptly after arrival at Basrah and after inspection by merchants". The appellant shipowner did not know this, but he was aware of the fact that there was a market for sugar at Basrah. The sugar was in fact sold at Basrah in lots between Dec. 12 and 22 but shortly before that time the market price had fallen partly by reason of the arrival of another cargo of sugar. It was found by the umpire that if there had not been this delay of nine days the sugar would have fetched £32 10s. per ton. The actual price realized was only £31 2s.9d. per ton. The charterers claim that they are entitled to recover the difference as damage for breach of contract. The shipowner admits that he is liable to pay interest for nine days on the value of the sugar and [plaintiff's cable] expenses but denies that fall in market value can be taken into account in assessing damages in this case.

All of the judges agreed that on these facts the shipowner was liable for damages measured by the fall in the sugar price. Again, Lord Reid:

> ... There is no finding that [the charterers] had in mind any particular date as the likely date of arrival at Basrah or that they had any knowledge or expectation that in late November or December there would be a rising or a falling market. The shipowner was given no information about these matters by the charterers. He did not know what the charterers intended to do with the sugar. But he knew there was a market in sugar at Basrah, and it appears to me that, if he had thought about the matter, he must have realized that at least it was not unlikely that the sugar would be sold in the market at market price on arrival. And he must be held to have known that in any ordinary market prices are apt to fluctuate from day to day: but he had no reason to suppose it more probable that during the relevant period such fluctuation would be downwards rather than upwards—it was an even chance that the fluctuation would be downwards. . . .

While all the judges concurred in the result, they differed on how the principle of Hadley v. Baxendale should be expressed. The discussion in this regard centered around Asquith's opinion in *Victoria Laundry*. Asquith's use of the phrase "on the cards" brought reproof, but his use of the phrases "liable to result," "real danger," and "serious possibility," met general approval. Lord Reid somewhat querulously disagreed even with these phrases, but made some interesting comments:

> The modern rule of tort is quite different [from that in contract] and it imposes a much wider liability. The defendant will be liable for any type of damage which is reasonably foreseeable as liable to happen even in the most unusual case, unless the risk is so small that a reasonable man would in the whole circumstances feel justified in neglecting it. And there is good reason for the difference. In contract, if one party wishes to

protect himself against a risk which to the other party would appear unusual, he can direct the other party's attention to it before the contract is made, and I need not stop to consider in what circumstances the other party will then be held to have accepted responsibility in that event.... [I]n tort, there is no opportunity for the injured party to protect himself in that way, and the tortfeasor cannot reasonably complain if he has to pay for some very unusual but nevertheless foreseeable damage which results from his wrongdoing. I have no doubt that today a tortfeasor would be held liable for a type of damage as unlikely as was the stoppage of Hadley's Mill for lack of a crank shaft: to anyone with the knowledge the carrier had that may have seemed unlikely but the chance of it happening would have been seen to be far from negligible.

A passage in Lord Reid's opinion also suggests, by inference, some outer limits for determining whether an event should be reasonably foreseeable under the principle of Hadley v. Baxendale. "Suppose one takes a well-shuffled pack of cards, it is quite likely or not unlikely that the top card will prove to be a diamond: the odds are only three to one against. But most people would not say that it is quite likely to be the nine of diamonds for the odds are then fifty-one to one against." If this metaphor is to be taken seriously, it suggests that if, at the time of contract formation, there is a 25 percent chance that a given type of damage will occur in the event of breach, the damage will be compensable under Hadley v. Baxendale, but if there is only a 2 percent chance that a given type of damage will occur, the damage will not be compensable.

HECTOR MARTINEZ AND CO. v. SOUTHERN PACIFIC TRANSP. CO., 606 F.2d 106 (5th Cir.1979), cert. denied 446 U.S. 982, 100 S.Ct. 2962, 64 L.Ed.2d 838 (1980). Martinez shipped by rail a used dragline (strip-mining machinery) from Ohio to Eagle Pass, Texas. The dragline was loaded onto five separate railroad cars. The five cars were shipped separately, and the last car arrived in Eagle Pass on April 2, 1974. Martinez contended that the last of the cars should have arrived on March 1, and sued Southern Pacific, the responsible railroad, for the dragline's fair rental value during the period from March 1 until April 2. The trial court dismissed Martinez's claim, under Hadley v. Baxendale. Reversed.

"Martinez asserts that his loss resulting from the delay in shipment was reasonably foreseeable when he entered the contract to transport his dragline. *Hadley* held that the damages arising from an inoperative mill were not foreseeable results of delayed shipment of a shaft, without specific notice. It was not obvious that the shaft in *Hadley* was an indispensable element of a mill. In the instant case, however, it was obvious that the dragline is a machine which of itself has a use value. Some cases after *Hadley* have suggested that the injury resulting from loss of a machine's use are not foreseeable results of delayed transport, because it is not a usual consequence although it is a proximate consequence.... These decisions are unwarranted extension of *Hadley* and employ arbitrary and inflexible definitions of foreseeability. Capital goods such as machinery have a use value, which may equal the rental value of the equipment or may be an interest value. The latter is ordinarily interest at the market rate on the value of the machine. It might be quite foreseeable that deprivation of the machine's use because of a carriage delay will cause a loss of rental value or interest value during the delay period. . . . We must not lose sight of the basic common law rule, enunciated in *Hadley,* of damages for foreseeable loss. The amount of damages that was reasonably foreseeable involves a fact question that Martinez is entitled to present to a jury.

"Southern Pacific replies that it was as foreseeable that the goods were to be sold as that they were to be used. This contention proves too much because *Hadley* allows recovery for harms that should have been foreseen. The general rule does not require the plaintiff to show that the actual harm suffered was the *most* foreseeable of possible harms. He need only demonstrate that his harm was not so remote as to make it unforeseeable to a reasonable man at the time of contracting. Even if the dragline were being shipped for sale it does not follow that delay in shipment would cause no recoverable loss. . . .

"The common law employs a number of methods for computing damages recoverable for unreasonable delay in shipment. One of these is the market value test that measures damages by the diminution in the goods' value between the time of dispatch and the time of actual delivery. . . . That test, however, 'is merely a method,' and it 'is not applied in cases where . . . another rule will better compute actual damages.' . . . Lost rental value is frequently an appropriate measure of damages from a delay in shipment of machinery. . . . In deciding which measure of damage to apply, courts look to the actual loss suffered by the plaintiff and the common law rule of compensating that loss."

NOTE ON THE SCOPE OF HADLEY v. BAXENDALE

In most cases in which the principle of Hadley v. Baxendale is applied, the issue is whether at the time the contract was made it was reasonably foreseeable that a given type of loss would result from breach. Suppose, however, that while a given *type* of loss was reasonably foreseeable, the defendant claims that the *amount* of the loss was not? In *Victoria Laundry* the court held, in regard to the buyer's lost profits on potential very lucrative dying contracts, that even if a type of loss is reasonably foreseeable, the plaintiff can recover only that amount of loss of that type that was reasonably foreseeable.

A different view was taken in Wroth v. Tyler, [1974] Ch. 80. There, a husband had contracted to sell a house, but was unable to perform the contract because his wife legally prevented him from selling. The husband agreed to pay damages, but argued that he could not have foreseen a dramatic increase in property values between 1971 and 1973. Justice Megarry held that a defendant cannot escape liability because the amount or quantum of damages was unforeseeable. Once a contracting party is held liable for a type of damage, the party will be liable for the full extent of those damages:

> It was beyond question that a rise in the price of houses was in the contemplation of the parties when the contract was made in this case. But Mr. Lyndon–Stanford [the defendant's barrister] took it further. He contended that what a plaintiff must establish is not merely a contemplation of a particular head of damage, but also of the quantum under that

head. Here, the parties contemplated a rise in house prices, but not a rise of an amount approaching that which in fact took place. A rise which nearly doubled the market price of the property was, as the evidence showed, outside the contemplation of the parties, and so it could not be recovered. Thus ran the argument.

I do not think that this can be right. On principle, it seems to me to be quite wrong to limit damages flowing from a contemplated state of affairs to the amount that the parties can be shown to have had in contemplation, for to do this would require evidence of the calculation in advance of what is often incalculable until after the event. The function of the so-called "second rule" in Hadley v. Baxendale, 9 Exch. 341, seems to me to be not so much to add to the damages recoverable as to exclude from them any liability for any type or kind of loss which could not have been foreseen when the contract was made. No authority was put before me which appeared to me to provide any support for the alleged requirement that the quantum should have been in contemplation. So far as it went, the language used in the authorities that were cited seems to me to have been directed to the heads of damage rather than to quantum. Thus one finds phrases such as "special circumstances" and the "type" or "kind" of damage. I would therefore on principle reject the defendant's contention, and hold that a plaintiff invoking the so-called "second rule" in Hadley v. Baxendale, 9 Exch. 341, need show only a contemplation of circumstances which embrace the head or type of damage in question, and need not demonstrate a contemplation of the quantum of damages under that head or type.

Accord: Brown v. KMR Services Ltd. [1995] 4 All E.R. 598, [1995] 2 Lloyd's Rep 513.

RESTATEMENT, SECOND, CONTRACTS § 351

[See Selected Source Materials Supplement]

UCC §§ 2–713, 2–715(2)

[See Selected Source Materials Supplement]

PANHANDLE AGRI–SERVICE, INC. v. BECKER, 231 Kan. 291, 644 P.2d 413 (1982). "Consequential damages are limited under [UCC §] 2–715(2)(a) to those instances where it is established that the loss could not reasonably be prevented by cover or otherwise. A buyer does not have to cover under [UCC §] 2–712(3); however, on failure to attempt cover, consequential damages, including loss of profits, cannot be recovered. [UCC §] 2–715(2)(a)."

CISG ART. 74

[See Selected Source Materials Supplement]

UNIDROIT PRINCIPLES OF INTERNATIONAL COMMERCIAL CONTRACTS ART. 7.4.4

[See Selected Source Materials Supplement]

PRINCIPLES OF EUROPEAN CONTRACT LAW ART. 9.503

[See Selected Source Materials Supplement]

NOTE—LIMITATIONS ON CONTRACT DAMAGES

According to Fuller and Perdue, The Reliance Interest in Contract Damages, 46 Yale L.J. 52, 84 (1936), Hadley v. Baxendale "may be said to stand for two propositions: (1) that it is not always wise to make the defaulting promisor pay for all the damage which follows as a consequence of his breach, and (2) that specifically the proper test for determining whether particular items of damage should be compensable is to inquire whether they should have been foreseen by the promisor at the time of the contract. The first aspect of the case is much more important than the second. In its first aspect the case bears an integral relation to the very bases of contract liability. It declares in effect that just as it is wise to refuse enforcement altogether to some promises (considerationless, unaccepted, 'social' promises, etc.) so it is wise not to go too far in enforcing those promises which are deemed worthy of legal sanction." As the cases in this Chapter frequently illustrate, many of the principles governing damages for breach of contract reflect a tension between that idea and the idea that contract damages should put the injured party "in as good a position as that in which he would have been put by full performance of the contract."

NOTE ON CAUSATION

A principle related to that expressed in Hadley v. Baxendale is that damages "must in fact be caused by the defendant's breach." This may seem obvious, but what if several factors contribute to the same result? In Krauss v. Greenbarg, 137 F.2d 569 (3d Cir.1943), cert. denied, 320 U.S. 791, 64 S.Ct. 207, 88 L.Ed. 477, a buyer sued for consequential damages for delay in delivery of webbing to be used in making Army leggings. The seller claimed that other contributing causes of the buyer's damages were "a landlord's [seizure of buyer's property for nonpayment of rent,] and eviction at the buyer's factory, a removal by the [buyer] of its plant, a shortage of eyelets necessary to the manufacture of the leggings, and excessive delay by the manufacturer even after all the webbing had been delivered." The trial judge charged the jury that the seller's breach must be the "chief" cause, "sufficient in itself." The Court of Appeals affirmed a judgment for the buyer, saying that the charge may have been too favorable to the seller. It cited the Restatement of Torts as supporting a legal test that the defendant's breach "shall have been a substantial factor in bringing about the harm," having "such an effect in procuring the harm as to lead reasonable men to regard it as a cause." "If a number of factors are operating one may so predominate in bringing about the harm as to make the effect produced by others so negligible that they cannot be considered substantial factors and hence legal causes of the harm produced."

INDEPENDENT MECHANICAL CONTRACTORS, INC. v. GORDON T. BURKE & SONS, 138 N.H. 110, 635 A.2d 487 (1993). "Burke apparently argues that its breach did not justify the jury's award of damages because other events may have contributed to IMC's injuries. While we recognize the plausibility of Burke's premise, we point out that no one event is the sole cause of another. 'In all cases involving problems of causation and responsibility for harm, a good many factors have united in producing the result. . . .' 5 Corbin ... § 999, at 24. 'In order to establish liability the plaintiff must [merely] show that the defendant's breach "a substantial factor" in causing the injury.' 5 Corbin ... § 999, at 25. IMC has done this."

S.J. GROVES & SONS CO. v. WARNER CO., 576 F.2d 524 (3d Cir.1978). As part of a highway improvement program, Pennsylvania undertook the erection of the Girard Point Bridge in southwest Philadelphia. Groves was awarded a subcontract for the placement of the bridge's concrete decks and parapets, and contracted with Warner for the delivery of ready-mixed concrete for use at the Girard Point site. Subsequently, Groves sued. Among other things, Warner claimed extensive losses because of Warner's failure to properly perform. In particular, Groves claimed that it was entitled to the loss it sustained as a result of a defective slab poured on July 9, 1970, which had to be removed and replaced. There was an inadequate amount of retarder in the concrete, which caused premature solidification, and some of the concrete was too dry. There was also a failure to observe instructions as to delivery times. Furthermore, the first truck was late in reaching the job site and the following two trucks arrived too soon. On the other hand, Groves's crews, having a case of "first day jitters," functioned inefficiently, and weather conditions were extremely unfavorable. The court determined that Warner's poor performance was "a substantial cause," but not the only cause, of the defective slab, and awarded Groves one-fourth of the damages it sought in regard to the slab. Affirmed.

"Groves contends that Warner did not meet its contractual obligations on July 9 and should be liable for the entire loss. But the court's analysis of the incident demonstrates that the conduct of both parties contributed in some degree to the loss. The burden is on the plaintiff to establish proximate cause between breach and damage and if the loss caused by a breach cannot be isolated from that attributable to other factors, no damages may be award-ed....

"... The action of the trial judge in dividing the loss between the parties was a fair solution to a difficult problem and is not reversible in the circumstances here."

SECTION 5. CERTAINTY

KENFORD CO. v. ERIE COUNTY

New York Court of Appeals, 1986.
67 N.Y.2d 257, 502 N.Y.S.2d 131, 493 N.E.2d 234.

Per Curiam.

The issue in this appeal is whether a plaintiff, in an action for breach of contract, may recover loss of prospective profits for its contemplated 20–year operation of a domed stadium which was to be constructed by defendant County of Erie (County).

On August 8, 1969, pursuant to a duly adopted resolution of its legisla-ture, the County of Erie entered into a contract with Kenford Company, Inc. (Kenford) and Dome Stadium, Inc. (DSI) for the construction and operation of a domed stadium facility near the City of Buffalo. The contract provided that construction of the facility by the County would commence within 12 months of the contract date and that a mutually acceptable 40–year lease between the County and DSI for the operation of said facility would be negotiated by the parties and agreed upon within three months of the receipt by the County of preliminary plans, drawings and cost estimates. It was further provided that in the event a mutually acceptable lease could not be agreed upon within the three-month period, a separate management contract between the County and DSI, as appended to the basic agreement, would be executed by the parties, providing for the operation of the stadium facility by DSI for a period of 20 years from the completion of the stadium and its availability for use.

Although strenuous and extensive negotiations followed, the parties never agreed upon the terms of a lease, nor did construction of a domed facility begin within the one-year period or at any time thereafter. A breach of the contract thus occurred and this action was commenced in June 1971 by Kenford and DSI.

Prolonged and extensive pretrial and preliminary proceedings transpired throughout the next 10 years, culminating with the entry of an order which affirmed the grant of summary judgment against the County on the issue of liability and directed a trial limited to the issue of damages (*Kenford Co. v. County of Erie*, 88 A.D.2d 758, *lv dismissed* 58 N.Y.2d 689). The ensuing trial ended some nine months later with a multimillion dollar jury verdict in plaintiffs' favor. An appeal to the Appellate Division resulted in a modification of the judgment. That court reversed portions of the judgment awarding damages for loss of profits and for certain out-of-pocket expenses incurred, and directed a new trial upon other issues (*Kenford Co. v. County of Erie,* 108 A.D.2d 132). On appeal to this court, we are concerned only with that portion of the verdict which awarded DSI money damages for loss of prospective profits during the 20–year period of the proposed management contract, as appended to the basic contract. That portion of the verdict was set aside by the Appellate Division and the cause of action dismissed. The court concluded that the use of expert opinion to present statistical projections of future business operations involved the use of too many variables to provide a rational basis upon which lost profits could be calculated and, therefore, such projections were insufficient as a matter of law to support an award of lost profits. We agree with this ultimate conclusion, but upon different grounds.

Loss of future profits as damages for breach of contract have been permitted in New York under long-established and precise rules of law. First, it must be demonstrated with certainty that such damages have been caused by the breach and, second, the alleged loss must be capable of proof with reasonable certainty. In other words, the damages may not be merely speculative, possible or imaginary, but must be reasonably certain and directly traceable to the breach, not remote or the result of other intervening causes (*Wakeman v. Wheeler & Wilson Mfg. Co.,* 101 N.Y. 205). In addition, there must be a showing that the particular damages were fairly within the contemplation of the parties to the contract at the time it was made (*Witherbee v. Meyer,* 155 N.Y. 446). If it is a new business seeking to recover for loss of future profits, a stricter standard is imposed for the obvious reason that there does not exist a reasonable basis of experience upon which to estimate lost profits with the requisite degree of reasonable certainty (*Cramer v. Grand Rapids Show Case Co.,* 223 N.Y. 63; 25 CJS, Damages, § 42[b]).

These rules must be applied to the proof presented by DSI in this case. We note the procedure for computing damages selected by DSI was in accord with contemporary economic theory and was presented through the testimony of recognized experts. Such a procedure has been accepted in this State and many other jurisdictions (*see, De Long v. County of Erie,* 60 N.Y.2d 296). DSI's economic analysis employed historical data, obtained from the operation of other domed stadiums and related facilities throughout the country, which was then applied to the results of a comprehensive study of the marketing prospects for the proposed facility in the Buffalo area. The quantity of proof is massive and, unquestionably, represents business and industry's most advanced and sophisticated method for predicting the probable results of contemplated projects. Indeed, it is difficult to conclude what additional relevant proof could have been submitted by DSI in support of its attempt to establish, with reasonable certainty, loss of prospective profits. Nevertheless, DSI's proof is insufficient to meet the required standard.

The reason for this conclusion is twofold. Initially, the proof does not satisfy the requirement that liability for loss of profits over a 20–year period was in the contemplation of the parties at the time of the execution of the basic contract or at the time of its breach (*see, Chapman v. Fargo,* 223 N.Y. 32; 36 N.Y.Jur.2d, Damages, §§ 39, 40, at 66–70). Indeed, the provisions in the contract providing remedy for a default do not suggest or provide for such a heavy responsibility on the part of the County. In the absence of any provision for such an eventuality, the commonsense rule to apply is to consider what the parties would have concluded had they considered the subject. The evidence here fails to demonstrate that liability for loss of profits over the length of the contract would have been in the contemplation of the parties at the relevant times.

Next, we note that despite the massive quantity of expert proof submitted by DSI, the ultimate conclusions are still projections, and as employed in the present day commercial world, subject to adjustment and modification. We of course recognize that any projection cannot be absolute, nor is there any such requirement, but it is axiomatic that the degree of certainty is dependent upon known or unknown factors which form the basis of the ultimate conclusion. Here, the foundations upon which the economic model was created undermine the certainty of the projections. DSI assumed that the facility was completed, available for use and successfully operated by it for 20 years, providing professional sporting events and other forms of entertainment, as well as hosting meetings, conventions and related commercial gatherings. At the time of the breach, there was only one other facility in this country to use as a basis of comparison, the Astrodome in Houston. Quite simply, the multitude of assumptions required to establish projections of profitability over the life of this contract require speculation and conjecture, making it beyond the capability of even the most sophisticated procedures to satisfy the legal requirements of proof with reasonable certainty.

The economic facts of life, the whim of the general public and the fickle nature of popular support for professional athletic endeavors must be given great weight in attempting to ascertain damages 20 years in the future. New York has long recognized the inherent uncertainties of predicting profits in the entertainment field in general (*see, Broadway Photoplay Co. v. World Film Corp.,* 225 N.Y. 104) and, in this case, we are dealing, in large part, with a new facility furnishing entertainment for the public. It is our view that the record in this case demonstrates the efficacy of the principles set forth by this court in *Cramer v. Grand Rapids Show Case Co.* (223 N.Y. 63, *supra*), principles to which we continue to adhere. In so doing, we specifically reject the "rational basis" test enunciated in *Perma Research & Dev. Co. v. Singer Co.* (542 F.2d 111, *cert. denied* 429 U.S. 987) and adopted by the Appellate Division.

Accordingly, that portion of the order of the Appellate Division being appealed from should be affirmed.

Chief Judge WACHTLER and Judges MEYER, ALEXANDER, TITONE and KANE* concur in Per Curiam opinion; Judges Simons, Kaye AND Hancock, Jr., TAKING NO PART.

Order insofar as appealed from affirmed, with costs.

NOTE ON KENFORD

At the end of the opinion in *Kenford,* the court stated that "we specifically reject the 'rational basis' test enunciated in *Perma Research* ... and adopted by the Appellate Division." The passage of the Appellate Division opinion to which the Court of Appeals referred reads as follows:

* Designated pursuant to N.Y. Constitution, article VI, § 2.

... In [Perma Research & Devel. Co. v. Singer Co., 402 F.Supp. 881, affd. 542 F.2d 111, cert. den. 429 U.S. 987, 97 S.Ct. 507, 50 L.Ed.2d 598, the court held that lost profits for a new venture] may be awarded if plaintiff establishes three elements: that the lost profits are the direct and proximate result of the breach; that profits were contemplated by the parties; and that there is a rational basis on which to calculate the lost profits (Perma Research & Devel. Co. v. Singer Co....). The first two criteria reflect the lost profits test applicable to established businesses as enunciated in Witherbee v. Meyer, 155 N.Y. 446, 449–450, 50 N.E. 58.... What the court did in *Perma Research,* in essence, was to add a third requirement for new businesses by requiring them to establish some rational basis on which to calculate the lost profits.... The *Perma Research* test has been subsequently employed in the Second Circuit (Lexington Prods. Ltd. v. B.D. Communications, 677 F.2d 251, 253; Western Geophysical Co. of Am. v. Bolt Assocs., 584 F.2d 1164, 1172 ... Contemporary Mission v. Famous Music Corp., 557 F.2d 918, 926....)

ASHLAND MANAGEMENT INC. v. JANIEN, 82 N.Y.2d 395, 604 N.Y.S.2d 912, 624 N.E.2d 1007 (1993). Ashland Management was a successful investment advisory company which managed over $1 billion in client funds. As part of its investment strategy, Ashland relied on a computerized mathematical stock-selection model, known as Alpha, to analyze selected financial information and make an initial determination of which stocks should be bought and sold. In 1985, Ashland and Janien entered into a contract for the development by Janien of a second investment model, Eta, to be used by Ashland. Paragraph C(12) of the contract projected the minimum sums expected to be under management by the Eta model for each year between 1988 and 1992. It also provided that if these minimum sums were not achieved, Ashland could terminate Janien's employment. Paragraph C(21) provided that if "for any reason" Janien left Ashland's employment, he was entitled to "a royalty of the higher of $50,000 or 15% of gross revenues per annum of any and all existing or future accounts" using the Eta Model or "any derivative thereof." (The gross revenue was a 1% fee charged customers by Ashland for the funds under management.) Thereafter, Ashland terminated Janien's employment. The trial court held that Janien was entitled to damages for lost profits based on the projections set forth in paragraph C(12). Affirmed.

"[The requirement that damages be reasonably certain] does not require absolute certainty. Damages resulting from the loss of future profits are often an approximation. The law does not require that they be determined with mathematical precision. It requires only that damages be capable of measurement based upon known reliable factors without undue speculation (see, Restatement [Second] of Contracts § 352; 3 Farnsworth, Contracts § 12.15 [2d ed. 1990]; see [Kenford Co. v. Erie County]....

"Lost profits must also be established with reasonable certainty. In *Kenford....* we determined that the evidence failed to meet the requirement of reasonable certainty because it rested on a host of speculative assumptions and few known factors.... Before accepting plaintiff's figures, the court was obliged to assume not only that the stadium had been completed, opened and operated successfully for 20 years, but that it also attracted professional sporting events, concerts and conventions fully supported by the public.

"The projection of future profits in this case requires no such speculation.

"First, defendant's claim rests on the parties' carefully studied professional judgments of what they believed were realistic estimates of future assets to be managed by the use of Eta. By applying Ashland's 1% management fee to these sums to determine the revenues derived from them and then allotting defendant 15% of those revenues, as paragraph C(21) provided, Janien's loss could be easily computed. Second, while the parties were launching a new investment strategy, they were not entering a new or unfamiliar business.... Ashland had been a substantial presence in the financial management field for several years. The introduction of Eta was viewed as an addition to and an enhancement of Ashland's existing Alpha strategy, which had been highly successful, and Ashland intended to rely on its experience in marketing Alpha to market Eta. Third, Ashland had a ready reservoir of customers for Eta because it intended to appeal not only to the market in general but also to its existing Alpha customers. Finally, although Eta had never been used in a commercial setting, it had been extensively back-tested over a number of years, and Ashland itself had enough confidence in its ability to perform to predict minimum amounts of funding which Eta would attract. It agreed to compensate Janien on that basis. Based on this evidence, the court properly relied on the projections of paragraph C(12) and the provisions of paragraph C(21) to hold that defendant had met his burden of proving his lost profits with reasonable certainty...."

NOTE ON THE NEW–BUSINESS RULE

In the past, a major application of the uncertainty principle was the "new-business rule." This rule prohibits recovery of lost profits that a plaintiff claims would have been generated by a proposed new business, on the ground that in such cases profits are too speculative. (In one typical fact-pattern, the plaintiff had leased premises for its new business from the defendant, who then broke the lease before the plaintiff even moved in.) The new-business rule still surfaces in some cases, but there is a definite trend toward abrogating the rule, and reconstruing the older cases as resting only on the particular facts involved, rather than on a special rule. For example, in Fera v. Village Plaza, Inc., 396 Mich. 639, 242 N.W.2d 372 (1976), plaintiffs executed a ten-year lease for a "book and bottle" shop in defendants' proposed shopping center. Later, plaintiffs were refused their space, because defendants had misplaced the lease and rented the space to other tenants. Plaintiffs brought suit, claiming lost profits. The jury returned a verdict against the defendants for $200,000. The Court of Appeals (an intermediate appellate court) reversed, partly on the basis of the new-business rule. The Michigan Supreme Court reinstated the jury verdict:

> [Earlier Michigan cases] should not be read as stating a rule of law which prevents *every* new business from recovering anticipated lost profits for breach of contract. The rule is merely an application of the doctrine that "[i]n order to be entitled to a verdict, or a judgment, for damages for breach of contract, the plaintiff must lay a basis for a

reasonable estimate of the extent of his harm, measured in money." 5 Corbin on Contracts, § 1020, p. 124. The issue becomes one of sufficiency of proof. . . .

The Court of Appeals based its opinion reversing the jury's award on two grounds: First, that a new business cannot recover damages for lost profits for breach of a lease. We have expressed our disapproval of that rule. Secondly, the Court of Appeals held plaintiffs barred from recovery because the proof of lost profits was entirely speculative. We disagree. . . .

While we might have found plaintiffs' proofs lacking had we been members of the jury, that is not the standard of review we employ. As a reviewing court we will not invade the fact finding of the jury or remand for entry of judgment unless the factual record is so clear that reasonable minds may not disagree. This is not the situation here. . . .

———

ROMBOLA v. COSINDAS, 351 Mass. 382, 220 N.E.2d 919 (1966). Rombola agreed to train, maintain, and race Cosindas's horse, Margy Sampson, for the period November 8, 1962, to December 1, 1963. Rombola was to pay all expenses and receive 75% of all gross purses, and Cosindas was to receive the remaining 25%. In the winter of 1962–63, Rombola maintained and trained the horse at his stable, and in the following spring and summer he raced her twenty-five times. In fall 1963, Rombola entered Margy Sampson in six stake races—races in which horses run against others in their own class, according to the amount of money they have won—to be held at a Suffolk Downs meet ending December 1. Before the meet began, Cosindas took possession of Margy Sampson, and thereby deprived Rombola of his right to race her. The horse was not raced again until after December 1. Rombola sued Cosindas for breach of contract, and the trial judge directed a verdict for Cosindas on the ground that Rombola's damages were too uncertain. Reversed.

. . . In the year of the contract, of the twenty-five races in which the horse was entered by Rombola, she had won ten and shared in the purse money in a total of twenty races, earning, in all, purses approximating $12,000. In the year following the expiration of Rombola's contract with Cosindas, the horse raced twenty-nine times and won money in an amount almost completely consistent percentagewise with the money won during the period of the contract. . . .

We think . . . that Rombola would be entitled to show substantial damages on the theory of loss of prospective profits. . . . [Margy Sampson] had already proved her ability both prior to and while under Rombola's management and training, over an extended period of time, against many competitors and under varying track conditions. Her consistent performance in the year subsequent to the breach negates any basis for an inference of a diminution in ability or in earning capacity at the time of the Suffolk Downs meet. While it is possible that no profits would have been realized if Margy Sampson had participated in the scheduled stake races, that possibility is inherent in any business venture. . . .

CONTEMPORARY MISSION, INC. v. FAMOUS MUSIC CORP., 557 F.2d 918 (2d Cir.1977). Famous Music failed to perform a contract with Contemporary Mission, under which Famous Music had agreed to pay a royalty to Contemporary Mission, in return for the master tape-recording of *Virgin* (a rock opera) and the exclusive right to manufacture and sell records made from the master. Under the agreement, Famous Music was obliged to release at least four separate single records from *Virgin.*

Under the doctrine of Wood v. Lucy (Chapter 2, Section 3, supra), Famous Music had an obligation to use reasonable efforts to promote *Virgin* on a nationwide basis. Prior to the breach, one of the singles from *Virgin* had reached number 80 on the hot soul record charts, and later it reached number 61. At the trial, Contemporary Mission offered a statistical analysis of every song that had reached number 61 during 1974. This analysis showed that 76 percent of the 324 songs that had reached number 61 ultimately reached the top 40; 65 percent reached the top 30; 51 percent reached the top 20; 34 percent reached the top 10; 21 percent reached the top 5; and 10 percent reached number 1. Contemporary Mission also was prepared to offer the testimony of an expert witness who could have converted these measures of success into projected sales figures and lost royalties. The trial judge excluded all this evidence on the ground that it was speculative. Held, the evidence should have been admitted.

". . . This is not a case in which the plaintiff sought to prove hypothetical profits from the sale of a hypothetical record at a hypothetical price in a hypothetical market. . . . [T]he record was real, the price was fixed, the market was buying and the record's success, while modest, was increasing. Even after the promotional efforts ended, [and] the record was withdrawn from the marketplace, it was carried, as a result of its own momentum, to an additional 10,000 sales and to a rise from approximately number 80 on the 'Hot Soul Singles' chart of Billboard magazine to number 61. It cannot be gainsaid that if someone had continued to promote it, and if it had not been withdrawn from the market, it would have sold more records than it actually did. Thus, it is certain that Contemporary suffered some damage in the form of lost royalties. . . ."

UCC § 1–106(1)

[See Selected Source Materials Supplement]

RESTATEMENT, SECOND, CONTRACTS § 352

[See Selected Source Materials Supplement]

UNIDROIT PRINCIPLES OF INTERNATIONAL
COMMERCIAL CONTRACTS ART. 7.4.3

[See Selected Source Materials Supplement]

———

NOTE ON UNCERTAINTY

A premise of the approach taken in cases like *Kenford* is that there is some level of likelihood—say 50%—such that if the injured party's proof of his total damages is just above that level, his damages are reasonably certain, and he is awarded all of his damages, but if his proof is just below the level, his damages are speculative and he is awarded nothing. Accordingly, this approach is often referred to as the all-or-nothing rule.

The all-or-nothing rule is dramatically out of touch with the reality of probability. For example, take a case where a contestant who has properly qualified for a contest is wrongfully disqualified by the contest's promoter, and it cannot be determined whether the contestant would have won a prize if he had not been disqualified. In such a case, the promoter's breach has clearly caused a loss to the contestant: Before the promoter acted wrongfully, the contestant had a chance to win the contest; after the promoter acted wrongfully, the contestant did not have the chance. As a result of the promoter's wrongful act, therefore, the contestant has lost an asset—the chance to win the contest—and the promoter should be liable for the value of that asset. By way of analogy, suppose that Burgle steals a lottery ticket owned by Jones. Burgle should be liable to Jones for the value of the ticket even though the ticket was not a winner. Similarly, if the promoter of a contest wrongfully disqualified a contestant, the promoter should be liable to the contestant for the value of the contestant's chance even though that chance was significantly less than 50%.

The leading case is Chaplin v. Hicks, [1911] 2 K.B. 786, decided by the English Court of Appeal in 1911. Hicks, a well-known actor and theater manager, ran a contest for actresses. The prizes were theatrical engagements. The not-very-appealing rules of the contest were as follows: Contestants would send photographs of themselves to Hicks, who would divide England into ten districts and would publish, in a newspaper in each district, photographs of the candidates he had selected. Newspaper readers would then vote for the contestants they considered to be the most beautiful. Hicks would thereafter interview fifty finalists, consisting of the five candidates in each district who had the highest votes. From these fifty finalists, Hicks would select twelve winning contestants, who would receive the theatrical engagements.

Chaplin became one of the fifty finalists, but Hicks did not give her an interview. Chaplin then brought an action against Hicks for the loss of her chance of being selected as one of the twelve winners. At trial, she was awarded damages of £ 100. The Court of Appeal affirmed. Lord Justice Moulton stated:

> Is expulsion from a limited class of competitors an injury? To my mind there can be only one answer to that question; it is an injury and

may be a very substantial one. Therefore the plaintiff starts with an unchallengeable case of injury, and the damages given in respect of it should be equivalent to the loss. . . .

. . . Is there any such rule as that, where the result of a contract depends on the volition of an independent party, the law shuts its eyes to the wrong and says that there are no damages? Such a rule, if it existed, would work great wrong. Let us take the case of a man under a contract of service to serve as a second-class clerk for five years at a salary of £200 a year, which expressly provides that, at the end of that period, out of every five second-class clerks two first-class clerks will be chosen at a salary of £500 a year. If such a clause is embodied in the contract, it is clear that a person thinking of applying for the position would reckon that he would have the advantage of being one of five persons from whom the two first-class clerks must be chosen, and that might be a very substantial portion of the consideration for his appointment. If, after he has taken the post and worked under the contract of service, the employers repudiate the obligation, is he to have no remedy? He has sustained a very real loss, and there can be no possible reason why the law should not leave it to the jury to estimate the value of that of which he has been deprived. Where by contract a man has a right to belong to a limited class of competitors, he is possessed of something of value, and it is the duty of the jury to estimate the pecuniary value of that advantage if it is taken from him.

Moulton's opinion did not state with precision how the value of a contestant's chance should be measured. In cases like lottery tickets, in which there is an established market for the chance, the value of the chance is normally its market price. When there is no established market, the value of the chance is the price that a willing buyer of the chance would pay to a willing seller. This approach was implied in the opinion of Lord Justice Vaughan Williams, concurring in Chaplin v. Hicks:

It is true that no market [for the chance to win the contest] can be said to exist. None of the fifty competitors could have gone into the market and sold her right; her right was a personal right and incapable of transfer. But a jury might well take the view that such a right, if it could have been transferred, would have been of such a value that every one would recognize that a good price could be obtained for it.

Typically, in the absence of a market price, what a willing buyer would pay a willing seller should be based on the expected value of the chance. So, for example, in Van Gulik v. Resource Development Council for Alaska, 695 P.2d 1071 (Alaska 1985), a promoter had staged a lottery. Under the lottery's rules, the contestants' tickets were to be drawn from a bin, one-by-one. The last ticket drawn would win the grand prize of $10,000. When only three tickets, owned by A, B, and C, remained in the bin, the lottery operators mistakenly, and in breach of the contest rules, drew the tickets owned by B and C simultaneously, and overlooked the fact that A's ticket was still in the bin. When they realized their mistake, the operators then compounded their breach by wrongfully drawing all the lottery tickets all over again. A brought suit. If the lottery operators had drawn only B's ticket, or only C's ticket, as they should have done, the last two tickets would have either been those of A and B or A and C. Accordingly, at the time of the breach A had a 50% chance of winning $10,000. The court gave A the choice of either (i) $5,000 in damages, based on the expected value of his chance at the time of the breach, or (ii) participation in a re-drawing involving only his ticket and one other.

A claim for the loss of profits is normally a special case of a claim for the loss of a chance, that is, the chance to make a profit. Just as the damages of a person who holds an explicit chance, like a contestant, should be measured by the value of the chance of winning at the time of breach, so too in the lost-profits case the plaintiff's damages should be measured by the value of the chance of profits at the time of breach. Accordingly, the plaintiff should recover the amount that a buyer would have paid for a pre-breach assignment of the plaintiff's right to earn profits under the contract.

The problem is how to measure the market value of such a right when, as in *Kenford*, there is no actual market in which identical rights are freely traded. The answer is that a right is an asset, and financial economics provides a well-established methodology, known as the Capital Asset Pricing Model (CAPM, pronounced cap-em) for determining the value of assets whose value is based on prospective returns. To apply CAPM, the *expected cash flow* of an income-producing asset (that is, roughly speaking, the income that can be expected to be generated by the asset, minus the expenses required to generate that income) is calculated by determining the various possible cash flows that the asset may yield, multiplying each cash flow by its probability, and summing the result. The value of the asset is then calculated, based on (i) the expected cash flow and (ii) a formula that turns in large part on the risk rates implicitly assigned by the stock market to corporations that are in the kind of business the asset involves. So, for example, in deciding how much to pay for a movie theater, an investor using CAPM basically would apply, to the theater's expected cash flow, the risk rate implicitly assigned by the stock market to corporations engaged in the movie-theater business.

As the methodology of financial economics shows, therefore, the fact that projected profits are risky and uncertain does not prevent the valuation of an income-producing asset—it could not; virtually all such assets have risky and uncertain returns. Instead, risk and uncertainty is impounded into the value of the assets, first in weighting the cash flows the asset may produce, and then in determining the risk rates to apply to the expected cash flow based on that weighting.

A contract is a special type of income-producing asset. Its value should be determined in the same way as the value of any other such asset. Thus if in *Kenford* there was a 40% probability of a $10 million cash flow to Dome over the twenty-year term of the management agreement, a 30% probability of a $30 million cash flow, and a 30% probability of a $40 million cash flow, the expected cash flow to Dome would be $25 million (40% of $10 million, plus 30% of $30 million, plus 30% of $40 million). Damages would be calculated by applying the appropriate risk rate to the expected cash flow. A court that believes profits under a contract to be uncertain should therefore not deny recovery of profits, but instead should assign very low probabilities to very unlikely cash flows, assign a high risk rate, or both.

As a second-best alternative, even a court that requires a relatively high degree of certainty should at least award the minimum amount of damages that are more probable than not. For example, suppose in *Kenford* there was 10% probability that the plaintiff would have earned $100 million under the contract with Erie County, a 15% probability that it would have earned $80 million, a 20% probability that it would have earned $60 million, and a 75% probability that it would have earned $40 million. Given these assumptions, the plaintiff should at least recover $40 million.

———

MEARS v. NATIONWIDE MUTUAL INS. CO., 91 F.3d 1118 (8th Cir. 1996). Mears won a contest in which the prize was two Mercedes–Benz automobiles. The promoter of the contest contended that the contract was too indefinite to enforce because there was a very wide range of Mercedes–Benz used and new models and no model had been specified. Held for Mears.

First, contract terms are interpreted with strong consideration for what is reasonable.... Under a reasonable interpretation of the contest contract, the jury could expect the automobiles to be new.

Second, when a minor ambiguity exists in a contract, Arkansas law allows the complaining party to insist on the reasonable interpretation that is least favorable to him.... These two factors, taken together, are sufficient to support the jury's conclusion that Nationwide owed Mears two of Mercedes–Benz's least expensive new automobiles as his contest prize."

———

SECTION 6.   DAMGES FOR MENTAL DISTRESS

———

HAWKINS v. McGEE

Chapter 5, supra

———

SULLIVAN v. O'CONNOR

Chapter 5, supra

———

VALENTINE v. GENERAL AMERICAN CREDIT, INC.

Supreme Court of Michigan, 1984.
420 Mich. 256, 362 N.W.2d 628

LEVIN, Justice.

Sharon Valentine seeks to recover mental distress damages arising out of the alleged breach of an employment contract. Valentine claims that, under the contract, she was entitled to job security and the peace of mind that is associated with job security. Because an employment contract providing for job security has a personal element, and breach of such a contract can be expected to result in mental distress, Valentine argues that she should be able to recover mental distress damages. She also asks for exemplary damages.

The Court of Appeals affirmed the decision of the trial court dismissing the claims for mental distress and exemplary damages.[1] We affirm.

I

In *Toussaint v. Blue Cross & Blue Shield of Michigan,* 408 Mich. 579, 292 N.W.2d 880 (1980), this Court held that an employment contract providing that an employee would not be terminated except for cause was enforceable although no definite term of employment was stated.

Toussaint makes employment contracts which provide that an employee will not be dismissed except for cause enforceable in the same manner as other contracts. It did not recognize employment as a fundamental right or create a new "special" right. The only right held in *Toussaint* to be enforceable was the right that arose out of the promise not to terminate except for cause.

Employers and employees remain free to provide, or not to provide, for job security. Absent a contractual provision for job security, either the employer or the employee may ordinarily terminate an employment contract at any time for any, or no, reason. The obligation which gave rise to this action is based on the agreement of the parties; it is not an obligation imposed on the employer by law. This is an action for breach of contract and not a tort action.

II

Valentine may not recover mental distress damages for breach of the employment contract, although such damages may have been foreseeable and she might not be "made whole" absent an award of mental distress damages.

Valentine relies on the rule of *Hadley v. Baxendale,* 9 Exch. 341, 156 Eng.Rep. 145 (1854), which provides that damages recoverable for a breach of contract are those that "may fairly and reasonably be considered either arising naturally, i.e., according to the usual course of things, from such breach of contract itself, or such as may reasonably be supposed to have been in the contemplation of both parties at the time they made the contract, as the probable result of the breach of it."

Although courts frequently begin analysis with a reference to the rule stated in *Hadley v. Baxendale,* that rule has not been applied scrupulously. As stated by Professor Dobbs in his treatise on remedies, a "difficulty in the *Hadley* type case is that the test of foreseeability [*i.e.,* whether damages 'arise naturally'] has little or no meaning. The idea is so readily subject to expansion or contraction that it becomes in fact merely a technical way in which the judges can state their conclusion."[7]

---

1. On April 11, 1980, Valentine filed an action alleging breach of a contract of employment and intentional infliction of mental distress. She sought mental distress damages and exemplary damages. On June 1, 1981, the trial court granted defendant General American Credit's motion for partial summary judgment on the issues of mental distress damages and exemplary damages. The Court of Appeals, dividing two-to-one, affirmed. *Valentine v. General American Credit, Inc.,* 123 Mich.App. 521, 332 N.W.2d 591 (1983).

7. Dobbs, Remedies, § 12.3, p. 814. See also Dobbs, § 12.3, p. 804; 5 Corbin, Contracts, § 1007, pp. 70–71.

Under the rule of *Hadley v. Baxendale,* literally applied, damages for mental distress would be recoverable for virtually every breach of contract. Professor Dobbs said:

"When a defendant breaches a contract, this may and often does cause pecuniary loss to the other party, at least temporarily. It is a common experience of mankind that pecuniary loss almost invariably causes some form and degree of mental distress."

In *Stewart v. Rudner,* 349 Mich. 459, 470, 84 N.W.2d 816 (1957), this Court said that "all breaches of contract do more or less" cause "vexation and annoyance"; similarly, see *Kewin v. Massachusetts Mutual Life Ins. Co.,* 409 Mich. 401, 417, 295 N.W.2d 50 (1980).

Yet the general rule, with few exceptions, is to "uniformly den[y]" recovery for mental distress damages although they are "foreseeable within the rule of *Hadley v. Baxendale.*"[10] The rule barring recovery of mental distress damages—a gloss on the generality of the rule stated in *Hadley v. Baxendale*—is fully applicable to an action for breach of an employment contract.

The denial of mental distress damages, although the result is to leave the plaintiff with less than a full recovery, has analogy in the law. The law does not generally compensate for all losses suffered. Recovery is denied for attorney's fees, for mental anguish not accompanied by physical manifestation, and "make-whole" or full recovery has been denied where the cost of performance exceeds the value to the promisee. The courts have not, despite "make whole" generalizations regarding the damages recoverable, attempted to provide compensation for all losses. Instead, specific rules have been established that provide for the calculation of the damages recoverable in particular kinds of actions. In contract actions, the market price is the general standard.

In determining what damages are recoverable, the courts of this state have qualified the general rule, pursuant to which mental distress damages for breach of contract are not recoverable, with a narrow exception. Rather than look to the foreseeability of loss to determine the applicability of the exception, the courts have considered whether the contract "has elements of personality"[19] and whether the "damage suffered upon the breach of the agreement is capable of adequate compensation by reference to the terms of the contract."[20]

The narrow scope of those verbal formulas appears on consideration of the limited situations in which this Court has allowed the recovery of mental distress damages for breach of contract. In *Vanderpool v. Richardson,* 52 Mich. 336, 17 N.W. 936 (1883), recovery was allowed for breach of a promise to marry. In *Stewart v. Rudner,* 349 Mich. 459, 84 N.W.2d 816 (1957), a

---

10. Grismore, Contracts (rev. ed.), § 203, p. 320. See also *Kewin, supra,* p. 414, 295 N.W.2d 50; Dobbs, Remedies, § 12.4, p. 819.

19. *Stewart, supra,* 349 Mich. p. 471, 84 N.W.2d 816. In *Stewart, supra,* p. 471, 84 N.W.2d 816, the Court also said that mental distress damages are recoverable in cases "where a contract is *made* to secure relief from a particular inconvenience or annoyance, or to confer a particular enjoyment." (Emphasis

supplied.) See also *Kewin, supra,* 409 Mich. p. 416, 295 N.W.2d 50, in which the Court emphasized that, for mental distress damages to be recoverable, the parties must have formed "a contract *meant* to secure [the] protection" of personal interests. (Emphasis supplied.)

20. *Kewin, supra,* 409 Mich. p. 417, 295 N.W.2d 50. See also *Stewart, supra,* 349 Mich. p. 470, 84 N.W.2d 816.

doctor who failed to fulfill his promise to deliver a child by caesarean section was required to pay mental distress damages. In *Miholevich v. Mid–West Mutual Auto Ins. Co.,* 261 Mich. 495, 246 N.W. 202 (1933), the plaintiff, who was jailed for failure to pay a liability judgment, recovered mental distress damages from an insurer who had failed to pay the judgment.[21]

Loss of a job is not comparable to the loss of a marriage or a child and generally results in estimable monetary damages. In *Miholevich,* the breach resulted in a deprivation of personal liberty.

An employment contract will indeed often have a personal element. Employment is an important aspect of most persons' lives, and the breach of an employment contract may result in emotional distress. The primary purpose in forming such contracts, however, is economic and not to secure the protection of personal interests. The psychic satisfaction of the employment is secondary.

Mental distress damages for breach of contract have not been awarded where there is a market standard by which damages can be adequately determined. Valentine's monetary loss can be estimated with reasonable certainty according to the terms of the contract and the market for, or the market value of, her service. Mental distress damages are not awarded an employee found to have been wrongfully discharged in violation of a collective bargaining agreement.

We conclude, because an employment contract is not entered into primarily to secure the protection of personal interests and pecuniary damages can be estimated with reasonable certainty, that a person discharged in breach of an employment contract may not recover mental distress damages.

III

Valentine has not separately argued her exemplary damage claim. In *Kewin, supra,* 409 Mich. pp. 420–421, 295 N.W.2d 50, this Court said that "absent allegation and proof of tortious conduct existing independent of the breach [citation omitted], exemplary damages may not be awarded in common-law actions brought for breach of a commercial contract." Valentine failed to plead the requisite purposeful tortious conduct, and therefore she may not recover exemplary damages.

Affirmed.

WILLIAMS, C.J., KAVANAGH, CAVANAGH, BRICKLEY, RYAN and BOYLE, JJ., concur.

––––––

LANE v. KINDERCARE LEARNING CENTERS, INC., 231 Mich. App. 689, 588 N.W.2d 715 (1998). Plaintiff enrolled her eighteen-month-old daughter in day care with defendant. On December 9, 1992, plaintiff dropped off her daughter at defendant's facility at lunch time. Plaintiff's daughter had been prescribed medication, and plaintiff filled out an authorization form granting defendant's employees permission to administer the medication to

21. *Humphrey v. Michigan United R. Co.,* 166 Mich. 645, 132 N.W. 447 (1911), concerned the duty of a common carrier to a passenger. This duty is imposed by law without regard to contract.

her daughter that day. Just after 5:00 p.m., one of defendant's employee's placed the child, who had fallen asleep, in a crib in the infant room. At approximately 6:00 p.m., defendant's employees locked the doors of the facility and went home for the day, apparently unaware that plaintiff's daughter was still sleeping in the crib. Shortly thereafter, plaintiff returned to the facility to pick up her daughter and found the facility locked and unlit. Plaintiff called 911. A police officer who responded to the call looked through a window of the facility, with the aid of a flashlight, and saw the child sleeping in the crib. Another officer then broke a window and retrieved the child from the building. The child was upset after the incident, but was not physically harmed. When plaintiff went into the facility to retrieve her daughter's belongings, she apparently found the medication authorization form and observed that it had not been initialed to indicate that the child had been given the medication.

Plaintiff sued defendant for breach of contract and negligence, claiming that she suffered emotional distress as a result of the incident. The trial court granted summary judgment for the defendant, on the ground that plaintiff failed to plead that she suffered a physical injury as a result of her emotional distress. Reversed.

> ... [I]t is generally held that damages for emotional distress cannot be recovered for the breach of a commercial contract.... However, ... damages for emotional distress may be recovered for the breach of a contract in cases that do not involve commercial or pecuniary contracts, but involve contracts of a personal nature....
>
> We believe that a contract to care for one's child is a matter of "mental concern and solicitude," rather than "pecuniary aggrandizement." ... Therefore, ... the contract involved in the instant case was personal in nature, rather than commercial. At the time the contract was executed, it was foreseeable that a breach of the contract would result in mental distress damages to plaintiff, which would extend beyond the mere "annoyance and vexation" that normally accompanies the breach of a contract.... Such damages are clearly within the contemplation of the parties to such a contract.
>
> ... [D]amages may be awarded for emotional distress caused by a breach of a personal contract even where the emotional distress does not result in a physical injury. ... We therefore conclude that the trial court erred in granting summary disposition of plaintiff's breach of contract claim....

RESTATEMENT, SECOND, CONTRACTS § 353

[See Selected Source Materials Supplement]

UNIDROIT PRINCIPLES OF INTERNATIONAL
COMMERCIAL CONTRACTS ART. 7.4.2

[See Selected Source Materials Supplement]

JARVIS v. SWAN TOURS, LTD., [1972] W.L.R. 954, Jarvis made a contract with Swan Tours, under which Jarvis agreed to pay £ 63.45 for a package holiday in Switzerland. The holiday that Swan provided was not the holiday promised in Swan's brochure, and in fact was a flop. Jarvis sued. The trial judge awarded Jarvis damages of £ 31.72, half the amount that Jarvis had paid. The Court of Appeals increased the damages to £ 125. Lord Denning said:

> What is the right way of assessing damages? It has often been said that on a breach of contract damages cannot be given for mental distress....
>
> I think that those limitations are out of date. In a proper case damages for mental distress can be recovered in contract, just as damages for shock can be recovered in tort. One such case is a contract for a holiday, or any other contract to provide entertainment and enjoyment. If the contracting party breaks his contract, damages can be given for the disappointment, the distress, the upset and frustration caused by the breach. I know that it is difficult to assess in terms of money, but it is no more difficult than the assessment which the courts have to make every day in personal injury cases for loss of amenities. Take the present case. Mr. Jarvis has only a fortnight's holiday in the year. He books it far ahead, and looks forward to it all that time. He ought to be compensated for the loss of it....
>
> ... I think the judge was in error in taking the sum paid for the holiday 63.45 and halving it. The right measure of damages is to compensate him for the loss of entertainment and enjoyment which he was promised, and which he did not get.

Judge Davies said:

> If in such circumstances travel agents fail to provide a holiday for the contracted quality, they are liable in damages. In assessing those damages the court is not, in my judgment, restricted by the 63.45 paid by the client for his holiday. Nor is it confined to matters of physical inconvenience and discomfort, or even to quantifying the difference between such items as the expected delicious Swiss cakes and the depressingly desiccated biscuits and crisps provided for tea, between ski-pack ordered and the miniature skis supplied, nor between the "very good ... houseparty arrangements" assured and the lone wolf second week of the unfortunate plaintiff's stay. The court is entitled, and indeed bound, to contrast the overall quality of the holiday so enticingly promised with that which the defendants in fact provided.
>
> In determining what would be proper compensation for the defendants' marked failure to fulfill their undertaking I am of the opinion that

... "vexation" and "being disappointed in a particular thing you have set your mind upon" are relevant considerations which afford the court a guide in arriving at a proper figure.

———

JACKSON v. HORIZON HOLIDAYS, LTD., [1975] 1 W.L.R. 1468 (1974). This case was similar to Jarvis v. Swan Tours, supra, except that the vacation was for a family of four—Mr. and Mrs. Jackson and their two children. The court that Mr. Jackson, who had made the contract to purchase the holiday package, was entitled to recover the damages for the mental distress suffered by the whole family, not just himself.

For other vacation cases, see Baltic Shipping Company v. Dillon, 67 ALJR 228, [1993] ASC 56–206 (Australia); Vorvis v. Insurance Corporation of British Columbia (1989) 58 D.L.R. (4th) 193 at 204, 213 (Canada); Byrne v. Auckland Irish Society Inc. [1979] 1 N.Z.L.R. 351 (New Zealand).

———

DEITSCH v. MUSIC CO., 6 Ohio Misc.2d 6, 453 N.E.2d 1302 (Mun.Ct. 1983). Music Co. agreed to provide a four-piece band at the Deitschs' wedding reception from 8:00 p.m. to midnight. The reception took place, but the four-piece band failed to arrive. Deitsch made several attempts to contact Music Co., but were not successful. After wailing and gnashing of teeth, Deitsch sent a friend to obtain stereo equipment to provide music; the equipment was set up at about 9:00 p.m. Held, plaintiffs were entitled to compensation of $750 for their distress and inconvenience, and the diminution in value of their reception.

———

RESTATEMENT, SECOND, CONTRACTS § 355

[See Selected Source Materials Supplement]

———

SECTION 7. LIQUIDATED DAMAGES

———

WASSERMAN'S INC. v. MIDDLETOWN
Supreme Court of New Jersey, 1994.
137 N.J. 238, 645 A.2d 100.

POLLOCK, J.

Pursuant to a public advertisement for bids, plaintiff Wasserman's Inc. (Wasserman's) and defendant, Township of Middletown (the Township or Middletown), entered into a commercial lease for a tract of municipally-owned property. The agreement contained a clause providing that if the Township cancelled the lease, it would pay the lessee, Wasserman's, a pro-rata reimbursement for any improvement costs and damages of twenty-five percent of the lessee's average gross receipts for one year. In 1989, the Township cancelled the lease and sold the property, but refused to pay the agreed damages. On cross-motions for summary judgment, the Law Division held that the ... cancellation clause [was] enforceable. It subsequently required the Township to pay damages in the amount of $346,058.44 plus interest. In an unreported opinion, the Appellate Division affirmed. We granted certification, 134 *N.J.* 478, 634 *A.*2d 525 (1993), and now on ... reverse and remand for a plenary trial on damages.... We affirm the award of renovation costs and remand to the Law Division the issue of the enforceability of the stipulated damages clause.

–I–

The Township owned a parcel of approximately 20,500 square feet in a commercial area at 89 Leonardville Road, in the Belford section of the Township. From 1948 to 1968, Wasserman's leased the property from the Township for a 3,200–square-foot general store. In 1969, the Township advertised for bids to lease the property, which the Township evaluated at $47,500. Wasserman's submitted the sole bid. After rejecting Wasserman's bid, the Township again advertised in May 1970. Once again, Wasserman's submitted the only bid. Subsequent negotiations resulted in the Township adopting a resolution approving the lease on September 22, 1970. The parties signed the lease on May 21, 1971.

At the center of the dispute is the cancellation clause in the lease. The bid specifications provided that if the Township cancelled the lease, it would pay the tenant a pro-rata reimbursement of improvement costs. Consistent with the specifications, the clause provides in part for reimbursement: "payment to be made shall be (1.) total value of all improvements made by lessee at time of construction (multiplied by) years remaining in Lease term (divided by) total number of years in Lease term." More controversial is the second half of the clause, the terms of which were not included in the original specifications. That provision requires the Township to pay "(2.) twenty-five percent of the lessee[']s average gross receipts for one year (to be computed by + (adding) the lessee[']s total gross receipts for the lessee[']s three full fiscal years immediately preceding the time of cancellation of the lease and (dividing by) 12 (twelve)[)]." The lease also provided for a fixed monthly rental of $458.33, with no escalation for the entire thirty-year term.

Wasserman's made the agreed improvements, spending $142,336.01 in 1971 on the expansion and renovation of the store, which now is approximately 5,600 square feet. In August 1973, Wasserman's sold "the business," presumably the corporate assets, and sublet the premises to Rocco Laurino doing business as Jo–Ro, Inc. (Jo–Ro). The sublease provided that Jo–Ro was to pay Wasserman's a monthly rent of $1,850. Wasserman's and Jo–Ro, jointly described as "plaintiffs," provided for an allocation of any payments made by the Township if it cancelled the lease.

In 1977, Samuel Krawet and Arnold Kornblum purchased from Laurino all of the Jo–Ro stock for $95,000. In connection with the sale, Laurino executed an affidavit, representing that the lease between Middletown and Wasserman's was in full force and effect. Additionally, the Township sent a letter to Wasserman's stating that the Township would permit subletting the property to Jo–Ro.

By letter dated December 7, 1987, the Township cancelled the lease effective December 31, 1988. Krawet and Kornblum vacated the premises, leaving them without a place for their business. In June 1989, the Township, after advertising the property at public auction, sold it for $610,000, nearly thirteen times the value of the property at the time the Township had leased it to Wasserman's in 1971. . . .

–II–

Plaintiffs sued for breach of contract, seeking in part damages under the terms of the lease. The Township filed an answer and counterclaim seeking a declaration of invalidity of that part of the cancellation clause that required the Township to pay as damages twenty-five percent of the lessee's gross receipts. Originally the Township also disputed its obligation to reimburse Wasserman's for a pro-rata portion of the cost of renovations, but it now concedes the validity of that provision. The parties filed cross-motions for summary judgment.

The Law Division initially granted plaintiffs a partial summary judgment according "full force and effect" to the lease and the cancellation clause. On a subsequent motion, the court awarded plaintiffs damages of $346,058.44 plus ten-percent prejudgment interest. The trial court calculated damages as follows:

> $142,336.01 (construction costs) multiplied by 11.75 (remaining years) divided by 30 years (term of lease) for a total of $55,748.27.

> $3,483,722.25 (Jo–Ro's gross receipts for the years 1985, 1986, 1987) divided by 12 equalling $290,310.18.

> | | |
> |---|---:|
> | Construction compensation | $ 55,748.27 |
> | Gross receipts compensation | + 290,310.18 |
> | | |
> | Total amount due | $346,058.45   . . . |

–IV–

The provision in the termination clause providing for damages based on the lessee's gross receipts presents a more difficult issue [than damages based on renovation costs]. The issue is whether that provision is an enforceable liquidated damages provision or is an unenforceable penalty clause.

Disapproval of penalty clauses originated at early common law when debtors bound themselves through sealed penalty bonds for twice the amount of their actual debts. Charles J. Goetz & Robert E. Scott, *Liquidated Damages, Penalties and the Just Compensation Principle: Some Notes on an Enforcement Model and a Theory of Efficient Breach*, 77 Colum.L.Rev., 554, 554 (1977) (hereinafter Goetz & Scott). Because clauses in penalty bonds "carried an unusual danger of oppression and extortion," equity courts refused to enforce them. *Id.* at 555. "This equitable rule, designed to prevent overreaching and to give relief from unconscionable bargains, was later adopted by courts of law." John D. Calamari & Joseph M. Perillo, *The Law of Contracts,* § 14–31 at 639 (3d ed. 1987) (hereinafter Calamari & Perillo). In a sense, judicial reluctance to enforce penalty clauses is a product of history.

For more than five centuries, courts have scrutinized contractual provisions that specify damages payable in the event of breach. *Wassenaar v. Panos,* 111 *Wis.*2d 518, 331 *N.W.*2d 357, 362 (1983); Goetz & Scott, *supra,* 77 *Colum.L.Rev.* at 554. The validity of these "stipulated damage clauses" has depended on a judicial assessment of the clauses as an unenforceable penalty or as an enforceable provision for "liquidated damage." Thus, " '[l]iquidated damages' and 'penalties' are terms used to reflect legal conclusions as to the enforceability or nonenforceability, respectively, of stipulated damage clauses." Kenneth W. Clarkson et al., *Liquidated Damages v. Penalties: Sense or Nonsense?,* 1978 *Wis.L.Rev.* 351, 351 n. 1 (hereinafter Clarkson).

Thirty years ago, the Appellate Division distinguished liquidated damages and penalty clauses:

> *Liquidated damages* is the sum a party to a contract agrees to pay if he breaks some promise, and which, having been arrived at by a good faith effort to estimate in advance the actual damages that will probably ensue from the breach, is legally recoverable as agreed damages if the breach occurs. A *penalty* is the sum a party agrees to pay in the event of a breach, but which is fixed, not as a pre-estimate of probable actual damages, but as a punishment, the threat of which is designed to prevent the breach.

Parties to a contract may not fix a penalty for its breach. The settled rule in this State is that such a contract is unlawful.

> [*Westmount Country Club v. Kameny,* 82 *N.J.Super.* 200, 205, 197 A.2d 379 (1964) (citations omitted).]

Stating the distinction, however, has been easier than describing its underlying rationale. " '[T]he ablest judges have declared that they felt themselves embarrassed in ascertaining the principle on which the decisions [distinguishing penalties from liquidated damages] were founded.' " E. Allan Farnsworth, *Contracts* § 12.18 at 937 (2d ed. 1990) (alterations in original) (quoting *Cotheal v. Talmage,* 9 *N.Y.* 551, 553 (1854)); *see also Giesecke v. Cullerton,* 280 *Ill.* 510, 117 *N.E.* 777, 778 (1917) (observing that "no branch of the law is involved in more obscurity by contradictory decisions").

As the law has evolved, a stipulated damage clause "must constitute a reasonable forecast of the provable injury resulting from breach; otherwise, the clause will be unenforceable as a penalty and the non-breaching party will be limited to conventional damage measures." Goetz & Scott, *supra,* 77 *Colum.L.Rev.* at 554. So viewed, "reasonableness" emerges as the standard for deciding the validity of stipulated damages clauses. *See Wassenaar, supra,* 331 N.W.2d at 361 (noting that "[t]he overall single test of validity is whether the clause is reasonable under the totality of circumstances").

The reasonableness test has developed as a compromise between two competing viewpoints concerning stipulated damages clauses. The Wisconsin Supreme Court has described the policy considerations underlying these viewpoints:

> Enforcement of stipulated damages clauses is urged because the clauses serve several purposes. The clauses allow the parties to control

their exposure to risk by setting the payment for breach in advance. They avoid the uncertainty, delay, and expense of using the judicial process to determine actual damages. They allow the parties to fashion a remedy consistent with economic efficiency in a competitive market, and they enable the parties to correct what the parties perceive to be inadequate judicial remedies by agreeing upon a formula which may include damage elements too uncertain or remote to be recovered under rules of damages applied by the courts. In addition to these policies specifically relating to stipulated damages clauses, considerations of judicial economy and freedom of contract favor enforcement of stipulated damages clauses.

A competing set of policies disfavors stipulated damages clauses, and thus courts have not been willing to enforce stipulated damages clauses blindly without carefully scrutinizing them. Public law, not private law, ordinarily defines the remedies of the parties. Stipulated damages are an exception to this rule. Stipulated damages allow private parties to perform the judicial function of providing the remedy in breach of contract cases, namely, compensation of the nonbreaching party, and courts must ensure that the private remedy does not stray too far from the legal principle of allowing compensatory damages. Stipulated damages substantially in excess of injury may justify an inference of unfairness in bargaining or an objectionable *in terrorem* agreement to deter a party from breaching the contract, to secure performance, and to punish the breaching party if the deterrent is ineffective. [*Wassenaar, supra,* 331 *N.W.*2d at 362.]

Consistent with the principle of reasonableness, New Jersey courts have viewed enforceability of stipulated damages clauses as depending on whether the set amount "is a reasonable forecast of just compensation for the harm that is caused by the breach" and whether that harm "is incapable or very difficult of accurate estimate." *Westmount Country Club, supra,* 82 *N.J.Super.* at 206, 197 *A.*2d 379; *accord Monmouth Park Ass'n v. Wallis Iron Works,* 55 *N.J.L.* 132, 140–41, 26 *A.* 140 (E. & A. 1892); *Wood v. City of Ocean City,* 85 *N.J.Eq.* 328, 330, 96 *A.* 489 (Ch.1915); *see 218–220 Market St. Corp. v. Krich–Radisco, Inc.,* 124 *N.J.L.* 302, 305, 11 *A.*2d 109 (E. & A.1939).

Uncertainty or difficulty in assessing damages is best viewed not as an independent test, Calamari and Perillo, *supra,* § 14–31 at 641; Goetz & Scott, *supra,* 77 *Colum.L.Rev.* at 559 (stating, "liquidated damages provisions have seldom been voided solely because the damages were easy to estimate"), but rather as an element of assessing the reasonableness of a liquidated damages clause, *Wassenaar, supra,* 331 *N.W.*2d at 363. Thus, "[t]he greater the difficulty of estimating or proving damages, the more likely the stipulated damages will appear reasonable." *Ibid.*

Some courts in other jurisdictions have also considered whether the parties intended the clause to be one for liquidated damages. Clarkson, *supra,* 1978 *Wis.L.Rev.* at 353. Even those courts recognize that "subjective intent has little bearing on whether the clause is objectively reasonable." *Wassenaar, supra,* 331 *N.W.*2d at 363. For the past eighty years, New Jersey courts have relied on the "circumstances of the case and not on the words used by the parties" in determining the enforceability of stipulated damages clauses. *Gibbs v. Cooper,* 86 *N.J.L.* 226, 227–28, 90 *A.* 1115 (E. & A.1914); *see also* Farnsworth, *supra,* § 12.18 at 939 ("the parties' own characterization of the sum as 'liquidated damages' or as a 'penalty' is not controlling"); Clarkson, *supra,* 1978 *Wis.L.Rev.* at 353 (same); *cf. Monmouth Park Ass'n, supra,* 55 *N.J.L.* at 141, 26 *A.* 140 (stating, "if it be doubtful on the whole agreement whether the sum is intended as a penalty or as liquidated damages, it will be construed as a penalty, because the law favors mere indemnity"). We conclude that the parties' characterization of stipulated damages as "liquidated damages" or as a "penalty" should not be dispositive.

Although the Appellate Division has indicated that courts should determine the enforceability of a stipulated damages clause as of the time of the making of the contract, *Westmount Country Club, supra,* 82 *N.J.Super.* at 206, 197 *A.*2d 379, the modern trend is towards assessing reasonableness either at the time of contract formation or at the time of the breach. Calamari & Perillo, *supra,* § 14–31 at 642 (stating, "there are two moments at which the liquidated damages clause may be judged rather than just one").

Actual damages, moreover, reflect on the reasonableness of the parties' prediction of damages. "If the damages provided for in the contract are grossly disproportionate to the actual harm sustained, the courts usually conclude that the parties' original expectations were unreasonable." *Wassenaar, supra,* 331 *N.W.*2d at 364; *see* 5A. *Corbin on Contracts* § 1063 (1951) (Corbin) ("It is to be observed that hindsight is frequently better than foresight, and that, in passing judgment upon the honesty and genuineness of the preestimate made by the parties, the court cannot help but be influenced by its knowledge of subsequent events."). Determining enforceability at the time either when the contract is made or when it is breached encourages more frequent enforcement of stipulated damages clauses. Calamari & Perillo, *supra,* § 14–31 at 642.

Two of the most authoritative statements concerning liquidated damages are contained in the Uniform Commercial Code and the *Restatement (Second) of Contracts,* both of which emphasize reasonableness as the touchstone. Farnsworth, *supra,* § 12.18 at 938. Thus, section 2–718 of the Uniform Commercial Code, adopted in New Jersey as *N.J.S.A.* 12A:2–718, provides:

> (1) Damages for breach by either party may be liquidated in the agreement but only at an amount which is reasonable in the light of the anticipated or actual harm caused by the breach, the difficulties of proof of loss, and the inconvenience or nonfeasibility of otherwise obtaining an adequate remedy.

Similarly, the Second Restatement of Contracts provides:

> Damages for breach by either party may be liquidated in the agreement but only at an amount that is reasonable in the light of the anticipated or actual loss caused by the breach and the difficulties of proof of loss. A term fixing unreasonably large liquidated damages is unenforceable on grounds of public policy as a penalty. [*Restatement (Second) of Contracts* § 356(1) (1981).]

Consistent with the trend toward enforcing stipulated damages clauses, the Appellate Division has recognized that such clauses should be deemed presumptively reasonable and that the party challenging such a clause should bear the burden of proving its unreasonableness.... Similarly, most courts today place the burden on the party challenging a stipulated damages clause....

In commercial transactions between parties with comparable bargaining power, stipulated damage provisions can provide a useful and efficient remedy. . . . Sophisticated parties acting under the advice of counsel often negotiate stipulated damages clauses to avoid the cost and uncertainty of litigation. Such parties can be better situated than courts to provide a fair and efficient remedy. Absent concerns about unconscionability, courts frequently need ask no more than whether the clause is reasonable. We do not reach the issue of the enforceability of liquidated damage clauses in consumer contracts. Notwithstanding the presumptive reasonableness of stipulated damage clauses, we are sensitive to the possibility that, as their history discloses, such clauses may be unconscionable and unjust. *Foont–Freedenfeld Corp. v. Electro–Protective Corp.*, 126 *N.J.Super.* 254, 258, 314 *A.*2d 69 (App.Div.1973), *aff'd o.b.*, 64 *N.J.* 197, 314 *A.*2d 68 (1974); *Westmount Country Club, supra,* 82 *N.J.Super.* at 206, 197 *A.*2d 379; Goetz & Scott, *supra,* 77 *Colum.L.Rev.* at 588 (stating that "in the absence of bargaining unfairness, a stipulated damage clause reflects equivalent value").

–V–

The purpose of a stipulated damages clause is not to compel the promisor to perform, but to compensate the promisee for non-performance. Farnsworth, *supra,* § 12.18 at 936. Accordingly, provisions for liquidated damages are enforceable only if "the amount so fixed is a reasonable forecast of just compensation for the harm that is caused by the breach." *Westmount Country Club, supra,* 82 *N.J.Super.* at 206, 197 *A.*2d 379; *see also Restatement (Second) of Contracts, supra,* § 356 comment a (stating, "The parties to a contract may effectively provide in advance the damages that are to be payable in the event of breach as long as the provision does not disregard the principle of just compensation."). One injured by a breach of contract is entitled only to just and adequate compensation. *McDaniel Bros. Constr. Co. v. Jordy,* 195 *So.*2d 922, 925 (Miss.1967). Thus, the subject cancellation clause is unreasonable if it does more than compensate plaintiffs for their approximate actual damages caused by the breach.

Whether measured from the time of execution of the contract or from the termination of the lease, *see Westmount Country Club, supra,* 82 *N.J.Super.* at 206, 197 *A.*2d 379, damages based on gross receipts run the risk of being found unreasonable. Generally speaking, gross receipts do not reflect actual losses incurred because of the cancellation. Gross receipts, unlike net profits, do not account for ordinary expenses; nor do they account for the expenses specifically attributable to the breach. Here, we cannot determine whether the stipulated amount was based on damages that would likely flow from a breach or whether it is an arbitrary figure unrelated to any such damages. . . .

Furthermore, basing damages on gross profits could award the plaintiff a windfall. . . .

We cannot determine from plaintiffs' gross receipts the losses they sustained because of the Township's cancellation of the lease. The subject clause requires the Township to pay damages of twenty-five percent of the lessee's average gross receipts for one year. Under the lease, average gross receipts are calculated by taking an average of the lessee's total gross receipts for three fiscal years immediately preceding the cancellation. So calculated, Jo–Ro's average yearly gross was $1,161,240.75. Twenty-five percent of this figure amounts to $290,310.18.

This amount, however, does not necessarily reflect plaintiffs' actual losses on considering operating expenses or relocation costs and other expenses attributable to defendant's breach. As reflected in Jo–Ro's income-tax returns, Jo–Ro earned a net profit of $3,649 in 1985, $414 in 1986, and sustained a loss of $323 in 1987. We recognize the difference between tax losses and actual losses. Yet, to the extent that tax returns reflect actual profit or loss, they demonstrate the unreasonableness of damages exceeding $290,000, which were calculated on the basis of gross receipts.

The decision whether a stipulated damages clause is enforceable is a question of law for the court. *218–220 Market St. Corp., supra,* 124 *N.J.L.* at 304, 11 A.2d 109; *Robinson v. Centenary Fund,* 68 *N.J.L.* 723, 725–26, 54 A. 416 (E. & A. 1902). Although the question is one of law, it may require resolution of underlying factual issues. *Highgate Assocs., Ltd. v. Merryfield,* 157 *Vt.* 313, 597 A.2d 1280, 1282 (1991).

On balance, we believe we should remand this matter to the trial court to consider the reasonableness of the clause in light of this opinion. In resolving that issue, the court should consider, among other relevant considerations, the reasonableness of the use of gross receipts as the measure of damages no matter when the cancellation occurs; the significance of the award of damages based on twenty-five percent of one year's average gross receipts, rather than on some other basis such as total gross receipts computed for each year remaining under the lease; the reasoning of the parties that supported the calculation of the stipulated damages; the lessee's duty to mitigate damages; and the fair market rent and availability of replacement space. We leave to the sound discretion of the trial court the extent to which additional proof is necessary on the reasonableness of the clause. Because stipulated damages clauses are presumptively reasonable, *supra* at 252–253, 645 A.2d at 108, the burden of production and of persuasion rests on the Township.

To summarize, we affirm the judgment of the Appellate Division that the Township is liable to plaintiffs for terminating the lease. We also affirm the judgment of the Appellate Division awarding plaintiffs damages of $55,748.27 for renovation costs. We remand to the Law Division the issue whether the clause requiring payment of stipulated damages based on the lessee's gross receipts is a valid liquidated damages clause.

The judgment of the Appellate Division is affirmed in part, reversed in part, and the matter is remanded to the Law Division.

For affirmance in part, reversal in part and remandment—Chief Justice WILENTZ, and Justices CLIFFORD, HANDLER, POLLOCK, O'HERN, GARIBALDI and STEIN—7.*

LEE OLDSMOBILE, INC. v. KAIDEN, 32 Md.App. 556, 363 A.2d 270 (1976). Lee Oldsmobile dealt in Rolls–Royces as part of its business operations. Kaiden learned that Lee had on order, as a part of its allotted 1973 quota of ten or eleven Rolls–Royces, a car of the style and color she wanted,

---

* Victor Goldberg reports that following the decision by the New Jersey Supreme Court, the parties settled for $360,000, "which, after taking into account the time value of money, comes to about sixty cents on the dollar." Goldberg, Framing Contract Law: An Economic Perspective 258. (Footnote by ed.)

and in August 1973 she sent Lee a $5,000 deposit on the purchase of this car for $29,500. Lee then sent Kaiden an order form, which she signed and returned. The order form contained a clause providing that Lee had the right, upon failure or refusal of the purchaser to accept delivery of the motor vehicle, to retain as liquidated damages any cash deposit made by the purchaser. Apparently there was a dispute concerning the date of delivery, and on November 21, Kaiden notified Lee that she had purchased another Rolls elsewhere, and instructed that her order be canceled. On November 29, Lee notified Kaiden that the car was ready for delivery. She declined to accept and demanded the return of her deposit. Lee refused, and later sold the Rolls to another purchaser. Held, Kaiden was entitled to recover the amount of her deposit, minus actual damages.

"We reject the application of the liquidated damage clause in the present case ... because it is clear that the actual damages are capable of accurate estimation. We do not say this from hindsight made possible because the actual figures claimed were in evidence. We say it because at the time the contract was made, it was clear that the nature of any damages which would result from a possible future breach was such that they would be easily ascertainable...."

HUTCHISON v. TOMPKINS, 259 So.2d 129 (Fla.1972). Plaintiffs agreed to sell certain land to the Tompkins for $125,000. Of this amount, $10,000 in cash was deposited with an escrow agent. The contract contained a liquidated damages clause, which provided that if the buyer failed to perform sellers could at their option elect to retain the $10,000 deposit. According to the complaint, the Tompkins breached the contract by refusing to complete the purchase, but the escrow agent improperly returned their $10,000 deposit to them. Plaintiffs brought suit against the Tompkins and the escrow agent to recover the $10,000. The trial court dismissed the complaint on the ground that the liquidated damages clause was invalid as a penalty, relying on a Florida Supreme Court case, Pembroke v. Caudill, 160 Fla. 948, 37 So.2d 538 (1948). On appeal, the Florida Supreme Court began by discussing *Pembroke* and a later case, Hyman v. Cohen, 73 So.2d 393 (Fla.1954):

> ... [T]he rationale of *Pembroke* may be stated as follows: if damages are readily ascertainable at the time of breach, then a liquidated damage clause will be construed as a penalty, even though the damages were not susceptible of ascertainment at the time the contract was entered into. Conversely, in *Hyman* the Court concluded that it was necessary for the damages to be readily ascertainable *at the time of the drawing of the contract* in order for a liquidated damage clause to constitute a penalty:

> We are convinced that the *Hyman* rationale provides the sounder approach to the problem of ascertainability of damages. Damages, especially in real estate transactions, are nearly always ascertainable at the time a contract is breached, because, as the *Pembroke* opinion points out, the measure of damages involves determining the difference between the agreed purchase price and the market value of the land as of the date of breach. Accordingly, the rule in *Pembroke* must have, when followed in letter and spirit ... a chilling effect on contract negotiations where the parties wish to include a provision for liquidated damages.

For centuries the concept of liquidated damages has been a part of our law. We have no wish to emasculate it now by following a rule which renders nearly all deposit receipt contracts invalid. The better result, in our judgment, as *Hyman* contemplates, is to allow the liquidated damage clause to stand if the damages are not readily ascertainable at the time the contract is drawn, but to permit equity to relieve against the forfeiture if it appears unconscionable in light of the circumstances existing at the time of breach. For instance, assume a situation in which damages were not readily ascertainable at the time the contract was drawn, and the parties agreed to a liquidated damage provision of $100,000. Purchaser later repudiated the contract; vendor resold the land to another party, which because of fluctuations in the real estate market, resulted in a loss to himself of only $2,000. In such a case a court following the *Hyman* theory would allow the liquidated damage clause to stand, because damages were not readily ascertainable at the time of drawing the contract, but would as a court of equity, relieve against the forfeiture as unconscionable. Under the *Pembroke* theory the liquidated damage clause would be struck down on its face without any consideration of vendor's actual damages.

The instant case falls squarely within *Hyman*. A contract for the sale of land generally suffers from the same uncertainty as to possible future damages as a lease agreement. The land sale market in Florida fluctuates from year to year and season to season, and it is generally impossible to say at the time a contract for sale is drawn what vendor's loss (if any) will be should the contract be breached by purchaser's failure to close. Accordingly, in the instant case we conclude that the damages which the parties could expect as a result of a breach were not readily ascertainable as of the time the contract was drawn up; therefore, under *Hyman*, ... the liquidated damage provision [was not] a penalty.... Moreover, because the definition of "readily ascertainable" in Pembroke v. Caudill, supra, is incompatible with the rationale of *Hyman*, we hereby recede from *Pembroke* to the extent of such conflict.

UCC § 2–718(1)*

[See Selected Source Materials Supplement]

---

* In 2003 the National Conference of Commissioners on State Laws and the American Law Institute promulgated an amended version of Article 2. Amended section 2–718(1) provides as follows:

§ 2–718. Liquidation or Limitation of Damages; Deposits.

(1) Damages for breach by either party may be liquidated in the agreement but only at an amount that is reasonable in the light of the anticipated or actual harm caused by the breach and, in a consumer contract, the difficulties of proof of loss, and the inconvenience or nonfeasibility of otherwise obtaining an adequate remedy. Section 2–719 [Contractual Modification or Liquidation of Remedy] determines the enforceability of a term that limits but does not liquidate damages.

For various reasons, as of early 2006 no state legislature has adopted the amended version of Article 2. At least for the present, therefore, liquidated-damages provisions in contracts for the sale of goods continue to be governed by the pre–2003 version of section 2–718.

RESTATEMENT, SECOND, CONTRACTS § 356

[See Selected Source Materials Supplement]

UNIDROIT PRINCIPLES OF INTERNATIONAL COMMERCIAL CONTRACTS ART. 7.4.13

[See Selected Source Materials Supplement]

PRINCIPLES OF EUROPEAN CONTRACT LAW ART. 9.509

[See Selected Source Materials Supplement]

NOTE ON LIQUIDATED DAMAGES

All courts agree on the principle that liquidated-damages provisions should be given special judicial scrutiny, although the formulation of the principle varies. In contrast, many commentators have criticized this principle. Most of the critiques have an implicit or explicit three-part structure: (1) They begin by assuming that the major justification for the principle that liquidated-damages provisions should be given special scrutiny is that such provisions lend themselves to blameworthy exploitation of one party by the other, and consequent one-sidedness, in a way that other types of contract provisions do not. (2) They then argue that this justification will not hold. (3) They conclude that the principle is therefore unjustified. So, for example, Goetz and Scott argue that the principle of special scrutiny of liquidated-damages provisions arose in a historical context in which protections against fraud and duress were not available. Given the modern development of unconscionability as a unifying unfairness principle, they suggest, the law should simply collapse the treatment of liquidated damages into that principle. Charles J. Goetz & Robert E. Scott, Liquidated Damages, Penalties and the Just Compensation Principle: Some Notes on an Enforcement Model and a Theory of Efficient Breach, 77 Colum. L. Rev. 554, 592 (1977).

The assumption that special scrutiny of liquidated-damages provisions is justified primarily by a special potential for blameworthy exploitation and one-sidedness does reflect the courts' rhetoric, which is cast in terms of whether or not such provisions are "penalties," and therefore suggests a concern with advantage-taking and oppression. In fact, however, the justification for the special scrutiny of liquidated-damages provisions is not that such provisions are specially amenable to blameworthy exploitation and one-sidedness, but that such provisions are systematically likely to reflect the limits of human cognition.

Classical contract law was based on a rational-actor model of psychology. Under this model, actors who make decisions in the face of uncertainty rationally maximize their subjective expected utility, with all future benefits and costs properly discounted to present value. A great body of theoretical and empirical work in cognitive psychology within the last thirty or forty years has shown that rational-actor psychology often lacks explanatory power. Although rational-actor psychology is the foundation of the standard *economic* model of choice, the empirical evidence shows that this model often diverges from the actual *psychology* of choice, due to limits of cognition. As Amos Tversky and Daniel Kahneman point out, expected-utility (rational-actor) theory "emerged from a logical analysis of games of chance rather than from a psychological analysis of risk and value. The theory was conceived as a normative model of an idealized decision maker, not as a description of the behavior of real people." Amos Tversky & Daniel Kahneman, Rational Choice and the Framing of Decisions, 59 J. Bus. S251 (1986).

In contrast to rational-actor psychology, modern cognitive psychology recognizes various limits of cognition. For purposes of contract law, three kinds of limits of cognition are especially salient: bounded rationality, irrational disposition, and defective capability.

1. *Bounded Rationality*

To begin with, an actor may not even consider the alternative that would maximize his utility, because actors limit their search for and their deliberation on alternatives. If the costs of searching for and processing (evaluating and deliberating on) information were zero, and human information-processing capabilities were perfect, then an actor contemplating a decision would make a comprehensive search for relevant information, would process perfectly all the information he acquired, and would then make the best possible substantive decision—the decision that, as of the time made, was better than all the alternative decisions the actor might have made if he had complete knowledge and perfect processing abilities, and which would therefore maximize the actor's subjective expected utility.

In reality, of course, searching for and processing information does involve costs, in the form of time, energy, and perhaps money. Most actors either do not want to expend the resources required for comprehensive search and processing or recognize that comprehensive search and processing would not be achievable at any realistic cost. Actors therefore put boundaries on the amount of search and processing they engage in before making decisions. To put it differently, actors often consciously choose to be in a state of *rational ignorance*—"rational," because the incremental cost of achieving complete knowledge about a decision would be more than the expected gain from making the decision with complete rather than partial knowledge. So, for example, a patient may seek a second or perhaps a third doctor's opinion about treatment, but no more, because he believes it unlikely that consulting an extra five, ten, or fifteen doctors will improve his treatment decision enough to justify spending the extra time and money.

Furthermore, our abilities to process information and solve problems are constrained by limitations of computational ability, ability to calculate consequences, ability to organize and utilize memory, and the like. Hence, actors will often process imperfectly even the information they do acquire. Such imperfections in human processing ability increase as decisions become more complex and involve more permutations.

Accordingly, human rationality is normally bounded both by limited information and limited information-processing ability.

2. *Irrational disposition*

Next, actors are unrealistically optimistic as a systematic matter. (Lawyers do not realize this, because they are trained to be systematically pessimistic.) The dispositional characteristic of undue optimism is strikingly illustrated in a study by Lynn Baker and Robert Emery, appropriately titled, When Every Relationship Is Above Average, 17 Law and Hum. Behav. 439 (1993). Baker and Emery asked subjects who were about to get married to report on their own divorce-related prospects as compared to the divorce-related prospects of the general population. The disparities between perceptions as to the prospects of the general population and the prospects of the subjects were enormous, and were almost invariably in the direction of optimism. For example, the subjects correctly estimated that fifty percent of American couples will eventually divorce. In contrast, the subjects estimated that their own chance of divorce was zero. Similarly, the subjects' median estimate of how often spouses pay all court-ordered alimony was that forty percent paid. In contrast, 100 percent of the subjects predicted that their own spouse would pay all court-ordered alimony.

3. *Defective Capability*

Finally, cognitive psychology has established that actors use certain decision-making rules (heuristics) that yield systematic errors: "[T]he deviations of actual behavior from the normative model are too widespread to be ignored, too systematic to be dismissed as random error, and too fundamental to be accommodated by relaxing the normative system." Tversky & Kahneman, supra, at S252. For example, actors make decisions on the basis of data that is readily available to their memory, rather than on the basis of all the relevant data. (This is known as the "availability heuristic.") In particular, actors systematically give undue weight to instantiated evidence as compared to general statements, to vivid evidence as compared to pallid evidence, and to concrete evidence as compared to abstract evidence. Similarly, actors are systematically insensitive to sample size, and erroneously take small samples as representative samples.

Another defect in capability concerns the ability of actors to make rational comparisons between present and future states. For example, the sample consisting of present events is often wrongly taken to be representative, and therefore unduly predictive, of future events. Actors also systematically give too little weight to future benefits and costs as compared to present benefits and costs. Thus Martin Feldstein concludes that "some or all individuals have, in Pigou's ... words, a 'faulty telescopic faculty' that causes them to give too little weight to the utility of future consumption." Feldstein, The Optimal Level of Social Security Benefits, 100 Q. J. Econ. 303, 307 (1985).

A defect of capability related to faulty telescopic faculties is the systematic underestimation of risks. Based on the work of cognitive psychologists, Kenneth Arrow observes that "[i]t is a plausible hypothesis that individuals are unable to recognize that there will be many surprises in the future; in short, as much other evidence tends to confirm, there is a tendency to underestimate uncertainties." Arrow, Risk Perception in Psychology and Economics, 20 Econ. Inquiry 1, 5 (1982). In fact, empirical evidence shows that actors often not only underestimate but ignore low-probability risks.

4. *Liquidated-damages provisions.*

The limits of cognition have a special bearing on liquidated-damages provisions. To begin with, bounded rationality and rational ignorance play an important role here. Contracting parties normally will find it relatively easy to evaluate proposed performance terms, such as subject matter, quantity, and price. In contrast, at the time a contract is made it is often impracticable, if not impossible, to imagine all the scenarios of breach. Similarly, the inherent complexity of determining the application of a liquidated-damages provision to every possible breach scenario will often exceed actors' information-processing abilities.

Even on the doubtful assumption that a contracting party could imagine all breach scenarios, and determine the application of a liquidated-damages provision to every possible scenario, the benefits of extensive search and information-processing on these issues will often seem to be very low as compared to the costs. A party who contracts to buy or sell a commodity normally expects to perform. Accordingly, the benefits to the party of deliberating very carefully on performance terms—terms that specify what performance the party is required to render—are compelling, and the costs of such deliberation usually do not outweigh the benefits. In contrast, a party often will not expect that a liquidated-damages provision will ever come into play against him, partly because he intends to perform, and partly because experience will tell him that in general there is a high rate of performance of contracts. For example, if contracts are performed at least ninety-five percent of the time (which observation suggests is likely), all the costs of processing the more remote applications of a liquidated-damages provision would have to be taken into account, but the benefits of such processing would have to be discounted by ninety-five percent. The resulting cost-benefit ratio will often provide a substantial disincentive for processing every possible application of a liquidated-damages provision, even if it were in fact possible to imagine every such application. As a result, contracting parties are often likely to not completely think through liquidated-damages provisions, and are therefore often unlikely to fully understand the implications of such provisions.

The problem of irrational disposition also bears significantly on liquidated-damages provisions. Because actors tend to be unrealistically optimistic, a contracting party probably will believe that his performance is more likely, and his breach less likely, than is actually the case. Accordingly, unrealistic optimism will reduce even further the deliberation that actors give to liquidated-damages provisions.

Finally, defective capabilities have particular relevance to liquidated-damages provisions. The availability heuristic may lead a contracting party to give undue weight to his present intention to perform, which is vivid and concrete, as compared with the abstract possibility that future circumstances may compel him to breach. Because actors tend to take the sample of present evidence as unduly representative of the future, a contracting party is apt to overestimate the extent to which his present intention to perform is a reliable predictor of his future intentions. Because actors have faulty telescopic faculties, a contracting party is likely to overvalue the benefit of the prospect of performance, which will normally begin to occur in the short term, as against the cost of breach, which will typically occur, if at all, only down the road. Because actors tend to underestimate risks, a contracting party is likely to underestimate the risk that a liquidated-damages provision will take effect.

The rationale for giving special scrutiny to liquidated damages provisions affects the point of time on which the scrutiny is focused. If the justification for giving special scrutiny to liquidated damages provisions is that such provisions are especially subject to blameworthy exploitation and one-sidedness, the scrutiny should be focused on the time the contract is made—a "forward looking" test. In contrast, if the justification for special scrutiny is that parties often make cognitive errors in adopting such provisions, the scrutiny should be focused on the time of breach—a "second look" approach, which compares the liquidated damages with actual loss—because a gross discrepancy between forecast and result suggests that the liquidated-damages provision was a product of limited or defective cognition.

About half the states hold that the enforceability of liquidated-damages provisions is to be determined at the time the contract is made, and about half the states hold that enforceability of such provisions is to be determined at the time of the breach. See Kelly v. Marx, 44 Mass.App.Ct. 825, 694 N.E.2d 869 (1998), reversed, Kelly v. Marx, 428 Mass. 877, 705 N.E.2d 1114 (1999). However, even courts that purport to employ a forward-looking test may apply a second-look test in the guise relief against forfeiture, unconscionability in application, or the like. See, e.g., Hutchison v. Tompkins, supra.

———

NOTE ON PROVISIONS THAT LIMIT DAMAGES

In a typical liquidated-damages case, the parties try to either (1) estimate the actual damages that will be suffered if a breach occurs, or (2) craft a penalty, in an amount that is greater than estimated actual damages, to deter breach. In contrast, in many cases the parties adopt a technique to limit damages to an amount that is *less* than estimated actual damages. Such provisions are known as *underliquidated-damages* provisions, and are normally enforced. See, e.g., Global Octanes Texas, L.P. v. BP Exploration & Oil Inc., 154 F.3d 518 (5th Cir.1998); Rassa v. Rollins Protective Services Co., 30 F.Supp.2d 538 (D.Md.1998).

A second technique is to limit or exclude liability for consequential damages.

A third technique is to provide that if the goods are defective, the seller's responsibility is limited to repair or replacement of the goods.

The second and third techniques are explicitly validated, subject to certain limitations, by U.C.C. § 2–719, which provides:

> (1) Subject to the provisions of subsections (2) and (3) of this section and of the preceding section on liquidation and limitation of damages,
>
> > (a) the agreement may provide for remedies in addition to or in substitution for those provided in this Article and may limit or alter the measure of damages recoverable under this Article, as by limiting the buyer's remedies to return of the goods and repayment of the price or to repair and replacement of nonconforming goods or parts; and

(b) resort to a remedy as provided is optional unless the remedy is expressly agreed to be exclusive, in which case it is the sole remedy.

(2) Where circumstances cause an exclusive or limited remedy to fail of its essential purpose, remedy may be had as provided in this Act.

(3) Consequential damages may be limited or excluded unless the limitation or exclusion is unconscionable. Limitation of consequential damages for injury to the person, in the case of consumer goods is prima facie unconscionable but limitation of damages where the loss is commercial is not.

Note that although repair-or-replace provisions are explicitly validated by Subsection 1(a), Subsection (2) provides that a provision that limits remedies is unenforceable where circumstances cause the limited remedy to "fail of its essential purpose." In a repair-or-replace case, this limitation comes into play where the seller either fails to repair or replace, or does so only in a very dilatory manner.

Frequently, a repair-or-replace provision is coupled with a provision that eliminates liability for consequential damages. The question often arises, if the repair-or-replace provision is held to be unenforceable because it fails of its essential purpose (for example, because of the seller's delay in making the repairs), does a companion provision that eliminates consequential damages remain enforceable, or should it be deemed so closely bound to the repair-or-replace provision that when the latter provision falls, so does the former? "[C]ourts are deeply divided on this issue, and ... about the same number of cases can be marshalled on either side of the question." International Financial Services, Inc. v. Franz, 534 N.W.2d 261 (Minn.1995).

Chapter 7

SPECIFIC PERFORMANCE

INTRODUCTORY NOTE

Chapter 7 concerns the remedy of specific performance. Under this remedy, the court, instead of ordering the breaching party to pay damages, orders the breaching party to perform the contract.

The historical background. For centuries the English administration of justice was characterized by the peculiarity that there were two systems of courts administering two different bodies of law. What may be called the "regular" court system consisted of the courts of common law, which had jurisdiction over "actions at law," and administered "regular" law. The other system consisted of courts of "equity" or "chancery," which had jurisdiction over "suits in equity," and applied a body of principles that came to be called "equity." (Note the double linguistic usages involved here. "Law" used: (1) in a broad sense to mean the principles for administering justice, which includes both common law and equity, or (2) in a narrower sense, to mean the principles applied by the common law courts. "Equity" used: (1) in a broad sense, to mean fairness, or (2) in a narrower sense, to mean the established principles administered by a specific system of courts.)

In general, the English equity or chancery courts acted to remedy defects in the rules administered by the common law courts. The equity courts did not have a general jurisdiction over all kinds of disputes; their function was to act in those cases where "the legal remedy was inadequate," that is, where according to the notions of the time, the regular or common law courts did not give the kind of relief that the plaintiff ought to have.

One of the great defects of common law courts was that except in certain extraordinary cases, the procedure in those courts did not contemplate *ordering* the defendant to do anything. If a creditor sued his debtor for £10 and was awarded a judgment at law, the judgment did not take the form of an order commanding the debtor to pay his debt. Instead, in its traditional form the judgement recited that it was "considered that the plaintiff do recover against the defendant his debt." Enforcement of the judgment was accomplished not by commanding the defendant to pay, but by directing the sheriff to levy execution on the defendant's property if the defendant did not pay, so that the plaintiff's claim could be satisfied out of this property.

Where the plaintiff was complaining of a breach of contract by the defendant, this defect prevented the courts from ordering the defendant to perform his promise. Thus, if Seller contracted to convey Blackacre to Buyer, and then broke his promise, there was no way in which Buyer, by appealing to the common law courts, could get a deed to Blackacre, even though Seller had a perfectly good title to the land and was wholly capable of carrying out her contract. Accordingly, the only relief Buyer could obtain from a common law court was an award of money damages.

However, in such a case Buyer could successfully appeal to a court of equity, alleging that his legal remedy (money damages) was inadequate. The equity court would issue a decree ordering Seller to execute a deed in Buyer's favor. If Seller refused to obey this order, she would put herself in contempt of court and be subject to fine or imprisonment.

There are other situations, though, where an appeal to equity to enforce a contract would fail. To put the plainest kind of case, suppose that Seller had sold and delivered a horse to Buyer for $500, and that Buyer, although having ample funds to do so, refused to pay the promised price of the horse. Here conceivably Seller might get a certain spiritual satisfaction out of an order commanding Buyer to pay his debt—an order that the common law courts would not issue. On the other hand, the common law courts would ensure the promised price for Seller through a levy of execution on Buyer's goods. Accordingly in this case the legal remedy was deemed to be adequate, and a suit by Seller in an equity court would be denied.

In other cases, equity refused to enforce contracts not because the legal remedy was adequate, but because it was considered unwise for one or another reasons to attempt specific enforcement. For example, a famous opera singer agrees to sing in the plaintiff's opera house for three months and then breaks her contract. Here the opera-house proprietor may with much justice assert that his legal remedy of damages is inadequate; an award of money can scarcely be treated as an adequate substitute for actual performance. At the same time, there are obvious objections to attempting to compel a star to sing against her will. Accordingly, this is a case where a court of equity would deny specific performance despite a recognition that the monetary relief granted by the common law courts is an inadequate form of relief.

The relation of law and equity in the United States today. The illustrations provided above give a general view of the way in which the English courts dealt with specific enforcement of contracts at the time the United States began its independent legal existence. Today, most American states no longer have separate courts of law and equity. Instead, in most states the same judges administer both bodies of principles. This does not mean, however, that the two bodies of principles are not to a considerable extent still kept distinct in the thinking of lawyers and judges. If a plaintiff asks the court to issue an order directing the defendant to perform her promise—say, to convey Blackacre—such a suit will be tested by principles called "equity" and derived historically from the English chancery courts. In some jurisdictions, the suit will in fact be labeled as a "suit in equity" even though the judge who tries the suit has the power to try "actions at law" as well. Even in those jurisdictions where no label is attached to the suit to indicate whether it is "at law" or "in equity," the rules applied to the suit will be "equity" rules if the case involves a demand for an order directing the defendant to specifically perform.

LONDON BUCKET CO. v. STEWART

Court of Appeals of Kentucky, 1951.
314 Ky. 832, 237 S.W.2d 509.

STANLEY, COMMISSIONER. This is an appeal from a judgment decreeing specific performance of a contract to properly furnish and install a heating system for a large motel. The basic contention of the appellant, London Bucket Company, is that the remedy of specific performance will not lie for breach of this type of contract.

The chancellor overruled a demurrer to the petition and this is the first assignment of error. Stewart's petition set out the contract, the pertinent parts of which are as follows: "The parties of the first part agree and bind themselves to furnish and install (subletting installation) in said building the following equipment...." The only standard as to the quality of work to be performed was that the defendant was to "guarantee to heat this said court to 75 degrees in winter, and to supervise all work," etc. The plaintiff alleged that the defendant "soon thereafter and within one year installed a plant in an incompleted, unskilled unworkmanlike manner, never finishing same, and of such size, type and inferior quality of materials that same does not to a reasonable degree perform the purpose contemplated." The petition further states: "Plaintiff here now demands of the court of equity that defendant be compelled to specifically perform the terms of said contract and complete said installation and furnish the type of furnace provided in said contract and all the things necessary to properly heat said building and rooms and same to be done forthwith, before the fall of cold weather."

The plaintiff prayed that "immediate specific performance be adjudged" and also asked $8,250 damages for faulty and negligent construction and resulting expense, loss of business, etc. On being required to elect his remedy, he chose specific performance and dismissed without prejudice his action for damages.

The defendant, among other defenses, pleaded there had been a mutual cancellation of the contract insofar as it covered the completion of the job. Upon sharply conflicting evidence, but with some documents strongly supporting the plaintiff's contention, the court found as a fact that there had been no such cancellation. This was an issue necessary to be decided before deciding there could be a decree of specific performance.

The court decreed: "The defendant is hereby mandatorily ordered and directed to comply with the terms of said contract, in its entirety. He shall proceed diligently so to do and continue its obligation, assumed by it under the said contract, therein specifically set out."

No matter what the evidence may have been, the plaintiff's legal right could be no greater than that which the basic facts pleaded authorized. So if the demurrer should have been sustained to his pleading which undertook to state his whole case, that is all the court need consider. In other words, if the plaintiff did not state a cause of action for specific performance, the demurrer should have been sustained instead of overruled. That is the way the trial court treated the case except to find that the work done was defective, the heating system was not properly functioning, and the job was incomplete. In his opinion, the court recognized the difficulty of the question whether the contract and the conditions were such as required specific performance. He considered the familiar principle that such an equitable decree will not be adjudged unless the ordinary common law remedy of damages for a breach of contract is an inadequate and incomplete remedy for injuries arising from the failure to carry out its terms. Edelen v. Samuels & Co., 126 Ky. 295, 103 S.W. 360. The court concluded, nevertheless, that this case was within Schmidt v. Louisville & N.R. Co., 101 Ky. 441, 41 S.W. 1015, 19 Ky.Law Rep. 666, 38 L.R.A. 809, and Pennsylvania Railroad Co. v. City of Louisville, 277 Ky. 402, 126 S.W.2d 840.

It seems to us the two cases are not altogether apt. In the *Schmidt* case it was held a decree of specific performance to operate the railroad under the terms of the lease for the benefit of both holders was proper since there was no adequate remedy at law. The *Pennsylvania Railroad* Case was a suit to declare the rights of the parties and to require several railroad companies to proceed with the elimination of grade crossings as they had contracted to do. Both cases involve matters of great magnitude and were of public interest and welfare. In each case the court in effect said, "Proceed to do what you contracted to do." There was no question of partial or incomplete or faulty performance of a building contract. The *Schmidt* case is distinguished in the leading case of Edelen v. Samuels & Co., supra. In the present case the decree was in effect to direct a building contractor to go back, correct defective work and complete its job. It is the general rule that contracts for building construction will not be specifically enforced because ordinarily damages are an adequate remedy and, in part, because of the incapacity of the court to superintend the performance. 9 Am.Jur., Building and Construction Contracts, § 124; 58 C.J. 1046. The case at bar is not within the exceptions to the rule or of the class where specific performance should be decreed. 49 Am.Jur., Specific Performance, § 12. That there may be difficulty in proving the damages as appellee suggests, is not enough to put the case within the exceptions.

Under our conclusion that specific performance should not have been decreed, the decision on the issue of cancellation of the contract must follow it. This will leave the question open in the common-law action for damages should it be filed.

Wherefore, the judgment is reversed.

———

RESTATEMENT, SECOND, CONTRACTS §§ 359, 360

[See Selected Source Materials Supplement]

———

UNIDROIT PRINCIPLES OF INTERNATIONAL COMMERCIAL CONTRACTS ARTS. 7.2.1, 7.2.2, 7.2.3

[See Selected Source Materials Supplement]

———

PRINCIPLES OF EUROPEAN CONTRACT
LAW ARTS. 9.101, 9.102, 9.103

[See Selected Source Materials Supplement]

WALGREEN CO. v. SARA CREEK PROPERTY CO.

United States Court of Appeals, Seventh Circuit, 1992.
966 F.2d 273.

POSNER, Circuit Judge.

This appeal from the grant of a permanent injunction raises fundamental issues concerning the propriety of injunctive relief. 775 F.Supp. 1192 (E.D.Wis.1991). The essential facts are simple. Walgreen has operated a pharmacy in the Southgate Mall in Milwaukee since its opening in 1951. Its current lease, signed in 1971 and carrying a 30–year, 6–month term, contains, as had the only previous lease, a clause in which the landlord, Sara Creek, promises not to lease space in the mall to anyone else who wants to operate a pharmacy or a store containing a pharmacy. . . .

In 1990, fearful that its largest tenant—what in real estate parlance is called the "anchor tenant"—having gone broke was about to close its store, Sara Creek informed Walgreen that it intended to buy out the anchor tenant and install in its place a discount store operated by Phar–Mor Corporation, a "deep discount" chain, rather than, like Walgreen, just a "discount" chain. Phar–Mor's store would occupy 100,000 square feet, of which 12,000 would be occupied by a pharmacy the same size as Walgreen's. The entrances to the two stores would be within a couple of hundred feet of each other.

Walgreen filed this diversity suit for breach of contract against Sara Creek and Phar–Mor and asked for an injunction against Sara Creek's letting the anchor premises to Phar–Mor. After an evidentiary hearing, the judge found a breach of Walgreen's lease and entered a permanent injunction against Sara Creek's letting the anchor tenant premises to Phar–Mor until the expiration of Walgreen's lease. He did this over the defendants' objection that Walgreen had failed to show that its remedy at law—damages—for the breach of the exclusivity clause was inadequate. Sara Creek had put on an expert witness who testified that Walgreen's damages could be readily estimated, and Walgreen had countered with evidence from its employees that its damages would be very difficult to compute, among other reasons because they included intangibles such as loss of goodwill.

Sara Creek reminds us that damages are the norm in breach of contract as in other cases. Many breaches, it points out, are "efficient" in the sense that they allow resources to be moved into a more valuable use. Patton v. Mid–Continent Systems, Inc., 841 F.2d 742, 750–51 (7th Cir.1988). Perhaps this is one—the value of Phar–Mor's occupancy of the anchor premises may exceed the cost to Walgreen of facing increased competition. If so, society will be better off if Walgreen is paid its damages, equal to that cost, and Phar–Mor is allowed to move in rather than being kept out by an injunction. That is why injunctions are not granted as a matter of course, but only when the plaintiff's damages remedy is inadequate. Northern Indiana Public Service Co. v. Carbon County Coal Co., 799 F.2d 265, 279 (7th Cir.1986). Walgreen's is not, Sara Creek argues; the projection of business losses due to increased competition is a routine exercise in calculation. Damages representing either the present value of lost future profits or (what should be the equivalent ...) the diminution in the value of the leasehold have either been awarded or deemed the proper remedy in a number of reported cases for breach of an exclusivity clause in a shopping-center lease.... Why, Sara Creek asks, should they not be adequate here?

Sara Creek makes a beguiling argument that contains much truth, but we do not think it should carry the day. For if, as just noted, damages have been awarded in some cases of breach of an exclusivity clause in a shopping-center lease, injunctions have been issued in others.... The choice between remedies requires a balancing of the costs and benefits of the alternatives. Hecht Co. v. Bowles, 321 U.S. 321, 329, 64 S.Ct. 587, 591, 88 L.Ed. 754 (1944); Yakus v. United States, 321 U.S. 414, 440, 64 S.Ct. 660, 674, 88 L.Ed. 834 (1944). The task of striking the balance is for the trial judge, subject to deferential appellate review in recognition of its particularistic, judgmental, fact-bound character. K–Mart Corp. v. Oriental Plaza, Inc., 875 F.2d 907, 915 (1st Cir.1989). As we said in an appeal from a grant of a preliminary injunction—but the point is applicable to review of a permanent injunction as well—"The question for us [appellate judges] is whether the [district] judge exceeded the bounds of permissible choice in the circumstances, not what we would have done if we had been in his shoes." Roland Machinery Co. v. Dresser Industries, Inc., 749 F.2d 380, 390 (7th Cir.1984).

The plaintiff who seeks an injunction has the burden of persuasion—damages are the norm, so the plaintiff must show why his case is abnormal.... [W]hen, as in this case, the issue is whether to grant a permanent injunction, ... the burden is to show that damages are inadequate....

The benefits of substituting an injunction for damages are twofold. First, it shifts the burden of determining the cost of the defendant's conduct from the court to the parties. If it is true that Walgreen's damages are smaller than the gain to Sara Creek from allowing a second pharmacy into the shopping mall, then there must be a price for dissolving the injunction that will make both parties better off. Thus, the effect of upholding the injunction would be to substitute for the costly processes of forensic fact determination the less costly processes of private negotiation. Second, a premise of our free-market system, and the lesson of experience here and abroad as well, is that prices and costs are more accurately determined by the market than by government. A battle of experts is a less reliable method of determining the actual cost to Walgreen of facing new competition than negotiations between Walgreen and Sara Creek over the price at which Walgreen would feel adequately compensated for having to face that competition.

That is the benefit side of injunctive relief but there is a cost side as well. Many injunctions require continuing supervision by the court, and that is costly.... This ground was ... stressed in Rental Development Corp. v. Lavery, 304 F.2d 839, 841–42 (9th Cir.1962), a case involving a lease. Some injunctions are problematic because they impose costs on third parties. Shondel v. McDermott, 775 F.2d 859, 868 (7th Cir.1985). A more subtle cost of injunctive relief arises from the situation that economists call "bilateral monopoly," in which two parties can deal only with each other: the situation that an injunction creates. Goldstick v. ICM Realty, 788 F.2d 456, 463 (7th Cir.1986) . . . . . The sole seller of widgets selling to the sole buyer of that product would be an example. But so will be the situation confronting Walgreen and Sara Creek if the injunction is upheld. Walgreen can "sell" its injunctive right only to Sara Creek, and Sara Creek can "buy" Walgreen's surrender of its right to enjoin the leasing of the anchor tenant's space to Phar–Mor only from Walgreen. The lack of alternatives in bilateral monopoly creates a bargaining range, and the costs of negotiating to a point within that range may be high. Suppose the cost to Walgreen of facing the competition of Phar–Mor at the Southgate Mall would be $1 million, and the benefit to Sara Creek of leasing to Phar–Mor would be $2 million. Then at any price between those figures for a waiver of Walgreen's injunctive right both parties would be better off, and we expect parties to bargain around a judicial assignment of legal rights if the assignment is inefficient. R.H. Coase, "The Problem of Social Cost," 3 J. Law & Econ. 1 (1960). But each of the parties would like to engross as much of the bargaining range as possible—Walgreen to press the price toward $2 million, Sara Creek to depress it toward $1 million. With so much at stake, both parties will have an incentive to devote substantial resources of time and money to the negotiation process. The process may even break down, if one or both parties want to create for future use a reputation as a hard bargainer; and if it does break down, the injunction will have brought about an inefficient result. All these are in one form or another costs of the injunctive process that can be avoided by substituting damages.

The costs and benefits of the damages remedy are the mirror of those of the injunctive remedy. The damages remedy avoids the cost of continuing supervision and third-party effects, and the cost of bilateral monopoly as well. It imposes costs of its own, however, in the form of diminished accuracy in the determination of value, on the one hand, and of the parties' expenditures on preparing and presenting evidence of damages, and the time of the court in evaluating the evidence, on the other. The weighing up of all these costs and benefits is the analytical procedure that is or at least should be employed by a judge asked to enter a permanent injunction, with the understanding that if the balance is even the injunction should be withheld. The judge is not required to explicate every detail of the analysis and he did not do so here, but as long we are satisfied that his approach is broadly consistent with a proper analysis we shall affirm; and we are satisfied here. The determination of Walgreen's damages would have been costly in forensic resources and inescapably inaccurate. . . . The lease had ten years to run. So Walgreen would have had to project its sales revenues and costs over the next ten years, and then project the impact on those figures of Phar–Mor's competition, and then discount that impact to present value. All but the last step would have been fraught with uncertainty.

. . . It is difficult to forecast the profitability of a retail store over a decade, let alone to assess the impact of a particular competitor on that profitability over that period. Of course one can hire an expert to make such predictions, Glen A. Stankee, "Econometric Forecasting of Lost Profits: Using High Technology to Compute Commercial Damages," 61 Fla.B.J. 83 (1987), and if injunctive relief is infeasible the expert's testimony may provide a tolerable basis for an award of damages. We cited cases in which damages have been awarded for the breach of an exclusivity clause in a shopping-center lease. But they are awarded in such circumstances not because anyone thinks them a clairvoyant forecast but because it is better to give a wronged person a crude remedy than none at all. It is the same theory on which damages are awarded for a disfiguring injury. No one thinks such injuries readily monetizable, City of Panama, 101 U.S. 453, 464, 25 L.Ed. 1061 (1880); McCarty v. Pheasant Run, Inc., 826 F.2d 1554, 1557 (7th Cir.1987); Marcus L. Plant, "Damages for Pain and Suffering," 19 Ohio St.L.J. 200, 205–06 (1958), but a crude estimate is better than letting the wrongdoer get off scot-free (which, not incidentally, would encourage more such injuries). Randall R. Bovbjerg et al., "Valuing Life and Limb in Tort: Scheduling 'Pain and Suffering,' " 83 Nw.U.L.Rev. 908 (1989). Sara Creek presented evidence of what happened (very little) to Walgreen when Phar–Mor moved into other shopping malls in which Walgreen has a pharmacy, and it was on the right track in putting in comparative evidence. But there was a serious question whether the other malls were actually comparable to the Southgate Mall, so we cannot conclude, in the face of the district judge's contrary conclusion, that the existence of comparative evidence dissolved the difficulties of computing damages in this case. Sara Creek complains that the judge refused to compel Walgreen to produce all the data that Sara Creek needed to demonstrate the feasibility of forecasting Walgreen's damages. Walgreen resisted, on grounds of the confidentiality of the data and the cost of producing the massive data that Sara Creek sought. Those are legitimate grounds; and the cost (broadly conceived) they expose of pretrial discovery, in turn presaging complexity at trial, is itself a cost of the damages remedy that injunctive relief saves.

Damages are not always costly to compute, or difficult to compute accurately. In the standard case of a seller's breach of a contract for the sale of goods where the buyer covers by purchasing the same product in the market, damages are readily calculable by subtracting the contract price from the market price and multiplying by the quantity specified in the contract. But this is not such a case and here damages would be a costly and inaccurate remedy; and on the other side of the balance some of the costs of an injunction are absent and the cost that is present seems low. The injunction here, like one enforcing a covenant not to compete (standardly enforced by injunction ..., is a simple negative injunction—Sara Creek is not to lease space in the Southgate Mall to Phar–Mor during the term of Walgreen's lease—and the costs of judicial supervision and enforcement should be negligible. There is no contention that the injunction will harm an unrepresented third party. It may harm Phar–Mor but that harm will be reflected in Sara Creek's offer to Walgreen to dissolve the injunction. (Anyway Phar–Mor is a party.) The injunction may also, it is true, harm potential customers of Phar–Mor—people who would prefer to shop at a deep-discount store than an ordinary discount store—but their preferences, too, are registered indirectly. The more business Phar–Mor would have, the more rent it will be willing to pay Sara Creek, and therefore the more Sara Creek will be willing to pay Walgreen to dissolve the injunction.

The only substantial cost of the injunction in this case is that it may set off a round of negotiations between the parties. In some cases, illustrated by Boomer v. Atlantic Cement Co., 26 N.Y.2d 219, 309 N.Y.S.2d 312, 257 N.E.2d 870 (1970), this consideration alone would be enough to warrant the denial of injunctive relief. The defendant's factory was emitting cement dust that caused the plaintiffs harm monetized at less than $200,000, and the only way to abate the harm would have been to close down the factory, which had cost $45 million to build. An injunction against the nuisance could therefore have created a huge bargaining range (could, not would, because it is unclear what the current value of the factory was), and the costs of negotiating to a point within it might have been immense. If the market value of the factory was actually $45 million, the plaintiffs would be tempted to hold out for a price to dissolve the injunction in the tens of millions and the factory would be tempted to refuse to pay anything more than a few hundred thousand dollars. Negotiations would be unlikely to break down completely, given such a bargaining range, but they might well be protracted and costly. There is nothing so dramatic here. Sara Creek does not argue that it will have to close the mall if enjoined from leasing to Phar–Mor. Phar–Mor is not the only potential anchor tenant. . . .

To summarize, the judge did not exceed the bounds of reasonable judgment in concluding that the costs (including forgone benefits) of the damages remedy would exceed the costs (including forgone benefits) of an injunction. We need not consider whether, as intimated by Walgreen, exclusivity clauses in shopping-center leases should be considered presumptively enforceable by injunctions. Although we have described the choice between legal and equitable remedies as one for case-by-case determination, the courts have sometimes picked out categories of case in which injunctive relief is made the norm. The best-known example is specific performance of contracts for the sale of real property. Anderson v. Onsager, 155 Wis.2d 504, 455 N.W.2d 885 (1990); Okaw Drainage District v. National Distillers & Chemical Corp., 882 F.2d 1241, 1248 (7th Cir.1989); Anthony T. Kronman, "Specific Performance," 45 U.Chi. L.Rev. 351, 355 and n. 20 (1978). The rule that specific performance will be ordered in such cases as a matter of course is a generalization of the considerations discussed above. Because of the absence of a fully liquid market in real property and the frequent presence of subjective values (many a homeowner, for example, would not sell his house for its market value), the calculation of damages is difficult; and since an order of specific performance to convey a piece of property does not create a continuing relation between the parties, the costs of supervision and enforcement if specific performance is ordered are slight. The exclusivity clause in Walgreen's lease relates to real estate, but we hesitate to suggest that every contract involving real estate should be enforceable as a matter of course by injunctions. Suppose Sara Creek had covenanted to keep the entrance to Walgreen's store free of ice and snow, and breached the covenant. An injunction would require continuing supervision, and it would be easy enough if the injunction were denied for Walgreen to hire its own ice and snow remover and charge the cost to Sara Creek. Cf. City of Michigan City v. Lake Air Corp., 459 N.E.2d 760 (Ind.App. 1984). On the other hand, injunctions to enforce exclusivity clauses are quite likely to be justifiable by just the considerations present here—damages are difficult to estimate with any accuracy and the injunction is a one-shot remedy requiring no continuing judicial involvement. So there is an argument for making injunctive relief presumptively appropriate in such cases, but we need not decide in this case how strong an argument.

AFFIRMED.

HARLINGTON WOOD, Jr., Senior Circuit Judge, concurring.

I gladly join in the affirmance reached in Judge Posner's expert analysis.

———

STOKES v. MOORE, 262 Ala. 59, 77 So.2d 331 (1955). Complainants entered into a contract with Stokes, which provided for his employment by them as manager of their business. The contract also provided that if Stokes's employment was terminated for any reason he would not engage in a similar line of business in Mobile for one year immediately following, and that if this covenant was breached "a restraining order or injunction may be issued and entered against me (employee) in any court of equity jurisdiction." The court stated, "We do not wish to express the view that an agreement for the issuance of an injunction, if and when a stipulated state of facts arises in the future, is binding on the court to that extent. Such an agreement would serve to oust the inherent jurisdiction of the court to determine whether an injunction is appropriate when applied for and to require its issuance even though to do so would be contrary to the opinion of the court.... But ... the provision for an injunction is important in its influence upon an exercise of the discretionary power of the court to grant a temporary injunction."

―――――

VAN WAGNER ADVERTISING CORP. v. S & M ENTERPRISES, 67 N.Y.2d 186, 501 N.Y.S.2d 628, 492 N.E.2d 756 (1986). Michaels leased space on the exterior wall of a building to Van Wagner Advertising. Van Wagner was in the business of erecting and leasing billboards, and the parties anticipated that Van Wagner would erect a sign on the leased space, which faced an exit ramp of the Midtown Tunnel in New York City and was therefore visible to vehicles entering Manhattan from the Tunnel. Michaels improperly terminated the contract, and Van Wagner sued for specific performance and damages. The trial court declined to order specific performance, because it found that Van Wagner "has an adequate remedy at law for damages." Affirmed.

"Van Wagner argues that specific performance must be granted in light of the trial court's finding that the 'demised space is unique as to location for the particular advertising purpose intended.' The word 'uniqueness' is not, however, a magic door to specific performance. A distinction must be drawn between physical difference and economic interchangeability. The trial court found that the leased property is physically unique, but so is every parcel of real property and so are many consumer goods. Putting aside contracts for the sale of real property, where specific performance has traditionally been the remedy for breach, uniqueness in the sense of physical difference does not itself dictate the propriety of equitable relief.

"By the same token, at some level all property may be interchangeable with money. Economic theory is concerned with the degree to which consumers are willing to substitute the use of one good for another (see, Kronman, Specific Performance, 45 U.Chi.L.Rev. 351, 359), the underlying assumption being that 'every good has substitutes, even if only very poor ones,' and that 'all goods are ultimately commensurable.' ... Such a view, however, could strip all meaning from uniqueness, for if all goods are ultimately exchangeable for a price, then all goods may be valued. Even a rare manuscript has an economic substitute in that there is a price for which any purchaser would likely agree to give up a right to buy it, but a court would in all probability order specific performance of such a contract on the ground that the subject matter of the contract is unique.

"The point at which breach of a contract will be redressable by specific performance thus must lie not in any inherent physical uniqueness of the property but instead in the uncertainty of valuing it: 'What matters, in measuring money damages, is the volume, refinement, and reliability of the available information about substitutes for the subject matter of the breached contract. When the relevant information is thin and unreliable, there is a substantial risk that an award of money damages will either exceed or fall short of the promisee's actual loss. Of course this risk can always be reduced—but only at great cost when reliable information is difficult to obtain. Conversely, when there is a great deal of consumer behavior generating abundant and highly dependable information about substitutes, the risk of error in measuring the promisee's loss may be reduced at much smaller cost. In asserting that the subject matter of a particular contract is unique and has no established market value, a court is really saying that it cannot obtain, at reasonable cost, enough information about substitutes to permit it to calculate an award of money damages without imposing an unacceptably high risk of undercompensation on the injured promisee. Conceived in this way, the uniqueness test seems economically sound.' (45 U.Chi.L.Rev., at 362.) This principle is reflected in the case law [see, e.g., Erie R.R. Co. v. City of Buffalo, 180 N.Y. 192, 73 N.E. 26], and is essentially the position of the Restatement (Second) of Contracts, which lists 'the difficulty of proving damages with reasonable certainty' as the first factor affecting adequacy of damages (Restatement [Second] of Contracts § 360[a]).

"Thus, the fact that the subject of the contract may be 'unique as to location for the particular advertising purpose intended' by the parties does not entitle a plaintiff to the remedy of specific performance."

UCC §§ 2–709, 2–716

[See Selected Source Materials Supplement]

CISG ARTS. 46, 62

[See Selected Source Materials Supplement]

NOTE ON THE TRADITIONAL RULE CONCERNING SPECIFIC PERFORMANCE OF CONTRACTS FOR THE SALE OF GOODS

Specific performance for contracts for the sale of goods is now largely governed by UCC § 2–716. Official Comment 1 to that Section refers to the "prior policy as to specific performance." The traditional, pre-UCC rule, inherited from the English legal system, was that in a contract for the sale of goods neither the buyer nor the seller could ordinarily get specific performance unless the goods were "unique." The explanation for this result was that monetary relief is normally adequate in a contract for the sale of goods. To take a simple case, if the seller has broken a contract to deliver 100 bushels of wheat to the buyer, the buyer can cover his needs by buying wheat on the market, and in an action at law the cost of cover is the measure of his right to money damages against the seller. On the other hand, where a contract is for the sale of a unique item, such as a painting or an heirloom, cover on the market was by hypothesis not possible, and specific performance would be granted by a court of equity. The next principal case considers the extent to which the traditional rule is modified by the UCC.

LACLEDE GAS CO. v. AMOCO OIL CO.

United States Court of Appeals, Eighth Circuit, 1975.
522 F.2d 33.

Ross, Circuit Judge. [In 1970, Amoco Oil and Laclede Gas (more accurately, the parties' predecessors in interests) entered into a master contract designed to allow Laclede to provide local propane-gas distribution systems to residential developments in Missouri until natural-gas mains were extended to a development. The master contract contemplated that residential developers would apply to Laclede for a local propane system. Laclede could then ask Amoco to supply propane to the development. Laclede would make these requests in supplemental letters whose form was prescribed by the master agreement. If Amoco decided to supply the propane, it would bind itself to do so by signing the letter. Laclede, for its part, agreed to pay Amoco's posted price for propane plus four cents per gallon. Once a letter agreement covering a given residential development was signed, Amoco was bound to deliver propane to Laclede for that development. In 1973, Amoco breached its letter agreements, by refusing to supply further propane. Laclede brought an action for specific performance.]

Generally the determination of whether or not to order specific performance of a contract lies within the sound discretion of the trial court. Landau v. St. Louis Public Service Co., 364 Mo. 1134, 273 S.W.2d 255, 259 (1954). However, this discretion is, in fact, quite limited; and it is said that when certain equitable rules have been met and the contract is fair and plain "specific performance goes as a matter of right." Miller v. Coffeen, 365 Mo. 204, 280 S.W.2d 100, 102 (1955), quoting, Berberet v. Myers, 240 Mo. 58, 77, 144 S.W. 824, 830 (1912). (Emphasis omitted.)

. . . [W]e have carefully reviewed the very complete record on appeal and conclude that the trial court should grant the injunctive relief prayed. We are satisfied that this case falls within that category in which specific performance should be ordered as a matter of right. See Miller v. Coffeen, supra, 280 S.W.2d at 102.

Amoco contends that four of the requirements for specific performance have not been met. Its claims are: (1) there is no mutuality of remedy in the contract; (2) the remedy of specific performance would be difficult for the court to administer without constant and long-continued supervision; (3) the contract is indefinite and uncertain; and (4) the remedy at law available to Laclede is adequate. The first three contentions have little or no merit and do not detain us for long.

There is simply no requirement in the law that both parties be mutually entitled to the remedy of specific performance in order that one of them be given that remedy by the court. . . .

While a court may refuse to grant specific performance where such a decree would require constant and long-continued court supervision, this is merely a discretionary rule of decision which is frequently ignored when the public interest is involved. See, e.g., Joy v. St. Louis, 138 U.S. 1, 47, 11 S.Ct. 243, 34 L.Ed. 843 (1891); Western Union Telegraph Co. v. Pennsylvania Co., 129 F. 849, 869 (3d Cir.1904). . . .

Here the public interest in providing propane to the retail customers is manifest, while any supervision required will be far from onerous.

Section 370 of the Restatement, Contracts (1932) provides:

Specific enforcement will not be decreed unless the terms of the contract are so expressed that the court can determine with reasonable certainty what is the duty of each party and the conditions under which performance is due.

We believe these criteria have been satisfied here. As discussed in part I of this opinion, as to all developments for which a supplemental agreement has been signed, Amoco is to supply all the propane which is reasonably foreseeably required, while Laclede is to purchase the required propane from Amoco and pay the contract price therefor. The parties have disagreed over what is meant by "Wood River Area Posted Price" in the agreement, but the district court can and should determine with reasonable certainty what the parties intended by this term and should mold its decree, if necessary accordingly.[3] Likewise, the fact that the agreement does not have a definite time of duration is not fatal since the evidence established that the last subdivision should be converted to natural gas in 10 to 15 years. This sets a reasonable time limit on performance and the district court can and should mold the final decree to reflect this testimony.

It is axiomatic that specific performance will not be ordered when the party claiming breach of contract has an adequate remedy at law. Jamison Coal & Coke Co. v. Goltra, 143 F.2d 889, 894 (8th Cir.), cert. denied, 323 U.S. 769, 65 S.Ct. 122, 89 L.Ed. 615 (1944). This is especially true when the contract involves personal property as distinguished from real estate.

However, in Missouri, as elsewhere, specific performance may be ordered even though personalty is involved in the "proper circumstances." Mo.Rev. Stat. § 400.2–716(1); Restatement, Contracts, supra, § 361. And a remedy at law adequate to defeat the grant of specific performance "must be as certain, prompt, complete, and efficient to attain the ends of justice as a decree of specific performance." National Marking Mach. Co. v. Triumph Mfg. Co., 13 F.2d 6, 9 (8th Cir.1926). Accord, Snip v. City of Lamar, 239 Mo.App. 824, 201 S.W.2d 790, 798 (1947).

---

3. The record indicates that Laclede has now accepted Amoco's interpretation and has agreed that "Wood River Area Posted Price" means Amoco's posted price for propane at its Wood River refinery.

One of the leading Missouri cases allowing specific performance of a contract relating to personalty because the remedy at law was inadequate is Boeving v. Vandover, 240 Mo.App. 117, 218 S.W.2d 175, 178 (1949). In that case the plaintiff sought specific performance of a contract in which the defendant had promised to sell him an automobile. At that time (near the end of and shortly after World War II) new cars were hard to come by, and the court held that specific performance was a proper remedy since a new car "could not be obtained elsewhere except at considerable expense, trouble or loss, which cannot be estimated in advance."

We are satisfied that Laclede has brought itself within this practical approach taken by the Missouri courts. As Amoco points out, Laclede has propane immediately available to it under other contracts with other suppliers. And the evidence indicates that at the present time propane is readily available on the open market. However, this analysis ignores the fact that the contract involved in this lawsuit is for a long-term supply of propane to these subdivisions. The other two contracts under which Laclede obtains the gas will remain in force only until March 31, 1977, and April 1, 1981, respectively; and there is no assurance that Laclede will be able to receive any propane under them after that time. Also it is unclear as to whether or not Laclede can use the propane obtained under these contracts to supply the Jefferson County subdivisions, since they were originally entered into to provide Laclede with propane with which to "shave" its natural gas supply during peak demand periods.[4] Additionally, there was uncontradicted expert testimony that Laclede probably could not find another supplier of propane willing to enter into a long-term contract such as the Amoco agreement, given the uncertain future of worldwide energy supplies. And, even if Laclede could obtain supplies of propane for the affected developments through its present contracts or newly negotiated ones, it would still face considerable expense and trouble which cannot be estimated in advance in making arrangements for its distribution to the subdivisions.

Specific performance is the proper remedy in this situation, and it should be granted by the district court.

CONCLUSION

For the foregoing reasons the judgment of the district court is reversed and the cause is remanded for the fashioning of appropriate injunctive relief in the form of a decree of specific performance as to those developments for which a supplemental agreement form has been signed by the parties.

WEATHERSBY v. GORE, 556 F.2d 1247 (5th Cir.1977). On March 6, 1973, Weathersby made a contract with Gore, a farmer, under which Gore agreed to sell Weathersby the cotton that Gore produced on 500 acres of land during the 1973 crop year, at 30 cents per pound. On May 3, Gore gave notice that he was cancelling the contract on the ground that Weathersby had failed to provide a required payment bond. Weathersby could have covered, then or later, but did not.

---

4. During periods of cold weather, when demand is high, Laclede does not receive enough natural gas to meet all this demand. It, therefore, adds propane to the natural gas it places in its distribution system. This practice is called "peak shaving."

Soon after the May 3 cancellation, cotton was selling for around 35 cents. On September 28, Weathersby sued for specific performance. By this time cotton had soared to 80 cents. The trial court found that Gore had breached the contract, and ordered specific performance. The Court of Appeals remanded for consideration of the issue whether Weathersby had furnished the bond within a reasonable time, but held that even if Gore had breached the contract, Weathersby was not entitled to specific performance.

"... The parties are in considerable disagreement over the meaning of [UCC § 2–716(1)]: 'Specific performance may be decreed where the goods are unique or in other proper circumstances.' Various authorities have been cited to the court indicating that crop contracts historically have been treated as susceptible to specific performance treatment more readily than other types of contracts.... However, cotton contracts have not been given such treatment in Mississippi when other cotton was readily available on the open market....

"... Other than to indicate that the Code is intended to 'further a more liberal attitude than some courts have shown in connection with the specific performance of contracts of sale,' the comments accompanying UCC § 2–716 are of little guidance. The comments also state that '[o]utput and requirements contracts involving a particularly or peculiarly available source of market present today the typical commercial specific performance situation,' but the interpretation of this language appears to range from suggesting all output contracts should be specifically enforceable to a mere observation that output contracts form a suitable factual background in most cases in which specific performance may be sought.

"The general rule applicable when specific performance is requested has been stated in Roberts v. Spence, 209 So.2d 623, 626 (Miss.1968): 'Specific performance of a contract will not be awarded where damages may be recovered and the remedy in a court of law is adequate to compensate the injured party.' ... Weathersby was adequately protected from any damages occasioned by Gore's breach of the contract, if any occurred. He could have acquired additional cotton on the open market when Gore informed him he would no longer perform under the contract. He did not do so and thus, if entitled to damages at all, must settle for the difference between the contract and the market price at the time Gore cancelled."

NOTE ON SPECIFIC PERFORMANCE OF CONTRACTS FOR THE SALE OF LAND AND EMPLOYMENT CONTRACTS

1. Contracts for the sale of land. It is well settled that in a contract for sale of land, the buyer can get a decree specifically ordering the seller to execute a deed in his favor. In most states, the seller can also get a decree ordering the buyer to take title to the land and pay the agreed price. Restatement Second § 360, Comment e.

The traditional rationale of the rule that a *buyer* of land can get specific performance has been that damages are inadequate in such cases because: (1) The value of land is always to some extent conjectural, since land usually does not have a clearly defined market price; and (2) Every piece of land is to some extent unique, and therefore the buyer cannot with an award of money damages go out on the market and buy a piece of land exactly like that promised him by the defaulting seller. Statutes now provide for self-executing decrees in such cases; such a decree has the effect of a deed, and can be recorded in the Registry of Deeds.

Today, the concept that every piece of real property is unique seems questionable. A few cases recognize this reality and criticize the traditional rule. For example, in Semelhago v. Paramadevan, [1996] 136 D.L.R. (4th) 1, decided by the Canadian Supreme Court, the seller breached a contract to sell a home. Although the case did not involve a decree of specific performance, the court forcefully pointed out that not all real estate is unique:

> While at one time the common law regarded every piece of real estate to be unique, with the progress of modern real estate development this is no longer the case. Both residential, business and industrial properties are mass produced much in the same way as other consumer products. If a deal falls through for one property, another is frequently, though not always, readily available. It is no longer appropriate, therefore, to maintain a distinction in the approach to specific performance as between realty and personalty. It cannot be assumed that damages for breach of contract for the purchase and sale of real estate will be an inadequate remedy in all cases. . . .

Similarly, in Watkins v. Paul, 95 Idaho 499, 511 P.2d 781 (1973), the court refused, on similar grounds, to order specific performance of an option to purchase a tract of land:

> The evidence fails to show that the plaintiffs need the land in question for any particular, unique purpose, which is one of the main reasons for granting specific performance; on the contrary, the plaintiffs' own evidence shows that they seek to obtain the land only so that they may resell it for profit. Under these circumstances, specific performance would bring the plaintiffs no greater relief than would damages in the amount of their lost profit.

The *seller's* right to specific performance was often rested on the "affirmative doctrine of mutuality of remedy"—that since the buyer can sue for specific performance, the seller should have a corresponding remedy. That doctrine is now generally discredited; better reasons are the uncertainty of damages measured by the difference between the contract price and the value of the land, and the need for a formal termination of the buyer's interest in the land to facilitate its resale. Partly because constitutional provisions forbid imprisonment for debt, a decree in favor of the seller ordering the buyer to pay money is not ordinarily enforced by contempt. Instead, the decree provides that if the money is not paid by a certain time, the right of the buyer to "redeem" the land by paying the debt is to be cut off, or "foreclosed."

2. Employment contracts. Employment contracts are not specifically enforced at the suit of either the employee or the employer. Restatement Second § 367(1). The objections to specific performance here do not lie in a notion that monetary relief is an adequate substitute for the promised performance. Rather, they stem from a belief that it is unwise to attempt to extract, from an unwilling party, a performance involving personal relations. In some cases, the courts, although they will not order the employee to work for the employer, will enjoin the employee from working for a competitor

Often, such an injunction could be tantamount to ordering specific perform-ance, because if the employee cannot work for a competitor, she will not be able to earn a living, and therefore will be indirectly forced to work for her original employer. Accordingly, Restatement Second § 367(2) adopts the rule that "[a] promise to render personal service exclusively for one employer will not be enforced by an injunction against serving another if its probable result will be to compel a performance involving personal relations the enforced continuance of which is undesirable or will be to leave the employee without other reasonable means of making a living."

———

Chapter 8

THE RELIANCE AND RESTITUTION MEASURES

This Chapter considers two damage measures that may be used in a bargain context as an alternative to the expectation measure.

Section 1 concerns the reliance measure as a remedy for breach in a bargain context. (Recall from Chapter 1 that the reliance measure may also be used in a donative context.) As pointed out earlier, the name of this measure is something of a misnomer. Calling it the *cost* measure would be more accurate, and would make it easier to understand the measure's dynamics.

Section 2(a) concerns the restitution measure as a remedy for breach of a bargain contract.

Section 2(b) concerns restitution in favor of a person who is herself in breach.

SECTION 1. RELIANCE DAMAGES IN A BARGAIN CONTEXT

SECURITY STOVE & MFG. CO. v. AMERICAN RYS. EXPRESS CO.

Kansas City Court of Appeals, Missouri, 1932.
227 Mo.App. 175, 51 S.W.2d 572.

BLAND, J. This is an action for damages for the failure of defendant to transport, from Kansas City to Atlantic City, New Jersey, within a reasonable time, a furnace equipped with a combination oil and gas burner. The cause was tried before the court without the aid of a jury, resulting in a judgment in favor of plaintiff in the sum of $801.50 and interest, or in a total sum of $1,000.00. Defendant has appealed.

The facts show that plaintiff manufactured a furnace equipped with a special combination oil and gas burner it desired to exhibit at the American

Gas Association Convention held in Atlantic City in October, 1926. The president of plaintiff testified that plaintiff engaged space for the exhibit for the reason "that the Henry L. Dougherty Company was very much interested in putting out a combination oil and gas burner; we had just developed one, after we got through, better than anything on the market and we thought this show would be the psychological time to get in contact with the Dougherty Company"; that "the thing wasn't sent there for sale but primarily to show"; that at the time the space was engaged it was too late to ship the furnace by freight so plaintiff decided to ship it by express, and, on September 18th, 1926, wrote the office of the defendant in Kansas City, stating that it had engaged a booth for exhibition purposes at Atlantic City, New Jersey, from the American Gas Association, for the week beginning October 11th; that its exhibit consisted of an oil burning furnace, together with two oil burners which weighed at least 1,500 pounds; that, "In order to get this exhibit in place on time it should be in Atlantic City not later than October the 8th. What we want you to do is to tell us how much time you will require to assure the delivery of the exhibit on time."

Mr. Bangs, chief clerk in charge of the local office of the defendant, upon receipt of the letter, sent Mr. Johnson, a commercial representative of the defendant, to see plaintiff. Johnson called upon plaintiff taking its letter with him. Johnson made a notation on the bottom of the letter giving October 4th, as the day that defendant was required to have the exhibit in order for it to reach Atlantic City on October 8th.

On October 1st, plaintiff wrote the defendant at Kansas City, referring to its letter of September 18th, concerning the fact that the furnace must be in Atlantic City not later than October 8th, and stating what Johnson had told it, saying: "Now Mr. Bangs, we want to make doubly sure that this shipment is in Atlantic City not later than October 8th and the purpose of this letter is to tell you that you can *have your truck call for the shipment between 12 and 1 o'clock on Saturday, October 2nd for this.*" (Italics plaintiff's.) On October 2nd, plaintiff called the office of the express company in Kansas City and told it that the shipment was ready. Defendant came for the shipment on the last mentioned day, received it and delivered the express receipt to plaintiff. The shipment contained 21 packages. Each package was marked with stickers backed with glue and covered with silica of soda, to prevent the stickers being torn off in shipping. Each package was given a number. They ran from 1 to 21.

Plaintiff's president made arrangements to go to Atlantic City to attend the convention and install the exhibit, arriving there about October 11th. When he reached Atlantic City he found the shipment had been placed in the booth that had been assigned to plaintiff. The exhibit was set up, but it was found that one of the packages shipped was not there. This missing package contained the gas manifold, or that part of the oil and gas burner that controlled the flow of gas in the burner. This was the most important part of the exhibit and a like burner could not be obtained in Atlantic City.

Wires were sent and it was found that the stray package was at the "over and short bureau" of defendant in St. Louis. Defendant reported that the package would be forwarded to Atlantic City and would be there by Wednesday, the 13th. Plaintiff's president waited until Thursday, the day the convention closed, but the package had not arrived at the time, so he closed up the exhibit and left. About a week after he arrived in Kansas City, the package was returned by the defendant. . . .

The petition upon which the case was tried alleges that "... relying upon defendant's promise and the promises of its agents and servants, that said parcels would be delivered at Atlantic City by October 8th, 1926, if delivered to defendant by October 4th, 1926, plaintiff herein hired space for an exhibit at the American Gas Association Convention at Atlantic City, and planned for an exhibit at said Convention and sent men in the employ of this plaintiff to Atlantic City to install, show and operate said exhibit, and that these men were in Atlantic City ready to set up this plaintiff's exhibit at the American Gas Association Convention on October 8th, 1926." ...

Plaintiff asked damages, which the court in its judgment allowed as follows: $147.00 express charges (on the exhibit); $45.12 freight on the exhibit from Atlantic City to Kansas City; $101.39 railroad and pullman fares to and from Atlantic City, expended by plaintiff's president and a workman taken by him to Atlantic City; $48.00 hotel room for the two; $150.00 for the time of the president; $40.00 for wages of plaintiff's other employee and $270.00 for rental of the booth, making a total of $801.51. . . .

We think, under the circumstances in this case, that it was proper to allow plaintiff's expenses as its damages. Ordinarily the measure of damages where the carrier fails to deliver a shipment at destination within a reasonable time is the difference between the market value of the goods at the time of the delivery and the time when they should have been delivered. But where the carrier has notice of peculiar circumstances under which the shipment is made, which will result in an unusual loss by the shipper in case of delay in delivery, the carrier is responsible for the real damage sustained from such delay if the notice given is of such character, and goes to such extent, in informing the carrier of the shipper's situation, that the carrier will be presumed to have contracted with reference thereto. Central Trust Co. of New York v. Savannah & W.R. Co. (C.C.) 69 F. 683, 685. . . .

Defendant contends that plaintiff "is endeavoring to achieve a return of the status quo in a suit based on a breach of contract. Instead of seeking to recover what he would have had, had the contract not been broken, plaintiff is trying to recover what he would have had, had there never been any contract of shipment"; that the expenses sued for would have been incurred in any event. It is no doubt, the general rule that where there is a breach of contract the party suffering the loss can recover only that which he would have had, had the contract not been broken, and this is all the cases decided upon which defendant relies, including C., M. & St. P. Ry. v. McCaull–Dinsmore Co., 253 U.S. 97, 100, 40 S.Ct. 504, 64 L.Ed. 801. But this is merely a general statement of the rule and is not inconsistent with the holdings that, in some instances, the injured party may recover expenses incurred in relying upon the contract, although such expenses would have been incurred had the contract not been breached. See Morrow v. Railroad, 140 Mo.App. 200, 212, 213, 123 S.W. 1034; Bryant v. Barton, 32 Neb. 613, 616, 49 N.W. 331; Woodbury v. Jones, 44 N.H. 206; Driggs v. Dwight, 17 Wend. (N.Y.) 71, 31 Am.Dec. 283.

In Sperry et al. v. O'Neill–Adams Co. (C.C.A.) 185 F. 231, the court held that the advantages resulting from the use of trading stamps as a means of increasing trade are so contingent that they cannot form a basis on which to rest a recovery for a breach of contract to supply them. In lieu of compensation based thereon the court directed a recovery in the sum expended in preparation for carrying on business in connection with the use of the stamps. The court said, loc. cit. 239:

> "Plaintiff in its complaint had made a claim for lost profits, but, finding it impossible to marshal any evidence which would support a finding of exact figures, abandoned that claim. Any attempt to reach a precise sum would be mere blind guesswork. Nevertheless a contract, which both sides conceded would prove a valuable one, had been broken and the party who broke it was responsible for resultant damage. In order to carry out this contract, the plaintiff made expenditures which otherwise it would not have made.... The trial judge held, as we think rightly, that plaintiff was entitled at least to recover these expenses to which it had been put in order to secure the benefits of a contract of which defendant's conduct deprived it." ...

The case at bar was [not] to recover damages for loss of profits by reason of the failure of the defendant to transport the shipment within a reasonable time, so that it would arrive in Atlantic City for the exhibit. There were no profits contemplated. The furnace was to be shown and shipped back to Kansas City. There was no money loss, except the expenses, that was of such a nature as any court would allow as being sufficiently definite or lacking in pure speculation. Therefore, unless plaintiff is permitted to recover the expenses that it went to, which were a total loss to it by reason of its inability to exhibit the furnace and equipment, it will be deprived of any substantial compensation for its loss. The law does not contemplate any such injustice. It ought to allow plaintiff, as damages, the loss in the way of expenses that it sustained, and which it would not have been put to if it had not been for its reliance upon the defendant to perform its contract. There is no contention that the exhibit would have been entirely valueless and whatever it might have accomplished defendant knew of the circumstances and ought to respond for whatever damages plaintiff suffered. In cases of this kind the method of estimating the damages should be adopted which is the most definite and certain and which best achieves the fundamental purpose of compensation. 17 C.J. p. 846; Miller v. Robertson, 266 U.S. 243, 257, 45 S.Ct. 73, 78, 69 L.Ed. 265. Had the exhibit been shipped in order to realize a profit on sales and such profits could have been realized, or to be entered in competition for a prize, and plaintiff failed to show loss of profits with sufficient definiteness, or that he would have won the prize, defendant's cases might be in point. But as before stated, no such situation exists here.

While it is true that plaintiff already had incurred some of these expenses, in that it had rented space at the exhibit before entering into the contract with defendant for the shipment of the exhibit and this part of plaintiff's damages, in a sense, arose out of a circumstance which transpired before the contract was even entered into, yet, plaintiff arranged for the exhibit knowing that it could call upon defendant to perform its common law duty to accept and transport the shipment with reasonable dispatch. The whole damage, therefore, was suffered in contemplation of defendant performing its contract, which it failed to do, and would not have been sustained except for the reliance by plaintiff upon defendant to perform it. It can, therefore, be fairly said that the damages or loss suffered by plaintiff grew out of the breach of the contract, for had the shipment arrived on time, plaintiff would have had the benefit of the contract, which was contemplated by all parties, defendant being advised of the purpose of the shipment.

The judgment is affirmed.

All concur.

———

ANGLIA TELEVISION LTD. v. REED, [1971] 3 All.E.R. 690 (C.A. 1971) (Lord Denning). Anglia Television Ltd wanted to make a film for television entitled "The Man in the Wood," which portrayed an American man married to an English woman. Before Anglia selected the leading man, it arranged for a place where the filming was to occur; employed a director, a designer, and a stage manager; and involved itself in much expense. For the leading man, Anglia required a strong actor capable of holding the film together. It eventually decided upon Robert Reed, an American with a very high reputation as an actor, and by telephone conversation the parties agreed that Reed would come to England and star in the film for a fee of $581,050 and expenses. Because of a mixup on his bookings, Reed later repudiated the contract. Anglia tried hard to find a substitute but could not do so, and abandoned the film. It then sued Reed for its out-of-pocket expenses on the film of $582,750, including almost $581,900 incurred before the contract was made. Held, Anglia was entitled to recover all of its expenses:

> [I]t is plain that, when Mr. Reed entered into this contract, he must have known perfectly well that much expenditure had already been incurred on director's fees and the like. He must have contemplated—or, at any rate, it is reasonably to be imputed to him—that if he broke his contract, all that expenditure would be wasted, whether or not it was incurred before or after the contract. He must pay damages for all the expenditure so wasted and thrown away.... It is true that, if the defendant had never entered into the contract, he would not be liable, and the expenditure would have been incurred by the plaintiff without redress; but, the defendant having made his contract and broken it, it does not lie in his mouth to say he is not liable, when it was because of his breach that the expenditure has been wasted.

———

BEEFY TRAIL, INC. v. BEEFY KING INT'L, INC., 267 So.2d 853 (Fla.Dist.App.1972) (Owen, J., concurring in part and dissenting in part). "Essentially, the rationale [for granting reliance damages in a bargain context] is this: Normally, had the contract's performance not been prevented by the defendant, and the contract had been a profitable one for the plaintiff, the plaintiff would have recovered over the life of the contract a gain, sufficient not only to fully reimburse him for his expenditures, but also to yield an excess which would be the profit. Since the amount of the gross receipts (i.e., the gain) cannot be determined with the requisite degree of certainty, the amount of the profit cannot be determined and therefore cannot be allowed in the recovery. *But the amount of the gain which would have reimbursed plaintiff for the expenditures incurred in preparation and part performance* *can be determined by and to the extent of these expenditures,* and therefore *this amount can be allowed in the recovery."* (Emphasis in original.)

L. ALBERT & SON v. ARMSTRONG RUBBER CO., 178 F.2d 182 (2d Cir.1949) (L. Hand, J.). Seller agreed to sell to Buyer four machines designed to recondition old rubber. Seller breached the contract, and Buyer claimed as damages the expenses that it had incurred in reliance upon Seller's promise, including the $3000 cost of a foundation that it had laid for the machines. In the course of his opinion, Hand discussed as follows the issues involved by the possibility that if the contract had been completed it would have resulted in a loss to the plaintiff:

> ... The Buyer ... asserts that it is ... entitled to recover the cost of the foundation upon the theory that what it expended in reliance upon the Seller's performance was a recoverable loss. In cases where the venture would have proved profitable to the promisee, there is no reason why he should not recover his expenses. On the other hand, on those occasions in which the performance would not have covered the promisee's outlay, such a result imposes the risk of the promisee's contract upon the promisor.... It is often very hard to learn what the value of the performance would have been; and it is a common expedient, and a just one, in such situations to put the peril of the answer upon that party who by his wrong has made the issue relevant to the rights of the other. On principle therefore the proper solution would seem to be that the promisee may recover his outlay in preparation for the performance, subject to the privilege of the promisor to reduce it by as much as he can show that the promisee would have lost, if the contract had been performed....

C.C.C. FILMS (LONDON) V. IMPACT QUADRANT FILMS LTD., [1985] 1 Q.B. 16. The court here considered the following issue: If a plaintiff seeks reliance damages in lieu of expectation damages for lost profits because the amount of lost profits is too uncertain, which party has the burden of proving whether the plaintiff would have had any profits if the contract had been performed? Hutchinson, J., held that the burden of proof should be on the defendant. "[I]n those cases where the plaintiff's decision to base his claim on abortive expenditure was dictated by the practical impossibility of proving loss of profit rather than by unfettered choice, [placing the burden of proof on the plaintiff] would largely, if not entirely, defeat the object of allowing this alternative method of formulating the claim. This is because, notwithstanding the distinction ... between proving a loss of net profit and proving in general terms the probability of sufficient returns to cover expenditure, in the majority of contested cases impossibility of proof of the first would probably involve like impossibility in the case of the second. It appears to me to be eminently fair that in such cases where the plaintiff has by the defendant's breach been prevented from exploiting ... the right contracted for and, therefore, putting to the test the question of whether he would have recouped his expenditure, the general rule as to the onus of proof of damage should be modified in this manner.''

SULLIVAN v. O'CONNOR

Chapter 1, supra

D & G STOUT, INC. v. BACARDI IMPORTS, INC.

Chapter 1, supra

WALTERS v. MARATHON OIL CO.

Chapter 1, supra

WESTSIDE GALVANIZING SERVICES, INC. v. GEORGIA–PACIFIC CORP., 921 F.2d 735 (8th Cir.1990). In 1987, Georgia–Pacific determined to build a chip-thickness screening facility at one of its paper mills. Southeastern contracted with Georgia–Pacific to furnish steel for the project, and Westside contracted with Southeastern to galvanize the steel before it was shipped. Westside was to ship the galvanized steel directly to the Georgia–Pacific worksite, but was to send its galvanizing invoices to Southeastern for payment.

Southeastern began defaulting on its contracts with both Georgia–Pacific and Westside. As a result, Westside stopped shipping the galvanized steel to Georgia–Pacific. However, Georgia–Pacific persuaded Westside to ship the steel in Westside's possession by indicating that Georgia–Pacific would make sure that Westside got paid.

Westside was not paid by either Southeastern or Georgia–Pacific, and sued Georgia–Pacific for the amount due to Westside from Southeastern, on the theory that Westside's action in shipping the galvanized steel to Georgia–Pacific, in reliance on Georgia–Pacific's promise that Westside would be paid, made the promise enforceable. Held, Westside could sue Georgia–Pacific, but only for its reliance damages, measured by the value of shipments made after Georgia–Pacific's promise, not for all of Southeastern's obligation to Westside.

''Westside contends that its claim for detrimental reliance should not be limited to the value of the shipment made after Georgia–Pacific promised Westside 'would be paid' and that it is entitled to recover the unpaid balance in full. Under Arkansas law, the relief awarded under the theory of detrimental reliance need not extend to the full amount stated in the representation.... As stated in Restatement (Second) of Contracts '90 comment d (1981), 'relief may sometimes be limited to restitution or to damages or specific relief measured by the extent of the promisee's reliance rather than by the terms of the promise.' " ...

SECTION 2. THE RESTITUTION MEASURE

The term "restitution" has both a substantive and a remedial sense. Substantively, restitution refers to the recapture of a benefit conferred on the defendant by the plaintiff, the retention of which would leave the defendant unjustly enriched. Remedially, restitution refers to remedies, including money remedies, that are based on the amount of a defendant's unjust enrichment.

(a) Restitutionary Damages for Breach of Contract

OSTEEN v. JOHNSON

Colorado Court of Appeals, 1970.
473 P.2d 184.

DUFFORD, JUDGE ... This was an action for breach of an oral contract. Trial was to the court, which found that the plaintiffs had paid the sum of $2,500. In exchange, the defendant had agreed to "promote" the plaintiffs' daughter, Linda Osteen, as a singer and composer of country-western music. More specifically, it was found that the defendant had agreed to advertise Linda through various mailings for a period of one year; to arrange and furnish the facilities necessary for Linda to record several songs; to prepare two records from the songs recorded; to press and mail copies of one of the records to disc jockeys throughout the country; and, if the first record met with any success, to press and mail out copies of the second record.

The trial court further found that the defendant did arrange for several recording sessions, at which Linda recorded four songs. A record was prepared of two of the songs, and 1,000 copies of the record were then pressed. Of the pressed records, 340 copies were mailed to disc jockeys, 200 were sent to the plaintiffs, and the remainder were retained by the defendant. Various mailings were made to advertise Linda; flyers were sent to disc jockeys throughout the country; and Linda's professional name was advertised in trade magazines. The record sent out received a favorable review and a high rating in a trade magazine.

Upon such findings the trial court concluded that the defendant had substantially performed the agreement. However, a judgment was entered in favor of the plaintiffs in the sum of $1.00 and costs on the basis that the defendant had wrongfully caused the name of another party to appear on the label of the record as co-author of a song which had been written solely by

Linda. The trial court also ordered the defendant to deliver to the plaintiffs certain master tapes and records in the defendant's possession.

1. RIGHT OF RESTITUTION

Although plaintiffs' reasons are not clearly defined, they argue here that the award of damages is inadequate, and that the trial court erred in concluding that the defendant had substantially performed the agreement. However, no evidence was presented during the trial of the matter upon which an award of other than nominal damages could be based. In our opinion, the remedy which plaintiffs proved and upon which they can rely is that of restitution. See 5 A. Corbin, Contracts § 996. This remedy is available where there has been a contract breach of vital importance, variously defined as a substantial breach or a breach which goes to the essence of the contract. See 5 A. Corbin, Contracts § 1104, where the author writes:

> "In the case of a breach by non-performance, . . . the injured party's alternative remedy by way of restitution depends upon the extent of the non-performance by the defendant. The defendant's breach may be nothing but a failure to perform some minor part of his contractual duty. Such a minor non-performance is a breach of contract and an action for damages can be maintained. The injured party, however, can not maintain an action for restitution of what he has given the defendant unless the defendant's non-performance is so material that it is held to go to the 'essence'. . . . A minor breach by one party does not discharge the contractual duty of the other party; and the latter being still bound to perform as agreed can not be entitled to the restitution of payments already made by him or to the value of other part performances rendered." . . .

2. BREACH OF CONTRACT

The essential question here then becomes whether any breach on the part of the defendant is substantial enough to justify the remedy of restitution. Plaintiffs argue that the defendant breached the contract in the following ways: First, the defendant did not promote Linda for a period of one year as agreed; secondly, the defendant wrongfully caused the name of another party to appear on the label as co-author of the song which had been composed solely by Linda; and thirdly, the defendant failed to press and mail out copies of the second record as agreed.

The first argument is not supported by the record. Plaintiffs brought the action within the one-year period for which the contract was to run. There was no evidence that during this period the defendant had not continued to promote Linda through the use of mailings and advertisements. Quite obviously the mere fact that the one-year period had not ended prior to the commencement of the action does not justify the conclusion that the defendant had breached the agreement. Plaintiffs' second argument overlooks the testimony offered on behalf of the defendant that listing the other party as co-author of the song would make it more likely that the record would be played by disc jockeys.

The plaintiffs' third argument does, however, have merit. It is clear from the record and the findings of the trial court that the first record had met with some success. It is also clear that copies of the second record were neither pressed nor mailed out. In our opinion the failure of the defendant to press and mail out copies of the second record after the first had achieved some success constituted a substantial breach of the contract and, therefore, justifies the remedy of restitution. Seale v. Bates, 145 Colo. 430, 359 P.2d 356; Colorado Management Corp. v. American Founders Life Insurance Co., 145 Colo. 413, 359 P.2d 665; Bridges v. Ingram, 122 Colo. 501, 223 P.2d 1051. Both parties agree that the essence of their contract was to publicize Linda as a singer of western songs and to make her name and talent known to the public. Defendant admitted and asserted that the primary method of achieving this end was to have records pressed and mailed to disc jockeys. . . .

3. DETERMINING DAMAGES

It is clear that the defendant did partially perform the contract and, under applicable law, should be allowed compensation for the reasonable value of his services. See 5 A. Corbin, Contracts § 1114, where the author writes:

> "[A]ll courts are in agreement that restitution by the defendant will not be enforced unless the plaintiff returns in some way what he has received as a part performance by the defendant."

It shall, therefore, be the ultimate order of this court that prior to restoring to the plaintiffs the $2,500 paid by them to the defendant further proceedings be held during which the trial court shall determine the reasonable value of the services which the defendant rendered on plaintiffs' behalf.

The judgment is reversed, and this case is remanded with directions that a new trial be held to determine the one issue of the amount to which the plaintiffs are entitled by way of restitution. Such amount shall be the $2,500 paid by plaintiffs to defendant less the reasonable value of the services which the defendant performed on behalf of plaintiffs.

COYTE and PIERCE, JJ., concur.

RESTATEMENT, SECOND, CONTRACTS §§ 344, 345, 370, 371

[See Selected Source Materials Supplement]

RESTATEMENT, SECOND, CONTRACTS § 370, ILLUSTRATIONS 2, 5

2. A contracts to sell B a machine for $100,000. After A has spent $40,000 on the manufacture of the machine but before its completion, B repudiates the contract. A cannot get restitution of the $40,000 because no benefit was conferred on B. . . .

5. A, a social worker, promises B to render personal services to C in return for B's promise to educate A's children. B repudiates the contract after A has rendered part of the services. A can get restitution from B for the services, even though they were not rendered to B, because they conferred a benefit on B. . . .

UNITED STATES v. ALGERNON BLAIR, INC.

United States Court of Appeals, Fourth Circuit, 1973.
479 F.2d 638.

CRAVEN, CIRCUIT JUDGE. May a subcontractor, who justifiably ceases work under a contract because of the prime contractor's breach, recover in quantum meruit the value of labor and equipment already furnished pursuant to the contract irrespective of whether he would have been entitled to recover in a suit on the contract? We think so, and, for reasons to be stated, the decision of the district court will be reversed.

The subcontractor, Coastal Steel Erectors, Inc., brought this action under the provisions of the Miller Act, 40 U.S.C.A. § 270a et seq., in the name of the United States against Algernon Blair, Inc., and its surety, United States Fidelity and Guaranty Company. Blair had entered a contract with the United States for the construction of a naval hospital in Charleston County, South Carolina. Blair had then contracted with Coastal to perform certain steel erection and supply certain equipment in conjunction with Blair's contract with the United States. Coastal commenced performance of its obligations, supplying its own cranes for handling and placing steel. Blair refused to pay for crane rental, maintaining that it was not obligated to do so under the subcontract. Because of Blair's failure to make payments for crane rental, and after completion of approximately 28 percent of the subcontract, Coastal terminated its performance. Blair then proceeded to complete the job with a new subcontractor. Coastal brought this action to recover for labor and equipment furnished.

The district court found that the subcontract required Blair to pay for crane use and that Blair's refusal to do so was such a material breach as to justify Coastal's terminating performance. This finding is not questioned on appeal. The court then found that under the contract the amount due Coastal, less what had already been paid, totaled approximately $37,000. Additionally, the court found Coastal would have lost more than $37,000 if it had completed performance. Holding that any amount due Coastal must be reduced by any loss it would have incurred by complete performance of the contract, the court denied recovery to Coastal. While the district court correctly stated the " 'normal' rule of contract damages,"[1] we think Coastal is entitled to recover in quantum meruit.

In United States for Use of Susi Contracting Co. v. Zara Contracting Co., 146 F.2d 606 (2d Cir.1944), a Miller Act action, the court was faced with a situation similar to that involved here—the prime contractor had unjustifiably breached a subcontract after partial performance by the subcontractor. The court stated:

> For it is an accepted principle of contract law, often applied in the case of construction contracts, that the promisee upon breach has the option to forego any suit on the contract and claim only the reasonable value of his performance.

---

1. Fuller & Perdue, The Reliance Interest in Contract Damages, 46 Yale L.J. 52 (1936);   Restatement of Contracts § 333 (1932).

146 F.2d at 610. The Tenth Circuit has also stated that the right to seek recovery under quantum meruit in a Miller Act case is clear.[3] Quantum meruit recovery is not limited to an action against the prime contractor but may also be brought against the Miller Act surety, as in this case. Further, that the complaint is not clear in regard to the theory of a plaintiff's recovery does not preclude recovery under quantum meruit. Narragansett Improvement Co. v. United States, 290 F.2d 577 (1st Cir.1961). A plaintiff may join a claim for quantum meruit with a claim for damages from breach of contract.

In the present case, Coastal has, at its own expense, provided Blair with labor and the use of equipment. Blair, who breached the subcontract, has retained these benefits without having fully paid for them. On these facts, Coastal is entitled to restitution in quantum meruit:

> The "restitution interest," involving a combination of unjust impoverishment with unjust gain, presents the strongest case for relief. If, following Aristotle, we regard the purpose of justice as the maintenance of an equilibrium of goods among members of society, the restitution interest presents twice as strong a claim to judicial intervention as the reliance interest, since if A not only causes B to lose one unit but appropriates that unit to himself, the resulting discrepancy between A and B is not one unit but two.

Fuller & Perdue, The Reliance Interest in Contract Damages, 46 Yale L.J. 52, 56 (1936).[6]

The impact of quantum meruit is to allow a promisee to recover the value of services he gave to the defendant irrespective of whether he would have lost money on the contract and been unable to recover in a suit on the contract. Scaduto v. Orlando, 381 F.2d 587, 595 (2d Cir.1967). The measure of recovery for quantum meruit is the reasonable value of the performance, Restatement of Contracts § 347 (1932); and recovery is undiminished by any loss which would have been incurred by complete performance. 12 Williston on Contracts § 1485, at 312 (3d ed. 1970). While the contract price may be evidence of reasonable value of the services, it does not measure the value of the performance or limit recovery. Rather, the standard for measuring the reasonable value of the services rendered is the amount for which such services could have been purchased from one in the plaintiff's position at the time and place the services were rendered.

Since the district court has not yet accurately determined the reasonable value of the labor and equipment use furnished by Coastal to Blair, the case must be remanded for those findings. When the amount has been determined, judgment will be entered in favor of Coastal, less payments already made under the contract. Accordingly, for the reasons stated above, the decision of the district court is

Reversed and remanded with instructions.

---

3. Southern Painting Co. v. United States, 222 F.2d 431, 433 (10th Cir.1955). See also Great Lakes Constr. Co. v. Republic Creosoting Co., 139 F.2d 456 (8th Cir.1943) (dealing with a prior statute).

6. This case also comes within the requirements of the Restatements for recovery in quantum meruit. Restatement, Restitution § 107 (1937); Restatement, Contracts §§ 347–357 (1932).

OLIVER v. CAMPBELL, 43 Cal.2d 298, 273 P.2d 15 (1954). Oliver, a lawyer, had agreed to represent Dr. Campbell in a separate-maintenance and divorce action until final judgment, for a fee of $850, including $100 for costs and incidentals. The trial lasted twenty-nine days. After the trial's conclusion, the court indicated its intention to give Mrs. Campbell a divorce. While Mrs. Campbell's proposed findings were under consideration, Dr. Campbell discharged Oliver. At that point, Oliver had been paid $550. Dr. Campbell refused to pay more, and Oliver brought this action to recover the reasonable value of his services, which the court below found to be $5,000. Held, that the trial court should enter a verdict of $300 in Oliver's favor. " 'It is well settled that one who is wrongfully discharged and prevented from further performance of his contract may elect as a general rule to treat the contract as rescinded, may sue upon a *quantum meruit* as if the special contract of employment had never been made and may recover the reasonable value of the services performed even though such reasonable value exceeds the contract price.' ... The question remains, however, of the application of the foregoing rules to the instant case. Plaintiff had performed practically all of the services he was employed to perform when he was discharged. The trial was at an end. The court had indicated its intention to give judgment against Dr. Campbell and all that remained was a signing of findings and judgment. The full sum called for in the contract was payable because the trial had ended. Under these circumstances it would appear that in effect, plaintiff had completed the performance of his service and the rule would apply that: 'the remedy of restitution in money is not available to one who has fully performed his part of a contract, if the only part of the agreed exchange for such performance that has not been rendered by the defendant is a sum of money constituting a liquidated debt.... Rest. Contracts, § 350....' "

Schauer, J., dissenting, was of the opinion that the trial court should be directed to enter a verdict of $5,000 in Oliver's favor on the ground that Oliver had not fully performed at the time of breach. *"The contract plaintiff made with Dr. Campbell did not limit his services to the trial of the case....* Under the contract he agreed to represent the doctor until final judgment, and he told the doctor he *'thought the case would be reversed on appeal.'* " (Emphasis in original.)

————

1 G. PALMER, THE LAW OF RESTITUTION 378–79 (1978). "When the plaintiff has fully performed his obligations under the contract and the defendant's obligation is to pay money, restitution of the value of the plaintiff's performance is regularly denied. The plaintiff's sole remedy is to recover the agreed price.... The principal basis for criticism of the decisions lies in the fact that, for part performance, restitution free of the contract price is recognized by the great weight of authority, and it seems somewhat incongruous that the price should be controlling after full performance. The incongruity is most evident when a plaintiff who has only partly performed is granted restitution of an amount in excess of the contract price for full performance, as has been allowed in numerous decisions."

————

NOTE ON RESTITUTIONARY AND RELIANCE DAMAGES

In theory, restitutionary and reliance damages are easily distinguishable: restitutionary damages are based on *benefit conferred;* reliance damages are based on *costs incurred.* In practice, however, the distinction is often not easy to maintain, because in an action for restitution the benefit conferred is often effectively measured by the plaintiff's costs. This is particularly true where the action is brought in "quantum meruit," the name of the traditional action that seeks recovery for the reasonable value of work, labor, and services performed at the defendant's request. For example, in Randolph v. Castle, 190 Ky. 776, 228 S.W. 418 (1921), defendant, the owner of a small coal mine, entered into an oral contract with plaintiffs, whereby plaintiffs agreed to work defendant's mine for three years, and defendant agreed to pay plaintiffs $2.10 per ton for coal removed. Defendant later repudiated the contract, and plaintiffs sued for damages. The court said, "... [T]he contract ... was within the statute of frauds.... [and] plaintiffs were entitled to recover, if at all, on the *quantum meruit.* This necessitated plaintiffs showing the value of the services performed.... If the plaintiffs at the instance of defendant's mine foreman remained at the mine, ready, willing and able to work, but were assigned no duties, and thereby lost time, the defendant is liable to them for the reasonable value thereof...."

NOTE ON EXPECTATION AS A CAP
ON RELIANCE DAMAGES

As reflected in *Algernon Blair*, the majority rule is that a promisee who has entered into a losing contract under which he has conferred a benefit on a promisor who has committed a material breach can recover the market value of the benefit even if that value exceeds the contract price. To put this differently, unless some exception applies, the expectation measure does not set a cap on restitutionary damages in a suit in unjust enrichment against a breaching promisor. Therefore, in the case of a losing contract the promisee may be better off suing for restitutionary damages than suing for expectation damages. Suppose that the promisee in a losing contract sues for reliance damages based on the cost the promisor has incurred, rather than for restitutionary damages based on the benefit the promisor has conferred. Will expectation damages set a cap on the promisee's recovery in that case?

Restatement Second § 349 states in unqualified terms that "As an alternative to the measure of damages stated in § 347 [expectation damages], the injured party has a right to damages based on his reliance interest ...." However, the Comment and Illustrations to § 349 suggest that despite the generality of the black-letter rule, the rule is intended to apply only where expectation damages are too uncertain to recover, or where damages should to be limited to less than full expectation in the interests of justice. The Comment states, "it is open to the party in breach to prove the amount of the loss, to the extent that he can do so with reasonable certainty under the standard stated in § 352, and have it subtracted from the injured party's damages. The resulting damages will then be the same as those under the rule stated in § 347. If the injured party's expenditures exceed the contract price, it is clear that at least to the extent of the excess, there would have been a loss. For this reason, recovery for expenditures under the rule stated in this section may not exceed the full contract price."

In L. Albert & Son v. Armstrong Rubber Co., section 1, supra, Learned Hand said that expectation sets a cap on reliance. The courts have not strayed from Hand's resolution of the question, notwithstanding the breadth of the text of the Restatement Second § 349. For example, in Lord's & Lady's Enters. v. John Paul Mitchell Sys., 46 Mass.App.Ct. 262, 705 N.E.2d 302, 307 (1999), the court referred to "the recognized principle that, 'where full performance of a contract would have given claimant no benefit, or at least less than the reliance damages claimed, this fact may justify limiting or disallowing reliance damages. The notion is that claimant should on no account get more than would have accrued if the contract had been performed.' DPJ Co. Ltd. Partnership v. Federal Deposit Ins. Corp., 30 F.3d [247,] at 250." See also Farnsworth, Contracts § 12.16 (4th ed. 2004); Doering Equip. Co. v. John Deere Co., 61 Mass.App.Ct. 850, 815 N.E.2d 234 (2004). Similarly, in his leading treatise on remedies, Dobbs states, "To allow reliance recovery in excess of the appropriate measure of expectancy would mean that the plaintiff would be better off by reason of the breach and recovery than he would have been upon full performance. Such a result might be justified if the reliance claim is properly regarded as a tort claim, or at any rate as something other than a contract claim. But if the reliance claim is to be justified as a contract claim, then a recovery that makes the plaintiff better off by reason of breach seems wrong.... In accord with this view, [Restatement section 349 cmt. a] and the leading decisions have taken the position that the expectancy is a ceiling on reliance damages." 3 D. Dobbs, Remedies § 12.3(2).

(b) Restitution in Favor of a Plaintiff in Default*

KUTZIN v. PIRNIE

Supreme Court of New Jersey, 1991.
124 N.J. 500, 591 A.2d 932.

CLIFFORD, J. This is an action on a contract for the sale of residential property. The sellers' real-estate agent prepared the contract, after which defendants, the prospective buyers, signed it, paid a deposit of nearly ten percent of the purchase price, and then decided not to go through with the purchase. In the trial court the buyers argued that the contract had been rescinded because attorneys for both parties had sought to amend it during the three-day period provided by the contract's attorney-review clause. The court found the contract to be valid and awarded the sellers compensatory damages, albeit in an amount less than the deposit. The Appellate Division agreed that the contract is binding but held that the sellers are entitled to keep the entire deposit as damages. We granted certification ... to determine whether the contract is enforceable and, if so, whether the sellers should be

---

* Logically, the subject-matter of Section 2(b) does not fit under the heading of Part II, because it does not concern a remedy for breach. The subject is nevertheless taken up at this point, partly because it is remedial in nature, and partly because of its close connection with Section 2(a).

allowed to keep the deposit. We affirm the Appellate Division holding that the contract is valid but modify that court's judgment on the issue of damages and reinstate the damage award of the trial court.

I

On September 1, 1987, defendants, Duncan and Gertrude Pirnie, and plaintiffs, Milton and Ruth Kutzin, signed a contract for the sale of the Kutzins' house in Haworth for $365,000. The contract, which is the standard-form real-estate sales contract adopted by the New Jersey Association of Realtors, had been prepared by Weichert Realtors (Weichert), the sellers' real-estate agent. Under its terms, the Pirnies agreed to pay a partial deposit of $1,000 on signing the contract and the remainder of the deposit, $35,000, within seven days. In compliance therewith, the Pirnies made out a check for $1,000 to the trust account of Russo Real Estate (Russo), their real-estate agent. The contract does not contain a "forfeiture" or "liquidated damages" clause; with reference to the disposition of the deposit should the sale not take place, the contract merely states, "If this contract is voided by either party, the escrow monies shall be disbursed pursuant to the written direction of both parties."

The contract also contains the following attorney-review provision:

1. *Study by Attorney*

The Buyer or the Seller may choose to have an attorney study this contract. If an attorney is consulted, the attorney must complete his or her review of the contract within a three-day period. This contract will be legally binding at the end of this three-day period unless an attorney for the Buyer or the Seller reviews and disapproves of the contract.

2. *Counting the Time*

You count the three days from the date of delivery of the signed contract to the Buyer and the Seller. You do not count Saturdays, Sundays or legal holidays. The Buyer and the Seller may agree in writing to extend the three-day period for attorney review.

3. *Notice of Disapproval*

If an attorney for the Buyer or the Seller reviews and disapproves of this contract, the attorney must notify the REALTOR(S) and the other party named in this contract within the three-day period. Otherwise this contract will be legally binding as written. The attorney must send the notice of disapproval to the REALTOR(S) by certified mail, by telegram, or by delivering it personally. The telegram or certified letter will be effective upon sending. The personal delivery will be effective upon delivery to the REALTOR(S) office. The attorney may also, but need not, inform the REALTOR(S) of any suggested revision(s) in the contract that would make it satisfactory.

The Kutzins' attorney, Marshall Kozinn, telephoned Russo on September 2nd to communicate his approval of the contract with one exception: he wanted to hold the deposit in his trust account pending closing. Kozinn followed up that conversation by mailing a letter to Russo dated September 3, 1987, with a copy to Joseph Maccarone, the Pirnies' attorney, which read:

As per our telephone conversation, the above contract is satisfactory to me as Attorney for the Seller with the exception that my clients have requested that I hold the deposit pending closing.

Would you please forward the One Thousand ($1,000.) Dollars to me, and arrange to have the $35,000 remaining deposit balance made payable to my attorney trust account.

Russo had already complied with Kozinn's request (without discussing the matter with Maccarone) by endorsing the Pirnies' check to Kozinn's trust account and sending it to him on September 2nd.

In a telephone conversation with Kozinn on September 4th, Maccarone agreed to allow Kozinn to hold the deposit but expressed his opinion that the contract prepared by Weichert did not provide adequate protection for the buyers. That same day Maccarone mailed to Kozinn the following letter:

This office shall be representing the Buyers, Duncan and Gertrude Pirnie with reference to [this] transaction.

I have reviewed the contracts prepared by the Realtor and I would like to propose the attached amendments which I have taken the liberty to prepare. If these forms meet with your approval, I would appreciate your having them executed by the Sellers and return them to me for execution by the Buyers.

I shall forward you the balance of the deposit shortly.

Maccarone enclosed with the letter his standard rider for protection of buyers of real estate. Significantly, the rider was silent on the issue of what would happen to the deposit if the sale were not completed.

On September 10th, Maccarone telephoned Kozinn to inquire if the terms of the rider were acceptable. When Kozinn indicated that they were not, the attorneys discussed their differences and eventually agreed on certain changes. During that conversation, Kozinn mentioned that he had not yet received the additional deposit of $35,000 and questioned whether the Pirnies intended to proceed with the purchase. Maccarone assured Kozinn of the Pirnies' intention to buy the house, stating that "if the deposit was to be any demonstration of good faith or what have you [Kozinn] would have the deposit." Kozinn received the Pirnies' check for the balance of the deposit the next day. Thus assured that the sale would occur, the Kutzins left for their Florida home on the 13th of September.

Maccarone revised the rider and on September 21st sent to Kozinn two copies, already signed by the Pirnies, for execution by the Kutzins. Kozinn received the copies of the modified rider on September 22nd and forwarded them to the Kutzins that same day. A letter accompanied the riders requesting, among other things, that the Kutzins sign and return the riders to Kozinn as soon as the couple returned from Florida. The Kutzins apparently received the letter when they returned to New Jersey on September 24th.

Shortly thereafter the Pirnies instructed their new attorney, Harold Goldman, to write Kozinn the following letter, which was mailed on September 28th:

Be advised the Purnies [sic: "Pirnies" or "Pirnie" throughout] have retained my office to represent them in their effort to negotiate the purchase of a home in Haworth owned by your client, Milton Kutzin.

Mrs. Purnie has indicated to me that the Purnies are no longer interested in purchasing the subject property. Therefore, please treat this letter as formal notice to withdraw the offer to purchase by the Purnies. I must add that the desire to withdraw the offer to purchase was communicated to Joan Harrison, the listing broker, yesterday by both Mrs. Purnie and [myself].

It is my understanding that you are presently holding in trust deposit monies remitted by the Purnies in regard to the proposed purchase. Please call [me] to arrange for the return of said monies.

The Kutzins refused to return the deposit and promptly sued for specific performance of the contract. The Pirnies counterclaimed for return of their $36,000 deposit, contending that the contract had been validly rescinded either pursuant to the attorney-review provision or by agreement of the parties. Because the Kutzins sold the house to another buyer for $352,500 while the case was pending, they amended their complaint to seek only damages.

The trial court ruled that the parties had entered into a binding contract that had not been rescinded either by agreement or pursuant to the attorney-review clause. Consequently, the court held that the sellers were entitled to $17,325 in damages. That amount consisted of the $12,500 difference between the $365,000 the Pirnies had contracted to pay and the $352,500 for which the house eventually sold; $3,825 in utilities, real-estate taxes, and insurance expenses the Kutzins had incurred during the six-month period between the originally-anticipated closing date and the date of actual sale; and $1,000 the Kutzins had paid for a new basement carpet, which their realtor had recommended they buy to enhance the attractiveness of their house to prospective buyers. The court denied recovery of interest the Kutzins contended they would have earned on the purchase price had the sale to the Pirnies gone through. It also refused to award damages for the increased capital-gains tax the Kutzins had paid as a result of the breach. The court ordered the Kutzins to return the $18,675 balance of the deposit to the Pirnies.

On appeal, the Kutzins argued that they should recover the lost interest and the increased capital-gains tax they had incurred, or, alternatively, that they should be allowed to retain the deposit. On cross-appeal the Pirnies claimed entitlement to the entire deposit, again asserting that the contract had been validly rescinded. In an unreported opinion, the Appellate Division found that the contract between the parties "was enforceable according to its terms" but that "the Kutzins' claims to compensation for their allegedly increased tax liability and lost interest were too speculative to be compensable." The court then noted that "the Kutzins' loss as determined by the trial court was less than the Pirnies' $36,000 deposit," and concluded that "the Kutzins are entitled to retain the [entire] deposit, but they may not recover any additional amount as damages." . . .

III

We [now] determine whether the Kutzins are entitled to retain the entire $36,000 deposit as damages. The issue of whether a seller should be entitled to retain a deposit when a buyer breaches a contract that does not contain a liquidated-damages or forfeiture clause has long troubled courts. As Professor Williston has observed, "Few questions in the law have given rise to more discussion and difference of opinion than that concerning the right of one who has materially broken his contract without legal excuse to recover for such benefit [here, the deposit] as he may have conferred on the other party...." 12 S. Williston, *A Treatise on the Law of Contracts* § 1473 at 220 (3d ed. 1961) (Williston).

-A-

"[T]he common-law rule, which has been very generally followed ..., [was] that where the vendee of real property makes a part payment on the purchase price, but fails to fulfill the contract without lawful excuse, he cannot recover the payment ... even though the vendor may have made a profit by reason of the default." *Quillen v. Kelley*, 216 *Md.* 396, 401–02, 140 A.2d 517, 520 (1958); *see, e.g.,* Annotation, *Modern Status of Defaulting Vendee's Right to Recover Contractual Payments Withheld by Vendor as Forfeited*, 4 A.L.R.4th 993, 997 (1981) (The general rule is that "a vendee in default cannot recover back the money he has paid on an executory contract to his vendor who is not himself in default."). The thought behind that rule is that "restitution should always be refused, for the good and sufficient reason that the [buyer] is guilty of a breach of contract and should never be allowed to have advantage from his own wrong." 5A A. Corbin, *Corbin on Contracts* § 1129 at 37 (1964) (Corbin); *see, e.g., Haslack v. Mayers,* 26 *N.J.L.* 284, 290–91 (Sup.Ct.1857) ("The plaintiff here has deliberately broken his covenant with the defendant.... For the court to aid him[ ] would be to lend its aid to an act of bad faith.... Let him perform his contract ... or ... the loss is the consequence of his own act.").

New Jersey traditionally has adhered to the common-law rule. As the Appellate Division stated in *Oliver v. Lawson,* 92 *N.J.Super.* 331, 333, 223 A.2d 355 (1966), *certif. denied,* 48 *N.J.* 574, 227 A.2d 133 (1967), "It has heretofore generally been held in New Jersey that ... the defaulting buyer may not recover his deposit, irrespective of the actual damages suffered by the seller and regardless of whether the contract contains a forfeiture provision or not." ...

Following [a] long line of cases, the Appellate Division held that the Kutzins are entitled to retain the deposit even though the court was "sympathetic to the trial judge's ruling that the Pirnies were entitled to the return of the balance of their $36,000 contract deposit in excess of the Kutzins' actual damages."

-B-

Despite the ample authority supporting the Appellate Division's disposition of the damages question, "there has been a growing recognition of the injustice that often results from the application of the rule permitting total forfeiture of part payments under a contract of sale." *Great United Realty Co. v. Lewis,* 203 *Md.* 442, 448, 101 A.2d 881, 883 (1954); *see also Quillen v. Kelley, supra,* 216 *Md.* at 402, 140 A.2d at 520 ("In applying [the common-law] rule, there have been instances of harshness and injustice, which have caused a reconsideration of the same, in recent years, by the courts and by learned and renowned scholars and text-writers on the subject of contracts.").

Professor Corbin led the movement favoring departure from the strict common-law rule. In *The Right of a Defaulting Vendee to the Restitution of*

Installments Paid, 40 *Yale L.J.* 1013, 1013 (1931) (*Defaulting Vendee*), he stated:

> If a contractor has committed a total breach of his contract, having rendered no performance whatever thereunder, no penalty or forfeiture will be enforced against him; he will be required to do no more than to make the injured party whole by paying full compensatory damages. In like manner, a contractor who commits a breach after he has rendered part performance must also make the injured party whole by payment of full compensatory damages. The part performance rendered, however, may be much more valuable to the defendant than the amount of the injury caused by the breach; and in such case, to allow the injured party to retain the benefit of the part performance so rendered, without making restitution of any part of such value, is the enforcement of a penalty or forfeiture against the contract-breaker.

Corbin went on to declare that if a plaintiff "can and does show by proper evidence that the defendant is holding an amount of money as a penalty rather than as compensation for injury, he should be given judgment for restitution of that amount." *Id.* at 1025–26 (footnote omitted). . . .

Professor Corbin's article . . . was used in the formulation of section 357 of the *Restatement of Contracts* (1932). Section 357 . . . states:

> (1) Where the defendant fails or refuses to perform his contract and is justified therein by the plaintiff's own breach of duty or non-performance of a condition, but the plaintiff has rendered a part performance under the contract that is a net benefit to the defendant, the plaintiff can get judgment, except as stated in Subsection (2), for the amount of such benefit in excess of the harm that he has caused to the defendant by his own breach, in no case exceeding a ratable proportion of the agreed compensation, if

> > (a) the plaintiff's breach or non-performance is not wilful and deliberate; or

> > (b) the defendant, with knowledge that the plaintiff's breach of duty or non-performance of condition has occurred or will thereafter occur, assents to the rendition of the part performance, or accepts the benefit of it, or retains property received although its return in specie is still not unreasonably difficult or injurious.

> (2) The plaintiff has no right to compensation for his part performance if it is merely a payment of earnest money, or if the contract provides that it may be retained and it is not so greatly in excess of the defendant's harm that the provision is rejected as imposing a penalty. . . .

Section 374(1) of the *Restatement (Second) of Contracts* is based on section 357 but "is more liberal in allowing recovery in accord with the policy behind Uniform Commercial Code § 2–718(2)." *Restatement (Second) of Contracts* § 374 reporter's note (1981). That section sets forth the rule as follows:

> [I]f a party justifiably refuses to perform on the ground that his remaining duties of performance have been discharged by the other party's breach, the party in breach is entitled to restitution for any benefit that he has conferred by way of part performance or reliance in excess of the loss that he has caused by his own breach. [*Id.* § 374(1).]

Particularly relevant to this case is the following illustration:

A contracts to sell land to B for $100,000, which B promises to pay in $10,000 installments before transfer of title. After B has paid $30,000 he fails to pay the remaining installments and A sells the land to another buyer for $95,000. B can recover $30,000 from A in restitution less $5,000 damages for B's breach of contract, or $25,000. If A does not sell the land to another buyer and obtains a decree of specific performance against B, B has no right to restitution. [*Id.* § 374 illustration 1.]

Since publication of the first *Restatement of Contracts* in 1932, few courts have followed the common-law rule refusing restitution. See 5A Corbin, *supra*, § 1129 at 37–38. The *Restatement* approach of allowing recovery "has steadily increased in favor and probably represents the weight of authority." 12 Williston, *supra*, § 1473 at 222 (footnote omitted). . . .

With the issue squarely presented in this case, we overrule those New Jersey cases adhering to the common-law rule and adopt the modern approach set forth in section 374(1) of the *Restatement (Second) of Contracts*. In Professor Williston's words, "to deny recovery [in this situation] often gives the [seller] more than fair compensation for the injury he has sustained and imposes a forfeiture (which the law abhors) on the [breaching buyer]." 12 Williston, *supra*, § 1473 at 222. The approach that we adopt is suggested to have the added benefit of promoting economic efficiency: penalties deter "efficient" breaches of contract "by making the cost of the breach to the contract breaker greater than the cost of the breach to the victim." R. Posner, *Economic Analysis of Law* § 4.10 at 116 (3d ed. 1986).

-C-

We conclude that the Pirnies are entitled, under the *Restatement* formulation of damages, to restitution for any benefit that they conferred by way of part performance or reliance in excess of the loss that they caused by their own breach. See *Restatement (Second) of Contracts, supra,* § 374(1). We stress, however, that "[o]ne who charges an unjust enrichment has the burden of proving it." *Oliver v. Lawson, supra*, 92 *N.J.Super.* at 336, 223 A.2d 355. . . .

The trial court found that the Kutzins had suffered $17,325 in damages, a figure that we accept because it is not challenged in this Court. The Pirnies' deposit of $36,000 exceeded the injury caused by their breach by $18,675, and they are thus entitled to recovery of that amount.

Our holding is not affected by the fact that the $36,000 deposit was less than ten percent of the $365,000 purchase price. *Cf. Krupnick v. Guerriero* . . ., 247 *N.J.Super.* [373,] at 380, 589 A.2d [620,] at 624 ("As a general rule a defaulting buyer may not recover a deposit which does not materially exceed 10%. . . ."). Whenever the breaching buyer proves that the deposit exceeds the seller's actual damages suffered as a result of the breach, the buyer may recover the difference.

III

To ensure that our opinion not be misread, we emphasize that the contract at issue does not contain a forfeiture or liquidated-damages clause; it merely states, "If this contract is voided by either party, the escrow monies shall be disbursed pursuant to the written direction of both parties." The contract is otherwise silent on the subject of what would happen to the deposit were the sale not to occur. Had the contract contained a liquidated-damages clause, this case would have been governed by section 374(2) of the *Restatement (Second) of Contracts,* which states:

> To the extent that, under the manifested assent of the parties, a party's performance is to be retained in the case of breach, that party is not entitled to restitution if the value of the performance as liquidated damages is reasonable in the light of the anticipated loss caused by the breach and the difficulties of proof of loss. . . .

IV

We hold that. . . . the Pirnies' refusal to proceed constituted a breach of contract entitling the Kutzins to recover compensatory damages for the loss they suffered as a result of the breach. We also hold that the Kutzins cannot retain the entire deposit as damages. The Pirnies are entitled to restitution of their deposit less the amount of the injury to the Kutzins caused by the Pirnies' breach. To allow retention of the entire deposit would unjustly enrich the Kutzins and would penalize the Pirnies contrary to the policy behind our law of contracts.

The judgment of the Appellate Division is modified to reinstate the trial court's damage award. As modified the judgment is:

Affirmed.

For affirmance—Chief Justice WILENTZ and Justices CLIFFORD, HANDLER, POLLOCK, O'HERN, GARIBALDI and STEIN—7.

Opposed—None.

––––––

UNITED STATES EX REL. PALMER CONSTRUCTION, INC. v. CAL STATE ELECTRIC, INC., 940 F.2d 1260 (9th Cir.1991). "As a matter of pure contract law it is generally true that if two individuals enter into a contract and one breaches, the breaching party cannot obtain a recovery from the innocent party. Rather, if the innocent party has suffered, a recovery against the party in breach is generally accorded.

"On the other hand, if the breaching party has conferred a benefit upon the innocent party rather than a detriment, it would unjustly enrich the innocent party and unduly punish the breaching party if the latter received nothing for its services. Quasi contract principles will supply the remedy for that.

"These policies appear to conflict to some extent, so anyone who considers them must reconcile their opposing tendencies. When faced with these propositions, the commentators have resolved them by stating that the breaching party is entitled to the reasonable value of its services less any damages caused by the breach. They have added that the breaching party should not, in any event, be able to recover more than the contract price, or perhaps even a ratable part of that contract price. . . .

. . . [The] effect is to preclude a recovery by the breaching party which will cause the innocent party to pay more than the contract price itself. . . .

"It is interesting to observe that treatise illustrations of the application of these principles demonstrate that the innocent party never winds up paying a total that is more than the contract price itself. That is sensible. Were it otherwise, there would be a powerful inducement to breach rather than complete any contract which did not turn out to be profitable. By doing so, the ultimate loss of the bargain would be shifted from the breaching party to the innocent party, which is precisely what would occur in the case at hand if the district court's judgement stands."

R.J. BERKE & CO. v. GRIFFIN, INC., 116 N.H. 760, 367 A.2d 583 (1976). "... [G]enerally quantum meruit recovery will not be awarded where the conduct has been 'wilful.' Corbin notes that the term is not easily defined, and that a breach is not ordinarily considered willful if there is involved an honest dispute as to contract obligation. See 5A A. Corbin, Contracts '1123 (1964). It has been suggested that the quality of the breach bears no logical relationship to the theory of quantum meruit recovery, and that the willful defaulter should thus not be denied relief."

VINES v. ORCHARD HILLS, INC., 181 Conn. 501, 435 A.2d 1022 (1980). "This case concerns the right of purchasers of real property, after their own default, to recover moneys paid at the time of execution of a valid contract of sale. The plaintiffs, Euel D. Vines and his wife Etta Vines, contracted, on July 11, 1973, to buy Unit No. 10, Orchard Hills Condominium, New Canaan, Connecticut, from the defendant Orchard Hills, Inc. for $78,800. On or before that date, they had paid the defendant $7880 as a down payment toward the purchase. Alleging that the sale of the property was never consummated, the plaintiffs sought to recover their down payment....

"... The purchasers decided not to take title to the condominium because Euel D. Vines was transferred by his employer to New Jersey; the Vines so informed the seller by a letter dated January 4, 1974. There has never been any claim that the seller has failed, in any respect, to conform to his obligations under the contract, nor does the complaint allege that the purchasers are legally excused from their performance under the contract. In short, it is the purchasers and not the seller whose breach precipitated the present cause of action....

"The right of a contracting party, despite his default, to seek restitution for benefits conferred and allegedly unjustly retained has been much disputed in the legal literature and in the case law.... Although earlier cases often refused to permit a party to bring an action that could be said to be based on his own breach ... many of the more recent cases support restitution in order to prevent unjust enrichment and to avoid forfeiture....

"A variety of considerations, some practical and some theoretical, underlie this shift in attitude toward the plaintiff in breach. As Professor Corbin pointed out in his seminal article, 'The Right of a Defaulting Vendee to the Restitution of Installments Paid,' 40 Yale L.J. 1013 (1931), the anomalous result of denying any remedy to the plaintiff in breach is to punish more severely the person who has partially performed, often in good faith, than the person who has entirely disregarded his contractual obligations from the outset. Only partial performance triggers a claim for restitution, and partial performance will not, in the ordinary course of events, have been more injurious to the innocent party than total nonperformance. Recognition of a claim in restitution is, furthermore, consistent with the economic functions that the law of contracts is designed to serve. See Kessler & Gilmore, Contracts, pp. 4–6 (1970). The principal purpose of remedies for the breach of contract is to provide compensation for loss; see Restatement (Second), Contracts, c. 16, Introductory Note (Tent.Draft No. 14, 1979); Farnsworth, 'Legal Remedies for Breach of Contract,' 70 Colum.L.Rev. 1145 (1970); and therefore a party injured by breach of contract is entitled to retain nothing in excess of that sum which compensates him for the loss of his bargain. . . .

"Recognition that there are circumstances under which a defaulting purchaser may be entitled to restitution for benefits conferred upon the innocent seller of land is consistent with parallel developments elsewhere in the law of contracts. Judicial resistance to enforcement of forfeitures has of course long been commonplace, particularly with regard to contract clauses purporting to liquidate damages. See 5 Corbin, Contracts § 1058 (1964); 5 Williston, Contracts § 788 (3d Ed.1961). Despite the deference afforded by nineteenth-century courts to freedom of contract in other areas; see Weisbrod, The Boundaries of Utopia, pp. 165–67, 210–11 (1980); clauses that might impose forfeitures were invariably carefully scrutinized and frequently denounced as penal. . . .

". . . We . . . conclude that a purchaser whose breach is not willful has a restitutionary claim to recover moneys paid that unjustly enrich his seller. In this case, no one has alleged that the purchasers' breach, arising out of a transfer to a more distant place of employment, should be deemed to have been willful. . . .

"The purchaser's right to recover in restitution requires the purchaser to establish that the seller has been unjustly enriched. The purchaser must show more than that the contract has come to an end and that the seller retains moneys paid pursuant to the contract. To prove unjust enrichment, in the ordinary case, the purchaser, because he is the party in breach, must prove that the damages suffered by his seller are less than the moneys received from the purchaser. *Schwasnick v. Blandin, 65 F.2d 354, 358 (2d Cir.1933);* Kitchin v. Mori, 84 Nev. 181, 437 P.2d 865, 866 (1968). It may not be easy for the purchaser to prove the extent of the seller's damages, it may even be strategically advantageous for the seller to come forward with relevant evidence of the losses he has incurred and may expect to incur on account of the buyer's breach. Nonetheless, only if the breaching party satisfies his burden of proof that the innocent party has sustained a net gain may a claim for unjust enrichment be sustained. Dobbs, Remedies '12.14 (1973); 1 Palmer, Restitution § 5.4 (1978)."

———

NELSON v. HAZEL, 91 Idaho 850, 433 P.2d 120 (1967). "Even where [a contract for construction] cannot be said to be substantially performed, the weight of authority allows a negligent contractor to recover for the benefits actually conferred, in order that a forfeiture be avoided. . . . If the defect is remediable, recovery will be based on [contract price, offset by amounts already paid and] the market price of completing or correcting the performance, and such will normally be shown by the cost of completing the work by another person. . . .

"If the defective performance, though less than substantial, has conferred benefits on the homeowner in excess of his injury, he is under a quasi-contractual duty to pay that excess. . . ."

––––––

UCC § 2–718(2), (3)

[See Selected Source Materials Supplement]

––––––

*

Part III

ASSENT

The most common forms of contracts are bargains. A bargain entails assent. What constitutes assent for purposes of the law of contracts is a very difficult issue. That issue is considered in Part III.

Part III begins with Chapter 9, which concerns the basic principles of interpretation in contract law. Although problems of interpretation run through all areas of contract law, they are most salient in the area of assent.

Although bargains can be formed in more than one way, they are most commonly formed by an offer followed by an acceptance. Chapters 10_12 concern problems of offer and acceptance—problems such as what constitutes an offer, whether and when offers are revocable, and what kind of acceptance an offer requires.

Chapter 13 concerns contracts that are formed by implied promises or by conduct, rather than by explicit promises.

Chapter 14 concerns the problems that arise where the terms of an agreement are indefinite or not final.

Finally, Chapter 15 concerns special rules of evidence and interpretation that apply when a contract is in writing.

Chapter 9

AN INTRODUCTION TO INTERPRETATION

This Chapter concerns the interpretation of contractual language. The Chapter consists of three Sections.

Section 1 introduces the role of subjective and objective elements in the principles of interpretation in contract law.

Section 2 concerns the problems of interpreting purposive language.

Section 3 introduces the role of usage, course of dealing, and course of performance in interpretation.

Special rules of interpretation are sometimes applied when a contract is in writing. These rules will be considered later, in Chapter 15, because they reflect policies other than the determination of the parties' intentions.

SECTION 1. SUBJECTIVE AND OBJECTIVE ELEMENTS IN THE PRINCIPLES OF INTERPRETATION IN CONTRACT LAW

INTRODUCTORY NOTE

It is very commonly asserted that a contract requires "a meeting of the minds." In many contexts this statement is scarcely objectionable. For example, if A offers to sell his bicycle to B for $40, and B says that he accepts, provided A will reduce the price to $36, it is obvious that no contract has as yet been entered. One may quite properly justify this conclusion by saying that there has been no "meeting of the minds." On the other hand, difficulties will arise if the requirement of a "meeting of the minds" is taken literally and applied indiscriminately. In Europe there has been much discussion of the problem of the "mental reservation." Could a defendant who had signed a contract with the apparent intention of binding himself escape liability by showing that at the time of the signing he had made a "mental reservation" that he should not be bound? It is obvious that this defense should not be allowed; so obvious is this conclusion that the question has not even been discussed in the case-oriented literature of the common law.

But there are questions of practical import that do present real difficulty, including cases where effective communication fails because one party misinterprets the intention of the others. In these cases, the question may arise whether an expression of intention may be affected by a state of mind that accompanied it. A major theme running through Part III is the tension, in such cases, between subjective intent (state of mind, or what a party "really" meant) and objective intent (what the party expressed, or "seemed" to have meant).

It is sometimes concluded that what a party objectively means is not a question of "intent" at all. That this conclusion rests on a confusion of thought concerning the meaning of intent may be shown by the analogy of legislation. Under our constitutional system, the courts are generally subservient to the legislature. If Congress has properly enacted a law falling within the field of its competence, the courts are bound to follow and apply this law. With respect to the statute, the court's function is conceived as being subordinate. This constitutional relation between courts and statutes is commonly expressed by saying that the "intent" of the legislature governs questions of interpretation of a statute. Yet it is generally recognized that the "intent" that the court must respect is a formalized thing, and not the "actual, inner" intent of particular legislators. A statute becomes law only after it has been enacted in accordance with certain rules; when these rules have been followed the statute stands as law even though Senator Sorghum confides to his dinner partner that he was asleep when the bill was read and did not know what he was voting for.

Similarly, it is sometimes concluded that by emphasizing objective intent, contract law makes no place for subjective intent. This conclusion is equally flawed. The attitude that our courts take toward private agreements rests upon a kind of tacitly accepted constitution. This constitution, like that which regulates the relation of the courts to statutes, is a multi-faceted concept. When this is recognized, there is no longer any need to be disturbed by the fact that judges sometimes hold a person to an agreement he did not subjectively intend and at the same time insist that their purpose in enforcing contracts is to carry out the intention of the parties. Similar paradoxes, proceeding from similar causes, are to be found in most human institutions. The rules of an athletic association, for example, may be intended to ensure that the official record shall go to the fastest runner. At the same time these rules may operate to exclude the fastest runner from the record because his achievement occurred under conditions not satisfying the association's standards of proof. No one argues from this that the association has placed itself in a self-contradictory position, and must either abandon its rules for establishing records or cease pretending that it is interested in the speed of runners. There is as little reason to force upon the law of contracts a similar "either-or" alternative with regard to the treatment of intent.

———

RESTATEMENT, [FIRST,] CONTRACTS § 227 "A Standard of Interpretation is the Test Applied by the Law to Words and to Other Manifestations of Intention in Order to Determine the Meaning to be Given to Them.

"*Comment: a.* [This comment lists six 'conceivable standards of interpretation,' as follows:]

"1. The standard of general usage;

"2. A standard of limited usage, which would attach the meaning given to language in a particular locality, or by ... those engaged in a particular occupation ... (the distinction between 1 and 2 is a difference in degree, since generality of usage does not necessarily imply universality);

"3. A mutual standard, which would allow only such meanings as conform to an intention common to both or all the parties, and would attach this meaning although it violates the usage of all other persons;

"4. An individual standard, which would attach to words or other manifestations of intention whatever meaning the person employing them intended them to express, or that the person receiving the communication understood from it;

"5. A standard of reasonable expectation, which would attach to words or other manifestations of intention the meaning which the party employing them should reasonably have apprehended that they would convey to the other party;

"6. A standard of reasonable understanding, which would attach to words or other manifestations of intention the meaning which the person to whom the manifestations are addressed might reasonably give to them."

LUCY v. ZEHMER

Supreme Court of Appeals of Virginia, 1954.
196 Va. 493, 84 S.E.2d 516.

BUCHANAN, JUSTICE. This suit was instituted by W.O. Lucy and J.C. Lucy, complainants, against A.H. Zehmer and Ida S. Zehmer, his wife, defendants, to have specific performance of a contract by which it was alleged the Zehmers had sold to W.O. Lucy a tract of land owned by A.H. Zehmer in Dinwiddie County containing 471.6 acres, more or less, known as the Ferguson farm, for $50,000. J.C. Lucy, the other complainant, is a brother of W.O. Lucy, to whom W.O. Lucy transferred a half interest in his alleged purchase.

The instrument sought to be enforced was written by A.H. Zehmer on December 20, 1952, in these words: "We hereby agree to sell to W.O. Lucy the Ferguson Farm complete for $50,000.00, title satisfactory to buyer," and signed by the defendants, A.H. Zehmer and Ida S. Zehmer.

The answer of A.H. Zehmer admitted that at the time mentioned W.O. Lucy offered him $50,000 cash for the farm, but that he, Zehmer considered that the offer was made in jest; that so thinking, and both he and Lucy having had several drinks, he wrote out "the memorandum" quoted above and induced his wife to sign it; that he did not deliver the memorandum to Lucy, but that Lucy picked it up, read it, put it in his pocket, attempted to offer

Zehmer $5 to bind the bargain, which Zehmer refused to accept, and realizing for the first time that Lucy was serious, Zehmer assured him that he had no intention of selling the farm and that the whole matter was a joke. Lucy left the premises insisting that he had purchased the farm.

Depositions were taken and the decree appealed from was entered holding that the complainants had failed to establish their right to specific performance, and dismissing their bill. The assignment of error is to this action of the court.

W.O. Lucy, a lumberman and farmer, thus testified in substance: He had known Zehmer for fifteen or twenty years and had been familiar with the Ferguson farm for ten years. Seven or eight years ago he had offered Zehmer $20,000 for the farm which Zehmer had accepted, but the agreement was verbal and Zehmer backed out. On the night of December 20, 1952, around eight o'clock, he took an employee to McKenney, where Zehmer lived and operated a restaurant, filling station and motor court. While there he decided to see Zehmer and again try to buy the Ferguson farm. He entered the restaurant and talked to Mrs. Zehmer until Zehmer came in. He asked Zehmer if he had sold the Ferguson farm. Zehmer replied that he had not. Lucy said, "I bet you wouldn't take $50,000.00 for that place." Zehmer replied, "Yes, I would too; you wouldn't give fifty." Lucy said he would and told Zehmer to write up an agreement to that effect. Zehmer took a restaurant check and wrote on the back of it, "I do hereby agree to sell to W.O. Lucy the Ferguson Farm for $50,000 complete." Lucy told him he had better change it to "We" because Mrs. Zehmer would have to sign it too. Zehmer then tore up what he had written, wrote the agreement quoted above and asked Mrs. Zehmer, who was at the other end of the counter ten or twelve feet away, to sign it. Mrs. Zehmer said she would for $50,000 and signed it. Zehmer brought it back and gave it to Lucy, who offered him $5 which Zehmer refused, saying, "You don't need to give me any money, you got the agreement there signed by both of us."

The discussion leading to the signing of the agreement, said Lucy, lasted thirty or forty minutes, during which Zehmer seemed to doubt that Lucy could raise $50,000. Lucy suggested the provision for having the title examined and Zehmer made the suggestion that he would sell it "complete, everything there," and stated that all he had on the farm was three heifers.

December 20 was on Saturday. Next day Lucy telephoned to J.C. Lucy and arranged with the latter to take a half interest in the purchase and pay half of the consideration. On Monday he engaged an attorney to examine the title. The attorney reported favorably on December 31 and on January 2 Lucy wrote Zehmer stating that the title was satisfactory, that he was ready to pay the purchase price in cash and asking when Zehmer would be ready to close the deal. Zehmer replied by letter, mailed on January 13, asserting that he had never agreed or intended to sell.

Mr. and Mrs. Zehmer were called by the complainants as adverse witnesses. Zehmer testified in substance as follows.

He bought this farm more than ten years ago for $11,000. He had had twenty-five offers, more or less, to buy it, including several from Lucy, who had never offered any specific sum of money. He had given them all the same answer, that he was not interested in selling it. On this Saturday night before Christmas it looked like everybody and his brother came by there to have a drink. He took a good many drinks during the afternoon and had a pint of his own. When he entered the restaurant around eight-thirty Lucy was there and he could see that he was "pretty high." He said to Lucy, "Boy, you got some good liquor, drinking, ain't you?" Lucy then offered him a drink. "I was already high as a Georgia pine, and didn't have any more better sense than to pour another great big slug out and gulp it down, and he took one too."

After they had talked a while Lucy asked whether he still had the Ferguson farm. He replied that he had not sold it and Lucy said, "I bet you wouldn't take $50,000.00 for it." Zehmer asked him if he would give $50,000 and Lucy said yes. Zehmer replied, "You haven't got $50,000.00 in cash." Lucy said he did and Zehmer replied that he did not believe it. They argued "pro and con for a long time," mainly about "whether he had $50,000 in cash that he could put up right then and buy that farm."

Finally, said Zehmer, Lucy told him if he didn't believe he had $50,000, "you sign that piece of paper here and say you will take $50,000.00 for the farm." He, Zehmer, "just grabbed the back off of a guest check there" and wrote on the back of it. At that point in his testimony Zehmer asked to see what he had written to "see if I recognize my own handwriting." He examined the paper and exclaimed, "Great balls of fire, I got 'Firgerson' for Ferguson. I have got satisfactory spelled wrong. I don't recognize that writing if I would see it, wouldn't know it was mine."

After Zehmer had, as he described it, "scribbled this thing off," Lucy said, "Get your wife to sign it." Zehmer walked over to where she was and she at first refused to sign but did so after he told her that he "was just needling him [Lucy], and didn't mean a thing in the world, that I was not selling the farm." Zehmer then "took it back over there . . . and I was still looking at the dern thing. I had the drink right there by my hand, and I reached over to get a drink, and he said, 'Let me see it.' He reached and picked it up, and when I looked back again he had it in his pocket and he dropped a five dollar bill over there, and he said, 'Here is five dollars payment on it.' . . . I said, 'Hell no, that is beer and liquor talking. I am not going to sell you the farm. I have told you that too many times before.' "[Mrs. Zehmer's testimony was comparable to that of Mr. Zehmer. She added that after Lucy said, "All right, get your wife to sign it." Zehmer came back to where she was standing and said, "You want to put your name to this?" She said "No," but he said in an undertone, "It is nothing but a joke," and she signed it.] . . .

The defendants insist that the evidence was ample to support their contention that the writing sought to be enforced was prepared as a bluff or dare to force Lucy to admit that he did not have $50,000; that the whole matter was a joke; that the writing was not delivered to Lucy and no binding contract was ever made between the parties. . . .

In his testimony Zehmer claimed that he "was high as a Georgia pine," and that the transaction "was just a bunch of two doggoned drunks bluffing to see who could talk the biggest and say the most." That claim is inconsistent with his attempt to testify in great detail as to what was said and what was done. It is contradicted by other evidence as to the condition of both parties. . . . It was in fact conceded by defendants' counsel in oral argument that under the evidence Zehmer was not too drunk to make a valid contract. . . .

The appearance of the contract, the fact that it was under discussion for forty minutes or more before it was signed; Lucy's objection to the first draft because it was written in the singular, and he wanted Mrs. Zehmer to sign it also; the rewriting to meet that objection and the signing by Mrs. Zehmer; the discussion of what was to be included in the sale, the provision for the examination of the title, the completeness of the instrument that was executed, the taking possession of it by Lucy with no request or suggestion by either of the defendants that he give it back, are facts which furnish persuasive evidence that the execution of the contract was a serious business transaction rather than a casual, jesting matter as defendants now contend. . . .

If it be assumed, contrary to what we think the evidence shows, that Zehmer was jesting about selling his farm to Lucy and that the transaction was intended by him to be a joke, nevertheless the evidence shows that Lucy did not so understand it but considered it to be a serious business transaction and the contract to be binding on the Zehmers as well as on himself. . . .

Not only did Lucy actually believe, but the evidence shows he was warranted in believing, that the contract represented a serious business transaction and a good faith sale and purchase of the farm.

In the field of contracts, as generally elsewhere, "We must look to the outward expression of a person as manifesting his intention rather than to his secret and unexpressed intention. 'The law imputes to a person an intention corresponding to the reasonable meaning of his words and acts.'" First Nat. Exchange Bank of Roanoke v. Roanoke Oil Co., 169 Va. 99, 114, 192 S.E. 764, 770.

At no time prior to the execution of the contract had Zehmer indicated to Lucy by word or act that he was not in earnest about selling the farm. They had argued about it and discussed its terms, as Zehmer admitted, for a long time. Lucy testified that if there was any jesting it was about paying $50,000 that night. The contract and the evidence show that he was not expected to pay the money that night. Zehmer said that after the writing was signed he laid it down on the counter in front of Lucy. Lucy said Zehmer handed it to him. In any event there had been what appeared to be a good faith offer and a good faith acceptance, followed by the execution and apparent delivery of a written contract. Both said that Lucy put the writing in his pocket and then offered Zehmer $5 to seal the bargain. Not until then, even under the defendants' evidence, was anything said or done to indicate that the matter was a joke. Both of the Zehmers testified that when Zehmer asked his wife to sign he whispered that it was a joke so Lucy wouldn't hear and that it was not intended that he should hear.

The mental assent of the parties is not requisite for the formation of a contract. If the words or other acts of one of the parties have but one reasonable meaning, his undisclosed intention is immaterial except when an unreasonable meaning which he attaches to his manifestations is known to the other party. Restatement of the Law of Contracts, Vol. I, § 71, p. 74. . . .

So a person cannot set up that he was merely jesting when his conduct and words would warrant a reasonable person in believing that he intended a real agreement. 17 C.J.S., Contracts, § 47, p. 390; Clark on Contracts, 4 ed., § 27, at p. 54.

Whether the writing signed by the defendants and now sought to be enforced by the complainants was the result of a serious offer by Lucy and a serious acceptance by the defendants, or was a serious offer by Lucy and an acceptance in secret jest by the defendants, in either event it constituted a binding contract of sale between the parties.

Defendants contend further, however, that even though a contract was made, equity should decline to enforce it under the circumstances. These circumstances have been set forth in detail above. They disclose some drinking by the two parties but not to an extent that they were unable to understand fully what they were doing. There was no fraud, no misrepresentation, no sharp practice and no dealing between unequal parties. The farm had been bought for $11,000 and was assessed for taxation at $6,300. The purchase price was $50,000. Zehmer admitted that it was a good price. There is in fact present in this case none of the grounds usually urged against specific performance. . . .

The complainants are entitled to have specific performance of the contract sued on. The decree appealed from is therefore reversed and the cause is remanded for the entry of a proper decree requiring the defendants to perform the contract in accordance with the prayer of the bill.

Reversed and remanded.

————

KELLER v. HOLDERMAN, 11 Mich. 248, 83 Am.Dec. 737 (1863). Suit against the maker of a check for $300, which had been given in return for an old silver watch, worth about $15. The court said, "when the court below found as a fact that 'the whole transaction between the parties was a frolic and a banter, the plaintiff not expecting to sell, nor the defendant to buy the watch at the sum for which the check was drawn,' the conclusion should have been that no contract was ever made by the parties, and the finding should have been that no cause of action existed upon the check to the plaintiff."

————

RAFFLES v. WICHELHAUS

In the Court of Exchequer, 1864.
2 Hurl. & C. 906.

Declaration. For that it was agreed between the plaintiff and the defendants, to wit, at Liverpool, that the plaintiff should sell to the defendants, and the defendants buy of the plaintiff, certain goods, to wit, 125 bales of Surat cotton, guaranteed middling fair merchant's dhollorah, to arrive ex Peerless from Bombay; and that the cotton should be taken from the quay, and that the defendants would pay the plaintiff for the same at a certain rate, to wit, at the rate of 17¼ d. per pound, within a certain time then agreed upon after the arrival of the said goods in England. Averments: that the said goods did arrive by the said ship from Bombay in England, to wit, at Liverpool, and the plaintiff was then and there ready and willing and offered to deliver the said goods to the defendants, etc. Breach: that the defendants refused to accept the said goods or pay the plaintiff for them.

Plea. That the said ship mentioned in the said agreement was meant and intended by the defendant to be the ship called the Peerless, which sailed from Bombay, to wit, in October; and that the plaintiff was not ready and willing, and did not offer to deliver to the defendants any bales of cotton which arrived by the last-mentioned ship, but instead thereof was only ready and willing, and offered to deliver to the defendants 125 bales of Surat cotton which arrived by another and different ship, which was also called the Peerless, and which sailed from Bombay, to wit, in December.

Demurrer, and joinder therein.

Milward, in support of the demurrer. The contract was for the sale of a number of bales of cotton of a particular description, which the plaintiff was ready to deliver. It is immaterial by what ship the cotton was to arrive, so that it was a ship called the Peerless. The words "to arrive ex Peerless," only mean that if the vessel is lost on the voyage, the contract is to be at an end. [Pollock, C.B. It would be a question for the jury whether both parties meant the same ship called the Peerless.] That would be so if the contract was for the sale of a ship called the Peerless; but it is for the sale of cotton on board a ship of that name. [Pollock, C.B. The defendant only bought that cotton which was to arrive by a particular ship. It may as well be said, that if there is a contract for the purchase of certain goods in warehouse A., that is satisfied by the delivery of goods of the same description in warehouse B.] In that case there would be goods in both warehouses; here it does not appear that the plaintiff had any goods on board the other Peerless. [Martin, B. It is imposing on the defendant a contract different from that which he entered into. Pollock, C.B. It is like a contract for the purchase of wine coming from a particular estate in France or Spain, where there are two estates of that name.] The defendant has no right to contradict by parol evidence, a written contract good upon the face of it. He does not impute misrepresentation or fraud, but only says that he fancied the ship was a different one. Intention is of no avail, unless stated at the time of the contract. [Pollock, C.B. One vessel sailed in October and the other in December.] The time of sailing is no part of the contract.

Mellish (Cohen with him), in support of the plea. There is nothing on the face of the contract to show that any particular ship called the Peerless was meant; but the moment it appears that two ships called the Peerless were about to sail from Bombay there is a latent ambiguity, and parol evidence may be given for the purpose of showing that the defendant meant one Peerless and the plaintiff another. That being so, there was no consensus ad idem, and therefore no binding contract. He was then stopped by the Court.

PER CURIAM. There must be judgment for the defendants.

Judgment for the defendants.

————

SIMPSON, CONTRACTS FOR COTTON TO ARRIVE: THE CASE OF THE TWO SHIPS *PEERLESS*, 11 Cardozo L. Rev. 287, 295 (1989). "There were reports of at least eleven ships called *Peerless* sailing the seven seas at the time [of the *Peeerless* case], for the name was a popular one. The *Mercantile Navy List* for 1863 lists nine British registered sailing vessels of that name, their ports of registration being London, Aberystwyth, Dartmouth,

Greennock, Halifax, Windsor (Nova Scotia), Hull, and Liverpool, which boasted two such ships. There were also two American ships named *Peerless* from Boston and Baltimore. The existence of so many vessels of the same or a similar name could obviously cause confusion in shipping movement reports. There was nothing unusual however in this state of affairs. Ships commonly shared the same name, particularly popular names such as *Annie*. But the two vessels with which we are concerned can readily be identified as the two which were registered at Liverpool. At the time it was the practice in the shipping press to differentiate vessels bearing the same name by the names of their captains, not, as one might expect, by using their unique registered number."

FRIGALIMENT IMPORTING CO. v. B.N.S. INTERN. SALES CORP.

United States District Court, Southern District of New York, 1960.
190 F.Supp. 116.

FRIENDLY, CIRCUIT JUDGE.

The issue is, what is chicken? Plaintiff says "chicken" means a young chicken, suitable for broiling and frying. Defendant says "chicken" means any bird of that genus that meets contract specifications on weight and quality, including what it calls "stewing chicken" and plaintiff pejoratively terms "fowl". Dictionaries give both meanings, as well as some others not relevant here. To support its, plaintiff sends a number of volleys over the net; defendant essays to return them and adds a few serves of its own. Assuming that both parties were acting in good faith, the case nicely illustrates Holmes' remark "that the making of a contract depends not on the agreement of two minds in one intention, but on the agreement of two sets of external signs— not on the parties" having meant the same thing but on their having said the same thing." The Path of the Law, in Collected Legal Papers, p. 178. I have concluded that plaintiff has not sustained its burden of persuasion that the contract used "chicken" in the narrower sense.

The action is for breach of the warranty that goods sold shall correspond to the description, New York Personal Property Law, McKinney"s Consol. Laws, c. 41, § 95. Two contracts are in suit. In the first, dated May 2, 1957, defendant, a New York sales corporation, confirmed the sale to plaintiff, a Swiss corporation, of

"US Fresh Frozen Chicken, Grade A, Government Inspected, Eviscerated

"2 1/2–3 lbs. and 1 1/2–2 lbs. each all chicken individually wrapped in cryovac, packed in secured fiber cartons or wooden boxes, suitable for export

"75,000 lbs. 2 1/2–3 lbs . . . . @\$33.00

"25,000 lbs. 1 1/2–2 lbs . . . . @\$36.50

"per 100 lbs. FAS New York

"scheduled May 10, 1957 pursuant to instructions from Penson & Co., New York."

The second contract, also dated May 2, 1957, was identical save that only 50,000 lbs. of the heavier "chicken" were called for, the price of the smaller birds was $37 per 100 lbs., and shipment was scheduled for May 30. The initial shipment under the first contract was short but the balance was shipped on May 17. When the initial shipment arrived in Switzerland, plaintiff found, on May 28, that the 2 1/2–3 lbs. birds were not young chicken suitable for broiling and frying but stewing chicken or "fowl"; indeed, many of the cartons and bags plainly so indicated. Protests ensued. Nevertheless, shipment under the second contract was made on May 29, the 2 1/2–3 lbs. birds again being stewing chicken. Defendant stopped the transportation of these at Rotterdam.

This action followed. Plaintiff says that, notwithstanding that its acceptance was in Switzerland, New York law controls under the principle of Rubin v. Irving Trust Co., 1953, 305 N.Y. 288, 305, 113 N.E.2d 424, 431; defendant does not dispute this, and relies on New York decisions. I shall follow the apparent agreement of the parties as to the applicable law.

Since the word "chicken" standing alone is ambiguous, I turn first to see whether the contract itself offers any aid to its interpretation. Plaintiff says the 1 1/2–2 lbs. birds necessarily had to be young chicken since the older birds do not come in that size, hence the 2 1/2–3 lbs. birds must likewise be young. This is unpersuasive—a contract for "apples" of two different sizes could be filled with different kinds of apples even though only one species came in both sizes. Defendant notes that the contract called not simply for chicken but for "US Fresh Frozen Chicken, Grade A, Government Inspected." It says the contract thereby incorporated by reference the Department of Agriculture's regulations, which favor its interpretation; I shall return to this after reviewing plaintiff's other contentions.

The first hinges on an exchange of cablegrams which preceded execution of the formal contracts. The negotiations leading up to the contracts were conducted in New York between defendant's secretary, Ernest R. Bauer, and a Mr. Stovicek, who was in New York for the Czechoslovak government at the World Trade Fair. A few days after meeting Bauer at the fair, Stovicek telephoned and inquired whether defendant would be interested in exporting poultry to Switzerland. Bauer then met with Stovicek, who showed him a cable from plaintiff dated April 26, 1957, announcing that they "are buyer" of 25,000 lbs. of chicken 2 1/2–3 lbs. weight, Cryovac packed, grade A Government inspected, at a price up to 33 cents per pound, for shipment on May 10, to be confirmed by the following morning, and were interested in further offerings. After testing the market for price, Bauer accepted, and Stovicek sent a confirmation that evening. Plaintiff stresses that, although these and subsequent cables between plaintiff and defendant, which laid the basis for the additional quantities under the first and for all of the second contract, were predominantly in German, they used the English word "chicken"; it claims this was done because it understood "chicken" meant young chicken whereas the German word, "Huhn," included both "Brathuhn" (broilers) and "Suppenhuhn" (stewing chicken), and that defendant, whose officers were thoroughly conversant with German, should have realized this. Whatever force this argument might otherwise have is largely drained away by Bauer's testimony that he asked Stovicek what kind of chickens were wanted, received the answer "any kind of chickens," and then, in German, asked whether the cable meant "Huhn" and received an affirmative response. . . .

Plaintiff's next contention is that there was a definite trade usage that "chicken" meant "young chicken." Defendant showed that it was only beginning in the poultry trade in 1957, thereby bringing itself within the principle that "when one of the parties is not a member of the trade or other circle, his acceptance of the standard must be made to appear" by proving either that he had actual knowledge of the usage or that the usage is "so generally known in the community that his actual individual knowledge of it may be inferred." 9 Wigmore, Evidence (3d ed. § 1940) 2464. Here there was no proof of actual knowledge of the alleged usage; indeed, it is quite plain that defendant's belief was to the contrary. In order to meet the alternative requirement, the law of New York demands a showing that "the usage is of so long continuance, so well established, so notorious, so universal and so reasonable in itself, as that the presumption is violent that the parties contracted with reference to it, and made it a part of their agreement." Walls v. Bailey, 1872, 49 N.Y. 464, 472–473.

Plaintiff endeavored to establish such a usage by the testimony of three witnesses and certain other evidence. Strasser, resident buyer in New York for a large chain of Swiss cooperatives, testified that "on chicken I would definitely understand a broiler." However, the force of this testimony was considerably weakened by the fact that in his own transactions the witness, a careful businessman, protected himself by using "broiler" when that was what he wanted and "fowl" when he wished older birds. Indeed, there are some indications, dating back to a remark of Lord Mansfield, Edie v. East India Co., 2 Burr. 1216, 1222 (1761), that no credit should be given "witnesses to usage, who could not adduce instances in verification." 7 Wigmore, Evidence (3d ed. 1940), § 1954; see McDonald v. Acker, Merrall & Condit Co., 2d Dept.1920, 192 App.Div. 123, 126, 182 N.Y.S. 607. While Wigmore thinks this goes too far, a witness' consistent failure to rely on the alleged usage deprives his opinion testimony of much of its effect. Niesielowski, an officer of one of the companies that had furnished the stewing chicken to defendant, testified that "chicken" meant "the male species of the poultry industry. That could be a broiler, a fryer or a roaster", but not a stewing chicken; however, he also testified that upon receiving defendant's inquiry for "chickens", he asked whether the desire was for "fowl or frying chickens" and, in fact, supplied fowl, although taking the precaution of asking defendant, a day or two after plaintiff's acceptance of the contracts in suit, to change its confirmation of its order from "chickens," as defendant had originally prepared it, to "stewing chickens." Dates, an employee of Urner–Barry Company, which publishes a daily market report on the poultry trade, gave it as his view that the trade meaning of "chicken" was "broilers and fryers." In addition to this opinion testimony, plaintiff relied on the fact that the Urner–Barry service, the Journal of Commerce, and Weinberg Bros. & Co. of Chicago, a large supplier of poultry, published quotations in a manner which, in one way or another, distinguish between "chicken," comprising broilers, fryers and certain other categories, and "fowl," which, Bauer acknowledged, included stewing chickens. This material would be impressive if there were nothing to the contrary. However, there was, as will now be seen.

Defendant's witness Weininger, who operates a chicken eviscerating plant in New Jersey, testified "Chicken is everything except a goose, a duck, and a turkey. Everything is a chicken, but then you have to say, you have to specify which category you want or that you are talking about." Its witness Fox said that in the trade "chicken" would encompass all the various classifications. Sadina, who conducts a food inspection service, testified that he would consider any bird coming within the classes of "chicken" in the Department of Agriculture's regulations to be a chicken. The specifications approved by the General Services Administration include fowl as well as broilers and fryers under the classification "chickens." Statistics of the Institute of American Poultry Industries use the phrases "Young chickens" and "Mature chickens," under the general heading "Total chickens." and the Department of Agriculture's daily and weekly price reports avoid use of the word "chicken" without specification.

Defendant advances several other points which it claims affirmatively support its construction. Primary among these is the regulation of the Department of Agriculture, 7 C.F.R. § 70.300–70.370, entitled, "Grading and Inspection of Poultry and Edible Products Thereof." and in particular 70.301 which recited:

"*Chickens*. The following are the various classes of chickens:

(a) Broiler or fryer . . .

(b) Roaster . . .

(c) Capon . . .

(d) Stag . . .

(e) Hen or stewing chicken or fowl . . .

(f) Cock or old rooster . . .

Defendant argues, as previously noted, that the contract incorporated these regulations by reference. Plaintiff answers that the contract provision related simply to grade and Government inspection and did not incorporate the Government definition of "chicken," and also that the definition in the Regulations is ignored in the trade. However, the latter contention was contradicted by Weininger and Sadina; and there is force in defendant's argument that the contract made the regulations a dictionary, particularly since the reference to Government grading was already in plaintiff's initial cable to Stovicek. Defendant makes a further argument based on the impossibility of its obtaining broilers and fryers at the 33 cents price offered by plaintiff for the 2 1/2–3 lbs. birds. There is no substantial dispute that, in late April, 1957, the price for 2 1/2–3 lbs. broilers was between 35 and 37 cents per pound, and that when defendant entered into the contracts, it was well aware of this and intended to fill them by supplying fowl in these weights. It claims that plaintiff must likewise have known the market since plaintiff had reserved shipping space on April 23, three days before plaintiff's cable to Stovicek, or, at least, that Stovicek was chargeable with such knowledge. It is scarcely an answer to say, as plaintiff does in its brief, that the 33 cents price offered by the 2 1/2–3 lbs. "chickens" was closer to the prevailing 35 cents price for broilers than to the 30 cents at which defendant procured fowl. Plaintiff must have expected defendant to make some profit—certainly it could not have expected defendant deliberately to incur a loss. . . .

When all the evidence is reviewed, it is clear that defendant believed it could comply with the contracts by delivering stewing chicken in the 2 1/2–3 lbs. size. Defendant's subjective intent would not be significant if this did not coincide with an objective meaning of "chicken." Here it did coincide with one of the dictionary meanings, with the definition in the Department of Agriculture Regulations to which the contract made at least oblique reference, with at least some usage in the trade, with the realities of the market, and with what plaintiff's spokesman had said. Plaintiff asserts it to be equally plain that plaintiff's own subjective intent was to obtain broilers and fryers; the only evidence against this is the material as to market prices and this may not have been sufficiently brought home. In any event it is unnecessary to determine that issue. For plaintiff has the burden of showing that "chicken" was used in the narrower rather than in the broader sense, and this it has not sustained.

This opinion constitutes the Court's findings of fact and conclusions of law. Judgment shall be entered dismissing the complaint with costs.

The following year, Judge Friendly stated that *Frigaliment* might better have been placed on the ground of failure of the minds to meet, under Raffles v. Wichelhaus, "with the loss still left on the plaintiff because defendant's not unjustifiable change of position...." Dadourian Export Corp. v. United States, 291 F.2d 178, 187 n. 4. (2d Cir.1961) (dissenting opinion).

OSWALD v. ALLEN, 417 F.2d 43 (2d Cir.1969). Dr. Oswald, a coin collector from Switzerland, was interested in Mrs. Allen's collection of Swiss coins. In April 1964 Dr. Oswald was in the United States, and the parties drove to the Newburgh Savings Bank, where two of Mrs. Allen's coin collections were located. Dr. Oswald first examined the coins in Mrs. Allen's Swiss Coin Collection, and was then shown several valuable Swiss coins from Mrs. Allen's Rarity Coin Collection. He took notes on each collection. On the parties' return from the bank, a price of $50,000 was agreed upon for Mrs. Allen's collection of Swiss coins. However, Dr. Oswald thought he was buying all of Mrs. Allen's Swiss coins, while Mrs. Allen thought she was selling only the Swiss Coin Collection, and not the Swiss coins in the Rarity Coin Collection. The evidence showed that each collection had its own key number, and was housed in a labeled cigar box. Dr. Oswald, however, testified that he did not know that some of the Swiss coins he examined were in a separate Collection. Held, no contract was formed. "Even though the mental assent of the parties is not requisite for the formation of a contract ... the facts ... clearly place this case within the small group of exceptional cases in which there is 'no sensible basis for choosing between conflicting understandings.' ... The rule of Raffles v. Wichelhaus is applicable here."

FALCK v. WILLIAMS, [1900] Appeal Cases 176. Plaintiff and Defendant used a code for business communications. Plaintiff received a telegraphic offer from Defendant which was ambiguous, the ambiguity arising because of the lack of a stop sign, which left it doubtful whether an important word of the code went with one sentence or the sentence following. Plaintiff accepted the offer. It turned out that the plaintiff's interpretation of the offer was not that which the Defendant put on it. Plaintiff sued for breach of contract, contending that his construction was the true one. Held, for Defendant. The court said that Defendant would equally have failed if he, as plaintiff, had sought to maintain his construction.

COLFAX ENVELOPE CORP. v. LOCAL NO. 458–3M, 20 F.3d 750 (7th Cir.1994). "*Raffles* and *Oswald* were cases in which neither party was blameable for the mistake.... If neither party can be assigned the greater blame for the misunderstanding, there is no nonarbitrary basis for deciding which party's understanding to enforce, so the parties are allowed to abandon the contract without liability.... These are not cases in which one party's understanding is more reasonable than the other's. Compare Restatement ... § 20(2)(b). If rescission were permitted in that kind of case, the enforcement of every contract would be at the mercy of a jury, which might be persuaded that one of the parties had genuinely held an idiosyncratic idea of its meaning, so that there had been, in fact, no meeting of the minds."

EMBRY v. HARGADINE, McKITTRICK DRY GOODS CO.

St. Louis Court of Appeals, Missouri, 1907.
127 Mo.App. 383, 105 S.W. 777.

Action by Charles R. Embry against the Hargadine–McKittrick Dry Goods Company. From a judgment for defendant, plaintiff appeals. Reversed and remanded.

GOODE, J. We dealt with this case on a former appeal (115 Mo.App. 130, 91 S.W. 170). It has been retried, and is again before us for the determination of questions not then reviewed. The appellant was an employee of the respondent company under a written contract to expire December 15, 1903, at a salary of $2,000 per annum. His duties were to attend to the sample department of respondent, of which he was given complete charge. It was his business to select samples for the traveling salesmen of the company, which is a wholesale dry goods concern, to use in selling goods to retail merchants.

Appellant contends that on December 23, 1903, he was re-engaged by respondent, through its president, Thos. H. McKittrick, for another year at the same compensation and for the same duties stipulated in his previous written contract. On March 1, 1904, he was discharged, having been notified in February that, on account of the necessity of retrenching expenses, his services and that of some other employees would no longer be required.

The respondent company contends that its president never re-employed appellant after the termination of his written contract, and hence that it had a right to discharge him when it chose. The point with which we are concerned requires an epitome of the testimony of appellant and the counter testimony of McKittrick, the president of the company, in reference to the alleged re-employment.

Appellant testified: That several times prior to the termination of his written contract on December 15, 1903, he had endeavored to get an understanding with McKittrick for another year, but had been put off from time to time. That on December 23d, eight days after the expiration of said contract, he called on McKittrick, in the latter's office, and said to him that as appellant's written employment had lapsed eight days before, and as there were only a few days between then and the 1st of January in which to seek employment with other firms, if respondent wished to retain his services longer he must have a contract for another year, or he would quit respondent's service then and there. That he had been put off twice before and wanted an understanding or contract at once so that he could go ahead without worry. That McKittrick asked him how he was getting along in his department, and appellant said he was very busy, as they were in the height of the season getting men out—had about 110 salesmen on the line and others in preparation. That McKittrick then said: "Go ahead, you're all right. Get your men out, and don't let that worry you." That appellant took McKittrick at his word and worked until February 15th without any question in his mind. It was on February 15th that he was notified his services would be discontinued on March 1st.

McKittrick denied this conversation as related by appellant, and said that, when accosted by the latter on December 23d he (McKittrick) was working on his books in order to get out a report for a stockholders' meeting, and, when appellant said if he did not get a contract he would leave, that he (McKittrick) said: "Mr. Embry, I am just getting ready for the stockholders' meeting to-morrow. I have no time to take it up now. I have told you before I would not take it up until I had these matters out of the way. You will have to see me at a later time. I said: 'Go back upstairs and get your men out on the road.' I may have asked him one or two other questions relative to the department, I don't remember. The whole conversation did not take more than a minute."

Embry also swore that, when he was notified he would be discharged, he complained to McKittrick about it, as being a violation of their contract, and McKittrick said it was due to the action of the board of directors, and not to any personal action of his, and that others would suffer by what the board had done as well as Embry. Appellant requested an instruction to the jury setting out, in substance, the conversation between him and McKittrick according to his version, and declaring that those facts, if found to be true, constituted a contract between the parties that defendant would pay plaintiff the sum of $2,000 for another year, provided the jury believed from the evidence that plaintiff commenced said work believing he was to have $2,000 for the year's work. This instruction was refused, but the court gave another embodying in substance appellant's version of the conversation, and declaring it made a contract "if you (the jury) find both parties thereby intended and did contract with each other for plaintiff's employment for one year from and including December 23, 1903, at a salary of $2,000 per annum." Embry swore that, on several occasions when he spoke to McKittrick about employment for the ensuing year, he asked for a renewal of his former contract, and that on December 23d, the date of the alleged renewal, he went into Mr. McKittrick's office and told him his contract had expired, and he wanted to renew it for a year, having always worked under year contracts. Neither the refused instruction nor the one given by the court embodied facts quite as strong as appellant's testimony, because neither referred to appellant's alleged statement to McKittrick that unless he was re-employed he would stop work for respondent then and there.

It is assigned for error that the court required the jury, in order to return a verdict for appellant, not only to find the conversation occurred as appellant swore, but that both parties intended by such conversation to contract with each other for plaintiff's employment for the year from December 1903, at a salary of $2,000. If it appeared from the record that there was a dispute between the parties as to the terms on which appellant wanted re-employment, there might have been sound reason for inserting this clause in the instruction; but no issue was made that they split on terms; the testimony of McKittrick tending to prove only that he refused to enter into a contract with appellant regarding another year's employment until the annual meeting of stockholders was out of the way. Indeed as to the proposed terms McKittrick agrees with Embry, for the former swore as follows: "Mr. Embry said he wanted to know about the renewal of his contract. Said if he did not have the contract made he would leave." As the two witnesses coincided as to the terms of the proposed re-employment, there was no reason for inserting the above mentioned clause in the instruction in order that it might be settled by the jury whether or not plaintiff, if employed for one year from December 23, 1903, was to be paid $2,000 a year. Therefore it remains to determine whether or not this part of the instruction was a correct statement of the law in regard to what was necessary to constitute a contract between the parties; that is to say, whether the formation of a contract by what, according to Embry, was said, depended on the intention of both Embry and McKittrick. Or, to put the question more precisely: Did what was said constitute a contract of re-employment on the previous terms irrespective of the intention or purpose of McKittrick?

Judicial opinion and elementary treatises abound in statements of the rule that to constitute a contract there must be a meeting of the minds of the parties, and both must agree to the same thing in the same sense. Generally speaking, this may be true; but it is not literally or universally true. That is to say, the inner intention of parties to a conversation subsequently alleged to create a contract cannot either make a contract of what transpired, or prevent one from arising, if the words used were sufficient to constitute a contract. In so far as their intention is an influential element, it is only such intention as the words or acts of the parties indicate; not one secretly cherished which is inconsistent with those words or acts. . . .

In Smith v. Hughes, L.R. 6 Q.B. 597, 607, it was said: "If, whatever a man's real intention may be, he so conducts himself that a reasonable man would believe that he was assenting to the terms proposed by the other party, and that other party upon that belief enters into the contract with him, the man thus conducting himself would be equally bound as if he had intended to agree to the other party's terms." . . .

In view of those authorities, we hold that, though McKittrick may not have intended to employ Embry by what transpired between them according to the latter's testimony, yet if what McKittrick said would have been taken by a reasonable man to be an employment, and Embry so understood it, it constituted a valid contract of employment for the ensuing year.

The next question is whether or not the language used was of that character, namely, was such that Embry, as a reasonable man, might consider that he was re-employed for the ensuing year on the previous terms, and act accordingly. We do not say that in every instance it would be for the court to pronounce on this question, because, peradventure, instances might arise in which there would be such an ambiguity in the language relied on to show an assent by the obligor to the proposal of the obligee that it would be for the jury to say whether a reasonable mind would take it to signify acceptance of the proposal. . . . Embry was demanding a renewal of his contract, saying he had been put off from time to time and that he had only a few days before the end of the year in which to seek employment from other houses, and that he would quit then and there unless he was re-employed. McKittrick inquired how he was getting along with the department, and Embry said they, i.e., the employees of the department, were very busy getting out salesmen. Whereupon McKittrick said: "Go ahead, you are all right. Get your men out, and do not let that worry you." We think no reasonable man would construe that answer to Embry's demand that he be employed for another year, otherwise than as an assent to the demand, and that Embry had the right to rely on it as an assent. . . . The answer was unambiguous, and we rule that if the conversation was according to appellant's version, and he understood he was employed, it constituted in law a valid contract of re-employment, and the court erred in making the formation of a contract depend on a finding that both parties intended to make one. . . .

The judgment is reversed, and the cause remanded. All concur.

––––––––

RESTATEMENT, SECOND, CONTRACTS §§ 20, 201

[See Selected Source Materials Supplement]

––––––––

CISG ART. 8

[See Selected Source Materials Supplement]

––––––––

UNIDROIT PRINCIPLES OF INTERNATIONAL COMMERCIAL CONTRACTS ARTS. 4.1, 4.2, 4.3

[See Selected Source Materials Supplement]

––––––––

PRINCIPLES OF EUROPEAN CONTRACT LAW ARTS. 5.101, 5.102

[See Selected Source Materials Supplement]

––––––––

MCC–MARBLE CERAMIC CENTER, INC. v. CERAMICA NUOVA D'AGOSTINO

United States Court of Appeals, Eleventh Circuit, 1998.
144 F.3d 1384.

BIRCH, Circuit Judge:

This case ... [concerns a] dispute governed by the United Nations Convention on Contracts for the International Sale of Goods ("CISG"). The district court granted summary judgment on behalf of the defendant-appellee, relying on certain terms and provisions that appeared on the reverse of a pre-printed form contract for the sale of ceramic tiles. The plaintiff-appellant sought to rely on a number of affidavits that tended to show both that the parties had arrived at an oral contract before memorializing their agreement in writing and that they subjectively intended not to apply the terms on the reverse of the contract to their agreements. The magistrate judge held that the affidavits did not raise an issue of material fact and recommended that the district court grant summary judgment based on the terms of the contract. The district court agreed with the magistrate judge's reasoning and entered summary judgment in the defendant-appellee's favor. We REVERSE.

BACKGROUND

The plaintiff-appellant, MCC–Marble Ceramic, Inc. ("MCC"), is a Florida corporation engaged in the retail sale of tiles, and the defendant-appellee, Ceramica Nuova d'Agostino S.p.A. ("D'Agostino") is an Italian corporation engaged in the manufacture of ceramic tiles. In October 1990, MCC's president, Juan Carlos Monzon, met representatives of D'Agostino at a trade fair in Bologna, Italy and negotiated an agreement to purchase ceramic tiles from D'Agostino based on samples he examined at the trade fair. Monzon, who spoke no Italian, communicated with Gianni Silingardi, then D'Agostino's commercial director, through a translator, Gianfranco Copelli, who was himself an agent of D'Agostino.[1] The parties apparently arrived at an oral agreement on the crucial terms of price, quality, quantity, delivery and payment. The parties then recorded these terms on one of D'Agostino's standard, pre-printed order forms and Monzon signed the contract on MCC's behalf. According to MCC, the parties also entered into a requirements contract in February 1991, subject to which D'Agostino agreed to supply MCC with high grade ceramic tile at specific discounts as long as MCC purchased sufficient quantities of tile. MCC completed a number of additional order forms requesting tile deliveries pursuant to that agreement.

MCC brought suit against D'Agostino claiming a breach of the February 1991 requirements contract when D'Agostino failed to satisfy orders in April, May, and August of 1991. In addition to other defenses, D'Agostino responded that it was under no obligation to fill MCC's orders because MCC had defaulted on payment for previous shipments. In support of its position, D'Agostino relied on the pre-printed terms of the contracts that MCC had executed. The executed forms were printed in Italian and contained terms and conditions on both the front and reverse. According to an English translation

---

1. Since this case is before us on summary judgment, we consider the facts in the light most favorable to MCC, the non-moving party, and grant MCC the benefit of every factual inference. See Welch v. Celotex Corp., 951 F.2d 1235, 1237 (11th Cir.1992).

of the October 1990 contract, the front of the order form contained the following language directly beneath Monzon's signature:

> [T]he buyer hereby states that he is aware of the sales conditions stated on the reverse and that he expressly approves of them with special reference to those numbered 1–2–3–4–5–6–7–8.

R2–126, Exh. 3 ¶ 5 ("Maselli Aff."). Clause 6(b), printed on the back of the form states:

> [D]efault or delay in payment within the time agreed upon gives D'Agostino the right to ... suspend or cancel the contract itself and to cancel possible other pending contracts and the buyer does not have the right to indemnification or damages.

Id. ¶ 6. D'Agostino also brought a number of counterclaims against MCC, seeking damages for MCC's alleged nonpayment for deliveries of tile that D'Agostino had made between February 28, 1991 and July 4, 1991. MCC responded that the tile it had received was of a lower quality than contracted for, and that, pursuant to the CISG, MCC was entitled to reduce payment in proportion to the defects.[2] D'Agostino, however, noted that clause 4 on the reverse of the contract states, in pertinent part:

> Possible complaints for defects of the merchandise must be made in writing by means of a certified letter within and not later than 10 days after receipt of the merchandise....

Maselli Aff. ¶ 6. Although there is evidence to support MCC's claims that it complained about the quality of the deliveries it received, MCC never submitted any written complaints.

MCC did not dispute these underlying facts before the district court, but argued that the parties never intended the terms and conditions printed on the reverse of the order form to apply to their agreements. As evidence for this assertion, MCC submitted Monzon's affidavit, which claims that MCC had no subjective intent to be bound by those terms and that D'Agostino was aware of this intent. MCC also filed affidavits from Silingardi and Copelli, D'Agostino's representatives at the trade fair, which support Monzon's claim that the parties subjectively intended not to be bound by the terms on the reverse of the order form. The magistrate judge held that the affidavits, even if true, did not raise an issue of material fact regarding the interpretation or applicability of the terms of the written contracts and the district court accepted his recommendation to award summary judgment in D'Agostino's favor. MCC then filed this timely appeal.

DISCUSSION

We review a district court's grant of summary judgment de novo and apply the same standards as the district court. See Harris v. H & W Contracting Co., 102 F.3d 516, 518 (11th Cir.1996). Summary judgment is appropriate when the pleadings, depositions, and affidavits reveal that no genuine issue of material fact exists and the moving party is entitled to judgment as a matter of law. See Fed.R.Civ.P. 56(c).

The parties to this case agree that the CISG governs their dispute because the United States, where MCC has its place of business, and Italy,

---

2. Article 50 of the CISG permits a buyer to reduce payment for nonconforming goods in proportion to the nonconformity under certain conditions. See CISG, art. 50.

where D'Agostino has its place of business, are both States Party to the Convention. See CISG, art. 1. Article 8 of the CISG governs the interpretation of international contracts for the sale of goods and forms the basis of MCC's appeal from the district court's grant of summary judgment in D'Agostino's favor.[3] MCC argues that the magistrate judge and the district court improperly ignored evidence that MCC submitted regarding the parties' subjective intent when they memorialized the terms of their agreement on D'Agostino's pre-printed form contract, and that the magistrate judge erred by applying the parol evidence rule in derogation of the CISG.

Subjective Intent Under the CISG

Contrary to what is familiar practice in United States courts, the CISG appears to permit a substantial inquiry into the parties' subjective intent, even if the parties did not engage in any objectively ascertainable means of registering this intent. Article 8(1) of the CISG instructs courts to interpret the "statements ... and other conduct of a party ... according to his intent" as long as the other party "knew or could not have been unaware" of that intent. The plain language of the Convention, therefore, requires an inquiry into a party's subjective intent as long as the other party to the contract was aware of that intent.

In this case, MCC has submitted three affidavits that discuss the purported subjective intent of the parties to the initial agreement concluded between MCC and D'Agostino in October 1990. All three affidavits discuss the preliminary negotiations and report that the parties arrived at an oral agreement for D'Agostino to supply quantities of a specific grade of ceramic tile to MCC at an agreed upon price. The affidavits state that the "oral agreement established the essential terms of quality, quantity, description of goods, delivery, price and payment." See R3–133 ¶ 9 ("Silingardi Aff."); R1–51 ¶ 7 ("Copelli Aff."); R1–47 ¶ 7 ("Monzon Aff."). The affidavits also note that the parties memorialized the terms of their oral agreement on a standard D'Agostino order form, but all three affiants contend that the parties *subjectively* intended not to be bound by the terms on the reverse of that form despite a provision directly below the signature line that expressly and specifically incorporated those terms.

The terms on the reverse of the contract give D'Agostino the right to suspend or cancel all contracts in the event of a buyer's non-payment and require a buyer to make a written report of all defects within ten days. As the magistrate judge's report and recommendation makes clear, if these terms applied to the agreements between MCC and D'Agostino, summary judgment would be appropriate because MCC failed to make any written complaints about the quality of tile it received and D'Agostino has established MCC's

---

3. Article 8 provides:

(1) For the purposes of this Convention statements made by and other conduct of a party are to be interpreted according to his intent where the other party knew or could not have been unaware what that intent was.

(2) If the preceding paragraph is not applicable, statements made by and conduct of a party are to be interpreted according to the understanding a reasonable person of the same kind as the other party would have had in the same circumstances.

(3) In determining the intent of a party or the understanding a reasonable person would have had, due consideration is to be given to all relevant circumstances of the case including the negotiations, any practices which the parties have established between themselves, usages and any subsequent conduct of the parties.

CISG, art. 8.

non-payment of a number of invoices amounting to $108,389.40 and 102,053,-846.00 Italian lira.

Article 8(1) of the CISG requires a court to consider this evidence of the parties' subjective intent. Contrary to the magistrate judge's report, which the district court endorsed and adopted, article 8(1) does not focus on interpreting the parties' statements alone. Although we agree with the magistrate judge's conclusion that no "interpretation" of the contract's *terms* could support MCC's position, article 8(1) also requires a court to consider subjective intent while interpreting the *conduct* of the parties. The CISG's language, therefore, requires courts to consider evidence of a party's subjective intent when signing a contract if the other party to the contract was aware of that intent at the time. This is precisely the type of evidence that MCC has provided through the Silingardi, Copelli, and Monzon affidavits, which discuss not only Monzon's intent as MCC's representative but also discuss the intent of D'Agostino's representatives and their knowledge that Monzon did not intend to agree to the terms on the reverse of the form contract. This acknowledgment that D'Agostino's representatives were aware of Monzon's subjective intent puts this case squarely within article 8(1) of the CISG, and therefore requires the court to consider MCC's evidence as it interprets the parties' conduct.[4]

II.   ...

... [All this] is not to say that parties to an international contract for the sale of goods cannot depend on written contracts or that ... evidence regarding subjective contractual intent need always prevent a party relying on a written agreement from securing summary judgment. To the contrary, most cases will not present a situation (as exists in this case) in which both parties to the contract acknowledge a subjective intent not to be bound by the terms of a pre-printed writing. In most cases, therefore, article 8(2) of the CISG will apply, and objective evidence will provide the basis for the court's decision. See Honnold, Uniform Law § 107 at 164–65. Consequently, a party to a contract governed by the CISG will not be able to avoid the terms of a contract and force a jury trial simply by submitting an affidavit which states that he or she did not have the subjective intent to be bound by the contract's terms.... Moreover, to the extent parties wish to avoid parol evidence problems they can do so by including a merger clause in their agreement that extinguishes any and all prior agreements and understandings not expressed in the writing.

Considering MCC's affidavits in this case, however, we conclude that the magistrate judge and the district court improperly granted summary judgment in favor of D'Agostino. Although the affidavits are, as D'Agostino observes, relatively conclusory and unsupported by facts that would objectively establish MCC's intent not to be bound by the conditions on the reverse of the form, article 8(1) requires a court to consider evidence of a party's subjective intent when the other party was aware of it, and the Silingardi and Copelli affidavits provide that evidence. This is not to say that the affidavits

---

4. Without this crucial acknowledgment, we would interpret the contract and the parties' actions according to article 8(2), which directs courts to rely on objective evidence of the parties' intent. On the facts of this case it seems readily apparent that MCC's affidavits provide *no evidence* that Monzon's actions would have made his alleged subjective intent not to be bound by the terms of the contract known to "the understanding that a reasonable person ... would have had in the same circumstances." CISG, art 8(2).

are conclusive proof of what the parties intended. A reasonable finder of fact, for example, could disregard testimony that purportedly sophisticated international merchants signed a contract without intending to be bound as simply too incredible to believe and hold MCC to the conditions printed on the reverse of the contract.[5] Nevertheless, the affidavits raise an issue of material fact regarding the parties' intent to incorporate the provisions on the reverse of the form contract. If the finder of fact determines that the parties did not intend to rely on those provisions, then the more general provisions of the CISG will govern the outcome of the dispute.[6] . . .

CONCLUSION

MCC asks us to reverse the district court's grant of summary judgment in favor of D'Agostino. The district court's decision rests on pre-printed contractual terms and conditions incorporated on the reverse of a standard order form that MCC's president signed on the company's behalf. Nevertheless, we conclude that the CISG, which governs international contracts for the sale of goods, precludes summary judgment in this case because MCC has raised an issue of material fact concerning the parties' subjective intent to be bound by the terms on the reverse of the pre-printed contract. . . . Accordingly, we REVERSE the district court's grant of summary judgment and REMAND this case for further proceedings consistent with this opinion.

MAYOL v. WEINER COMPANIES, LTD.,

Appellate Court of Illinois, Fourth District, 1981.
98 Ill.App.3d 985, 425 N.E.2d 45, 54 Ill.Dec. 533.

TRAPP, Presiding Justice:

This case primarily involves the interpretation of the parties' contract to purchase real estate. Essentially, both parties contend that based upon their interpretation the other breached the contract.

The evidence at the bench trial showed that Somers (hereinafter seller) desired to sell rental property located on South First Street in Champaign. Seller enlisted the aid of Steven Vance of the Weiner Companies, Ltd. to help him sell the property, which, at that time, had a tenant. Vance, acting as the seller's agent, showed the property to Mayol (hereinafter buyer), who subse-

---

5. D'Agostino attempts to explain and undermine the affidavit of its representatives during the transaction, by calling Silingardi a "disgruntled" former employee. Appellee's Br. at 11, 39. Silingardi's alleged feelings towards his former employer may indeed be relevant to undermine the credibility of his assertions, but that is a matter for the finder of fact, not for this court on summary judgment.

6. Article 50, which permits a buyer to reduce payment to a seller who delivers nonconforming goods, and article 39, which deprives the buyer of that right if the buyer fails to give the seller notice specifying the defect in the goods delivered within a reasonable time, will be of primary importance. Although we may affirm a district court's grant of summary judgment if it is correct for any reason, even if not relied upon below, see United States v. $121,100.00 in United States Currency, 999 F.2d 1503, 1507 (11th Cir.1993), and the parties have touched upon these articles in their briefs, they have not provided us with sufficient information to resolve their dispute under the CISG. MCC's affidavits indicate that MCC may have complained about the quality of the tile D'Agostino delivered, but they have provided no authority regarding what constitutes a reasonable time for such a complaint in this context. Accordingly, we decline to affirm the district court's grant of summary judgment on this basis.

quently informed Vance that he wanted to purchase the property. Consequently, the buyer and seller signed a contract to purchase real estate, which in relevant part, stated:

"Conditions of offer:

1.   Possession to be delivered on or before November 1, 1979 subject to tenant's rights. . . .

4.   Seller shall furnish merchantable abstract of title or owner's title insurance policy, in the amount of the purchase price, showing merchantable title of record in seller's name, subject only to encumbrances assumed herein.

5.   Seller shall convey title by warranty deed, subject only to encumbrances assumed herein. . . .

11.   Subject to existing restrictive covenants, easements and zoning regulations, if any."

(The underlined words indicate that they were typed onto the form contract.)

Pursuant to other terms of the contract to purchase, the buyer tendered $1,000, which was held in escrow by the Weiner Companies, Ltd.

After signing the contract, the buyer received a copy of the tenant's lease, and, for the first time, learned that the tenant had an option to purchase the property. As a result of this knowledge, the buyer refused to abide by the contract to purchase and sued the Weiner Companies, Ltd., for the $1,000 in escrow. The record shows that, in turn, the Weiner Companies, Ltd., sued the seller. Prior to trial, however, the Weiner Companies, Ltd., tendered $1,000 to the clerk of the circuit court, and the case proceeded as if the Weiner Companies, Ltd., had interpleaded the buyer and the seller.

After the evidence was presented, the trial court concluded that the crucial phrase in the parties' contract "possession to be delivered on or before November 1, 1979, subject to tenant's rights" was ambiguous. Thus, to ascertain what the parties meant by this phrase the trial court determined that it would consider extrinsic evidence. Based on the evidence presented, the trial court found that the parties intended the phrase to mean that the buyer was taking the property subject to all the tenant's rights contained in the lease, including the tenant's option to purchase. Accordingly, the trial court entered judgment in favor of the seller, awarding the seller the $1,000 as liquidated damages for buyer's breach of contract.

On appeal, the buyer argues: (1) The trial court's interpretation of the contract is against the manifest weight of the evidence, and (2) the seller is not entitled to judgment because he has not furnished the buyer a "merchantable abstract of title or owner's title insurance policy, . . . showing merchantable title of record in seller's name . . ." as required by the contract.

In Martindell v. Lake Shore National Bank (1958), 15 Ill.2d 272, 283–84, 154 N.E.2d 683, 689, the Illinois Supreme Court stated:

"A contract, however, is to be construed as a whole, giving meaning and effect to every provision thereof, if possible, since it will be presumed that everything in the contract was inserted deliberately and for a purpose. . . . The intention of the parties is not to be gathered from detached portions of a contract or from any clause or provision standing by itself, but each part of the instrument should be viewed in the light of the other parts....

The primary object of the construction of a contract is to give effect to the intention of the parties, greater regard being given to such intent, when clearly revealed, than to any particular words used in expression thereof.... In general, the intention of the parties is to be determined from the final agreement executed by them, rather than from preliminary negotiations and agreements ... but previous agreements, negotiations and circumstances may be considered in determining the meaning of specific words and clauses.... Similarly, under well recognized exceptions to the parol evidence rule, extrinsic evidence is admissible to show the meaning of words used in a contract where there is an ambiguity, or when the language is susceptible of more than one meaning...."

... Whether an ambiguity exists in a contract is a question of law. (Coney v. Rockford Life Insurance Co. (1966), 67 Ill.App.2d 395, 214 N.E.2d 1.) Here, the trial court determined that the phrase "subject to tenant's rights" was ambiguous. With this determination we agree. Thus, as the above quoted cases point out, the trial court properly considered extrinsic evidence in its determination of what the parties meant by the ambiguous phrase "subject to tenant's rights."

Accepting that the contract is ambiguous, both parties agree that the question of whether the trial court's interpretation of the ambiguous contract is correct is a question of fact. (See 12 Ill. L. & Prac. Contracts § 247 (1970).) The buyer contends that the trial court's interpretation is against the manifest weight of the evidence. We agree.

Even though the use of extrinsic evidence is proper in this case, the express wording of the contract to purchase also merits consideration. (See Martindell.) As previously stated, paragraph 1 of the contract states "possession to be delivered on or before November 1, 1979, subject to tenant's rights." Paragraph 11, on the other hand, specifically enumerates three encumbrances to which the title was subject; namely, easements, restrictive covenants and zoning regulations. If, as the trial court found, the parties had intended the phrase "subject to tenant's rights" to encompass the tenant's option to purchase the land the buyer was purchasing, then it is curious that the phrase "subject to tenant's rights" was not listed in paragraph 11 along with the other enumerated encumbrances on title.

An option to purchase is an atypical tenant's rights. Thus, the placement of the words "subject to tenant's rights" immediately after the words "possession to be delivered on or before November 1, 1979" does not readily suggest to the buyer, or for that matter anyone else reading the contract, that he is purchasing land which is subject to an option to purchase. The more common interpretation of these words, we believe, is that the buyer is purchasing land subject to the tenant's right to remain in possession. Although the phrase "subject to tenant's rights" is subject to different interpretations, the contract construed as a whole does not favor the trial court's interpretation.

Similarly, the extrinsic evidence also does not support the trial court's interpretation. The evidence is undisputed that the buyer did not know that the tenant had an option to purchase when he signed the contract. The testimony at trial shows that Vance, the seller's agent, showed the property in question to the buyer. The buyer knew that a tenant was living there subject to a lease. In fact, the buyer asked questions and talked to Vance concerning the tenant and his lease. Vance, as well as the buyer, testified that the buyer did not know that the property was subject to the tenant's option to purchase. The ineluctable conclusion was that neither the seller, nor his agent, informed the buyer of the tenant's option to purchase even though the buyer had inquired about the lease. Also, the buyer's unrefuted testimony indicates that he requested a copy of the lease, which he did not receive until after he signed the contract. After the buyer went over the lease with his attorney, he refused to go through with the contract.

Clearly, the buyer did not intend the phrase "subject to tenant's rights" to encompass the tenant's option to purchase. Further, there is nothing in the record to indicate that the seller thought that the buyer would interpret "subject to tenant's rights" to mean subject to tenant's option to purchase. This observation is underscored by the fact that the seller did not inform the buyer of the tenant's option to purchase even though the buyer inquired about the lease. Further, the fact that such a crucial encumbrance to the title was not disclosed to the buyer, or specifically enumerated in the contract, does not support the seller's position that the phrase "possession to be delivered on or before November 1, 1979, subject to tenant's rights" would be interpreted to mean that the buyer was purchasing land subject to an option to purchase held by the tenant.

In relevant part, Restatement (Second) of Contracts, section 21(a)(19), reads:

"(2) The manifestations of the parties are operative in accordance with the meaning attached to them by one of the parties if . . .

(b) that party has no reason to know of any different meaning attached by the other, and the other has reason to know the meaning attached by the first party."

In essence, the position taken by the Restatement (Second) is that if the parties' intent does not coincide on a material term, then there is not a contract unless one of the parties is more guilty than the other for the difference in the meaning attached. Or, in other words, if there is a misunderstanding a contract results on the terms understood by the party who is less at fault for the misunderstanding. Calamari, and Perillo, Contracts, at 93. For a similar pronouncement, see Coney v. Rockford Life Insurance Co.

We hold that the trial court's interpretation of the parties' contract was against the manifest weight of the evidence. The evidence showed that the buyer had no reason to know from the language used in the contract, or from the circumstances surrounding the contract's execution, that he was signing a contract to purchase land subject to an option to purchase; and the seller had no reason to believe that the buyer thought he was purchasing land subject to the tenant's option to purchase. For such reason we hold that the buyer is entitled to the return of the $1,000 payment deposited in escrow. Upon such determination it is unnecessary to examine the second issue argued by the buyer.

The judgment is reversed and the cause is remanded to the trial court with directions to enter judgment not inconsistent with the views expressed.

Reversed and remanded with directions.

MILLS and LONDRIGAN, JJ., concur.

———

NOTE ON OBJECTIVE AND SUBJECTIVE
ELEMENTS IN INTERPRETATION

Recall that one difference between classical contract law and modern contract law is that classical contract law tended to be objective and standardized, while modern contract law tends to include subjective and individualized elements as well. This difference is particularly striking in the area of interpretation. Classical contract law adopted a theory of interpretation that was purely, or almost purely, objective. As stated in Woburn National Bank v. Woods, 77 N.H. 172, 89 A. 491 (1914):

> A contract involves what is called a meeting of the minds of the parties. But this does not mean that they must have arrived at a common mental state touching the matter in hand. The standard by which their conduct is judged and their rights are limited is not internal but external. In the absence of fraud or incapacity, the question is: What did the party say and do? "The making of a contract does not depend upon the state of the parties' minds; it depends upon their overt acts."

The strict objectivism of classical contract law is also reflected in well-known passages by Williston and Learned Hand. According to Williston:

> It is even conceivable that a contract shall be formed which is in accordance with the intention of neither party. If a written contract is entered into, the meaning and effect of the contract depends on the construction given the written language by the court, and the court will give that language its natural and appropriate meaning; and, if it is unambiguous, will not even admit evidence of what the parties may have thought the meaning to be.

1 Samuel Williston, The Law of Contracts § 95, at 181–82 (1st ed. 1920.)

And according to Learned Hand:

> A contract has, strictly speaking, nothing to do with the personal, or individual, intent of the parties. A contract is an obligation attached by the mere force of law to certain acts of the parties, usually words, which ordinarily accompany and represent a known intent. If, however, it were proved by twenty bishops that either party, when he used the words, intended something else than the usual meaning which the law imposes upon them, he would still be held, unless there were some mutual mistake, or something else of the sort. Of course, if it appear by other words, or acts, of the parties, that they attribute a peculiar meaning to such words as they use in the contract, that meaning will prevail, but only by virtue of the other words, and not because of their unexpressed intent.
>
> ... [W]hatever was the understanding in fact of the banks [in this case] ... of the legal effect of this practice between them, it is of not the slightest consequence, unless it took form in some acts or words, which, being reasonably interpreted, would have such meaning to ordinary men .... Yet the question always remains for the court to interpret the

reasonable meaning to the acts of the parties, by word or deed, and no characterization of its effect by either party thereafter, however truthful, is material. . . .

Hotchkiss v. National City Bank, 200 F. 287, 293–94 (S.D.N.Y.1911), aff'd 201 F. 664 (2d Cir.1912), aff'd 231 U.S. 50, 34 S.Ct. 20, 58 L.Ed. 115 (1913).

However, contract law is a functional instrument, whose purpose is to effectuate the objectives of parties to a promissory transaction, provided appropriate conditions (such as consideration) are satisfied, and subject to appropriate constraints (such as unconscionability). Accordingly, the principles of interpretation should be responsive not only to objective elements but, where appropriate, to the parties' subjective intentions. Under modern contract law, that is just the case, as illustrated by four central modern principles of interpretation:

Principle I: If the parties subjectively attach different meanings to an expression, neither party knows that the other attaches a different meaning, and the two meanings are not equally reasonable, the more reasonable meaning prevails.

Principle I is adopted in Restatement Second § 201(2)(b):

Where the parties have attached different meanings to a promise or agreement or a term thereof, it is interpreted in accordance with the meaning attached by one of them if at the time the agreement was made. . . .

(b) that party had no reason to know of any different meaning attached by the other, and the other had reason to know the meaning attached by the first party.

Principle I is based in significant part on the concept of liability for fault. A is at fault—is negligent—if he uses an expression that he should realize would lead a reasonable person in B's position to understand that A attaches a given meaning, Beta, to the expression, when in fact A attaches meaning Alpha to the expression. If B attaches meaning Beta to the expression, and thereby suffers wasted reliance or the defeat of a legitimate expectation when A insists on meaning Alpha, A should compensate B.

Although *Principle I* is primarily objective, it has a subjective element as well. The more reasonable meaning will prevail only if one of the parties has actually (subjectively) attached that meaning to the expression.

Principle II: If the parties subjectively attach different meanings to an expression, neither party knows that the other attaches a different meaning, and the two meanings are equally reasonable, neither meaning prevails.

Principle II is adopted in the Restatement Second § 20(1):

There is no manifestation of mutual assent to an exchange if the parties attach materially different meanings to their manifestations and

(a) neither party knows or has reason to know the meaning attached by the other; or

(b) each party knows or each party has reason to know the meaning attached by the other.

Principle II is consistent with *Principle I*. If parties to a promissory transaction subjectively attach different meanings to their expressions, and in attaching these different meanings both parties are either equally fault-free or equally at fault, there is no reason why one meaning rather than the other should prevail. *Principle II* is associated with Raffles v. Wichelhaus, the *Peerless* case. To preserve the classical–school program, Holmes argued that the result in *Peerless* could be explained by objective theory. "The true ground of the decision was not that each party meant a different thing from the other … but that each said a different thing. The plaintiff offered one thing, the defendant expressed his assent to another." Holmes, The Common Law 309 (1881). But if both parties subjectively meant the December Peerless, Buyer should have been deemed in breach; and if both parties subjectively meant the October Peerless, Seller should have been deemed in breach. Holmes had it backwards: the result in *Peerless* is correct because the parties meant different things, not because the parties said different things.

Principle III: If the parties subjectively attach the same meaning to an expression, that meaning prevails even though it is unreasonable. Principle III squarely reverses the strict objectivism of classical contract law, under which the subjective intention of the parties was irrelevant, even if mutually held. Again, the objectivists had it wrong. Where both parties attach the same, unreasonable, meaning to an expression, both parties may have been at fault in their use of language, but the fault caused no injury. Indeed, a party who in litigation presses a meaning that he did not attach to his expression at the time of contract–formation is himself at fault.

Principle III is adopted in Restatement Second § 201(1). That section provides that "[w]here the parties have attached the same meaning to a promise or agreement or a term thereof, it is interpreted in accordance with that meaning." Under section 201(1), reasonableness becomes relevant only where there is not a mutually held subjective meaning. Thus, Restatement Second stands the classical school's position on its head, by giving primacy to mutually held subjective interpretation, and resorting to an objective or reasonable meaning only in the absence of a mutually held subjective meaning.

Principle IV: If the parties, A and B, attach different meanings, Alpha and Beta, to an expression, and A knows that B attaches meaning Beta, but B does not know that A attaches meaning Alpha, the meaning Beta prevails even if it is less reasonable than the meaning Alpha.

Principle IV is adopted in Restatement Second § 201(2):

> Where the parties have attached different meanings to a promise or agreement or a term thereof, it is interpreted in accordance with the meaning attached by one of them if at the time the agreement was made
>
> (a) that party did not know of any different meaning attached by the other, and the other knew the meaning attached by the first party....

Principle IV is largely subjective. It is supported by a fault analysis. B may have been at fault in attaching meaning Beta to the expression, but A was more at fault in allowing B to proceed on the basis of an interpretation that A knew B held, at least when B did not know that A held a different interpretation.

———

BERKE MOORE CO. v. PHOENIX BRIDGE CO., 98 N.H. 261, 98 A.2d 150 (1953). "The rule which precludes the use of the understanding of one party alone is designed to prevent imposition of his private understanding upon the other party to a bilateral transaction. IX Wig.Ev., 3d Ed., § 2460; Smart v. Huckins, 82 N.H. 342, 348, 134 A. 520. But when it appears that the understanding of one is the understanding of both, no violation of the rule results from determination of the mutual understanding according to that of one alone.

"Where the understanding is mutual, it ceases to be the 'private' understanding of one party. Having thus determined the mutual understanding of the parties, the Court properly interpreted the contract accordingly."

NOTE ON "INTENTION" AS A TEST
OF LEGAL CONSEQUENCES

Legal consequences can be said to be directly derived from "the intention of the parties" only where that intention runs in terms that roughly coincide with the categories of the law—when, in other words, the parties' intention is capable of answering the question that the law proposes. The difficulties that are often encountered in attempting to make legal results hinge on the parties' intention are illustrated in the following passage, taken from an essay on legal reasoning: "A young woman becomes engaged to a young man who is a business clerk. To enable them to establish an independent household, the young woman gives the young man her savings. A business, founded with this money and run jointly by the two young people, now living together, goes badly, and the engagement disintegrates. The young woman sues for the return of her money, to which the young man responds that the money was lost in the business. The judge must determine whether the original furnishing of the money was intended by the young woman as a loan, or as marital assets, or whether she basically intended to direct the use the money (so that the business was to belong to the young woman herself), or whether the money had the character of an investment in a partnership, etc. The judge has to answer these questions, even though possibly, indeed, *probably*, the intent of the parties was completely unsettled, and even though the parties were completely unaware of the legal side of their actions. Their entire conscious meaning exhausted itself in that they loved each other, had complete trust in one another, and were to be married. It was irrelevant in whose pocket the money was kept. [In short, the judge has to place the couple's relationship in regard to the young woman's money into a conventional legal category] despite the fact that their thinking and intending did not take shape within conventional legal forms." (Translated by Sean Callagy from Wurzel, Das juristische Denken, 82 (1904). A different translation will be found in The Science of Legal Method, the Modern Legal Philosophy Series, 339 (1921), where the whole essay is printed, at pp. 286–428.)

SECTION 2. PROBLEMS OF INTERPRETING PURPOSIVE LANGUAGE

WILLIAMS, LANGUAGE AND THE LAW—PART IV
61 L.Q.Rev. 384, 400–404 (1945).

[A distinction must] be made between (a) the literal or primary meaning of the words, and (b) the ulterior meaning i.e., the meaning, other than the literal meaning, intended to be conveyed by the speaker when he uttered the words, or the meaning, other than the literal meaning, attributed by a hearer to the speaker. . . .

. . . For example a tactless host looks out of the window and says to his guest: "It has stopped raining." The guest mistakenly takes this to be an oblique hint that he is desired to leave. Here it may be said that while the meaning of the words to the host is "It has stopped raining" . . . the meaning to the guest is both this . . . and also "Please go". . . .

It has already been remarked that the Courts will generally enforce consequences logically implied in the language of contracts, wills, statutes, and other legal documents and transactions. The point now to be noticed is that the legal doctrine of implied terms goes much farther than this. Judges are accustomed to read into documents and transactions many terms that are not logically implied in them. As an academic matter non-logical implication may be classified into three kinds: (i) of terms that the parties (the plural shall throughout include the singular) probably had in mind but did not trouble to express; (ii) of terms that the parties, whether or not they actually had them in mind, would probably have expressed if the question had been brought to their attention; and (iii) of terms that the parties, whether or not they had them in mind or would have expressed them if they had foreseen the difficulty, are implied by the Court because of the Court's view of fairness or policy or in consequence of rules of law. Of these three kinds of non-logical implication (i) is an effort to arrive at actual intention; (ii) is an effort to arrive at hypothetical or conditional intention—the intention that the parties would have had if they had foreseen the difficulty; (iii) is not concerned with the intention of the parties except to the extent that the term implied by the Court may be excluded by an expression of positive intention to the contrary.

. . . [O]nly in case (i) does the implication amount to a declaration by the Court of ulterior meaning in the sense already defined; in the other two cases the so-called implication is in reality an addition by the Court to the meaning of the parties. . . .

We pass to a consideration of . . . types (ii) and (iii). It is common form among judges to deny that they ever read into a contract or other document anything other than what, in their view, the parties actually intended; and occasionally they have even gone so far as to say that the implication must be collected from the words of the document itself. These statements cannot be taken seriously. It is true that the declaration of presumed actual intention is the commonest form of implication; but it is not the only form. Courts frequently import into a document terms that are not logically implied in it, and that the parties probably did not think about: or, to say the least, such terms are imported whether or not in the particular case it is probable that the parties thought about them. . . .

The view may perhaps be held that this particular process is not very happily called "implication." It is not so much the interpretation of a pre-existing and expressed intent as legislation amending or supplementing the expressed intent. Terms so read into the contract might better be called "constructive" than "implied." However, this is simply a question of nomenclature; and in any case no fixed nomenclature can be maintained in practice, because terms of classes (i) (ii) and (iii) merge into each other. . . .

This brings me to my last point, which is that it is a matter of taste whether implied terms of classes (ii) and (iii) be styled implied terms or rules of law. They are in fact merely rules of law that apply in the absence of an expression of contrary intent: whether we choose to call them implied terms or not is simply a matter of terminology. . . .

FISH, NORMAL CIRCUMSTANCES, LITERAL LANGUAGE, DIRECT SPEECH ACTS, THE ORDINARY, THE EVERYDAY, THE OBVIOUS, WHAT GOES WITHOUT SAYING, AND OTHER SPECIAL CASES

4 Critical Inquiry 625 (Summer 1978).

. . . [A]s Kenneth Abraham observes,

A statute without a purpose would be meaningless . . . to speak of the literal meaning of a statute . . . is already to have read it in the light of some purpose, to have engaged in an interpretation.

In other words, any reading that is plain and obvious in the light of some assumed purpose (and it is impossible not to assume one) is a literal reading, but no reading is *the* literal reading in the sense that it is available apart from any purpose whatsoever.

A sentence is never not in a context. We are never not in a situation. . . . A set of interpretive assumptions is always in force. A sentence that seems to need no interpretation is already the product of one. . . .

[Suppose student X says to student Y, "Let's go to the movies tonight," and student Y replies, "I have to study for an exam." The statement by student X seems to be a proposal, and the statement by student Y seems to be rejection of the proposal. Now suppose student Y replies instead, "I have to eat popcorn tonight" or "I have to tie my shoes." In most circumstances, those statements would not be regarded as a rejection of the proposal. But] is it possible to imagine a set of circumstances in which "I have to eat popcorn tonight" would immediately and without any chain of inference be heard as a rejection of X's proposal? It is not only possible; it is easy. Let us suppose that student Y is passionately fond of popcorn and that it is not available in any of the local movie theaters. If student X knows these facts (if he and student Y mutually share background information), then he will hear "I have to eat popcorn tonight" as a rejection of his proposal. Or, let us suppose that student Y is by profession a popcorn taster; that is, he works in a popcorn manufacturing plant and is responsible for quality control. Again if student X knows this, he will hear "I have to eat popcorn tonight" as a rejection of his proposal because it will mean "Sorry, I have to work." Or, let us suppose that student Y owns seventy-five pairs of shoes and that he has been ordered by a dormitory housemother to retrieve them from various corners, arrange them neatly in one place, and tie them together in pairs so that they will not again be separated and scattered. In such a situation "I have to tie my shoes" will constitute a rejection of student X's proposal and will be so heard. Moreover it is not just "I have to eat popcorn" and "I have to tie my shoes" that could be heard as a rejection of the proposal; given the appropriate circumstances *any* sentence ("The Russians are coming," "My pen is blue," "Why do you behave like that?") could be so heard....

The argument will also hold for "Let's go to the movies tonight." ... Thus if speakers X and Y are trapped in some wilderness, and one says to the other, "Let's go to the movies tonight," it will be heard not as a proposal, but as a joke; or if student X is confined to his bed or otherwise immobilized, and student Y says, "Let's go to the movies tonight," it will be heard not as a proposal, but as a dare....

It is important to realize what my argument does *not* mean. It does not mean that [a] sentence can mean anything at all.... A sentence ... is never in the abstract; it is always in a situation, and the situation will already have determined the purpose for which it can be used. So it is not that any sentence can be used as a request to open the window, but that given any sentence, there are circumstances under which it would be heard as a request to open the window. A sentence neither means anything at all, nor does it always mean the same thing; it always has the meaning that has been conferred on it by the situation in which it is uttered.

HAINES v. NEW YORK

Court of Appeals of New York, 1977.
41 N.Y.2d 769, 396 N.Y.S.2d 155, 364 N.E.2d 820.

GABRIELLI, JUDGE.

In the early 1920's, respondent City of New York and intervenors Town of Hunter and Village of Tannersville embarked upon negotiations for the construction of a sewage system to serve the village and a portion of the town. These negotiations were prompted by the city's need and desire to prevent the discharge of untreated sewage by residents of the area into Gooseberry Creek, a stream which fed a reservoir of the city's water supply system in the Schoharie watershed.

In 1923, the Legislature enacted enabling legislation authorizing the city to enter into contracts with municipalities in the watershed area "for the purpose of providing, maintaining [and] operating systems and plants for the collection and disposal of sewage" (L.1923, ch. 630, § 1). The statute further provided that any such contracts would be subject to the approval of the New York City Board of Estimate and Apportionment.

The negotiations culminated in an agreement in 1924 between the city and intervenors. By this agreement, the city assumed the obligation of constructing a sewage system consisting of a sewage disposal plant and sewer mains and laterals, and agreed that "all costs of construction and subsequent operation, maintenance and repair of said sewage system with the house connections thereof and said disposal works shall be at the expense" of the city. The agreement also required the city to extend the sewer lines when "necessitated by future growth and building constructions of the respective communities". The village and town were obligated to and did obtain the necessary easements for the construction of the system and sewage lines.

The Board of Estimate, on December 9, 1926, approved the agreement and authorized the issuance of $500,000 of "corporate stock" of the City of New York for construction of the system by appropriate resolution. It is interesting to here note that a modification of the original agreement occurred in 1925 wherein the village agreed to reimburse the city for a specified amount representing the expense of changing the location of certain sewer lines. The plant was completed and commenced operation in 1928. The city has continued to maintain the plant through the ensuing years and in 1958 expended $193,000 to rehabilitate and expand the treatment plant and facilities.

Presently, the average flow of the plant has increased from an initial figure of 118,000 gallons per day to over 600,000 gallons daily and the trial court found that the plant "was operating substantially in excess of design capacity". The city asserts, and it is not disputed by any of the parties in this action, that the system cannot bear any significant additional "loadings" because this would result in inadequate treatment of all the sewage and consequently harm the city's water supply. The instant controversy arose when plaintiff, who is the owner of a tract of unimproved land which he seeks to develop into 50 residential lots, applied to the city for permission to connect houses, which he intends to construct on the lots, to existing sewer lines. The city refused permission on the ground that it had no obligation to further expand the plant, which is presently operating at full capacity, to accommodate this new construction.

Plaintiff then commenced this action for declaratory and injunctive relief, in which intervenors town and village joined as plaintiffs, maintaining that the 1924 agreement is perpetual in duration and obligates the city to expend additional capital funds to enlarge the existing plant or build a new one to accommodate the present and future needs of the municipalities. Both the trial court and the Appellate Division, by a divided court, held in favor of plaintiff and intervenors concluding, that, while the contract did not call for perpetual performance, the city was bound to construct additional facilities to meet increased demand until such time as the village or town is legally obligated to maintain a sewage disposal system. Two members of the court dissented in part stating that the agreement should not be construed as requiring the city to construct new or additional facilities.

We conclude that the city is presently obligated to maintain the existing plant but is not required to expand that plant or construct any new facilities to accommodate plaintiff's substantial, or any other, increased demands on the sewage system. The initial problem encountered in ascertaining the nature and extent of the city's obligation pursuant to the 1924 agreement, is its duration. We reject, as did the courts below, the plaintiff's contention that the city is perpetually bound under the agreement. The contract did not expressly provide for perpetual performance and both the trial court and the Appellate Division found that the parties did not so intend. Under these circumstances, the law will not imply that a contract calling for continuing performance is perpetual in duration (*Mitler v. Friedeberg,* 32 Misc.2d 78, 85, 222 N.Y.S.2d 480, 488; *Warner–Lambert Pharm. Co. v. John J. Reynolds, Inc.,* 178 F.Supp. 655, affd. 2 Cir., 280 F.2d 197; *Holt v. St. Louis Union Trust Co.,* 4 Cir., 52 F.2d 1068, 1069; *Town of Readsboro v. Hoosac Tunnel & Wilmington R.R. Co.,* 2 Cir., 6 F.2d 733 [L. Hand, J.]; *Borough of West Caldwell v. Borough of Caldwell,* 26 N.J. 9, 28–29, 138 A.2d 402, 1 Williston, Contracts [3d ed.], § 38, p. 113).

On the other hand, the city's contention that the contract is terminable at will because it provides for no express duration should also be rejected. In the absence of an express term fixing the duration of a contract, the courts may inquire into the intent of the parties and supply the missing term if a duration may be fairly and reasonably fixed by the surrounding circumstances and the parties' intent (*Warner–Lambert Pharm. Co. v. John J. Reynolds, Inc., supra,* p. 661; *Benham v. World Airways,* 9 Cir., 432 F.2d 359, 361; *Town of Readsboro v. Hoosac Tunnel & Wilmington R.R. Co., supra,* p. 735). It is generally agreed that where a duration may be fairly and reasonably supplied by implication, a contract is not terminable at will (1 Williston, *op. cit.,* p. 112; 10 N.Y.Jur., Contracts, § 412, p. 426; 17 Am.Jur.2d, Contracts, § 487, p. 957; 17A C.J.S. Contracts § 398, p. 480; see, also, Restatement, Contracts 2d [Tent. Draft No. 7], § 230).

While we have not previously had occasion to apply it, the weight of authority supports the related rule that where the parties have not clearly expressed the duration of a contract, the courts will imply that they intended performance to continue for a reasonable time (*Colony Liq. Distrs. v. Daniel Distillery–Lem Motlow Prop.,* 22 A.D.2d 247, 249–250, 254 N.Y.S.2d 547, 549, 550 [Aulisi, J.]; *Metal Assoc. v. East Side Metal Spinning & Stamping Corp.,* 2 Cir., 165 F.2d 163, 165; *Borough of West Caldwell v. Borough of Caldwell, supra,* 138 A.2d p. 412; Simpson, Contracts, § 48, p. 74; 1 Williston, *op. cit.,* pp. 116–117; 10 N.Y.Jur., Contracts, § 413, p. 427). For compelling policy reasons, this rule has not been, and should not be, applied to contracts of employment or exclusive agency, distributorship, or requirements contracts which have been analogized to employment contracts.... The considerations relevant to such contracts do not obtain here. Thus, we hold that it is reasonable to infer from the circumstances of the 1924 agreement that the parties intended the city to maintain the sewage disposal facility until such time as the city no longer needed or desired the water, the purity of which the plant was designed to insure. The city argues that it is no longer obligated to maintain the plant because State law now prohibits persons from discharging raw sewage into streams such as Gooseberry Creek. However, the parties did not contemplate the passage of environmental control laws which would prohibit individuals or municipalities from discharging raw, untreated sewage into certain streams. Thus, the city agreed to assume the obligation of assuring that its water supply remained unpolluted and it may not now avoid that obligation for reasons not contemplated by the parties when the agreement was executed, and not within the purview of their intent, expressed or implied.

Having determined the duration of the city's obligation, the scope of its duty remains to be defined. By the agreement, the city obligated itself to build a specifically described disposal facility and to extend the lines of that facility to meet future increased demand. At the present time, the extension of those lines would result in the overloading of the system. Plaintiff claims that the city is required to build a new plant or expand the existing facility to overcome the problem. We disagree. The city should not be required to extend the lines to plaintiffs' property if to do so would overload the system and result in its inability to properly treat sewage. In providing for the extension of sewer lines, the contract does not obligate the city to provide sewage disposal services for properties in areas of the municipalities not presently served or even to new properties in areas which are presently served where to do so could reasonably be expected to significantly increase the demand on present plant facilities.

Thus, those paragraphs of the judgment which provide that the city is obligated to construct any additional facilities required to meet increased demand and that plaintiff is entitled to full use of the sewer lines should be stricken.

Accordingly, the order of the Appellate Division should be modified and the case remitted to Supreme Court, Greene County, for the entry of judgment in accordance with the opinion herein and, as so modified, affirmed, with costs to appellants against plaintiffs-respondents only.

BREITEL, C.J., and JASEN, JONES, WACHTLER, FUCHSBERG and COOKE, JJ., concur.

Order modified, etc.

———

RESTATEMENT, SECOND, CONTRACTS § 204

[See Selected Source Materials Supplement]

———

UNIDROIT PRINCIPLES OF INTERNATIONAL COMMERCIAL CONTRACTS ART. 4.8

[See Selected Source Materials Supplement]

———

SPAULDING v. MORSE

Supreme Judicial Court of Massachusetts, 1947.
322 Mass. 149, 76 N.E.2d 137.

DOLAN, JUSTICE. [George and Ruth Morse were married in 1921. In 1932, Ruth obtained a decree of divorce which made provision for the custody and support of the Morse's two children, Richard and Merilyn. Subsequently, disputes arose between the Morses. As a result, in 1937 they entered into an agreement "intended to supersede in so far as the provisions herein contained are concerned" the provisions made in the decree for the benefit of Ruth, Richard, and Merilyn. The agreement provided that George would make a lump sum payment to Ruth, in installments, as alimony, that Ruth would have custody of Richard, and that George would have custody of Merilyn. In addition, a trustee was appointed for Richard, and it was agreed that George "shall and will pay to the said trustee in trust for his said minor son Richard the sum of twelve hundred dollars ($1,200) per year ... until the entrance of Richard D. Morse into some college, university or higher institution of learning beyond the completion of the high school grades, and thereupon, instead of said payments, amounting to twelve hundred dollars ($1,200) yearly, he shall and will then pay to the trustee payments in the sum of twenty-two hundred dollars ($2,200) per year for a period of said higher education but not more than four years...."

[Richard completed high school in February 1946, and was immediately inducted into the Army. The trustee brought this action to require George to continue paying $100 a month for Richard while he was in the Army. The trial court held for the trustee, and ordered George to pay $1,500 (the amount which had accrued since Richard's induction) and to continue paying $100 per month to the trustee "until such time, if any, as [Richard] enters college, and, thereupon, and for a period not to exceed four (4) years thereafter, to pay the sum of twenty-two hundred dollars ($2,200) per year to the ... [plaintiff] payable in monthly payments." George appealed.]

"Every instrument in writing is to be interpreted, with a view to the material circumstances of the parties at the time of the execution, in the light of the pertinent facts within their knowledge and in such manner as to give effect to the main end designed to be accomplished.... [The] instrument is to be so construed as to give effect to the intent of the ... [parties] as manifested by the words used illumined by all the attendant factors, unless inconsistent with some positive rule of law or repugnant to other terms of the instrument. An omission to express an intention cannot be supplied by conjecture. But, if the instrument as a whole produces a conviction that a particular result was fixedly desired although not expressed by formal words, that defect may be supplied by implication and the underlying intention ... may be effectuated, provided it is sufficiently declared by the entire instrument." Dittemore v. Dickey, 249 Mass. 95, 104, 105, 144 N.E. 57, 60....

Examining the instrument before us, guided by the settled rule of interpretation set forth above, it is manifest that the main purpose of the parents of Richard was to arrive at an agreement for his maintenance and education and to provide security therefor. At the time of the execution of the agreement he was almost ten years of age. His custody had already been awarded to his mother by the decree of divorce of the Nevada court, concerning the validity of which no question is raised. This being so, it is a fair inference that in so far as Richard was concerned his maintenance and education were the main purposes sought to be accomplished by the trust agreement, the parties to the agreement having in mind his age and recognizing the necessity of his being supported during the years to come, and of his being properly educated in a manner appropriate to the defendant's financial ability and station in life. The instrument specifically provided that the payments to be made by the defendant to the trustee for Richard's benefit should "be applied by ... [his mother] or the trustee upon or toward the maintenance and education and benefit of said Richard, so long as she shall maintain and educate said Richard to the satisfaction of the said trustee." But, as appears by the agreed facts and the record, the education of Richard was interrupted by the second World War and his induction into the armed forces of the United States on February 6, 1946, the day following the completion of his high school grades on February 5, 1946. Since then he had been continuously, and at the time of the hearing and order for decree in the court below was, in the service of the armed forces of the nation. Thus he was actually under the command of his superior officers in that service, his maintenance was provided for during the period here involved by the government, and he was not in the actual custody of his mother and was not a student in any higher institution of learning. Thus neither of the main objects for which the defendant had bound himself to provide existed within the meaning of the trust instrument during the period for which the plaintiff claims payment. In these circumstances we are of opinion that the proper construction of the trust instrument is that the defendant is not required under its terms to perform provisions for the maintenance and education of Richard while he was or is in the armed service of the United States....

It follows from what we have said that the decree entered by the judge must be reversed and that instead a final decree must be entered after rescript dismissing the bill with costs of the appeal.

So ordered.

———

LAWSON v. MARTIN TIMBER CO., 238 La. 467, 115 So.2d 821 (1959). Lawson and Timber Company entered into an agreement on October 14, 1948, which provided that Timber Company had two years to cut and remove timber from Lawson's land, and that "in event of high water after this time [i.e., during the two–year period], ... Timber Co. is to get additional one year's time." Timber Company cut and removed certain timber from Lawson's land in July 1951, after the original two–year period had expired. Lawson brought an action to recover the value of that timber. The evidence indicated that there was high water during approximately half of the two–year period, but that all the lumber on Lawson's land could have easily been cut and removed during the other half.

The issue was whether the one–year extension was applicable under these circumstances. On the original hearing, a majority of the court held that it was. "[W]hether or not the defendant was prevented from removing the timber within two years from the date of the contract on account of high water ... is immaterial under the very wording contained in the contract granting defendant an additional year within which to remove the timber 'in event of high water after this time.' The language used in this provision of the contract is clear and unambiguous and we cannot go beyond it with the view of seeking the intention of the parties."

Justice Simon dissented. "The words in the clause standing alone are meaningless. But when taken in context with the preceding language of the contract wherein it is stated that the defendant is given two years in which to cut and remove all of said timber, this clause can have but one objective meaning.... It is manifest that, taking the clause as written in the language preceding, it can only mean that if there existed any overflow or high water during the period of two years which would have *prevented* the cutting and removal of this timber within the stated primary term, then the defendant enjoyed the right of so doing during the period of one additional year...."

On rehearing, the court adopted Justice Simon's position.

———

LIEBER, LEGAL AND POLITICAL HERMENEUTICS 17–19 (3d ed. 1880). "Let us take an instance of the simplest kind, to show in what degree we are continually obliged to resort to interpretation. By and by we shall find that the same rules which common sense teaches every one to use, in order to understand his neighbor in the most trivial intercourse, are necessary likewise, although not sufficient, for the interpretation of documents or texts of the highest importance, constitutions as well as treaties between the greatest nations.

"Suppose a housekeeper says to a domestic: 'fetch some soupmeat,' accompanying the act with giving some money to the latter; he will be unable to execute the order without interpretation, however easy and, consequently, rapid the performance of the process may be. Common sense and good faith tell the domestic, that the housekeeper's meaning was this: 1. He should go immediately, or as soon as his other occupations are finished; or, if he be directed to do so in the evening, that he should go the next day at the *usual* hour; 2. that the money handed him by the housekeeper is intended to pay for the meat thus ordered, and not as a present to him; 3. that he should buy such meat and of such parts of the animal, as, to his knowledge, has commonly been used in the house he stays at, for making soups; 4. that he buy the best meat he can obtain, for a fair price; 5. that he go to that butcher who usually provides the family, with whom the domestic resides, with meat, or to some convenient stall, and not to any unnecessarily distant place; 6. that he return the rest of the money; 7. that he bring home the meat in good faith, neither adding any thing disagreeable nor injurious; 8. that he fetch the meat for the use of the family and not for himself. Suppose, on the other hand, the housekeeper, afraid of being misunderstood, had mentioned these eight specifications, she would not have obtained her object, if it were to exclude all *possibility* of misunderstanding. For, the various specifications would have required new ones. Where would be the end? We are constrained then, always, to leave a considerable part of our meaning to be found out by interpretation, which, in many cases must necessarily cause greater or less obscurity with regard to the exact meaning, which our words were intended to convey."

———

SECTION 3. THE ROLE OF USAGE, COURSE OF DEALING, AND COURSE OF PERFORMANCE IN INTERPRETATION

FOXCO INDUSTRIES, LTD. v. FABRIC WORLD, INC.

United States Court of Appeals, Fifth Circuit, 1979.
595 F.2d 976.

TJOFLAT, Circuit Judge:

In this diversity action Foxco Industries, Ltd. (Foxco), a Delaware corporation, following a jury trial recovered a $26,000 judgment against Fabric World, Inc. (Fabric World), an Alabama corporation, for breaching a contract to purchase certain knitted fabric goods and refusing to pay for merchandise previously purchased. [On appeal, Fabric World argues that] the district court erred in admitting into evidence published standards of the Knitted Textile Association to establish the meaning of a disputed contract term. For the reasons set forth below, we reject the [argument] of Fabric World and affirm.

I

Foxco is in the business of manufacturing knitted fabrics for sale to retail fabric stores and the garment industry. Foxco's principal place of business is in New York City; it has never formally qualified to do business in Alabama. Fabric World is engaged in the retail fabric business and operates a chain of stores in a number of states; its headquarters is in Huntsville, Alabama.

There are two seasons in the fabric industry, a spring season and a fall season. Before the beginning of each season Foxco displays for customers samples of the line of fabrics it will manufacture that season. Customer orders are accepted only from the fabric shown on display. Foxco's manufacturing operation is limited to filling these orders; no fabrics are manufactured merely to be held as inventory. There was some conflict in the testimony as to whether fabric specially knit for one customer, such as Fabric World, could be resold to another customer.

Foxco sells some of its goods to retail fabric stores through manufacturers' representatives, operating on a commission basis, who sell the lines of numerous manufacturers. Foxco furnishes each representative with samples and a price list. Larger retail store customers, such as Fabric World, are handled personally by Foxco's sales manager, Allen Feller, a salaried employee, who supervises all retail fabric store sales. He has responsibility over the approximately twenty-six manufacturers' representatives carrying the Foxco line.

Foxco has never maintained an office in Alabama. At the time of the transactions giving rise to this action, its manufacturers' representative in Alabama was a resident of the state. Foxco's sales manager, Feller, made periodic trips to Alabama to meet with this representative and to obtain orders from Fabric World and Kennemer Company, another large fabric retailer. At the beginning of each season Feller would meet with the manufacturers' representative for two or three days so that the new line of fabrics could be previewed and discussed. In 1974, Foxco's gross sales approximated $14,000,000; Alabama accounted for in excess of $100,000 of that amount. A substantial portion of the Alabama business was with Fabric World, from which three separate orders were obtained.

On April 22, 1974, Feller traveled to Huntsville to show Fabric World the new fall line. His meeting with Glenn Jameson, Fabric World's president, culminated in a written order for "first quality" goods. A dispute subsequently arose regarding the quality of the goods sent to fill the order, and Fabric World refused to pay for the portion of the goods it considered defective.

On October 21, 1974, Feller returned to Huntsville to show Jameson the line for the following spring season. Jameson voiced no complaint about the quality of the goods received pursuant to the previous April 22 order. In fact, he gave Feller a new order, in writing, for 12,000 yards of first quality fabric, at a price of $36,705, to be delivered by January 15, 1975.

A few weeks after the October 21 order was placed, the textile industry began to experience a precipitous decline in the price of yarn. Because of a drop in the price of finished goods, Fabric World wrote Foxco on November 15, 1974, and cancelled its October 21 order. Foxco immediately replied, stating that the manufacture of the order was substantially completed and that it could not accept the cancellation. On November 27, 1974, Foxco's attorney wrote Fabric World that if the goods were not accepted they would be finished and sold and Fabric World sued for the difference between the contract price and the sales price received by Foxco. On December 3, 1974, Fabric World agreed to accept the order, but threatened to return the entire shipment if it contained one flaw. Foxco, believing that it was impossible to produce an order of this magnitude without a single flaw, decided it would not ship the order (which was completed a short time later).

Fabric World established that in December 1974 the fair market value of the October order was approximately 20% less than the contract price. However, Foxco made no attempt to sell the goods from the time Fabric World cancelled the order until September 1975, when the goods had dropped 50% In value. In that month Foxco sold at a private sale without notice to Fabric World approximately 7,000 yards from the order for an average price of between $1.50 and $1.75 per yard, a total consideration of $10,119.50. By the time of trial in April 1976, Foxco had on hand about 5,000 yards of the order worth between $1.25 and $1 per yard, or about $6,250.

During the course of the trial there was much testimony regarding the meaning of the term first quality goods used in the contracts between Foxco and Fabric World. The testimony on behalf of Fabric World was that it meant fabric containing no flaws. Foxco introduced evidence, over the objection of Fabric World, in the form of an exhibit containing standards for finished knitted goods promulgated by the Knitted Textile Association, a large textile industry group to which Foxco belongs. These standards indicated that certain types and amounts of flaws were permissible in first quality fabric. Fabric World is not a member of that association and claimed it had no knowledge of the standards adopted by the association's members. One ground for Fabric World's present appeal is its contention that the standards of a trade association of which it had no knowledge are not admissible to show the meaning of the undefined and disputed contract term "first quality" goods. . . .

Fabric World's [claims] that the district court erred in admitting into evidence the definition of first quality goods contained in the Standards for Finished Knitted Fabrics of the Knitted Textile Association. It contends that it is not a member of the Knitted Textile Association, was unaware of its existence until the time of trial, and that that group's standards were inadmissible because they were a custom or usage of the trade of which Fabric World had no knowledge. We find no error in the trial court's ruling.

A major issue in this case is what was meant by the term "first quality." Under the traditional application of the parol evidence rule, Fabric World's contention may have merit: the private, subjective intent of one party to a contract may well be irrelevant in determining the meaning of a contract term unless it is shown that that intent was communicated to the other party. See Levie, Trade Usage and Custom under the Common Law and the Uniform Commercial Code, 40 N.Y.U.L.Rev. 1101 (1965). In this case there is no direct evidence, as Fabric World argues, that it was put on notice that usage and custom, as embodied in the industry standards, would be used to define the meaning of first quality. Under Alabama sales law, however, that Fabric World did not know of the industry's usage and custom or of the standards in question is of no moment; the parties to a contract such as the one in issue are presumed to have intended the incorporation of trade usage in striking their bargain. U.C.C. section 2–202, Ala.Code tit. 7, § 7–2–202 (1977), explicitly provides that trade usages may help explain or supplement contract terms.[8] As stated in the comment to that provision,

> [Section 2–202(a)] makes admissible evidence of course of dealing, usage of trade and course of performance to explain or supplement the terms of any writing stating the agreement of the parties in order that the true understanding of the parties as to the agreement may be reached. *Such writings are to be read on the assumption that* the course of prior dealings between the parties *and the usages of trade were taken for granted when the document was phrased. Unless carefully negated they have become an element of the meaning of the words used.*

Id., Official Comment (emphasis added). Section 1–205(2) . . . defines trade usages. It provides in part that

> A usage of trade is any practice or method of dealing having such regularity of observance in a place, vocation or trade as to justify an expectation that it will be observed with respect to the transaction in question. The existence and scope of such a usage are to be proved as facts.

It further states: "A course of dealing between parties and any usage of trade in the vocation or trade in which they are engaged or of which they are or should be aware give particular meaning to and supplement or qualify terms of an agreement." . . . There was uncontroverted testimony that the Knitted Textile Association is an industry group with over 1500 members. Its standards could certainly qualify as trade usages, and thus were admissible notwithstanding Fabric World's unawareness of them. Loeb & Co. v. Martin, 295 Ala. 262, 327 So.2d 711, 715 (1976). See Columbia Nitrogen Corp. v.

8. Section 2–202 states:

Final written expression: Parol or extrinsic evidence.

Terms with respect to which the confirmatory memoranda of the parties agree or which are otherwise set forth in a writing intended by the parties as a final expression of their agreement with respect to such terms as are included therein may not be contradicted by evidence of any prior agreement or of a contemporaneous oral agreement but may be explained or supplemented:

(a) By course of dealing or usage of trade (section 7–1–205) or by course of performance (section 7–2–208); and

(b) By evidence of consistent additional terms unless the court finds the writing to have been intended also as a complete and exclusive statement of the terms of the agreement.

Royster Co., 451 F.2d 3 (4th Cir. 1971); Chase Manhattan Bank v. First Marion Bank, 437 F.2d 1040 (5th Cir. 1971); Southern Concrete Services, Inc. v. Mableton Contractors, Inc., 407 F.Supp. 581 (N.D.Ga.1975), aff'd 569 F.2d 1154 (5th Cir. 1978).

. . . Accordingly, the judgment of the district court is AFFIRMED.

RESTATEMENT, SECOND, CONTRACTS
§ 221, ILLUSTRATION 2

2. A, an ordained rabbi, is employed by B, an orthodox Jewish congregation, to officiate as cantor at specified religious services. At the time the contract is made, it is the practice of such congregations to seat men and women separately at services, and a contrary practice would violate A's religious beliefs. At a time when it is too late for A to obtain substitute employment, B adopts a contrary practice. A refuses to officiate. The practice is part of the contract, and A is entitled to the agreed compensation.

RESTATEMENT, SECOND, CONTRACTS § 222

[See Selected Source Materials Supplement]

RESTATEMENT, SECOND, CONTRACTS
§ 222, ILLUSTRATIONS 1–3

1. A contracts to sell B 10,000 shingles. By usage of the lumber trade, in which both are engaged, two packs of a certain size constitute 1,000, though not containing that exact number. Unless otherwise agreed, 1,000 in the contract means two packs.

2. A contracts to sell B 1,000 feet of San Domingo mahogany. By usage of dealers in mahogany, known to A and B, good figured mahogany of a certain density is known as San Domingo mahogany, though it does not come from San Domingo. Unless otherwise agreed, the usage is part of the contract. . . .

3. A and B enter into a contract for the purchase and sale of "No. 1 heavy book paper guaranteed free from ground wood." Usage in the paper trade may show that this means paper not containing over 3% ground wood.

HURST v. W.J. LAKE & CO., 141 Or. 306, 16 P.2d 627 (1932). Buyer and Seller made a contract for the sale of 350 tons of horse meat scraps, "minimum 50% protein," for $50 per ton. Under the contract, if any of the scraps tested at "less than 50% of protein" Buyer was to receive a discount of $5.00 per ton. About 170 tons contained less than 50% protein; of these, 140 tons contained 49.53 to 49.96% protein. Buyer took a $5.00 discount on the entire 170 tons. Seller claimed that Buyer was entitled to a discount on only

30 tons, because under a usage of trade the terms "minimum 50% protein" and "less than 50% protein," when used in a contract for the sale of horse meat scraps, meant that a protein content of not less than 49.5% was equal to a content of 50% protein. The trial court granted Buyer's motion for judgment on the pleadings. Reversed.

"The flexibility of or multiplicity in the meaning of words is the principal source of difficulty in the interpretation of language. Words are the conduits by which thoughts are communicated, yet scarcely any of them have such a fixed and single meaning that they are incapable of denoting more than one thought. In addition to the multiplicity in meaning of words set forth in the dictionaries there are the meanings imparted to them by trade customs, local uses, dialects, telegraphic codes, etc. One meaning crowds a word full of significance, while another almost empties the utterance of any import. The various groups above indicated are constantly amplifying our language; in fact, they are developing what may be called languages of their own. Thus one is justified in saying that the language of the dictionaries is not the only language spoken in America. For instance, the word, 'thousand' as commonly used has a very specific meaning; it denotes ten hundreds or fifty scores, but the language of the various trades and localities has assigned to it meanings quite different from that just mentioned. Thus in the bricklaying trade a contract which fixes the bricklayer's compensation at "$5.25 a thousand" does not contemplate that he need lay actually one thousand bricks in order to earn $5.25 but that he should build a wall of a certain size: Brunold v. Glasser, 25 Misc. 285 (53 N.Y.S. 1021); Walker v. Syms, 118 Mich. 183 (76 N.W. 320). In the lumber industry a contract requiring the delivery of 4,000 shingles will be fulfilled by the delivery of only 2,500 when it appears that by trade custom two packs of a certain size are regarded as 1,000 shingles and that, hence, the delivery of eight packs fulfills the contract, even though they contain only 2,500 shingles by actual count: Soutier v. Kellerman, 18 Mo. 509. And where the custom of locality considers 100 dozen as constituting a thousand, one who has 19,200 rabbits upon a warren under an agreement for their sale at the price of 60 pounds for each thousand rabbits will be paid for only 16,000 rabbits: Smith v. Wilson, 3 Barn. & Adol. 728. . . .

". . . We believe that it is safe to assume, in the absence of evidence to the contrary, that when tradesmen employ trade terms they attach to them their trade significance. If, when they write their trade terms into their contracts, they mean to strip the terms of their special significance and demote them to their common import, it would seem reasonable to believe that they would so state in their agreement. Otherwise, they would refrain from using the trade term and express themselves in other language."

———

RESTATEMENT, SECOND, CONTRACTS § 220, Illustration 9: ". . . A promises to sell and B to buy a certain quantity of 'white arsenic' for a stated price. The parties contract with reference to a usage of trade that 'white arsenic' includes arsenic colored with lamp black. The usage is part of the contract."

———

FLOWER CITY PAINTING CONTRACTORS, INC. v. GUMINA, 591 F.2d 162 (2d Cir.1979). Gumina Construction Company was a general contractor. Flower City Painting was a newly formed painting contracting firm, which was owned and managed by minority personnel. In March 1973, Gumina entered into a contract for the construction of FIGHT City, a garden-apartment project. The project was federally funded and developed under the auspices of the Department of Housing and Urban Development (HUD). Pursuant to HUD regulations, the terms of the prime contract obliged Gumina to recruit and hire minority subcontractors. Part of that obligation was satisfied by Gumina's award of a painting contract to Flower.

The terms of the Gumina–Flower subcontract included the following Schedule:

The painting of the above mentioned project in accordance with the painting specifications and plans for this project.

1.	One bedroom units	$*335.00 per unit	$*17,420.00
2.	Two bedroom units	$*371.00 per unit	$*28,196.00
3.	Three bedroom units	$*428.00 per unit	$*29,960.00
4.	Four bedroom units	$*477.58 per unit	$*22,923.84
		A Total of:	$*98,499.84

In March 1974, a year after Flower entered into its contract with Gumina, Flower asserted that the contract only required Flower to paint interior walls of the individual apartment units, not laundry rooms, storage rooms, hallways, exterior doors, or exterior trim, and that the latter items would require additional payment. Gumina responded that the work in question was covered under Flower's contract, and cancelled that contract. Flower sued Gumina for damages. Held, for Gumina, on the ground that no contract had been formed.

" . . . [T]he habitual or customary practice of the construction industry in Rochester, New York, [was] that painting subcontracts be awarded on an entire project basis [that is, at a price that covered all the painting required for the entire project] . . . .

" . . . [I]n an ordinary situation involving the painting subcontract on a construction job in Rochester, the court could find as a fact that a painting contractor 'knows or has reason to know of [this usage's] existence and nature.' It seems clear enough that Flower actually did *not* know the usage, as its President testified, and the [trial] court made no finding to the contrary. The question whether Flower had 'reason to know' is the issue.

" . . . Flower was a neophyte minority painting contractor. This was its first substantial subcontract on a construction job. It would be unrealistic to hold it strictly to a 'reason to know' standard of trade usage. . . . Each party, in fact, held a different and reasonable view of the undertaking, Flower on the basis of its literal reading of the word 'units' and Gumina because of its suppositions concerning trade practice and its awareness that Flower was to be paid virtually the entire sum allocated to painting the FIGHT City project.

"Though the setting is new, the problem is old. In two nineteenth century cases, Raffles v. Wichelhaus, 159 Eng.Rep. 375 (Ex.1864) (the famous 'Peerless' case) and Kyle v. Kavanagh, 103 Mass. 356 (1869), courts, when faced with an arguably material contract term that could mean or represent two different things, found that no contract existed.''

————

UCC §§ 1–201(3), (11), 1–205, 2–208

[See Selected Source Materials Supplement]

————

RESTATEMENT, SECOND, CONTRACTS §§ 219–223

[See Selected Source Materials Supplement]

————

CISG ART. 9

[See Selected Source Materials Supplement]

————

UNIDROIT PRINCIPLES OF INTERNATIONAL COMMERCIAL CONTRACTS ART. 1.9

[See Selected Source Materials Supplement]

————

PRINCIPLES OF EUROPEAN CONTRACT LAW ART. 1.105

[See Selected Source Materials Supplement]

————

J. WHITE & R. SUMMERS, UNIFORM COMMERCIAL CODE § 1–2 (5th ed. 2000). "Some of the Article 2 provisions on the formation of contracts for the sale of goods have not only radically altered sales law but have influenced the new Restatement (Second) of Contracts as well. In most fundamental terms, Article Two expands our conception of contract....

"Article Two contracts are ... more expansive in content than before. Thus 1–201(11) defines 'contract' as the 'total legal obligation which results from the parties' agreement,' and 1_201(3) defines 'agreement' to mean 'the bargain of the parties in fact as found in their language or by implication from other circumstances including course of dealing or usage of trade or course of performance as provided in this Act.' ... The Code therefore adds to sales agreements much that is not made express by the parties.''

————

Chapter 10

THE MECHANICS OF A BARGAIN (I)—OFFER AND REVOCATION

Most bargains are formed by the process of offer and acceptance. Because a bargain is enforceable by expectation damages at the moment it is formed, without regard to whether it has been relied upon, the rules that govern the offer-and-acceptance process often play a central role in contract disputes. These issues are the subject of Chapters 10–12.

Chapter 10 focuses on offers. It consists of three Sections:

Section 1 concerns the issue, what constitutes an offer. If it is determined that a party has made an offer, the legal consequence is to create in the offeree a power of acceptance—that is, a power to conclude a bargain (and therefore a legally enforceable contract) by accepting the offer. Section 2 concerns three kinds of events that can terminate a power of acceptance: lapse of the offer; rejection of the offer; and the making of a counter-offer (or some legal equivalent) by the offeree. Finally, Section 3 concerns the power of an offeror to terminate the offeree's power of acceptance by revoking the offer.

SECTION 1. WHAT CONSTITUTES AN OFFER

RESTATEMENT, SECOND, CONTRACTS § 24

[See Selected Source Materials Supplement]

CISG ART. 14(1)

[See Selected Source Materials Supplement]

UNIDROIT PRINCIPLES OF INTERNATIONAL
COMMERCIAL CONTRACTS ART. 2.1.2

[See Selected Source Materials Supplement]

PRINCIPLES OF EUROPEAN CONTRACT LAW § 2.201(1)

[See Selected Source Materials Supplement]

LONERGAN v. SCOLNICK

California Court of Appeal, Fourth District, 1954.
129 Cal.App.2d 179, 276 P.2d 8.

BARNARD, PRESIDING JUSTICE. This is an action for specific performance or for damages in the event specific performance was impossible.

The complaint alleged that on April 15, 1952, the parties entered into a contract whereby the defendant agreed to sell, and plaintiff agreed to buy a 40–acre tract of land for $2,500; that this was a fair, just and reasonable value of the property; that on April 28, 1952, the defendant repudiated the contract and refused to deliver a deed; that on April 28, 1952, the property was worth $6,081; and that plaintiff has been damaged in the amount of $3,581. The answer denied that any contract had been entered into, or that anything was due to the plaintiff.

By stipulation the issue of whether or not a contract was entered into between the parties was first tried, reserving the other issues for a further trial if that became necessary. The issue as to the existence of a contract was submitted upon an agreed statement, including certain letters between the parties, without the introduction of other evidence.

The stipulated facts are as follows: During March, 1952, the defendant placed an ad in a Los Angeles paper reading, so far as material here, "Joshua Tree vic. 40 acres, ... need cash, will sacrifice." In response to an inquiry resulting from this ad the defendant, who lived in New York, wrote a letter to the plaintiff dated March 26, briefly describing the property, giving directions as to how to get there, stating that his rock-bottom price was $2,500 cash, and further stating that "This is a form letter." On April 7, the plaintiff wrote a letter to the defendant saying that he was not sure he had found the property, asking for its legal description, asking whether the land was all level or whether it included certain jutting rock hills, and suggesting a certain bank as escrow agent "should I desire to purchase the land." On April 8, the defendant wrote to the plaintiff saying "From your description you have found the property"; that this bank "is O.K. for escrow agent"; that the land was fairly level; giving the legal description; and then saying, "If you are really interested, you will have to decide fast, as I expect to have a buyer in the next week or so." On April 12, the defendant sold the property to a third party for $2,500. The plaintiff received defendant's letter of April 8 on April

14. On April 15 he wrote to the defendant thanking him for his letter "confirming that I was on the right land", stating that he would immediately proceed to have the escrow opened and would deposit $2,500 therein "in conformity with your offer", and asking the defendant to forward a deed with his instructions to the escrow agent. On April 17, 1952, the plaintiff started an escrow and placed in the hands of the escrow agent $100, agreeing to furnish an additional $2,400 at an unspecified time, with the provision that if the escrow was not closed by May 15, 1952, it should be completed as soon thereafter as possible unless a written demand for a return of the money or instruments was made by either party after that date. It was further stipulated that the plaintiff was ready and willing at all times to deposit the $2,400.

The matter was submitted on June 11, 1953. On July 10, 1953, the judge filed a memorandum opinion stating that it was his opinion that the letter of April 8, 1952, when considered with the previous correspondence, constituted an offer of sale which offer was, however, qualified and conditioned upon prompt acceptance by the plaintiff; that in spite of the condition thus imposed, the plaintiff delayed more than a week before notifying the defendant of his acceptance; and that since the plaintiff was aware of the necessity of promptly communicating his acceptance to the defendant his delay was not the prompt action required by the terms of the offer. Findings of fact were filed on October 2, 1953, finding that each and all of the statements in the agreed statement are true, and that all allegations to the contrary in the complaint are untrue. As conclusions of law, it was found that the plaintiff and defendant did not enter into a contract as alleged in the complaint or otherwise, and that the defendant is entitled to judgment against the plaintiff. Judgment was entered accordingly, from which the plaintiff has appealed.

The appellant contends that the judgment is contrary to the evidence and to the law since the facts, as found, do not support the conclusions of law upon which the judgment is based. It is argued that there is no conflict in the evidence, and this court is not bound by the trial court's construction of the written instruments involved; that the evidence conclusively shows that an offer was made to the plaintiff by the defendant, which offer was accepted by the mailing of plaintiff's letter of April 15; that upon receipt of defendant's letter of April 8 the plaintiff had a reasonable time within which to accept the offer that had been made; that by his letter of April 15 and his starting of an escrow the plaintiff accepted said offer; and that the agreed statement of facts establishes that a valid contract was entered into between the parties. In his briefs the appellant assumes that an offer was made by the defendant, and confined his argument to contending that the evidence shows that he accepted that offer within a reasonable time.

There can be no contract unless the minds of the parties have met and mutually agreed upon some specific thing. This is usually evidenced by one party making an offer which is accepted by the other party. Section 25 of the Restatement, Law on Contracts reads:

"If from a promise, or manifestation of intention, or from the circumstances existing at the time, the person to whom the promise or manifestation is addressed knows or has reason to know that the person making it does not intend it as an expression of his fixed purpose until he has given a further expression of assent, he has not made an offer."

The language used in Niles v. Hancock, 140 Cal. 157, 73 P. 840, 842, "It is also clear from the correspondence that it was the intention of the defendant that the negotiations between him and the plaintiff were to be purely preliminary," is applicable here. The correspondence here indicates an intention on the part of the defendant to find out whether the plaintiff was interested, rather than an intention to make a definite offer to the plaintiff. The language used by the defendant in his letters of March 26 and April 8 rather clearly discloses that they were not intended as an expression of fixed purpose to make a definite offer, and was sufficient to advise the plaintiff that some further expression of assent on the part of the defendant was necessary.

The advertisement in the paper was a mere request for an offer. The letter of March 26 contains no definite offer, and clearly states that it is a form letter. It merely gives further particulars, in clarification of the advertisement, and tells the plaintiff how to locate the property if he was interested in looking into the matter. The letter of April 8 added nothing in the way of a definite offer. It merely answered some questions asked by the plaintiff, and stated that if the plaintiff was really interested he would have to act fast. The statement that he expected to have a buyer in the next week or so indicated that the defendant intended to sell to the first-comer, and was reserving the right to do so. From this statement, alone, the plaintiff knew or should have known that he was not being given time in which to accept an offer that was being made but that some further assent on the part of the defendant was required. Under the language used the plaintiff was not being given a right to act within a reasonable time after receiving the letter; he was plainly told that the defendant intended to sell to another, if possible, and warned that he would have to act fast if he was interested in buying the land.

Regardless of any opinion previously expressed, the court found that no contract had been entered into between these parties, and we are in accord with the court's conclusion on that controlling issue. The court's construction of the letters involved was a reasonable one, and we think the most reasonable one, even if it be assumed that another construction was possible.

The judgment is affirmed.

Griffin and Mussell, JJ., concur.

REGENT LIGHTING CORP. v. CMT CORP., 1997 WL 441297 (M.D.N.C. 1997). On September 1, 1994, Defendant sent a letter to Plaintiff requesting a "firm quotation for winding equipment." The first sentence in this letter stated, "[w]e enclose the following proposal. . . ." The proposal that followed contained a description of the machine, and the price. Included with the proposal was Defendant's "standard terms and conditions." These standard terms stated that "no order shall be binding on SELLER until and unless accepted by SELLER in writing. SELLER may refuse to accept any order for any cause which SELLER deems sufficient and shall not be liable for any claims of any nature because of failure to accept." Held, this term prevented the proposal from being an offer. "An offer 'must be made under circumstances evidencing an express or implied intention that its acceptance shall constitute a binding contract.' Because Defendant reserved the right to not accept an order, its proposal was merely an invitation to submit an offer. Therefore, the proposal sent on September 1, 1994 was not an offer."

———————

LEFKOWITZ v. GREAT MINNEAPOLIS SURPLUS STORE

Supreme Court of Minnesota, 1957.
251 Minn. 188, 86 N.W.2d 689.

MURPHY, JUSTICE. This is an appeal from an order of the Municipal Court of Minneapolis denying the motion of the defendant for amended findings of fact, or, in the alternative, for a new trial. The order for judgment awarded the plaintiff the sum of $138.50 as damages for breach of contract.

This case grows out of the alleged refusal of the defendant to sell to the plaintiff a certain fur piece which it had offered for sale in a newspaper advertisement. It appears from the record that on April 6, 1956, the defendant published the following advertisement in a Minneapolis newspaper:

> "Saturday 9 A.M. Sharp
>
> 3 Brand New
>
> Fur Coats
>
> Worth to $100
>
> First Come
>
> First Served
>
> $1 Each"

On April 13, the defendant again published an advertisement in the same newspaper as follows:

> "Saturday 9 A.M.
>
> 2 Brand New Pastel
>
> Mink 3–Skin Scarfs
>
> Selling for $89.50
>
> Out they go
>
> Saturday.
>
> Each.... $1.00
>
> 1 Black Lapin Stole
>
> Beautiful,
>
> worth $139.50.... $1.00
>
> First Come
>
> First Served"

The record supports the findings of the court that on each of the Saturdays following the publication of the above-described ads the plaintiff was the first to present himself at the appropriate counter in the defendant's store and on each occasion demanded the coat and the stole so advertised and indicated his readiness to pay the sale price of $1. On both occasions, the defendant refused to sell the merchandise to the plaintiff, stating on the first occasion that by a "house rule" the offer was intended for women only and sales would not be made to men, and on the second visit that plaintiff knew defendant's house rules.

The trial court properly disallowed plaintiff's claim for the value of the fur coats since the value of these articles was speculative and uncertain. The only evidence of value was the advertisement itself to the effect that the coats were "Worth to $100.00," how much less being speculative especially in view of the price for which they were offered for sale. With reference to the offer of the defendant on April 13, 1956, to sell the "1 Black Lapin Stole . . . worth $139.50 . . ." the trial court held that the value of this article was established and granted judgment in favor of the plaintiff for that amount less the $1 quoted purchase price.

1.   The defendant contends that a newspaper advertisement offering items of merchandise for sale at a named price is a "unilateral offer" which may be withdrawn without notice. He relies upon authorities which hold that, where an advertiser publishes in a newspaper that he has a certain quantity or quality of goods which he wants to dispose of at certain prices and on certain terms, such advertisements are not offers which become contracts as soon as any person to whose notice they may come signifies his acceptance by notifying the other that he will take a certain quantity of them. Such advertisements have been construed as an invitation for an offer of sale on the terms stated, which offer, when received, may be accepted or rejected and which therefore does not become a contract of sale until accepted by the seller; and until a contract has been so made, the seller may modify or revoke such prices or terms. . . .

The defendant relies principally on Craft v. Elder & Johnston Co. supra. In that case, the court discussed the legal effect of an advertisement offering for sale, as a one-day special, an electric sewing machine at a named price. The view was expressed that the advertisement was (38 N.E.2d 417, 34 Ohio L.A. 605) "not an offer made to any specific person but was made to the public generally. Thereby it would be properly designated as a unilateral offer and not being supported by any consideration could be withdrawn at will and without notice." It is true that such an offer may be withdrawn before acceptance. Since all offers are by their nature unilateral because they are necessarily made by one party or on one side in the negotiation of a contract, the distinction made in that decision between a unilateral offer and a unilateral contract is not clear. On the facts before us we are concerned with whether the advertisement constituted an offer, and, if so, whether the plaintiff's conduct constituted an acceptance.

There are numerous authorities which hold that a particular advertisement in a newspaper or circular letter relating to a sale of articles may be construed by the court as constituting an offer, acceptance of which would complete a contract. . . .

The test of whether a binding obligation may originate in advertisements addressed to the general public is "whether the facts show that some performance was promised in positive terms in return for something requested." 1 Williston, Contracts (Rev. ed.) § 27.

The authorities above cited emphasize that, where the offer is clear, definite, and explicit, and leaves nothing open for negotiation, it constitutes an offer, acceptance of which will complete the contract. The most recent case on the subject is Johnson v. Capital City Ford Co., La.App., 85 So.2d 75, in which the court pointed out that a newspaper advertisement relating to the purchase and sale of automobiles may constitute an offer, acceptance of which will consummate a contract and create an obligation in the offeror to perform according to the terms of the published offer.

Whether in any individual instance a newspaper advertisement is an offer rather than an invitation to make an offer depends on the legal intention of the parties and the surrounding circumstances. Annotation, 157 A.L.R. 744, 751; 77 C.J.S. Sales § 25b; 17 C.J.S. Contracts § 389. We are of the view on the facts before us that the offer by the defendant of the sale of the Lapin fur was clear, definite, and explicit, and left nothing open for negotiation. The plaintiff having successfully managed to be the first one to appear at the seller's place of business to be served, as requested by the advertisement, and having offered the stated purchase price of the article, he was entitled to performance on the part of the defendant. We think the trial court was correct in holding that there was in the conduct of the parties a sufficient mutuality of obligation to constitute a contract of sale.

2. The defendant contends that the offer was modified by a "house rule" to the effect that only women were qualified to receive the bargains advertised. The advertisement contained no such restriction. This objection may be disposed of briefly by stating that, while an advertiser has the right at any time before acceptance to modify his offer, he does not have the right, after acceptance, to impose new or arbitrary conditions not contained in the published offer....

Affirmed.

———

FORD MOTOR CREDIT CO. v. RUSSELL, 519 N.W.2d 460 (Minn. Ct. App. 1994). In March 1988, Monticello Ford, an independent dealer, advertised a 1988 Ford Escort Pony in a local newspaper for $7,826, with monthly payments of $159.29, based on 11% financing. On March 15, Dawn Russell sought to purchase a 1988 Escort Pony at the advertised sales price. Monticello Ford contacted three finance companies in an attempt to obtain 11% financing for Russell. Two companies refused to extend credit because of Russell's limited credit history. Ford Motor Credit Company, a subsidiary of Ford Motor Manufacturing Company, offered to finance the purchase at a 13.75% interest rate under a special retail plan for persons with limited or poor credit. Monticello Ford drew up a contract, which Russell signed, providing for the sale of the automobile at a cash price of $7,826 together with the financing arrangements. Monticello Ford subsequently assigned its rights under the contract to Ford Credit. The contract provided that upon default, Ford Credit could accelerate the balance due and repossess the vehicle. In 1990, Russell defaulted on numerous payments. Eventually, Ford Credit repossessed the car, sold it for less than the amount Russell still owed, and sued her for the difference. Russell counterclaimed that the advertisement constituted an offer, which Russell accepted, and therefore Ford Credit breached its contract to sell her a 1988 Ford Escort at 11% financing. Held, for Ford Credit:

> Generally, if goods are advertised for sale at a certain price, it is not an offer and no contract is formed; such an advertisement is merely an invitation to bargain rather than an offer. The test of whether a binding obligation may originate in advertisements addressed to the general public is "whether the facts show that some performance was promised in positive terms in return for something requested." Lefkowitz v. Great Minneapolis Surplus Store, Inc., 251 Minn. 188, 191, 86 N.W.2d 689, 691 (1957). . . .

> We conclude that the advertisement here did not constitute an offer of sale to the general public. Because not everyone qualifies for financing and Monticello Ford does not have an unlimited number of Ford Escorts to sell, it was unreasonable for appellants to believe that the advertisement was an offer binding the advertiser.

DONOVAN v. RRL CORP., 26 Cal.4th 261, 109 Cal.Rptr.2d 807, 27 P.3d 702 (2001). "Some courts have stated that an advertisement or other notice disseminated to the public at large generally does not constitute an offer, but rather is presumed to be an invitation to consider, examine, and negotiate. . . . Nevertheless, certain advertisements have been held to constitute offers where they invite the performance of a specific act without further communication and leave nothing for negotiation. Advertisements for rewards typically fall within this category, because performing the requested act (e.g., returning a lost article or supplying particular information) generally is all that is necessary to accept the offer and conclude the bargain. . . .

"Various advertisements involving transactions in goods also have been held to constitute offers where they invite particular action. For example, a merchant's advertisement that listed particular goods at a specific price and included the phrase 'First Come First Served' was deemed to be an offer, because it constituted a promise to sell to a customer at that price in exchange for the customer's act of arriving at the store at a particular time. (*Lefkowitz v. Great Minneapolis Surplus Store* (1957) 251 Minn. 188, 86 N.W.2d 689, 691; Rest.2d Contracts, § 26, com. b, illus. 1, p. 76.) Similarly, external wording on the envelope of an item of bulk rate mail promising to give the recipient a watch "just for opening the envelope" before a certain date was held to constitute an operative offer accepted by performance of the act of opening the envelope. (*Harris v. Time, Inc.,* . . . 191 Cal.App.3d 449, 455–456, 237 Cal.Rptr. 584.) In addition, an advertisement stating that anyone who purchased a 1954 automobile from a dealer could exchange it for a 1955 model at no additional cost constituted an offer that was accepted when the plaintiff purchased the 1954 vehicle. (*Johnson v. Capital City Ford Co.* (La.Ct.App. 1955) 85 So.2d 75, 79–80; see also *Cobaugh v. Klick–Lewis* (1989) 385 Pa.Super. 587, 561 A.2d 1248, 1249–1250 [sign at golf course stated 'hole-in-one wins' an automobile at a specified price].) In such cases, courts have considered whether the advertiser, in clear and positive terms, promised to render performance in exchange for something requested by the advertiser, and whether the recipient of the advertisement reasonably might have concluded that by acting in accordance with the request a contract would be formed.... [S]ee, e.g., *Chang v. First Colonial Sav. Bank* (1991) 242 Va. 388, 410 S.E.2d 928, 929–930 [bank's newspaper advertisement stating 'Deposit $14,000 and receive ... $20,136.12 upon maturity in 3 1/2 years' constituted an offer that was accepted by the plaintiffs' deposit of that sum for the specified period].)

"Relying upon these decisions, defendant contends that its advertisement for the 1995 Jaguar XJ6 Vanden Plas [which included the price] did not constitute an offer, because the advertisement did not request the performance of a specific act that would conclude the bargain. According to defendant, plaintiff's assertion that the advertisement was an offer conflicts with the generally accepted 'black-letter' rule that an advertisement that simply identifies goods and specifies a price is an invitation to negotiate.

"This court has not previously applied the common law rules upon which defendant relies, including the rule that advertisements generally constitute invitations to negotiate rather than offers. Plaintiff observes that such rules governing the construction of advertisements have been criticized on the ground that they are inconsistent with the reasonable expectations of consumers and lead to haphazard results. (See Eisenberg, *Expression Rules in Contract Law and Problems of Offer and Acceptance* (1994) 82 Cal. L.Rev. 1127, 1166–1172.) Plaintiff urges this court to reject the black-letter advertising rule.

"In the present case, however, we need not consider the viability of the black-letter rule regarding the interpretation of advertisements *in general*. [Vehicle Code section 11713.1(e), provides that it is a violation of the Vehicle Code for the holder of any dealer's license to "[f]ail to sell a vehicle to any person at the advertised total price ... while the vehicle remains unsold, unless the advertisement states the advertised total price is good only for a specified time and the time has elapsed. We] conclude that a licensed automobile dealer's advertisement for the sale of a particular vehicle at a specific price—when construed in light of Vehicle Code section 11713.1, subdivision (e)—reasonably justifies a consumer's understanding that the dealer intends the advertisement to constitute an offer and that the consumer's assent to the bargain is invited and will conclude it."

FISHER v. BELL, [1961] 1 Q.B. 394 (1960). The Restriction of Offensive Weapons Act made it unlawful to "offer for sale" a switchblade knife. Defendant, who owned a store known as Bell's Music Shop, was prosecuted under the Act for having displayed such a knife in his shop window accompanied by a ticket upon which the words "Ejector knife–4s. [shillings]" were printed. Held, for defendant. "The sole question is whether the exhibition of that knife in the window with the ticket constituted an offer for sale within the statute. I confess that I think most lay people and, indeed, I myself when I first read the papers, would be inclined to the view that to say that if a knife was displayed in a window like that with a price attached to it was not offering it for sale was just nonsense. In ordinary language it is there inviting people to buy it, and it is for sale; but any statute must of course be looked at in the light of the general law of the country. Parliament in its wisdom in passing an Act must be taken to know the general law. It is perfectly clear that according to the ordinary law of contract the display of an article with a price on it in a shop window is merely an invitation to treat.''

———

RESTATEMENT, SECOND, CONTRACTS § 26

[See Selected Source Materials Supplement]

———

CISG ARTICLE 14(2)

[See Selected Source Materials Supplement]

———

PRINCIPLES OF EUROPEAN CONTRACT LAW ART. 2.201(2), (3)

[See Selected Source Materials Supplement]

———

UNIFORM DECEPTIVE TRADE PRACTICES ACT

[See Selected Source Materials Supplement]

———

FEDERAL TRADE COMMISSION REGULATIONS— RETAIL FOOD STORE ADVERTISING AND MARKETING PRACTICES

[See Selected Source Materials Supplement]

———

UCC § 2–328

[See Selected Source Materials Supplement]

———

HOFFMAN v. HORTON, 212 Va. 565, 186 S.E.2d 79 (1972). In this case, the Virginia Supreme Court held that the rule embodied in the second sentence of UCC § 2–328(2) would also be applied to auctions for the sale of land. ''[W]hile the Uniform Commercial Code is not controlling here, we think it appropriate to borrow from it to establish the rule applicable to the transaction at hand. To vest the auctioneer crying a sale of land with the same discretion to reopen bidding that he has in the sale of goods is to achieve uniformity and, of more importance, to recognize a rule which is both necessary and fair."

———

NOTE ON AUCTIONS

The basic rule governing auctions is that the act of an auctioneer in putting an item up for sale is not an offer, but only an invitation to bid. Accordingly, the auctioneer normally is not legally bound to sell the item if the highest bid is unsatisfactory. Under a related rule, a would-be seller at auction can choose to become legally bound to sell an item, once it has been put up for auction, by stating that the auction is "without reserve." (The term "reserve," in this context, refers to a reservation price—that is, a price below which a would-be seller is not willing to sell. Similarly, a would-be buyer may have a reservation price above which he is not willing to buy.) In effect, therefore, the basic rule that governs auctions is a default rule under which the auction of an item is with reserve unless it is declared to be without reserve.

Reserves can take various forms. The reserve price may be publicly announced, but usually is not. If in a normal auction (one with reserve) the highest bid does not equal the reserve price, the auctioneer may state that the reserve price has not been met, or may purport to recognize a fictitious bid equal to the reserve price.

At least at first glance, the rule governing auctions seems incongruent with the result that would follow from application of the general principles of interpretation, because a casual auction-goer would probably believe that auctioned items are offered for sale to the highest bidder. Thus Williston stated, in the first edition of his treatise:

> As an original question it seems fairly open to argument whether an auctioneer by putting up goods for sale makes an offer which ripens into a contract or sale when the highest bidder accepts the offer; or whether putting up the goods for sale is merely an invitation to those present to make offers which they do by making bids, one of which is ultimately accepted by the fall of the hammer.

Nevertheless, the rule may be justified. To begin with, most, although not all, bidders at an auction are likely to know the rules that govern the auction. Taking auctions as a whole, the great bulk of dollar volume is undoubtedly accounted for not by casual auction-goers, but by sophisticated bidders who are repeat players. This is most obviously true of auctions to the trade, such as auctions of tobacco or freshly landed fish. Even those auctions that are open to all comers often involve knowledgeable repeat players, as in the case of art or antique auctions dominated by collectors and dealers. As a result, the auction rule is unlikely to frustrate the expectations of most bidders.

Reserve rules also appear to be justified within the social practice of auctions. Reserve rules cannot be taken in isolation, but rather are part of a web of interrelated rules that define and constitute any given auction. Reserves may be set for a number of reasons. Among these are a seller's concern that the highest bid at an auction may be unduly low because not enough interested buyers will show up, or because the bidding will be held down by tacit or explicit collusion among potential bidders. These problems may be accentuated when buyers rather than sellers control an institutionalized auction, as where buyers have organized the auction, or a group of buyers participates in the auction on a regular basis while any given seller participates on only an episodic basis. From this perspective, reserves are part of a complex of rules through which the relative needs and power of the members of various auction communities can be accommodated.

NOTE ON OFFER AND ACCEPTANCE

Everyday life gives rise to recurring kinds of arrangements that might or might not be considered to be contracts. For example, a hotel reservation has been held to be a contract binding on the hotel, even where the guest has not guaranteed the reservation. Wells v. Holiday Inns, Inc., 522 F.Supp. 1023 (W.D.Mo.1981). On the other hand, in Glass Service Co. v. State Farm Mutual Auto. Ins. Co., 530 N.W.2d 867 (Minn.App.1995), the court held that appointments made by customers with an auto glass-repair company did not constitute contracts. In the course of its opinion the court said, "We do not believe people intend to be legally bound when they make reservations at a restaurant, or schedule appointments to have their car repaired, their hair cut, or their teeth checked. Nor is it likely that the providers of such services perceive the customers to be bound or intend to be legally bound themselves by scheduling appointments."

SECTION 2. TERMINATION OF THE OFFEREE'S POWER OF ACCEPTANCE: LAPSE, REJECTION, AND COUNTER–OFFER

AKERS v. J.B. SEDBERRY, INC.
Court of Appeals of Tennessee, 1955.
39 Tenn.App. 633, 286 S.W.2d 617, cert. denied by Tenn.S.Ct.

Felts, Judge. These two consolidated causes are before us upon a writ of error sued out by J.B. Sedberry, Inc., and Mrs. M.B. Sedberry, defendants below, to review a decree of the Chancery Court, awarding a recovery against them in favor of each of the complainants, Charles William Akers and William Gambill Whitsitt, for damages for breach of a contract of employment....

J.B. Sedberry, Inc., was a Tennessee corporation with its principal place of business at Franklin, Tennessee. Mrs. M.B. Sedberry owned practically all of its stock and was its president and in active charge of its affairs. It was engaged in the business of distributing "Jay Bee" hammer mills, which were manufactured for it under contract by Jay Bee Manufacturing Company, a Texas corporation, whose plant was in Tyler, Texas, and whose capital stock was owned principally by L.M. Glasgow and B.G. Byars.

On July 1, 1947, J.B. Sedberry, Inc., by written contract, employed complainant Akers as Chief Engineer for a term of five years at a salary of $12,000 per year, payable $1,000 per month, plus 1% of its net profits for the first year, 2% the second, 3% the third, 4% the fourth, and 5% the fifth year. His duties were to carry on research for his employer, and to see that the Jay Bee Manufacturing Company, Tyler, Texas, manufactured the mills and parts according to proper specifications. Mrs. M.B. Sedberry guaranteed the employer's performance of this contract.

On August 1, 1947, J.B. Sedberry, Inc., by written contract, employed complainant Whitsitt as Assistant Chief Engineer for a term of five years at a salary of $7,200 per year, payable $600 per month, plus 1% of the corporation's net profits for the first year, 2% for the second, 3% for the third, 4% for the fourth, and 5% for the fifth year. His duties were to assist in the work done by the Chief Engineer. Mrs. M.B. Sedberry guaranteed the employer's performance of this contract.

Under Mrs. Sedberry's instructions, Akers and Whitsitt moved to Tyler, Texas, began performing their contract duties in the plant of the Jay Bee Manufacturing Company, continued working there, and were paid under the contracts until October 1, 1950, when they ceased work, under circumstances hereafter stated . . . .

[After the employment contracts were made, Mrs. Sedberry acquired the stock of Jay Bee from Glasgow and Byars, and installed a new manager, A.M. Sorenson.] There soon developed considerable friction between Sorenson and complainants Akers and Whitsitt. The Jay Bee Manufacturing Company owed large sums to the Tyler State Bank & Trust Co.; and the bank's officers, fearing the company might fail under Sorenson's management, began talking to Akers and Whitsitt about the company's financial difficulties . . . .

While these matters were pending, Akers and Whitsitt flew to Nashville and went to Franklin to talk with Mrs. Sedberry about them. They had a conference with her at her office on Friday, September 29, 1950, lasting from 9:30 a.m. until 4:30 p.m. As they had come unannounced, and unknown to Sorenson, they felt Mrs. Sedberry might mistrust them; and at the outset to show their good faith, they offered to resign, but she did not accept their offer. Instead, she proceeded with them in discussing the operation and refinancing of the business.

Testifying about this conference, Akers said that, at the very beginning, to show their good faith, he told Mrs. Sedberry that they would offer their resignations on a ninety-day notice, provided they were paid according to the contract for that period; that she pushed the offers aside—"would not accept them", but went into a full discussion of the business; that nothing was thereafter said about the offers to resign; and that they spent the whole day discussing the business, Akers making notes of things she instructed him to do when he got back to Texas.

Whitsitt testified that . . . [Mrs. Sedberry] . . . . did not accept the offer, but proceeded with the business, and nothing further was said about resigning.

Mrs. Sedberry testified that Akers and Whitsitt came in and "offered their resignations"; that they said they could not work with Sorenson and did not believe the bank would go along with him; and that "they said if it would be of any help to the organization they would be glad to tender their resignation and pay them what was due them." She further said that she "did not accept the resignation", that she "felt it necessary to contact Mr. Sorenson and give consideration to the resignation offer." But she said nothing to complainants about taking the offer under consideration.

On cross-examination she said that in the offer to resign "no mention was made of any ninety-day notice". Asked what response she made to the offer she said, "I treated it rather casually because I had to give it some thought and had to contact Mr. Sorenson." She further said she excused herself from the conference with complainants, went to another room, tried to telephone Sorenson in Tyler, Texas, but was unable to locate him.

She then resumed the conference, nothing further was said about the offers to resign, nothing was said by her to indicate that she thought the offers were left open or held under consideration by her. But the discussion proceeded as if the offers had not been made. She discussed with complainants future plans for refinancing and operating the business, giving them instructions, and Akers making notes of them.

Following the conference, complainants, upon Mrs. Sedberry's request, flew back to Texas to proceed to carry out her instructions. . . .

On Monday, October 2, 1950, Mrs. Sedberry sent to complainants similar telegrams, signed by "J.B. Sedberry, Inc., by M.B. Sedberry, President", stating that their resignations were accepted, effective immediately. We quote the telegram to Akers, omitting the formal parts:

> "Account present unsettled conditions which you so fully are aware we accept your kind offer of resignation effective immediately. Please discontinue as of today with everyone employed in Sedberry, Inc., Engineering Department, discontinuing all expenses in this department writing." . . .

While this said she was "writing", she did not write. . . .

[Akers then wrote] that he was amazed to get her telegram, and called her attention to the fact that no offer to resign by him was open or outstanding when she sent the telegram; that while he had made a conditional offer to resign at their conference on September 29, she had immediately rejected the offer, and had discussed plans for the business and had instructed him and Whitsitt as to things she wanted them to do in the business on their return to Tyler.

This letter further stated that Akers was expecting to be paid according to the terms of his contract until he could find other employment that would pay him as much income as that provided in his contract, and that if he had to accept a position with less income, he would expect to be paid the difference, or whatever losses he suffered by her breach of the contract. [Whitsitt wrote a similar letter.] . . .

As it takes two to make a contract, it takes two to unmake it. It cannot be changed or ended by one alone, but only by mutual assent of both parties. A contract of employment for a fixed period may be terminated by the employee's offer to resign, provided such offer is duly accepted by the employer. . . .

An employee's tender of his resignation, being a mere offer is, of course, not binding until it has been accepted by the employer. Such offer must be accepted according to its terms and within the time fixed. The matter is governed by the same rules as govern the formation of contracts. . . .

An offer may be terminated in a number of ways, as, for example, where it is rejected by the offeree, or where it is not accepted by him within the time fixed, or, if no time is fixed, within a reasonable time. An offer terminated in either of these ways ceases to exist and cannot thereafter be accepted. 1 Williston on Contracts (1936), secs. 50A, 51, 53, 54; 1 Corbin on Contracts (1950), secs. 35, 36; 1 Restatement, Contracts, §§ 35, 40.

The question what is a reasonable time, where no time is fixed, is a question of fact, depending on the nature of the contract proposed, the usages of business and other circumstances of the case. Ordinarily, an offer made by one to another in a face to face conversation is deemed to continue only to the close of their conversation, and cannot be accepted thereafter.

The rule is illustrated by Restatement Contracts § 40, Illustration 2, as follows:

> "2. While A and B are engaged in conversation, A makes B an offer to which B then makes no reply, but a few hours later meeting A again, B states that he accepts the offer. There is no contract unless the offer or the surrounding circumstances indicate that the offer is intended to continue beyond the immediate conversation." . . .

Professor Corbin says:

> "When two negotiating parties are in each other's presence, and one makes an offer to the other without indicating any time for acceptance, the inference that will ordinarily be drawn by the other party is that an answer is expected at once. . . . If, when the first reply is not an acceptance, the offeror turns away in silence, the proper inference is that the offer is no longer open to acceptance." 1 Corbin on Contracts (1950), section 36, p. 111.

The only offer by Akers and Whitsitt to resign was the offer made by them in their conversation with Mrs. Sedberry. They made that offer at the outset, and on the evidence it seems clear that they expected an answer at once. Certainly, there is nothing in the evidence to show that they intended the offer to continue beyond that conversation; and on the above authorities, we think the offer did not continue beyond that meeting.

Indeed, it did not last that long, in our opinion, but was terminated by Mrs. Sedberry's rejection of it very early in that meeting. While she did not expressly reject it, and while she may have intended, as she says, to take the offer under consideration, she did not disclose such an intent to complainants; but, by her conduct, led them to believe she rejected the offer, brushed it aside, and proceeded with the discussion as if it had not been made.

> "An offer is rejected when the offeror is justified in inferring from the words or conduct of the offeree that the offeree intends not to accept the offer or to take it under further advisement (Rest. Contracts sec. 36)." 1 Williston on Contracts, section 51.

So, we agree with the Trial Judge that when defendants sent the telegrams, undertaking to accept offers of complainants to resign, there was no such offer in existence; and that this attempt of defendants to terminate their contract was unlawful and constituted a breach for which they are liable to complainants....

Finally, defendants contend that if complainants are entitled to any recovery at all, such recovery should have been limited to the ninety-day period from and after October 2, 1950, because complainants themselves admitted that they had offered to resign upon ninety days notice with pay for that period.

The answer to this contention is that their offer to resign on ninety days notice was not accepted, but had terminated, and there was no offer in existence when Mrs. Sedberry undertook to accept their offers of resignation. Such attempt by defendants to terminate their contract was unlawful and was a breach for which they become liable for the measure of recovery as above stated....

All of the assignments of error are overruled and the decree of the Chancellor is affirmed....

The causes are remanded to the Chancery Court for further proceedings not inconsistent with this opinion.

HICKERSON and SHRIVER, JJ., concur.

————

RESTATEMENT, SECOND, CONTRACTS §§ 38, 41

[See Selected Source Materials Supplement]

————

CISG ART. 17

[See Selected Source Materials Supplement]

————

UNIDROIT PRINCIPLES OF INTERNATIONAL COMMERCIAL CONTRACTS ARTS. 2.1.5, 2.1.7

[See Selected Source Materials Supplement]

————

PRINCIPLES OF EUROPEAN CONTRACT LAW ARTS. 2.203, 2.206

[See Selected Source Materials Supplement]

————

NOTE ON THE EFFECT OF THE REJECTION OF AN OFFER

A recurring problem in the area of offer and acceptance concerns the issue whether an expression by the offeree, in response to an offer, terminates the offeree' s power of acceptance. The underlying question in determining whether an offeree's expression terminates his power of acceptance is whether the offeror would reasonably understand that the expression serves to take the offer off the table. If an offer is off the table, the offeree has nothing to accept, any more than if the offer had never been made or if it had lapsed. Furthermore, an offeror is likely to rely on his understanding that the offer is off the table. For example, suppose an offer states that it will be open for ten days. During those ten days, the offeror may take steps to prepare for performance based on his assessment of the probability of acceptance. Suppose now that as a result of an expression used by the offeree on the second day, the offeror reasonably believes the offer is off the table. In that case, the offeror will take no further steps to prepare for performance, and may arrange his affairs on the basis that he will not be entering into a contract. Alternatively, the offeror may make a new offer to a third party that he would not have made in the absence of the offeree's expression. If the offeree then tries to accept on the tenth day, the offeror would be caught short. Moreover, it would be difficult if not impossible for the offeror to prove that he would have acted differently in the absence of the offeree's expression, because the offeror's response to the expression may consist of nonaction or of action that is not related to the expression in an obvious way.

The issue then is, what kinds of expressions by an offeree will lead an offeror to reasonably believe that the offer is off the table. To a very large extent, the law of offer and acceptance deals with this issue through a series of categorical rules, rather than by application of the general principles of interpretation on a case-by-case basis. Under one of these rules, a rejection terminates the offeree's power of acceptance, even if the rejection is communicated before the offer would otherwise have lapsed. It is easy to justify this rule, because it seems virtually certain that under the general principles of interpretation a rejection would be understood by the offeror to take the offer off the table. Although it is conceivable that in a few cases the general principles of interpretation would lead to a different result—because, for example, neither party subjectively viewed the rejection as taking the offer off the table—such a scenario is so unlikely that a categorical rule is supported by administrative justifications. It should be stressed, however, that even in this relatively easy case the categorical rule represents a choice. If the rule is that a rejection terminates the power of acceptance, this is not because a rejection must logically terminate the power of acceptance, but because the rule is perceived to be justified by prudential considerations.

———

ARDENTE v. HORAN

Supreme Court of Rhode Island, 1976.
117 R.I. 254, 366 A.2d 162.

DORIS, JUSTICE. Ernst P. Ardente, the plaintiff, brought this civil action in Superior Court to specifically enforce an agreement between himself and William A. and Katherine L. Horan, the defendants, to sell certain real property. The defendants filed an answer together with a motion for summary judgment pursuant to Super.R.Civ.P. 56. Following the submission of affidavits by both the plaintiff and the defendants and a hearing on the motion, judgment was entered by a Superior Court justice for the defendants. The plaintiff now appeals.

In August 1975, certain residential property in the city of Newport was offered for sale by defendants. The plaintiff made a bid of $250,000 for the property which was communicated to defendants by their attorney. After defendants' attorney advised plaintiff that the bid was acceptable to defendants, he prepared a purchase and sale agreement at the direction of defendants and forwarded it to plaintiff's attorney for plaintiff's signature. After investigating certain title conditions, plaintiff executed the agreement. Thereafter plaintiff's attorney returned the document to defendants along with a check in the amount of $20,000 and a letter dated September 8, 1975, which read in relevant part as follows:

> "My clients are concerned that the following items remain with the real estate: a) dining room set and tapestry wall covering in dining room; b) fireplace fixtures throughout; c) the sun parlor furniture. I would appreciate your confirming that these items are a part of the transaction, as they would be difficult to replace."

The defendants refused to agree to sell the enumerated items and did not sign the purchase and sale agreement. They directed their attorney to return the agreement and the deposit check to plaintiff and subsequently refused to sell the property to plaintiff. This action for specific performance followed.

In Superior Court, defendants moved for summary judgment on the ground that the facts were not in dispute and no contract had been formed as a matter of law.[1] The trial justice ruled that the letter quoted above constituted a conditional acceptance of defendants' offer to sell the property and consequently must be construed as a counteroffer. Since defendants never accepted the counteroffer, it followed that no contract was formed, and summary judgment was granted. . . .

The plaintiff assigns several grounds for appeal in his brief. He urges first that summary judgment was improper because there existed a genuine issue of fact. The factual question, according to plaintiff, was whether the oral agreement which preceded the drafting of the purchase and sale agreement was intended by the parties to take effect immediately to create a binding oral contract for the sale of the property.

---

1. Although the contract would appear to be within the statute of frauds, defendants did not raise this defense in the trial court, nor do they raise it here. Where a party makes no claim to the benefit of the statute, the court sua sponte will not interpose it for him. Conti v. Fisher, 48 R.I. 33, 36, 134 A. 849, 850 (1926).

We cannot agree with plaintiff's position. A review of the record shows that the issue was never raised before the trial justice. The plaintiff did not, in his affidavit in opposition to summary judgment or by any other means, bring to the attention of the trial court any facts which established the existence of a relevant factual dispute. Indeed, at the hearing on the motion plaintiff did not even mention the alleged factual dispute which he now claims the trial justice erred in overlooking. The only issue plaintiff addressed was the proper interpretation of the language used in plaintiff's letter of acceptance. This was solely a question of law. . . .

The plaintiff's second contention is that the trial justice incorrectly applied the principles of contract law in deciding that the facts did not disclose a valid acceptance of defendants' offer. Again we cannot agree.

The trial justice proceeded on the theory that the delivery of the purchase and sale agreement to plaintiff constituted an offer by defendants to sell the property. Because we must view the evidence in the light most favorable to the party against whom summary judgment was entered, in this case plaintiff, we assume as the trial justice did that the delivery of the agreement was in fact an offer.[2]

The question we must answer next is whether there was an acceptance of that offer. The general rule is that where, as here, there is an offer to form a bilateral contract, the offeree must communicate his acceptance to the offeror before any contractual obligation can come into being. A mere mental intent to accept the offer, no matter how carefully formed, is not sufficient. The acceptance must be transmitted to the offeror in some overt manner. Bullock v. Harwick, 158 Fla. 834, 30 So.2d 539 (1947); Armstrong v. Guy H. James Constr. Co., 402 P.2d 275 (Okl.1965); 1 Restatement, Contracts § 20 (1932). See generally 1 Corbin, Contracts § 67 (1963). A review of the record shows that the only expression of acceptance which was communicated to defendants was the delivery of the executed purchase and sale agreement accompanied by the letter of September 8. Therefore it is solely on the basis of the language used in these two documents that we must determine whether there was a valid acceptance. Whatever plaintiff's unexpressed intention may have been in sending the documents is irrelevant. We must be concerned only with the language actually used, not the language plaintiff thought he was using or intended to use.

There is no doubt that the execution and delivery of the purchase and sale agreement by plaintiff, without more, would have operated as an acceptance. The terms of the accompanying letter, however, apparently conditioned the acceptance upon the inclusion of various items of personalty. In assessing the effect of the terms of that letter we must keep in mind certain generally accepted rules. To be effective, an acceptance must be definite and unequivocal. "An offeror is entitled to know in clear terms whether the offeree accepts his proposal. It is not enough that the words of a reply justify a probable inference of assent." 1 Restatement, Contracts § 58, comment a (1932). The acceptance may not impose additional conditions on the offer, nor may it add

---

2. The conclusion that the delivery of the agreement was an offer is not unassailable in view of the fact that defendants did not sign the agreement before sending it to plaintiff, and the fact that plaintiff told defendants' attorney after the agreement was received that he would have to investigate certain conditions of title before signing the agreement. If it was not an offer, plaintiff's execution of the agreement could itself be no more than an offer, which defendants never accepted.

limitations. "An acceptance which is equivocal or upon condition or with a limitation is a counteroffer and requires acceptance by the original offeror before a contractual relationship can exist." John Hancock Mut. Life Ins. Co. v. Dietlin, 97 R.I. 515, 518, 199 A.2d 311, 313 (1964). Accord, Cavanaugh v. Conway, 36 R.I. 571, 587, 90 A. 1080, 1086 (1914).

However, an acceptance may be valid despite conditional language if the acceptance is clearly independent of the condition. Many cases have so held. Williston states the rule as follows:

> "Frequently an offeree, while making a positive acceptance of the offer, also makes a request or suggestion that some addition or modification be made. So long as it is clear that the meaning of the acceptance is positively and unequivocally to accept the offer whether such request is granted or not, a contract is formed." 1 Williston, Contracts § 79 at 261–62 (3d ed.1957).

Corbin is in agreement with the above view. 1 Corbin, supra, § 84 at 363–65. Thus our task is to decide whether plaintiff's letter is more reasonably interpreted as a qualified acceptance or as an absolute acceptance together with a mere inquiry concerning a collateral matter.

In making our decision we recognize that, as one text states, "The question whether a communication by an offeree is a conditional acceptance or counter-offer is not always easy to answer. It must be determined by the same common-sense process of interpretation that must be applied in so many other cases." 1 Corbin, supra § 82 at 353. In our opinion the language used in plaintiff's letter of September 8 is not consistent with an absolute acceptance accompanied by a request for a gratuitous benefit. We interpret the letter to impose a condition on plaintiff's acceptance of defendants' offer. The letter does not unequivocally state that even without the enumerated items plaintiff is willing to complete the contract. In fact, the letter seeks "confirmation" that the listed items "are a part of the transaction". Thus, far from being an independent, collateral request, the sale of the items in question is explicitly referred to as a part of the real estate transaction. Moreover, the letter goes on to stress the difficulty of finding replacements for these items. This is a further indication that plaintiff did not view the inclusion of the listed items as merely collateral or incidental to the real estate transaction.

A review of the relevant case law discloses that those cases in which an acceptance was found valid despite an accompanying conditional term generally involved a more definite expression of acceptance than the one in the case at bar. E.g., Moss v. Cogle, 267 Ala. 208, 101 So.2d 314 (1958); Jaybe Constr. Co. v. Beco, Inc., 3 Conn.Cir. 406, 216 A.2d 208, 212 (1965); Katz v. Pratt Street Realty Co., 257 Md. 103, 262 A.2d 540 (1970); Nelson v. Hamlin, 258 Mass. 331, 155 N.E. 18 (1927); Duprey v. Donahoe, 52 Wash.2d 129, 323 P.2d 903 (1958).

Accordingly, we hold that since the plaintiff's letter of acceptance dated September 8 was conditional, it operated as a rejection of the defendants' offer and no contractual obligation was created.

The plaintiff's appeal is denied and dismissed, the judgment appealed from is affirmed and the case is remanded to the Superior Court.

PAOLINO, J., did not participate.

———

RHODE ISLAND DEP'T OF TRANSPORTATION v. PROVIDENCE & WORCESTER R.R., 674 A.2d 1239 (R.I.1996). P & W owned a parcel of waterfront property in East Providence, Rhode Island. There were railroad tracks on the property. A statute, Rhode Island G.L. § 39–6.1–9, provided that "All rail properties within the state offered for sale by any railway corporation ... shall be offered for sale to the state in the first instance at the lowest price at which the railway corporation is willing to sell.... The state shall have a period of not more than thirty (30) days from receipt of the notification to accept the offer." P & W entered into a Real Estate Sales Agreement to sell the property to Promet for $100,000, subject to the State's option. Under the agreement with Promet, P & W was required to remove the tracks from the property. Pursuant to the statute, P & W then offered the property to the State for $100,000. The relevant State official accepted the offer in writing, but added, "Of course, you understand that certain wording in the Real Estate Sales Agreement [with Promet] relating to 'buyer' and obligations concerning the removal of track would be inappropriate to the purpose of the State's purchase." P & W claimed that no contract had been formed because the State's response was a conditional acceptance. Held, for the State:

> This Court has held that a valid acceptance "must be definite and unequivocal," Ardente v. Horan, 117 R.I. 254, 259, 366 A.2d 162, 165 (1976), and that an "acceptance which is equivocal or upon condition or with a limitation is a counteroffer and requires acceptance by the original offeror before a contractual relationship can exist." John Hancock Mutual Life Insurance Co. v. Dietlin, 97 R.I. 515, 518, 199 A.2d 311, 313 (1964). It is not equivocation, however, "if the offeree merely puts into words that which was already reasonably implied in the terms of the offer." 1 Corbin on Contracts, S 3.32 at 478–79 (rev. ed.1993). It is further the case that "an acceptance must receive a reasonable construction" and that "the mere addition of a collateral or immaterial [matter] will not prevent the formation of a contract." Raydon Exploration, Inc. v. Ladd, 902 F.2d 1496, 1500 (10th Cir.1990). See also Hoyt R. Matise Co. v. Zurn, 754 F.2d 560, 566 (5th Cir.1985) ("[t]o transmogrify a purported acceptance into a counteroffer, it must be shown that the acceptance differs in some material respect from the offer").

> The state's letter of acceptance points out that the name of the buyer in the original agreement would have to be changed. In our opinion, this statement simply reflected the obvious necessity to replace "the state" for "Promet" as the named buyer in the deed. Moreover, the letter's reference to P & W's obligation to Promet to remove tracks from the property as "inappropriate to the purpose of the State's purchase" did not add any terms or conditions to the contract but, instead, constituted a clear benefit to P & W. In pointing out that the "wording" that obligated P & W to remove tracks would be "inappropriate" in an agreement between P & W and the state, the state, in fact, relieved P & W from the obligation and expense it otherwise would have incurred in selling the property to Promet. When an offeree, in its acceptance of an offer, absolves the

offeror of a material obligation, the "rules of contract construction and the 'rules of common sense' " preclude construing that absolution as an additional term that invalidates the acceptance. Textron, Inc. v. Aetna Casualty and Surety Co., 638 A.2d 537, 541 (R.I.1994)....

Therefore, we concur with the trial justice who found that the state validly accepted the option extended to it by P & W.

———

RESTATEMENT, SECOND, CONTRACTS § 39

[See Selected Source Materials Supplement]

———

RESTATEMENT, SECOND, CONTRACTS § 39, ILLUSTRATIONS 1–3

1. A offers B to sell him a parcel of land for $5,000, stating that the offer will remain open for thirty days. B replies, "I will pay $4800 for the parcel," and on A's declining that, B writes, within the thirty day period, "I accept your offer to sell for $5,000." There is no contract unless A's offer was [an option supported by consideration], or unless A's reply to the counter-offer manifested an intention to renew his original offer.

2. A makes the same offer to B as that stated in Illustration 1, and B replies, "Won't you take less?" A answers, "No." An acceptance thereafter by B within the thirty-day period is effective. B's inquiry was not a counter-offer, and A's original offer stands.

3. A makes the same offer to B as that stated in Illustration 1. B replies "I am keeping your offer under advisement, but if you wish to close the matter at once I will give you $4800." A does not reply, and within the thirty-day period B accepts the original offer. B's acceptance is effective.

———

PRICE v. OKLAHOMA COLLEGE OF OSTEOPATHIC MEDICINE AND SURGERY, 733 P.2d 1357 (Okla. Ct. App. 1986). Oklahoma College wrote a letter to Price, a member of its faculty, offering a one-year renewal of Price's appointment at an annual salary of $47,117. In the letter, the College asked Price to indicate his acceptance of the offer by signing and returning a copy. The words, "I accept the responsibilities of the appointment under the terms outlined above" were typed at the end of the letter, above a space for Price's signature. Price signed and returned a copy of the letter, but underneath his signature he wrote, "Signed under protest that salary does not reflect guarantees under present and past Personnel Policies and that proper evaluation procedures were not followed." The College responded that Price's reply was not an acceptance, and that his appointment was terminated. Price sued for breach of contract. Held, for Price.

"The protest language did not in tenor or letter alter or purport to alter any term of the offer; it merely articulated the offeree's opinion that one term of the offer—the salary—had not been determined in accord with 'present and past personnel policies.' Execution of the acceptance was precisely in the manner directed by the offeror. The note added below the acceptance was a precative protest not substantially unlike he had written on the acceptance letter in prior years. The notation amounted to no more than saying I don't like your offer, I don't think it's right or fair, but I accept it. That and nothing more."

RESTATEMENT, SECOND, CONTRACTS § 59

[See Selected Source Materials Supplement]

CISG ART. 19

[See Selected Source Materials Supplement]

UNIDROIT PRINCIPLES OF INTERNATIONAL COMMERCIAL CONTRACTS ART. 2.1.11

[See Selected Source Materials Supplement]

PRINCIPLES OF EUROPEAN CONTRACT LAW ART. 2.208

[See Selected Source Materials Supplement]

NOTE ON THE MIRROR–IMAGE RULE

Under classical contract law, the rule that a conditional acceptance terminates the power of acceptance was accompanied by a closely connected rule known as the mirror-image or ribbon-matching rule. Under that rule, if a purported acceptance varied from the offer in any respect, no matter how minor, no contract was formed. Under modern contract law, the bite of this rule has been softened in two respects. First, UCC § 2–207 applies a special rule in the case of contracts for the sale of goods. Although section 2–207 is not limited in terms to form offers and form acceptances, it is obviously designed primarily to deal with the problems presented by forms, and normally is applied only to forms. UCC § 2–207 will be considered in Chapter 16, infra. Second, Comment a to Restatement Second § 59, which builds on UCC § 2–207, and is supported by some case law, provides that "a definite and seasonal expression of acceptance is operative despite the statement of additional or different terms if the acceptance is not made to depend on assent to the additional or different terms." This leaves open how a court is to determine whether in any given case the acceptance is or is not made to depend on assent to the additional or different terms.

————

LIVINGSTONE v. EVANS, Alberta Supreme Court, [1925] 4 D.L.R. 769. The correspondence between the parties was as follows: (1) A letter from Seller to Buyer offering to sell certain land for $1800 on terms specified. (2) A telegram from Buyer to Seller: "Send lowest cash price. Will give $1600 cash. Wire." (3) A telegraphic answer from Seller reading simply, "Cannot reduce price." (4) An acceptance from Buyer of the offer contained in Seller's letter, posted after the receipt of Seller's telegram. Held, there was a contract. Buyer's telegram (no. 2 above) being a counter—offer terminated Buyer's power of acceptance until Seller's telegraphic answer (no. 3 above) by implication renewed the offer.

————

CULTON v. GILCHRIST, 92 Iowa 718, 61 N.W. 384 (1894). A landlord offered his tenant a renewal of a lease on premises then occupied by the tenant. The tenant replied accepting the offer and adding, "Mr. Culton ... I would like to put a small cookroom at the south side, so we could have some place to cook, wash, as it is very hard for my wife to only have one room. We have stood it quite a while through hot weather. I would like to do this myself, if in the lease you will give me the privilege of taking the same away providing I do not buy." The court stated, "All that is said about this cookroom, and the taking it away is a mere request, which [the landlord] might comply with or not at his election. The acceptance is complete and absolute, and depended in no way upon the matter relating to this cookroom."

————

RESTATEMENT, SECOND, CONTRACTS § 37

[See Selected Source Materials Supplement]

————

NOTE ON THE EFFECT OF THE OFFEROR'S DEATH
OR INCAPACITY BEFORE ACCEPTANCE

Under a traditional rule of contract law, the death or incapacity of an offeror terminates the offeree's power of acceptance if the offer is revocable when the death or incapacity occurs. This rule is unexceptionable where the offeree knows or has reason to know of the offeror's death or incapacity before he accepts the offer. The rule is also unexceptionable where, even in the absence of the rule, if a contract is formed the offeror's estate will be excused under the doctrine of changed circumstances. (An example is a contract that involves personal services by the offeror.) The bite of the rule, therefore, is that it applies even when (1) the offeree accepts at a time when he neither knows nor has reason to know of the offeror's death or incapacity and (2) in the absence of the rule, the offeror's death or incapacity would not excuse her estate from performance.

The bite of the rule should not be exaggerated. The rule would normally be inapplicable to offers made by entities that have perpetual existence, such as corporations and governmental bodies. Indeed, the rule would probably be deemed inapplicable to an offer made by most types of business organizations other than sole entrepreneurships—even those types that do not have perpetual existence. Probably too, the rule would be deemed inapplicable to persons who contract in a representative rather than an individual role, such as trustees and executors. Therefore, the principal application of the rule is to cases in which the offer is made by an individual and if a contract was formed, the individual's estate would not be excused by her death or incapacity.

The traditional rule has been criticized on the ground that it defeats the reasonable expectations of offerees who accept when they neither know nor have reason to know of the offeror's death or incapacity. Section 48 of Restatement Second adopts the traditional rule in the black letter, but criticizes the rule in the Comment. "This rule," the Comment states, "seems to be a relic of the obsolete view that a contract requires a 'meeting of minds,' and it is out of harmony with the modern doctrine that a manifestation of assent is effective without regard to actual mental assent."

Occasional cases have rejected the rule. In Swift & Co. v. Smigel, 115 N.J.Super. 391, 279 A.2d 895, 896, 899–900 (App.Div. 1971), aff'd, 60 N.J. 348, 289 A.2d 793 (1972), the offeror had been declared incompetent before the offeree, who did not know of the incompetence, accepted. The contract was held valid. The offer in *Swift* was a guaranty of payment for merchandise supplied to a corporation in which the offeror had a substantial interest. The court stated:

> In the present instance decedent promised plaintiff to make good any bills for provisions incurred by a corporate business enterprise in which he had a one-half stock interest. Had he not done so plaintiff presumably would not have taken on the business risk of selling to the corporation. It would seem to us that if plaintiff neither knew nor had any reason to know of decedent's later adjudication as an incompetent during any portion of the time it was making the deliveries which gave rise to the debts here sued on, plaintiff's reasonable expectations based on decedent's original continuing promise would be unjustifiably defeated by denial of recovery.

> If the situation is judged in terms of relative convenience, it would seem easier and more expectable for the guardian of the incompetent to notify at least those people with whom the incompetent had been doing business of the fact of adjudication than for the holder of a guaranty such as here to have to make a specific inquiry as to competency of the guarantor on each occasion of an advance of credit to the principal debtor.

The great majority of the cases, however, have upheld the rule that an offeror's death or incapacity terminates the offeree's power of acceptance. It is easy to understand why this should be so, if the application of the rule was limited to cutting off expectation damages against an individual's estate for nonperformance of a wholly executory contract. As a practical matter, a contract entered into by an individual will normally be worthless to her estate if she dies before performance is to occur, because there will be no practical way for the estate to perform. Think here of a sole entrepreneur who makes an offer in the ordinary course of business and then dies or becomes incapacitated. Consider also that there may be no one who can timely perform the contract on the estate's behalf, because it almost invariably takes time before a representative of an estate is appointed. Accordingly, the courts might understandably be reluctant to saddle an offeror's estate with liability for expectation damages where the offeror died or became incompetent before the offeree accepted.

On the other hand, as Richard Craswell points out, it is often in an offeror's interest that the offeree's power of acceptance not be terminated by the death or incapacity of the offeror unbeknown to the offeree. See Craswell, Offer, Acceptance, and Efficient Reliance, 48 Stan. L. Rev. 481, 515–16 (1996). In particular, in certain cases it is in the offeror's interest to empower the offeree to reliably take an action that the offer is intended to induce. An obvious case of this sort is one like *Swift*, in which the offer consists of a guarantee for an extension of credit by the offeree to a third party, which will benefit the offeror.

The competing considerations that bear on the effect of the death or incapacity of an offeror could be reconciled by a rule that if an offeree accepts an offer that was made by an individual who, unbeknown to the offeree, died or became incompetent after making the offer, the offeree should not be entitled to recover expectation damages against the individual's estate, but should be entitled to recover damages for any justifiable reliance that occurred between the time the offeree accepted and the time he learned of the offeror's death or incompetence.

SECTION 3. TERMINATION OF THE OFFEREE'S POWER OF ACCEPTANCE: REVOCATION

DICKINSON v. DODDS

In the Court of Appeal, Chancery Division, 1876.
2 Ch.Div. 463.

On Wednesday, the 10th of June, 1874, the defendant John Dodds signed and delivered to the plaintiff, George Dickinson, a memorandum, of which the material part was as follows:

"I hereby agree to sell to Mr. George Dickinson the whole of the dwellinghouses, garden ground, stabling, and outbuildings thereto belonging, situate at Croft, belonging to me, for the sum of £800. As witness my hand this tenth day of June, 1874.

"£800. [Signed] John Dodds."

"P.S.—This offer to be left over until Friday, 9 o'clock a.m. J.D. (the twelfth), 12th June, 1874.

[Signed] J. Dodds."

The bill alleged that Dodds understood and intended that the plaintiff should have until Friday, 9 a.m., within which to determine whether he would or would not purchase, and that he should absolutely have until that time the refusal of the property at the price of £800, and that the plaintiff in fact determined to accept the offer on the morning of Thursday, the 11th of June, but did not at once signify his acceptance to Dodds, believing that he had the power to accept it until 9 a.m. on the Friday.

In the afternoon of the Thursday the plaintiff was informed by a Mr. Berry that Dodds had been offering or agreeing to sell the property to Thomas Allan, the other defendant. Thereupon the plaintiff, at about half past seven in the evening, went to the house of Mrs. Burgess, the mother-in-law of Dodds, where he was then staying, and left with her a formal acceptance in writing of the offer to sell the property. According to the evidence of Mrs. Burgess this document never in fact reached Dodds, she having forgotten to give it to him.

On the following (Friday) morning, at about seven o'clock, Berry, who was acting as agent for Dickinson, found Dodds at the Darlington railway station, and handed to him a duplicate of the acceptance by Dickinson, and explained to Dodds its purport. He replied that it was too late, as he had sold the property. A few minutes later Dickinson himself found Dodds entering a railway carriage, and handed him another duplicate of the notice of acceptance, but Dodds declined to receive it, saying: "You are too late. I have sold the property."

It appeared that on the day before, Thursday, the 11th of June, Dodds had signed a formal contract for the sale of the property to the defendant Allan for £800, and had received from him a deposit of £40.

The bill in this suit prayed that the defendant Dodds might be decreed specifically to perform the contract of the 10th of June, 1874; that he might be restrained from conveying the property to Allan; that Allan might be restrained from taking any such conveyance; that, if any such conveyance had been or should be made, Allan might be declared a trustee of the property for, and might be directed to convey the property to, the plaintiff; and for damages.

The cause came on for hearing before Vice Chancellor Bacon on the 25th of January, 1876. [It was his opinion that Dodds could withdraw only by giving notice to Dickinson, in spite of Cooke v. Oxley, 3 T.R. 653, and that the contract took effect by the doctrine of relation back as of the time of the offer and hence was prior to the sale to Allan. He therefore decreed specific performance in favor of the plaintiff. From the decision both of the defendants appealed.]

JAMES, L.J., after referring to the document of the 10th of June, 1874, continued:

The document, though beginning "I hereby agree to sell," was nothing but an offer, and was only intended to be an offer, for the plaintiff himself tells us that he required time to consider whether he would enter into an agreement or not. Unless both parties had then agreed, there was no concluded agreement then made; it was in effect and substance only an offer to sell. The plaintiff, being minded not to complete the bargain at that time, added this memorandum: "This offer to be left over until Friday, 9 o'clock a.m. 12th

June, 1874." That shows it was only an offer. There was no consideration given for the undertaking or promise, to whatever extent it may be considered binding, to keep the property unsold until 9 o'clock on Friday morning; but apparently Dickinson was of opinion, and probably Dodds was of the same opinion, that he (Dodds) was bound by that promise, and could not in any way withdraw from it, or retract it, until 9 o'clock on Friday morning, and this probably explains a good deal of what afterwards took place. But it is clear settled law, on one of the clearest principles of law, that this promise, being a mere nudum pactum, was not binding, and that at any moment before a complete acceptance by Dickinson of the offer, Dodds was as free as Dickinson himself.

Well, that being the state of things, it is said that the only mode in which Dodds could assert that freedom was by actually and distinctly saying to Dickinson, "Now I withdraw my offer." It appears to me that there is neither principle nor authority for the proposition that there must be an express and actual withdrawal of the offer, or what is called a retraction. It must, to constitute a contract, appear that the two minds were at one, at the same moment of time, that is, that there was an offer continuing up to the time of the acceptance. If there was not such a continuing offer, then the acceptance comes to nothing. Of course it may well be that the one man is bound in some way or other to let the other man know that his mind with regard to the offer has been changed; but in this case, beyond all question, the plaintiff knew that Dodds was no longer minded to sell the property to him as plainly and clearly as if Dodds had told him in so many words, "I withdraw the offer." This is evident from the plaintiff's own statements in the bill.

The plaintiff says in effect that, having heard and knowing that Dodds was no longer minded to sell to him and that he was selling or had sold to some one else, thinking that he could not in point of law withdraw his offer, meaning to fix him to it, and endeavoring to bind him: "I went to the house where he was lodging, and saw his mother-in-law, and left with her an acceptance of the offer, knowing all the while that he had entirely changed his mind. I got an agent to watch for him at 7 o'clock the next morning, and I went to the train just before 9 o'clock, in order that I might catch him and give him my notice of acceptance just before 9 o'clock, and when that occurred he told my agent, and he told me, 'You are too late,' and he then threw back the paper." It is to my mind quite clear that before there was any attempt at acceptance by the plaintiff, he was perfectly well aware that Dodds had changed his mind, and that he had in fact agreed to sell the property to Allan. It is impossible, therefore, to say there was ever that existence of the same mind between the two parties which is essential in point of law to the making of an agreement. I am of opinion, therefore, that the plaintiff has failed to prove that there was any binding contract between Dodds and himself. . . .

[The bill] will be dismissed with costs.

[The concurring opinion of MELLISH, L.J., is omitted.]

————

RESTATEMENT, SECOND, CONTRACTS §§ 42, 43

[See Selected Source Materials Supplement]

CISG ART. 16

[See Selected Source Materials Supplement]

UNIDROIT PRINCIPLES OF INTERNATIONAL COMMERCIAL CONTRACTS ART. 2.1.4

[See Selected Source Materials Supplement]

PRINCIPLES OF EUROPEAN CONTRACT LAW ART. 2.202

[See Selected Source Materials Supplement]

NOTE ON CONTRACT PRACTICE

In 1988, Professor Russell Weintraub sent a questionaire to the general counsels of 182 corporations of various sizes, asking for their company's views on certain contracts issues. Weintraub, A Survey of Contract Practice and Policy, 1992 Wisc.L.Rev. 1. Several questions in the survey concerned firm offers. The results were as follows: 76% of the respondents reported that their companies received firm offers. Of these, 95% reported that they relied on the firm offers they received. Correspondingly, 73% percent of the respondents reported that their companies made firm offers to other companies. Of these, 97% reported that they expected offerees to rely on their firm offers.

NOTE ON WHAT CONSTITUTES RECEIPT OF A WRITTEN ACCEPTANCE

What was the legal effect of leaving a written acceptance with Dodds's mother-in-law, assuming Dickinson still had power to accept? Restatement, Second, Contracts § 68 provides that "A written revocation, rejection, or acceptance is received when the writing comes into the possession of the person addressed, or of some person authorized by him to receive it for him, or when it is deposited in some place which he has authorized as the place for this or similar communications to be deposited for him." Illustration 1 to § 68 is as follows:

A sends B by mail an offer dated from A's house and states as a condition of the offer that an acceptance must be received within three days. B mails an acceptance which reaches A's house and is delivered to a servant or is deposited in a mail box at the door within three days; but A has been called away from home and does not personally receive the letter for a week. There is a contract.

Under UCC § 1–201(27), "[A] notice or notification received by an organization is effective for a particular transaction from the time when it is brought to the attention of the individual conducting that transaction, and in any event from the time when it would have been brought to his attention if the organization had exercised due diligence. . . ."

See also Note on Transacting by Electronic Commerce, Chapter 11, infra.

RESTATEMENT, SECOND, CONTRACTS § 45

[See Selected Source Materials Supplement]

RAGOSTA v. WILDER

Supreme Court of Vermont, 1991.
156 Vt. 390, 592 A.2d 367.

Before ALLEN, C.J., and PECK, GIBSON, DOOLEY and MORSE, JJ.

PECK, JUSTICE.

Defendant appeals from a judgment ordering him to convey to plaintiffs a piece of real property known as "The Fork Shop." Defendant argues that the court improperly found that a binding contract existed and that it misapplied the doctrine of equitable estoppel. He also contends that the ruling cannot be upheld under promissory estoppel principles since the court failed to examine the extent to which enforcement of defendant's promise to sell was required to prevent injustice. Because the trial court's ruling cannot stand on contract or equitable estoppel grounds and because the court's analysis of promissory estoppel is inextricably bound in its contractual analysis, we reverse and remand the cause for further proceedings consistent with the principles expressed herein.

In 1985, plaintiffs became interested in purchasing "The Fork Shop" from defendant, but preliminary negotiations between the parties were fruitless. In 1987, plaintiffs learned that defendant was again considering selling "The Fork Shop," [and] mailed him a letter offering to purchase the property along with a check for $2,000 and began arrangements to obtain the necessary financing. By letter dated September 28, 1987, defendant returned the $2,000 check explaining that he had two properties "up for sale" and that he would not sign an acceptance to plaintiffs' offer because "that would tie up both these properties until [there was] a closing." In the letter, he also made the following counter-offer:

> I will sell you The Fork Shop and its property as listed in book 35, at page 135 of the Brookfield Land Records on 17 April 1972, for $88,-000.00—(Eighty-eight thousand dollars), at anytime up until the 1st of

November 1987 that you appear with me at the Randolph National Bank with said sum. At which time they will give you a certified deed to this property or to your agent as directed, providing said property has not been sold.

On October 1st, the date plaintiffs received the letter, they called defendant. The court found that during the conversation plaintiffs told defendant that "the terms and conditions of his offer were acceptable and that they would in fact prepare to accept the offer." Defendant assured plaintiffs that there was no one else currently interested in purchasing "The Fork Shop."

On October 6th, plaintiffs informed defendant that they would not close the sale on October 8th as discussed previously but that they would come to Vermont on October 10th. On October 8th, defendant called plaintiffs and informed them that he was no longer willing to sell "The Fork Shop." The trial court found that, at that time, defendant was aware plaintiffs "had processed their loan application and were prepared to close." Plaintiffs informed defendant that they would be at the Randolph National Bank at 10:00 a.m. on October 15th with the $88,000 purchase price and in fact appeared. Defendant did not. Plaintiffs claim they incurred $7,499.23 in loan closing costs.

Plaintiffs sued for specific performance arguing that defendant had contracted to sell the property to them. They alleged moreover that defendant knew they would have to incur costs to obtain financing for the purchase but assured them that the sale would go through and that they relied on his assurances.

The trial court concluded that defendant "made an offer in writing which could only be accepted by performance prior to the deadline." It concluded further that defendant could not revoke his offer on October 8th because plaintiffs, relying on the offer, had already begun performance and that defendant should be estopped from revoking the offer on a theory of equitable estoppel. It ordered defendant to convey to plaintiffs "The Fork Shop" for $88,000. This appeal followed.

I.

Plaintiffs claim that defendant's letter of September 28, 1987 created a contract to sell "The Fork Shop" to them unless the property was sold to another buyer. Rather, defendant's letter contains an offer to sell the property for $88,000, which the trial court found could only be accepted "by performance prior to the deadline," and a promise to keep the offer open unless the property were sold to another buyer. Defendant received no consideration for either promise. In fact, defendant returned plaintiffs' check for $2,000 which would have constituted consideration for the promise to keep the offer open, presumably because he did not wish to make a firm offer. Thus, the promise to keep the offer to sell open was not enforceable and, absent the operation of equitable estoppel, defendant could revoke the offer to sell the property at any time before plaintiffs accepted it. See *Buchannon v. Billings,* 127 Vt. 69, 75, 238 A.2d 638, 642 (1968) ("An option is a continuing offer, and *if supported by a consideration,* it cannot be withdrawn before the time limit.") (emphasis added).

Plaintiffs argue that the actions they undertook to obtain financing, which were detrimental to them, could constitute consideration for the promise to keep the offer to sell open. Their argument is unconvincing. Although plaintiffs are correct in stating that a detriment may constitute consideration, they ignore the rule that "[t]o constitute consideration, a performance or a return promise must be bargained for." Restatement (Second) of Contracts § 71(1) (1981). "A performance or return promise is bargained for if it is sought by the promisor in exchange for his promise and is given by the promisee in exchange for that promise." *Id.* at § 71(2). Plaintiffs began to seek financing even before defendant made a definite offer to sell the property. Whatever detriment they suffered was not in exchange for defendant's promise to keep the offer to sell open.

The trial court ruled that the offer to sell "The Fork Shop" could only be accepted by performance but concluded that in obtaining financing plaintiffs began performance and that therefore defendant could not revoke the offer to sell once plaintiffs incurred the cost of obtaining financing. Section 45 of the Restatement (Second) of Contracts provides that "[w]here an offer invites an offeree to accept by rendering a performance and does not invite a promissory acceptance, an option contract is created when the offeree tenders or begins the invited performance or tenders a beginning of it." However, "[w]hat is begun or tendered must be part of the actual performance invited in order to preclude revocation under this Section." *Id.* at comment f.

Here, plaintiffs were merely engaged in preparation for performance. The court itself found only that "plaintiffs had changed their position in order to tender performance." At most, they obtained financing and assured defendant that they would pay; plaintiffs never tendered to defendant or even began to tender the $88,000 purchase price. Thus, they never accepted defendant's offer and no contract was ever created. See *Multicare Medical Center v. State Social & Health Services,* 114 Wash.2d 572, 584, 790 P.2d 124, 131 (1990) ("under a unilateral contract, an offer cannot be accepted by promising to perform; rather, the offeree must accept, if at all, by performance, and the contract then becomes executed").*

II.

Defendant claims next that the court was not justified in applying equitable estoppel in this case. We agree.

> One who invokes the doctrine of equitable estoppel has the burden of establishing each of its constituent elements. Four essential elements must be established: first, the party to be estopped must know the facts; second, the party being estopped must intend that his conduct shall be acted upon or the acts must be such that the party asserting the estoppel has a right to believe it is so intended; third, the latter must be ignorant of the true facts; and finally, the party asserting the estoppel must rely on the conduct of the party to be estopped to his detriment.

Fisher v. Poole, 142 Vt. 162, 168, 453 A.2d 408, 411–12 (1982) (citations omitted).

---

* Because defendant specified that the manner of acceptance would be performance, plaintiffs' argument that they accepted defendant's offer over the telephone must fail. In fact, plaintiffs admitted in their depositions that they were very worried that the property would be sold to someone else prior to closing. Thus, they should have understood that they had no enforceable contract until closing.

Equitable estoppel is inapplicable here because there were no facts known to defendant but unknown to plaintiffs. Plaintiffs cannot have acted on an understanding that defendant would definitely convey the property to them. On its face, defendant's offer stated only that he would convey the property to plaintiffs if he did not convey it to another party first. The trial court acknowledged that if defendant had sold "The Fork Shop" to another party plaintiffs would not have been entitled to relief. Thus, plaintiffs had no assurance that defendant would definitely convey the property to them even if on October 1st defendant told them that there was no one else interested in buying the property at that time. Moreover, plaintiffs engaged in obtaining financing for the purchase even before defendant made any offer to them whatsoever. They understood, at the time they obtained financing for the transaction, that they were assuming a risk that they would be unable to purchase the property in question. Since the plaintiffs had not tendered performance and did not establish the elements for the application of equitable estoppel, defendant was entitled to withdraw his offer when he did.

III.

In the course of analyzing the case under part performance and equitable estoppel theories, the trial court cited promissory estoppel principles. It noted, "Plaintiffs relied on the conduct of the Defendant to their detriment when they prepared for and tendered performance" and concluded that defendant's conduct induced plaintiffs to begin performance by obtaining financing.

> A promise which the promisor should reasonably expect to induce action or forbearance on the part of the promisee or a third person and which does induce such action or forbearance is binding if injustice can be avoided only by enforcement of the promise. The remedy granted for breach may be limited as justice requires.

Restatement (Second) of Contracts § 90(1). This principle is distinct from part performance since the action or forbearance involved need not constitute part performance. While the court's order cannot be upheld under a part performance theory, its ruling may be appropriate on promissory estoppel grounds. We cannot affirm the order on those grounds, however, because the trial court, in ruling that the promise must be enforced, erroneously relied on a part performance theory. Cf. *Price v. Price,* 149 Vt. 118, 122, 541 A.2d 79, 82 (1987) (order must be reversed and remanded where court may have relied on inappropriate considerations for its ruling). Under promissory estoppel, plaintiffs are entitled to enforcement of defendant's promise only if the promise induced them to take action "of a definite and substantial character," and if "injustice [*can*] *be avoided only* by enforcement of the promise." *Stacy v. Merchants Bank,* 144 Vt. 515, 521, 482 A.2d 61, 64 (1984) (emphasis added) (citing Restatement (Second) of Contracts § 90).

On remand the court shall consider the case under promissory estoppel only and determine what remedy, if any, is necessary to prevent injustice. In making this determination the court should consider the fact that plaintiffs incurred the expense of obtaining financing although they could not be certain that the property would be sold to them . . . .

Reversed and the cause remanded for further proceedings consistent with the principles expressed herein.

———————

NOTE ON OFFERS FOR UNILATERAL CONTRACTS

The court in *Ragosta* drew a sharp distinction between *preparing* to perform an act pursuant to an offer for a unilateral contract and *beginning* to perform the act. To understand why the court drew this distinction, it is necessary to briefly trace the doctrinal history concerning offers for a unilateral contract—that is, an offer for a contract to be formed by the exchange of a promise (in the form of an offer) and an act, rather than an offer for a contract to be formed by an exchange of promises.

It was a rule of classical contract law that an offer for a unilateral contract could be revoked at any time before the designated act had been completed, even if performance of the act had begun. This rule was exemplified in a pair of famous hypotheticals. In one, A says to B, "I will give you $100 if you walk across the Brooklyn Bridge." After B has walked halfway across the bridge, A overtakes B and revokes. In the other, A offers B $50 to climb a flagpole. After B has climbed halfway up the flagpole, A calls out to B and revokes. The result under classical contract law was the same in both hypotheticals: the revocation was effective, on the ground that an offer for a unilateral contract is revocable until performance of the act has been completed, even if performance had begun. Too bad for B.

The rule that an offer for a unilateral contract is revocable until the act has been completed was justified almost exclusively on the basis of deductive reasoning. The major premises of this reasoning were that only a bargained-for promise was enforceable, and that an offer could be revoked at any time prior to acceptance unless the offeror had made a bargained-for promise to hold the offer open. The minor premises were that an offer for a unilateral contract is not bargained for, and is not accepted until the act of performance that the offer calls for has occurred, that is, has been completed. The deductive conclusion was that an offer for a unilateral contract is revocable until performance has been completed.

The unilateral-contract rule defeated the reasonable expectations of offerees. Tiersma has put this point very well:

> [N]o reasonable person would intentionally create the sort of agreement that the traditional theory of unilateral contracts assumes. Suppose that a person, asserting his freedom to contract and his mastery over his offer, specifically intends to make a promise that will bind him not at the time he makes it, but only after the other party has completed a particular act in exchange. In other words, this promisor wishes to create the traditional unilateral contract. For example, he might tell the offeree that if she paints his house, he will—once she is finished—commit himself to paying her $1000. He makes it clear that he does not wish to be bound until she is completely finished, explaining to her that before she is finished he may revoke with impunity. What rational person would even buy the paint if she believed the speaker had not committed himself? The fact of the matter ... is that very reasonable people spend substantial time and money doing the sorts of things that unilateral contracts attempt to induce them to do. The only rational explanation for such behavior is that people believe the speaker is in fact committed then and there to paying the price if the conditions of the offer are met.

Peter Meijes Tiersma, Reassessing Unilateral Contracts: The Role of Offer, Acceptance and Promise, 26 U.C. Davis L. Rev. 1, 29 (1992).

Furthermore, the unilateral-contract rule was against the interests of offerors as a class. An actor makes an offer for a unilateral contract because she thinks her interests are best served by such an offer. It is in the interests of an actor who makes an offer for a unilateral contract that the offeree act under the offer—otherwise, the offer would not be made—and correspondingly that the offeree begin acting as quickly as reasonably possible. If, however, offers for unilateral contracts were revocable before performance was completed, offerees would not act under such offers, or at least would act at a much lower rate, because of the substantial risks of forfeiture that such action would entail if the offeror revokes before the act has been completed.

The framers of Restatement First—in particular, Williston, as the Reporter—understood that the unilateral-contract rule was unsatisfactory. However, because classical contract law was conceived as an axiomatic system, and the unilateral-contract rule seemed to flow inexorably from some of the axioms, Williston had trouble in figuring out how to break away from the rule without breaking away from the axioms on which he conceived contract law to rest. Williston was willing to bend, but not to break. The result was Section 45 of the First Restatement, which provided:

> If an offer for a unilateral contract is made, and part of the consideration requested in the offer is given or tendered by the offeree in response thereto, the offeror is bound by a contract, the duty of immediate performance of which is conditional on the full consideration being given or tendered within the time stated in the offer, or, if no time is stated therein, within a reasonable time.

Despite the fact that Section 45 liability was triggered only if the offeree took a certain kind of action, Section 45 was not conceptualized as reliance-based. If it had been conceptualized that way, then the section would have been unnecessary, because the problem it addressed could have been solved by its even more famous cousin, Section 90. Instead, the beginning of performance was—and under Restatement Second still is—conceptualized as completing an option contract, enforceable by expectation damages. The theory is as follows: an offer for a unilateral contract carries with it an implied promise that if part of the requested performance is given or tendered, the offeror will not revoke the offer. Rendering (or tendering) part performance completes a bargain for that promise. This makes the promise enforceable as an option under the bargain theory of consideration.

In order to maintain this conceptualization, the text and comment of Section 45, as formulated in both the First and Second Restatements, drew a sharp distinction between beginning to perform and preparing to perform. Under Section 45 of Restatement First, beginning to perform completed a bargain and therefore made the offeror's promise to hold the offer open enforceable. In contrast, action by the offeree other than beginning to perform had no effect under Section 45, because it would not complete a Section 45 bargain—although the Comment to Restatement First added that such action could have an effect under Section 90, which is not bargain-based:

> The main offer [for a unilateral contract] includes as a subsidiary promise, necessarily implied, that if part of the requested performance is given, the offeror will not revoke his offer.... Part performance ... may thus

furnish consideration for the subsidiary [promise]. Moreover, merely acting in justifiable reliance on an offer may in some cases serve as sufficient reason for making a promise binding (see § 90).

Section 45 of Restatement Second carries forward the approach of the First Restatement.

The distinction drawn in Section 45, and Ragosta v. Wilder, between beginning to perform and preparing to perform, is not easy to justify. For example, suppose A offers B $10,000 to B if B produces a solution to a famous mathematical problem. B begins by developing some new techniques that will be needed to solve the problem, but will also have independent significance. Has B prepared to perform or has he begun to perform? And why should it matter? As James Gordley observes, under the preparation-versus-performance distinction if the offeree takes one step on the Brooklyn Bridge, the offeror is bound, but if the offeree engages in massive preparations to get ready to cross the Bridge, the offeror is not bound. James Gordley, Enforcing Promises, 82 Cal. L. Rev. 547, 605 (1995).

DRENNAN v. STAR PAVING CO.

Supreme Court of California, 1958.
51 Cal.2d 409, 333 P.2d 757.

TRAYNOR, JUSTICE. Defendant appeals from a judgment for plaintiff in an action to recover damages caused by defendant's refusal to perform certain paving work according to a bid it submitted to plaintiff.

On July 28, 1955, plaintiff, a licensed general contractor, was preparing a bid on the "Monte Vista School Job" in the Lancaster school district. Bids had to be submitted before 8:00 p.m. Plaintiff testified that it was customary in that area for general contractors to receive the bids of subcontractors by telephone on the day set for bidding and to rely on them in computing their own bids. Thus on that day plaintiff's secretary, Mrs. Johnson, received by telephone between fifty and seventy-five subcontractors' bids for various parts of the school job. As each bid came in, she wrote it on a special form, which she brought into plaintiff's office. He then posted it on a master cost sheet setting forth the names and bids of all subcontractors. His own bid had to include the names of subcontractors who were to perform one-half of one per cent or more of the construction work, and he had also to provide a bidder's bond of ten per cent of his total bid of $317,385 as a guarantee that he would enter the contract if awarded the work.*

Late in the afternoon, Mrs. Johnson had a telephone conversation with Kenneth R. Hoon, an estimator for defendant. He gave his name and telephone number and stated that he was bidding for defendant for the paving work at the Monte Vista School according to plans and specifications and that his bid was $7,131.60. At Mrs. Johnson's request he repeated his bid. Plaintiff listened to the bid over an extension telephone in his office and posted it on

---

* Under a "bidder's" or "bid" bond, a Surety promises the person who is receiving bids (the "Obligee"), that if the bidder is awarded the contract but refuses to enter into it, the Surety will pay damages up to a stipulated amount (called "the penalty") that is set in the bond. (Footnote by ed.)

the master sheet after receiving the bid form from Mrs. Johnson. Defendant's was the lowest bid for the paving. Plaintiff computed his own bid accordingly and submitted it with the name of defendant as the subcontractor for the paving. When the bids were opened on July 28th, plaintiff's proved to be the lowest, and he was awarded the contract.

On his way to Los Angeles the next morning plaintiff stopped at defendant's office. The first person he met was defendant's construction engineer, Mr. Oppenheimer. Plaintiff testified: "I introduced myself and he immediately told me that they had made a mistake in their bid to me the night before, they couldn't do it for the price they had bid, and I told him I would expect him to carry through with their original bid because I had used it in compiling my bid and the job was being awarded them. And I would have to go and do the job according to my bid and I would expect them to do the same."

Defendant refused to do the paving work for less than $15,000. Plaintiff testified that he "got figures from other people" and after trying for several months to get as low a bid as possible engaged L & H Paving Company, a firm in Lancaster, to do the work for $10,948.60.

The trial court found on substantial evidence that defendant made a definite offer to do the paving on the Monte Vista job according to the plans and specifications for $7,131.60, and that plaintiff relied on defendant's bid in computing his own bid for the school job and naming defendant therein as the subcontractor for the paving work. Accordingly, it entered judgment for plaintiff in the amount of $3,817.00 (the difference between defendant's bid and the cost of the paving to plaintiff) plus costs.

Defendant contends that there was no enforceable contract between the parties on the ground that it made a revocable offer and revoked it before plaintiff communicated his acceptance to defendant.

There is no evidence that defendant offered to make its bid irrevocable in exchange for plaintiff's use of its figures in computing his bid. Nor is there evidence that would warrant interpreting plaintiff's use of defendant's bid as the acceptance thereof, binding plaintiff, on condition he received the main contract, to award the subcontract to defendant. In sum, there was neither an option supported by consideration nor a bilateral contract binding on both parties.

Plaintiff contends, however, that he relied to his detriment on defendant's offer and that defendant must therefore answer in damages for its refusal to perform. Thus the question is squarely presented: Did plaintiff's reliance make defendant's offer irrevocable?

Section 90 of the Restatement of Contracts states: "A promise which the promisor should reasonably expect to induce action or forbearance of a definite and substantial character on the part of the promisee and which does induce such action or forbearance is binding if injustice can be avoided only by enforcement of the promise." This rule applies in this state. . . .

Defendant's offer constituted a promise to perform on such conditions as were stated expressly or by implication therein or annexed thereto by operation of law. (See 1 Williston, Contracts [3rd ed.], § 24A, p. 56, § 61, p. 196.) Defendant had reason to expect that if its bid proved the lowest it would be used by plaintiff. It induced "action . . . of a definite and substantial character on the part of the promisee."

Had defendant's bid expressly stated or clearly implied that it was revocable at any time before acceptance we would treat it accordingly. It was silent on revocation, however, and we must therefore determine whether there are conditions to the right of revocation imposed by law or reasonably inferable in fact. In the analogous problem of an offer for a unilateral contract, the theory is now obsolete that the offer is revocable at any time before complete performance. Thus section 45 of the Restatement of Contracts provides: "If an offer for a unilateral contract is made, and part of the consideration requested in the offer is given or tendered by the offeree in response thereto, the offeror is bound by a contract, the duty of immediate performance of which is conditional on the full consideration being given or tendered within the time stated in the offer, or, if no time is stated therein, within a reasonable time." In explanation, comment b states that the "main offer includes as a subsidiary promise, necessarily implied, that if part of the requested performance is given, the offeror will not revoke his offer, and that if tender is made it will be accepted. Part performance or tender may thus furnish consideration for the subsidiary promise. Moreover, merely acting in justifiable reliance on an offer may in some cases serve as sufficient reason for making a promise binding (see § 90)."

Whether implied in fact or law, the subsidiary promise serves to preclude the injustice that would result if the offer could be revoked after the offeree had acted in detrimental reliance thereon. Reasonable reliance resulting in a foreseeable prejudicial change in position affords a compelling basis also for implying a subsidiary promise not to revoke an offer for a bilateral contract.

The absence of consideration is not fatal to the enforcement of such a promise. It is true that in the case of unilateral contracts the Restatement finds consideration for the implied subsidiary promise in the part performance of the bargained-for exchange, but its reference to section 90 makes clear that consideration for such a promise is not always necessary. The very purpose of section 90 is to make a promise binding even though there was no consideration "in the sense of something that is bargained for and given in exchange." (See 1 Corbin, Contracts 634 et seq.) Reasonable reliance serves to hold the offeror in lieu of the consideration ordinarily required to make the offer binding. In a case involving similar facts the Supreme Court of South Dakota stated that "we believe that reason and justice demand that the doctrine [of section 90] be applied to the present facts. We cannot believe that by accepting this doctrine as controlling in the state of facts before us we will abolish the requirement of a consideration in contract cases, in any different sense than an ordinary estoppel abolishes some legal requirement in its application. We are of the opinion, therefore, that the defendants in executing the agreement [which was not supported by consideration] made a promise which they should have reasonably expected would induce the plaintiff to submit a bid based thereon to the Government, that such promise did induce this action, and that injustice can be avoided only by enforcement of the promise." Northwestern Engineering Co. v. Ellerman, 69 S.D. 397, 408, 10 N.W.2d 879, 884; see also, Robert Gordon, Inc. v. Ingersoll–Rand Co., 7 Cir., 117 F.2d 654, 661; cf. James Baird Co. v. Gimbel Bros., 2 Cir., 64 F.2d 344.

When plaintiff used defendant's offer in computing his own bid, he bound himself to perform in reliance on defendant's terms. Though defendant did not bargain for this use of its bid neither did defendant make it idly, indifferent to whether it would be used or not. On the contrary it is reasonable to suppose that defendant submitted its bid to obtain the subcontract. It was bound to realize the substantial possibility that its bid would be the lowest, and that it would be included by plaintiff in his bid. It was to its own interest that the contractor be awarded the general contract; the lower the subcontract bid, the lower the general contractor's bid was likely to be and the greater its chance of acceptance and hence the greater defendant's chance of getting the paving subcontract. Defendant had reason not only to expect plaintiff to rely on its bid but to want him to. Clearly defendant had a stake in plaintiff's reliance on its bid. Given this interest and the fact that plaintiff is bound by his own bid, it is only fair that plaintiff should have at least an opportunity to accept defendant's bid after the general contract has been awarded to him.

It bears noting that a general contractor is not free to delay acceptance after he has been awarded the general contract in the hope of getting a better price. Nor can he reopen bargaining with the subcontractor and at the same time claim a continuing right to accept the original offer. See, R.J. Daum Const. Co. v. Child, Utah, 247 P.2d 817, 823. In the present case plaintiff promptly informed defendant that plaintiff was being awarded the job and that the subcontract was being awarded to defendant.

Defendant contends, however, that its bid was the result of mistake and that it was therefore entitled to revoke it. It relies on the rescission cases of M.F. Kemper Const. Co. v. City of Los Angeles, 37 Cal.2d 696, 235 P.2d 7, and Brunzell Const. Co. v. G.J. Weisbrod, Inc., 134 Cal.App.2d 278, 285 P.2d 989. See also, Lemoge Electric v. San Mateo County, 46 Cal.2d 659, 662, 297 P.2d 638. In those cases, however, the bidder's mistake was known or should have been known to the offeree, and the offeree could be placed in status quo. Of course, if plaintiff had reason to believe that defendant's bid was in error, he could not justifiably rely on it, and section 90 would afford no basis for enforcing it. Robert Gordon, Inc. v. Ingersoll–Rand, Inc., 7 Cir., 117 F.2d 654, 660. Plaintiff, however, had no reason to know that defendant had made a mistake in submitting its bid, since there was usually a variance of 160 per cent between the highest and lowest bids for paving in the desert around Lancaster. He committed himself to performing the main contract in reliance on defendant's figures. Under these circumstances defendant's mistake, far from relieving it of its obligation, constitutes an additional reason for enforcing it, for it misled plaintiff as to the cost of doing the paving. Even had it been clearly understood that defendant's offer was revocable until accepted, it would not necessarily follow that defendant had no duty to exercise reasonable care in preparing its bid. It presented its bid with knowledge of the substantial possibility that it would be used by plaintiff; it could foresee the harm that would ensue from an erroneous underestimate of the cost. Moreover, it was motivated by its own business interest. Whether or not these considerations alone would justify recovery for negligence had the case been tried on that theory (see Biakanja v. Irving, 49 Cal.2d 647, 650, 320 P.2d 16), they are persuasive that defendant's mistake should not defeat recovery under the rule of section 90 of the Restatement, Contracts. As between the subcontractor who made the bid and the general contractor who reasonably relied on it, the loss resulting from the mistake should fall on the party who caused it. . . .

There is no merit in defendant's contention that plaintiff failed to state a cause of action, on the ground that the complaint failed to allege that plaintiff attempted to mitigate the damages or that they could not have been mitigated. Plaintiff alleged that after defendant's default, "plaintiff had to procure the services of the L & H Co. to perform said asphaltic paving for the sum of $10,948.60." Plaintiff's uncontradicted evidence showed that he spent several months trying to get bids from other subcontractors and that he took the lowest bid. Clearly he acted reasonably to mitigate damages. In any event any uncertainty in plaintiff's allegation as to damages could have been raised by special demurrer. Code Civ.Proc. § 430, subd. 9. It was not so raised and was therefore waived. Code Civ.Proc. § 434.

The judgment is affirmed.

GIBSON, C.J., and SHENK, SCHAUER, SPENCE and McCOMB, JJ., concur.

PAVEL ENTERPRISES, INC. v. A.S. JOHNSON CO., 342 Md. 143, 674 A.2d 521 (1996). "The *Drennan* decision has been very influential. Many states have adopted the reasoning used by Justice Traynor. . . .

"Despite the popularity of the *Drennan* reasoning, the case has subsequently come under some criticism. The criticism centers on the lack of symmetry of detrimental reliance in the bid process, in that subcontractors are bound to the general, but the general is not bound to the subcontractors. The result is that the general is free to bid shop,[3] bid chop,[4] and to encourage bid peddling,[5] to the detriment of the subcontractors. One commentator described the problems that these practices create:

'Bid shopping and peddling have long been recognized as unethical by construction trade organizations. These "unethical," but common practices have several detrimental results. First, as bid shopping becomes common within a particular trade, the subcontractors will pad their initial bids in order to make further reductions during post-award negotiations. This artificial inflation of subcontractor's offers makes the bid process less effective. Second, subcontractors who are forced into post-award negotiations with the general often must reduce their sub-bids in order to avoid losing the award. Thus, they will be faced with a Hobson's choice between doing the job at a loss or doing a less than adequate job. Third, bid shopping and peddling tend to increase the risk of loss of the time and money used in preparing a bid. This occurs because generals and subcontractors who engage in these practices use, without expense, the bid estimates prepared by others. Fourth, it is often impossible for a general to obtain bids far enough in advance to have sufficient time to properly prepare his own bid because of the practice, common among many subcontractors, of holding sub-bids until the last possible moment in order to avoid pre-award bid shopping by the general. Fifth, many

---

3. Bid shopping is the use of the lowest subcontractor's bid as a tool in negotiating lower bids from other subcontractors post-award.

4. "The general contractor, having been awarded the prime contract, may pressure the subcontractor whose bid was used for a particular portion of the work in computing the overall bid on the prime contract to reduce the amount of the bid." . . .

5. An unscrupulous subcontractor can save estimating costs, and still get the job by not entering a bid or by entering an uncompetitive bid. After bid opening, this unscrupulous subcontractor, knowing the price of the low sub-bid, can then offer to perform the work for less money, precisely because the honest subcontractor has already paid for the estimate and included that cost in the original bid. This practice is called bid peddling.

subcontractors refuse to submit bids for jobs on which they expect bid shopping. As a result, competition is reduced, and, consequently, construction prices are increased. Sixth, any price reductions gained through the use of post-award bid shopping by the general will be of no benefit to the awarding authority, to whom these price reductions would normally accrue as a result of open competition before the award of the prime contract. Free competition in an open market is therefore perverted because of the use of post-award bid shopping.'

" . . . These problems have caused at least one court to reject promissory estoppel in the contractor-subcontractor relationship. Home Elec. Co. v. Underdown Heating & Air Conditioning Co., 86 N.C.App. 540, 358 S.E.2d 539 (1987). . . . But other courts, while aware of the limitations of promissory estoppel, have adopted it nonetheless. . . ."

UCC § 2–205

[See Selected Source Materials Supplement]

DODGE, TEACHING THE CISG IN CONTRACTS, 50 J. Leg. Ed. 72 (2000). "Under the common law, an offer is freely revocable, even if the offeror has promised to hold it open, unless that promise is supported by consideration or reliance. The UCC, of course, changes this rule, allowing a merchant to make an irrevocable offer—a "firm offer"—without the need for consideration. But the UCC's firm-offer rule contains a number of restrictions: the offeror must be a merchant; the offer must be in a signed writing; the offer must contain an "assurance that it will be held open"; and the period of irrevocability may not exceed three months.

"CISG Article 16 allows an offeror to make a firm offer without these limitations:

> (1) Until a contract is concluded an offer may be revoked if the revocation reaches the offeree before he has dispatched an acceptance.

> (2) However, an offer cannot be revoked:

>> (a) if it indicates, whether by stating a fixed time for acceptance or otherwise, that it is irrevocable; or

>> (b) if it was reasonable for the offeree to rely on the offer as being irrevocable and the offeree has acted in reliance on the offer.

"As one can see, Article 16 does not require that the offeror be a merchant or that the offer be in a signed writing, and there is no limit on the period of irrevocability. Article 16 does not even require an express assurance that the offer will be held open. It requires only that the offer 'indicate that it is irrevocable' and it makes clear that an offer may do this 'by stating a fixed time for acceptance.' If an offer simply stated that it would expire after thirty days, the UCC would not treat the offer as 'firm' and would allow the offeror to revoke before the thirty days were up. The CISG, on the other hand, would treat the offer as being irrevocable during the thirty-day period. Article

16(2)(b), like Restatement (Second) § 87(2), provides for an offer to become irrevocable because of the offeree's reliance.

"Article 16 reflects a compromise between the civil law tradition, which presumes that offers are irrevocable, and the common law tradition, which presumes the opposite. Article 16(1) provides that offers are revocable, as under the common law, but Article 16(2) creates broad exceptions that will lead many offers to be irrevocable in practice."

———

PRELOAD TECHNOLOGY, INC. v. A.B. & J. CONSTRUCTION CO., INC., 696 F.2d 1080, 1089 (5th Cir.1983). "Another limitation on the doctrine of promissory estoppel in [suits by a general contractor alleging reliance on a subcontractor's bid] is the prohibition against 'bid shopping,' 'bid chiseling' and related practices sometimes engaged in by general contractors after they have been awarded the general contract and before they subcontract the particular part of the work in dispute.... 'Bid shopping' commonly refers to a general contractor's seeking of bids from subcontractors other than the one whose bid amount the general used in calculating its own bid, and often involves the general's informing the other subcontractors of the amount of the low bid and inviting them to undercut it. 'Bid chiseling' usually refers to the general contractor's attempt to negotiate a lower price than that bid from the subcontractor whose bid figure the general employed in calculating its own bid, frequently by threatening to subcontract the work to a third party.... When these practices are engaged in, recovery by the general contractor under § 90 may be denied on a variety of theories, viz: that the general contractor did not in fact rely on the subcontractor's bid, or failed to accept it within a reasonable time, or rejected it by a counter-offer, or, perhaps more persuasively, because in such circumstances there is a failure to meet § 90's requirement that 'injustice can be avoided only by enforcement of the promise.' "

———

ALLEN M. CAMPBELL CO. v. VIRGINIA METAL INDUSTRIES, INC., 708 F.2d 930 (4th Cir.1983). Campbell, a general contractor, proposed to bid on a contract to construct housing. In that connection, Virginia Metal telephoned Campbell and quoted a price to supply hollow metal doors and frames that were required by the contract plans and specification. Campbell was awarded the contract, but Virginia Metal backed out of its bid. Campbell sued. The case was governed by North Carolina law. Held, Virginia Metal was bound to its bid under the theory of promissory estoppel. Although the bid was oral, the UCC Statute of Frauds was not a defense, because under North Carolina law promissory estoppel overcomes the Statute of Frauds.

———

RESTATEMENT, SECOND, CONTRACTS § 87(2)

[See Selected Source Materials Supplement]

———

NOTE ON RESTATEMENT SECOND § 87(2)

At first glance, it is not easy to see how the operation of Restatement Second § 87(2) differs from that of § 45, since both sections concern offers that have been relied upon. At least in the view of those who prepared Restatement Second, the difference is rooted in the distinction discussed in the Note on Offers for Unilateral Contracts, supra, between beginning to perform and preparing to perform. According to the Comment to Section 45, that section (which in any event only applies to offers for unilateral contracts) is applicable to beginning to perform, but not to preparing to perform. The Comment goes on to say, however, that "Preparations to perform may ... constitute justifiable reliance sufficient to make the offeror's promise binding under Section 87(2)."

Thus the framers of the Restatement apparently believed that where an offeree has actually *begun* to perform pursuant to an offer for a unilateral contract, he should automatically be entitled to expectation damages, while in other cases of reliance on an offer, the offeree may appropriately be limited to reliance damages. According to the Comment to Section 87(2), "[i]f the beginning of performance is a reasonable mode of acceptance, it makes the offer *fully enforceable* under § 45 ...; if not, the offeror commonly has no reason to expect part performance before acceptance. But circumstances may be such that the offeree must undergo substantial expense, or undertake substantial commitments, or forego alternatives, in order to put himself in a position to accept by either promise or performance.... Full-scale enforcement of the offered contract is not necessarily appropriate in such cases." (Emphasis added.)

Chapter 11

THE MECHANICS OF A BARGAIN (II)—TRANSACTING AT A DISTANCE

INTRODUCTORY NOTE

The issue often arises in contract law whether a given type of communication is effective when it is dispatched or when it is received. The rules that govern this issue were formulated when the basic modes of communication were usually face-to-face or by mail, and somewhat later, by telephone or telegram. In general, the traditional rule in the contexts of these modes is that a communication is effective when received. However, acceptances have been treated in a special way. Under the traditional rule, if an acceptance is transmitted in a face-to-face context, then like other communications it is effective when received. That is also true if the acceptance is transmitted "by telephone or other medium of substantially instantaneous two-way communication." See Restatement Second § 64. However, if the acceptance is transmitted through a medium that is not substantially instantaneous, such as regular mail, then the acceptance is effective when dispatched, unless the offeror specifies otherwise. (Presumably, the same rule would apply to private express-mail services, such as FedEx.) This rule is known as the *mailbox rule* or the *dispatch rule*. The rule is often associated with a famous English case, Adams v. Lindsell, 1 Barn. & Ald. 681 (K.B. 1818).

Application of the mailbox rule arises in a variety of contexts.

1. *Crossed revocation and acceptance.* The paradigm case for application of the mailbox rule is a crossed revocation and acceptance. For example, assume that A makes an offer by mail to B on June 1. The course of post is two days, so that B receives the offer on June 3. B promptly accepts by mail that day, and his acceptance reaches A on June 5. Meanwhile, on June 2, A has sent B a revocation, which reaches B on June 4. Here A's revocation was dispatched before B's acceptance was dispatched, and was received before B's acceptance was received. Nevertheless, under the mailbox rule a contract is formed, because a revocation is effective only when received (on June 4) while an acceptance is effective when dispatched (on June 3).

An argument in favor of the mailbox rule in this context is that it pushes up the beginning of performance to the earliest possible date. Suppose, for example, that, as in the hypothetical, the course of post is two days, and the offeree is to perform before the offeror. Under the mailbox rule, an offeree can safely begin to perform as soon as he dispatches his acceptance. If we assume that, as seems likely, most offerors do not revoke, then offerors as a class may prefer the mailbox rule, because it is in the interests of offerors that performance begin as soon as possible.

2. *Delay or failure of transmission.* A different question is presented when a mailed acceptance is either delayed or fails to reach the offeror. For example, suppose that Seller offers by mail to sell Blackacre to Buyer, and gives Buyer five days in which to accept. Buyer promptly dispatches a letter of acceptance, but the letter miscarries and never reaches Seller. Seller waits ten days, and having had no word from Buyer, assumes that Buyer is no longer interested and sells Blackacre to someone else. Buyer, who has no reason to anticipate that his acceptance will fail to reach Seller, disposes of premises now in his possession, in the expectation of occupying Blackacre. Is there a contract?

Delay or failure cases are commonly dealt with under the mailbox rule, on the theory that the cases turn on the same issue as crossed-revocation-and-acceptance cases—namely, the issue when does an acceptance take effect. It is apparent, however, that delay or failure cases involve different considerations than those involved in the crossed-revocation-and-acceptance context. In crossed-revocation-and-acceptance cases, the offeror knows that the offeree decided to accept. In delay or failure cases, the offeror is likely to believe that the offeree decided not to accept. Accordingly, if an acceptance takes effect on dispatch in the delay or failure cases, it must either be for reasons other than those that apply to the crossed-revocation-and-acceptance case, or because it is thought wise to avoid nuances and complexities by establishing a categorical rule to cover all types of cases in which the issue is, when does an acceptance take effect.

3. *The date on which contractual liability* arises. Another question involves determining the date on which contractual liability arises. An offer to provide fire insurance is made by mail, and the offeree mails back an acceptance. The property involved is destroyed by fire while the letter of acceptance is en route. Is the loss covered by the insurance contract? A leading case holding that the insurance company is liable under these circumstances is Tayloe v. Merchants' Fire Insurance Co., 50 U.S. (9 How.) 390, 13 L.Ed. 187 (1850).

4. *Interpretation of the* offer. Assume the following facts: On April 1, A makes an offer to B by mail. By its terms, the offer is open until April 5. The course of post is two days. B receives the offer on April 3, and mails an acceptance on April 4. B's acceptance arrives on April 6—that is, B's acceptance is dispatched before April 5, but received after April 5. Should A's offer be interpreted to mean that the acceptance has to be dispatched by April 5, or received by April 5? In such cases, too, the mailbox rule has been applied, so that the offer in the hypothetical is interpreted to mean that the acceptance must be dispatched by April 5, not received by April 5. Falconer v. Mazess, 403 Pa. 165, 168 A.2d 558 (1961). On a companion issue of interpretation, it has been held that where the offeror gives the offeree a fixed period in which to accept the offer, the period begins to run from the date the offer is received, not from the date it is posted. Caldwell v. Cline, 109 W.Va. 553, 156 S.E. 55 (1930).

———

RESTATEMENT, SECOND, CONTRACTS §§ 30, 49, 60, 63–68

[See Selected Source Materials Supplement]

UCC § 2–206(1)

[See Selected Source Materials Supplement]

CISG ARTS. 15, 16, 18(2), 20, 22, 23, 24

[See Selected Source Material Supplement]

UNIDROIT PRINCIPLES OF INTERNATIONAL COMMERCIAL CONTRACTS ARTS. 2.1.3, 2.1.6(2), 2.1.7, 2.1.8, 2.1.10

[See Selected Source Materials Supplement]

PRINCIPLES OF EUROPEAN CONTRACT LAW ARTS. 2.205(1), 2.206

[See Selected Source Materials Supplement]

DODGE, TEACHING THE CISG IN CONTRACTS, 50 J. Leg. Ed. 72 (2000). "Under the common law, acceptances are effective upon dispatch, even if they never reach the offeror. This rule performs two functions: it protects the offeree against the possibility of revocation once the acceptance is dispatched, and it places the risk of a lost communication on the offeror. In contrast to the common law mailbox rule, Article 18(2) of the CISG adopts a receipt rule: 'An acceptance of an offer becomes effective at the moment the indication of assent reaches the offeror.' But this provision must be read in conjunction with Article 16(1), which says that 'an offer may be revoked if the revocation reaches the offeree before he has dispatched an acceptance' (emphasis added). In other words, once the offeree has dispatched an acceptance, the offeror may no longer revoke, but if the acceptance is lost in the mail there is no contract. So the CISG and the common law both protect the offeree against the possibility of revocation once the acceptance is dispatched, but the CISG places the risk of a lost communication on the offeree rather than the offeror.

NOTE ON ELECTRONIC COMMERCE

Many contracts are now formed by electronic means. For example, consumers often purchase products from electronic retailers, like Amazon. Similarly, many commercial contracts are undoubtedly formed by an exchange of emails, or by other electronic transactions. One issue raised by electronic contracting concerns the time at which an acceptance is effective. Originally, the paradigmatic means of making an offer were face-to-face and by mail. Where the issue when an acceptance is effective has arisen in the context of a new technology, contract law has often mechanically pigeonholed the technology into one of these two classic paradigms, largely according to whether the technology resembles face-to-face communication, because it involves substantially instantaneous transmission and direct and immediate interaction, or resembles communication through the mail, because it does not inherently involve substantially instantaneous communication and immediate interaction. Thus Restatement Second § 64 provides that "Acceptance given by telephone or other medium of substantially instantaneous two-way communication is governed by the principles applicable to acceptances where the parties are in the presence of each other."

There are relatively few cases concerning new technologies other than telegrams, which are no longer offered in the United States by the basic carrier, Western Union. Of the few cases involving new technologies other than telegrams, most involved telex—which itself has probably been superseded by electronic communications—and concerned the question, where is a contract deemed to be formed for choice-of-law purposes if an acceptance is telexed. American cases held that at least for this purpose a telexed acceptance was effective, and a contract formed, on dispatch.[1]

If a relatively mechanical approach was applied to electronic transmissions, they would seem to fall under the mailbox rule. Although it is true that electronic messages can be transmitted on a virtually instantaneous basis, and that parties using electronic means can engage in direct and immediate interaction, as a practical matter interaction through electronic means usually will not be direct and immediate. Messages sent by electronic messages are not always instantaneously received, are often not read until some time after they have been received, and are often not responded to immediately upon being read. On the other hand, transmission is usually close to instantaneous, and the parties usually have an opportunity for almost-instantaneous interaction.

It is an open question whether the dispatch rule will be applied to electronic acceptances. Section 15 of the Uniform Electronic Transactions Act

---

1. For example, in General Time Corp. v. Eye Encounter, Inc., 50 N.C.App. 467, 274 S.E.2d 391 (1981), the court held that where a telexed acceptance was sent from North Carolina, the contract was made in North Carolina, so that suit could be brought in that state. In Norse Petroleum A/S v. LVO International, Inc., 389 A.2d 771 (Del.Super.1978), the court held that if a telexed acceptance was sent from Norway, Norwegian law governed. Two English cases look the other way. In Entores Ld. v. Miles Far East Corp., [1985] 2 Q.B. 327, the court held that where a contract is made by instantaneous communication, such as by telex, the contract is complete only when the acceptance is received by the offeror, so that where a telexed acceptance was sent from Amsterdam to London, the contract was made in England, and an action therefore could be brought on the contract in England. A comparable result was reached in Brinkibon Ltd. v. Stahag Stahl und Stahlwarenhandels GmbH, [1982] All E.R. 293 (H.L.).

specifies in detail when an electronic record is considered to be sent. However, the Comment to Section 15 provides that although Section 15(a) furnishes rules for determining when an electronic record is sent, "The *effect* of its sending and its import are determined by other law once it is determined that a sending has occurred." (Emphasis added.) Presumably, "other law" includes contract law. In contrast, Section 215 of the Uniform Computer Information Transactions Act (UCITA) is intended to substitute a time-of-receipt rule for the mailbox rule in this case of electronic communication. However, UCITA has only been adopted in two states.

NOTE ON THE CONCEPT OF "RECORD"

With the advent of electronic contracting, the term "record" has been introduced into contract discourse. Under the Electronic Signatures in Global and National Commerce Act and the Uniform Electronic Transactions Act, "record" means "information that is inscribed on a tangible medium or that is stored in an electronic or other medium and is retrievable in perceivable form." "Electronic record," a special type of record, means "a record created, generated, sent, communicated, received, or stored by electronic means." The Comments to Section 2 (Definitions) of the Uniform Electronic Transactions Act state:

10. **"Record."** This is a standard definition designed to embrace all means of communicating or storing information except human memory. It includes any method for storing or communicating information, including "writings." A record need not be indestructible or permanent, but the term does not include oral or other communications which are not stored or preserved by some means. Information that has not been retained other than through human memory does not qualify as a record ...

6. **"Electronic record."** An electronic record is a subset of the broader defined term "record." It is any record created, used or stored in a medium other than paper....

Information processing systems, computer equipment and programs, electronic data interchange, electronic mail, voice mail, facsimile, telex, telecopying, scanning, and similar technologies all qualify as electronic under this Act. Accordingly information stored on a computer hard drive or disc, faxes, voice mail messages, messages on a telephone answering machine, audio and video tape recordings, among other records, all would be electronic records under this Act.

Chapter 12

THE MECHANICS OF A BARGAIN (III)—MODES OF ACCEPTANCE

NOTE ON THE CONSEQUENCES OF UTILIZING THE WRONG MODE OF ACCEPTANCE

Often it is ambiguous how an offer is to be accepted. If, in such a case, the offeree uses the wrong mode of acceptance (for example, makes an acceptance by promise when the offer requires an acceptance by act), there may be significant consequences. These consequences may occur in the context of a variety of scenarios.

In one scenario, after Offeree accepts an offer, Offeror revokes, claiming that the offer is still revocable, despite the purported acceptance, because Offeree used the wrong mode of acceptance.

In another scenario, after Offeree accepts an offer, some event occurs that would terminate Offeree's power of acceptance by operation of law if a contract has not already been concluded—for example the Offeror dies or becomes incapacitated. Offeror's estate or guardian claims that the acceptance was ineffective because it was in the wrong mode, and that it is now too late to accept because the power of acceptance was terminated by the relevant event.

Typically, although not invariably, issues concerning the consequences of using the wrong mode of acceptance arise where the question is whether the offer was to be accepted by an act, so that it was an offer for a unilateral contract, or by a promise, so that it was an offer for a bilateral contract. Restatement First § 31 provided that "In case of doubt it is presumed that an offer invites the formation of a bilateral contract." That rule was criticized, and in its place Restatement Second § 32 provides that "In case of doubt an offer is interpreted as inviting the offeree to accept either by promising to perform what the offer requests or by rendering the performance, as the offeree chooses." Similarly, UCC § 2–206(1) provides that "Unless otherwise unambiguously indicated by the language or circumstances ... an offer to make a contract shall be construed as inviting acceptance by any manner ... reasonable under the circumstances."

The balance of this Chapter will concern issues that arise in connection with acceptance by act (Section 1), subjective acceptance (Section 2), acceptance by conduct (Section 3), the effect of using a subcontractor's bid (Section

461

4), the effect of failing to reject an offer (Section 5), silence as acceptance (Section 6), and acceptance by electronic agent (Section 7).

————

RESTATEMENT, SECOND, CONTRACTS § 32

[See Selected Source Materials Supplement]

————

UCC § 2–206(1)

[See Selected Source Materials Supplement]

————

SECTION 1. ACCEPTANCE BY ACT

————

KLOCKNER v. GREEN

Supreme Court of New Jersey, 1969.
54 N.J. 230, 254 A.2d 782.

SCHETTINO, J. Plaintiffs, Richard Klockner and Frances Klockner, the stepson and stepgranddaughter respectively of the late Edyth Klockner, brought suit to enforce an alleged oral contract between the deceased and the plaintiffs obligating the deceased to bequeath her estate to the plaintiffs in return for their services to her during her lifetime. Named as defendants were Harry Green, the executor of the estate, William Rhodes, Elizabeth Sylvania and Margaret Rhodes, the surviving next of kin of decedent, and Carolyn Wolf Field, a legatee under decedent's last executed will. (Carolyn Wolf Field did not answer nor appear in this case.)

At the conclusion of plaintiffs' case, the trial court granted defendants' motion to dismiss, holding that the proofs did not reveal the making of a contract because no offer and acceptance nor consideration had been established. The Appellate Division affirmed, holding that since there was no reliance by plaintiffs upon decedent's promise, the statute of frauds barred enforcement of that promise under N.J.S.A. 25:1–5. We granted certification. 53 N.J. 272, 250 A.2d 136 (1969).

Plaintiffs' uncontradicted proofs (as stated above, the motion to dismiss was granted before defendants introduced their case) established that Edyth Klockner, the deceased, and her husband, Richard Klockner's father, executed wills in favor of each other. Although her husband predeceased her, Edyth never revised her will. Accordingly, at her death, approximately three years later, her testamentary disposition had lapsed, and, but for this suit, the bulk of her estate would apparently pass by intestacy to her sole surviving relatives, defendants herein.

Richard Klockner's relationship with decedent, his stepmother, was like that of a natural child to his parent. He performed numerous services for her both before and after his father's death, doing as much and more than could be expected from even one's natural child. On an average, Richard attended to her needs once or twice a week from 1963 to her death in 1966.

Plaintiff, Frances Klockner (daughter of plaintiff, Richard Klockner), similarly spent much time with decedent, having a relationship more like that of mother and daughter than stepgrandmother and stepgranddaughter. Frances spent numerous nights with decedent when the latter felt fearful or alone, and also accompanied her on trips whenever she was needed.

In the early part of 1965 decedent approached Mr. Green, who had represented both her and her husband for many years, to discuss drawing a will. She indicated she wanted to leave her real property to Richard and her personal property to Frances. At Mr. Green's suggestion she prepared a draft of a will, modeled after her earlier will, leaving the bulk of her estate to Richard and Frances. This draft was revised pursuant to suggestions from Mr. Green. Neither was ever executed, however.

Subsequently, in June 1965, decedent discussed with Richard the disposition of her estate. She informed him that she wanted to compensate him for being so helpful, and that if he would agree to continue to look after her and continue to let Frances visit her, she would leave the real property to him and the balance of the estate to Frances. Frances testified that the decedent discussed with her the understanding she had with Richard.

Decedent again contacted Mr. Green and informed him of the understanding she had with plaintiff regarding the disposition of her estate. Using decedent's second draft as a guide, Mr. Green redrafted her will and mailed it to decedent on November 24, 1965. Apparently because of decedent's belief that a will was a premonition of death, this draft remained unexecuted. Decedent became ill suddenly and died in February 1966, never having executed a will subsequent to the mutual will drawn with her husband in 1940.

Both the trial court and the Appellate Division held for defendants because, when questioned on cross-examination, both Richard and Frances testified that they would have continued to perform the services for decedent even if she had not made the promises to compensate them.

It is not disputed that a valid, enforceable contract can be made obligating a person to bequeath property in a specified manner. Accord Davison v. Davison, 13 N.J.Eq. 246 (Ch.1861) (upholding a parol agreement to bequeath real estate in exchange for services); Johnson v. Hubbell, 10 N.J.Eq. 332 (Ch.1855) (holding valid an oral agreement by a father to bequeath property in exchange for a son's conveyance of property to his sister). The question is: was such a contract entered into here?

Although we recognize that alleged agreements to make a particular disposition of one's estate must be subjected to close scrutiny, we have no doubt that decedent here intended to obligate herself to bequeath her property to plaintiffs so long as they continued to serve her as they had prior to her promise. Such a promise, when acted upon, becomes a binding obligation. Decedent bargained for plaintiffs' services and obligated herself to bequeath the property to them when they performed. See 1 Corbin, Contracts, § 63 (1963).

The performance by plaintiffs need not have been induced solely by the offer of compensation. In the Restatement, Contracts § 55 (1932), it is indicated that if an act is requested by the offeror as consideration for a unilateral contract, the act need only be given with the intent of accepting the offer. The examples which illustrate that rule clearly encompass the instant case.

> "A offers a reward for information leading to the conviction of a criminal.... B, ... induced by motives of fear or public duty, would have given the information without hope of reward, but as there is an offer of reward he intends when he gives the information to accept the offer. There is a contract."

In the only New Jersey case discussing this rule, the Court of Errors and Appeals noted that once the contract has been legally concluded, in giving effect to that contract "the motive which induced the party to make the contract or perform it must always be immaterial." Mayor, etc. of Hoboken v. Bailey, 36 N.J.L. 490, 497 (E. & A. 1873). See also 1 Corbin, Contracts § 58 (1963) (recognizing the complexity of motivating causes in human action); Restatement, Second, Contracts § 55 (Tent. Draft No. 1, April 13, 1964) and § 84 (Tent. Draft No. 2, April 30, 1965).

In reviewing the facts of the instant case for purposes of the motion for judgment of dismissal, we must accept as true all the evidence which supports the view of the party against whom the motion is made, and should give him the benefit of all legitimate inferences which may be drawn in his favor. De Rienzo v. Morristown Airport Corp., 28 N.J. 231, 146 A.2d 127 (1958); Cauco v. Galante, 6 N.J. 128, 77 A.2d 793 (1951).

We have no doubt that in the instant case a valid contract was entered into between plaintiffs and Edyth Klockner. Nothing in Richard's testimony indicated that he did not intend to accept the offer notwithstanding his statement that he would have served his stepmother anyway. The testimony of Frances similarly reveals no rejection of the offer despite a similar statement. These statements were merely the normal expressions of affection which naturally flow from the type of relationship which existed between plaintiffs and decedent.

The evidence also fully supports the existence of a bargain by decedent and her belief that she had contracted with plaintiff. Her attempt to execute a will (stymied only by her superstitions), and the testimony of her attorney, while not conclusive, present strong evidence of her intent to carry out her end of the bargain. See Laune v. Chandless, 99 N.J.Eq. 186, 131 A. 634 (Ch.1926) (where the court interpreted the evidence of decedent's attempt to execute a will as indicative of decedent's belief that he had a moral and legal obligation to satisfy the contract); Vreeland v. Vreeland, 53 N.J.Eq. 387, 32 A. 3 (Ch.1895) (where testimony and an undelivered deed were deemed sufficient corroboration of the alleged contract).

Regardless of the apparent existence of a contract, the Appellate Division nevertheless affirmed on the basis that the statute of frauds barred enforcement of the contract. We do not agree that the contract is unenforceable. The rule that a statute of frauds should not be used to work a fraud is well settled.

Oral contracts which have been performed by one party are frequently enforced where to do otherwise would work an inequity on the party who has performed. Thus, the cases hold that such performance takes the contract out of the statute of frauds. E.g., Poloha v. Ruman, 137 N.J.Eq. 167, 44 A.2d 411 (Ch.1945) (specifically enforcing parol agreement to leave plaintiff her home if plaintiff would continue to care for decedent and her husband), affirmed per curiam 140 N.J.Eq. 396, 54 A.2d 775 (E. & A.1947); Davison v. Davison, supra 13 N.J.Eq. 246 (holding that plaintiff's part performance took the oral contract out of the statute of frauds)....

We also find no reason on the present record for penalizing plaintiffs because of their professed willingness to serve the widow. Plaintiffs have fully performed, and decedent has received the full benefit of her bargain. Because the decedent has received the full benefit of her bargain, the policy reasons justifying the development of the part performance exception to the statute of frauds have been satisfied. Since at this stage of the proceedings there is no real doubt as to the existence of the contract, the courts should not allow defendants to use the statute of frauds as a device to work a fraud on both plaintiffs and the decedent who at no time gave any indication that her estate should go to someone other than the plaintiffs.

Our discussion of course assumes the truth of the testimony of the plaintiffs and the inferences most favorable to them. We do so, because, as stated at the outset, judgment was granted on motion at the close of plaintiffs' case. We of course do not intend by this opinion to suggest how the testimony should be viewed at the close of the entire case.

We reverse and remand for further proceedings not inconsistent with this opinion.

For reversal and remandment: CHIEF JUSTICE WEINTRAUB and JUSTICES JACOBS, FRANCIS, PROCTOR, HALL, SCHETTINO and HANEMAN–7.

For affirmance: None.

DE CICCO v. SCHWEIZER, 221 N.Y. 431, 117 N.E. 807 (1917) (Cardozo, J.) "It will not do to divert the minds of others from a given line of conduct, and then to urge that because of the diversion the opportunity has gone by to say how their minds would otherwise have acted. If the tendency of the promise is to induce them to persevere, reliance and detriment may be inferred from the mere fact of performance. The springs of conduct are subtle and varied. One who meddles with them must not insist upon too nice a measure of proof that the spring which he released was effective to the exclusion of all others."

SIMMONS v. UNITED STATES, 308 F.2d 160 (4th Cir.1962). American Brewery sponsored a well–publicized annual American Beer Fishing Derby. Under the Derby rules, the Brewery tagged one of the millions of rockfish in Chesapeake Bay, and named the fish Diamond Jim III. Anyone who caught Diamond Jim III and presented the fish to the brewery, together with the identification tag and an affidavit that the fish was caught on hook and line, would be entitled to a cash prize of $25,000. Simmons caught Diamond Jim III about six weeks after the fish was tagged, and soon thereafter received the cash prize. Simmons knew about the contest, but as an experienced fisherman he also knew that his chances of landing Diamond Jim III were minuscule, and he did not have the fish in mind when he set out to go fishing. Subsequently, the Internal Revenue Service taxed the prize as income. Simmons then filed a claim for refund, on the ground that the payment to him was a gift and therefore was not taxable under § 102 of the Internal Revenue Code, which provides that "Gross income does not include the value of property acquired by gift, bequests, devise, or inheritance." Held, the prize was not a gift.

> ... [U]nder accepted principles of contract law ... the company was legally obligated to award the prize once Simmons had caught the fish and complied with the remaining conditions precedent. The offer of a prize or reward for doing a specified act, like catching a criminal, is an offer for a unilateral contract. For the offer to be accepted and the contract to become binding, the desired act must be performed with knowledge of the offer. The evidence is clear that Simmons knew about the Fishing Derby the morning he caught Diamond Jim III. It is not fatal to his claim for refund that he did not go fishing for the express purpose of catching one of the prize fish. So long as the outstanding offer was known to him, a person may accept an offer for a unilateral contract by rendering performance, even if he does so primarily for reasons unrelated to the offer.

STEPHENS v. MEMPHIS, 565 S.W.2d 213 (Tenn.App.1977) (Nearn, J., dissenting): " ... [T]o base the payment of a reward on 'prior knowledge' ought to be against the public policy of this state.... What policy could be more fraught with impediments to justice and with fraud than one that says to the public, 'Citizens, if you come forward and do your civic duty promptly as you should without knowledge or thought of reward, you shall forfeit all claims to any funds which have been offered by other public-minded citizens to induce the citizenry to come forward and do their duty as they should. However, citizen, if you do not do your duty as you should, but on the contrary, wait until the "pot is right" and you are assured that top dollar will be paid for the information which you ought to have promptly given in the first instance, then you may come forward with your concealed information and you will be amply rewarded for your delay of justice and personal avarice.' To hold 'prior knowledge' necessary for recovery is to make that statement to the people of this state."

CARLILL v. CARBOLIC SMOKE BALL CO.
Court of Appeal, 1892.
[1893] 1 Q.B. 256.

Appeal from a decision of Hawkins, J. [1892] 2 Q.B. 484.

The defendants, who were the proprietors and vendors of a medical preparation called "The Carbolic Smoke Ball," inserted in the Pall Mall

Gazette of November 13, 1891, and in other newspapers, the following advertisement:

> "£ 100 reward will be paid by the Carbolic Smoke Ball Company to any person who contracts the increasing epidemic influenza, colds, or any disease caused by taking cold, after having used the ball three times daily for two weeks according to the printed directions supplied with each ball. £1000 is deposited with the Alliance Bank, Regent Street, shewing our sincerity in the matter.

> "During the last epidemic of influenza many thousand carbolic smoke balls were sold as preventives against this disease, and in no ascertained case was the disease contracted by those using the carbolic smoke ball.

> "One carbolic smoke ball will last a family several months, making it the cheapest remedy in the world at the price, 10s., post free. The ball can be refilled at a cost of 5s. Address, Carbolic Smoke Ball Company, 27 Princes Street, Hanover Square, London."

The plaintiff, a lady, on the faith of this advertisement, bought one of the balls at a chemist's and used it as directed, three times a day, from November 20, 1891, to January 17, 1892, when she was attacked by influenza. Hawkins, J., held that she was entitled to recover the £100. The defendants appealed.

LINDLEY, L.J. ... We must first consider whether this was intended to be a promise at all, or whether it was a mere puff which meant nothing. Was it a mere puff? My answer to that question is "No," and I base my answer upon this passage: "£1000 is deposited with the Alliance Bank, shewing our sincerity in the matter." Now, for what was that money deposited or that statement made except to negative the suggestion that this was a mere puff and meant nothing at all? The deposit is called in aid by the advertiser as a proof of his sincerity in the matter—that is, the sincerity of his promise to pay this £100 in the event which he has specified. I say this for the purpose of giving point to the observation that we are not inferring a promise; there is the promise, as plain as words can make it.

Then it is contended that it is not binding. In the first place, it is said that it is not made with anybody in particular. Now that point is common to the words of this advertisement and to the words of all other advertisements offering rewards. They are offers to anybody who performs the conditions named in the advertisement, and anybody who does perform the condition accepts the offer. In point of law this advertisement is an offer to pay £100 to anybody who will perform these conditions, and the performance of the conditions is the acceptance of the offer. That rests upon a string of authorities, the earliest of which is Williams v. Carwardine, 4 Barn. & Adol. 621, which has been followed by many other decisions upon advertisements offering rewards.

But then it is said, "Supposing that the performance of the conditions is an acceptance of the offer, that acceptance ought to have been notified." Unquestionably, as a general proposition, when an offer is made, it is necessary in order to make a binding contract, not only that it should be accepted, but that the acceptance should be notified. But is that so in cases of this kind? I apprehend that they are an exception to that rule, or, if not an exception, they are open to the observation that the notification of the acceptance need not precede the performance. This offer is a continuing offer. It was never revoked, and if notice of acceptance is required,—which I doubt very much, for I rather think the true view is that which was expressed and explained by Lord Blackburn in the case of Brogden v. Railway Co., 2 App.Cas. 666, 691,—if notice of acceptance is required, the person who makes the offer gets the notice of acceptance contemporaneously with his notice of the performance of the condition. If he gets notice of the acceptance before his offer is revoked, that in principle is all you want. I, however, think that the true view, in a case of this kind, is that the person who makes the offer shows by his language and from the nature of the transaction that he does not expect and does not require notice of the acceptance apart from notice of the performance. . . .

I come now to the last point which I think requires attention: that is, the consideration. It has been argued that this is nudum pactum—that there is no consideration. We must apply to that argument the usual legal tests. Let us see whether there is no advantage to the defendants. It is said that the use of the ball is no advantage to them, and that what benefits them is the sale; and the case is put that a lot of these balls might be stolen, and that it would be no advantage to the defendants if the thief or other people used them. The answer to that, I think, is as follows: It is quite obvious that in the view of the advertisers a use by the public of their remedy, if they can only get the public to have confidence enough to use it, will react and produce a sale which is directly beneficial to them. Therefore, the advertisers get out of the use an advantage which is enough to constitute a consideration.

But there is another view. Does not the person who acts upon this advertisement and accepts the offer put himself to some inconvenience at the request of the defendants? Is it nothing to use this ball three times daily for two weeks according to the directions at the request of the advertiser? Is that to go for nothing? It appears to me that there is a distinct inconvenience, not to say a detriment to any person who so uses the smoke ball. I am of opinion, therefore, that there is ample consideration for the promise. . . .

[The concurring opinions of Bowen, L.J., and Smith, L.J., are omitted.]

Appeal dismissed.

————

A.W.B. SIMPSON, QUACKERY AND CONTRACT LAW: THE CASE OF THE CARBOLIC SMOKE BALL, 14 J. Leg. Stud. 345, 348–352 (1985). "[As described in the patent application for the carbolic smoke ball, the device] 'comprises a compressible hollow ball or receptacle of India Rubber or other suitable elastic material, having an orifice or nozzle provided with a porous or perforated disc or diaphragm consisting of muslin, silk, wire or gauze, perforated sheet metal or the like, though which, when the ball or receptacle is compressed, the powder will be forced *in a cloud of infinitesimally small particles resembling smoke.*' . . . By a fortunate chance the directions for use of the ball as marketed survive . . . :

> Hold the ball by the loose end below the silk floss, with the thumb and forefinger in front of the mouth. Snap or flip rapidly on the side of the ball, on the place marked "S" and a fine powder resembling smoke will arise. Inhale this smoke or powder as it arises, as shown in the above

illustration. This will cause sneezing and for a few moments you will feel as if you were taking cold. This feeling will soon pass away and the cure has commenced. If you do not feel the effects at the first inhalation by it making you sneeze, take a second in the same manner....

"Carbolic acid, though not at the time a scheduled poison, could be fatal if taken internally in more than small amounts. Inhaling the powder through the nostrils must certainly have produced a numbing and astringent effect and been somewhat disagreeable and, as the directions for use indicate, caused sneezing."

BISHOP v. EATON

Supreme Judicial Court of Massachusetts, 1894.
161 Mass. 496, 37 N.E. 665.

Contract, on a guaranty. Writ dated February 2d, 1892. Trial in the Superior Court without a jury, before Braley, J., who found the following facts:

The plaintiff in 1886 was a resident of Sycamore in the State of Illinois, and was to some extent connected in business with Harry H. Eaton, a brother of the defendant. In December, 1886, the defendant in a letter to the plaintiff said, "If Harry needs more money, let him have it, or assist him to get it, and I will see that it is paid."

On January 7th, 1887, Harry Eaton gave his promissory note for two hundred dollars to one Stark, payable in one year. The plaintiff signed the note as surety relying on the letter of the defendant and looked to the defendant solely for reimbursement, if called upon to pay the note. Shortly afterward the plaintiff wrote to the defendant a letter stating that the note had been given and its amount, and deposited the letter in the mail at Sycamore, postage prepaid, and properly addressed to the defendant at his home in Nova Scotia. The letter, according to the testimony of the defendant, was never received by him. At the maturity of the note the time for its payment was extended for a year, but whether with the knowledge or consent of the defendant was in dispute. In August, 1889, in an interview between them, the plaintiff asked the defendant to take up the note still outstanding, and pay it, to which the defendant replied: "Try to get Harry to pay it. If he don't, I will. It shall not cost you anything."

On October 1st, 1891, the plaintiff paid the note, and thereafter made no effort to collect it from Harry Eaton, the maker. The defendant testified that he had no notice of the payment of the note by the plaintiff until December 22d, 1891....

The judge ... ruled, as matter of law upon the findings of fact, that the plaintiff was entitled to recover, and ordered judgment for him; and the defendant alleged exceptions.

KNOWLTON, J. ... The defendant requested many rulings in regard to the law applicable to contracts of guaranty, most of which it becomes necessary to consider. The language relied on was an offer to guarantee, which the plaintiff might or might not accept. Without acceptance of it there was no contract, because the offer was conditional and there was no consideration for the promise. But this was not a proposition which was to become a contract only upon the giving of a promise for the promise, and it was not necessary that the plaintiff should accept it in words, or promise to do anything before acting upon it. It was an offer which was to become effective as a contract upon the doing of the act referred to. It was an offer to be bound in consideration of an act to be done, and in such a case the doing of the act constitutes the acceptance of the offer and furnishes the consideration. Ordinarily there is no occasion to notify the offerer of the acceptance of such an offer, for the doing of the act is a sufficient acceptance, and the promisor knows that he is bound when he sees that action has been taken on the faith of his offer. But if the act is of such a kind that knowledge of it will not quickly come to the promisor, the promisee is bound to give him notice of his acceptance within a reasonable time after doing that which constitutes the acceptance. In such a case it is implied in the offer that, to complete the contract, notice shall be given with due diligence, so that the promisor may know that a contract has been made. But where the promise is in consideration of an act to be done, it becomes binding upon the doing of the act so far that the promisee cannot be affected by a subsequent withdrawal of it, if within a reasonable time afterward he notifies the promisor. In accordance with these principles, it has been held in cases like the present, where the guarantor would not know of himself, from the nature of the transaction, whether the offer has been accepted or not, that he is not bound without notice of the acceptance, seasonably given after the performance which constitutes the consideration. Babcock v. Bryant, 12 Pick. 133; Whiting v. Stacy, 15 Gray, 270; Schlessinger v. Dickinson, 5 Allen, 47.

In the present case the plaintiff seasonably mailed a letter to the defendant, informing him of what he had done in compliance with the defendant's request, but the defendant testified that he never received it, and there is no finding that it ever reached him. The judge ruled, as matter of law, that upon the facts found, the plaintiff was entitled to recover, and the question is thus presented whether the defendant was bound by the acceptance when the letter was properly mailed, although he never received it.

When an offer of guaranty of this kind is made, the implication is that notice of the act which constitutes an acceptance of it shall be given in a reasonable way. What kind of a notice is required depends upon the nature of the transaction, the situation of the parties, and the inferences fairly to be drawn from their previous dealings, if any, in regard to the matter. If they are so situated that communication by letter is naturally to be expected, then the deposit of a letter in the mail is all that is necessary. If that is done which is fairly to be contemplated from their relations to the subject-matter and from their course of dealing, the rights of the parties are fixed, and a failure actually to receive the notice will not affect the obligation of the guarantor.

The plaintiff in the case now before us resided in Illinois, and the defendant in Nova Scotia. The offer was made by letter, and the defendant must have contemplated that information in regard to the plaintiff's acceptance or rejection of it would be by letter. It would be a harsh rule which would subject the plaintiff to the risk of the defendant's failure to receive the letter giving notice of his action on the faith of the offer. We are of opinion that the plaintiff, after assisting Harry to get the money, did all that he was required to do when he seasonably sent the defendant the letter by mail informing him of what had been done.

How far such considerations are applicable to the case of an ordinary contract made by letter, about which some of the early decisions are conflicting, we need not now consider. . . .

[A new trial was granted on the ground that when the note became due, it was extended without the consent of the defendant. Because a surety is discharged by an extension of time to the principal debtor, unless the surety consents to the extension, the trial judge should have determined whether the evidence warranted the conclusion that the defendant had consented to the extension.]

RESTATEMENT, SECOND, CONTRACTS § 54

[See Selected Source Materials Supplement]

UCC § 2–206(2)

[See Selected Source Materials Supplement]

SECTION 2. SUBJECTIVE ACCEPTANCE

INTERNATIONAL FILTER CO. v. CONROE GIN, ICE & LIGHT CO.

Texas Commission of Appeals, 1925.
277 S.W. 631.

NICKELS, J. Plaintiff in error, an Illinois corporation, is a manufacturer of machinery, apparatus, etc., for the purification of water in connection with the manufacture of ice, etc., having its principal office in the city of Chicago. Defendant in error is a Texas corporation engaged in the manufacture of ice, etc., having its plant, office, etc., at Conroe, Montgomery county, Tex.

On February 10, 1920, through its traveling solicitor, Waterman, plaintiff in error, at Conroe, submitted to defendant in error, acting through Henry Thompson, its manager, a written instrument, addressed to defendant in error, which (with immaterial portions omitted) reads as follows:

"Gentlemen:

"We propose to furnish, f.o.b. Chicago, one No. two Junior (steel tank) International water softener and filter to purify water of the character shown by sample to be submitted. . . . Price: Twelve hundred thirty ($1,230.00) dollars. . . . This proposal is made in duplicate and becomes a contract when accepted by the purchaser and approved by an executive officer of the International Filter Company, at its office in

Chicago. Any modification can only be made by duly approved supplementary agreement signed by both parties.

"This proposal is submitted for prompt acceptance, and unless so accepted is subject to change without notice.

"Respectfully submitted,

"International Filter Co.

"W.W. Waterman."

On the same day the "proposal" was accepted by defendant in error through notation made on the paper by Thompson reading as follows:

"Accepted Feb. 10, 1920.

"Conroe Gin, Ice & Light Co.,

"By Henry Thompson, Mgr."

The paper as thus submitted and "accepted" contained the notation, "Make shipment by Mar. 10." The paper, in that form, reached the Chicago office of plaintiff in error, and on February 13, 1920, P.N. Engel, its president and vice president, indorsed thereon: "O.K. Feb. 13, 1920, P.N. Engel." February 14, 1920, plaintiff in error wrote and mailed, and in due course defendant in error received, the following letter:

"Feb. 14, 1920.

"Attention of Mr. Henry Thompson, Manager.

"Conroe Gin, Ice & Light Co., Conroe, Texas—Gentlemen: This will acknowledge and thank you for your order given Mr. Waterman for a No. 2 Jr. steel tank International softener and filter, for 110 volt, 60 cycle, single phase current—for shipment March 10th.

"Please make shipment of the sample of water promptly so that we may make the analysis and know the character of the water before shipment of the apparatus. Shipping tag is [**inclosed**], and please note the instructions to pack to guard against freezing.

"Yours very truly,

"International Filter Co.,

"M.B. Johnson."

By letter of February 28, 1920, defendant in error undertook to countermand the "order," which countermand was repeated and emphasized by letter of March 4, 1920. By letter of March 2, 1920 (replying to the letter of February 28th), plaintiff in error denied the right of countermand, etc., and insisted upon performance of the "contract." The parties adhered to the respective positions thus indicated, and this suit resulted.

Plaintiff in error sued for breach of the contract alleged to have been made in the manner stated above. The defense is that no contract was made because: (1) Neither Engel's indorsement of "O.K.," nor the letter of February 14, 1920, amounted to approval "by an executive officer of the International Filter Company, at its office in Chicago." (2) Notification of such approval, or acceptance, by plaintiff in error was required to be communicated to defendant in error; it being insisted that this requirement inhered in the terms of the proposal and in the nature of the transaction and, also, that Thompson, when he indorsed "acceptance" on the paper stated to Waterman, as agent of plaintiff in error, that such notification must be promptly given; it being insisted further that the letter of February 14, 1920, did not constitute such acceptance or notification of approval, and therefore defendant in error, on February 28, 1920, etc., had the right to withdraw, or countermand, the unaccepted offer. Thompson testified in a manner to support the allegation of his statement to Waterman. There are other matters involved in the suit which must be ultimately determined, but the foregoing presents the issues now here for consideration.

The case was tried without a jury, and the judge found the facts in favor of defendant in error on all the issues indicated above, and upon other material issues. The judgment was affirmed by the Court of Civil Appeals, 269 S.W. 210.

Opinion.

We agree with the honorable Court of Civil Appeals upon the proposition that Mr. Engel's indorsement of "O.K." amounted to an approval "by an executive officer of the International Filter Company, at its office in Chicago," within the meaning of the so-called "proposal" of February 10th. The paper then became a "contract," according to its definitely expressed terms, and it became then, and thereafter it remained, an enforceable contract, in legal contemplation, unless the fact of approval by the filter company was required to be communicated to the other party and unless, in that event, the communication was not made.

We are not prepared to assent to the ruling that such communication was essential. There is no disposition to question the justice of the general rules stated in support of that holding, yet the existence of contractual capacity imports the right of the offerer to dispense with notification; and he does dispense with it "if the form of the offer," etc., "shows that this was not to be required." 9 Cyc. 270, 271; Carlill v. Carbolic Smoke Ball Co., 1 Q.B. 256 (and other references in note 6, 9 Cyc. 271).... The Conroe Gin, Ice & Light Company executed the paper for the purpose of having it transmitted, as its offer, to the filter company at Chicago. It was so transmitted and acted upon. Its terms embrace the offer, and nothing else, and by its terms the question of notification must be judged, since those terms are not ambiguous.

The paper contains two provisions which relate to acceptance by the filter company. One is the declaration that the offer shall "become a contract * * * when approved by an executive officer of the International Filter Company, at its Chicago office." The other is thus stated: "This proposal is submitted for prompt acceptance, and unless so accepted is subject to change without notice." The first provision states "a particular mode of acceptance as sufficient to make the bargain binding," and the filter company (as stated above) followed "the indicated method of acceptance." When this was done, so the paper declares, the proposal "became a contract." The other provision does not in any way relate to a different method of acceptance by the filter company. Its sole reference is to the time within which the act of approval must be done; that is to say, there was to be a "prompt acceptance," else the offer might be changed "without notice." The second declaration merely required the approval thereinbefore stipulated for to be done promptly; if the act was so done, there is nothing in the second provision to militate against, or to conflict with, the prior declaration that, thereupon, the paper should become "a contract."

The offerer said that the contract should be complete if approval be promptly given by the executive officer at Chicago; the court cannot properly restate the offer so as to make the offerer declare that a contract shall be made only when the approval shall have been promptly given at Chicago and that fact shall have been communicated to the offerer at Conroe. In our opinion, therefore, notice of the approval was not required.

The letter of February 14th, however, sufficiently communicated notice, if it was required.... Here the fact of acceptance in the particular method prescribed by the offerer is established aliunde [from outside] the letter— Engel's "O.K." indorsed on the paper at Chicago did that. The form of notice, where notice is required, may be quite a different thing from the acceptance itself; the latter constitutes the meeting of the minds, the former merely relates to that pre-existent fact. The rules requiring such notice, it will be marked, do not make necessary any particular form or manner, unless the parties themselves have so prescribed. Whatever would convey, by word or fair implication, notice of the fact would be sufficient. And this letter, we think, would clearly indicate to a reasonably prudent person, situated as was the defendant in error, the fact of previous approval by the filter company. If the Gin, Ice & Light Company had acted to change its position upon it as a notification of that fact, it must be plain that the filter company would have been estopped to deny its sufficiency.

There are other questions in the case which must be determined on the appeal. Those questions were pretermitted by the honorable Court of Civil Appeals because of its holdings that communication of notice of the filter's company's approval was necessary, that such notice was not given—the letter of February 14th being thought insufficient for that purpose—and that defendant in error, therefore, had the right to countermand the proposal as it did (rather, attempted to do) on February 28th.

We recommend that the judgment of the Court of Civil Appeals be reversed, and that the cause be remanded to that court for its disposition of all questions not passed upon by it heretofore and properly before it for determination.

CURETON, C.J. [of the Texas Supreme Court]. Judgment of the Court of Civil Appeals reversed, and cause remanded to the Court of Civil Appeals for further consideration by that court, as recommended by the Commission of Appeals.

———

RESTATEMENT, SECOND, CONTRACTS § 56, ILLUSTRATION 2. "A makes written application for life insurance through an agent for B Insurance Company, pays the first premium, and is given a receipt stating that the insurance "shall take effect as of the date of approval of the application" at B's home office. Approval at the home office in accordance with B's usual practice is an acceptance of A's offer even though no steps are taken to notify A."

———

SECTION 3.   ACCEPTANCE BY CONDUCT

POLAROID CORP. v. ROLLINS ENVIRONMENTAL SERVICES (NJ), INC.

Supreme Judicial Court of Massachusetts, 1993.
416 Mass. 684, 624 N.E.2d 959.

Before LIACOS, C.J., and WILKINS, ABRAMS, LYNCH and GREANEY, JJ.

LYNCH, JUSTICE.

The defendant appeals from a Superior Court judgment granting the plaintiffs' motion for declaratory relief and ruling that the defendant is obligated to indemnify the plaintiffs for costs associated with a hazardous waste cleanup performed pursuant to the Comprehensive Environmental Response Compensation and Liability Act (CERCLA), 42 U.S.C. §§ 9601 et seq. (1988 & Supp. III 1991). The defendant, Rollins Environmental Services (NJ), Inc. (Rollins), operates a waste disposal facility in Bridgeport, New Jersey, where it disposes of hazardous waste materials through incineration and other chemical and biological processes for customers throughout the country. Polaroid Corporation (Polaroid) and Hooker Chemical Corporation (Hooker), the predecessor company of the plaintiff Occidental Chemical Corporation (Occidental), were customers of Rollins during the 1970's, whereby Rollins disposed of their hazardous wastes.

The plaintiffs' action sought a determination that Rollins was contractually obliged to indemnify them against liability for hazardous waste spills at a temporary storage facility, Bridgeport Rental and Oil Service, Inc. (Bridgeport). Although the complaint sets forth several counts, only the declaratory judgment count is presently before this court. The parties filed cross motions for summary judgment and agreed that there was no dispute as to the material facts.

In her well-reasoned opinion, the trial judge concluded that Polaroid and Occidental have valid, binding, and enforceable indemnification contracts with Rollins under which Rollins is to indemnify and to save the plaintiffs harmless from all liability and loss for releases or a substantial threat of release of hazardous substances at the Bridgeport site. . . . We transferred this case from the Appeals Court on our own motion and we now affirm.

The judge set forth the following undisputed facts from the pleadings, depositions, affidavits, and exhibits. In early 1976, Polaroid and Rollins entered into an agreement whereby Rollins agreed to perform waste disposal services for Polaroid. Polaroid gave Rollins a copy of Polaroid's "Supplemental General Conditions for Chemical Waste Disposal Services" (supplemental general conditions) and informed Rollins that agreement to the supplemental conditions was an essential condition to any contract between the parties. Rollins made a number of handwritten and initialed changes and then both Rollins and Polaroid signed the supplemental general conditions which provide in pertinent part:

"8. *Precautions*

"You shall perform all services hereunder in a careful and workman-like manner in full compliance with all applicable federal, state and local laws and shall utilize your best efforts to avoid injuries to persons, damage to property or damage to the environment. You further agree to comply with all safety and environmental standards adopted by Polaroid with respect to the handling and transportation, while on Polaroid premises. You further agree to issue certificates of disposal to Polaroid signifying environmentally proper disposal has been accomplished. . . .

"10. *Indemnification*

"You hereby agree to indemnify and save Polaroid harmless from all liability and loss arising from services performed by you or your employees hereunder except where such liability or loss is the result of the negligence of Polaroid or its employees."

From May, 1976, until at least 1980, Rollins provided chemical waste disposal services to Polaroid and transported materials from Polaroid's Massachusetts plants to Rollins' New Jersey plant for treatment. Routinely, Polaroid sent Rollins a completed waste data sheet, a written description, and a sample of the waste to enable Rollins to determine whether its facility could properly treat the waste. Rollins would analyze the waste and return a written proposal with the treatment price and shipping cost to Polaroid. Polaroid would then execute a purchase order and Rollins would pick up the waste. All of Polaroid's purchase orders referenced the supplemental general conditions in a list of "documents which constitute this contract." Copies exist only of the fronts of Polaroid's purchase orders, which include the supplemental general conditions. However, the backs of purchase order forms of that general time period, which contain other terms and conditions, are available.

The Occidental Purchase Orders.

Hooker, the predecessor to Occidental, entered into a similar business arrangement with Rollins in late 1970 or early 1971. Hooker operated a chemical manufacturing plant in Hicksville, New York, and contracted with Rollins for waste removal and treatment. Routinely, Hooker submitted purchase orders which contained the following indemnity clause typed on their fronts:

"Rollins–Purle (Seller) shall assume all responsibility for injury or damage to the seller, or others, based on or arising out of possession, handling, or use by seller, or by others of any such material for any purpose whatsoever. The seller shall hold and save the buyer harmless of and from any and all claims, demands, damages, actions, and causes of action whatsoever arising from or growing out of possession, handling, or use by seller or by others of materials purchased."

The purchase orders also stated:

"IMPORTANT: ALL TERMS AND CONDITIONS ON THE FACE AND REVERSE SIDE HEREOF ARE A PART OF THIS CONTRACT.

"INSTRUCTIONS:

"1. INVOICE IN DUPLICATE

"2. INCLUDE PACKING LIST WITH ALL SHIPMENTS

"3. FILL IN ACKNOWLEDGMENT COPY AND RETURN IMMEDIATELY

"4. ADVISE AT ONCE IF YOU CANNOT DELIVER ON DATE SPECIFIED

"5. PREPAY AND ADD ALL FREIGHT

"6. NO SHIPMENTS ACCEPTED AFTER 3 P.M."

Although Occidental has produced copies of the fronts of the purchase orders with the preceding language, they have not produced the reverse side of the documents. From 1971 through 1976, thirteen of the fourteen purchase orders issued by Hooker contained the preceding indemnity clause and instructions. Rollins never returned the acknowledgement copies of an order containing the indemnity language. This indemnity language was used on Hooker's purchase orders without objection from Rollins until January 6, 1977, when Rollins refused a Hooker purchase order because it objected to the typed indemnity clause. At Rollins' behest, the parties thereafter adopted an indemnification clause which provided indemnification only for Rollins' negligent acts.

During the course of doing business with both Polaroid and Hooker, Rollins sometimes stored the plaintiffs' waste materials in the Bridgeport "tank farm" until Rollins' facility was able to process the waste. Several hazardous waste spills occurred at Bridgeport during the 1970's. In August of 1988, the United States Environmental Protection Agency (EPA) notified Polaroid and Occidental that, as waste generators, they were potentially responsible parties under CERCLA and would be held jointly and severally liable for investigation and remediation costs incurred by the government. The EPA asserted that Polaroid was potentially responsible as the generator of waste shipped to Bridgeport on October 17, 1973, and seven additional shipments made between August 11, 1976, and April 2, 1977. Occidental is listed as the generator of waste shipped on June 27, 1974, and August 2, 1974.

The New Jersey Department of Environmental Protection has requested potentially responsible parties voluntarily to contribute $9,224,189 to the remediation efforts at the Bridgeport site. Polaroid has paid a small portion but Occidental has paid nothing. Both Polaroid and Occidental requested Rollins to defend and to indemnify them with regard to the Bridgeport site spills but Rollins has refused. . . .

Rollins argues . . . that it rejected the indemnification language by not returning the acknowledgment copy of the purchase agreement as requested. Although the purchase orders requested acknowledgement of the terms of the contract, Rollins routinely completed performance pursuant to the terms of the purchase order without returning an acknowledgement and without objecting to the indemnity clause. If an offeror prescribes an exclusive method of acceptance, only an acceptance in the manner prescribed will bind the offeror; but if an offeror merely suggests a permitted method of acceptance, other methods of acceptance are not precluded. Restatement (Second) of Contracts § 30 comment b (1981).

There is no suggestion from the purchase order that acknowledgement and return of the purchase order was the sole means of acceptance. Although silence does not ordinarily manifest assent, the relationship between the parties or other circumstances may justify the assumption that silence indicates assent to the proposal. *Weichert Co. Realtors v. Ryan,* 128 N.J. 427, 436, 608 A.2d 280 (1992). Moreover, when an offeree accepts the offeror's services without expressing any objection to the offer's essential terms, the offeree has manifested assent to those terms. *Id.* Prior to 1977, Rollins did not give any indication that it rejected the indemnification clause, and it performed pursuant to all of the other terms of the purchase orders issued by Hooker. Although Rollins did object to the indemnification clause in 1977 and negotiated a change with Hooker, there is no indication that the parties understood that the change would be retroactive or otherwise affect past course of dealings. Accordingly, Rollins' performance in compliance with the terms of the agreement without objecting to the indemnity clause constitutes acceptance of the offer's terms. Accord *Allied Steel & Conveyors, Inc. v. Ford Motor Co.,* 277 F.2d 907, 911–913 (6th Cir.1960); *U.S. Ore Corp. v. Commercial Transp. Corp.,* 369 F.Supp. 792, 796 (E.D.La.1974); *Joseph v. Atlantic Basin Iron Works Inc.,* 132 N.Y.S.2d 671, 672–673 (1954), aff'd, 285 A.D. 1147, 143 N.Y.S.2d 601 (1955). . . .

Judgment affirmed.

SECTION 4. THE EFFECT OF USING A SUBCONTRACTOR'S BID

HOLMAN ERECTION CO. v. ORVILLE E. MADSEN & SONS, INC.

Supreme Court of Minnesota, 1983.
330 N.W.2d 693.

YETKA, JUSTICE.

Plaintiff-appellant Holman Erection Company (Holman) commenced an action against Orville Madsen & Sons, Inc., (Madsen), alleging that Madsen had breached a construction contract. Holman claims that Madsen accepted Holman's bid on a subcontract, and thereby formed a contract, by listing Holman as a proposed subcontractor in a general contract bid Madsen submitted to the City of Moorhead. Holman sought the profits it argued it had lost when Madsen awarded the subcontract to a different construction company.

The Clay County District Court granted Madsen's motion for summary judgment. Holman appeals from the order and judgment dismissing Holman's claim. We affirm.

The facts of this case are undisputed. The City of Moorhead, Minnesota, advertised for bids to build a wastewater treatment facility. Bids from general contractors were to be opened at a public meeting of the governing body on January 22, 1981, pursuant to Minn.Stat. § 471.705 (1982). Madsen decided to bid on the general contract for the project. It sent bid invitations to potential subcontractors, including Holman. Shortly before the general contract bids were due to the City of Moorhead, Madsen received a bid from Holman. The bid was taken over the telephone. It is normal practice in the construction industry for subcontractors to submit bids shortly before the general bid is due, as was done here. This procedure is intended to prevent the general contractor from "bid shopping," a practice whereby the general takes a subcontractor's bid and uses it as leverage to obtain lower bids from other potential subcontractors. *See* Closen & Weiland, *The Construction Industry Bidding Cases: Application of Traditional Contract, Promissory Estoppel, and Other Theories to the Relations Between General Contractors and Subcontractors,* 13 J.Mar.L.Rev. 565, 574–77 (1980).

When Holman phoned in its bid, information on the total price and work included in the bid was written down on a note pad by someone at Madsen's office in Hudson, Wisconsin, and relayed to Madsen's representatives in Moorhead. The bid was received 2–3 hours before the general bid was due to the city. Holman also submitted bids to six other general contractors that were bidding on the same project. The identical bid was made to each general. The work and expense involved in developing a bid is not segregated by subcontractors to individual general contractors.

Madsen utilized Holman's bid, as well as past experience, in preparing its bid for the general contract. The city required general contractors to list all proposed subcontractors on their prime bids to the city. Holman was listed on Madsen's bid as the subcontractor for the steel erection portion of the project. This portion accounted for 2% of the total project. Other than taking Holman's bid over the telephone, no one at Madsen ever spoke to Holman about the bid, any potential contract or the project in general until Holman called Madsen after the subcontracts had already been awarded.

The bids of all the general contractors were opened by the city on January 22, 1981. On February 2, 1981, Madsen was awarded the prime contract.

Following award of the contract, Madsen began entering into subcontracts with various subcontractors. At this stage of the process, limited negotiation takes place with the subcontractors. Items are clarified and written contracts are executed. Instead of contacting Holman to finalize arrangements for steel erection, Madsen discussed this aspect of the contract with Van Knight Steel Erection, Inc. (Van Knight), a different steel erection subcontract bidder. Madsen sent Van Knight a letter, stating that Van Knight's bid was being reviewed. Madsen requested information on Van Knight's status and qualification as a minority business. The contract with the City of Moorhead required that an effort be made to have a portion of the work done by minority business enterprises, pursuant to federal regulations.

Madsen eventually awarded the steel erection subcontract to Van Knight. Van Knight also agreed to supply a substantial amount of materials and some labor not included in Holman's bid.

Holman learned from one of the other general contract bidders that Madsen had been the low general bidder and that Holman had been the low sub-bidder for steel erection. When Holman also discovered that it had been listed as a proposed subcontractor in Madsen's bid, it called Madsen and was told that the subcontract was going to a different company. Madsen at no time indicated to Holman that Holman was to get the contract. Other than the two phone conversations—the first when Holman called in its bid; the second after Holman's discovery—no other communication, written or oral, occurred between Holman and Madsen.

Holman brought suit against Madsen, alleging that Madsen had accepted Holman's sub-bid on the wastewater treatment project and had thus formed a binding contract which it breached by awarding the subcontract to a different company.

The Clay County District Court found that no contract had been created between the parties and granted summary judgment.

The two issues on appeal are:

1. Is a contract formed between a general contractor and a subcontractor when the general submits a bid on a public construction project and lists the subcontractor as the proposed subcontractor for one aspect of the project as required by the awarding authority and the general subsequently wins the contract and awards the subcontract to a different subcontractor?

2. Did the lower court err in granting summary judgment in favor of the general contractor?

Appellant Holman argues that a binding contractual relationship was created between it and Madsen when Madsen utilized Holman's sub-bid in its general bid for the waste treatment plant project and listed Holman as a proposed subcontractor for steel erection work. Does the act of listing Holman in the general bid constitute an acceptance of Holman's offer to do the work when no other communication occurred after the offer and prior to the substitution of a different subcontractor? We think not.

To constitute an acceptance, Madsen's acts must be deemed a manifestation of assent when evaluated under an objective standard. *See Capital Warehouse Co. v. McGill–Warner–Farnham Co.,* 276 Minn. 108, 114, 149 N.W.2d 31, 35 (1967). The form of the assent, whether it be written, oral, or by conduct, is not relevant as long as objective standards are applied and the essential finding of mutual assent is made. *See Bergstedt, Wahlberg, Berquist Associates, Inc. v. Rothchild,* 302 Minn. 476, 479, 225 N.W.2d 261, 263 (1975). The Restatement (Second) of Contracts § 19 (1979) provides:

(1) The manifestation of assent may be made wholly or partly by written or spoken words or by other acts or by failure to act.

(2) The conduct of a party is not effective as a manifestation of his assent unless he intends to engage in the conduct and knows or has reason to know that the other party may infer from his conduct that he assents.

Comment c to section 19 provides:

[E]ven though the intentional conduct of a party creates an appearance of assent on his part, he is not responsible for that appearance unless he knows or has reason to know that his conduct may cause the other party to understand that he assents.

Holman argues that listing Holman as a subcontractor, as required by the awarding authority, constitutes an acceptance because: 1) there is no other reasonable explanation for the act; 2) it is unfair to bind Holman to its bid without binding Madsen to use it; and 3) Madsen knew the general bid was public record pursuant to statutes. Since Madsen knew Holman could discover that Holman had been listed in the general bid, Holman argues that the inference can be drawn that Madsen intended to accept Holman's offer and communicated the assent by listing Holman in the general bid.

Appellant's argument flies in the face of a large body of precedent holding that no contract is formed by the listing of a subcontractor in a general contractor's bid. There is no case in Minnesota that deals precisely with the issue presented. This court has held, however, that the subcontractor may be bound to his bid as submitted to the general contractor by operation of promissory estoppel. *See Constructors Supply Co. v. Bostrom Sheet Metal Works, Inc.,* 291 Minn. 113, 190 N.W.2d 71 (1971)....

California courts have addressed the precise issue presented here in several cases. The only significant distinguishing characteristic is that a statute required the listing of proposed subcontractors. In the present case, the listing was required by the awarding authority, but not by statute. In *Klose v. Sequoia Union High School District,* 118 Cal.App.2d 636, 258 P.2d 515 (1953), the general contractor mistakenly included the wrong subcontractor in its bid and, after winning the contract, substituted a different subcontractor for the one listed. A member of the school district sued the general contractor, seeking imposition of the statutory penalty for wrongful substitution. The court stated:

> Petitioner's arguments are necessarily predicated upon the concept that a subcontractor, whose name is submitted with the bid of the general contractor, in some undefined way, secures some legal rights when the general contractor's bid is accepted by the awarding authority. In the absence of statute that is not the law. A subcontractor bidder merely makes an offer that is converted into a contract by a regularly communicated acceptance conveyed to him by the general contractor. No contractual relationship is created between the subcontractor and the general contractor even though the bid is used as part of the general overall bid by the general contractor and accepted by the awarding authority.

Id. at 640–41, 258 P.2d at 517.

In *Southern Cal. Acoustics Co. v. C.V. Holder, Inc.,* 71 Cal.2d 719, 79 Cal.Rptr. 319, 456 P.2d 975 (1969), the California Supreme Court reaffirmed *Klose,* holding that the listing of a subcontractor does not constitute an acceptance or confer any contract rights. The court did, however, leave open a possible statutory remedy if the substitution was in violation of the governing statute. *See also Interior Systems, Inc. v. Del E. Webb Corp.,* 121 Cal.App.3d 312, 175 Cal.Rptr. 301 (1981).

In *Milone & Tucci, Inc. v. Bona Fide Builders, Inc.,* 49 Wash.2d 363, 301 P.2d 759 (1956), the Washington Supreme Court held that the mere use of the subcontractor's figures did not constitute an acceptance of the subcontractor's offer, despite the fact that the general requested the subcontractor's bid. In *Corbin–Dykes Electric Co. v. Burr,* 18 Ariz.App. 101, 500 P.2d 632 (1972), the Arizona Court of Appeals held that a subcontractor's bid was nothing more than an offer to perform, not ripening into a contract until voluntarily accepted, and that the use of the subcontractor's bid in the general bid did not constitute a manifestation of assent....

Holman attempts to distinguish the vast authority that holds in opposition to its position by pointing to factual differences between those cases and the instant case. While mistake, inadvertence, and other distinguishing facts are present in the cases, the courts' decisions did not turn on these elements. The holdings applied the general law of contracts, not resting on the types of facts highlighted by appellant. In the present case, the subcontractor has shown no reliance, additional communications or detriment stemming from the substitution of a different subcontractor. Further, Madsen had a legitimate reason for substituting a different subcontractor for Holman, that is, complying with federal Minority Business Enterprise (MBE) regulations. The mere absence of mistake, fraud or incapability of the subcontractor has no determinative effect on the resolution of the contract formation issue.

While commentators have urged that a general contractor be bound to a listed subcontractor upon the mere listing or use of the subcontractor's bid in the general bid on several theories, we do not adopt the reasoning. *See, e.g.,* Note, *Another Look at Construction Bidding and Contracts at Formation,* 53 Va.L.Rev. 1720 (1967); Note, *Once Around the Flag Pole: Construction Bidding and Contracts at Formation,* 39 N.Y.U.L.Rev. 816 (1964); *see also* Closen & Weiland, *supra* at 605 (urging legislative action to regulate the public bidding process). One theory requires a factual inquiry into the circumstances surrounding the relationship of the general contractor and subcontractor. It would find that a contract exists unless: 1) the sub-bid is not responsive to the plans and specifications embodied in the overall project; or 2) the subcontractor is shown to be unreliable or incapable of performing his side of the bargain without unreasonably complicating the general's position. This approach rests on a supposedly objective and realistic examination of construction industry bidding practices and emphasizes "factual realities." The dominant policy justification is said to be the avoidance of bid-shopping while not unnecessarily restricting the freedom of general contractors.

A second analysis rests on an analogy to the Uniform Commercial Code. The UCC provides a more liberal standard for formation of contracts than does the common law of contracts and allows any reasonable manner of acceptance to bind both promisor and promisee. *See* Minn.Stat. § 336.2–206 (1982). It is argued that the court must look to the "fulcrum point of agreement" to determine when the parties are bound. The factual context of general/subcontractor agreements is said to compel the conclusion that since the parties consider themselves bound at the time the general utilizes the subcontractor's bid, this intent should be enforceable.

The broad policy justifications advanced for binding the general to the subcontractor upon utilization or listing of the subcontractor in the general bid include:

> (1) limiting bargaining to the pre-award stage to put the general and the sub on equal footing as to any subsequent negotiation or modification of the initial agreement;

> (2) providing certainty in the industry;

> (3) avoiding bid-shopping;

> (4) providing formality and allowing the commercial context to supply the necessary fact basis; and

> (5) allowing for necessary negotiation on open terms, the only binding terms being the price and the nature of the work bid on.

Underlying all of the above justifications is a superficial equity notion. In Minnesota, as well as most other jurisdictions, the subcontractor may be obligated to perform by application of promissory estoppel. The general, however, remains free to avoid the listed subcontractor and negotiate with other subcontractors. This one-sided arrangement seems, on its face, unfair. Why should one party be bound and [the] other not? A close examination of the construction business and the nature of the bidding process, however, reveals several justifications for the unequal treatment of generals and subcontractors.

First, the reason a subcontractor is bound by its bid is the existence of justifiable reliance by the general on the subcontractor's price for specified work. The general makes his bid after gathering and evaluating a number of subcontract bids. Once the general wins the prime contract from the awarding authority, he is bound to his own bid. For the subcontractor to be able to refuse to perform would subject the general to a financial detriment. *See Constructors Supply Co. v. Bostrom Sheet Metal Works, Inc.*, 291 Minn. 113, 120, 190 N.W.2d 71, 75–76 (1971).

In contrast, the subcontractor does not rely on the general and suffers no detriment. A subcontractor submits bids to all or most of the general contractors that it knows are bidding on a project. The subcontractor receives invitations to bid from some generals and submits bids to others without invitation. The time and expense involved in preparing the bid is not segregated to any particular general. The total cost is part of the overhead of doing business. The same bid is submitted to each general. Thus, whether or not any particular general wins the contract is of little or no concern to the subcontractor. The subcontractor engages in the same work and expense in preparing its bid regardless of who wins the general contract and whether the subcontractor wins the contract on which it bid. No further expense is incurred until a formal agreement is reached with the general and actual work commences. Clearly, the promissory estoppel concept is not applicable in this situation. *Bostrom* bound the subcontractor to his bid not on the basis of a contract, but on the basis of estoppel. With no detrimental reliance, there can be no estoppel claim. Ample justification exists for binding the subcontractor and not binding the general. The two situations are very different.

Second, the nature of the bidding process compels allowing the general sufficient leeway to maintain its flexibility in executing subcontracts and selecting the subcontractors it will hire for a project. Typically, subcontractors submit their bids only a few hours before the general bid must be submitted to the awarding authority. The general's representatives take the bids over the telephone and hurriedly compile their own bid. This period of time is hectic and complex. The bids received consist of the contract price and a listing of work included. Specifics are left for future negotiation and clarification.

The last-minute procedure is designed to prevent bid-shopping. This court has recognized the undesirable nature of bid-shopping, *Bostrom*, 291 Minn. at 121, 190 N.W.2d at 76, and the last-minute bidding process seems well entrenched in the construction industry. *See Hoel–Steffen Construction Co. v. United States*, 684 F.2d 843, 849 (Ct.Cl.1982).

The bidding process puts the subcontractor and the general in very different positions as to the content of the subcontract. The subcontractors have the luxury of preparing their bids on their own timetable, subject only to the deadline for submitting their bids to the general contractors. The same bid goes to all the general contractors and covers the same work. The generals, on the other hand, are dealing with all the various construction aspects of the project and with numerous potential subcontractors. They compile their bids, as the various subcontractor bids are received, within a few hours of the deadline for submission of the prime bid. Specifics are necessarily given less than thorough consideration and are left for future negotiations. Finally, the lowest dollar amount bidder is not always the one chosen to do the work or the one listed as the potential subcontractor. Reliability, quality of work, and capability to handle the job are all considerations weighed by the general in choosing subcontractors. MBE regulations requiring an effort to use a percentage of minority contractors are another potential consideration.

Binding general contractors to subcontractors because a particular bid was listed in the general bid or was utilized in making the bid would remove a considerable degree of needed flexibility. The present case illustrates the consequences quite well. Because the project involved was a public project, MBE regulations required that an effort be made to use minority contractors. When Madsen began to put the specifics of the project together, it was forced to juggle the subcontracts in order to comply with the MBE regulations. Van Knight, the subcontractor chosen instead of Holman, qualified as a minority business and offered to supply materials and supplies not included in Holman's bid. Despite a slightly higher cost, Madsen selected Van Knight as the steel erection subcontractor.

If Madsen was bound to the bids listed in its prime bid, there is a possibility that the contract would have been lost due to failure to comply with MBE regulations. The next highest qualifying bidder would then have been selected, to the awarding authority's greater expense and to Madsen's detriment. Such a result imposes a greater cost on the project and a loss to the general contractor. The result under the prevailing law in most jurisdictions, and which we adopt here, would not impose any additional expenses on the rejected subcontractor.

A decision in favor of the subcontractor on this issue would place Minnesota in a minority position as perhaps the sole state to hold that a contract is formed by the mere listing of a subcontractor in a general contractor's bid to the awarding authority. Although supplying some certainty and symmetry to the construction industry, such a decision would also impose a rigidity on the process and result in greater cost to awarding authorities and potential detriment to general contractors. If such a change is to take place, it is one properly brought before the legislature.

Appellant argues that despite the lack of dispute over the facts, summary judgment is inappropriate because the fact-finder could infer that a contract had been formed.

The lower court concluded that the mere listing of a subcontractor's name by a general contractor in its bid to the awarding authority does not create a contract between the subcontractor and the general contractor. Since that conclusion is affirmed by this court, summary judgment was clearly appropriate. The facts are not in dispute and no inferences can be drawn from those facts that change the result. The trial court is thus affirmed.

NOTE ON SOUTHERN CALIFORNIA ACOUSTICS
CO. v. C.V. HOLDER, INC.

In Holman Erection Co. v. Orville E. Madsen & Sons, Inc., supra, the Minnesota court referred to a California decision, *Southern California Acoustics Co. v. C. V. Holder, Inc.*, 71 Cal.2d 719, 79 Cal.Rptr. 319, 456 P.2d 975 (1969). The *Holman* opinion states that in *Southern California Acoustics* "the California Supreme Court reaffirmed [Klose v. Sequoia Union High School District, 118 Cal.App.2d 636, 258 P.2d 515 (1953)], holding that the listing of a subcontractor does not constitute an acceptance or confer any contract rights. The court did, however, leave open a possible statutory remedy if the substitution was in violation of the governing statute." This description of *Southern California Acoustics* is literally accurate, but substantively misleading.

The plaintiff in *Klose* had argued that if a general contractor listed the name of a subcontractor, then under both contract law and a California statute that required subcontractors to be listed and seemed to prohibit substitution, the prime contractor could not substitute another subcontractor in place of the listed subcontractor. The court in *Klose* rejected both arguments. The court held that (1) as a matter of contract law, listing a subcontractor is not an implied acceptance of the subcontractor's bid, and (2) the statute did not give the subcontractor a right to prevent substitution. The major ground of the statutory ruling was that because the statute did not in terms permit substitution where the contractor was unable or unwilling to perform, if the statute was interpreted to give the subcontractor a right to prevent substitution, then a subcontractor could not be replaced even if it was unable or unwilling to perform.

After the decision in *Klose* the statute was amended to address those concerns, by providing that substitution of a listed subcontractor was prohibited unless the subcontractor was unable or unwilling to perform. The preamble to the amended statute stated that the purpose of the statute was to protect the public and subcontractors from bid shopping and bid peddling. The court in *Southern California Acoustics* agreed with *Klose* that a listed subcontractor did not have a right against a prime under contract law. However, based on the revisions to the statute and the preamble, the court held that the amended statute conferred upon a listed subcontractor a right not to be substituted for unless the statutory grounds for a valid substitution existed, and this right could be enforced by an action against the prime contractor for expectation damages.

WILLIAMS v. FAVRET, 161 F.2d 822 (5th Cir.1947). Favret, a general contractor, was about to bid on a Federal Government project at Gulfport. At Favret's invitation, Williams submitted a telegraphic bid on June 4 for the electrical work in connection with the project. Williams's bid stated, "If our estimate used wire us collect prior to June 6 [the date for the opening of bids on the project] or else same is withdrawn." On June 6, Favret telegraphed Williams, "We used your bid for wiring on barracks and dispensary Gulfport." Favret was awarded the general contract, but gave the electrical work to another subcontractor, and Williams sued for breach of contract. Held, no contract had been formed. "Defendant's telegram of the 6th ... contained nothing from which an acceptance of the [plaintiff's] offer ... can be implied." McCord, J., dissented. "I think the exchange of telegrams, viewed in their proper setting, clearly demonstrates that it was the purpose and intention of the parties to create an effective and binding contract between them, conditioned only on Favret being awarded the general contract. Williams made his offer, and after Favret advised him within the time limit that he was using it in his general bid, Williams was bound; and after Favret was awarded the government contract, Williams could not withdraw his offer, he could not change his price, *he had to do the work at Favret's call.* The testimony of Harold Favret clearly shows that the telegram was sent to Williams for the purpose of holding him to his bid: 'Q. You were wanting to hold Mr. Williams to his bid? Correct? A. Here is the point. Mr. Williams threatened to withdraw that bid prior to the time we submitted our bids, which, *if we banked on his bid entirely,* and he withdrew it, it would cause us to be in error in our estimate.' Could Williams be bound and Favret remain free to do as he pleased? I know of no such one—sided application, hornbook or otherwise, of the law of contracts.... If the exchange of telegrams did not establish offer and acceptance, what was their purpose and meaning?" (Emphasis in original.)

———

ELECTRICAL CONSTRUCTION & MAINTENANCE CO. v. MAEDA PACIFIC CORP., 764 F.2d 619 (9th Cir.1985). The government of Guam awarded Maeda the prime contract on a project to expand and modernize Guam's port facilities. Prior to bidding on the project, Maeda solicited proposals from various subcontractors, including ECM, to perform the electrical work. ECM claimed that when Maeda solicited ECM's bid (1) ECM told Maeda that it was unwilling to bid unless Maeda agreed to award ECM the subcontract if Maeda was the successful bidder on the prime contract and ECM was the lowest bidder on the subcontract, and (2) Maeda accepted ECM's proposal. The trial court held that ECM's complaint failed to state a claim for relief. Reversed.

"Generally, the mere use of a subcontractor's bid by a general contractor bidding on a prime contract does not constitute acceptance of the subcontractor's bid and imposes no obligation upon the prime contractor to accept the subcontractor's bid. See Merritt–Chapman & Scott Corp. v. Gunderson Bros. Engineering Corp., 305 F.2d 659 (9th Cir.), cert. denied, 371 U.S. 935, 83 S.Ct. 307, 9 L.Ed.2d 271 (1962); Southern Cal. Acoustics Co. v. C.V. Holder, Inc., 71 Cal.2d 719, 456 P.2d 975, 79 Cal.Rptr. 319 (1969); Williams v. Favret, 161 F.2d 822 (5th Cir.1947). Moreover, ECM concedes that the mere solicitation of bids by a general contractor is not an offer and does not impose any obligations upon the general contractor. But ECM points out that even if it were obligated not to revoke its bid, it was not obligated to bid in the first place. ECM alleged in its complaint that it initially refused Maeda's solicitation to bid and only subsequently bid because Maeda promised that if ECM undertook the time and expense to prepare and submit an electrical subcontractor's bid, Maeda would award ECM the subcontract if its bid were the lowest. While this is an issue of first impression, we believe that where a subcontractor allegedly agreed to bid only after receiving the general contractor's promise to accept the bid if it were the low bid and if the general contractor were awarded the prime contract, there is consideration for the general contractor's promise. The consideration for Maeda's promise was ECM's submission of a bid—an act for which Maeda bargained and that ECM was not under a legal duty to perform."

INDUSTRIAL ELECTRIC–SEATTLE, INC. v. BOSKO, 67 Wash.2d 783, 410 P.2d 10 (1966). Bosko, a general contractor, used the bid of Industrial Electric, an electrical subcontractor, and was awarded the general contract, but failed to award the electrical contract to Industrial Electric. Industrial Electric sued. The trial court entered judgment for Industrial Electric, finding that a custom existed among contractors in the community that if a general contractor requested and obtained a subcontractor's price for a portion of the work, and used that price in preparing his bid for the prime contract, the general contractor was bound to use the subcontractor's services. Affirmed. "We believe ... [custom] is admissable to show the meaning of the words and acts of the parties in the sense that we normally mean by the term 'objective manifestations of intent.' "

LORANGER CONST. CORP. v. E.F. HAUSERMAN COMPANY, 376 Mass. 757, 384 N.E.2d 176 (1978). A general contractor sued a subcontractor who had made an "estimate" and then refused to enter into a contract in accordance with the estimate. The court treated the estimate as an offer, and said that acceptance might have been found in several ways, one of which was that "the offer might have been accepted by the doing of an act, using the defendant's estimate in submitting the plaintiff's bid. Acceptance in this way might be complete without notification to the offeror. Bishop v. Eaton, 161 Mass. 496, 499, 37 N.E. 665 (1894)."

PAVEL ENTERPRISES, INC. v. A.S. JOHNSON CO., 342 Md. 143, 674 A.2d 521 (1996). "Courts and commentators have ... suggested [solutions to the subcontractor-bidding problem] intended to bind the parties without the use of detrimental reliance theory....

" ... [W]e now clarify that Maryland courts are to apply the test of the Restatement (Second) of Contracts § 90(1) (1979), which we have recast as a four-part test:

"1. a clear and definite promise;

"2. where the promisor has a reasonable expectation that the offer will induce action or forbearance on the part of the promisee;

"3. which does induce actual and reasonable action or forbearance by the promisee; and

"4. causes a detriment which can only be avoided by the enforcement of the promise...."

"As to the third element, a general contractor must prove that he actually and reasonably relied on the subcontractor's sub-bid. We decline to provide a checklist of potential methods of proving this reliance, but we will make several observations. First, a showing by the subcontractor, that the general contractor engaged in 'bid shopping,' or actively encouraged 'bid chopping,' or 'bid peddling' is strong evidence that the general did not rely on the sub-bid. Second, prompt notice by the general contractor to the subcontractor that the general intends to use the sub on the job, is weighty evidence that the general did rely on the bid. Third, if a sub-bid is so low that a reasonably prudent general contractor would not rely upon it, the trier of fact may infer that the general contractor did not in fact rely upon the erroneous bid. . . .

"Finally, as to the fourth prima facie element, the trial court, and not a jury, must determine that binding the subcontractor is necessary to prevent injustice. This element is to be enforced as required by common law equity courts—the general contractor must have 'clean hands.' This requirement includes, as did the previous element, that the general did not engage in bid shopping, chopping or peddling, but also requires the further determination that justice compels the result."

SECTION 5. THE EFFECT OF FAILING TO NOTIFY AN OFFEREE THAT HIS ACCEPTANCE IS TOO LATE

PHILLIPS v. MOOR

Supreme Judicial Court of Maine, 1880.
71 Me. 78.

BARROWS, J. Negotiations by letter, looking to the purchase by the defendant of a quantity of hay in the plaintiff's barn, had resulted in the pressing of the hay by the defendant's men, to be paid for at a certain rate if the terms of sale could not be agreed on; and in written invitations from plaintiff's guardian to defendant, to make an offer for the hay, in one of which he says: "If the price is satisfactory I will write you on receipt of it;" and in the other: "If your offer is satisfactory I shall accept it; if not, I will send you the money for pressing." Friday, June 14th, defendant made an examination of the hay after it had been pressed, and wrote to plaintiff's guardian, same day . . . "Will give $9.50 per ton, for all but three tons, and for that I will give $5.00." Plaintiff's guardian lived in Carmel, 14 miles from Bangor where defendant lived, and there is a daily mail communication each way between the two places. The card containing defendant's offer was mailed at Bangor, June 15, and probably received by plaintiff in regular course, about nine o'clock A.M., that day. The plaintiff does not deny this, though he says he does not always go to the office, and the mail is sometimes carried by. Receiving no better offer, and being offered less by another dealer, on Thursday, June 20th, he went to Bangor, and there, not meeting the defendant, sent him through the post office a card, in which he says he was in hopes defendant would have paid him $10.00 for the best quality: "But you can take the hay at your offer, and when you get it hauled in, if you can pay the $10.00 I would like to have you do it, if the hay proves good enough for the price." Defendant received this card that night or the next morning, made no reply, and Sunday morning the hay was burnt in the barn. Shortly after, when the parties met, the plaintiff claimed the price of the hay and defendant denied his liability, and asserted a claim for the pressing. Hence this suit.

The guardian's acceptance of the defendant's offer was absolute and unconditional. It is not in any legal sense qualified by the expression of his hopes, as to what the defendant would have done, or what he would like to have him do, if the hay when hauled proved good enough. Aside from all this, the defendant was told that he could take the hay at his own offer. It seems to have been the intention and understanding of both the parties that the property should pass. The defendant does not deny what the guardian testifies he told him at their conference after the hay was burned,—that he had agreed with a man to haul the hay for sixty cents a ton. The guardian does not seem to have claimed any lien for the price, or to have expected payment until the hay should have been hauled by the defendant. But the defendant insists that the guardian's acceptance of his offer was not seasonable; that in the initiatory correspondence the guardian had in substance promised an immediate acceptance or rejection of such offer as he might make, and that the offer was not, in fact, accepted within a reasonable time.

If it be conceded that for want of a more prompt acceptance the defendant had the right to retract his offer, or to refuse to be bound by it when notified of its acceptance, still the defendant did not avail himself of such right. Two days elapsed before the fire after the defendant had actual notice that his offer was accepted, and he permitted the guardian to consider it sold, and made a bargain with a third party to haul it.

It is true that an offer, to be binding upon the party making it, must be accepted within a reasonable time. Peru v. Turner, 10 Maine, 185; but if the party to whom it is made, makes known his acceptance of it to the party making it, within any period which he could fairly have supposed to be reasonable, good faith requires the maker, if he intends to retract on account of the delay, to make known that intention promptly. If he does not, he must be regarded as waiving any objection to the acceptance as being too late.

The question here is,—In whom was the property in the hay at the time of its destruction? . . .

Chancellor Kent, 2 Com. 492, states the doctrine thus: "When the terms of sale are agreed on and the bargain is struck, and everything that the seller has to do with the goods is complete, the contract of sale becomes absolute without actual payment or delivery, and the property and risk of accident to the goods vest in the buyer." That doctrine was expressly approved by this court in Wing v. Clark, 24 Maine, 366, 372, where its origin in the civil law is referred to. And this court went farther in Waldron v. Chase, 37 Maine, 414; and held that when the owner of a quantity of corn in bulk, sold a certain number of bushels therefrom and received his pay, and the vendee had taken away a part only, the property in the whole quantity sold, vested in the buyer, although it had not been measured and separated from the heap, and that it thenceforward remained in charge of the seller at the buyer's risk.

In the case at bar all the hay was sold. The quality had been ascertained by the defendant. The price was agreed on. The defendant had been told that he might take it and had nothing to do but to send the man whom he had engaged to haul it, and appropriate it to himself without any further act on the part of the seller. . . .

Judgment for plaintiff.

––––––––

NOTE ON THE RISK OF LOSS

UCC § 2–509 now governs risk of loss under a contract for the sale of goods where neither party is in breach and the contract does not specifically cover the risk of loss. Subdivision (3), which would apply to facts such as those in Phillips v. Moor, provides that "the risk of loss passes to the buyer on his receipt of the goods if the seller is a merchant; otherwise, the risk passes to the buyer on tender of delivery."

––––––––

RESTATEMENT, SECOND, CONTRACTS §§ 69, 70

[See Selected Source Materials Supplement]

––––––––

CISG ART. 21

[See Selected Source Materials Supplement]

––––––––

UNIDROIT PRINCIPLES OF INTERNATIONAL COMMERCIAL CONTRACTS ART. 2.1.9

[See Selected Source Materials Supplement]

––––––––

PRINCIPLES OF EUROPEAN CONTRACT LAW ART. 2.207

[See Selected Source Materials Supplement]

––––––––

SECTION 6. SILENCE AS ACCEPTANCE

VOGT v. MADDEN

Court of Appeals of Idaho, 1985
110 Idaho 6, 713 P.2d 442

WALTERS, Chief Judge.

Harold and Betty Vogt sued Bob and Neva Madden for damages allegedly resulting from the Maddens' breach, as landlords, of a sharecrop agreement. A jury returned a verdict in favor of the Vogts. The Maddens appeal from the judgment entered on the verdict, presenting three issues. They contend . . . that the evidence was insufficient to support the jury's implicit finding that a sharecrop agreement existed between the parties for the year 1981. We agree with the Maddens that it was not proven that a contract existed between the parties for the year 1981 . . .

It was undisputed that Harold Vogt had an oral sharecrop agreement with Bob Madden to farm seventy acres of land owned by the Maddens, for the year 1979. It also was undisputed that the parties renewed the agreement for the year 1980. Under their agreement, certain expenses would be borne solely by Vogt, other expenses would be shared equally between Vogt and Madden, and the net profits derived from crops grown on the land would be divided equally between them. When the Vogts eventually filed suit contending a sharecrop agreement existed for the year 1981, Vogt also sought recovery from Madden of $2,000 for the Maddens' share of expenses incurred by Vogt in the years 1979 and 1980.

The dispositive issue in this appeal is whether Vogt and Madden had a sharecrop agreement that Vogt could continue to farm the seventy acres, during 1981. Vogt testified that because no profits had been realized from wheat crops grown on the property in 1979 and 1980, he planned to raise beans on the land in 1981. He testified that he met with Madden several times in August and September, after the wheat crop had been harvested in 1980, concerning the expenses remaining for the years 1979 and 1980. He testified:

> [W]e also discussed the 1981 crop, of what to do then. We had several discussions on this. I met with him two or three, four times—I'm not sure how many—and we both agreed it wasn't the best ground. It isn't number one soil out there, because of the steepness, but I had raised grain for two years, and I had left the straw and stubble on the ground. And I had raised a—let the volunteer grain grow, watered it and plowed it under the first year. And I anticipated plowing under the second year and at that point I told him I thought it would raise a fairly decent crop of pinto beans.
>
> And at that time I told Bob [Madden] that I'd raised two years of grain, plowed under this straw and stubble, and I thought it would raise a crop of pinto beans. And at that time I had decided to do that. I was going to raise the pinto beans on there, along with possibly a few acres of garden beans.
>
> Q: And as a result of that conversation, it was your understanding that you were to farm that; is that correct?
>
> A: Yes.

Q: And when you were discussing the fact of growing the bean crop with Mr. Madden, did he have any objection to that type of crop being grown on his ground?

A: No, not at all.

On cross-examination, Vogt testified as follows:

Q: You talked about beans, then?

A: Yes, sir.

Q: But Mr. Madden never told you that he wanted to grow beans, did he?

A: No.

Q: He never expressly told you that he would enter into another agreement in the spring of '81?

A: Yes. What we done, we just—I told him I had raised this crop, the wheat and grain for two years, and the third year we could raise a crop of pintos, a crop of beans. And the price of beans at that time was good, and as far as I know that was the way the discussion ended.

Q: But Mr. Madden never agreed one way or another, right?

A: I would say I was under the impression that we had an agreement.

Q: But he never said anything to give you that indication?

A: Honestly, I don't think he said, "Yes, go ahead." No, he didn't say that.

Madden disputed that he and Vogt had agreed to a sharecrop arrangement for the year 1981. He testified that, following one of their discussions over the expense bills for 1979 and 1980,

And I said at that time, I told him, I said, "I just had it. I don't want you to farm it any more. I'll send you what I think is right."

"Harold," I said, "Life's too short to argue over these things, let's just—we're through."

In respect to that same discussion, Vogt denied on rebuttal that Madden had made any statement about Vogt not farming the Maddens' land the next year. In the late fall of 1980, Madden leased the property to another party for the 1981 crop year, thus preventing Vogt from pursuing his plan to raise beans on the land. This lawsuit for damages followed.

By its verdict in favor of Vogt for $18,540, the jury concluded that a sharecrop agreement existed between Vogt and Madden for the year 1981.[1] In order to reach such a conclusion the jury must have disbelieved Madden when he testified he informed Vogt that their relationship was "through," and that he, Madden, did not want Vogt to farm the property any longer. Otherwise, had the jury believed Madden, then clearly the parties would not have had a contract for 1981. If Madden were disbelieved, then the only evidence regarding the creation of a contract between Vogt and Madden for the year 1981

---

1.   Vogt testified that, had he been allowed to farm the Maddens' property in 1981 under the same sharecrop arrangement as in 1979 and 1980, he would have realized a net profit of $16,540. That figure, when added to the $2,000 owed by Madden to Vogt for the 1979–80 expenses, totals $18,540, the amount of the verdict.

would be Vogt's testimony that he informed Madden of his intent to raise beans on the property in 1981, that Madden did not say "yes" to this proposal, but that Vogt nonetheless was left with the "impression" that a contract had been created.

The question whether silence or inaction may constitute acceptance of an offer was an issue in this case. Over Madden's objection, the jury was given an instruction, No. 18, concerning silence as an acceptance of an offer, creating a contract between the offeror, Vogt, and the offeree, Madden. The instruction was requested by Vogt, demonstrating that Vogt was pursuing a theory that the evidence showed the creation of a sharecrop agreement for 1981 arising because of silence on Madden's part.

The instruction stated:

Silence and inaction may constitute acceptance of an offer to contract, where a party is under a duty to speak or to reject the offer. Such a duty may arise under any one of the following circumstances.

1. Where because of previous dealings it is reasonable that the offeree should notify the offeror if the offeree does not intend to accept.

2. Where an offeree takes the benefit of offered services with reasonable opportunity to reject them and reason to believe the offeror thought the offer was accepted.

3. Where the offeror has stated or given the offeree reason to understand that assent may be manifested by silence or inaction, and the offeree in remaining silent and inactive intends to accept the offer.

This instruction was a slightly modified version of the Restatement (Second) Of Contracts § 69 (1981).[2] The Restatement explains that silence by an offeree ordinarily does not operate as an acceptance of an offer. "The exceptional cases where silence is acceptance fall into two main classes: those where the offeree silently takes offered benefits, and those where one party relies on the other party's manifestation of intention that silence may operate as acceptance." Id. comment a, at 165.

Here, two of the exceptions stated in § 69, and in the court's instruction No. 18, are patently inapplicable because they are wholly unsupported by the evidence. There was no evidence that Madden received "the benefit of offered services" for which Vogt expected to be compensated. See, id. comment b, at 165 ("when the recipient knows or has reason to know that services are being rendered with an expectation of compensation, and by a word could prevent the mistake, his privilege of inaction gives way; under Subsection (1)(a) he is held to an acceptance if he fails to speak."). Vogt did not, in fact, farm the property in 1981. Nor does the evidence show that Vogt stated or gave Madden reason to understand that assent to Vogt's expectation to farm the

---

2. In relevant part, Restatement (Second) of Contracts § 69, at 165 provides:

(1) Where an offeree fails to reply to an offer, his silence and inaction operate as an acceptance in the following cases only:

(a) Where an offeree takes the benefit of offered services with reasonable opportunity to reject them and reason to know that they were offered with the expectation of compensation.

(b) Where the offeror has stated or given the offeree reason to understand that assent may be manifested by silence or inaction, and the offeree in remaining silent and inactive intends to accept the offer.

(c) Where because of previous dealings or otherwise, it is reasonable that the offeree should notify the offeror if he does not intend to accept.

property might be manifested by silence or inaction, and the evidence does not show that Madden, by remaining silent and inactive intended to accept Vogt's offer. Id. § 69(1)(b).

Finally, the exception arising from "previous dealings" between the parties is inapposite. In their prior dealings, 1979 and 1980, the parties expressly reached oral agreements for sharecropping the farm. After completion of the contract for 1979, a new contract for 1980 did not automatically follow. It was preceded by discussions between Vogt and Madden resulting in an express understanding that Vogt could farm the property in 1980 on a sharecrop basis. We do not believe those previous transactions could give rise to a legitimate conclusion that Vogt's offer to farm the property in 1981 would be accepted in the absence of affirmative notification from Madden that the offer would not be accepted. To the contrary, the previous dealings always resulted in a contract only when both parties expressly agreed.

Absent the applicability of the exceptions stated in Restatement § 69, it is a general rule of law that silence and inaction, or mere silence or failure to reject an offer when it is made, does not constitute an acceptance of the offer. See generally 17 Am.Jur.2d, Contracts § 47, at 385–86 (1964); J. Calamari and J. Perillo, The Law of Contracts § 2–21, at 63–68 (1977). Because none of the exceptions is applicable in this case, we conclude as a matter of law that no contract to sharecrop the Maddens' property in 1981 was created by Madden's silence in response to Vogt's offer to farm the property. We therefore set aside that portion of the judgment awarding damages to the Vogts based on the alleged 1981 contract. . . .

The judgment is reversed in respect to award of any damages for breach of the alleged 1981 contract. . . .

Swanstrom, J., concurs. Burnett, J., voted to grant the petition for rehearing.

————

RESTATEMENT, SECOND, CONTRACTS § 69

[See Selected Source Materials Supplement]

————

CISG ART. 18(1), (3)

[See Selected Source Materials Supplement]

————

UNIDROIT PRINCIPLES OF INTERNATIONAL COMMERCIAL CONTRACTS ART. 2.1.6(3)

[See Selected Source Materials Supplement]

————

PRINCIPLES OF EUROPEAN CONTRACT LAW ART. 2.204(2)

[See Selected Source Materials Supplement]

LAUREL RACE COURSES v. REGAL CONST. CO., 274 Md. 142, 333 A.2d 319 (1975). Regal agreed to construct a racetrack for Laurel. Disputes arose concerning the quality of the track, and Regal did additional work. Regal's president claimed that when he met with Laurel's president in an effort to resolve their disputes, he proposed that if the additional work turned out to be necessitated by defective workmanship on Regal's part, Regal would absorb the cost, but if the additional work was occasioned for any other reason, Regal would be paid for the work on a cost-plus basis. Regal's president conceded that this proposal was greeted with silence, but insists that the silence was taken by everyone present as Laurel's assent. Regal immediately ordered men and equipment onto the job, and though Laurel was aware that the work was in progress, it never rejected the proposal. Held, Laurel was bound to the terms that Regal had proposed:

> The question presented here, therefore is whether estoppel based upon silence is sufficient to constitute assent. As a general rule, mere silence will not raise an estoppel. . . . Where, however, the circumstances are such as to require a silent party to speak, so that an injured party may take steps to protect himself against a loss which might otherwise result, the silent party will be estopped from asserting the defense he would have had but for his silence. . . .

> This principle has been approved by the commentators and text writers. See, e. g., 1 Williston on Contracts, § 91 (3rd Edition 1957); 1 Corbin on Contracts, § 75 (1963); Restatement of Contracts, 2d, § 72 (1973). These authorities recognize, as one of the limited exceptions to the general rule that silence does not operate as an acceptance of an offer, this proposition: Where the offeree with reasonable opportunity to reject offered services takes the benefit of them under circumstances which would indicate to a reasonable person that they were offered with the expectation of compensation, he assents to the terms proposed and thus accepts the offer. This principle is clearly applicable here; therefore, an oral contract was created.

COLE–McINTYRE–NORFLEET CO. v. HOLLOWAY

Supreme Court of Tennessee, 1919.
141 Tenn. 679, 214 S.W. 817, 7 A.L.R. 1683.

LANDSDEN, C.J. This case presents a question of law, which, so far as we are advised, has not been decided by this court in its exact phases. March 26, 1917, a traveling salesman of plaintiff in error [the defendant originally] solicited and received from defendant in error [the plaintiff originally], at his country store in Shelby county, Tenn., an order for certain goods, which he was authorized to sell. Among these goods were 50 barrels of meal. The meal was to be ordered out by defendant in error by the 31st day of July, and afterwards 5 cents per barrel per month was to be charged him for storage.

After the order was given, the defendant in error heard nothing from it until the 26th of May, 1917, when he was in the place of business of plaintiff in error, and told it to begin shipment of the meal on his contract. He was informed by plaintiff in error that it did not accept the order of March 26th, and for that reason the defendant had no contract for meal.

The defendant in error never received confirmation or rejection from plaintiff in error, or other refusal to fill the order. The same traveling salesman of plaintiff in error called on defendant as often as once each week, and this order was not mentioned to defendant, either by him or by his principals, in any way. Between the day of the order and the 26th of May, the day of its alleged rejection, prices on all of the articles in the contract greatly advanced. All of the goods advanced about 50 per cent in value.

Some jobbers at Memphis received orders from their drummers, and filled the orders or notified the purchaser that the orders were rejected; but this method was not followed by plaintiff in error.

The contract provided that it was not binding until accepted by the seller at its office in Memphis, and that the salesman had no authority to sign the contract for either the seller or buyer. It was further stipulated that the order should not be subject to countermand.

It will be observed that plaintiff in error was silent upon both the acceptance and rejection of the contract. It sent forth its salesman to solicit this and other orders. The defendant in error did not have the right to countermand orders and the contract was closed, if and when it was accepted by plaintiff in error. The proof that some jobbers in Memphis uniformly filled such orders unless the purchaser was notified to the contrary is of no value because it does not amount to a custom.

The case, therefore, must be decided upon its facts. The circuit court and the court of civil appeals were both of opinion that the contract was completed because of the lapse of time before plaintiff in error rejected it. The time intervening between the giving of the order by defendant and its alleged repudiation by plaintiff in error was about 60 days. Weekly opportunities were afforded the salesman of plaintiff in error to notify the defendant in error of the rejection of the contract, and, of course, daily occasions were afforded plaintiff in error to notify him by mail or wire. The defendant believed the contract was in force on the 26th of May, because he directed plaintiff in error to begin shipment of the meal on that day. Such shipments were to have been completed by July 31st, or defendant to pay storage charges. From this evidence the circuit court found as an inference of fact that plaintiff in error had not acted within a reasonable time, and therefore its silence would be construed as an acceptance of the contract. The question of whether the delay of plaintiff in error was reasonable or unreasonable was one of fact, and the circuit court was justified from the evidence in finding that the delay was unreasonable. Hence the case, as it comes to us, is whether delay upon the part of plaintiff in error for an unreasonable time in notifying the defendant in error of its action upon the contract is an acceptance of its terms.

We think such delay was unreasonable, and effected an acceptance of the contract. It should not be forgotten that this is not the case of an agent exceeding his authority, or acting without authority. Even in such cases the principal must accept or reject the benefits of the contract promptly and within a reasonable time. Williams v. Storm, 6 Cold. 207.

Plaintiff's agent in this case was authorized to do precisely that which he did do, both as to time and substance. The only thing which was left open by the contract was the acceptance or rejection of its terms by plaintiff in error. It will not do to say that a seller of goods like these could wait indefinitely to decide whether or not he will accept the offer of the proposed buyer. This was all done in the usual course of business, and the articles embraced within the contract were consumable in the use, and some of them would become unfitted for the market within a short time.

It is undoubtedly true that an offer to buy or sell is not binding until its acceptance is communicated to the other party. The acceptance, however, of such an offer, may be communicated by the other party either by a formal acceptance, or acts amounting to an acceptance. Delay in communicating action as to the acceptance may amount to an acceptance itself. When the subject of a contract, either in its nature or by virtue of conditions of the market, will become unmarketable by delay, delay in notifying the other party of his decision will amount to an acceptance by the offerer [offeree?] Otherwise, the offerer [offeree?] could place his goods upon the market, and solicit orders, and yet hold the other party to the contract, while he reserves time to himself to see if the contract will be profitable.

Writ denied.

Response to Petition to Rehear.

An earnest petition to rehear has been filed, and we have re-examined the question with great care. The petition quotes the text of 13 Corpus Juris, p. 276, as follows:

"An offer made to another, either orally or in writing, cannot be turned into an agreement because the person to whom it is made or sent makes no reply, even though the offer states that silence will be taken as consent, for the offerer cannot prescribe conditions of rejection, so as to turn silence on the part of the offeree into acceptance."

And further:

"In like manner mere delay in accepting or rejecting an offer cannot make an agreement." . . .

It is a general principle of the law of contracts that, while an assent to an offer is requisite to the formation of an agreement, yet such assent is a condition of the mind, and may be either express or evidenced by circumstances from which the assent may be inferred. Hartford et al. v. Jackson, 24 Conn. 514, 63 Am.Dec. 177; 6 Ruling Case Law, 605; 13 Corpus Juris, 276, 9 Cyc. 258. And see the cases cited in the notes of these authorities. They all agree that acceptance of an offer may be inferred from silence. This is only where the circumstances surrounding the parties afford a basis from which an inference may be drawn from silence. There must be the right and the duty to speak, before the failure to do so can prevent a person from afterwards setting up the truth. We think it is the duty of a wholesale merchant, who sends out his drummers to solicit orders for perishable articles, and articles consumable in the use, to notify his customers within a reasonable time that the orders are not accepted; and if he fails to do so, and the proof shows that he had ample opportunity, silence for an unreasonable length of time will amount to an acceptance, if the offerer is relying upon him for the goods.

The petition to rehear is denied.

———

KUKUSKA v. HOME MUT. HAIL–TORNADO INS. CO., 204 Wis. 166, 235 N.W. 403 (1931). On July 3, Kukuska, a farmer, applied to an agent of the Home Mutual Hail–Tornado Insurance Company for hail insurance. Kukuska received no communication from the company or its agent until 11 A.M. on August 1, when he was informed that his application was declined. That afternoon, Kukuska's crops were severely damaged by hail. "Other insurance companies were writing hail insurance, and, if the plaintiff had been notified of the rejection of his application within a reasonable time, he could have protected himself against such loss. It is well known that the months of July and August constitute the most hazardous period for hail-storms in the locality where plaintiff's crops were situated." Kukuska brought suit against the company for the loss occasioned by the hailstorm. Held, for Kukuska:

> It is significant that the insured does not take the first step in the process which leads to the making of a contract of insurance.... [The insurer in this case] required the application to be made upon blanks furnished by it. By the terms of the application, which was required to be made according to the by-laws, the applicant agreed to pay all just assessments and to be governed and abide by the rules, regulations, and by-laws of the company. He was required to pay the amount of the premium in advance. If the application were accepted, he agreed that the policy should run from the date of the application, July 2, 1928, rather than from the date of the acceptance when made. By the soliciting, making and receiving of the application, the parties had entered into some kind of a consensual relationship....

> Under such circumstances, having in view the nature of the risk against which the insurer seeks protection, is there not a duty upon the insurer to act upon the application within a reasonable time? Can the insurer, having preempted the field, retain control of the situation and the applicant's funds indefinitely? Does not the very nature of the transaction impose upon the insurer a duty to act? It is considered that there is a duty. If the insurer is under such a duty and fails to perform the duty within a reasonable time and, as a consequence, the applicant sustains damage, it is not vastly important that the legal relationship be placed in a particular category. If we say it is contractual, that is, there is an implied agreement under the circumstances on the part of the insurer to act within a reasonable time, or, having a duty to act, the insurer negligently fails in the performance of that duty, or that the duty springs out of a consensual relationship, and is therefore in the nature of a quasi contractual liability, is not vitally important. Each view finds some support in the cases....

HOBBS v. MASSASOIT WHIP CO., 158 Mass. 194, 33 N.E. 495 (1893). Without receiving any specific order for them, the plaintiff had on four or five occasions shipped eelskins to the defendant, for which the defendant had paid. The plaintiff then shipped further eelskins. The defendant retained these eelskins for some months without communicating with the plaintiff, but after a destruction of the skins, the defendant refused to pay for them. The plaintiff sued for the price of the skins. Held, for the plaintiff. The past dealings of the parties were such that the plaintiff had a kind of "standing offer" for eelskins. "... Even if the offer was not such that the contract was made as soon as skins corresponding to its terms were sent, sending them did impose on the defendant a duty to act about them; and silence on its part, coupled with a retention of the skins for an unreasonable time, might be found by the jury to warrant the plaintiff in assuming that they were accepted, and thus to amount to an acceptance."

————

LOUISVILLE TIN & STOVE CO. v. LAY, 251 Ky. 584, 65 S.W.2d 1002 (1933). Mrs. Lay operated Lay's Variety Store. Her husband, who was insolvent and without credit, operated an independent business known as Lay's Electric Shop. Mr. Lay ordered goods from the plaintiff to be consigned to Lay's Variety Store. When Mrs. Lay was informed that the goods consigned to her store had arrived at the railway depot, she "became angry and said it was her husband's doings." Mrs. Lay directed a drayman to take the goods from the depot to Lay's Electric Shop. Held, when Mrs. Lay assumed control over the disposition of the goods, her acts constituted an acceptance of the shipment, and she became liable to the plaintiff for the price of the goods.

————

AUSTIN v. BURGE, 156 Mo.App. 286, 137 S.W. 618 (1911). This was an action for the subscription price of a newspaper. The defendant's father-in-law had given him a two-year subscription to the newspaper, but the publisher continued mailing the newspaper to defendant after the subscription expired. The defendant twice paid bills for the subscription price, but each time he directed the newspaper to be stopped. The publisher nevertheless continued to mail the newspaper to the defendant, and the defendant continued to receive and read the newspaper, until finally he moved to another state. The trial court gave judgment for the defendant. Reversed:

> It is certain that one cannot be forced into contractual relations with another and that therefore he cannot, against his will, be made the debtor of a newspaper publisher. But it is equally certain that he may cause contractual relations to arise by necessary implication from his conduct.... In this case defendant admits that, notwithstanding he ordered the paper discontinued at the time when he paid a bill for it, yet plaintiff continued to send it, and he continued to take it from the post office to his home. This was an acceptance and use of the property, and, there being no pretense that a gratuity was intended, an obligation arose to pay for it....

> The preparation and publication of a newspaper involves much mental and physical labor, as well as an outlay of money. One who accepts the paper, by continuously taking it from the post office, receives a benefit and pleasure arising from such labor and expenditure as fully as

if he had appropriated any other product of another's labor, and by such act he must be held liable for the subscription price.

---

39 U.S.C. § 3009 [MAILING OF UNORDERED MERCHANDISE]

[See Selected Source Materials Supplement]

NOTE ON NEGATIVE–OPTION PLANS

A promotional technique that is similar in some respects to the sending of unordered merchandise is the negative-option plan. This type of plan is defined in a Federal Trade Commission rule to mean "a contractual plan or arrangement under which a seller periodically sends to subscribers an announcement which identifies merchandise (other than annual supplements to previously acquired merchandise) it proposes to send to subscribers to such plan, and the subscribers thereafter receive and are billed for the merchandise identified in each such announcement, unless by a date or within a time specified by the seller with respect to each such announcement the subscribers, in conformity with the provisions of such plan, instruct the seller not to send the identified merchandise." 16 C.F.R. § 425.1. Among the most familiar examples are book and record clubs. In contract-law terms, negative-option plans differ significantly from the sending of unordered merchandise, because the consumer normally contracts in advance, for consideration (in the form of a "bonus" for joining), to be bound by the plan's terms. The FTC's rule does not prohibit such plans. Instead, the rule requires clear disclosure of the plan's material terms, and imposes certain minimal regulation, such as a requirement that the subscriber be given at least ten days in which to instruct the seller not to mail the selection.

NOTE ON THE SIGNIFICANCE OF UNJUST ENRICHMENT AND LOSS THROUGH RELIANCE IN CASES WHERE SILENCE IS TREATED AS ACCEPTANCE

Three kinds of cases in which an offeree remains silent after receiving an offer may be distinguished: (1) Cases where the offeree silently appropriates to himself the benefit of something offered to him. (2) Cases where the offeror changes her position either (a) because she assumes that her offer has been accepted, or (b) because, as in the *Kukuska* case, supra, the very act of making the offer requires her to forgo other opportunities of covering her needs. (3) Cases where there is no enrichment of the offeree, and no detrimental reliance by the offeror, but where the offeror forms an expectation of profit on the assumption that a contract has been concluded through the offeree's silence. Assuming that the facts bearing on the apparent meaning of silence are in other respects the same in all three situations, it is clear that a court will be more likely to give relief in (1) than in (2), and that (2) in turn makes a stronger appeal to judicial sympathy than (3). The problem of silence as acceptance is analyzed in these terms in Laufer, Silence as Acceptance: A Critique, 1939, 7 Duke Bar Ass'n Jour. 87.

SECTION 7. ACCEPTANCE BY ELECTRONIC AGENT

Until several years ago, it may have been open to question whether an electronic writing and an electronic signature satisfied the Statute of Frauds. That issue has now been resolved by the Uniform Electronic Transactions Act ("VETA") and the Electronic Signatures in Global and National Communications Act ("E–Sign"), both of which validate electronic records and signatures for Statute of Frauds purposes.

One form of electronic commerce is known as EDI. The term "EDI" (Electronic Data Intercharge) refers to a method by which business data can be communicated electronically between computers in standardized formats. These formats can include purchase orders, invoices (bills), shipping notices, and all other types of documents routinely used in sales transactions.

Transmissions of EDI messages may be made either directly between the parties or through "Providers". Providers are businesses that serve as a channel of communication for EDI transmissions, and function as electronic-mail-processing systems. They may maintain electronic mailboxes, into which communications of trading partners can be placed. They may also interconnect with other Providers to permit communications between the providers' respective customers.

Here is an example of the manner in which EDI frequently is implemented to effect commercial sales transactions:

ABC and XYZ have a long-standing purchase and sale relationship. Recognizing the economic and administrative benefits attributed to EDI, ABC announces to its vendors, including XYZ, that ABC will require, or provide incentives for, the use of EDI in future transactions. ABC engages a [Provider] to receive, transmit, and sort the various EDI transmissions of ABC. In addition, ABC determines which paper-based documents will be replaced by EDI formats, as well as which industry standards will be adopted around which all transmissions will be structured, and implements certain security procedures for assuring the authenticity and integrity of the electronic communications. All of this information is communicated to ABC's vendors, one of which is XYZ, who must implement EDI accordingly to keep ABC's business (or obtain the available incentives, as the case may be) ...

In a fully automated EDI environment, trading partners have developed applications software programs which eliminate human decision making with respect to particular transactions. For example, in the event that reported inventory reaches a certain level, ABC's computer might automatically generate an appropriate purchase order, including terms as to price, quantity, and similar items predefined to be within the parameters of the business relationship with XYZ. Similarly, XYZ's computer may be programmed to automatically accept any purchase order whose terms fall within predefined parameters. This process may be sufficient, if fully established, to permit ordering, shipping, invoicing, and payment to occur electronically, with human review and intervention, if it occurs at all, limited to supervisory summaries of daily activity.

Electronic Messaging Task Force, The Commercial Use of Electronic Data Interchange—A Report and Model Trading Partner Agreement, 45 Bus.Law. 1645, 1655–57 (1990).

UETA and E–SIGN make clear that contracts can be formed by communications between a person and a computer, or even between two computers. For example, Comments 2 and 5 to UETA § 3 (Definitions) state:

2. "Automated Transaction."

An automated transaction is a transaction performed or conducted by electronic means in which machines are used without human intervention to form contracts and perform obligations under existing contracts. Such broad coverage is necessary because of the diversity of transactions to which this Act may apply.

As with electronic agents, this definition addresses the circumstance where electronic records may result in action or performance by a party although no human review of the electronic records is anticipated. Section 14 provides specific rules to assure that where one or both parties do not review the electronic records, the resulting agreement will be effective.

The critical element in this definition is the lack of a human actor on one or both sides of a transaction. For example, if one orders books from Bookseller.com through Bookseller's website, the transaction would be an automated transaction because Bookseller took and confirmed the order via its machine. Similarly, if Automaker and supplier do business through Electronic Data Interchange, Automaker's computer, upon receiving information within certain pre-programmed parameters, will send an electronic order to supplier's computer. If Supplier's computer confirms the order and processes the shipment because the order falls within pre-programmed parameters in Supplier's computer, this would be a fully automated transaction. If, instead, the Supplier relies on a human employee to review, accept, and process the Buyer's order, then only the Automaker's side of the transaction would be automated. In either case, the entire transaction falls within this definition.

5. "Electronic agent."

This definition establishes that an electronic agent is a machine ...

An electronic agent, such as a computer program or other automated means employed by a person, is a tool of that person. As a general rule, the employer of a tool is responsible for the results obtained by the use of that tool since the tool has no independent volition of its own. However, an electronic agent, by definition, is capable within the parameters of its programming, of initiating, responding or interacting with other parties or their electronic agents once it has been activated by a party, without further attention of that party.

While this Act proceeds on the paradigm that an electronic agent is capable of performing only within the technical strictures of its preset programming, it is conceivable that, within the useful life of this Act, electronic agents may be created with the ability to act autonomously, and not just automatically. That is, through developments in artificial intelligence, a computer may be able to "learn through experience, modify the instructions in their own programs, and even devise new instructions." Allen and Widdison, "Can Computers Make Contracts?" *9 Harv. J.L. & Tech 25* (Winter, 1996). If such developments occur, courts may construe the definition of electronic agent accordingly, in order to recognize such new capabilities.

The examples involving Bookseller.com and Automaker in the Comment to the definition of Automated Transaction are equally applicable here. Bookseller acts through an electronic agent in processing an order for books. Automaker and the supplier each act through electronic agents in facilitating and effectuating the just-in-time inventory process through EDI.

A contract or other record relating to a transaction in or affecting interstate or foreign commerce may not be denied legal effect, validity, or enforceability solely because its formation, creation, or delivery involved the action of one or more electronic agents so long as the action of any such electronic agent is legally attributable to the person to be bound.

———

Chapter 13

IMPLIED–IN–LAW AND IMPLIED–IN–FACT CONTRACTS; UNILATERAL CONTRACTS REVISITED

NURSING CARE SERVICES, INC. v. DOBOS

District Court of Appeal of Florida, Fourth District, 1980.
380 So.2d 516.

HURLEY, JUDGE.

Plaintiff, Nursing Care Services, Inc., appeals from that part of a final judgment which disallowed compensation for certain nursing care services. Our review of the record reveals substantial uncontradicted testimony supporting plaintiff's theory of recovery and thus we remand for entry of an amended final judgment.

Mary Dobos, the defendant, was admitted to Boca Raton Community Hospital with an abdominal aneurysm. Her condition was sufficiently serious to cause her doctor to order around-the-clock nursing care. The hospital implemented this order by calling upon the plaintiff which provides individualized nursing services.

Mrs. Dobos received nursing care which in retrospect can be divided into three periods: (1) two weeks of in-hospital care; (2) forty-eight hour post-release care; and (3) two weeks of at-home care. The second period of care (the forty-eight hour post-release care) was removed as an issue at trial when Mrs. Dobos conceded that she or her daughter authorized that period of care. The total bill for all three periods came to $3,723.90; neither the reasonableness of the fee, the competency of the nurses, nor the necessity for the services was contested at trial.

The gist of the defense was that Mrs. Dobos never signed a written contract nor orally agreed to be liable for the nursing services. Testifying about the in-hospital care, she said, "Dr. Rosen did all the work. I don't know what he done (sic), and he says, I needed a nurse." It is undisputed that Mrs. Dobos was mentally alert during her at-home recuperation period. Asked if she ever tried to fire the nurses or dispense with their care, she replied, "I didn't. I didn't know who—I thought maybe if they insist, the doctors insist so much, I thought the Medicare would take care of it, or whatever. I don't know."

After a non-jury trial, the court granted judgment for the plaintiff in the sum of $248.00, the cost of the forty-eight hour post-release care. It declined to allow compensation for the first and third periods of care, saying,

"... [T]here certainly was a service rendered, but based on the total surrounding circumstances, I don't think there is sufficient communications and dealings with Mrs. Dobos to make sure that she knew that she would be responsible for those services rendered...."

We concur in the trial court's determination that the plaintiff failed to prove an express contract or a contract implied in fact. It is our view, however, that the uncontradicted testimony provided by plaintiff and defendant alike, clearly established a contract implied in law which entitles the plaintiff to recover.

Contracts implied in law, or as they are more commonly called "quasi contracts", are obligations imposed by law on grounds of justice and equity. Their purpose is to prevent unjust enrichment. Unlike express contracts or contracts implied in fact, quasi contracts do not rest upon the assent of the contracting parties. See generally, 28 Fla.Jur., Restitution and Implied Contracts.

One of the most common areas in which recovery on a contract implied in law is allowed is that of work performed or services rendered. The rationale is that the defendant would be unjustly enriched at the expense of the plaintiff if she were allowed to escape payment for services rendered or work performed. There is, however, an important limitation. Ordinarily liability is imposed to pay for services rendered by another only when the person for whose benefit they were rendered requested the services or knowingly and voluntarily accepted their benefits. *Yeats v. Moody,* 128 Fla. 658, 175 So. 719 (1937); *Strano v. Carr & Carr, Inc.,* 97 Fla. 150, 119 So. 864 (1929); *Taylor v. Thompson,* 359 So.2d 14 (Fla. 1st DCA 1978); and *Tobin & Tobin Insurance Agency, Inc. v. Zeskind,* 315 So.2d 518 (Fla. 3d DCA 1975).

The law's concern that needless services not be foisted upon the unsuspecting has led to the formulation of the "officious intermeddler doctrine." It holds that where a person performs labor for another without the latter's request or implied consent, however beneficial such labor may be, he cannot recover therefor. *Tipper v. Great Lakes Chemical Company,* 281 So.2d 10 (Fla.1973). A notable exception to this rule, however, is that of emergency aid:

A person who has supplied things or services to another, although acting without the other's knowledge or consent, is entitled to restitution therefore from the other if he acted unofficiously and with intent to charge therefore, and the things or services were necessary to prevent the other from suffering serious bodily harm or pain, and the person supplying them had no reason to know that the other would not consent to receiving them, if mentally competent, and it was impossible for the other to give consent or, because of extreme youth or mental impairment, the other's consent would have been immaterial. 66 Am.Jur.2d, Restitution and Implied Contract, § 23.

In the case at bar it is unclear whether Mrs. Dobos, during the period of in-hospital care, understood or intended that compensation be paid. Her condition was grave. She had been placed in the hospital's intensive care unit and thereafter had tubes and other medical equipment attached to her body which necessitated special attention. She was alone, unable to cope and without family assistance. It is worthy of note that at no point during the litigation was there any question as to the propriety of the professional judgment that the patient required special nursing care. To the contrary, the record demonstrates that the in-hospital nursing care was essential to Mrs. Dobos' health and safety. Given these circumstances it would be unconscionable to deny the plaintiff recovery for services which fall squarely within the emergency aid exception. *Tipper v. Great Lakes Chemical Company,* supra.

The third period of care is less difficult. It is unquestioned that during the at-home recuperation, Mrs. Dobos was fully aware of her circumstances and readily accepted the benefits conferred. Given such facts, we believe the rule set down in *Symon v. J. Rolfe Davis, Inc.,* 245 So.2d 278, 279 (Fla. 4th DCA 1971) must govern:

> It is well settled that where services are rendered by one person for another which are knowingly and voluntarily accepted, the law presumes that such services are given and received in expectation of being paid for, and will imply a promise to pay what they are reasonably worth.

A patient's unannounced misconception that the cost of accepted services will be paid by an insurer or Medicare does not absolve her of responsibility to bear the cost of the services.

As a postscript we note that Mrs. Dobos' home recuperation was interrupted by her readmission to the hospital with an apparent heart attack. In this age of burgeoning malpractice actions it is not idle conjecture to ponder what her legal position might have been had the plaintiff unilaterally terminated its services at a time of vital need. To its credit, it did not and therefore it is entitled to just compensation. Accordingly, we remand the cause to the trial court with instructions to enter an amended final judgment for the plaintiff in the sum of $3,723.90 plus interest and court costs.

It is so ordered.

ANSTEAD and LETTS, JJ., concur.

SCEVA v. TRUE, 53 N.H. 627 (1873), "We regard it as well settled by the cases referred to in the briefs of counsel, many of which have been commented on at length by Mr. Shirley for the defendant, that an insane person, an idiot, or a person utterly bereft of all sense and reason by the sudden stroke of accident or disease, may be held liable, in assumpsit, for necessaries furnished to him in good faith while in that unfortunate and helpless condition. And the reasons upon which this rests are too broad, as well as too sensible and humane, to be overborne by any deductions which a refined logic may make from the circumstance that in such cases there can be no contract or promise in fact,—no meeting of the minds of the parties. The cases put it on the ground of an implied contract; and by this is not meant, as the defendant's counsel seems to suppose, an actual contract,—that is, an actual meeting of the minds of the parties, an actual, mutual understanding, to be inferred from language, acts, and circumstances, by the jury,—but a contract and promise, said to be implied by the law, where, in point of fact, there was no contract, no mutual understanding, and so no promise. The defendant's counsel says it is usurpation for the court to hold, as matter of law, that there is a contract and a promise, when all the evidence in the case shows that there was not a contract, nor the semblance of one. It is doubtless a legal fiction, invented and used for the sake of the remedy. If it was originally usurpation, certainly it has now become very inveterate, and firmly fixed in the body of the law."

NOTE ON TERMINOLOGY

Three overlapping terms are used in the law to denote cases that involve a recovery based on benefit conferred: restitution, unjust enrichment, and quasi-contract. Because the terms are often used in an imprecise manner, any attempt at precision is somewhat artificial. Within that constraint, however, the following definitions are generally consistent with modern usage:

Unjust enrichment is the general principle that one person should not be unjustly enriched at another's expense.

Restitution has two meanings.

First, restitution is a catchall *substantive* term to describe the body of specific rules that give effect to the principle that one person should not be enriched at another's expense. A typical example would be a case where plaintiff had paid money to defendant by mistake (for example, an overpayment in a settlement of accounts, resulting from a mistake in addition), both parties assuming that the amount paid was the amount actually due. Here defendant has neither committed a tort (the payment was voluntary and there was no fraud), nor expressly or impliedly promised to repay the mistaken overpayment. Certainly, however, she should be required to do so.

Second, restitution is a catchall *remedial* term to describe *remedies* based on a right to recover on the ground of unjust enrichment.

Quasi-contract ("as if it were a contract") is the name given to describe actions at law, as opposed to actions in equity, that are based on unjust enrichment. Those actions are called by a name that includes the word "contract," even though there is often nothing contractual about them, because for historical reasons, discussed in the following Note, the actions were originally brought under a writ, known as assumpsit, that was basically contractual. In general it is said that a quasi-contractual obligation will be imposed when—but only when—two factors are present in the case: (1) the defendant has received a benefit, and (2) retention of the benefit is inequitable. See Woodward, The Law of Quasi Contracts § 7 (1913). Thus, if Uncle freely gives Nephew $1000, he cannot, on later repenting of his generosity, recover the sum given. Nephew has been benefited, but his retention of the benefit is not unjust, because he received the benefit as a gift. Or suppose Meddle decides that the house of his neighbor, Peel, is in need of a coat of paint. During Peel's absence, and without consulting him, Meddle paints the house, and later brings a suit for the value of his services. Peel has perhaps been benefited, but his retention of the benefit would probably not be regarded as unjust, because the benefit was thrust upon Peel without his consent and under circumstances offering no justification for Meddle's interference in Peel's affairs.

NOTE ON IMPLIED–IN–FACT AND IMPLIED– IN–LAW CONTRACTS

In principle, there is a sharp distinction between implied-in-fact and implied-in-law contracts. An *implied-in-fact* contract is a true contract, which differs from a run-of-the-mill contract only in the fact that the parties' assent, while real, is implicit rather than explicit. For example, a winning bidder at an auction, who made her bid by raising her hand, may be said to have made an implied-in-fact contract: the bidder did not expressly say "I bid," or "I offer," or the like, but that is what is implied when she raised her hand in the context of an auction. Or suppose that every day Janet Jones passes a produce store and buys an apple for lunch. One day Jones is in a hurry to catch her bus, so she takes an apple from a bin outside the store, catches the owner's eye, waves the apple at him, and runs off. Here Jones has not explicitly said "I am buying an apple from you, which I will pay for later," but that is implied.

In contrast, an *implied-in-law* contract is not a contract at all. Instead, it is a label given to certain kinds of conduct that gives rise to liability for unjust enrichment. In large part, contract terminology is applied to such cases only as a result of legal history. At an early time, the English common law settled into a *formulary* system. Under this system, a plaintiff could obtain a judicial remedy only if the transaction giving rise to his grievance came within (or could, through a legal fiction, be made to come within) an established form of action or *writ*. Originally, there were only two writs for actions in contract, covenant and debt: *Covenant* could be brought for cases in which the contract was under seal. *Debt* could be brought for cases in which the plaintiff had fully performed a contract that involved (i) a quid pro quo and (ii) a promise to pay a "sum certain," which the defendant had refused to pay. Accordingly, covenant was a *formal* contract action, because it was based on a form—the seal—while debt was an action based on a *half-completed exchange*.

Covenant and debt were burdened with archaic procedures, and were gradually superseded by a new form of action, known as *assumpsit*. Assumpsit had two advantages over debt and covenant. First, it was not burdened with archaic procedures. Second, it was not restricted to contracts under seal or half-completed exchanges, but instead was potentially applicable to all contracts. See Appendix B. At least in the beginning, however, assumpsit apparently had to be based on an express promise.

Because the procedural elements of the old forms of action were archaic, there was constant pressure to expand assumpsit at their expense. Blocking the path of such expansion was a supposed early common-law rule that the same set of facts could not give rise to more than one form of action. Under this rule, if A refused to pay for goods that B had delivered to A pursuant to a contract of sale, the action of debt would lie, and therefore assumpsit would not. But a way was developed to bypass this roadblock. It came to be held, during the sixteenth century, that if a debtor, *after* her debt had been incurred, made a *new* express promise to pay the debt, the action of debt would not lie on the new promise, because there was no "quid pro quo." Since an action of debt would not lie, an action of assumpsit could lie. This action was called *indebitatus assumpsit*, after the key allegation in the complaint, which was that defendant, already being indebted, made a new undertaking (promise) to pay the debt.

A comparable development led to the use of indebitatus assumpsit where a person had made an implied-in-fact promise to pay for a benefit and later made an express promise to pay. For example, suppose that a tailor, at the request of his customer, made and delivered a suit, there being no agreement on the amount the customer would pay. Here the tailor could not bring an action of covenant, because there was no promise under seal; could not bring an action of debt, because there was no "sum certain"; and, at first, could not bring an action of assumpsit, because there was no express promise by the customer—although such a promise could readily be implied in fact, since it is implicit in the customer's request. That being so, the tailor was left remediless. Of this result, Ames wrote, "The lawyer of today, familiar with the ethical character of the law as now administered, can hardly fail to be startled when he discovers how slowly the conception of a promise implied in fact, as the equivalent of an express promise, made its way in our law."

The injustice of denying a remedy to one in the tailor's position was so manifest that it could be expected that the English courts would, despite the restrictions of the formulary system, find some way of protecting his interest. For understandable reasons, the development occurred along the following lines: It was first held that if the customer *later* made an express promise to pay a certain amount, this promise could be enforced in assumpsit—the benefit conferred in the past, at the customer's request, being treated as consideration for this promise. For some time, it was held that assumpsit would not lie against a debtor who had *not* made a separate and later promise to pay her debt, "for if he assumed at the time of the contract then debt lies, and not assumpsit; but if he assumed after the contract, then an action lies upon the assumpsit." (Manwood, C.B. in Anon., Dailson 84 pl. 35, 1572.) However, the pressure for a more complete release from the archaic restrictions of the action of debt continued, and was reinforced by the desire of the King's Bench court to increase its powers by expanding the scope of assumpsit (that court being excluded from jurisdiction over actions in debt). Accordingly, King's Bench began to allow assumpsit in cases where the action of debt would lie, even in the absence of a later promise by the debtor to pay.

This attempt to relieve the plaintiff in assumpsit from the burden of proving a later promise was for a while thwarted by the Exchequer Chamber, but finally "all the justices of England" were brought together to consider *Slade's Case* (4 Coke 92b.), and decided, in 1602, that the practice of King's Bench should be upheld. To bring this result within the cover of previous practice, it became customary after *Slade's Case* to include an allegation in the complaint that the defendant *being indebted, undertook to pay* ("indebitatus assumpsit"). The allegation that the defendant had made a new promise to pay was treated as a legal fiction, which the defendant was not permitted to deny and the plaintiff was not required to prove. However, the defendant could deny that the transaction that was claimed to be the basis of the defendant's obligation occurred, or could argue that even if the transaction did occur, it gave rise to no legal obligation. These developments are elaborated upon in Appendix C.

Once the later promise was treated as a fiction, the way was open to bringing the principle of unjust enrichment within assumpsit. The plaintiff would allege that: (1) As a result of certain conduct (for example, the payment of money to the defendant by mistake), the defendant had been unjustly enriched at the plaintiff's expense; and (2) the defendant had thereafter promised to pay the plaintiff the amount of this enrichment. The defendant could deny that the conduct described in the first allegation had occurred, or could deny that the conduct resulted in the defendant's being unjustly enriched. However, the defendant was not permitted to deny the second allegation, that the defendant had later made a new promise to pay, because that allegation was fictional. Hence the name *contracts implied in law*, that is, transactions that are *not* contractual but are brought in assumpsit—a contract action—through the legal fiction that the defendant made a new promise to pay the amount by which she had been unjustly enriched.

Although implied-in-fact and implied-in-law contracts are clearly distinguishable in principle, and although strictly speaking implied-in-law contracts are not contracts at all, nevertheless there are strong connections between implied-in-law contracts and implied-in-fact contracts. First, in practice it is sometimes not easy to say whether a court is concluding that a party to a voluntary transaction gave a real although not explicit consent, giving rise to an implied-in-fact contract, or that the party is to be held liable because of an obligation imposed upon him by law, giving rise to an implied-in-law contract). Second, when a true contract (whether explicit or implied-in-fact) fails—for example, because of the Statute of Frauds—a party who had received benefits under the contract from her contracting counterparty is liable in unjust enrichment for the value of those benefits.

MARY JANE MORRISON, I IMPLY WHAT YOU INFER UNLESS YOU ARE A COURT, 35 Okla. L. Rev. 708 (1982). "The major difference between *infer* and *imply* is focus: What I imply you can infer, and what you infer is what I imply. You can infer only what is there by implication, i.e., only what follows [from my words or conduct].

"Of course, the more I *say*, the less I imply; hence, the less you can infer. Within a certain range, I leave greater room for your inferences—and multiply my implications—by not making my remarks fully explicit. There is a continuum from the explicit to the implicit, and there is a parallel continuum from the blunt remark to the too-indefinite-to-mean-anything remark. But always, what legitimates your inferring that I have said that so-and-so in saying "such-and-such" is that I have implied that so-and-so when I said "such-and-such." If we are interested in *your* role, we will talk about inferences. If we are interested in *my* role, we will talk about implications. There is merely a difference of focus here....

"A contract implied in fact simply is a contract. Compare this with a contract implied in law, a quasi-contract, which is not a contract at all. Just as the term 'quasi' sucks all the meaning out of 'contract,' so too does the phrase 'implied in law.' A quasi-contract or contract implied in law is a device courts use to avoid unjust enrichment of one of the parties. Here nothing the parties say or do implies a contract exists, and nothing the parties say or do warrants our inferring a contract exists. Whether the parties had any subjective or objective intention of contracting is irrelevant for these implied-in-law cases....

" . . . [T]he fundamental theoretical difference between contracts implied in fact and quasi-contracts is exactly a matter of who bears the ultimate responsibility for how we characterize the relationship between the parties: For contracts implied in fact, the parties themselves bear this responsibility. *They*, through their behavior, say there is an actual contract, and they thus legitimate our inference that they intended to contract. With quasi-contracts, the court bears the responsibility. The *court* imposes a contract-like remedy even when one of the parties correctly protests that he has done nothing that warrants saying he implied the existence of an actual contract. Further, any of us, individuals or courts, can make the contract-implied-in-fact inference, but only a court can find a contract implied in law."

DAY v. CATON

Supreme Judicial Court of Massachusetts, 1876.
119 Mass. 513.

Contract to recover the value of one-half of a brick party wall built by the plaintiff upon and between the adjoining estates, 27 and 29 Greenwich Park, Boston.

At the trial in the Superior Court, before Allen, J., it appeared that, in 1871, the plaintiff, having an equitable interest in lot 29, built the wall in question, placing one half of it on the vacant lot 27, in which the defendant then had an equitable interest. The plaintiff testified that there was an express agreement on the defendant's part to pay him one half the value of the wall when the defendant should use it in building upon lot 27. The defendant denied this, and testified that he never had any conversation with the plaintiff about the wall; and there was no other direct testimony on this point.

The defendant requested the judge to rule that: "(1) The plaintiff can recover in this case only upon an express agreement. (2) If the jury find there was no express agreement about the wall, but the defendant knew that the plaintiff was building upon land in which the defendant had an equitable interest, the defendant's rights would not be affected by such knowledge, and his silence and subsequent use of the wall would raise no implied promise to pay anything for the wall."

The judge refused so to rule, but instructed the jury as follows: "A promise would not be implied from the fact that the plaintiff, with the defendant's knowledge, built the wall and the defendant used it, but it might be implied from the conduct of the parties. If the jury find that the plaintiff undertook and completed the building of the wall with the expectation that the defendant would pay him for it, and the defendant had reason to know that the plaintiff was so acting with that expectation, and allowed him so to act without objection, then the jury might infer a promise on the part of the defendant to pay the plaintiff."

The jury found for the plaintiff, and the defendant alleged exceptions.

Devens, J. The ruling that a promise to pay for the wall would not be implied from the fact that the plaintiff, with the defendant's knowledge, built the wall, and that the defendant used it, was substantially in accordance with the request of the defendant, and is conceded to have been correct. Chit.Cont. (11th Ed.) 86; Wells v. Banister, 4 Mass. 514; Knowlton v. Plantation No. 4, 14 Me. 20; Davis v. School Dist., 24 Me. 349.

The [defendant], however, contends that the presiding judge incorrectly ruled that such promise might be inferred from the fact that the plaintiff undertook and completed the building of the wall with the expectation that the defendant would pay him for it, the defendant having reason to know that the plaintiff was acting with that expectation, and allowed him thus to act without objection.

The fact that the plaintiff expected to be paid for the work would certainly not be sufficient of itself to establish the existence of a contract, when the question between the parties was whether one was made. Taft v. Dickinson, 6 Allen, 553. It must be shown that in some manner the party sought to be charged assented to it. If a party, however, voluntarily accepts and avails himself of valuable services rendered for his benefit, when he has the option whether to accept or reject them, even if there is no distinct proof that they were rendered by his authority or request, a promise to pay for them may be inferred. His knowledge that they were valuable, and his exercise of the option to avail himself of them, justify this inference. Abbot v. Hermon, 7 Greenl. (Me.) 118; Hayden v. Madison, 7 Greenl. (Me.) 76. And when one stands by in silence, and sees valuable services rendered upon his real estate by the erection of a structure (of which he must necessarily avail himself afterwards in his proper use thereof), such silence, accompanied with the knowledge on his part that the party rendering the services expects payment therefor, may fairly be treated as evidence of an acceptance of it, and as tending to show an agreement to pay for it.

The maxim, "Qui tacet consentire videtur," is to be construed indeed as applying only to those cases where the circumstances are such that a party is fairly called upon either to deny or admit his liability.* But, if silence may be interpreted as assent where a proposition is made to one which he is bound to deny or admit, so also it may be if he is silent in the face of facts which fairly call upon him to speak. Lamb v. Bunce, 4 Maule & S. 275; Connor v. Hackley, 2 Metc. (Mass.) 613; Preston v. Linen Co., 119 Mass. 400.

If a person saw day after day a laborer at work in his field doing services, which must of necessity inure to his benefit, knowing that the laborer expected pay for his work, when it was perfectly easy to notify him if his services were not wanted, even if a request were not expressly proved, such a request, either previous to or contemporaneous with the performance of the services, might fairly be inferred. But if the fact was merely brought to his attention upon a single occasion and casually, if he had little opportunity to notify the other that he did not desire the work and should not pay for it, or could only do so at the expense of much time and trouble, the same inference might not be made. The circumstances of each case would necessarily determine whether silence with a knowledge that another was doing valuable work for his benefit and with the expectation of payment indicated that consent which would give rise to the inference of a contract. The question would be

---

* According to Black's Law Dictionary, the Latin maxim "Qui tacet consentire videtur, ubi tractatur de ejus commodo" means "He who is silent is considered as assenting, when his interest is at stake." (Footnote by ed.)

one for the jury, and to them it was properly submitted in the case before us by the presiding judge.

Exceptions overruled.

———

NOTE ON DAY v. CATON

Day v. Caton was decided on a contract theory. Some cases analyze fact-situations comparable to those in Day v. Caton on an unjust-enrichment theory, although the analysis and even the remedy may not differ much. An example is Sparks v. Gustafson, 750 P.2d 338 (Alaska 1988). There, Gustafson had managed the Nome Center for his friend, Sparks, until Sparks's death, and continued to manage the Center for two years after Sparks's death. Gustafson had not been compensated by either Sparks or Sparks's Estate. Gustafson sued the Estate for the value of his services. Held, for Gustafson:

... In this case Gustafson made substantial repairs and improvements to the Nome Center, provided management services that kept Nome Center operating, and paid debts incurred by Nome Center, all arguably on the Estate's behalf. There is no question that Gustafson conferred a benefit upon the Estate.

Even where a person has conferred a benefit upon another, however, he is entitled to compensation only if it would be just and equitable to require compensation under the circumstances. Restatement of the Law of Restitution § 1, comment c (1937). Courts will allow the defendant to retain a benefit without compensating plaintiff in several situations, one of which is relevant to the case at hand: where the benefit was given gratuitously without expectation of payment ..... Appellants argue that this situation is present in the case before us.

This court has not yet addressed the circumstances which give rise to a finding of gratuitous intent. A good discussion of this issue in the context of a decedent's estate can be found in Kershaw v. Tracy Collins Bank & Trust Co., 561 P.2d 683 (Utah 1977). In that case the decedent's best friend provided a variety of services to the decedent's widow, including chauffeuring, buying groceries, running errands, and performing minor repair work. Id. at 684. The court looked at the extent of the services provided to the widow, the closeness of the relationship between the parties, and the fact that the plaintiff never sought compensation until after the widow died. The court found that the widow had not been unjustly enriched, since plaintiff's services were not necessary for the widow's existence and were of the sort which could reasonably be expected from a long time friend. Id. at 687.

In this case there was a similarly close relationship between the plaintiff and the decedent. It appears that Gustafson managed the Nome Center Building for the decedent without requesting compensation, in recognition of many long years of friendship and business association together. At trial, the executor testified that he thought Gustafson would continue to manage the building for two years after Sparks' death out of the goodness of his heart, without expectation of payment....

... [T]he services that Gustafson performed for the Estate were not the sort which one would ordinarily expect to receive from a friend as a mere gratuity. Gustafson spent approximately five hours a day for two years collecting rents for Nome Center, soliciting new tenants, making repairs and improvements, paying utility, insurance and mortgage bills out of his own pocket when rental income fell short of expenses, and performing other general maintenance and management services for the Estate. These are the types of extensive business services for which one would ordinarily expect to be paid. We therefore agree with the trial court that Gustafson's services were not offered gratuitously [and that Gustafson should be compensated].

BASTIAN v. GAFFORD

Supreme Court of Idaho, 1977.
98 Idaho 324, 563 P.2d 48.

DONALDSON, JUSTICE. On appeal, plaintiff-appellant contends that because the trial court in its decision failed to distinguish between contracts implied in fact and quasi-contracts, the court did not decide this case on the theory alleged in appellant's complaint. We agree and therefore reverse the judgment and remand this case for a new trial.

During March, 1972, the defendant-respondent V.H. Gafford asked plaintiff-appellant Leo Bastian if he would be interested in constructing an office building upon a parcel of respondent's real property located in Twin Falls, Idaho. After several discussions between the parties, appellant orally agreed to construct the building and began drafting the plans therefor. After the plans were substantially completed, respondent contacted First Federal Savings and Loan Association of Twin Falls to seek financing for the building. He was informed that First Federal required a firm bid by a contractor and would not finance the project on a cost-plus basis. Respondent told appellant of the need for a firm bid, but appellant refused to submit one stating that he would only construct the building on a cost-plus basis. Respondent thereafter hired an architect to prepare a second set of plans, and employed another contractor to construct the building using those plans. On June 29, 1972, appellant filed a materialmen's lien upon respondent's real property in the amount of $3,250 for goods and services rendered in preparing the plans. He then commenced this action to foreclose that lien, alleging an implied-in-fact contract to compensate him for his services. After a trial on the merits, however, the court entered judgment for respondent on the ground that respondent had not been unjustly enriched. Since he did not use appellant's plans in constructing the office building, respondent received no benefit from them and was therefore not required to compensate appellant for drafting them.

In basing its decision on unjust enrichment, the trial court failed to distinguish between a quasi-contract and a contract implied in fact. Although unjust enrichment is necessary for recovery based upon quasi-contract, it is irrelevant to a contract implied in fact. *Continental Forest Products, Inc. v. Chandler Supply Co.*, 95 Idaho 739, 518 P.2d 1201 (1974). For appellant to recover under the latter theory, it is not necessary that respondent either use the plans or derive any benefit from them. *Clements v. Jungert,* 90 Idaho 143,

408 P.2d 810 (1965). It is enough that he requested and received them under circumstances which imply an agreement that he pay for appellant's services.

It is apparent from the record that the requested performance may not have been limited to the drafting of the building plans. We express no opinion on what performance was requested, on whether the requested performance was tendered, and on whether the circumstances imply an agreement to compensate appellant.

The judgment is reversed and the cause is remanded for a new trial. Costs to appellants.

McFADDEN, C.J., and SHEPARD, BAKES and BISTLINE, JJ., concur.

HILL v. WAXBERG, 237 F.2d 936 (9th Cir.1956). "An 'implied in fact' contract is essentially based on the intentions of the parties. It arises where the court finds from the surrounding facts and circumstances that the parties intended to make a contract but failed to articulate their promises and the court merely implies what it feels the parties really intended. It would follow then that the general contract theory of compensatory damages should be applied. Thus, if the court can in fact imply a contract for services, the compensation therefor is measured by the going contract rate.

"An 'implied in law' contract, on the other hand, is a fiction of the law which is based on the maxim that one who is unjustly enriched at the expense of another is required to make restitution to the other. The intentions of the parties have little or no influence on the determination of the proper measure of damages. In the absence of fraud or other tortious conduct on the part of the person enriched, restitution is properly limited to the value of the benefit which was acquired.

"The distinction is based on sound reason, too, for where a contract is all but articulated, the expectations of the parties are very nearly mutually understood, and the Court has merely to protect those expectations as men in the ordinary course of business affairs would expect them to be protected, whereas in a situation where one has acquired benefits, without fraud and in a non-tortious manner, with expectations so totally lacking in such mutuality that no contract in fact can be implied, the party benefited should not be required to reimburse the other party on the basis of such party's losses and expenditures, but rather on a basis limited to the benefits, which the benefited party has actually acquired."

RAMSEY v. ELLIS, 168 Wis.2d 779, 484 N.W.2d 331 (1992). "The common law action for quantum meruit . . . was founded upon the principle of unjust enrichment. Seegers v. Sprague, 70 Wis.2d 997, 1003–04, 236 N.W.2d 227 (1975). However, quantum meruit is a distinct cause of action from an action for unjust enrichment, with distinct elements and a distinct measure of damages. While recovery for unjust enrichment is based upon the inequity of allowing the defendant to retain a benefit without paying for it, recovery in quantum meruit is based upon an implied contract to pay reasonable compensation for services rendered. No contract is implied in an action for unjust enrichment. Accordingly, damages in an unjust enrichment claim are measured by the benefit conferred upon the defendant, while damages in a quantum meruit claim are measured by the reasonable value of the plaintiff's services."

———

PAFFHAUSEN v. BALANO, 708 A.2d 269 (Me.1998). "We have recently explained the difference between quantum meruit and unjust enrichment. Quantum meruit, also sometimes labelled 'contract implied in fact,' involves recovery for services or materials provided under an implied [-in-fact] contract. See Aladdin Elec. Assoc. v. Old Orchard Beach, 645 A.2d 1142, 1145 (Me.1994). See also United States ex rel. Modern Elec., Inc. v. Ideal Elec. Sec. Co., 81 F.3d 240, 246 (D.C.Cir.1996) ('[Q]uantum meruit ... rests on a contract implied in fact, that is, a contract inferred from the conduct of the parties.'). Unjust enrichment describes recovery for the value of the benefit retained when there is no contractual relationship, but when, on the grounds of fairness and justice, the law compels performance of a legal and moral duty to pay, and the 'damages analysis is based on principles of equity, not contract.[1]' Aladdin Elec. Assoc., 645 A.2d at 1145.

"Damages in unjust enrichment are measured by the value of what was inequitably retained. Id. In quantum meruit, by contrast, the damages are not measured by the benefit realized and retained by the defendant, but rather are based on the value of the services provided by the plaintiff. See Siciliani v. Connolly, 651 A.2d 386, 387 (Me.1994) (plaintiff's labor rather than enhanced value of property is the proper measure in quantum meruit claim); William Mushero, Inc. v. Hull, 667 A.2d 853, 855 (Me.1995) (quantum meruit damages are equal to the reasonable value of the services rendered)."

———

WAGENSELLER v. SCOTTSDALE MEMORIAL HOSPITAL

Supreme Court of Arizona, In Banc, 1985.
147 Ariz. 370, 710 P.2d 1025.

FELDMAN, Justice.

Catherine Sue Wagenseller petitioned this court to review a decision of the court of appeals affirming in part the trial court's judgment in favor of Scottsdale Memorial Hospital and certain Hospital employees (defendants). The trial court had dismissed all causes of action on defendants' motion for

1. ... [C]onfusion has resulted from our use of the term "quasi-contract" both to describe unjust enrichment ... and to describe *quantum meruit....*

The association of quasi-contract and quantum meruit ... is not helpful, because it suggests that the quantum meruit recovery is not based upon contract principles, as we have said that it must be. Cf. Restatement (Second) of Contracts § 4 com. b (1981) ("[U]nlike true contracts, quasi contracts are not based on the apparent intention of the parties to undertake the performances in question, nor are they promises. They are obligations created by law for reasons of justice.")....

Given the relative clarity that we have achieved in our distinction between quantum meruit and unjust enrichment, see Aladdin, 645 A.2d at 1145, and the ambiguity inherent in the term "quasi-contract," the latter term may have limited usefulness in our analytical framework.

summary judgment. The court of appeals affirmed in part and remanded, ruling that the only cause of action available to plaintiff was the claim against her supervisor, Kay Smith. *Wagenseller v. Scottsdale Memorial Hospital,* 148 Ariz. 242, 714 P.2d 412 (1984).... We granted review to consider the law of this state with regard to the employment-at-will doctrine. The issues we address are:

1.   Is an employer's right to terminate an at-will employee limited by any rules which, if breached, give rise to a cause of action for wrongful termination?

2.   If "public policy" or some other doctrine does form the basis for such an action, how is it determined?

3.   Did the trial court err, in view of *Leikvold v. Valley View Community Hospital,* 141 Ariz. 544, 688 P.2d 170 (1984), when it determined as a matter of law that the terms of Scottsdale Memorial Hospital's personnel policy manual were not part of the employment contract?

4.   Do employment contracts contain an implied covenant of "good faith and fair dealing," and, if so, what is the nature of the covenant? ...

FACTUAL BACKGROUND

Catherine Wagenseller began her employment at Scottsdale Memorial Hospital as a staff nurse in March 1975, having been personally recruited by the manager of the emergency department, Kay Smith. Wagenseller was an "at-will" employee—one hired without specific contractual term. Smith was her supervisor. In August 1978, Wagenseller was assigned to the position of ambulance charge nurse, and approximately one year later was promoted to the position of paramedic coordinator, a newly approved management position in the emergency department. Three months later, on November 1, 1979, Wagenseller was terminated.

Most of the events surrounding Wagenseller's work at the Hospital and her subsequent termination are not disputed, although the parties differ in their interpretation of the inferences to be drawn from and the significance of these events. For more than four years, Smith and Wagenseller maintained a friendly, professional, working relationship. In May 1979, they joined a group consisting largely of personnel from other hospitals for an eight-day camping and rafting trip down the Colorado River. According to Wagenseller, "an uncomfortable feeling" developed between her and Smith as the trip progressed—a feeling that Wagenseller ascribed to "the behavior that Kay Smith was displaying." Wagenseller states that this included public urination, defecation and bathing, heavy drinking, and "grouping up" with other rafters. Wagenseller did not participate in any of these activities. She also refused to join in the group's staging of a parody of the song "Moon River," which allegedly concluded with members of the group "mooning" the audience. Smith and others allegedly performed the "Moon River" skit twice at the Hospital following the group's return from the river, but Wagenseller declined to participate there as well.

Wagenseller contends that her refusal to engage in these activities caused her relationship with Smith to deteriorate and was the proximate cause of her termination. She claims that following the river trip Smith began harassing her, using abusive language and embarrassing her in the company of other staff. Other emergency department staff reported a similar marked change in Smith's behavior toward Wagenseller after the trip, although Smith denied it.

Up to the time of the river trip, Wagenseller had received consistently favorable job performance evaluations. Two months before the trip, Smith completed an annual evaluation report in which she rated Wagenseller's performance as "exceed[ing] results expected," the second highest of five possible ratings. In August and October 1979, Wagenseller met first with Smith and then with Smith's successor,[2] Jeannie Steindorff, to discuss some problems regarding her duties as paramedic coordinator and her attitude toward the job. On November 1, 1979, following an exit interview at which Wagenseller was asked to resign and refused, she was terminated.

She appealed her dismissal in letters to her supervisor and to the Hospital administrative and personnel department, answering the Hospital's stated reasons for her termination, claiming violations of the disciplinary procedure contained in the Hospital's personnel policy manual, and requesting reinstatement and other remedies. When this appeal was denied, Wagenseller brought suit against the Hospital, its personnel administrators, and her supervisor, Kay Smith.

Wagenseller, an "at-will" employee, contends that she was fired for reasons which contravene public policy and without legitimate cause related to job performance. She claims that her termination was wrongful, and that damages are recoverable under both tort and contract theories. The Hospital argues that an "at-will" employee may be fired for cause, without cause, or for "bad" cause. We hold that in the absence of contractual provision such an employee may be fired for good cause or for no cause, but not for "bad" cause.

THE EMPLOYMENT–AT–WILL DOCTRINE

History

As early as 1562, the English common law presumed that an employment contract containing an annual salary provision or computation was for a one-year term. Murg & Scharman, *Employment at Will: Do the Exceptions Overwhelm the Rule?* 23 B.C.L.Rev. 329, 332 (1982). Originally designed for the protection of seasonal farm workers, the English rule expanded over the years to protect factory workers as well. Workers were well protected under this rule, for the one-year presumption was not easy to overcome. *Id.* English courts held an employer liable for breaching the employment contract if he terminated an employee at any time during the year without "reasonable cause to do so." 1 *W. Blackstone, Commentaries* *413. To uphold an employer's discharge of an employee without a showing of "good cause," the courts required a clear expression of a contrary intent as evidenced either on the face of the contract or by a clearly defined custom of the industry. Murg & Scharman, *supra,* at 332.

In the early nineteenth century, American courts borrowed the English rule. The legal rationale embodied in the rule was consistent with the nature of the predominant master-servant employment relationship at the time because it reflected the master's duty to make provision for the general well-being of his servants. *Id.* at 334 and n. 22. In addition, the master was under a duty to employ the servant for a term, either a specified or implied time of

---

2. Smith left the emergency department on October 1, 1979.

service, and could not terminate him strictly at will. Hermann & Sor, *Property Rights in One's Job: The Case for Limiting Employment-at-Will,* 24 Ariz. L.Rev. 763, 770 (1982). The late nineteenth century, however, brought the Industrial Revolution; with it came the decline of the master-servant relationship and the rise of the more impersonal employer-employee relationship. In apparent response to the economic changes sweeping the country, American courts abandoned the English rule and adopted the employment-at-will doctrine. Murg & Scharman, *supra,* at 334. This new doctrine gave the employer freedom to terminate an at-will employee for any reason, good or bad.

The at-will rule has been traced to an 1877 treatise by H.G. Wood, in which he wrote:

> With us the rule is inflexible, that a general or indefinite hiring is *prima facie* a hiring at will, and if the servant seeks to make it out a yearly hiring, the burden is upon him to establish it by proof.... [I]t is an indefinite hiring and is determinable at the will of either party....

H.G. Wood, Law of Master and Servant § 134 at 273 (1877). As commentators and courts later would point out, none of the four cases cited by Wood actually supported the rule....

However unsound its foundation, Wood's at-will doctrine was adopted by the New York courts in *Martin v. New York Life Insurance Co.,* 148 N.Y. 117, 42 N.E. 416 (1895), and soon became the generally accepted American rule. In 1932, this court first adopted the rule for Arizona: "The general rule in regard to contracts for personal services, ... where no time limit is provided, is that they are terminable at pleasure by either party, or at most upon reasonable notice." *Dover Copper Mining Co. v. Doenges,* 40 Ariz. 349, 357, 12 P.2d 288, 291–92 (1932). Thus, an employer was free to fire an employee hired for an indefinite term "for good cause, for no cause, or even for cause morally wrong, without being thereby guilty of legal wrong." ...

Present-Day Status of the At–Will Rule

In recent years there has been apparent dissatisfaction with the absolutist formulation of the common law at-will rule. The Illinois Supreme Court is representative of courts that have acknowledged a need for a less mechanical application of the rule:

> With the rise of large corporations conducting specialized operations and employing relatively immobile workers who often have no other place to market their skills, recognition that the employer and employee do not stand on equal footing is realistic. In addition, unchecked employer power, like unchecked employee power, has been seen to present a distinct threat to the public policy carefully considered and adopted by society as a whole. As a result, it is now recognized that a proper balance must be maintained among the employer's interest in operating a business efficiently and profitably, the employee's interest in earning a livelihood, and society's interest in seeing its public policies carried out.

Palmateer v. International Harvester Co., 85 Ill.2d 124, 129, 52 Ill.Dec. 13, 15, 421 N.E.2d 876, 878 (1981) (citation omitted). Today, courts in three-fifths of the states have recognized some form of a cause of action for wrongful discharge. Lopatka, *The Emerging Law of Wrongful Discharge—A Quadrennial Assessment of the Labor Law Issue of the 80s,* 40 Bus.Law. 1 (1984).

The trend has been to modify the at-will rule by creating exceptions to its operation. Three general exceptions have developed. The most widely accepted approach is the "public policy" exception, which permits recovery upon a finding that the employer's conduct undermined some important public policy. The second exception, based on contract, requires proof of an implied-in-fact promise of employment for a specific duration, as found in the circumstances surrounding the employment relationship, including assurances of job security in company personnel manuals or memoranda. Under the third approach, courts have found in the employment contract an implied-in-law covenant of "good faith and fair dealing" and have held employers liable in both contract and tort for breach of that covenant. Wagenseller raises all three doctrines.

THE PUBLIC POLICY EXCEPTION

The public policy exception to the at-will doctrine began with a narrow rule permitting employees to sue their employers when a statute expressly prohibited their discharge. *See Kouff v. Bethlehem–Alameda Shipyard,* 90 Cal.App.2d 322, 202 P.2d 1059 (1949) (statute prohibiting discharge for serving as an election officer). This formulation was then expanded to include any discharge in violation of a statutory expression of public policy. *See Petermann v. Teamsters Local 396,* 174 Cal.App.2d 184, 344 P.2d 25 (1959) (discharge for refusal to commit perjury). Courts later allowed a cause of action for violation of public policy, even in the absence of a specific statutory prohibition. *See Nees v. Hocks,* 272 Or. 210, 536 P.2d 512 (1975) (discharge for being absent from work to serve on jury duty). The New Hampshire Supreme Court announced perhaps the most expansive rule when it held an employer liable for discharging an employee who refused to go out with her foreman. The court concluded that termination "motivated by bad faith or malice or based on retaliation is not [in] the best interest of the economic system or the public good and constitutes a breach of the employment contract." *Monge v. Beebe Rubber Co.,* 114 N.H. 130, 133, 316 A.2d 549, 551 (1974).[3] Although no other court has gone this far, a majority of the states have now either recognized a cause of action based on the public policy exception or have indicated their willingness to consider it, given appropriate facts.[4] The key to an employee's claim in all of these cases is the proper definition of a public policy that has been violated by the employer's actions.

Before deciding whether to adopt the public policy exception, we first consider what kind of discharge would violate the rule. The majority of courts require, as a threshold showing, a "clear mandate" of public policy. *E.g., Parnar v. Americana Hotels,* 65 Hawaii 370, 652 P.2d 625, 631 (1982); *Geary v. United States Steel Corp.,* 456 Pa. 171, 184, 319 A.2d 174, 180 (1974);

3. Although *Monge* held that the aggrieved employee had a cause of action for breach of her employment contract based on the employer's "bad faith," the New Hampshire Supreme Court later restricted the reach of *Monge,* construing it to apply "only to a situation where an employee is discharged because he performed an act that public policy would encourage, or refused to do that which public policy condemned." *Howard v. Dorr Woolen Co.,* 120 N.H. 295, 297, 414 A.2d 1273, 1274 (1980).

4. Twelve states have recognized a wrongful discharge cause of action for violation of public policy; fifteen additional states have acknowledged a willingness to consider it, if presented with appropriate facts. *See* Shepard & Moran, *"Wrongful" Discharge Litigation,* ILR Report (Fall 1982) and cases decided since the issuance of that report, including *Meredith v. C.E. Walther,* 422 So.2d 761 (Ala.1982); *Parnar v. Americana Hotels,* 65 Hawaii 370, 652 P.2d 625 (1982); *Brockmeyer v. Dun & Bradstreet,* 113 Wis.2d 561, 335 N.W.2d 834 (1983).

Thompson v. St. Regis Paper Co., 102 Wash.2d 219, 685 P.2d 1081 (1984). The leading case recognizing a public policy exception to the at-will doctrine is *Palmateer v. International Harvester Co., supra,* which holds that an employee stated a cause of action for wrongful discharge when he claimed he was fired for supplying information to police investigating alleged criminal violations by a co-employee. Addressing the issue of what constitutes "clearly mandated public policy," the court stated:

> There is no precise definition of the term. In general, it can be said that public policy concerns what is right and just and what affects the citizens of the State collectively. It is to be found in the State's constitution and statutes and, when they are silent, in its judicial decisions. Although there is no precise line of demarcation dividing matters that are the subject of public policies from matters purely personal, a survey of cases in other States involving retaliatory discharges shows that a matter must strike at the heart of a citizen's social rights, duties, and responsibilities before the tort will be allowed.

85 Ill.2d at 130, 52 Ill.Dec. at 15–16, 421 N.E.2d at 878–79 (citation omitted).

Other courts have allowed a cause of action where an employee was fired for refusing to violate a specific statute. *E.g., Petermann v. Teamsters Local 396, supra* (declined to commit perjury before a legislative committee); *Tameny v. Atlantic Richfield Co.,* 164 Cal.Rptr. 839, 164 Cal.Rptr. 839, 610 P.2d 1330 (1980) (would not engage in price-fixing); *Sheets v. Teddy's Frosted Foods,* 179 Conn. 471, 427 A.2d 385 (1980) (insisted that employer comply with state Food, Drug, and Cosmetic Act); *Trombetta v. Detroit, Toledo & Ironton Railroad Co.,* 81 Mich.App. 489, 265 N.W.2d 385 (1978) (refused to alter state-mandated pollution control reports); *O'Sullivan v. Mallon,* 160 N.J.Super. 416, 390 A.2d 149 (1978) (would not perform medical procedure for which she was not licensed); *Harless v. First National Bank,* 162 W.Va. 116, 246 S.E.2d 270 (1978) (would not violate consumer protection law). Failure to perform an act which would violate provisions of the Oregon state constitution formed the basis for a cause of action in *Delaney v. Taco Time International,* 297 Or. 10, 681 P.2d 114 (1984) (declined to sign a false and arguably tortious statement regarding a co-employee). Similarly, courts have found terminations improper where to do otherwise would have impinged on the employee's exercise of statutory rights or duties. *E.g., Glenn v. Clearman's Golden Cock Inn,* 192 Cal.App.2d 793, 13 Cal.Rptr. 769 (1961) (right to join a union); *Midgett v. Sackett–Chicago,* 105 Ill.2d 143, 85 Ill.Dec. 475, 473 N.E.2d 1280 (1984) (filing of a workers' compensation claim by a union member protected by a collective bargaining agreement); *Frampton v. Central Indiana Gas Co.,* 260 Ind. 249, 297 N.E.2d 425 (1973) (filing of a workers' compensation claim); *Nees v. Hocks, supra* (requesting not to be excused from jury duty). A division of our court of appeals recently adopted the public policy exception, ruling that the discharge of an at-will employee who refused to conceal a violation of Arizona's theft statute was contrary to public policy. *Vermillion v. AAA Pro Moving & Storage* 146 Ariz. 215 at 216, 704 P.2d 1360 at 1361. (App.1985). The court's ruling, it stated, was the "logical conclusion" to draw from previous decisions of the court of appeals. *Id. See Daniel v. Magma Copper Co.,* 127 Ariz. 320, 620 P.2d 699 (App.1980); *Larsen v. Motor Supply Co.,* 117 Ariz. 507, 573 P.2d 907 (App.1977).

It is difficult to justify this court's further adherence to a rule which permits an employer to fire someone for "cause morally wrong." So far as we can tell, no court faced with a termination that violated a "clear mandate of public policy" has refused to adopt the public policy exception. Certainly, a court would be hard-pressed to find a rationale to hold that an employer could with impunity fire an employee who refused to commit perjury. Why should the law imply an agreement which would give the employer such power? It may be argued, of course, that our economic system functions best if employers are given wide latitude in dealing with employees. We assume that it is in the public interest that employers continue to have that freedom. We also believe, however, that the interests of the economic system will be fully served if employers may fire for good cause or without cause. The interests of society as a whole will be promoted if employers are forbidden to fire for cause which is "morally wrong."

We therefore adopt the public policy exception to the at-will termination rule. We hold that an employer may fire for good cause or for no cause. He may not fire for bad cause—that which violates public policy.

We turn then to the questions of where "public policy" may be found and how it may be recognized and articulated. As the expressions of our founders and those we have elected to our legislature, our state's constitution and statutes embody the public conscience of the people of this state. It is thus in furtherance of their interests to hold that an employer may not with impunity violate the dictates of public policy found in the provisions of our statutory and constitutional law.

We do not believe, however, that expressions of public policy are contained only in the statutory and constitutional law, nor do we believe that all statements made in either a statute or the constitution are expressions of public policy. Turning first to the identification of other sources, we note our agreement with the following:

> Public policy is usually defined by the political branches of government. Something "against public policy" is something that the Legislature has forbidden. But the Legislature is not the only source of such policy. In common-law jurisdictions the courts too have been sources of law, always subject to legislative correction, and with progressively less freedom as legislation occupies a given field. It is the courts, to give one example, that originated the whole doctrine that certain kinds of businesses—common carriers and innkeepers—must serve the public without discrimination or preference. In this sense, then, courts make law, and they have done so for years.

Lucas v. Brown & Root, 736 F.2d 1202, 1205 (8th Cir.1984). Other state courts have similarly recognized judicial decisions as a source of public policy. *E.g., Palmateer v. International Harvester Co.,* 85 Ill.2d at 130, 52 Ill.Dec. at 15, 421 N.E.2d at 878; *Pierce v. Ortho Pharmaceutical Corp.,* 84 N.J. 58, 72, 417 A.2d 505, 512 (1980); *Thompson v. St. Regis Paper Co.,* 102 Wash.2d at 232—233, 685 P.2d at 1089. Thus, we believe that reliance on prior judicial decisions, as part of the body of applicable common law, is appropriate, although we agree with the Hawaii Supreme Court that "courts should proceed cautiously if called upon to declare public policy absent some prior legislative or judicial expression on the subject." *Parnar v. Americana Hotels,* 65 Hawaii at 380, 652 P.2d at 631. Thus, we will look to the pronouncements of our founders, our legislature, and our courts to discern the public policy of this state.

All such pronouncements, however, will not provide the basis for a claim of wrongful discharge. Only those which have a singularly *public* purpose will have such force. Lord Truro set forth the classic formulation of the public policy doctrine nearly 150 years ago:

> Public policy is that principle of the law which holds that no subject can lawfully do that which has a tendency to be injurious to the public, or against the public good, which may be termed, as it sometimes has been, the policy of the law, or public policy in relation to the administration of the law.

Egerton v. Earl Brownlow, 4 H.L.Cas. 1, 196 (1853). Where the interest involved is merely private or proprietary, the exception does not apply. In *Pierce v. Ortho Pharmaceutical Corp., supra,* for instance, the court held that the plaintiff did not have a cause of action for wrongful discharge based on her refusal to do certain research, where she had failed to articulate a clear public policy that had been violated. Citing the personal nature of Dr. Pierce's opposition, the court stated:

> Chaos would result if a single doctor engaged in research were allowed to determine, according to his or her individual conscience, whether a project should continue. An employee does not have a right to continued employment when he or she refuses to conduct research simply because it would contravene his or her personal morals. An employee at will who refuses to work in answer to a call of conscience should recognize that other employees and their employer might heed a different call.

84 N.J. at 75, 417 A.2d at 514 (citation omitted). Although an employee facing such a quandary may refuse to do the work believed to violate her moral philosophy, she may not also claim a right to continued employment. *Id.* . . .

However, some legal principles, whether statutory or decisional, have a discernible, comprehensive public purpose. A state's criminal code provides clear examples of such statutes. Thus, courts in other jurisdictions have consistently recognized a cause of action for a discharge in violation of a criminal statute. In a seminal case involving the public policy exception, *Petermann v. International Brotherhood of Teamsters Local 396,* 174 Cal. App.2d 184, 344 P.2d 25 (1959), the California Court of Appeals upheld an employee's right to refuse to commit perjury, stating:

> The public policy of this state as reflected in the Penal Code . . . would be seriously impaired if it were to be held that one could be discharged by reason of his refusal to commit perjury. To hold that one's continued employment could be made contingent upon his commission of a felonious act at the instance of his employer would be to encourage criminal conduct upon the part of both the employee and employer and would serve to contaminate the honest administration of public affairs. This is patently contrary to the public welfare.

Id. at 189, 344 P.2d at 27.

Although we do not limit our recognition of the public policy exception to cases involving a violation of a criminal statute, we do believe that our duty will seldom be clearer than when such a violation is involved. We agree with the Illinois Supreme Court that "[t]here is no public policy more basic, nothing more implicit in the concept of ordered liberty, than the enforcement of a State's criminal code." *Palmateer v. International Harvester Co.*, 85 Ill.2d at 132, 52 Ill.Dec. at 16, 421 N.E.2d at 879 (citations omitted).

In the case before us, Wagenseller refused to participate in activities which arguably would have violated our indecent exposure statute, A.R.S. § 13–1402. She claims that she was fired because of this refusal. The statute provides:

§ 13–1402. Indecent exposure; classifications

A. A person commits indecent exposure if he or she exposes his or her genitals or anus or she exposes the areola or nipple of her breast or breasts and another person is present, and the defendant is reckless about whether such other person, as a reasonable person, would be offended or alarmed by the act.

B. Indecent exposure is a class 1 misdemeanor. Indecent exposure to a person under the age of fifteen years is a class 6 felony.

While this statute may not embody a policy which "strikes at the heart of a citizen's social right, duties and responsibilities" (*Palmateer, supra*) as clearly and forcefully as a statute prohibiting perjury, we believe that it was enacted to preserve and protect the commonly recognized sense of public privacy and decency. The statute does, therefore, recognize bodily privacy as a "citizen's social right." We disagree with the court of appeals' conclusion that a minor violation of the statute would not violate public policy. (Slip op. at 6.) The nature of the act, and not its magnitude, is the issue. The legislature has already concluded that acts fitting the statutory description contravene the public policy of this state. We thus uphold this state's public policy by holding that termination for refusal to commit an act which might violate A.R.S. § 13–1402 may provide the basis of a claim for wrongful discharge. The relevant inquiry here is not whether the alleged "mooning" incidents were either felonies or misdemeanors or constituted purely technical violations of the statute, but whether they contravened the important public policy interests embodied in the law.... We are compelled to conclude that termination of employment for refusal to participate in public [mooning] ... is a termination contrary to the policy of this state, even if, for instance, the employer might have grounds to believe that all of the onlookers were voyeurs and would not be offended. In this situation, there might be no crime, but there would be a violation of public policy to compel the employee to do an act ordinarily proscribed by the law.

From a theoretical standpoint, we emphasize that the "public policy exception" which we adopt does not require the court to make a new contract for the parties. In an at-will situation, the parties have made no express agreement regarding the duration of employment or the grounds for discharge. The common law has presumed that in so doing the parties have intended to allow termination at any time, with or without good cause. It might be more properly argued that the law has recognized an implied covenant to that effect. Whether it be presumption or implied contractual covenant, we do not disturb it. We simply do not raise a presumption or imply a covenant that would require an employee to do that which public policy forbids or refrain from doing that which it commands.

Thus, in an at-will hiring we continue to recognize the presumption or to imply the covenant of termination at the pleasure of either party, whether with or without cause. Firing for bad cause—one against public policy articulated by constitutional, statutory, or decisional law—is not a right inherent in the at-will contract, or in any other contract, even if expressly provided. *See 1 A. Corbin, Contracts* § 7; 6A *A. Corbin, Contracts* §§ 1373–75 (1962). Such a termination violates rights guaranteed to the employee by law and is tortious. *See Prosser & Keeton on Torts* § 92 at 655 (5th ed. 1984).

THE "PERSONNEL POLICY MANUAL" EXCEPTION

Although an employment contract for an indefinite term is presumed to be terminable at will, that presumption, like any other presumption, is rebuttable by contrary evidence. *See* Restatement (Second) of Agency § 442; *Leikvold v. Valley View Community Hospital,* 141 Ariz. 544, 547, 688 P.2d 170, 173 (1984). Thus, in addition to relying on the public policy analysis to restrict the operation of the terminable-at-will rule, courts have turned to the employment contract itself, finding in it implied terms that limit the employer's right of discharge. Two types of implied contract terms have been recognized by the courts: implied-in-law terms and implied-in-fact terms. An implied-in-law term arises from a duty imposed by law where the contract itself is silent; it is imposed even though the parties may not have intended it, and it binds the parties to a legally enforceable duty, just as if they had so contracted explicitly. 1 *A. Corbin, Contracts* § 17, at 38 (1960). The covenant of good faith and fair dealing, discussed [below], is an implied-in-law contract term that has been recognized by a small number of courts in the employment-at-will context.

An implied-in-fact contract term, on the other hand, is one that is inferred from the statements or conduct of the parties. *Id.* It is not a promise defined by the law, but one made by the parties, though not expressly. Courts have found such terms in an employer's policy statements regarding such things as job security and employee disciplinary procedures, holding that by the conduct of the parties these statements may become part of the contract, supplementing the verbalized at-will agreement, and thus limiting the employer's absolute right to discharge an at-will employee. *Toussaint v. Blue Cross & Blue Shield of Michigan, supra; Pine River State Bank v. Mettille,* 333 N.W.2d 622 (Minn.1983). Arizona is among the jurisdictions that have recognized the implied-in-fact contract term as an exception to the at-will rule. In *Leikvold v. Valley View Community Hospital, supra,* this court held that a personnel manual can become part of an employment contract and remanded the cause for a jury determination as to whether the particular manual given to Leikvold had become part of her employment contract with Valley View. 141 Ariz. at 548, 688 P.2d at 174.

The relevant facts in the case before us are not dissimilar to those in *Leikvold.* In October 1978, Scottsdale Memorial Hospital established a four-step disciplinary procedure to achieve the Hospital's stated policy of "provid[ing] fair and consistent discipline as required to assist with the improvement of employees' behavior or performance." Subject to 32 listed exceptions, prior to being terminated a Hospital employee must be given a verbal warning, a written performance warning, a letter of formal reprimand, and a notice of dismissal. The manual further qualifies the mandatory procedure by providing that the 32 exceptions "are not inclusive and are only guidelines."

In appealing her dismissal, Wagenseller cited violations of this procedure, but the trial court ruled as a matter of law that the manual had not become part of the employment contract between Wagenseller and the Hospital. The court of appeals held that the Hospital's failure to follow the four-step disciplinary procedure did not violate Wagenseller's contract rights because she failed to prove her reliance on the procedure as a part of her employment contract. (Slip op. at 14.) We disagree with both of these rulings.

First, we need look only to *Leikvold* for the rule governing the determination of whether a particular statement by an employer becomes a part of an employment contract:

> Whether any particular personnel manual modifies any particular employment-at-will relationship and becomes part of the particular employment contract is a *question of fact.* Evidence relevant to this factual decision includes the language used in the personnel manual as well as the employer's course of conduct and oral representations regarding it.

141 Ariz. at 548, 688 P.2d at 174 (emphasis added). Thus, we held in *Leikvold* that entry of summary judgment was inappropriate "[b]ecause a material question—whether the policies manual was incorporated into and became part of the terms of the employment contract—remain[ed] in dispute." *Id.* The court may determine as a matter of law the proper construction of contract terms which are "clear and unambiguous." *Id.* Here, the court of appeals ruled, in effect, that the Hospital had adequately disclaimed any liability for failing to follow the procedure it had established. It found this disclaimer in the final item in the Hospital's list of exceptions to its disciplinary procedure: "20. These major and minor infractions are not inclusive and are only guidelines." The court concluded that the effect of this "clear" and "conspicuous" provision was "to create, by its terms, no rights at all." (Slip op. at 14.)

We do not believe this document, read in its entirety, has the clarity that the court of appeals attributed to its individual portions. One reading the document might well infer that the Hospital had established a procedure that would generally apply in disciplinary actions taken against employees. Although such a person would also note the long list of exceptions, he might not conclude from reading the list that an exception would apply in every case so as to swallow the general rule completely. We do not believe that the provision for unarticulated exceptions destroys the entire articulated general policy as a matter of law. Not only does such a result defy common sense, it runs afoul of our reasoning in *Leikvold,* where we addressed this problem directly:

> Employers are certainly free to issue no personnel manual at all or to issue a personnel manual that clearly and conspicuously tells their employees that the manual is not part of the employment contract and that their jobs are terminable at the will of the employer with or without reason. Such actions, either not issuing a personnel manual or issuing one with clear language of limitation, instill no reasonable expectations of job security and do not give employees any reason to rely on representations in the manual. However, if an employer does choose to issue a policy statement, in a manual or otherwise, and, by its language or by the employer's actions, encourages reliance thereon, the employer cannot be free to only selectively abide by it. Having announced a policy, the employer may not treat it as illusory.

141 Ariz. at 548, 688 P.2d at 174.

We emphasize here that the rule set forth in *Leikvold* is merely a reiteration of employment law as it has existed for centuries, exemplified by the English common law one-year presumption ... and the at-will employment doctrine itself. The right of discharge without cause is an implied contractual term which is said to exist in an at-will relationship when there are no factual indications to the contrary. The intent to create a different relationship, as well as the parameters of that relationship, are to be discerned from the totality of the parties' statements and actions regarding the employment relationship. *Leikvold,* 141 Ariz. at 548, 688 P.2d at 174.

The general rule is that the determination whether in a particular case a promise should be implied in fact is a question of fact. 1 A. *Corbin, supra,* § 17 at 38; *see also Leikvold,* 141 Ariz. at 548, 688 P.2d at 174. Where reasonable minds may draw different conclusions or inferences from undisputed evidentiary facts, a question of fact is presented. *Dietz v. Waller,* 141 Ariz. 107, 110–111, 685 P.2d 744, 747–48 (1984). "[T]he very essence of [the jury's] function is to select from among conflicting inferences and conclusions that which it considers most reasonable." *Apache Railway Co. v. Shumway,* 62 Ariz. 359, 378, 158 P.2d 142, 150 (1945). We believe that reasonable persons could differ in the inferences and conclusions they would draw from the Hospital's published manual regarding disciplinary policy and procedure. Thus, there are questions of fact as to whether this policy and procedure became a part of Wagenseller's employment contract. *See Leikvold,* 141 Ariz. at 548, 688 P.2d at 174. The trial court therefore erred in granting summary judgment on this issue.

The court of appeals' resolution of the reliance issue also was incorrect. A party may enforce a contractual provision without showing reliance. *Leikvold* does not require a plaintiff employee to show reliance in fact. The employee's reliance on an announced policy is only one of several factors that are relevant in determining whether a particular policy was intended by the parties to modify an at-will agreement. The employer's course of conduct and oral representations regarding the policy, as well as the words of the policy itself, also may provide evidence of such a modification. *Leikvold,* 141 Ariz. at 548, 688 P.2d at 174.

THE "GOOD FAITH AND FAIR DEALING" EXCEPTION

We turn next to a consideration of implied-in-law contract terms which may limit an employer's right to discharge an at-will employee. Wagenseller claims that discharge without good cause breaches the implied-in-law covenant of good faith and fair dealing contained in every contract. *See* Restatement (Second) of Contracts § 205; *Savoca Masonry Co. v. Homes & Son Construction Co.,* 112 Ariz. 392, 396, 542 P.2d 817, 821 (1975). *See also* 3 A. *Corbin, supra,* § 541 at 97; 5 S. *Williston, The Law of Contracts* § 670 at 159 (3d ed. 1961). In the context of this case, she argues that discharge without good cause violates the covenant of good faith and is, therefore, wrongful. The covenant requires that neither party do anything that will injure the right of the other to receive the benefits of their agreement. *Comunale v. Traders & General Insurance Co.,* 50 Cal.2d 654, 658, 328 P.2d 198, 200 (1958); *Fortune v. National Cash Register Co.,* 373 Mass. 96, 104, 364 N.E.2d 1251, 1257 (1977).[7] The duty not to act in bad faith or deal unfairly thus becomes a part

---

7. Some courts trace the recognition of the good faith covenant in employment-at-will contracts to *Fortune v. National Cash Register Co.,* 373 Mass. 96, 364 N.E.2d 1251 (1977). We of the contract, and, as with any other element of the contract, the remedy for its breach generally is on the contract itself. *Zancanaro v. Cross,* 85 Ariz. 394, 339 P.2d 746 (1959). In certain circumstances, breach of contract, including breach of the covenant of good faith and fair dealing, may provide the basis for a tort claim. *Noble v. National American Life Insurance Co.,* 128 Ariz. 188, 190, 624 P.2d 866, 868 (1981); *Seamen's Direct Buying Service v. Standard Oil Co. of California,* 36 Cal.3d 752, 206 Cal.Rptr. 354, 686 P.2d 1158 (1984)....

The question whether a duty to terminate only for good cause should be implied into all employment-at-will contracts has received much attention in the case law and other literature. *See, e.g., Pugh v. See's Candies,* 116 Cal.App.3d 311, 171 Cal.Rptr. 917 (1981); *Fortune v. National Cash Register Co., supra; Thompson v. St. Regis Paper Co., supra....* Courts have generally rejected the invitation to imply such a duty in employment contracts, voicing the concern that to do so would place undue restrictions on management and would infringe the employer's "legitimate exercise of management discretion." *Pugh v. See's Candies,* 116 Cal.App.3d at 330, 171 Cal.Rptr. at 928. ....

California has come closer than any other jurisdiction to implying a good cause duty in all employment-at-will contracts. ...

We find neither the logic of the California cases nor their factual circumstances compelling for recognition of so broad a rule in the case before us. Were we to adopt such a rule, we fear that we would tread perilously close to abolishing completely the at-will doctrine and establishing by judicial fiat the benefits which employees can and should get *only* through collective bargaining agreements or tenure provisions. *Cf. Fleming v. Pima County,* 141 Ariz. 149, 685 P.2d 1301 (1984) (county employee protected by a merit system was permitted to bring a tort action for wrongful discharge). While we do not reject the propriety of such a rule, we are not persuaded that it should be the result of judicial decision.

In reaching this conclusion, however, we do not feel that we should treat employment contracts as a special type of agreement in which the law refuses to imply the covenant of good faith and fair dealing that it implies in all other contracts. As we noted above, the implied-in-law covenant of good faith and fair dealing protects the right of the parties to an agreement to receive the benefits of the agreement that they have entered into. The denial of a party's right to those benefits, whatever they are, will breach the duty of good faith implicit in the contract. Thus, the relevant inquiry always will focus on the contract itself, to determine what the parties did agree to. In the case of an employment-at-will contract, it may be said that the parties have agreed, for example, that the employee will do the work required by the employer and

do not read *Fortune* so broadly. In *Fortune,* the plaintiff salesman received a notice of termination the first working day after the company received a $5 million order on which plaintiff was entitled to a substantial commission. By the terms of an express "bonus" agreement between the salesman and the company, he was not eligible to receive the full bonus until actual delivery and installation of the product, which occurred well after his termination. Plaintiff brought suit to recover the commissions allegedly due to him. In upholding the jury's award of the commissions to plaintiff, the Supreme Judicial Court of Massachusetts relied, not on the implied covenant of good faith, but upon the express contract itself, stating that it need not "speculate as to whether the good faith requirement is implicit in every contract for employment at will." *Id.* at 104, 364 N.E.2d at 1257. (Footnote relocated by ed.)

that the employer will provide the necessary working conditions and pay the employee for work done. What cannot be said is that one of the agreed benefits to the at-will employee is a guarantee of continued employment or tenure. The very nature of the at-will agreement precludes any claim for a prospective benefit. Either employer or employee may terminate the contract at any time.

We do, however, recognize an implied covenant of good faith and fair dealing in the employment-at-will contract, although that covenant does not create a duty for the employer to terminate the employee only for good cause. The covenant does not protect the employee from a "no cause" termination because tenure was never a benefit inherent in the at-will agreement. The covenant does protect an employee from a discharge based on an employer's desire to avoid the payment of benefits already earned by the employee, such as the sales commissions in *Fortune, supra,* but not the tenure required to earn ... pension and retirement benefits .... Thus, plaintiff here has a right to receive the benefits that were a part of her employment agreement with defendant Hospital. To the extent, however, that the benefits represent a claim for prospective employment, her claim must fail. The terminable-at-will contract between her and the Hospital made no promise of continued employment. To the contrary, it was, by its nature, subject to termination by either party at any time, subject only to the legal prohibition that she could not be fired for reasons which contravene public policy.

Thus, because we are concerned not to place undue restrictions on the employer's discretion in managing his workforce and because tenure is contrary to the bargain in an at-will contract, we reject the argument that a no cause termination breaches the implied covenant of good faith and fair dealing in an employment-at-will relationship....

SUMMARY AND CONCLUSIONS

The trial court granted summary judgment against Wagenseller on the count alleging the tort of wrongful discharge in violation of public policy. We adopt the "public policy" exception to the at-will termination rule and hold that the trial court erred in granting judgment against plaintiff on this theory. On remand plaintiff will be entitled to a jury trial if she can make a prima facie showing that her termination was caused by her refusal to perform some act contrary to public policy, or her performance of some act which, as a matter of public policy, she had a right to do. The obverse, however, is that mere dispute over an issue involving a question of public policy is not equivalent to establishing causation as a matter of law and will not automatically entitle plaintiff to judgment. In the face of conflicting evidence or inferences as to the actual reason for termination, the question of causation will be a question of fact.

The trial court granted summary judgment against Wagenseller on the count alleging breach of implied-in-fact provisions of the contract. We hold that this was error. On this record, there is a jury question as to whether the provisions of the employment manual were part of the contract of employment.

We affirm the grant of summary judgment on the count seeking recovery for breach of the implied covenant of good faith and fair dealing. We recognize that covenant as part of this and other contracts, but do not construe it to give either party to the contract rights—such as tenure—different from those for which they contracted. . . .

For the foregoing reasons, we affirm in part and reverse in part. The decision of the court of appeals is vacated and the case remanded to the trial court for proceedings not inconsistent with this opinion.

GORDON, V.C.J., and HAYS and CAMERON, JJ., concur.

HOLOHAN, C.J., concurred in the result except as to the personnel-manual issue. As to that issue, Holohan, C.J. concluded that the personnel manual "was not, as a matter of law, part of the employment contract."]

NOTE ON EMPLOYMENT AT WILL

As the court in *Wagenseller* points out, one exception to the at-will rule is that employers cannot discharge an at-will employee for a reason that is prohibited by statute. For example, federal statutes provide that an employee cannot be discharged on the basis of race, religion, gender, age, or disability. See, e.g., Age Discrimination in Employment Act of 1967 § 4(a), 29 U.S.C: § 623(a)(*l*); Civil Rights Act of 1964 § 703(a), 42 U.S.C. § 2000e–2(a)(1); Americans with Disabilities Act, 42 U.S.C. § 12112. A recently adopted federal statute, the Sarbanes–Oxley Act, protects whistleblowers by prohibiting the discharge of an employee of a public company because the employee provided information about, assisted in an investigation of, or testified in a proceeding concerning conduct that the employee reasonably believes violates Securities and Exchange Commission regulations or other relevant laws. 18 U.S.C. § 1514A.

At-will employment is also protected against improper interference by third persons. In Haddle v. Garrison, 525 U.S. 121, 119 S.Ct. 489, 142 L.Ed.2d 502 (1998), a federal statute, 42 U.S.C. § 1985(2), proscribed conspiracies to "deter, by force, intimidation, or threat, any party or witness in any court of the United States from attending such court, or from testifying to any matter pending therein, freely, fully, and truthfully, or to injure such party or witness in his person or property on account of his having so attended or testified." Haddle, an at-will employee, sued Healthmaster, his employer, and Garrison and Kelley, who were Healthmaster officers, on the ground that the three had conspired to have him fired in retaliation for obeying a federal grand jury subpoena, and to deter him from testifying at their upcoming criminal trial for Medicare fraud, and that their acts had "injured [him] in his person or property" in violation of § 1985(2). The District Court dismissed Haddle's suit, on the ground that an at-will employee discharged pursuant to a conspiracy proscribed by § 1985(2) suffers no actual injury, because he has no constitutionally protected interest in continued employment. The Eleventh Circuit affirmed. The Supreme Court reversed:

> . . . [T]he fact that employment at will is not "property" for purposes of the Due Process Clause . . . does not mean that loss of at-will employment may not "injur[e] [petitioner] in his person or property" for purposes of § 1985(2). . . .

We hold that the sort of harm alleged by petitioner here—essentially third-party interference with at-will employment relationships—states a claim for relief under § 1985(2). Such harm has long been a compensable injury under tort law, and we see no reason to ignore this tradition in this case....

This Court ... recognized in *Truax v. Raich,* 239 U.S. 33, 36 S.Ct. 7, 60 L.Ed. 131 (1915):

> "The fact that the employment is at the will of the parties, respectively, does not make it one at the will of others. The employee has manifest interest in the freedom of the employer to exercise his judgment without illegal interference or compulsion and, by the weight of authority, the unjustified interference of third persons is actionable although the employment is at will." *Id.,* at 38, 36 S.Ct. 7....

———

PINE RIVER STATE BANK v. METTILLE, 333 N.W.2d 622 (Minn. 1983). "[The employer-defendant argues that the job-security provisions in its personnel handbook] lack enforceability because mutuality of obligation is lacking. Since under a contract of indefinite duration the employee remains free to go elsewhere, why should the employer be bound to its promise not to terminate unless for cause or unless certain procedures are followed? The demand for mutuality of obligation, although appealing in its symmetry, is simply a species of the forbidden inquiry into the adequacy of consideration, an inquiry in which this court has, by and large, refused to engage. *See Estrada v. Hanson,* 215 Minn. 353, 10 N.W.2d 223 (1943). 'If the requirement of consideration is met, there is no additional requirement of ... equivalence in the values exchanged; or ... "mutuality of obligation".' Restatement (Second) of Contracts § 79 (1981). We see no merit in the lack of mutuality argument; as we pointed out in *Cardinal Consulting Co. v. Circo Resorts,* 297 N.W.2d 260, 266 (Minn.1980), the concept of mutuality in contract law has been widely discredited and the right of one party to terminate a contract at will does not invalidate the contract...."

———

NOTE ON MODIFICATION OF EMPLOYEE HANDBOOKS

The cases have differed on an employer's right to modify provisions of an employee handbook that have contractual force. In Asmus v. Pacific Bell, 23 Cal.4th 1, 999 P.2d 71, 96 Cal.Rptr.2d 179 (2000), Pacific Bell had issued the following Management Employment Security Policy (MESP) in 1986: "It will be Pacific Bell's policy to offer all management employees who continue to meet our changing business expectations employment security through reassignment to and retraining for other management positions, even if their present jobs are eliminated. This policy will be maintained so long as there is no change that will materially affect Pacific Bell's business plan achievement."

In January 1990, Pacific Bell notified its managers that industry conditions could force it to discontinue its MESP. In October 1991, Pacific Bell announced it would terminate its MESP on April 1, 1992, so that it could achieve more flexibility in conducting its business and compete more successfully in the marketplace. That same day, Pacific Bell announced it was adopting a new layoff policy (the Management Force Adjustment Program (MFAP)) that replaced the MESP. Employees who chose to continue working for Pacific Bell would receive enhanced pension benefits. Employees who opted to retire in December 1991 would receive additional enhanced pension benefits. Employees who chose to resign in November 1991 would receive these and other benefits, and severance pay equaling the employee's salary and bonus multiplied by a percentage of the employee's years of service.

Former Pacific Bell management employees who were affected by the MESP cancellation brought a suit challenging the cancellation. The plaintiffs had remained with the Pacific Bell for several years after the policy termination, and had received increased pension benefits for their continued employment while working under the new MFAP. Held, for Pacific Bell:

> In a unilateral contract, there is only one promisor, who is under an enforceable legal duty. (1 Corbin on Contracts (1993) § 1.23, p. 87.) The promise is given in consideration of the promisee's act or forbearance. As to the promisee, in general, any act or forbearance, including continuing to work in response to the unilateral promise, may constitute consideration for the promise. (1 Witkin, Summary of Cal. Law, supra, Contracts, § 213, p. 221; 2 Corbin on Contracts (1995) § 5.9, pp. 40–46; Rest.2d Contracts, §§ 71, 72; Civ.Code, § 1584.) . . .

> . . . The parties here disagree on how employers may terminate or modify a unilateral contract that has been accepted by the employees' performance. Plaintiffs assert that Pacific Bell was not entitled to terminate its MESP until it could demonstrate a change materially affecting its business plan, i.e., until the time referred to in a clause in the contract. Pacific Bell asserts that because it formed the contract unilaterally, it could terminate or modify that contract as long as it did so after a reasonable time, gave affected employees reasonable notice, and did not interfere with the employees' vested benefits (e.g., pension and other retirement benefits). . . .

> . . . [T]he majority of other jurisdictions that have addressed the question conclude that an employer may terminate or modify a contract with no fixed duration period after a reasonable time period, if it provides employees with reasonable notice, and the modification does not interfere with vested employee benefits. . . .

> . . . Just as employers must accept the employees' continued employment as consideration for the original contract terms, employees must be bound by amendments to those terms, with the availability of continuing employment serving as adequate consideration from the employer. When Pacific Bell terminated its original MESP and then offered continuing employment to employees who received notice and signed an acknowledgement to that effect, the employees accepted the new terms, and the subsequent modified contract, by continuing to work. Continuing to work after the policy termination and subsequent modification constituted acceptance of the new employment terms. . . .

In Demasse v. ITT Corp., 194 Ariz. 500, 984 P.2d 1138 (1999), the Arizona Supreme Court reached a different conclusion concerning the modification of employee handbooks:

ITT [the employer] argues that it had the legal power to unilaterally modify the contract by simply publishing a new [1989] handbook. But as with other contracts, an implied-in-fact contract term cannot be modified unilaterally.... Once an employment contract is formed—whether the method of formation was unilateral, bilateral, express, or implied—a party may no longer unilaterally modify the terms of that relationship....

The cases ITT cites hold that continued work alone both manifested the Demasse employees' assent to the modification and constituted consideration for it. We disagree with both contentions and the cases that support them. Separate consideration, beyond continued employment, is necessary to effect a modification....

Continued employment after issuance of a new handbook does not constitute acceptance, otherwise the "illusion (and the irony) is apparent: to preserve their right under the [existing contract] ... plaintiffs would be forced to quit." Doyle, 237 Ill.Dec. 100, 708 N.E.2d at 1145.... It is "too much to require an employee to preserve his or her rights under the original employment contract by quitting working." Brodie, 934 P.2d at 1268; see Robinson, 19 F.3d at 364; Torosyan v. Boehringer Ingelheim Pharmaceuticals, Inc., 234 Conn. 1, 662 A.2d 89, 99 (1995). Thus, the employee does not manifest consent to an offer modifying an existing contract without taking affirmative steps, beyond continued performance, to accept....

When ITT distributed the 1989 handbook containing the provisions permitting unilateral modification or cancellation, it did not bargain with those pre–1989 employees who had seniority rights under the old handbooks, did not ask for or obtain their assent, and did not provide consideration other than continued employment. The employees signed a receipt for the "1989 handbook stating that they had received the handbook[,] understood that it was their responsibility to read it, comply with its contents, and contact Personnel if they had any questions concerning the contents." ... The Demasse employees were not informed that continued employment—showing up for work the next day—would manifest assent, constitute consideration, and permit cancellation of any employment rights to which they were contractually entitled. Thus, even if we were to agree that continued employment could provide consideration for rescission of the job security term, that consideration would not have been bargained for and would not support modification.... Our courts have not adopted any conflicting principle.

———

NOTE ON THE EFFECT OF DISCLAIMERS
IN EMPLOYEE HANDBOOKS

An employee handbook that would otherwise give rise to contractual liability may not do so if it includes a disclaimer against such liability. Some cases have been relatively quick to give effect to such a disclaimer. See, e.g., Abney v. Baptist Medical Centers, 597 So.2d 682, 683 (Ala. 1992); Lobosco v. N.Y. Tel. Company/NYNEX, 96 N.Y.2d 312, 727 N.Y.S.2d 383, 751 N.E.2d 462

(2001). Other cases, however, have held that such a disclaimer will be effective only if it satisfies very demanding conditions of clarity and notice. For example, in Sanchez v. Life Care Centers of America, Inc., 855 P.2d 1256 (Wyo.1993), reaffirmed, Life Care Centers of America v. Dexter, 65 P.3d 385 (Wyo.2003), an employee handbook contained the following disclaimer on the second page:

HANDBOOK DISCLAIMER

The guidelines outlined in this handbook are for the mutual benefit of this nursing center and its associates. These guidelines include methods of procedure which, when implemented, can effectively enhance the management of a successful nursing center. The executive director and supervisors must therefore reserve all the customary rights of management, including the right to supervise and control all operations; direct all work; interpret, change or cancel all personnel policies with or without notice; hire, schedule, terminate, layoff, transfer, promote, reward, discipline, or otherwise manage associates and select the manner, method and means of doing so. This handbook is not a contract and contains no promises, guarantees, representations, agreements, or warranties upon which any prospective, current or prior associates of this nursing center can reasonably maintain or create any expectations of such.

The court held that the disclaimer was ineffective because it was not sufficiently conspicuous to maintain the at-will nature of employment:

In the case before us, the disclaimer is in the "Introduction" section of the handbook, subtitled "Handbook Disclaimer." The language of the disclaimer speaks in terms of "mutual benefit," management "enhancement" and the right to supervise. It does not say that the employer retains the right to deviate from the terms of the handbook at its own caprice. It does not say that the employer remains free to change wages and all other working conditions without consulting the employee or obtaining his agreement, nor that the employer retains absolute power to fire anyone with or without good cause. Instead, there is an inference in the disclaimer that it is a guide for "mutual benefit," that certain procedures contained therein would be "implemented" to "enhance the management of a successful nursing center," and that the "customary rights" of the employer were set forth in the handbook.

The operative language in the disclaimer is not bold lettered; it is buried in introductory paragraphs. It is not designed to attract attention and is stated in language which does not tell the employee what he needs to know....

See also, e.g., Nicosia v. Wakefern Food Corp., 136 N.J. 401, 643 A.2d 554 (1994); Swanson, LeDuc v. Liquid Air Corp., 118 Wash.2d 512, 826 P.2d 664 (1992); McDonald v. Mobil Coal Producing, Inc., 820 P.2d 986 (Wyo.1991).

PETTIT, MODERN UNILATERAL CONTRACTS, 63 Boston U.L.Rev. 551 (1983). "[An] important reason for the continued use of unilateral contract analysis in contemporary litigation is that it has proved adaptable to the needs of judges and lawyers in areas unforeseen by [Karl] Llewellyn and apparently by the drafters of the *Second Restatement*. Relatively few of the modern unilateral contracts cases involve traditional commercial exchanges (sales of goods), and it was primarily the traditional commercial context that Llewellyn had in mind when he unleashed his attack on the unilateral contract idea. Llewellyn did not foresee the usefulness in a highly organized society of a concept that allows a plaintiff to assert the defendant's promissory obligation and at the same time preempt the argument that he himself did not undertake any obligation. Many of the modern unilateral contracts cases involve claims by an individual offeree against an organizational offeror—the little guy against the big organization. In this context courts often are quite willing to conclude that the organization made a promise even though the individual did not. . . .

"... [L]awyers and judges recently have been choosing unilateral contract analysis with remarkable and increasing frequency. In assessing this trend toward the unilateral contract, however, it is important to recognize an important change in the way that unilateral contract is being used. In Llewellyn's time, unilateral contract was predominantly a defendant's theory; the plaintiff pressed a bilateral contract argument and the defendant claimed to have made an offer for a unilateral contract which he revoked before the plaintiff's acceptance by performance. In modern times, unilateral contract is predominantly a plaintiff's theory. With some exceptions, courts employ unilateral contract analysis when they find liability and reject it when they deny liability.

"The crucial, difficult question facing the courts in the modern cases is not whether to choose unilateral or bilateral contract analysis, but whether to employ any contractual analysis at all. Judges and lawyers have been expanding contract analysis into new areas and situations. It is no coincidence that they have resorted to unilateral contract in this process. The need to find an enforceable return promise provides some limitation on the use of bilateral contract theory to impose liability. Plaintiffs pursuing a bilateral theory have to prove, and sometimes subject themselves to, their own promissory obligation. Plaintiffs using the unilateral contract device, like tort plaintiffs, have to prove only the defendant's obligation.

"More often than not, the source of the defendant's obligation in modern unilateral contracts cases is an implied, rather than an express, promise. Moreover, the implied promise often takes the following form: 'As long as you keep doing what you've been doing, or are about to do, I'll keep doing what I've been doing, or am about to do.' In other words, the defendant's alleged promise is a promise to maintain the status quo, and the plaintiff's performance is simply continuing the status quo. The only limit on the use of unilateral contract theory is the court's willingness to find the alleged implied promise. Any assessment, therefore, of the appropriateness of modern judicial use of unilateral contract theory must focus on the promissory basis of the asserted obligation: Did the defendant really make a promise and, if so, should that promise serve as the basis for determining the existence and extent of liability?"

Chapter 14

PRELIMINARY NEGOTIATIONS, IN-DEFINITENESS, AND THE DUTY TO BARGAIN IN GOOD FAITH

One of the axioms of classical contract law was that a contract is formed by offer and acceptance. This axiom was at the center of several clusters of rules. One of these clusters concerned preliminary negotiations, indefiniteness, further-document-to-follow provisions, agreements to agree, and the duty to negotiate in good faith. The rules in this cluster are the subject of this Chapter.

One set of these rules concerned the characterization and effect of expressions used in a bargaining context. Under classical contract law, such expressions were characterized as either an offer or acceptance, on the one hand, or as preliminary negotiations, on the other. This was a binary characterization, in which an expression either had immediate legal effect or no legal effect. An offer had the immediate legal effect of creating a power of acceptance in the offeree, and an acceptance had the immediate legal effect of concluding a contract. In contrast, preliminary negotiations had no legal effect. This binary characterization was reflected in binary outcomes: no liability up to the time at which an acceptance of an offer occurred; full liability for expectation damages thereafter.

Another set of rules in this cluster concerned the indefiniteness of agreements. The relationship between the basic rules of offer and acceptance and the rules concerning indefiniteness was not always clear. A basic rule of offer and acceptance is that an expression will not constitute an offer unless it is sufficiently definite. But why then should contract law have another rule about the indefiniteness of *agreements*? If an expression is not sufficiently definite to constitute an offer, no contract can be formed. If an expression is sufficiently definite to constitute an offer, and the offeree assents, what room is left to argue that a resulting agreement is too indefinite?

One possible answer to this question is that the concept of indefiniteness of agreements reflects the brute fact that in reality many contracts are not formed by an offer-and-acceptance sequence. Instead, many contracts are probably formed by simultaneous actions, like signing, shaking hands, concurring that "It's a deal," or the like. In such cases, whether one of the parties used an expression that was sufficiently definite to constitute an offer is usually irrelevant. Instead, indefiniteness bears on whether parties to a joint expression that *looks like* an agreement believed that (1) they had concluded the bargaining process or (2) instead they were still in preliminary negotiations—preliminary, that is, to the conclusion of a bargain. In addition, indefiniteness may be relevant because even if the parties believed they had concluded the bargaining process, the resulting bargain they made may be too indefinite to allow the courts to fashion a remedy for its breach.

Still another set of rules involved fact patterns in which the parties have made an agreement that would look as if it were a completed bargain except for the fact that the parties included in the agreement a provision that contemplated a further, more elaborate agreement. Often, the original agreement would be sufficiently definite to be enforceable but for the presence of such a provision. The question then is, what is the legal significance of the provision? The rule of classical contract law again was binary and static: If the parties intended the further agreement to be only an evidentiary memorial of the terms of their original agreement (for example, to tie together various pieces of correspondence), and the original agreement was otherwise sufficiently definite, then the original agreement was enforceable. If, however, the parties intended not to be bound unless and until the further agreement was executed, so that the further agreement was to be the consummation of their negotiations, then the original agreement was unenforceable. Accordingly, the parties' contemplation of a further document either (1) prevented the formation of a contract, in which case there was no liability, or (2) did not, in which case there was a contract on the terms of the original agreement.

Finally, classical contract law did not recognize a duty to negotiate in good faith. On the contrary, it adopted the rule that an agreement to agree was unenforceable, which by implication precluded an obligation to negotiate in good faith.

As will be seen in this Chapter, in regard to these issues modern contract law has made important dynamic departures from the static offer-and-acceptance model of classical contract law.

ACADEMY CHICAGO PUBLISHERS v. CHEEVER

Supreme Court of Illinois, 1991.
144 Ill.2d 24, 161 Ill.Dec. 335, 578 N.E.2d 981.

JUSTICE HEIPLE delivered the opinion of the court:

This is a suit for declaratory judgment. It arose out of an agreement between the widow of the widely published author, John Cheever, and Academy Chicago Publishers. Contact between the parties began in 1987 when the publisher approached Mrs. Cheever about the possibility of publishing a collection of Mr. Cheever's short stories which, though previously published, had never been collected into a single anthology. In August of that year, a publishing agreement was signed which provided, in pertinent part:

> "Agreement made this 15th day of August 1987, between Academy Chicago Publishers or any affiliated entity or imprint (hereinafter re-

ferred to as the Publisher) and Mary W. Cheever and Franklin H. Dennis of the USA (hereinafter referred to as Author).

Whereas the parties are desirous of publishing and having published a certain work or works, tentatively titled *The Uncollected Stories of John Cheever* (hereinafter referred to as the Work):

* * * * * *

2. The Author will deliver to the Publisher on a mutually agreeable date one copy of the manuscript of the Work as finally arranged by the editor and satisfactory to the Publisher in form and content.

* * * * * *

5. Within a reasonable time and a mutually agreeable date after delivery of the final revised manuscript, the Publisher will publish the Work at its own expense, in such style and manner and at such price as it deems best, and will keep the Work in print as long as it deems it expedient; but it will not be responsible for delays caused by circumstances beyond its control."

Academy and its editor, Franklin Dennis, assumed the task of locating and procuring the uncollected stories and delivering them to Mrs. Cheever. Mrs. Cheever and Mr. Dennis received partial advances for manuscript preparation. By the end of 1987, Academy had located and delivered more than 60 uncollected stories to Mrs. Cheever. Shortly thereafter, Mrs. Cheever informed Academy in writing that she objected to the publication of the book and attempted to return her advance.

Academy filed suit in the circuit court of Cook County in February 1988, seeking a declaratory judgment: (1) granting Academy the exclusive right to publish the tentatively titled, "The Uncollected Stories of John Cheever"; (2) designating Franklin Dennis as the book's editor; and (3) obligating Mrs. Cheever to deliver the manuscript from which the work was to be published. The trial court entered an order declaring, *inter alia:* (1) that the publishing agreement executed by the parties was valid and enforceable; (2) that Mrs. Cheever was entitled to select the short stories to be included in the manuscript for publication; (3) that Mrs. Cheever would comply with her obligations of good faith and fair dealing if she delivered a manuscript including at least 10 to 15 stories totaling at least 140 pages; (4) Academy controlled the design and format of the work to be published, but control must be exercised in cooperation with Mrs. Cheever.

Academy appealed the trial court's order, challenging particularly the declaration regarding the minimum story and page numbers for Mrs. Cheever's compliance with the publishing agreement, and the declaration that Academy must consult with defendant on all matters of publication of the manuscript.

The appellate court affirmed the decision of the trial court with respect to the validity and enforceability of the publishing agreement and the minimum story and page number requirements for Mrs. Cheever's compliance with same. The appellate court reversed the trial court's declaration regarding control of publication, stating that the trial court erred in considering extrinsic evidence to interpret the agreement regarding control of the publication, given the explicit language of the agreement granting exclusive control to Academy. (200 Ill.App.3d 677, 146 Ill.Dec. 386, 558 N.E.2d 349.) Appeal is taken in this court pursuant to Supreme Court Rule 315(a) (134 Ill.2d R. 315(a)).

The parties raise several issues on appeal; this matter, however, is one of contract and we confine our discussion to the issue of the validity and enforceability of the publishing agreement.

While the trial court and the appellate court agreed that the publishing agreement constitutes a valid and enforceable contract, we cannot concur. The principles of contract state that in order for a valid contract to be formed, an "offer must be so definite as to its material terms or require such definite terms in the acceptance that the promises and performances to be rendered by each party are reasonably certain." (1 Williston, Contracts §§ 38 through 48 (3d ed. 1957); 1 Corbin, Contracts §§ 95 through 100 (1963).) Although the parties may have had and manifested the intent to make a contract, if the content of their agreement is unduly uncertain and indefinite no contract is formed. 1 Williston § 37; 1 Corbin § 95.

The pertinent language of this agreement lacks the definite and certain essential terms required for the formation of an enforceable contract. (*Midland Hotel Corp. v. Reuben H. Donnelley Corp.* (1987), 118 Ill.2d 306, 113 Ill.Dec. 252, 515 N.E.2d 61.) A contract "is sufficiently definite and certain to be enforceable if the court is enabled from the terms and provisions thereof, under proper rules of construction and applicable principles of equity, to ascertain what the parties have agreed to do." (*Morey v. Hoffman* (1957), 12 Ill.2d 125, 145 N.E.2d 644.) The provisions of the subject publishing agreement do not provide the court with a means of determining the intent of the parties.

Trial testimony reveals that a major source of controversy between the parties is the length and content of the proposed book. The agreement sheds no light on the minimum or maximum number of stories or pages necessary for publication of the collection, nor is there any implicit language from which we can glean the intentions of the parties with respect to this essential contract term. The publishing agreement is similarly silent with respect to who will decide which stories will be included in the collection. Other omissions, ambiguities, unresolved essential terms and illusory terms are: No date certain for delivery of the manuscript. No definition of the criteria which would render the manuscript satisfactory to the publisher either as to form or content. No date certain as to when publication will occur. No certainty as to style or manner in which the book will be published nor is there any indication as to the price at which such book will be sold, or the length of time publication shall continue, all of which terms are left to the sole discretion of the publisher.

A contract may be enforced even though some contract terms may be missing or left to be agreed upon, but if the essential terms are so uncertain that there is no basis for deciding whether the agreement has been kept or broken, there is no contract. (*Champaign National Bank v. Landers Seed Co.* (1988), 165 Ill.App.3d 1090, 116 Ill.Dec. 742, 519 N.E.2d 957, Restatement (Second) of Contracts § 33 (1981).) Without setting forth adequate terms for compliance, the publishing agreement provides no basis for determining when breach has occurred, and, therefore, is not a valid and enforceable contract.

An enforceable contract must include a meeting of the minds or mutual assent as to the terms of the contract. (*Midland Hotel,* 118 Ill.2d at 313, 113 Ill.Dec. 252, 515 N.E.2d 61.) It is not compelling that [whether?] the parties share a subjective understanding as to the terms of the contract; the parties' conduct may indicate an agreement to the terms of same. (*Steinberg v. Chicago Medical School* (1977), 69 Ill.2d 320, 13 Ill.Dec. 699, 371 N.E.2d 634.) In the instant case, however, no mutual assent has been illustrated. The parties did not and do not share a common understanding of the essential terms of the publishing agreement.

In rendering its judgment, the trial court supplied minimum terms for Mrs. Cheever's compliance, including story and page numbers. It is not uncommon for a court to supply a missing material term, as the reasonable conclusion often is that the parties intended that the term be supplied by implication. However, where the subject matter of the contract has not been decided upon and there is no standard available for reasonable implication, courts ordinarily refuse to supply the missing term. (1 Williston § 42; 1 Corbin § 100.) No suitable standard was available for the trial court to apply. It is our opinion that the trial court incorrectly supplied minimum compliance terms to the publishing agreement, as the agreement did not constitute a valid and enforceable contract to begin with. As noted above, the publishing agreement contains major unresolved uncertainties. It is not the role of the court to rewrite the contract and spell out essential elements not included therein.

In light of our decision that there was no valid and enforceable contract between the parties, we need not address other issues raised on appeal. For the foregoing reasons, the decisions of the trial and appellate courts in this declaratory judgment action are reversed.

Reversed.

JUSTICES CLARK and FREEMAN took no part in the consideration or decision of this opinion.

PETER KURTH, BOOK REVIEW OF ANITA MILLER, UNCOL-LECTING CHEEVER, THE FAMILY OF JOHN CHEEVER v. ACADE-MY CHICAGO PUBLISHER, Salon, November 25, 1998. " 'Uncollecting Cheever' is the blow-by-blow account of the Cheevers' famous legal battle with Academy Chicago, a small Midwestern publishing house owned and run by [Anita] Miller and her husband, Jordan, who in 1988 hoped to publish a volume of Cheever's previously uncollected short stories. The idea for the book came from Franklin Dennis, a New York book publicist who did work for the Millers and was also a neighbor of the Cheevers in Ossining. Mary Cheever at first agreed to the project, signing a contract and receiving half of a $1,500 token advance for what she later insisted she had envisioned as 'a small edition for libraries, for students,' and not a major commercial work. Only when Franklin Dennis had unearthed more than 60 Cheever stories from magazines and anthologies, and when paperback rights to the collection were sold for $225,500 in advance of publication, did the Cheevers—and, for that matter, the Millers—realize that they might have 'a gold mine' on their hands. Mary Cheever tried to break the contract; the Millers responded with a lawsuit to enforce its terms; the Cheevers countered with a suit to protect their copyright, and one of the great literary court battles was born."

RIDGWAY v. WHARTON, 6 Clark's H.L. Cases 238, 305–306 (1856). Lord Wensleydale said: "An agreement to be finally settled must comprise all the terms which the parties intend to introduce into the agreement. An agreement to enter into an agreement upon terms to be afterwards settled between the parties is a contradiction in terms. It is absurd to say that a man enters into an agreement till the terms of that agreement are settled. Until those terms are settled he is perfectly at liberty to retire from the bargain."

BERG AGENCY v. SLEEPWORLD—WILLINGBORO, INC., 136 N.J.Super. 369, 346 A.2d 419 (1975). On May 11, Bressman and Lustwig signed a document that set out terms for renting a vacant commercial building to Lustwig. Bressman claimed the document was binding; Lustwig claimed it was only a preliminary proposal. Held, the document was binding.

"The May 11 document sets forth in substantial detail the essential elements of a commercial lease as applicable to the particular premises and the intended use by the tenant . . .

"[Bressman] asserts that there are no provisions relating to maintenance, insurance, repairs, assignment, etc. It is apparent that such provisions were not made. However it is not necessary for a writing to contain every possible contractual provision to cover every contingency in order to qualify as a completed binding agreement. . . . Some of these issues may be determined by the operation of law, or the parties may resolve such differences by subsequent agreement, or a contract may be silent in those respects. In any event, a contract is no less a contract because some preferable clauses may be omitted either deliberately or by neglect. So long as the basic essentials are sufficiently definite, any gaps left by the parties should not frustrate their intention to be bound. Such is the just and fair result."

REGO v. DECKER, 482 P.2d 834 (Alaska 1971). "Regarding the rule requiring reasonable certainty and its application to particular factual situations, [our cases] demonstrate that:

> The dream of a mechanical justice is recognized for what it is—only a dream and not even a rosy or desirable one.

"In general it has been said that the primary underlying purpose of the law of contracts is the attempted 'realization of reasonable expectations that have been induced by the making of a promise.' In light of this underlying purpose, two general considerations become relevant to solution of reasonable certainty-specific performance problems. On the one hand, courts should fill gaps in contracts to ensure fairness where the reasonable expectations of the parties are fairly clear. The parties to a contract often cannot negotiate and draft solutions to all the problems which may arise. Except in transactions involving very large amounts of money or adhesion contracts to be imposed on many parties, contracts tend to be skeletal, because the amount of time and money needed to produce a more complete contract would be disproportionate to the value of the transaction to the parties. Courts would impose too great a burden on the business community if the standards of certainty were set too high. On the other hand, the courts should not impose on a party any performance to which he did not and probably would not have agreed. Where the character of a gap in an agreement manifests failure to reach an agreement rather than a sketchy agreement, or where gaps cannot be filled with confidence that the reasonable expectations of the parties are being fulfilled, then specific enforcement should be denied for lack of reasonable certainty.

"Several other considerations affect the standard of certainty. A greater degree of certainty is required for specific performance than for damages, because of the difficulty of framing a decree specifying the performance required, as compared with the relative facility with which a breach may be perceived for purposes of awarding damages. Less certainty is required where the party seeking specific performance has substantially shifted his position in reliance on the supposed contract, than where the contract is wholly unperformed on both sides."

AROK CONSTRUCTION CO. v. INDIAN CONSTRUCTION SERVICES, 174 Ariz. 291, 848 P.2d 870 (1993). "The enforcement of incomplete agreements is a necessary fact of economic life. Business people are not soothsayers, and can neither provide in advance for every unforeseen contingency nor answer every unasked question regarding a commercial agreement. This is especially so with a complex contract for a major construction project. Nor are entrepreneurs perfect at drafting legal documents. Finally, parties may want to bind themselves and at the same time desire to leave some matters open for future resolution in order to maintain flexibility. Thus, courts are often presented with incomplete bargains when the parties intend and desire to be bound.... Refusing the enforcement of obligations the parties intended to create and that marketplace transactions require hardly seems the solution."

SALIBA–KRINGLEN CORP. v. ALLEN ENGINEERING CO., 15 Cal.App.3d 95, 92 Cal.Rptr. 799 (1971). Saliba, a general contractor, was awarded a freeway-construction contract. Allen, an electrical subcontractor, had submitted the low bid to Saliba for the electrical work, but refused to honor its bid, and Saliba was forced to subcontract out the electrical work at a price in excess of Allen's bid. Saliba sued Allen, who defended on the ground that its bid was too indefinite to form the basis of a contract, since it stated only price. Held, for Saliba:

It is undisputed that the customary practice in the construction industry is for the general contractor who is awarded a contract to enter into a written contract with the subcontractor, which written contract embraces far more than the price which the subcontractor has bid by telephone. The additional matters would include such things as whether the subcontractor would furnish a bond, who would provide for insurance, how payments would be made and many other matters. Although the provisions other than price are not identical in all subcontracts generally or in electrical subcontracts particularly, price is the principal item as is evident from the fact (as shown by the evidence) that seldom does a general contractor fail to reach an agreement with the subcontractor whose bid is low. Defendant asserts that it should not be held to its bid price because the general contractor could not have known that the general contractor and defendant would have reached an agreement on the terms of the subcontract.

While a prospective subcontractor could submit a bid by way of a written proposed subcontract including not only the price but all other details, we are not aware that this is ever done. The customary bid is made, as it was here, by a brief telephone call in which only the price is stated. If defendant's position is correct, there would never be an occasion to invoke section 90 of the Restatement, Contracts by a general contractor against a prospective subcontractor. Even a subcontractor who did not make a mistake in his bid price but who desired to avoid doing the work because of increased costs, other commitments or any other reason could claim that his bid is not binding because it is incomplete. But California has not taken that position. In *Drennan* the bid was one of price only and it is obvious that the general contractor would have entered into a written subcontract with the prospective subcontractor containing terms other than price. The Supreme Court nevertheless held that the subcontractor's bid was binding. The same rule must be applied here.

It should be noted that here the lack of an electrical subcontract between the general contractor and defendant was not due to the failure of the parties negotiating in good faith to arrive at the terms other than price. We do not intimate what our conclusion would be had that been the case. Here, as in *Drennan,* the parties did not get around to discussing contract provisions because defendant made it clear that it would not do the work at the price bid regardless of the other contractual provisions.

CROOK v. MORTENSON–NEAL, 727 P.2d 297 (Alaska 1986). This was another case in which a general contractor sued a subcontractor on the ground that it had relied on the subcontractor's bid. The subcontractor argued that the general contractor did not rely on the bid, but instead continued to negotiate with the subcontractor for the purpose of extracting a better bargain. In particular, the subcontractor argued that the written subcontract proffered by the general contractor after the bid contained many additional terms, involving such matters as time for performance, payment schedule, and lien waivers, that were not described in the bidding documents. Held, for the general contractor.

"Resolution of the parties' dispute requires an appreciation of the complexities of construction bidding. A general contractor's addition to the formal subcontract of terms not present in the bidding documents does not necessarily impose materially different duties. The bidding documents in this case did not purport to express completely the relationship between the general and its subcontractors. Rather, they described the respective duties assumed by the project owner and the general contractor and specifically required the general contractor to include certain provisions in any subcontract. The documents contemplated a contractual relationship between general and subcontractor distinct from the relationship between owner and general.

"The bidding documents ... did not purport to be the exclusive agreement between general and subcontractor. Rather, they provided [the subcontractor] with enough information to calculate its bid within the owner's requirements. The documents only outlined the duties owed by [the subcontractor to the general contractor] and left the task of detailing the parties' respective obligations for a separate agreement. At the time [the subcontractor] bid on its subcontract, it should have expected to be bound by reasonable additional terms governing standard conditions implicit in the relationship between subcontractor and general contractor. Both industry custom, as expressed in standard form subcontracts, and the circumstances surrounding the particular project, dictate the kinds of provisions [the subcontractor] should reasonably have expected in its final subcontract."

The court distinguished cases in which the general contractors had attempted to expand the scope of the duties required of the subcontractor beyond that reasonably to be inferred or required by custom.

RESTATEMENT, SECOND, CONTRACTS §§ 33, 34

[See Selected Source Materials Supplement]

UCC §§ 2–204, 2–305, 2–308, 2–309, 2–310

[See Selected Source Materials Supplement]

CISG ARTS. 14(1), 31, 33, 55, 57, 58

[See Selected Source Materials Supplement]

UNIDROIT PRINCIPLES OF INTERNATIONAL COMMERCIAL CONTRACTS ARTS. 2.1.2, 2.1.13, 2.1.14, 5.1.7, 5.1.8, 6.1.1, 6.6.6

[See Selected Source Materials Supplement]

PRINCIPLES OF EUROPEAN CONTRACT LAW
§§ 2.201(1), 6.104, 6.109, 7.01, 7.102

[See Selected Source Materials Supplement]

NOTE ON GAP–FILLERS

The UCC provisions cross-referenced above are generally referred to as *gap-fillers*, because they fill gaps that parties may leave in a contract for the sale of goods. The UCC gap-filler provisions are *default rules*; that is, background rules that the law reads into a contract in the absence of, but only in the absence of, the parties' actual agreement on the relevant issues. (In contrast, *mandatory rules,* such as the principles of consideration, cannot be supplanted by the parties' agreement.)

The theory of how default rules should be constructed is contested. Most commentators take the position that, with certain exceptions, default rules should be based on the agreement that probably would have been reached if the relevant issue had been specifically addressed. This approach leaves open two possible conceptions. Under one conception, the default rule should be the term that *reasonable persons in the positions of the parties* probably would have agreed to if they had specifically addressed the relevant issue when they made the contract. Under an alternative conception, the default rule should be the term that the *actual parties* probably would have agreed to if they had specifically addressed the issue. The second conception takes into account the bargaining power and risk-averseness of the actual parties, the intensity with which those parties hold various positions, and the like. The first conception seems much more attractive, in part because it would be extremely difficult to determine the actual parties' relative bargaining power, degree of risk-averseness, intensity, and the like, at the time they made the contract; and even if those elements could be determined, it would be highly problematic how those elements would have played out in the negotiation of any given issue if the parties had chosen to address that issue when they made the contract.

HAWKLAND, SALES CONTRACT TERMS UNDER THE UCC, 17 U.C.C.L.J. 195, 207 (1985). "The rationale underlying the use of statutory [gap–filler] terms is that they represent ordinary understanding about common matters and therefore most likely would have been used by the parties had they considered the term when they made their agreement. In short, statutory terms presuppose that the parties have omitted, through haste, ignorance, or forgetfulness, a routine term that subsequently has become important and that the fairest method to fill that missing term is to impose upon them the kind of term that normally is used by most parties in common, unexceptional deals."

JOSEPH MARTIN, JR., DELICATESSEN, INC. v. SCHUMACHER,
52 N.Y.2d 105, 436 N.Y.S.2d 247, 417 N.E.2d 541 (1981). In 1973, Landlord leased a retail store to Tenant for a five–year term at a rent that graduated upwards, from $500 per month for the first year to $650 for the fifth. A renewal clause stated that "[t]he Tenant may renew this lease for an additional period of five years at annual rentals to be agreed upon; Tenant shall give Landlord thirty (30) days written notice, to be mailed certified mail, return receipt requested, of the intention to exercise such right." Tenant gave timely notice of its desire to renew, but after Landlord made it clear that he would renew only at a rental starting at $900 a month, Tenant engaged an appraiser, who opined that a fair market rental value would be $545.41.

Tenant then began an action for specific performance to compel Landlord to extend the lease for the additional term at the appraiser's figure, or such other sum as the court would decide was reasonable. For his part, Landlord brought a proceeding to evict Tenant. The trial court dismissed Tenant's complaint on the ground that an agreement to agree on a future rental was unenforceable for uncertainty. The Appellate Division reinstated Tenant's complaint. It reasoned that "a renewal clause in a lease providing for future agreement on the rent to be paid during the renewal term is enforceable if it is established that the parties' intent was not to terminate in the event of a failure to agree." It went on to state that, if Tenant met that burden, the trial court could proceed to set a "reasonable rent." On appeal, the New York Court of Appeals held that the Appellate Division's disposition of the case was incorrect.

" . . . [I]t is rightfully well settled in the common law of contracts in this State that a mere agreement to agree, in which a material term is left for future negotiations, is unenforceable. . . .

"This is not to say that the requirement for definiteness in the case before us now could only have been met by explicit expression of the rent to be paid. The concern is with substance, not form. It certainly would have sufficed, for instance, if a methodology for determining the rent was to be found within the four corners of the lease, for a rent so arrived at would have been the end product of agreement between the parties themselves. Nor would the agreement have failed for indefiniteness because it invited recourse to an objective extrinsic event, condition or standard on which the amount was made to depend. All of these, inter alia, would have come within the embrace of the maxim that what can be made certain is certain. . . .

"But the renewal clause here in fact contains no such ingredients. Its unrevealing, unamplified language speaks to no more than 'annual rentals to be agreed upon'. Its simple words leave no room for legal construction or resolution of ambiguity. Neither tenant nor landlord is bound to any formula. There is not so much as a hint at a commitment to be bound by the 'fair market rental value' which the tenant's expert reported or the 'reasonable rent' the Appellate Division would impose, much less any definition of either. Nowhere is there an inkling that either of the parties directly or indirectly assented, upon accepting the clause, to subordinate the figure on which it ultimately would insist, to one fixed judicially . . . or, for that matter, by an arbitrator or other third party."

MOOLENAAR v. CO–BUILD COMPANIES INC., 354 F.Supp. 980 (D.Vi.1973) In October 1967, Moolenaar, a sheep-and-goat farmer, leased 150 acres of land from Correa. The lease was to run for a period of five years, and Moolenaar had an option to renew for an additional five years. Moolenaar was to pay $375 per month during the initial term. The lease provided that the rent for the renewal period "shall be renegotiated." Later, Correa sold the land to Co–Build Companies. Co-build purchased the land subject to Moolenaar's rights under the lease.

In April 1972, six months before the first five-year term expired, Moolenaar informed Co–Build of his intention to exercise the renewal option. Co–Build expressed its willingness to extend the lease at a "renegotiated" rent of $17,000 per month. Co–Build justified this figure by the high price it had paid for the land, and by the land's unquestionably great value if put to industrial use. Such a rent, however, was beyond the resources of the less profitable goat-husbandry business. Moolenaar therefore proposed a considerably lower figure, and indicated his desire to meet for direct negotiations. All such offers were declined. Upon Co–Build's refusal to recede from its initial position, Moolenaar filed an action for a declaratory judgement of the rights of the parties under the lease. Held, Moolenaar had a right to renew at a reasonable rent.

"The threshold question is, of course, whether Moolenaar possesses a renewal option at all. A number of jurisdictions would hold that he does not, reasoning that a clause which neglects to stipulate the rent is void for uncertainty and indefiniteness. . . . The better view, however, would hold that such a clause intends renewal at a 'reasonable' rent, and would find that market conditions are ascertainable with sufficient certainty to make the clause specifically enforceable. A number of policy considerations support this result. First, it will probably effectuate the intent of the parties better than would striking out the clause altogether. A document should be construed where possible to give effect to every term, on the theory that the signatories inserted each for a reason and if one party had agreed to the clause only in the secret belief that it would prove unenforceable, he should be discouraged from such paths. Secondly, a renewal option has a more sympathetic claim to enforcement than do most vague contractual terms, since valuable consideration will often have already been paid for it. The option of renewal is one factor inducing the tenant to enter into the lease, or to pay as high a rent as he did during the initial period. To this extent the landlord benefited from the tenant's reliance on the clause, and so the tenant has a stronger claim to receive the reciprocal benefit of the option.[1] . . .

" . . . The rule which I have followed here is admittedly the minority view. . . . I think it is appropriate to give greater weight to recent decisions rather than weighing the authorities on a strictly numerical basis. . . . Briefly, the common law is in a state of perpetual evolution and recent decisions will more accurately reflect the current understanding on an issue. For the issue at hand the minority view is nonetheless a widely followed one, . . . and has been gaining adherents at a rate which indicates that the common law is

---

1. Contrary to Co–Build's assertion that such a clause may benefit either the landlord or the tenant, depending on market conditions, it benefits only the tenant. He has the choice of whether or not to exercise the option, while the landlord would be in a corresponding position only if he could elect to renew the lease and thereby bind the tenant for rent during the additional period.

moving in that direction. Compare, e. g., 30 A.L.R. 572 (1924) (few cases cited for minority view) with 6 A.L.R.2d 448, 454 (1949) (many such cases). And while, of course, not controlling here, the U.C.C. provisions on the Sale of Goods also illustrate the approach of the modern law, with its emphasis on reasonable commercial dealings and its rejection of technical requirements."

CHANNEL HOME CENTERS v. GROSSMAN
United States Court of Appeals, Third Circuit, 1986.
795 F.2d 291.

Before WEIS, HIGGINBOTHAM, BECKER, CIRCUIT JUDGES.

Opinion of the Court

BECKER, CIRCUIT JUDGE.

This diversity case presents the question whether, under Pennsylvania law, a property owner's promise to a prospective tenant, pursuant to a detailed letter of intent, to negotiate in good faith with the prospective tenant and to withdraw the lease premises from the marketplace during the negotiation, can bind the owner for a reasonable period of time where the prospective tenant has expended significant sums of money in connection with the lease negotiations and preparation and where there was evidence that the letter of intent was of significant value to the property owner. We hold that it may. We therefore vacate and reverse the district court's determination that there was no enforceable agreement, and remand the case for trial.

I.

Appellant Channel Home Centers ("Channel"), a division of Grace Retail Corporation, operates retail home improvement stores throughout the Northeastern United States, including Philadelphia and its suburbs. Appellee Frank Grossman, a real estate broker and developer, with his sons Bruce and Jeffrey Grossman, either owns or has a controlling interest in appellees Tri–Star Associates ("Tri–Star"), Baker Investment Corporation ("Baker"), and Cedarbrook Associates, a Pennsylvania Limited Partnership ("Cedarbrook").

Between November, 1984 and February, 1985, the Grossmans, through Baker, were in the process of acquiring ownership of Cedarbrook Mall ("the mall") located in Cheltenham Township, Pennsylvania, a northern suburb of Philadelphia. During these months, Baker was the equitable owner of the mall, Tri–Star was acting as the mall's leasing agent, and legal title was in Equitable Life Assurance Society. It was anticipated that, upon closing in February, 1985, Baker would become both legal and equitable owner of the mall. App. at 218a–219a, 496a. The Grossmans intended to revitalize the mall, which had fallen on hard times prior to their acquisition, through an aggressive rehabilitation and leasing program.

In the third week of November, 1984, Tri–Star wrote to Richard Perkowski, Director of Real Estate for Channel, informing him of the availability of a store location in Cedarbrook Mall which Tri–Star believed Channel would be interested in leasing. Perkowski expressed some interest, and met the Grossmans on November 28, 1984. After Perkowski was given a tour of the premises, the terms of a lease were discussed. App. at 457a, 496a. Frank

Grossman testified that "we discussed various terms, and these terms were, some were loose, some were more or less terms." App. at 364a, 496a–497a.

In a memorandum dated December 7, 1984, to S. Charles Tabak, Channel's senior vice-president for general administration, Perkowski outlined the salient lease terms that he had negotiated with the Grossmans. App. at 97a. On or about the same date, Tabak and Leon Burger, President of Channel, visited the mall site with the Grossmans. They indicated that Channel desired to lease the site. App. at 413a–415a. Frank Grossman then requested that Channel execute a letter of intent that, as Grossman put it, could be shown to "other people, banks or whatever." App. at 366a–367a. Tabak testified that the Grossmans wanted to get Channel into the site because it would give the mall four "anchor" stores. App. at 414a. Apparently, Frank Grossman was anxious to get Channel's signature on a letter of intent so that it could be used to help Grossman secure financing for his purchase of the mall. App. at 366a–367a, 497a.

On December 11, 1984, in response to Grossman's request, Channel prepared, executed, and submitted a detailed letter of intent setting forth a plethora of lease terms which provided, *inter alia,* that

> [t]o induce the Tenant [Channel] to proceed with the leasing of the Store, you [Grossman] will withdraw the Store from the rental market, and only negotiate the above described leasing transaction to completion.

Please acknowledge your intent to proceed with the leasing of the store under the above terms, conditions and understanding by signing the enclosed copy of the letter and returning it to the undersigned within ten (10) days from the date hereof.

App. at 31a.[2]

2. The full December 11, 1984 letter, on Channel stationery, reads as follows:

Dear Mr. Grossman:

The Channel Home Centers Division of Grace Retail Corporation has approved the leasing of a store at the above described location subject to the terms and conditions of this letter. The purpose of this letter is to express the understanding under which an Agreement of Lease, prepared by Tenant, but in a mutually satisfactory form, is to be executed by the owner of the Shopping Center, as Landlord and Grace Retail Corporation, as Tenant.

The Landlord will lease to the Tenant the following described Store located in the captioned Shopping Center, all as shown and described on the copy of your leasing brochure attached to this letter and on the following terms:

1. *Store:* Existing 70,400 sq. ft. area designated in the attached leasing brochure as space "1" on lower level of mall beneath Jamesway Department Store, together with use of outdoor area for storage and sales. Such area located in portion of parking lot adjacent to space "1".

2. *Term & Rent:* Term of twenty-five (25) years commencing the date Tenant opens for business during which Tenant will pay Annual Rent in the amounts set forth below plus Percentage Rent of two (2) percent of Gross Sales during each lease year in excess of the Gross Sales Break Point set forth below:

Lease Year	Annual Rent	Gross Sales Break Point
1– 5	$112,500	$10.0 MM
6–10	137,500	11.0 MM
11–15	162,500	12.1 MM
16–20	187,500	13.3 MM
20–25	212,500	14.6 MM

3. *Option Periods:* Tenant's right to extend for four (4) option periods of five (5) years each, on the same terms as during the initial term, except that during each exercised option period, the Annual Rent shall be increased once by $25,000 per year, and the Gross Sales Break Point shall be increased by 10% over the sums in effect for the prior 5–year period (i.e. during Lease Years 26–30 of first option period, Annual Rent shall be $237,500 per year and Gross Sales Break Point shall be $16.06 million);

4. *Real Estate Taxes:* Landlord's obligation, Tenant does not make contributions;

5. *Common Area Maintenance:* Landlord's obligation to maintain and repair existing 850 car parking lot in northeast portion of

Frank Grossman promptly signed the letter of intent and returned it to Channel. App. at 499a. Grossman contends that Perkowski and Tabak also agreed orally that a draft lease be submitted within thirty (30) days. App. at 331a–332a, 365–366a. Perkowski and Tabak denied telling Grossman that a lease would be forthcoming within 30 days or any finite period of time. App. at 445a, 473a.

Thereafter, both parties initiated procedures directed toward satisfaction of lease contingencies. The letter of intent specified that execution of the lease was expressly subject to each of the following: (1) approval by Channel's parent corporation, W.R. Grace & Company ("Grace"), of the essential business terms of the lease; (2) approval by Channel of the status of title for the site; and (3) Channel's obtaining, with Frank Grossman's cooperation, all necessary permits and zoning variances for the erection of Channel's identification signs. App. at 30a; *see supra* note 2.

On December 14, 1984, Channel directed the Grace legal department to prepare a lease for the premises. Channel's real estate committee approved the lease site on December 20, 1984. App. at 472a. Channel planning representatives visited the premises on December 21, 1984, to obtain measurements for architectural alterations, renovations and related construction. App. at 379a. Detailed marketing plans were developed, building plans drafted, delivery schedules were prepared and materials and equipment deemed neces-

---

Shopping Center, which will be the Tenant's primary parking area, and other common areas of the Shopping Center; Tenant does not make contributions;

6. *Landlord's Pre-term Responsibilities:* Landlord will deliver Store empty and broom clean including the removal of all partitions, and with HVAC system in working order. The Landlord will submeter and locate the major electric service to the area of the Store, as Channel designates. Landlord will remove the existing escalator and provide escape stairs as per fire code, and will insure that the building is free of any asbestos hazard. The service elevator and two receiving bays on the lower level, will be boxed-out from the Tenant's Store, to serve the upper levels of the Shopping Center.

7. *Maintenance & Repairs:* Landlord will maintain repair and replace if necessary the HVAC system, roof and structural and exterior portions of the building. Tenant responsible for building interior and store front and will pay its prorate share of HVAC usage.

Execution of the Agreement of Lease by Landlord and Tenant is specifically subject to each of the following:

a. *Tenant's authority:* Approval by Tenant's parent corporation, W.R. Grace & Co., and its Retail Group, of the essential business terms of the Agreement of Lease;

b. *Legal Title:* Approval by the Tenant of the status of title for the site, including any access easements.

c. *Sign Contingency:* The Tenants obtaining all necessary permits with the [Landlord's] cooperation (including obtaining any

sign variances) for the erection of Tenant's identification signs, on two (2) pylons located on Cheltenham Ave. and Easton Ave., respectively, and two building signs on the front of the mall and the front of the Store.

The Tenant has and will not incur any brokerage fees in connection with this proposed lease. Any expenditure by the Landlord or Tenant prior to execution of the Agreement of Lease shall be at the party's own risk.

A store opening date during the first half of 1985 is planned. Lease preparation, obtaining the sign permits and approvals described above and delivery of possession of the Store to Tenant would commence immediately and proceed to achieve that estimated opening date. To induce the Tenant to proceed with the leasing of this Store, you will withdraw the Store from the rental market, and only negotiate the above described leasing transaction to completion.

Please acknowledge your intent to proceed with the leasing of the captioned store under the above terms, conditions and understanding by signing the enclosed copy of this letter and returning it to the undersigned within ten (10) days from the date hereof.

Very truly yours,
s/s/
S.C. Tabak
Senior Vice President
Channel Home Center
Division

App. at 29a–31a.

sary for the store were purchased. App. at 91a–96a, 99a–135a, 422a–423a, 517a–547a. The Grossmans applied to the Cheltenham Township building and zoning committee for permission to erect commercial signs for Channel and other tenants of the mall. App. at 15a.

On January 11, 1985, Frank Shea, Esquire, of the Grace legal department sent to Frank Grossman two copies of a forty-one (41) page draft lease and, in a cover letter, requested copies of several documents to be used as exhibits to the lease. App. at 43a–44a. On January 16, 1985, Frank Shea received the following letter from Bruce Grossman:

Dear Mr. Shea:

As you requested, enclosed please find the following documents:

    1) A copy of a recent title report for the Cedarbrook Mall (the "Mall"),

    2) A legal description of the Mall,

    3) A site plan of the Mall, and

    4) A description of the Landlord's construction.

As we discussed, we have commenced work on the Channel location at the Mall and would, therefore, appreciate your assistance in expediting the execution of the Channel lease.

I look forward to hearing from you soon.

> Very truly yours,
>
> BAKER INVESTMENT
> CORPORATION
>
> /s/
>
> Bruce S. Grossman,
>
> Executive Vice President

App. at 16a. On January 21, 1985, Frank Shea received a copy of a letter from Frank Grossman to Richard Perkowski dated January 17, 1985. It provided:

    At Frank Shea's request, enclosed is a site plan for the Cedarbrook Mall and also a copy of the proposed pylon sign design.

    We look forward to executing the lease agreement in the very near future. If you have any questions, please feel free to call me.

App. at 46a.

Bruce Grossman called Shea on January 23, 1985 to discuss the lease. The only item Grossman could recall discussing pertained to the "use" clause in the lease, specifically whether Channel could use the site for warehouse facilities at some future point. App. at 286a–287a, 502a. Apparently, Grossman then related other areas of concern and Shea suggested that a telephone conference be arranged with all parties the following week. App. at 382a, 502a. Grossman agreed. According to Grossman, Shea was supposed to initiate the conference call; however, when the call was not forthcoming, Grossman did not attempt to reach Shea or anyone else at Channel. App. at

389a–390a. Shea understood that the Grossmans were going to discuss the lease among themselves and get back to him. App. at 448a.

On or about January 22, 1985, Stephen Erlbaum, Chairman of the Board of Mr. Good Buys of Pennsylvania, Inc. ("Mr. Good Buys"), contacted Frank Grossman. Like Channel, Mr. Good Buys is a corporation engaged in the business of operating retail home improvement centers; it is a major competitor of Channel in the Philadelphia area. App. at 20a–21a. Erlbaum advised Grossman that Mr. Good Buys would be interested in leasing space at Cedarbrook Mall, and sent Grossman printed information about Mr. Good Buys. App. at 202a.

On January 24, 1985, construction representatives from Channel met at the mall site to go over building alterations and designs. App. at 287a–288a, 503a. The next day, January 25, 1985, Erlbaum and other representatives from Mr. Good Buys met with the Grossmans and toured Channel's proposed lease location. App. at 503a. When Erlbaum expressed an interest in leasing this site, lease terms were discussed. *Id.*

On February 6, 1985, Frank Grossman notified Channel that "negotiations terminated as of this date" due to Channel's failure to submit a signed and mutually acceptable lease for the mall site within thirty days of the December 11, 1984 letter of intent. App. at 42a. (This was the first and only written evidence of the purported thirty-day time limit. The letter of intent contained no such term. . . .) On February 7, 1985, Mr. Good Buys and Frank Grossman executed a lease for the Cedarbrook Mall. App. at 147a–196a. Mr. Good Buys agreed to make base-level annual rental payments which were substantially greater than those agreed to by Channel in the December 11, 1984 letter of intent. App. at 147a.[3] Channel's corporate parent, Grace, approved the terms of Channel's proposed lease on February 13, 1985. App. at 443a–444a.

II.

Channel commenced this diversity action, 28 U.S.C. § 1332(a), in the district court for the Eastern District of Pennsylvania on February 15, 1985. Count I of Channel's complaint alleged that appellees' conduct violated the December 11, 1984 letter of intent and constituted a breach of contract. . . . In a supporting affidavit, S. Charles Tabak averred that Channel had substantially completed all tasks necessary to meet the opening date contemplated in the letter of intent and that it had made out-of-pocket expenditures to this end in the sum of $25,000. . . .

Thereafter, on March 26, 1985, the district court filed a Memorandum Opinion and Order. . . .

In its opinion, the district court rejected Channel's arguments that the letter of intent constituted either a valid unilateral or a valid bilateral

---

3. Channel had agreed to rental payments of $112,500 for years 1–5; $137,500 for years 6–10; $162,500 for years 11–15; $187,500 for years 16–20, and $212,500 for years 20–25. Additionally, Channel agreed to pay percentage rent of two (2) percent of gross sales above the following gross sales break points: $10,000,000 for years 1–5; $11,000,000 for years 6–10; $12,100,000 for years 11–15; $13,300,000 for years 16–20, and $14,600,000 for years 20–25. *See supra* note 3. Mr. Good Buys agreed to rental payments of $249,750 for years 1–5; $360,750 for years 6–10; $388,500 for years 11–15; $416,250 for years 6–20; and $444,000 for years 21–25. App. at 147a. Mr. Good Buys did not have to pay additional percentage rent based on gross sales, however. *Id.*

agreement. The court concluded that the letter of intent (1) did not bind the parties to any obligation; (2) was unenforceable for lack of consideration....

IV.

[Channel contends] that the district court erred in holding that the letter of intent was unenforceable and did not bind the parties to any obligation. Channel argues that the letter, coupled with the surrounding circumstances, constitutes a binding agreement to negotiate in good faith. Appellees rejoin that a promise to negotiate in good faith or to use best efforts to reduce to formal writing an agreement between the parties is enforceable only if the parties have in fact reached agreement on the underlying transaction. Because it is conceded that the letter of intent did not constitute a final agreement between the parties, appellees contend that it is merely evidence of preliminary negotiations and, as such, is unenforceable at law. Appellees further argue that even if the agreement were an otherwise enforceable contract, the letter of intent and any promises contained therein are unenforceable by virtue of Channel's lack of consideration. The parties agree that Pennsylvania law applies to the case.

It is hornbook law that evidence of preliminary negotiations or an agreement to enter into a binding contract in the future does not alone constitute a contract. *See Goldman v. McShain,* 432 Pa. 61, 68, 247 A.2d 455, 458 (1968); *Lombardo v. Gasparini Excavating Co.,* 385 Pa. 388, 392, 123 A.2d 663, 666 (1956); *Kazanjian v. New England Petroleum Corp.,* 332 Pa.Super. 1, 7, 480 A.2d 1153, 1157 (1984); *see* Restatement (Second) of Contracts § 26 (1979). Appellees believe that this doctrine settles this case, but, in so arguing, appellees misconstrue Channel's contract claim. Channel does not contend that the letter of intent is binding as a lease or an agreement to enter into a lease. Rather, it is Channel's position that this document is enforceable as a mutually binding obligation *to negotiate in good faith.*[4] By unilaterally terminating negotiations with Channel and precipitously entering into a lease agreement with Mr. Good Buys, Channel argues, Grossman acted in bad faith and breached his promise to "withdraw the Store from the rental market and only negotiate the above-described leasing transaction to completion." *See supra* note 2.

Under Pennsylvania law, the test for enforceability of an agreement is whether both parties have manifested an intention to be bound by its terms and whether the terms are sufficiently definite to be specifically enforced. *Lombardo v. Gasparini Excavating Co.,* 385 Pa. 388, 393, 123 A.2d 663, 666; *Linnet v. Hitchcock,* 324 Pa.Super. 209, 214, 471 A.2d 537, 540. Additionally, of course, there must be consideration on both sides. *Stelmack v. Glen Alden Coal Co.,* 339 Pa. 410, 14 A.2d 127 (1940); *Cardamone v. University of Pittsburgh,* 253 Pa.Super. 65, 384 A.2d 1228 (1978). Consideration "confers a benefit upon the promisor or causes a detriment to the promisee and must be an act, forbearance or return promise bargained for and given in exchange for the original promise." *Curry v. Estate of Thompson,* 332 Pa.Super. 364, 371, 481 A.2d 658, 661 (1984).

---

4. Because Channel does not argue that the letter of intent is enforceable as a lease between the parties, appellees' reliance upon the district court's conclusion that the letter of intent is insufficient to satisfy the Pennsylvania Statute of Frauds for Leases, Pa.Stat.Ann. tit. 68, §§ 250.202–203 (Purdon 1965 & Supp. 1986), is misplaced. The district court therefore erred in holding that the letter of intent was insufficient to satisfy the Statute of Frauds for leases.

Although no Pennsylvania court has considered whether an agreement to negotiate in good faith may meet these conditions, the jurisdictions that have considered the issue have held that such an agreement, if otherwise meeting the requisites of a contract, is an enforceable contract. *See, e.g., Thompson v. Liquichimica of America, Inc.*, 481 F.Supp. 365, 366 (E.D.N.Y.1979); ("Unlike an agreement to agree, which does not constitute a closed proposition, an agreement to use best efforts [or to negotiate in good faith] is a closed proposition, discrete and actionable."); *accord Reprosystem, B.V. v. SCM Corp.*, 727 F.2d 257, 264 (2d Cir.1984); *Chase v. Consolidated Foods Corp.*, 744 F.2d 566, 571 (7th Cir.1984); *Arnold Palmer Golf Co. v. Fuqua Industries Inc.*, 541 F.2d 584 (6th Cir.1976); *Itek Corp. v. Chicago Aerial Industries, Inc.*, 248 A.2d 625 (Del.1968); Restatement (Second) of Contracts § 205 comment (c) (1979) ("Good faith in negotiation"); *see generally* Kessler and Fine, *Culpa in Contrahendo, Bargaining in Good Faith, and Freedom of Contract; a Comparative Study,* 77 Harv.L.Rev. 401 (1964).[5] We are satisfied that Pennsylvania would follow this rule. Applying Pennsylvania law, then, we must ask (1) whether both parties manifested an intention to be bound by the agreement; (2) whether the terms of the agreement are sufficiently definite to be enforced; and (3) whether there was consideration.

In determining the parties' intentions concerning the letter of intent, we must examine the entire document and the relevant circumstances surrounding its adoption. *United Refining Co. v. Jenkins*, 410 Pa. 126, 137, 189 A.2d 574, 580 (1963); *Hillbrook Apartments, Inc. v. Nyce Crete Co.*, 237 Pa.Super. 565, 572, 352 A.2d 148, 151 (1975). The letter of intent, signed by both parties, provides that "[t]o induce the Tenant [Channel] to proceed with the leasing of the Store, you [Grossman] will withdraw the Store from the rental market, and only negotiate the above described leasing transaction to completion." *See supra* note 2. The agreement thus contains an unequivocal promise by Grossman to withdraw the store from the rental market and to negotiate the proposed leasing transaction with Channel to completion.

Evidence of record supports the proposition that the parties intended this promise to be binding. After the letter of intent was executed, both Channel and the Grossmans initiated procedures directed toward satisfaction of lease contingencies. Channel directed its parent corporation to prepare a draft lease; Channel planning representatives visited the lease premises to obtain measurements for architectural alterations, renovations, and related construction. Channel developed extensive marketing plans; delivery schedules were prepared and material and equipment deemed necessary for the store were purchased. The Grossmans applied to the township zoning committee for permission to erect Channel signs at various locations on the mall property. Channel submitted a draft lease on January 11, 1985, and the parties, through correspondence and telephone conversations and on-site visits, exhibited an intent to move toward a lease as late as January 23, 1985.... Accordingly, the letter of intent and the circumstances surrounding its

---

5. Good faith in the bargaining or formation stages of the contracting process is distinguishable from the common law duty to perform in good faith. *See* Restatement of Contracts (Second) § 205 (1979) ("Every contract imposes upon each party a duty of good faith and fair dealing in its performance and its enforcement."); *Baker v. Lafayette College,* 350 Pa.Super. 68, 84, 504 A.2d 247, 255 (1986); *Germantown Manufacturing Co. v. Rawlinson,* 341 Pa.Super. 42, 60, 491 A.2d 138, 148 (1985); *see generally* Burton, *Breach of Contract and the Common Law Duty to Perform in Good Faith,* 94 Harv.L.Rev. 369 (1980).

adoption both support a finding that the parties intended to be bound by an agreement to negotiate in good faith.

We also believe that Grossman's promise to "withdraw the Store from the rental market and only negotiate the above described leasing transaction to completion," viewed in the context of the detailed letter of intent (which covers most significant lease terms, *see supra* n. 2), is sufficiently definite to be specifically enforced, provided that Channel submitted sufficient legal consideration in return.

Appellees argue that "[n]o money or thing of value was paid, either at the time of the letter or at any other time that would convert an agreement to negotiate into some enforceable type of contract." Brief of Appellees at 16. We disagree. It seems clear that the execution and tender of the letter of intent by Channel was of substantial value to Frank Grossman. At the time the letter of intent was executed, Grossman was in the process of obtaining financing for his purchase of the mall. When it became apparent to Grossman that Channel—a major corporate tenant—was seriously interested in leasing the mall site, he requested that Channel sign a letter of intent which, as Grossman put it, could be shown to "other people, banks or whatever with a view to getting permanent financing." App. at 366a–367a. Fully aware of Grossman's desire to obtain financing, Channel sought to solidify its bargaining position by requesting that Grossman also sign the letter of intent and promise to "withdraw the store from the rental market and only negotiate the above-described leasing transaction to completion." There being evidence that value passed from each party to the other, we conclude that the record would support a finding that Channel's execution and tender of the letter of intent conferred a bargained for benefit on Grossman which was valid consideration for Grossman's return promise to negotiate in good faith.

V.

In sum, we agree with Channel that the record contains evidence that supports a finding that the parties intended to enter into a binding agreement to negotiate in good faith. We further hold that the agreement had sufficient specificity to make it an enforceable contract if the parties so intended, and that consideration passed between the parties. We will therefore remand this case to the district court for trial.

At least two significant issues must be resolved at trial. First, although our review of the record reveals that there is sufficient evidence to support a finding that the parties intended to be bound by the letter of intent, we do not hold that the evidence requires this conclusion. At trial, evidence will presumably be brought to light that will aid the trier of fact in deciding this issue.

As noted above, there is also some dispute over whether there was a time limit on the negotiations that was not specified in the letter of intent. Because the district court erroneously concluded that the letter of intent was unenforceable as a matter of law, it made no factual findings with regard to this critical term. If, as appellees suggest, Channel orally agreed to forward a draft lease within 30 days of the date on which the letter of intent was executed, Channel's failure to do so could have terminated the agreement. Alternatively, if, as Channel argues, the parties did not fix a definite time for the duration of negotiations, then a reasonable time would be applicable. *See Darlington v. General Electric Corp.,* 350 Pa.Super. 183, 192–93, 504 A.2d 306, 310–11

(1986), and a determination must be made as to what constitutes a reasonable time under all the circumstances.

The judgment of the district court will therefore be reversed, and the case remanded for further proceedings consistent with this opinion.

———

A/S APOTHEKERNES LABORATORIUM FOR SPECIALPRAE-PARATER v. I.M.C. CHEMICAL GROUP, INC., 873 F.2d 155 (7th Cir. 1989). This case concerned the legal effect of a letter of intent, signed by both parties, for a purchase and sale of assets. The Court of Appeals began by approving the District Court's finding that the letter of intent did not constitute a binding contract: "[A]s we recently stated, ... the purpose and function of a preliminary letter of intent is not to bind the parties to their ultimate contractual objective. Instead, it is only 'to provide the initial framework from which the parties might later negotiate a final ... agreement, if the deal works out.' "

The Court of Appeals then approved the district court's conclusion that the letter of intent did impose upon the parties an obligation to negotiate in good faith:

"We agree that that conclusion was proper; a number of courts, including this court, have held that the terms of a letter of intent may impose such a duty. . . .

"The obligation to negotiate in good faith has been generally described as preventing one party from, 'renouncing the deal, abandoning the negotiations, or insisting on conditions that do not conform to the preliminary agreement.' ... For instance, a party might breach its obligation to bargain in good faith by unreasonably insisting on a condition outside the scope of the parties' preliminary agreement, especially where such insistence is a thinly disguised pretext for scotching the deal because of an unfavorable change in market conditions. ... The full extent of a party's duty to negotiate in good faith can only be determined, however, from the terms of the letter of intent itself."

———

UNIDROIT PRINCIPLES OF INTERNATIONAL COMMERCIAL CONTRACTS ART. 2.1.15

[See Selected Source Materials Supplement]

———

PRINCIPLES OF EUROPEAN CONTRACT LAW ART. 2.301

[See Selected Source Materials Supplement]

———

TEACHERS INSURANCE AND ANNUITY ASSOCIATION OF AMERICA v. TRIBUNE CO.

United States District Court, Southern District of New York, 1987.
670 F.Supp. 491.

LEVAL, DISTRICT JUDGE. . . .

[To raise cash that it needed for a number of purposes, including the operation of its newspaper, The New York Daily News, Tribune Company decided to sell the News Building. To this end, Tribune entered negotiations to sell the News Building to LaSalle Partners as part of a complex three-party transaction. The concept of the transaction was as follows: LaSalle would pay for the News Building by giving Tribune a mortgage note secured by a mortgage on the building. This note was to be "nonrecourse," meaning that LaSalle would have no liability under the mortgage note, although the noteholder could foreclose on the Building under the mortgage if the note was not paid.

[Because LaSalle would give Tribune only a nonrecourse note, the LaSalle transaction, taken in itself, would produce no immediate cash for Tribune. However, Tribune would proceed to borrow from a lending institution an amount of money equal to the mortgage note, and in exchange would give the lending institution Tribune's own note for that amount. The loan agreement with the lending institution would provide that Tribune could pay off its own note to the institution by "putting" (delivering to the institution), in place of its own note, the nonrecourse mortgage note that Tribune would receive from LaSalle. To compensate the lending institution for the additional risk inherent in the possible put, Tribune would pay the lender a premium above market interest rates.

[The complex nature of the proposed transaction was largely driven by tax considerations, but there was also an accounting element to the transaction. Tribune believed that because it would have the right to put the mortgage note to the lending institution in full satisfaction of its debt to the institution, it would not be required to include its debt to the institution as a liability on its balance sheet. Instead, Tribune believed, it could employ offset accounting, under which it would set off its debt to the lending institution against the mortgage note, eliminate both its debt and the mortgage note from its balance sheet, and instead describe the debt and mortgage note in the footnotes to its financial statements. This would make Tribune's balance sheet look better, because Tribune would show the cash infusion, but not the debt.

[For tax reasons, it was important that the transaction be completed during 1982. Tribune prepared a list of six leading institutions, including Teachers Insurance and Annuity Association of America ("Teachers" or "TIAA"), that it believed would have the means and flexibility to make a loan with the required specifications. All but Teachers promptly rejected Tribune's proposal. On August 20, Scott Smith, Tribune's Vice President and Treasurer, sent Martha Driver, of Teachers, an Offering Circular, including a term sheet, which described the proposed transaction. Smith's letter stated, "While we are flexible on funds delivery, our objective is to have a firm commitment from a lender by September 15, 1982. Consequently, we need to move the due diligence and negotiation process along very quickly." On September 16, Teachers' Finance Committee met and approved the Tribune loan. Driver then told Smith that TIAA would promptly issue a commitment letter, committing TIAA to make the loan.

[The commitment letter was mailed by TIAA on September 22. It included a two-page term sheet, which was drawn from Tribune's own term sheet and ensuing conversations. TIAA's term sheet covered all the basic economic terms of a loan. Neither TIAA's term sheet nor its commitment letter made reference to the availability of offset accounting. TIAA's letter stated that the loan agreement was "contingent upon the preparation, execution and delivery of documents ... in form and substance satisfactory to TIAA and to TIAA's special counsel," and that the transaction documents would contain the usual and customary representations and warranties, closing conditions, other covenants, and events of default "as we and our special counsel may deem reasonably necessary to accomplish this transaction." The letter concluded by inviting Tribune to "evidence acceptance of the conditions of this letter by having it executed below by a duly authorized officer," and added that "Upon receipt by TIAA of an accepted counterpart of this letter, our agreement to purchase from you and your agreement to issue sell and deliver to us ... the captioned securities, shall become a binding agreement between us."

[The "binding agreement" language in the TIAA commitment letter caused serious concern to Tribune's lawyers. Tribune's outside counsel advised Smith, Tribune's Vice President and Treasurer, not to sign a letter containing "binding agreement" language. But having been turned down by five other lending institutions, Smith did not want to risk losing TIAA's commitment. Therefore, he did not raise a question with TIAA concerning the "binding agreement" language. Instead, he executed the commitment letter on Tribune's behalf, and added a notation that the commitment letter was subject to certain modifications outlined in his covering letter. In the covering letter, Smith wrote that "[O]ur acceptance and agreement is subject to approval by the Company's Board of Directors and the preparation and execution of legal documentation satisfactory to the Company." Smith's covering letter, like TIAA's commitment letter, made no mention of offset accounting.

[On October 28, Tribune's board resolved "that the proper officers of the Company be and they hereby are authorized" to effect the borrowing "with all of the actual terms and conditions to be subject to the prior approval by resolution of the Finance Committee." In the meantime, however, interest rates had dropped rapidly, and were now substantially below the rates that prevailed when TIAA and Tribune had entered into the commitment letter. In addition, Tribune began to be concerned that its accountants would not approve Tribune's use of offset accounting for the transaction.

[On December 6, Tribune closed the sale of the building to LaSalle. TIAA then became concerned that Tribune, which could now borrow at substantially lower rates, was seeking to back out of the transaction, and pressed Tribune to put the loan documents into final form. To this end, TIAA dropped a demand it had made imposing conditions on Tribune's exercise of the put, and it asked for a meeting to iron out all open issues. But the drop in interest rates, together with doubts as to the availability of offset accounting, now made the deal much less attractive to Tribune. Smith therefore replied that there was no point in meeting unless TIAA was willing to agree that Tribune's obligation to close the TIAA loan would be conditional on Tribune's ability to use offset accounting. TIAA responded that Tribune's accounting was not part of the deal. When Tribune exhibited no further interest in pursuing the transaction, TIAA brought suit.]

DISCUSSION

The primary contested issue is as to the nature of the obligations that arose out of the commitment letter agreement:

Tribune contends that although the commitment letter was an undertaking to negotiate, it did not obligate either side to enter into a loan contract that was adverse to its interest. Pointing out that the commitment letter agreement left many terms open, that both sides had reserved the right of approval of satisfactory documentation, and that Tribune had furthermore made its obligation conditioned on the approval of its Board of Directors, it argues that it had no binding commitment to the loan agreement, especially if it found the terms adverse to its interests.

Teachers [TIAA] argues that although the commitment letter did not constitute a concluded *loan agreement,* it was nonetheless a binding commitment which obligated both sides to negotiate in good faith toward a final contract conforming to the agreed terms; it thus committed both sides not to abandon the deal, nor to break it by a demand that was outside the scope of the agreement. Although Teachers recognizes that the letter agreement left many points unspecified, it argues that the open terms were of minor economic significance and were covered by the provision that "[t]he documents shall contain such representations and warranties, closing conditions, other covenants, events of default and remedies, requirements for delivery of financial statements, and other information and provisions *as are usual and customary in this type of transaction . . . .*" (Emphasis supplied.) . . . It argues that these minor open terms did not render the contract illusory or unenforceable. Nor did they indicate an intention of the parties not to be bound when taken together with the express language of "binding agreement." Although it was of course possible for the deal to break without liability on either side by reason of inability of the parties to reach agreement on the open terms, Teachers argues that neither side was free to break the deal over conditions which were either inconsistent with the agreed terms or outside the scope of provisions that would be "usual and customary in this type of transaction."

. . .

There has been much litigation over preliminary agreements. It is difficult to generalize about their legal effect. They cover a broad scope ranging in innumerable forms and variations from letters of intent which presuppose that no binding obligations will be placed upon any party until final contract documents have been signed, to firm binding commitments which, notwithstanding a need for a more detailed documentation of agreement, can bind the parties to adhere in good faith to the deal that has been agreed. As is commonly the case with contract disputes, prime significance attaches to the intentions of the parties and to their manifestations of intent. Labels such as "letter of intent" or "commitment letter" are not necessarily controlling although they may be helpful indicators of the parties' intentions. Notwithstanding the intention of the parties at the time, if the agreement is too fragmentary, in that it leaves open terms of too fundamental importance, it may be incapable of sustaining binding legal obligation. Furthermore, the conclusion that a preliminary agreement created binding obligations does not necessarily resolve disputes because it leaves open the further question of the nature, scope and extent of the binding obligations.

A primary concern for courts in such disputes is to avoid trapping parties in surprise contractual obligations that they never intended. Ordinarily in contract negotiations, enforceable legal rights do not arise until either the expression of mutual consent to be bound, or some equivalent event that marks acceptance of offer. Contractual liability, unlike tort liability, arises from consent to be bound (or in any event from the manifestation of consent). It is fundamental to contract law that mere participation in negotiations and discussions does not create binding obligation, even if agreement is reached on all disputed terms. More is needed than agreement on each detail, which is overall agreement (or offer and acceptance) to enter into the binding contract.[6] Nor is this principle altered by the fact that negotiating parties may have entered into letters of intent or preliminary agreements if those were made with the understanding that neither side would be bound until final agreement was reached. The Court of Appeals in several recent cases has stressed the importance of recognizing the freedom of negotiating parties from binding obligations, notwithstanding their having entered into various forms of non-binding preliminary assent. Those decisions have underlined various indicia that can be helpful in making the determination whether a manifestation of preliminary assent amounted to a legally binding agreement.*

Notwithstanding the importance of protecting negotiating parties from involuntary judicially imposed contract, it is equally important that courts enforce and preserve agreements that were intended as binding, despite a need for further documentation or further negotiation. It is, of course, the aim of contract law to gratify, not to defeat, expectations that arise out of intended contractual agreement, despite informality or the need for further proceedings between the parties.

Preliminary contracts with binding force can be of at least two distinct types. One occurs when the parties have reached complete agreement (including the agreement to be bound) on all the issues perceived to require negotiation. Such an agreement is preliminary only in form—only in the sense that the parties desire a more elaborate formalization of the agreement. The second stage is not necessary; it is merely considered desirable. As the Court of Appeals stated with respect to such preliminary agreements in *V'Soske v. Barwick,* 404 F.2d 495, 499 (2d Cir.), *cert. denied,* 394 U.S. 921, 89 S.Ct. 1197, 22 L.Ed.2d 454 (1969), "the mere fact that the parties contemplate memorializing their agreement in a formal document does not prevent their informal

---

6. *See Winston v. Mediafare Entertainment Corp.,* 777 F.2d 78 (2d Cir.1985); *R.G. Group v. Horn & Hardart Co.,* 751 F.2d 69 (2d Cir. 1984); *Reprosystem, B.V. v. SCM Corp.,* 727 F.2d 257 (2d Cir.), *cert. denied,* 469 U.S. 828, 105 S.Ct. 110, 83 L.Ed.2d 54 (1984).

*. [These factors were summarized as follows in *Winston,* supra note 7.

... We have articulated several factors that help determine whether the parties intended to be bound in the absence of a document executed by both sides. The court is to consider (1) whether there has been an express reservation of the right not to be bound in the absence of a writing; (2) whether there has been partial performance of the contract; (3) whether all of the terms of the alleged contract have been agreed upon; and (4) whether the agreement at issue is the type of contract that is usually committed to writing.

(Footnote by ed.)]

agreement from taking effect prior to that event.... Restatement (Second) of Contracts, § 26 (then Tent.Draft No. 1, 1964); 1 Corbin on Contracts § 30 (1950); 1 Williston on Contracts § 28 (3d ed. 1957)."

The second and different sort of preliminary binding agreement is one that expresses mutual commitment to a contract on agreed major terms, while recognizing the existence of open terms that remain to be negotiated. Although the existence of open terms generally suggests that binding agreement has not been reached, that is not necessarily so. For the parties can bind themselves to a concededly incomplete agreement in the sense that they accept a mutual commitment to negotiate together in good faith in an effort to reach final agreement within the scope that has been settled in the preliminary agreement. To differentiate this sort of preliminary agreement from the first, it might be referred to as a binding preliminary commitment. Its binding obligations are of a different order than those which arise out of the first type discussed above. The first type binds both sides to their ultimate contractual objective in recognition that that contract has been reached, despite the anticipation of further formalities. The second type—the binding preliminary commitment—does not commit the parties to their ultimate contractual objective but rather to the obligation to negotiate the open issues in good faith in an attempt to reach the alternate objective within the agreed framework. In the first type, a party may lawfully demand performance of the transaction even if no further steps have been taken following the making of the "preliminary" agreement. In the second type, he may not. What he may demand, however, is that his counter-party negotiate the open terms in good faith toward a final contract incorporating the agreed terms. This obligation does not guarantee that the final contract will be concluded if both parties comport with their obligation, as good faith differences in the negotiation of the open issues may prevent a reaching of final contract. It is also possible that the parties will lose interest as circumstances change and will mutually abandon the negotiation. The obligation does, however, bar a party from renouncing the deal, abandoning the negotiations, or insisting on conditions that do not conform to the preliminary agreement.

It may often be difficult for a court to determine whether a preliminary manifestation of assent should be found to be a binding commitment. The factors mentioned by the Court of Appeals in *Winston,* 777 F.2d 78, and *R.G. Group,* 751 F.2d 69, as relevant to a determination whether final contracts had been reached in preliminary form are also relevant to determination whether preliminary commitments are to be considered binding. But, for this different inquiry, the factors must be applied in a different way. For example, in *R.G. Group,* 751 F.2d at 76, the court identified the ... factor ... "whether there was literally nothing left to negotiate or settle, so that all that remained to be done was to sign what had already been fully agreed to." The existence of open terms is always a factor tending against the conclusion that the parties have reached a binding agreement. But open terms obviously have a somewhat different significance where, unlike *R.G. Group,* the nature of the contract alleged is that it commits the parties in good faith to negotiate the open terms. To consider the existence of open terms as fatal would be to rule, in effect, that preliminary binding commitments cannot be enforced. That is not the law.

In seeking to determine whether such a preliminary commitment should be considered binding, a court's task is, once again, to determine the intentions of the parties at the time of their entry into the understanding, as well as their manifestations to one another by which the understanding was reached. Courts must be particularly careful to avoid imposing liability where binding obligation was not intended. There is a strong presumption against finding binding obligation in agreements which include open terms, call for future approvals and expressly anticipate future preparation and execution of contract documents. Nonetheless, if that is what the parties intended, courts should not frustrate their achieving that objective or disappoint legitimately bargained contract expectations.

Giving legal recognition to preliminary binding commitments serves a valuable function in the marketplace, particularly for relatively standardized transactions like loans. It permits borrowers and lenders to make plans in reliance upon their preliminary agreements and present market conditions. Without such legal recognition, parties would be obliged to expend enormous sums negotiating every detail of final contract documentation before knowing whether they have an agreement, and if so, on what terms. At the same time, a party that does not wish to be bound at the time of the preliminary exchange of letters can very easily protect itself by not accepting language that indicates a "firm commitment" or "binding agreement."

*   *   *   *   *   *

Upon careful consideration of the circumstances and the express terms of this commitment letter, I conclude that it represented a binding preliminary commitment and obligated both sides to seek to conclude a final loan agreement upon the agreed terms by negotiating in good faith to resolve such additional terms as are customary in such agreements. I reject Tribune's contention that its reservation of the right of approval to its Board of Directors left it free to abandon the transaction.

Expression of Intent

The Court of Appeals' first and most important factor looks to the language of the preliminary agreement for indication whether the parties considered it binding or whether they intended not to be bound until the conclusion of final formalities. This factor strongly supports Teachers. The exchange of letters constituting the commitment was replete with the terminology of binding contract, for example:

> If the foregoing properly sets forth your understanding of this transaction, please evidence acceptance of the conditions of this letter by having it executed below by a duly authorized officer ... and by returning one executed counterpart....

> Upon receipt by [Teachers] of an accepted counterpart of this letter, our agreement to purchase from you and your agreement to issue, sell and deliver to us ... the captioned securities, shall become a binding agreement between us.

In signing, Tribune used the words "Accepted and agreed to." Tribune's additional letter of acceptance began "Attached is an executed copy of the Commitment Letter ... for a $76 million loan." The intention to create mutually binding contractual obligations is stated with unmistakable clarity, in a manner not comfortably compatible with Tribune's contention that either side was free to walk away from the deal if it decided its interests were not served thereby.

Tribune argues that this language of binding agreement was effectively contradicted by its statement that "our acceptance and agreement is subject to approval by the Company's Board of Directors and the preparation and execution of legal documentation satisfactory to the Company," as well as by similar reservations in Teachers' letter.

Contracts of preliminary commitment characteristically contain language reserving rights of approval and establishing conditions such as the preparation and execution of documents satisfactory to the contracting party. Although such reservations, considered alone, undoubtedly tend to indicate an intention not to be finally bound, they do not necessarily require that conclusion. Such terms are not to be considered in isolation, but in the context of the overall agreement. Such terms are by no means incompatible with intention to be bound. Since the parties recognize that their deal will involve further documentation and further negotiation of open terms, such reservations make clear the right of a party, or of its Board, to insist on appropriate documentation and to negotiate for or demand protections which are customary for such transactions. In *Reprosystem,* 727 F.2d at 262, and *R.G. Group,* 751 F.2d at 75, the court reasoned that a term stating the agreement would be effective "when executed" could conclusively establish that no binding force was intended prior to execution. That reasoning is of diminished force, however, where the inquiry is not whether the parties had concluded their deal, but only whether they had entered into a binding preliminary commitment which required further steps. Here, the reservation of Board approval and the expressed "contingen[cy] upon the preparation, execution and delivery of documents" did not override and nullify the acknowledgement that a "binding agreement" had been made on the stated terms; those reservations merely recognized that various issues and documentation remained open which also would require negotiation and approval. If full consideration of the circumstances and the contract language indicates that there was a mutual intent to be bound to a preliminary commitment, the presence of such reservations does not free a party to walk away from its deal merely because it later decides that the deal is not in its interest.

The Context of the Negotiations

These conclusions are further reinforced by the particular facts of the negotiation. As Smith's proposal letter of August 20 advised Teachers, Tribune wanted "to have a firm commitment from a lender by September 15, 1982." If such a "firm commitment" meant nothing more than Tribune now contends it does, such a commitment would have been of little value, as the lender would have remained free to abandon the loan if it decided at anytime that the transaction did not suit its purposes, whether because of changed interest rates or for any reason: Tribune wanted a firm commitment because it felt it needed to be sure the transaction would be concluded by the end of the year.

This same thinking governed Tribune's conduct a month later when it received the Teachers' commitment letter. Tribune's lawyers, recognizing that the form of agreement committed Tribune to a "binding" obligation, warned about the consequences of signing it. Tribune, however, wanted Teachers' binding commitment to make the loan. Tribune had been turned down by the five other lenders it considered eligible, and it did not want to risk losing Teachers' commitment. Accordingly, Smith refrained from raising any question about the "binding agreement" language. If he intended by adding the reservation of approval of Tribune's Board of Directors to change the deal fundamentally by freeing Tribune from binding obligations without Teachers noticing the change, he did not accomplish this. Tribune remained committed, as Teachers did. That is to say each was obligated to seek in good faith to conclude a final agreement within the terms specified in the commitment letter, supplemented by such representations, warranties and other conditions as are customary in such transactions. Teachers would not have been free to walk away from the loan by reason of a subsequent decision that the transaction was not in Teachers' interest. Nor could Tribune.

Tribune further contends that, given the uncertainties implicit in the three-cornered deal, neither party could have considered the loan commitment as binding. The agreed terms required Tribune to pay a premium over the prevailing interest rates for the privilege of its option to put the mortgage to Teachers. If Tribune had failed to conclude its deal with LaSalle for the sale of the Building, there would have been no purchase money mortgage and no reason for paying an interest premium.

The argument is not frivolous, but nor is it compelling. If Tribune had failed to sell the News Building and Teachers had nonetheless sought to compel it to take down the loan, Tribune might have succeeded in arguing that the sale of the Building was a mutually agreed implicit condition of the enforceability of the loan agreement. Tribune's argument in those circumstances would have been supported by the references in the commitment letter to the purchase money mortgage resulting from the Building sale.

But, however that dispute would have been resolved had it arisen, it does not compel the conclusion that there was no binding obligation. The Building sale did not fall through. It was concluded on the anticipated terms. If the sale of the Building was an implicit condition of the borrowing, that condition was fulfilled.

Open Terms

Tribune contends that the commitment letter agreement included so many open terms that it could not be deemed a binding contract. It argues also that the numerous open terms indicate a lack of intention on either side to be bound. Neither contention is convincing. Tribune does cite reputable authority to the effect that, notwithstanding language of binding agreement, if a contract fails to include agreement on basic terms of prime importance, it can be considered a nullity. This principle, however, has no application to the present facts. The two page term sheet attached to the commitment letter covered the important economic terms of a loan. The fact that countless pages of relatively conventional minor clauses remained to be negotiated does not render the agreement unenforceable.

The contention is superficially appealing with respect to the mortgage. The commitment letter, although referring to Tribune's optional right to put a mortgage to Teachers in satisfaction of its obligations, did not specify any of the terms of such a mortgage. Absence of agreement on so important a specification as the basic terms of the mortgage would render this agreement illusory. There was, however, no absence of agreement on the basic terms of the mortgage. The references in the commitment letter to the mortgage were understood by both parties as references to the mortgage term sheet that Tribune had furnished to Teachers in its Offering Circular. [The commitment letter stated that the mortgage to be tendered by Tribune "shall preserve the economics proposed for the present Mortgagee (Tribune Company)."] That two-page term sheet described the important economic terms of the proposed LaSalle purchase money mortgage. Notwithstanding its silence as to countless pages of secondary conventional mortgage clauses which remained to be negotiated, it sufficiently specified the important terms to make the commitment letter agreement meaningful and enforceable.

Nor did the existence of open secondary terms compel the conclusion that the parties did not intend to be bound. In support of this argument, Tribune cites the implication of the Court of Appeals in *R.G. Group,* 751 F.2d at 76–77 and *Winston,* 777 F.2d at 80, 82, that the existence of any single open term requires the conclusion that a binding contract had not yet been reached. This takes the Court's observation out of context and distorts its meaning. If the issue is whether the parties have reached final agreement requiring only formal memorialization, the recognized existence of open terms may be a strong indication that they have not. If, on the other hand, as here, the question is whether a preliminary expression of commitment was intended to bind the parties to negotiate the open terms in good faith, the mere fact of the existence of open terms is, of course, far less persuasive. Although the existence of open terms may always be a factor that suggests intention not to be bound, it is by no means conclusive. Where the parties have manifested intention to make a binding agreement, the mere fact of open terms will not permit them to disavow it.

Partial Performance

The factor of partial performance slightly favors Teachers. The evidence shows that for Teachers, its "commitment" to lend involved a budgeting of the funds, albeit somewhat informal. Teachers was in the business of lending its funds. The amount it had available for placement in long-term loans was finite, if large. In its loan budgeting process, Teachers would informally allocate funds which had been so committed. Such allocation reduced the net amount considered available for commitments to new loans. In fact, Teachers advised Tribune that it had only $25 million remaining available to be advanced in 1982 and that the rest would be advanced in 1983.

Tribune argues that because there was no formal segregation, it was of no significance. This misses the point. However informally it was done, the allocation of the loan commitment effectively reserved the funds for the Tribune loan. It reduced the amount of Teachers' funds that it would consider available to competing borrowers. It meant that Teachers would forgo opportunities to procure commitments from other borrowers when its own commitments exhausted its available funds.

In urgently seeking Teachers' "firm commitment" by September 15, Tribune well understood that the commitment would involve a partial performance on Teachers' part. By virtue of the commitment given in September, Tribune was assured that when the time came in December for concluding final documents and drawdown, it would not be told that Teachers had nothing left to lend. Tribune was negotiating to reserve those funds. Teachers acceded and issued the commitment. That constituted a partial performance.

A party's partial performance does not necessarily indicate a belief that the other side is bound. A party may make some partial performance merely to further the likelihood of consummation of a transaction it considers advantageous. This factor was not the subject of highly focused evidence. I have not attached great importance to it and mention it primarily because it is listed among the factors suggested by the Court of Appeals in *R.G. Group* and *Winston.* I conclude, however, that this factor favors the conclusion that both sides considered the commitment binding.

The Customary Form for Such Transactions

The fourth factor mentioned in *R.G. Group,* and *Winston,* is "whether the agreement at issue is the type of contract that is usually committed to writing." 777 F.2d at 80. *See also* 751 F.2d at 77. Of course, the agreement here, unlike those cases, was in writing, but that does not dispose of the issue. To give this factor a broader application, it would better be put in terms of whether in the relevant business community, it is customary to accord binding force to the type of informal or preliminary agreement at issue. The evidence on that question tends to favor Teachers.

Of course it is true, as Tribune argues, that $80 million loans involving mortgages are generally not concluded by means of a four-page letter. But that is not the issue. The question is rather whether the customary practices of the relevant financial community include according such binding force as Teachers here advocates to such preliminary commitment agreements. Teachers' expert evidence showed that it is within the recognized practices of the financial community to accept that preliminary commitments can be binding. Not all preliminary commitments are binding. Some are not. Some are binding on only one side: Where, for example, the borrower pays a commitment fee for the purpose of binding the lender, the agreement may be in the nature of an option to the borrower to decide by a specified date whether to go ahead with the transaction. In such cases the seller has been paid for its one-sided commitment. Some such preliminary agreements are properly seen as merely letters of intent which leave both sides free to abandon the transaction. The point is that the practices of the marketplace are not rigid or uniform. They encompass a considerable variety of transactions negotiated to suit the needs of the parties, including mutually binding preliminary commitments. Each transaction must be examined carefully to determine its characteristics.

Tribune has failed to show to the court's satisfaction that such binding commitments are outside the usages of the marketplace.

Action by Tribune's Board of Directors

The parties disagree as to whether the Teachers' loan was or was not approved by Tribune's Board of Directors. Tribune contends that the resolutions adopted by its Board on October 28th did not involve any approval whatsoever, but merely a delegation of responsibility to the Finance Committee to approve or disapprove the transaction. Teachers contends that the action of the Board did approve the loan in concept, while delegating to the Finance Committee the right and authority to pass on the particular loan documents. Teachers contends that its interpretation is reinforced by Smith's statement to Driver, when she inquired in late November, that the Board had given "general approval" to the transaction at the October 28 meeting (a statement Smith denies having made).

I need not rule on whether the resolutions adopted by the Board of Directors did or did not constitute approval of the transaction, because nothing turns on this. As noted above, although Tribune had reserved the right of approval of the final transaction to its Board of Directors, this did not mean Tribune could defeat its obligations under the binding agreement of commitment merely by having its Board do nothing. The commitment agreement called for conclusion of the transaction and a $25 million first drawdown before the end of the year. Even if I were to accept Tribune's contention that its Board took no action other than to delegate responsibility to the Finance Committee, that would not justify Tribune's backing out of its binding agreement to negotiate in good faith to reach a complete final contract.

Tribune's argument would construe the commitment letter agreement either as a free option to Tribune to decide over the next three months whether to hold Teachers to its commitment to make the loan, or alternatively as a nonbinding statement of mutual intention. Neither is consistent with either the written agreement or the conduct of the parties. Tribune had requested the "firm commitment" of Teachers to make the loan. Teachers' firm commitment was not given for free but in exchange for Tribune's similarly binding commitment. The reservations as to preparation and execution of documents and as to the satisfaction of Teachers' counsel and Tribune's Board permitted each side to negotiate the implementation of the agreement and to require the inclusion of customary terms in a form which it deemed necessary or appropriate to its protection. But those reservations did not authorize either side to escape its obligation simply by declining to negotiate or to give approval.

In any event, I conclude that Tribune's Board did give approval within the meaning of the agreement. The Minutes reflect that the proper officers were expressly authorized to arrange for the borrowing at a maximum interest rate of 15.25%, "with all of the actual terms and conditions to be subject to the prior approval by resolution of the Finance Committee...." The Resolution went on to say that the "authority granted by this resolution shall expire if not utilized prior to April 30, 1983." (DX 19.) This express authorization to "the proper officers ... to arrange for" the borrowing (which would expire if not acted on by April 30, 1983), surely went beyond a mere delegation to the Finance Committee of the Board's responsibility to approve or disapprove. The fact that the authorization was "subject to" Finance Committee approval recognized rather that there were terms and documents that remained to be negotiated, calling for Board level approval. It did not mean that the Board had done nothing but delegate. On consideration of the minutes and resolutions, as well as the testimony of Tribune officers and directors who were present at the meeting, I find, as Smith later told Driver, that the Board gave "general approval" to the transaction.

Tribune's October 6 letter reserving approval to Tribune's Board did not specify any particular form of Board approval, nor did it require that approval be of the final loan documents. Indeed, it distinguished between the requirements of "*approval* by the Company's Board of Directors" and "the preparation and execution of legal documentation *satisfactory to the Company*." The general approval given was sufficient under the contract.

*Tribune's Right to Condition the Loan
on Offset Accounting*

Tribune contends that its right to carry the loan off-balance-sheet by offset accounting was always deemed an essential condition of the deal. It points out that the Offering Circular which it delivered to Teachers, and the Price Waterhouse background memoranda, which also were delivered to Teachers during the early due diligence and discussion phase, all underlined offset accounting as an important Tribune concern. Nor does Teachers deny that in the early discussions, Smith spoke of Tribune's accounting and tax objectives. The witnesses disagree along predictable lines as to whether Driver told Smith that Teachers would not take the risk of Tribune's accounting treatment. The conflict need not be resolved. For regardless whether Driver orally refused to have Teachers assume the risk of Tribune's right to satisfactory accounting, the signed agreement did not provide for any such condition. The written agreement between the parties contains no basis whatever for the proposition that Tribune's obligation was conditioned on satisfactory assurance that it could report the loan off balance sheet. The fact that Tribune considered this significant is not disputed, but it is not determinative.

Both parties were aware of Tribune's objectives as to both the tax and accounting for the proposed deal. Tribune could, of course, have demanded as a condition of its commitment that it receive satisfactory assurances (in the form of opinion letters of counsel and auditors, or otherwise) as to both deferred taxation and offset accounting. It could have offered to pay a fee for Teachers' commitment on terms that would have left Tribune free to proceed with the loan or not, at its option. Alternatively, it could have negotiated for the option to prepay if the Internal Revenue Service or the SEC disallowed the desired tax or accounting consequences. The problem was that in September of 1982, Tribune believed that it needed an immediate "firm commitment" from Teachers to be sure of its ability to conclude the transaction as planned within 1982. Had Tribune made such demands, Teachers might well have turned down Tribune's proposal (as the five other institutions had done). Indeed, Tribune was so sensitive to its need for Teachers' firm commitment that when its counsel warned of the consequences of signing the commitment letter with its "binding agreement" language, Tribune disregarded this advice so as not to lose the lender's commitment. Neither the language of the agreement, nor the negotiations of the parties give any support to the contention that offset accounting was a condition of the agreement.

There was perhaps an additional reason why Tribune did not negotiate for offset accounting as a condition of the deal, being that in September and early October it did not have the doubts that it later developed as to the availability of offset accounting. It had received a prior opinion of Price Waterhouse to the effect that the unconditional put would make offset accounting appropriate. Only after the FASB's mid-October exposure draft did Price Waterhouse begin to emphasize doubts about offset accounting and about the position the SEC might take in the event Tribune offered public securities under an SEC registration statement.

Whether the reason was that Tribune was afraid to lose Teachers prompt firm commitment, or that Tribune had not yet worried, as it later did, about the availability of its accounting objective, or simply that Tribune was willing to take the risk to secure this important deal, the fact is that Tribune did not negotiate for and did not obtain its right to offset accounting as a condition of its bargain.

By December of 1982 Tribune faced a completely different set of factors. Interest rates had declined very substantially. The loan agreement that it negotiated with Teachers was no longer to its benefit since it could now borrow money at substantially cheaper cost. Price Waterhouse's newly expressed doubts about the availability of offset accounting gave it further reason to question whether the deal it had made was a good one. With the benefit of two months' hindsight, Tribune most likely would not have entered into the commitment agreement it made in early October. That was, however, the agreement it made.

Conditions Precedent to Enforcement

Tribune contends that even if the commitment letter constituted a valid, enforceable contract, there were conditions precedent to its enforcement that were never satisfied. Teachers' commitment letter stated that the authorization of the loan was "contingent upon the preparation, execution and delivery of" final contract documents; Tribune's response, likewise, stated that "our acceptance and agreement is subject to . . . the preparation and execution of legal documentation satisfactory to the Company." Tribune contends that since final contract documents were never prepared, the conditions precedent to the enforceability of the agreement were never satisfied and, accordingly, Tribune cannot be charged with breach. This argument misconceives the meaning of these clauses. The preliminary agreement envisions and requires further and final contract documents without which the loan will not be made; if, through no fault on either party, no final contract were reached, either because the parties in good faith failed to agree on the open secondary terms, or because, as often happens in business, the parties simply lost interest in the transaction and by mutual tacit consent abandoned it without having reached final contract documents, no enforceable rights would survive based on the preliminary commitment. This does not mean that the language of reservation authorized one party to kill the deal simply by refusing to negotiate or to sign the contract documents. Such an interpretation would render language like "binding agreement" and "firm commitment" meaningless.

Tribune's point would be well taken if the negotiations had aborted over inability to reach agreement on the terms of the purchase money mortgage or the put. Indeed, if they had aborted because Teachers had insisted on imposing conditions on the exercise of the put that were incompatible with the initial agreement, Tribune might properly have charged Teachers with breach of the commitment letter agreement.

What in fact happened was the other way around. Tribune broke off contract negotiations by insisting on a condition (satisfactory accounting) that was not within the scope of the agreement. Although Tribune's refusal to go ahead with the contract may well have been motivated in part by doubts as to the availability of offset accounting, I find that that decline in interest rates also substantially influenced Tribune's decision.

Of course it is true that numerous issues remained open at this time. The basic loan agreement was in draft form, recently circulated by Teachers, without any negotiations having taken place over its form and minor terms.

Although I find (as a matter of disputed fact) that Teachers had expressed its agreement to a put on terms that were acceptable to Tribune, it is less clear that Teachers had ever stated its acceptance of the form of mortgage that Tribune had concluded with LaSalle. (Teacher's counsel Tencza of the Debevoise firm had recently sent Tribune a letter specifying 35 problematic points in the LaSalle purchase money mortgage.) But the existence of those open points is of no consequence because they did not break the deal. Teachers offered in mid-December to sit down with Tribune and resolve all open issues so that the first drawdown could be made before the end of the year as contemplated in the commitment letter; Tribune declined stating that such a meeting would be of no value unless Teachers was prepared to agree that Tribune's satisfaction as to its accounting would be a condition of its obligation to draw down the loans.

Whatever Teachers' past posture had been as to the mortgage put and terms, there is every reason to believe that it would have acceded to Tribune's demands so long as they were within the terms of the commitment agreement. Given the fact that interest rates had dropped precipitously from the time of the commitment letter, it would have been bad business judgment for Teachers to lose the deal by refusing to agree on points of minor importance. Driver's testimony that Teachers was prepared to agree to Tribune's terms on the purchase money mortgage and the put is entirely credible. But the issue does not depend on a finding as to the likelihood of Teachers acceding to Tribune's demands on those open issues. The point is simply that Teachers, in conformity with its contract obligations, was asking Tribune to sit down and negotiate in good faith towards agreement on the open points, while Tribune refused to negotiate unless Teachers agreed to add a condition that was outside the scope of the bargain. The existence of open points and the failure of the parties to satisfy the condition of execution of final documentation is, therefore, chargeable to Tribune. It cannot rely on those circumstances to escape its contract obligation. . . .

Judgment is granted to the plaintiff.

SO ORDERED.

———

VENTURE ASSOCIATES CORP. v. ZENITH DATA SYSTEMS CORP., 96 F.3d 275 (7th Cir.1996) (Posner, J.). "Damages for breach of an agreement to negotiate may be, although they are unlikely to be, the same as the damages for breach of the final contract that the parties would have signed had it not been for the defendant's bad faith. If, quite apart from any bad faith, the negotiations would have broken down, the party led on by the other party's bad faith to persist in futile negotiations can recover only his reliance damages—the expenses he incurred by being misled, in violation of the parties' agreement to negotiate in good faith, into continuing to negotiate futilely. But if the plaintiff can prove that had it not been for the defendant's bad faith the parties would have made a final contract, then the loss of the benefit of the contract is a consequence of the defendant's bad faith, and, provided that it is a foreseeable consequence, the defendant is liable for that loss—liable, that is, for the plaintiffs consequential damages. . . . The difficulty, which may well be insuperable, is that since by hypothesis the parties had not agreed on *any* of the terms of their contract, it may be impossible to determine what those terms would have been and hence what profit the victim of bad faith would have had.... But this goes to the practicality of the remedy, not the principle of it. Bad faith is deliberate misconduct, whereas many breaches of 'final' contracts are involuntary—liability for breach of contract being, in general, strict liability. It would be a paradox to place a lower ceiling on damages for bad faith than on damages for a perfectly innocent breach, though a paradox that the practicalities of proof may require the courts in many or even all cases to accept."

————

KANSAS MUNICIPAL GAS AGENCY v. VESTA ENERGY CO., 843 F.Supp. 1401 (D. Kan. 1994). In early April 1992, Vesta Energy Co. entered into three letter agreements to begin supplying gas to Kansas Municipal Gas Agency (KMGA) from three designated pipelines at agreed-upon prices. The letter agreements were for one-year terms, but each agreement provided that "This Letter Agreement shall remain valid until the execution of a mutually agreeable contract. Should Buyer and Seller fail to reach a mutually agreeable contract, this Letter Agreement shall become null and void." Following the execution of the letter agreements, the parties entered into negotiations for a finalized written contract. Over the next several months, the parties exchanged several draft contracts and had numerous telephone contacts in an attempt to arrive at a mutually agreeable contract. Several issues remained unresolved. On August 17, 1992, KMGA prepared yet another draft contract and sent it to Vesta. On September 8, however, Vesta sent a letter to KMGA declaring the letter agreements null and void due to the parties' failure to reach agreement on a mutually acceptable contract. KMGA brought suit. The court held that Vesta had violated an obligation to negotiate in good faith, and was liable for expectation damages.

"The court is persuaded that Vesta terminated the agreement because it was a bad business deal and it could not extricate itself otherwise. Its stated reasons for terminating were pretextual. The evidence on which the court relies in arriving at this conclusion is best understood in the context of Vesta's demand for a force majeure clause in the final contract that was not limited to conditions generally accepted in the natural gas supply business, but rather one which would have provided it with a way out of the contract in the event of a broadly defined 'loss of supply.'

"The RFP [request for proposal] sent out by KMGA specifically set forth that KMGA was seeking a 'firm supply' of gas. Having a firm supply of gas was of the utmost importance to KMGA. This is due to the fact that its member cities use the gas for residential heating and cooling, and an interruption of gas supply would have a traumatic effect on the member cities. It made this point clear to Vesta and the court has no difficulty finding as a matter of fact that the mutual intention of the parties was that the letter agreements were for a firm supply. Within the natural gas industry, 'firm supply' generally means that the supplier guarantees that it will meet its supply requirements. This is typically done by providing specific well dedications in the case of a producer or, in the case of a marketer such as Vesta, by warranting that it has gas supply in sufficient quantities to meet its obligations under a gas supply contract. In contrast, a 'best efforts' arrangement requires that a gas supplier use its 'best efforts' to supply gas, but typically imposes no penalty for a failure to do so. A firm supply contract creates a much greater commitment on the part of a supplier to supply gas than does a best efforts contract.

"Although a firm supply contract puts a great onus on the supplier to deliver the specified quantity of gas, firm supply contracts typically contain a provision limiting the supplier's obligation in cases of 'force majeure.' A contractual force majeure provision provides that a supplier is not obligated to supply gas when certain events, beyond the control of a supplier, make such supply impossible. Typical force majeure events in a gas supply contract consist of various events that are beyond the supplier's control, including, among other things, such conditions as acts of God, strikes, lockouts, wars, blockades, government regulatory intervention, explosions, sabotage, freezeup and line collapse. As one of its reasons for canceling the letter agreements, Vesta points to the failure of KMGA to agree to force majeure language in the contract to the effect that Vesta would not be obligated to produce gas in cases of 'failure of supply.' The court finds that this broad loss of supply provision demanded by Vesta is totally contradictory to the notion of a firm supply contract, and the court relies on the testimony of expert witness William Giese that such a provision would not be generally accepted force majeure language in a firm supply contract. . . .

". . . Natural gas is covered by the definition of 'goods' contained in [UCC §] 2–105. There can be no doubt that, at the time of the execution of the letter agreements, the parties fully intended that performance under the letter agreements included attempting to arrive at a mutually agreeable final written contract governing the gas purchase. The parties were therefore obligated under . . . [UCC §] 1–203 to conduct themselves in good faith in endeavoring to negotiate and finalize the final written contract. Because the parties fit the UCC definition of merchants contained in . . . UCC § 2–104(1), the duty of good faith applicable here is defined in . . . [§] 2–103(b).

". . . Vesta's demand for a broad 'failure of supply provision' in the force majeure section of the contract was totally contradictory to the notion of a firm supply contract and . . . such a provision would not be generally accepted language in a firm supply contract. Consequently, the court finds that Vesta's insistence on such a broad force majeure provision was not consistent with 'the observance of reasonable commercial standards of fair dealing in the trade,' as required by [§] 2–103(b) and therefore was not a valid justification for Vesta's termination of the letter agreements. . . .

"Following Vesta's breach of the letter agreements, KMGA proceeded to purchase substitute gas from another supplier. Pursuant to [UCC §] 2–712(1), following a breach by a seller the buyer may 'cover' by making in good faith and without unreasonable delay any reasonable purchase of or contract to purchase goods in substitution for those from the seller. The buyer is then entitled to recover from the seller as damages the difference between the cost of cover and the contract price."

HOFFMAN v. RED OWL STORES, INC.

Supreme Court of Wisconsin, 1965.
26 Wis.2d 683, 133 N.W.2d 267.

Action by Joseph Hoffman (hereinafter "Hoffman") and wife, plaintiffs, against defendants Red Owl Stores, Inc. (hereinafter "Red Owl") and Edward Lukowitz.

The complaint alleged that Lukowitz, as agent for Red Owl, represented to and agreed with plaintiffs that Red Owl would build a store building in Chilton and stock it with merchandise for Hoffman to operate in return for which plaintiffs were to put up and invest a total sum of $18,000; that in reliance upon the above mentioned agreement and representations plaintiffs sold their bakery building and business and their grocery store and business; also in reliance on the agreement and representations Hoffman purchased the building site in Chilton and rented a residence for himself and his family in Chilton; plaintiffs' actions in reliance on the representations and agreement disrupted their personal and business life; plaintiffs lost substantial amounts of income and expended large sums of money as expenses. Plaintiffs demanded recovery of damages for the breach of defendants' representations and agreements.

The action was tried to a court and jury. The facts hereafter stated are taken from the evidence adduced at the trial. Where there was a conflict in the evidence the version favorable to plaintiffs has been accepted since the verdict rendered was in favor of plaintiffs.

Hoffman assisted by his wife operated a bakery at Wautoma from 1956 until sale of the building late in 1961. The building was owned in joint tenancy by him and his wife. Red Owl is a Minnesota corporation having its home office at Hopkins, Minnesota. It owns and operates a number of grocery supermarket stores and also extends franchises to agency stores which are owned by individuals, partnerships and corporations. Lukowitz resides at Green Bay and since September, 1960, has been divisional manager for Red Owl in a territory comprising Upper Michigan and most of Wisconsin in charge of 84 stores. Prior to September, 1960, he was district manager having charge of approximately 20 stores.

In November, 1959, Hoffman was desirous of expanding his operations by establishing a grocery store and contacted a Red Owl representative by the name of Jansen, now deceased. Numerous conversations were had in 1960 with the idea of establishing a Red Owl franchise store in Wautoma. In September, 1960, Lukowitz succeeded Jansen as Red Owl's representative in the negotiations. Hoffman mentioned that $18,000 was all the capital he had available to invest and he was repeatedly assured that this would be sufficient to set him up in business as a Red Owl Store. About Christmastime, 1960, Hoffman thought it would be a good idea if he bought a small grocery store in Wautoma and operated it in order that he gain experience in the grocery business prior to operating a Red Owl store in some larger community. On February 6, 1961, on the advice of Lukowitz and Sykes, who had succeeded Lukowitz as Red Owl's district manager, Hoffman bought the inventory and fixtures of a small grocery store in Wautoma and leased the building in which it was operated.

After three months of operating this Wautoma store, the Red Owl representatives came in and took inventory and checked the operations and found the store was operating at a profit. Lukowitz advised Hoffman to sell the store to his manager, and assured him that Red Owl would find a larger store for him elsewhere. Acting on this advice and assurance, Hoffman sold the fixtures and inventory to his manager on June 6, 1961. Hoffman was reluctant to sell at that time because it meant losing the summer tourist business, but he sold on the assurance that he would be operating in a new location by fall and that he must sell this store if he wanted a bigger one. Before selling, Hoffman told the Red Owl representatives that he had $18,000 for "getting set up in business" and they assured him that there would be no problems in establishing him in a bigger operation. The makeup of the $18,000 was not discussed; it was understood plaintiff's father-in-law would furnish part of it. By June, 1961, the towns for the new grocery store had been narrowed down to two, Kewaunee and Chilton. In Kewaunee, Red Owl had an option on a building site. In Chilton, Red Owl had nothing under option, but it did select a site to which plaintiff obtained an option at Red Owl's suggestion. The option stipulated a purchase price of $6,000 with $1,000 to be paid on election to purchase and the balance to be paid within 30 days. On Lukowitz's assurance that everything was all set plaintiff paid $1,000 down on the lot on September 15th.

On September 27, 1961, plaintiff met at Chilton with Lukowitz and Mr. Reymund and Mr. Carlson from the home office who prepared a projected financial statement. Part of the funds plaintiffs were to supply as their investment in the venture were to be obtained by sale of their Wautoma bakery building.

On the basis of this meeting Lukowitz assured Hoffman: " ... [E]verything is ready to go. Get your money together and we are set." Shortly after this meeting Lukowitz told plaintiffs that they would have to sell their bakery business and bakery building, and that their retaining this property was the only "hitch" in the entire plan. On November 6, 1961, plaintiffs sold their bakery building for $10,000. Hoffman was to retain the bakery equipment as he contemplated using it to operate a bakery in connection with his Red Owl store. After sale of the bakery Hoffman obtained employment on the night shift at an Appleton bakery.

The record contains different exhibits which were prepared in September and October, some of which were projections of the fiscal operation of the business and others were proposed building and floor plans. Red Owl was to procure some third party to buy the Chilton lot from Hoffman, construct the building, and then lease it to Hoffman. No final plans were ever made nor were bids let or a construction contract entered. Some time prior to November 20, 1961, certain of the terms of the lease under which the building was to be rented by Hoffman were understood between him and Lukowitz. The lease was to be for 10 years with a rental approximating $550 a month calculated on the basis of 1 percent per month on the building cost, plus 6 percent of the land cost divided on a monthly basis. At the end of the 10–year term he was to have an option to renew the lease for an additional 10–year period or to buy the property at cost on an instalment basis. There was no discussion as to what the instalments would be or with respect to repairs and maintenance.

On November 22nd or 23rd, Lukowitz and plaintiffs met in Minneapolis with Red Owl's credit manager to confer on Hoffman's financial standing and on financing the agency. Another projected financial statement was there drawn up entitled, "Proposed Financing For An Agency Store." This showed Hoffman contributing $24,100 of cash capital of which only $4,600 was to be cash possessed by plaintiffs. Eight thousand was to be procured as a loan from a Chilton bank secured by a mortgage on the bakery fixtures, $7,500 was to be obtained on a 5 percent loan from the father-in-law, and $4,000 was to be obtained by sale of the lot to the lessor at a profit.

A week or two after the Minneapolis meeting Lukowitz showed Hoffman a telegram from the home office to the effect that if plaintiff could get another $2,000 for promotional purposes the deal could go through for $26,000. Hoffman stated he would have to find out if he could get another $2,000. He met with his father-in-law, who agreed to put $13,000 into the business provided he could come into the business as a partner. Lukowitz told Hoffman the partnership arrangement "sounds fine" and that Hoffman should not go into the partnership arrangement with the "front office." On January 16, 1962, the Red Owl credit manager teletyped Lukowitz that the father-in-law would have to sign an agreement that the $13,000 was either a gift or a loan subordinate to all general creditors and that he would prepare the agreement. On January 31, 1962, Lukowitz teletyped the home office that the father-in-law would sign one or other of the agreements. However, Hoffman testified that it was not until the final meeting some time between January 26th and February 2nd, 1962, that he was told that his father-in-law was expected to sign an agreement that the $13,000 he was advancing was to be an outright gift. No mention was then made by the Red Owl representatives of the alternative of the father-in-law signing a subordination agreement. At this meeting the Red Owl agents presented Hoffman with the following projected financial statement:

"Capital required in operation:

"Cash	$ 5,000.00	
"Merchandise	20,000.00	
"Bakery	18,000.00	
"Fixtures	17,500.00	
"Promotional Funds	1,500.00	
TOTAL:		$62,000.00

"Source of funds:

"Red Owl 7–day terms	$ 5,000.00	
"Red Owl Fixture contract (Term 5 years)	14,000.00	
"Bank loans (Term 9 years)		
Union State Bank of Chilton	8,000.00	
"(Secured by Bakery Equipment)		
"Other loans (Term No-pay)		
No interest	13,000.00	
"Father-in-law		
"(Secured by None)		
"(Secured by Mortgage on		
"Wautoma Bakery Bldg.)	2,000.00	
"Resale of land	6,000.00	
"Equity Capital: $ 5,000.00-Cash		
"Amount owner has 17,500.00-Bakery Equip.		
"to invest:	22,500.00	
TOTAL:		$70,500.00"

Hoffman interpreted the above statement to require of plaintiffs a total of $34,000 cash made up of $13,000 gift from his father-in-law, $2,000 on mortgage, $8,000 on Chilton bank loan, $5,000 in cash from plaintiff, and $6,000 on the resale of the Chilton lot. Red Owl claims $18,000 is the total of the unborrowed or unencumbered cash, that is, $13,000 from the father-in-law and $5,000 cash from Hoffman himself. Hoffman informed Red Owl he could not go along with this proposal, and particularly objected to the requirement that his father-in-law sign an agreement that his $13,000 advancement was an absolute gift. This terminated the negotiations between the parties.

The case was submitted to the jury on a special verdict with the first two questions answered by the court. This verdict, as returned by the jury, was as follows:

"Question No. 1: Did the Red Owl Stores, Inc. and Joseph Hoffman on or about mid-May of 1961 initiate negotiations looking to the establishment of Joseph Hoffman as a franchise operator of a Red Owl Store in Chilton? Answer: Yes. (Answered by the Court.)

"Question No. 2: Did the parties mutually agree on all of the details of the proposal so as to reach a final agreement thereon? Answer: No. (Answered by the Court.)

"Question No. 3: Did the Red Owl Stores, Inc., in the course of said negotiations, make representations to Joseph Hoffman that if he fulfilled certain conditions that they would establish him as a franchise operator of a Red Owl Store in Chilton? Answer: Yes.

"Question No. 4: If you have answered Question No. 3 'Yes,' then answer this question: Did Joseph Hoffman rely on said representations and was he induced to act thereon? Answer: Yes.

"Question No. 5: If you have answered Question No. 4 'Yes,' then answer this question: Ought Joseph Hoffman, in the exercise of ordinary care to have relied on said representations? Answer: Yes.

"Question No. 6: If you have answered Question No. 3 'Yes' then answer this question: Did Joseph Hoffman fulfill all the conditions he was required to fulfill by the terms of the negotiations between the parties up to January 26, 1962? Answer: Yes.

"Question No. 7: What sum of money will reasonably compensate the plaintiffs for such damages as they sustained by reason of:

"(a) The sale of the Wautoma store fixtures and inventory?

"Answer: $16,735.00.

"(b) The sale of the bakery building?

"Answer: $2,000.00.

"(c) Taking up the option on the Chilton lot?

"Answer: $1,000.00.

"(d) Expenses of moving his family to Neenah?

"Answer: $140.00.

"(e) House rental in Chilton?

"Answer: $125.00."

Plaintiffs moved for judgment on the verdict while defendants moved to change the answers to Questions 3, 4, 5, and 6 from "Yes" to "No", and in the alternative for relief from the answers to the subdivisions of Question 7 or a new trial. On March 31, 1964, the circuit court entered the following order:

"It is ordered in accordance with said decision on motions after verdict hereby incorporated herein by reference:

"1. That the answer of the jury to Question No. 7(a) be and the same is hereby vacated and set aside and that a new trial be had on the sole issue of the damages for loss, if any, on the sale of the Wautoma store, fixtures and inventory.

"2. That all other portions of the verdict of the jury be and hereby are approved and confirmed and all after-verdict motions of the parties inconsistent with this order are hereby denied."

Defendants have appealed from this order and plaintiffs have cross-appealed from paragraph 1. thereof. . . .

CURRIE, CHIEF JUSTICE. The instant appeal and cross-appeal present these questions:

(1) Whether this court should recognize causes of action grounded on promissory estoppel as exemplified by sec. 90 of Restatement, 1 Contracts?

(2) Do the facts in this case make out a cause of action for promissory estoppel?

(3) Are the jury's findings with respect to damages sustained by the evidence?

[The court began by adopting the doctrine of promissory estoppel as stated in section 90 of the Restatement of Contracts.]

APPLICABILITY OF DOCTRINE TO FACTS OF THIS CASE

The record here discloses a number of promises and assurances given to Hoffman by Lukowitz in behalf of Red Owl upon which plaintiffs relied and acted upon to their detriment.

Foremost were the promises that for the sum of $18,000 Red Owl would establish Hoffman in a store. After Hoffman had sold his grocery store and paid the $1,000 on the Chilton lot, the $18,000 figure was changed to $24,100. Then in November, 1961, Hoffman was assured that if the $24,100 figure were increased by $2,000 the deal would go through. Hoffman was induced to sell his grocery store fixtures and inventory in June, 1961, on the promise that he would be in his new store by fall. In November, plaintiffs sold their bakery building on the urging of defendants and on the assurance that this was the last step necessary to have the deal with Red Owl go through.

We determine that there was ample evidence to sustain the answers of the jury to the questions of the verdict with respect to the promissory representations made by Red Owl, Hoffman's reliance thereon in the exercise of ordinary care, and his fulfillment of the conditions required of him by the terms of the negotiations had with Red Owl.

There remains for consideration the question of law raised by defendants that agreement was never reached on essential factors necessary to establish a contract between Hoffman and Red Owl. Among these were the size, cost, design, and layout of the store building; and the terms of the lease with respect to rent, maintenance, renewal, and purchase options. This poses the question of whether the promise necessary to sustain a cause of action for promissory estoppel must embrace all essential details of a proposed transaction between promisor and promisee so as to be the equivalent of an offer that would result in a binding contract between the parties if the promisee were to accept the same.

Originally the doctrine of promissory estoppel was invoked as a substitute for consideration rendering a gratuitous promise enforceable as a contract. See Williston, Contracts (1st ed.), p. 307, sec. 139. In other words, the acts of reliance by the promisee to his detriment provided a substitute for consideration. If promissory estoppel were to be limited to only those situations where the promise giving rise to the cause of action must be so definite with respect to all details that a contract would result were the promise supported by consideration, then the defendants' instant promises to Hoffman would not meet this test. However, sec. 90 of Restatement, 1 Contracts, does not impose the requirement that the promise giving rise to the cause of action must be so comprehensive in scope as to meet the requirements of an offer that would ripen into a contract if accepted by the promisee. Rather the conditions imposed are:

(1) Was the promise one which the promisor should reasonably expect to induce action or forbearance of a definite and substantial character on the part of the promisee?

(2) Did the promise induce such action or forbearance?

(3) Can injustice be avoided only by enforcement of the promise?

We deem it would be a mistake to regard an action grounded on promissory estoppel as the equivalent of a breach of contract action. As Dean Boyer points out, it is desirable that fluidity in the application of the concept be maintained. 98 University of Pennsylvania Law Review (1950), 459, at page 497. While the first two of the above listed three requirements of promissory estoppel present issues of fact which ordinarily will be resolved by a jury, the third requirement, that the remedy can only be invoked where necessary to avoid injustice, is one that involves a policy decision by the court. Such a policy decision necessarily embraces an element of discretion.

We conclude that injustice would result here if plaintiffs were not granted some relief because of the failure of defendants to keep their promises which induced plaintiffs to act to their detriment.

Damages

Defendants attack all the items of damages awarded by the jury.

The bakery building at Wautoma was sold at defendants' instigation in order that Hoffman might have the net proceeds available as part of the cash capital he was to invest in the Chilton store venture. The evidence clearly establishes that it was sold at a loss of $2,000. Defendants contend that half of this loss was sustained by Mrs. Hoffman because title stood in joint tenancy. They point out that no dealings took place between her and defendants as all negotiations were had with her husband. Ordinarily only the promisee and not third persons are entitled to enforce the remedy of promissory estoppel against the promisor. However, if the promisor actually foresees, or has reason to foresee, action by a third person in reliance on the promise, it may be quite unjust to refuse to perform the promise. 1A Corbin, Contracts, p. 220, sec. 200. Here not only did defendants foresee that it would be necessary for Mrs. Hoffman to sell her joint interest in the bakery building, but defendants actually requested that this be done. We approve the jury's award of $2,000 damages for the loss incurred by both plaintiffs in this sale.

Defendants attack on two grounds the $1,000 awarded because of Hoffman's payment of that amount on the purchase price of the Chilton lot. The first is that this $1,000 had already been lost at the time the final negotiations with Red Owl fell through in January, 1962, because the remaining $5,000 of purchase price had been due on October 15, 1961. The record does not disclose that the lot owner had foreclosed Hoffman's interest in the lot for failure to pay this $5,000. The $1,000 was not paid for the option, but had been paid as part of the purchase price at the time Hoffman elected to exercise the option. This gave him an equity in the lot which could not be legally foreclosed without affording Hoffman an opportunity to pay the balance. The second ground of attack is that the lot may have had a fair market value of $6,000, and Hoffman should have paid the remaining $5,000 of purchase price. We determine that it would be unreasonable to require Hoffman to have invested an additional $5,000 in order to protect the $1,000 he had paid. Therefore, we find no merit to defendants' attack upon this item of damages.

We also determine it was reasonable for Hoffman to have paid $125 for one month's rent of a home in Chilton after defendants assured him everything would be set when plaintiff sold the bakery building. This was a proper item of damage.

Plaintiffs never moved to Chilton because defendants suggested that Hoffman get some experience by working in a Red Owl store in the Fox River Valley. Plaintiffs, therefore, moved to Neenah instead of Chilton. After moving, Hoffman worked at night in an Appleton bakery but held himself available for work in a Red Owl store. The $140 moving expense would not have been incurred if plaintiffs had not sold their bakery building in Wautoma in reliance upon defendants' promises. We consider the $140 moving expense to be a proper item of damage.

We turn now to the damage item with respect to which the trial court granted a new trial, i.e., that arising from the sale of the Wautoma grocery store fixtures and inventory for which the jury awarded $16,735. The trial court ruled that Hoffman could not recover for any loss of future profits for the summer months following the sale on June 6, 1961, but that damages would be limited to the difference between the sales price received and the fair market value of the assets sold, giving consideration to any goodwill attaching thereto by reason of the transfer of a going business. There was no direct evidence presented as to what this fair market value was on June 6, 1961. The evidence did disclose that Hoffman paid $9,000 for the inventory, added $1,500 to it and sold it for $10,000 or a loss of $500. His 1961 federal income tax return showed that the grocery equipment had been purchased for $7,000 and sold for $7,955.96. Plaintiffs introduced evidence of the buyer that during the first eleven weeks of operation of the grocery store his gross sales were $44,000 and his profit was $6,000 or roughly 15 per cent. On cross-examination he admitted that this was gross and not net profit. Plaintiffs contend that in a breach of contract action damages may include loss of profits. However, this is not a breach of contract action.

The only relevancy of evidence relating to profits would be with respect to proving the element of goodwill in establishing the fair market value of the grocery inventory and fixtures sold. Therefore, evidence of profits would be admissible to afford a foundation for expert opinion as to fair market value.

Where damages are awarded in promissory estoppel instead of specifically enforcing the promisor's promise, they should be only such as in the opinion of the court are necessary to prevent injustice. Mechanical or rule of thumb approaches to the damage problem should be avoided. . . .

At the time Hoffman bought the equipment and inventory of the small grocery store at Wautoma he did so in order to gain experience in the grocery store business. At that time discussion had already been had with Red Owl representatives that Wautoma might be too small for a Red Owl operation and that a larger city might be more desirable. Thus Hoffman made this purchase more or less as a temporary experiment. Justice does not require that the damages awarded him, because of selling these assets at the behest of defendants, should exceed any actual loss sustained measured by the difference between the sales price and the fair market value.

Since the evidence does not sustain the large award of damages arising from the sale of the Wautoma grocery business, the trial court properly ordered a new trial on this issue.

Order affirmed. Because of the cross-appeal, plaintiffs shall be limited to taxing but two-thirds of their costs.

———

COMMENT, ONCE MORE INTO THE BREACH: PROMISSORY ESTOPPEL AND TRADITIONAL CONTRACT DOCTRINE, 37 U.Chi. L.Rev. 559, 573–75 (1970). "Traditional wisdom of Anglo—American contract law is that private autonomy in the market place best regulates the terms of exchange. [By virtue of the requirement of consideration—a bargained—for equivalent—the] law will not normally intervene to enforce a commercial promise unless it is embodied in an agreement containing an exchange of economic values. . . .

"The net effect . . . is to identify the point of contract formation as one at which the consequences of transactional conduct are altered. Until that point is reached the promisor is encouraged to consider the consequences of entering into the agreement. Until that time he also remains free to deal with the other parties at arm's length, acting in his own best interests. Most important is the fact that the point at which the bargain is struck is usually mutually identifiable to the parties. They themselves are aware of the extent to which they may act in their own interests, and of the point at which their conduct has led to a binding obligation. The requirement of consideration thus operates to delineate an identifiable sphere of precontractual conduct free of legal restraint. . . .

"But since action-in-reliance designates a promise enforceable at some point prior to the moment of normal contract formation, it impliedly represents a departure from the notion that private autonomy determines what promises will be enforced. To the extent that the imposition of liability occurs during the course of precontractual negotiations, reliance enforcement also represents an intrusion on that sphere of activity left free of legal restraint by the requirement of consideration. . . . ''

GRUEN INDUSTRIES, INC. v. BILLER, 608 F.2d 274 (7th Cir.1979). Biller and Hersch owned 340,000 of Windsor's 400,000 outstanding shares. Gruen Industries, represented by Evans, its Vice President, approached Biller and Hersch in early 1975 to discuss a possible acquisition of Windsor. In May, Biller and Hersch orally agreed to a sale of their stock. At the time of the oral agreement, Gruen informed Hersch that it would not incur the expenses for preparation of the written agreement unless he would assure Gruen that it had a firm commitment. Hersch assured Gruen that it did. Gruen then retained lawyers and the drafting process began. The date to sign the written agreement was set for the middle of July.

The drafting of the agreement was virtually complete by early July. However, on July 17 a third party, PCA, made a written proposal to purchase the Windsor shares for a higher price. Biller and Hersch sold their shares to PCA, and the draft agreement with Gruen was never signed. Gruen sued in federal court for expectation damages on the ground of breach of contract, and alternatively for reliance damages on the ground of promissory estoppel. The suit was governed by the law of Wisconsin. The Seventh Circuit first held that the breach of contract claim was barred by the Statute of Frauds. It then turned to the claim based on promissory estoppel, which had been dismissed by the trial court on a motion for summary judgment.

". . . The plaintiffs seek to recover various preparation expenses incurred, comprising primarily substantial attorneys' fees for drafting the agreement and supplemental documents. As the basis for this theory of recovery the plaintiff has alleged that the defendants orally assured them that they had a firm commitment and then consented to the plaintiffs' procuring legal counsel for the purpose of drafting the necessary documents.

"In *Hoffman v. Red Owl Stores, Inc.*, 26 Wis.2d 683, 133 N.W.2d 267 (1965), the Wisconsin Supreme Court established three conditions for application of promissory estoppel:

(1) Was the promise one which the promisor should reasonably expect to induce action or forbearance of a definite and substantial character on the part of the promisee?

(2) Did the promise induce such action or forbearance?

(3) Can injustice be avoided only by enforcement of the promise?

The first two conditions present questions of fact; the third presents a policy question for the court to decide, and necessarily embraces an element of discretion. . . .

"More recently, in *Silberman v. Roethe,* 64 Wis.2d 131, 218 N.W.2d 723 (1974), the Wisconsin Supreme Court discussed in detail for the first time the factors to be considered by the trial court in deciding whether a plaintiff has satisfied the third condition. The factor receiving primary consideration in *Silberman* was the certainty 'that the plaintiff has actually suffered from his action in reliance.' In *Silberman* the plaintiff reduced a debt owed to him by a corporation in reliance on a promise by the defendant to purchase the corporation and to strengthen it financially. The defendant did not keep its promise, and the corporation failed. Nevertheless, the plaintiff did not prevail against the defendant because it was speculative that the plaintiff ever could have collected the full debt had it tried.

"Similarly, the alleged agreement here was subject to numerous conditions, some of which were under the control of third parties. If any of these conditions were not satisfied, the buyers or sellers would have been able to terminate the agreement unilaterally prior to the sale and purchase of the stock. Had the defendants kept the alleged promises, as they are embodied in the unsigned Agreement, the sale may very well have failed on the basis of the many contingencies, and the plaintiffs would not have been entitled to any reimbursement of their expenses. We agree with the district court that summary judgment is appropriate here. To avoid injustice, it clearly is not necessary that plaintiffs be placed in a better position for the alleged breach than they may have been had the promise been kept. The conditional promise alleged is not a reasonable basis for reliance and thus not a proper basis for estoppel. . . .

"In addition to the conditional nature of the promise, other circumstances of this case militate against recovery on an estoppel theory. The alleged promises were made informally; indeed even under the plaintiffs' theory of the case, the written Agreement was intended as a formal and more detailed record of the agreement of the parties. *See Silberman, supra,* 64 Wis.2d at 146, 218 N.W.2d at 730. Furthermore, the plaintiffs were represented by sophisticated businessmen, and therefore '[t]his is not a situation of an individual taken advantage of by a corporation or individual with superior knowledge of legal and business practices.' *Id.* Finally, there is no allegation that the defendants were in any way unjustly enriched because of the plaintiff's reliance. In fact, the defendants also retained attorneys in connection with the preparation of the agreement and no doubt paid a substantial sum for their services."

———

NEISS v. EHLERS, 135 Or.App. 218, 899 P.2d 700 (1995). "In our view, the better reasoning supports the conclusion that promissory estoppel can apply, under appropriate circumstances, to promises that are indefinite or incomplete, including agreements to agree. The cases that take the contrary view appear to rest on the premise that that application of the doctrine is a bootstrap operation by which promises that are illusory, in that they lack the precision to be enforceable through normal contract remedies, can be enforced in a different guise. That premise is flawed, for at least two reasons. First, promissory estoppel would not generally entail "enforcement" of the same kind or extent that the traditional remedies provide. As indicated in the current section 90, . . . promissory estoppel remedies are more flexible in nature than contract remedies and are aimed at compensating the promisee for damages that result from actions in reliance on the promise, rather than providing comprehensive contract relief for the breach of the indefinite promise itself.

"The second reason for our rejection of the premise is related: The evil to be rectified through promissory estoppel is not the breach of the promise, but the harm that results from the promisor's inducement and the promisee's actions in reliance. The fact that a promise is indefinite, incomplete or even incapable of enforcement according to its own terms, does not mean that no redress should be possible for the damage that directly flows from the promisee's reliance on the promise.

"Nothing that we find in the stated rationales for a different rule, and nothing that occurs to us, persuades us that the applicability of promissory estoppel should depend generally on why the promise is contractually unenforceable, or that the indefiniteness of a promise makes it inappropriate to apply promissory estoppel as a remedy. Obviously, "indefiniteness" is a question of degree, and the facts of specific cases may be such that the promise is not only too indefinite for enforcement as a contract, but is so illusory that it could not reasonably have been acted on or foreseen as an inducement to action."

RACINE & LARAMIE, LTD. v. CALIFORNIA DEPT. OF PARKS & RECREATION, 11 Cal.App.4th 1026, 14 Cal.Rptr.2d 335 (1992). "To recapitulate: The fact that parties commence negotiations looking to a contract, or to the amendment of an existing contract, does not by itself impose any duty on either party not to be unreasonable or not to break off negotiations, for any reason or for no reason. During the course of negotiations [, however,] things may be done which *do* then impose a duty of continued bargaining only in good faith.

"For instance, a preexisting agreement may impose an obligation of good faith bargaining with respect to the modification of some term of the agreement. The preexisting agreement which vests a discretionary power of alteration of the terms of the agreement may impliedly require that such be done in good faith. Or, in anticipation of an agreement the parties may, by letter of intent or otherwise, agree that they will bargain in good faith for the purpose of reaching an agreement. Finally, in the course of negotiations it is possible for a party to so mislead another by promises or representations, upon which the second party detrimentally relies, as to bring into play the concept of promissory estoppel.

"Absent the existence of such special circumstances or conditions, however, there is no obligation in California to bargain for a new or amended contract in good faith."

Chapter 15

THE PAROL EVIDENCE RULE AND THE INTERPRETATION OF WRITTEN CONTRACTS

This Chapter takes up three related issues.

Section 1 concerns cases in which A and B have admittedly entered into a written contract, but A claims that prior to, or contemporaneously with, making the written contract, the parties entered into a separate agreement that concerned the same subject matter as the written contract, but was not intended to be superseded by the written contract. The treatment of such alleged separate agreements—and more specifically, the issue whether evidence concerning such agreements is admissible—is governed by the *parol evidence rule*. This rule is the subject of Section 1 of this chapter.

Section 2 considers the issue whether, in the admissibility of evidence concerning the *interpretation* of a contract, it should make a difference that the contract is in writing; and if so, what difference it should make. This issue is analytically separate from the issue governed by the parol evidence rule, which concerns the admissibility of evidence concerning whether the parties had a *separate agreement*. The two issues are considered together in this Chapter, partly because courts often run the two issues together, and partly because in practice both issues typically (although not invariably) involve oral evidence that seems to qualify a written contract.

Section 3 further considers the extent to which trade usage, course of performance, and course of dealing may be part of a written contract.

SECTION 1. THE PAROL EVIDENCE RULE

MITCHILL v. LATH
Court of Appeals of New York, 1928.
247 N.Y. 377, 160 N.E. 646, 68 A.L.R. 239.

Action by Catherine C. Mitchill against Charles Lath and another. Judgment of Special Term in plaintiff's favor, directing specific performance of an agreement to remove an icehouse, was affirmed by the Appellate Division (220 App.Div. 776, 221 N.Y.S. 864), and defendants appeal. Judgments of Appellate Division and Trial Term reversed, and complaint dismissed.

ANDREWS, J. In the fall of 1923 the Laths owned a farm. This they wished to sell. Across the road, on land belonging to Lieutenant Governor Lunn, they had an icehouse which they might remove. Mrs. Mitchell looked over the land with a view to its purchase. She found the icehouse objectionable. Thereupon "the defendants orally promised and agreed, for and in consideration of the purchase of their farm by the plaintiff, to remove the said icehouse in the spring of 1924." Relying upon this promise, she made a written contract to buy the property for $8,400, for cash and a mortgage and containing various provisions usual in such papers. Later receiving a deed, she entered into possession, and has spent considerable sums in improving the property for use as a summer residence. The defendants have not fulfilled their promise as to the icehouse, and do not intend to do so. We are not dealing, however, with their moral delinquencies. The question before us is whether their oral agreement may be enforced in a court of equity.

This requires a discussion of the parol evidence rule—a rule of law which defines the limits of the contract to be construed. Glackin v. Bennett, 226 Mass. 316, 115 N.E. 490. It is more than a rule of evidence, and oral testimony, even if admitted, will not control the written contract (O'Malley v. Grady, 222 Mass. 202, 109 N.E. 829), unless admitted without objection (Brady v. Nally, 151 N.Y. 258, 45 N.E. 547). It applies, however, to attempts to modify such a contract by parol. It does not affect a parol collateral contract distinct from and independent of the written agreement. It is, at times, troublesome to draw the line. Williston, in his work on Contracts (section 637) points out the difficulty. "Two entirely distinct contracts," he says, "each for a separate consideration, may be made at the same time, and will be distinct legally. Where, however, one agreement is entered into wholly or partly in consideration of the simultaneous agreement to enter into another, the transactions are necessarily bound together.... Then if one of the agreements is oral and the other in writing, the problem arises whether the bond is sufficiently close to prevent proof of the oral agreement." That is the situation here. It is claimed that the defendants are called upon to do more than is required by their written contract in connection with the sale as to which it deals.

The principle may be clear, but it can be given effect by no mechanical rule. As so often happens, it is a matter of degree, for, as Prof. Williston also says, where a contract contains several promises on each side it is not difficult to put any one of them in the form of a collateral agreement. If this were enough, written contracts might always be modified by parol. Not form, but substance, is the test.

In applying this test, the policy of our courts is to be considered. We have believed that the purpose behind the rule was a wise one, not easily to be abandoned. Notwithstanding injustice here and there, on the whole it works for good. Old precedents and principles are not to be lightly cast aside, unless it is certain that they are an obstruction under present conditions. New York has been less open to arguments that would modify this particular rule, than some jurisdictions elsewhere. Thus in Eighmie v. Taylor, 98 N.Y. 288, it was held that a parol warranty might not be shown, although no warranties were contained in the writing.

Under our decisions before such an oral agreement as the present is received to vary the written contract, at least three conditions must exist: (1) The agreement must in form be a collateral one; (2) it must not contradict express or implied provisions of the written contract; (3) it must be one that parties would not ordinarily be expected to embody in the writing, or, put in another way, an inspection of the written contract, read in the light of surrounding circumstances, must not indicate that the writing appears "to contain the engagements of the parties, and to define the object and measure the extent of such engagement." Or, again, it must not be so clearly connected with the principal transaction as to be part and parcel of it.

The respondent does not satisfy the third of these requirements. It may be, not the second. We have a written contract for the purchase and sale of land. The buyer is to pay $8,400 in the way described. She is also to pay her portion of any rents, interest on mortgages, insurance premiums, and water meter charges. She may have a survey made of the premises. On their part, the sellers are to give a full covenant deed of the premises as described, or as they may be described by the surveyor, if the survey is had, executed, and acknowledged at their own expense; they sell the personal property on the farm and represent they own it; they agree that all amounts paid them on the contract and the expense of examining the title shall be a lien on the property; they assume the risk of loss or damage by fire until the deed is delivered; and they agree to pay the broker his commissions. Are they to do more? Or is such a claim inconsistent with these precise provisions? It could not be shown that the plaintiff was to pay $500 additional. Is it also implied that the defendants are not to do anything unexpressed in the writing?

That we need not decide. At least, however, an inspection of this contract shows a full and complete agreement, setting forth in detail the obligations of each party. On reading it, one would conclude that the reciprocal obligations of the parties were fully detailed. Nor would his opinion alter if he knew the surrounding circumstances. The presence of the icehouse, even the knowledge that Mrs. Mitchill thought it objectionable, would not lead to the belief that a separate agreement existed with regard to it. Were such an agreement made it would seem most natural that the inquirer should find it in the contract. Collateral in form it is found to be, but it is closely related to the subject dealt with in the written agreement—so closely that we hold it may not be proved. . . .

We do not ignore the fact that authorities may be found that would seem to support the contention of the appellant. Such are Erskine v. Adeane (1873) L.R. 8 Ch.App. 756, and Morgan v. Griffith (1871) L.R. 6 Exch. 70, where although there was a written lease a collateral agreement of the landlord to reduce the game was admitted. In this state, Wilson v. Deen might lead to the contrary result. Neither are they approved in New Jersey. Naumberg v. Young, 44 N.J.Law, 331, 43 Am.Rep. 380. Nor in view of later cases in this court can Batterman v. Pierce, 3 Hill, 171, be considered an authority. A line of cases in Massachusetts, of which Durkin v. Cobleigh, 156 Mass. 108, 30 N.E. 474, 17 L.R.A. 270, 32 Am.St.Rep. 436, is an example, have to do with collateral contracts made before a deed is given. But the fixed form of a deed makes it inappropriate to insert collateral agreements, however closely connected with the sale. This may be cause for an exception. Here we deal with the contract on the basis of which the deed to Mrs. Mitchill was given subsequently, and we confine ourselves to the question whether its terms may be modified. . . .

It is argued that what we have said is not applicable to the case as presented. The collateral agreement was made with the plaintiff. The contract of sale was with her husband, and no assignment of it from him appears. Yet the deed was given to her. It is evident that here was a transaction in which she was the principal from beginning to end. We must treat the contract as if in form, as it was in fact, made by her.

Our conclusion is that the judgment of the Appellate Division and that of the Special Term should be reversed and the complaint dismissed, with costs in all courts.

LEHMAN, J. (dissenting). I accept the general rule as formulated by Judge Andrews. I differ with him only as to its application to the facts shown in the record. The plaintiff contracted to purchase land from the defendants for an agreed price. A formal written agreement was made between the sellers and the plaintiff's husband. It is on its face a complete contract for the conveyance of the land. It describes the property to be conveyed. It sets forth the purchase price to be paid. All the conditions and terms of the conveyance to be made are clearly stated. I concede at the outset that parol evidence to show additional conditions and terms of the conveyance would be inadmissible. There is a conclusive presumption that the parties intended to integrate in that written contract every agreement relating to the nature or extent of the property to be conveyed, the contents of the deed to be delivered, the consideration to be paid as a condition precedent to the delivery of the deeds, and indeed all the rights of the parties in connection with the land. The conveyance of that land was the subject-matter of the written contract, and the contract completely covers that subject.

The parol agreement which the court below found the parties had made was collateral to, yet connected with, the agreement of purchase and sale. It has been found that the defendants induced the plaintiff to agree to purchase the land by a promise to remove an icehouse from land not covered by the agreement of purchase and sale. No independent consideration passed to the defendants for the parol promise. To that extent the written contract and the alleged oral contract are bound together. The same bond usually exists wherever attempt is made to prove a parol agreement which is collateral to a written agreement. Hence "the problem arises whether the bond is sufficiently close to prevent proof of the oral agreement." See Judge Andrews' citation from Williston on Contracts, § 637.

Judge Andrews has formulated a standard to measure the closeness of the bond. Three conditions, at least, must exist before an oral agreement may be proven to increase the obligation imposed by the written agreement. I think we agree that the first condition that the agreement "must in form be a collateral one" is met by the evidence. I concede that this condition is met in most cases where the courts have nevertheless excluded evidence of the collateral oral agreement. The difficulty here, as in most cases, arises in connection with the two other conditions.

The second condition is that the "parol agreement must not contradict express or implied provisions of the written contract." Judge Andrews voices doubt whether this condition is satisfied. The written contract has been carried out. The purchase price has been paid; conveyance has been made; title has passed in accordance with the terms of the written contract. The mutual obligations expressed in the written contract are left unchanged by the alleged oral contract. When performance was required of the written contract, the obligations of the parties were measured solely by its terms. By the oral agreement the plaintiff seeks to hold the defendants to other obligations to be performed by them thereafter upon land which was not conveyed to the plaintiff. The assertion of such further obligation is not inconsistent with the written contract, unless the written contract contains a provision, express or implied, that the defendants are not to do anything not expressed in the writing. Concededly there is no such express provision in the contract, and such a provision may be implied, if at all, only if the asserted additional obligation is "so clearly connected with the principal transaction as to be part and parcel of it," and is not "one that the parties would not ordinarily be expected to embody in the writing." The hypothesis so formulated for a conclusion that the asserted additional obligation is inconsistent with an implied term of the contract is that the alleged oral agreement does not comply with the third condition as formulated by Judge Andrews. In this case, therefore, the problem reduces itself to the one question whether or not the oral agreement meets the third condition.

I have conceded that upon inspection the contract is complete. "It appears to contain the engagements of the parties, and to define the object and measure the extent of such engagement;" it constitutes the contract between them, and is presumed to contain the whole of that contract. Eighmie v. Taylor, 98 N.Y. 288. That engagement was on the one side to convey land; on the other to pay the price. The plaintiff asserts further agreement based on the same consideration to be performed by the defendants after the conveyance was complete, and directly affecting only other land. It is true, as Judge Andrews points out, that "the presence of the icehouse, even the knowledge that Mrs. Mitchill thought it objectionable, would not lead to the belief that a separate agreement existed with regard to it"; but the question we must decide is whether or not, *assuming* an agreement was made for the removal of an unsightly icehouse from one parcel of land as an inducement for the purchase of another parcel, the parties would ordinarily or naturally be expected to embody the agreement for the removal of the icehouse from one parcel in the written agreement to convey the other parcel. Exclusion of proof of the oral agreement on the ground that it varies the contract embodied in the writing may be based only upon a finding or presumption that the written contract was intended to cover the oral negotiations for the removal of the icehouse which lead up to the contract of purchase and sale. To determine what the writing was intended to cover, "the document alone will not suffice. What it was intended to cover cannot be known till we know what there was to cover. The question being whether certain subjects of negotiation were intended to be covered, we must compare the writing and the negotiations before we can determine whether they were in fact covered." Wigmore on Evidence (2d Ed.) § 2430.

The subject-matter of the written contract was the conveyance of land. The contract was so complete on its face that the conclusion is inevitable that the parties intended to embody in the writing all the negotiations covering at least the conveyance. The promise by the defendants to remove the icehouse from other land was not connected with their obligation to convey except that one agreement would not have been made unless the other was also made. The plaintiff's assertion of a parol agreement by the defendants to remove the icehouse was completely established by the great weight of evidence. It must prevail unless that agreement was part of the agreement to convey and the entire agreement was embodied in the writing.

The fact that in this case the parol agreement is established by the overwhelming weight of evidence is, of course, not a factor which may be considered in determining the competency or legal effect of the evidence. Hardship in the particular case would not justify the court in disregarding or emasculating the general rule. It merely accentuates the outlines of our problem. The assumption that the parol agreement was made is no longer obscured by any doubts. The problem, then, is clearly whether the parties are presumed to have intended to render that parol agreement legally ineffective and nonexistent by failure to embody it in the writing. Though we are driven to say that nothing in the written contract which fixed the terms and conditions of the stipulated conveyance suggests the existence of any further parol agreement, an inspection of the contract, though it is complete on its face in regard to the subject of the conveyance, does not, I think, show that it was intended to embody negotiations or agreements, if any, in regard to a matter so loosely bound to the conveyance as the removal of an icehouse from land not conveyed.

The rule of integration undoubtedly frequently prevents the assertion of fraudulent claims. Parties who take the precaution of embodying their oral agreements in a writing should be protected against the assertion that other terms of the same agreement were not integrated in the writing. The limits of the integration are determined by the writing, read in the light of the surrounding circumstances. A written contract, however complete, yet covers only a limited field. I do not think that in the written contract for the conveyance of land here under consideration we can find an intention to cover a field so broad as to include prior agreements, if any such were made, to do other acts on other property after the stipulated conveyance was made.

In each case where such a problem is presented, varying factors enter into its solution. Citation of authority in this or other jurisdictions is useless, at least without minute analysis of the facts. The analysis I have made of the decisions in this state leads me to the view that the decision of the courts below is in accordance with our own authorities and should be affirmed.

CARDOZO, C.J., and POUND, KELLOGG and O'BRIEN, JJ., concur with ANDREWS, J.

LEHMAN, J., dissents in opinion in which CRANE, J., concurs.

Judgment accordingly.

––––––––

VON MEHREN, CIVIL LAW ANALOGUES TO CONSIDERATION: AN EXERCISE IN COMPARATIVE ANALYSIS, 72 Harv.L.Rev. 1009, 1011–1012 (1959). "One or more of the interested parties often think that a contractual obligation will be more readily enforced if it is formally divorced from the environment and the motives that produced it. Civil-law theorists, especially the German writers, have discussed such a divorcement in terms of whether the legal system permits an 'abstract' obligation.... [I]n all jurisdictions, a transaction can also be rendered partially abstract by embodying it in an integrating agreement."

JAMES BRADLEY THAYER, A PRELIMINARY TREATISE ON EVIDENCE 428–429 (1898). Commenting on an opinion of Chief Justice Holt, Thayer remarked: "The Chief Justice here retires into that lawyer's Paradise where all words have a fixed, precisely ascertained meaning; where men may express their purposes, not only with accuracy, but with fulness; and where, if the writer has been careful, a lawyer, having a document referred to him, may sit in his chair, inspect the text, and answer all questions without raising his eyes. Men have dreamed of attaining for their solemn muniments of title such an absolute security; and some degree of security they have encompassed by giving strict definitions and technical meanings to words and phrases, and by rigid rules of construction. But the fatal necessity of looking outside the text in order to identify persons and things, tends steadily to destroy such illusions and to reveal the essential imperfection of language, whether spoken or written."

CALAMARI & PERILLO, A PLEA FOR A UNIFORM PAROL EVIDENCE RULE AND PRINCIPLES OF INTERPRETATION

42 Indiana L.J. 333 (1967).

Any reader of advance sheets is well aware that most of the contract decisions reported do not involve offer and acceptance or other subjects usually explored in depth in a course in contracts but rather involve the parol evidence rule and questions of interpretation, topics given scant attention in most courses in contracts.... Much of the fog and mystery surrounding these subjects stems from the fact that there is basic disagreement as to the meaning and effect of the parol evidence rule and as to the appropriate goals to be achieved by the process of contractual interpretation. The cases and treatises of the contract giants tend to conceal this conflict. While frequently masking disagreement by using the same terminology, Professors Williston and Corbin are often poles apart in the meaning they attach to the same term. Often starting from what superficially appear to be the same premises, they frequently advocate different results in similar fact situations. The polarity of their views reflects conflicting value judgments as to policy issues that are as old as our legal system and that are likely to continue as long as courts of law exist. Although many writers and courts have expressed their views on the subject and have made major contributions to it, concentration on the analyses of Professors Williston and Corbin will point up the fundamental bases upon which the conflicting cases and views rest.

THE AREA OF SUBSTANTIAL AGREEMENT

There is a rule of substantive law which states that whenever contractual intent is sought to be ascertained from among several expressions of the parties, an earlier tentative expression will be rejected in favor of a later expression that is final. More simply stated, the contract made by the parties supersedes tentative promises made in earlier negotiations. Consequently, in determining the content of the contract, the earlier tentative promises are irrelevant.

The parol evidence rule comes into play only when the last expression is in writing. Professor Corbin states the rule as follows: "When two parties have made a contract and have expressed it in a writing to which they have both assented as the complete and accurate integration of that contract, evidence, whether parol or otherwise, of antecedent understandings and negotiations will not be admitted for the purpose of varying or contradicting the writing." Professor Williston's formulation is not to the contrary: "Briefly stated," he writes, "this rule requires, in the absence of fraud, duress, mutual mistake, or something of the kind, the exclusion of extrinsic evidence, oral or written, where the parties have reduced their agreement to an integrated writing." Both agree that this, too, is a rule of substantive law that also operates as an exclusionary rule of evidence merely because prior understandings are irrelevant to the process of determining the content of the final contract. The similarity between the parol evidence rule and the rule stated in the preceding paragraph is obvious. The main and important difference is that where the last expression is not in writing the jury determines whether the parties intended the second expression to supersede the first. This is to say that this question of intention is determined as is any other question of intention stemming from oral transactions. Where the later expression is in writing, however, this question is usually determined by the trial judge. At an early date it was felt (and the feeling strongly remains) that writings require the special protection that is afforded by removing this issue from the province of unsophisticated jurors.

The Parol Evidence Rule: The Major Area of Conflict

Apparent agreement by Professors Williston and Corbin, except as noted, on the rules stated above conceals real conflict. The battleground upon which they express disagreement is a major one: the concept of total integration. This, of course, is the area in which most of the cases arise. Both assert that the existence of a total integration depends on the intention of the parties. . . . It appears, however, that in this context they use the term "intent" in ways that are remarkably dissimilar. A typical fact situation will illustrate this. A agrees to sell and B agrees to purchase Blackacre for $10,000. The contract is in writing and in all respects appears complete on its face. Prior to the signing of the contract A, in order to induce B's assent, orally promises him in the presence of a number of reputable witnesses that if B will sign the contract, A will remove an unsightly shack on A's land across the road from Blackacre. May this promise be proved and enforced? This depends upon whether the writing is a total integration.

Williston argues that if the intention to have a total integration were to be determined by the ordinary process of determining intention, the parol evidence rule would be emasculated. He points out that the mere existence of the collateral oral agreement would conclusively indicate that the parties intended only a partial integration and that the only question that would be presented is whether the alleged prior or contemporaneous agreement was actually made. This would be a question of fact for the jury, thus eliminating the special protection which the trial judge should afford the writing. . . .

. . . [Williston therefore suggests that] where the writing appears to be a complete instrument expressing the rights and obligations of both parties, it is deemed a total integration unless the alleged additional terms were such as might naturally be made as a separate agreement by parties situated as were the parties to the written contract.

Professor Corbin has an easy task in demolishing the Willistonian approach. In treating the matter of integration as a question of intent, as Professor Williston purports to do, he shows the absurdity of excluding all relevant evidence of intent except the writing itself. But . . . Williston, and [courts that follow his view] are unconcerned about the true intention of the parties. Rather, shorn of rote language of fiction indicating a search for intention, they are advocating and applying a rule of form. Since (and even before) the common law had its genesis, there has been a deeply-felt belief that transactions will be more secure, litigation will be reduced, and the temptation to perjury will be removed, if everyone will only use proper forms for his transactions. The Statute of Wills and the Statute of Frauds are but examples of this belief. Professor Corbin, by attacking the apparent arguments of Williston's position has not expressly come to grips with the substance of his position. This is not to suggest that either he or Professor Williston have been unaware of the true nature of their disagreement. Rather, they seem for the most part to have been content not to make explicit the basis of their differing views. . . .

The debate involves the question: is the public better served by giving effect to the parties' entire agreement written and oral, even at the risk of injustice caused by the possibility of perjury and the possibility that superseded documents will be treated as operative, or does the security of transactions require that, despite occasional injustices, persons adopting a formal writing be required, on the penalty of voidness of their oral and written side agreements, to put their entire agreement in the formal writing. . . .

RESTATEMENT, FIRST, CONTRACTS §§ 228, 237, 239, 240

§ 228. What is Integration

An agreement is integrated where the parties thereto adopt a writing or writings as the final and complete expression of the agreement. An integration is the writing or writings so adopted.

§ 237. Parol Evidence Rule; Effect of Integration on Prior or Contemporaneous Agreements

Except as stated in [§ 240] the integration of an agreement makes inoperative to add to or to vary the agreement all contemporaneous oral agreements relating to the same subject-matter; and . . . all prior oral or written agreements relating thereto. . . .

§ 239. Effect of Partial Integration

Where there is integration of part of the terms of a contract prior written agreements and contemporaneous oral agreements are operative to vary these terms only to the same extent as if the whole contract had been integrated.

§ 240. In What Cases Integration Does Not Affect Prior or Contemporaneous Agreements

(1) An oral agreement is not superseded or invalidated by a subsequent or contemporaneous integration, nor a written agreement by a subsequent integration relating to the same subject-matter, if the agreement is not inconsistent with the integrated contract, and

(a) is made for separate consideration, or

(b) is such an agreement as might naturally be made as a separate agreement by parties situated as were the parties to the written contract. . . .

RESTATEMENT, SECOND, CONTRACTS
§§ 209, 210, 213, 214, 215, 216

[See Selected Source Materials Supplement]

BRAUCHER, INTERPRETATION AND LEGAL EFFECT IN THE SECOND RESTATEMENT OF CONTRACTS, 81 Colum.L.Rev. 13, 17 (1981). "The core of the 'parol evidence rule' is stated in section 213: a binding integrated agreement discharges inconsistent prior agreements, and a binding completely integrated agreement discharges prior agreements within its scope. These statements, however, merely point to the obvious conclusion; the difficulties arise in determining whether there is an integrated agreement, whether, if so, it is completely or only partially integrated, and whether the prior agreement is consistent with the integrated agreement or within its scope. Those determinations are made in accordance with all relevant evidence, and require interpretation both of the integrated agreement and of the prior agreement. They are made by the court, not by the trier of fact."

HATLEY v. STAFFORD, 284 Or. 523, 534, 588 P.2d 603, 609 (1978). "In determining whether or not an oral term is one that 'naturally' would have been included in the writing, the trial court is not limited to a consideration of the face of the document. This court has recognized that 'the surrounding circumstances, as well as the written contract, may be considered.' Blehm v. Ringering, 260 Or. 46, 50, 488 P.2d 798 (1971). When considering the surrounding circumstances, the trial court should be aware of the fact that parties with business experience are more likely to reduce their entire agreement to writing than parties without such experience[,] . . . and that this is especially true when the parties are represented by counsel on both sides. . . . The relative bargaining strength of the parties also should be considered, since a transaction not negotiated at arm's length may result in a writing that omits essential terms. . . . And, of course, the apparent completeness and detail of the writing itself may lead the court to conclude the parties intended the writing to be a complete integration of their agreement. . . . This is not to say, however, that the trial court should readily admit parol evidence whenever one of the parties claims a writing does not include all the terms of an agreement. The court should presume that the writing was intended to be a complete integration, at least when the writing is complete on its face, and should admit evidence of consistent additional terms only if there is substantial evidence that the parties did not intend the writing to embody the entire agreement...."

INTERFORM CO. v. MITCHELL CONSTR. CO., 575 F.2d 1270, 1275–77 (9th Cir.1978). "In practice ... the difference between the [Corbin and Williston] views is less significant than one might imagine. A writing, which ordinarily and naturally would be an integrated one, generally is one the parties thereto intended to be integrated. Also, the meaning to which the reasonably intelligent person would subscribe generally is that to which the parties did subscribe....

"There are, however, significant differences between the two views. To suggest none exist would reduce the debate between their respective leading protagonists, Williston with regard to the first and Corbin the second, to a triviality. The debate is not that. It relates, as indicated, to the attitude with which judges should approach written contracts. Williston requires the judge to ascertain the legal relations between the parties by reference to those associated with the 'forms' (that is, the natural and normal integration practices and the meaning of words that reasonably intelligent people would employ) to which they should adhere and from which they depart at their peril. Calamari & Perillo 104–05; Williston §§ 633, 638–39. Corbin, on the other hand, directs the judge to fix the legal relations between the parties in accordance with their intention even when the 'forms' they employed suggest otherwise. Corbin §§ 538–42A. A judge, guided by Williston ... would impose upon the parties the terms of the [contractual documents] as understood by the reasonably intelligent person if [those documents] appear complete and any additional terms ordinarily and naturally would have been included therein. Williston §§ 638–39; Calamari & Perillo 105. A judge, guided by Corbin, would impose upon the parties the agreement that the evidence indicates they in fact reached....

"It is unlikely that any jurisdiction will inflexibly adopt one approach to the exclusion of the other; each is likely to influence the conduct of judges and the disposition of cases. However, it must be acknowledged that the influence of Corbin's way is stronger now ..., than when he and Williston grappled during the drafting of the American Law Institute's first Restatement, Contracts...."

MURRAY, THE PAROL EVIDENCE PROCESS AND STANDARDIZED AGREEMENTS UNDER THE RESTATEMENT, SECOND, CONTRACTS, 123 U.Pa.L.Rev. 1342 (1975). "The first indication of the test suggested in the *Restatement, Second* is found in comment *c* to the first section of topic three, [section 209]: 'Whether a writing has been adopted as an integrated agreement is a question of fact to be determined in accordance with all relevant evidence.' That the question is 'one of fact' has long been generally conceded. The significance of the statement is its direction that the integration determination be made 'in accordance with all relevant evidence.' The flavor of Corbin is here so strong as to mask any others. Professor Corbin has suggested that '[o]n this issue of fact, no relevant testimony should be excluded.' Here, at the outset of the *Restatement, Second,* Corbin appears to win the first and probably the decisive battle...."

CISG ART. 8(3)

[See Selected Source Materials Supplement]

DODGE, TEACHING THE CISG IN CONTRACTS, 50 J. Leg. Ed. 72 (2000). "Under the parol evidence rule found in both the common law and the UCC, the parties may not contradict the terms of a final written agreement with evidence of prior or contemporaneous negotiations or agreements. CISG Article 8(3), by contrast, directs a court interpreting a contract to give 'due consideration ... to all relevant circumstances of the case including the negotiations, any practices which the parties have established between themselves, usages and any subsequent conduct of the parties.' In other words, the CISG lacks a parol evidence rule and allows a court interpreting a written contract to consider not just trade usage, course of dealing, and course of performance, but even the parties' prior negotiations."

UNIDROIT PRINCIPLES OF INTERNATIONAL LAW ART. 4.3

[See Selected Source Materials Supplement]

MASTERSON v. SINE

Supreme Court of California, 1968.
68 Cal.2d 222, 65 Cal.Rptr. 545, 436 P.2d 561.

TRAYNOR, CHIEF JUSTICE.

Dallas Masterson and his wife Rebecca owned a ranch as tenants in common. On February 25, 1958, they conveyed it to Medora and Lu Sine by a grant deed "Reserving unto the Grantors herein an option to purchase the above described property on or before February 25, 1968" for the "same consideration as being paid heretofore plus their depreciation value of any improvements Grantees may add to the property from and after two and a half years from this date." Medora is Dallas' sister and Lu's wife. Since the conveyance Dallas has been adjudged bankrupt. His trustee in bankruptcy and Rebecca brought this declaratory relief action to establish their right to enforce the option.

The case was tried without a jury. Over defendants' objection the trial court admitted extrinsic evidence that by "the same consideration as being paid heretofore" both the grantors and the grantees meant the sum of $50,000 and by "depreciation value of any improvements" they meant the depreciation value of improvements to be computed by deducting from the total amount of any capital expenditures made by defendants grantees the amount of depreciation allowable to them under United States income tax regulations as of the time of the exercise of the option.

The court also determined that the parol evidence rule precluded admission of extrinsic evidence offered by defendants to show that the parties wanted the property kept in the Masterson family and that the option was therefore personal to the grantors and could not be exercised by the trustee in bankruptcy.

The court entered judgment for plaintiffs, declaring their right to exercise the option, specifying in some detail how it could be exercised, and reserving jurisdiction to supervise the manner of its exercise and to determine the amount that plaintiffs will be required to pay defendants for their capital expenditures if plaintiffs decide to exercise the option.

Defendants appeal. They contend that the option provision is too uncertain to be enforced and that extrinsic evidence as to its meaning should not have been admitted. The trial court properly refused to frustrate the obviously declared intention of the grantors to reserve an option to repurchase by an overly meticulous insistence on completeness and clarity of written expression. (See California Lettuce Growers v. Union Sugar Co. (1955) 45 Cal.2d 474, 481, 289 P.2d 785, 49 A.L.R.2d 496; Rivers v. Beadle (1960) 183 Cal.App.2d 691, 695–697, 7 Cal.Rptr. 170.) It properly admitted extrinsic evidence to explain the language of the deed. . . . to the end that the consideration for the option would appear with sufficient certainty to permit specific enforcement. . . . The trial court erred, however, in excluding the extrinsic evidence that the option was personal to the grantors and therefore nonassignable.

When the parties to a written contract have agreed to it as an "integration"—a complete and final embodiment of the terms of an agreement—parol evidence cannot be used to add to or vary its terms. . . . When only part of the agreement is integrated, the same rule applies to that part, but parol evidence may be used to prove elements of the agreement not reduced to writing. . . .

California cases have stated that whether there was an integration is to be determined solely from the face of the instrument . . . and that the question for the court is whether it "appears to be a complete . . . agreement. . . ." . . . Neither of these strict formulations of the rule, however, has been consistently applied. The requirement that the writing must appear incomplete on its face has been repudiated in many cases where parol evidence was admitted "to prove the existence of a separate oral agreement as to any matter on which the document is silent and which is not inconsistent with its terms"—even though the instrument appeared to state a complete agreement. . . . Even under the rule that the writing alone is to be consulted, it was found necessary to examine the alleged collateral agreement before concluding that proof of it was precluded by the writing alone. (See 3 Corbin, Contracts (1960) § 582, pp. 444–446.) It is therefore evident that "The conception of a writing as wholly and intrinsically self-determinative of the parties' intent to make it a sole memorial of one or seven or twenty-seven subjects of negotiation is an impossible one." (9 Wigmore, Evidence (3d ed. 1940) § 2431, p. 103.) For example, a promissory note given by a debtor to his creditor may integrate all their present contractual rights and obligations, or it may be only a minor part of an underlying executory contract that would never be discovered by examining the face of the note.

In formulating the rule governing parol evidence, several policies must be accommodated. One policy is based on the assumption that written evidence is more accurate than human memory.... This policy, however, can be adequately served by excluding parol evidence of agreements that directly contradict the writing. Another policy is based on the fear that fraud or unintentional invention by witnesses interested in the outcome of the litigation will mislead the finder of facts....

Evidence of oral collateral agreements should be excluded only when the fact finder is likely to be misled. The rule must therefore be based on the credibility of the evidence. One such standard, adopted by section 240(1)(b) of the Restatement [First] of Contracts, permits proof of a collateral agreement if it "is such an agreement as might *naturally* be made as a separate agreement by parties situated as were the parties to the written contract." (Italics added; see McCormick, Evidence (1954) § 216, p. 441; see also 3 Corbin, Contracts (1960) § 583, p. 475, § 594, pp. 568–569; 4 Williston, Contracts (3d ed. 1961) § 638, pp. 1039–1045.) The draftsmen of the Uniform Commercial Code would exclude the evidence in still fewer instances: "If the additional terms are such that if agreed upon, they would *certainly* have been included in the document in the view of the court, then evidence of their alleged making must be kept from the trier of fact." (Com. 3, § 2–202, italics added.)[1]

The option clause in the deed in the present case does not explicitly provide that it contains the complete agreement, and the deed is silent on the question of assignability. Moreover, the difficulty of accommodating the formalized structure of a deed to the insertion of collateral agreements makes it less likely that all the terms of such an agreement were included. (See 3 Corbin, Contracts (1960) § 587; 4 Williston, Contracts (3d ed. 1961) § 645; 70 A.L.R. 752, 759 (1931); 68 A.L.R. 245 (1930).) The statement of the reservation of the option might well have been placed in the recorded deed solely to preserve the grantors' rights against any possible future purchasers and this function could well be served without any mention of the parties' agreement that the option was personal. There is nothing in the record to indicate that the parties to this family transaction, through experience in land transactions or otherwise, had any warning of the disadvantages of failing to put the whole agreement in the deed. This case is one, therefore, in which it can be said that a collateral agreement such as that alleged "might naturally be made as a

---

1. Corbin suggests that, even in situations where the court concludes that it would not have been natural for the parties to make the alleged collateral oral agreement, parol evidence of such an agreement should nevertheless be permitted if the court is convinced that the unnatural actually happened in the case being adjudicated. (3 Corbin, Contracts, § 485, pp. 478, 480; cf. Murray, The Parol Evidence Rule: A Clarification (1966) 4 Duquesne L.Rev. 337, 341–342.) This suggestion may be based on a belief that judges are not likely to be misled by their sympathies. If the court believes that the parties intended a collateral agreement to be effective, there is no reason to keep the evidence from the jury.

separate agreement." *A fortiori*, the case is not one in which the parties "would certainly" have included the collateral agreement in the deed.

It is contended, however, that an option agreement is ordinarily presumed to be assignable if it contains no provisions forbidding its transfer or indicating that its performance involves elements personal to the parties. (Mott v. Cline (1927) 200 Cal. 434, 450, 253 P. 718; Altman v. Blewett (1928) 93 Cal.App. 516, 525, 269 P. 751.) The fact that there is a written memorandum, however, does not necessarily preclude parol evidence rebutting a term that the law would otherwise presume. In American Industrial Sales Corp. v. Airscope, Inc., supra, 44 Cal.2d 393, 397–398, 282 P.2d 504, we held it proper to admit parol evidence of a contemporaneous collateral agreement as to the place of payment of a note, even though it contradicted the presumption that a note, silent as to the place of payment, is payable where the creditor resides. (For other examples of this approach, see Richter v. Union Land etc. Co. (1900) 129 Cal. 367, 375, 62 P. 39 [presumption of time of delivery rebutted by parol evidence]; Wolters v. King (1897) 119 Cal. 172, 175–176, 51 P. 35 [presumption of time of payment rebutted by parol evidence]; Mangini v. Wolfschmidt, Ltd., supra, 165 Cal.App.2d 192, 198–201, 331 P.2d 728 [presumption of duration of an agency contract rebutted by parol evidence]; Zinn v. Ex–Cell–O Corp. (1957) 148 Cal.App.2d 56, 73–74, 306 P.2d 1017; see also Rest., Contracts, § 240, com. c.)[2] Of course a statute may preclude parol evidence to rebut a statutory presumption.... Here, however, there is no such statute. In the absence of a controlling statute the parties may provide that a contract right or duty is nontransferable.... Moreover, even when there is no explicit agreement—written *or* oral—that contractual duties shall be personal, courts will effectuate a presumed intent to that effect if the circumstances indicate that performance by substituted person would be different from that contracted for....

In the present case defendants offered evidence that the parties agreed that the option was not assignable in order to keep the property in the Masterson family. The trial court erred in excluding that evidence.

The judgment is reversed.

PETERS, TOBRINER, MOSK, and SULLIVAN, JJ., concur.

Dissenting Opinion

BURKE, JUSTICE.

I dissent....

2. Counsel for plaintiffs direct our attention to numerous cases that they contend establish that parol evidence may never be used to show a collateral agreement contrary to a term that the law presumes in the absence of an agreement. In each of these cases, however, the decision turned upon the court's belief that the writing was a complete integration and was no more than an application of the rule that parol evidence cannot be used to vary the terms of a completely integrated agreement....

In Standard Box Co. v. Mutual Biscuit Co. (1909) 10 Cal.App. 746, 750, 103 P. 938, 940, the [court excluded] evidence of an agreement for a time of performance other than the "reasonable time" implied by law in a situation where the writing, although stating no time of performance, was "clear and complete when aided by that which is imported into it by legal implication." This decision was simply an application of the then-current theory regarding integration. The court regarded the instrument as a complete integration, and it therefore precluded proof of collateral agreements. Since it is now clear that integration cannot be determined from the writing alone, the decision is not authoritative insofar as it finds a complete integration. There is no reason to believe that the court gave any independent significance to implied terms. Had the court found from the writing alone that there was no integration, there is nothing to indicate that it would have excluded proof contrary to terms it would have otherwise presumed....

The court properly admitted parol evidence to explain the intended meaning of the "same consideration" and "depreciation value" phrases of the written option to purchase defendants' land, as the intended meaning of those phrases was not clear. However, there was nothing ambiguous about the *granting* language of the option and not the slightest suggestion in the document that the option was to be nonassignable. Thus, to permit such words of limitation to be added by parol is to *contradict* the absolute nature of the grant, and to directly violate the parol evidence rule.

Just as it is unnecessary to state in a deed to "lot X" that the house located thereon goes with the land, it is likewise unnecessary to add to "I grant an option to Jones" the words *"and his assigns"* for the option to be assignable.... California statutes expressly declare that it *is* assignable, and only if I add language in writing showing my intent to withhold or restrict the right of assignment may the grant be so limited. Thus, to seek to restrict the grant by parol is to *contradict* the written document in violation of the parol evidence rule....

McComb, J., concurs.

Rehearing denied; McComb and Burke, JJ., dissenting.

UCC § 2–202

[See Selected Source Materials Supplement]

INTERFORM v. MITCHELL CONSTR. CO., 575 F.2d 1270, 1277 (9th Cir. 1978). "... [UCC § 2–202] reflects Corbin's influence. It precludes contradiction of 'confirmatory memoranda' by prior or contemporaneous oral agreements when the writing was '*intended* by the parties as a final expression of their agreement' and permits the introduction of consistent additional terms 'unless the court finds the writing to have been *intended* also as a complete and exclusive statement of the terms of the agreement.' (Italics added). The focus plainly is on the intention of the parties, not the integration practices of reasonable persons acting normally and naturally. This is Corbin's focus. Furthermore, [Official Comment 1 rejects] certain rules more applicable to Williston's approach than to Corbin's...."

HUNT FOODS AND INDUSTRIES, INC. v. DOLINER

Supreme Court of New York, Appellate Division, First Department 1966.
26 A.D.2d 41, 270 N.Y.S.2d 937.

Before Breitel, J.P., and Rabin, Stevens, Steuer and Capozzoli, JJ.

Steuer, Justice. In February 1965 plaintiff corporation undertook negotiations to acquire the assets of Eastern Can Company. The stock of the latter is owned by defendant George M. Doliner and his family to the extent of 73%. The balance is owned by independent interests. At a fairly early stage of the negotiations agreement was reached as to the price to be paid by plaintiff ($5,922,500 if in cash, or $5,730,000 in Hunt stock), but several important items, including the form of the acquisition, were not agreed upon. At this point it was found necessary to recess the negotiations for several weeks. The Hunt negotiators expressed concern over any adjournment and stated that they feared that Doliner would use their offer as a basis for soliciting a higher bid from a third party. To protect themselves they demanded an option to purchase the Doliner stock. Such an option was prepared and signed by George Doliner and the members of his family and at least one other person associated with him who were stockholders. It provides that Hunt has the option to buy all of the Doliner stock at $5.50 per share. The option is to be exercised by giving notice on or before June 1, 1965, and if notice is not given the option is void. If given, Hunt is to pay the price and the Doliners to deliver their stock within seven days thereafter. The agreement calls for Hunt to pay $1,000 for the option, which was paid. To this point there is substantial accord as to what took place.

Defendant claims that when his counsel called attention to the fact that the option was unconditional in its terms, he obtained an understanding that it was only to be used in the event that he solicited an outside offer; and that plaintiff insisted that unless the option was signed in unconditional form negotiations would terminate. Plaintiff contends there was no condition. Concededly, on resumption of negotiations the parties failed to reach agreement and the option was exercised. Defendants declined the tender and refused to deliver the stock.

Plaintiff moved for summary judgment for specific performance. We do not believe that summary judgment lies. Plaintiff's position is that the condition claimed could not be proved under the parol evidence rule, and, eliminating that, there is no defense to the action.

The parol evidence rule, at least as that term refers to contracts of sale,[3] is now contained in Section 2–202 of the Uniform Commercial Code, which reads:

> "Terms with respect to which the confirmatory memoranda of the parties agree or which are otherwise set forth in a writing intended by the parties as a final expression of their agreement with respect to such terms as are included therein may not be contradicted by evidence of any prior agreement or of a contemporaneous oral agreement but may be explained or supplemented
>
> " * * *
>
> "(b) by evidence of consistent additional terms unless the court finds the writing to have been intended also as a complete and exclusive statement of the terms of the agreement."

The term (that the option was not to be exercised unless Doliner sought outside bids), admittedly discussed but whose operative effect is disputed, not

---

3. While article 2 of the Uniform Commercial Code which contains this section does not deal with the sale of securities, this section applies to article 8, dealing with securities. Cf. Agar v. Orda, 264 N.Y. 248, 190 N.E. 479, 90 A.L.R. 269; Official Comment, McKinney's Uniform Commercial Code, Part 1, pp. 96–97; Note, 65 Col.L.Rev. 880, 890–1. All parties and Special Term so regarded it.

being set out in the writing, is clearly "additional" to what is in the writing. So the first question presented is whether that term is "consistent" with the instrument. In a sense any oral provision which would prevent the ripening of the obligations of a writing is inconsistent with the writing. But that obviously is not the sense in which the word is used (Hicks v. Bush, 10 N.Y.2d 488, 491, 225 N.Y.S.2d 34, 180 N.E.2d 425). To be inconsistent the term must contradict or negate a term of the writing. A term or condition which has a lesser effect is provable.

The Official Comment prepared by the drafters of the Code contains this statement:

> "If the additional terms are such that, if agreed upon, they would certainly have been included in the document in the view of the court, then evidence of their alleged making must be kept from the trier of fact." (McKinney's Uniform Commercial Code, Part 1, p. 158)

Special Term interpreted this language as not only calling for an adjudication by the court in all instances where proof of an "additional oral term" is offered, but making that determination exclusively the function of the court. We believe the proffered evidence to be inadmissible only where the writing contradicts the existence of the claimed additional term (Meadow Brook Nat. Bank v. Bzura, 20 A.D.2d 287, 290, 246 N.Y.S.2d 787, 790). The conversations in this case, some of which are not disputed, and the expectation of all the parties for further negotiations, suggest that the alleged oral condition precedent cannot be precluded as a matter of law or as factually impossible. It is not sufficient that the existence of the condition is implausible. It must be impossible (cf. Millerton Agway Coop. v. Briarcliff Farms, 17 N.Y.2d 57, 63–64, 268 N.Y.S.2d 18, 215 N.E.2d 341).

The order should be reversed on the law and the motion for summary judgment denied with costs and disbursements to abide the event.

Order and judgment ... unanimously reversed, on the law, with $50 costs and disbursements to abide the event, and plaintiff's motion for summary judgment denied. All concur.

────────

ALASKA NORTHERN DEVELOPMENT, INC. v. ALYESKA PIPELINE SERVICE CO., 666 P.2d 33 (Alaska 1983), cert. denied, 464 U.S. 1041, 104 S.Ct. 706, 79 L.Ed.2d 170 (1984). "The narrow view of consistency expressed in *Hunt Foods* has been criticized. In Snyder v. Herbert Greenbaum & Associates, Inc., 38 Md.App. 144, 380 A.2d 618 (Md.App.1977), the court held that the parol evidence of a contractual right to unilateral rescission was inconsistent with a written agreement for the sale and installation of carpeting. The court defined 'inconsistency' as used in section 2–202(b) as 'the absence of reasonable harmony in terms of the language and respective obligations of the parties.' Id. 380 A.2d at 623 (emphasis in original) (citing U.C.C. § 1–205(4)). Accord: Luria Brothers & Co. v. Pielet Brothers Scrap Iron & Metal, Inc., 600 F.2d 103, 111 (7th Cir.1979); Southern Concrete Services, Inc. v. Mableton Contractors, Inc., 407 F.Supp. 581 (N.D.Ga.1975), aff'd mem., 569 F.2d 1154 (5th Cir.1978).

"We agree with this view of inconsistency and reject the view expressed in *Hunt Foods*.[4] Under this definition of inconsistency, it is clear that the proffered parol evidence limiting the owner committee's right of final approval to price is inconsistent with the integrated term that unconditionally gives the committee the right to approval. Therefore, the superior court was correct in refusing to admit parol evidence on this issue."

NOTE ON MERGER CLAUSES

Many written contracts contain provisions that state that the written contract is the entire contract between the parties. These provisions are known as "merger" or "integration" clauses because they say, in effect, that all agreements between the parties have been merged or integrated into the writing. Typically these are "boilerplate" provisions—that is, they are standardized provisions that are routinely inserted by the drafting lawyer into every contract the lawyer writes—even when the principals have not specifically negotiated such a provision—and usually appear at the end of the contract with other standardized provisions, like provisions that set out the addresses to which notices should be sent.

The law on what effect should be given to merger clauses is messy. In some cases they have been given a great deal of weight; in some they have been given little weight; and in some the courts have said that the weight to be given such provisions depends on the circumstances. The muddiness of the case-law is reflected in the muddiness of Restatement Second § 216, Comment e:

> e. *Written term excluding oral terms ("merger" clause)*. Written agreements often contain clauses stating that there are no representations, promises or agreements between the parties except those found in the writing. Such a clause may negate the apparent authority of an agent to vary orally the written terms, and if agreed to is likely to conclude the issue whether the agreement is completely integrated. Consistent additional terms may then be excluded even though their omission would have been natural in the absence of such a clause. But such a clause does not control the question whether the writing was assented to as an integrated agreement, the scope of the writing if completely integrated, or the interpretation of the written terms.

ARB (AMERICAN RESEARCH BUREAU), INC. v. E–SYSTEMS, INC., 663 F.2d 189, 198–99 (D.C.Cir.1980). "We believe that the written contract was 'intended . . . as a complete and exclusive statement of the terms of the agreement.' Two factors support this conclusion: first and most important is that the written contract contains an integration clause, and

---

4. *Hunt Foods* was implicitly rejected in Johnson v. Curran, 633 P.2d 994, 996–97 (Alaska 1981) (parol evidence concerning an early termination right based on nightclub owner's dissatisfaction with the band's per- formance was inconsistent with parties' written contract specifying definite time without mention of any right of early termination and thus inadmissible).

integration clauses are generally to be given effect under section 2–202. . . . The integration clause in question here is not susceptible of any other reasonable interpretation; it states: 'This contract . . . constitutes the entire agreement between Buyer and Seller.' . . .

"This decision to give effect to the integration clause is consistent with non-U.C.C. Maryland law, which holds that integration clauses, although not 'absolutely conclusive,' are 'indicative of the intention of the parties to finalize their complete understanding in the written contract . . . that there was no other prior or contemporaneous agreement not included in the written contract.' Pumphrey v. Kehoe, 261 Md. 496, 505, 276 A.2d 194, 199 (1971). Maryland law further requires, however, that the circumstances surrounding the making of the contract be considered to discover whether the integration clause in question does, in fact, express the genuine intention of the parties to make the written contract the complete and exclusive statement of their agreement. Shoreham Developers, Inc. v. Randolph Hills, Inc., 248 Md. 267, 271–72, 235 A.2d 735, 739 (1967); Rinaudo v. Bloom, 209 Md. 1, 9, 120 A.2d 184, 190 (1956). Thus, the issue is not whether the deletion of a given sentence antecedent to the making of the written contract was an agreement as to the matter deleted, but whether the integration clause, at the time it was agreed upon, represented the intentions of the parties. Here, the bulk of the evidence suggests that the parties intended the written contract to be the complete and exclusive statement of the terms of their agreement. The length of the contract, its exhaustive detail, and the prolonged period of negotiation preceding its signing, collectively considered, support this conclusion. At the same time, E–Systems has offered no persuasive evidence supporting a determination that the parties intended, at the time of contracting, that non-written terms be part of the overall agreement."

———

SEIBEL v. LAYNE & BOWLER, INC., 56 Or.App. 387, 641 P.2d 668 (1982). "Defendant contends that the contract cannot be supplemented, because it contains a merger clause which indicates that it was intended to be a complete and exclusive expression of their agreement. [UCC § 2–202] requires, however, that the *parties* intend for the agreement to be their complete expression. Because the merger clause is as inconspicuous as the disclaimers, it provides little or no evidence of the parties' intentions, regardless of the defendant's intentions. Moreover, under the UCC, courts are to limit the application of contract provisions so as to avoid any unconscionable result. [UCC § 2–302] Official Comment 1 for this section indicates that a principle underlying unconscionability is the prevention of unfair surprise. . . . We think that it would be unconscionable to permit an inconspicuous merger clause to exclude evidence of an express oral warranty—especially in light of the policy expressed by [UCC § 2–316]. That is, a disclaimer of the implied warranties of fitness and merchantability must be conspicuous to prevent surprise. We think that a merger clause which would deny effect to an express warranty must be conspicuous to prevent an even greater surprise."

———

UNIDROIT PRINCIPLES OF INTERNATIONAL COMMERCIAL CONTRACTS ART. 2.1.17

[See Selected Source Materials Supplement]

NOTE ON THE FRAUD EXCEPTION TO THE PAROL EVIDENCE RULE

It is a well-established exception to the parol evidence rule that evidence of speech or conduct that occurred prior to or contemporaneous with the adoption of a writing is admissible, notwithstanding the rule, if the evidence shows an "invalidating cause" of the written agreement, such as lack of consideration, duress, mistake, illegality, or fraud. Restatement Second § 214(d). The fraud exception raises special problems in the context of promissory fraud, especially when the written agreement includes a merger clause.

1. *Promissory Fraud.* Normally, fraud involves a misrepresentation of *fact*. Under the doctrine of promissory fraud, however, a *promise* is fraudulent if the promisor makes the promise with a present intent not to perform it. Under the fraud exception to the parol evidence rule, therefore, evidence of a side agreement that would otherwise be barred under the rule may be admissible if the promisor made the agreement with a present intent not to perform it. For example, in Sabo v. Delman, 3 N.Y.2d 155, 164 N.Y.S.2d 714, 143 N.E.2d 906 (1957), Sabo had assigned to Delman applications for letters patent on a machine he had invented, and had entered into written contracts with Delman concerning the assignment and the sharing of proceeds realized therefrom. Thereafter, Sabo brought an action to rescind these transactions, on the ground that Delman had induced Sabo to enter into them by fraudulently making promises that he would finance manufacture of the machine and use his best efforts to promote its sale or lease, when in fact he had no intention to do so. The Court of Appeals held that evidence of these promises was admissible under the fraud exception.

> While "Mere promissory statements as to what will be done in the future are not actionable" (Adams v. Clark, 239 N.Y. 403, 410, 146 N.E. 642, 644), it is settled that, if a promise was actually made with a preconceived and undisclosed intention of not performing it, it constitutes a misrepresentation of "a material existing fact" upon which an action for rescission may be predicated.

The court stressed that the action was for rescission, not for damages for breach:

> ... [I]t is well to bear in mind that the complaint before us neither asserts a breach of contract nor attempts to enforce any promise made by defendants. On the contrary, ... the plaintiff seeks to set aside the arrangements between defendants and himself on the ground of fraud in the inception....

Because a promisor will seldom if ever admit that she made an agreement with an intent not to perform, such an intent normally must be established through circumstantial evidence. The result is that a promisee may be able to avoid the bite of the parol evidence rule if the circumstances support a plausible claim that an otherwise-inadmissible parol agreement was made with an intent not to perform it.

In applying the promissory-fraud exception, courts may either (1) restrict relief to rescission, (2) award damages measured on a tort theory, based on the extent to which the promisee was made worse off by the promise, or (3) award damages measured on a contract theory, based on the value of the promise. Professor Sweet points out that:

> In many instances the courts have allowed the victim of a false promise to either sue for damages in a tort action of deceit, or affirm the contract and sue for its breach. If it could be said that an action for damages does not amount to enforcement of the false promise, limiting the remedies to rescission or damages would fit neatly into the [rationale that the parol evidence rule is inapplicable to promissory fraud because such fraud undermines the validity of the alleged integration]. Such an approach might be realistic where damages for fraud are based on out-of-pocket loss. But in most jurisdictions, damages are based on what the defrauded party would have received had the promise been performed, and in such cases it is difficult to argue that the promise is not being enforced.

Sweet, Promissory Fraud and the Parol Evidence Rule, 49 Calif.L.Rev. 877, 900 (1961).

2. *Merger Clauses.* The issue of promissory fraud becomes even more complex when the written contract has a merger clause that provides that the parties made no representations or agreements other than those in the writing. As in the case of merger clauses generally, the judicial reaction to merger clauses in the promissory-fraud context has been mixed. In Sabo v. Delman, supra, a general merger clause was held not to bar rescission for promissory fraud:

> The agreements being attached to the complaint, we are brought to a consideration of the impact of the recital in each of them that "No verbal understanding or conditions, not herein specified, shall be binding on either party."

> ... [Just as the parol evidence] rule is ineffectual to exclude evidence of fraudulent representations, so [the merger clause in this contract] may not be invoked to keep out such proof. Indeed, if it were otherwise, a defendant would have it in his power to perpetrate a fraud with immunity, depriving the victim of all redress, if he simply has the foresight to include a merger clause in the agreement. Such, of course, is not the law.

However, the New York Court took a different position in Danann Realty Corp. v. Harris, 5 N.Y.2d 317, 184 N.Y.S.2d 599, 157 N.E.2d 597 (1959), where the merger clause related much more specifically to the parol evidence sought to be introduced. In *Danann,* the purchaser of a lease on a building brought an action for damages against the seller, claiming that the seller had orally misrepresented the building's operating expenses and the profits to be derived from the purchaser's investment. The contract of sale contained the following merger clause:

The Purchaser has examined the premises agreed to be sold and is familiar with the physical condition thereof. The Seller has not made and does not make any representations as to the physical condition, rents, leases, *expenses, operation* or any other matter or thing affecting or related to the aforesaid premises, except as herein specifically set forth, and the Purchaser hereby *expressly acknowledges that no such representations have been made, and the Purchaser further acknowledges that it has inspected the premises and agrees to take the premises 'as is'*.... It is understood and agreed that all understandings and agreements heretofore had between the parties hereto are merged in this contract, which alone fully and completely expresses their agreement, and that the same is entered into after full investigation, neither party relying upon any statement or representation, not embodied in this contract, made by the other. The Purchaser has inspected the buildings standing on said premises and is thoroughly acquainted with their condition.

Held, on these facts no cause of action was stated:

Here ... plaintiff has in the plainest language announced and stipulated that it is not relying on any representations as to the very matter as to which it now claims it was defrauded. Such a specific disclaimer destroys the allegations in plaintiff's complaint that the agreement was executed in reliance upon these contrary oral representations.... The *Sabo* case ... dealt with the usual merger clause. The present case ... additionally, includes a disclaimer as to specific representations....

NOTE ON THE CONDITION–TO–LEGAL–EFFECTIVENESS EXCEPTION TO THE PAROL EVIDENCE RULE

A standard exception to the parol evidence rule is that the rule does not apply to a parol agreement under which the occurrence or nonoccurrence of some state of events is a condition to making the written agreement binding or effective. The exception is illustrated as follows in Restatement Second § 217, Illustration 5:

A and B make and sign an elaborate written agreement for the merger of their corporate holdings into a single new company. The writing provides that all obligations under it will terminate unless agreed subscriptions to the stock of the new company are accepted within twenty days. It is also orally agreed that the project is not to be operative unless the parties raise $600,000 additional capital. If the additional capital is not raised, there is no contract.

Although the condition-to-legal-effectiveness exception is well-established, it is subject to two related criticisms.

First, the exception turns on verbal form, rather than on substance. If the parties characterize a parol agreement as a condition to *the performance* of a written agreement, the agreement will be inadmissible under the parol evidence rule, because the written agreement is then admittedly a binding contract. However, if the parties characterize their parol agreement as a condition to *the legal effectiveness* of the written agreement, under the exception the parol agreement is not subject to the parol evidence rule, even though the parties clearly had concluded a deal, and therefore had made a contract.

Second, in practice it is not easy to reconcile the exception and the rule. The rationale of the exception is that (i) the parol evidence rule applies only where a writing is a contract, and (ii) if there was a parol agreement that a writing was not to be legally effective as a contract unless and until some condition is fulfilled, then the writing is not a contract prior to that time, so the parol evidence rule does not apply. The problem with this rationale is that in most cases where the exception is applied, it is usually clear that the writing *is* a contract, and that the parol agreement was a condition to the obligation of performance under the contract, not a condition to the legal effectiveness of the writing as a contract. For example, in Illustration 5 to Restatement Second § 217, supra, despite the phrasing of the oral agreement it is likely that A would be in breach of contract if A walked away from the deal before B had a chance to raise $600,000 additional capital.

UCC § 2–209(2), (4), (5)

[See Selected Source Materials Supplement]

UNIDROIT PRINCIPLES OF INTERNATIONAL COMMERCIAL CONTRACTS ART. 2.1.18

[See Selected Source Materials Supplement]

PRINCIPLES OF EUROPEAN CONTRACT LAW ART. 2.106

[See Selected Source Materials Supplement]

NOTE ON NO–ORAL–MODIFICATION CLAUSES

The parol evidence rule applies only to agreements made before or, in certain cases, contemporaneously with, a written contract that constitutes an integration. The rule therefore is inapplicable to a *later* agreement that modifies an integration. Such a modification may, however, be unenforceable under the legal-duty rule, or, if it is oral and is required to be in writing, under the Statute of Frauds.

Often, a written contract includes a provision that the contract cannot be modified except by a writing—a sort of private Statute of Frauds. Such provisions are sometimes referred to as n.o.m. (no oral modification) clauses. The general rule at common law was that an oral modification was enforceable, notwithstanding an n.o.m. clause—assuming there were no legal-duty rule or true Statute of Frauds problems. The theory was that: (1) Parties can, by later contracts, change their earlier contracts. (2) An oral modification is a later contract. (3) An implied provision of the later contract is to abrogate the n.o.m. provision of the earlier contract.

As to contracts for the sale of goods, UCC § 2–209 makes two critical changes in the common law rules concerning modifications. From the perspective of enforceability, these two changes go in opposite directions. In one direction, Section 2–209(1) provides that a modification needs no consideration to be enforceable, so that the legal-duty rule does not apply. In the other direction, Section 2–209(2) provides that if a contract for the sale of goods includes an n.o.m. clause, then modifications of the contract must be in writing.

The force of Section 2–209(2) is moderated by Section 2–209(4), which provides that "Although an attempt at modification does not satisfy [Section 2–209(2)] it can operate as a waiver." The inference is that when a modification "operate[s] as a waiver" it *will* be legally effective. However, Section 2–209(4) may be limited by Section 2–209(5), which provides that "[a] party who has made a waiver affecting an *executory* [unperformed] portion of the contract may retract the waiver by reasonable notification received by the other party that strict performance will be required of any term waived, unless the retraction would be unjust in view of a material change of position in reliance on the waiver." (Emphasis added.)

SECTION 2. THE INTERPRETATION OF WRITTEN CONTRACTS

STEUART v. McCHESNEY

Supreme Court of Pennsylvania, 1982.
498 Pa. 45, 444 A.2d 659.

Before O'BRIEN, C.J., and ROBERTS, NIX, LARSEN, FLAHERTY, McDERMOTT and HUTCHINSON, JJ.

OPINION OF THE COURT

FLAHERTY, JUSTICE.

This is an appeal from an Order of the Superior Court which reversed a Decree of the Court of Common Pleas of the Thirty–Seventh Judicial District construing a Right of First Refusal affecting the sale of certain real property.

On June 8, 1968, the appellant, Lepha I. Steuart, and her husband, James A. Steuart (now deceased), executed an agreement granting to the appellees, William C. McChesney and Joyce C. McChesney, husband and wife, a Right of First Refusal on a parcel of improved farmland. The agreement provided:

(a) During the lifetime of said Steuarts, should said Steuarts obtain a Bona Fide Purchaser for Value, the said McChesneys may exercise their right to purchase said premises at a value equivalent to the market value of the premises according to the assessment rolls as maintained by the County of Warren and Commonwealth of Pennsylvania for the levying and assessing of real estate taxes; provided, however, that the date of valuation shall be that upon which the said Steuarts notify said McChesneys, in writing, of the existence of a Bona Fide Purchaser.

On July 6, 1977, the subject property was appraised by a real estate broker at a market value of $50,000. Subsequently, on October 10, 1977 and October 13, 1977 respectively, appellant received bona fide offers of $35,000 and $30,000 for the land. Upon receiving notice of these offers, the appellees sought to exercise their right to purchase the property by tendering $7,820. This amount was exactly twice the assessed value of the property as listed on the tax rolls maintained in Warren County, it being the practice in that County to value real estate for tax assessment purposes at 50% of market value. The tender was refused, however, by appellant, who then commenced an action in equity seeking to cancel the Right of First Refusal, or, in the alternative, to have the agreement construed as requiring that the exercise price be that of a bona fide third party offer or fair market value as determined independently of assessed value. Appellees, requesting a conveyance of the subject premises for $7,820, sought specific performance.

The primary issue on appeal concerns the price at which the Right of First Refusal may be exercised. The Court of Common Pleas, after hearing testimony, held that the formula of twice the assessed value was intended to serve as "a mutual protective minimum price for the premises rather than to be the controlling price without regard to a market third party offer." The agreement was, therefore, construed as granting appellees a preemptive right to purchase the land for $35,000, the amount of the first bona fide offer received. The Superior Court reversed, holding that the plain language of the agreement required that assessed market value, alone, determine the exercise price. We agree.

It is well established that the intent of the parties to a written contract is to be regarded as being embodied in the writing itself, and when the words are clear and unambiguous the intent is to be discovered only from the express language of the agreement. *Estate of Breyer,* 475 Pa. 108, 379 A.2d 1305 (1977); *Felte v. White,* 451 Pa. 137, 302 A.2d 347 (1973).... As this Court stated in *East Crossroads Center, Inc. v. Mellon–Stuart Co.,* 416 Pa. at 230–231, 205 A.2d at 866, "[w]hen a written contract is clear and unequivocal, its meaning must be determined by its contents alone. It speaks for itself and a meaning cannot be given to it other than that expressed. Where the intention of the parties is clear, there is no need to resort to extrinsic aids or evidence." Hence, where language is clear and unambiguous, the focus of interpretation is upon the terms of the agreement as *manifestly expressed,* rather than as, perhaps, silently intended.

Application of the plain meaning rule of interpretation has, however, been subjected to criticism as being unsound in theory. "The fallacy consists in assuming that there is or ever can be *some one real* or absolute meaning." 9 Wigmore, *Evidence* § 2462 (Chadbourn rev. 1981). "[S]ome of the surrounding circumstances always must be known before the meaning of the words can be plain and clear; and proof of the circumstances may make a meaning plain and clear when in the absence of such proof some other meaning may also have seemed plain and clear." 3 Corbin, *Contracts* § 542 (1960). "It is indeed desirable that it be made as difficult as is reasonably feasible for an unscrupulous person to establish a meaning that was foreign to what was in fact understood by the parties to the contract. However, this result can be achieved without the aid of an inflexible rule." Murray, *Contracts,* § 110 (1974).

While adhering to the plain meaning rule of construction, this Court, too, has cautioned:

> We are not unmindful of the dangers of focusing only upon the words of the writing in interpreting an agreement. A court must be careful not to "retire into that lawyer's Paradise where all words have a fixed, precisely ascertained meaning; where men may express their purposes, not only with accuracy, but with fullness; and where, if the writer has been careful, a lawyer, having a document referred to him, may sit in his chair inspect the text, and answer all questions without raising his eyes." Thayer, Preliminary Treatise on Evidence 428, quoted in 3 Corbin on Contracts § 535 n. 16 (1960).

Estate of Breyer, 475 Pa. at 115, 379 A.2d at 1309 n. 5 (1977). Indeed, whether the language of an agreement is clear and unambiguous may not be apparent without cognizance of the context in which the agreement arose:

> The flexibility of or multiplicity in the meaning of words is the principal source of difficulty in the interpretation of language. Words are the conduits by which thoughts are communicated, yet scarcely any of them have such a fixed and single meaning that they are incapable of denoting more than one thought. In addition to the multiplicity in meaning of words set forth in the dictionaries there are the meanings imparted to them by trade customs, local uses, dialects, telegraphic codes, etc. One meaning crowds a word full of significance, while another almost empties the utterance of any import.

Hurst v. Lake & Co., Inc., 141 Or. 306, 310, 16 P.2d 627, 629 (1932), quoted in 4 Williston, *Contracts* § 609 (3d ed. 1961).

Nevertheless, the rationale for interpreting contractual terms in accord with the plain meaning of the language expressed is multifarious, resting in part upon what is viewed as the appropriate role of the courts in the interpretive process: "[T]his Court long ago emphasized that '[t]he parties [have] the right to make their own contract, and it is not the function of this Court to re-write it, or to give it a construction in conflict with ... the accepted and plain meaning of the language used.' *Hagarty v. William Akers, Jr. Co.,* 342 Pa. 236, 20 A.2d 317 (1941)." *Felte v. White,* 451 Pa. at 144, 302 A.2d at 351. " 'It is not the province of the court to alter a contract by construction or to make a new contract for the parties; its duty is confined to the interpretation of the one which they have made for themselves, without regard to its wisdom or folly.' [13 C.J. § 485, p. 524]" *Moore v. Stevens Coal Co.,* 315 Pa. 564, 568, 173 A. 661, 662 (1934).

In addition to justifications focusing upon the appropriate role of the courts in the interpretive process, the plain meaning approach to construction has been supported as generally best serving the ascertainment of the contracting parties' mutual intent. "When the parties have reduced their agreement to writing, the writing is to be taken to be the final expression of their intention." 17A C.J.S. *Contracts* § 296(2). "Where the contract evidences care in its preparation, it will be presumed that its words were employed deliberately and with intention." 17A C.J.S. *Contracts* § 296(2). "In determining what the parties intended by their contract, the law must look to what they clearly expressed. Courts in interpreting a contract do not assume that its language was chosen carelessly." *Moore v. Stevens Coal Co.,* 315 Pa. at 568, 173 A. at 662. Neither can it be assumed that the parties were ignorant of the meaning of the language employed. *See Fogel Refrigerator Co. v. Oteri,* 391 Pa. 188, 137 A.2d 225, 231 (1958).

Accordingly, the plain meaning approach enhances the extent to which contracts may be relied upon by contributing to the security of belief that the final expression of *consensus ad idem* will not later be construed to import a meaning other than that clearly expressed. *Cf.* McCormick, *The Parol Evidence Rule as a Procedural Device for Control of the Jury,* 41 Yale L.J. 365, 365–366 (1932). Likewise, resort to the plain meaning of language hinders parties dissatisfied with their agreement from creating a myth as to the true meaning of the agreement through subsequently exposed extrinsic evidence. Absent the plain meaning rule, nary an agreement could be conceived, which, in the event of a party's later disappointment with his stated bargain, would not be at risk to having its true meaning obfuscated under the guise of examining extrinsic evidence of intent. Even if the dissatisfied party in good faith believed that the agreement, as manifest, did not express the *consensus ad idem,* his post hoc judgment would be inclined to be colored by belief as to what should have been, rather than what strictly was, intended. Hence, the plain meaning approach to interpretation rests upon policies soundly based, and the judiciousness of that approach warrants reaffirmation.

In the instant case, the language of the Right of First Refusal, viewed in context, is express and clear and is, therefore, not in need of interpretation by reference to extrinsic evidence. The plain meaning of the agreement in question is that if, during the lifetime of the appellant, a bona fide purchaser for value should be obtained, the appellees may purchase the property "at a value equivalent to the market value of the premises according to the assessment rolls as maintained by the County of Warren and Commonwealth of Pennsylvania for the levying and assessing of real estate taxes." Indeed, a more clear and unambiguous expression of the Right of First Refusal's exercise price would be onerous to conceive. By conditioning exercise of the Right of First Refusal upon occurrence of the triggering event of there being obtained a bona fide offer, protection was afforded against a sham offer, made not in good faith, precipitating exercise of the preemptive right. The clear language of the agreement, however, in no manner links determination of the exercise price to the magnitude of the bona fide offer received through that triggering mechanism.

Were the present agreement to be regarded as ambiguous, so as to enable a court to consider extrinsic evidence of the meaning intended, as was done in the Court of Common Pleas, the policy of resorting to extrinsic evidence only when confronted with unclear or ambiguous language would be enervated. Certainly, the words of the Right of First Refusal are not indefinite, doubtful, or uncertain in their signification, so as to be regarded as unclear. Nor is the language reasonably or fairly susceptible to being understood in more than one sense so as to be regarded as ambiguous. "A patent ambiguity is that which appears on the face of the instrument, and arises from the defective, obscure, or insensible language used." *Black's Law Dictionary* 105 (rev. 4th ed. 1968). In contrast, a latent ambiguity arises from extraneous or collateral facts which make the meaning of a written agreement uncertain although the language thereof, on its face, appears clear and unambiguous. *Easton v. Washington County Insurance Co.,* 391 Pa. 28, 137 A.2d 332 (1957). "The usual instance of a latent ambiguity is one in which a writing refers to a particular person or thing and is thus apparently clear on its face, but upon application to external objects is found to fit two or more of them equally." *Id.* at 35, 137 A.2d at 336. In holding that an ambiguity is present in an agreement, a court must not rely upon a strained contrivancy to establish one; scarcely an agreement could be conceived that might not be unreasonably contrived into the appearance of ambiguity. Thus, the meaning of language cannot be distorted to establish the ambiguity. *Anstead v. Cook,* 291 Pa. 335, 337, 140 A. 139, 140, (1927). The instant agreement, not being reasonably susceptible to being understood in more than one sense, whether by patent or latent ambiguity, does not present language in need of extrinsic clarification.

By construing the clause in question to merely signify that the exercise price be, *in effect, "not less than"* the market value of the premises according to the assessment rolls, the Court of Common Pleas ignored the clearly expressed intent that the exercise price be *"equivalent* to the market value of the premises according to the assessment rolls." To no extent is the term "equivalent", meaning "equal",[5] interchangeable with "not less than", and, since the parties specified the former, they shall be deemed to have intended the same. Hence, any divergence between the exercise price and the bona fide offer cannot be eliminated by construction where no ambiguity exists. Nor is there freedom, under the guise of construction, to redraft the Right of First Refusal simply because of the realization, at the time when rights under the agreement are to be exercised, that the market price according to the assessment rolls falls substantially short of the bona fide offers received.

Appellant contends that, based upon equitable considerations, specific performance at the assessed market value of $7,820 should be denied; in particular, the divergence between assessed market value and the amount of the bona fide offers assertedly renders an award of specific performance inequitable. As this Court has established, however, " '[i]nadequacy of consideration is not ground for refusing to decree specific performance of a contract to convey real estate, unless there is evidence of fraud or unfairness in the transaction sufficient to make it inequitable to compel performance ...' *Welsh v. Ford,* 282 Pa. 96, 99, 127 A. 431, 432 (1925)...."....Appellant alleges that an attorney employed solely by the appellees drafted the Right of First Refusal agreement, and that she was unfairly induced to enter the agreement without representation of her interests. This position ignores, however, an express finding of fact by the Court of Common Pleas, amply supported by testimony of record, that at the time of the preliminary negotiation and drafting of the agreement the parties were all represented by the same attorney. Hence, appellant's assertion is without merit.

5. "Equivalent carries with it the idea of value in some way (Latin *aequus,* equal, plus *valere,* to be strong or valuable). When something adds up to something else in value or worth or significance or importance, the two are said to be equivalent the one to the other; when two or more things are exactly the same they are properly said to be equal. *Equal* is the simpler term, and applies to simpler considerations." J.B. Opdycke, *Mark My Words,* at 568–569 (1940).

Order affirmed.

ROBERTS, J., files a dissenting opinion in which LARSEN, J., joins.

ROBERTS, JUSTICE, dissenting.

I dissent. Although the contract at issue mandates that appellees may purchase appellant's property at "the market value of the premises according to the assessment rolls as maintained by the County of Warren ...," it is by no means clear that $7,820 is the price which appellees should pay.

The omission from the contract of a specific future purchase price was intentional because, according to the draftsman, the parties "wanted to reflect either increase or decrease of the assessed value as of [the] time" of appellees' exercise of the option to buy. To assure the accuracy and currency of this "reflection" of the change in assessed value, the parties provided that "the date of valuation shall be that upon which the said Steuarts notify said McChesneys, in writing, of the existence of a Bona Fide purchaser."

Written notice of appellant's receipt of an offer for the property was delivered to appellees on or about October 25, 1977. At that time, the assessed value of the property, as recorded on the tax rolls of Warren County, was $3,910, or 50% of the "market value" of $7,820. However, from the testimony of the draftsman, it would appear that the property had not been reassessed since 1972, when the assessed value was increased by only $405.

Section 602 of the Fourth to Eighth Class County Assessment Law provides:

> "It shall be the duty of the chief assessor to assess, rate and value all subjects and objects of local taxation ... according to the actual value thereof.... [R]eal property shall be assessed at a value based upon an established predetermined ratio ... not exceeding seventy-five per centum (75%) of its actual value or the price for which the same would separately bona fide sell...."

72 P.S. § 5453.602(a) (1964). As this Court stated in *Brooks Building Tax Assessment Case,* 391 Pa. 94, 97, 137 A.2d 273, 274 (1958),

> "[t]he term 'actual value' means 'market value' [citing cases]. And market value has been defined as the price which a purchaser, willing but not obliged to buy, would pay an owner, willing but not obliged to sell, taking into consideration all uses to which the property is adapted and might in reason be applied."

Accord, *Buhl Foundation v. Board of Property Assessment,* 407 Pa. 567, 570, 180 A.2d 900, 902 (1962).

Here, where appellant received bona fide offers of $30,000, $35,000, and $50,000 for her property, there can be no doubt that the actual value of appellant's property in 1977 was at least four times greater than the value according to the outdated assessment on the Warren County tax rolls. It is the height of unfairness to grant appellees' requested decree for specific performance at a price based on a valuation which took place in 1972. In effect, appellees are receiving a substantial windfall simply because Warren County has apparently failed to maintain accurate assessments "according to the actual value" of appellant's property, as required by law.

In these circumstances, I would remand this case to the Court of Common Pleas of Warren County for a determination of what the proper assessed value of appellant's property would have been on October 25, 1977, the "date of valuation," with directions to enter a decree of specific performance in favor of appellees at a "market value" based upon that determination.

LARSEN, J., joins in this dissenting opinion.

———

MELLON BANK, N.A. v. AETNA BUSINESS CREDIT, INC., 619 F.2d 1001, 1011 (3d Cir.1980). "A court must have a reference point to determine if words may reasonably admit of different meanings. Under a 'four corners' approach a judge sits in chambers and determines from his point of view whether the written words before him are ambiguous. An alternative approach is for the judge to hear the proffer of the parties and determine if there is objective indicia that, from the linguistic reference point of the parties, the terms of the contract are susceptible of differing meanings. We believe the latter to be the correct approach.

"It is the role of the judge to consider the words of the contract, the alternative meaning suggested by counsel, and the nature of the objective evidence to be offered in support of that meaning. The trial judge must then determine if a full evidentiary hearing is warranted. If a *reasonable* alternative interpretation is suggested, even though it may be alien to the judge's linguistic experience, objective evidence in support of that interpretation should be considered by the fact finder."

———

AMOCO PRODUCTION CO. v. WESTERN SLOPE GAS CO., 754 F.2d 303, 308 (10th Cir. 1985). "Under the UCC, the lack of facial ambiguity in the contract language is basically irrelevant to whether extrinsic evidence ought to be considered by the court as an initial matter. A judge first must consider the circumstances and purposes surrounding the making of the writing before he or she can determine whether it is in fact ambiguous. '[I]t is proper to consider the contract's commercial setting even though the contract is not facially ambiguous.' ...

"[U]nder section 2–202, there is no longer an assumption that the parties intended a writing to be the complete expression of their agreement. In fact, the assumption is to the contrary unless the court expressly finds that the parties intended the contract to be completely integrated.... See generally, Interform Co. v. Mitchell, 575 F.2d 1270, 1274–78 (9th Cir.1978). Only if in light of the circumstances and purposes of the contract the judge finds it unambiguous should he or she prohibit parol evidence to explain its meaning."

———

PACIFIC GAS & ELECTRIC CO. v. G.W. THOMAS DRAYAGE & RIGGING CO.

Supreme Court of California, 1968.
69 Cal.2d 33, 69 Cal.Rptr. 561, 442 P.2d 641.

TRAYNOR, CHIEF JUSTICE. Defendant appeals from a judgment for plaintiff in an action for damages for injury to property under an indemnity clause of a contract.

In 1960 defendant entered into a contract with plaintiff to furnish the labor and equipment necessary to remove and replace the upper metal cover of plaintiff's steam turbine. Defendant agreed to perform the work "at [its] own risk and expense" and to "indemnify" plaintiff "against all loss, damage, expense and liability resulting from ... injury to property, arising out of or in any way connected with the performance of this contract." Defendant also agreed to procure not less than $50,000 insurance to cover liability for injury to property. Plaintiff was to be an additional named insured, but the policy was to contain a cross-liability clause extending the coverage to plaintiff's property.

During the work the cover fell and injured the exposed rotor of the turbine. Plaintiff brought this action to recover $25,144.51, the amount it subsequently spent on repairs. During the trial it dismissed a count based on negligence and thereafter secured judgment on the theory that the indemnity provision covered injury to all property regardless of ownership.

Defendant offered to prove by admissions of plaintiff's agents, by defendant's conduct under similar contracts entered into with plaintiff, and by other proof that in the indemnity clause the parties meant to cover injury to property of third parties only and not to plaintiff's property.[6] Although the trial court observed that the language used was "the classic language for a third party indemnity provision" and that "one could very easily conclude that ... its whole intendment is to indemnify third parties," it nevertheless held that the "plain language" of the agreement also required defendant to indemnify plaintiff for injuries to plaintiff's property. Having determined that the contract had a plain meaning, the court refused to admit any extrinsic evidence that would contradict its interpretation.

When a court interprets a contract on this basis, it determines the meaning of the instrument in accordance with the " ... extrinsic evidence of the judge's own linguistic education and experience." (3 Corbin on Contracts (1960 ed.) [1964 Supp. § 579, p. 225, fn. 56].) The exclusion of testimony that might contradict the linguistic background of the judge reflects a judicial belief in the possibility of perfect verbal expression. (9 Wigmore on Evidence (3d ed. 1940) § 2461, p. 187.) This belief is a remnant of a primitive faith in the inherent potency and inherent meaning of words.

The test of admissibility of extrinsic evidence to explain the meaning of a written instrument is not whether it appears to the court to be plain and unambiguous on its face, but whether the offered evidence is relevant to prove

6. Although this offer of proof might ordinarily be regarded as too general to provide a ground for appeal ... since the court repeatedly ruled that it would not admit extrinsic evidence to interpret the contract and sustained objections to all questions seeking to elicit such evidence, no formal offer of proof was required....

a meaning to which the language of the instrument is reasonably susceptible. . . .

A rule that would limit the determination of the meaning of a written instrument to its four-corners merely because it seems to the court to be clear and unambiguous, would either deny the relevance of the intention of the parties or presuppose a degree of verbal precision and stability our language has not attained.

Some courts have expressed the opinion that contractual obligations are created by the mere use of certain words, whether or not there was any intention to incur such obligations.[7] Under this view, contractual obligations flow, not from the intention of the parties but from the fact that they used certain magic words. Evidence of the parties' intention therefore becomes irrelevant.

In this state, however, the intention of the parties as expressed in the contract is the source of contractual rights and duties.[8] A court must ascertain and give effect to this intention by determining what the parties meant by the words they used. Accordingly, the exclusion of relevant, extrinsic evidence to explain the meaning of a written instrument could be justified only if it were feasible to determine the meaning the parties gave to the words from the instrument alone.

If words had absolute and constant referents, it might be possible to discover contractual intention in the words themselves and in the manner in which they were arranged. Words, however, do not have absolute and constant referents. "A word is a symbol of thought but has no arbitrary and fixed meaning like a symbol of algebra or chemistry, ..." (Pearson v. State Social Welfare Board (1960) 54 Cal.2d 184, 195, 5 Cal.Rptr. 553, 559, 353 P.2d 33, 39.) The meaning of particular words or groups of words varies with the " . . . verbal context and surrounding circumstances and purposes in view of the linguistic education and experience of their users and their hearers or readers (not excluding judges). . . . A word has no meaning apart from these factors; much less does it have an objective meaning, one true meaning." (Corbin, The Interpretation of Words and the Parol Evidence Rule (1965) 50 Cornell L.Q. 161, 187.) Accordingly, the meaning of a writing " . . . can only be found by interpretation in the light of all the circumstances that reveal the sense in which the writer used the words. The exclusion of parol evidence regarding such circumstances merely because the words do not appear ambiguous to the reader can easily lead to the attribution to a written instrument of a meaning that was never intended. [Citations omitted.]" (Universal Sales Corp. v. Cal. Press Mfg. Co., supra, 20 Cal.2d 751, 776, 128 P.2d 665, 679 (concurring opinion); see also, e.g., Garden State Plaza Corp. v. S.S. Kresge Co. (1963) 78 N.J.Super. 485, 189 A.2d 448, 454. . . .

Although extrinsic evidence is not admissible to add to, detract from, or vary the terms of a written contract, these terms must first be determined before it can be decided whether or not extrinsic evidence is being offered for

---

7. "A contract has, strictly speaking, nothing to do with the personal, or individual, intent of the parties. A contract is an obligation attached by the mere force of law to certain acts of the parties, usually words, which ordinarily accompany and represent a known intent." (Hotchkiss v. National City Bank of New York (S.D.N.Y.1911) 200 F. 287, 293. . . .)

8. "A contract must be so interpreted as to give effect to the mutual intention of the parties as it existed at the time of contracting, so far as the same is ascertainable and lawful." (Civ.Code, § 1636 . . .)

a prohibited purpose. The fact that the terms of an instrument appear clear to a judge does not preclude the possibility that the parties chose the language of the instrument to express different terms. That possibility is not limited to contracts whose terms have acquired a particular meaning by trade usage, but exists whenever the parties' understanding of the words used may have differed from the judge's understanding.

Accordingly, rational interpretation requires at least a preliminary consideration of all credible evidence offered to prove the intention of the parties.[9] (Civ.Code, § 1647; Code Civ.Proc. § 1860; see also 9 Wigmore on Evidence, op. cit. supra, § 2470, fn. 11, p. 227.) Such evidence includes testimony as to the "circumstances surrounding the making of the agreement ... including the object, nature and subject matter of the writing ..." so that the court can "place itself in the same situation in which the parties found themselves at the time of contracting." (Universal Sales Corp. v. Cal. Press Mfg. Co., supra, 20 Cal.2d 751, 761, 128 P.2d 665, 671; Lemm v. Stillwater Land & Cattle Co., supra, 217 Cal. 474, 480–481, 19 P.2d 785.) If the court decides, after considering this evidence, that the language of a contract, in the light of all the circumstances, is "fairly susceptible of either one of the two interpretations contended for...." ... extrinsic evidence relevant to prove either of such meanings is admissible.[10]

In the present case the court erroneously refused to consider extrinsic evidence offered to show that the indemnity clause in the contract was not intended to cover injuries to plaintiff's property. Although that evidence was not necessary to show that the indemnity clause was reasonably susceptible of the meaning contended for by defendant, it was nevertheless relevant and admissible on that issue. Moreover, since that clause was reasonably susceptible of that meaning, the offered evidence was also admissible to prove that the clause had that meaning and did not cover injuries to plaintiff's property.[11] Accordingly, the judgment must be reversed....

PETERS, MOSK, BURKE, SULLIVAN, and PEEK, JJ., concur.

McCOMB, J., dissents.

---

9. When objection is made to any particular item of evidence offered to prove the intention of the parties, the trial court may not yet be in a position to determine whether in the light of all of the offered evidence, the item objected to will turn out to be admissible as tending to prove a meaning of which the language of the instrument is reasonably susceptible or inadmissible as tending to prove a meaning of which the language is not reasonably susceptible. In such case the court may admit the evidence conditionally by either reserving its ruling on the objection or by admitting the evidence subject to a motion to strike. (See Evid.Code, § 403.)

10. Extrinsic evidence has often been admitted in such cases on the stated ground that the contract was ambiguous (e.g., Universal Sales Corp. v. Cal. Press Mfg. Co., supra, 20 Cal.2d 751, 761, 128 P.2d 665). This statement of the rule is harmless if it is kept in mind that the ambiguity may be exposed by extrinsic evidence that reveals more than one possible meaning.

11. The court's exclusion of extrinsic evidence in this case would be error even under a rule that excluded such evidence when the instrument appeared to the court to be clear and unambiguous on its face. The controversy centers on the meaning of the word "indemnify" and the phrase "all loss, damage, expense and liability." The trial court's recognition of the language as typical of a third party indemnity clause and the double sense in which the word "indemnify" is used in statutes and defined in dictionaries demonstrate the existence of an ambiguity. (Compare Civ.Code, § 2772, "Indemnity is a contract by which one engages to save another from a legal consequence of the conduct of one of the parties, or of some other person," with Civ.Code, § 2527, "Insurance is a contract whereby one undertakes to indemnify another against loss, damage, or liability, arising from an unknown or contingent event." Black's Law Dictionary (4th ed. 1951) defines "indemnify" as "A collateral contract or assurance, by which one person engages to secure another against an anticipated loss or to prevent him from being damnified by the legal consequences of an act or forbearance on the part of one of the parties or of some third person." Stroud's Judicial Dictionary (2d ed.

GARDEN STATE PLAZA CORP. v. S.S. KRESGE CO., 78 N.J.Super. 485, 189 A.2d 448 (1963). "[T]he parol evidence rule does not even come into play until it is first determined what the true agreement of the parties is—i.e., what they meant by what they wrote down. Only when that is determined is one in an appropriate position to raise the bar of the parol evidence rule to prevent alteration or impugnment of the agreement by the asserted contradictory prior or contemporaneous agreement. In other words, interpretation and construction must necessarily precede protection against forbidden contradiction or modification. And in the process of interpretation and construction of the integrated agreement all relevant evidence pointing to meaning is admissible because experience teaches that language is so poor an instrument for communication or expression of intent that ordinarily all surrounding circumstances and conditions must be examined before there is any trustworthy assurance of derivation of contractual intent, even by reasonable judges of ordinary intelligence, from any given set of words which the parties have committed to paper as their contract. Construing a contract of debatable meaning by resort to surrounding and antecedent circumstances and negotiations for light as to the meaning of the words used is never a violation of the parol evidence rule. And debatability of meaning is not always discernible at the first reading of a contract by a new mind. More often it becomes manifest upon exposure of the specific disputed interpretations in the light of the attendant circumstances.... Of course, in order to justify the use of evidence of extrinsic circumstances to establish a contended—for interpretation of disputed contractual language, that interpretation must be one 'which the written words will bear.' ... As stated in the Restatement, Contracts (1932), § 242, comment, p. 342, 'Previous negotiations cannot give to an integrated agreement a meaning completely alien to anything its words can possibly express.' "

1903) defines it as a "Contract ... to indemnify against a liability...." One of the definitions given to "indemnify" by Webster's Third New Internat. Dict. (1961 ed.) is "to exempt from incurred penalties or liabilities.")

Plaintiff's assertion that the use of the word "all" to modify "loss, damage, expense and liability" dictates an all inclusive interpretation is not persuasive. If the word "indemnify" encompasses only third-party claims, the word "all" simply refers to all such claims. The use of the words "loss," "damage," and "expense" in addition to the word "liability" is likewise inconclusive. These words do not imply an agreement to reimburse for injury to an indemnitee's property since they are commonly inserted in third-party indemnity clauses, to enable an indemnitee who settles a claim to recover from his indemnitor without proving his liability. (Carpenter Paper Co. v. Kellogg (1952) 114 Cal.App.2d 640, 651, 251 P.2d 40....

The provision that defendant perform the work "at his own risk and expense" and the provisions relating to insurance are equally inconclusive. By agreeing to work at its own risk defendant may have released plaintiff from liability for any injuries to defendant's property arising out of the contract's performance, but this provision did not necessarily make defendant an insurer against injuries to plaintiff's property. Defendant's agreement to procure liability insurance to cover damages to plaintiff's property does not indicate whether the insurance was to cover all injuries or only injuries caused by defendant's negligence.

TRIDENT CENTER v. CONNECTICUT GENERAL LIFE INS. CO.,
847 F.2d 564 (9th Cir.1988). In 1983, an insurance company and two large law
firms formed a partnership, Trident Center, for the purpose of constructing
an office-building complex in West Los Angeles. The partnership obtained
financing for the project from Connecticut General Life Insurance Company.
The loan documents provided for a loan of $56,500,000 at 12 1/4 percent
interest for a term of 15 years, secured by a deed of trust on the project. The
promissory note provided that "[m]aker [Trident Center] shall not have the
right to prepay the principal amount hereof in whole or in part" for the first
twelve years. In years thirteen to fifteen, the loan could be prepaid, subject to
a sliding prepayment fee. The promissory note also provided that in case of a
default during years one to twelve, Connecticut General had the option of
accelerating the note and adding a 10 percent prepayment fee.

By 1987, interest rates began to drop, and the 12 1/4 percent rate
compared unfavorably with 1987 market rates. Trident started looking for
ways of refinancing the loan to take advantage of the lower rates. Connecticut
General was unwilling to oblige, insisting that the loan could not be prepaid
for the first twelve years of its life, that is, until January 1996.

Trident then brought suit seeking a declaration that it was entitled to
prepay the loan, subject only to a 10 percent prepayment fee. Connecticut
General brought a motion to dismiss, claiming that the loan documents
clearly and unambiguously precluded prepayment during the first twelve
years. The district court agreed and dismissed Trident's complaint. The Ninth
Circuit reversed, in an opinion by Judge Kozinski.

". . . It is difficult to imagine language that more clearly or unambiguously expresses the idea that Trident may not unilaterally prepay the loan during
its first 12 years. Trident, however, argues that there is an ambiguity because
another clause of the note provides that '[i]n the event of a prepayment
resulting from a default hereunder or the Deed of Trust prior to January 10,
1996 the prepayment fee will be ten percent (10%).' . . . Trident interprets
this clause as giving it the option of prepaying the loan if only it is willing to
incur the prepayment fee.

"We reject Trident's argument out of hand. In the first place, its
proffered interpretation would result in a contradiction between two clauses
of the contract; the default clause would swallow up the clause prohibiting
Trident from prepaying during the first 12 years of the contract. The normal
rule of construction, of course, is that courts must interpret contracts, if
possible, so as to avoid internal conflict. . . .

"Trident nevertheless argues that it is entitled to precipitate a default
and insist on acceleration by tendering the balance due on the note plus the
10 percent prepayment fee. The contract language . . . leaves no room for this
construction. It is true, of course, that Trident is free to stop making
payments, which may then cause Connecticut General to declare a default and
accelerate. But that is not to say that Connecticut General would be required
to so respond. The contract quite clearly gives Connecticut General other
options: It may choose to waive the default, or to take advantage of some
other remedy such as the right to collect 'all the income, rents, royalties,
revenue, issues, profits, and proceeds of the Property.' Deed of Trust § 1.18,
at 22. By interpreting the contract as Trident suggests, we would ignore those
provisions giving Connecticut General, not Trident, the exclusive right to

decide how, when and whether the contract will be terminated upon default during the first 12 years. . . .

"In effect, Trident is attempting to obtain judicial sterilization of its intended default. But defaults are messy things; they are supposed to be. Once the maker of a note secured by a deed of trust defaults, its credit rating may deteriorate; attempts at favorable refinancing may be thwarted by the need to meet the trustee's sale schedule; its cash flow may be impaired if the beneficiary takes advantage of the assignment of rents remedy; default provisions in its loan agreements with other lenders may be triggered. Fear of these repercussions is strong medicine that keeps debtors from shirking their obligations when interest rates go down and they become disenchanted with their loans. That Trident is willing to suffer the cost and delay of a lawsuit, rather than simply defaulting, shows far better than anything we might say that these provisions are having their intended effect. We decline Trident's invitation to truncate the lender's remedies and deprive Connecticut General of its bargained-for protection. . . ."

"Trident argues in the alternative that, even if the language of the contract appears to be unambiguous, the deal the parties actually struck is in fact quite different. It wishes to offer extrinsic evidence that the parties had agreed Trident could prepay at any time within the first 12 years by tendering the full amount plus a 10 percent prepayment fee. As discussed above, this is an interpretation to which the contract, as written, is not reasonably susceptible. Under traditional contract principles, extrinsic evidence is inadmissible to interpret, vary or add to the terms of an unambiguous integrated written instrument. See 4 S. Williston, supra p. 5, § 631, at 948–49; 2 B. Witkin, California Evidence § 981, at 926 (3d ed. 1986).

Trident points out, however, that California does not follow the traditional rule. Two decades ago the California Supreme Court in Pacific Gas & Electric Co. v. G.W. Thomas Drayage & Rigging Co., 69 Cal.2d 33, 442 P.2d 641, 69 Cal.Rptr. 561 (1968), turned its back on the notion that a contract can ever have a plain meaning discernible by a court without resort to extrinsic evidence. . . .

"*Pacific Gas* casts a long shadow of uncertainty over all transactions negotiated and executed under the law of California. As this case illustrates, even when the transaction is very sizeable, even if it involves only sophisticated parties, even if it was negotiated with the aid of counsel, even if it results in contract language that is devoid of ambiguity, costly and protracted litigation cannot be avoided if one party has a strong enough motive for challenging the contract. While this rule creates much business for lawyers and an occasional windfall to some clients, it leads only to frustration and delay for most litigants and clogs already overburdened courts.

"It also chips away at the foundation of our legal system. By giving credence to the idea that words are inadequate to express concepts, Pacific Gas undermines the basic principle that language provides a meaningful constraint on public and private conduct. If we are unwilling to say that parties, dealing face to face, can come up with language that binds them, how can we send anyone to jail for violating statutes consisting of mere words lacking 'absolute and constant referents'? How can courts ever enforce decrees, not written in language understandable to all, but encoded in a dialect reflecting only the 'linguistic background of the judge'? Can lower courts ever be faulted for failing to carry out the mandate of higher courts when 'perfect verbal expression' is impossible? Are all attempts to develop the law in a reasoned and principled fashion doomed to failure as 'remnant[s] of a primitive faith in the inherent potency and inherent meaning of words'? Be that as it may. While we have our doubts about the wisdom of *Pacific Gas*, we have no difficulty understanding its meaning, even without extrinsic evidence to guide us. As we read the rule in California, we must reverse and remand to the district court in order to give plaintiff an opportunity to present extrinsic evidence as to the intention of the parties in drafting the contract. It may not be a wise rule we are applying, but it is a rule that binds us."

FISH, THE LAW WISHES TO HAVE A FORMAL EXISTENCE

We may see what is at stake in disputes about formalism by turning to a recent ... opinion delivered by Judge Alex Kozinski of the United States Court of Appeals for the Ninth Circuit [Trident Center v. Connecticut General Life Insurance Co., 847 F.2d 564 (9th Cir.1988)]. The case involved the desire of a construction partnership called Trident Center to refinance a loan at rates more favorable than those originally secured. Unfortunately (or so it seemed) language in the original agreement expressly blocked such an action, to wit that the "maker shall not have the right to prepay the principal amount hereof in whole or in part" for the first twelve years. Trident's attorneys, however, pointed to another place in the writing where it is stipulated that "in the event of a prepayment resulting from a default ... prior to January 10, 1996 the prepayment fee will be ten percent" and argued that this clause gives Trident the option of prepaying the loan provided that it is willing to incur the penalty as stated. Kozinski is singularly unimpressed by this reasoning, and, as he himself says, dismisses it "out of hand," citing as his justification the clear and unambiguous language of the contract. Referring to Trident's contention that it is entitled to precipitate a default by tendering the balance plus the ten percent fee, Kozinski declares that "the contract language, cited above, leaves no room for this construction," a judgment belied by the fact that Trident's lawyers managed to make room for just that construction in their arguments. It is a feature of cases like this that turn on the issue of what is and is not "expressly" said that the proclamation of an undisputed meaning always occurs in the midst of a dispute about it. Given Kozinski's rhetorical stance, the mere citation (his word and a very dangerous one for his position) of the contract language should be sufficient to end all argument, but what he himself immediately proceeds to do is argue, offering a succession of analyses designed to buttress his contention that it "is difficult to imagine language that more clearly or unambiguously expresses the idea that Trident may not unilaterally ... prepay the loan during its first twelve years." If this were in fact so it would be difficult to imagine why Kozinski should feel compelled to elaborate his opinion again and again. I shall not take up his points except to say that in general they are not particularly persuasive and usually function to open up just the kind of interpretive room he declares unavailable. Thus, for example, he reasons that Trident's interpretation "would result in a contradiction between two clauses of the contract" whereas the "normal rule of construction ... is that courts must interpret contracts if possible to avoid internal conflict." But it is no trick at all (or at least not a hard one) to treat the two clauses so that they refer to different anticipated situations and are not contradictory (indeed that is what Trident's lawyers do): in the ordinary course of things, as defined by the rate and schedule of payments set down in the contract, Trident will not have the option of pre-paying; but in the extraordinary event of a default, the prepayment penalty clause will then kick in. To be sure Kozinski is ready with objections to this line of argument, but those objections themselves trace out a line of argument and operate no less than do the interpretations he rejects to fill out the language whose self-sufficiency he repeatedly invokes.

In short ... Kozinski's assertion of ready made formal constraints is belied by his efforts to stabilize what he supposedly relies on, the plain meaning of absolutely clear language. The act of construction for which he says there is no room is one he is continually performing. Moreover, he performs it in a way no different from the performance he castigates. Trident, he complains, is attempting "to obtain judicial sterilization of its intended default," and the reading its lawyers propose is an extension of that attempt rather than a faithful rendering of what the document says. The implication is that *his* reading is the extension of nothing, proceeds from no purpose except the purpose to be scrupulously literal. But his very next words reveal another, less disinterested purpose: "But defaults are messy things and they are supposed to be ... Fear of repercussion is [the] strong medicine that keeps debtors from shirking their obligations." And he is, of course, now administering that strong medicine through his reading, a reading that is produced not by the agreement, but by his antecedent determination to enforce contracts whenever he can. The contrast then is not (as he attempts to draw it) between a respect for what "the contract clearly does ... provide" and the bending of the words to an antecedently held purpose, but between two bendings....

———

HOLMES, THE THEORY OF LEGAL INTERPRETATION, 12 Harv. L.Rev. 417 (1899). "I do not suppose that you could prove, for purposes of construction as distinguished from avoidance, an oral declaration or even an agreement that words in a dispositive instrument making sense as they stand should have a different meaning from the common one; for instance, that the parties to a contract orally agreed that when they wrote five hundred feet it should mean one hundred inches, or that Bunker Hill Monument should signify Old South Church."

———

WILLISTON ON CONTRACTS, 3d ed., § 95. "It is even conceivable that a contract may be formed which is in accordance with the intention of neither party. If a written contract is entered into, the meaning and effect of the contract depends on the interpretation given the written language by the court. The court will give that language its natural and appropriate meaning; and, if the words are unambiguous, will not even admit evidence of what the parties may have thought the meaning to be."

———

RESTATEMENT, [FIRST,] CONTRACTS § 231, Illustration 2: "A and B are engaged in buying and selling shares of stock from one another and agree orally for the purpose of concealing the nature of their dealings that in transactions between them the word 'buy' shall be used to mean 'sell,' and that the word 'sell' shall be used to mean 'buy.' A sends a written offer to B to 'sell' certain shares of stock. B, having in mind the oral agreement, accepts the offer and tenders the shares to A. On A's refusal to accept the tender, B brings an action against him. B cannot recover, unless reformation is had of the writings. The private oral agreement cannot make 'buy' mean 'sell,' though a private agreement may give to a word which has no inconsistent meaning, a meaning in accordance with the agreement."

―――――

CORBIN ON CONTRACTS, Supp. § 572b (1971). "No contract should ever be interpreted and enforced with a meaning that neither party gave it."

―――――

RESTATEMENT, SECOND, CONTRACTS § 212, Illustration 4: "A and B are engaged in buying and selling shares of stock from each other, and agree orally to conceal the nature of their dealings by using the word 'sell' to mean 'buy' and using the word 'buy' to mean 'sell.' A sends a written offer to B to 'sell' certain shares, and B accepts. The parties are bound in accordance with the oral agreement."

―――――

BERG v. HUDESMAN, 115 Wash.2d 657, 801 P.2d 222 (1990) (en banc). "Despite the accuracy of the conclusion that seldom will any word or phrase carry only a single meaning which is readily discernible by any reader, this court on occasion has embraced the 'plain meaning rule.'

> The Plain Meaning Rule states that if a writing, or the term in question, appears to be plain and unambiguous on its face, its meaning must be determined from the four corners of the instrument without resort to extrinsic evidence of any nature.

(Footnote omitted.) J. Calamari & J. Perillo, *Contracts* § 3–10, at 166–67 (3d ed. 1987). In following this rule, this court has held that only if a contract is ambiguous on its face will the court look to evidence of the parties' intent as shown by the contract as a whole, its subject matter and objective, the circumstances of its making, the subsequent conduct of the parties, and the reasonableness of their interpretations. . . .

"The plain meaning rule has been criticized by leading commentators. *See, e.g.,* 3 A. Corbin § 542; 9 J. Wigmore, *Evidence* §§ 2461–2462 (1981); 4 S. Williston § 629; 2 E. Farnsworth, *Contracts* § 7.12, at 277–78 (1990); J. Calamari & J. Perillo § 3–10. The rule has been rejected by the Uniform Commercial Code, U.C.C. § 2–202 comment 2, and the Restatement (Second) of Contracts §§ 200–04 (1981).

"As Professor Shattuck notes, however, even while sometimes following the plain meaning rule, this court has not consistently applied it. Instead, the court has also sometimes held that a trial court may, in interpreting contract language, consider the surrounding circumstances leading to execution of the agreement, including the subject matter of the contract as well as the subsequent conduct of the parties, not for the purpose of contradicting what is in the agreement, but for the purpose of determining the parties' intent.... This analytic framework for interpreting written contract language has been called the 'context rule.' Eagle Ins. Co. v. Albright, 3 Wash.App. 256, 474 P.2d 920 (1970). *See* Pacific Gas & Elec. Co. v. G.W. Thomas Drayage & Rigging Co., 69 Cal.2d 33, 442 P.2d 641, 69 Cal.Rptr. 561, 40 A.L.R.3d 1373 (1968) for an excellent articulation of the rationale of the context principle. Other courts have allowed evidence of the circumstances of the making of a contract for the purpose of interpreting the contract. *E.g.,* Darner Motor Sales, Inc. v. Universal Underwriters Ins. Co., 140 Ariz. 383, 682 P.2d 388 (1984); Admiral Builders Sav. & Loan Ass'n v. South River Landing, Inc., 66 Md.App. 124, 502 A.2d 1096 (1986); Keating v. Stadium Mgt. Corp., 24 Mass.App.Ct. 246, 508 N.E.2d 121 (1987).

"The instant case presents a clear opportunity for this court to resolve the longstanding confusion engendered by inconsistent holdings in this area.

"We now hold that extrinsic evidence is admissible as to the entire circumstances under which the contract was made, as an aid in ascertaining the parties' intent. We adopt the Restatement (Second) of Contracts §§ 212, 214(c) (1981). Section 212 provides:

(1) The interpretation of an integrated agreement is directed to the meaning of the terms of the writing or writings in the light of the circumstances, in accordance with the rules stated in this Chapter.

(2) A question of interpretation of an integrated agreement is to be determined by the trier of fact if it depends on the credibility of extrinsic evidence or on a choice among reasonable inferences to be drawn from extrinsic evidence. Otherwise a question of interpretation of an integrated agreement is to be determined as a question of law.

"As explained in comment b to this section:

It is sometimes said that extrinsic evidence cannot change the plain meaning of a writing, but meaning can almost never be plain except in a context. Accordingly, the rule stated in Subsection (1) is not limited to cases where it is determined that the language used is ambiguous. Any determination of meaning or ambiguity should only be made in the light of the relevant evidence of the situation and relations of the parties, the subject matter of the transaction, preliminary negotiations and statements made therein, usages of trade, and the course of dealing between the parties....

"Comment b to [§ 214] explains:

Words, written or oral, cannot apply themselves to the subject matter. The expressions and general tenor of speech used in negotiations are admissible to show the conditions existing when the writing was made, the application of the words, and the meaning or meanings of the parties. Even though words seem on their face to have only a single possible meaning, other meanings often appear when the circumstances are disclosed. In cases of misunderstanding, there must be inquiry into the meaning attached to the words by each party and into what each knew or had reason to know."

———

NOTE—IS THE INTERPRETATION OF WRITTEN CONTRACTS A QUESTION FOR THE JUDGE OR FOR THE JURY?

It is commonly said that questions of fact are for the jury and questions of law are for the judge. A more realistic statement would be that questions that the legal system assigns to the jury are *called* "questions of fact," and questions that the legal system assigns to the judge are *called* "questions of law." Within this verbal framework, it has long been the general rule that the interpretation of written contracts is a question of law even though "in actuality [such interpretation involves] a factual, not a legal, decision.... This fact-finding function exercised by the court is denominated a 'question of law' ... not because analytically it is a question of law but rather to indicate that it is the trial judge, not the jury, to whom the law assigns the responsibility for deciding the matter." Community College v. Community College, Society of the Faculty, 473 Pa. 576, 375 A.2d 1267 (1977).

Traditionally, there has been an exception to this general rule—that is, the interpretation of written contracts has been given to the trier of fact— where the court deems the agreement ambiguous; the meaning of the agreement turns on evidence extrinsic to the agreement; and the credibility of that evidence is at issue. In Meyers v. Selznick Co., 373 F.2d 218 (2d Cir.1966), Judge Friendly forcefully supported a liberalization of this exception. Under this liberalization, questions of interpretation are for the trier of fact *whenever* evidence extrinsic to the written instrument is relevant to its interpretation, even though there is no issue as to the credibility of the evidence, but merely as to its significance:

> Whether determination of meaning be regarded as a question of fact, a question of law, or just itself, reliance on the jury to resolve ambiguities in the light of extrinsic evidence seems quite as it should be, save where the form or subject-matter of a particular contract outruns a jury's competence.... Resolution of [issues involving the determination of meaning] may hinge in no small degree on notions of fairness—the very kind of decision laymen are ideally equipped to make.

This view is adopted in Restatement Second § 212(2), which provides that "A question of interpretation of an integrated agreement is to be determined by the trier of fact if it depends on the credibility of extrinsic evidence or on a choice among reasonable inferences to be drawn from extrinsic evidence. Otherwise a question of interpretation of an integrated agreement is to be determined as a question of law."

Some courts go even further in determining what issues of interpretation are for the jury. In C.R. Anthony Co. v. Loretto Mall Partners, 112 N.M. 504, 817 P.2d 328 (1991), the court said, "New Mexico courts long have held that the question of whether a contractual term or provision is susceptible to reasonable but conflicting meanings, *i.e.*, whether there is ambiguity, is one of law.... We also have held, however, that if the court finds ambiguity, the jury (or the court as the fact finder in the absence of a jury) resolves the ambiguity as an issue of ultimate fact before deciding issues of breach and damages.... The question of interpretation of language and conduct (the question of the meaning to be given the words of the contract) is a question of fact where that meaning depends on reasonable but conflicting inferences to be drawn from events occurring or circumstances existing before, during, or after negotiation of the contract. There is, as Professor Corbin points out, 'no "legal" meaning, separate and distinct from some person's meaning in fact.' ... It may be that the evidence presented is so clear that no reasonable person would determine the issue before the court in any way but one. In that case, to the extent the court decides the issue, the question then may be described as one of law. [Furthermore, a court may employ the many rules of contract interpretation that do not depend on evidence extrinsic to the contract. *See, e.g., Smith v. Tinley,* 100 N.M. 663, 665, 674 P.2d 1123, 1125 (1984) (reasonable interpretation of contract is favored); *Schultz & Lindsay Constr. Co. v. State,* 83 N.M. 534, 536, 494 P.2d 612, 614 (1972) (uncertainties construed strictly against drafter); *Id.* at 535, 494 P.2d at 613 (each part of contract is to be given significance according to its place in the contract so as to give effect to the intentions of the parties). To the extent a court resolves an issue of contract interpretation solely by reference to such aids, or by traditional rules of grammar and punctuation, without resort to evidence of surrounding facts and circumstances, then that issue, as well, may be described as one of law.] ... However, if the proffered evidence is in dispute, turns on witness credibility, or is susceptible of conflicting inferences, the ultimate factual issues must be resolved by the appropriate fact finder with the benefit of a full evidentiary hearing. To hold otherwise would be to relegate to judicial divination the determinative issues of many contract disputes."

SECTION 3. TRADE USAGE, COURSE OF PERFORMANCE AND COURSE OF DEALING AS PART OF A WRITTEN CONTRACT

NANAKULI PAVING AND ROCK CO. v. SHELL OIL CO.

United States Court of Appeals, Ninth Circuit, 1981.
664 F.2d 772.

Before BROWNING, CHIEF JUDGE, and KENNEDY, CIRCUIT JUDGE, and HOFFMAN,* DISTRICT JUDGE.

HOFFMAN, DISTRICT JUDGE:

[Prior to 1963, there were two major paving contractors on Oahu: Nanakuli and Hawaiian Bitumals ("H.B."). Of these, H.B. was by far the largest, in part because it had a special relationship with Chevron, which supplied asphalt, a major element in paving construction. Shell Oil, like

---

* Honorable Walter E. Hoffman, Senior United States District Judge for the Eastern District of Virginia, sitting by designation.

Chevron, was a major worldwide oil company, but partly because of the relationship between H.B. and Chevron, Shell had only a small percentage of the asphalt market in Hawaii and had no asphalt terminals in Hawaii.

[In 1963, Nanakuli and Shell entered into a five-year contract under which Nanakuli agreed to buy its asphalt requirements from Shell, and Shell agreed to supply these requirements. The contract gave Nanakuli an assured source of supply, so that it could compete on equal terms with H.B., and gave Shell the potential for drastically expanding its asphalt sales in Hawaii. In 1969, a new contract was executed. The term of this contract was until December 31, 1975, at which point each party had an option to cancel on 6 months' notice.

[In February 1976, Nanakuli sued Shell for breach of the 1969 contract. That contract provided that the price of asphalt to Nanakuli would be "Shell's posted price at the time of delivery"—that is, the price Shell posted, at the time of delivery, for sale to all buyers. Nanakuli argued that notwithstanding this price term, Nanakuli was entitled to "price protection" under both trade usage and course of performance, and that Shell had breached the contract by refusing to give such protection. "Price protection" means that a supplier will not increase the price charged to a contractor, despite an increase in the supplier's posted price, without advance notice, and instead will apply the posted price that is in place at the time the contractor made a bid, and that is incorporated by the contractor into its bid, long enough to allow the contractor to order the asphalt needed on the job. Nanakuli claimed that Shell breached the 1969 contract in January 1974 by failing to price protect Nanakuli on 7,200 tons of asphalt when Shell raised the price for asphalt from $44 to $76. The jury returned a verdict of $220,800 for Nanakuli. The district court set aside this verdict, and granted Shell's motion for judgment n.o.v.]

... We reinstate the jury verdict because we find that, viewing the evidence as a whole, there was substantial evidence to support a finding by reasonable jurors that Shell breached its contract by failing to provide protection for Nanakuli in 1974....

[W]e hold that, under the facts of this case, a jury could reasonably have found that Shell's acts on two occasions to price protect Nanakuli were not ambiguous and therefore indicated Shell's understanding of the terms of the agreement with Nanakuli rather than being a waiver by Shell of those terms.[12]

[We also] hold that, although the express price terms of Shell's posted price of delivery may seem, at first glance, inconsistent with a trade usage of price protection at time of increases in price, a closer reading shows that the jury could have reasonably construed price protection as consistent with the express term. We reach this holding for several reasons. First, we are persuaded by a careful reading of the U.C.C., one of whose underlying purposes is to promote flexibility in the expansion of commercial practices and which rather drastically overhauls this particular area of the law. The Code would have us look beyond the printed pages of the contract to usages and the entire commercial context of the agreement in order to reach the "true

---

12. In addition, Shell's Bohner volunteered on direct for Shell that Shell price protected Nanakuli again after 1974 on the only two occasions of later price increases in 1977 and 1978. Although not constituting a course of performance, since the occasions took place under different contracts, these two additional instances of price protection could have reinforced the jury's impression that Shell's earlier actions were a carrying out of the price term.

understanding" of the parties. Second, decisions of other courts in similar situations have managed to reconcile such trade usages with seemingly contradictory express terms where the prior course of dealings between the parties, trade usages, and the actual performance of the contract by the parties showed a clear intent by the parties to incorporate those usages into the agreement or to give to the express term the particular meaning provided by those usages, even at times varying the apparent meaning of the express terms. Third, the delineation by thoughtful commentators of the degree of consistency demanded between express terms and usage is that a usage should be allowed to modify the apparent agreement, as seen in the written terms, as long as it does not totally negate it. We believe the usage here falls within the limits set forth by commentators and generally followed in the better reasoned decisions. The manner in which price protection was actually practiced in Hawaii was that it only came into play at times of price increases and only for work committed prior to those increases on non-escalating contracts. Thus, it formed an exception to, rather than a total negation of, the express price term of "Shell's Posted Price at time of delivery." Our decision is reinforced by the overwhelming nature of the evidence that price protection was routinely practiced by all suppliers in the small Oahu market of the asphaltic paving trade and therefore was known to Shell; that it was a realistic necessity to operate in that market and thus vital to Nanakuli's ability to get large government contracts and to Shell's continued business growth on Oahu; and that it therefore constituted an intended part of the agreement, as that term is broadly defined by the Code, between Shell and Nanakuli....

II

Trade Usage Before and After 1969

The key to price protection being so prevalent in 1969 that both parties would intend to incorporate it into their contract is found in one reality of the Oahu asphaltic paving market: the largest paving contracts were let by government agencies and none of the three levels of government—local, state, or federal—allowed escalation clauses for paving materials. If a paver bid at one price and another went into effect before the award was made, the paving company would lose a great deal of money, since it could not pass on increases to any government agency or to most general contractors. Extensive evidence was presented that, as a consequence, aggregate suppliers routinely price protected paving contractors in the 1960's and 1970's, as did the largest asphaltic supplier in Oahu, Chevron. Nanakuli presented documentary evidence of routine price protection by aggregate suppliers as well as two witnesses: Grosjean, Vice–President for Marketing of Ameron H.C. & D., and Nihei, Division Manager of Lone Star Industries for Pacific Cement and Aggregate (P.C. & A.). Both testified that price protection to their knowledge had always been practiced: at H.C. & D. for many years prior to Grosjean's arrival in 1962 and at P.C. & A. routinely since Nihei's arrival in 1960. Such protection consisted of advance notices of increases, coupled with charging the old price for work committed at that price or for enough time to order the tonnage committed. The smallness of the Oahu market led to complete trust among suppliers and pavers. H.C. & D. did not demand that Nanakuli or other pavers issue purchase orders or sign contracts for aggregate before incorporating its aggregate prices into bids. Nanakuli would merely give H.C.

& D. a list of projects it had bid at the time H.C. & D. raised its prices, without documentation. "Their word and letter is good enough for us," Grosjean testified. Nihei said P.C. & A. at the time of price increases would get a list of either particular projects bid by a paver or simply total tonnage bid at the old price. "We take either one. We take their word for it." None of the aggregate companies had a contract with Nanakuli expressly stating price protection would be given; Nanakuli's contract with P.C. & A. merely set out that P.C. & A. would not charge Nanakuli more than it charged its other customers.

The evidence about Chevron's practice of price protection came in the form of an affidavit by Bery Jameyson, Chevron's Division Manager–Asphalt in California. He stated that Chevron had routinely price protected H.B. on work bid for many years, the last occasion prior to the signing of the 1969 contracts between Nanakuli and Shell being a price increase put into effect on March 7, 1969, with the understanding that H.B. would be protected on work bid, which amounted to 12,000 tons. In answer to Shell's protest that such evidence was not relevant without the contract itself, Nanakuli introduced the contract into evidence. Much like the contract at issue here, it provided that the price to H.B. would be a given percentage of the price Chevron set for a specified crude oil in California. No mention was made of price protection in the written contract between H.B. and Chevron.

In addition to evidence of trade usages existing in 1969 when the contract at issue was signed, the District Judge let in evidence of the continuation of that trade usage after 1969, over Shell's protest. He stated that, giving a liberal reading to Section 1–205, he felt that later evidence was relevant to show that the expectation of the parties that a given usage would be observed was justified. The basis for incorporating a trade usage into a contract under the U.C.C. is the justifiable expectation of the parties that it will be observed. That later evidence consisted here of more price protection by the aggregate companies on Oahu, as well as continued asphalt price protection. Chevron after 1969 continued price protecting H.B. on Oahu and, on raising prices in 1979, price protected Nanakuli on the island of Molokai, where Nanakuli purchased its asphalt from Chevron. Additionally, Shell price protected Nanakuli in 1977 and 1978 on Oahu.[13]

III

Shell's Course of Performance of the 1969 Contract

The Code considers actual performance of a contract as the most relevant evidence of how the parties interpreted the terms of that contract. In 1970 and 1971, the only points at which Shell raised prices between 1969 and 1974, it price protected Nanakuli by holding its old price for four and three months, respectively, after announcing a price increase. In the late summer of 1970, Shell had announced a price increase from $35 to $40 a ton effective September 1, 1970. When Nanakuli protested to Bohner [Shell's Hawaiian representative] that it should be price protected on work already committed,

---

13. We do not need to decide whether usage evidence after a contract was signed is admissible to show that a party's reliance on a given usage was justifiable, given its continuation, because part of that evidence dealing with asphalt prices was admissible to show the rea-sonably commercial standards of fair dealing prevalent in the trade in 1974 and the part dealing with the continuation of price protection by aggregate suppliers, after 1969 was not so extensive as to be prejudicial to Shell. . . .

Blee [a Shell asphalt official in San Francisco, to whom Bohner reported] wrote Bohner an in-house memo that, if Bohner could not "convince" Nanakuli to go along with the price increase on September 1, he should try to "bargain" to get Nanakuli to accept the price raise by at least the first of the year, which was what was finally agreed upon. During that four-month period, Nanakuli bought 3,300 tons. Shell announced a second increase in October, 1970, from $40 to $42 effective December 31st. Before that increase went into effect, on November 25 Shell increased the [amount of the] raise to $4, making the price $44 as of the first of the year.[14] Shell again agreed to price protect Nanakuli by holding the price at $40, which had been the official price since September 1, for three months from January to March, 1971. Shell did not actually raise prices again until January, 1974, but at several points it believed that increases would be necessary and gave several months' advance notice of those possible increases. Those actions were in accord with Shell's own policy, as professed by Bohner, and that of other asphalt and aggregate suppliers: to give at least several months' advance notice of price increases. On January 14, 1971, Shell wrote its asphalt customers that the maximum 1971 increase would be to $46. On July 9, 1971, another letter promised the price would not go over $50 in 1972. In addition, Bohner volunteered on direct the information that Shell price protected Nanakuli on the only two occasions of price increases after 1974 by giving 6 months' advance notice in 1977 and 3 or 4 months' advance notice in 1978, a practice he described as "in effect carryover pricing," his term for price protection. By its actions, Bohner testified, Shell allowed Nanakuli time to make arrangements to buy up tonnage committed at the old price, that is, to "chew up" tonnage bid or contracted. Shell apparently offered this testimony to impress the jury with its subsequent good faith toward Nanakuli. In fact, it also may have reinforced the impression of the universality of price protection in the asphaltic paving trade on Oahu and, by showing Shell's adherence to that practice on every relevant occasion except 1974, have highlighted for the jury what was the commercially reasonable standard of fair dealing in effect on Oahu in 1974. . . .

VI

Waiver or Course of Performance

Course of performance under the Code is the action of the parties in carrying out the contract at issue, whereas course of dealing consists of relations between the parties *prior* to signing that contract. Evidence of the latter was excluded by the District Judge; evidence of the former consisted of Shell's price protection of Nanakuli in 1970 and 1971. Shell protested that the jury could not have found that those two instances of price protection amounted to a course of performance of its 1969 contract, relying on two Code comments. First, one instance does not constitute a course of performance. "A single occasion of conduct does not fall within the language of this section. . . ." Haw.Rev.Stat. § 490:2–208, Comment 4. Although the Comment rules out one instance, it does not further delineate how many acts are needed to form a course of performance. The prior occasions here were only two, but they constituted the only occasions before 1974 that would call for such

---

14. That November letter also announced a "new pricing policy" of Shell, setting out a requirement that firm contractual commit- ments be made with Shell within 15 days of accepting a bid.

conduct. In addition, the language used by a top asphalt official of Shell in connection with the first price protection of Nanakuli indicated that Shell felt that Nanakuli was entitled to some form of price protection. On that occasion in 1970 Blee, who had negotiated the contract with Nanakuli and was familiar with exactly what terms Shell was bound to by that agreement, wrote of the need to "bargain" with Nanakuli over the extent of price protection to be given, indicating that some price protection was a legal right of Nanakuli's under the 1969 agreement.

Shell's second defense is that the Comment expresses a preference for an interpretation of waiver.

> 3.   Where it is difficult to determine whether a particular act merely sheds light on the meaning of the agreement or represents a waiver of a term of the agreement, the preference is in favor of "waiver" whenever such construction, plus the application of the provisions on the reinstatement of rights waived ..., is needed to preserve the flexible character of commercial contracts and to prevent surprise or other hardship.

Id., Comment 3. The preference for waiver only applies, however, where acts are ambiguous. It was within the province of the jury to determine whether those acts were ambiguous, and if not, whether they constituted waivers or a course of performance of the contract. The jury's interpretation of those acts as a course of performance was bolstered by evidence offered by Shell that it again price protected Nanakuli on the only two occasions of post–1974 price increases, in 1977 and 1978.[15]

VII

Express Terms as Reasonably Consistent With Usage In Course of Performance

Perhaps one of the most fundamental departures of the Code from prior contract law is found in the parol evidence rule and the definition of an agreement between two parties. Under the U.C.C., an agreement goes beyond the written words on a piece of paper. " 'Agreement' means the bargain of the parties in fact as found in their language or by implication from other circumstances including course of dealing or usage of trade or course of performance as provided in this chapter (sections 490:1–205 and 490:2–208)." *Id.* § 490:1–201(3). Express terms, then, do not constitute the entire agreement, which must be sought also in evidence of usages, dealings, and performance of the contract itself. The purpose of evidence of usages, which are defined in the previous section, is to help to understand the entire agreement.

> [Usages are] a factor in reaching the commercial meaning of the agreement which the parties have made. The language used is to be interpreted as meaning what it may fairly be expected to mean to parties involved in the particular commercial transaction in a given locality or in a given vocation or trade.... Part of the agreement of the parties ... is to be sought for in the usages of trade which furnish the background and

---

15. Bohner testified on direct for Shell at the 1978 trial that the two later instances of price protection occurred "this" year and "last" year, by which he could have meant 1976 and 1977. Bohner's testimony was that on those later occasions Shell gave Nanakuli six and three or four months' notice of an increase to allow Nanakuli to buy tonnage it had committed at the old price. He defined Shell's actions as "in effect carryover pricing." The jury's finding was reasonable in light of the circumstances of universal price protection by asphalt and aggregate suppliers, as well as by Shell on all price increases except 1974.

give particular meaning to the language used, and are the framework of common understanding controlling any general rules of law which hold only when there is no such understanding.

Id. § 490:1–205, Comment 4. Course of dealings is more important than usages of the trade, being specific usages between the two parties to the contract. "[C]ourse of dealing controls usage of trade." *Id.* § 490:1–205(4). It "is a sequence of previous conduct between the parties to a particular transaction which is fairly to be regarded as establishing a common basis of understanding for interpreting their expressions and other conduct." *Id.* § 490:1–205(1). Much of the evidence of prior dealings between Shell and Nanakuli in negotiating the 1963 contract and in carrying out similar earlier contracts was excluded by the court.[16]

A commercial agreement, then, is broader than the written paper and its meaning is to be determined not just by the language used by them in the written contract but "by their action, read and interpreted in the light of commercial practices and other surrounding circumstances. The measure and background for interpretation are set by the commercial context, which may explain and supplement even the language of a formal or final writing." *Id.,* Comment 1. Performance, usages, and prior dealings are important enough to be admitted always, even for a final and complete agreement; only if they cannot be reasonably reconciled with the express terms of the contract are they not binding on the parties. "The express terms of an agreement and an applicable course of dealing or usage of trade shall be construed wherever reasonable as consistent with each other; but when such construction is unreasonable express terms control both course of dealing and usage of trade and course of dealing controls usage of trade." *Id.* § 490:1–205(4).

Of these three, then, the most important evidence of the agreement of the parties is their actual performance of the contract. *Id.* The operative definition of course of performance is as follows: "Where the contract for sale involves repeated occasions for performance by either party with knowledge of the nature of the performance and opportunity for objection to it by the other, any course of performance accepted or acquiesced in without objection shall be relevant to determine the meaning of the agreement." *Id.* § 490:2–208(1). "Course of dealing ... is restricted, literally, to a sequence of conduct between the parties previous to the agreement. However, the provisions of the Act on course of performance make it clear that a sequence of conduct after or under the agreement may have equivalent meaning (Section 2–208)." *Id.* 490:1–205, Comment 2. The importance of evidence of course of performance is explained: "The parties themselves know best what they have meant by their words of agreement and their action under that agreement is the best indication of what that meaning was. This section thus rounds out the set of factors which determines the meaning of the 'agreement' ..." *Id.* § 490:2–208, Comment 1. "Under this section a course of performance is always relevant to determine the meaning of the agreement." *Id.,* Comment 2.

Our study of the Code provisions and Comments, then, form the first basis of our holding that a trade usage to price protect pavers at times of price increases for work committed on nonescalating contracts could reasonably be construed as consistent with an express term of seller's posted price at delivery. Since the agreement of the parties is broader than the express terms

---

16. *See* footnote 31, *supra.*

and includes usages, which may even add terms to the agreement,[17] and since the commercial background provided by those usages is vital to an understanding of the agreement, we follow the Code's mandate to proceed on the assumption that the parties have included those usages unless they cannot reasonably be construed as consistent with the express terms.

Federal courts usually have been lenient in not ruling out consistent additional terms or trade usage for apparent inconsistency with express terms. The leading case on the subject is *Columbia Nitrogen Corp. v. Royster Co.*, 451 F.2d 3 (4th Cir.1971). Columbia, the buyer, had in the past primarily produced and sold nitrogen to Royster. When Royster opened a new plant that produced more phosphate than it needed, the parties reversed roles and signed a sales contract for Royster to sell excess phosphate to Columbia. The contract terms set out the price that would be charged by Royster and the amount to be sold. It provided for the price to go up if certain events occurred but did not provide for price declines. When the price of nitrogen fell precipitously, Columbia refused to accept the full amount of nitrogen specified in the contract after Royster refused to renegotiate the contract price. The District Judge's exclusion of usage of the trade and course of dealing to explain the express quantity term in the contract was reversed. Columbia had offered to prove that the quantity set out in the contract was a mere projection to be adjusted according to market forces. Ambiguity was not necessary for the admission of evidence of usage and prior dealings.[18] Even though the lengthy contract was the result of long and careful negotiations and apparently covered every contingency, the appellate court ruled that "the test of admissibility is not whether the contract appears on its face to be complete in every detail, but whether the proffered evidence of course of dealing and trade usage reasonably can be construed as consistent with the express terms of the agreement." *Id.* at 9. The express quantity term could be reasonably construed as consistent with a usage that such terms would be mere projections for several reasons: (1) the contract did not expressly state that usage and dealings evidence would be excluded; (2) the contract was silent on the adjustment of price or quantities in a declining market; (3) the minimum tonnage was expressed in the contract as Products Supplied, not Products Purchased; (4) the default clause of the contract did not state a penalty for failure to take delivery; and (5) apparently most important in the court's view, the parties had deviated from similar express terms in earlier contracts in times of declining market. *Id.* at 9–10. As here, the contract's merger clause said that there were no oral agreements. The court explained that its ruling "reflects the reality of the marketplace and avoids the overly legalistic interpretations which the Code seeks to abolish." *Id.* at 10. The Code assigns dealing and usage evidence "unique and important roles" and

---

17. "The agreement of the parties includes that part of their bargain found in course of dealing, usage of trade, or course of performance. These sources are relevant not only to the interpretation of express contract terms, but may themselves constitute contract terms." White & Summers, *supra*, § 3–3 at 84.

18. As discussed earlier, the District Judge here mistakenly equated ambiguity with admissibility. He said, "I think this is a close case. On the face of the contract it would seem to be unambiguous," although acknowledging

that liberal commentators on the Code would let in evidence of usage and performance even without ambiguity. He only let in usage evidence because Shell's answer to interrogatory 11 provided some ambiguity, ... saying "I think if these can be consistently used to explain the apparently unambiguous terms, they should be allowed in." In fact, this court has ruled that ambiguity is not necessary to admit usage evidence. *Board of Trade of San Francisco v. Swiss Credit Bank*, 597 F.2d 146, 148 (9th Cir.1979).

therefore "overly simplistic and overly legalistic interpretation of a contract should be shunned." *Id.* at 11.

Usage and an oral understanding led to much the same interpretation of a quantity term specifying delivery of 500 tons of stainless-steel solids in *Michael Schiavone & Sons, Inc. v. Securalloy Co.,* 312 F.Supp. 801 (D.Conn. 1970). In denying summary judgment for plaintiff-buyer, the court ruled that defendant-seller could attempt to prove that the quantity term was modified by an oral understanding, in line with a trade usage, that seller would only supply as many tons as he could, with 500 tons the upper limit. The court reasoned that an additional term with a lesser effect than total contradiction or negation of a contract term can be a consistent term and "[e]vidence that the quantity to be supplied by defendant was orally understood to be up to 500 tons cannot be said to be inconsistent with the terms of the written contract which specified the quantity as '500 Gross Ton.'" *Id.* at 804. . . .

Probably the two leading cases that have rejected usage evidence as inconsistent with express terms are *Southern Concrete Services, Inc. v. Mableton Contractors, Inc.,* 407 F.Supp. 581 (N.D.Ga.1975), *aff'd,* 569 F.2d 1154 (5th Cir.1978) (unpublished opinion), and *Division of Triple T Service, Inc. v. Mobil Oil Corp.,* 60 Misc.2d 720, 304 N.Y.S.2d 191 (Sup.Ct.1969). In *Southern Concrete* the District Court, distinguishing its facts from those in *Columbia Nitrogen, supra,* held that evidence of a trade usage and an agreement to additional terms was not admissible. The usage allegedly was that contract quantity specifications were not mandatory on either buyer or seller. The court acknowledged that U.C.C. § 2–202 "was meant to liberalize the common law parol evidence rule to allow evidence of agreements outside the contract, without a prerequisite finding that the contract was ambiguous" and "requires that contracts be interpreted in light of the commercial context in which they were written and not by the rules on legal construction." *Southern Concrete, supra,* at 582–83. Nevertheless, the court held, the express quantity term in the contract and the usage could not be construed as reasonably consistent. "A construction which negates the express terms of the contract by allowing unilateral abandonment of its specifications is patently unreasonable." *Id.* at 585. The court's attempt to differentiate its facts from those in *Columbia Nitrogen* was unsuccessful; the distinctions discussed were very minor. The difference between the two results should depend less on such subtle variations in contract language and more on the strength of the usage evidence and whether the parties are or should be aware of the usage and thus should be bound by it. The court in *Southern Concrete* acknowledged that *Columbia Nitrogen* is not the only case at odds with its holding that a usage that quantities are projections cannot modify a seemingly unambiguous quantity term. *Southern Concrete, supra,* at 585–86.

The other leading case cited by Shell is a New York case, *Triple T, supra.* Because the express term of the franchise agreement gave either party the right to terminate 90–days' notice, the court refused to find as reasonably consistent with that term a usage of the trade that a gasoline franchisor could only terminate a dealer for "cause". "[T]he express terms of the contract cover the entire area of termination and negate plaintiff's argument that the custom or usage in the trade implicitly adds the words 'with cause' in the termination clause. The contract is unambiguous and no sufficient basis appears for a construction which would insert words to limit the effect of the termination clause." *Id.* at 203. The court then held that only consistent usages are admissible, which is an incorrect reading of the Code. Usage is always admissible, even though the express term controls in the event of inconsistency, which is a jury question.

Higher New York courts have not been as quick to reject evidence of additional terms for inconsistency as was the Supreme Court in *Triple T* in rejecting usage evidence.... *Hunt Foods & Industries, Inc. v. Doliner,* 26 App.Div.2d 41, 270 N.Y.S.2d 937 (1966) [p. 541, supra]....

... Here the evidence was overwhelming that all suppliers to the asphaltic paving trade price protected customers under the same types of circumstances. Chevron's contract with H.B. was a similar long-term supply contract between a buyer and seller with very close relations, on a form supplied by the seller, covering sales of asphalt, and setting the price at seller's posted price, with no mention of price protection....

> Because the stock printed forms cannot always reflect the changing methods of business, members of the trade may do business with a standard clause in the forms that they ignore in practice. If the trade consistently ignores obsolete clauses at variance with actual trade practices, a litigant can maintain that it is reasonable that the courts also ignore the clauses....

Kirst, [Usage of Trade and Course of Dealing: Subversion of the UCC Theory, [1977] U.Ill.L. Forum 811] at 824. *Levie,* [Trade Usage and Custom ..., 40 N.Y.U.L.Rev. 1101 (1965)], at 1112, writes, "Astonishing as it will seem to most practicing attorneys, under the Code it will be possible in some cases to use custom to contradict the written agreement.... Therefore usage may be used to 'qualify' the agreement, which presumably means to 'cut down' express terms although not to negate them entirely." Here, the express price term was "Shell's Posted Price at time of delivery." A total negation of that term would be that the buyer was to set the price. It is a less than complete negation of the term that an unstated exception exists at times of price increases, at which times the old price is to be charged, for a certain period or for a specified tonnage, on work already committed at the lower price on nonescalating contracts. Such a usage forms a broad and important exception to the express term, but does not swallow it entirely. Therefore, we hold that, under these particular facts, a reasonable jury could have found that price protection was incorporated into the 1969 agreement between Nanakuli and Shell and that price protection was reasonably consistent with the express term of seller's posted price at delivery....

[The court also held that in light of the universal practice in the asphaltic paving trade of giving advance notice of a price increase, Shell could not have exercised good faith in raising its price by $32, effective January 1, in a letter written on December 31 and only received on January 4.]

Because the jury could have found for Nanakuli on its price protection claim under either theory, we reverse the judgment of the District Court and reinstate the jury verdict for Nanakuli in the amount of $220,800, plus interest according to law.

REVERSED AND REMANDED WITH DIRECTIONS TO ENTER FINAL JUDGMENT.

KENNEDY, CIRCUIT JUDGE, concurring specially:

The case involves specific pricing practices, not an allegation of unfair dealing generally. Our opinion should not be interpreted to permit juries to import price protection or a similarly specific contract term from a concept of good faith that is not based on well-established custom and usage or other objective standards of which the parties had clear notice. Here, evidence of custom and usage regarding price protection in the asphaltic paving trade was not contradicted in major respects, and the jury could find that the parties knew or should have known of the practice at the time of making the contract. In my view, these are necessary predicates for either theory of the case, namely, interpretation of the contract based on the course of its performance or a finding that good faith required the seller to hold the price. With these observations, I concur.

C-THRU CONTAINER CORP. v. MIDLAND MFG. CO., 533 N.W.2d 542 (Iowa 1995). C–Thru and Midland entered into a contract under which Midland purchased bottle-making equipment from C–Thru. Under the contract, Midland could pay for the equipment by supplying commercially acceptable bottles to C–Thru. If Midland failed to supply the bottles, C–Thru could demand the purchase price of the equipment in cash. C–Thru claimed that Midland had breached the contract by being incapable of producing commercially acceptable bottles, and demanded that Midland pay the purchase price of the equipment. Midland contended that it had not breached the contract because C–Thru had not ordered any bottles. C–Thru responded that the practice in the bottling industry was that before the purchaser places an order, the bottle manufacturer provides sample bottles to verify that it is capable of producing commercially acceptable bottles, and that C–Thru had not provided such samples. C–Thru argued that evidence of this practice was inadmissible under the parol evidence rule, because the contract was complete and unambiguous. Held, evidence that there was such a practice was admissible.

We first reject Midland's argument that evidence of trade usage is admissible only when the contract is ambiguous. There is no such requirement in [UCC § 2–202]. Moreover, the official comment to [§ 2–202] ... states that this section "definitely rejects" a requirement that the language of the contract be ambiguous as a condition precedent to the admission of trade-usage evidence....

We also hold that even a "complete" contract may be explained or supplemented by parol evidence of trade usages.[19] ... As the official comment to section 2–202 states, commercial sales contracts "are to be read on the assumption that the course of prior dealings between the parties and the usages of trade were taken for granted when the document was phrased." U.C.C. § 2–202 cmt. 2 (1977). Therefore, even a completely integrated contract may be supplemented by practices in the industry that do not contradict express terms of the contract.

That brings us to the remaining argument made by Midland—that C–Thru may not use parol evidence to add a new term to the agreement. Section [2–202] says that when parol evidence shows a usage of trade that

19. The contract here stated that "[t]his agreement constitutes the entire agreement between C–Thru and Midland and supersedes any and all prior agreements between them."

does not contradict a contract term, the evidence is admissible to "supplement" the contract. We look to the common meaning of the word "supplement." ... "Supplement" means "to add ... to." Webster's Third New Int'l Dictionary 2297 (1993). Consequently, the trade-usage evidence upon which C–Thru relies is admissible even though it adds a new term to the contract. White & Summers, § 3–3 (usage of trade may itself constitute a contract term).

———

NOTE ON THE PLAIN–MEANING RULE
AND THE PAROL EVIDENCE RULE

Strictly speaking, the plain meaning (or "four corners") rule, that extrinsic evidence cannot be introduced to help interpret a written contract unless the contract is ambiguous on its face, is not the same as the parol evidence rule. At least in theory, the plain meaning rule is a principle of interpretation; the parol evidence rule is not. Furthermore, the term *extrinsic evidence* is broader than the term *parol evidence*, because extrinsic evidence includes not only evidence of other agreements, but evidence of the circumstances surrounding the making of a contract. Thus many plain-meaning-rule opinions, like Steuart v. McChesney, don't even mention the parol evidence rule.

However, the two rules are similar in certain fundamental respects. Both aim, properly or misguidedly, to preserve what proponents of the rules perceive to be the integrity of writings. Both operate to preclude the introduction of evidence concerning, but not contained in, a written contract. Both focus largely on the exclusion of oral evidence, which is often referred to as parol evidence even in plain-meaning-rule cases. The two rules differ in that the parol evidence rule normally does not preclude evidence of the *circumstances* under which a written contract was made, as opposed to evidence of *agreements* not embodied in the written contract, while the plain-meaning rule may preclude even evidence concerning circumstances.

Although in principle the parol evidence rule applies only to alleged parol agreements, in practice courts often apply the rule to exclude interpretive evidence that in the courts' view would lead to an interpretation that the writing "cannot bear."

*

Part IV

FORM CONTRACTS IN COMMERCIAL AND CONSUMER CONTEXTS

The problems raised by form contracts have been a major preoccupation of contract–law scholars since the middle of the twentieth century. The primary areas of concern have been the enforceability of preprinted terms and the import of preprinted terms in determining whether a form sent in response to an offer constitutes an acceptance.

The phenomenon of rational ignorance plays a powerful role in both concerns. The provisions of a contract can be divided into performance and nonperformance terms. Performance terms specify the performance each party must render. All other provisions are normally nonperformance terms. The most important types of performance terms concern the description of the subject-matter of the contract, quantity, price, delivery terms, and payment terms. Nonperformance terms cover a wide range of issues, such as how and when notice of default must be given, limitations on warranties, excuse, and so forth. Most preprinted terms are nonperformance terms that concern low-probability future risks. Call a party who prepares a form contract a form-giver, and a party who receives a form contract a form-taker. A form-giver typically offers a package consisting of a commodity (using that term in a broadly defined manner, to include goods, realty, and services) and a form contract that states the terms on which the commodity will be purchased or sold. Each part of the package, in turn, consists of a number of attributes: The commodity has physical attributes, such as size, shape, and color. The form contract has business and legal attributes, most of which are nonperformance terms. Typically, the most important performance terms—description, quantity, price, delivery, payment—will be custom-tailored to each transaction, and individually filled into the form. In contrast, the nonperformance terms and the less important performance terms (such as provisions concerning crating or notice of shipment) will typically be preprinted.

To make an optimum substantive decision, a form-taker who is choosing between a variety of commodities of a given type would carefully deliberate not only on the characteristics of the commodities, but also on the business and legal attributes of each form contract that is coupled with each commodity that he is considering. Analyzing all the terms of a form contract in this manner, however, will often be unduly costly. First, a form contract often contains a very large number of terms. Form insurance contracts, for example, often contain forty, fifty, or more terms. Moreover, the meaning and effect of the preprinted terms will very often be inaccessible to laypersons. In part, this is because the terms are often written in highly technical prose. Even if the terms are written clearly, however, the form-taker usually will be unable fully to understand their effects, because preprinted terms characteristically vary the form-taker's baseline legal rights, and most form-takers do not know their baseline legal rights. The verbal and legal obscurity of preprinted terms renders the cost of searching out and deliberating on the preprinted terms of various form contracts exceptionally high. In contrast, the low probability that these nonperformance terms will ever come into play heavily discounts the benefits of search and deliberation.

Furthermore, the length and complexity of a form contract is often not correlated to the dollar value of the transaction. Often, therefore, the cost of thorough search and deliberation on preprinted terms, let alone the cost of legal advice about the meaning and effect of the terms, would be prohibitive in relation to the benefits. A rational form-taker faced with preprinted terms whose effect he knows he will find difficult or impossible to fully understand, which involve risks that probably will never mature, which are unlikely to be worth the cost of search and deliberation, and which probably aren't subject to negotiation in any event, will typically decide to remain ignorant of many or most preprinted terms.

There is, however, a fundamental imbalance in this respect between the form-taker and the form-giver. For the form-taker, any given form contract is normally a one-shot transaction. This is one reason why the costs of searching and deliberating on the preprinted terms, or of retaining a lawyer to evaluate them, will normally far exceed the benefits of search and deliberation. For the form-giver, however, a form contract is a high-volume, repeat transaction. Thus, a rational form-giver will spend a significant amount of time and money, including money for legal services, to prepare a form contract that is optimal from his perspective. These asymmetrical incentives almost always work to heavily slant form contracts in favor of form-givers.

The law has responded to these problems through Section 2–207(1) of the Uniform Commercial Code, and through the common law doctrines of unfair surprise and reasonable expectations, which sharply limit the effect of preprinted terms in the contexts of contract formation and contract enforceability, respectively. The former issue is the subject of Chapter 16; the latter issue is the subject of Chapter 17.

————

Chapter 16

CONTRACT FORMATION IN A FORM–CONTRACT SETTING

1. BATTLE OF THE FORMS: THE BASIC ISSUES

NOTE ON THE BATTLE OF THE FORMS

When goods are supplied by a commercial seller to a commercial buyer, in most cases there is no document covering the transaction that is called on its face a "contract." Often the buyer will send to the seller a form the buyer calls a "purchase order." At the bottom of this form, or on the reverse side, there will appear certain preprinted terms, often loosely designated in the form as "conditions." These terms may be fairly extensive, and include shipping instructions, provisions making the order cancellable for delays in delivery, provisions covering crating charges, provisions for the arbitration of disputes, etc. Usually the purchase-order form will state that the order is given "subject to" the conditions stated. Generally the purchase order will request an "acknowledgment," although occasionally the word "acceptance" is used. The buyer sometimes hopefully provides a tear sheet or a separate form, requesting the seller to sign and return this form as an "acknowledgment" of the order.

Often the seller, instead of accepting the buyer's purchase order, or returning the buyer's "acknowledgment" form, sends the buyer the seller's own form, frequently called a "sales order." Or the first document may be a "sales order" sent by the seller to the buyer. This will be like the buyer's "purchase order," and will itself be "subject to" certain preprinted terms or "conditions" printed at the bottom or on the back.

The chances that the preprinted terms in the sales order will coincide with those in the purchase order are negligible. Sometimes, to strengthen its position, the seller will repeat its terms (or perhaps a different set of terms) on the invoice that is sent when the goods are shipped, stating in this form that the goods are shipped "subject to the following conditions." The buyer, anticipating that the seller will decorate the back of its invoice with fine print, may stipulate in its purchase order that if the terms stated in the invoice do not agree with the buyer's purchase order, the terms of the purchase order will control.

The result is that instead of an orderly negotiation of the terms of the sale, we have the parties engaged in a battle of forms, each jockeying for position and each attempting to get the other to indicate assent to its form. Sometimes a seller's sales order is signed by the buyer, and a buyer's purchase order is signed by the seller. Thus, the same transaction is covered by two different forms, stipulating inconsistent terms. More commonly, neither party is willing to sign the other's form, so that each party states in writing its terms of the sale, but neither expressly indicates assent to the terms proposed by the other.

The battle of the forms had a special bite under the *mirror-image* (or *ribbon-matching*) rule of classical contract law. Under this rule, any difference between an offer and a purported acceptance, no matter how minor, prevented the formation of a contract. Since the seller's form and the buyer's form seldom if ever matched, the exchange of a purchase order and a sales order (or counterpart forms) would seldom if ever constitute a contract under the mirror-image rule.

But the matter did not end there. Under another rule, an offer can be accepted by conduct. Putting the two rules together, if no contract was formed by the exchange of forms, but the seller shipped the goods and the buyer accepted them, a contract was deemed to have been made, consisting of the terms in whichever form was sent last. The theory was that the first form was an offer, the responding form was a counter-offer, and the goods were shipped and accepted pursuant to that counter-offer. For example, suppose the buyer began a transaction by sending a purchase order, and the seller responded by sending back a nonconforming sales order. Under the mirror-image rule, there would be no contract at that point. However, the sales order would not be without legal effect; instead, under traditional principles it would be a counter-offer. Now suppose the seller shipped the goods and the buyer accepted the shipment. The buyer was deemed to have accepted pursuant to the sales order/counter-offer, so that the terms of the resulting contract were those set by the seller. Similarly, suppose the seller began a transaction be sending a sales order, the buyer responded with a nonconforming purchase order, the seller shipped the goods, and the buyer accepted the shipment. In that case, the terms of the contract would be those set in the purchase order, because the buyer's nonconforming purchase order would be a counter-offer, and the seller's shipment would be deemed an acceptance of that counter-offer. This analysis was often called the "last-shot" approach, because if the goods were shipped and accepted, the terms of the contract were those set by whichever party fired the last shot in the battle of the forms.

UCC §§ 2–204(1), 2–204, 2–207

[See Selected Source Materials Supplement]

ABA TASK FORCE REPORT ON ARTICLE 2, 16 Del.J.Corp.Law. 981, 1063–64 (1991). "The premise that underlies [UCC] section 2–207 is that pre–printed boilerplate terms in each party's form are not read. Indeed, they cannot reasonably be expected to be read by the other party."

————

NOTE ON WHAT CONSTITUTES AN ACCEPTANCE UNDER UCC § 2–207

UCC § 2–207 applies only if there has been a "definite and [seasonable] expression of acceptance," but leaves open what constitutes a definite and seasonable expression of acceptance. In most cases under § 2–207 the offeror has sent a form to the offeree; the offeree has returned to the offeror another form whose individualized (non-preprinted) terms match the individualized terms of the offer; virtually no other terms match; and the courts have explicitly or implicitly held that the return form nevertheless constitutes an "expression of acceptance" under § 2–207. Indeed, that is the paradigm case at which § 2–207 was directed.

Where, however, the parties don't employ forms, even a small difference between the offer and the response may prevent a response from being an acceptance under § 2–207, at least if the parties have been bargaining about that difference.

For example, in Koehring Co. v. Glowacki, 77 Wis.2d 497, 253 N.W.2d 64 (1977), Koehring circulated a letter listing nine items of surplus machinery that were available for sale at its plant on an "as is, where is" basis. The term "as is, where is" meant that the buyer would bear the cost and risk of loading the machinery onto its truck. Glowacki telephoned Koehring, inquiring as to price. Koehring responded that Glowacki must bid $16,500, and that the bid must be in the form of a telegram. Glowacki telegraphed a bid of only $16,000. Koehring called Glowacki, reiterating that the bid must be $16,500. Glowacki then sent a second telegram, which bid $16,500, but including the statement "FOB [free on board], our truck, your plant, loaded." The term "FOB . . . loaded" meant that the seller would bear the cost and risk of loading the machinery onto the buyer's truck. Koehring responded with a telegram "accepting" the bid, but restating that the machinery was sold "as is, where is." In a suit by Koehring, the court held that no contract had been formed:

> As the trial court properly held in the present case, before we reach the question of additional or different terms added to a contract, we must first inquire whether or not any contract ever existed. Here the defendant's telegram was an offer to purchase at a price of $16,500 "FOB, our truck, your plant, loaded." Plaintiff's response was a counteroffer to sell at the price of $16,500 on an "as is, where is" basis. There was no "meeting of the minds" or agreement of the parties prior to the exchange of telegrams. No such "meeting of the minds" or agreement resulted from the exchange of telegrams. This being so, we do not reach the issue as to whether additional or differing terms do or do not destroy an agreement of the parties since there is no valid contract in the first place.

> In the case before us, we deal with an initial and continuing absence of agreement between the parties as to whether the sales price included loading risks and costs. The second telegram of defendant, offering $16,500 "FOB, our truck, your plant, loaded," was an offer. The respond-

ing telegram of plaintiff, all tools sold on an "as is, where is" basis, while labeled an acceptance, was actually a rejection of the defendant's offer and a counteroffer. This being the situation, it follows, as the trial court concluded, that there was here no contract or agreement between these two parties either preceding or derived from their exchange of telegrams.

COLUMBIA HYUNDAI, INC. v. CARLL HYUNDAI, INC., 326 S.C. 78, 484 S.E.2d 468 (1997). In early 1993, Gibbes negotiated with Carll to purchase Carll's Hyundai automobile dealership. After several months of negotiations, and numerous drafts, Carll submitted an "Agreement for Purchase and Sale of Assets" to Gibbes. Paragraph I(a) of the proposed agreement provided for the purchase by Gibbs of "All of Seller's right title and interest in and to all saleable new Hyundai vehicles in existence at the close of business on the last business day before final closing date...." Gibbes signed the proposed agreement but added the words "current year" before the words "Hyundai vehicles." This meant that Gibbes would not be obliged to purchase any of Carll's saleable new Hyundi vehicles that had been manufactured before the current year. Upon receipt of the agreement from Gibbes, Carll advised Gibbes that its "counter-offer" was rejected. Gibbes instituted suit for breach of contract and specific performance. The trial judge submitted the issue to the jury, which found there was no contract. Gibbes appealed. Affirmed.

"Adoption of § 2–207 resulted from what is commonly known as 'the battle of the forms' in which parties exchange preprinted, standardized forms to finalize their bargain, which forms tend to use 'boilerplate language' and omit material terms'....

"However, there are some situations which simply do not warrant application of § 2–207. It has been noted by Professors White and Summers that in the case of non-form agreements, there is no pattern of exchange of printed forms. Under such circumstances, when the parties fully negotiate each provision of a contract, a contract may be 'beyond the reach of 2–207 and adrift on the murky sea of common law.' White and Summers, § 1–3 at p. 29.... We find the present case presents such a situation. The parties met and negotiated the provisions of their contract, through their attorneys, for several months. They exchanged at least four draft proposals, making numerous changes....

"Under the limited factual circumstances presented here, we find this is simply not a 'battle of the forms' case; on the contrary, this was merely one more in a series of contract negotiations. Accordingly, we find section 2–207 inapplicable to the present facts. Therefore, we find the matter of the existence of a contract was properly submitted to the jury."

CISG ART. 19

[See Selected Source Materials Supplement]

UNIDROIT PRINCIPLES OF INTERNATIONAL COMMERCIAL CONTRACTS ARTS. 2.1.12, 2.1.22

[See Selected Source Materials Supplement]

PRINCIPLES OF EUROPEAN CONTRACT LAW ART. 2.209

[See Selected Source Materials Supplement]

GARDNER ZEMKE CO. v. DUNHAM BUSH, INC.

Supreme Court of New Mexico, 1993.
115 N.M. 260, 850 P.2d 319.

Franchini, Justice.

This case involves a contract for the sale of goods and accordingly the governing law is the Uniform Commercial Code—Sales, as adopted in New Mexico. NMSA 1978, §§ 55-2-101 to-2-725 (Orig.Pamp. & Cum.Supp.1992) (Article 2). In the course of our discussion, we will also refer to pertinent general definitions and principles of construction found in NMSA 1978, Sections 55-1-101 to-1-209 (Orig.Pamp. & Cum.Supp.1992). Section 55-2-103(4). The case presents us with our first opportunity to consider a classic "battle of the forms" scenario arising under Section 55-2-207. Appellant Gardner Zemke challenges the trial court's judgment that a Customer's Acknowledgment (Acknowledgment) sent by appellee manufacturer Dunham Bush, in response to a Gardner Zemke Purchase Order (Order), operated as a counteroffer, thereby providing controlling warranty terms under the contract formed by the parties. We find merit in appellants' argument and remand for the trial court's reconsideration.

I.

Acting as the general contractor on a Department of Energy (DOE) project, Gardner Zemke issued its Order to Dunham Bush for air-conditioning equipment, known as chillers, to be used in connection with the project. The Order contained a one-year manufacturer's warranty provision and the requirement that the chillers comply with specifications attached to the Order. Dunham Bush responded with its preprinted Acknowledgment containing extensive warranty disclaimers, a statement that the terms of the Acknowledgment controlled the parties' agreement, and a provision deeming silence to be acquiescence to the terms of the Acknowledgment.

The parties did not address the discrepancies in the forms exchanged and proceeded with the transaction. Dunham Bush delivered the chillers, and Gardner Zemke paid for them. Gardner Zemke alleges that the chillers provided did not comply with their specifications and that they incurred additional costs to install the nonconforming goods. Approximately five or six months after start up of the chillers, a DOE representative notified Gardner Zemke of problems with two of the chillers. In a series of letters, Gardner

Zemke requested on-site warranty repairs. Through its manufacturer's representative, Dunham Bush offered to send its mechanic to the job site to inspect the chillers and absorb the cost of the service call only if problems discovered were within any component parts it provided. Further, Dunham Bush required that prior to the service call a purchase order be issued from the DOE, to be executed by Dunham Bush for payment for their services in the event their mechanic discovered problems not caused by manufacturing defects. Gardner Zemke rejected the proposal on the basis that the DOE had a warranty still in effect for the goods and would not issue a separate purchase order for warranty repairs.

Ultimately, the DOE hired an independent contractor to repair the two chillers. The DOE paid $24,245.00 for the repairs and withheld $20,000.00 from its contract with Gardner Zemke.[1] This breach of contract action then ensued, with Gardner Zemke alleging failure by Dunham Bush to provide equipment in accordance with the project plans and specifications and failure to provide warranty service.

II.

On cross-motions for summary judgment, the trial court granted partial summary judgment in favor of Dunham Bush, ruling that its Acknowledgment was a counteroffer to the Gardner Zemke Order and that the Acknowledgment's warranty limitations and disclaimers were controlling. Gardner Zemke filed an application for interlocutory appeal from the partial summary judgment in this Court, which was denied. A bench trial was held in December 1991, and the trial court again ruled the Acknowledgment was a counteroffer which Gardner Zemke accepted by silence and that under the warranty provisions of the Acknowledgment, Gardner Zemke was not entitled to damages.

On appeal, Gardner Zemke raises two issues: (1) the trial court erred as a matter of law in ruling that the Acknowledgment was a counteroffer; and (2) Gardner Zemke proved breach of contract and contract warranty, breach of code warranties, and damages.

III.

Karl N. Llewellyn, the principal draftsman of Article 2, described it as "[t]he heart of the Code." Karl N. Llewellyn, *Why We Need the Uniform Commercial Code,* 10 U.Fla.L.Rev. 367, 378 (1957). Section 2–207 is characterized by commentators as a "crucial section of Article 2" and an "iconoclastic Code section." *Bender's Uniform Commercial Code Service* (Vol. 3, Richard W. Duesenberg & Lawrence P. King, Sales & Bulk Transfers Under The Uniform Commercial Code) § 3.01 at 3–2 (1992). Recognizing its innovative purpose and complex structure Duesenberg and King further observe Section 2–207 "is one of the most important, subtle, and difficult in the entire Code, and well it may be said that the product as it finally reads is not altogether satisfactory." *Id.* § 3.02 at 3–13.

---

1. The government has the right to set off the remaining $4,245.00 from any other Gardner Zemke government contract. *See Project* *Map, Inc. v. United States,* 203 Ct.Cl. 52, 486 F.2d 1375 (1973) (per curiam).

Section 55–2–207 provides:

(1) A definite and seasonable expression of acceptance or a written confirmation which is sent within a reasonable time operates as an acceptance even though it states terms additional to or different from those offered or agreed upon, unless acceptance is expressly made conditional on assent to the additional or different terms.

(2) The additional terms are to be construed as proposals for addition to the contract. Between merchants such terms become part of the contract unless:

(a) the offer expressly limits acceptance to the terms of the offer;

(b) they materially alter it; or,

(c) notification of objection to them has already been given or is given within a reasonable time after notice of them is received.

(3) Conduct by both parties which recognizes the existence of a contract is sufficient to establish a contract for sale although the writings of the parties do not otherwise establish a contract. In such case the terms of the particular contract consist of those terms on which the writings of the parties agree, together with any supplementary terms incorporated under any other provisions of this act [this chapter].

Relying on Section 2–207(1), Gardner Zemke argues that the trial court erred in concluding that the Dunham Bush Acknowledgment was a counteroffer rather than an acceptance. Gardner Zemke asserts that even though the Acknowledgment contained terms different from or in addition to the terms of their Order, it did not make acceptance expressly conditional on assent to the different or additional terms and therefore should operate as an acceptance rather than a counteroffer.

At common law, the "mirror image" rule applied to the formation of contracts, and the terms of the acceptance had to exactly imitate or "mirror" the terms of the offer. *Idaho Power Co. v. Westinghouse Elec. Corp.*, 596 F.2d 924, 926 (9th Cir.1979). If the accepting terms were different from or additional to those in the offer, the result was a counteroffer, not an acceptance. *Id.; see also Silva v. Noble*, 85 N.M. 677, 678–79, 515 P.2d 1281, 1282–83 (1973). Thus, from a common law perspective, the trial court's conclusion that the Dunham Bush Acknowledgment was a counteroffer was correct.

However, the drafters of the Code "intended to change the common law in an attempt to conform contract law to modern day business transactions." *Leonard Pevar Co. v. Evans Prods. Co.*, 524 F.Supp. 546, 551 (D.Del.1981). As Professors White and Summers explain:

The rigidity of the common law rule ignored the modern realities of commerce. Where preprinted forms are used to structure deals, they rarely mirror each other, yet the parties usually assume they have a binding contract and act accordingly. Section 2–207 rejects the common law mirror image rule and converts many common law counteroffers into acceptances under 2–207(1).

James J. White & Robert S. Summers, *Handbook of the Law Under the Uniform Commercial Code* § 1–3 at 29–30 (3d ed. 1988) (footnotes omitted).

On its face, Section 2–207(1) provides that a document responding to an offer and purporting to be an acceptance will be an acceptance, despite the presence of additional and different terms. Where merchants exchange pre-printed forms and the essential contract terms agree, a contract is formed under Section 2–207(1). Duesenberg & King, § 3.04 at 3–47 to–49. A responding document will fall outside of the provisions of Section 2–207(1) and convey a counteroffer, only when its terms differ radically from the offer, or when "acceptance is expressly made conditional on assent to the additional or different terms"—whether a contract is formed under Section 2–207(1) here turns on the meaning given this phrase.

Dunham Bush argues that the language in its Acknowledgment makes acceptance expressly conditional on assent to the additional or different terms set forth in the Acknowledgment. The face of the Acknowledgment states:

> IT IS UNDERSTOOD THAT OUR ACCEPTANCE OF THIS ORDER IS SUBJECT TO THE TERMS AND CONDITIONS ENUMERATED ON THE REVERSE SIDE HEREOF, IT BEING STRICTLY UNDERSTOOD THAT THESE TERMS AND CONDITIONS BECOME A PART OF THIS ORDER AND THE ACKNOWLEDGMENT THEREOF.

The following was among the terms and conditions on the reverse side of the Acknowledgment.

> Failure of the Buyer to object in writing within five (5) days of receipt thereof to Terms of Sale contained in the Seller's acceptance and/or acknowledgment, or other communications, shall be deemed an acceptance of such Terms of Sale by Buyer.

In support of its contention that the above language falls within the "expressly conditional" provision of Section 2–207, Dunham Bush urges that we adopt the view taken by the First Circuit in *Roto–Lith, Ltd. v. F.P. Bartlett & Co.*, 297 F.2d 497 (1st Cir.1962). There, Roto–Lith sent an order for goods to Bartlett, which responded with an acknowledgment containing warranty disclaimers, a statement that the acknowledgment reflected the terms of the sale, and a provision that if the terms were unacceptable Roto–Lith should notify Bartlett at once. *Id.* at 498–99. Roto–Lith did not protest the terms of the acknowledgment and accepted and paid for the goods. The court held the Bartlett acknowledgment was a counteroffer that became binding on Roto–Lith with its acceptance of the goods, reasoning that "a response which states a condition materially altering the obligation solely to the disadvantage of the offeror" falls within the "expressly conditional" language of 2–207(1). *Id.* at 500.

Dunham Bush suggests that this Court has demonstrated alliance with the principles of *Roto–Lith* in *Fratello v. Socorro Electric Cooperative, Inc.*, 107 N.M. 378, 758 P.2d 792 (1988). *Fratello* involved the terms of a settlement agreement in which one party sent the other party a proposed stipulated order containing an additional term. In the context of the common law, we cited *Roto–Lith* in support of the proposition that the additional term made the proposed stipulation a counteroffer. *Fratello,* 107 N.M. at 381, 758 P.2d at 795.

We have never adopted *Roto–Lith* in the context of the Code and decline to do so now. While ostensibly interpreting Section 2–207(1), the First Circuit's analysis imposes the common law doctrine of offer and acceptance on language designed to avoid the common law result. *Roto–Lith* has been almost uniformly criticized by the courts and commentators as an aberration on

Article 2 jurisprudence. *Leonard Pevar Co.,* 524 F.Supp. at 551 (and cases cited therein); Duesenberg & King, § 3.05[1] at 3–61 to–62; White & Summers, § 1–3 at 36–37.

Mindful of the purpose of Section 2–207 and the spirit of Article 2, we find the better approach suggested in *Dorton v. Collins & Aikman Corp.,* 453 F.2d 1161 (6th Cir.1972). In *Dorton,* the Sixth Circuit considered terms in acknowledgment forms sent by Collins & Aikman similar to the terms in the Dunham Bush Acknowledgment. The Collins & Aikman acknowledgments provided that acceptance of orders was subject to the terms and conditions of their form, together with at least seven methods in which a buyer might acquiesce to their terms, including receipt and retention of their form for ten days without objection. *Id.* at 1167–68.

Concentrating its analysis on the concept of the offeror's "assent," the Court reasoned that it was not enough to make acceptance expressly conditional on additional or different terms; instead, the expressly conditional nature of the acceptance must be predicated on the offeror's "assent" to those terms. *Id.* at 1168. The Court concluded that the "expressly conditional" provision of Section 2–207(1) "was intended to apply only to an acceptance which clearly reveals that the offeree is unwilling to proceed with the transaction unless he is assured of the offeror's assent to the additional or different terms therein." *Id.* This approach has been widely accepted. *Diatom, Inc. v. Pennwalt Corp.,* 741 F.2d 1569, 1576–77 (10th Cir.1984); *Reaction Molding Technologies, Inc. v. General Elec. Co.,* 588 F.Supp. 1280, 1288 (E.D.Pa.1984); *Idaho Power Co.,* 596 F.2d at 926–27.

We agree with the court in *Dorton* that the inquiry focuses on whether the offeree clearly and unequivocally communicated to the offeror that its willingness to enter into a bargain was conditioned on the offeror's "assent" to additional or different terms. An exchange of forms containing identical dickered terms, such as the identity, price, and quantity of goods, and conflicting undickered boilerplate provisions, such as warranty terms and a provision making the bargain subject to the terms and conditions of the offeree's document, however worded, will not propel the transaction into the "expressly conditional" language of Section 2–207(1) and confer the status of counteroffer on the responsive document.

While *Dorton* articulates a laudable rule, it fails to provide a means for the determination of when a responsive document becomes a counteroffer. We adopt the rule in *Dorton* and add that whether an acceptance is made expressly conditional on assent to different or additional terms is dependent on the commercial context of the transaction. Official Comment 2 to Section 55–2–207 suggests that "[u]nder this article a proposed deal which in commercial understanding has in fact been closed is recognized as a contract." While the comment applies broadly and envisions recognition of contracts formed under a variety of circumstances, it guides us to application of the concept of "commercial understanding" to the question of formation. *See* 2 William D. Hawkland, *Uniform Commercial Code Series* § 2–207:02 at 160 (1992) ("The basic question is whether, in commercial understanding, the proposed deal has been closed.").

Discerning whether "commercial understanding" dictates the existence of a contract requires consideration of the objective manifestations of the parties' understanding of the bargain. It requires consideration of the parties' activities and interaction during the making of the bargain; and when available, relevant evidence of course of performance, Section 55–2–208; and course of dealing and usage of the trade, Section 55–1–205. The question guiding the inquiry should be whether the offeror could reasonably believe that in the context of the commercial setting in which the parties were acting, a contract had been formed. This determination requires a very fact specific inquiry. *See* John E. Murray, Jr., *Section 2–207 Of The Uniform Commercial Code: Another Word About Incipient Unconscionability,* 39 U.Pitt.L.Rev., 597, 632–34 (1978) (discussing *Dorton* and identifying the commercial understanding of the reasonable buyer as the "critical inquiry").

Our analysis does not yield an iron clad rule conducive to perfunctory application. However, it does remain true to the spirit of Article 2, as it calls the trial court to consider the commercial setting of each transaction and the reasonable expectations and beliefs of the parties acting in that setting. *Id.* at 600; § 55–1–102(2)(b) (stating one purpose of the act is "to permit the continued expansion of commercial practices through custom, usage and agreement of the parties").

The trial court's treatment of this issue did not encompass the scope of the inquiry we envision. We will not attempt to make the factual determination necessary to characterize this transaction on the record before us. Not satisfied that the trial court adequately considered all of the relevant factors in determining that the Dunham Bush Acknowledgment functioned as a counteroffer, we remand for reconsideration of the question.

In the event the trial court concludes that the Dunham Bush Acknowledgment constituted an acceptance, it will face the question of which terms will control in the exchange of forms. In the interest of judicial economy, and because this determination is a question of law, we proceed with our analysis.

IV.

The Gardner Zemke Order provides that the "[m]anufacturer shall replace or repair all parts found to be defective during initial year of use at no additional cost." Because the Order does not include any warranty terms, Article 2 express and implied warranties arise by operation of law. Section 55–2–313 (express warranties), § 55–2–314 (implied warranty of merchantability), § 55–2–315 (implied warranty of fitness for a particular purpose). The Dunham Bush Acknowledgment contains the following warranty terms.

WARRANTY: We agree that the apparatus manufactured by the Seller will be free from defects in material and workmanship for a period of one year under normal use and service and when properly installed: and our obligation under this agreement is limited solely to repair or replacement at our option, at our factories, of any part or parts thereof which shall within one year from date of original installation or 18 months from date of shipment from factory to the original purchaser, whichever date may first occur be returned to us with transportation charges prepaid which our examination shall disclose to our satisfaction to have been defective. THIS AGREEMENT TO REPAIR OR REPLACE DEFECTIVE PARTS IS EXPRESSLY IN LIEU OF AND IS HEREBY DISCLAIMER OF ALL OTHER EXPRESS WARRANTIES, AND IS IN LIEU OF AND IN DISCLAIMER AND EXCLUSION OF ANY IMPLIED WARRANTIES OF MERCHANTABILITY AND FITNESS FOR A PAR-

TICULAR PURPOSE, AS WELL AS ALL OTHER IMPLIED WARRAN-
TIES, IN LAW OR EQUITY, AND OF ALL OTHER OBLIGATIONS OR
LIABILITIES ON OUR PART. THERE ARE NO WARRANTIES WHICH
EXTEND BEYOND THE DESCRIPTION HEREOF.... Our obligation
to repair or replace shall not apply to any apparatus which shall have
been repaired or altered outside our factory in any way.

The one proposition on which most courts and commentators agree at
this point in the construction of the statute is that Section 2–207(3) applies
only if a contract is not found under Section 2–207(1). *Dorton,* 453 F.2d at
1166; Duesenberg & King, § 3.03[1] at 3–40; 2 Hawkland, § 2–207:04 at 178–
79; White & Summers, § 1–3 at 35. However, there are courts that disagree
even with this proposition. *See Westinghouse Elec. Corp. v. Nielsons, Inc.,* 647
F.Supp. 896 (D.Colo.1986) (dealing with different terms, finding a contract
under 2–207(1) and proceeding to apply 2–207(2) and 2–207(3)).

The language of the statute makes it clear that "additional" terms are
subject to the provisions of Section 2–207(2). However, a continuing controversy rages among courts and commentators concerning the treatment of
"different" terms in a Section 2–207 analysis. While Section 2–207(1) refers to
both "additional or different" terms, Section 2–207(2) refers only to "additional" terms. The omission of the word "different" from Section 55–2–207(2)
gives rise to the questions of whether "different" terms are to be dealt with
under the provisions of Section 2–207(2), and if not, how they are to be
treated. That the terms in the Acknowledgment are "different" rather than
"additional" guides the remainder of our inquiry and requires that we join
the fray. Initially, we briefly survey the critical and judicial approaches to the
problem posed by "different" terms.

One view is that, in spite of the omission, "different" terms are to be
analyzed under Section 2–207(2). 2 Hawkland, § 2–207:03 at 168. The foundation for this position is found in Comment 3, which provides "[w]hether or
not additional or different terms will become part of the agreement depends
upon the provisions of Subsection (2)." Armed with this statement in Comment 3, proponents point to the ambiguity in the distinction between "different" and "additional" terms and argue that the distinction serves no clear
purpose. *Steiner v. Mobil Oil Corp.,* 20 Cal.3d 90, 141 Cal.Rptr. 157, 165–66 n.
5, 569 P.2d 751, 759–60 n. 5 (1977); *Boese–Hilburn Co. v. Dean Machinery
Co.,* 616 S.W.2d 520, 527 (Mo.Ct.App.1981). Following this rationale in this
case, and relying on the observation in Comment 4 that a clause negating
implied warranties would "materially alter" the contract, the Dunham Bush
warranty terms would not become a part of the contract, and the Gardner
Zemke warranty provision, together with the Article 2 warranties would
control. § 55–2–207(2)(b).

Another approach is suggested by Duesenberg and King who comment
that the ambiguity found in the treatment of "different" and "additional"
terms is more judicially created than statutorily supported. While conceding
that Comment 3 "contributes to the confusion," they also admonish that "the
Official Comments do not happen to be the statute." Duesenberg & King,
§ 3.05 at 3–52. Observing that "the drafters knew what they were doing, and
that they did not sloppily fail to include the term 'different' when drafting
subsection (2)," Duesenberg and King postulate that a "different" term in a
responsive document operating as an acceptance can never become a part of

the parties' contract under the plain language of the statute. *Id.* § 3.03[1] at 3–38.

The reasoning supporting this position is that once an offeror addresses a subject it implicitly objects to variance of that subject by the offeree, thereby preventing the "different" term from becoming a part of the contract by prior objection and obviating the need to refer to "different" terms in Section 55–2–207(2). *Id.* § 3.05[1] at 3–77; *Air Prods. & Chems. Inc. v. Fairbanks Morse, Inc.,* 58 Wis.2d 193, 206 N.W.2d 414, 423–25 (1973). Professor Summers lends support to this position. White & Summers, § 1–3 at 34. Although indulging a different analysis, following this view in the case before us creates a result identical to that flowing from application of the provisions of Section 2–207(2) as discussed above—the Dunham Bush warranty provisions fall out, and the stated Gardner Zemke and Article 2 warranty provisions apply.

Yet a third analysis arises from Comment 6, which in pertinent part states:

> Where clauses on confirming forms sent by both parties conflict each party must be assumed to object to a clause of the other conflicting with one on the confirmation sent by himself. As a result the requirement that there be notice of objection which is found in Subsection (2) is satisfied and the conflicting terms do not become a part of the contract. The contract then consists of the terms originally expressly agreed to, terms on which the confirmations agree, and terms supplied by this act, including Subsection (2).

The import of Comment 6 is that "different" terms cancel each other out and that existing applicable code provisions stand in their place. The obvious flaws in Comment 6 are the use of the words "confirming forms," suggesting the Comment applies only to variant confirmation forms and not variant offer and acceptance forms, and the reference to Subsection 55–2–207(2)—arguably dealing only with "additional" terms—in the context of "different" terms. Of course, Duesenberg and King remind us that Comment 6 "is only a comment, and a poorly drawn one at that." Duesenberg & King, § 3.05[1] at 3–79.

The analysis arising from Comment 6, however, has found acceptance in numerous jurisdictions including the Tenth Circuit. *Daitom, Inc. v. Pennwalt Corp.,* 741 F.2d 1569, 1578–79 (10th Cir.1984). Following a discussion similar to the one we have just indulged, the court found this the preferable approach. *Id.* at 1579; *accord Southern Idaho Pipe & Steel Co. v. Cal–Cut Pipe & Supply, Inc.,* 98 Idaho 495, 567 P.2d 1246, 1254–55 (1977), *appeal dismissed and cert. denied,* 434 U.S. 1056, 98 S.Ct. 1225, 55 L.Ed.2d 757 (1978). Professor White also finds merit in this analysis. White & Summers, § 1–3 at 33–35. Application of this approach here cancels out the parties' conflicting warranty terms and allows the warranty provisions of Article 2 to control.

We are unable to find comfort or refuge in concluding that any one of the three paths drawn through the contours of Section 2–207 is more consistent with or true to the language of the statute. We do find that the analysis relying on Comment 6 is the most consistent with the purpose and spirit of the Code in general and Article 2 in particular. We are mindful that the overriding goal of Article 2 is to discern the bargain struck by the contracting parties. However, there are times where the conduct of the parties makes realizing that goal impossible. In such cases, we find guidance in the Code's commitment to fairness, Section 55–1–102(3); good faith, Sections 55–1–203 & –2–103(1)(b); and conscionable conduct, Section 55–2–302.

While Section 2–207 was designed to avoid the common law result that gave the advantage to the party sending the last form, we cannot conclude that the statute was intended to shift that advantage to the party sending the first form. Such a result will generally follow from the first two analyses discussed. We adopt the third analysis as the most even-handed resolution of a difficult problem. We are also aware that under this analysis even though the conflicting terms cancel out, the Code may provide a term similar to one rejected. We agree with Professor White that "[a]t least a term so supplied has the merit of being a term that the draftsmen considered fair." White & Summers, § 1–3 at 35.

Due to our disposition of this case, we do not address the second issue raised by Gardner Zemke. On remand, should the trial court conclude a contract was formed under Section 2–207(1), the conflicting warranty provisions in the parties' forms will cancel out, and the warranty provisions of Article 2 will control.

IT IS SO ORDERED.

Baca, J., and Patricio M. Serna, District Judge (sitting by designation).

NOTE ON GARDNER ZEMKE

The rule approved in *Gardner Zemke,* that when a contract is formed under UCC § 2–207 conflicting terms in the offer and acceptance cancel each other out, is commonly referred to as the "knockout" rule, because under the rule conflicting terms knock each other out of the parties' agreement. In Dorton v. Collins & Aikman Corp., 453 F.2d 1161 (6th Cir.1972), the court applied the knockout rule where one of the conflicting terms was implied, rather than express.

NOTE ON THE MEANING OF "MATERIALLY ALTER" UNDER UCC § 2–207(2)(b)

Notwithstanding the knockout rule, a contract formed under UCC § 2–207(1) may include important terms that are neither in both forms, supplied by other provisions of Article 2, nor supplied by trade usage. In particular, important terms may be added by an acceptance, if the offeror fails to either expressly limit acceptance to the terms of the offer under subsection (2)(a), object to the added terms in the acceptance under subsection (2)(c), or include contrary terms in the offer so that both the offeror's terms and the offeree's added terms drop away under the knockout rule.

It is true that under subsection (2)(b), a term that is added by an acceptance does not become part of the contract if the term would "materially alter" the contract. Furthermore, in general usage a term in a contract would be considered "material" if it had economic significance or would be likely to affect a party's decision whether to enter into the contract. Accordingly, if the language of subsection (2)(b) was given its ordinary meaning, an added term that is economically significant or would be likely to affect a party's decision whether to enter into the contract would be excluded under that subsection. However, the Official Comment to section 2–207 utilizes a different test for materiality—whether the added term would result in "surprise or hardship":

> 4. Examples of typical clauses which would normally "materially alter" the contract and so result in surprise or hardship if incorporated without express awareness by the other party are: a clause negating such standard warranties as that of merchantability or fitness for a particular purpose in circumstances in which either warranty normally attaches ... [or] a clause requiring that complaints be made in a time materially shorter than customary or reasonable.

> 5. Examples of clauses which involve no element of unreasonable surprise and which therefore are to be incorporated in the contract unless notice of objection is seasonably given are: a clause setting forth and perhaps enlarging slightly upon the seller's exemption due to supervening causes beyond his control, similar to those covered by the provision of this Article on merchant's excuse by failure of presupposed conditions or ... a clause fixing a reasonable time for complaints within customary limits ... ; a clause providing for interest on overdue invoices or fixing the seller's standard credit terms where they are within the range of trade practice and do not limit any credit bargained for; a clause limiting the right of rejection for defects which fall within the customary trade tolerances for acceptance "with adjustment" or otherwise limiting remedy in a reasonable manner (see Sections 2–718 and 2–719).

Relying on the test and illustrations set out in the Official Comment, a number of cases have upheld the inclusion of additional terms in an acceptance, even though the terms were material in the ordinary sense of that term, on the ground that they did not result in surprise or hardship. For example, in Aceros Prefabricados, S.A. v. TradeArbed, Inc., 282 F.3d 92 (2d Cir. 2002), the court held that an added term in the acceptance that required all disputes to be arbitrated did not result in a material alteration of the contract under subsection (b)(2):

> A material alteration is one that would "result in surprise or hardship if incorporated without express awareness by the other party." ... U.C.C. § 2–207 cmt. 4; *Bayway Ref. [Co. v. Oxygenated Mktg. & Trading A.G.*, 215 F.3d 219,] 224 (2d. Cir. 2000). Surprise includes both a subjective element of what a party actually knew and an objective element of what a party should have known. *Id.* We have stated that "[a] profession of surprise and raised eyebrows are not enough." *Id.* Instead, "[t]o carry [its] burden ... [the nonassenting] party must establish that, under the circumstances, it cannot be presumed that a reasonable merchant would have consented to the additional term." *Id.*

Similarly, in Southern Illinois Riverboat Casino Cruises, Inc. v. Triangle Insulation and Sheet Metal Co., 302 F.3d 667 (7th Cir. 2002), the court held that the addition of a term in an acceptance that significantly limited the buyer's remedies did not result in a material alteration of the contract under subsection 2(b).

Another issue in this context is the meaning of the "hardship" test in the Comment to section 2–207. Most cases have treated "hardship" as a criterion that is independent of surprise in determining whether a term constitutes a material alteration under UCC § 2–207(2)(b). For example, in Maxon Corp. v. Tyler Pipe Industries, Inc., 497 N.E.2d 570 (Ind.App. 1986), the court said:

... [E]ven if Tyler [the offeror] was not surprised by the indemnity clause in Maxon's invoice, the clause is nevertheless a material alteration if its incorporation without Tyler's express awareness would result in hardship.

There can be no doubt that Maxon's indemnity clause would impose serious hardship if incorporated without Tyler's express awareness. By its very nature, a clause which shifts liability from a negligent party to an innocent party imposes hardship. Accordingly, we hold that Maxon's indemnity clause constitutes a material alteration as a matter of law.

Similarly, in Horning Co. v. Falconer Glass Industries, Inc., 730 F.Supp. 962 (S.D.Ind.1990), the court held that although a term limiting consequential damages was not surprising, because of industry practice, the term did not become part of the contract, because it would result in hardship.

Some cases, however, suggest or imply that if an added term is not surprising it will not be deemed to cause hardship. Union Carbide Corp. v. Oscar Mayer Foods Corp., 947 F.2d 1333 (7th Cir. 1991); cf *Aceros*, supra.

NOTE ON THE "EXPRESSLY MADE CONDITIONAL" CLAUSE

Under section 2–207, the inclusion of an "expressly made conditional" or "conditional-assent" provision in a response to offer can have significant consequences. The question then arises, what kind of language is necessary to constitute such a provision. Some courts have effectively held that unless language in a response to an offer virtually tracks the "expressly made conditional" clause of UCC § 2–207(1), it will not be treated as a conditional assent under that section. In Dorton v. Collins & Aikman Corp., 453 F.2d 1161 (6th Cir.1972), cited with approval in *Gardner Zemke,* the court said, "In order to fall within [the conditional-assent] proviso, it is not enough that an acceptance is expressly conditional on additional or different terms; rather, an acceptance must be *expressly* conditional on the offeror's *assent* to those terms. Viewing the Subsection (1) proviso within the context of the rest of that Subsection and within the policies of Section 2–207 itself, we believe that it was intended to apply only to an acceptance which clearly reveals that the offeree is unwilling to proceed with the transaction unless he is assured of the offeror's assent to the additional or different terms therein.... That the acceptance is predicated on the offeror's assent must be 'directly and distinctly stated or expressed rather than implied or left to inference.' Webster's Third International Dictionary (defining 'express')." (Emphasis by the court.)

Other courts have taken a less stringent view. For example, in Step–Saver Data Systems, Inc. v. Wyse Technology, 939 F.2d 91 (3d Cir.1991), the court said:

To determine whether a writing constitutes a conditional acceptance, courts have established [various] tests....

[Under one approach an acceptance is] conditional when certain key words or phrases are used, such as a written confirmation stating that "the terms of the confirmation are the only ones upon which we will accept orders." [Another] approach requires the offeree to demonstrate an unwillingness to proceed with the transaction unless the additional or different terms are included in the contract.

Although we are not certain that these ... two approaches would generate differing answers, we adopt the [latter] approach for our analysis because it best reflects the understanding of commercial transactions developed in the UCC....

NOTE ON THE EFFECT OF CONFIRMATIONS WITH ADDITIONAL TERMS

It's important to bear in mind that under UCC § 2–207 it is possible for additional terms to become part of a contract even if the terms are not proposed until after the contract is made. As pointed out in Aceros Prefabricados, S.A. v. TradeArbed ["TA"], 282 F.3d 92 (2d Cir. 2002):

Under [the UCC] an expression of acceptance or written confirmation that sets forth terms in addition to those initially agreed upon will not defeat formation of a binding contract. Instead, a contract will be found and the additional terms ... are then treated as "proposals" for addition to the contract.... [Emphasis added.] An Official Comment to section 2–207 makes clear the applicability of that provision to these two situations:

Under this Article a proposed deal which in commercial understanding has in fact been closed is recognized as a contract. Therefore, any additional matter contained *either in the writing intended to close the deal or in a later confirmation* falls within subsection (2) and must be regarded as a proposal for an added term....

... U.C.C. § 2–207 cmt. 2. Therefore, were we to find that the contract between Aceros and TA was formed on January 12, as Aceros claims and as the district court held, then the three confirmation orders would constitute written confirmations stating terms additional to the January 12 agreement, and analysis would proceed under section 2–207(2).*

Were we to agree instead with TA's argument that each of its order confirmations served as a separate acceptance of individual prior offers by Aceros to purchase steel, the confirmations would then constitute acceptances proposing additional terms and analysis would likewise proceed under section 2–207(2), albeit of three individual contracts. Both contract formation scenarios lead us to the same conclusion regarding the [effect of the additional term].

---

* Emphasis by the court. (Footnote by ed.)

Of course, an additional term in a confirmation, like an additional term in an acceptance, will not become part of a contract if it is excluded under section 2–207(2)(a), (b), or (c), or by the knockout rule.

DIAMOND FRUIT GROWERS, INC. v. KRACK CORP.

United States Court of Appeals, Ninth Circuit, 1986.
794 F.2d 1440.

Before FLETCHER, ALARCON, and WIGGINS, CIRCUIT JUDGES.

WIGGINS, CIRCUIT JUDGE:

Metal–Matic, Inc. (Metal–Matic) appeals from judgment entered after a jury verdict in favor of Krack Corporation (Krack) on Krack's third-party complaint against Metal–Matic. Metal–Matic also appeals from the district court's denial of its motion for judgment n.o.v. We have jurisdiction under 28 U.S.C. § 1291 (1982) and affirm.

FACTS AND PROCEEDINGS BELOW

Krack is a manufacturer of cooling units that contain steel tubing it purchases from outside suppliers. Metal–Matic is one of Krack's tubing suppliers. At the time this dispute arose, Metal–Matic had been supplying tubing to Krack for about ten years. The parties followed the same course of dealing during the entire ten years. At the beginning of each year, Krack sent a blanket purchase order to Metal–Matic stating how much tubing Krack would need for the year. Then, throughout the year as Krack needed tubing, it sent release purchase orders to Metal–Matic requesting that tubing be shipped. Metal–Matic responded to Krack's release purchase orders by sending Krack an acknowledgment form and then shipping the tubing.[2]

Metal–Matic's acknowledgment form disclaimed all liability for consequential damages and limited Metal–Matic's liability for defects in the tubing to refund of the purchase price or replacement or repair of the tubing. As one would expect, these terms were not contained in Krack's purchase order. The following statement was printed on Metal–Matic's form: "Metal–Matic, Inc.'s acceptance of purchaser's offer or its offer to purchaser is hereby expressly made conditional to purchaser's acceptance of the terms and provisions of the acknowledgment form." This statement and the disclaimer of liability were on the back of the acknowledgment form. However, printed at the bottom of the front of the form in bold-face capitals was the following statement: "SEE REVERSE SIDE FOR TERMS AND CONDITIONS OF SALE."

On at least one occasion during the ten-year relationship between Metal–Matic and Krack, Allen Zver, Krack's purchasing manager, discussed the limitation of warranty and disclaimer of liability terms contained in Metal–Matic's acknowledgment form with Robert Van Krevelen, Executive Vice President of Metal–Matic. Zver told Van Krevelen that Krack objected to the terms and tried to convince him to change them, but Van Krevelen refused to

---

2. The blanket purchase order apparently did no more than establish Krack's willingness to purchase an amount of tubing during the year. The parties' conduct indicates that they intended to establish their contract based on Krack's release purchase orders and Metal–Matic's acknowledgments sent in response to those purchase orders.

do so. After the discussions, Krack continued to accept and pay for tubing from Metal–Matic.[3]

In February 1981, Krack sold one of its cooling units to Diamond Fruit Growers, Inc. (Diamond) in Oregon, and in September 1981, Diamond installed the unit in a controlled-atmosphere warehouse. In January 1982, the unit began leaking ammonia from a cooling coil made of steel tubing.

After Diamond discovered that ammonia was leaking into the warehouse, Joseph Smith, the engineer who had been responsible for building Diamond's controlled-atmosphere warehouses, was called in to find the source of the leak. Smith testified that he found a pinhole leak in the cooling coil of the Krack cooling unit. Smith inspected the coil while it was still inside the unit. He last inspected the coil on April 23, 1982. The coil then sat in a hall at Diamond's warehouse until May, 1984, when John Myers inspected the coil for Metal–Matic.

Myers cut the defective tubing out of the unit and took it to his office. At his office, he did more cutting on the tubing. After Myers inspected the tubing, it was also inspected by Bruce Wong for Diamond and Paul Irish for Krack.

Diamond sued Krack to recover the loss in value of fruit that it was forced to remove from the storage room as a result of the leak. Krack in turn brought a third-party complaint against Metal–Matic and Van Huffel Tube Corporation (Van Huffel), another of its tubing suppliers, seeking contribution or indemnity in the event it was held liable to Diamond. At the close of the evidence, both Metal–Matic and Van Huffel moved for a directed verdict on the third party complaint. The court granted Van Huffel's motion based on evidence that the failed tubing was not manufactured by Van Huffel. The court denied Metal–Matic's motion.

The jury returned a verdict in favor of Diamond against Krack. It then found that Krack was entitled to contribution from Metal–Matic for thirty percent of Diamond's damages. Metal–Matic moved for judgment n.o.v. The court denied that motion and entered judgment on the jury verdict.

Metal–Matic raises two grounds for reversal. First, Metal–Matic contends that as part of its contract with Krack, it disclaimed all liability for consequential damages and specifically limited its liability for defects in the tubing to refund of the purchase price or replacement or repair of the tubing. Second, Metal–Matic asserts that the evidence does not support a finding that it manufactured the tubing in which the leak developed or that it caused the leak. We address each of these contentions in turn. . . .

DISCUSSION

. . .

If the contract between Metal–Matic and Krack contains Metal–Matic's disclaimer of liability, Metal–Matic is not liable to indemnify Krack for part of Diamond's damages. Therefore, the principal issue before us on this appeal is whether Metal–Matic's disclaimer of liability became part of the contract between these parties.

---

3. Krack contends that there is no evidence of when these discussions took place. That is not the case. Van Krevelen testified that at least some discussions were held before this incident arose. That testimony is not contradicted.

Relying on Uniform Commercial Code (U.C.C.) § 2–207, Or.Rev.Stat. § 72.2070 (1985), Krack argues that Metal–Matic's disclaimer did not become part of the contract. Metal–Matic, on the other hand, argues that section 2–207 is inapplicable to this case because the parties discussed the disclaimer, and Krack assented to it.

Krack is correct in its assertion that section 2–207 applies to this case. One intended application of section 2–207 is to commercial transactions in which the parties exchange printed purchase order and acknowledgment forms. *See* U.C.C. § 2–207 comment 1. The drafters of the U.C.C. recognized that "[b]ecause the [purchase order and acknowledgment] forms are oriented to the thinking of the respective drafting parties, the terms contained in them often do not correspond." *Id.* Section 2–207 is an attempt to provide rules of contract formation in such cases. In this case, Krack and Metal–Matic exchanged purchase order and acknowledgment forms that contained different or additional terms. This, then, is a typical section 2–207 situation. The fact that the parties discussed the terms of their contract after they exchanged their forms does not put this case outside section 2–207. *See* 3 R. Duesenburg & L. King, *Sales and Bulk Transfers under the Uniform Commercial Code* (Bender's U.C.C. Service) § 3.05[2] (1986). Section 2–207 provides rules of contract formation in cases such as this one in which the parties exchange forms but do not agree on all the terms of their contract.

Generally, section 2–207(1) "converts a common law counteroffer into an acceptance even though it states additional or different terms." *Idaho Power,* 596 F.2d at 926; *see* U.C.C. § 2–207(1). The only requirement under section 2–207(1) is that the responding form contain a definite and seasonable expression of acceptance. The terms of the responding form that correspond to the offer constitute the contract. Under section 2–207(2), the additional terms of the responding form become proposals for additions to the contract. Between merchants the additional terms become part of the contract unless the offer is specifically limited to its terms, the offeror objects to the additional terms, or the additional terms materially alter the terms of the offer. U.C.C. § 2–207(2); *see* J. White & R. Summers, § 1–2 at 32.

However, section 2–207(1) is subject to a proviso. If a definite and seasonable expression of acceptance expressly conditions acceptance on the offeror's assent to additional or different terms contained therein, the parties' differing forms do not result in a contract unless the offeror assents to the additional terms. *See* J. White & R. Summers, § 1–2 at 32–33. If the offeror assents, the parties have a contract and the additional terms are a part of that contract. If, however, the offeror does not assent, but the parties proceed with the transaction as if they have a contract, their performance results in formation of a contract. U.C.C. § 2–207(3). In that case, the terms of the contract are those on which the parties' forms agree plus any terms supplied by the U.C.C. *Id.; see Boise Cascade Corp. v. Etsco, Ltd.,* 39 U.C.C.Rep.Serv. (Callaghan) 410, 414 (D.Or.1984); J. White & R. Summers, § 1–2 at 34.

In this case, Metal–Matic expressly conditioned its acceptance on Krack's assent to the additional terms contained in Metal–Matic's acknowledgment form. That form tracks the language of the section 2–207(1) proviso, stating that "Metal–Matic, Inc.'s acceptance ... is hereby *expressly made conditional* to purchaser's acceptance of the terms and provisions of the acknowledgment form." (emphasis added). *See C. Itoh & Co.,* 552 F.2d at 1235. Therefore, we must determine whether Krack assented to Metal–Matic's limitation of liability term.

Metal–Matic argues that Krack did assent to the limitation of liability term. This argument is based on the discussions between Zver for Krack and Van Krevelen for Metal–Matic. Some time during the ten-year relationship between the companies, these two men discussed Krack's objections to the warranty and liability limitation terms in Metal–Matic's acknowledgment form. Krack attempted to persuade Metal–Matic to change its form, but Metal–Matic refused to do so. After the discussions, the companies continued to do business as in the past. Metal–Matic contends that Krack assented to the limitation of liability term when it continued to accept and pay for tubing after Metal–Matic insisted that the contract contain its terms.

To address Metal–Matic's argument, we must determine what constitutes assent to additional or different terms for purposes of section 2–207(1). The parties have not directed us to any cases that analyze this question and our research has revealed none. We therefore look to the language and structure of section 2–207 and to the purposes behind that section to determine the correct standard.

One of the principles underlying section 2–207 is neutrality. If possible, the section should be interpreted so as to give neither party to a contract an advantage simply because it happened to send the first or in some cases the last form. *See* J. White & R. Summers, § 1–2 at 26–27. Section 2–207 accomplishes this result in part by doing away with the common law's "last shot" rule. *See* 3 R. Duesenberg & L. King, § 3.05[1][a][iii] at 3–73. At common law, the offeree/counterofferor gets all of its terms simply because it fired the last shot in the exchange of forms. Section 2–207(3) does away with this result by giving neither party the terms it attempted to impose unilaterally on the other. *See id.* at 3–71. Instead, all of the terms on which the parties' forms do not agree drop out, and the U.C.C. supplies the missing terms.

Generally, this result is fair because both parties are responsible for the ambiguity in their contract. The parties could have negotiated a contract and agreed on its terms, but for whatever reason, they failed to do so. Therefore, neither party should get its terms. *See* 3 R. Duesenberg & L. King, § 3.05[2] at 3–88. However, as White and Summers point out, resort to section 2–207(3) will often work to the disadvantage of the seller because he will "wish to undertake less responsibility for the quality of his goods than the Code imposes or else wish to limit his damages liability more narrowly than would the Code." J. White & R. Summers, § 1–2 at 34. Nevertheless, White and Summers recommend that section 2–207(3) be applied in such cases. *Id.* We agree. Application of section 2–207(3) is more equitable than giving one party its terms simply because it sent the last form. Further, the terms imposed by the code are presumably equitable and consistent with public policy because they are statutorily imposed. *See* 3 R. Duesenberg & L. King, § 3.05[2] at 3–88.

With these general principles in mind, we turn now to Metal–Matic's argument that Krack assented to the disclaimer when it continued to accept and pay for tubing once Metal–Matic indicated that it was willing to sell tubing only if its warranty and liability terms were part of the contract. Metal–Matic's argument is appealing. Sound policy supports permitting a seller to control the terms on which it will sell its products, especially in a case in which the seller has indicated both in writing and orally that those are the only terms on which it is willing to sell the product. Nevertheless, we reject Metal–Matic's argument because we find that these considerations are outweighed by the public policy reflected by Oregon's enactment of the U.C.C.

If we were to accept Metal–Matic's argument, we would reinstate to some extent the common law's last shot rule. To illustrate, assume that the parties in this case had sent the same forms but in the reverse order and that Krack's form contained terms stating that Metal–Matic is liable for all consequential damages and conditioning acceptance on Metal–Matic's assent to Krack's terms. Assume also that Metal–Matic objected to Krack's terms but Krack refused to change them and that the parties continued with their transaction anyway. If we applied Metal–Matic's argument in that case, we would find that Krack's term was part of the contract because Metal–Matic continued to ship tubing to Krack after Krack reaffirmed that it would purchase tubing only if Metal–Matic were fully liable for consequential damages. Thus, the result would turn on which party sent the last form, and would therefore be inconsistent with section 2–207's purpose of doing away with the last shot rule.

That result is avoided by requiring a specific and unequivocal expression of assent on the part of the offeror when the offeree conditions its acceptance on assent to additional or different terms. If the offeror does not give specific and unequivocal assent but the parties act as if they have a contract, the provisions of section 2–207(3) apply to fill in the terms of the contract. Application of section 2–207(3) is appropriate in that situation because by going ahead with the transaction without resolving their dispute, both parties are responsible for introducing ambiguity into the contract. Further, in a case such as this one, requiring the seller to assume more liability than it intends is not altogether inappropriate. The seller is most responsible for the ambiguity because it inserts a term in its form that requires assent to additional terms and then does not enforce that requirement. If the seller truly does not want to be bound unless the buyer assents to its terms, it can protect itself by not shipping until it obtains that assent. *See C. Itoh & Co.,* 552 F.2d at 1238.

We hold that because Krack's conduct did not indicate unequivocally that Krack intended to assent to Metal–Matic's terms, that conduct did not amount to the assent contemplated by section 2–207(1). *See* 3 R. Duesenberg & L. King, § 3.05[1][a][iii] at 3–74. . . .

[The court also concluded that the evidence supported the findings that Metal–Matic manufactured the tubing that failed, and caused the defect.]

The jury verdict is supported by the evidence and consistent with the U.C.C. Therefore, the district court did not err in denying Metal–Matic's motion for a directed verdict.

AFFIRMED.

———

C. ITOH & CO. (AMERICA), INC. v. JORDAN INTERNATIONAL CO., 552 F.2d 1228 (7th Cir.1977). " . . . [W]e find that the 'supplementary terms' contemplated by section 2–207(3) are limited to those supplied by the standardized 'gapfiller' provisions of [UCC] Article Two. . . .

"We are convinced that this conclusion does not result in any unfair prejudice to a seller who elects to insert in his standard sales acknowledgement form the statement that acceptance is expressly conditional on buyer's assent to additional terms contained therein. Such a seller obtains a substantial benefit under Section 2–207(1) through the inclusion of an 'expressly conditional' clause. If he decides after the exchange of forms that the particular transaction is not in his best interest, Subsection (1) permits him to walk away from the transaction without incurring any liability so long as the buyer has not in the interim expressly assented to the additional terms. Moreover, whether or not a seller will be disadvantaged under Subsection (3) as a consequence of inserting an 'expressly conditional' clause in his standard form is within his control. If the seller in fact does not intend to close a particular deal unless the additional terms are assented to, he can protect himself by not delivering the goods until such assent is forthcoming. If the seller does intend to close a deal irrespective of whether or not the buyer assents to the additional terms, he can hardly complain when the contract formed under Subsection (3) as a result of the parties' conduct is held not to include those terms. Although a seller who employs such an 'expressly conditional' clause in his acknowledgement form would undoubtedly appreciate the dual advantage of not being bound to a contract under Subsection (1) if he elects not to perform and of having his additional terms imposed on the buyer under Subsection (3) in the event that performance is in his best interest, we do not believe such a result is contemplated by Section 2–207. Rather, while a seller may take advantage of an 'expressly conditional' clause under Subsection (1) when he elects not to perform, he must accept the potential risk under Subsection (3) of not getting his additional terms when he elects to proceed with performance without first obtaining buyer's assent to those terms. Since the seller injected ambiguity into the transaction by inserting the 'expressly conditional' clause in his form, he, and not the buyer, should bear the consequence of that ambiguity under Subsection (3)."

TRANSWESTERN PIPELINE CO. v. MONSANTO CO., 46 Cal. App.4th 502, 53 Cal.Rptr.2d 887 (1996). Monsanto sold a lubricant called Turbinol to Texas Eastern during a twelve-year period. The Turbinol was sold for use by Texas Eastern's subsidiary, Transwestern, a pipeline company. It turned out that Turbinol contained PCBs, a chemical that poses a substantial risk of environmental contamination. Some of the PCBs ended up in a pipeline owned by SoCalGas. Transwestern paid SoCalGas's cleanup costs, and then sued Monsanto for indemnification.

Monsanto's acceptances of Texas Eastern's purchase orders for Turbinol had been expressly made conditional on Turbinol's assent to the additional terms in Monsanto's sales-invoice forms. These forms disclaimed liability for consequential damages, and limited the buyer's damages to the purchase price. Monsanto contended that no contract was formed under UCC §§ 2–207(1) and (2), because of the expressly-made-conditional provisions, and that under § 2–207 (3) the provisions in the sales invoices became "supplementary terms" of the contracts as a result of the parties' course of dealing over a twelve-year period. Held, for Transwestern:

"We agree with Monsanto [that] the 'supplementary terms' referred to in section [2–207(3)] may include terms incorporated as a result of the parties' course of dealing. Subdivision (3) refers to 'supplementary terms incorporated under any other provisions of this code.' Section [1–201], subdivision (3) defines an 'agreement' as: "[T]he bargain of the parties in fact as found in their language or by implication from other circumstances including course of dealing . . .

"Thus, the issue boils down to whether the exchange of forms containing inconsistent provisions as to liability and remedies, over a long period of time, can 'fairly be regarded as establishing a common basis of understanding' between the parties as to their respective liability and remedies.

"Common sense tells us the mere exchange of forms containing inconsistent terms, for however long a period, cannot establish a common understanding between the parties as to which set of conflicting terms is part of their contract. Although Monsanto repeatedly stated in its invoices its acceptance was conditioned on assent to its liability limiters, Texas Eastern never expressed such assent. Moreover, Texas Eastern's purchase orders repeatedly stated terms and conditions which contained no limitations on Monsanto's liability. Under these circumstances, we see no reason why Monsanto's form disclaiming liability and limiting Texas Eastern's remedies should be accepted over Texas Eastern's form which contained no such limitations. Each party is equally entitled to claim its terms and conditions constituted the parties' 'course of dealing.' . . . Furthermore, the fact this battle of the forms went on for 12 years makes Monsanto's argument even less tenable. The longer such a battle continues, the more obvious it is the parties have not reached an agreement over the terms in dispute."

JOM, INC. v. ADELL PLASTICS, INC., 193 F.3d 47, 53 (1st Cir. 1999). "Section 2–207 . . . affords three main avenues to contract formation. . . . First, if the parties exchange forms with divergent terms, yet the seller's invoice does not state that its acceptance is made 'expressly conditional' on the buyer's assent to any additional or different terms in the invoice, a contract is formed, and its precise terms are determined through recourse to the three-part test in § 2–207(2).

"Second, if the seller does make its acceptance 'expressly conditional' on the buyer's assent to any additional or divergent terms in the seller's invoice, the invoice is merely a counteroffer, and a contract is formed [under § 2–207(1)] only when the buyer expresses its affirmative acceptance of the seller's counteroffer. Unlike the 'mirror image' rule at common law, however, the seller's invoice is not deemed 'expressly conditional' under § 2–207 merely because its terms do not *match* the terms of the buyer's offer. Rather, to be deemed 'expressly conditional,' the seller's invoice must place the buyer on unambiguous notice that the invoice is a mere counteroffer. *See* 1 James J. White & Robert S. Summers, Uniform Commercial Code § 1–3 at 20 (4th ed. 1995) (noting that 'express conditionality' is '*not* easily invoked').

"Finally, where for any reason the exchange of forms does not result in contract formation (*e.g.,* the buyer 'expressly limits acceptance to the terms of [its offer]' under § 2–207(2)(a), or the buyer does not accept the seller's counteroffer under the second clause of § 2–207(1)), a contract nonetheless is formed [under § 2–207(3)] if their *subsequent conduct*—for instance, the seller ships and the buyer accepts the goods—demonstrates that the parties *believed* that a binding agreement had been formed. The terms of their agreement would then be determined under the 'default' test in § 2–207(3), which implicitly incorporates the criteria prescribed in § 2–207(2)."

SECTION 2. "ROLLING CONTRACTS"

ProCD, INC. v. ZEIDENBERG

United States Court of Appeals, Seventh Circuit, 1996.
86 F.3d 1447.

EASTERBROOK, Circuit Judge.

Must buyers of computer software obey the terms of shrinkwrap licenses? The district court held not ... [on the ground that] they are not contracts because the licenses are inside the box rather than printed on the outside.... [W]e disagree with the district judge's conclusion.... Shrinkwrap licenses are enforceable unless their terms are objectionable on grounds applicable to contracts in general (for example, if they violate a rule of positive law, or if they are unconscionable). Because no one argues that the terms of the license at issue here are troublesome, we remand with instructions to enter judgment for the plaintiff.

I

ProCD, the plaintiff, has compiled information from more than 3,000 telephone directories into a computer database. We may assume that this database cannot be copyrighted, although it is more complex, contains more information (nine-digit zip codes and census industrial codes), is organized differently, and therefore is more original than the single alphabetical directory at issue in Feist Publications, Inc. v. Rural Telephone Service Co., 499 U.S. 340, 111 S.Ct. 1282, 113 L.Ed.2d 358 (1991). See Paul J. Heald, The Vices of Originality, 1991 Sup.Ct. Rev. 143, 160–68. ProCD sells a version of the database, called SelectPhone (trademark), on CD–ROM discs. (CD–ROM means "compact disc—read only memory." The "shrinkwrap license" gets its name from the fact that retail software packages are covered in plastic or cellophane "shrinkwrap," and some vendors, though not ProCD, have written licenses that become effective as soon as the customer tears the wrapping from the package. Vendors prefer "end user license," but we use the more common term.) A proprietary method of compressing the data serves as effective encryption too. Customers decrypt and use the data with the aid of an application program that ProCD has written. This program, which is copyrighted, searches the database in response to users' criteria (such as "find all people named Tatum in Tennessee, plus all firms with 'Door Systems' in the corporate name"). The resulting lists (or, as ProCD prefers, "listings") can be read and manipulated by other software, such as word processing programs.

The database in SelectPhone (trademark) cost more than $10 million to compile and is expensive to keep current. It is much more valuable to some users than to others. The combination of names, addresses, and SIC codes enables manufacturers to compile lists of potential customers. Manufacturers and retailers pay high prices to specialized information intermediaries for such mailing lists; ProCD offers a potentially cheaper alternative. People with nothing to sell could use the database as a substitute for calling long distance information, or as a way to look up old friends who have moved to unknown towns, or just as an electronic substitute for the local phone book. ProCD decided to engage in price discrimination, selling its database to the general public for personal use at a low price (approximately $150 for the set of five discs) while selling information to the trade for a higher price. It has adopted some intermediate strategies too: access to the SelectPhone (trademark) database is available via the America Online service for the price America Online charges to its clients (approximately $3 per hour), but this service has been tailored to be useful only to the general public.

If ProCD had to recover all of its costs and make a profit by charging a single price—that is, if it could not charge more to commercial users than to the general public—it would have to raise the price substantially over $150. The ensuing reduction in sales would harm consumers who value the information at, say, $200. They get consumer surplus of $50 under the current arrangement but would cease to buy if the price rose substantially. If because of high elasticity of demand in the consumer segment of the market the only way to make a profit turned out to be a price attractive to commercial users alone, then all consumers would lose out—and so would the commercial clients, who would have to pay more for the listings because ProCD could not obtain any contribution toward costs from the consumer market.

To make price discrimination work, however, the seller must be able to control arbitrage. An air carrier sells tickets for less to vacationers than to business travelers, using advance purchase and Saturday-night-stay requirements to distinguish the categories. A producer of movies segments the market by time, releasing first to theaters, then to pay-per-view services, next to the videotape and laserdisc market, and finally to cable and commercial tv. Vendors of computer software have a harder task. Anyone can walk into a retail store and buy a box. Customers do not wear tags saying "commercial user" or "consumer user." Anyway, even a commercial-user-detector at the door would not work, because a consumer could buy the software and resell to a commercial user. That arbitrage would break down the price discrimination and drive up the minimum price at which ProCD would sell to anyone.

Instead of tinkering with the product and letting users sort themselves— for example, furnishing current data at a high price that would be attractive only to commercial customers, and two-year-old data at a low price—ProCD turned to the institution of contract. Every box containing its consumer product declares that the software comes with restrictions stated in an enclosed license. This license, which is encoded on the CD–ROM disks as well as printed in the manual, and which appears on a user's screen every time the software runs, limits use of the application program and listings to non-commercial purposes.

Matthew Zeidenberg bought a consumer package of SelectPhone (trademark) in 1994 from a retail outlet in Madison, Wisconsin, but decided to ignore the license. He formed Silken Mountain Web Services, Inc., to resell the information in the SelectPhone (trademark) database. The corporation makes the database available on the Internet to anyone willing to pay its price—which, needless to say, is less than ProCD charges its commercial customers. Zeidenberg has purchased two additional SelectPhone (trademark) packages, each with an updated version of the database, and made the latest information available over the World Wide Web, for a price, through his corporation. ProCD filed this suit seeking an injunction against further dissemination that exceeds the rights specified in the licenses (identical in each of the three packages Zeidenberg purchased). The district court held the licenses ineffectual because their terms do not appear on the outside of the packages. The court added that the second and third licenses stand no different from the first, even though they are identical, because they might have been different, and a purchaser does not agree to—and cannot be bound by—terms that were secret at the time of purchase. 908 F.Supp. at 654.

II

Following the district court, we treat the licenses as ordinary contracts accompanying the sale of products, and therefore as governed by the common law of contracts and the Uniform Commercial Code. Whether there are legal differences between "contracts" and "licenses" (which may matter under the copyright doctrine of first sale) is a subject for another day. See Microsoft Corp. v. Harmony Computers & Electronics, Inc., 846 F.Supp. 208 (E.D.N.Y. 1994). Zeidenberg does not argue that Silken Mountain Web Services is free of any restrictions that apply to Zeidenberg himself, because any effort to treat the two parties as distinct would put Silken Mountain behind the eight ball on ProCD's argument that copying the application program onto its hard disk violates the copyright laws. Zeidenberg does argue, and the district court held, that placing the package of software on the shelf is an "offer," which the customer "accepts" by paying the asking price and leaving the store with the goods. Peeters v. State, 154 Wis. 111, 142 N.W. 181 (1913). In Wisconsin, as elsewhere, a contract includes only the terms on which the parties have agreed. One cannot agree to hidden terms, the judge concluded. So far, so good—but one of the terms to which Zeidenberg agreed by purchasing the software is that the transaction was subject to a license. Zeidenberg's position therefore must be that the printed terms on the outside of a box are the parties' contract—except for printed terms that refer to or incorporate other terms. But why would Wisconsin fetter the parties' choice in this way? Vendors can put the entire terms of a contract on the outside of a box only by using microscopic type, removing other information that buyers might find more useful (such as what the software does, and on which computers it works), or both. The "Read Me" file included with most software, describing system requirements and potential incompatibilities, may be equivalent to ten pages of type; warranties and license restrictions take still more space. Notice on the outside, terms on the inside, and a right to return the software for a refund if the terms are unacceptable (a right that the license expressly extends), may be a means of doing business valuable to buyers and sellers alike. See E. Allan Farnsworth, 1 Farnsworth on Contracts § 4.26 (1990); Restatement (2d) of Contracts § 211 comment a (1981) ("Standardization of agreements serves many of the same functions as standardization of goods and services; both are essential to a system of mass production and distribution. Scarce and costly time and skill can be devoted to a class of transactions rather than the details of individual transactions.''). Doubtless a state could forbid the use of standard contracts in the software business, but we do not think that Wisconsin has done so.

Transactions in which the exchange of money precedes the communication of detailed terms are common. Consider the purchase of insurance. The buyer goes to an agent, who explains the essentials (amount of coverage, number of years) and remits the premium to the home office, which sends back a policy. On the district judge's understanding, the terms of the policy are irrelevant because the insured paid before receiving them. Yet the device of payment, often with a "binder" (so that the insurance takes effect immediately even though the home office reserves the right to withdraw coverage later), in advance of the policy, serves buyers' interests by accelerating effectiveness and reducing transactions costs. Or consider the purchase of an airline ticket. The traveler calls the carrier or an agent, is quoted a price, reserves a seat, pays, and gets a ticket, in that order. The ticket contains elaborate terms, which the traveler can reject by canceling the reservation. To use the ticket is to accept the terms, even terms that in retrospect are disadvantageous. See Carnival Cruise Lines, Inc. v. Shute, 499 U.S. 585, 111 S.Ct. 1522, 113 L.Ed.2d 622 (1991); see also Vimar Seguros y Reaseguros, S.A. v. M/V Sky Reefer, 515 U.S. 528, 115 S.Ct. 2322, 132 L.Ed.2d 462 (1995) (bills of lading). Just so with a ticket to a concert. The back of the ticket states that the patron promises not to record the concert; to attend is to agree. A theater that detects a violation will confiscate the tape and escort the violator to the exit. One could arrange things so that every concertgoer signs this promise before forking over the money, but that cumbersome way of doing things not only would lengthen queues and raise prices but also would scotch the sale of tickets by phone or electronic data service.

Consumer goods work the same way. Someone who wants to buy a radio set visits a store, pays, and walks out with a box. Inside the box is a leaflet containing some terms, the most important of which usually is the warranty, read for the first time in the comfort of home. By Zeidenberg's lights, the warranty in the box is irrelevant; every consumer gets the standard warranty implied by the UCC in the event the contract is silent; yet so far as we are aware no state disregards warranties furnished with consumer products. Drugs come with a list of ingredients on the outside and an elaborate package insert on the inside. The package insert describes drug interactions, contraindications, and other vital information—but, if Zeidenberg is right, the purchaser need not read the package insert, because it is not part of the contract.

Next consider the software industry itself. Only a minority of sales take place over the counter, where there are boxes to peruse. A customer may place an order by phone in response to a line item in a catalog or a review in a magazine. Much software is ordered over the Internet by purchasers who have never seen a box. Increasingly software arrives by wire. There is no box; there is only a stream of electrons, a collection of information that includes data, an application program, instructions, many limitations ("MegaPixel 3.14159 cannot be used with BytePusher 2.718"), and the terms of sale. The user purchases a serial number, which activates the software's features. On Zeidenberg's arguments, these unboxed sales are unfettered by terms—so the seller has made a broad warranty and must pay consequential damages for any shortfalls in performance, two "promises" that if taken seriously would drive prices through the ceiling or return transactions to the horse-and-buggy age.

According to the district court, the UCC does not countenance the sequence of money now, terms later. (Wisconsin's version of the UCC does not differ from the Official Version in any material respect, so we use the regular numbering system. Wis. Stat. § 402.201 corresponds to UCC § 2–201, and other citations are easy to derive.) One of the court's reasons—that by proposing as part of the draft Article 2B a new UCC § 2–2203 that would explicitly validate standard-form user licenses, the American Law Institute and the National Conference of Commissioners on Uniform Laws have conceded the invalidity of shrinkwrap licenses under current law, see 908 F.Supp. at 655–56—depends on a faulty inference.

To propose a change in a law's *text* is not necessarily to propose a change in the law's *effect*. New words may be designed to fortify the current rule with a more precise text that curtails uncertainty. To judge by the flux of law review articles discussing shrinkwrap licenses, uncertainty is much in need of reduction—although businesses seem to feel less uncertainty than do scholars, for only three cases (other than ours) touch on the subject, and none directly addresses it. See Step–Saver Data Systems, Inc. v. Wyse Technology, 939 F.2d 91 (3d Cir.1991); Vault Corp. v. Quaid Software Ltd., 847 F.2d 255, 268–70 (5th Cir.1988); Arizona Retail Systems, Inc. v. Software Link, Inc., 831 F.Supp. 759 (D.Ariz.1993). As their titles suggest, these are not consumer transactions. *Step–Saver* is a battle-of-the-forms case, in which the parties exchange incompatible forms and a court must decide which prevails. See Northrop Corp. v. Litronic Industries, 29 F.3d 1173 (7th Cir.1994) (Illinois law); Douglas G. Baird & Robert Weisberg, Rules, Standards, and the Battle of the Forms: A Reassessment of § 2–207, 68 Va. L.Rev. 1217, 1227–31 (1982). Our case has only one form; UCC § 2–207 is irrelevant. *Vault* holds that Louisiana's special shrinkwrap-license statute is preempted by federal law, a question to which we return. And *Arizona Retail Systems* did not reach the question, because the court found that the buyer knew the terms of the license before purchasing the software. What then does the current version of the UCC have to say? We think that the place to start is § 2–204(1): "A contract for sale of goods may be made in any manner sufficient to show agreement, including conduct by both parties which recognizes the existence of such a contract." A vendor, as master of the offer, may invite acceptance by conduct, and may propose limitations on the kind of conduct that constitutes acceptance. A buyer may accept by performing the acts the vendor proposes to treat as acceptance. And that is what happened. ProCD proposed a contract that a buyer would accept by *using* the software after having an opportunity to read the license at leisure. This Zeidenberg did. He had no choice, because the software splashed the license on the screen and would not let him proceed without indicating acceptance. So although the district judge was right to say that a contract can be, and often is, formed simply by paying the price and walking out of the store, the UCC permits contracts to be formed in other ways. ProCD proposed such a different way, and without protest Zeidenberg agreed. Ours is not a case in which a consumer opens a package to find an insert saying "you owe us an extra $10,000" and the seller files suit to collect. Any buyer finding such a demand can prevent formation of the contract by returning the package, as can any consumer who concludes that the terms of the license make the software worth less than the purchase price. Nothing in the UCC requires a seller to maximize the buyer's net gains.

Section 2–606, which defines "acceptance of goods", reinforces this understanding. A buyer accepts goods under § 2–606(1)(b) when, after an opportunity to inspect, he fails to make an effective rejection under § 2–602(1). ProCD extended an opportunity to reject if a buyer should find the license terms unsatisfactory; Zeidenberg inspected the package, tried out the software, learned of the license, and did not reject the goods. We refer to § 2–606 only to show that the opportunity to return goods can be important; acceptance of an offer differs from acceptance of goods after delivery, see Gillen v. Atalanta Systems, Inc., 997 F.2d 280, 284 n. 1 (7th Cir.1993); but the UCC consistently permits the parties to structure their relations so that the buyer has a chance to make a final decision after a detailed review.

Some portions of the UCC impose additional requirements on the way parties agree on terms. A disclaimer of the implied warranty of merchantability must be "conspicuous." UCC § 2–316(2), incorporating UCC § 1–201(10). Promises to make firm offers, or to negate oral modifications, must be "separately signed." UCC §§ 2–205, 2–209(2). These special provisos reinforce the impression that, so far as the UCC is concerned, other terms may be as inconspicuous as the forum-selection clause on the back of the cruise ship ticket in *Carnival Lines*. Zeidenberg has not located any Wisconsin case—for that matter, any case in any state—holding that under the UCC the ordinary terms found in shrinkwrap licenses require any special prominence, or otherwise are to be undercut rather than enforced. In the end, the terms of the license are conceptually identical to the contents of the package. Just as no court would dream of saying that SelectPhone (trademark) must contain 3,100 phone books rather than 3,000, or must have data no more than 30 days old, or must sell for $100 rather than $150—although any of these changes would be welcomed by the customer, if all other things were held constant—so, we believe, Wisconsin would not let the buyer pick and choose among terms. Terms of use are no less a part of "the product" than are the size of the database and the speed with which the software compiles listings. Competition among vendors, not judicial revision of a package's contents, is how consumers are protected in a market economy. Digital Equipment Corp. v. Uniq Digital Technologies, Inc., 73 F.3d 756 (7th Cir.1996). ProCD has rivals, which may elect to compete by offering superior software, monthly updates, improved terms of use, lower price, or a better compromise among these elements. As we stressed above, adjusting terms in buyers' favor might help Matthew Zeidenberg today (he already has the software) but would lead to a response, such as a higher price, that might make consumers as a whole worse off. . . .

REVERSED AND REMANDED.

———

NOTE

Stewart MacCauley, a noted Contracts scholar at the University of Wisconsin, posted the following message concerning *ProCD* on a Contracts listserve: "We have a box of the ProCD disks that were involved in that case. The notice that you were to look inside was in yellow type in a sentence mixed in with others. The typeface is very very small, and the notice is on the bottom flap of the box next to the bar code. I cannot believe that many people would see it. The few who did wouldn't understand that they were buying far less than it might seem.

"However, the defendant in the case was a graduate student in computer sciences at the UW–Madison. He had consulted my colleague John Kidwell about the assertion of a copyright to telephone book listings. He might have known apart from what he read on the box. Of course, there is no evidence of that in the record."

HILL v. GATEWAY 2000, 105 F.3d 1147 (7th Cir. 1997) (Easterbrook, J.). "A customer picks up the phone, orders a computer, and gives a credit card number. Presently a box arrives, containing the computer and a list of terms, said to govern unless the customer returns the computer within 30 days. Are these terms effective as the parties' contract, or is the contract term-free because the order-taker did not read any terms over the phone and elicit the customer's assent?

"One of the terms in the box containing a Gateway 2000 system was an arbitration clause. Rich and Enza Hill, the customers, kept the computer more than 30 days before complaining about its components and performance. They filed suit in federal court. . . . Gateway asked the district court to enforce the arbitration clause; the judge refused. . . .

"ProCD, Inc. v. Zeidenberg, 86 F.3d 1447 (7th Cir. 1996), holds that terms inside a box of software bind consumers who use the software after an opportunity to read the terms and to reject them by returning the product. . . . Gateway shipped computers with the same sort of accept-or-return offer ProCD made to users of its software. . . .

"Plaintiffs ask us to limit *ProCD* to software, but where's the sense in that? *ProCD* is about the law of contract, not the law of software. Payment preceding the revelation of full terms is common for air transportation, insurance, and many other endeavors. Practical considerations support allowing vendors to enclose the full legal terms with their products. Cashiers cannot be expected to read legal documents to customers before ringing up sales. If the staff at the other end of the phone for direct-sales operations such as Gateway's had to read the four-page statement of terms before taking the buyer's credit card number, the droning voice would anesthetize rather than enlighten many potential buyers. Others would hang up in a rage over the waste of their time. And oral recitation would not avoid customers' assertions (whether true or feigned) that the clerk did not read term X to them, or that they did not remember or understand it. Writing provides benefits for both sides of commercial transactions. Customers as a group are better off when vendors skip costly and ineffectual steps such as telephonic recitation, and use instead a simple approve-or-return device. Competent adults are bound by such documents, read or unread. . . .

"For their second sally, the Hills contend that *ProCD* should be limited to executory contracts (to licenses in particular), and therefore does not apply because both parties' performance of this contract was complete when the box arrived at their home. This is legally and factually wrong: legally because the question at hand concerns the *formation* of the contract rather than its *performance*, and factually because both contracts were incompletely performed. *ProCD* did not depend on the fact that the seller characterized the transaction as a license rather than as a contract; we treated it as a contract for the sale of goods and reserved the question whether for other purposes a "license" characterization might be preferable. 86 F.3d at 1450. All debates about characterization to one side, the transaction in *ProCD* was no more executory than the one here: Zeidenberg paid for the software and walked out of the store with a box under his arm, so if arrival of the box with the product ends the time for revelation of contractual terms, then the time ended in *ProCD* before Zeidenberg opened the box. But of course *ProCD* had not completed performance with delivery of the box, and neither had Gateway. One element of the transaction was the warranty, which obliges sellers to fix defects in their products. The Hills have invoked Gateway's warranty and are not satisfied with its response, so they are not well positioned to say that Gateway's obligations were fulfilled when the motor carrier unloaded the box. What is more, both ProCD and Gateway promised to help customers to use their products. Long-term service and information obligations are common in the computer business, on both hardware and software sides. Gateway offers 'lifetime service' and has a round-the-clock telephone hotline to fulfil this promise. Some vendors spend more money helping customers use their products than on developing and manufacturing them. The document in Gateway's box includes promises of future performance that some consumers value highly; these promises bind Gateway just as the arbitration clause binds the Hills. . . .

"At oral argument the Hills propounded still another distinction: the box containing ProCD's software displayed a notice that additional terms were within, while the box containing Gateway's computer did not. The difference is functional, not legal. Consumers browsing the aisles of a store can look at the box, and if they are unwilling to deal with the prospect of additional terms can leave the box alone, avoiding the transactions costs of returning the package after reviewing its contents. Gateway's box, by contrast, is just a shipping carton; it is not on display anywhere. Its function is to protect the product during transit, and the information on its sides is for the use of handlers (Fragile! "This Side Up!") rather than would-be purchasers.

"Perhaps the Hills would have had a better argument if they were first alerted to the bundling of hardware and legal-ware after opening the box and wanted to return the computer in order to avoid disagreeable terms, but were dissuaded by the expense of shipping. What the remedy would be in such a case—could it exceed the shipping charges?—is an interesting question, but one that need not detain us because the Hills knew before they ordered the computer that the carton would include *some* important terms, and they did not seek to discover these in advance. Gateway's ads state that their products come with limited warranties and lifetime support. How limited was the warranty—30 days, with service contingent on shipping the computer back, or five years, with free onsite service? What sort of support was offered? Shoppers have three principal ways to discover these things. First, they can ask the vendor to send a copy before deciding whether to buy. The Magnuson–Moss Warranty Act requires firms to distribute their warranty terms on request, 15 U.S.C. § 2302(b)(1)(A); the Hills do not contend that Gateway would have refused to enclose the remaining terms too. Concealment would be bad for business, scaring some customers away and leading to excess returns from others. Second, shoppers can consult public sources (computer magazines, the Web sites of vendors) that may contain this information. Third, they may inspect the documents after the product's delivery. Like Zeidenberg, the Hills took the third option. By keeping the computer beyond 30 days, the Hills accepted Gateway's offer, including the arbitration clause.''

M.A. MORTENSON, CO. v. TIMBERLINE SOFTWARE CORP., 140 Wash.2d 568, 998 P.2d 305 (2000). ''We find the approach of the *ProCD* [and] *Hill* . . . courts persuasive and adopt it to guide our analysis under [UCC § 2–204]. We conclude because [UCC § 2–204] allows a contract to be formed 'in any manner sufficient to show agreement . . . even though the moment of its making is undetermined,' it allows the formation of 'layered contracts' similar to those envisioned by *ProCD* [and] *Hill* . . . .''

KLOCEK v. GATEWAY, INC., 104 F.Supp.2d 1332 (D. Kan. 2000). ''The Court is not persuaded that Kansas or Missouri courts would follow the Seventh Circuit reasoning in *Hill* and *ProCD*. In each case the Seventh Circuit concluded without support that UCC § 2–207 was irrelevant because the cases involved only one written form. *See ProCD,* 86 F.3d at 1452 (citing no authority); *Hill,* 105 F.3d at 1150 (citing *ProCD*). This conclusion is not supported by the statute or by Kansas or Missouri law. Disputes under § 2–207 often arise in the context of a ''battle of forms,'' . . . but nothing in its language precludes application in a case which involves only one form. The statute provides:

Additional terms in acceptance or confirmation.

    (1) A definite and seasonable expression of acceptance or a written confirmation which is sent within a reasonable time operates as an acceptance even though it states terms additional to or different from those offered or agreed upon, unless acceptance is expressly made conditional on assent to the additional or different terms.

    (2) The additional terms are to be construed as proposals for addition to the contract [if the contract is not between merchants]. . . .

''. . . By its terms, § 2–207 applies to an acceptance or written confirmation. It states nothing which requires another form before the provision becomes effective.''

CHATEAU DES CHARMES WINES LTD. v. SABATE USA INC.

United States Court of Appeals, Ninth Circuit, 2003.
328 F.3d 528.

OPINION

PER CURIAM.

    Chateau des Charmes Wines, Ltd. (''Chateau des Charmes''), a Canadian company, appeals the dismissal of its action for breach of contract and related claims arising out of its purchase of wine corks from Sabaté, S.A. ("Sabaté France"), a French company, and Sabaté USA, Inc. ("Sabaté USA"), a wholly owned California subsidiary. The district court held that forum selection clauses in the invoices that Sabaté France sent to Chateau des Charmes were part of the contract between the parties and dismissed the case in favor of adjudication in France. Because we conclude that the forum selection clauses in question were not part of any agreement between the parties, we reverse.

FACTUAL BACKGROUND AND PROCEDURAL HISTORY

The material facts pertinent to this appeal are not disputed. Sabaté France manufactures and sells special wine corks that it claims will not cause wines to be spoiled by "cork taint," a distasteful flavor that some corks produce. It sells these corks through a wholly owned California subsidiary, Sabaté USA.

In February 2000, after some preliminary discussions about the characteristics of Sabaté's corks, Chateau des Charmes, a winery from Ontario, Canada, agreed by telephone with Sabaté USA to purchase a certain number of corks at a specific price. The parties agreed on payment and shipping terms. No other terms were discussed, nor did the parties have any history of prior dealings. Later that year, Chateau des Charmes placed a second telephone order for corks on the same terms. In total, Chateau des Charmes ordered 1.2 million corks.

Sabaté France shipped the corks to Canada in eleven shipments. For each shipment, Sabaté France also sent an invoice. Some of the invoices arrived before the shipments, some with the shipments, and some after the shipments. On the face of each invoice was a paragraph in French that specified that "Any dispute arising under the present contract is under the sole jurisdiction of the Court of Commerce of the City of Perpignan." On the back of each invoice a number of provisions were printed in French, including a clause that specified that "any disputes arising out of this agreement shall be brought before the court with jurisdiction to try the matter in the judicial district where Seller's registered office is located." Chateau des Charmes duly took delivery and paid for each shipment of corks. The corks were then used to bottle Chateau des Charmes' wines.

Chateau des Charmes claims that, in 2001, it noticed that the wine bottled with Sabaté's corks was tainted by cork flavors. Chateau des Charmes filed suit in federal district court in California against Sabaté France and Sabaté USA alleging claims for breach of contract, strict liability, breach of warranty, false advertising, and unfair competition. Sabaté France and Sabaté USA filed a motion to dismiss based on the forum selection clauses. The district court held that the forum selection clauses were valid and enforceable and dismissed the action. This appeal ensued.

DISCUSSION

I. . . .

The question before us is whether the forum selection clauses in Sabaté France's invoices were part of any agreement between the parties. The disputes in this case arise out of an agreement for a sale of goods from a

French party and a United States party to a Canadian party. Such international sales contracts are ordinarily governed by a multilateral treaty, the United Nations Convention on Contracts for the International Sale of Goods ("C.I.S.G."), which applies to "contracts of sale of goods between parties whose places of business are in different States ... when the States are Contracting States." C.I.S.G., art. 1(1)(a), 15 U.S.C.App., 52 Fed.Reg. 6262 (March 2, 1987). The United States, Canada, and France are all contracting states to the C.I.S.G....

II.

Under the C.I.S.G., it is plain that the forum selection clauses were not part of any agreement between the parties. The Convention sets out a clear regime for analyzing international contracts for the sale of goods: "A contract of sale need not be concluded in or evidenced by writing and is not subject to any other requirement as to form." C.I.S.G., art. 11. A proposal is an offer if it is sufficiently definite to "indicate[ ] the goods and expressly or implicitly fix[ ] or make[ ] provision for determining the quantity and the price," *id.*, art. 14, and it demonstrates an intention by the offeror to be bound if the proposal is accepted. *Id.* In turn, an offer is accepted if the offeree makes a "statement ... or other conduct ... indicating assent to an offer." *Id.*, art. 18. Further, "A contract is concluded at the moment when an acceptance of an offer becomes effective." *Id.*, art. 23. Within such a framework, the oral agreements between Sabaté USA and Chateau des Charmes as to the kind of cork, the quantity, and the price were sufficient to create complete and binding contracts.[3]

The terms of those agreements did not include any forum selection clause. Indeed, Sabaté France and Sabaté USA do not contend that a forum selection clause was part of their oral agreements, but merely that the clauses in the invoices became part of a binding agreement. The logic of this contention is defective. Under the Convention, a "contract may be modified or terminated by the mere agreement of the parties." *Id.*, art. 29(1). However, the Convention clearly states that "[a]dditional or different terms relating, among other things, to ... the settlement of disputes are considered to alter the terms of the offer materially." *Id.*, art. 19(3). There is no indication that Chateau des Charmes conducted itself in a manner that evidenced any affirmative assent to the forum selection clauses in the invoices. Rather, Chateau des Charmes merely performed its obligations under the oral contract.

Nothing in the Convention suggests that the failure to object to a party's unilateral attempt to alter materially the terms of an otherwise valid agreement is an "agreement" within the terms of Article 29. *Cf.* C.I.S.G., art. 8(3) ("In determining the intent of a party or the understanding a reasonable person would have had, due consideration is to be given to all relevant circumstances of the case including the negotiations, any practices which the parties have established between themselves, usages and any subsequent conduct of the parties."). Here, no circumstances exist to conclude that Chateau des Charmes's conduct evidenced an "agreement." We reject the contention that because Sabaté France sent multiple invoices it created an

---

3. In this respect, the regime of the C.I.S.G. differs from that of the Uniform Commercial Code, which would require a contract for the sale of corks for the value involved here to be evidenced by a writing. *See* U.C.C. § 2–201.

agreement as to the proper forum with Chateau des Charmes. The parties agreed in two telephone calls to a purchase of corks to be shipped in eleven batches. In such circumstances, a party's multiple attempts to alter an agreement unilaterally do not so effect. *See In re CFLC, Inc.,* 166 F.3d 1012, 1019 (9th Cir.1999).

CONCLUSION

Because the contract for the sale of corks did not contain the forum selection clauses in Sabaté France's invoices, there was nothing for the district court to enforce, and its dismissal of this action was an abuse of discretion. The action is reinstated.

REVERSED and REMANDED.

ARIZONA CARTRIDGE REMANUFACTURERS' ASS'N. v. LEXMARK INT'L INC., 421 F.3d 981 (9th Cir. 2005). Lexmark made and sold laser printers and printer cartridges. Arizona Cartridge Remanufacturers' Association (ACRA) represented wholesalers that remanufactured depleted Lexmark printer cartridges for re-use. Before 1997, Lexmark did not compete against ACRA's members, because it sold only new cartridges. In 1997, however, Lexmark began to remanufacture its own cartridges, and launched an aggressive new strategy to market those cartridges. In particular, Lexmark introduced a "Prebate" program, which gave consumers an upfront 20% discount on cartridges but required the consumer to return the depleted cartridge to Lexmark. An outside surface of the packaging for the Prebate cartridges set forth the following license agreement:

RETURN EMPTY CARTRIDGE TO LEXMARK

FOR REMANUFACTURING AND RECYCLING.

> Please read before opening. Opening of this package or using the patented cartridge inside confirms your acceptance of the following license agreement. The patented cartridge is sold at a special price subject to a restriction that it may be used only once. Following this initial use, you agree to return the empty cartridge only to Lexmark for remanufacturing and recycling. If you don't accept these terms, return the unopened package to your point of purchase. A regular price cartridge without these terms is available.

ACRA sued Lexmark for violation of the antitrust laws. For technical reasons, one element of ACRA's case was that Lexmark did not have a valid contract with consumers to limit the post-sale use of the Lexmark cartridges that were sold on a Prebate basis. The court rejected this position:

> California law, adopting the relevant Uniform Commercial Code provisions, establishes that a "contract for sale of goods may be made in any manner sufficient to show agreement, including conduct by both parties which recognizes the existence of such a contract." [U.C.C. § 2–]204(1). Additionally, California law provides that an "agreement sufficient to constitute a contract for sale may be found even though the moment of its making is undetermined." Id. at § [2–]204(2).

... Lexmark has presented sufficient unrebutted evidence to show that it has a facially valid contract with the consumers who buy and open its cartridges. Specifically, the language on the outside of the cartridge package specifies the terms under which a consumer may use the purchased item. The consumer can read the terms and conditions on the box before deciding whether to accept them or whether to opt for the non-Prebate cartridges that are sold without any restrictions.

The district court found that the ultimate purchasers of the cartridge—consumers—had notice of the restrictions on use and had a chance to reject the condition before opening the clearly marked cartridge container.... These findings support the conclusion that the consumer accepts the terms placed on usage of the Prebate cartridge by opening the box.

The court added, in a footnote:

This case is different from those instances in which a consumer lacks notice of the condition at the time of purchase. *See, e.g., Step–Saver Data Sys. v. Wyse Tech., Inc.*, 939 F.2d 91, 105 (3d Cir. 1991) (treating box-top license as an additional term not incorporated into the parties' contract where the term's addition to the contract would materially alter the agreement and the consumer did not see license until after paying for product). Another variant involves "shrinkwrap licenses" on software, which impose restrictions that a consumer may discover only after opening and installing the software. *See, e.g., ProCD v. Zeidenberg*, 86 F.3d 1447, 1452–53 (7th Cir. 1996)....

SPECHT v. NETSCAPE COMMUNICATIONS CORP.

United States Court of Appeals, Second Circuit, 2002.
306 F.3d 17.

Before McLAUGHLIN, LEVAL, and SOTOMAYOR, Circuit Judges.

SOTOMAYOR, Circuit Judge.

This is an appeal from a judgment of the Southern District of New York denying a motion by defendants-appellants Netscape Communications Corporation and its corporate parent, America Online, Inc. (collectively, "defendants" or "Netscape"), to compel arbitration and to stay court proceedings. In order to resolve the central question of arbitrability presented here, we must address issues of contract formation in cyberspace. Principally, we are asked to determine whether plaintiffs-appellees ("plaintiffs"), by acting upon defendants' invitation to download free software made available on defendants' webpage, agreed to be bound by the software's license terms (which included the arbitration clause at issue), even though plaintiffs could not have learned of the existence of those terms unless, prior to executing the download, they had scrolled down the webpage to a screen located below the download button. We agree with the district court that a reasonably prudent Internet user in circumstances such as these would not have known or learned of the existence of the license terms before responding to defendants' invitation to download the free software, and that defendants therefore did not provide reasonable notice of the license terms. In consequence, plaintiffs' bare act of downloading the software did not unambiguously manifest assent to the arbitration provision contained in the license terms.

We also agree with the district court that plaintiffs' claims relating to the software at issue—a "plug-in" program entitled SmartDownload ("Smart-Download" or "the plug-in program"), offered by Netscape to enhance the functioning of the separate browser program called Netscape Communicator ("Communicator" or "the browser program")—are not subject to an arbitration agreement contained in the license terms governing the use of Communicator. . . .

We therefore affirm the district court's denial of defendants' motion to compel arbitration and to stay court proceedings.

BACKGROUND

. . . FACTS

In three related putative class actions, plaintiffs alleged that, unknown to them, their use of SmartDownload transmitted to defendants private information about plaintiffs' downloading of files from the Internet, thereby effecting an electronic surveillance of their online activities in violation of two federal statutes, the Electronic Communications Privacy Act, 18 U.S.C. § § 2510 *et seq.*, and the Computer Fraud and Abuse Act, 18 U.S.C. § 1030.

Specifically, plaintiffs alleged that when they first used Netscape's Communicator—a software program that permits Internet browsing—the program created and stored on each of their computer hard drives a small text file known as a "cookie" that functioned "as a kind of electronic identification tag for future communications" between their computers and Netscape. Plaintiffs further alleged that when they installed SmartDownload—a separate software "plug-in"[2] that served to enhance Communicator's browsing capabilities—SmartDownload created and stored on their computer hard drives another string of characters, known as a "Key," which similarly functioned as an identification tag in future communications with Netscape. According to the complaints in this case, each time a computer user employed Communicator to download a file from the Internet, SmartDownload "assume[d] from Communicator the task of downloading" the file and transmitted to Netscape the address of the file being downloaded together with the cookie created by Communicator and the Key created by SmartDownload. These processes, plaintiffs claim, constituted unlawful "eavesdropping" on users of Netscape's software products as well as on Internet websites from which users employing SmartDownload downloaded files.

In the time period relevant to this litigation, Netscape offered on its website various software programs, including Communicator and SmartDownload, which visitors to the site were invited to obtain free of charge. It is undisputed that five of the six named plaintiffs—Michael Fagan, John Gibson, Mark Gruber, Sean Kelly, and Sherry Weindorf—downloaded Communicator from the Netscape website. These plaintiffs acknowledge that when they

---

2. Netscape's website defines "plug-ins" as "software programs that extend the capabilities of the Netscape Browser in a specific way—giving you, for example, the ability to play audio samples or view video movies from within your browser." (http://wp.net-scape.com/plugins/) SmartDownload purported-ly made it easier for users of browser programs like Communicator to download files from the Internet without losing their progress when they paused to engage in some other task, or if their Internet connection was severed. *See Specht,* 150 F.Supp.2d at 587.

proceeded to initiate installation[3] of Communicator, they were automatically shown a scrollable text of that program's license agreement and were not permitted to complete the installation until they had clicked on a "Yes" button to indicate that they accepted all the license terms.[4] If a user attempted to install Communicator without clicking "Yes," the installation would be aborted. All five named user plaintiffs[5] expressly agreed to Communicator's license terms by clicking "Yes." The Communicator license agreement that these plaintiffs saw made no mention of SmartDownload or other plug-in programs, and stated that "[t]hese terms apply to Netscape Communicator and Netscape Navigator"[6] and that "all disputes relating to this Agreement (excepting any dispute relating to intellectual property rights)" are subject to "binding arbitration in Santa Clara County, California."

Although Communicator could be obtained independently of SmartDownload, all the named user plaintiffs, except Fagan, downloaded and installed Communicator in connection with downloading SmartDownload.[7] Each of these plaintiffs allegedly arrived at a Netscape webpage[8] captioned "Smart-Download Communicator" that urged them to "Download With Confidence Using SmartDownload!" At or near the bottom of the screen facing plaintiffs was the prompt "Start Download" and a tinted button labeled "Download." By clicking on the button, plaintiffs initiated the download of SmartDownload. Once that process was complete, SmartDownload, as its first plug-in task, permitted plaintiffs to proceed with downloading and installing Communicator, an operation that was accompanied by the clickwrap display of Communicator's license terms described above.

---

3. There is a difference between downloading and installing a software program. When a user downloads a program from the Internet to his or her computer, the program file is stored on the user's hard drive but typically is not operable until the user installs or executes it, usually by double-clicking on the file and causing the program to run.

4. This kind of online software license agreement has come to be known as "clickwrap" (by analogy to "shrinkwrap," used in the licensing of tangible forms of software sold in packages) because it "presents the user with a message on his or her computer screen, requiring that the user manifest his or her assent to the terms of the license agreement by clicking on an icon. The product cannot be obtained or used unless and until the icon is clicked." *Specht*, 150 F.Supp.2d at 593–94 (footnote omitted). Just as breaking the shrinkwrap seal and using the enclosed computer program after encountering notice of the existence of governing license terms has been deemed by some courts to constitute assent to those terms in the context of tangible software, *see, e.g., ProCD, Inc. v. Zeidenberg*, 86 F.3d 1447, 1451 (7th Cir.1996), so clicking on a webpage's clickwrap button after receiving notice of the existence of license terms has been held by some courts to manifest an Internet user's assent to terms governing the use of downloadable intangible software, *see, e.g., Hotmail Corp. v. Van$ Money Pie Inc.*, 47 U.S.P.Q.2d 1020, 1025 (N.D.Cal.1998).

5. The term "user plaintiffs" here and elsewhere in this opinion denotes those plaintiffs who are suing for harm they allegedly incurred as computer users, in contrast to plaintiff Specht, who alleges that he was harmed in his capacity as a website owner. [Ed.—The portion of the opinion concerning Specht is omitted.]

6. While Navigator was Netscape's "standalone" Internet browser program during the period in question, Communicator was a "software suite" that comprised Navigator and other software products. All five named user plaintiffs stated in affidavits that they had obtained upgraded versions of Communicator. . . .

7. Unlike the four other user plaintiffs, Fagan chose the option of obtaining Netscape's browser program without first downloading SmartDownload. As discussed below, Fagan allegedly obtained SmartDownload from a separate "shareware" website unrelated to Netscape. [Ed.—In a subsequent portion of the opinion, the court held that Fagan's legal position was the same as that of the other user plaintiffs. This portion of the opinion is omitted.]

8. For purposes of this opinion, the term "webpage" or "page" is used to designate a document that resides, usually with other webpages, on a single Internet website and that contains information that is viewed on a computer monitor by scrolling through the document. To view a webpage in its entirety, a user typically must scroll through multiple screens.

The signal difference between downloading Communicator and downloading SmartDownload was that no clickwrap presentation accompanied the latter operation. Instead, once plaintiffs Gibson, Gruber, Kelly, and Weindorf had clicked on the "Download" button located at or near the bottom of their screen, and the downloading of SmartDownload was complete, these plaintiffs encountered no further information about the plug-in program or the existence of license terms governing its use.[9] The sole reference to SmartDownload's license terms on the "SmartDownload Communicator" webpage was located in text that would have become visible to plaintiffs only if they had scrolled down to the next screen.

Had plaintiffs scrolled down instead of acting on defendants' invitation to click on the "Download" button, they would have encountered the following invitation: "Please review and agree to the terms of the *Netscape SmartDownload software license agreement* before downloading and using the software." Plaintiffs Gibson, Gruber, Kelly, and Weindorf averred in their affidavits that they never saw this reference to the SmartDownload license agreement when they clicked on the "Download" button. They also testified during depositions that they saw no reference to license terms when they clicked to download SmartDownload, although under questioning by defendants' counsel, some plaintiffs added that they could not "remember" or be "sure" whether the screen shots of the SmartDownload page attached to their affidavits reflected precisely what they had seen on their computer screens when they downloaded SmartDownload.[10]

In sum, plaintiffs Gibson, Gruber, Kelly, and Weindorf allege that the process of obtaining SmartDownload contrasted sharply with that of obtaining Communicator. Having selected SmartDownload, they were required neither to express unambiguous assent to that program's license agreement nor even to view the license terms or become aware of their existence before proceeding with the invited download of the free plug-in program. Moreover, once these plaintiffs had initiated the download, the existence of SmartDownload's license terms was not mentioned while the software was running or at any later point in plaintiffs' experience of the product.

Even for a user who, unlike plaintiffs, did happen to scroll down past the download button, SmartDownload's license terms would not have been immediately displayed in the manner of Communicator's clickwrapped terms. Instead, if such a user had seen the notice of SmartDownload's terms and then clicked on the underlined invitation to review and agree to the terms, a hypertext link would have taken the user to a separate webpage entitled "License & Support Agreements." The first paragraph on this page read, in pertinent part:

> The use of each Netscape software product is governed by a license agreement. You must read and agree to the license agreement terms

9. Plaintiff Kelly, a relatively sophisticated Internet user, testified that when he clicked to download SmartDownload, he did not think that he was downloading a software program at all, but rather that SmartDownload "was merely a piece of download technology." He later became aware that SmartDownload was residing as software on his hard drive when he attempted to download electronic files from the Internet.

10. In the screen shot of the SmartDownload webpage attached to Weindorf's affidavit, the reference to license terms is partially visible, though almost illegible, at the bottom of the screen. In the screen shots attached to the affidavits of Gibson, Gruber, and Kelly, the reference to license terms is not visible.

BEFORE acquiring a product. Please click on the appropriate link below to review the current license agreement for the product of interest to you before acquisition. For products available for download, you must read and agree to the license agreement terms BEFORE you install the software. If you do not agree to the license terms, do not download, install or use the software.

Below this paragraph appeared a list of license agreements, the first of which was *"License Agreement for Netscape Navigator and Netscape Communicator Product Family* (Netscape Navigator, Netscape Communicator and Netscape SmartDownload)." If the user clicked on that link, he or she would be taken to yet another webpage that contained the full text of a license agreement that was identical in every respect to the Communicator license agreement except that it stated that its "terms apply to Netscape Communicator, Netscape Navigator, and Netscape SmartDownload." The license agreement granted the user a nonexclusive license to use and reproduce the software, subject to certain terms:

> BY CLICKING THE ACCEPTANCE BUTTON OR INSTALLING OR USING NETSCAPE COMMUNICATOR, NETSCAPE NAVIGATOR, OR NETSCAPE SMARTDOWNLOAD SOFTWARE (THE "PRODUCT"), THE INDIVIDUAL OR ENTITY LICENSING THE PRODUCT ("LICENSEE") IS CONSENTING TO BE BOUND BY AND IS BECOMING A PARTY TO THIS AGREEMENT. IF LICENSEE DOES NOT AGREE TO ALL OF THE TERMS OF THIS AGREEMENT, THE BUTTON INDICATING NON–ACCEPTANCE MUST BE SELECTED, AND LICENSEE MUST NOT INSTALL OR USE THE SOFTWARE.

Among the license terms was a provision requiring virtually all disputes relating to the agreement to be submitted to arbitration:

> Unless otherwise agreed in writing, all disputes relating to this Agreement (excepting any dispute relating to intellectual property rights) shall be subject to final and binding arbitration in Santa Clara County, California, under the auspices of JAMS/EndDispute, with the losing party paying all costs of arbitration. . . .

II. PROCEEDINGS BELOW

In the district court, defendants moved to compel arbitration and to stay court proceedings pursuant to the Federal Arbitration Act ("FAA"), 9 U.S.C. § 4, arguing that the disputes reflected in the complaints, like any other dispute relating to the SmartDownload license agreement, are subject to the arbitration clause contained in that agreement. Finding that Netscape's webpage, unlike typical examples of clickwrap, neither adequately alerted users to the existence of SmartDownload's license terms nor required users unambiguously to manifest assent to those terms as a condition of downloading the product, the court held that the user plaintiffs had not entered into the SmartDownload license agreement. *Specht,* 150 F.Supp.2d at 595–96.

The district court also ruled that the separate license agreement governing use of Communicator, even though the user plaintiffs had assented to its terms, involved an independent transaction that made no mention of SmartDownload and so did not bind plaintiffs to arbitrate their claims relating to SmartDownload. *Id.* at 596. . . .

DISCUSSION

I. STANDARD OF REVIEW AND APPLICABLE LAW

A district court's denial of a motion to compel arbitration is reviewed *de novo*....

The FAA provides that a "written provision in any ... contract evidencing a transaction involving commerce to settle by arbitration a controversy thereafter arising out of such contract or transaction ... shall be valid, irrevocable, and enforceable, save upon such grounds as exist at law or in equity for the revocation of any contract." 9 U.S.C. § 2. It is well settled that a court may not compel arbitration until it has resolved "the question of the very existence" of the contract embodying the arbitration clause. *Interocean Shipping Co. v. Nat'l Shipping & Trading Corp.*, 462 F.2d 673, 676 (2d Cir.1972). "[A]rbitration is a matter of contract and a party cannot be required to submit to arbitration any dispute which he has not agreed so to submit."

The district court properly concluded that in deciding whether parties agreed to arbitrate a certain matter, a court should generally apply state-law principles to the issue of contract formation.... The district court further held that California law governs the question of contract formation here; the parties do not appeal that determination....

In sum, we conclude that the district court properly decided the question of reasonable notice and objective manifestation of assent as a matter of law on the record before it, and we decline defendants' request to remand for a full trial on that question....

III. WHETHER THE USER PLAINTIFFS HAD REASONABLE NOTICE OF AND MANIFESTED ASSENT TO THE SMARTDOWNLOAD LICENSE AGREEMENT

Whether governed by the common law or by Article 2 of the Uniform Commercial Code ("UCC"), a transaction, in order to be a contract, requires a manifestation of agreement between the parties. *See Windsor Mills, Inc. v. Collins & Aikman Corp.*, 25 Cal.App.3d 987, 991, 101 Cal.Rptr. 347, 350 (1972) ("[C]onsent to, or acceptance of, the arbitration provision [is] necessary to create an agreement to arbitrate."); *see also* Cal. Com.Code § 2204(1) ("A contract for sale of goods may be made in any manner sufficient to show agreement, including conduct by both parties which recognizes the existence of such a contract.").[13] Mutual manifestation of assent, whether by written or spoken word or by conduct, is the touchstone of contract. *Binder v. Aetna Life Ins. Co.*, 75 Cal.App.4th 832, 848, 89 Cal.Rptr.2d 540, 551 (1999); *cf.* Restatement (Second) of Contracts § 19(2) (1981) ("The conduct of a party is not effective as a manifestation of his assent unless he intends to engage in the conduct and knows or has reason to know that the other party may infer from

---

13. The district court concluded that the SmartDownload transactions here should be governed by "California law as it relates to the sale of goods, including the Uniform Commercial Code in effect in California." *Specht*, 150 F.Supp.2d at 591. It is not obvious, however, that UCC Article 2 ("sales of goods") applies to the licensing of software that is downloadable from the Internet. *Cf. Advent Sys. Ltd. v. Unisys Corp.*, 925 F.2d 670, 675 (3d Cir.1991)...

We need not decide today whether UCC Article 2 applies to Internet transactions in downloadable products. The district court's analysis and the parties' arguments on appeal show that, for present purposes, there is no essential difference between UCC Article 2 and the common law of contracts. We therefore apply the common law, with exceptions as noted.

his conduct that he assents.''). Although an onlooker observing the disputed transactions in this case would have seen each of the user plaintiffs click on the SmartDownload "Download" button, *see Cedars Sinai Med. Ctr. v. Mid–West Nat'l Life Ins. Co.,* 118 F.Supp.2d 1002, 1008 (C.D.Cal.2000) ("In California, a party's intent to contract is judged objectively, by the party's outward manifestation of consent."), a consumer's clicking on a download button does not communicate assent to contractual terms if the offer did not make clear to the consumer that clicking on the download button would signify assent to those terms, *see Windsor Mills,* 25 Cal.App.3d at 992, 101 Cal.Rptr. at 351 ("[W]hen the offeree does not know that a proposal has been made to him this objective standard does not apply."). California's common law is clear that "an offeree, regardless of apparent manifestation of his consent, is not bound by inconspicuous contractual provisions of which he is unaware, contained in a document whose contractual nature is not obvious." *Id.; see also Marin Storage & Trucking, Inc. v. Benco Contracting & Eng'g, Inc.,* 89 Cal.App.4th 1042, 1049, 107 Cal.Rptr.2d 645, 651 (2001) (same).

Arbitration agreements are no exception to the requirement of manifestation of assent. "This principle of knowing consent applies with particular force to provisions for arbitration." *Windsor Mills,* 101 Cal.Rptr. at 351. Clarity and conspicuousness of arbitration terms are important in securing informed assent. "If a party wishes to bind in writing another to an agreement to arbitrate future disputes, such purpose should be accomplished in a way that each party to the arrangement will fully and clearly comprehend that the agreement to arbitrate exists and binds the parties thereto." *Commercial Factors Corp. v. Kurtzman Bros.,* 131 Cal.App.2d 133, 134–35, 280 P.2d 146, 147–48 (1955) (internal quotation marks omitted). Thus, California contract law measures assent by an objective standard that takes into account both what the offeree said, wrote, or did and the transactional context in which the offeree verbalized or acted.

A. The Reasonably Prudent Offeree of Downloadable Software

Defendants argue that plaintiffs must be held to a standard of reasonable prudence and that, because notice of the existence of SmartDownload license terms was on the next scrollable screen, plaintiffs were on "inquiry notice" of those terms.[14] We disagree with the proposition that a reasonably prudent offeree in plaintiffs' position would necessarily have known or learned of the existence of the SmartDownload license agreement prior to acting, so that plaintiffs may be held to have assented to that agreement with constructive notice of its terms. *See* Cal. Civ.Code § 1589 ("A voluntary acceptance of the benefit of a transaction is equivalent to a consent to all the obligations arising from it, so far as the facts are known, or ought to be known, to the person accepting."). It is true that "[a] party cannot avoid the terms of a contract on the ground that he or she failed to read it before signing." *Marin Storage & Trucking,* 89 Cal.App.4th at 1049, 107 Cal.Rptr.2d at 651. But courts are quick to add: "An exception to this general rule exists when the writing does not appear to be a contract and the terms are not called to the attention of the recipient. In such a case, no contract is formed with respect to the undisclosed term." *Id.; cf. Cory v. Golden State Bank,* 95 Cal.App.3d 360, 364,

---

14. "Inquiry notice" is "actual notice of circumstances sufficient to put a prudent man upon inquiry." *Cal. State Auto. Ass'n Inter–* *Ins. Bureau v. Barrett Garages, Inc.,* 257 Cal. App.2d 71, 64 Cal.Rptr. 699, 703 (Cal.Ct.App. 1967) (internal quotation marks omitted).

157 Cal.Rptr. 538, 541 (1979) ("[T]he provision in question is effectively hidden from the view of money order purchasers until after the transactions are completed. . . . Under these circumstances, it must be concluded that the Bank's money order purchasers are not chargeable with either actual or constructive notice of the service charge provision, and therefore cannot be deemed to have consented to the provision as part of their transaction with the Bank.").

Most of the cases cited by defendants in support of their inquiry-notice argument are drawn from the world of paper contracting. *See, e.g., Taussig v. Bode & Haslett,* 134 Cal. 260, 66 P. 259 (1901) (where party had opportunity to read leakage disclaimer printed on warehouse receipt, he had duty to do so); *In re First Capital Life Ins. Co.,* 34 Cal.App.4th 1283, 1288, 40 Cal. Rptr.2d 816, 820 (1995) (purchase of insurance policy after opportunity to read and understand policy terms creates binding agreement); *King v. Larsen Realty, Inc.,* 121 Cal.App.3d 349, 356, 175 Cal.Rptr. 226, 231 (1981) (where realtors' board manual specifying that party was required to arbitrate was "readily available," party was "on notice" that he was agreeing to mandatory arbitration); *Cal. State Auto. Ass'n Inter–Ins. Bureau v. Barrett Garages, Inc.,* 257 Cal.App.2d 71, 76, 64 Cal.Rptr. 699, 703 (1967) (recipient of airport parking claim check was bound by terms printed on claim check, because [an] "ordinarily prudent" person would have been alerted to the terms); *Larrus v. First Nat'l Bank,* 122 Cal.App.2d 884, 888, 266 P.2d 143, 147 (1954) ("clearly printed" statement on bank card stating that depositor agreed to bank's regulations provided sufficient notice to create agreement, where party had opportunity to view statement and to ask for full text of regulations, but did not do so); *see also Hux v. Butler,* 339 F.2d 696, 700 (6th Cir.1964) (constructive notice found where "slightest inquiry" would have disclosed relevant facts to offeree); *Walker v. Carnival Cruise Lines,* 63 F.Supp.2d 1083, 1089 (N.D.Cal.1999) (under California and federal law, "conspicuous notice" directing the attention of parties to existence of contract terms renders terms binding) (quotation marks omitted); *Shacket v. Roger Smith Aircraft Sales, Inc.,* 651 F.Supp. 675, 691 (N.D.Ill.1986) (constructive notice found where "minimal investigation" would have revealed facts to offeree).

As the foregoing cases suggest, receipt of a physical document containing contract terms or notice thereof is frequently deemed, in the world of paper transactions, a sufficient circumstance to place the offeree on inquiry notice of those terms. "Every person who has actual notice of circumstances sufficient to put a prudent man upon inquiry as to a particular fact, has constructive notice of the fact itself in all cases in which, by prosecuting such inquiry, he might have learned such fact." Cal. Civ.Code § 19. These principles apply equally to the emergent world of online product delivery, pop-up screens, hyperlinked pages, clickwrap licensing, scrollable documents, and urgent admonitions to "Download Now!". What plaintiffs saw when they were being invited by defendants to download this fast, free plug-in called SmartDownload was a screen containing praise for the product and, at the very bottom of the screen, a "Download" button. Defendants argue that under the principles set forth in the cases cited above, a "fair and prudent person using ordinary care" would have been on inquiry notice of SmartDownload's license terms. *Shacket,* 651 F.Supp. at 690.

We are not persuaded that a reasonably prudent offeree in these circumstances would have known of the existence of license terms. Plaintiffs were responding to an offer that did not carry an immediately visible notice of the existence of license terms or require unambiguous manifestation of assent to those terms. Thus, plaintiffs' "apparent manifestation of . . . consent" was to terms "contained in a document whose contractual nature [was] not obvious." *Windsor Mills,* 25 Cal.App.3d at 992, 101 Cal.Rptr. at 351. Moreover, the fact that, given the position of the scroll bar on their computer screens, plaintiffs may have been aware that an unexplored portion of the Netscape webpage remained below the download button does not mean that they reasonably should have concluded that this portion contained a notice of license terms. In their deposition testimony, plaintiffs variously stated that they used the scroll bar "[o]nly if there is something that I feel I need to see that is on—that is off the page," or that the elevated position of the scroll bar suggested the presence of "mere[ ] formalities, standard lower banner links" or "that the page is bigger than what I can see." Plaintiffs testified, and defendants did not refute, that plaintiffs were in fact unaware that defendants intended to attach license terms to the use of SmartDownload.

We conclude that in circumstances such as these, where consumers are urged to download free software at the immediate click of a button, a reference to the existence of license terms on a submerged screen is not sufficient to place consumers on inquiry or constructive notice of those terms.[15] The SmartDownload webpage screen was "printed in such a manner that it tended to conceal the fact that it was an express acceptance of [Netscape's] rules and regulations." *Larrus,* 266 P.2d at 147. Internet users may have, as defendants put it, "as much time as they need[ ]" to scroll through multiple screens on a webpage, but there is no reason to assume that viewers will scroll down to subsequent screens simply because screens are there. When products are "free" and users are invited to download them in the absence of reasonably conspicuous notice that they are about to bind themselves to contract terms, the transactional circumstances cannot be fully analogized to those in the paper world of arm's-length bargaining. In the next two sections, we discuss case law and other legal authorities that have addressed the circumstances of computer sales, software licensing, and online transacting. Those authorities tend strongly to support our conclusion that plaintiffs did not manifest assent to SmartDownload's license terms.

B. Shrinkwrap Licensing and Related Practices

Defendants cite certain well-known cases involving shrinkwrap licensing and related commercial practices in support of their contention that plaintiffs became bound by the SmartDownload license terms by virtue of inquiry notice. For example, in *Hill v. Gateway 2000, Inc.,* 105 F.3d 1147 (7th Cir.1997), the Seventh Circuit held that where a purchaser had ordered a computer over the telephone, received the order in a shipped box containing the computer along with printed contract terms, and did not return the computer within the thirty days required by the terms, the purchaser was bound by the contract. *Id.* at 1148–49. In *ProCD, Inc. v. Zeidenberg,* the same court held that where an individual purchased software in a box containing license terms which were displayed on the computer screen every time the

---

15. We do not address the district court's alternative holding that notice was further vitiated by the fact that the reference to Smart-Download's license terms, even if scrolled to, was couched in precatory terms ("a mild request") rather than mandatory ones. *Specht,* 150 F.Supp.2d at 596.

user executed the software program, the user had sufficient opportunity to review the terms and to return the software, and so was contractually bound after retaining the product. *ProCD,* 86 F.3d at 1452; *cf. Moore v. Microsoft Corp.,* 293 A.D.2d 587, 587, 741 N.Y.S.2d 91, 92 (2d Dep't 2002) (software user was bound by license agreement where terms were prominently displayed on computer screen before software could be installed and where user was required to indicate assent by clicking "I agree"); *Brower v. Gateway 2000, Inc.,* 246 A.D.2d 246, 251, 676 N.Y.S.2d 569, 572 (1st Dep't 1998) (buyer assented to arbitration clause shipped inside box with computer and software by retaining items beyond date specified by license terms); *M.A. Mortenson Co. v. Timberline Software Corp.,* 93 Wash.App. 819, 970 P.2d 803, 809 (1999) (buyer manifested assent to software license terms by installing and using software), *aff'd,* 140 Wash.2d 568, 998 P.2d 305 (2000); *see also I.Lan Sys.,* 183 F.Supp.2d at 338 (business entity "explicitly accepted the clickwrap license agreement [contained in purchased software] when it clicked on the box stating 'I agree' ").

These cases do not help defendants. To the extent that they hold that the purchaser of a computer or tangible software is contractually bound after failing to object to printed license terms provided with the product, *Hill* and *Brower* do not differ markedly from the cases involving traditional paper contracting discussed in the previous section. Insofar as the purchaser in *ProCD* was confronted with conspicuous, mandatory license terms every time he ran the software on his computer, that case actually undermines defendants' contention that downloading in the absence of conspicuous terms is an act that binds plaintiffs to those terms. In *Mortenson,* the full text of license terms was printed on each sealed diskette envelope inside the software box, printed again on the inside cover of the user manual, and notice of the terms appeared on the computer screen every time the purchaser executed the program. *Mortenson,* 970 P.2d at 806. In sum, the foregoing cases are clearly distinguishable from the facts of the present action.

C. Online Transactions

Cases in which courts have found contracts arising from Internet use do not assist defendants, because in those circumstances there was much clearer notice than in the present case that a user's act would manifest assent to contract terms. *See, e.g., Hotmail Corp. v. Van$ Money Pie Inc.,* 47 U.S.P.Q.2d 1020, 1025 (N.D.Cal.1998) (granting preliminary injunction based in part on breach of "Terms of Service" agreement, to which defendants had assented); *America Online, Inc. v. Booker,* 781 So.2d 423, 425 (Fla.Dist.Ct.App.2001) (upholding forum selection clause in "freely negotiated agreement" contained in online terms of service); *Caspi v. Microsoft Network, L.L.C.,* 323 N.J.Super. 118, 732 A.2d 528, 530, 532–33 (N.J.Super.Ct.App.Div.1999) (upholding forum selection clause where subscribers to online software were required to review license terms in scrollable window and to click "I Agree" or "I Don't Agree"); *Barnett v. Network Solutions, Inc.,* 38 S.W.3d 200, 203–04 (Tex.App.2001) (upholding forum selection clause in online contract for registering Internet domain names that required users to scroll through terms before accepting or rejecting them); *cf. Pollstar v. Gigmania, Ltd.,* 170 F.Supp.2d 974, 981–82 (E.D.Cal.2000) (expressing concern that notice of license terms had appeared in small, gray text on a gray background on a linked webpage, but concluding that it was too early in the case to order dismissal).

After reviewing the California common law and other relevant legal authority, we conclude that under the circumstances here, plaintiffs' downloading of SmartDownload did not constitute acceptance of defendants' license terms. Reasonably conspicuous notice of the existence of contract terms and unambiguous manifestation of assent to those terms by consumers are essential if electronic bargaining is to have integrity and credibility. We hold that a reasonably prudent offeree in plaintiffs' position would not have known or learned, prior to acting on the invitation to download, of the reference to SmartDownload's license terms hidden below the "Download" button on the next screen. We affirm the district court's conclusion that the user plaintiffs, including Fagan, are not bound by the arbitration clause contained in those terms.

IV. Whether Plaintiffs' Assent to Communicator's License Agreement Requires Them To Arbitrate Their Claims Regarding SmartDownload

Plaintiffs do not dispute that they assented to the license terms governing Netscape's Communicator. The parties disagree, however, over the scope of that license's arbitration clause. Defendants contend that the scope is broad enough to encompass plaintiffs' claims regarding SmartDownload, even if plaintiffs did not separately assent to SmartDownload's license terms and even though Communicator's license terms did not expressly mention Smart-Download. Thus, defendants argue, plaintiffs must arbitrate. . . .

After careful review of these allegations, we conclude that plaintiffs' claims "present no question involving construction of the [Communicator license agreement], and no questions in respect of the parties' rights and obligations under it." *Collins & Aikman,* 58 F.3d at 23. It follows that the claims of the five user plaintiffs are beyond the scope of the arbitration clause contained in the Communicator license agreement. Because those claims are not arbitrable under that agreement or under the SmartDownload license agreement, to which plaintiffs never assented, we affirm the district court's holding that the five user plaintiffs may not be compelled to arbitrate their claims. . . .

CONCLUSION

For the foregoing reasons, we affirm the district court's denial of defendants' motion to compel arbitration and to stay court proceedings.

REGISTER.COM, INC. v. VERIO, INC.

United States Court of Appeals, Second Circuit, 2004.
356 F.3d 393.

Before: LEVAL, Circuit Judge, and J.F. KEENAN, District Judge.*

LEVAL, Circuit Judge.

Defendant, Verio, Inc. ("Verio") appeals from an order of the United States District Court for the Southern District of New York (Barbara S.

---

*The Honorable John F. Keenan, United States District Judge for the Southern District of New York, sitting by designation. The Honorable Fred I. Parker was a member of the panel but died on August 12, 2003. Judge Par-ker would have voted to reverse the district court's order. This appeal is being decided by the two remaining members of the panel, who are in agreement. . . .

Jones, J.) granting the motion of plaintiff Register.com, Inc. ("Register") for a preliminary injunction. The court's order enjoined Verio from, [among other things,] using data obtained from Register's database of contact information of registrants of Internet domain names to solicit the registrants for the sale of web site development services by electronic mail, telephone calls, or direct mail. We affirm.

BACKGROUND

This plaintiff Register is one of over fifty companies serving as registrars for the issuance of domain names on the world wide web. As a registrar, Register issues domain names to persons and entities preparing to establish web sites on the Internet. Web sites are identified and accessed by reference to their domain names.

Register was appointed a registrar of domain names by the Internet Corporation for Assigned Names and Numbers, known by the acronym "ICANN." ICANN is a private, non-profit public benefit corporation which was established by agencies of the U.S. government to administer the Internet domain name system. To become a registrar of domain names, Register was required to enter into a standard form agreement with ICANN, designated as the ICANN Registrar Accreditation Agreement, November 1999 version (referred to herein as the "ICANN Agreement").

Applicants to register a domain name submit to the registrar contact information, including at a minimum, the applicant's name, postal address, telephone number, and electronic mail address. The ICANN Agreement, referring to this registrant contact information under the rubric "WHOIS information," requires the registrar, under terms discussed in greater detail below, to preserve it, update it daily, and provide for free public access to it through the Internet as well as through an independent access port, called port 43. *See* ICANN Agreement § II.F.1....

In compliance with § II.F.1 of the ICANN Agreement, Register updated the WHOIS information on a daily basis and established Internet and port 43 service, which allowed free public query of its WHOIS information. An entity making a WHOIS query through Register's Internet site or port 43 would receive a reply furnishing the requested WHOIS information, captioned by a legend devised by Register, which stated,

> By submitting a WHOIS query, you agree that you will use this data only for lawful purposes and that under no circumstances will you use this data to ... support the transmission of mass unsolicited, commercial advertising or solicitation via email.

... Subsequently, as explained below, Register amended the terms of this legend to impose more stringent restrictions on the use of the information gathered through such queries.

In addition to performing the function of a registrar of domain names, Register also engages in the business of selling web-related services to entities that maintain web sites. These services cover various aspects of web site development. In order to solicit business for the services it offers, Register sends out marketing communications. Among the entities it solicits for the sale of such services are entities whose domain names it registered. However, during the registration process, Register offers registrants the opportunity to elect whether or not they will receive marketing communications from it.

The defendant Verio, against whom the preliminary injunction was issued, is engaged in the business of selling a variety of web site design, development and operation services. In the sale of such services, Verio competes with Register's web site development business. To facilitate its pursuit of customers, Verio undertook to obtain daily updates of the WHOIS information relating to newly registered domain names. To achieve this, Verio devised an automated software program, or robot, which each day would submit multiple successive WHOIS queries through the port 43 accesses of various registrars. Upon acquiring the WHOIS information of new registrants, Verio would send them marketing solicitations by email, telemarketing and direct mail. To the extent that Verio's solicitations were sent by email, the practice was inconsistent with the terms of the restrictive legend Register attached to its responses to Verio's queries....

In the meantime, Register changed the restrictive legend it attached to its responses to WHOIS queries.... [I]ts new legend undertook to bar mass solicitation "via direct mail, electronic mail, or by telephone." ...

Register wrote to Verio demanding that it cease using WHOIS information derived from Register not only for email marketing, but also for marketing by direct mail and telephone. Verio ceased using the information in email marketing, but refused to stop marketing by direct mail and telephone.

Register brought this suit on August 3, 2000, and moved for a temporary restraining order and a preliminary injunction.... On December 8, 2000, the district court entered a preliminary injunction. The injunction barred Verio from ... [using any data currently in Verio's possession, custody or control, that using its best efforts, Verio can identify as having been obtained from Register.com's computers and computer networks, to enable the transmission of unsolicited commercial electronic mail, telephone calls, or direct mail to the individuals listed in said data.] Verio appeals from that order.

DISCUSSION ...

... Verio contends that it ... never became contractually bound to the conditions imposed by Register's restrictive legend because, in the case of each query Verio made, the legend did not appear until after Verio had submitted the query and received the WHOIS data. Accordingly, Verio contends that in no instance did it receive legally enforceable notice of the conditions Register intended to impose. Verio therefore argues it should not be deemed to have taken WHOIS data from Register's systems subject to Register's conditions.

Verio's argument might well be persuasive if its queries addressed to Register's computers had been sporadic and infrequent. If Verio had submitted only one query, or even if it had submitted only a few sporadic queries, that would give considerable force to its contention that it obtained the WHOIS data without being conscious that Register intended to impose conditions, and without being deemed to have accepted Register's conditions. But Verio was daily submitting numerous queries, each of which resulted in its receiving notice of the terms Register exacted. Furthermore, Verio admits that it knew perfectly well what terms Register demanded. Verio's argument fails.

The situation might be compared to one in which plaintiff P maintains a roadside fruit stand displaying bins of apples. A visitor, defendant D, takes an apple and bites into it. As D turns to leave, D sees a sign, visible only as one turns to exit, which says "Apples—50 cents apiece." D does not pay for the apple. D believes he has no obligation to pay because he had no notice when he bit into the apple that 50 cents was expected in return. D's view is that he never agreed to pay for the apple. Thereafter, each day, several times a day, D revisits the stand, takes an apple, and eats it. D never leaves money.

P sues D in contract for the price of the apples taken. D defends on the ground that on no occasion did he see P's price notice until after he had bitten into the apples. D may well prevail as to the first apple taken. D had no reason to understand upon taking it that P was demanding the payment. In our view, however, D cannot continue on a daily basis to take apples for free, knowing full well that P is offering them only in exchange for 50 cents in compensation, merely because the sign demanding payment is so placed that on each occasion D does not see it until he has bitten into the apple.

Verio's circumstance is effectively the same. Each day Verio repeatedly enters Register's computers and takes that day's new WHOIS data. Each day upon receiving the requested data, Verio receives Register's notice of the terms on which it makes the data available—that the data not be used for mass solicitation via direct mail, email, or telephone. Verio acknowledges that it continued drawing the data from Register's computers with full knowledge that Register offered access subject to these restrictions. Verio is no more free to take Register's data without being bound by the terms on which Register offers it, than D was free, in the example, once he became aware of the terms of P's offer, to take P's apples without obligation to pay the 50 cent price at which P offered them.

Verio seeks support for its position from cases that have dealt with the formation of contracts on the Internet. An excellent example, although decided subsequent to the submission of this case, is *Specht v. Netscape Communications Corp.*, 306 F.3d 17 (2d Cir.2002). The dispute was whether users of Netscape's software, who downloaded it from Netscape's web site, were bound by an agreement to arbitrate disputes with Netscape, where Netscape had posted the terms of its offer of the software (including the obligation to arbitrate disputes) on the web site from which they downloaded the software. We ruled against Netscape and in favor of the users of its software because the users would not have seen the terms Netscape exacted without scrolling down their computer screens, and there was no reason for them to do so. The evidence did not demonstrate that one who had download-ed Netscape's software had necessarily seen the terms of its offer.

Verio, however, cannot avail itself of the reasoning of *Specht*. In *Specht*, the users in whose favor we decided visited Netscape's web site one time to download its software. Netscape's posting of its terms did not compel the conclusion that its downloaders took the software subject to those terms because there was no way to determine that any downloader had seen the terms of the offer. There was no basis for imputing to the downloaders of Netscape's software knowledge of the terms on which the software was offered. This case is crucially different. Verio visited Register's computers daily to access WHOIS data and each day saw the terms of Register's offer;

Verio admitted that, in entering Register's computers to get the data, it was fully aware of the terms on which Register offered the access.

Verio's next argument is that it was not bound by Register's terms because it rejected them. Even assuming Register is entitled to demand compliance with its terms in exchange for Verio's entry into its systems to take WHOIS data, and even acknowledging that Verio was fully aware of Register's terms, Verio contends that it still is not bound by Register's terms because it did not agree to be bound. In support of its claim, Verio cites a district court case from the Central District of California, *Ticketmaster Corp. v. Tickets.com, Inc.,* No. CV99–7654, 2000 WL 1887522 (C.D.Cal. Aug.10, 2000), in which the court rejected Ticketmaster's application for a preliminary injunction to enforce posted terms of use of data available on its website against a regular user. Noting that the user of Ticketmaster's web site is not required to check an "I agree" box before proceeding, the court concluded that there was insufficient proof of agreement to support a preliminary injunction. *Id.* at *5.

We acknowledge that the *Ticketmaster* decision gives Verio some support, but not enough. In the first place, the *Ticketmaster court* was not making a definitive ruling rejecting Ticketmaster's contract claim. It was rather exercising a district court's discretion to deny a preliminary injunction because of a doubt whether the movant had adequately shown likelihood of success on the merits.

But more importantly, we are not inclined to agree with the *Ticketmaster* court's analysis. There is a crucial difference between the circumstances of *Specht,* where we declined to enforce Netscape's specified terms against a user of its software because of inadequate evidence that the user had seen the terms when downloading the software, and those of *Ticketmaster,* where the taker of information from Ticketmaster's site knew full well the terms on which the information was offered but was not offered an icon marked, "I agree," on which to click. Under the circumstances of *Ticketmaster,* we see no reason why the enforceability of the offeror's terms should depend on whether the taker states (or clicks), "I agree."

We recognize that contract offers on the Internet often require the offeree to click on an "I agree" icon. And no doubt, in many circumstances, such a statement of agreement by the offeree is essential to the formation of a contract. But not in all circumstances. While new commerce on the Internet has exposed courts to many new situations, it has not fundamentally changed the principles of contract. It is standard contract doctrine that when a benefit is offered subject to stated conditions, and the offeree makes a decision to take the benefit with knowledge of the terms of the offer, the taking constitutes an acceptance of the terms, which accordingly become binding on the offeree. *See, e.g.,* Restatement (Second) of Contracts § 69(1)(a) (1981) ("[S]ilence and inaction operate as an acceptance ... [w]here an offeree takes the benefit of offered services with reasonable opportunity to reject them and reason to know that they were offered with the expectation of compensation."); 2 Richard A. Lord, Williston on Contracts § 6:9 (4th ed. 1991) ("[T]he acceptance of the benefit of services may well be held to imply a promise to pay for them if at the time of acceptance the offeree has a reasonable opportunity to reject the service and knows or has reason to know that compensation is expected."); Arthur Linton Corbin, Corbin on Contracts § 71 (West 1 vol. ed.

1952) ("The acceptance of the benefit of the services is a promise to pay for them, if at the time of accepting the benefit the offeree has a reasonable opportunity to reject it and knows that compensation is expected."); *Jones v. Brisbin,* 41 Wash.2d 167, 172, 247 P.2d 891 (1952) ("Where a person, with reasonable opportunity to reject offered services, takes the benefit of them under circumstances which would indicate, to a reasonable man, that they were offered with the expectation of compensation, a contract, complete with mutual assent, results."); *Markstein Bros. Millinery Co. v. J.A. White & Co.,* 151 Ark. 1, 235 S.W. 39 (1921) (buyer of hats was bound to pay for hats when buyer failed to return them to seller within five days of inspection as seller requested in clear and obvious notice statement).

Returning to the apple stand, the visitor, who sees apples offered for 50 cents apiece and takes an apple, owes 50 cents, regardless whether he did or did not say, "I agree." The choice offered in such circumstances is to take the apple on the known terms of the offer or not to take the apple. As we see it, the defendant in *Ticketmaster* and Verio in this case had a similar choice. Each was offered access to information subject to terms of which they were well aware. Their choice was either to accept the offer of contract, taking the information subject to the terms of the offer, or, if the terms were not acceptable, to decline to take the benefits.

We find that the district court was within its discretion in concluding that Register showed likelihood of success on the merits of its contract claim....

CONCLUSION

The ruling of the district court is hereby AFFIRMED....

———

Chapter 17

INTERPRETATION AND UNCON-
SCIONABILITY IN A FORM–
CONTRACT SETTING

SARDO v. FIDELITY & DEPOSIT CO.

Court of Errors and Appeals of New Jersey, 1926.
100 N.J.Eq. 332, 134 A. 774.

Suit by Thomas Sardo against the Fidelity & Deposit Company of Maryland to reform a policy of insurance. From a decree for plaintiff (98 N.J.Eq. 22, 131 A. 73), defendant appeals. Reversed.

Kays, J. The bill in this case was filed by the complainant-respondent for the purpose of having a policy of insurance reformed which had been issued by the defendant, the Fidelity & Deposit Company of Maryland, to Thomas Sardo, the complainant-respondent. It appears from the proofs in this case that Thomas Sardo, the complainant, desired to obtain insurance against theft on his stock of jewelry in a store in the city of Paterson, N.J., which business was there conducted by him. Sardo applied for such insurance to one Lederer, who took him to a man named Mellor Newman. Newman, whose office was in the city of Paterson, was an agent for the defendant company. Newman told the complainant that he had authority to write burglary insurance only, and that he would confer with the company concerning the kind of policy which Sardo desired. It appears that the issuing office of the company for the Paterson district was under the management of one Brush at Newark, N.J. Brush, prior to the issuance of the policy, visited the complainant's place of business for the purpose of investigating the risk. The company, after these negotiations with the complainant, through the several agents issued a policy of insurance covering money and securities of the complainant, but not including jewelry. Mellor Newman received the policy, examined it, observed its language and scope, but concluded that, as he had applied to the company for a policy covering jewelry, the words "money and securities" embraced within their meaning also jewelry. Newman turned over this policy to Lederer, who was not an agent of the company, but evidently an insurance broker with whom Sardo transacted business. Lederer did not examine the policy, but gave it to Sardo, and Sardo did not read it, but assumed that it covered jewelry. In this policy, which was delivered to Sardo, the word "securities" is defined as follows:

" 'Securities' as used in this policy shall mean only such bonds, debentures, checks, coupons, demand and time drafts, promissory notes, bills of exchange, warehouse receipts, bills of lading, express and postal money orders, certificates of stock and deposit, and other instruments as are negotiable, and as respects which when negotiated the assured has no recourse against the innocent holder."

Sardo paid the agent the usual premium or charge made by the company for the kind of policy which was actually issued to him.

Subsequently there was a robbery of Sardo's store, and a considerable amount of jewelry was stolen therefrom. It further appeared that, when the complainant, Sardo, applied to the agent of the company for the issuing of the policy, the agent had knowledge that there were no securities in the complainant's store. Basing his opinion largely upon this fact, the Vice Chancellor concluded that Sardo, the complainant, was entitled to have the policy of insurance reformed to include the item of jewelry. Thereupon a decree was made, striking from the policy the word "securities" and inserting therein the word "jewelry," so that the said policy should read "money and jewelry" instead of "money and securities." From this decree the defendant appeals.

We think the conclusion of the Vice Chancellor was erroneous. It is not contended in this case that there was fraud practiced by the defendant upon the complainant, nor did the complainant attempt to rescind the contract. There is no suggestion that the officers of the company or any agent representing them in the writing of this policy understood the policy was to cover anything more than was expressed in it, to wit, money and securities. The rule laid down in this state is that, in order to reform a contract of insurance or other written contract in the absence of fraud on the part of the defendant, it must appear that the minds of the parties to said contract have met, and that a mutual mistake of the contracting parties has been made in writing out the contract, so that the parties appear to have entered into a contract which they have not entered into. The reformation, therefore, of such a contract must be to make the written contract to conform to that upon which the minds of the parties have met. It cannot be said in this case that, because the complainant assumed that the word "securities" included jewelry, or because he did not read the policy, the defendant intended that the word "securities" was to include the word "jewelry." . . .

The most that can be said in this case is that it was the opinion of the agent Newman that this policy covered jewelry, although this opinion was not even expressed to the complainant, Sardo, or his broker; and, even though this were so, it would not bind the company. The assumption of Sardo that the word "securities" included jewelry, or that the policy included the word "jewelry," was, of course, without foundation, and he cannot now obtain the relief he seeks by reason of his unwarranted assumption, nor upon the ground that there was a mutual mistake. The word "securities" as above mentioned was very clearly defined in the policy, and a reading of the policy would immediately show that jewelry was not embraced within the term "securities." There is no evidence in this case which would indicate that a mutual mistake had been made, or that the company intended to issue any other policy than the policy which was actually issued.

The decree of the Court of Chancery will therefore be reversed.

For affirmance: JUSTICES MINTURN, KALISCH, and LLOYD, and JUDGES VAN BUSKIRK, and HETFIELD.

For reversal: THE CHIEF JUSTICE, JUSTICES TRENCHARD, PARKER, BLACK, KATZEN-BACH, and CAMPBELL, and JUDGES WHITE, GARDNER, MCGLENNON, and KAYS.

LLEWELLYN, THE COMMON LAW TRADITION: DECIDING APPEALS

362–371 (1960).

The impetus to the form-pad is clear, for any business unit: by standardizing terms, and by standardizing even the spot on the form where any individually dickered term appears, one saves all the time and skill otherwise needed to dig out and record the meaning of variant language; one makes check-up, totaling, follow-through, etc., into routine operations; one has duplicates (in many colors) available for the administration of a multidepartment business; and so on more. The content of the standardized terms accumulates experience, it avoids or reduces legal risks and also confers all kinds of operating leeways and advantages, all without need of either consulting counsel from instance to instance or of bargaining with the other parties. Not to be overlooked, either, is the tailoring of the crude misfitting hand-me-down pattern of the "general law" "in the absence of agreement" to the particular detailed working needs of your own line of business—whether apartment rentals, stock brokerage, international grain trade, installment selling of appliances, flour milling, sugar beet raising, or insurance. It would be a heartwarming scene, a triumph of private attention to what is essentially private self-government in the lesser transactions of life or in those areas too specialized for the blunt, slow tools of the legislature—if only all businessmen and all their lawyers would be reasonable.

But power, like greed, if it does not always corrupt, goes easily to the head. So that the form-agreements tend either at once or over the years, and often by whole lines of trade, into a massive and almost terrifying jug-handled character; the one party lays his head into the mouth of a lion—either, and mostly, without reading the fine print, or occasionally in hope and expectation (not infrequently solid) that it will be a sweet and gentle lion. The more familiar instances, perhaps, are the United Realtors' Standard Lease, almost any bank's collateral note or agreement, almost any installment sale form, an accident insurance policy, a steamship ticket, a beet sugar refinery contract with a farmer or a flour miller's with its customer; or, on a lesser scale, the standard nonwarranty given by seed companies or auto manufacturers. In regard to such, one notes four things: (1) sometimes language which seems at first sight horrifying may have good human and economic stimulus; thus, suits for loss of crop before a farmer jury are pretty terrible things to face for the price of a few bags of seed; and (2) there are crooked claims and there are irrationally unreasonable ones—each with its jury risk—as well as solid ones; and only a clause which in law bars the claim absolutely can free an outfit like an insurance company to deal fairly though "in its discretion" with the latter class. On the other hand, (3) boiler-plate clauses can and often do run far beyond any such need or excuse, sometimes ... involving flagrant trickery;

and (4) not all "dominant" parties are nice lions, and even nice lions can make mistakes.

There is a fifth and no less vital thing to note: Where the form is drawn with a touch of Mr. Dooley's "gentlemanly restraint," or where, as with the overseas grain contracts or the Pacific Coast dried fruit contracts or the Worth Street Rules on textiles, two-fisted bargainers on either side have worked out in the form a balanced code to govern the particular line or trade or industry, there is every reason for a court to assume both fairness and wisdom in the terms, and to seek in first instance to learn, understand, and fit both its own thinking and its action into the whole design. Contracts of this kind (so long as reasonable in the net) are a road to better than official-legal regulation of our economic life. . . .

. . . [T]he true answer to the whole problem seems, amusingly, to be one which could occur to any court or any lawyer, at any time, as readily as to a scholar who had spent a lifetime on the subject—though I doubt if it could occur to anyone without the inquiry and analysis in depth which we owe to the scholarly work.

The answer, I suggest, is this: Instead of thinking about "assent" to boilerplate clauses, we can recognize that so far as concerns the specific, there is no assent at all. What has in fact been assented to, specifically, are the few dickered terms, and the broad type of the transaction, and but one thing more. That one thing more is a blanket assent (not a specific assent) to any not unreasonable or indecent terms the seller may have on his form, which do not alter or eviscerate the reasonable meaning of the dickered terms. The fine print which has not been read has no business to cut under the reasonable meaning of those dickered terms which constitute the dominant and only real expression of agreement. . . .

The queer thing is that where the transaction occurs without the fine print present, courts do not find this general line of approach too hard to understand: thus . . . [I cannot] see a court having trouble, where a short memo agrees in due course to sign "our standard contract," in rejecting an outrageous form as not being fairly within the reasonable meaning of the term. The clearest case to see is the handing over of a blank check: no court, judging as between the parties, would fail to reach for the circumstances, in determining whether the amount filled in had gone beyond the reasonable.

Why, then, can we not face the fact where boiler-plate is present? There has been an arm's length deal, with dickered terms. There has been accompanying that basic deal another which, if not on any fiduciary basis, at least involves a plain expression of confidence, asked and accepted, with a corresponding limit on the powers granted: the boiler-plate is assented to en bloc, "unsight, unseen," on the implicit assumption and to the full extent that (1) it does not alter or impair the fair meaning of the dickered terms when read alone, and (2) that its terms are neither in the particular nor in the net manifestly unreasonable and unfair. Such is the reality, and I see nothing in the way of a court's operating on that basis, to truly effectuate the only intention which can in reason be worked out as common to the two parties, granted good faith. And if the boiler-plate party is not playing in good faith, there is law enough to bar that fact from benefiting it. We had a hundred years of sales law in which any sales transaction with explicit words resulted in two several contracts for the one consideration: that of sale, and the collateral one of warranty. The idea is applicable here, for better reason: any contract with boiler-plate results in *two* several contracts: the *dickered* deal, and the collateral one of *supplementary* boiler-plate.

Rooted in sense, history, and simplicity, it is an answer which could occur to anyone.

WEAVER v. AMERICAN OIL CO.

Supreme Court of Indiana, 1971.
257 Ind. 458, 276 N.E.2d 144.

Action for a declaratory judgment to determine whether exculpatory and indemnity clauses of gas station lease were enforceable. The Circuit Court, Marshall County, Roy Sheneman, J., upheld enforceability, and lessee appealed. The Appellate Court, 261 N.E. 99, reversed and remanded. On rehearing, 262 N.E.2d 663, the prior opinion was modified, and petition to transfer appeal was granted. . . .

ARTERBURN, CHIEF JUSTICE. In this case the appellee oil company presented to the appellant-defendant leasee, a filling station operator, a printed form contract as a lease to be signed, by the defendant, which contained, in addition to the normal leasing provisions, a "hold harmless" clause which provided in substance that the leasee operator would hold harmless and also indemnify the oil company for any negligence of the oil company occurring on the leased premises. The litigation arises as a result of the oil company's own employee spraying gasoline over Weaver and his assistant and causing them to be burned and injured on the leased premises. This action was initiated by American Oil and Hoffer (Appellees) for a declaratory judgment to determine the liability of appellant Weaver, under the clause in the lease. The trial court entered judgment holding Weaver liable under the lease.

Clause three [3] of the lease reads as follows:

"Lessor, its agents and employees shall not be liable for any loss, damage, injuries, or other casualty of whatsoever kind or by whomsoever caused to the person or property of anyone (including Lessee) on or off the premises, arising out of or resulting from Lessee's use, possession or operation thereof, or from defects in the premises whether apparent or hidden, or from the installation[,] existence, use, maintenance, condition, repair, alteration, removal or replacement of any equipment thereon, whether due in whole or in part to negligent acts or omissions of Lessor, its agents or employees; and Lessee for himself, his heirs, executors, administrators, successors and assigns, hereby agrees to indemnify and hold Lessor, its agents and employees, harmless from and against all claims, demands, liabilities, suits or actions (including all reasonable expenses and attorneys' fees incurred by or imposed on the Lessor in connection therewith) for such loss, damage, injury or other casualty. Lessee also agrees to pay all reasonable expenses and attorneys' fees incurred by Lessor in the event that Lessee shall default under the provisions of this paragraph."

It will be noted that this lease clause not only exculpated the lessor oil company from its liability for its negligence, but also compelled Weaver to indemnify them for any damages or loss incurred as a result of its negligence. The appellate court held the exculpatory clause invalid, 261 N.E.2d 99, but the indemnifying clause valid, 262 N.E.2d 663. In our opinion, both these provisions must be read together since one may be used to effectuate the result obtained through the other. We find no ground for any distinction and we therefore grant the petition to transfer the appeal to this court.

This is a contract, which was submitted (already in printed form) to a party with lesser bargaining power. As in this case, it may contain unconscionable or unknown provisions which are in fine print. Such is the case now before this court.

The facts reveal that Weaver had left high school after one and a half years and spent his time, prior to leasing the service station, working at various skilled and unskilled labor oriented jobs. He was not one who should be expected to know the law or understand the meaning of technical terms. The ceremonious activity of signing the lease consisted of nothing more than the agent of American Oil placing the lease in front of Mr. Weaver and saying "sign", which Mr. Weaver did. There is nothing in the record to indicate that Weaver read the lease; that the agent asked Weaver to read it; or that the agent, in any manner, attempted to call Weaver's attention to the "hold harmless" clause in the lease. Each year following, the procedure was the same. A salesman, from American Oil, would bring the lease to Weaver, at the station, and Weaver would sign it. The evidence showed that Weaver had never read the lease prior to signing and that the clauses in the lease were never explained to him in a manner from which he could grasp their legal significance. The leases were prepared by the attorneys of American Oil Company, for the American Oil Company, and the agents of the American Oil Company never attempted to explain the conditions of the lease nor did they advise Weaver that he should consult legal counsel, before signing the lease. The superior bargaining power of American Oil is patently obvious and the significance of Weaver's signature upon the legal document amounted to nothing more than a mere formality to Weaver for the substantial protection of American Oil.

Had this case involved the sale of goods it would have been termed an "unconscionable contract" under sec. 2–302 of the Uniform Commercial Code. . . .

> "It is not the policy of the law to restrict business dealings or to relieve a party of his own mistakes of judgment, but where one party has taken advantage of another's necessities and distress to obtain an unfair advantage over him, and the latter, owing to his condition, has encumbered himself with a heavy liability or an onerous obligation for the sake of a small or inadequate present gain, there will be relief granted." Stiefler v. McCullough (1933), 97 Ind.App. 123, 174 N.E. 823.

The facts of this case reveal that in exchange for a contract which, if the clause in question is enforceable, may cost Mr. Weaver potentially thousands of dollars in damages for negligence of which he was not the cause, Weaver must operate the service station seven days a week for long hours, at a total yearly income of $5,000–$6,000. The evidence also reveals that *the clause was in fine print and contained no title heading* which would have identified it as an indemnity clause. It seems a deplorable abuse of justice to hold a man of poor education, to a contract prepared by the attorneys of American Oil, for the benefit of American Oil which was presented to Weaver on a "take it or leave it basis".

Justice Frankfurter of the United States Supreme Court spoke on the question of inequality of bargaining power in his dissenting opinion in United States v. Bethlehem Steel Corp. (1942), 315 U.S. 289, 326, 62 S.Ct. 581, 599, 86 L.Ed. 855, 876.

> "(I)t is said that familiar principles would be outraged if Bethlehem were denied recovery on these contracts. But is there any principle which is more familiar or more firmly embedded in the history of Anglo–American law than the basic doctrine that the courts will not permit themselves to be used as instruments of inequity and injustice? Does any principle in our law have more universal application than the doctrine that courts will not enforce transactions in which the relative positions of the parties are such that one has unconscionably taken advantage of the necessities of the other?" . . .

The traditional contract is the result of free bargaining of parties who are brought together by the play of the market, and who meet each other on a footing of approximate economic equality. In such a society there is no danger that freedom of contract will be a threat to the social order as a whole. But in present-day commercial life the standardized mass contract has appeared. It is used primarily by enterprises with strong bargaining power and position. The weaker party, in need of the good or services, is frequently not in a position to shop around for better terms, either because the author of the standard contract has a monopoly (natural or artificial) or because all competitors use the same clauses.

Judge Frankfurter's dissent was written nearly twenty years ago. It represents a direction and philosophy which the law . . . at that time was taking and is now compelled to accept in our modern society over the old principle known as the *parol evidence rule*. The parol evidence rule states that an agreement or contract, signed by the parties, is *conclusively presumed* to represent an integration or meeting of the minds of the parties. This is an archaic rule from the old common law. The objectivity of the rule has as its only merit its simplicity of application which is far outweighed by its failure in many cases to represent the actual agreement, particularly where a printed form prepared by one party [which] contains hidden clauses unknown to the other party is submitted and signed. The law should seek the truth or the subjective understanding of the parties in this more enlightened age. The burden should be on the party submitting such "a package" in printed form to show that the other party had knowledge of any unusual or unconscionable terms contained therein. The principle should be the same as that applicable to implied warranties, namely that a package of goods sold to a purchaser is fit for the purposes intended and contains no harmful materials other than that represented. Caveat lessee is no more the current law than caveat emptor. Only in this way can justice be served and the true meaning of freedom of contract preserved. The analogy is rational. We have previously pointed out a similar situation in the Uniform Commercial Code, which prohibits unconscionable contract clauses in sales agreements.

When a party can show that the contract, which is sought to be enforced, was in fact an unconscionable one, due to a prodigious amount of bargaining power on behalf of the stronger party, which is used to the stronger party's advantage and is unknown to the lesser party, causing a great hardship and risk on the lesser party, the contract provision, or the contract as a whole, if the provision is not separable, should not be enforceable on the grounds that the provision is contrary to public policy. The party seeking to enforce such a contract has the burden of showing that the provisions were explained to the other party and *came to his knowledge* and there was in fact *a real and voluntary meeting of the minds and not merely an objective meeting.* . . .

We do not mean to say or infer that parties may not make contracts exculpating one of his negligence and providing for indemnification, but it must be done *knowingly* and *willingly* as in insurance contracts made for that very purpose.

It is the duty of the courts to administer justice and that role is not performed, in this case, by enforcing a written instrument, not really an agreement of the parties as shown by the evidence here, although signed by the parties. The parol evidence rule must yield to the equities of the case. The appeal is transferred to this court and the judgment of the trial court is reversed with direction to enter judgment for the appellant.

GIVAN, DeBRULER and HUNTER, JJ., concur.

[The dissenting opinion of Justice Prentice is omitted.]

———

RESTATEMENT, SECOND, CONTRACTS § 211

[See Selected Source Materials Supplement]

———

UNIDROIT PRINCIPLES OF INTERNATIONAL COMMERCIAL CONTRACTS ARTS. 2.1.19, 2.1.22

[See Selected Source Materials Supplement]

———

PRINCIPLES OF EUROPEAN CONTRACT LAW ART. 4.110

[See Selected Source Materials Supplement]

———

DARNER MOTOR SALES v. UNIVERSAL UNDERWRITERS

Supreme Court of Arizona, En Banc, 1984.
140 Ariz. 383, 682 P.2d 388.

FELDMAN, JUSTICE.

Darner Motor Sales, Inc., dba Darner Leasing Co. (Darner Motors), petitions for review of a memorandum decision of the court of appeals (Darner

Motor Sales, Inc. v. Universal Underwriters Insurance Company, No. 1 CA–CIV 5796, filed February 22, 1983). That decision affirmed a summary judgment in favor of Universal Underwriters Insurance Company (Universal) and their agent, John Brent Doxsee (Doxsee), who were the third party defendants impleaded by Darner Motors. We granted review because we believe that the issues presented call into question the clarity and consistency of a large body of Arizona law dealing with insurance coverage. We have jurisdiction pursuant to Ariz. Const. Art. 6, § 5(3) and Rule 23, Rules of Civ.App.P., 17A A.R.S.

FACTS

Darner Motors is in the automobile sales, service and leasing business. Prior to transacting business with Universal, Darner Motors' various operations were insured under several policies issued by The Travelers Company (Travelers). In October of 1973, Doxsee, an insurance agent who was a full-time employee of Universal, contacted Joel Darner to solicit insurance business. The following month, Darner purchased a Universal "U–Drive policy" through Doxsee. This policy insured Darner Motors and the lessees of its cars for automobile liability risk. Darner Motors was covered in limits of $100,000 for any one injury and $300,000 (100/300) for all injuries arising out of any one accident. The lessees were covered in limits of 15/30. The rest of Darner Motors' business risks continued to be insured under a "dealership package policy" issued by Travelers.

It is unclear from the record, but this situation presumably continued until April of 1975, a renewal date of the Travelers policy. In April of 1975, Universal "picked up" the entire insurance "package" for Darner Motors' various business activities. This "package" consisted of a Universal "Unicover" policy which included coverage for garagekeeper's liability, premises liability, property coverage, crime coverage, customer car coverage, and plate glass insurance. The parties describe this as an "umbrella policy," so it is possible that, in addition to covering multiple risks, it also contained excess coverage over other policies which provided primary coverage.[1] In addition to the umbrella policy, Universal also renewed the U–Drive policy, which provided coverage to the lessees of Darner Motors.[2]

Substantial controversy exists with regard to many of the factual allegations. However, according to Darner, he informed Doxsee that renewal of lessee coverage was to be in the same limits as applied to Darner Motors in the original U–Drive policy. When the new U–Drive policy arrived after renewal in April of 1975, Darner examined it and noticed that the limits of coverage for lessees were 15/30. After reading this, Darner claims that he called Doxsee. He was concerned because his rental contract contained a representation of greater coverage (100/300) and because he felt that it would be better for his business operation if his lessees had the higher coverage. Darner told Doxsee that the liability limits of the U–Drive policy did not conform to their prior agreement, and asked Doxsee to come to Darner

---

1. It is difficult to tell just what was or was not insured under this "umbrella policy" since a copy of the policy is not part of the record, even though the coverage contained in that policy is the precise issue in the case.

2. Lessors are required to provide such insurance to their lessees, A.R.S. § 28–324. The statute also provides that if the lessor fails to do so, it is jointly and severally liable for all damages caused by the lessee while driving the leased vehicle.

Motors and discuss the matter. Doxsee did call upon Mr. Darner at the latter's office. Although Doxsee could not recall the subsequent conversation, both Darner and his former sales manager, Jack Hadley, testified about the discussion. Their deposition testimony would support a finding that Doxsee told Darner not to worry about the limits because, although the U–Drive policy provided only 15/30 coverage, the all-risk clause of the umbrella policy would provide additional coverage to limits of 100/300.[3]

At some time after he received the U–Drive policy and, presumably, also after his discussions with Doxsee, Darner did receive a copy of the umbrella policy. That policy was evidently quite lengthy and forbidding. Darner admits never reading it; he explained this omission by pointing out that "it's like reading a book" and stating that, following his conversations with Doxsee, "I didn't think I needed to." Darner's office manager testified that she never really read the policy either and saw little need to do so in view of the fact that Doxsee would occasionally appear, remove pages from the loose-leaf binder and insert new pages. So far as the record shows, the printed, boiler-plate provisions contained in the loose-leaf type, "book length," all-risk policy were neither negotiated before nor discussed after the policy was delivered. The parties seem to have confined themselves to a discussion of the objectives that would be realized from the purchase of the policy rather than an attempt to negotiate the wording of the policy.

Approximately twenty months after the conversation between Darner and Doxsee concerning coverage under the Universal policies, Darner Motors rented a car to Dwayne Crawford. The transaction was in the ordinary course of business, except that the form used for the rental agreement was the "old type," which contained a representation of coverage in the amount of 100/300. While driving the vehicle under this rental contract, Crawford negligently injured a pedestrian and caused severe injuries. The pedestrian sued Craw-ford, who looked to Universal for coverage. Universal claimed that lessee's coverage on the "U–Drive" policy was limited to 15/30. Crawford then sued Darner Motors under the rental agreement warranty that coverage was provided in limits of 100/300. Darner Motors called upon Universal to provide additional coverage under the umbrella policy. The umbrella policy did contain the higher limits, but Universal claimed that lessees were not parties "insured" as that term was defined in the all-risk policy. Universal was therefore unwilling to provide coverage in excess of the $15,000 limit of the U–Drive policy. Darner Motors then filed a third-party complaint, naming Universal and Doxsee as third party defendants.

Eventually, the pedestrian recovered $60,000 from Crawford. Universal paid $15,000 of this amount, and Darner Motors has either paid or is liable to Crawford for the remainder. Darner Motors claims that Universal and Doxsee are obligated to indemnify it against that loss. To support that contention, Darner Motors advances the following theories:

---

3. As might be expected, although Doxsee does not remember the substance of the con-versation, he is quite sure he could have told Darner no such thing. Darner's testimony was impeached by evidence that he subsequently reduced the limits on his rental forms from 100/300 to 15/30. Darner explains this by stat-ing that Doxsee told him that it was better to represent the coverage limits at the minimum required by the state so as to discourage plain-tiffs' lawyers from pursuing claims for their badly injured clients. As in most such cases, who told what to whom is hotly contested, and there is much to be said for both versions of the facts.

(1) Universal is estopped to deny coverage for lessees under the umbrella policy in amounts less than 100/300;

(2) The umbrella policy should be reformed so that it does contain such coverage;

(3) If no coverage is found through estoppel or reformation, then the loss incurred by Darner Motors was caused by the negligence of Universal and its agent, Doxsee, and should be borne by them;

(4) If no coverage exists by way of estoppel or reformation, then the loss incurred by Darner Motors is the result of fraud committed by Universal and its agent, Doxsee.

After considerable discovery, Universal and Doxsee moved for summary judgment, contending that there was no genuine issue of fact and that they were entitled to judgment as a matter of law. The motion was granted and judgment entered against Darner Motors. The court of appeals affirmed; pointing out that Darner Motors had not claimed that the umbrella policy was ambiguous, the court held that the insured's failure to read the policy prevented recovery on any theory, even though the contents of the policy did not comport with the representations of the insurance agent and those same representations were a part of the reason that the insured failed to read the policy.

The court of appeals stated that under Arizona law an insured who had received a copy of an unambiguous policy could not "expand the insurer's liability beyond the terms of the ... policy issued...." We believe this statement is too broad, though we acknowledge that the law is, at best, confused on this subject. In an attempt to bring some clarity and logic to the question, we have reviewed our cases and will discuss each of the theories advanced by Darner Motors. Before doing so, however, we must consider the inherent nature of an insurance contract and of the issues presented by the fact situation before us.

CONTRACT LAW AND INSURANCE POLICIES

Since this is an appeal from summary judgment, we must view the facts in the light most favorable to the party against whom judgment was taken. *Gulf Insurance Co. v. Grisham,* 125 Ariz. 123, 124, 613 P.2d 283, 284 (1980). Taking the facts in that light, the question we must decide is whether the courts will enforce an unambiguous provision contrary to the negotiated agreement made by the parties because, after the insurer's representations of coverage, the insured failed to read the insurance contract which was in his possession.[4]

Implicit in the reasoning of the court of appeals is the concept that the insurance policies purchased by Darner constitute *the* contract between Dar-

---

4. In characterizing the issue in this manner, we acknowledge that the insured did read the terms of the policy covering lessees and did discover the error in that policy. He was told by the agent that the umbrella policy provided the additional coverage. He did not read the provisions of the umbrella policy. Although that policy is not part of the record, we assume that it contains a clause or clauses defining the word "insured" in such a manner that lessees are excluded from the class of persons insured by the policy. We assume further that this definitional exclusion is clear and unambiguous. Therefore, it could have been found, read and understood by Darner. Of course we have no way of knowing that these assumptions are correct; however, it was the appellant's burden to make an adequate record on appeal. Since the appellant failed to offer the policy in evidence at the trial, we settle all factual uncertainty in favor of supporting the judgment of the trial court.

ner and Universal. Darner is considered to be bound by the terms contained within the documents. The court of appeals held:

> Because Mr. Darner received a copy of the umbrella policy and made no contention that it was ambiguous or confusing, he cannot expand the insurer's liability beyond the terms of the umbrella policy issued by Universal.

(slip op. at 7). Basic to this holding is the principle that the oral agreement between Doxsee and Darner cannot be shown to vary the terms of the insurance policy. This, indeed, was at one time the majority view. See cases cited in 12 Appleman, *Insurance Law and Practice* § 7155 (1981); similar language is contained in *Parks v. American Casualty Co. of Reading, Pa.,* 117 Ariz. 339, 572 P.2d 801 (1977); *Sellers v. Allstate Insurance Company,* 113 Ariz. 419, 422, 555 P.2d 1113, 1116 (1976); *see also Western Farm Bureau Mut. Ins. Co. v. Barela,* 79 N.M. 149, 441 P.2d 47 (1968). Some cases, including those from our own state, hold that since insurance policies are like other contracts, where the meaning and intent of the parties is "clear" from the words used in the instrument, the courts cannot "rewrite" the policy by considering the actual "words" used in striking the bargain. Thus, the rule of interpretation is stated to be that the intention of the parties as derived from the language used within the four corners of the instrument must prevail. *See, e.g., Rodemich v. State Farm Mutual Auto. Insurance Co.,* 130 Ariz. 538, 539, 637 P.2d 748, 749 (App.1981) (a vehicle which turned over and was damaged when the driver swerved to avoid an animal was not covered under the "upset" clause of a comprehensive risk policy because "upsets" resulting from attempts to avoid collision with animals were not covered unless there was actual contact)....

 . . . Artificial results derived from application of ordinary rules of contract construction to insurance policies have made courts struggle to find some method of reaching a sensible resolution within the conceptual bounds of treating standardized, formal contracts as if they were traditional "agreements," reached by bargaining between the parties. This difficult task is often accomplished by the use of various constructs which enable courts to reach a desired result by giving lip service to traditional contract rules. One of the most prominent of these methods is the well recognized principle of resolving ambiguities against the insurer. *See Almadova v. State Farm Mutual Automobile Ins. Co.,* 133 Ariz. 81, 649 P.2d 284 (1982). The limitations of this principle have been discussed by Professor Robert Keeton, who comments that

> [t]he principle of resolving ambiguities against the draftsman is simply an inadequate explanation of the results of some cases. The conclusion is inescapable that courts have sometimes invented ambiguity where none existed, then resolved the invented ambiguity contrary to the plainly expressed terms of the contract document.

Keeton, *Insurance Law Rights at Variance with Policy Provisions,* 83 Harv. L.Rev. 961, 972 (1970) (footnotes omitted). Our court of appeals has attempted to avoid the problem of invented ambiguity by stating the principle that courts should not create ambiguities in order to rewrite the policy. Cf. *Barber v. Old Republic Life Ins. Co.,* 132 Ariz. 602, 604, 647 P.2d 1200, 1202 (App.1982) with *State Farm v. Gibbs, supra.* However, we also follow the rule of construction that where different jurisdictions reach different conclusions regarding the language of an insurance contract "ambiguity is established," *Federal Insurance Co. v. P.A.T. Homes, Inc.,* 113 Ariz. 136, 138, 547 P.2d 1050, 1052 (1976); thus, we may find ourselves justly criticized for accepting the inventions of other courts. It is also illogical to hold that an unexpected, unknown ambiguity in a clause which the parties did not negotiate, write or read should permit them to show the true terms of the agreement, but that the lack of such an ambiguity prevents them from so doing.

Such systems of logic—or illogic—have been criticized by Keeton, *supra,* and others for failing to recognize the realities of the insurance business and the methods used in modern insurance practice. *See, e.g., Zuckerman v. Transamerica Ins. Co.,* 133 Ariz. 139, 144–46, 650 P.2d 441, 446–48 (1982); *Harr v. Allstate Insurance Co.,* 54 N.J. 287, 301–04, 255 A.2d 208, 216–18 (1969); Restatement of Contracts (Second) § 211, comment b, and authorities cited in the reporter's note thereto; Abraham, *Judge–Made Law and Judge–Made Insurance: Honoring the Reasonable Expectations of the Insured,* 67 Va.L.Rev. (1981); Murray, *The Parol Evidence Process and Standardized Agreements under the Restatement (Second) of Contracts,* 123 U.Pa.L.Rev. 1342 (1975).

Abraham, *supra,* argues that "insurance law should be brought into the mainstream of our jurisprudence," and notes that "in many states, a principle authorizing the courts to honor the 'reasonable expectations' of the insured is emerging." *Id.* at 1151. "Emergence" is probably an inaccurate description of the use of the reasonable expectations test since, if correctly understood, that doctrine has long been a basic principle in the law of contracts.

> That portion of the field of law that is classified and described as the law of contracts attempts the realization of *reasonable expectations that have been induced* by the making of a promise.

1 Corbin, *Contracts* § 1, at 2 (1963) (emphasis supplied). We have previously recognized the doctrine of "reasonable expectations." *Zuckerman v. Transamerica Ins. Co.,* 133 Ariz. at 146, 650 P.2d at 448; *Sparks v. Republic Nat. Life Ins. Co.,* 132 Ariz. 529, 536–37, 647 P.2d 1127, 1134–35, *cert. denied,* 459 U.S. 1070, 74 L.Ed.2d 632, 103 S.Ct. 490 (1982). Of course, if not put in proper perspective, the reasonable expectations concept is quite troublesome, since most insureds develop a "reasonable expectation" that every loss will be covered by their policy. Therefore, the reasonable expectation concept must be limited by something more than the fervent hope usually engendered by loss. Such a limitation is easily found in the postulate contained in Corbin's work— that the expectations to be realized are those that "have been induced by the making of a promise." 1 Corbin, *supra* § 1 at 2.

We think it better, then, to start the analysis by attempting to determine what expectations have been induced. We note the concept that contracts are not merely printed words. The words, of course, are usually of paramount importance. However, other matters are also significant. 3 Corbin, *supra* §§ 538, 549. It is important to recognize that although the writing "may be coextensive with the agreement, it is not the agreement but only evidence thereof." Murray, *supra,* 123 U.Pa.L.Rev. at 1389. Murray adds that "if the writing is normally executed absent understanding of its fine print provisions, it is less worthy as evidence of the true agreement." *Id.* at 1373. Llewellyn puts the proposition another way:

The fine print which has not been read has no business to cut under the reasonable meaning of those dickered terms which constitute the dominant and only real expression of agreement, but much of [the writing] commonly belongs in [the contract].

Llewellyn, *The Common Law Tradition* 370 (1960). Thus, Llewellyn concludes, "any contract with boiler-plate results in *two* several contracts: the *dickered* deal and the collateral one of *supplementary* boiler-plate." *Id.* at 371 (emphasis in original).

If we continue to look at an insurance policy as a contract between the insured and insurer, the foregoing analysis compels the conclusion that the problem is simply the application of the parol evidence rule. The traditional view of the law of contracts is that a written agreement adopted by the parties will be viewed as an integrated contract which binds those parties to the terms expressed within the four corners of the agreement. Thus, the parties may not vary or expand the agreement by introducing parol evidence to show understandings or antecedent agreements which are in some way contrary to the terms of the contract. *Restatement (Second) of Contracts* § 215. This rule is applied with varying degrees of exactitude to insurance policies. Cases from this state reflect that attitude. *See Sparks v. Republic Nat. Life Ins. Co., supra; Isaak v. Massachusetts Indemnity Life Ins. Co.,* 127 Ariz. 581, 623 P.2d 11 (1981); *Dairyland Mutual Ins. Co. v. Andersen,* 102 Ariz. 515, 433 P.2d 963 (1967); *but see Southern Casualty v. Hughes,* 33 Ariz. 206, 263 P. 584 (1928); *Ranger Insurance Co. v. Phillips,* 25 Ariz.App. 426, 544 P.2d 250 (1976).

When faced with harsh or illogical results, such as those produced by application of the parol evidence rule to most insurance contracts, the law usually reacts by recognizing exceptions which permit courts to avoid injustice. The ambiguity rule is, of course, one of those exceptions. Others, advanced with varying success, are the doctrines of waiver and estoppel. In our view, a better rationale is to be found by application of *established principles of contract law.* In so doing, however, we must remember that the usual insurance policy is a special kind of contract. It is largely adhesive; some terms are bargained for, but most terms consist of boilerplate, not bargained for, neither read nor understood by the buyer, and often not even fully understood by the selling agent. In contracts, as in other fields, the common law has evolved to accommodate the practices of the marketplace. Thus, in insurance law, as in other areas of contract law, the parol evidence rule has not been strictly applied to enforce an illusory "bargain" set forth in a *standardized contract* when that "bargain" was never really made and would, if applied, defeat the true agreement which was supposedly contained in the policy. *Sparks v. Republic National Life Insurance Co.,* 132 Ariz. at 537, 647 P.2d at 1135. *See also Zuckerman v. Transamerica Insurance Co.,* 133 Ariz. at 144, 650 P.2d at 446.

Sparks and *Zuckerman* reflect this court's attempt to bring some degree of logic and predictability into the field of insurance. What is needed, however, is recognition of a general rule of contract law. We believe that the current formulation of the *Restatement (Second) of Contracts* contains a workable resolution of the problem. The Restatement approach is basically a modification of the parol evidence rule when dealing with contracts containing boilerplate provisions which are not negotiated, and often not even read by the parties.

Standardized Agreements

(1) Except as stated in Subsection (3), where a party to an agreement signs or otherwise manifests assent to a writing and has reason to believe that like writings are regularly used to embody terms of agreements of the same type, he adopts the writing as an integrated agreement with respect to the terms included in the writing.

(2) Such a writing is interpreted wherever reasonable as treating alike all those similarly situated, without regard to their knowledge or understanding of the standard terms of the writing.

(3) Where the other party has reason to believe that the party manifesting such assent would not do so if he knew that the writing contained a particular term, the term is not part of the agreement.

Restatement (Second) of Contracts § 211. We believe that the comments to this section of the Restatement support the wisdom of the rule formulated. Comment (a) points out that standardization of agreements is essential

> to a system of mass production and distribution. Scarce and costly time and skill can be devoted to a class of transactions rather than to details of individual transactions.... Sales personnel and customers are freed from attention to numberless variations and can focus on meaningful choice among a limited number of significant features: transaction-type, style, quantity, price, or the like. Operations are simplified and costs reduced, to the advantage of all concerned.

Subsections (1) and (2) of § 211 reflect the reality of the marketplace. Thus, those who make use of a standardized form of agreement neither expect nor desire their customers "to understand or even to read the standard terms." *Id.* comment (b). On the other hand, customers "trust to the good faith of the party using the form [and] ... understand that they are assenting to the terms not read or not understood, subject to such limitations as the law may impose." *Id.* The limitations that the law may impose are that standard terms

> may be superseded by separately negotiated or added terms (§ 203), they are construed against the draftsman (§ 206), and they are subject to the overriding obligation of good faith (§ 205) and to the power of the court to refuse to enforce an unconscionable contract or term (§ 208).

Id. comment (c).[5]

Subsection (3) of § 211 is the Restatement's codification of and limitation on the "reasonable expectation" rule as applied to standardized agreements. The comment reads as follows:

> Although customers typically adhere to standardized agreements and are bound by them without even appearing to know the standard terms in detail, they are not bound to unknown terms which are beyond the range of reasonable expectation.... [An insured] who adheres to the [insurer's] standard terms does not assent to a term if the [insurer] has reason to believe that the [insured] would not have accepted the agreement if he had known that the agreement contained the particular term. Such a belief or assumption may be shown by the prior negotiations or

---

5. The Section numbers in this quote refer to sections in the Restatement (Second) of Contracts.

inferred from the circumstances. Reason to believe may be inferred from the fact that the term is bizarre or oppressive, from the fact that it eviscerates the non-standard terms explicitly agreed to, or from the fact that it eliminates the dominant purpose of the transaction. The inference is reinforced if the adhering party never had an opportunity to read the term, or if it is illegible or otherwise hidden from view. This rule is closely related to the policy against unconscionable terms and the rule of interpretation against the draftsman.

Id. comment (f). We believe the analysis contained in the comments to the cited sections in the Restatement is a sensible rationale for interpretation of the usual type of insuring agreement.[6]

This treatment of insurance law is neither radical nor new. All that is new in the "changed" Restatement is the articulation of the rule. Some cases long ago recognized the underlying principles. . . .

. . . Missing has been the articulation or formulation of some general rule to explain results of many past cases and to provide a pragmatic, honest approach to the resolution of future disputes. Hopefully, the adoption of § 211 of the Restatement as the rule for standardized contracts will provide greater predictability and uniformity of results—a benefit to both the insurance industry and the consumer.

In adopting this rule, we do not create a special field of contract law, we merely adopt a rule of integration which recognizes the method by which people do business. Indeed, the law pertaining to nonstandardized, negotiated contracts long ago began to move in the same direction. "Ordinary" contract law now recognizes that an agreement may be "partially integrated," or "completely integrated," depending upon "the degree to which the parties intended the writing to express their agreement." E. Farnsworth, *Contracts,* § 7.3 at 452 (1982). The relationship between the degree of integration and the application of the parol evidence rule has been the subject of much scholarly controversy. The authors of the leading contract treatises, Williston and Corbin, present differing views. "The point in dispute is whether the fact that the writing appears on its face to be a complete and exclusive statement of the terms of the agreement establishes conclusively that the agreement is completely integrated." Farnsworth, *supra* at 455. If it does, Williston would restrict interpretation to the four corners of the document. *Id.; See 4 Williston on Contracts* §§ 600A, 629, 633 (3d ed. 1961). Corbin argues that account should always be taken of all the surrounding circumstances to determine the extent of the integration *and* the interpretation of the agreement. Farnsworth, *supra* at 456; 3 Corbin, *supra,* § 582.

Recent decisions, the Uniform Commercial Code and the Restatement (Second) of Contracts have all favored Corbin's view. Farnsworth, *supra* at 453. *See also* Braucher, *Interpretation and Legal Effect in the Second Restate-*

---

6. It would, of course, also be applicable to other transactions handled in a similar manner. We note, for example, that contracts for transport by rail, airline or bus; for rental of cars, trucks and other equipment; credit card and charge account "rules" and terms; bills of lading, invoices and many other commercial documents are "sold" or "made" in the same manner as most insurance policies. On the other hand, there are some insurance transactions which are still the product of negotiation which includes the terms of the policy. Such contracts are not affected by § 211 because it applies only to standardized agreements such as the average automobile, general liability, or fire policy.

ment of Contracts, 81 Colum.L.Rev. 12 (1981). Arizona has followed the modern trend and adopted the Corbin view. . . .

It would be anomalous, indeed, to follow this view for contracts with bargained terms but to cling to the rejected rule in cases involving standardized form contracts. It would be even more anomalous if reasonable expectations induced by promises or conduct of a party are to be considered in determining integration or interpreting the words of a negotiated . . . agreement but disregarded when dealing with boilerplate, so that regardless of intent or even actual agreement, the parties are bound by provisions that were never discussed, examined, read or understood.

The general rule of contract interpretations adopted by the Restatement and based on Corbin's viewpoint is a modern view which takes into account the realities of present day commercial practice. See, Trakman, *Interpreting Contracts: A Common Law Dilemma,* 59 Canadian Bar Review 241 (1981). The rule which we adopt today for interpretation of standardized contracts recognizes modern commercial practice by business entities which use automated equipment to effect a large volume of transactions through use of standardized forms. It parallels the general rule which applies to all contracts by attempting to discover the intent of the parties, in so far as intent existed, and attempts to ascertain the real agreement so far as it was expressed or conveyed by implication. However, it recognizes that most provisions of standardized agreements are not the result of negotiation; often, neither customer nor salesperson are aware of the contract provisions. The rule adopted today recognizes reality and the needs of commerce; it allows businesses that use such forms to write their own contract. It charges the customer with knowledge that the contract being "purchased" is or contains a form applied to a vast number of transactions and includes terms which are unknown (or even unknowable); it binds the customer to such terms. However, the rule stops short of granting the drafter of the contract license to accomplish any result. It holds the drafter to good faith and terms which are conscionable; it requires drafting of provisions which can be understood if the customer does attempt to check on his rights; it does not give effect to boilerplate terms which are contrary to either the expressed agreement or the purpose of the transaction as known to the contracting parties. From the standpoint of the judicial system, the rule recognizes the true origin of standardized contract provisions, frees the courts from having to write a contract for the parties, and removes the temptation to create ambiguity or invent intent in order to reach a result.

The rule does not set a premium on failure to read. Those who negotiate their transactions will be held to the same rules as have previously obtained with regard to the duty to read. The rule which we adopt applies to contracts (or parts of contracts) made up of standardized forms which, because of the nature of the enterprise, customers will not be expected to read and over which they have no real power of negotiation.[7]

---

7. It cannot be seriously contended, for instance, that airline companies, car rental agencies, and the like expect their customers to line up, demand copies of the various instruments which set forth the "contract" and require explanations of the various terms. The usual "contract" for air transportation provides an example; it begins as follows:

Conditions of Contract

As used in this contract "ticket" means this passenger ticket and baggage check, of which these conditions and the notices form part, "carriage" is equivalent to "transporta-

To apply the old rule and interpret such contracts according to the imagined intent of the parties is to perpetuate a fiction which can do no more than bring the law into ridicule. To those troubled by the change in the law, we point out that the fundamental change occurred first in business practice. The change in legal analysis does no more than reflect the change in methods of doing business. To acknowledge standardized contracts for what they are—rules written by commercial enterprises—and to enforce them as written, subject to those reasonable limitations provided by law, is to recognize the reality of the marketplace as it now exists, while imposing just limits on business practice. These, we think, have always been the proper functions of contract law.

We turn, then, to the facts of this case. We have adopted a rule of law which, in proper circumstances, will relieve the insured from certain clauses of an agreement which he did not negotiate, probably did not read, and probably would not have understood had he read them. Does this case present a proper circumstance? If so, by what process is this to be accomplished? How is the restatement rule to be given effect?

Equitable Estoppel

The elements of estoppel are "conduct by which one . . . induces another to believe . . . in certain material facts, which inducement results in acts in reliance thereon, justifiably taken, which cause injury. . . ." *Sahlin v. American Casualty Company of Reading,* 103 Ariz. 57, 59, 436 P.2d 606, 608 (1968) (quoting *Builders Supply Corp. v. Marshall,* 88 Ariz. 89, 94, 352 P.2d 982, 985 (1960)).

The majority rule is considered to be "that the doctrines of waiver and estoppel are not available to bring within the coverage of an insurance policy risks not covered by its terms, or expressly excluded therefrom." Annot. 1 A.L.R.3d 1149, 1147 (1965). Indeed, the annotation lists only two jurisdictions (Idaho and South Dakota) that clearly take the contrary view. *Id.* at 1150–51. However, since the annotation was published several other states have adopted the view that estoppel may be available under certain circumstances. *Harr v. Allstate Insurance Co.,* 54 N.J. 287, 255 A.2d 208 (1969); *King v. Travelers Ins. Co.,* 84 N.M. 550, 505 P.2d 1226 (1973); *Hunter v. Farmers Insurance Group,* 554 P.2d 1239, 1243 (Wyo.1976).

. . . The "majority rule" is eroding. *See* 16C Appleman, *supra,* § 9166 at 153–58, § 9167 at 162–65 (1981). Given our view of contract theory and the policy considerations in *Sparks* and *Zuckerman,* there are strong reasons to recognize a rule which allows an insured to raise the issue of estoppel to establish coverage contrary to the limitations in the boiler-plate policy when the insurer's agent had represented the coverage as greater than the language found in the printed policy. The fact that the insured has not read the

tion", "carrier" means all air carriers that carry or undertake to carry the passenger or his baggage hereunder or perform any other service incidental to such air carriage, "Warsaw Convention" means the convention for the unification of certain rules relating to international carriage by air signed at Warsaw, 12th of October, 1929, or that convention as amended at the Hague, 28th September, 1955, whichever may be applicable.

Uniform Passenger Ticket and Baggage Check, ATC version, printed on the back of the standard form of ticket in general use by airlines in the United States. Fortunately, we have not yet been required to interpret this contract by conjuring up some supposed intent of the passenger.

insurance policy "word for word" is not, as a matter of law, an absolute bar to his theory of estoppel. *See Northwestern National Ins. Co. v. Chambers*, 24 Ariz. 86, 94, 206 P. 1081, 1084 (1922) (disapproving of the rule of *caveat emptor* in insurance transactions). It is for the trier of fact to determine whether, under circumstances such as this, the appellant had a duty to read. *Heiner*, 74 Ariz. at 156, 245 P.2d at 418. *See generally,* Macaulay, *Private Legislation and the Duty to Read—Business Run by IBM Machine, the Law of Contracts and Credit Cards,* 19 Vand.L.Rev. 1051, 1051–69 (1966).

The facts of the case at bench are within the exception to interpretation contained in subsection (3) to *Restatement (Second) of Contracts,* § 211. The coverage limits for lessees were separately negotiated. The standard boiler-plate definition of the word "insured", excluding lessees, was not bargained for, not written by and not read by the parties. It need not be allowed to "undercut the dickered deal." We therefore adopt the rationale of the New Jersey Supreme Court in *Harr*[8] and recognize equitable estoppel as a device to prevent enforcement of those boiler-plate terms of the insurance contract which are more limited than the coverage expressly agreed upon by the parties. As applied to this case, the rule adopted means simply that if the fact finder determines that Darner and Doxsee did agree upon lessee's coverage in limits of 100/300, and if, by justifiably relying on Doxsee's assurances or for some other justifiable reason, Darner was unaware of the limitation in the umbrella policy, Universal would be estopped to assert the definitional exclusion which eliminates Darner's lessee from the class of persons insured. Thus, we do not limit the assertion of estoppel by the insured to cases in which an insurance policy has not been delivered prior to the loss. Since the parol evidence rule does not necessarily prevent establishing the true agreement, estoppel may apply where, from the nature of the transaction, the fact finder is able to determine that the insured acted reasonably in not reading the particular provision of the policy.[9]

Reformation

"Where reformation is sought because of the mistake of one party only, it is essential that fraud or inequitable conduct be found in the other." *Korrick v. Tuller*, 42 Ariz. 493, 498, 27 P.2d 529, 531 (1933). "Inequitable conduct which would justify reformation when there is unilateral mistake takes the form of knowledge on the part of one party of the other's mistake." *Isaak v. Massachusetts Indemnity Life Ins. Co.*, 127 Ariz. at 584, 623 P.2d at 14.

---

8. ... where an insurer or its agent misrepresents, even though innocently, the coverage of an insurance contract or the exclusions therefrom, to an insured before or at the inception of the contract, and the insured reasonably relies thereupon to his ultimate detriment, the insurer is estopped to deny coverage after a loss on a risk or from a peril actually not covered by the terms of the policy. The proposition is one of elementary and simple justice. By justifiably relying on the insurer's superior knowledge, the insured has been prevented from procuring the desired coverage elsewhere. To reject this approach because a new contract is thereby made for the parties would be an unfortunate triumph of form over substance. . . .

9. The jury could find, for instance, that the insured acted reasonably in failing to read standard boilerplate which defined insured—particularly in view of Doxsee's assurances regarding the limits. On the other hand, if the limit problem is clearly disclosed in the declaration page, and Darner also failed to read that, the fact finder might find that estoppel was not applicable under the principles of § 211. The key question is whether the clause or provision was one bargained for and agreed upon, in which case it is enforced as written and interpreted, or whether it was part of the standardized form which the customer would not ordinarily be expected to read, in which case it would be enforced as written, subject to the constraints and limitations of § 211.

"Ordinarily, the terms of the policy should control, although the statement of an agent well may ground an action for reformation." 16C Appleman, *supra,* § 9167 at 165. Moreover, one whose inequitable conduct has caused the instrument to be "accepted with provisions at variance with the true agreement may not set up the other party's negligence in failing to read the instrument. * * *" *Lane v. Mathews,* 75 Ariz. 1, 5, 251 P.2d 303 (1952) (quoting 76 C.J.S., Reformation of Instruments, § 46 at 400).

According to Universal, Darner was simply mistaken about the extent of coverage under his umbrella policy. Darner avers that, if so, this resulted from Doxsee's failure to properly explain the terms of the policy. There is no dispute that Darner told Doxsee he was concerned about having only 15/30 coverage for lessees. There is clearly a factual dispute regarding Doxsee's appreciation of Darner's concern. Arguably, Doxsee had knowledge of Darner's "mistaken" understanding of the agreement. Thus it may be that "the true contract of insurance in this case . . . arose out of the oral agreement between the parties and not that as evidenced by the written policy." *Ranger Insurance Co. v. Phillips,* 25 Ariz.App. 426, 430, 544 P.2d 250, 254 (1976); *See also A.I.D. Ins. Services v. Riley,* 25 Ariz.App. 132, 135, 541 P.2d 595, 598 (1975).

The same disputed material facts which demand trial on the merits regarding the estoppel remedy can also be marshalled under the reformation theory. Under the provisions of *Restatement (Second) of Contracts,* § 211 the form provisions at variance with the bargained deal or contrary to the dominant purpose of the transaction are "not part of the agreement." They should be eliminated, so that the bargains made will be realized. The written agreement may be reformed to state the true agreement. Accordingly, summary judgment on reformation was error.

[As to Darner's negligence theory, the court held that an insurance agent owes a duty to the insured to exercise reasonable care, skill, and prudence in procuring insurance; that whether the insured's not reading the policies constitutes contributory negligence turns on the reasonableness of not reading the policies and relying on the agent's statements; and that the issue was one for the trier of fact. As to Darner's fraud theory, the court held that it could not say that the allegations on which the fraud count was based were wholly without merit.]

For the foregoing reasons we vacate the decision of the court of appeals and reverse the trial court's summary judgment as to the counts of equitable estoppel, reformation of the contract, negligent misrepresentation and fraud. Because of this disposition of the substantive matters, the court of appeals' award of attorney's fees is vacated.

GORDON, V.C.J., and HAYS, J., concur.

[The concurring opinion of Cameron, J., and the dissenting opinion of Holohan, C.J., are omitted.]

––––––

GORDINIER v. AETNA CASUALTY & SURETY CO., 154 Ariz. 266, 742 P.2d 277 (1987). The Arizona Court here elaborated on *Darner* as follows: " . . . As a synthesis of the cases and authorities demonstrates, Arizona courts will not enforce even unambiguous boilerplate terms in standardized insurance contracts in a *limited* variety of situations:

"1. Where the contract terms, although not ambiguous to the court, cannot be understood by the reasonably intelligent consumer who might check on his or her rights, the court will interpret them in light of the objective, reasonable expectations of the average insured (*see* ... *Wainscott v. Ossenkop,* 633 P.2d 237 (Alaska 1981) (application of "resident of same household" definition, while not technically ambiguous, defeats reasonable expectations of spouse));

"2. Where the insured did not receive full and adequate notice of the term in question, and the provision is either unusual or unexpected, or one that emasculates apparent coverage ... ;

"3. Where some activity which can be reasonably attributed to the insurer would create an objective impression of coverage in the mind of a reasonable insured ... ;

"4. Where some activity reasonably attributable to the insurer has induced a particular insured reasonably to believe that he has coverage, although such coverage is expressly and unambiguously denied by the policy....

FARM BUREAU MUTUAL INSURANCE CO. v. SANDBULTE, 302 N.W.2d 104 (Iowa 1981). "The rationale of the reasonable expectation doctrine is that, in a contract of adhesion, such as an insurance policy, form must not be exalted over substance, and that the reasonable expectations of the insured may not be frustrated 'even though painstaking study of the policy provisions would have negated those expectations.' Rodman v. State Farm Mutual Insurance Co., 208 N.W.2d at 906 (quoting Keeton, Insurance Law— Basic Text § 6.3(a), at 351 (1971)); *see also* C & J Fertilizer, Inc., 227 N.W.2d at 176–77. Reasonable expectations giving rise to application of the doctrine may be established by proof of the underlying negotiations or inferred from the circumstances. Restatement (Second) of Contracts § 237, at 541 (comment f). The doctrine will apply here if the exclusion (1) is bizarre or oppressive, (2) eviscerates terms explicitly agreed to, or (3) eliminates the dominant purpose of the transaction. *Id.* The doctrine is well illustrated by C & J Fertilizer: Under the terms of a burglary policy the insurer agreed '[t]o pay for loss by burglary or by robbery of a watchman, while the premises are not open for business....' In the definition section of the policy, however, burglary was defined in such a way as to exclude any occurrence which was not evidenced by marks left on the exterior of the premises. This definition was not consistent with a layman's concept of the crime, nor with its legal interpretation. In effect, the definition overrode the dominant purpose for purchasing the policy and in effect eviscerated the coverage specifically bargained for, protecting against burglary. 227 N.W.2d at 176–77."

Part V

MISTAKE AND UNEXPECTED CIRCUMSTANCES

Chapter 18

MISTAKE

Suppose that A and B enter into a contract that is either based on or reflects some kind of mistake made by A, or by A and B jointly. After the mistake is discovered, A claims that because of the mistake the contract should either be unenforceable, if it has not been performed, or reversible, if it has been.

The problems raised by claims of this kind have been a source of persistent difficulty in contract law. In part this difficulty results from the complex nature of the underlying issues. Intuitively, there seems to be a serious tension between the concept that a mistake may be a ground for relief in contractual transactions, on the one hand, and such basic ideas of contract law as risk-shifting, the security of transactions, and rewards for knowledge, skill, and diligence, on the other. Much of the difficulty, however, results from the use of legal categories and doctrinal rules that are not based on a functional analysis.

Traditionally, the subject of mistake in contract law has been divided into four categories: misunderstanding, mutual mistake, unilateral mistake, and mistake in transcription. These names are somewhat misleading, because often they are not descriptive of the kind of mistake cases that normally fall within each category. Despite the somewhat misleading nature of the names of these categories, they will be used as Section headings in this Chapter. In part, this is because the names of the categories are traditional. Another reason is that the traditional *categories* are functional, even if their names are not. The cases in each traditional category concern a different kind of mistake, even though the kind of mistake each category concerns may not be the kind described in the category's title.

This Chapter will consider four types of mistake: mechanical errors, mistranscriptions, shared mistaken factual assumptions, and unshared mistaken factual assumptions. ("Misunderstanding" cases have been considered in Chapter 9, Section 1, supra.)

SECTION 1. UNILATERAL MISTAKES (MECHANICAL ERRORS)

A common kind of mistake in everyday life consists of physical blunders, like spilling coffee. This kind of mistake, although manifested externally, normally results from an error in the mechanics of an actor's internal machinery, such as a lapse of concentration, a loss of balance, or an error in hand-eye coordination. Such errors are almost invariably transient. If an actor spilled every cup of coffee he handled, we would not characterize his spills as mistakes, but instead would conclude that he had a disability.

A counterpart to transient physical blunders consists of intellectual blunders that result from transient errors in the mechanics of an actor's internal machinery. For example, as a result of a transient error in the mechanics of an actor's mental machinery, the actor may write "65" when he intends to write "56" or may incorrectly add a column of figures.

Mistakes of this kind—that is, physical or intellectual blunders that result from transient errors in the mechanics of an actor's internal machinery—may be thought of as *mechanical errors*. Mechanical errors resemble the kind of mistake sometimes made in the transcription of DNA. Almost invariably, that transcription is correct. Every once in a while, it goes transiently awry.

Although contract law does not use the term "mechanical errors," in fact virtually all cases that are categorized as involving "unilateral mistakes" are essentially mechanical-error cases.

DONOVAN v. RRL CORP.

Supreme Court of California, 2001.
26 Cal.4th 261, 109 Cal.Rptr.2d 807, 27 P.3d 702.

GEORGE, C.J.

Defendant RRL Corporation is an automobile dealer doing business under the name Lexus of Westminster. Because of typographical and proofreading errors made by a local newspaper, defendant's advertisement listed a price for a used automobile that was significantly less than the intended sales price. Plaintiff Brian J. Donovan read the advertisement and, after examining the vehicle, attempted to purchase it by tendering the advertised price. Defendant refused to sell the automobile to plaintiff at that price, and plaintiff brought this action against defendant for breach of contract. The municipal court entered judgment for defendant on the ground that the mistake in the advertisement precluded the existence of a contract. The appellate department of the superior court and the Court of Appeal reversed, relying in part upon Vehicle Code section 11713.1, subdivision (e), which makes it unlawful for an automobile dealer not to sell a motor vehicle at the advertised price while the vehicle remains unsold and before the advertisement expires.

We conclude that a contract satisfying the statute of frauds arose from defendant's advertisement and plaintiff's tender of the advertised price, but that defendant's unilateral mistake of fact provides a basis for rescinding the contract. Although Vehicle Code section 11713.1, subdivision (e), justifies a reasonable expectation on the part of consumers that an automobile dealer intends that such an advertisement constitute an offer, and that the offer can be accepted by paying the advertised price, this statute does not supplant governing common law principles authorizing rescission of a contract on the ground of mistake. As we shall explain, rescission is warranted here because the evidence establishes that defendant's unilateral mistake of fact was made in good faith, defendant did not bear the risk of the mistake, and enforcement of the contract with the erroneous price would be unconscionable. Accordingly, we shall reverse the judgment of the Court of Appeal.

I

While reading the April 26, 1997, edition of the Costa Mesa Daily Pilot, a local newspaper, plaintiff noticed a full-page advertisement placed by defendant. The advertisement promoted a "PRE–OWNED COUP–A–RAMA SALE!/ 2–DAY PRE–OWNED SALES EVENT" and listed, along with 15 other used automobiles, a 1995 Jaguar XJ6 Vanden Plas. The advertisement described the color of this automobile as sapphire blue, included a vehicle identification number, and stated a price of $25,995. The name Lexus of Westminster was displayed prominently in three separate locations in the advertisement, which included defendant's address along with a small map showing the location of the dealership. The following statements appeared in small print at the bottom of the advertisement: "All cars plus tax, lic., doc., smog & bank fees. On approved credit. Ad expires 4/27/97[.]"

Also on April 26, 1997, plaintiff visited a Jaguar dealership that offered other 1995 Jaguars for sale at $8,000 to $10,000 more than the price specified in defendant's advertisement. The following day, plaintiff and his spouse drove to Lexus of Westminster and observed a blue Jaguar displayed on an elevated ramp. After verifying that the identification number on the sticker was the same as that listed in defendant's April 26 Daily Pilot advertisement, they asked a salesperson whether they could test drive the Jaguar. Plaintiff mentioned that he had seen the advertisement and that the price "looked really good." The salesperson responded that, as a Lexus dealer, defendant might offer better prices for a Jaguar automobile than would a Jaguar dealer. At that point, however, neither plaintiff nor the salesperson mentioned the specific advertised price.

After the test drive, plaintiff and his spouse discussed several negative characteristics of the automobile, including high mileage, an apparent rust problem, and worn tires. In addition, it was not as clean as the other Jaguars they had inspected. Despite these problems, they believed that the advertised price was a very good price and decided to purchase the vehicle. Plaintiff told the salesperson, "Okay. We will take it at your price, $26,000." When the salesperson did not respond, plaintiff showed him the advertisement. The salesperson immediately stated, "That's a mistake."

After plaintiff asked to speak with an individual in charge, defendant's sales manager also told plaintiff that the price listed in the advertisement was a mistake. The sales manager apologized and offered to pay for plaintiff's fuel, time, and effort expended in traveling to the dealership to examine the automobile. Plaintiff declined this offer and expressed his belief that there had been no mistake. Plaintiff stated that he could write a check for the full purchase price as advertised. The sales manager responded that he would not sell the vehicle at the advertised price. Plaintiff then requested the sales price. After performing some calculations, and based upon defendant's $35,000 investment in the automobile, the sales manager stated that he would sell it to plaintiff for $37,016. Plaintiff responded, "No, I want to buy it at your advertised price, and I will write you a check right now." The sales manager again stated that he would not sell the vehicle at the advertised price, and plaintiff and his spouse left the dealership.

Plaintiff subsequently filed this action against defendant for breach of contract, fraud, and negligence. In addition to testimony consistent with the facts set forth above, the following evidence was presented to the municipal court, which acted as the trier of fact.

Defendant's advertising manager compiles information for placement in advertisements in several local newspapers, including the Costa Mesa Daily Pilot. Defendant's advertisement published in the Saturday, April 19, 1997, edition of the Daily Pilot listed a 1995 Jaguar XJ6 Vanden Plas but did not specify a price for that automobile; instead, the word "Save" appeared in the space where a price ordinarily would have appeared. The following Thursday afternoon, defendant's sales manager instructed the advertising manager to delete the 1995 Jaguar from all advertisements and to substitute a 1994 Jaguar XJ6 with a price of $25,995. The advertising manager conveyed the new information to a representative of the Daily Pilot that same afternoon.

Because of typographical and proofreading errors made by employees of the Daily Pilot, however, the newspaper did not replace the description of the 1995 Jaguar with the description of the 1994 Jaguar, but did replace the word "Save" with the price of $25,995. Thus, the Saturday, April 26, edition of the Daily Pilot erroneously advertised the 1995 Jaguar XJ6 Vanden Plas at a price of $25,995. The Daily Pilot acknowledged its error in a letter of retraction sent to defendant on April 28. No employee of defendant reviewed a proof sheet of the revised Daily Pilot advertisement before it was published, and defendant was unaware of the mistake until plaintiff attempted to purchase the automobile.

Except for the 1995 Jaguar XJ6 Vanden Plas, defendant intended to sell each vehicle appearing in the April 26, 1997, Daily Pilot advertisement at the advertised price. Defendant's advertisements in the April 26 editions of several other newspapers correctly listed the *1994* Jaguar XJ6 with a price of $25,995. In May 1997, defendant's advertisements in several newspapers listed the 1995 Jaguar XJ6 Vanden Plas for sale at $37,995. Defendant subsequently sold the automobile for $38,399.

The municipal court entered judgment for defendant. During the trial, the court ruled that plaintiff had not stated a cause of action for negligence, and it precluded plaintiff from presenting evidence in support of such a claim. After the close of evidence and presentation of argument, the municipal court concluded as a matter of law that a newspaper advertisement for an automobile generally constitutes a valid contractual offer that a customer may accept by tendering payment of the advertised price. The court also determined that such an advertisement satisfies the requirements of the statute of frauds when the dealer's name appears in the advertisement. Nevertheless, the municipal court held that in the present case there was no valid offer because defendant's unilateral mistake of fact vitiated or negated contractual intent.

The court made factual findings that defendant's mistake regarding the advertisement was made in good faith and was not intended to deceive the public. The municipal court also found that plaintiff was unaware of the mistake before it was disclosed to him by defendant's representatives....

[T]he Court of Appeal reversed the judgment of the municipal court and held that defendant's advertisement constituted a contractual offer that invited acceptance by the act of tendering the advertised price, which plaintiff performed. Acknowledging that the question was close, ... the Court of Appeal reasoned that Vehicle Code section 11713.1, subdivision (e), "tips the scale in favor of ... construing the advertisement as an offer...." The court disagreed with the municipal court's conclusion that defendant's unilateral mistake of fact, unknown to plaintiff at the time he tendered the purchase price, precluded the existence of a valid offer. With regard to the contention that defendant should not bear the risk of an error resulting solely from the negligence of the newspaper, the Court of Appeal made a factual finding based upon the appellate record (Code Civ. Proc., § 909) that defendant's failure to review a proof sheet for the Daily Pilot advertisement constituted negligence that contributed to the placement of the erroneous advertisement.

We granted defendant's petition for review...

IV

[The court first concluded that defendant's advertisement for the sale of the Jaguar automobile constituted an offer that was accepted by plaintiff's tender of the advertised price (this portion of the case is set out in Chapter 10, Section 1, supra), and that the resulting contract satisfied the statute of frauds.]

[W]e next consider whether defendant can avoid enforcement of the contract on the ground of mistake....

A party may rescind a contract if his or her consent was given by mistake. (Civ.Code, § 1689, subd. (b)(1).) A factual mistake by one party to a contract, or unilateral mistake, affords a ground for rescission in some circumstances. Civil Code section 1577 states in relevant part: "Mistake of fact is a mistake, not caused by the neglect of a legal duty on the part of the person making the mistake, and consisting in: [¶] 1. An unconscious ignorance or forgetfulness of a fact past or present, material to the contract...." ....

Under the first Restatement of Contracts, unilateral mistake did not render a contract voidable unless the other party knew of or caused the mistake. (1 Witkin, ... Contracts, § 370, p. 337; see Rest., Contracts, § 503.) In *Germain etc. Co. v. Western Union etc. Co.* (1902) 137 Cal. 598, 602, 70 P. 658, this court endorsed a rule similar to that of the first Restatement. Our opinion indicated that a seller's price quotation erroneously transcribed and delivered by a telegraph company contractually could bind the seller to the incorrect price, unless the buyer knew or had reason to suspect that a mistake had been made. Some decisions of the Court of Appeal have adhered to the approach of the original Restatement. (See, e.g., *Conservatorship of O'Connor* (1996) 48 Cal.App.4th 1076, 1097–1098, 56 Cal.Rptr.2d 386, and cases cited therein.) Plaintiff also advocates this approach and contends that rescission is unavailable to defendant, because plaintiff was unaware of the mistaken price in defendant's advertisement when he accepted the offer.

The Court of Appeal decisions reciting the traditional rule do not recognize that in *M.F. Kemper Const. Co. v. City of L.A.* (1951) 37 Cal.2d 696, 701, 235 P.2d 7 (*Kemper*), we acknowledged but rejected a strict application of the foregoing Restatement rule regarding unilateral mistake of fact. The plaintiff in *Kemper* inadvertently omitted a $301,769 item from its bid for the defendant city's public works project—approximately one-third of the total contract price. After discovering the mistake several hours later, the plaintiff immediately notified the city and subsequently withdrew its bid. Nevertheless, the city accepted the erroneous bid, contending that rescission of the offer was unavailable for the plaintiff's unilateral mistake.

Our decision in *Kemper* recognized that the bid, when opened and announced, resulted in an irrevocable option contract conferring upon the city a right to accept the bid, and that the plaintiff could not withdraw its bid unless the requirements for rescission of this option contract were satisfied. (*Kemper, supra,* 37 Cal.2d at pp. 700, 704, 235 P.2d 7.) We stated: "Rescission may be had for mistake of fact if the mistake is material to the contract and was not the result of neglect of a legal duty, if enforcement of the contract as made would be unconscionable, and if the other party can be placed in statu quo. [Citations.]" (*Id.* at p. 701, 235 P.2d 7.) Although the city knew of the plaintiff's mistake before it accepted the bid, and this circumstance was relevant to our determination that requiring the plaintiff to perform at the mistaken bid price would be unconscionable (*id.* at pp. 702–703, 235 P.2d 7), we authorized rescission of the city's option contract even though the city had not known of or contributed to the mistake before it opened the bid.

Similarly, in *Elsinore Union etc. Sch. Dist. v. Kastorff* (1960) 54 Cal.2d 380, 6 Cal.Rptr. 1, 353 P.2d 713 (*Elsinore*), we authorized the rescission of an erroneous bid even where the contractor had assured the public agency, after the agency inquired, that his figures were accurate, and where the agency already had accepted the bid before it was aware of the mistake. In this situation, the other party clearly had no reason to know of the contractor's mistake before it accepted the bid.

The decisions in *Kemper* and *Elsinore* establish that California law does not adhere to the original Restatement's requirements for rescission based upon unilateral mistake of fact—i.e., only in circumstances where the other party knew of the mistake or caused the mistake. Consistent with the decisions in *Kemper* and *Elsinore,* the Restatement Second of Contracts authorizes rescission for a unilateral mistake of fact where "the effect of the mistake is such that enforcement of the contract would be unconscionable." (Rest.2d Contracts, § 153, subd. (a).)[6] The comment following this section recognizes "a growing willingness to allow avoidance where the consequences of the mistake are so grave that enforcement of the contract would be unconscionable." (*Id.,* com. a, p. 394.) Indeed, two of the illustrations recognizing this additional ground for rescission in the Restatement Second of Contracts are based in part upon this court's decisions in *Kemper* and *Elsinore.* (Rest.2d Contracts, § 153, com. c, illus. 1, 3, pp. 395, 396, and

6. Section 153 of the Restatement Second of Contracts states: "Where a mistake of one party at the time a contract was made as to a basic assumption on which he made the contract has a material effect on the agreed exchange of performances that is adverse to him, the contract is voidable by him if he does not bear the risk of the mistake under the rule stated in § 154, and [¶] (a) the effect of the mistake is such that enforcement of the contract would be unconscionable, or [¶] (b) the other party had reason to know of the mistake or his fault caused the mistake."

Reporter's Note, pp. 400–401.... Although the most common types of mistakes falling within this category occur in bids on construction contracts, section 153 of the Restatement Second of Contracts is not limited to such cases. (Rest.2d Contracts, § 153, com. b, p. 395.)

Because the rule in section 153, subdivision (a), of the Restatement Second of Contracts, authorizing rescission for unilateral mistake of fact where enforcement would be unconscionable, is consistent with our previous decisions, we adopt the rule as California law. As the author of one treatise recognized more than 40 years ago, the decisions that are inconsistent with the traditional rule "are too numerous and too appealing to the sense of justice to be disregarded." (3 Corbin, Contracts (1960) § 608, p. 675, fn. omitted.) We reject plaintiff's contention and the Court of Appeal's conclusion that, because plaintiff was unaware of defendant's unilateral mistake, the mistake does not provide a ground to avoid enforcement of the contract.

Having concluded that a contract properly may be rescinded on the ground of unilateral mistake of fact as set forth in section 153, subdivision (a), of the Restatement Second of Contracts, we next consider whether the requirements of that provision, construed in light of our previous decisions, are satisfied in the present case. Where the plaintiff has no reason to know of and does not cause the defendant's unilateral mistake of fact, the defendant must establish the following facts to obtain rescission of the contract: (1) the defendant made a mistake regarding a basic assumption upon which the defendant made the contract; (2) the mistake has a material effect upon the agreed exchange of performances that is adverse to the defendant; (3) the defendant does not bear the risk of the mistake; and (4) the effect of the mistake is such that enforcement of the contract would be unconscionable. We shall consider each of these requirements below.

A significant error in the price term of a contract constitutes a mistake regarding a basic assumption upon which the contract is made, and such a mistake ordinarily has a material effect adverse to the mistaken party. (See, e.g., *Elsinore, supra,* 54 Cal.2d at p. 389, 6 Cal.Rptr. 1, 353 P.2d 713 [7 percent error in contract price]; *Lemoge Electric v. County of San Mateo* (1956) 46 Cal.2d 659, 661–662, 297 P.2d 638 [6 percent error]; *Kemper, supra,* 37 Cal.2d at p. 702, 235 P.2d 7 [28 percent error]; *Brunzell Const. Co. v. G.J. Weisbrod, Inc.* (1955) 134 Cal.App.2d 278, 286, 285 P.2d 989 [20 percent error]; Rest.2d Contracts, § 152, com. b, illus. 3, p. 387 [27 percent error].) In establishing a material mistake regarding a basic assumption of the contract, the defendant must show that the resulting imbalance in the agreed exchange is so severe that it would be unfair to require the defendant to perform. (Rest.2d Contracts, § 152, com. c, p. 388.) Ordinarily, a defendant can satisfy this requirement by showing that the exchange not only is less desirable for the defendant, but also is more advantageous to the other party. (*Ibid.*)

Measured against this standard, defendant's mistake in the contract for the sale of the Jaguar automobile constitutes a material mistake regarding a basic assumption upon which it made the contract. Enforcing the contract with the mistaken price of $25,995 would require defendant to sell the vehicle to plaintiff for $12,000 less than the intended advertised price of $37,995—an error amounting to 32 percent of the price defendant intended. The exchange of performances would be substantially less desirable for defendant and more desirable for plaintiff. Plaintiff implicitly concedes that defendant's mistake was material.

The parties and amici curiae vigorously dispute, however, whether defendant should bear the risk of its mistake. Section 154 of the Restatement Second of Contracts states: "A party bears the risk of a mistake when [¶] (a) the risk is allocated to him by agreement of the parties, or [¶] (b) he is aware, at the time the contract is made, that he has only limited knowledge with respect to the facts to which the mistake relates but treats his limited knowledge as sufficient, or [¶] (c) the risk is allocated to him by the court on the ground that it is reasonable in the circumstances to do so." Neither of the first two factors applies here. Thus, we must determine whether it is reasonable under the circumstances to allocate to defendant the risk of the mistake in the advertisement.

Civil Code section 1577, as well as our prior decisions, instructs that the risk of a mistake must be allocated to a party where the mistake results from that party's neglect of a legal duty. (*Kemper, supra,* 37 Cal.2d at p. 701, 235 P.2d 7.) It is well established, however, that ordinary negligence does not constitute neglect of a legal duty within the meaning of Civil Code section 1577. (*Kemper, supra,* 37 Cal.2d at p. 702, 235 P.2d 7.) For example, we have described a careless but significant mistake in the computation of the contract price as the type of error that sometimes will occur in the conduct of reasonable and cautious businesspersons, and such an error does not necessarily amount to neglect of legal duty that would bar equitable relief. (*Ibid.;* see also *Sun 'n Sand, Inc. v. United California Bank* (1978) 21 Cal.3d 671, 700–701, 148 Cal.Rptr. 329, 582 P.2d 920 (plur. opn. of Mosk, J.); *Elsinore, supra,* 54 Cal.2d at pp. 388–389, 6 Cal.Rptr. 1, 353 P.2d 713.)

A concept similar to neglect of a legal duty is described in section 157 of the Restatement Second of Contracts, which addresses situations in which a party's fault precludes relief for mistake. Only where the mistake results from "a failure to act in good faith and in accordance with reasonable standards of fair dealing" is rescission unavailable. (Rest.2d Contracts, § 157.) This section, consistent with the California decisions cited in the preceding paragraph, provides that a mistaken party's failure to exercise due care does not necessarily bar rescission under the rule set forth in section 153.

"The mere fact that a mistaken party could have avoided the mistake by the exercise of reasonable care does not preclude ... avoidance ... [on the ground of mistake]. Indeed, since a party can often avoid a mistake by the exercise of such care, the availability of relief would be severely circumscribed if he were to be barred by his negligence. Nevertheless, in *extreme cases* the mistaken party's fault is a proper ground for denying him relief for a mistake that he otherwise could have avoided.... [T]he rule is stated in terms of good faith and fair dealing.... [A] failure to act in good faith and in accordance with reasonable standards of fair dealing during pre-contractual negotiations does not amount to a breach. Nevertheless, under the rule stated in this Section, the failure bars a mistaken party from relief based on a mistake that otherwise would not have been made. During the negotiation stage each party is held to a degree of responsibility appropriate to the justifiable expectations of the other. The terms 'good faith' and 'fair dealing' are used, in this context, in much the same sense as in ... Uniform Commercial Code § 1–203." (Rest.2d Contracts, § 157, com. a, pp. 416–417, italics added.) Section 1201, subdivision (19), of the California Uniform Commercial Code defines "good faith," as used in section 1203 of that code, as "honesty in fact in the conduct or transaction concerned." . . .

[The municipal court made an express finding of fact that "the mistake on the part of [defendant] was made in good faith[;] it was an honest mistake, not intended to deceive the public. . . ." The Court of Appeal correctly recognized that "[w]e must, of course, accept the trial court's finding that there was a 'good faith' mistake that caused the error in the advertisement." The evidence presented at trial compellingly supports this finding.]

Defendant regularly advertises in five local newspapers. Defendant's advertising manager, Crystal Wadsworth, testified that ordinarily she meets with Kristen Berman, a representative of the Daily Pilot, on Tuesdays, Wednesdays, and Thursdays to review proof sheets of the advertisement that will appear in the newspaper the following weekend. When Wadsworth met with Berman on Wednesday, April 23, 1997, defendant's proposed advertisement listed a 1995 Jaguar XJ6 Vanden Plas without specifying a price, as it had the preceding week. On Thursday, April 24, a sales manager instructed Wadsworth to substitute a 1994 Jaguar XJ6 with a price of $25,995. The same day, Wadsworth met with Berman and conveyed to her this new information. Wadsworth did not expect to see another proof sheet reflecting this change, however, because she does not work on Friday, and the Daily Pilot goes to press on Friday and the edition in question came out on Saturday, April 26.

Berman testified that the revised advertisement was prepared by the composing department of the Daily Pilot. Berman proofread the advertisement, as she does all advertisements for which she is responsible, but Berman did not notice that it listed the 1995 Jaguar XJ6 Vanden Plas for sale at $25,995, instead of listing the 1994 Jaguar at that price. Both Berman and Wadsworth first learned of the mistake on Monday, April 28, 1997. Defendant's sales manager first became aware of the mistake after plaintiff attempted to purchase the automobile on Sunday, April 27. Berman confirmed in a letter of retraction that Berman's proofreading error had led to the mistake in the advertisement.

Defendant's erroneous advertisement in the Daily Pilot listed 16 used automobiles for sale. Each of the advertisements prepared for several newspapers in late April 1997, except for the one in the Daily Pilot, correctly identified the 1994 Jaguar XJ6 for sale at a price of $25,995. In May 1997, defendant's advertisements in several newspapers listed the 1995 Jaguar XJ6 Vanden Plas for sale at $37,995, and defendant subsequently sold the automobile for $38,399. Defendant had paid $35,000 for the vehicle.

Evidence at trial established that defendant adheres to the following procedures when an incorrect advertisement is discovered. Defendant immediately contacts the newspaper and requests a letter of retraction. Copies of any erroneous advertisements are provided to the sales staff, the error is explained to them, and the mistake is circled in red and posted on a bulletin board at the dealership. The sales staff informs customers of any advertising errors of which they are aware.

No evidence presented at trial suggested that defendant knew of the mistake before plaintiff attempted to purchase the automobile, that defendant intended to mislead customers, or that it had adopted a practice of deliberate indifference regarding errors in advertisements. Wadsworth regularly reviews proof sheets for the numerous advertisements placed by defendant, and representatives of the newspapers, including the Daily Pilot, also proofread defendant's advertisements to ensure they are accurate. Defendant follows procedures for notifying its sales staff and customers of errors of which it becomes aware. The uncontradicted evidence established that the Daily Pilot made the proofreading error resulting in defendant's mistake.

Defendant's fault consisted of failing to review a proof sheet reflecting the change made on Thursday, April 24, 1997, and/or the actual advertisement appearing in the April 26 edition of the Daily Pilot—choosing instead to rely upon the Daily Pilot's advertising staff to proofread the revised version. Although, as the Court of Appeal found, such an omission might constitute negligence, it does not involve a breach of defendant's duty of good faith and fair dealing that should preclude equitable relief for mistake. In these circumstances, it would not be reasonable for this court to allocate the risk of the mistake to defendant.

As indicated above, the Restatement Second of Contracts provides that during the negotiation stage of a contract "each party is held to a degree of responsibility appropriate to the justifiable expectations of the other." (Rest.2d Contracts, § 157, com. a, p. 417.) No consumer reasonably can expect 100 percent accuracy in each and every price appearing in countless automobile advertisements listing numerous vehicles for sale. The degree of responsibility plaintiff asks this court to impose upon automobile dealers would amount to strict contract liability for any typographical error in the price of an advertised automobile, no matter how serious the error or how blameless the dealer. We are unaware of any other situation in which an individual or business is held to such a standard under the law of contracts. Defendant's good faith, isolated mistake does not constitute the type of extreme case in which its fault constitutes the neglect of a legal duty that bars equitable relief. Therefore, ... defendant's conduct in the present case does not preclude rescission.

The final factor defendant must establish before obtaining rescission based upon mistake is that enforcement of the contract for the sale of the 1995 Jaguar XJ6 Vanden Plas at $25,995 would be unconscionable. Although the standards of unconscionability warranting rescission for mistake are similar to those for unconscionability justifying a court's refusal to enforce a contract or term, the general rule governing the latter situation (Civ.Code, § 1670.5) is inapplicable here, because unconscionability resulting from mistake does not appear at the time the contract is made. (Rest.2d Contracts, § 153, com. c, p. 395; 1 Witkin, *supra,* Contracts, § 370, pp. 337–338.)

An unconscionable contract ordinarily involves both a procedural and a substantive element: (1) oppression or surprise due to unequal bargaining power, and (2) overly harsh or one-sided results. (*Armendariz v. Foundation Health Psychcare Services, Inc.* (2000) 24 Cal.4th 83, 114, 99 Cal.Rptr.2d 745, 6 P.3d 669.) Nevertheless, " 'a sliding scale is invoked which disregards the regularity of the procedural process of the contract formation, that creates the terms, in proportion to the greater harshness or unreasonableness of the substantive terms themselves.' [Citations.]" (*Ibid.*) For example, the Restatement Second of Contracts states that "[i]nadequacy of consideration does not of itself invalidate a bargain, but gross disparity in the values exchanged may be an important factor in a determination that a contract is unconscionable and may be sufficient ground, without more, for denying specific performance." (Rest.2d Contracts, § 208, com. c, p. 108.) In ascertaining whether rescission is warranted for a unilateral mistake of fact, substantive unconscionability often will constitute the determinative factor, because the oppression and surprise ordinarily results from the mistake—not from inequality in bargaining power. Accordingly, even though defendant is not the weaker party to the contract and its mistake did not result from unequal bargaining power, defendant was surprised by the mistake, and in these circumstances overly harsh or one-sided results are sufficient to establish unconscionability entitling defendant to rescission.

Our previous cases support this approach. In *Kemper, supra,* 37 Cal.2d 696, 235 P.2d 7, we held that enforcement of the city's option to accept a construction company's bid, which was 28 percent less than the intended bid, would be unconscionable. Our decision reasoned that (1) the plaintiff gave prompt notice upon discovering the facts entitling it to rescind, (2) the city therefore was aware of the clerical error before it exercised the option, (3) the city already had awarded the contract to the next lowest bidder, (4) the company had received nothing of value it was required to restore to the city, and (5) "the city will not be heard to complain that it cannot be placed in statu quo because it will not have the benefit of an inequitable bargain." (*Id.* at p. 703, 235 P.2d 7.) Therefore, "under all the circumstances, it appears that it would be unjust and unfair to permit the city to take advantage of the company's mistake." (*Id.* at pp. 702–703, 235 P.2d 7.) Nothing in our decision in *Kemper* suggested that the mistake resulted from surprise related to inequality in the bargaining process. (Accord, *Farmers Sav. Bank, Joice v. Gerhart* (Iowa 1985) 372 N.W.2d 238, 243–245 [holding unconscionable the enforcement of sheriff's sale against bank that overbid because of a mistake caused by negligence of its own attorney].) Similarly, in *Elsinore, supra,* 54 Cal.2d 380, 6 Cal.Rptr. 1, 353 P.2d 713, we authorized rescission of a bid based upon a clerical error, without suggesting any procedural unconscionability, even where the other party afforded the contractor an opportunity to verify the accuracy of the bid before it was accepted.

In the present case, enforcing the contract with the mistaken price of $25,995 would require defendant to sell the vehicle to plaintiff for $12,000 less than the intended advertised price of $37,995—an error amounting to 32 percent of the price defendant intended. Defendant subsequently sold the automobile for slightly more than the intended advertised price, suggesting that that price reflected its actual market value. Defendant had paid $35,000 for the 1995 Jaguar and incurred costs in advertising, preparing, displaying, and attempting to sell the vehicle. Therefore, defendant would lose more than $9,000 of its original investment in the automobile. Plaintiff, on the other hand, would obtain a $12,000 windfall if the contract were enforced, simply because he traveled to the dealership and stated that he was prepared to pay the advertised price.

These circumstances are comparable to those in our prior decisions authorizing rescission on the ground that enforcing a contract with a mistaken price term would be unconscionable. Defendant's 32 percent error in the price exceeds the amount of the errors in cases such as *Kemper* and *Elsinore.* For example, in *Elsinore, supra,* 54 Cal.2d at page 389, 6 Cal.Rptr. 1, 353 P.2d 713, we authorized rescission for a $6,500 error in a bid that was intended to be $96,494—a mistake of approximately 7 percent in the intended contract price. As in the foregoing cases, plaintiff was informed of the mistake as soon as defendant discovered it. Defendant's sales manager, when he first learned of the mistake in the advertisement, explained the error to plaintiff, apologized, and offered to pay for plaintiff's fuel, time, and effort expended in traveling to the dealership to examine the automobile. Plaintiff refused this offer to be restored to the status quo. Like the public agencies in *Kemper* and *Elsinore,* plaintiff should not be permitted to take advantage of defendant's honest mistake that resulted in an unfair, one-sided contract. (Cf. *Drennan v. Star Paving Co.* (1958) 51 Cal.2d 409, 415–416, 333 P.2d 757 [no rescission of mistaken bid where other party detrimentally altered his position in reasonable reliance upon the bid and could not be restored to the status quo].) . . .

. . . [U]nder the circumstances, enforcement of the contract for the sale of the 1995 Jaguar XJ6 Vanden Plas at the $25,995 mistaken price would be unconscionable. The other requirements for rescission on the ground of unilateral mistake have been established. Defendant entered into the contract because of its mistake regarding a basic assumption, the price. The $12,000 loss that would result from enforcement of the contract has a material effect upon the agreed exchange of performances that is adverse to defendant. Furthermore, defendant did not neglect any legal duty within the meaning of Civil Code section 1577 or breach any duty of good faith and fair dealing in the steps leading to the formation of the contract. Plaintiff refused defendant's offer to compensate him for his actual losses in responding to the advertisement. "The law does not penalize for negligence beyond requiring compensation for the loss it has caused." (3 Corbin, Contracts, *supra,* § 609, p. 684.) In this situation, it would not be reasonable for this court to allocate the risk of the mistake to defendant.

Having determined that defendant satisfied the requirements for rescission of the contract on the ground of unilateral mistake of fact, we conclude that the municipal court correctly entered judgment in defendant's favor.

V

The judgment of the Court of Appeal is reversed.

KENNARD, J., CHIN, J., and BROWN, J., concur.

[The dissenting Opinion by WERDEGAR, J. in which Baxter, J., concurred, is omitted. Judge Werdegar agreed that an enforceable contract was formed between the parties but dissented from the grant of rescission on the ground that the defendant had not sought rescission either in the trial court or on appeal.]

———

SPECKEL v. PERKINS, 364 N.W.2d 890 (Minn. Ct. App. 1985). Speckel had been injured in an automobile accident involving a collision between a car driven by Perkins and a truck in which Speckel was a passenger. Spreckel sued Perkins. During the course of the litigation, Perkins's attorney, Wheat, wrote to Speckel's attorney, Eckman, as follows:

In reviewing my file concerning this claim and the upcoming trial, I note that we have a demand in our file [from you for a settlement at the] policy limits of $50,000.00. While I agree that the case has some value, I cannot agree that this is a limits case.

At this point in time I have authority to offer you $50,000.00 in settlement of your claim against my client.... I would appreciate hearing from you at your earliest convenience and would be pleased to carry any offer you may wish to make back to my client's insurance company for their consideration.

Eckman replied, "Your offer of $50,000 to settle this case ... is hereby ACCEPTED."

Perkins and his insurance company claimed that no contract had been formed. In support of this claim, Perkins's attorney, Wheat, stated in an affidavit that he intended to offer a settlement of $15,000 in his letter, not $50,000. Wheat explained that he was engaged in a trial in another matter at the time, and dictated the letter to his assistant, who misheard the term that Wheat dictated, "$15,000," as "$50,000." The assistant signed the letter on Wheat's behalf, so Wheat didn't notice the mistake.

The court held that no contract had been formed because Eckman should have known that it was not Wheat's intention to settle for $50,000:

> Several aspects of the offer ... negate its validity. A duty to inquire may be imposed on the person receiving the offer when there are factors that reasonably raise a presumption of error. An offeree "will not be permitted to snap up an offer that is too good to be true; no agreement based on such an offer can ... be enforced by the acceptor."

> In this case Wheat's letter is internally inconsistent. After stating that the case is not worth the policy limits, it proceeds to offer precisely that amount. We find that this internal inconsistency raises a presumption of error and imposed upon Eckman a consequent duty to inquire, particularly in this context—the policy limits, requested when negotiations began, were offered on the eve of trial when the parties were presumably prepared and circumstances had not changed. Finally, the letter expressly states that Wheat "would be pleased to carry any offer [Eckman] may wish to make back to [Wheat's] client's insurance company for their consideration." Despite offering the full amount of the demand, the language does not indicate that an acceptance is anticipated, but rather calls for a counter-offer. We cannot agree that it is an offer enforceable upon acceptance.

THE NOLAN RYAN BASEBALL CARD CASE.* In April 1990, Joe Irmen opened a baseball-card store named Ball–Mart. One of the cards Ball–Mart offered for sale was a 1968 Jerry Koosman/Nolan Ryan rookie card in almost perfect condition. A rookie card is the first published baseball card featuring a given player. The rookie card of a player who later becomes a superstar, like Nolan Ryan, normally commands a very high price. Irmen had obtained the card on consignment from its owner, and was required to pay the

* The account of the case is drawn largely from media reports. See Lisa Twyman Bessone, What a Card, Sports Illustrated, Mar. 18, 1991, at 9; Mark Hansen, Major League Dispute, A.B.A. J., June 1991, at 24; John Leptich, Boy Sued over Baseball Card, Chi. Trib., Nov. 10, 1990, § 1, at 1; John Leptich, Charity Delivers Winning Pitch in Baseball–Card Suit, Chi. Trib., Apr. 23, 1991, § 3, at 1; John Leptich, Finally, It's Bottom of 9th in Baseball Card Case, Chi. Trib., Apr. 5, 1991, § 3, at 2. Some of these reports vary in certain details. Where that occurs, the version that seems most plausible has been adopted.

owner $1,000 if the card was sold. A subsequent issue of a monthly price guide listed the price of a Nolan Ryan rookie card as $800–$1,200.

Bryan Wrzesinski was a twelve-year-old boy who had a collection of 40,000–50,000 baseball cards. On April 20, a few days after Ball–Mart had been opened, Bryan came into the Ball–Mart store. At that point, Irmen had more people in Ball–Mart than he could serve. Irmen owned a jewelry store next door to Ball–Mart, and he asked Kathleen Braker, a salesperson in that store, to help out. Braker had no knowledge of baseball cards. Bryan saw the Nolan Ryan card, showed it to Braker, and said, "Is this card worth twelve dollars?" According to a newspaper account of testimony Braker gave a year later, the Nolan Ryan card was marked "1200" but Braker was not sure, when she gave her testimony, "if the number contained other marks such as a comma, decimal, or dollar sign." Bryan said the card was marked "1200," without any other marks.

In response to Bryan's question whether the card was worth twelve dollars, Braker said yes, and Bryan bought the card for that amount. When Irmen found out what happened, he offered Bryan $100 for return of the card. Bryan declined, and Irmen sued to recover either the card or damages. The case was settled in mid-trial. The settlement provided that the card would be auctioned off and each party would donate his half of the proceeds to charity. (Because of the notoriety the card had acquired, by the time of the settlement the card was worth $3,000–$5,000 and possibly more. Accordingly, Irmen's tax deduction for his charitable contribution might have approached or exceeded his $1,000 cost. In addition, by this time Bryan had sued Irmen for libel on the ground that Irmen had stated publicly that Bryan had stolen the card. The settlement included a dismissal of the libel action.)

Because the case was settled, it did not result in an opinion. However, the case has been widely discussed. The facts are ambiguous concerning how the price was marked. Consider three possible scenarios.

Suppose first that the price was marked "$1,200" or "1,200." The case would then be pretty easy: Bryan would have actively misled Braker about the price by saying to her "Is this card worth $12.00?"

Suppose next that the card was marked "$1200" or "1200." As the owner of 40,000–50,000 baseball cards, Bryan almost certainly would know or should have known that in this context "1200" did not mean "12.00." On these facts too, therefore, Bryan probably would have misled Braker if he said to her, "Is this card worth $12.00?"

Suppose, finally, that the card was marked "$12.00" or "12.00." Given the size of Bryan's collection and the true value of the card, Bryan would almost certainly have known that the $12.00 price was based on a mechanical error. On these facts too, therefore, Bryan should not have been able to retain the card, under the rule reflected in *Donovan* and Restatement Second.

RESTATEMENT, SECOND, CONTRACTS §§ 153, 154

[See Selected Source Materials Supplement]

NOTE ON UNILATERAL MISTAKE

It is sometimes said that relief for unilateral mistake will not be granted unless the parties "can be placed in status quo in the equity sense, i.e. rescission must not result in prejudice to the other party except for the loss of his bargain." James T. Taylor & Son, Inc. v. Arlington Independent School District, 160 Tex. 617, 335 S.W.2d 371 (1960). Taken literally, this would preclude relief when there has been *any* reliance by the nonmistaken party. Such a rule would be unnecessary to serve the purposes intended, and expressions like that in *James T. Taylor* should be read to mean that relief will not be granted unless the other party has either not relied *or* cannot be restored to his precontractual position by the award of reliance damages.

SECTION 2. MISTAKES IN TRANSCRIPTION; REFORMATION

TRAVELERS INS. CO. v. BAILEY

Supreme Court of Vermont, 1964.
124 Vt. 114, 197 A.2d 813.

BARNEY, JUSTICE. The plaintiff insurance company has come into equity asking for reformation of the annuity provisions of a life insurance policy on the basis of mistake. Thirty years after issuance of the original policy it tendered the defendant insured an amended policy which he refused. On trial, the chancellor found that the amended policy represented the true insuring agreement originally entered into by the parties and allowed reformation. The defendant appealed.

At the instance of his mother, the defendant, when nineteen, submitted an application to an agent of the plaintiff for a life insurance policy. The plan requested in the application was one insuring the defendant's life for five thousand dollars, with an annuity at age sixty-five for five hundred dollars a year for the balance of his life, ten years certain. When the application was accepted and the policy prepared in the home office of the plaintiff, the correct descriptive information was inserted on the wrong policy form. The printed portion of the form used yielded the correct life insurance contract, but produced an annuity obligation to pay five hundred dollars a month for life, one hundred months certain. The application was made a part of the policy, by its terms. In accordance with its usual practice, the plaintiff did not retain a copy of the policy itself but kept a record of the information permitting reproduction of the policy if the occasion demanded.

The premiums were regularly paid on the policy issued in 1931, and about the middle of 1961 the actual policy came into the possession of the defendant for the first time. The semi-annual premiums charged and paid were identical with the prescribed premium for five thousand dollars of life insurance with annuity at age sixty-five of five hundred dollars annually, with payment for ten years certain. This $40.90 semi-annual premium was applicable only to that policy plan, issued at the defendant's then age of nineteen, and no other. The plaintiff had no rate for and did not sell a policy for five thousand dollars life insurance with an annuity at age sixty-five of five hundred dollars monthly, payment for one hundred months certain.

After being told by a third party that his policy could not have the provisions he claimed for it, the defendant took the policy to the office of the defendant's agent that sold the policy and made inquiry. Shortly thereafter, in late 1961, the amended policy was tendered. There is no evidence that the defendant then knew that his original policy provided for an annuity payment larger than he was entitled to in view of the premium paid and the life insurance coverage purchased.

Vermont law, like that of many jurisdictions, imposes upon the party seeking reformation the duty of establishing, beyond a reasonable doubt, the true agreement to which the contract in question is to be reformed. deNeergaard v. Dillingham, 123 Vt. 327, 331, 187 A.2d 494. That this was accomplished, in the judgment of the chancellor, is demonstrated by this finding in particular:

> "The only agreement that the plaintiff and defendant made was for $5000 insurance with annuity of $500 per year at attained age 65, ten years certain."

Adequate evidentiary support for all findings of fact, including this one, made in this case by the chancellor, appears from the transcript of the evidence.

Indeed, in his appeal, the defendant does not question any of the findings relating to the facts already recited. His principal attack on the decision relates to the chancellor's finding that the mistake in issuing the policy furnished the defendant came about through no fault of the defendant, but solely through the negligence and inattention of the plaintiff. This, says the defendant, is a finding of unilateral mistake, and therefore, under the authority of New York Life Insurance Co. v. Kimball, 93 Vt. 147, 153, 106 A. 676, is not grounds for reformation. . . .

In [that case] Justice Miles commented . . . "The law of a case cannot be determined from a brief quotation of portions of the opinion separate from the facts of a case, especially where the law upon the subject has many exceptions, as in the subject now under consideration." This thought is particularly applicable to cases dealing with mistake and reformation. . . .

One variety of classification [of cases involving mistake] is suggested by the difference between a subsequent erroneous recording or transcription of a contract already in fact agreed to by the parties, and a mistake or misunderstanding [which] occurs while the parties are seeking to arrive at or believe they are arriving at an agreement. In the first case an agreement already exists, while in the second considerations of mutuality, together with knowledge of and responsibility for the mistake, weigh heavily in determining whether or not an enforceable agreement, or a right to relief, exists. Unfortunately, language appropriate to the second situation has sometimes been transposed to the first, where it may be both inappropriate and misleading. See 3 Corbin on Contracts § 608 (1960).

Where, as here, an antecedent contract has been established by the requisite measure of proof, equity will act to bring the erroneous writing into conformity with the true agreement. Burlington Building & Loan Ass'n v. Cummings, 111 Vt. 447, 453, 17 A.2d 319. On the basis of the maxim, "Equity regards that as done which ought to be done," equity will deal generously with the correction of mistakes. Stone v. Blake, 118 Vt. 424, 427, 110 A.2d 702, 704. This power has been regularly and frequently invoked in connection with real estate transactions, but there is nothing that requires that equity limit its application to that kind of case.

Other courts have exercised the equitable power of reformation in similar cases. In New England Mutual Life Insurance Co. v. Jones, D.C., 1 F.Supp. 984, a clerical mistake in the policy was discovered after the death of the insured when a double indemnity benefit claim for accidental death was made. The policy provided for double indemnity on the basis of the face amount of the policy, but in the blank space stating the obligation the figure $5000.00 had been entered. This considerably increased the double indemnity figure above that computed on the face amount of the policy. Premiums had been assessed and paid on the basis of the correct figure. Reformation was allowed.

In Stamen v. Metropolitan Life Insurance Co., 41 N.J.Super. 135, 124 A.2d 328, the insured received a policy, after a series of policy conversions, which inadvertently included a provision for disability benefits. The original application accepted by the company requested a policy without such provision, and the premiums had been assessed on the basis that no such benefits were payable. Reformation was allowed. . . .

Each of these cases speak of the reformation as justified either because there was "mutuality" of mistake or because the policy holder knew or ought to have known that there was a variation between the policy described in the accepted application and the one handed the insured. To insist on enforcement of the contract once knowledge of the error is acquired by the insured is held to be unconscionable, and classified as then a unilateral mistake known to the other party, which supports reformation. If the mistake exists in the writing unknown to both parties, it is classified as "mutual" and reformation is allowed.

Since these cases support reformation irrespective of the insured's knowledge of the existence of the mistake conferring a benefit on him beyond the bargain, talk of "mutual" or "unilateral" mistake seems to be of little help in this kind of situation. . . .

If, in this kind of case, talk of "mutuality" of mistake is unnecessary, much confusion can be avoided. Invariably, two mistakes are involved. There is a natural tendency to concentrate on the making of the clerical error in the writing as the critical mistake involved, when the true crucial error is mistaken belief of the parties about the correctness of the written instrument. When a test of "mutuality" is applied to the clerical error, the confusion is compounded, since the concern of the court should be with the belief or knowledge of the parties. The concept of "mutuality" adds nothing to the right to a remedy in this type of case. It is important as a concept in other, different, reformation situations. Applying to all the common linguistic label of "mutuality" gives to unlike situations an illusion of similarity. This invites the misapplication of principles, sound for one type of situation, to a different type, for which they are unsound.

Accordingly, we hold that where there has been established beyond a reasonable doubt a specific contractual agreement between parties, and a subsequent erroneous rendition of the terms of the agreement in a material particular, the party penalized by the error is entitled to reformation, if there has been no prejudicial change of position by the other party while ignorant of the mistake. If such change of position can equitably be taken into account and adjusted for in the decree, reformation may be possible even then. Mutual Life Ins. Co. of Baltimore v. Metzger, 167 Md. 27, 172 A. 610; see also Brown v. Lamphear, 35 Vt. 252. Mistakes generally occur through some carelessness, and failure to discover a mistake may be in some degree negligent, but unless some prejudice to the other party's rights under the true contract results, so as to make its enforcement inequitable, reformation will not be refused because of the presence of some negligence. Ward v. Lyman, 108 Vt. 464, 471, 188 A. 892; Mutual Life Insurance Co. of Baltimore v. Metzger, supra, 167 Md. 27, 30, 172 A. 610.

Change of position is raised as an issue by the defendant. It cannot be said that the defendant acted in reliance on the terms of the policy which, he testified, were not exactly known by him until he received the policy in 1961. But he argues that the mere passage of time, in this case thirty years, should overcome the chancellor's finding to the contrary and establish a change of position. But clearly this aging process was inevitable, and not a prejudicial act induced by the mistaken term in the policy. The defendant has not demonstrated that he was prejudiced by the existence of the error. Ward v. Lyman, supra, 108 Vt. 464, 471, 188 A. 892.

Reformation was properly granted.

Decree affirmed.

RESTATEMENT, SECOND, OF CONTRACTS § 155

[See Selected Source Materials Supplement]

CHIMART ASSOCIATES v. PAUL, 66 N.Y.2d 570, 498 N.Y.S.2d 344, 489 N.E.2d 231 (1986). "Because the thrust of a reformation claim is that a writing does not set forth the actual agreement of the parties, generally neither the parol evidence rule nor the Statute of Frauds applies to bar proof, in the form of parol or extrinsic evidence, of the claimed agreement.... However, this obviously recreates the very danger against which the parol evidence rule and Statute of Frauds were supposed to protect—the danger that a party, having agreed to a written contract that turns out to be disadvantageous, will falsely claim the existence of a different, oral contract.... To this end ... reformation has been limited both substantively and procedurally. Substantively, for example, reformation based upon mistake is not available where the parties purposely contract based upon uncertain or contingent events....

"Procedurally, there is a 'heavy presumption that a deliberately prepared and executed written instrument [manifests] the true intention of the parties' ... and a correspondingly high order of evidence is required to overcome that presumption.... The proponent of reformation must 'show in no uncertain terms, not only that mistake or fraud exists, but exactly what was really agreed upon between the parties'...."

SECTION 3. MUTUAL MISTAKES (SHARED MISTAKEN ASSUMPTIONS)

Another important type of mistake in contract law consists of a mistaken factual assumption about the present state of the world outside the mind of the actor who holds the assumption. Mistaken factual assumptions differ from mechanical errors, because they do not involve blunders that result from transient errors in a party's mental or physical machinery. They differ from mistranscriptions, because they do not turn on whether a writing is erroneous.

A mistaken factual assumption may either be shared by both parties to a contract or held by only one of the parties. Traditionally, shared mistaken factual assumptions have been treated under the heading of *mutual mistake*, meaning a mistake that is shared by both parties. This terminology fails to differentiate among shared mistakes according to their functional characteristics. Some kinds of shared mistakes should provide a basis for relief, while others should not. For example, if Team A trades Player P to Team B, and both teams share a mistake about just how fast or how strong P is, that mistake should not and would not give either team the right to rescind the trade. Even shared mistakes that should provide a basis for relief fall into different functional categories that require differing treatment. For example, in mistranscription cases the parties both mistakenly believe that the writing properly transcribes the bargain. The appropriate remedy here normally is reformation, not recission.

In short, that a mistake is shared is relevant but it is not critical. What is critical is the character of the shared mistake. That character is captured in the term *shared mistaken factual assumptions* or, for short, *shared mistaken assumptions*.

In analyzing shared assumptions from the perspective of mistake, it is useful to begin with shared assumptions that are made explicit in a contract. If a contract is explicitly based on a shared assumption that turns out to have been mistaken, normally the mistake should furnish a basis for relief under a relatively straightforward interpretation of the language of the contract. For example, suppose A agrees to sell a plot of land, Tenacre, to B, and the contract provides, "This agreement is made on the assumption that Tenacre is zoned for commercial use." If it turns out that Tenacre is not zoned for commercial use, it is pretty clear that under the contract, B should be entitled to rescission.

Now suppose a shared mistaken assumption is tacit rather than explicit. The concept of a tacit assumption has been explicated as follows by Lon Fuller: Words like "intention," "assumption," "expectation" and "understanding" all seem to imply a conscious state involving an awareness of alternatives and a deliberate choice among them. It is, however, plain that there is a psychological state that can be described as a "tacit assumption", which does not involve a consciousness of alternatives. The absent-minded professor stepping from his office into the hall as he reads a book "assumes" that the floor of the hall will be there to receive him. His conduct is conditioned and directed by this assumption, even though the possibility that the floor has been removed does not "occur" to him, that is, is not present in his conscious mental processes.

A more colloquial expression that captures the concept of a tacit assumption is "taken for granted." A tacit assumption is so deeply embedded in an actor's mind that it simply doesn't occur to the actor to make the assumption explicit—any more than it occurs to Fuller's professor to think to himself, every time he is about to walk through a door, "Remember to check that the floor is still in place." Of course, if actors had infinite time and no costs, they would ransack their minds to think through every one of their tacit assumptions, and make each of those assumptions explicit. But actors do not have infinite time and they do have costs. Normally, it would be irrational for a potential contracting party to take the time to determine, and make explicit, every tacit assumption that he holds, because the costs of doing so would often approach or exceed the expected profit from the contract. It would also normally be virtually impossible to make such a determination. As Randy Barnett has stated:

> [When we add] to the infinity of knowledge about the present world the inherent uncertainty of future events ... we immediately can see that the seductive idea that a contract can ... articulate every contingency that might arise before ... performance is sheer fantasy. For this reason, contracts must be silent on an untold number of items. And many of these silent assumptions that underlie every agreement are as basic as the assumption that the sun will rise tomorrow. They are simply too basic to merit mention.

Randy E. Barnett, Contracts: Cases and Doctrine 1163 (2d ed. 1999).

WITTGENSTEIN, PHILOSOPHICAL INVESTIGATIONS 33 (1953 tr.) "Someone says to me: 'Show the children a game.' I teach them gaming with dice, and the other says, 'I didn't mean that sort of game.' Must the exclusion of the game with dice have come before his mind when he gave the order?"

SHERWOOD v. WALKER

Supreme Court of Michigan, 1887.
66 Mich. 568, 33 N.W. 919, 11 Am.St.Rep. 531.

MORSE, J. Replevin for a cow. Suit commenced in justice's court; judgment for plaintiff; appealed to circuit court of Wayne county, and verdict and judgment for plaintiff in that court. The defendants bring error, and set out 25 assignments of the same.

The main controversy depends upon the construction of a contract for the sale of the cow. The plaintiff claims that the title passed, and bases his action upon such claim. The defendants contend that the contract was executory, and by its terms no title to the animal was acquired by plaintiff. The defendants reside at Detroit, but are in business at Walkerville, Ontario, and have a farm at Greenfield, in Wayne county, upon which were some blooded cattle supposed to be barren as breeders. The Walkers are importers and breeders of polled Angus cattle. The plaintiff is a banker living at Plymouth, in Wayne county. He called upon the defendants at Walkerville for the purchase of some of their stock, but found none there that suited him. Meeting one of the defendants afterwards, he was informed that they had a few head upon their Greenfield farm. He was asked to go out and look at them, with the statement at the time that they were probably barren, and would not breed. May 5, 1886, plaintiff went out to Greenfield and saw the cattle. A few days thereafter, he called upon one of the defendants with the view of purchasing a cow, known as "Rose 2d of Aberlone." After considerable talk it was agreed that defendants would telephone Sherwood at his home in Plymouth in reference to the price. The second morning after this talk he was called up by telephone, and the terms of the sale were finally agreed upon. He was to pay five and one-half cents per pound, live weight, fifty pounds shrinkage. He was asked how he intended to take the cow home, and replied that he might ship her from King's cattle-yard. He requested defendants to confirm the sale in writing, which they did by sending him the following letter:

"Walkerville, May 15, 1886.

"T.C. Sherwood, President, etc.—Dear Sir: We confirm sale to you of the cow Rose 2d of Aberlone, lot 56 of our catalogue, at five and a half cents per pound, less fifty pounds shrink. We inclose herewith order on Mr. Graham for the cow. You might leave check with him, or mail to us here, as you prefer.

"Yours truly,
Hiram Walker & Sons."

The order upon Graham enclosed in the letter read as follows:

"Walkerville, May 15, 1886.

"George Graham: You will please deliver at King's cattle-yard to Mr. T.C. Sherwood, Plymouth, the cow Rose 2d of Aberlone, lot 56 of our catalogue. Send halter with the cow, and have her weighed.

"Yours truly,
Hiram Walker & Sons."

On the twenty-first of the same month the plaintiff went to defendants' farm at Greenfield, and presented the order and letter to Graham, who informed him that the defendants had instructed him not to deliver the cow. Soon after, the plaintiff tendered to Hiram Walker, one of the defendants, $80, and demanded the cow. Walker refused to take the money or deliver the cow. The plaintiff then instituted this suit. After he had secured possession of the cow under the writ of replevin, the plaintiff caused her to be weighed by the constable who served the writ, at a place other than King's cattle-yard. She weighed 1,420 pounds.

When the plaintiff, upon the trial in the circuit court, had submitted his proofs showing the above transaction, defendants moved to strike out and exclude the testimony from the case, for the reason that it was irrelevant and did not tend to show that the title to the cow passed, and that it showed that the contract of sale was merely executory. The court refused the motion, and an exception was taken.

The defendants then introduced evidence tending to show that at the time of the alleged sale it was believed by both the plaintiff and themselves that the cow was barren and would not breed; that she cost $850, and if not barren would be worth from $750 to $1,000; that after the date of the letter, and the order to Graham, the defendants were informed by said Graham that in his judgment the cow was with calf, and therefore they instructed him not to deliver her to plaintiff, and on the twentieth of May, 1886, telegraphed plaintiff what Graham thought about the cow being with calf, and that consequently they could not sell her. The cow had a calf in the month of October following.

On the nineteenth of May, the plaintiff wrote Graham as follows:

"Plymouth, May 19, 1886

"Mr. George Graham, Greenfield—Dear Sir: I have bought Rose or Lucy from Mr. Walker, and will be there for her Friday morning, nine or ten o'clock. Do not water her in the morning.

"Yours, etc., T.C. Sherwood"

Plaintiff explained the mention of the two cows in this letter by testifying that, when he wrote this letter, the order and letter of defendants was at his home, and, writing in a hurry, and being uncertain as to the name of the cow, and not wishing his cow watered, he thought it would do no harm to name them both, as his bill of sale would show which one he had purchased. Plaintiff also testified that he asked defendants to give him a price on the balance of their herd at Greenfield, as a friend thought of buying some, and received a letter dated May 17, 1886, in which they named the price of five cattle, including Lucy, at $90, and Rose 2d at $80. When he received the letter he called defendants up by telephone, and asked them why they put Rose 2d in the list, as he had already purchased her. They replied that they knew he had, but thought it would make no difference if plaintiff and his friend concluded to take the whole herd.

The foregoing is the substance of all the testimony in the case.

The circuit judge instructed the jury that if they believed the defendants, when they sent the order and letter to plaintiff, meant to pass the title to the cow, and that the cow was intended to be delivered to plaintiff, it did not matter whether the cow was weighed at any particular place, or by any particular person; and if the cow was weighed afterwards, as Sherwood testified, such weighing would be a sufficient compliance with the order. If they believed that defendants intended to pass the title by writing, it did not matter whether the cow was weighed before or after suit brought, and the plaintiff would be entitled to recover.

The defendants submitted a number of requests which were refused. The substance of them was that the cow was never delivered to plaintiff, and the title to her did not pass by the letter and order; and that under the contract, as evidenced by these writings, the title did not pass until the cow was weighed and her price thereby determined; and that, if the defendants only agreed to sell a cow that would not breed, then the barrenness of the cow was a condition precedent to passing title, and plaintiff cannot recover. The court also charged the jury that it was immaterial whether the cow was with calf or not. It will therefore be seen that the defendants claim that, as a matter of law, the title of this cow did not pass, and that the circuit judge erred in submitting the case to the jury, to be determined by them, upon the intent of the parties as to whether or not the title passed with the sending of the letter and order by the defendants to the plaintiff. . . .

It appears from the record that both parties supposed this cow was barren and would not breed, and she was sold by the pound for an insignificant sum as compared with her real value if a breeder. She was evidently sold and purchased on the relation of her value for beef, unless the plaintiff had learned of her true condition, and concealed such knowledge from the defendants. Before the plaintiff secured the possession of the animal, the defendants learned that she was with calf, and therefore of great value, and undertook to rescind the sale by refusing to deliver her. The question arises whether they had a right to do so. The circuit judge ruled that this fact did not avoid the sale and it made no difference whether she was barren or not. I am of the opinion that the court erred in this holding. I know that this is a close question, and the dividing line between the adjudicated cases is not easily discerned. But it must be considered as well settled that a party who has given an apparent consent to a contract of sale may refuse to execute it, or he may avoid it after it has been completed, if the assent was founded, or the contract made, upon the mistake of a material fact,—such as the subject-matter of the sale, the price, or some collateral fact materially inducing the agreement; and this can be done when the mistake is mutual. . . .

If there is a difference or misapprehension as to the substance of the thing bargained for; if the thing actually delivered or received is different in substance from the thing bargained for, and intended to be sold,—then there is no contract; but if it be only a difference in some quality or accident, even though the mistake may have been the actuating motive to the purchaser or seller, or both of them, yet the contract remains binding. "The difficulty in every case is to determine whether the mistake or misapprehension is as to the substance of the whole contract, going, as it were, to the root of the matter, or only to some point, even though a material point, an error as to which does not affect the substance of the whole consideration." Kennedy v. Panama, etc., Mail Co., L.R. 2 Q.B. 580, 588. It has been held, in accordance with the principles above stated, that where a horse is bought under the belief that he is sound, and both vendor and vendee honestly believe him to be sound, the purchaser must stand by his bargain, and pay the full price, unless there was a warranty.

It seems to me, however, in the case made by this record, that the mistake or misapprehension of the parties went to the whole substance of the agreement. If the cow was a breeder, she was worth at least $750; if barren, she was worth not over $80. The parties would not have made the contract of sale except upon the understanding and belief that she was incapable of breeding, and of no use as a cow. It is true she is now the identical animal that they thought her to be when the contract was made; there is no mistake as to the identity of the creature. Yet the mistake was not of the mere quality of the animal, but went to the very nature of the thing. A barren cow is substantially a different creature than a breeding one. There is as much difference between them for all purposes of use as there is between an ox and a cow that is capable of breeding and giving milk. If the mutual mistake had simply related to the fact whether she was with calf or not for one season, then it might have been a good sale, but the mistake affected the character of the animal for all time, and for its present and ultimate use. She was not in fact the animal, or the kind of animal, the defendants intended to sell or the plaintiff to buy. She was not a barren cow, and, if this fact had been known, there would have been no contract. The mistake affected the substance of the whole consideration, and it must be considered that there was no contract to sell or sale of the cow as she actually was. The thing sold and bought had in fact no existence. She was sold as a beef creature would be sold; she is in fact a breeding cow, and a valuable one. The court should have instructed the jury that if they found that the cow was sold, or contracted to be sold, upon the understanding of both parties that she was barren, and useless for the purpose of breeding, and that in fact she was not barren, but capable of breeding, then the defendants had a right to rescind, and refuse to deliver, and the verdict should be in their favor.

The judgment of the court below must be reversed, and a new trial granted, with costs of this court to defendants.

CAMPBELL, C.J., and CHAMPLIN, J., concurred.

SHERWOOD, J. (dissenting). I do not concur in the opinion given by my brethren in this case....

As has already been stated by my brethren, the record shows that the plaintiff is a banker and a farmer as well, carrying on a farm, and raising the best breeds of stock, and lived in Plymouth, in the county of Wayne, 23 miles from Detroit; that the defendants lived in Detroit, and were also dealers in stock of the higher grades; that they had a farm at Walkerville, in Canada, and also one in Greenfield in said county of Wayne, and upon these farms the defendants kept their stock. The Greenfield farm was about 15 miles from the plaintiff's. In the spring of 1886 the plaintiff, learning that the defendants had some "polled Angus cattle" for sale, was desirous of purchasing some of that breed, and meeting the defendants, or some of them, at Walkerville, inquired about them, and was informed that they had none at Walkerville, "but had a few head left on their farm in Greenfield, and asked the plaintiff to go and see them, stating that in all probability they were sterile and would not breed." ... The record further shows that the defendants, when they sold the cow, believed the cow was not with calf, and barren; that from what the plaintiff had been told by defendants (for it does not appear he had any other knowledge or facts from which he could form an opinion) he believed the cow was farrow, but still thought she could be made to breed. The foregoing shows the entire interview and treaty between the parties as to the sterility and qualities of the cow sold to the plaintiff. The cow had a calf in the month of October.

There is no question but that the defendants sold the cow representing her of the breed and quality they believed the cow to be, and that the purchaser so understood it. And the buyer purchased her believing her to be of the breed represented by the sellers, and possessing all the qualities stated, and even more. He believed she would breed. There is no pretense that the plaintiff bought the cow for beef, and there is nothing in the record indicating that he would have bought her at all only that he thought she might be made to breed. Under the foregoing facts,—and these are all that are contained in the record material to the contract,—it is held that because it turned out that the plaintiff was more correct in his judgment as to one quality of the cow than the defendants, and a quality, too, which could not by any possibility be positively known at the time by either party to exist, the contract may be annulled by the defendants at their pleasure. I know of no law, and have not been referred to any, which will justify any such holding, and I think the circuit judge was right in his construction of the contract between the parties.

It is claimed that a mutual mistake of a material fact was made by the parties when the contract of sale was made. There was no warranty in the case of the quality of the animal. When a mistaken fact is relied upon as ground for rescinding, such fact must not only exist at the time the contract is made, but must have been known to one or both of the parties. Where there is no warranty, there can be no mistake of fact when no such fact exists, or, if in existence, neither party knew of it, or could know of it; and that is precisely this case. If the owner of a Hambletonian horse had speeded him, and was only able to make him go a mile in three minutes, and should sell him to another, believing that was his greatest speed, for $300, when the purchaser believed he could go much faster, and made the purchase for that sum, and a few days thereafter, under more favorable circumstances, the horse was driven a mile in 2 min. 16 sec., and was found to be worth $20,000, I hardly think it would be held, either at law or in equity, by any one, that the seller in such case could rescind the contract. The same legal principles apply in each case.

In this case neither party knew the actual quality and condition of this cow at the time of the sale. The defendants say, or rather said, to the plaintiff, "they had a few head left on their farm in Greenfield, and asked plaintiff to go and see them, stating to plaintiff that in all probability they were sterile and would not breed." Plaintiff did go as requested, and found there these cows, including the one purchased, with a bull. The cow had been exposed, but neither knew she was with calf or whether she would breed. The defendants thought she would not, but the plaintiff says that he thought she could be made to breed, but believed she was not with calf. The defendants sold the cow for what they believed her to be, and the plaintiff bought her as he believed she was, after the statements made by the defendants. No conditions whatever were attached to the terms of sale by either party. It was in fact as absolute as it could well be made, and I know of no precedent as authority by which this court can alter the contract thus made by these parties in writing, and interpolate in it a condition by which, if the *defendants should be mistaken in their belief that the cow was barren,* she could be returned to them and their contract should be annulled. It is not the duty of courts to destroy contracts when called upon to enforce them, after they have been legally made. There was no mistake of any material fact by either of the parties in the case as would license the vendors to rescind. There was no difference between the parties, nor misapprehension, as to the substance of the thing bargained for, which was a cow supposed to be barren by one party, and believed not to be by the other. As to the quality of the animal, subsequently developed, both parties were equally ignorant, and as to this each party took his chances. If this were not the law, there would be no safety in purchasing this kind of stock.

I entirely agree with my brethren that the right to rescind occurs whenever "the thing actually delivered or received is different in substance from the thing bargained for, and intended to be sold; but if it be only a difference in some quality or accident, even though the misapprehension may have been the actuating motive" of the parties in making the contract, yet it will remain binding. In this case the cow sold was the one delivered. What might or might not happen to her after the sale formed no element in the contract. . . .

NESTER v. MICHIGAN LAND & IRON CO., 69 Mich. 290, 37 N.W. 278 (1888). In September 1885, Michigan Land entered into a written contract with Nester, under which Michigan Land sold to Nester all the merchantable pine on certain land. Michigan Land made no representation to Nester that it intended Nester to rely upon, or that he did rely upon, in making his purchase. Prior to the sale, Michigan Land's agent told Nester that if he purchased the timber he had to do so on the basis of his own estimate. Nester had such an estimate made, and knew that an estimate could not be made with any degree of certainty—to use the language of his estimate, that "it is all guesswork any way." After the purchase, Nester sued to reduce the purchase price by 50% on the ground that both parties were mistaken in their estimate of the quality of the timber on the land; that a large portion of the timber was unsound; and that in consequence of the amount of decayed timber, the yield of merchantable pine furnished only about half the quantity of such pine that was anticipated or estimated. The case was decided by the Michigan Supreme Court, one year after Sherwood v. Walker. The opinion was written by Judge Sherwood, who had dissented in Sherwood v. Walker, and then had become Chief Judge of the Court. Held, for Michigan Land.

"We know of no case which will sustain the complainant's case upon the facts before us. That of *Sherwood v. Walker* . . . will come the nearest to it of any referred to. That is, however, somewhat different upon its facts, and the rule applied in that case can never be resorted to except in a case where all the facts and circumstances are precisely the same as in that." There were no dissents.

GRIFFITH v. BRYMER

King's Bench Div., 1903.
19 T.L.R. 434.

This was an action brought by Mr. Murray Griffith, of 8, Seamoreplace, Park-lane against Colonel W.E. Brymer, M.P., of 8, St. James's-street to recover the sum of £100 paid on an agreement to hire a certain room at 8, St. James's-street for the purpose of viewing the Coronation Procession on June 26, 1902.

The facts, so far as material, were as follows:—At 11 a.m. on June 24, 1902, the plaintiff entered into a verbal agreement with Messrs. Pope, Roach, and Co., the defendant's agents, to take the room for the purpose of viewing the procession on June 26, and handed over his cheque for £100. It was admitted that the decision to operate on the King, which rendered the procession impossible, had been reached at about 10 a.m. that morning. But neither party was aware of this fact when the agreement was entered into and the cheque given; and it was contended for the plaintiff that, as both parties were under a misconception with regard to the existing state of facts about which they were contracting, the plaintiff was entitled to the return of his money. In the course of the argument Clark v. Lindsay, 19 T.L.R. 202, 88 L.T. 198, and Blakeley v. Muller, 19 T.L.R. 186, were cited.

Mr. Justice Wright held that the principle of such cases as Coutourier v. Hastie, 8 Ex., 40, applied to this case, and expressed his agreement with the law as laid down by Mr. Justice Channell in Clark v. Lindsay. The agreement was made on the supposition by both parties that nothing had happened which made performance impossible. This was a missupposition of the state of facts which went to the whole root of the matter. The contract was therefore void, and the plaintiff was entitled to recover his £100.

WOOD v. BOYNTON, 64 Wis. 265, 25 N.W. 42 (1885). Wood had found a small stone about the size of a canary egg. Subsequently, she sold the stone for $1 to Boynton, who was in the jewelry business. Afterwards, it was ascertained that the stone was a rough diamond, worth about $700. After learning this fact, Wood tendered $1 plus 10¢ interest to Boynton, and demanded a return of the stone. Boynton refused, and Wood brought an action for rescission.

At the trial, Wood testified: "The first time Boynton saw that stone he was talking about buying the topaz, or whatever it is, in September or October. I went into the store to get a little pin mended, and I had it in a small box,—the pin,—a small ear–ring; . . . this stone, and a broken sleeve–button were in the box. Mr. Boynton turned to give me a check for my pin. I thought I would ask him what the stone was, and I took it out of the box and asked him to please tell me what that was. He took it in his hand and seemed some time looking at it. I told him I had been told it was a topaz, and he said it might be. He says, 'I would buy this; would you sell it?' I told him I did not know but what I would. What would it be worth? And he said he did not know; he would give me a dollar and keep it as a specimen, and I told him I would not sell it. . . . Afterwards, and about the twenty–eighth of December, I needed money pretty badly, and thought every dollar would help, and I took it back to Mr. Boynton and told him I had brought back the topaz, and he says, 'Well, yes; what did I offer you for it?' and I says, 'One dollar;' and he stepped to the change drawer and gave me the dollar, and I went out." Boynton testified that at the time he bought the stone he had never seen an uncut diamond; "he had no idea this was a diamond, and it never entered his brain at the time." Held, for Boynton:

> In this case, upon the plaintiff's own evidence, there can be no just ground for alleging that she was induced to make the sale she did by any fraud or unfair dealings on the part of Mr. Boynton. Both were entirely ignorant at the time of the character of the stone and of its intrinsic value. Mr. Boynton was not an expert in uncut diamonds, and had made

no examination of the stone, except to take it in his hand and look at it before he made the offer of one dollar, which was refused at the time, and afterwards accepted without any comment or further examination made by Mr. Boynton. The appellant had the stone in her possession for a long time, and it appears from her own statement that she had made some inquiry as to its nature and qualities. If she chose to sell it without further investigation as to its intrinsic value to a person who was guilty of no fraud or unfairness which induced her to sell it for a small sum, she cannot repudiate the sale because it is afterwards ascertained that she made a bad bargain. Kennedy v. Panama, etc., Mail Co., L.R. 2 Q.B. 580. There is no pretense of any mistake as to the identity of the thing sold. It was produced by the plaintiff and exhibited to the vendee before the sale was made, and the thing sold was delivered to the vendee when the purchase price was paid.... Suppose the appellant had produced the stone, and said she had been told it was a diamond, and she believed it was, but had no knowledge herself as to its character or value, and Mr. Boynton had given her $500 for it, could he have rescinded the sale if it had turned out to be a topaz or any other stone of very small value? Could Mr. Boynton have rescinded the sale on the ground of mistake? Clearly not....

It is urged, with a good deal of earnestness, on the part of the counsel for the appellant that, because it has turned out that the stone was immensely more valuable than the parties at the time of the sale supposed it was, such fact alone is a ground for the rescission of the sale, and that fact was evidence of fraud on the part of the vendee. Whether inadequacy of price is to be received as evidence of fraud, even in a suit in equity to avoid a sale, depends upon the facts known to the parties at the time the sale is made. When this sale was made the value of the thing sold was open to the investigation of both parties, neither knowing its intrinsic value, and, so far as the evidence in this case shows, both supposed that the price paid was adequate. How can fraud be predicated upon such a sale, even though after-investigation showed that the intrinsic value of the thing sold was hundreds of times greater than the price paid? It certainly shows no such fraud as would authorize the vendor to rescind the contract and bring an action at law to recover the possession of the thing sold. Whether that fact would have any influence in an action in equity to avoid the sale we need not consider....

We can find nothing in the evidence from which it could be justly inferred that Mr. Boynton, at the time he offered the plaintiff one dollar for the stone, had a knowledge of the real value of the stone, or that he entertained even a belief that the stone was a diamond. It cannot, therefore, be said that there was a suppression of knowledge on the part of the defendant as to the value of the stone which a court of equity might seize upon to avoid the sale.... However unfortunate the plaintiff may have been in selling this valuable stone for a mere nominal sum, she has failed entirely to make out a case either of fraud or mistake in the sale such as will entitle her to a rescission of such sale so as to recover the property sold in an action at law.

———

FIRESTONE & PARSON, INC. v. UNION LEAGUE OF PHILA-DELPHIA, 672 F.Supp. 819 (E.D.Pa.1987), aff'd without opinion, 833 F.2d 304 (3d Cir.1987). For many years, the Union League Club was the owner of an oil painting, "The Bombardment of Fort Sumter," which was generally regarded in art circles as being a major work of Albert Bierstadt, a renowned American landscape artist. In 1981, Firestone & Parson purchased that painting from the Club for $500,000. At that time, the parties all believed that the painting was Bierstadt's work. In Spring 1985, however, some art historians began to express doubts about the accuracy of the attribution. In February 1986, an article published in *Antiques* magazine by a noted art historian expressed the opinion that a Confederate artist, John Ross Key, had done the painting. This view came to be generally accepted among art experts.

In 1988, Firestone & Parson brought suit for rescission and damages, asserting that as a Bierstadt the painting was worth more than $500,000, but as the work of Key it was worth only about $50,000. The court held that the claim of Firestone & Parson, if any, accrued at the time of sale, and was therefore barred by a four-year statute-of-limitations period. The court added, "[The] ruling that plaintiffs' claims are time-barred should not be interpreted as suggesting that plaintiffs' claims would otherwise have been valid: in the arcane world of high-priced art, market value is affected by market perceptions; the market value of a painting is determined by the prevailing views of the marketplace concerning its attribution. Post-sale fluctuations in generally accepted attributions do not necessarily establish that there was a mutual mistake of fact at the time of the sale. If both parties correctly believed at that time that the painting was generally believed to be a Bierstadt, and in fact it was then generally regarded as a Bierstadt, it seems unlikely that plaintiff could show that there was a mutual mistake of fact."

EVERETT v. ESTATE OF SUMSTAD, 95 Wash.2d 853, 631 P.2d 366 (1981). The Mitchells owned a small secondhand store. In August 1978, they attended Alexander's Auction, where they frequently shopped to obtain merchandise for their own use and for use as inventory in their business. At the auction, the Mitchells purchased for $50 a used safe that had a locked inside compartment. Several days after the auction, the Mitchells took the safe to a locksmith to have the locked compartment opened. The locksmith found $32,207 inside, and a controversy arose whether the Mitchells were entitled to the money. An affidavit of the Mitchells stated:

> [W]e saw that the top outer-most door with a combination lock was open, and that the inner door was locked shut. That inner door required a key to open, and we learned that the safe would have to be taken to a locksmith to get the inner door opened because no key was available. We also learned that the combination for the outer lock was unknown. The auctioneer told the bidders that both this and the other safe had come from an estate, that both were still locked, that neither had been opened, and that the required combinations and key were unavailable for either.

The auctioneer's affidavit stated:

> I told the crowd at the auction that [the safes] were from an estate, that they were still locked and had never been opened by me and that I didn't have the combinations.

Held, for the Mitchells.

"A sale is a consensual transaction. The subject matter which passes is to be determined by the intent of the parties as revealed by the terms of their agreement in light of the surrounding circumstances. . . .

" . . . Under these circumstances, we hold reasonable persons would conclude that the auctioneer manifested an objective intent to sell the safe and its contents and that the parties mutually assented to enter into that sale of the safe and the contents of the locked compartment."

RESTATEMENT, SECOND, CONTRACTS §§ 151, 152, 154

[See Selected Source Materials Supplement]

UNIDROIT PRINCIPLES OF INTERNATIONAL COMMERCIAL CONTRACTS ARTS. 3.4, 3.5, 3.18

[See Selected Source Materials Supplement]

PRINCIPLES OF EUROPEAN CONTRACT LAW ART. 4.103

[See Selected Source Materials Supplement]

LENAWEE COUNTY BOARD OF HEALTH v. MESSERLY

Supreme Court of Michigan, 1982.
417 Mich. 17, 331 N.W.2d 203.

Ryan, Justice.

In March of 1977, Carl and Nancy Pickles, appellees, purchased from appellants, William and Martha Messerly, a 600–square-foot tract of land upon which is located a three-unit apartment building. Shortly after the transaction was closed, the Lenawee County Board of Health condemned the property and obtained a permanent injunction which prohibits human habitation on the premises until the defective sewage system is brought into conformance with the Lenawee County sanitation code.

We are required to determine whether appellees should prevail in their attempt to avoid this land contract on the basis of mutual mistake and failure of consideration. We conclude that the parties did entertain a mutual misapprehension of fact, but that the circumstances of this case do not warrant rescission.

I

The facts of the case are not seriously in dispute. In 1971, the Messerlys acquired approximately one acre plus 600 square feet of land. A three-unit apartment building was situated upon the 600–square–foot portion. The trial court found that, prior to this transfer, the Messerlys' predecessor in title, Mr. Bloom, had installed a septic tank on the property without a permit and in violation of the applicable health code. The Messerlys used the building as an income investment property until 1973 when they sold it, upon [a] land contract, to James Barnes who likewise used it primarily as an income-producing investment.

Mr. and Mrs. Barnes, with the permission of the Messerlys, sold approximately one acre of the property in 1976, and the remaining 600 square feet and building were offered for sale soon thereafter when Mr. and Mrs. Barnes defaulted on their land contract. Mr. and Mrs. Pickles evidenced an interest in the property, but were dissatisfied with the terms of the Barnes–Messerly land contract. Consequently, to accommodate the Pickleses' preference to enter into a land contract directly with the Messerlys, Mr. and Mrs. Barnes executed a quit-claim deed which conveyed their interest in the property back to the Messerlys. After inspecting the property, Mr. and Mrs. Pickles executed a new land contract with the Messerlys on March 21, 1977. It provided for a purchase price of $25,500. A clause was added to the end of the land contract form which provides:

> "17. Purchaser has examined this property and agrees to accept same in its present condition. There are no other or additional written or oral understandings."

Five or six days later, when the Pickleses went to introduce themselves to the tenants, they discovered raw sewage seeping out of the ground. Tests conducted by a sanitation expert indicated the inadequacy of the sewage system. The Lenawee County Board of Health subsequently condemned the property and initiated this lawsuit in the Lenawee Circuit Court against the Messerlys as land contract vendors, and the Pickleses, as vendees, to obtain a permanent injunction proscribing human habitation of the premises until the property was brought into conformance with the Lenawee County sanitation code. The injunction was granted, and the Lenawee County Board of Health was permitted to withdraw from the lawsuit by stipulation of the parties.

When no payments were made on the land contract, the Messerlys filed a cross-complaint against the Pickleses seeking foreclosure, sale of the property, and a deficiency judgment. Mr. and Mrs. Pickles then counterclaimed for rescission against the Messerlys, and filed a third-party complaint against the Barneses, which incorporated, by reference, the allegations of the counterclaim against the Messerlys. In count one, Mr. and Mrs. Pickles alleged failure of consideration. Count two charged Mr. and Mrs. Barnes with willful concealment and misrepresentation as a result of their failure to disclose the condition of the sanitation system. Additionally, Mr. and Mrs. Pickles sought to hold the Messerlys liable in equity for the Barneses' alleged misrepresentation. The Pickleses prayed that the land contract be rescinded.

After a bench trial, the court concluded that the Pickleses had no cause of action against either the Messerlys or the Barneses as there was no fraud or misrepresentation. This ruling was predicated on the trial judge's conclusion that none of the parties knew of Mr. Bloom's earlier transgression or of the resultant problem with the septic system until it was discovered by the Pickleses, and that the sanitation problem was not caused by any of the parties. The trial court held that the property was purchased "as is", after inspection and, accordingly, its "negative * * * value cannot be blamed upon an innocent seller". Foreclosure was ordered against the Pickleses, together with a judgment against them in the amount of $25,943.09.[1]

Mr. and Mrs. Pickles appealed from the adverse judgment. The Court of Appeals unanimously affirmed the trial court's ruling with respect to Mr. and Mrs. Barnes but, in a two-to-one decision, reversed the finding of no cause of action on the Pickleses' claims against the Messerlys. *Lenawee County Board of Health v. Messerly,* 98 Mich.App. 478, 295 N.W.2d 903 (1980). It concluded that the mutual mistake between the Messerlys and the Pickleses went to a basic, as opposed to a collateral, element of the contract,[2] and that the parties intended to transfer income-producing rental property but, in actuality, the vendees paid $25,500 for an asset without value.[3]

We granted the Messerlys' application for leave to appeal. 411 Mich. 900 (1981).[4]

II

We must decide initially whether there was a mistaken belief entertained by one or both parties to the contract in dispute and, if so, the resultant legal significance.[5]

A contractual mistake "is a belief that is not in accord with the facts". 1 Restatement Contracts, 2d, § 151, p. 383. The erroneous belief of one or both of the parties must relate to a fact in existence at the time the contract is executed. *Richardson Lumber Co. v. Hoey,* 219 Mich. 643, 189 N.W. 923 (1922); *Sherwood v. Walker,* 66 Mich. 568, 580, 33 N.W. 919 (1887) (Sherwood, J., dissenting). That is to say, the belief which is found to be in error may not be, in substance, a prediction as to a future occurrence or non-occurrence. *Henry v. Thomas,* 241 Ga. 360, 245 S.E.2d 646 (1978); *Hailpern v. Dryden,* 154 Colo. 231, 389 P.2d 590 (1964). But see *Denton v. Utley,* 350 Mich. 332, 86 N.W.2d 537 (1957).

The Court of Appeals concluded, after a *de novo* review of the record, that the parties were mistaken as to the income-producing capacity of the property in question. 98 Mich.App. 487–488, 295 N.W.2d 903. We agree. The vendors and the vendees each believed that the property transferred could be utilized

---

1. The parties stipulated that this amount was due on the land contract, assuming that the contract was valid and enforceable.

2. Mr. and Mrs. Pickles did not appeal the trial court's finding that there was no fraud or misrepresentation by the Messerlys or Mr. and Mrs. Barnes. Likewise, the propriety of that ruling is not before this Court today.

3. The trial court found that the only way that the property could be put to residential use would be to pump and haul the sewage, a method which is economically unfeasible, as the cost of such a disposal system amounts to double the income generated by the property. There was speculation by the trial court that the adjoining land might be utilized to make the property suitable for residential use, but, in the absence of testimony directed at that point, the court refused to draw any conclusions. The trial court and the Court of Appeals both found that the property was valueless, or had a negative value.

4. The Court of Appeals decision to affirm the trial court's finding of no cause of action against Mr. and Mrs. Barnes has not been appealed to this Court and, accordingly, the propriety of that ruling is not before us today.

5. We emphasize that this is a bifurcated inquiry. Legal or equitable remedial measures are not mandated in every case in which a mutual mistake has been established.

as income-generating rental property. All of the parties subsequently learned that, in fact, the property was unsuitable for any residential use.

Appellants assert that there was no mistake in the contractual sense because the defect in the sewage system did not arise until after the contract was executed. The appellees respond that the Messerlys are confusing the date of the inception of the defect with the date upon which the defect was discovered.

This is essentially a factual dispute which the trial court failed to resolve directly. Nevertheless, we are empowered to draw factual inferences from the facts found by the trial court. GCR 1963, 865.1(6).

An examination of the record reveals that the septic system was defective prior to the date on which the land contract was executed. The Messerlys' grantor installed a nonconforming septic system without a permit prior to the transfer of the property to the Messerlys in 1971. Moreover, virtually undisputed testimony indicates that, assuming ideal soil conditions, 2,500 square feet of property is necessary to support a sewage system adequate to serve a three-family dwelling. Likewise, 750 square feet is mandated for a one-family home. Thus, the division of the parcel and sale of one acre of the property by Mr. and Mrs. Barnes in 1976 made it impossible to remedy the already illegal septic system within the confines of the 600–square–foot parcel.

Appellants do not dispute these underlying facts which give rise to an inference contrary to their contentions.

Having determined that when these parties entered into the land contract they were laboring under a mutual mistake of fact, we now direct our attention to a determination of the legal significance of that finding.

A contract may be rescinded because of a mutual misapprehension of the parties, but this remedy is granted only in the sound discretion of the court. *Harris v. Axline,* 323 Mich. 585, 36 N.W.2d 154 (1949). Appellants argue that the parties' mistake relates only to the quality or value of the real estate transferred, and that such mistakes are collateral to the agreement and do not justify rescission, citing *A & M Land Development Co. v. Miller,* 354 Mich. 681, 94 N.W.2d 197 (1959).

In that case, the plaintiff was the purchaser of 91 lots of real property. It sought partial rescission of the land contract when it was frustrated in its attempts to develop 42 of the lots because it could not obtain permits from the county health department to install septic tanks on these lots. This Court refused to allow rescission because the mistake, whether mutual or unilateral, related only to the value of the property. . . .

Appellees contend, on the other hand, that in this case the parties were mistaken as to the very nature of the character of the consideration and claim that the pervasive and essential quality of this mistake renders rescission appropriate. They cite in support of that view *Sherwood v. Walker,* 66 Mich. 568, 33 N.W. 919 (1887), the famous "barren cow" case. . . .

As the parties suggest, the foregoing precedent arguably distinguishes mistakes affecting the essence of the consideration from those which go to its quality or value, affording relief on a per se basis for the former but not the latter. See, *e.g., Lenawee County Board of Health v. Messerly,* 98 Mich.App. 478, 492, 295 N.W.2d 903 (1980) (Mackenzie, J., concurring in part).

However, the distinctions which may be drawn from *Sherwood* and *A & M Land Development Co.* do not provide a satisfactory analysis of the nature of a mistake sufficient to invalidate a contract. Often, a mistake relates to an underlying factual assumption which, when discovered, directly affects value, but simultaneously and materially affects the essence of the contractual consideration. It is disingenuous to label such a mistake collateral. *McKay v. Coleman,* 85 Mich. 60, 48 N.W. 203 (1891). Corbin, Contracts (One Vol. ed.), § 605, p. 551.

Appellant and appellee both mistakenly believed that the property which was the subject of their land contract would generate income as rental property. The fact that it could not be used for human habitation deprived the property of its income-earning potential and rendered it less valuable. However, this mistake, while directly and dramatically affecting the property's value, cannot accurately be characterized as collateral because it also affects the very essence of the consideration. "The thing sold and bought [income generating rental property] had in fact no existence". *Sherwood v. Walker,* 66 Mich. 578, 33 N.W. 919.

We find that the inexact and confusing distinction between contractual mistakes running to value and those touching the substance of the consideration serves only as an impediment to a clear and helpful analysis for the equitable resolution of cases in which mistake is alleged and proven. Accordingly, the holdings of *A & M Land Development Co.* and *Sherwood* with respect to the material or collateral nature of a mistake are limited to the facts of those cases.

Instead, we think the better-reasoned approach is a case-by-case analysis whereby rescission is indicated when the mistaken belief relates to a basic assumption of the parties upon which the contract is made, and which materially affects the agreed performances of the parties. *Denton v. Utley,* 350 Mich. 332, 86 N.W.2d 537 (1957); *Farhat v. Rassey,* 295 Mich. 349, 294 N.W. 707 (1940); *Richardson Lumber Co. v. Hoey,* 219 Mich. 643, 189 N.W. 923 (1922). 1 Restatement Contracts, 2d, § 152, pp. 385–386. Rescission is not available, however, to relieve a party who has assumed the risk of loss in connection with the mistake. *Denton v. Utley,* 350 Mich. 344–345, 86 N.W.2d 537; *Farhat v. Rassey,* 295 Mich. 352, 294 N.W. 707; Corbin, Contracts (One Vol. ed.), § 605, p. 552; 1 Restatement Contracts, 2d, §§ 152, 154, pp. 385–386, 402–406.

All of the parties to this contract erroneously assumed that the property transferred by the vendors to the vendees was suitable for human habitation and could be utilized to generate rental income. The fundamental nature of these assumptions is indicated by the fact that their invalidity changed the character of the property transferred, thereby frustrating, indeed precluding, Mr. and Mrs. Pickles' intended use of the real estate. Although the Pickleses are disadvantaged by enforcement of the contract, performance is advantageous to the Messerlys, as the property at issue is less valuable absent its income-earning potential. Nothing short of rescission can remedy the mistake. Thus, the parties' mistake as to a basic assumption materially affects the agreed performances of the parties.

Despite the significance of the mistake made by the parties, we reverse the Court of Appeals because we conclude that equity does not justify the remedy sought by Mr. and Mrs. Pickles.

Rescission is an equitable remedy which is granted only in the sound discretion of the court. *Harris v. Axline,* 323 Mich. 585, 36 N.W.2d 154 (1949); *Hathaway v. Hudson,* 256 Mich. 694, 239 N.W. 859 (1932). A court need not grant rescission in every case in which the mutual mistake relates to a basic assumption and materially affects the agreed performance of the parties.

In cases of mistake by two equally innocent parties, we are required, in the exercise of our equitable powers, to determine which blameless party should assume the loss resulting from the misapprehension they shared.[6] Normally that can only be done by drawing upon our "own notions of what is reasonable and just under all the surrounding circumstances".[7]

Equity suggests that, in this case, the risk should be allocated to the purchasers. We are guided to that conclusion, in part, by the standards announced in § 154 of the Restatement of Contracts 2d, for determining when a party bears the risk of mistake.... Section 154(a) suggests that the court should look first to whether the parties have agreed to the allocation of the risk between themselves. While there is no express assumption in the contract by either party of the risk of the property becoming uninhabitable, there was indeed some agreed allocation of the risk to the vendees by the incorporation of an "as is" clause into the contract which, we repeat, provided:

> "Purchaser has examined this property and agrees to accept same in its present condition. There are no other or additional written or oral understandings."

That is a persuasive indication that the parties considered that, as between them, such risk as related to the "present condition" of the property should lie with the purchaser. If the "as is" clause is to have any meaning at all, it must be interpreted to refer to those defects which were unknown at the time that the contract was executed.[8] Thus, the parties themselves assigned the risk of loss to Mr. and Mrs. Pickles.

We conclude that Mr. and Mrs. Pickles are not entitled to the equitable remedy of rescission and, accordingly, reverse the decision the Court of Appeals.

WILLIAMS, C.J., and COLEMAN, FITZGERALD, KAVANAGH and LEVIN, JJ., concur.

RILEY, J., not participating.

---

6. This risk-of-loss analysis is absent in both *A & M Land Development Co.* and *Sherwood,* and this omission helps to explain, in part, the disparate treatment in the two cases. Had such an inquiry been undertaken in *Sherwood,* we believe that the result might have been different. Moreover, a determination as to which party assumed the risk in *A & M Land Development Co.* would have alleviated the need to characterize the mistake as collateral so as to justify the result denying rescission. Despite the absence of any inquiry as to the assumption of risk in those two leading cases, we find that there exists sufficient precedent to warrant such an analysis in future cases of mistake.

7. *Hathaway v. Hudson,* 256 Mich. 702, 239 N.W. 859, quoting 9 C.J., p. 1161.

8. An "as is" clause waives those implied warranties which accompany the sale of a new home, *Tibbitts v. Openshaw,* 18 Utah 2d 442, 425 P.2d 160 (1967), or the sale of goods. M.C.L. § 440.2316(3)(a); M.S.A. § 19.2316(3)(a). Since implied warranties protect against latent defects, an "as is" clause will impose upon the purchaser the assumption of the risk of latent defects, such as an inadequate sanitation system, even when there are no implied warranties.

BEACHCOMBER COINS, INC. v. BOSKETT, 166 N.J.Super. 442, 400 A.2d 78 (1979). Plaintiff, a retail dealer in coins, bought a coin for $500 from defendant, a part–time coin dealer. The coin was a dime purportedly minted at Denver in 1916. A dime minted at Denver in 1916 was a rarity. After the purchase, plaintiff learned that the "D" on the coin, which signified Denver mintage, had been counterfeited. Plaintiff brought an action for rescission on the ground of mutual mistake. The trial judge, sitting without a jury, held for defendant on the ground that customary coin–dealing procedures called for a dealer purchasing a coin to make his own investigation of the genuineness of the coin, and to assume the risk of his purchase if his investigation was faulty. Reversed.

" '[N]egligent failure of a party to know or to discover the facts as to which both parties are under a mistake does not preclude rescission or reformation on account thereof.' ... It is undisputed that both parties believed that the coin was a genuine Denver-minted one. The mistake was mutual in that both parties were laboring under the same misapprehension as to this particular, essential fact. The price asked and paid was directly based on that assumption. That plaintiff may have been negligent in his inspection of the coin (a point not expressly found but implied by the trial judge) does not, as noted above, bar its claim for rescission. . . .

"Defendant's contention that plaintiff assumed the risk that the coin might be of greater or lesser value than that paid is not supported by the evidence. It is well established that a party to a contract can assume the risk of being mistaken as to the value of the thing sold. . . . However, for the stated rule to apply, the parties must be conscious that the pertinent fact may not be true and make their agreement at the risk of that possibility. . . . In this case both parties were certain that the coin was genuine. They so testified. Plaintiff's principal thought so after his inspection, and defendant would not have paid nearly $450 for it otherwise. A different case would be presented if the seller were uncertain either of the genuineness of the coin or of its value [if] genuine, and had accepted the expert buyer's judgment on these matters."

––––––

UCC §§ 2–312, 2–313, 2–314, 2–315

[See Selected Source Materials Supplement]

––––––

SECTION 4. NONDISCLOSURE

MELVIN A. EISENBERG, DISCLOSURE IN CONTRACT LAW

91 Cal. L. Rev. 1645 (2003).*

Suppose that A and B propose to enter into a contract for the purchase and sale of a commodity (by which I mean anything that can be bought or sold). A knows a material fact, F, concerning the commodity. B does not know F. The problem raised by such a case is whether A must disclose the relevant fact, F, to B. I will call this the *disclosure problem*.

I.   INTRODUCTION

Traditionally, the issue raised by the disclosure problem has been cast in terms of whether the knowing party, A, has a duty to disclose. This terminology is functional and convenient. However, if we focus on the unknowing party, B, the issue is mistake, because in the paradigmatic nondisclosure case in contract law, A knows F is the case while B tacitly and mistakenly assumes that Not–F is the case.

Several paradigm cases exemplify the disclosure problem. Here are two of them.

Illustration 1. Brown owns an income-producing apartment house that she knows has an illegal septic tank. Brown offers to sell the property to Andrews for $400,000, a price that is based on the sale of comparable properties in the area. Andrews tacitly assumes that the apartment house is lawful income-producing property and agrees to purchase it for $400,000. If the illegality of the septic tank was known, the apartment house would be worth only one-tenth that price. Brown does not disclose to Andrews the problem with the septic tank, and Andrews purchases the property for $400,000.[6]

Illustration 2. Beta Mineral Co. is in the business of mining, smelting, and selling minerals. Beta's geologists identify promising sectors of public lands, and farmland areas, that have not previously been thought to have minerals. If a sector of public land seems promising, Beta's geologists make further investigation by going onto the land. If a sector of farmland seems promising, Beta overflies the land with a plane that has instruments that detect magnetic anomalies in the earth below. A magnetic anomaly is a sign of mineralization, but many anomalies are caused by minerals that have no commercial value, or by ore that cannot be economically mined because the ore body is not rich enough to justify the costs of mining it. If the geologists find a promising anomaly on farmland, Beta purchases the relevant farm at a farmland price through its wholly owned subsidiary, Sigma Farmland Company, and then begins exploratory drilling. Usually, this drilling finds only noncommercial or non-mineable minerals (in which case Beta resells the land at the farmland price), but periodically Beta finds a mineable body of ore. Beta finds an extremely promising magnetic anomaly under Farmer Adams's farm, and Sigma purchases the farm at the market price for farmland in the area. Sigma

---

* Minor stylistic revisions and omissions have been made in the text as it appears here. (Footnote by ed.)

6.   This Illustration is a variant of Lenawee County Board of Health v. Messerly.

does not disclose to Adams the existence or significance of the anomaly beneath his land. If the anomaly was known, the property would be worth significantly more than the price Sigma paid.[7]

Whether the knowing party is under a duty to disclose in cases like Illustrations 1 and 2 is one of the most intractable issues in contract law. A major reason is this: In most issues in contract law, morality and policy point in the same direction. In the disclosure problem, however, morality and policy often point in different directions.

Begin with morality. At least when actors are dealing face-to-face on an individual basis—rather than, say, through institutional intermediaries in a relatively anonymous market, like an auction or a stock market—social morality indicates that if one actor knows a material fact that is relevant to the transaction, and knows that the other actor does not know the fact, nondisclosure is sharp dealing, or a kind of moral fraud. For example, in Smith v. Hughes, Chief Justice Cockburn considered a hypothetical like Illustration 2 and said, "The case put of the purchase of an estate, in which there is a mine under the surface, but the fact is unknown to the seller, is one in which [the contract would be binding, but] a man of tender conscience or high honour would be unwilling to take advantage of the ignorance of the seller."[8]

In addition to the moral obligation, there are strong efficiency reasons for requiring disclosure.

To begin with, the principle that bargains should be enforced according to their terms rests most securely on a foundation of complete information. As Michael Trebilcock puts this point, quoting Milton Friedman:

> Even the most committed proponents of free markets and freedom of contracts recognize that certain information preconditions must be met for a given exchange to possess Pareto superior qualities. For example, to recall the statement of Milton Friedman: "The possibility of coordination through voluntary cooperation rests on the elementary—yet frequently

---

7. This Illustration is a variant of the facts underlying SEC v. Texas Gulf Sulphur Co., 401 F.2d 833 (2d Cir. 1968), a leading insider-trading case. Insider trading is itself a paradigm disclosure problem, although it is governed largely by federal law, primarily Rule 10b–5 under the Securities Exchange Act.

8. 6 L.R.-Q.B. 597, 604 (1871) (Eng.)... Cf. Michael J. Trebilcock, The Limits of Freedom of Contract 117–18 (1993):

> [A difficulty with a nondisclosure rule is revealed acutely in cases such as that of a prospector who through research of various kinds, including flying over vast expanses of farmland taking magnetic soundings, develops a well-informed hunch that a particular block of farmland may have serious potential as a mineral reserve or an oil-drilling site, and does not disclose this fact to the incumbent farmer before purchasing the land at a price that reflects only agricultural uses.] Although welfare considerations seem fairly unambiguously to militate in favor of non-

disclosure by the buyer, ... the deliberate exploitation by the buyer of the farmer's ignorance of a crucially important fact bearing on the real value of his property seems to involve the taking of advantage of a less that fully autonomous choice by the farmer if one views as pre-conditions for fully autonomous choices, as even Milton Friedman does, lack of coercion and full information. It may be plausible to argue that the buyer's conduct violates the Kantian categorical imperative of equal concern and respect in that if roles were reversed ... the buyer would not wish his ignorance to be exploited by the seller in this fashion, even though such a precept may come at a cost in terms of long-run community welfare. ... [T]he farmer might reasonably ask why his interests should be sacrificed to this greater social end (without his informed consent); that is, why should he be used as a means to the ends of others?

denied—proposition that both parties to an economic transaction benefit from it, *provided the transaction is bilaterally voluntary and informed.*"[9]

Furthermore, requiring disclosure may save socially wasteful costs of searching for information that the other party already has, or of making duplicate searches to generate the same information. Trebilcock writes:

> One might also reasonably argue that requiring disclosure [often] avoids various forms of socially wasteful transaction costs, such as a succession of prospective buyers hiring mechanics to inspect cars before purchase or, in the event of purchase in the absence of accurate information, further transactions that might be entailed in moving the goods to their socially most valuable uses, given the now fully revealed condition of the goods.
>
> . . . .
>
> . . . [Absent a requirement] of disclosure of material facts known to one party and unknown to the other . . . the second party and other prospective contracting parties may be induced to invest in wasteful precautions to generate information about the asset that is already possessed by the first party and can be transmitted at trivial marginal social cost.[10]

Finally, as stated by Anthony Kronman, nondisclosure "is a cost to the contracting parties themselves and to society as a whole since the actual occurrence of a mistake always (potentially) increases the resources which must be devoted to the process of allocating goods to their highest-valuing users,"[14] if only by potentially adding transaction costs.

On the other hand, at least in some kinds of cases there are efficiency arguments against a duty of disclosure. This is exemplified by Illustration 2. Suppose Beta (or its subsidiary, Sigma) was required to disclose the magnetic anomaly to Farmer Adams before concluding a contract. Then Farmer Adams might contact other mineral companies, tell them what Beta has found, and begin an auction for his land. In that case, Beta would have incurred very significant exploration costs from which it would derive no benefits, and might stop pursuing this kind of exploration. Since exploration for minerals is a socially valuable activity, to the extent that a duty of disclosure had such an effect it would be undesirable on efficiency grounds. Furthermore, in cases like Illustration 2 the knowing party's gain is typically earned as a return on its investment in acquiring information. While the size of the return may look very large when we focus on the single transaction taken in isolation, the return may in fact be moderate if we take into account the actor's total investment in acquiring information, much of which may be nonproductive. Accordingly, if Beta finds a body of mineable ore on Farmer Adams's property it will reap a huge return on its investment in that property, but Beta's return will be much more modest if measured against all of Beta's investment in acquiring information. . . .

---

9. Trebilcock, *supra* note 8, at 117 (1993) (quoting Milton Friedman, Capitalism and Freedom 13 (1962)) (emphasis by Trebilcock).

10. *Id.* at 108, 112. . . .

14. Anthony T. Kronman, *Mistake, Disclosure, Information, and the Law of Contracts*, 7 J. Legal Stud. 1, 2–3 (1978). Despite these arguments, neither Trebilcock nor Kronman advocate a general duty of disclosure.

II. Information that is Adventitiously Acquired

A. Information that is Not Acquired by a Deliberate Investment Made for that Purpose

The stage-setting work on the disclosure problem is Anthony Kronman's 1978 article, *Mistake, Disclosure, Information, and the Law of Contracts*. Kronman developed two concepts to govern the problem. Under the first concept, disclosure *should* be required if the relevant information was acquired by the actor casually. Information is acquired casually if the costs that were incurred to engage in the activity that produced the information were not incurred for the purpose of acquiring information. To put this differently, information is acquired casually if it is acquired in the course of an activity engaged in for purposes other than acquiring the information. In contrast, under the second concept disclosure *should not* be required if the relevant information was acquired as the result of the actor's deliberate and costly search for information. Kronman illustrated the two concepts as follows:

> In some cases, the individuals who supply information have obtained it by a deliberate search; in other cases, their information has been acquired casually. A securities analyst, for example, acquires information about a particular corporation in a deliberate fashion—by carefully studying evidence of its economic performance. By contrast, a businessman who acquires a valuable piece of information when he accidentally overhears a conversation on a bus acquires the information casually.

In discussing the casual acquisition of information, Kronman points out that "by being denied the [right not to disclose], one who has casually acquired information will not be discouraged from doing what—for independent reasons—he would have done in any case." This point, however, is not an affirmative reason for requiring disclosure. After all, the law could take the position that an actor who has acquired information casually is simply lucky, and is entitled to make use of the information without disclosing it. Kronman's affirmative reasons for the casual-acquisition concept seem to be as follows: (1) Mistakes are costs and disclosure will prevent those costs. (2) Since an actor who acquires information casually makes no investment in its acquisition, subjecting him to a duty to disclose is not likely to reduce the production of socially useful information.

To summarize, one strand of the rule that should govern the disclosure problem is that an actor should be required to disclose information that was casually or adventitiously acquired.

B. Information that is Acquired by a Deliberate Investment Made for that Purpose

Under Kronman's deliberate-acquisition concept, disclosure should not be required in the case of "information whose acquisition entails costs which would not have been incurred but for the likelihood, however great, that the information in question would actually be produced." The basic reason that Kronman advances to support this concept is that requiring disclosure of information that was acquired through a deliberate investment would significantly diminish the incentive to make such an investment, and therefore would significantly diminish production of valuable information. The idea here is that if contract law required disclosure of information that was acquired by deliberate investment, actors would not make such investments, because the investments would not generate a return.

In developing this concept, Kronman refers briefly to the exploration case on which Illustration 2 is based, but he emphasizes a very different paradigm case, Laidlaw v. Organ.[26] This case was decided by the United States Supreme Court in 1817, in an opinion by Chief Justice Marshall, in the days when the Court was still extensively engaged with commercial issues. The opinions in both the Supreme Court and in the federal district court are exceptionally brief, and as a result some of the facts in the case are unclear. The following account of the case is based on the district court opinion, the bill of exceptions to that opinion, the arguments of counsel, and a few straightforward inferences based on those sources. In keeping with the approach usually taken by commentators, I will focus only on the nondisclosure issue in the case.[28]

In early 1815, a British fleet was blockading New Orleans as part of the War of 1812. (Indeed, the greatest battle of the war was fought at New Orleans at this time.) On Saturday, February 18, 1815, three Americans, White, Shepard, and Livingston, were for some reason with the British fleet, and there got news that the war had been ended some time earlier by a peace treaty signed at Ghent. News of the end of the war had been published in British newspapers. It seems likely that the news was imparted to the fleet through delivery of these newspapers, although perhaps the news was imparted by delivery of letters from England. White quickly prepared a handbill with news of the peace treaty for distribution in New Orleans. The handbill was published in New Orleans at 8:00 a.m. on Sunday, February 19.

The price of tobacco in New Orleans would immediately rise when news of the peace became generally known there, because tobacco shipments would no longer be blockaded. Sometime after sunrise on Sunday, but before 8:00 a.m., when White's handbill was published, Shepard conveyed news of the peace privately to Organ, a merchant, and Organ then purchased 111 hogsheads of tobacco from Peter Laidlaw & Co., at the then-going (pre-news) price. As a result of the news of the peace treaty, the price of tobacco in New Orleans increased 30–50%. Laidlaw then either refused to deliver or seized back the tobacco. Organ brought suit for specific performance, damages, or both. The district court instructed the jury to find for Organ.

The Supreme Court concluded that Organ was not under a duty to disclose the news of the peace to Laidlaw:

> The question in this case is, whether the intelligence of extrinsic circumstances, which might influence the price of the commodity, and which was exclusively within the knowledge of the vendee, ought to have been communicated by him to the vendor? The court is of opinion that he

---

26. 15 U.S. (2 Wheat.) 178 (1817).

28. There was an added element in the case.... During the discussions leading up to the contract, Organ was asked if there was any news that was calculated to enhance the price or value of tobacco. It is unclear exactly how, if at all, Organ responded, although it seems that he either remained silent or was evasive. The district court instructed the jury to find for Organ. Laidlaw appealed not only on the ground that Organ was under a duty to disclose, but also on the grounds that Organ's response or lack of response to the question was wrongful, and that the issue was a mixed question of law and fact that should have been left to the jury. The outcome was that the Supreme Court reversed and remanded the case for a new trial, on the ground that "the absolute instruction of the judge was erroneous, and that the question, whether any imposition was practised by the vendee upon the vendor ought to have been submitted to the jury." *Id.* at 195.

was not bound to communicate it. It would be difficult to circumscribe the contrary doctrine within proper limits, where the means of intelligence are equally accessible to both parties. But at the same time, each party must take care not to say or do any thing tending to impose upon the other.

Laidlaw v. Organ is the centerpiece of Kronman's argument that the law should not require the disclosure of information that has been deliberately acquired. In fact, however, . . . in several important classes of cases the law should require the disclosure of information that has been deliberately acquired, and Laidlaw falls squarely within one of those classes, *foreknowledge*.

III. FOREKNOWLEDGE

One way to look at Kronman's approach to the problem of disclosure is as a process approach. Under Kronman's analysis, whether disclosure is required depends upon the process by which the relevant information was acquired. If the information was acquired by a deliberative process, disclosure is not required; if the information was acquired by a casual or adventitious process, disclosure is required. This process approach works for casual or adventitious acquisition, but this approach is too broad when it comes to deliberate acquisition.

In contrast to Kronman's process approach, several leading economists have adopted a substantive approach to the disclosure problem, under which the permissibility of nondisclosure would turn on the character of the relevant information, rather than on the process through which the information was obtained. The most notable contributions are Jack Hirshleifer's 1971 article, The Private Value of Information and the Reward to Inventive Activity;[31] Robert Cooter and Thomas Ulen's book, Law and Economics,[32] first published in 1987; and Steven Shavell's 1994 article, Acquisition and Disclosure of Information Prior to Sale.[33]

A. *Hirshleifer, Cooter and Ulen, and Shavell*

Hirshleifer's seminal contribution was to draw a critical distinction between "foreknowledge," on the one hand, and "discovery," on the other. Discovery is the "recognition of something that possibly already exists, though [it will be] hidden from view" unless and until the discovery is made. Here, "Nature's secret will not be autonomously revealed but must be extracted by man." Discovered knowledge can bring gains from allocating resources more efficiently. Such knowledge "makes the 'pie' larger." Discovered information brings gains to an actor who has privately acquired the information, but more importantly it can increase social wealth—it "increases ex ante each person's potential share."

In contrast, foreknowledge is knowledge that "will, in due time, be evident to all"; it is information that "Nature will . . . autonomously reveal." Foreknowledge involves "only the value of priority in time of superior knowledge." Foreknowledge of information can bring gains to an actor who

---

31. Jack Hirshleifer, *The Private and Social Value of Information and the Reward to Inventive Activity*, 61 Am. Econ. Rev. 561 (1971).

32. Robert Cooter & Thomas Ulen, Law and Economics 270–76 (3d ed. 2000).

33. Steven Shavell, *Acquisition and Disclosure of Information Prior to Sale*, 25 RAND J. Econ. 20 (1994).

privately acquires the information. As a result, actors may deliberately invest in acquiring foreknowledge. But the gains from foreknowledge are often only redistributive, not social. The information then "does not increase the pie's share, only the shares of those who have the relevant information." The cost of acquiring such foreknowledge will exceed the social value of the foreknowledge. In such cases, the law should not provide incentives for the deliberate acquisition of information.

Hirshleifer did not specifically address the disclosure problem. His interest was in the general issue of whether and when an investment in acquiring information is inefficient, and in the specific issue of patent-law policy. Unlike Hirshleifer, Cooter and Ulen developed a principle that distinguishes between different kinds of information for the specific purpose of dealing with the disclosure problem. Their analysis is comparable in its nature to Hirshleifer's, but it differs in significant ways. Rather than distinguishing between foreknowledge and discovery, Cooter and Ulen distinguish between productive information and redistributive information:

> Productive information can be used to produce more wealth. To illustrate, the discovery of a vaccine for polio and the discovery of a water route between Europe and China were productive.... In contrast, redistributive information creates a bargaining advantage that can be used to redistribute wealth in favor of the informed party. To illustrate, knowing before anyone else where the state will locate a new highway conveys a powerful advantage in real-estate markets.

Cooter and Ulen conclude that searching for redistributive information is socially wasteful, and therefore the law should discourage the expenditure of resources on this type of search. One important means to that end is to impose a duty of disclosure on an actor who has acquired such information:

> Efficiency demands giving people strong incentives to discover productive facts. Transmitting information is so easy that the person who discovers productive information seldom captures its full value. Consequently, the state must take special measures to reward people who discover productive information....

> ... Investment in discovering redistributive information wastes resources. In addition, investment in redistributive information induces defensive expenditures by people trying not to lose their wealth to better-informed people. Defensive expenditures prevent redistribution, rather than produce something. Thus, investment in redistributive information wastes resources directly and indirectly. The state should not create incentives to discover redistributive information. Instead, the state should discourage investment in discovering redistributive information....

> These considerations prompt ... [the formulation of the following] economic principle.... Contracts based upon one party's knowledge of productive information should be enforced, whereas contracts based upon one party's knowledge of purely redistributive information should not be enforced. This principle rewards investment in discovering productive information and discourages investment in discovering redistributive information.

Finally, Shavell, who also focuses on the disclosure problem, draws a distinction, comparable to those drawn by Hirshleifer and Cooter and Ulen, between information that is mere foreknowledge and information that is socially valuable because it allows action to be taken that will raise the value of a commodity to an actor who possesses the commodity and the information. Shavell concludes that an actor should be required to disclose private information that is mere foreknowledge, to reduce the incentive to wastefully acquire information that does not have social value.

Although there are substantive differences between the formulations of Hirshleifer, Cooter and Ulen, and Shavell, the common theme is much stronger than the differences. The common theme is that certain kinds of information are not socially valuable; that the costs of acquiring the information therefore represent a social waste; and that accordingly the law should not provide incentives for the acquisition of such information. On the contrary, the law should provide disincentives, including a requirement of disclosure.

HILL v. JONES

Arizona Court of Appeals, 1986.
151 Ariz. 81, 725 P.2d 1115.

MEYERSON, Judge.

Must the seller of a residence disclose to the buyer facts pertaining to past termite infestation? This is the primary question presented in this appeal. Plaintiffs Warren G. Hill and Gloria R. Hill (buyers) filed suit to rescind an agreement to purchase a residence. Buyers alleged that Ora G. Jones and Barbara R. Jones (sellers) had made misrepresentations concerning termite damage in the residence and had failed to disclose to them the existence of the damage and history of termite infestation in the residence. . . .

. . . The trial court granted summary judgment, finding that there was "no genuinely disputed issue of material fact and that the law favors the . . . defendants." . . . Buyers have appealed from the judgment and sellers have cross-appealed from the trial court's ruling on attorney's fees.

I. FACTS

In 1982, buyers entered into an agreement to purchase sellers' residence for $72,000. The agreement was entered after buyers made several visits to the home. The purchase agreement provided that sellers were to pay for and place in escrow a termite inspection report stating that the property was free from evidence of termite infestation. Escrow was scheduled to close two months later.

One of the central features of the house is a parquet teak floor covering the sunken living room, the dining room, the entryway and portions of the halls. On a subsequent visit to the house, and when sellers were present, buyers noticed a small "ripple" in the wood floor on the step leading up to the dining room from the sunken living room. Mr. Hill asked if the ripple could be termite damage. Mrs. Jones answered that it was water damage. A few years previously, a broken water heater in the house had in fact caused water damage in the area of the dining room and steps which necessitated that some repairs be made to the floor. No further discussion on the subject, however, took place between the parties at that time or afterwards.

Mr. Hill, through his job as maintenance supervisor at a school district, had seen similar "ripples" in wood which had turned out to be termite damage. Mr. Hill was not totally satisfied with Mrs. Jones's explanation, but he felt that the termite inspection report would reveal whether the ripple was due to termites or some other cause.

The termite inspection report stated that there was no visible evidence of infestation. The report failed to note the existence of physical damage or evidence of previous treatment. The realtor notified the parties that the property had passed the termite inspection. Apparently, neither party actually saw the report prior to close of escrow.

After moving into the house, buyers found a pamphlet left in one of the drawers entitled "Termites, the Silent Saboteurs." They learned from a neighbor that the house had some termite infestation in the past. Shortly after the close of escrow, Mrs. Hill noticed that the wood on the steps leading down to the sunken living room was crumbling. She called an exterminator who confirmed the existence of termite damage to the floor and steps and to wood columns in the house. The estimated cost of repairing the wood floor alone was approximately $5,000.

Through discovery after their lawsuit was filed, buyers learned the following. When sellers purchased the residence in 1974, they received two termite guarantees that had been given to the previous owner by Truly Nolen, as well as a diagram showing termite treatment at the residence that had taken place in 1963. The guarantees provided for semi-annual inspections and annual termite booster treatments. The accompanying diagram stated that the existing damage had not been repaired. The second guarantee, dated 1965, reinstated the earlier contract for inspection and treatment. Mr. Jones admitted that he read the guarantees when he received them. Sellers renewed the guarantees when they purchased the residence in 1974. They also paid the annual fee each year until they sold the home.

On two occasions during sellers' ownership of the house but while they were at their other residence in Minnesota, a neighbor noticed "streamers" evidencing live termites in the wood tile floor near the entryway. On both occasions, Truly Nolen gave a booster treatment for termites. On the second incident, Truly Nolen drilled through one of the wood tiles to treat for termites. The neighbor showed Mr. Jones the area where the damage and treatment had occurred. Sellers had also seen termites on the back fence and had replaced and treated portions of the fence.

Sellers did not mention any of this information to buyers prior to close of escrow. They did not mention the past termite infestation and treatment to the realtor or to the termite inspector. There was evidence of holes on the patio that had been drilled years previously to treat for termites. The inspector returned to the residence to determine why he had not found evidence of prior treatment and termite damage. He indicated that he had not seen the holes in the patio because of boxes stacked there. It is unclear whether the boxes had been placed there by buyers or sellers. He had not found the damage inside the house because a large plant, which buyers had purchased from sellers, covered the area. After investigating the second time, the inspector found the damage and evidence of past treatment. He acknowledged that this information should have appeared in the report. He complained, however, that he should have been told of any history of termite infestation and treatment before he performed his inspection and that it was customary for the inspector to be given such information.

Other evidence presented to the trial court was that during their numerous visits to the residence before close of escrow, buyers had unrestricted access to view and inspect the entire house. Both Mr. and Mrs. Hill had seen termite damage and were therefore familiar with what it might look like. Mr. Hill had seen termite damage on the fence at this property. Mrs. Hill had noticed the holes on the patio but claimed not to realize at the time what they were for. Buyers asked no questions about termites except when they asked if the "ripple" on the stairs was termite damage. Mrs. Hill admitted she was not "trying" to find problems with the house because she really wanted it. . . .

III. DUTY TO DISCLOSE

The principal legal question presented in this appeal is whether a seller has a duty to disclose to the buyer the existence of termite damage in a residential dwelling known to the seller, but not to the buyer, which materially affects the value of the property. For the reasons stated herein, we hold that such a duty exists.

This is not the place to trace the history of the doctrine of caveat emptor. Suffice it to say that its vitality has waned during the latter half of the 20th century. E.g., Richards v. Powercraft Homes, Inc., 139 Ariz. 242, 678 P.2d 427 (1984) (implied warranty of workmanship and habitability extends to subsequent buyers of homes); see generally Quashnock v. Frost, 299 Pa.Super. 9, 445 A.2d 121 (1982); Ollerman v. O'Rourke Co., 94 Wis.2d 17, 288 N.W.2d 95 (1980). The modern view is that a vendor has an affirmative duty to disclose material facts where:

> 1. Disclosure is necessary to prevent a previous assertion from being a misrepresentation or from being fraudulent or material;

> 2. Disclosure would correct a mistake of the other party as to a basic assumption on which that party is making the contract and if nondisclosure amounts to a failure to act in good faith and in accordance with reasonable standards of fair dealing;

> 3. Disclosure would correct a mistake of the other party as to the contents or effect of a writing, evidencing or embodying an agreement in whole or in part;

> 4. The other person is entitled to know the fact because of a relationship of trust and confidence between them.

Restatement (Second) of Contracts § 161 (1981) (Restatement); See Restatement (Second) of Torts § 551 (1977).

Arizona courts have long recognized that under certain circumstances there may be a "duty to speak." Van Buren v. Pima Community College Dist. Bd., 113 Ariz. 85, 87, 546 P.2d 821, 823 (1976); Batty v. Arizona State Dental Bd., 57 Ariz. 239, 254, 112 P.2d 870, 877 (1941). As the supreme court noted in the context of a confidential relationship, "[s]uppression of a material fact which a party is bound in good faith to disclose is equivalent to a false representation." Leigh v. Loyd, 74 Ariz. 84, 87, 244 P.2d 356, 358 (1952);

National Housing Indus. Inc. v. E.L. Jones Dev. Co., 118 Ariz. 374, 379, 576 P.2d 1374, 1379 (1978).

Thus, the important question we must answer is whether under the facts of this case, buyers should have been permitted to present to the jury their claim that sellers were under a duty to disclose their (sellers') knowledge of termite infestation in the residence. This broader question involves two inquiries. First, must a seller of residential property advise the buyer of material facts within his knowledge pertaining to the value of the property? Second, may termite damage and the existence of past infestation constitute such material facts?

The doctrine imposing a duty to disclose is akin to the well-established contractual rules pertaining to relief from contracts based upon mistake. Although the law of contracts supports the finality of transactions, over the years courts have recognized that under certain limited circumstances it is unjust to strictly enforce the policy favoring finality. Thus, for example, even a unilateral mistake of one party to a transaction may justify rescission. Restatement § 153.

There is also a judicial policy promoting honesty and fair dealing in business relationships. This policy is expressed in the law of fraudulent and negligent misrepresentations. Where a misrepresentation is fraudulent or where a negligent misrepresentation is one of material fact, the policy of finality rightly gives way to the policy of promoting honest dealings between the parties. See Restatement § 164(1).

Under certain circumstances nondisclosure of a fact known to one party may be equivalent to the assertion that the fact does not exist. For example "[w]hen one conveys a false impression by the disclosure of some facts and the concealment of others, such concealment is in effect a false representation that what is disclosed is the whole truth." State v. Coddington, 135 Ariz. 480, 481, 662 P.2d 155, 156 (App.1983). Thus, nondisclosure may be equated with and given the same legal effect as fraud and misrepresentation. One category of cases where this has been done involves the area of nondisclosure of material facts affecting the value of property, known to the seller but not reasonably capable of being known to the buyer.

Courts have formulated this "duty to disclose" in slightly different ways. For example, the Florida Supreme Court recently declared that "where the seller of a home knows of facts materially affecting the value of the property which are not readily observable and are not known to the buyer, the seller is under a duty to disclose them to the buyer." Johnson v. Davis, 480 So.2d 625, 629 (Fla.1985) (defective roof in three-year old home). In California, the rule has been stated this way:

> [W]here the seller knows of facts materially affecting the value or desirability of the property which are known or accessible only to him and also knows that such facts are not known to, or within the reach of the diligent attention and observation of the buyer, the seller is under a duty to disclose them to the buyer.

Lingsch v. Savage, 213 Cal.App.2d 729, 735, 29 Cal.Rptr. 201, 204 (1963); contra Ray v. Montgomery, 399 So.2d 230 (Ala.1980); see generally W. Prosser & W. Keeton, The Law of Torts § 106 (5th ed.1984). We find that the Florida formulation of the disclosure rule properly balances the legitimate interests of the parties in a transaction for the sale of a private residence and accordingly adopt it for such cases.

As can be seen, the rule requiring disclosure is invoked in the case of material facts.[22] Thus, we are led to the second inquiry—whether the existence of termite damage in a residential dwelling is the type of material fact which gives rise to the duty to disclose. The existence of termite damage and past termite infestation has been considered by other courts to be sufficiently material to warrant disclosure. See generally Annot., 22 A.L.R.3d 972 (1968). . . .

Although sellers have attempted to draw a distinction between live termites[23] and past infestation, the concept of materiality is an elastic one which is not limited by the termites' health. "A matter is material if it is one to which a reasonable person would attach importance in determining his choice of action in the transaction in question." Lynn v. Taylor, 7 Kan.App.2d at 371, 642 P.2d at 134–35. For example, termite damage substantially affecting the structural soundness of the residence may be material even if there is no evidence of present infestation. Unless reasonable minds could not differ, materiality is a factual matter which must be determined by the trier of fact. The termite damage in this case may or may not be material. Accordingly, we conclude that buyers should be allowed to present their case to a jury.

Sellers argue that even assuming the existence of a duty to disclose, summary judgment was proper because the record shows that their "silence . . . did not induce or influence" the buyers. This is so, sellers contend, because Mr. Hill stated in his deposition that he intended to rely on the termite inspection report. But this argument begs the question. If sellers were fully aware of the extent of termite damage and if such information had been disclosed to buyers, a jury could accept Mr. Hill's testimony that had he known of the termite damage he would not have purchased the house.

Sellers further contend that buyers were put on notice of the possible existence of termite infestation and were therefore "chargeable with the knowledge which [an] inquiry, if made, would have revealed." Godfrey v. Navratil, 3 Ariz.App. 47, 51, 411 P.2d 470 (1966) (quoting Luke v. Smith, 13 Ariz. 155, 162, 108 P. 494, 496 (1910)). It is also true that "a party may . . . reasonably expect the other to take normal steps to inform himself and to draw his own conclusions." Restatement § 161 comment d. Under the facts of this case, the question of buyers' knowledge of the termite problem (or their diligence in attempting to inform themselves about the termite problem) should be left to the jury.[24]

. . . Reversed and remanded.

CONTRERAS, P.J., and YALE McFATE, J. (Retired), concur.

———

22. Arizona has recognized that a duty to disclose may arise where the buyer makes an inquiry of the seller, regardless of whether or not the fact is material. Universal Inv. Co. v. Sahara Motor Inn, Inc., 127 Ariz. 213, 215, 619 P.2d 485, 487 (1980). The inquiry by buyers whether the ripple was termite damage imposed a duty upon sellers to disclose what information they knew concerning the existence of termite infestation in the residence.

23. Sellers acknowledge that a duty of disclosure would exist if live termites were present. Obde v. Schlemeyer, 56 Wash.2d 449, 353 P.2d 672 (1960).

24. Sellers also contend that they had no knowledge of any existing termite damage in the house. An extended discussion of the facts on this point is unnecessary. Simply stated, the facts are in conflict on this issue.

WEINTRAUB v. KROBATSCH, 64 N.J. 445, 317 A.2d 68 (1974). The Krobatschs agreed to purchase a house from Mrs. Weintraub. After making the contract, but before the closing, the Krobatschs discovered that the house was badly infested with roaches. The Krobatschs sought to rescind, and Mrs. Weintraub sued to recover a deposit of $4,250 that the Krobatschs had put into escrow. In their suit, the Krobatschs claimed that Mrs. Weintraub was aware of the infestation and had kept every room in the house illuminated while the Krobatschs inspected the house, to keep the roaches, which are nocturnal, from appearing. The trial court granted summary judgment for Mrs. Weintraub. The New Jersey Supreme Court reversed:

"[T]he purchasers here were entitled to withstand the seller's motion for summary judgment. They should have been permitted to proceed with their efforts to establish by testimony that they were equitably entitled to rescind because the house was extensively infested in the manner described by them, the seller was well aware of the infestation, and the seller deliberately concealed or failed to disclose the condition because of the likelihood that it would defeat the transaction. . . .

"If the trial judge finds such deliberate concealment or nondisclosure of the latent infestation not observable by the purchasers on their inspection, he will still be called upon to determine whether, in the light of the full presentation before him, the concealment or nondisclosure was of such significant nature as to justify rescission. Minor conditions which ordinary sellers and purchasers would reasonably disregard as of little or no materiality in the transaction would clearly not call for judicial intervention. While the described condition may not have been quite as major as in the termite cases which were concerned with structural impairments, to the purchasers here it apparently was of such magnitude and was so repulsive as to cause them to rescind immediately though they had earlier indicated readiness that there be adjustment at closing for damage resulting from a fire which occurred after the contract was signed. We are not prepared at this time to say that on their showing they acted either unreasonably or without equitable justification."

RESTATEMENT, SECOND, CONTRACTS §§ 159, 161

[See Selected Source Materials Supplement]

RESTATEMENT, SECOND, CONTRACTS
§ 161, ILLUSTRATIONS 7, 10, 11

7. A, seeking to induce B to make a contract to sell land, knows that B does not know that the land has appreciably increased in value because of a proposed shopping center but does not disclose this to B. B makes the

contract. Since B's mistake is not one as to a basic assumption ... A's non-disclosure is not equivalent to an assertion that the value of the land has not appreciably increased. . . . The contract is not voidable by B. . . .

10.   A, seeking to induce B to make a contract to sell A land, learns from government surveys that the land contains valuable mineral deposits and knows that B does not know this, but does not disclose this to B. B makes the contract. A's non-disclosure does not amount to a failure to act in good faith and in accordance with reasonable standards of fair dealing and is therefore not equivalent to an assertion that the land does not contain valuable mineral deposits. The contract is not voidable by B.

11.   The facts being otherwise as stated in Illustration 10, A learns of the valuable mineral deposits from trespassing on B's land and not from government surveys. A's non-disclosure is equivalent to an assertion that the land does not contain valuable mineral deposits, and this assertion is a misrepresentation. . . .

RESTATEMENT, SECOND, TORTS
§ 551, ILLUSTRATIONS 6, 8

6.   A is a violin expert. He pays a casual visit to B's shop, where second-hand musical instruments are sold. He finds a violin which, by reason of his expert knowledge and experience, he immediately recognizes as a genuine Stradivarius, in good condition and worth at least $50,000. The violin is priced for sale at $100. Without disclosing his information or his identity, A buys the violin from B for $100. A is not liable to B. . . .

8.   B has a shop in which he sells second-hand musical instruments. In it he offers for sale for $100 a violin, which he knows to be an imitation Stradivarius and worth at most $50. A enters the shop, looks at the violin and is overheard by B to say to his companion that he is sure that the instrument is a genuine Stradivarius. B says nothing, and A buys the violin for $100. B is not liable to A. . . .

UNITED STATES v. DIAL, 757 F.2d 163 (7th Cir.1985), cert. denied, 474 U.S. 838, 106 S.Ct. 116, 88 L.Ed.2d 95 (1985) (Posner, J.). "Fraud in the common law sense of deceit is committed by deliberately misleading another by words, by acts, or, in some instances—notably where there is a fiduciary relationship, which creates a duty to disclose all material facts—by silence. Liability is narrower for nondisclosure than for active misrepresentation, since the former sometimes serves a social purpose; for example, someone who bought land from another thinking that it had oil under it would not be required to disclose the fact to the owner, because society wants to encourage people to find out the true value of things, and it does this by allowing them to profit from their knowledge. . . . But if someone asks you to break a $10 bill, and you give him two $1 bills instead of two $5's because you know he cannot read and won't know the difference, that is fraud. Even more clearly is it fraud to fail to 'level' with one to whom one owes fiduciary duties. The essence of a fiduciary relationship is that the fiduciary agrees to act as his principal's alter ego rather than to assume the standard arm's length stance of traders in a market. Hence the principal is not armed with the usual wariness that one has in dealing with strangers; he trusts the fiduciary to deal with him as frankly as he would deal with himself—he has bought candor."

Chapter 19

THE EFFECT OF UNEXPECTED CIRCUMSTANCES

INTRODUCTORY NOTE

The issue considered in this Chapter is when, and to what extent, unexpected circumstances bear on the parties' rights under a contract. In many crucial respects, the modern legal rules that govern this issue are comparable to the rules that govern mutual mistake, in that both sets of rules focus on assumptions and risk. A major difference between the two kinds of cases is practical: In general, mutual-mistake cases usually involve attempts to either rescind the contract, or justify nonperformance, before either party has done much under the contract. In contrast, in unexpected-circumstances cases the relevant circumstances usually become salient only after performance has begun. The legal treatment of unexpected-circumstances cases is often rendered more complex and difficult as a result of this practical difference.

The cases considered in this chapter are generally dealt with under the legal rubrics *impossibility*, *impracticability*, and *frustration*. Roughly speaking, the three doctrines arose in that order: First, the courts recognized that impossibility might be a defense; next, that impracticability might be a defense; and finally, that frustration of the purpose of a contract might be a defense. In this Chapter, these three doctrines will be taken up more or less in that order ("more or less," because the doctrines overlap), under the general heading of unexpected circumstances.

TAYLOR v. CALDWELL
In the Queen's Bench, 1863.
3 Best & S. 826.

BLACKBURN, J. In this case the plaintiffs and defendants had, on May 27th, 1861, entered into a contract by which the defendants agreed to let the plaintiffs have the use of The Surrey Gardens and Music Hall on four days then to come, viz., June 17th, July 15th, August 5th, and August 19th, for the purpose of giving a series of four grand concerts, and day and night fêtes, at the Gardens and Hall on those days respectively; and the plaintiffs agreed to take the Gardens and Hall on those days, and pay £100 for each day.

765

The parties inaccurately call this a "letting," and the money to be paid, a "rent"; but the whole agreement is such as to show that the defendants were to retain the possession of the Hall and Gardens so that there was to be no demise of them, and that the contract was merely to give the plaintiffs the use of them on those days. Nothing, however, in our opinion, depends on this. The agreement then proceeds to set out various stipulations between the parties as to what each was to supply for these concerts and entertainments, and as to the manner in which they should be carried on. The effect of the whole is to show that the existence of the Music Hall in the Surrey Gardens in a state fit for a concert was essential for the fulfilment of the contract,—such entertainments as the parties contemplated in their agreement could not be given without it.

After the making of the agreement, and before the first day on which a concert was to be given, the Hall was destroyed by fire. This destruction, we must take it on the evidence, was without the fault of either party, and was so complete that in consequence the concerts could not be given as intended. And the question we have to decide is whether, under these circumstances, the loss which the plaintiffs have sustained is to fall upon the defendants. [The damages claimed in the declaration were for moneys paid by the plaintiffs in advertising the concerts and for sums expended and expenses incurred by them in preparing for the concerts.] The parties when framing their agreement evidently had not present to their minds the possibility of such a disaster, and have made no express stipulation with reference to it, so that the answer to the question must depend upon the general rules of law applicable to such a contract.

There seems no doubt that where there is a positive contract to do a thing, not in itself unlawful, the contractor must perform it or pay damages for not doing it, although in consequence of unforeseen accidents the performance of his contract has become unexpectedly burdensome or even impossible. The law is so laid down in 1 Roll.Abr. 450, Condition (G), and in the note (2) to Walton v. Waterhouse (2 Wms.Saund. 421a, 6th Ed.) and is recognized as the general rule by all the judges in the much discussed case of Hall v. Wright (E.B. & E. 746). But this rule is only applicable when the contract is positive and absolute, and not subject to any condition either express or implied; and there are authorities which, as we think, establish the principle that where, from the nature of the contract, it appears that the parties must from the beginning have known that it could not be fulfilled unless when the time for the fulfilment of the contract arrived some particular specified thing continued to exist, so that, when entering into the contract, they must have contemplated such continuing existence as the foundation of what was to be done; there, in the absence of any express or implied warranty that the thing shall exist, the contract is not to be construed as a positive contract, but as subject to an implied condition that the parties shall be excused in case, before breach, performance becomes impossible from the perishing of the thing without default of the contractor.

There seems little doubt that this implication tends to further the great object of making the legal construction such as to fulfill the intention of those who entered into the contract. For in the course of affairs men in making such contracts in general would, if it were brought to their minds, say that there should be such a condition. . . .

There is a class of contracts in which a person binds himself to do something which requires to be performed by him in person; and such promises, e.g. promises to marry, or promises to serve for a certain time, are never in practice qualified by an express exception of the death of the party; and therefore in such cases the contract is in terms broken if the promisor dies before fulfilment. Yet it was very early determined that, if the performance is personal, the executors are not liable; Hyde v. The Dean of Windsor (Cro.Eliz. 552, 553). See 2 Wms.Exors. 1560 (5th Ed.), where a very apt illustration is given. "Thus," says the learned author, "if an author undertakes to compose a work, and dies before completing it, his executors are discharged from this contract; for the undertaking is merely personal in its nature, and by the intervention of the contractor's death, has become impossible to be performed." For this he cites a dictum of Lord Lyndhurst in Marshall v. Broadhurst (1 Tyr. 348, 349) and a case mentioned by Patteson, J., in Wentworth v. Cock (10 A. & E. 42, 45–46). In Hall v. Wright (E.B. & E. 746, 749), Crompton, J., in his judgment, puts another case. "Where a contract depends upon personal skill, and the act of God renders it impossible, as, for instance, in the case of a painter employed to paint a picture who is struck blind, it may be that the performance might be excused."

It seems that in those cases the only ground on which the parties or their executors can be excused from the consequences of the breach of the contract, is, that from the nature of the contract there is an implied condition of the continued existence of the life of the contractor, and perhaps in the case of the painter, of his eyesight. In the instances just given the person, the continued existence of whose life is necessary to the fulfilment of the contract, is himself the contractor, but that does not seem in itself to be necessary to the application of the principle, as is illustrated by the following example. In the ordinary form of an apprentice deed, the apprentice binds himself in unqualified terms to "serve until the full end and term of seven years to be fully complete and ended," during which term it is covenanted that the apprentice his master "faithfully shall serve," and the father of the apprentice in equally unqualified terms binds himself for the performance by the apprentice of all and every covenant on his part. (See the form, 2 Chitty on Pleading, 370 [7th Ed.] by Greening.) It is undeniable that if the apprentice dies within the seven years, the covenant of the father that he shall perform his covenant to serve for seven years is not fulfilled, yet surely it cannot be that an action would lie against the father. Yet the only reason why it would not is that he is excused because of the apprentice's death.

These are instances where the implied condition is of the life of a human being, but there are others in which the same implication is made as to the continued existence of a thing. For example, where a contract of sale is made amounting to a bargain and sale, transferring presently the property in specific chattels, which are to be delivered by the vendor at a future day; there, if the chattels, without the fault of the vendor, perish in the interval, the purchaser must pay the price, and the vendor is excused from performing his contract to deliver, which has thus become impossible.

That this is the rule of the English law is established by the case of Rugg v. Minett (11 East, 210), where the article that perished before delivery was turpentine, and it was decided that the vendor was bound to refund the price of all those lots in which the property had not passed; but was entitled to retain without deduction the price of those lots in which the property had passed, though they were not delivered, and though in the conditions of sale, which are set out in the report, there was no express qualification of the promise to deliver on payment. It seems in that case rather to have been taken for granted than decided that the destruction of the thing sold before delivery excused the vendor from fulfilling his contract to deliver on payment. . . .

It may, we think, be safely asserted to be now English law, that in all contracts of loan of chattels or bailments if the performance of the promise of the borrower or bailee to return the things lent or bailed, becomes impossible because it has perished, this impossibility (if not arising from the fault of the borrower or bailee from some risk which he has taken upon himself) excuses the borrower or bailee from the performance of his promise to redeliver the chattel.

The great case of Coggs v. Bernard (1 Smith's L.C. 171 [5th Ed.] 2 L.Raym. 909) is now the leading case on the law of bailments, and Lord Holt, in that case, referred so much to the civil law that it might perhaps be thought that this principle was there derived direct from the civilians, and was not generally applicable in English law except in the case of bailments; but the case of Williams v. Lloyd (W. Jones, 179), above cited, shows that the same law had been already adopted by the English law as early as the Book of Assizes. The principle seems to us to be that, in contracts in which the performance depends on the continued existence of a given person or thing, a condition is implied that the impossibility of performance arising from the perishing of the person or thing shall excuse the performance.

In none of these cases is the promise in words other than positive, nor is there any express stipulation that the destruction of the person or thing shall excuse the performance; but that excuse is by law implied, because from the nature of the contract it is apparent that the parties contracted on the basis of the continued existence of the particular person or chattel. In the present case, looking at the whole contract, we find that the parties contracted on the basis of the continued existence of the Music Hall at the time when the concerts were to be given, that being essential to their performance.

We think, therefore, that the Music Hall having ceased to exist, without fault of either party, both parties are excused, the plaintiffs from taking the gardens and paying the money, the defendants from performing their promise to give the use of the Hall and Gardens and other things. Consequently the rule must be absolute to enter the verdict for the defendants.

Rule absolute.

TACIT ASSUMPTIONS—CONTINUED

In *Taylor v. Caldwell* the court says that when framing their agreement the parties "had not present to their minds the possibility" of a disaster affecting the Music Hall, and concludes that the parties "must have contemplated" the "continuing existence" of the Hall "as the foundation" of their agreement.

Is there a contradiction here? The court seems to say that the parties did not think of the possibility of the Hall's burning and therefore assumed that it would not burn. But how can the parties assume that no fire will occur when the possibility of a fire was never present to their minds? If this possibility was not present to their minds, would it not be more accurate to say that they assumed nothing about a fire, either that it would or would not occur?

The difficulty here can be resolved through the concept of tacit assumptions discussed in the previous Chapter. As pointed out in that Chapter, words like "intention," "assumption," "expectation" and "understanding" all seem to imply a *conscious* state involving an awareness of alternatives and a deliberate choice among them. It is, however, plain that there is a psychological state that can be described as a "tacit assumption," which does not involve a consciousness of alternatives. In experiments with animals the relative strength of such "assumptions" can be roughly measured. If a rat is trained for months to run through a particular maze, the sudden interposition of a barrier in one of the paths will have a very disruptive effect on its behavior. For some time after encountering the barrier, the rat will be likely to engage in random and apparently pointless behavior, running in circles, scratching itself, etc. The degree to which the barrier operates disruptively reflects the strength of the "assumption" made by the rat that the barrier would not be there. If the maze has been frequently changed, and the rat has only recently become accustomed to the maze's present form, the introduction of a barrier will act less disruptively. In such a case, after a relatively short period of random behavior the rat will begin to act purposively, will retrace its steps, seek other outlets, etc. In this situation the "assumption" that the path would not be obstructed has not been deeply etched into the rat's nervous system; the rat behaves as if it "half-expected" some such impediment.

In a similar way, where parties have entered into a contract, an unexpected obstacle to performance may operate disruptively in varying degrees depending on the context. To one who has contracted to carry goods by truck over a road traversing a mountain pass, a landslide filling the pass may be a very disruptive and unexpected event. But one who contracts to build a road through the mountains might view the same event, occurring during the course of construction, as a temporary set-back and a challenge to her resourcefulness. One who contracts to deliver goods a year from now at a fixed price certainly "takes into account" the possibility of some fluctuation in price levels, but may feel that a ten-fold inflation is contrary to an "assumption" or "expectation" that price variations would occur within the "normal" range, and that this expectation was "the foundation of the agreement."

In spite of hopeful beginnings that promise a more comprehensive psychological treatment of human behavior, for the time being the only methods available for dealing with problems like that raised by Taylor v. Caldwell are essentially those resting on intuition and introspection. We "just know" that the burning of a music hall violates a tacit assumption of the parties who executed a contract for hiring it for a few days; we "just know" that a two per cent increase in the price of beans does not violate a tacit assumption underlying a contract to deliver a ton of beans for a fixed price.

———

OCEAN TRAMP TANKERS CORP. v. V/O SOVFRACHT, [1964] 2 Q.B. 226 (1963) (Denning, M.R.). "It was originally said that the doctrine of frustration was based on an implied term. In short, that the parties, if they had foreseen the new situation, would have said to one another: 'If that happens, of course, it is all over between us.' But the theory of an implied term has now been discarded by everyone, or nearly everyone, for the simple reason that it does not represent the truth. The parties would not have said: 'It is all over between us.' They would have differed about what was to happen. Each would have sought to insert reservations or qualifications of one kind or another."

MINERAL PARK LAND CO. v. HOWARD, 172 Cal. 289, 156 P. 458 (1916). Plaintiff owned certain land in a ravine. Defendants had made a contract with public authorities to construct a concrete bridge across the ravine. In August 1911, the parties made a contract under which plaintiff granted defendants the right to haul gravel and earth from its land, and defendants agreed to take from that land all the gravel and earth necessary for the fill and cement work on the bridge. Defendants used 101,000 cubic yards in this work but procured 50,869 of those cubic yards from persons other than plaintiff, and plaintiff sued for breach of contract. The trial court found as follows: Plaintiff's land contained earth and gravel far in excess of 101,000 cubic yards of earth and gravel, but only 50,131 of these cubic yards, the amount taken by defendants, was above the water level. No greater quantity could have been taken by ordinary means, but only by employing a steam dredger, and earth and gravel taken in this way could not have been used without first having been dried. Defendants removed all the earth and gravel from plaintiff's land "that was practical to take and remove from a financial standpoint." Any greater amount could have been taken only at an expense of 10 or 12 times the usual cost per yard. It was not "advantageous or practical" to have taken more material from plaintiff's land, although it was not impossible. Held, defendant was excused:

> ... When [the parties] stipulated that all of the earth and gravel needed for this purpose should be taken from plaintiff's land, they contemplated and assumed that the land contained the requisite quantity, available for use. The defendants were not binding themselves to take what was not there. And, in determining whether the earth and gravel were "available," we must view the conditions in a practical and reasonable way. Although there was gravel on the land, it was so situated that the defendants could not take it by ordinary means, nor except at a prohibitive cost. To all fair intents then, it was impossible for defendants to take it.

> "... A thing is impossible in legal contemplation when it is not practicable; and a thing is impracticable when it can only be done at an excessive and unreasonable cost." 1 Beach on Contr. § 216. We do not mean to intimate that the defendants could excuse themselves by showing the existence of conditions which would make the performance of their obligation more expensive than they had anticipated, or which would entail a loss upon them. But, where the difference in cost is so great as here, and has the effect, as found, of making performance impracticable,

the situation is not different from that of a total absence of earth and gravel.

UNITED STATES v. WEGEMATIC CORP.

United States Court of Appeals, Second Circuit, 1966.
360 F.2d 674.

Before LUMBARD, CHIEF JUDGE, and FRIENDLY and ANDERSON, CIRCUIT JUDGES.

FRIENDLY, CIRCUIT JUDGE. The facts developed at trial in the District Court for the Southern District of New York, fully set forth in a memorandum by Judge Graven, can be briefly summarized: In June 1956 the Federal Reserve Board invited five electronics manufacturers to submit proposals for an intermediate-type, general-purpose electronic digital computing system or systems; the invitation stressed the importance of early delivery as a consideration in determining the Board's choice. Defendant, a relative newcomer in the field, which had enjoyed considerable success with a smaller computer known as the ALWAC III–E, submitted a detailed proposal for the sale or lease of a new computer designated as the ALWAC 800. It characterized the machine as "a truly revolutionary system utilizing all of the latest technical advances," and featured that "maintenance problems are minimized by the use of highly reliable magnetic cores for not only the high speed memory but also logical elements and registers." Delivery was offered nine months from the date the contract or purchase order was received. In September the Board acted favorably on the defendant's proposal, ordering components of the ALWAC 800 with an aggregate cost of $231,800. Delivery was to be made on June 30, 1957, with liquidated damages of $100 per day for delay. The order also provided that in the event the defendant failed to comply "with any provision" of the agreement, "the Board may procure the services described in the contract from other sources and hold the Contractor responsible for any excess cost occasioned thereby." Defendant accepted the order with enthusiasm.

The first storm warning was a suggestion by the defendant in March 1957 that the delivery date be postponed. In April it informed the Board by letter that delivery would be made on or before October 30 rather than as agreed, the delay being due to the necessity of "a redesign which we feel has greatly improved this equipment"; waiver of the stipulated damages for delay was requested. The Board took the request under advisement. On August 30 defendant wrote that delivery would be delayed "possibly into 1959"; it suggested use of ALWAC III–E equipment in the interim and waiver of the $100 per day "penalty." The Board also took this request under advisement but made clear it was waiving no rights. In mid-October defendant announced that "due to engineering difficulties it has become impracticable to deliver the ALWAC 800 Computing System at this time"; it requested cancellation of the contract without damages. The Board set about procuring comparable equipment from another manufacturer; on October 6, 1958, International Business Machines Corporation delivered an IBM 650 computer, serving substantially the same purpose as the ALWAC 800, at a rental of $102,000 a year with an option to purchase for $410,450.

In July 1958 the Board advised defendant of its intention to press its claim for damages; this suit followed. The court awarded the United States $46,300 for delay under the liquidated damages clause, $179,450 for the excess cost of the IBM equipment, and $10,056 for preparatory expenses useless in operating the IBM system—a total of $235,806, with 6% interest from October 6, 1958.

The principal point of the defense, which is the sole ground of this appeal, is that delivery was made impossible by "basic engineering difficulties" whose correction would have taken between one and two years and would have cost a million to a million and a half dollars, with success likely but not certain. Although the record does not give an entirely clear notion what the difficulties were, two experts suggested that they may have stemmed from the magnetic cores, used instead of transistors to achieve a solid state machine, which did not have sufficient uniformity at this stage of their development. Defendant contends that under federal law, which both parties concede to govern, see Cargill, Inc. v. Commodity Credit Corp., 275 F.2d 745, 751–753 (2 Cir.1960), the "practical impossibility" of completing the contract excused its defaults in performance. . . .

We find persuasive the defendant's suggestion of looking to the Uniform Commercial Code as a source for the "federal" law of sales. . . .

Section 2–615 of the UCC, entitled "Excuse by failure of presupposed conditions," provides that:

> "Except so far as a seller may have assumed a greater obligation . . . delay in delivery or non-delivery . . . is not a breach of his duty under a contract for sale if performance as agreed has been made impracticable by the occurrence of a contingency the nonoccurrence of which was a basic assumption on which the contract was made". . . .

The latter part of the test seems a somewhat complicated way of putting Professor Corbin's question of how much risk the promisor assumed. Recent Developments in the Law of Contracts, 50 Harv.L.Rev. 449, 465–66 (1937); 2 Corbin, Contracts § 1333, at 371. We see no basis for thinking that when an electronics system is promoted by its manufacturer as a revolutionary break-through, the risk of the revolution's occurrence falls on the purchaser; the reasonable supposition is that it has already occurred or, at least, that the manufacturer is assuring the purchaser that it will be found to have when the machine is assembled. As Judge Graven said: "The Board in its invitation for bids did not request invitations to conduct a development program for it. The Board requested invitations from manufacturers for the furnishing of a computer machine." Acceptance of defendant's argument would mean that though a purchaser makes his choice because of the attractiveness of a manufacturer's representation and will be bound by it, the manufacturer is free to express what are only aspirations and gamble on mere probabilities of fulfillment without any risk of liability. In fields of developing technology, the manufacturer would thus enjoy a wide degree of latitude with respect to performance while holding an option to compel the buyer to pay if the gamble should pan out. See Austin Co. v. United States, 314 F.2d 518, 521, 161 Ct.Cl. 76, cert. denied, 375 U.S. 830, 84 S.Ct. 75, 11 L.Ed.2d 62 (1963). We do not think this the common understanding—above all as to a contract where the manufacturer expressly agreed to liquidated damages for delay and authorized the purchaser to resort to other sources in the event of non-delivery. Contrast

National Presto Industries, Inc. v. United States, 338 F.2d 99, 106–112, 167 Ct.Cl. 749 (1964), cert. denied, 380 U.S. 962 (1965). If a manufacturer wishes to be relieved of the risk that what looks good on paper may not prove so good in hardware, the appropriate exculpatory language is well known and often used.

Beyond this the evidence of true impracticability was far from compelling. The large sums predicted by defendant's witnesses must be appraised in relation not to the single computer ordered by the Federal Reserve Board, evidently for a bargain price, but to the entire ALWAC 800 program as originally contemplated. Although the record gives no idea what this was, even twenty-five machines would gross $10,000,000 if priced at the level of the comparable IBM equipment. While the unanticipated need for expending $1,000,000 or $1,500,000 on redesign might have made such a venture unattractive, as defendant's management evidently decided, the sums are thus not so clearly prohibitive as it would have them appear. What seemingly did become impossible was on-time performance; the issue whether if defendant had offered prompt rectification of the design, the Government could have refused to give it a chance and still recover not merely damages for delay but also the higher cost of replacement equipment, is not before us.

Affirmed.

————

DILLS v. TOWN OF ENFIELD, 210 Conn. 705, 557 A.2d 517 (1989). The Town of Enfield, through its development agency, solicited developers for an industrial park on land owned by the Town. Dills entered into a contract with the Town to purchase, for $985,000, the land that was to be developed, and paid a deposit of $100,000 toward the purchase price. Under the terms of the contract, the development agency agreed to convey the property to Dills sixty days after the fulfillment of two conditions: the submission and approval of construction plans in accordance with the contract, and the submission of evidence of financial capacity. Section 702(b) of the contract allowed Dills to withdraw, and reclaim his deposit, if, after the preparation of construction plans satisfactory to the agency, Dills could not obtain the necessary mortgage financing. Section 703(b) allowed the agency to terminate the contract, and retain the deposit as liquidated damages, if Dills failed to submit acceptable construction plans. Dills never submitted acceptable construction plans because despite diligent effort he was unable to obtain financing. Dills brought suit to recover his $100,000 deposit on the ground that his inability to obtain financing made submitting construction plans a futile and useless act, and accordingly his duty to submit the plans was discharged by the doctrine of supervening impracticability. Held, for the Town.

"In this case the contingency upon which fulfilling the contract allegedly depended was Dills' obtaining the requisite financing. We cannot conclude, however, that Dills' failure to obtain financing was 'an event the non-occurrence of which was a basic assumption on which the contract was made.' Indeed, section 702(b) of the contract of sale demonstrates that the parties expressly contemplated that Dills might encounter financial difficulties. The contract allowed Dills to terminate for this reason [only] 'after preparation of Construction Plans satisfactory to the Agency.' . . .

"... 'Since impossibility and related doctrines are devices for shifting risk in accordance with the parties' presumed intentions, which are to minimize the costs of contract performance, one of which is the disutility created by risk, they have no place when the contract explicitly assigns a particular risk to one party or the other.' Northern Indiana Public Service Co. v. Carbon County Coal Co., 799 F.2d 265, 278 (7th Cir.1986).... Where, as in this case, sophisticated contracting parties have negotiated termination provisions, courts should be slow to invent additional ways to excuse performance. We exercise such caution in this case...."

TRANSATLANTIC FINANCING CORP. v. UNITED STATES

United States Court of Appeals, District of Columbia Circuit, 1966.
363 F.2d 312.

Before DANAHER, WRIGHT and McGOWAN, CIRCUIT JUDGES.

J. SKELLY WRIGHT, CIRCUIT JUDGE. This appeal involves a voyage charter between Transatlantic Financing Corporation, operator of the SS CHRISTOS, and the United States covering carriage of a full cargo of wheat from a United States Gulf port to a safe port in Iran. The District Court dismissed a libel filed by Transatlantic against the United States for costs attributable to the ship's diversion from the normal sea route caused by the closing of the Suez Canal. We affirm.

On July 26, 1956, the Government of Egypt nationalized the Suez Canal Company and took over operation of the Canal. On October 2, 1956, during the international crisis which resulted from the seizure, the voyage charter in suit was executed between representatives of Transatlantic and the United States. The charter indicated the termini of the voyage but not the route. On October 27, 1956, the SS CHRISTOS sailed from Galveston for Bandar Shapur, Iran, on a course which would have taken her through Gibraltar and the Suez Canal. On October 29, 1956, Israel invaded Egypt. On October 31, 1956, Great Britain and France invaded the Suez Canal Zone. On November 2, 1956, the Egyptian Government obstructed the Suez Canal with sunken vessels and closed it to traffic.

On or about November 7, 1956, Beckmann, representing Transatlantic, contacted Potosky, an employee of the United States Department of Agriculture, who appellant concedes was unauthorized to bind the Government, requesting instructions concerning disposition of the cargo and seeking an agreement for payment of additional compensation for a voyage around the Cape of Good Hope. Potosky advised Beckmann that Transatlantic was expected to perform the charter according to its terms, that he did not believe Transatlantic was entitled to additional compensation for a voyage around the Cape, but that Transatlantic was free to file such a claim. Following this discussion, the CHRISTOS changed course for the Cape of Good Hope and eventually arrived in Bandar Shapur on December 30, 1956.

Transatlantic's claim is based on the following train of argument. The charter was a contract for a voyage from a Gulf port to Iran. Admiralty principles and practices, especially stemming from the doctrine of deviation, require us to imply into the contract the term that the voyage was to be performed by the "usual and customary" route. The usual and customary route from Texas to Iran was, at the time of contract, via Suez, so the contract was for a voyage from Texas to Iran via Suez. When Suez was closed this contract became impossible to perform. Consequently, appellant's argument continues, when Transatlantic delivered the cargo by going around the Cape of Good Hope, in compliance with the Government's demand under claim of right, it conferred a benefit upon the United States for which it should be paid in *quantum meruit*.

The doctrine of impossibility of performance has gradually been freed from the earlier fictional and unrealistic strictures of such tests as the "implied term" and the parties' "contemplation." Page, The Development of the Doctrine of Impossibility of Performance, 18 Mich.L.Rev. 589, 596 (1920). See generally 6 Corbin, Contracts §§ 1320–1372 (rev. ed. 1962); 6 Williston, Contracts §§ 1931–1979 (rev. ed. 1938). It is now recognized that " 'A thing is impossible in legal contemplation when it is not practicable; and a thing is impracticable when it can only be done at an excessive and unreasonable cost.' " Mineral Park Land Co. v. Howard, 172 Cal. 289, 293, 156 P. 458, 460, L.R.A. 1916F, 1 (1916). Accord, Whelan v. Griffith Consumers Company, D.C.Mun.App., 170 A.2d 229 (1961); Restatement, Contracts § 454 (1932); Uniform Commercial Code (U.L.A.) § 2–615, comment 3. The doctrine ultimately represents the ever-shifting line, drawn by courts hopefully responsive to commercial practices and mores, at which the community's interest in having contracts enforced according to their terms is outweighed by the commercial senselessness of requiring performance.[1] When the issue is raised, the court is asked to construct a condition of performance based on the changed circumstances, a process which involves at least three reasonably definable steps. First, a contingency—something unexpected—must have occurred. Second, the risk of the unexpected occurrence must not have been allocated either by agreement or by custom. Finally, occurrence of the contingency must have rendered performance commercially impracticable.[2] Unless the court finds these three requirements satisfied, the plea of impossibility must fail.

The first requirement was met here. It seems reasonable, where no route is mentioned in a contract, to assume the parties expected performance by the usual and customary route at the time of contract. Since the usual and customary route from Texas to Iran at the time of contract[3] was through

---

1. While the impossibility issue rarely arises, as it has here, in a suit to recover the cost of an alternative method of performance, compare Annot., 84 A.L.R.2d 12, 19 (1962), there is nothing necessarily inconsistent in claiming commercial impracticability for the method of performance actually adopted; the concept of impracticability assumes performance was physically possible. Moreover, a rule making nonperformance a condition precedent to recovery would unjustifiably encourage disappointment of expectations.

2. Compare Uniform Commercial Code § 2–615(a)....

3. ... It may be that very often the availability of a customary route at the time of

performance other than the route expected to be used at the time of contract should result in denial of relief under the impossibility theory; certainly if *no* customary route is available at the time of performance the contract is rendered impossible. But the same customarily used alternative route may be practicable in one set of circumstances and impracticable in another, as where the goods are unable to survive the extra journey. Moreover, ... the alternative route, in our case around the Cape, may be practicable at some time during performance, for example while the vessel is still in the Atlantic Ocean, and impracticable at another time during performance, for example after the vessel has traversed most of the Mediterranean Sea....

Suez, closure of the Canal made impossible the expected method of performance. But this unexpected development raises rather than resolves the impossibility issue, which turns additionally on whether the risk of the contingency's occurrence had been allocated and, if not, whether performance by alternative routes was rendered impracticable.

Proof that the risk of a contingency's occurrence has been allocated may be expressed in or implied from the agreement. Such proof may also be found in the surrounding circumstances, including custom and usages of the trade. See 6 Corbin, supra, § 1339, at 394–397; 6 Williston, supra, § 1948, at 5457–5458. The contract in this case does not expressly condition performance upon availability of the Suez route. Nor does it specify "via Suez" or, on the other hand, "via Suez or Cape of Good Hope." Nor are there provisions in the contract from which we may properly imply that the continued availability of Suez was a condition of performance.[4] Nor is there anything in custom or trade usage, or in the surrounding circumstances generally, which would support our constructing a condition of performance. The numerous cases requiring performance around the Cape when Suez was closed, see e.g., Ocean Tramp Tankers Corp. v. V/O Sovfracht (The Eugenia), [1964] 2 Q.B. 226, and cases cited therein, indicate that the Cape route is generally regarded as an alternative means of performance. So the implied expectation that the route would be via Suez is hardly adequate proof of an allocation to the promisee of the risk of closure. In some cases, even an express expectation may not amount to a condition of performance.[5] The doctrine of deviation supports our assumption that parties normally expect performance by the usual and customary route, but it adds nothing beyond this that is probative of an allocation of the risk.[6]

If anything, the circumstances surrounding this contract indicate that the risk of the Canal's closure may be deemed to have been allocated to Transatlantic. We know or may safely assume that the parties were aware, as were most commercial men with interests affected by the Suez situation, see The Eugenia, supra, that the Canal might become a dangerous area. No doubt the tension affected freight rates, and it is arguable that the risk of closure

4. The charter provides that the vessel is "in every way fitted for *the voyage*" (emphasis added), and the "P. & I. Bunker Deviation Clause" refers to "the contract voyage" and the "direct and/or customary route." Appellant argues that these provisions require implication of a voyage by the direct and customary route. Actually they prove only what we are willing to accept—that the parties expected the usual and customary route would be used. The provisions in no way condition performance upon nonoccurrence of this contingency....

5. [The court here quoted UCC § 2–614(1).]

6. The deviation doctrine, drawn principally from admiralty insurance practice, implies into all relevant commercial instruments naming the termini of voyages the usual and customary route between those points. 1 Arnould, Marine Insurance and Average § 376, at 522 (10th ed. 1921). Insurance is cancelled when a ship unreasonably "deviates" from this course, for example by extending a voyage or by putting in at an irregular port, and the shipowner forfeits the protection of clauses of exception which might otherwise have protected him from his common law insurer's liability to cargo. See Gilmore & Black [on Admiralty] § 2–6, at 59–60. This practice, properly qualified see id. § 3–41, makes good sense, since insurance rates are computed on the basis of the implied course, and deviations in the course increasing the anticipated risk make the insurer's calculations meaningless. Arnould, supra, § 14, at 26. Thus the route, so far as insurance contracts are concerned, is crucial, whether express or implied. But even here, the implied term is not inflexible. Reasonable deviations do not result in loss of insurance, at least so long as established practice is followed ... The doctrine's only relevance, therefore, is that it provides additional support for the assumption we willingly make that merchants agreeing to a voyage between two points expect that the usual and customary route between those points will be used. The doctrine provides no evidence of an allocation of the risk of the route's unavailability.

became part of the dickered terms. Uniform Commercial Code § 2–615, comment 8. We do not deem the risk of closure so allocated, however. Foreseeability or even recognition of a risk does not necessarily prove its allocation.[7] Compare Uniform Commercial Code § 2–615, Comment 1; Restatement, Contracts § 457 (1932). Parties to a contract are not always able to provide for all the possibilities of which they are aware, sometimes because they cannot agree, often simply because they are too busy. Moreover, that some abnormal risk was contemplated is probative but does not necessarily establish an allocation of the risk of the contingency which actually occurs. In this case, for example, nationalization by Egypt of the Canal Corporation and formation of the Suez Users Group did not necessarily indicate that the Canal would be blocked even if a confrontation resulted.[8] The surrounding circumstances do indicate, however, a willingness by Transatlantic to assume abnormal risks, and this fact should legitimately cause us to judge the impracticability of performance by an alternative route in stricter terms than we would were the contingency unforeseen.

We turn then to the question whether occurrence of the contingency rendered performance commercially impracticable under the circumstances of this case. The goods shipped were not subject to harm from the longer, less temperate Southern route. The vessel and crew were fit to proceed around the Cape. Transatlantic was no less able than the United States to purchase insurance to cover the contingency's occurrence. If anything, it is more reasonable to expect owner-operators of vessels to insure against the hazards of war. They are in the best position to calculate the cost of performance by alternative routes (and therefore to estimate the amount of insurance required), and are undoubtedly sensitive to international troubles which uniquely affect the demand for and cost of their services. The only factor operating here in appellant's favor is the added expense, allegedly $43,972.00 above and beyond the contract price of $305,842.92, of extending a 10,000 mile voyage by approximately 3,000 miles. While it may be an overstatement to say that increased cost and difficulty of performance never constitute impracticability, to justify relief there must be more of a variation between expected cost and the cost of performing by an available alternative than is present in this case, where the promisor can legitimately be presumed to have accepted some degree of abnormal risk, and where impracticability is urged on the basis of added expense alone.

We conclude, therefore, as have most other courts considering related issues arising out of the Suez closure, that performance of this contract was not rendered legally impossible. Even if we agreed with appellant, its theory of relief seems untenable. When performance of a contract is deemed impossible it is a nullity. In the case of a charter party involving carriage of goods, the carrier may return to an appropriate port and unload its cargo, The Malcolm

---

7. See Note, The Fetish of Impossibility in the Law of Contracts, 53 Colum.L.Rev. 94, 98 n. 23 (1953), suggesting that foreseeability is properly used "as a *factor* probative of assumption of the risk of impossibility." (Emphasis added.)

8. Sources cited in the briefs indicate formation of the Suez Canal Users Association on October 1, 1956, was viewed in some quarters as an implied threat of force. See N.Y. Times,

Oct. 2, 1956, p. 1, col. 1, noting, on the day the charter in this case was executed, that "Britain has declared her freedom to use force as a last resort if peaceful methods fail to achieve a satisfactory settlement." Secretary of State Dulles was able, however, to view the statement as evidence of the canal users' "dedication to a just and peaceful solution." The Suez Problem 369–370 (Department of State Pub. 1956).

Baxter, Jr., 277 U.S. 323, 48 S.Ct. 516, 72 L.Ed. 901 (1928), subject of course to required steps to minimize damages. If the performance rendered has value, recovery in *quantum meruit* for the entire performance is proper. But here Transatlantic has collected its contract price, and now seeks *quantum meruit* relief for the additional expense of the trip around the Cape. If the contract is a nullity, Transatlantic's theory of relief should have been *quantum meruit* for the entire trip, rather than only for the extra expense. Transatlantic attempts to take its profit on the contract, and then force the Government to absorb the cost of the additional voyage. When impracticability without fault occurs, the law seeks an equitable solution, see 6 Corbin, supra, § 1321, and *quantum meruit* is one of its potent devices to achieve this end. There is no interest in casting the entire burden of commercial disaster on one party in order to preserve the other's profit. Apparently the contract price in this case was advantageous enough to deter appellant from taking a stance on damages consistent with its theory of liability. In any event, there is no basis for relief.

Affirmed.

AMERICAN TRADING & PRODUCTION CORP. v. SHELL INT'L MARINE LTD., 453 F.2d 939 (2d Cir.1972). American chartered the vessel Washington Trader to Shell for a voyage with a full cargo of lube oil from Beaumont, Texas to Bombay, India. The charter provided for a freight rate in accordance with the then–prevailing American Tanker Rate Schedule of $14.25 per long ton of cargo, plus seventy–five percent. In addition, there was a charge of $.85 per long ton for passage through the Suez Canal. On May 14, 1967, the Washington Trader departed from Beaumont with a cargo of 16,183.32 long tons of lube oil. Freight of $417,327.36 was paid to American in advance. American advised the Washington Trader by radio to bunker (take on additional fuel) at Ceuta in Spanish Morocco at the Strait of Gibraltar due to possible diversion because of the Suez Canal crisis. The vessel arrived at Ceuta on May 30, bunkered, and sailed for the Canal on May 31. On June 5, American cabled the ship's master, advised him of reports of trouble in the Canal, and suggested delay in entering it pending clarification. That day the Canal was closed due to the state of war which had developed. The vessel then proceeded westward, back through the Strait of Gibraltar and around the Cape, and eventually arrived in Bombay on July 15th, some 30 days later than initially expected, traveling a total of 18,055 miles, instead of the 9,709 miles that it would have sailed if the Canal had been open. American billed Shell $131,978.44 as extra compensation. Shell refused to pay, and American brought suit. Held, for Shell:

> Appellant . . . seeks to distinguish *Transatlantic* because in that case the change in course was in the mid-Atlantic and added some 300 miles to the voyage while in this case the WASHINGTON TRADER had traversed most of the Mediterranean and thus had added some 9000 miles to the contemplated voyage. It should be noted that although both the time and the length of the altered passage here exceeded those in the *Transatlantic,* the additional compensation sought here is just under one third of the contract price. Aside from this however, it is a fact that the master of the WASHINGTON TRADER was alerted by radio on May 29th, 1967 of

a "possible diversion because of Suez Canal crisis," but nevertheless two days later he had left Ceuta (opposite Gibraltar) and proceeded across the Mediterranean. While we may not speculate about the foreseeability of a Suez crisis at the time the contract was entered, there does not seem to be any question but that the master here had been actually put on notice before traversing the Mediterranean that diversion was possible. Had the WASHINGTON TRADER then changed course, the time and cost of the Mediterranean trip could reasonably have been avoided, thereby reducing the amount now claimed.

RESTATEMENT, SECOND, CONTRACTS § 261, Illustration 10: "[Several months after the nationalization of the Suez Canal, during the international crisis resulting from its seizure, A contracts to carry a cargo of B's wheat on A's ship from Galveston, Texas to Bandar Shapur, Iran, for a flat rate. The contract does not specify the route, but the voyage would normally be through the Strait of Gibraltar and the Suez Canal. The] Suez Canal is closed while A's ship is in the Canal, preventing the completion of the voyage. A's duty to carry B's cargo is discharged, and A is not liable to B for breach of contract."

JOSKOW, COMMERCIAL IMPOSSIBILITY, THE URANIUM MARKET AND THE WESTINGHOUSE CASE

6 J.Leg.Stud. 119, 153–162 (1977).

... [A] well designed rule of discharge can facilitate the process of exchange and reduce its cost. It would be costly if not impossible to lay out a complete contingent claims contract.* There are a number of possible contingencies, the occurrence of which can be contemplated by both parties, and provision for the effects of which would be desirable to one or both of the parties. Wars, embargoes, changes in government rules and regulations, destruction of key supply facilities, hyperinflation, etc., can all lead to effects on the supply and demand of the commodity in question which would make performance by one or both parties unattractive. These contingencies could all conceivably be listed in a contract along with the possible occurrences of each and the nature of performance in each instance. It may facilitate the contracting process, however, if it is understood or implied in the contract that when events such as this occur *and* lead to dramatic increases in the cost of performance or the impossibility of performance that the contract will simply be discharged or renegotiated. . . .

The foreseeability requirement may only make sense if we introduce the concept of "bounded rationality." Following Simon and Williamson, the concept of bounded rationality recognizes that human beings cannot evaluate all possible states of the world or all available information that might affect a particular situation. One way of thinking about the foreseeability doctrine is

---

* That is, a contract which sets out every contingency whose occurrence or nonoccurrence the parties contemplate as a condition to performance.

as delineating the boundary between those contingencies that are reasonably part of the decisionmaking process and those that are not. This recognizes that most contracts are not complete contingent claims contracts, commonly including only some subset of all possible occurrences. . . .

In essence the impracticability doctrine says that contracts will be enforced . . . unless it really hurts. Other things being equal, the seller bears all of the risk unless performance is extremely burdensome, in which case the buyer bears all of the risk. Superficially, this requirement appears to imply sharp boundaries between similar physical occurrences, some of which are "impracticable" and some of which are not. For example, if we had two similar occurrences, let's say embargoes, the seller would have to perform if the price rise were small, but would not be required to perform if the resulting cost increase were very large. Such asymmetric treatment of differing consequences from similar events only appears to make sense if we expand our notion of possible contingencies to include elements identified by both event and consequence, and assume that, given a particular type of occurrence, the size of the consequence and the probability of the consequence occurring are negatively correlated. That is to say, given the set of possible embargoes, those with small consequences are much more probable than those with large consequences. Then we could appeal to the notions of bounded rationality discussed above and argue that the low-probability events are outside of the boundary and not legally part of the contract. . . .

MISHARA CONSTR. CO. v. TRANSIT–MIXED CONCRETE CORP., 365 Mass. 122, 310 N.E.2d 363 (1974). "With respect to the requirement that performance must have been impracticable, the Official Code Comment to the section stresses that the reference is to 'commercial impracticability' as opposed to strict impossibility. G.L. c. 106, § 2–615, comments 3–4. This is not a radical departure from the common law of contracts as interpreted by this court. Although a strict rule was originally followed denying any excuse for accident or 'inevitable necessity,' e.g., Adams v. Nichols, 19 Pick. 275 (1837), it has long been assumed that circumstances drastically increasing the difficulty and expense of the contemplated performance may be within the compass of 'impossibility.' See Rowe v. Peabody, 207 Mass. 226, 233–234, 93 N.E. 604 (1911) (dictum); Fauci v. Denehy, 332 Mass. 691, 696–697, 127 N.E.2d 477 (1955). By adopting the term 'impracticability' rather than 'impossibility' the drafters of the Code appear to be in accord with Professor Williston who stated that 'the essence of the modern defense of impossibility is that the promised performance was at the making of the contract, or thereafter became, impracticable owing to some extreme or unreasonable difficulty, expense, injury, or loss involved, rather than that it is scientifically or actually impossible.' Williston, Contracts (Rev. ed.) § 1931 (1938). See Restatement: Contracts, § 454 (1932); Corbin, Contracts, § 1339 (1962).

"The second criterion of the excuse, that the intervening circumstance be one which the parties assumed would not occur, is also familiar to the law of Massachusetts. Baetjer v. New England Alcohol Co., 319 Mass. 592, 600, 66 N.E.2d 798 (1946). Boston Plate & Window Glass Co. v. John Bowen Co., Inc., 335 Mass. 697, 699–700, 141 N.E.2d 715 (1957). The rule is essentially aimed at the distribution of certain kinds of risks in the contractual relationship. By directing the inquiry to the time when the contract was first made, we really seek to determine whether the risk of the intervening circumstance was one which the parties may be taken to have assigned between themselves. It is, of course, the very essence of contract that it is directed at the elimination of some risks for each party in exchange for others. Each receives the certainty of price, quantity, and time, and assumes the risk of changing market prices, superior opportunity, or added costs. It is implicit in the doctrine of impossibility (and the companion rule of 'frustration of purpose') that certain risks are so unusual and have such severe consequences that they must have been beyond the scope of the assignment of risks inherent in the contract, that is, beyond the agreement made by the parties. To require performance in that case would be to grant the promisee an advantage for which he could not be said to have bargained in making the contract. 'The important question is whether an unanticipated circumstance has made performance of the promise vitally different from what should reasonably have been within the contemplation of both parties when they entered into the contract. If so, the risk should not fairly be thrown upon the promisor.' Williston, Contracts (Rev. ed.) § 1931 (1938). The emphasis in contracts governed by the Uniform Commercial Code is on the commercial context in which the agreement was made. The question is, given the commercial circumstances in which the parties dealt: Was the contingency which developed one which the parties could reasonably be thought to have foreseen as a real possibility which could affect performance? Was it one of that variety of risks which the parties were tacitly assigning to the promisor by their failure to provide for it explicitly? If it were, performance will be required. If it could not be so considered, performance is excused. The contract cannot be reasonably thought to govern in these circumstances, and the parties are both thrown upon the resources of the open market without the benefit of their contract."

UCC §§ 1–103, 2–509, 2–510, 2–613, 2–614, 2–615, 2–616

[See Selected Source Materials Supplement]

RESTATEMENT, SECOND, CONTRACTS §§ 261–272

[See Selected Source Materials Supplement]

CISG ARTS. 66–69

[See Selected Source Materials Supplement]

UNIDROIT PRINCIPLES OF INTERNATIONAL COMMERCIAL CONTRACTS ARTS. 6.2.1, 6.2.2, 6.2.3, 7.1.7

[See Selected Source Materials Supplement]

––––––––

PRINCIPLES OF EUROPEAN CONTRACT LAW ARTS. 4.102, 6.111, 8.108

[See Selected Source Materials Supplement]

––––––––

ABA TASK FORCE REPORT ON ARTICLE 2, 16 Del.J.Corp.Law 981, 1201 (1991). "The comments [to UCC § 2–615] should make clear that the section adopts the limited obligation theory of contract. That is, the parties ordinarily do not intend to allocate the risk of unforeseen events, thus leaving a gap in the contract. Should the unforeseen event occur, a court is to fill the gap. More specifically, the court should allocate the risk of the event based on what is fair under the circumstances, not on some supposed implicit agreement–based risk allocation which never occurred."

––––––––

J. WHITE & R. SUMMERS, UNIFORM COMMERCIAL CODE § 3.10 (5th ed. 2000). "The Doctrines of Impossibility, Commercial Impracticability or as the Uniform Commercial Code knows it, Excuse by Failure of Presupposed Conditions, comprise unclimbed peaks of contract doctrine. Clearly, all of the famous early and mid-twentieth century mountaineers, Corbin, Williston, Farnsworth and many lesser persons have made assaults on this topic but none has succeeded in conquering the very summit. The topic inheres in 2–615 of the UCC, in section 261 of the Restatement (Second) of Contracts and in a series of Anglo–American cases. In spite of attempts by all of the contract scholars and even in the face of eloquent and persuasive general statements, it remains impossible to predict with accuracy how the law will apply to a variety of relatively common cases. Both the cases and the Code commentary are full of weasel words such as 'severe' shortage, 'marked' increase, 'basic' assumptions, and 'force majeure.' "

––––––––

AMERICAN INSTITUTE OF ARCHITECTS, GENERAL CONDITIONS OF THE CONTRACT FOR CONSTRUCTION, AIA DOC A201, ARTICLES 4, 11 (1987)

[See Selected Source Materials Supplement]

––––––––

ALBRE MARBLE & TILE CO. v. JOHN BOWEN CO.

Supreme Judicial Court of Massachusetts, 1959.
338 Mass. 394, 155 N.E.2d 437.

Before SPALDING, WILLIAMS, COUNIHAN and WHITTEMORE, JJ.

SPALDING, JUSTICE. The declaration in this action of contract contains four counts. The plaintiff in counts 1 and 2 seeks damages for the defendant's alleged breach of two subcontracts under which the plaintiff agreed to supply labor and materials to the defendant as general contractor of the Chronic Disease Hospital and Nurses' Home in Boston.[12] In counts 3 and 4 the plaintiff seeks to recover the value of work and labor furnished by it to the defendant at the defendant's request. The defendant's substitute answer in defence to the first two counts states that the performance of the subcontracts became impossible when the defendant's general contract with the Commonwealth was declared invalid by this court in Gifford v. Commissioner of Public Health, 328 Mass. 608, 105 N.E.2d 476. The defendant's answer to counts 3 and 4 (based on quantum meruit) states that no payment could be demanded because the plaintiff did not possess an architect's certificate for the work done. . . .

The defendant filed a motion, accompanied by an affidavit, for the immediate entry of judgment in its favor. . . . The plaintiff filed a counter affidavit. After hearing, the motion was allowed, and the plaintiff duly claimed an exception.

[The court concluded that the granting of defendant's motion for judgment on counts 1 and 2 was proper.]

We turn now to counts 3 and 4 by which the plaintiff seeks a recovery for the fair value of work and labor furnished to the defendant prior to the termination of the general contract. The plaintiff seeks recovery in count 3 for "preparation of samples, shop drawings, tests and affidavits" in connection with the tile work; in count 4 recovery for similar work in connection with the marble contract is sought.

The defendant in its affidavit maintains that the tile and marble work to be furnished by the plaintiff could not have been done until late in the construction process; that no tile or marble was actually installed in the building; and that the expenses incurred by the plaintiff prior to the time the general contract was declared invalid consisted solely of expenditures in preparation for performance. Relying on the decision in Young v. Chicopee, 186 Mass. 518, 72 N.E. 63, the defendant maintains that where a building contract has been rendered impossible of performance a plaintiff may not recover for expenses incurred in preparation for performance, but may recover only for the labor and materials "wrought into" the structure. Therefore, the defendant says, the plaintiff should take nothing here.

The plaintiff places its reliance upon a clause appearing in both contracts which provides in part: "It is agreed you [the plaintiff] will furnish and submit all necessary or required samples, shop drawings, tests, affidavits, etc., for approval, all as ordered or specified. . . ." The plaintiff in effect concedes that no labor or materials were actually wrought into the structure, but

---

12. Count 1 relates to tile work and count
2 relates to marble work.

argues that the contract provision quoted above placed its preparatory efforts under the supervision of the defendant, and that this circumstance removes this case from the ambit of those decisions which apply the "wrought-in" principle....

The problem of allocating losses where a building contract has been rendered impossible of performance by a supervening act not chargeable to either party is a vexed one. In situations where the part performance of one party measurably exceeds that of the other the tendency has been to allow recovery for the fair value of work done in the actual performance of the contract and to deny recovery for expenditures made in reliance upon the contract or in preparing to perform. This principle has sometimes been expressed in terms of "benefit" or "lack of benefit." In other words, recovery may be had only for those expenditures which, but for the supervening act, would have enured to the benefit of the defendant as contemplated by the contract. See, e.g. Young v. Chicopee, 186 Mass. 518, 520, 72 N.E. 63. The "wrought-in" principle applied in building contract cases is merely a variant of this principle. It has long been recognized that this theory is unworkable if the concept of benefit is applied literally. In M. Ahern Co. v. John Bowen Co. Inc., 334 Mass. 36, 41, 133 N.E.2d 484, 487, we quoted with approval the statement of Professor Williston that "It is enough that the defendant has actually received in part performance of the contract something for which when completed he had agreed to pay a price." Williston on Contracts (Rev. ed.) § 1976.

Although the matter of denial of reliance expenditures in impossibility situations seems to have been discussed but little in judicial opinions, it has, however, been the subject of critical comment by scholars. See Fuller and Perdue, The Reliance Interest in Contract Damages, 46 Yale L.J. 52, 373, 379–383. Note, 46 Mich.L.Rev. 401. In England the recent frustrated contracts legislation provides that the court may grant recovery for expenditures in reliance on the contract or in preparation to perform it where it appears *"just to do so having regard to all the circumstances of the case"* (emphasis supplied). 6 & 7 George VI, c. 40.

We are of opinion that the plaintiff here may recover for those expenditures made pursuant to the specific request of the defendant as set forth in the contract clause quoted above. A combination of factors peculiar to this case justifies such a holding without laying down the broader principle that in every case recovery may be had for payments made or obligations reasonably incurred in preparation for performance of a contract where further performance is rendered impossible without fault by either party. See Boston Plate & Window Glass Co. v. John Bowen Co. Inc., 335 Mass. 697, 702, 141 N.E.2d 715.

The factors which determine the holding here are these: First, this is not a case of mere impossibility by reason of a supervening act. The opinion of this court in M. Ahern Co. v. John Bowen Co. Inc., 334 Mass. 36, 133 N.E.2d 484, points out that the defendant's involvement in creating the impossibility was greater than that of its subcontractors. The facts regarding the defendant's conduct are set forth in that opinion and need not be restated.* Although the defendant's conduct was not so culpable as to render it liable for

---

* The defendant had presented its bid for the hospital construction project in such a manner   as to cause the bid to appear to be the lowest although in fact it was not. (Footnote by ed.)

breach of contract (Boston Plate & Window Glass Co. v. John Bowen Co. Inc., 335 Mass. 697, 141 N.E.2d 715), nevertheless, it was a contributing factor to a loss sustained by the plaintiff which as between the plaintiff and the defendant the latter ought to bear to the extent herein permitted.

We attach significance to the clause in the contract, which was prepared by the defendant, specifically requesting the plaintiff to submit samples, shop drawings, tests, affidavits, etc., to the defendant. This is not a case in which all efforts in preparation for performance were solely within the discretion and control of the subcontractor. We are mindful that in Young v. Chicopee, 186 Mass. 518, 72 N.E. 63, recovery of the value of materials brought to the construction site at the specific request of the defendant therein was denied. But in that case the supervening act rendering further performance impossible was a fire not shown to have been caused by the fault of either party. We are not disposed to extend that holding to a situation in which the defendant's fault is greater than the plaintiff's.

Moreover, the acts requested here by their very nature could not be "wrought into" the structure. In Angus v. Scully, 176 Mass. 357, 57 N.E. 674, 49 A.L.R. 562, recovery for the value of services rendered by house movers was allowed although the house was destroyed midway in the moving. The present case comes nearer to the rationale of the *Angus* case than to that of the *Young* case. . . .

We hold that the damages to be assessed are limited solely to the fair value of those acts done in conformity with the specific request of the defendant as contained in the contract. Expenses incurred prior to the execution of the contract, such as those arising out of preparing the plaintiff's bid, are not to be considered.

The plaintiff's exceptions as to counts 1 and 2 are overruled and are sustained as to counts 3 and 4; as to those counts the case is remanded to the Superior Court for further proceedings in conformity with this opinion. The appeal is dismissed.

So ordered.

NOTE ON THE EQUITABLE APPORTIONMENT
OF LOSSES FOLLOWING IMPOSSIBILITY

Restatement First seemed to adopt the assumption that the reimbursement of reliance is not a proper function of the courts except in tort cases. It was assumed that in contract cases a court has a choice, subject to the applicable rules of law, of (1) denying relief; (2) granting relief measured by the value of the performance promised by the defendant; or (3) granting relief measured by the value of the benefit conferred by the plaintiff on the defendant. The possibility of measuring relief by the plaintiff's losses through reliance was completely passed over, except insofar as it crept in, perhaps unintentionally, in certain of the illustrative cases. As applied to changed-circumstances cases, this meant that courts had to go whole hog or none in dealing with the problem of remedies. It is difficult to see anything in the American case law that compelled that assumption. If a court has power to impose an obligation to return benefits, it would seem also to have power to impose equitable conditions and limitations on this obligation. If a court has power to relieve a person from a promise because of an unexpected event, it would seem also to have power to relieve the person on condition that she reimburse all or a part of the other party's reliance on the contract.

Restatement Second takes a considerably different view on this matter than Restatement First. Under Restatement Second § 272:

> (1) In any case governed by the rules stated in this Chapter [Impracticability and Frustration], either party may have a claim for relief including restitution . . .

> (2) In any case governed by the rules stated in this Chapter, if those rules together with the rules stated in [the chapter on remedies] will not avoid injustice, the court may grant relief on such terms as justice requires, including protection of the parties' reliance interests.

To the same effect is Official Comment 6 to UCC § 2–615 (the principal UCC section dealing with the problem of changed circumstances):

> In situations in which neither sense nor justice is served by either answer when the issue is posed in flat terms of "excuse" or "no excuse," adjustment under the various provisions of this Article is necessary, especially the sections on good faith, on insecurity and assurance and on the reading of all provisions in the light of their purposes, and the general policy of this Act to use equitable principles in furtherance of commercial standards and good faith.

––––––––––

MISSOURI PUBLIC SERVICE CO. v. PEABODY COAL CO.

Missouri Court of Appeals, Western District, 1979.
583 S.W.2d 721, cert. denied, 444 U.S. 865, 100 S.Ct. 135, 62 L.Ed.2d 88.

Before SHANGLER, P.J., SWOFFORD, C.J., and TURNAGE, J.

SWOFFORD, CHIEF JUDGE.

This is an appeal from a decree of specific performance involving a contract between the parties wherein the appellant (Peabody) agreed to supply the respondent (Public Service) with coal for the production of electricity at the power plants of Public Service in Jackson County, Missouri over a long term. Faced with escalating costs, Peabody unsuccessfully attempted to negotiate a higher price per ton for coal furnished under the contract, and failing in such attempts, declared its intention to discontinue coal shipments. Public Service thereupon elected to consider this position of Peabody to be an anticipatory breach of the contract and thereafter instituted this action to require specific performance of the contract as it was written.

The resolution of this appeal depends upon the underlying basic facts concerning the contractual relationship of the parties. Public Service is a state-regulated public utility supplying electricity and serving the consumers in 28 Missouri counties. In anticipation of need for expanded capacity, it constructed a large coal burning power plant at Sibley, Missouri in Jackson County, and simultaneously undertook negotiations with several coal suppliers, including Peabody, for a 10–year coal supply agreement to meet the requirements of the plant. Letters of intent were signed in 1966 with Peabody and one other coal supplier. At that time, the supply of coal was described as a "buyers market" in which coal suppliers and natural gas companies competed vigorously for the business of energy producers.

Negotiations progressed between the parties to the point where Peabody made an offer to Public Service to supply its coal needs at the Sibley plant for a period of ten years at a base price of $5.40 per net ton, subject to certain price adjustments from time to time relating to costs of labor, taxes, compliance with government regulations, and increase in transportation costs, as reflected in railroad tariffs. Peabody's offer also contained an inflation escalator clause based upon the Consumer Price Index published by the United States Department of Labor. Public Service rejected this offer because of the price adjustment features, but negotiations continued and ultimately resulted in the drafting by Peabody of an agreement essentially the same as the original offer in the area of price adjustments except that the inflation escalator clause was changed so that it would be based upon the Industrial Commodities Index, also published by the United States Department of Labor, but unlike the Consumer Price Index, based, in large part, upon material production costs. This final agreement was formally executed by the parties on December 22, 1967.

Performance under the agreement was profitable for Peabody during the first two years of operation thereunder. Thereafter, production costs began to outpace the price adjustment features of the contract to the extent that in 1974, Peabody requested modification of the price adjustment features. Public Service rejected all proposed modifications in this area but did offer a modification to provide for an increase of $1.00 in the original cost per net ton. This proposal was rejected by Peabody.

On September 16, 1974, a meeting was held between officials of Public Service and Peabody at the Jackson County, Missouri home office of Public Service. At this meeting Public Service again flatly rejected Peabody's proposed modifications of the contract. Peabody thereupon declared that unless these proposed modifications were met, coal shipments to Public Service would cease and the contract would be considered by Peabody to be inoperative. Contact and negotiations continued during which Public Service adamantly refused to agree to the proposed modifications and declared its intentions to hold Peabody to the terms of the original contract. Peabody, by letter dated May 6, 1975, mailed from its principal office in St. Louis, Missouri, advised Public Service that upon the expiration of 60 days all coal shipments under the contract would cease, if the contract modifications were not agreed to by Public Service.

It is undisputed that Peabody possessed adequate coal supplies and ability to perform the contract. Rather, excuse from performance is claimed upon the basis of excessive economic loss under the agreement, absent modification; that excuse from performance was lawful upon the doctrine of "commercial impracticability" under Section 400.2–615 RSMo 1969.

Peabody claimed and the evidence tended to establish that the loss was occasioned largely because the escalation clause in the contract was based upon the Industrial Commodities Index which in years prior to the execution of the contract had been an accurate measure of inflation but had ceased to be an effective measure due to the 1973 oil embargo, runaway inflation and the enactment of new and costly mine safety regulations. Public Service conceded a weakening of this significant function of the Industrial Commodities Index but introduced evidence, including admissions by Peabody, that the events bringing this about were foreseeable at the time of the execution of the contract.

Peabody introduced evidence that its losses under the contract were in excess of 3.4 million dollars at the time of the trial. Peabody's evidence showed that 60% of these claimed losses were not due to inadequacy of the price adjustment features of the contract to track inflation, but rather to reduction in price caused by lower calorific and higher waste content of the coal received than that originally contemplated under the terms of the contract. It is apparently not disputed that had the escalation clause been based upon the Consumer Price Index, Peabody's purported losses would have been substantially reduced.

That Peabody sustained loss under the contract seems clear, although the extent and cause thereof was in sharp dispute. Public Service, over objection, was permitted to show that since performance of the contract began, Peabody had experienced an approximate three-fold increase in the value of its coal reserves, presumably brought about by the same inflationary trend and other causes to which it ascribes its loss under the contract.

This cause was tried without a jury and the court entered its decree of specific performance, from which judgment Peabody appealed. Under such circumstances, the judgment must be affirmed unless there is no substantial evidence to support it, or it is against the weight of the evidence, or erroneously declares or applies the law. Rule 73.01; *Murphy v. Carron,* 536 S.W.2d 30, 32[1] (Mo. banc 1976). The issues upon this appeal are essentially legal in nature, and are, in part at least, issues of first impression in Missouri. These legal issues are governed by the terms and provisions of Chapter 400, Uniform Commercial Code, RSMo 1969 (effective July 1, 1965) (U.C.C.) and in force at the time of the execution of the sales contract here involved. . . .

. . . Peabody strongly urges, as a ground for reversal of the decree, that the court erred in entering the decree because Public Service acted in bad faith in its refusal to accede to a price modification of the contract and thus Public Service breached the contract. In so doing, Peabody relies upon the U.C.C. provisions imposing the obligation of good faith upon both buyer and seller as an inherent part of all contracts for the sale of goods. Section 400.1–203 under General Provisions of U.C.C. provides:

"Obligation of good faith

"Every contract or duty within this chapter imposes an obligation of good faith in its performance or enforcement."

Section 400.2–103(1)(b) under the provisions of U.C.C. relating to Sales, [provides] in part:

"Definitions and index of definitions . . .

" 'Good faith' in the case of a merchant means honesty in fact and the observance of reasonable commercial standards of fair dealing in the trade. . . ."

Such good faith, honesty and adherence to commercial or business standards are also inherent in the right to maintain an equitable action for specific performance of a contract as in the case at bar. There is no evidence or present claim that Public Service acted in any particular outside the boundaries thus imposed in the original negotiations, offer and counteroffers and final execution of the sales contract here in question nor in the performance of the obligations thereunder preceding the breach by repudiation. Peabody's charge is based entirely upon the refusal of Public Service to accede to Peabody's demands for price modification, which refusal, it asserts, constituted bad faith and thus placed the onus of breach upon Public Service. Neither the law of contracts generally nor the terms of U.C.C. relied upon by Peabody lend support to this theory. The contract here involved was settled as a result of arm's length dealing with no cloud of dishonesty, lack of good faith or failure to adhere to standard business or commercial practice upon the part of either party. The fact that foreseeable economic trends or developments resulted in loss of anticipated profits or, as here claimed, actual financial loss, does not prevent Public Service from refusal of a modification of price and to take advantage of a good bargain. Such is particularly true here, for the reason that Public Service is a utility impressed with public interest and any increase in its cost in producing electricity would reflect in its rates to its public and private consumers. For this reason, its good faith, if it had agreed to a gratuitous modification upward of its costs, might properly be called into question. Indeed, in the case of *U.S. for the Use and Benefit of Crane Co. v. Progressive Enterprises, Inc.*, 418 F.Supp. 662 (E.D.Va.1976), strongly relied upon by Peabody, the court held in similar circumstances that the purchaser "possessed the contractual right to refuse to modify and to demand performance on the original terms" (at l.c. 664). Where an enforceable, untainted contract exists, refusing modification of price and seeking specific performance of valid covenants does not constitute bad faith or breach of contract, and the trial court properly so held.

The appellant's final allegation of error is that the trial court erred in refusing to relieve or excuse it from its obligations under the contract upon the basis of "commercial impracticability" under Section 400.2–615 RSMo 1969 (U.C.C.), which section reads, in part:

"Excuse by failure of presupposed conditions

"Except so far as a seller may have assumed a greater obligation and subject to the preceding section on substituted performance:

"(a) Delay in delivery or nondelivery in whole or in part by a seller who complies with paragraphs (b) and (c)[13] is not a breach of his duty under a contract for sale *if performance as agreed has been made impracticable by the occurrence of a contingency the nonoccurrence of which was a basic assumption on which the contract was made* or by compliance in good faith with any applicable foreign or domestic governmental regulation or order whether or not it later proves to be invalid...." (Emphasis supplied)

The comments accompanying this section treat it as dealing with the doctrine of "commercial impracticability" and central to this concept is that the doctrine may be applicable upon the occurrence of a supervening, unfore-

---

13. Subparagraphs (b) and (c) cover situations where a seller's capacity to perform the contract is only partially impaired and for allo-cation of his curtailed production among all of his customers and notice to the buyers. These provisions are not applicable here.

seen event not within the reasonable contemplation of the parties at the time the contract was made. Such occurrence must go to the heart of the contract.

Further light is shed upon the provisions of Section 400.2–615, in Comment No. 4, accompanying that section, which states:

> "4. *Increased cost alone does not excuse performance* unless the rise in cost is due to some unforeseen contingency which alters *the essential nature of the performance.* Neither is a rise or a collapse in the market in itself a justification, *for that is exactly the type of business risk which business contracts made at fixed prices are intended to cover.* But a severe shortage of raw materials or of supplies due to a contingency such as war, embargo, local crop failure, unforeseen shutdown of major sources of supply or the like, which either causes a marked increase in cost or altogether prevents the seller from securing supplies necessary to his performance, is within the contemplation of this section." (Emphasis added)

In the case of *Transatlantic Financing Corp. v. United States*, 124 U.S.App.D.C. 183, 186, 363 F.2d 312, 315[3] (1966) the court articulates the ingredients necessary to establish the claim of "commercial impracticability" as (1) the occurrence of a contingency; (2) the nonoccurrence of which was a *basic assumption* upon which the contract was made; and (3) by which occurrence further performance has become commercially impracticable. The ... statute is drawn in such general terms ... to provide flexibility in its application and full scope for the application of equitable principles and considerations with which the doctrine of commercial impracticability is imbued, as recognized in the *Transatlantic Financing Corp.* decision, *supra.* When so viewed and applied, a wide variety of commercial situations often unique to the particular case under consideration are subject to scrutiny. This is particularly true in a case such as the one at bar, where the claim of commercial impracticability is based primarily upon the fact that the performance of the contract results in great financial loss to Peabody due to increase in cost of production (due to the causes enumerated) which were not foreseeable at the time the contract was made. In this connection, Peabody argues that in the resolution of this issue, only the contract in litigation should be considered by the court and that the factors of Peabody's financial condition, experience in the production of coal, resources, availability of the raw material (coal reserves) and other factors should be disregarded. This argument is without merit and Peabody cites no authority in support thereof. Those factors have a direct bearing and evidentiary value in determining the question of foreseeability of the occurrence triggering the loss. See e.g. *Eastern Airlines, Inc. v. Gulf Oil Corp.*, 415 F.Supp. 429 (S.D.Fla.1975). A commercial, governmental or business trend affecting a contract's value which would be foreseeable to a party with wide experience and knowledge in the field and, perhaps, not [foreseeable] to a party with less; a loss to a party with vast resources and ample supply of raw materials to perform a bad bargain would be less harmful than to a party without them; and, the application of the doctrine and the equitable principles inherent therein might call for relief in one instance and not another based upon these factors, and others, outside the strict confines of the contract itself.

Further, the trial court is put upon inquiry and finding (under the statute) that the nonoccurrence of the event was a "basic assumption on which the contract was made" and that the occurrence of such event "alters the essential nature of the performance thereunder." See: *Eastern Airlines v. Gulf Oil Corp., supra; United States v. Wegematic Corp.,* 360 F.2d 674 (2d Cir.1966); *Neal–Cooper Grain Co. v. Texas Gulf Sulphur Co.,* 508 F.2d 283 (7th Cir.1974); 6 Corbin on Contracts, Section 1333 (Rev.Ed.1962); 6 Williston on Contracts, Section 1952 (Rev.Ed.1938).

A recent case which is strikingly similar to the case at bar is *Iowa Electric Light & Power Co. v. Atlas Corporation,* 23 U.C.C.Rep.Service (U.S., N.D.Iowa 5/4/78). In that case, the Iowa Electric entered into a contract in 1973 whereby it was to purchase approximately 700,000 pounds of uranium concentrate from Atlas, at a beginning price per pound of $7.10, over an extended period for use in the production of electric energy. The contract contained an escalation clause providing for an automatic inflationary price per pound increase of $0.12329 cents per day or [3.75¢] per month on July 15th of each year so that the contract price by 1978 would be approximately $8.45 per pound. Because of late deliveries, Iowa Electric by way of a proceeding in injunction, in the nature of specific performance, sought to insure deliveries under the terms and at the price established in the contract, and Atlas counterclaimed seeking to reform the contract by judicial decree so as to provide a higher price per pound for the product upon the basis of commercial impracticability. The case was tried upon the counterclaim by stipulation of the parties and the court denied Atlas the relief sought and dismissed its counterclaim.

The basis upon which Atlas sought relief was that unforeseen factors had so drastically increased its costs and resulted in burdensome losses amounting to approximately $1,800,000.00 in 1976 and projected to losses of approximately $4,000,000.00 in fiscal years 1977–1979. Atlas attributed the increase in its costs to the Arab oil embargo and OPEC cartel, unexpected federal environmental and occupational safety regulations, inflation in wages and costs of chemicals and equipment, and certain uranium market conditions. Atlas produced evidence that its costs had increased to $17.40 per pound and that the open market price per pound in 1977 was $43.00 per pound. The court held, among other things:

(1) That the term " 'impracticable' as used in U.C.C. § 2–615 does not mean impossible and each situation should be viewed in the context of reasonable commercial relationships"; that "Atlas must show that the increase is more than onerous or expensive and that it had no part in stimulating that increase"; and that the "burden of proving each element of impracticability is on the party claiming excuse".

(2) That, although some of the factors which resulted in the increased cost of production may have been unforeseen and the total impact was not contemplated by the parties during contract negotiations, prior to contract there was good reason to anticipate rising costs and drastically increased expense arising from inflation and governmental environmental and safety regulations.

(3) It was not clear that Atlas was not in a position to protect itself contractually from some of the risks; that some of the increased costs resulted from internal corporate decisions; and, that increased costs were partially due to rise in the market price of uranium, the fact that Atlas' reserve in Alkaline ores used in processing uranium were rapidly becom-

ing exhausted, facts known to Atlas at the time the contract was negotiated.

The court in *Iowa Electric* refused to reform the contract principally upon the basis of the failure of Atlas to sustain its burden of proof to establish "commercial impracticability", but the facts there are so similar the case stands for an acceptable precedent in the case at bar.

It should again be emphasized that in the negotiations leading to the contract now before this Court an escalator clause was agreed upon to cover the contingencies of increase in Peabody's costs due to wages reflected by labor contracts; payments for unemployment, social security taxes and Workmen's Compensation insurance premiums; costs of compliance with federal, state and local laws, regulations or orders; railroad tariffs; and, increase in the costs of material and supplies, explosives, electric power and administrative and supervisory expense based upon the Industrial Commodities Index of the Department of Labor. There is no evidence nor, indeed, serious claim, that Public Service did not abide by the letter of these provisions, and in addition, prior to suit, agreed to a further price increase of $1.00 per net ton, which Peabody rejected.

The facts as shown by the record lead to the conclusion that at least some of the loss resulted from the fact that for some unexplained reason the Industrial Commodities Index lagged behind the Consumer Price Index, the measuring factor first proposed by Peabody, in reflecting inflationary cost increases. That such indexes were based upon different commercial and economic factors was presumably known by both parties since each was skilled and experienced in those areas and the divergence between the indexes could not be said to be unforeseeable. Be that as it may, Peabody agreed to the use of the Industrial Commodities Index factor.

The other claim made by Peabody alleged to bring it within the doctrine of "commercial impracticability", is the Arab oil embargo. Such a possibility was common knowledge and had been thoroughly discussed and recognized for many years by our government, media economists and business, and the fact that the embargo was imposed during the term of the contract here involved was foreseeable. Peabody failed to demonstrate that this embargo affected its ability to secure oil or petroleum products necessary to its mining production albeit at inflated cost. In fact, as previously stated, this embargo can reasonably be said to have, at least indirectly, contributed to the marked appreciation to the value of Peabody's coal reserves by forcing the market value of that alternative source of energy upward in this country.

It is apparent that Peabody did make a bad bargain and an unprofitable one under its contract with Public Service resulting in a loss, the cause and size of which is disputed. But this fact alone does not deal with either the "basic assumption" on which the contract was negotiated or alter the "essential nature of the performance" thereunder so as to constitute "commercial impracticability". The court below properly decreed specific performance.

The judgment is affirmed.

All concur.

———

GEORGIA POWER CO. v. CIMARRON COAL CORP., 526 F.2d 101 (6th Cir.1975), cert. denied, 425 U.S. 952, 96 S.Ct. 1727, 48 L.Ed.2d 195 (1976). Georgia Power and Cimarron Coal entered into a coal supply agreement which provided that for a period of ten years beginning January 1, 1970, Cimarron would sell and Georgia Power would purchase designated quantities of coal. The Agreement provided for a base price of $4.03 per ton, subject to adjustment from time to time. Specific provisions of the Agreement provided formulas or methods for adjusting the base price for changes in certain labor costs, supplies, and governmental requirements. The Agreement also contained the following provisions:

20.01 *Arbitration.* Any unresolved controversy between the parties, arising under this Agreement shall, at the request of either party, be submitted to arbitration under the rules of the American Arbitration Association. . . .

26.01 *Adjustments for Gross Inequities.* Any gross proven inequity that may result in unusual economic conditions not contemplated by the parties at the time of the execution of this Agreement may be corrected by mutual consent. Each party shall in the case of a claim of gross inequity furnish the other with whatever documentary evidence may be necessary to assist in affecting a settlement.

Nothing contained in this section shall be construed as relieving either the Purchaser or Seller from any of its respective obligations hereunder solely because of the existence of a claim of inequity or the failure of the parties to reach an agreement with respect thereto.

During 1973 and 1974, there was a rapid escalation in the market price of coal. In 1974, Cimarron requested adjustments in the base price under the gross-inequities provision of the Agreement, claiming that a gross inequity had resulted from the disparity between the market price of coal and the price being paid under the Agreement. Cimarron pointed out that the current adjusted base price under the Agreement was $10.00 per ton, while coal of the same quality was selling for $19.00 to $32.00 per ton on the open market. Georgia Power refused to make the requested adjustment, and Cimarron petitioned for arbitration on the ground that the parties had an "unresolved controversy" within the meaning of § 20.01. Held, Cimarron had a right to require a dispute under the gross-inequities provision to be resolved by arbitration.

". . . The gross inequities provision deals with a possible adjustment in price which might be required because of unforeseeable changes in the economic climate of the coal industry. This provision lacks the specific details of the other portions of the Agreement dealing with price adjustment, but that arises from the fact that it is something of a 'catch-all' provision designed to take care of the kinds of changes which cannot be predicted in detail, but which experience teaches do occur. In the absence of language withdrawing this provision from the arbitration requirement it is the duty of the court to resolve any doubts in favor of arbitration."

NOTE ON THE EFFECT OF SIGNIFICANTLY INCREASED COSTS UNDER UCC § 2–615

In the 1970s and '80s, a number of cases arose in which sellers sought relief under UCC § 2–615 based on significantly increased costs resulting from dramatic changes in the energy markets. Generally speaking, the sellers in these cases were unsuccessful. See, e.g., Iowa Electric Light and Power Co. v. Atlas Corp., 467 F.Supp. 129 (N.D.Iowa 1978), rev'd on other grounds, 603 F.2d 1301 (8th Cir.1979); Eastern Air Lines, Inc. v. Gulf Oil Corp., 415 F.Supp. 429 (S.D.Fla.1975).

A notable exception was Aluminum Co. of America ["ALCOA"] v. Essex Group, 499 F.Supp. 53 (W.D.Pa.1980). In December 1967, ALCOA and Essex entered a contract under which ALCOA would convert alumina supplied by Essex into aluminum. The contract was to run until the end of 1983, but Essex had the option to extend the contract until the end of 1988. The price for each pound of aluminum was calculated by a complex indexing formula: (1) Labor costs were to be escalated in proportion to changes in ALCOA's average hourly labor cost. (2) Non-labor costs were to be escalated in accordance with the Wholesale Price Index for Industrial Commodities, published by the U.S. Bureau of Labor Statistics (the "WPI–IC"). (3) The price as escalated by (1) and (2) was subject to an over-all cap of 65% of the price of a specified type of aluminum as published in a designated trade journal. This indexing formula was developed by ALCOA with the aid of Alan Greenspan, later Chairman of the Federal Reserve Bank, then a well-known economist.

Electric power is the principal non-labor cost factor in converting alumina into aluminum. Beginning in 1973, OPEC actions to increase oil prices, and unanticipated pollution-control costs, greatly increased ALCOA's cost for electricity, and electric power rates rose much more rapidly than did the WPI–IC. As a result, ALCOA stood to lose $75 million during the remaining term of the contract. ALCOA claimed excuse on the ground that the WPI–IC was incapable of reasonably reflecting ALCOA's changes in non-labor costs. The District Court held that ALCOA was entitled to relief on the grounds of mistake, impossibility, and frustration:

". . . ALCOA contends that both parties were mistaken in their estimate of the suitability of the WPI–IC as an objective index of ALCOA's non-labor production costs, and that their mistake is legally sufficient to warrant modification or avoidance of ALCOA's promise. . . .

". . . At the time the contract was made both parties. . . . [knew] that ALCOA sought a formula which would cover its out of pocket costs over the years and which would yield it a return of around four cents a pound. Both parties to the contract carefully examined the past performance of the WPI–IC before agreeing to its use. The testimony was clear that each assumed the Index was adequate to fulfill its purpose. This mistaken assumption was essentially a present actuarial error. . . .

"The cases clearly establish that mutual mistake lies in error concerning mutually understood material facts. . . .

"When ALCOA proposed the price formula which appears in the contract, Essex's management examined the past behavior of the indices for stability to assure they would not cause their final aluminum cost to deviate unacceptably from the going market rate. ALCOA's management was equally attentive to risk limitation. They went so far as to retain the noted economist Dr. Alan Greenspan as a consultant to advise them on the drafting of an objective pricing formula. They selected the WPI–IC as a pricing element for this long-term contract only after they assured themselves that it had closely tracked ALCOA's non-labor production costs for many years in the past and was highly likely to continue to do so in the future. In the context of the formation of the contract, it is untenable to argue that ALCOA implicitly or expressly assumed a limitless, if highly improbable, risk. On this record, the absence of an express floor limitation can only be understood to imply that the parties deemed the risk too remote and their meaning too clear to trifle with additional negotiation and drafting. . . .

"In the present case ALCOA has [also] satisfied the requirements of both [impossibility and frustration]. The impracticability of its performance is clear. The increase in its cost of performance is severe enough to warrant relief, and the other elements necessary for the granting of relief have been proven. . . ."

Based on these conclusions, the court reformed the contract so that the price to Essex would be the lesser of (A) the cap price stated in the contract (65% of a price of a specified type of aluminum published in a trade journal), or (B) the greater of (1) the price specified in the contract, computed according to its terms, or (2) a price that yielded ALCOA a profit of one cent per pound of aluminum converted from alumina.

Although *ALCOA* was seen by some commentators as either the brilliant dawn of a golden age or an awful descent into the fiery pit (depending on the commentator's perspective), it seems to have turned out to be an isolated judicial event. According to Wladis, Impracticability as Risk Allocation: The Effect of Changed Circumstances Upon Contract Obligations for the Sale of Goods, 22 Georgia L.Rev. 503, 586 n. 333 (1988), the procedural developments in the case after the District Court opinion were as follows: The case was appealed to the United States Court of Appeals for the Third Circuit, but the parties settled before the appeal was decided. The parties then made a joint motion requesting voluntary dismissal of the appeal, vacation of the District Court's judgment, and remand of the case to the District Court with directions to dismiss. The Third Circuit granted this relief, and District Court Judge Teitelbaum dismissed the action. Wladis reports that on the basis of this procedural history, the *ALCOA* opinion was characterized to him by judges of the Third Circuit as having only the precedential value of a law review article.

ALAMANCE COUNTY BOARD OF EDUCATION
v. BOBBY MURRAY CHEVROLET, INC.

Court of Appeals of North Carolina, 1996.
121 N.C.App. 222, 465 S.E.2d 306.

JOHN, Judge.

Defendant Bobby Murray Chevrolet, Inc. (Bobby Murray) appeals the trial court's entry of summary judgment in favor of plaintiffs, a number of

North Carolina school boards (plaintiffs; school boards), on their respective claims for breach of contract. Defendant contends application of N.C.G.S. § 25–2–615 (1995) regarding commercial impracticability operates under the facts of the case *sub judice* to excuse its performance under the contracts with plaintiffs. We disagree.

Pertinent factual and procedural information is as follows: Bobby Murray, a General Motors franchisee, received an invitation on or about 7 April 1989 to bid on approximately 1200 school bus chassis from the North Carolina Department of Administration's Division of Purchase and Contract (the Division). The Division assumes responsibility for contracting with various vendors of supplies and equipment on behalf of state entities, including boards of education. As is customary, the Division on this occasion sent bid invitations containing the required chassis specifications to a number of motor vehicle dealers.

After consulting with the GMC Truck Division (GM Truck) of defendant General Motors Corporation (GM) regarding prices and availability, Bobby Murray proposed to supply several different sizes of chassis at specified prices. The chassis were described as "Chevrolet" brand in the bid, but were to be manufactured by GM Truck.

Bobby Murray's bid was accepted by the Division, and the initial deadline for orders pursuant to the contract was set at 31 July 1990. All orders submitted prior to this date were properly filled by Bobby Murray and are not the subject of the instant litigation.

On 26 July 1990, the Environmental Protection Agency (EPA) enacted Federal Emissions Standards changes for heavy duty diesel engines, thereby rendering the 8.2N diesel engine described in Bobby Murray's bid out of compliance with the regulations effective 1 January 1991.

In mid-July 1990, GM tendered an extension of time for ordering chassis from 31 July to 31 August 1990. Bobby Murray conveyed this option to the Division, which accepted the extension. Shortly thereafter, GM requested the cut-off date for orders be moved forward to 14 August. The Division agreed and plaintiffs' orders were transmitted to Bobby Murray between 1 August 1990 and 14 August 1990. There is no contention these orders were not timely received by Bobby Murray or GM.

On 10 August 1990, Bobby Murray received a message from GM through its Dealer Communication System (DCS), a computer network linking GM with its dealers, setting the final chassis buildout date at the week of 10 December 1990, but warning that estimated production dates could be pushed back due to a potential shortage of the requisite brand of automatic transmission (Allison automatic transmissions). On 24 August 1990, in a DCS message to Bobby Murray, GM reiterated that due to "the uncertainty of major component availability," no further orders for school bus chassis would be accepted.

On 30 November 1990, another DCS message to Bobby Murray indicated that the chassis orders placed between 1 August and 14 August 1990 would not be filled due to unavailability of Allison automatic transmissions. Bobby Murray contacted GMC Truck on or about 11 December 1990 and learned that none of the chassis were to be built prior to the end of December because the Allison transmissions would not be provided until February or March

1991. At that point, however, installation of the 8.2N diesel engines would be illegal in consequence of the modified EPA regulations. On or about 11 December 1990, Bobby Murray notified the Division the chassis could not be supplied.

On or about 23 January 1991, the Division informed Bobby Murray the chassis were being purchased from another source, and that it intended to hold Bobby Murray liable for any excess in cost. The substitute chassis were later obtained by plaintiffs, who subsequently filed suit against Bobby Murray for a total of $150,152.94, representing the difference between the bid prices and the actual amounts expended by plaintiffs in purchasing similar chassis. In its answer and third-party complaint against GM, Bobby Murray claimed, *inter alia,* that GM breached its contract with Bobby Murray to provide the chassis at issue.... Thereafter, ... the plaintiffs ... filed motions for summary judgment.

Summary judgment was entered against Bobby Murray and in favor of plaintiffs 18 April 1994 by Judge F. Fetzer Mills in the amount of $150,152.94 plus interest at 8% per annum from 11 December 1990 until paid....

Bobby Murray admits the bus chassis ordered by plaintiff school boards were never delivered. However, Bobby Murray contends its lack of performance should be excused pursuant to N.C.G.S. § 25–2–615 (1995) which reads:

> (a) Delay in delivery or nondelivery in whole or in part by a seller who complies with paragraphs (b) and (c) is not a breach of his duty under a contract for sale *if performance as agreed has been made impracticable by the occurrence of a contingency the nonoccurrence of which was a basic assumption on which the contract was made or by compliance in good faith with any applicable foreign or domestic governmental regulation* or order whether or not it later proves to be invalid....

> (c) The seller must notify the buyer seasonably that there will be delay or nondelivery....

Bobby Murray asserts two arguments based upon the foregoing statute. It contends the failure of GM to supply the bus chassis was "a contingency the nonoccurrence of which" was a basic assumption of the underlying contracts between Bobby Murray and plaintiffs. Second, Bobby Murray claims governmental regulation prohibiting the installation of the 8.2N engine after 1 January 1991 was an intervening factor which should operate as an excuse....

Initially, Bobby Murray contends an implied condition of its contract with plaintiffs was the ability of GM to manufacture and supply the ordered bus chassis. We agree that when an exclusive source of supply is specified in a contract or may be implied by circumstances to have been contemplated by the parties, failure of that source may excuse the promisor from performance. N.C.G.S. § 25–2–615, Official Comment 5. However, neither contingency is reflected in the record herein.

Bobby Murray insists in its brief that "[a]ppellant disclosed in the bid that the chassis would be manufactured by Chevrolet and Plaintiff–Appellees had knowledge that Appellant's sole source of supply was General Motors." However, Bobby Murray points to no record evidence of such knowledge on the part of plaintiffs, and appears to rely solely upon its status as a GM franchisee to support its assertion.

By contrast, we note that the "General Contract Terms and Conditions" on Form TC–1, incorporated into the bid document, contain the following section entitled "MANUFACTURER'S NAMES":

> Any manufacturers' names, trade names, brand names, information and/or catalog numbers used herein are for purpose(s) of description and establishing general quality levels. Such references are not intended to be restrictive and products of any manufacturer may be offered.

Further, no clause in the contract between plaintiffs and Bobby Murray conditioned the latter's performance on its ability to obtain bus chassis from its manufacturer. *See* William H. Henning & George I. Wallach, *The Law of Sales Under the Uniform Commercial Code,* ¶ 5.10[2], S5–4 (1994 Supplement) (generally, where seller fails to make contract with buyer contingent on adequate supply, courts reluctant to excuse seller). Plaintiffs aptly point to Richard M. Smith and Donald F. Clifford, Jr., *North Carolina Practice, Uniform Commercial Code Forms Annotated,* Vol. 1, § 2–615, Form 3 (1968), which indicates a seller of goods may limit its liability by inclusion of the following "Single Source Clause":

> It is expressly understood that the seller has available only one source, [*name of single source*], of [*address*], for the [*name or identify the raw materials obtained by the seller from the single source*] used by the seller in the manufacture of the goods for the buyer under this contract. In the event of any interference or cessation of the supply from the seller's source of supply, the seller shall be temporarily, proportionately, or permanently relieved of liability under this contract, depending upon whether the interruption of the source of supply is a temporary interruption, a reduced delivery of materials, or a permanent cessation of supply.

Moreover, assuming *arguendo* GM *was* contemplated by the parties as Bobby Murray's exclusive source, the record reflects that Bobby Murray assumed the risk of its failure to supply the vehicles, as it was foreseeable that GM might not supply the bus chassis. Failure to make express provision for a foreseeable contingency in a sales contract implicitly places the burden of loss on the seller when the contingency comes to fruition. *Barbarossa & Sons, Inc. v. Iten Chevrolet, Inc.,* 265 N.W.2d 655, 659 (Minn.1978) (contingency that seller would be unable to procure truck from General Motors "was clearly . . . foreseen . . . before entering the contract," and thus seller not excused).

Foreseeability under § 2–615 is an objective standard; it matters not whether the seller thought a certain event would or would not occur, but what contingencies were reasonably foreseeable at the time the contract was made. Henning & Wallach, *supra,* at ¶ 5.10[2], 5–36 (1992). Examination of the record reveals that cancellation of chassis orders by GM was a risk reasonably foreseeable to Bobby Murray.

For example, the "Dealer Sales and Service Agreement" between Bobby Murray and GM provides as follows:

> Dealer's order for . . . Motor Vehicles are not binding on . . . [GM] until accepted by [GM]. . . . Orders are accepted by [GM] when Released to Production.

Vehicle orders thus bind GM only upon "Release to Production" of the subject vehicles. The bus chassis at issue herein were never "released to production."

The same document also suggests numerous factors which might affect the availability of vehicles, including "component availability" and "governmental regulations," and indicates that GM reserved the discretion to distribute vehicles based upon its own judgment.

Official Comment 5 of N.C.G.S. § 25–2–615, regarding failure of sources of supply, warns: "There is no excuse under this section, however, unless the seller has employed all due measures to assure himself that his source will not fail." The comment cites *Canadian Industrial Alcohol Co. v. Dunbar Molasses Co.,* 179 N.E. 383 (1932), in which a middleman contracted to supply a buyer with molasses. When the middleman's source was unable to deliver the required amount of molasses, the former claimed the excuse of impossibility. The court declined "to accept this defense because the middleman had not even bothered to obtain a contract from the refinery to cover his obligations." Henning & Wallach, *supra,* at ¶ 5.10[1], 5–35 (1992); *cf. Lane v. Coe,* 262 N.C. 8, 136 S.E.2d 269 (1964) (when defendant's ability to perform depends upon cooperation of third party, defendant cannot rely on third party's later refusal to cooperate to claim impossibility).

Similarly, the record herein contains no evidence of a contract between Bobby Murray and GM to ensure delivery of the ordered chassis. Robin J. Fleming, fleet sales manager of Bobby Murray, in deposition simply claimed GM had never before failed to produce vehicles for which it had taken orders while he had been with Bobby Murray, notwithstanding provisions in the "Dealer Sales and Service Agreement" to the effect that orders did not bind GM until the vehicles were "Released to Production" and that certain specified factors might affect production.

Moreover, during the time orders were accepted from plaintiffs, Bobby Murray also received a DCS message revealing that GM was experiencing shortages of Allison automatic transmissions. Bobby Murray therefore also had actual notice its source of supply might fail.

We next examine Bobby Murray's contention its performance should be excused in consequence of intervening governmental regulations. Generally, governmental regulations do not excuse performance under a contract where a party has assumed the risk of such regulation. Henning & Wallach, *supra,* at ¶ 5.10, 5–33 (1992). The contract between the parties *sub judice,* in its "General Contract Terms and Conditions", Form TC–1, provided as follows:

> GOVERNMENTAL RESTRICTIONS: In the event any Governmental restrictions may be imposed which would necessitate alteration of the material, quality, workmanship or performance of the items offered on this proposal prior to their delivery, it shall be the responsibility of the successful bidder to notify this Division at once, indicating in his letter the specific regulation which required such alterations. The State reserves the right to accept any such alterations, including any price adjustments occasioned thereby, or to cancel the contract.

Bobby Murray, by terms of the parties' agreement, accepted responsibility for keeping abreast of governmental regulations bearing upon the contract.

In addition, Bobby Murray was on notice 26 July 1990 that new emissions standards would preclude, effective 1 January 1991, production of bus chassis using the 8.2N engine specified in its bid. Nothing in the record indicates that this information was conveyed to plaintiffs. Bobby Murray was further notified 10 August 1990 that production dates could be pushed beyond December 1990. The record contains no evidence that Bobby Murray explored with plaintiffs, or otherwise, alternative methods of meeting its contractual obligations. Under these circumstances, equity dictates that excuse by governmental regulation be unavailable to Bobby Murray. *See* N.C.G.S. § 25–1–103 (1995) ("Unless displaced by the particular provisions of this chapter, the principles of law and equity ... shall supplement its provisions."). "The absence of fault is ... an important part of a Section 2–615 defense." Henning & Wallach, *supra,* at ¶ 5.10[1], 5–34 (1992). In sum, governmental regulations do not supervene in this case.

Bobby Murray also argues that there is a material issue of fact whether seasonable notice was given plaintiffs that Bobby Murray would be unable to perform. However, in that we have determined Bobby Murray does not succeed under N.C.G.S. § 25–2–615(a), it is unnecessary to address N.C.G.S. § 25–2–615(c), dealing with the requirement that timely notice be given a buyer....

Affirmed.

JOHNSON and MARK D. MARTIN, JJ., concur.

———

SELLAND PONTIAC–GMC, INC. v. KING, 384 N.W.2d 490 (Minn. App.1986). Selland Pontiac had lined up a customer to buy four buses that Selland would supply. To fill the customer's order, Selland entered into a written contract with George King. Under that contract, Selland would supply four chassis to King, and King would furnish bodies which he would attach to the chassis. The contract between Selland and King indicated that the bodies would be manufactured for King by Superior Manufacturing in Morris, Manitoba. In reliance on the contract, Selland ordered four bus chassis from General Motors. Soon thereafter, Superior went out of business, and the bodies were never manufactured. In December 1983, Selland's customer cancelled its order. Selland then sold the four chassis at a loss, and sued King for damages. Held, for King.

" ... Supply of Superior bus bodies was a basic assumption on which the contract was made. These became impracticable to supply when Superior ceased manufacturing.

"Appellant argues that the trial court improperly applied [UCC § 2–615]. In *Barbarossa & Sons v. Iten Chevrolet, Inc.,* 265 N.W.2d 655 (Minn.1978) the supreme court applied [§ 2–615] and affirmed judgment for the buyer where the manufacturer's supply of seller's order was not a basic assumption of the contract and the contract contained no escape clause. The manufacturer, General Motors, was not mentioned in the contract as the source of supply. General Motors had cancelled several orders at this time due to a shortage. The court stated:

A partial failure of a seller's source of supply generally has been treated as a foreseeable contingency, the risk of which is allocated to the seller absent a specific provision to the contrary in the contract.

Id. at 659–60 (citations omitted).

"The trial court's finding of no breach of contract here is consistent with *Barbarossa's* holding that the contract was breached under [§ 2–615]. Here the seller's supplier was specified in the contract. Superior was also specified in King's price quotation to Selland. In *Barbarossa* the supplier did not cease to manufacture, but simply cancelled the orders of some of its dealers. Here both parties testified that they had no knowledge of Superior's questionable financial circumstances when they contracted and King did not expressly assume the risk of Superior's ceasing production."

NOTE ON CONTRACTS TO SELL CROPS

In a recurring type of case, a farmer contracts to sell a specified amount of an agricultural product. The farmer fails to deliver part or all of the specified amount, and the buyer brings suit. The farmer claims, as a defense, that the crops he raised on his farm were insufficient to satisfy the contract because of drought, disease, or the like. Typically in these cases there is a written contract, which does not explicitly provide that the product to be delivered will be from a specific farm.

The results in the cases are divided, but farmers seem to lose these cases more often than they win them. See, e.g., Bunge Corporation v. Recker, 519 F.2d 449 (8th Cir.1975) (buyer wins); Campbell v. Hostetter Farms, Inc., 251 Pa.Super. 232, 380 A.2d 463 (1977) (farmer wins); Bunge Corp. v. Miller, 381 F.Supp. 176 (W.D.Tenn.1974) (buyer wins); Wickliffe Farms, Inc. v. Owensboro Grain Co., 684 S.W.2d 17 (Ky.App.1984) (buyer wins); Colley v. Bi–State, Inc., 21 Wash.App. 769, 586 P.2d 908 (1978) (buyer wins); Paymaster Oil Mill Co. v. Mitchell, 319 So.2d 652 (Miss.1975) (farmer wins).

In some of the cases, the decision is tipped by a trade usage in the local region or by some phrase in the contract. In fact, the rhetoric of these cases is often as much or more in terms of the parol evidence rule as in terms of the rules governing the effect of unexpected circumstances. The farmer argues that although the written contract simply provided for delivery of a specified amount of some agricultural product, evidence of the prior negotiations shows that the parties contemplated that the product would consist of a crop raised on the farmer's own land. (In particular, the farmer may try to show that the amount of product to be delivered under the contract was arrived at by an agreed-upon calculation in which the number of acres in his farm was multiplied by the expected yield per acre.) The buyer counters that this evidence is inadmissible under the parol evidence rule. If the court holds the evidence is admissible, the farmer wins; if the court holds the evidence is inadmissible, the buyer wins. Another, perhaps more realistic way of putting this is that if the court thinks the farmer should win, it holds that the parol evidence rule is inapplicable; if the court thinks the buyer should win, it holds that the farmer's evidence is barred by the parol evidence rule.

WICKLIFFE FARMS, INC. v. OWENSBORO GRAIN CO., 684 S.W.2d 17 (1984). Seller, a farmer, entered into a contract with Buyer for the sale of corn. Seller failed to deliver the corn, and Buyer sued for breach. Seller defended on the ground that his crop had failed. In holding for Buyer, the court stressed that Buyer had purchased the corn for resale immediately after the contract was made:

> The undisputed admissible material facts before the trial court prove the ordinary "futures contract" of an agreement to buy and sell a quantity of grain at a given price per bushel, to be delivered at a future date, the purchaser thereafter arranging a "back to back" sale of the commodity. The sellers in such a transaction gamble the market price will not be greater at the time of delivery and the buyers gamble that it will not be lower. All [the purchaser] was interested in was buying 35,000 bushels of No. 2 white corn from Wickliffe at $3.70 per bushel and nothing more. Its business was not to speculate either in the weather, crop yield or fluctuation of market price. It guaranteed its profit by selling immediately. Wickliffe's only interest was to sell it. It chose to contract to deliver the corn at a given price at a given future date and failed to do so.

KRELL v. HENRY

In the Court of Appeal, 1903.
[1903] 2 K.B. 740.

Appeal from a decision of DARLING, J.

The plaintiff, Paul Krell, sued the defendant, C.S. Henry, for £50, being the balance of a sum of £75, for which the defendant had agreed to hire a flat at 56A, Pall Mall on the days of June 26 and 27, for the purpose of viewing the processions to be held in connection with the coronation of His Majesty. The defendant denied his liability, and counterclaimed for the return of the sum of £25, which had been paid as a deposit, on the ground that, the processions not having taken place owing to the serious illness of the King, there had been a total failure of consideration for the contract entered into by him.

The facts, which were not disputed, were as follows. The plaintiff on leaving the country in March, 1902, left instructions with his solicitor to let his suite of chambers at 56A, Pall Mall on such terms and for such period (not exceeding six months) as he thought proper. On June 17, 1902, the defendant noticed an announcement in the windows of the plaintiff's flat to the effect that windows to view the coronation processions were to be let. The defendant interviewed the housekeeper on the subject, when it was pointed out to him what a good view of the procession could be obtained from the premises, and he eventually agreed with the housekeeper to take the suite for the two days in question for a sum of £75.

On June 20 the defendant wrote the following letter to the plaintiff's solicitor:—

> "I am in receipt of yours of the 18th instant, inclosing form of agreement for the suite of chambers on the third floor at 56A, Pall Mall, which I have agreed to take for the two days, the 26th and 27th instant, for the sum of £75. For reasons given you I cannot enter into the agreement, but as arranged over the telephone I inclose herewith cheque for £25 as deposit, and will thank you to confirm to me that I shall have

the entire use of these rooms during the days (not the nights) of the 26th and 27th instant. You may rely that every care will be taken of the premises and their contents. On the 24th inst. I will pay the balance, viz., £50, to complete the £75 agreed upon."

On the same day the defendant received the following reply from the plaintiff's solicitor:—

"I am in receipt of your letter of today's date inclosing cheque for £25 deposit on your agreeing to take Mr. Krell's chambers on the third floor at 56A, Pall Mall for the two days, the 26th and 27th June, and I confirm the agreement that you are to have the entire use of these rooms during the days (but not the nights), the balance, £50, to be paid to me on Tuesday next the 24th instant."

The processions not having taken place on the days originally appointed, namely, June 26 and 27, the defendant declined to pay the balance of £50 alleged to be due from him under the contract in writing of June 20 constituted by the above two letters. Hence the present action.

Darling J., on August 11, 1902, held upon the authority of Taylor v. Caldwell and The Moorcock (1889, 14 P.D. 64), that there was an implied condition in the contract that the procession should take place, and gave judgment for the defendant on the claim and counterclaim.

The plaintiff appealed.

Spencer Bower, K.C., and Holman Gregory, for the plaintiff. In the contract nothing is said about the coronation procession, but it is admitted that both parties expected that there would be a procession, and that the price to be paid for the rooms was fixed with reference to the expected procession. Darling J. held that both the claim and the counterclaim were governed by Taylor v. Caldwell, and that there was an implied term in the contract that the procession should take place. It is submitted that the learned judge was wrong. If he was right, the result would be that in every case of this kind an unremunerated promisor will be in effect an insurer of the hopes and expectations of the promisee.... In order that the person who has contracted to pay the price should be excused from doing so, there must be (1) no default on his part; (2) either the physical extinction or the not coming into existence of the subject-matter of the contract; (3) the performance of the contract must have been thereby rendered impossible.

In the present case there has been no default on the part of the defendant. But there has been no physical extinction of the subject-matter, and the performance of the contract was quite possible....

VAUGHAN WILLIAMS, L.J. read the following written judgment:—The real question in this case is the extent of the application in English law of the principle of the Roman law which has been adopted and acted on in many English decisions, and notably in the case of Taylor v. Caldwell.... It is said, on the one side, that the specified thing, state of things, or condition the continued existence of which is necessary for the fulfilment of the contract, so that the parties entering into the contract must have contemplated the continued existence of that thing, condition, or state of things as the foundation of what was to be done under the contract, is limited to things which are either the subject-matter of the contract or a condition or state of things, present or anticipated, which is expressly mentioned in the contract. But, on the other side, it is said that the condition or state of things need not be expressly specified, but that it is sufficient if that condition or state of things clearly appears by extrinsic evidence to have been assumed by the parties to be the foundation or basis of the contract, and the event which causes the impossibility is of such a character that it cannot reasonably be supposed to have been in the contemplation of the contracting parties when the contract was made. In such a case the contracting parties will not be held bound by the general words which, though large enough to include, were not used with reference to a possibility of a particular event rendering performance of the contract impossible. I do not think that the principle of the civil law as introduced into the English law is limited to cases in which the event causing the impossibility of performance is the destruction or nonexistence of some thing which is the subject-matter of the contract or of some condition or state of things expressly specified as a condition of it. I think that you first have to ascertain, not necessarily from the terms of the contract, but, if required, from necessary inferences, drawn from surrounding circumstances recognized by both contracting parties, what is the substance of the contract, and then to ask the question whether that substantial contract needs for its foundation the assumption of the existence of a particular state of things. If it does, this will limit the operation of the general words, and in such case, if the contract becomes impossible of performance by reason of the nonexistence of the state of things assumed by both contracting parties as the foundation of the contract, there will be no breach of the contract thus limited. . . .

In my judgment [in this case] the use of the rooms was let and taken for the purpose of seeing the Royal procession. It was not a demise of the rooms, or even an agreement to let and take the rooms. It is a licence to use rooms for a particular purpose and none other. And in my judgment the taking place of those processions on the days proclaimed along the proclaimed route, which passed 56A, Pall Mall, was regarded by both contracting parties as the foundation of the contract; and I think that it cannot reasonably be supposed to have been in the contemplation of the contracting parties, when the contract was made, that the coronation would not be held on the proclaimed days, or the processions not take place on those days along the proclaimed route; and I think that the words imposing on the defendant the obligation to accept and pay for the use of the rooms for the named days, although general and unconditional, were not used with reference to the possibility of the particular contingency which afterwards occurred.

It was suggested in the course of the argument that if the occurrence, on the proclaimed days, of the coronation and the procession in this case were the foundation of the contract, and if the general words are thereby limited or qualified, so that in the event of the non-occurrence of the coronation and procession along the proclaimed route they would discharge both parties from further performance of the contract, it would follow that if a cabman was engaged to take some one to Epsom on Derby Day at a suitable enhanced price for such a journey, say £10, both parties to the contract would be discharged in the contingency of the race at Epsom for some reason becoming impossible; but I do not think this follows, for I do not think that in the cab case the happening of the race would be the foundation of the contract. No doubt the purpose of the engager would be to go to see the Derby, and the price would be proportionately high; but the cab had no special qualifications for the purpose which led to the selection of the cab for this particular occasion. Any other cab would have done as well. Moreover, I think, that under the cab contract, the hirer, even if the race went off, could have said, "Drive me to Epsom; I will pay you the agreed sum; you have nothing to do with the purpose for which I hired the cab," and that if the cabman refused he would have been guilty of a breach of contract, there being nothing to qualify his promise to drive the hirer to Epsom on a particular day. Whereas in the case of the coronation, there is not merely the purpose of the hirer to see the coronation procession, but it is the coronation procession and the relative position of the rooms which is the basis of the contract as much for the lessor as the hirer; and I think that if the King, before the coronation day and after the contract, had died, the hirer could not have insisted on having the rooms on the days named. It could not in the cab case be reasonably said that seeing the Derby race was the foundation of the contract, as it was of the licence in this case. Whereas in the present case, where the rooms were offered and taken, by reason of their peculiar suitability from the position of the rooms for a view of the coronation procession, surely the view of the coronation procession was the foundation of the contract, which is a very different thing from the purpose of the man who engaged the cab—namely, to see the race—being held to be the foundation of the contract.

Each case must be judged by its own circumstances. In each case one must ask oneself, first, what, having regard to all the circumstances, was the foundation of the contract? Secondly, was the performance of the contract prevented? Thirdly, was the event which prevented the performance of the contract of such a character that it cannot reasonably be said to have been in the contemplation of the parties at the date of the contract? If all these questions are answered in the affirmative (as I think they should be in this case), I think both parties are discharged from further performance of the contract. . . .

This disposes of the plaintiff's claim for £50 unpaid balance of the price agreed to be paid for the use of the rooms. The defendant at one time set up a cross-claim for the return of the £25 he paid at the date of the contract. As that claim is now withdrawn it is unnecessary to say anything about it. . . . I think this appeal ought to be dismissed.

[The concurring opinions of Romer, L.J., and Stirling, L.J., are omitted.]

Appeal dismissed.

––––––––

WLADIS, COMMON LAW AND UNCOMMON EVENTS: THE DE-VELOPMENT OF THE DOCTRINE OF IMPOSSIBILITY OF PER-FORMANCE IN ENGLISH CONTRACT LAW, 75 Geo.L.J. 1575, 1609, 1618 (1987). "The facts giving rise to the coronation cases may be stated briefly: Edward VII was to be crowned on Thursday, June 26, 1902, in Westminster Abbey. There was to be a coronation procession that day between the royal residence at Buckingham Palace and the Abbey, and a lengthier one [on June 27] throughout the city of London. In addition, on Saturday, June 28, a naval review of the fleet was to take place. Flats were let, grandstands erected, and seats sold along the routes of the processions. Boats were also chartered to take the public to the naval review. However, during the morning of June 24 it was determined that Edward, who had been suffering from appendicitis, needed to undergo surgery. Later that day it was announced that the coronation would be postponed and the naval review not held. . . .

" . . . The coronation events were not canceled, but only postponed. The procession [scheduled for] June 26 eventually took place on August 9 and proceeded along the same route as had originally been planned. The procession scheduled for June 27 occurred on October 25 and followed as nearly as possible the original route. Even the naval review that had been canceled was rescheduled and held on August 16."

LLOYD v. MURPHY, 25 Cal.2d 48, 153 P.2d 47 (1944) (Traynor, J.). "The question in cases involving frustration is whether the equities of the case, considered in the light of sound public policy, require placing the risk of a disruption or complete destruction of the contract equilibrium on defendant or plaintiff under the circumstances of a given case . . . and the answer depends on whether an unanticipated circumstance, the risk of which should not be fairly thrown on the promisor, has made performance vitally different from what was reasonably to be expected."

ALFRED MARKS REALTY CO. v. HOTEL HERMITAGE CO., 170 App.Div. 484, 156 N.Y.S. 179 (1915). In January 1914, plaintiff undertook the publication of a "Souvenir and Program of International Yacht Races," the races being scheduled to take place in September. Defendant contracted for an advertisement in this program. Under its contract, defendant was to pay for the advertisement "upon publication and delivery of one copy." Early in August, plaintiff put out an anticipatory issue of about 3000 copies. In mid-August, the races were cancelled because of the outbreak of the European war. On August 25, a copy of the program was sent to defendant, with a demand for payment. Defendant did not pay, and plaintiff sued for the agreed price of the advertisement. Held, for defendant. Cancellation of the races frustrated the entire design of the project; a souvenir cannot recall what has not taken place. The partial and anticipatory issue of the program before the cancellation of the races did not constitute "publication" in the sense of the contract.

LA CUMBRE GOLF & COUNTRY CLUB v. SANTA BARBARA HOTEL CO., 205 Cal. 422, 271 P. 476 (1928). Santa Barbara Hotel Co. owned and operated the Ambassador Hotel. Under a contract between Santa Barbara and the La Cumbre Golf and Country Club, La Cumbre extended privileges at its club to guests at the Ambassador. In 1920, Santa Barbara wanted to purchase and operate a bus between the Ambassador and the club, provided the golf privileges were extended over an additional period of time. Accordingly, the parties made a contract for a period ending December 31, 1923, under which La Cumbre agreed that it would grant all the privileges of membership to guests at the Ambassador, and Santa Barbara agreed to be responsible for the guests' greens fees and to pay La Cumbre $300 a month. In April 1921, the Ambassador burned down. Santa Barbara stopped making payments under the contract, and La Cumbre sued for the balance due, $7200. Held, for Santa Barbara. It was an implied condition of the contract that there would be guests in the Ambassador.

CHASE PRECAST CORP. v. JOHN J. PAONESSA CO., 409 Mass. 371, 566 N.E.2d 603 (1991). In 1982, the Commonwealth of Massachusetts, through the Department of Public Works (the department), entered into two contracts with Paonessa for resurfacing and improvements to two stretches of Route 128. Part of each contract called for replacing a grass median strip between the north– and south–bound lanes with concrete surfacing and precast concrete median barriers. Paonessa then entered into two contracts with Chase, under which Chase was to supply 25,800 linear feet of precast concrete median barriers according to the specifications of the department for highway construction. The quantity and type of barriers to be supplied were specified in two purchase orders prepared by Chase.

The highway reconstruction began in the spring of 1983. By late May, the department was receiving protests from angry residents who objected to use of the concrete median barriers and removal of the grass median strip. Paonessa and Chase became aware of the protest around June 1. On June 6, a group of about 100 citizens filed an action in the Superior Court to stop installation of the concrete median barriers and other aspects of the work. On June 7, anticipating modification by the department, Paonessa notified Chase by letter to stop producing concrete barriers for the projects. Chase did so upon receipt of the letter the following day. On June 17, the department and the citizens' group entered into a settlement which provided, in part, that no additional concrete median barriers would be installed. On June 23, the department deleted the permanent concrete median barriers item from its contracts with Paonessa.

Before stopping production on June 8, Chase had produced approximately one-half of the concrete median barriers called for by its contracts with Paonessa, and had delivered most of them to the construction sites. Paonessa paid Chase, at the contract price, for all the barriers that Chase had produced. Chase suffered no out-of-pocket expense as a result of cancellation of the remaining portion of barriers.

Chase brought an action against Paonessa to recover its anticipated profit on the amount of median barriers called for by its supply contracts with Paonessa but not produced. After a jury-waived trial, a Superior Court judge ruled for Paonessa on the basis of impossibility of performance. The Appeals Court affirmed, noting that the doctrine of frustration of purpose more accurately described the basis of the trial judge's decision than the doctrine of impossibility. The Massachusetts Supreme Judicial Court agreed:

> Paonessa bore no responsibility for the department's elimination of the median barriers from the projects. Therefore, whether it can rely on the defense of frustration turns on whether elimination of the barriers was a risk allocated by the contracts to Paonessa. *Mishara Constr. Co.,*

supra, 365 Mass. [122,] at 129, 310 N.E.2d 363 [1974], articulates the relevant test:

> "The question is, given the commercial circumstances in which the parties dealt: Was the contingency which developed one which the parties could reasonably be thought to have foreseen as a real possibility which could affect performance? Was it one of that variety of risks which the parties were tacitly assigning to the promisor by their failure to provide for it explicitly? If it was, performance will be required. If it could not be so considered, performance is excused."

This is a question for the trier of fact. *Id.* at 127, 130, 310 N.E.2d 363.

————

POWER ENGINEERING & MANUFACTURING, LTD. v. KRUG INTERNATIONAL, 501 N.W.2d 490 (Iowa 1993). Tripod Laing had contracted to deliver to Iraqi Airways, in Iraq, an aeromedical equipment laboratory. One part of the laboratory was a human centrifuge to train jet pilots, and Tripod Laing contracted with Krug to build the centrifuge. Krug, in turn, contracted with Power Engineering for the construction of a gear box, to be used as a part of the centrifuge, for $149,700. Power Engineering did not know the identity of either Krug's buyer (Tripod Laing) or the ultimate consumer (Iraqi Airways). During the initial manufacturing stages, Krug paid Power Engineering $75,000. The gear box was completed in late July, and a minor adjustment requested by Krug was completed in early August. On August 7, Krug authorized Power Engineering to ship the gear box.

The Gulf War with Iraq broke out on or about August 6, 1990. The United Nations immediately implemented an embargo against all shipments to Iraq. Reacting to the embargo, on August 7 Tripod Laing directed Krug to carry out no more work and expend no more money until further notice. Several days later, Krug learned that Power Engineering had not yet shipped the gear box, and directed Power Engineering not to ship it. The gear box remained in storage, because Krug refused to have it shipped. Power Engineering then brought suit for the balance of the purchase price. Held, for Power Engineering.

"Under [UCC § 2–615] a buyer wishing to escape from liability for nonperformance must make a three-pronged showing:

(1) Its performance has become commercially impracticable,

(2) By either

(a) the occurrence of an unforeseen contingency the nonoccurrence of which was a basic assumption on which the contract was made, or

(b) compliance in good faith with any applicable foreign or domestic governmental regulation or order whether or not it later proves to be invalid, and

(3) It had not assumed the risk of the contingency or governmental regulation.

"We think the theory has no application here. In the first place Krug's performance cannot truly be said to be commercially impracticable.... The embargo does not prevent Krug from fulfilling its contractual obligations with

Power Engineering. Although the embargo prevents products from being shipped to Iraq, it does not prohibit a domestic purchaser from buying, from a domestic manufacturer, a machinery component part intended for shipment there.

"We do not believe that the stop order further up the chain of contracts in this case constitutes an 'occurrence of a contingency the nonoccurrence of which was a basic assumption on which the contract was made.' Although Krug may have made assumptions regarding such unforeseen contingencies, Power Engineering was not privy to Krug's planned use of the gear box. Under the circumstances Krug must be found to have assumed the risk that its purchaser would not, or could not, perform."

*

Part VI

PROBLEMS INVOLVING
PERSONS OTHER THAN
THE PARTIES TO THE
ORIGINAL CONTRACT

Chapter 20

THIRD–PARTY BENEFICIARIES

PRELIMINARY ANALYSIS OF THE
PROBLEM OF THIS CHAPTER

The basic situation dealt with in this Chapter can be stated as follows: A promises B for a valid consideration that A will render a designated performance. The performance will benefit C. To what extent shall the law protect C's interest in the contract between A and B?

This problem can be attacked in two different ways: In a formal way, as a problem of legal doctrine, or in a substantive way, as a problem of policy, morals, and experience. Under a formal methodology, the problem is one of deducing C's rights, or lack of rights, from some general premise. Under a substantive methodology, the problem is one of developing the best set of rules by applying the relevant policy, moral, and empirical propositions. The crucial inquiries from a substantive point of view are: Is there a need to grant legal protection to C's interest in the contract? If so, what undesirable consequences, if any, would be entailed in granting that protection?

When the question is raised in this form, it is at once apparent that it is necessary to know something about the objectives of the parties. For example, in exacting the promise from A, B's motive may have been that of conferring a gift on C, who is perhaps a favorite nephew or other relative. If B dies before A has conferred the promised benefit on C, then if C is denied a right to enforce the contract, it may not be carried out at all, because B's executor, who may represent legatees who are in competition with C, will have no incentive to bring a suit on C's behalf. In this particular situation, therefore, there is a sound reason for permitting a suit by C, because otherwise B's intent may be defeated. On the other hand, to grant a broad and unlimited protection to C's interest in the agreement may be going too far. For example, if B has not died but is still alive and now wishes to rescind or modify the agreement between himself and A, how shall we resolve a possible conflict of interest between B and C? A has promised only one performance, and in that sense is subject to one claim only. But B is interested in that claim as promisee and as the one who furnished the consideration for it, while C is interested in it as the designated recipient of the benefit. How shall we partition the control over this claim between B and C when they come in conflict?

A closer study of these concrete problems must be postponed until actual cases are presented. It is apparent, however, that substantive methodology for resolving this problem inevitably drives the courts in the direction of a close inquiry into the objectives and motives of the parties. That is not true of formal methodology. The formal methodology of classical contract law assumed that before any inquiry is made concerning the advisability of permitting or denying a suit by C, weight, perhaps decisive weight, must be given to an obstacle supposedly thought to be presented by an axiomatic premise, namely, that only a person who is a party to a contract can sue on it or have rights under it.

The objection that C is not "a party to the contract" was more specifically defined in three different ways: (1) The promise by A was not made *to* C, but to B. (The objection that C was not the promisee is one that was chiefly raised in American jurisdictions.) (2) The *consideration* did not move from C, but from B. (This seems to have been the controlling objection in England.) (3) C did not *assent* to the contract, because the expression of agreement ran between A and B. (This is the objection that has been most bothersome for legal theorists in the civil law.) The first objection assumes that only one to whom a promise is made can enforce the promise; the second, that only one who furnishes the consideration has rights under a contract; the third, that only one who has joined in the expression of mutual assent has rights under a contract.

None of these axiomatic objections involves any conscious weighing of the advantages or disadvantages of allowing suit by C, nor is there any such weighing even of the premise that only one who is a party to a contract can have rights on it. Rather, this premise is, in Holmes's expression, taken on inspiration and authority.

––––––

Nomenclature is important in analyzing third-party beneficiary problems. In the Notes in this Chapter, the term *third-party beneficiary* will be used to mean a person who is not a party to a contract, but who would benefit from its performance. The term *promisor* will be used to mean a person who has made a legally enforceable promise, the performance of which would benefit a third-party beneficiary. The term *promisee* will be used to mean the person to whom this promise is made. The term *contract* will be used to mean an enforceable agreement between a promisor and a promisee, the performance of which would benefit a third party. The term *contracting parties* will be used to refer to the promisor and the promisee, taken together. This nomenclature is somewhat artificial, because in bilateral contracts each party is both a promisor and a promisee. Typically, however, a third-party beneficiary would be benefited only by the performance of one of the parties—the party who will be called the promisor.

––––––

RESTATEMENT, SECOND, OF CONTRACTS
§ 302, ILLUSTRATIONS 16–19

16. B contracts with A to erect an expensive building on A's land. C's adjoining land would be enhanced in value by the performance of the contract. C is [only] an incidental beneficiary [and cannot bring suit under the contract].

17. B contracts with A to buy a new car manufactured by C. C is [only] an incidental beneficiary [and cannot bring suit under the contract], even though the promise can only be performed if money is paid to C.

18. A, a labor union, promises B, a trade association, not to strike against any member of B during a certain period. One of the members of B charters a ship from C on terms under which such a strike would cause financial loss to C. C is [only] an incidental beneficiary of A's promise [and cannot bring suit under the contract].

19. A contracts to erect a building for C. B then contracts with A to supply lumber needed for the building. C is [only] an incidental beneficiary of B's promise, and B is [only] an incidental beneficiary of C's promise to pay A for the building [and neither can bring suit under the other's contract].

LAWRENCE v. FOX

Court of Appeals of New York, 1859.
20 N.Y. 268.

Appeal from the Superior Court of the City of Buffalo. On the trial before Mr. Justice Masten, it appeared by the evidence of a bystander that one Holly, in November, 1857, at the request of the defendant, loaned and advanced to him $300, stating at the time that he owed that sum to the plaintiff for money borrowed of him, and had agreed to pay it to him the then next day; that the defendant in consideration thereof, at the time of receiving the money, promised to pay it to the plaintiff the then next day. Upon this state of facts the defendant moved for a nonsuit, upon three several grounds, viz.: That there was no proof tending to show that Holly was indebted to the plaintiff, that the agreement by the defendant with Holly to pay the plaintiff was void for want of consideration, and that there was no privity between the plaintiff and defendant. The court overruled the motion, and the counsel for the defendant excepted. The cause was then submitted to the jury, and they found a verdict for the plaintiff for the amount of the loan and interest, $344.66, upon which judgment was entered, from which the defendant appealed to the Superior Court, at General Term, where the judgment was affirmed, and the defendant appealed to this court. The cause was submitted on printed arguments.

H. Gray, J. The first objection raised on the trial amounts to this: That the evidence of the person present, who heard the declarations of Holly giving directions as to the payment of the money he was then advancing to the defendant, was mere hearsay and, therefore, not competent. Had the plaintiff sued Holly for this sum of money no objection to the competency of this evidence would have been thought of; and if the defendant had performed his promise by paying the sum loaned to him to the plaintiff, and Holly had afterward sued him for its recovery, and this evidence had been offered by the defendant, it would doubtless have been received without an objection from any source. All the defendant had the right to demand in this case was evidence which, as between Holly and the plaintiff, was competent to establish the relation between them of debtor and creditor. For that purpose the evidence was clearly competent; it covered the whole ground and warranted the verdict of the jury.

But it is claimed that notwithstanding this promise was established by competent evidence, it was void for the want of consideration. It is now more than a quarter of a century since it was settled by the Supreme Court of this state—in an able and painstaking opinion by the late Chief Justice Savage, in which the authorities were fully examined and carefully analyzed—that a promise in all material respects like the one under consideration was valid; and the judgment of that court was unanimously affirmed by the Court for the Correction of Errors. Farley v. Cleveland, 4 Cow. 432, 15 Am.Dec. 387; s.c. in error, 9 Cow. 639.

In that case one Moon owed Farley and sold to Cleveland a quantity of hay, in consideration of which Cleveland promised to pay Moon's debt to Farley; and the decision in favor of Farley's right to recover was placed upon the ground that the hay received by Cleveland from Moon was a valid consideration for Cleveland's promise to pay Farley, and that the subsisting liability of Moon to pay Farley was no objection to the recovery.

The fact that the money advanced by Holly to the defendant was a loan to him for a day, and that it thereby became the property of the defendant, seemed to impress the defendant's counsel with the idea that because the defendant's promise was not a trust fund placed by the plaintiff [Holly?] in the defendant's hands, out of which he was to realize money as from the sale of a chattel or the collection of a debt, the promise although made for the benefit of the plaintiff could not inure to his benefit. The hay which [Moon] delivered to [Cleveland] was not to be paid to Farley, but the debt incurred by Cleveland for the purchase of the hay, like the debt incurred by the defendant for money borrowed, was what was to be paid.

That case has been often referred to by the courts of this state, and has never been doubted as sound authority for the principle upheld by it. Barker v. Bucklin, 2 Denio, 45, 43 Am.Dec. 726; Canal Co. v. Westchester County Bank, 4 Denio, 97. It puts to rest the objection that the defendant's promise was void for want of consideration. The report of that case shows that the promise was not only made to Moon but to the plaintiff Farley. In this case the promise was made to Holly and not expressly to the plaintiff; and this difference between the two cases presents the question, raised by the defendant's objection, as to the want of privity between the plaintiff and defendant. As early as 1806 it was announced by the Supreme Court of this state, upon what was then regarded as the settled law of England, "That where one person makes a promise to another for the benefit of a third person, that third person may maintain an action upon it." Schemerhorn v. Vanderheyden, 1 Johns. 140, 3 Am.Dec. 304, has often been reasserted by our courts and never departed from....

The same principle is adjudged in several cases in Massachusetts. I will refer to but a few of them.... In Hall v. Marston [1822, 17 Mass. 575], the court say: "It seems to have been well settled that if A promises B for a valuable consideration to pay C, the latter may maintain assumpsit for the money;" and in Brewer v. Dyer [1851, 7 Cush. 337, 340], the recovery was upheld, as the court said, "upon the principle of law *long recognized and clearly* established, that when one person, for a valuable consideration, engages with another, by a simple contract, to do some act for the benefit of a third, the latter, who would enjoy the benefit of the act, may maintain an action for the breach of such engagement; that it does not rest upon the ground of any actual or supposed relationship between the parties as some of the earlier cases would seem to indicate, but upon the broader and more satisfactory basis, that the law operating on the act of the parties creates the duty, establishes a privity, and implies the promise and obligation on which the action is founded." ...

But it is urged that because the defendant was not in any sense a trustee of the property of Holly for the benefit of the plaintiff, the law will not imply a promise. I agree that many of the cases where a promise was implied were cases of trusts, created for the benefit of the promisor [beneficiary?]. The case of Felton v. Dickinson, 10 Mass. 287, and others that might be cited are of that class; but concede them all to have been cases of trusts, and it proves nothing against the application of the rule to this case. The duty of the trustee to pay the cestui que trust, according to the terms of the trust, implies his promise to the latter to do so. In this case the defendant, upon ample consideration received from Holly, promised Holly to pay his debt to the plaintiff; the consideration received and the promise to Holly made it as plainly his duty to pay the plaintiff as if the money had been remitted to him for that purpose, and as well implied a promise to do so as if he had been made a trustee of property to be converted into cash with which to pay. The fact that a breach of the duty imposed in the one case may be visited, and justly, with more serious consequences than in the other, by no means disproves the payment to be a duty in both. The principle illustrated by the example so frequently quoted (which concisely states the case in hand) "that a promise made to one for the benefit of another, he for whose benefit it is made may bring an action for its breach," has been applied to trust cases, not because it was exclusively applicable to those cases, but because it was a principle of law, and as such applicable to those cases.

It was also insisted that Holly could have discharged the defendant from his promise, though it was intended by both parties for the benefit of the plaintiff, and, therefore, the plaintiff was not entitled to maintain this suit for the recovery of a demand over which he had no control. It is enough that the plaintiff [Holly?] did not release the defendant from his promise, and whether he could or not is a question not now necessarily involved; but if it was, I think it would be found difficult to maintain the right of Holly to discharge a judgment recovered by the plaintiff upon confession or otherwise, for the breach of the defendant's promise; and if he could not, how could he discharge the suit before judgment, or the promise before suit, made as it was for the plaintiff's benefit and in accordance with legal presumption accepted by him (Berly v. Taylor, 5 Hill, 577–584 et seq.), until his dissent was shown.

The cases cited, and especially that of Farley v. Cleveland, established the validity of a parol promise; it stands then upon the footing of a written one. Suppose the defendant had given his note in which for value received of Holly, he had promised to pay the plaintiff and the plaintiff had accepted the promise, retaining Holly's liability. Very clearly Holly could not have discharged that promise, be the right to release the defendant as it may. No one can doubt that he owes the sum of money demanded of him, or that in accordance with his promise it was his duty to have paid it to the plaintiff; nor can it be doubted that whatever may be the diversity of opinion elsewhere, the adjudications in this state, from a very early period, approved by experience, have established the defendant's liability; if, therefore, it could be shown that a more strict and technically accurate application of the rules applied, would lead to a different result (which I by no means concede), the effort should not be made in the face of manifest justice.

The judgment should be affirmed.

JOHNSON, CH. J., DENIO, SELDEN, ALLEN and STRONG, Js. concurred. JOHNSON, CH. J., and DENIO, J., were of opinion that the promise was to be regarded as made to the plaintiff through the medium of his agent, whose action he could ratify when it came to his knowledge, though taken without his being privy thereto.

COMSTOCK, J. (Dissenting). The plaintiff had nothing to do with the promise on which he brought this action. It was not made to him, nor did the consideration proceed from him. If he can maintain the suit, it is because an anomaly has found its way into the law on this subject. In general, there must be privity of contract. The party who sues upon a promise must be the promisee, or he must have some legal interest in the undertaking. In this case, it is plain that Holly, who loaned the money to the defendant, and to whom the promise in question was made, could at any time have claimed that it should be performed to himself personally. He had lent the money to the defendant, and at the same time directed the latter to pay the sum to the plaintiff. This direction he could countermand, and if he had done so, manifestly the defendant's promise to pay according to the direction would have ceased to exist. The plaintiff would receive a benefit by a complete execution of the arrangement, but the arrangement itself was between other parties, and was under their exclusive control. If the defendant had paid the money to Holly, his debt would have been discharged thereby. So Holly might have released the demand or assigned it to another person, or the parties might have annulled the promise now in question, and designated some other creditor of Holly as the party to whom the money should be paid. It has never been claimed that in a case thus situated the right of a third person to sue upon the promise rested on any sound principle of law. We are to inquire whether the rule has been so established by positive authority. . . .

The cases in which some trust was involved are also frequently referred to as authority for the doctrine now in question, but they do not sustain it. If A. delivers money or property to B., which the latter accepts upon a trust for the benefit of C., the latter can enforce the trust by an appropriate action for that purpose. Berly v. Taylor, 5 Hill, 577. If the trust be of money, I think the beneficiary may assent to it and bring the action for money had and received to his use. If it be of something else than money, the trustee must account for it according to the terms of the trust, and upon principles of equity. There is some authority even for saying that an express promise founded on the possession of a trust fund may be enforced by an action at law in the name of the beneficiary, although it was made to the creator of the trust. Thus, in Comyn's Digest (Action on the Case upon Assumpsit, B, 15), it is laid down that if a man promise a pig of lead to A., and his executor give lead to make a pig to B., who assumes to deliver it to A., an assumpsit lies by A. against him. The case of Delaware & H. Canal Co. v. Westchester County Bank, 4 Denio, 97, involved a trust because the defendants had received from a third party a bill of exchange under an agreement that they would endeavor to collect it, and would pay over the proceeds when collected to the plaintiffs. A fund received under such an agreement does not belong to the person who receives it. He must account for it specifically; and perhaps there is no gross violation of principle in permitting the equitable owner of it to sue upon an express promise to pay it over. Having a specific interest in the thing, the undertaking to account for it may be regarded as in some sense made with him through the author of the trust. But further than this we cannot go without violating plain rules of law. In the case before us there was nothing in the nature of a trust or agency. The defendant borrowed the money of Holly and received it as his own. The plaintiff had no right in the fund, legal or equitable. The promise to repay the money created an obligation in favor of the lender to whom it was made and not in favor of any one else. . . .

The question was also involved in some confusion by the earlier cases in Massachusetts. Indeed, the Supreme Court of that State seems at one time to have made a nearer approach to the doctrine on which this action must rest, than the courts of this State have ever done. (10 Mass., 287; 17 id., 400.) But in the recent case of Mellen, Administratrix, v. Whipple (1854, 1 Gray, 317) the subject was carefully reviewed and the doctrine utterly overthrown. . . .

The judgment of the court below should, therefore, be reversed, and a new trial granted.

GROVER, J., also dissented.

Judgment affirmed.

————

NOTE ON LAWRENCE v. FOX

An obvious question in *Lawrence v. Fox* is why Holly engaged in the relatively unusual transaction described in the case—a one-day loan of what was then a relatively large amount of money—and why Lawrence followed the winding path of suing Fox rather than the straight path of suing Holly. On the basis of historical spadework and some leaps of deduction, Professor Jon Waters has suggested that Lawrence may have sued Fox rather than Holly because Holly's debt to Lawrence was a gambling debt, unenforceable at law. A gambling milieu might also, perhaps, explain the unusual nature of the Holly–Fox transaction. Waters, The Property in the Promise, 98 Harv.L.Rev. 1109 (1985). More conventional explanations of why Lawrence sued Fox would be that Holly was insolvent or outside the jurisdiction.

————

SEAVER v. RANSOM

Court of Appeals of New York, 1918.
224 N.Y. 233, 120 N.E. 639, 2 A.L.R. 1187.

Action by Marion E. Seaver against Matt C. Ransom and another, as executors, etc., of Samuel A. Beman, deceased. From a judgment of the Appellate Division (180 App.Div. 734, 168 N.Y.S. 454), affirming judgment for plaintiff, defendants appeal. Affirmed.

POUND, J. Judge Beman and his wife were advanced in years. Mrs. Beman was about to die. She had a small estate, consisting of a house and lot in Malone and little else. Judge Beman drew his wife's will according to her instructions. It gave $1,000 to plaintiff, $500 to one sister, plaintiff's mother, and $100 each to another sister and her son, the use of the house to her husband for life, and remainder to the American Society for the Prevention of Cruelty to Animals. She named her husband as residuary legatee and executor. Plaintiff was her niece, 34 years old, in ill health, sometimes a member of the Beman household. When the will was read to Mrs. Beman she said that it was not as she wanted it; she wanted to leave the house to plaintiff. She had no other objection to the will, but her strength was waning, and, although the judge offered to write another will for her, she said she was afraid she would not hold out long enough to enable her to sign it. So the judge said, if she would sign the will he would leave plaintiff enough in his will to make up the difference. He avouched the promise by his uplifted hand with all solemnity and his wife then executed the will. When he came to die, it was found that his will made no provision for the plaintiff.

This action was brought and plaintiff recovered judgment in the trial court on the theory that Beman had obtained property from his wife and induced her to execute the will in the form prepared by him by his promise to give plaintiff $6,000, the value of the house, and that thereby equity impressed his property with a trust in favor of plaintiff. Where a legatee promises the testator that he will use property given him by the will for a particular purpose, a trust arises. O'Hara v. Dudley, 95 N.Y. 403, 47 Am.Rep. 53; Trustees of Amherst College v. Ritch, 151 N.Y. 282, 45 N.E. 876, 37 L.R.A. 305; Ahrens v. Jones, 169 N.Y. 555, 62 N.E. 666, 88 Am.St.Rep. 620. Beman received nothing under his wife's will but the use of the house in Malone for life. Equity compels the application of property thus obtained to the purpose of the testator, but equity cannot so impress a trust, except on property obtained by the promise. Beman was bound by his promise, but no property was bound by it; no trust in plaintiff's favor can be spelled out.

An action on the contract for damages, or to make the executors trustees for performance, stands on different ground. Farmers' Loan & Trust Co. v. Mortimer, 219 N.Y. 290, 294, 295, 114 N.E. 389, Ann.Cas.1918E, 1159. The Appellate Division properly passed to the consideration of the question whether the judgment could stand upon the promise made to the wife, upon a valid consideration, for the sole benefit of plaintiff. The judgment of the trial court was affirmed by a return to the general doctrine laid down in the great case of Lawrence v. Fox, 20 N.Y. 268, which has since been limited as herein indicated.

Contracts for the benefit of third persons have been the prolific source of judicial and academic discussion. Williston, Contracts for the Benefit of a

Third Person, 15 Harvard Law Review, 767; Corbin, Contracts for the Benefit of Third Persons, 27 Yale Law Journal, 1008. The general rule, both in law and equity (Phalen v. United States Trust Co., 186 N.Y. 178, 186, 78 N.E. 943, 7 L.R.A., N.S., 734, 9 Ann.Cas. 595), was that privity between a plaintiff and a defendant is necessary to the maintenance of an action on the contract. The consideration must be furnished by the party to whom the promise was made. The contract cannot be enforced against the third party, and therefore it cannot be enforced by him. On the other hand, the right of the beneficiary to sue on a contract made expressly for his benefit has been fully recognized in many American jurisdictions, either by judicial decision or by legislation, and is said to be "the prevailing rule in this country." Hendrick v. Lindsay, 93 U.S. 143, 23 L.Ed. 855; Lehow v. Simonton, 3 Colo. 346. It has been said that "the establishment of this doctrine has been gradual and is a victory of practical utility over theory, of equity over technical subtlety." Brantly on Contracts (2d Ed.) p. 253. The reasons for this view are that it is just and practical to permit the person for whose benefit the contract is made to enforce it against one whose duty it is to pay. Other jurisdictions still adhere to the present English rule (7 Halsbury's Laws of England, 342, 343; Jenks' Digest of English Civil Law, § 229) that a contract cannot be enforced by or against a person who is not a party (Exchange Bank v. Rice, 107 Mass. 37, 9 Am.Rep. 1). But see, also Forbes v. Thorpe, 209 Mass. 570, 95 N.E. 955; Gardner v. Denison, 217 Mass. 492, 105 N.E. 359, 51 L.R.A., N.S., 1108.

In New York the right of the beneficiary to sue on contracts made for his benefit is not clearly or simply defined. It is at present confined, first, to cases where there is a pecuniary obligation running from the promisee to the beneficiary, "a legal right founded upon some obligation of the promisee in the third party to adopt and claim the promise as made for his benefit." Farley v. Cleveland, 4 Cow. 432, 15 Am.Dec. 387; Lawrence v. Fox, supra; Garnsey v. Rogers, 47 N.Y. 233, 7 Am.Rep. 440; Vrooman v. Turner, 69 N.Y. 280, 25 Am.Rep. 195; Lorillard v. Clyde, 122 N.Y. 498, 25 N.E. 917, 10 L.R.A. 113; Durnherr v. Rau, 135 N.Y. 219, 32 N.E. 49; Townsend v. Rackham, 143 N.Y. 516, 38 N.E. 731; Sullivan v. Sullivan, 161 N.Y. 554, 56 N.E. 116. Secondly, to cases where the contract is made for the benefit of the wife (Buchanan v. Tilden, 158 N.Y. 109, 52 N.E. 724, 44 L.R.A. 170, 70 Am.St.Rep. 454; Bouton v. Welch, 170 N.Y. 554, 63 N.E. 539), affianced wife (De Cicco v. Schweizer, 221 N.Y. 431, 117 N.E. 807, L.R.A.1918E, 1004, Ann.Cas.1918C, 816), or child (Todd v. Weber, 95 N.Y. 181, 193, 47 Am.Rep. 20; Matter of Kidd, 188 N.Y. 274, 80 N.E. 924) of a party to the contract. The close relationship cases go back to the early King's Bench Case (1677), long since repudiated in England, of Dutton v. Poole, 2 Lev. 211. See Schemerhorn v. Vanderheyden, 1 Johns. 139, 3 Am.Dec. 304. The natural and moral duty of the husband or parent to provide for the future of wife or child sustains the action on the contract made for their benefit. "This is the farthest the cases in this state have gone," says Cullen, J., in the marriage settlement case of Borland v. Welch, 162 N.Y. 104, 110, 56 N.E. 556.

The right of the third party is also upheld, in, thirdly, the public contract cases (Little v. Banks, 85 N.Y. 258; Pond v. New Rochelle Water Co., 183 N.Y. 330, 76 N.E. 211, 1 L.R.A., N.S., 958, 5 Ann.Cas. 504; Smyth v. City of New York, 203 N.Y. 106, 96 N.E. 409; Farnsworth v. Boro Oil & Gas Co., 216 N.Y. 40, 48, 109 N.E. 860; Rigney v. N.Y.C. & H.R.R.R. Co., 217 N.Y. 31, 111 N.E. 226; Matter of International Ry. Co. v. Rann, 224 N.Y. 83, 120 N.E. 153. Cf.

German Alliance Ins. Co. v. Home Water Supply Co., 226 U.S. 220, 33 S.Ct. 32, 57 L.Ed. 195, 42 L.R.A., N.S., 1000), where the municipality seeks to protect its inhabitants by covenants for their benefit; and, fourthly the cases where, at the request of a party to the contract, the promise runs directly to the beneficiary although he does not furnish the consideration (Rector, etc., v. Teed, 120 N.Y. 583, 24 N.E. 1014; F.N. Bank of Sing Sing v. Chalmers, 144 N.Y. 432, 439, 39 N.E. 331; Hamilton v. Hamilton, 127 App.Div. 871, 875, 112 N.Y.S. 10). It may be safely said that a general rule sustaining recovery at the suit of the third party would include but few classes of cases not included in these groups, either categorically or in principle.

The desire of the childless aunt to make provision for a beloved and favorite niece differs imperceptibly in law or in equity from the moral duty of the parent to make testamentary provision for a child. The contract was made for the plaintiff's benefit. She alone is substantially damaged by its breach. The representatives of the wife's estate have no interest in enforcing it specifically. It is said in Buchanan v. Tilden that the common law imposes moral and legal obligations upon the husband and the parent not measured by the necessaries of life. It was, however, the love and affection or the moral sense of the husband and the parent that imposed such obligations in the cases cited, rather than any common-law duty of husband and parent to wife and child. If plaintiff had been a child of Mrs. Beman, legal obligation would have required no testamentary provision for her, yet the child could have enforced a covenant in her favor identical with the covenant of Judge Beman in this case. De Cicco v. Schweizer, supra. The constraining power of conscience is not regulated by the degree of relationship alone. The dependent or faithful niece may have a stronger claim than the affluent or unworthy son. No sensible theory of moral obligation denies arbitrarily to the former what would be conceded to the latter. We might consistently either refuse or allow the claim of both, but I cannot reconcile a decision in favor of the wife in Buchanan v. Tilden based on the moral obligations arising out of near relationship with a decision against the niece here on the ground that the relationship is too remote for equity's ken. No controlling authority depends upon so absolute a rule. In Sullivan v. Sullivan, supra, the grandniece lost in a litigation with the aunt's estate, founded on a certificate of deposit payable to the aunt "or in case of her death to her niece"; but what was said in that case of the relations of plaintiff's intestate and defendant does not control here, any more than what was said in Durnherr v. Rau, supra, on the relation of husband and wife, and the inadequacy of mere moral duty, as distinguished from legal or equitable obligation, controlled the decision in Buchanan v. Tilden. Borland v. Welch, supra, deals only with the rights of volunteers under a marriage settlement not made for the benefit of collaterals. Kellogg, P.J., writing for the court below well said: "The doctrine of Lawrence v. Fox is progressive, not retrograde. The course of the late decisions is to enlarge, not to limit, the effect of that case."

The court in that leading case attempted to adopt the general doctrine that any third person, for whose direct benefit a contract was intended, could sue on it. The headnote thus states the rule. Finch, J., in Gifford v. Corrigan, 117 N.Y. 257, 262, 22 N.E. 756, 6 L.R.A. 610, 15 Am.St.Rep. 508, says that the case rests upon that broad proposition; Edward T. Bartlett, J., in Pond v. New Rochelle Water Co., 183 N.Y. 330, 337, 76 N.E. 211, 213, 1 L.R.A., N.S., 958, 5 Ann.Cas. 504, calls it "the general principle"; but Vrooman v. Turner, supra, confined its application to the facts on which it was decided. "In every case in which an action has been sustained," says Allen, J., "there has been a debt or duty owing by the promisee to the party claiming to sue upon the promise." 69 N.Y. 285, 25 Am.Rep. 195. As late as Townsend v. Rackham, 143 N.Y. 516, 523, 38 N.E. 731, 733, we find Peckham, J., saying that, "to maintain the action by the third person, there must be this liability to him on the part of the promisee." Buchanan v. Tilden went further than any case since Lawrence v. Fox in a desire to do justice rather than to apply with technical accuracy strict rules calling for a legal or equitable obligation. In Embler v. Hartford Steam Boiler Inspection & Ins. Co., 158 N.Y. 431, 53 N.E. 212, 44 L.R.A. 512, it may at least be said that a majority of the court did not avail themselves of the opportunity to concur with the views expressed by Gray, J., who wrote the dissenting opinion in Buchanan v. Tilden, to the effect that an employee could not maintain an action on an insurance policy issued to the employer which covered injuries to employees. In Wright v. Glen Telephone Co., 48 Misc. 192, 195, 95 N.Y.S. 101, the learned presiding justice who wrote the opinion in this case said at Trial Term: "The right of a third person to recover upon a contract made by other parties for his benefit must rest upon the peculiar circumstances of each case rather than upon the law of some other case." "The case at bar is decided upon its peculiar facts." Edward T. Bartlett, J., in Buchanan v. Tilden.

But, on principle, a sound conclusion may be reached. If Mrs. Beman had left her husband the house on condition that he pay the plaintiff $6,000, and he had accepted the devise, he would have become personally liable to pay the legacy, and plaintiff could have recovered in an action at law against him, whatever the value of the house. Gridley v. Gridley, 24 N.Y. 130; Brown v. Knapp, 79 N.Y. 136, 143; Dinan v. Coneys, 143 N.Y. 544, 547, 38 N.E. 715; Blackmore v. White [1899] 1 Q.B. 293, 304. That would be because the testatrix had in substance bequeathed the promise to plaintiff, and not because close relationship or moral obligation sustained the contract. The distinction between an implied promise to a testator for the benefit of a third party to pay a legacy and an unqualified promise on a valuable consideration to make provision for the third party by will is discernible, but not obvious. The tendency of American authority is to sustain the gift in all such cases and to permit the donee beneficiary to recover on the contract. Matter of Edmundson's Estate (1918) 259 Pa. 429, 103 A. 277, 2 A.L.R. 1150. The equities are with the plaintiff, and they may be enforced in this action, whether it be regarded as an action for damages or an action for specific performance to convert the defendants into trustees for plaintiff's benefit under the agreement.

The judgment should be affirmed with costs.

HOGAN, CARDOZO, and CRANE, JJ., concur. HISCOCK, C.J., and COLLIN and ANDREWS, JJ., dissent.

Judgment affirmed.

———

RESTATEMENT, FIRST, CONTRACTS § 133

§ 133. Definition of Donee Beneficiary, Creditor Beneficiary, Incidental Beneficiary

(1) Where performance of a promise in a contract will benefit a person other than the promisee, that person is, except as stated in Subsection (3):

(a) a donee beneficiary if it appears from the terms of the promise in view of the accompanying circumstances that the purpose of the promisee in obtaining the promise of all or part of the performance thereof is to make a gift to the beneficiary or to confer upon him a right against the promisor to some performance neither due nor supposed or asserted to be due from the promisee to the beneficiary;

(b) a creditor beneficiary if no purpose to make a gift appears from the terms of the promise in view of the accompanying circumstances and performance of the promise will satisfy an actual or supposed or asserted duty of the promisee to the beneficiary, or a right of the beneficiary against the promisee which has been barred by the Statute of Limitations or by a discharge in bankruptcy, or which is unenforceable because of the Statute of Frauds;

(c) an incidental beneficiary if neither the facts stated in Clause (a) nor those stated in Clause (b) exist....

[Ed. note: Under §§ 135 and 136, a donee or creditor beneficiary has legally enforceable rights under the contract; an incidental beneficiary does not.]

———

RESTATEMENT, SECOND, CONTRACTS §§ 302, 304, 315

[See Selected Source Materials Supplement]

———

EISENBERG, THIRD–PARTY BENEFICIARIES

92 Colum.L.Rev. 1358 (1992).

It is easy to see why not every third-party beneficiary should be allowed to enforce a contract. The reasons for enforcing bargain promises are complex, but the most important is that bargains enhance the wealth of the contracting parties by creating value through exchange and allowing the contracting parties to make reliable plans. At its core, therefore, contract law seeks to facilitate the power of self-governing parties to further their own interests by contracting. Allowing enforcement of contracts by third-party beneficiaries often conflicts with those interests.

For example, suppose Martial is a manufacturer of specialty toy soldiers, and Access is a toy distributor. Martial purchases special paint for her soldiers from Color, and employs skilled workers on an hourly basis. At a time when Martial would have otherwise had to idle her plant for lack of business, Access places a large order with Martial for highly detailed Civil War toy soldiers to take advantage of a special surge of interest in that war. Access plans to resell the toy soldiers to large retailers, including Toys "R" We. Martial designs the soldiers and draws engineering plans for the necessary dies and then enters into a contract with Diemaker, who agrees to produce the dies. At the time this contract is made, Diemaker knows that Martial requires the dies to fill her contract with Access, that Access plans to resell to Toys "R" We and other retailers, and that Martial has no other business in prospect.

In breach of his contract, Diemaker fails to deliver the dies. As a result, Martial, in turn, is in breach of her contract with Access and also is forced to idle her plant for six weeks, until new orders begin to come in. Access and Toys "R" We sue Diemaker for their lost profits on resale of the toy soldiers. Color sues Diemaker for its lost profits on sales of paint. Martial's workers sue Diemaker for their lost wages. Access, Toys "R" We, Color, and the workers are all third-party beneficiaries of the contract between Diemaker and Martial, but intuitively it seems clear that none of these beneficiaries should be able to bring suit against Diemaker.

The source of the intuition lies in considerations that might be thought of as remedial, that is, considerations concerning the promisor's liability and the impact of that liability on the contracting parties. In the hypothetical, Martial is entitled to expectation damages against Diemaker as a result of Diemaker's breach, and these damages would be measured in large part by Martial's lost profits. It can be assumed that the prospect of such damages affected the price Diemaker charged. If Martial had initially agreed to forgo expectation damages in the event of Diemaker's breach, Diemaker presumably would have agreed to a lower price. If Martial did not agree to forgo those damages, presumably that was partly because she wanted full compensation if Diemaker breached, and partly because she would have viewed the contract with Diemaker as unreliable if the contract was not backed by the sanction of expectation damages. Suppose now that the parties had directly addressed the issue of the third parties' rights. If Diemaker was to be exposed to liability to the third parties, as well as liability to Martial, Diemaker would certainly have demanded a higher price from Martial. Martial, however, would almost certainly have been unwilling to pay that higher price, because she would receive little or no corresponding benefit in return. We can therefore be fairly confident that if Martial and Diemaker had directly addressed the issue, they would have agreed that the third parties should not be able to enforce the contract. Accordingly, if the interests of the contracting parties, Martial and Diemaker, are measured by what they would have agreed to if they had addressed the issue, allowing the third parties in the hypothetical to enforce the contract would conflict with those interests.

In short, although social propositions [that is, propositions of policy, morals, and experience] ... do not support a rule that no third-party beneficiaries should be allowed to enforce contracts in their favor, neither do such propositions support a rule that all third-party beneficiaries should be allowed to enforce contracts in their favor....

... What principle ... should determine whether a given third-party beneficiary should be permitted to enforce a contract?

To answer this question, recall the reason why not every third-party beneficiary should have power to enforce contracts: in some cases, such enforcement would conflict with the interests of the contracting parties. The same reason points the way to the principle that should determine whether any given third-party beneficiary should have power to enforce a contract. This principle, which I will call the third-party-beneficiary principle, is as follows:

A third-party beneficiary should have power to enforce a contract if, but only if:

> (I) allowing the beneficiary to enforce the contract is a necessary or important means of effectuating the contracting parties' performance objectives, as manifested in the contract read in the light of surrounding circumstances; or

> (II) allowing the beneficiary to enforce the contract is supported by reasons of policy or morality independent of contract law and would not conflict with the contracting parties' performance objectives.

The term "the contracting parties' performance objectives" needs some exegesis. Normally, a third-party beneficiary will bring suit only if the promisor has breached. Obviously, it is not an objective of the promisor at that point to perform. Furthermore, in one sense it is never an objective of a promisor to perform, but only to obtain what is promised to her if she agrees to and does perform. Such a characterization of the promisor's objectives, however, would be too narrow, because the promisor can attain what she is promised only by joining in the enterprise that is embodied in the contract—an enterprise designed to fulfill various objectives, some shared, some dearer to the heart of the promisor, some dearer to the heart of the promisee. Accordingly, by the contracting parties' performance objectives I mean those objectives of the enterprise embodied in the contract, read in the light of surrounding circumstances, that the promisor either knew or should have known at the time the contract was made.

I will call the two elements of the third-party-beneficiary principle the first and second branches of that principle. The first branch of the principle reflects the concept that at its core contract law seeks to facilitate the power of self-governing parties to further their own interests by contracting. Under this branch, therefore, the purpose of allowing suit by a third party is not to ensure that the third party realizes a benefit, but to ensure that the contracting parties' performance objectives are effectuated.... To put this differently, under the first branch of the third-party-beneficiary principle, the law of third-party beneficiaries is largely conceived as remedial, rather than substantive. The question addressed by the first branch of the principle is not whether the contract creates a "right" in the third party, but whether empowering the third party to enforce the contract is a necessary or important means of effectuating the contracting parties' performance objectives.

Like other remedial problems, this question is seldom answered by the literal terms of the contract itself. In part, this is because it is costly to write contract terms, and it is likely to be more efficient for the parties to focus on terms that describe the performance they expect rather than on terms that describe the consequences that are to result if an expected performance is not rendered. Furthermore, although it is relatively easy for contracting parties to specify the performance they want, it is often extremely difficult to specify remedies in advance of knowing the nature of the breach and the circumstances of the world at the time of the breach.

Nevertheless, a court asked to determine a remedial problem would normally do well to ask what the parties would have provided if they had bargained under ideal conditions—that is, where foresight was perfect and negotiation and drafting were cost-free. The rules that the courts apply to fill in contracts should be both fair and efficient. Contracts negotiated under ideal conditions will be efficient, and enforcing the terms of such contracts will usually be regarded as fair. Thus, a remedial rule is fair and efficient if it corresponds to the terms that rational parties situated like the contracting parties would have reached when bargaining under ideal conditions. That determination, in turn, rests largely on whether the promisee will realize the objectives he bargained for if the [third party's] suit is not allowed; whether the promisor's risk of liability will be extended if the suit is allowed; and, if that liability will be extended, whether the parties have implicitly bargained for that risk. . . .

Unlike the first branch of the third-party-beneficiary principle, which focuses exclusively on effectuation of the contracting parties' performance objectives, the second branch of the principle reflects the concept that contract law properly may give effect to policy and moral concerns that are independent of the contracting parties' performance objectives. Policy and morality have traditionally entered into contract law in a variety of ways. For example, these elements help shape the rules of contract law on such issues as what kinds of promises the law should enforce, the extent to which the law should recognize limits (such as unconscionability) on the enforcement of bargain promises, and what remedies contract law should afford when enforceable promises are broken. Policy and morality also openly figure in the interpretation of contracts. Restatement Second Section 207 provides: "In choosing among the reasonable meanings of a promise or agreement or a term thereof, a meaning that serves the public interest is generally preferred." Similarly, Restatement Second Section 204, Comment d states: "[W]here there is in fact no agreement [on a matter that falls within the ambit of a contract], the courts should supply a term that comports with community standards of fairness and policy rather than analyze a hypothetical model of the bargaining process."

. . . Given the primacy of the contracting parties' performance objectives, as manifested in their contract, enforcement by the third-party beneficiary should not be permitted if it would conflict with those objectives. If, however, there is no such conflict, and the interests of policy or morality would be served by allowing the third party to enforce the contract, the rules of contract law should be shaped to allow such enforcement, just as they are shaped by policy and morality in other cases. . . .

HALE v. GROCE

Supreme Court of Oregon, 1987.
304 Or. 281, 744 P.2d 1289.

Before PETERSON, C.J., and LENT, LINDE, CAMPBELL, CARSON and GILLETTE, JJ.

LINDE, JUSTICE.

Defendant, who is an attorney, was directed by a client to prepare testamentary instruments and to include a bequest of a specified sum to plaintiff. After the client's death, it was discovered that the gift was not included either in the will or in a related trust instrument. After an unsuccessful attempt to obtain judicial reformation of the will and trust, plaintiff brought the present action for damages against the attorney.

The complaint alleged as two separate claims, first, that defendant was negligent in a number of particulars and, second, that he failed to carry out a contractual promise to his client, the decedent, which the decedent had intended specifically for the benefit of plaintiff. In other states plaintiffs in such cases have sometimes been allowed to recover on one or both of these theories, as negligently injured parties or as third-party beneficiaries under a contract. It is a new question in this court.

Defendant moved to dismiss the complaint on grounds that the stated facts did not constitute a claim under either theory and that, at least as to the tort theory, the action was not commenced within the time limited by the applicable statute. The circuit court held that the action was not time-barred but allowed defendant's motion to dismiss both claims. On plaintiff's appeal, the Court of Appeals reinstated plaintiff's negligence claim, and it also remanded for trial her allegations that defendant was estopped from invoking the statute of limitations. *Hale v. Groce,* 83 Or.App. 55, 57–58, 730 P.2d 576 (1986).

Both parties petitioned this court for review. Defendant asserts that a lawyer owes a professional duty of care only to his client and cannot be sued for malpractice by others who are injured by the way he performs that duty. Plaintiff asks us to reinstate her contract claim as a third-party beneficiary. We hold that the complaint states claims for damages under both theories, a claim as the intended beneficiary of defendant's professional contract with the decedent and a derivative tort claim based on breach of the duty created by that contract to the plaintiff as its intended beneficiary.

The two claims are related, but they differ in important respects. Standing alone, without a duty to plaintiff derived from defendant's contractual undertaking, plaintiff's tort claim would confront the rule that one ordinarily is not liable for negligently causing a stranger's purely economic loss without injuring his person or property. ... It does not suffice that the harm is a foreseeable consequence of negligent conduct that may make one liable to someone else, for instance to a client. Some source of a duty outside the common law of negligence is required. Even then, tort rules such as comparative fault may apply that do not apply to contract claims. *Compare Greycas, Inc. v. Proud,* 826 F.2d 1560, 1566 (7th Cir.1987) (no negligence in relying on lawyer's report that assets were free of liens). A contract claim, on the other hand, does not necessarily depend on showing negligence.

Similar claims were made in *Currey v. Butcher,* 37 Or. 380, 61 P. 631 (1900), in which attorneys were charged with a faulty search of a title. This court held that they were entitled to an instruction that they would not be liable to a person for whom their client may have acted unbeknownst to them. *Id.* at 388–89, 61 P. 631. That holding was reaffirmed in *Metzker v. Slocum,* 272 Or. 313, 537 P.2d 74 (1975). A chief precedent for *Currey* was *Buckley v. Gray,* 110 Cal. 339, 42 P. 900 (1895), which the court cited for the proposition that "an attorney employed to draw a will is not liable to a person who, through the attorney's ignorance or negligence in the discharge of his professional duties, was deprived of the portion of the estate which the testator instructed the attorney should be given such person by the will." *Currey,* 37 Or. at 389, 61 P. 631.

Since 1900, many courts have reconsidered that proposition, some preferring a contract analysis, some negligence, and at least one "a definite maybe." *Kirgan v. Parks,* 60 Md.App. 1, 3, 478 A.2d 713, 714 (1984). *Cf. Flaherty v. Weinberg,* 303 Md. 116, 131, 492 A.2d 618, 625 (1985) (clarifying *Kirgan*). *Buckley v. Gray* itself was overruled in *Lucas v. Hamm,* 56 Cal.2d 583, 588, 15 Cal.Rptr. 821, 823, 364 P.2d 685, 687 (1961). The California Supreme Court stated that a lawyer might be liable to an intended testamentary beneficiary either for negligence or for breach of the lawyer's contract with the testator, though the court balked at recognizing professional negligence in a lawyer's failure to meet the state's rule against perpetuities and restraints on alienation. 56 Cal.2d at 592, 15 Cal.Rptr. at 826, 364 P.2d at 690. After *Lucas,* the California court treated contract liability as superfluous and settled on negligence theory, which in California calls for applying "public policy" by "balancing" half a dozen "factors" in each case. *See Heyer v. Flaig,* 70 Cal.2d 223, 227, 74 Cal.Rptr. 225, 228, 449 P.2d 161, 164 (1969). . . .

The Pennsylvania Supreme Court chose the contrary course in *Guy v. Liederbach,* 501 Pa. 47, 459 A.2d 744 (1983), a claim by a beneficiary who lost a legacy because the testator's lawyer let her subscribe as a witness to the will. The court rejected both open-ended tort liability to foreseeably injured third parties and what it considered the "unworkable" California standard, *id.* at 57, 459 A.2d at 749, noting that:

> " * * * although a plaintiff on a third party beneficiary theory in contract may in some cases have to show a deviation from the standard of care, as in negligence, to establish breach, the class of persons to whom the defendant may be liable is restricted by principles of contract law, not negligence principles relating to foreseeability or scope of the risk."

Id. at 62, 459 A.2d at 752. Citing dictum in an early Pennsylvania decision, *Lawall v. Groman,* 180 Pa. 532, 37 A. 98 (1897), the court settled instead on liability to the intended beneficiary under Restatement (Second) Contracts section 302(1) (1981).

The Connecticut Supreme Court similarly allowed a disappointed beneficiary of a testamentary trust to proceed against the testatrix's lawyer on a contract theory over an objection that the lawyer's promise obligated him only to the client and not to the intended beneficiary, because the benefit to the plaintiff also was the essence of the benefit promised to the testatrix. *Stowe v. Smith,* 184 Conn. 194, 441 A.2d 81 (1981). *See also Ogle v. Fuiten,* 102 Ill.2d 356, 80 Ill.Dec. 772, 466 N.E.2d 224 (1984) (allowing action on both contract and tort theories).

We agree that the beneficiary in these cases is not only a plausible but a classic "intended" third-party beneficiary of the lawyer's promise to his client within the rule of Restatement section 302(1)(b) and may enforce the duty so created, as stated *id.* section 304. *See, e.g., Johnson v. Doughty,* 236 Or. 78, 83, 385 P.2d 760 (1963), *Parker v. Jeffery,* 26 Or. 186, 189, 37 P. 712 (1894) (stating rule that a contract may be enforced by one for whose benefit it was intended). The promise, of course, was not that the lawyer would pay plaintiff the stipulated sum, and it is too late for the lawyer to perform the promise that he did make, but this does not preclude an action for damages for the nonperformance. In principle, such an action is available to one in plaintiff's position.

Because under third-party analysis the contract creates a "duty" not only to the promisee, the client, but also to the intended beneficiary, negligent nonperformance may give rise to a negligence action as well. Not every such contract will support either claim. A contract to prepare a will or other instrument may promise different things. It may undertake to make a particular disposition by means specified by the client (for instance, in trust, or by a gift of identified property), or to accomplish the intended gift by specified means of the lawyer's choosing. Failure to do what was promised then would be a breach of contract regardless of any negligence. On the other hand, the lawyer's promise might be to use his best professional efforts to accomplish the specified result with the skill and care customary among lawyers in the relevant community. Because negligence liability of this kind arises only from the professional obligation to the client, it does not threaten to divide a lawyer's loyalty between the client and a potentially injured third party, as defendant argues.

Whether breach of that kind of promise is properly characterized as a breach of contract or as negligence, we have said, depends on the legal rule for which its character is at issue. *See Securities–Intermountain v. Sunset Fuel,* 289 Or. 243, 252 n. 6, 611 P.2d 1158 (1980). That case, like this one, involved an issue whether the action was commenced in time. We cited *Currey v. Butcher, supra,* to illustrate that a breach of professional duty could give rise to an action "either in assumpsit, for a breach of the implied promise, or in case, for the neglect of the duty." *Securities–Intermountain,* 289 Or. at 254, 611 P.2d 1158. We also noted Justice O'Connell's observation, in *Bales for Food v. Poole,* 246 Or. 253, 424 P.2d 892 (1967), that the different statutory time limitations for tort and contract claims deserved legislative reconsideration. 289 Or. at 260, 611 P.2d 1158.

In the present case, the Court of Appeals held that plaintiff's complaint pleaded only a tort claim. In the court's view, the complaint alleged no more than that the alleged professional contract "merely incorporate[d] by reference or by implication a general standard of skill and care to which the defendant would be bound independent of the contract." 83 Or.App. at 58, 730 P.2d 576, *quoting Securities–Intermountain,* 289 Or. at 259, 611 P.2d 1158. Quoting the same paragraph, plaintiff's brief contends, to the contrary, that defendant and his client "spelled out the performance expected by the [client] and promised by the defendant in terms that commit the defendant to this performance without reference to and irrespective of any general standard." 289 Or. at 259, 611 P.2d 1158.

The complaint alleged as follows:

> "4. In March 1982, Robert Rogers instructed defendant to draft documents to accomplish certain dispositions of Rogers' money and property. Rogers identified for defendant Rogers' intended beneficiaries and the bequests he intended to make.

> "5. Defendant assumed the duty of ensuring that the documents defendant drafted accomplished the distribution of Rogers' money and property that Rogers wanted to occur on his death. Defendant's duty extended to the persons Rogers identified as his intended beneficiaries.

"6. Rogers identified plaintiff to defendant as Rogers' intended beneficiary. Rogers also told defendant that he wanted plaintiff to receive a $300,000 gift at Rogers' death.

"7. Defendant failed to include, in either a trust or a will that defendant drafted for Robert Rogers in March 1982, a provision giving plaintiff $300,000 upon Rogers' death, as directed by Rogers."

These paragraphs adequately allege a claim that defendant was to use his professional skill to accomplish the donor's objectives and failed to do so. That is a tort claim for purposes of the statute of limitations.

The pertinent allegations of the contract claim were:

"18. Relying on defendant's promise to select a better legal mechanism by which to give plaintiff the gift, Rogers refrained during his lifetime from giving plaintiff his Cooper Industries stock. Defendant specifically told Rogers that defendant would prepare a trust document wherein Rogers and plaintiff would be co-trustees and through which plaintiff would receive the gift Rogers' [sic] intended her to have. Rogers specifically directed defendant to draft the trust and to include plaintiff's $300,000 gift.

"19. On March 8, 1982, defendant presented a trust document to Rogers for Rogers to execute. Defendant told Rogers and plaintiff, who were co-trustees of the trust, that the document included the $300,000 gift to plaintiff. Relying on defendant's representations, Rogers and plaintiff executed the trust without reading it.

"20. Defendant and Rogers specifically contracted for defendant to draft the trust document with plaintiff's gift in it. Defendant breached that contract by failing to include the provision for plaintiff to receive the $300,000 gift."

These paragraphs allege breach of a specific promise "that defendant would prepare a trust document wherein Rogers and plaintiff would be co-trustees and through which plaintiff would receive the gift Rogers intended her to have," a "trust document with plaintiff's gift in it." They allege, not that defendant performed this promise negligently, but that he did not perform it at all. As far as these allegations went, he might have broken the promise purposely, or under circumstances that might be a partial or entire defense to a negligence claim.

The allegations of the terms of the contract are not as detailed as those in the architect's contract annexed to the complaint in *Securities-Intermountain.* Whether this agreement in fact was sufficiently specific to go beyond a general promise by defendant to use his professional skills to carry out the assigned project is a matter for proof. Lacking a detailed written contract like that in *Securities-Intermountain,* it may depend on correspondence, memoranda, or testimony. When an alleged contract does not lend itself to incorporation of a writing in the complaint, the issue at least may have to await affidavits and possible counteraffidavits on motion for summary judgment. ORCP 47 D. It should not have been decided on a motion under ORCP 21 to dismiss the complaint. For this reason, we reverse so much of the decision of the Court of Appeals as affirmed the dismissal of the contract claim. We agree with the court's decision to leave to the circuit court plaintiff's allegations asserting that defendant waived the time limit for the negligence claim or is estopped to assert it.

The decision of the Court of Appeals is affirmed in part and reversed in part, the trial court's judgment is reversed, and the case is remanded to the trial court for further proceedings.

SCARPITTI v. WEBORG

Supreme Court of Pennsylvania, 1992.
530 Pa. 366, 609 A.2d 147.

Before NIX, C.J., and LARSEN, FLAHERTY, McDERMOTT, ZAPPALA, PAPADAKOS and CAPPY, JJ.

LARSEN, Justice.

This case presents the question of whether purchasers of lots in a residential subdivision, who are required by subdivision restrictions recorded of public record to have their house construction plans reviewed and approved by an architect retained by the subdivision developer, are intended beneficiaries of the implied contract between the developer and the architect, and, as a result, have a cause of action against the architect for any breach of said contract for his alleged failure to properly review and approve the plans of other lot purchasers in the subdivision.

Appellees, lot owners in the Winchester subdivision, instituted an action against appellant, architect William Weborg, seeking damages for his arbitrary enforcement of the subdivision restrictions. Appellant's preliminary objections in the nature of a demurrer were sustained by the trial court and appellees' complaint dismissed with prejudice. On appeal, the Superior Court reversed, 400 Pa.Super. 632, 576 A.2d 1144, and held that appellees had a cause of action as third party beneficiaries of the implied contract between appellant and the subdivision developer. We agree.

We begin by noting that for purposes of review of a dismissal on the pleadings in the nature of a demurrer, the averments of the petition, except to the extent they constitute conclusions of law, must be taken as true. *Cianfrani v. Com., State Employees' Retirement Bd.*, 505 Pa. 294, 479 A.2d 468 (1984). The question presented by a demurrer is whether, on the facts averred, the law says with certainty that no recovery is possible, and where a doubt exists as to whether a demurrer should be sustained, this doubt should be resolved in favor of overruling it. *Muhammad v. Strassburger, et al.*, 526 Pa. 541, 587 A.2d 1346 (1991), *cert. denied*, 502 U.S. 867, 112 S.Ct. 196, 116 L.Ed.2d 156 (1991).

Viewed in light of the aforementioned standards, the complaint avers that appellees William and Susan Scarpitti and Joseph and Judith Hines purchased residential lots located in the Winchester South Subdivision in Erie, Pennsylvania, from Winchester Development Company, Inc. (Winchester), the successor in interest to the original developer Red Dog Realty Partnership (Partnership). Each of the lots purchased by the Scarpittis and the Hineses are, and were at the time of purchase, subject to certain recorded deed restrictions. Restriction No. 2 provides that:

No more than one single family dwelling with no less than a two car nor more than a two and one-half car attached garage, shall be erected on any lot in the subdivision.

Restriction No. 7 provides that:

No dwelling, tennis court, swimming pool, fence, or other structure shall be erected or maintained on any lot in the subdivision unless the plans therefore, showing the nature, kind, shape, height, material, color scheme, and location of said structure, and the elevation and grading plans of the lot to be built upon, shall have been submitted to and approved in writing by the architectural firm of William Weborg Associates or such other authority as the Partnership, by a duly recorded amendment to these Restrictions, may designate for that purpose.

In accordance with Restriction No. 7, appellees submitted their construction plans to William Weborg, appellant, for approval. Appellees' plans were disapproved by appellant because their plans contained three car garages in violation of Restriction No. 2. Subsequently, based upon appellant's denial, appellees constructed homes with two or two and one-half car garages in accordance with Restriction No. 2. Some time later, however, appellant approved plans of other lot owners in the Winchester South Subdivision for homes with three car garages.[1]

Appellant asserts that no privity of contract existed between the parties thereby precluding a contract claim, and no legal duty existed between the parties thereby precluding a tort claim. Appellees contend that a cause of action exists against appellant under a contractual third party beneficiary theory. Under this analysis, appellees assert that they were intended beneficiaries of the implied contract which retained appellant for the purpose of approving construction plans and enforcing the recorded restrictions of the Winchester South Subdivision, pursuant to Restriction No. 7.

The current rule in Pennsylvania for designation of a party as a third party beneficiary was first articulated in the seminal case of *Spires v. Hanover Fire Insurance Co.,* 364 Pa. 52, 70 A.2d 828 (1950) (plurality opinion). In *Spires,* we held that in order for a third party beneficiary to have standing to recover on a contract, both contracting parties must have expressed an intention that the third party be a beneficiary, and that intention must have affirmatively appeared in the contract itself. *Spires v. Hanover Fire Insurance Co.,* 364 Pa. at 57, 70 A.2d at 830–31. But, in *Guy v. Liederbach,* 501 Pa. 47, 459 A.2d 744 (1983), we carved out an exception to the *Spires* rule, and allowed the beneficiary of a will to recover for legal malpractice against an attorney, despite the fact that the beneficiary was not in privity of contract with the attorney and was not named specifically as an intended beneficiary of the contract. In so doing, we adopted the Restatement (Second) of Contracts, § 302 (1979), as a guide for analysis of third party beneficiary claims in Pennsylvania. Restatement (Second) of Contracts, § 302 (1979) states:

INTENDED AND INCIDENTAL BENEFICIARIES

(1) Unless otherwise agreed between promisor and promisee, a beneficiary of a promise is an intended beneficiary if recognition of a right to

---

1. These plans that were approved by appellant which included three car garages were designed by appellant in his private capacity as a professional architect, and then approved by appellant in his capacity as the subdivision architect charged with reviewing construction plans and enforcing deed restrictions.

performance in the beneficiary is appropriate to effectuate the intentions of the parties and either

> (a) the performance of the promise will satisfy an obligation of the promisee to pay money to the beneficiary; or

> (b) the circumstances indicate that the promisee intends to give the beneficiary the benefit of the promised performance.

> (2) An incidental beneficiary is a beneficiary who is not an intended beneficiary.

Restatement (Second) of Contracts § 302 (1979).

Consequently, this Court in *Guy* concluded:

> There is thus a two part test for determining whether one is an intended third party beneficiary: (1) the recognition of the beneficiary's right must be "appropriate to effectuate the intention of the parties," and (2) the performance must "satisfy an obligation of the promisee to pay money to the beneficiary" or "the circumstances indicate that the promisee intends to give the beneficiary the benefit of the promised performance."

Guy v. Liederbach, 501 Pa. at 60, 459 A.2d at 751. The first part of the test sets forth a standing requirement which leaves discretion with the court to determine whether recognition of third party beneficiary status would be appropriate. The second part defines the two types of claimants who may be intended as third party beneficiaries. If a party satisfies both parts of the test, a claim may be asserted under the contract. *Id.*

Appellant argues that the holding in *Guy* was intended to have very limited application, and that the Restatement (Second) of Contracts, § 302 (1979) applies only where the court is faced with a legatee of a will as a possible third party beneficiary. Appellant cites numerous Superior Court opinions refusing to extend *Guy* to a new class of beneficiaries, contending that these cases stand for the proposition that *Guy* was intended to apply only to cases sufficiently similar on the facts. . . . In all of these cases, the Superior Court, although refusing to extend *Guy,* found that the third party was not an intended beneficiary either because there was no underlying contract, recognition of a right to performance was not appropriate to effectuate the intentions of the parties, or there was no clear intention to benefit the third party at the time the contract was entered into. Additionally, this Court never limited its holding in *Guy* to the facts of the case; rather, what this Court said in *Guy* was that "We believe that Restatement (Second) of Contracts § 302 (1979) provides an analysis of third party beneficiaries which permits a properly restricted cause of action for beneficiaries such as appellee. In adopting this standard, . . ." *Guy v. Liederbach,* 501 Pa. at 59, 459 A.2d at 751. It is clear from the language of the opinion in *Guy* that this Court was adopting the Restatement (Second) of Contracts § 302 (1979) as the law of Pennsylvania. Nothing in the holding of *Guy* precludes appellees from being included in the narrow class of third party beneficiaries envisioned by this Court, if they show that they meet the requirements of § 302.

Accordingly, we hold that a party becomes a third party beneficiary only where both parties to the contract express an intention to benefit the third party in the contract itself, *Spires, supra, unless,* the circumstances are so compelling that recognition of the beneficiary's right is appropriate to effectuate the intention of the parties, and the performance satisfies an obligation of the promisee to pay money to the beneficiary or the circumstances indicate that the promisee intends to give the beneficiary the benefit of the promised performance. *Guy, supra.*

Applying these principles to the case at bar, we find that appellees are intended third party beneficiaries of the implied contract between appellant and Winchester. The underlying contract is between appellant [promisor] and Winchester [promisee], whereby appellant promises to review all building plans and enforce the recorded subdivision restrictions. Obviously, the purpose of this agreement was to make the lots more attractive to prospective purchasers by assuring that other homeowners in the subdivision would be required to abide by the recorded subdivision restrictions. The third party beneficiary relationship, therefore, was within the contemplation of the promisor and the promisee at the time of contracting. It is the homeowners who have the greatest interest in uniform enforcement of restrictions and it is the homeowners who were benefitted by the establishment of a vehicle to enforce the restrictions. Hence, they were reasonable in relying upon the promise as manifesting an intention to confer a right on them. Although the agreement between appellant and Winchester does not expressly manifest an intent to benefit the subdivision homeowners, we find that recognition of a right to uniform enforcement of the deed restrictions in appellees is appropriate to effectuate the intention of the parties.

In this case, the architect is the promisor, promising to enforce deed restrictions which carry out the developer's intention to benefit the homeowners. The developer, the promisee, intends that the homeowners have the benefit of the architect's performance. Thus, it is patently clear that the parties, by establishing a vehicle for the enforcement of deed restrictions, intended to benefit the homeowners who purchased lots in the Winchester South Subdivision, at the time the contract was entered into. Although not individually named, appellee homeowners were part of a limited class of persons intended to benefit from the agreement between appellant and Winchester, thus satisfying the second prong of *Guy* and subsection (b) of § 302 Restatement (Second) of Contracts (1979). In fact, we have not been informed of any other purpose for the employment of appellant to review construction plans, but for the benefit of the homeowners in the subdivision. Accordingly, we find that appellees, as third party beneficiaries, have a cause of action in accord with the principles of the Restatement (Second) of Contracts § 302 (1979), and *Guy.*

Appellant also contends that the availability to appellees of alternative sources of redress takes the case out of the holding of *Guy.* Appellant suggests that appellees institute suit against either Winchester or the offending homeowners in the subdivision. Although part of what made a cause of action appropriate in *Guy* was the fact that Mrs. Guy would have been left without recourse or remedy if we denied her third party beneficiary status, the critical point in *Guy* was that the beneficiary was an *intended* beneficiary, intended by the promisee to receive the benefit of the promised performance. Nevertheless, the Superior Court found, and we agree, that subdivision Restriction No. 23 precludes homeowners from bringing suit against the developer. Said subdivision restriction reads as follows:

No delay or omission on the part of the Partnership or the owner of any other lot in the subdivision in exercising any right, power, or remedy herein provided for in the event of breach of any part of the provisions, conditions, restrictions, and covenants herein contained shall be construed as a waiver thereof or acquiescence therein; and no right of action shall accrue nor shall any action be brought or maintained by anyone whomsoever against the Partnership for or on account of the failure or neglect of the Partnership to exercise any right, power, or remedy herein provided for in the event of such breach.

Pursuant to this provision, the developer has no duty to enforce the subdivision restrictions and is essentially insulated from liability by virtue of this disclaimer. However, there is no such disclaimer that applies to appellant. Appellant, pursuant to his agreement with Winchester, assumed the duty of enforcing the subdivision restrictions and cannot now try to insulate himself from liability by bringing himself within the ambit of Restriction No. 23.[2]

We find, therefore, that the circumstances of this case are sufficiently compelling to warrant the application of the exception created in *Guy v. Liederbach*. Accordingly, the judgment of the Superior Court is affirmed. The case is remanded to the trial court with instructions to reinstate the complaint and proceed consistent with this opinion.

NIX, C.J., and FLAHERTY and ZAPPALA, JJ., concur in the result.

———

UCC § 2–318

[See Selected Source Materials Supplement]

———

RESTATEMENT, SECOND, CONTRACTS § 313

[See Selected Source Materials Supplement]

———

MARTINEZ v. SOCOMA COMPANIES, INC.

Supreme Court of California, 1974.
11 Cal.3d 394, 113 Cal.Rptr. 585, 521 P.2d 841.

WRIGHT, CHIEF JUSTICE. Plaintiffs brought this class action on behalf of themselves and other disadvantaged unemployed persons, alleging that defendants failed to perform contracts with the United States government under which defendants agreed to provide job training and at least one year of employment to certain numbers of such persons. Plaintiffs claim that they and the other such persons are third party beneficiaries of the contracts and as such are entitled to damages for defendants' nonperformance. General

---

2. We do not decide the propriety of a suit against the offending homeowners, since the existence of an alternative remedy does not preclude one from being a third party beneficiary, entitled to assert a claim under the contract.

demurrers to the complaint were sustained without leave to amend, apparently on the ground that plaintiffs lacked standing to sue as third party beneficiaries. Dismissals were entered as to the demurring defendants, and plaintiffs appeal.

We affirm the judgments of dismissal. As will appear, the contracts nowhere state that either the government or defendants are to be liable to persons such as plaintiffs for damages resulting from the defendants' nonperformance. The benefits to be derived from defendants' performance were clearly intended not as gifts from the government to such persons but as a means of executing the public purposes stated in the contracts and in the underlying legislation. Accordingly, plaintiffs were only incidental beneficiaries and as such have no right of recovery.

The complaint names as defendants Socoma Companies, Inc. ("Socoma"), Lady Fair Kitchens, Incorporated ("Lady Fair"), Monarch Electronics International, Inc. ("Monarch"), and eleven individuals of whom three are alleged officers or directors of Socoma, four of Lady Fair, and four of Monarch. Lady Fair and the individual defendants associated with it, a Utah corporation and Utah residents respectively, did not appear in the trial court and are not parties to this appeal.

The complaint alleges that under 1967 amendments to the Economic Opportunity Act of 1964 (81 Stat. 688–690, 42 U.S.C.A. §§ 2763–2768, repealed by 86 Stat. 703 (1972)) "the United States Congress instituted Special Impact Programs with the intent to benefit the residents of certain neighborhoods having especially large concentrations of low income persons and suffering from dependency, chronic unemployment and rising tensions." Funds to administer these programs were appropriated to the United States Department of Labor. The department subsequently designated the East Los Angeles neighborhood as a "Special Impact area" and made federal funds available for contracts with local private industry for the benefit of the "hard-core unemployed residents" of East Los Angeles.

On January 17, 1969, the corporate defendants allegedly entered into contracts with the Secretary of Labor, acting on behalf of the Manpower Administration, United States Department of Labor (hereinafter referred to as the "Government"). Each such defendant entered into a separate contract and all three contracts are made a part of the complaint as exhibits. Under each contract the contracting defendant agreed to lease space in the then vacant Lincoln Heights jail building owned by the City of Los Angeles, to invest at least $5,000,000 in renovating the leasehold and establishing a facility for the manufacture of certain articles, to train and employ in such facility for at least 12 months, at minimum wage rates, a specified number of East Los Angeles residents certified as disadvantaged by the Government, and to provide such employees with opportunities for promotion into available supervisorial-managerial positions and with options to purchase stock in their employer corporation. Each contract provided for the lease of different space in the building and for the manufacture of a different kind of product. As consideration, the Government agreed to pay each defendant a stated amount in installments. Socoma was to hire 650 persons and receive $950,000; Lady Fair was to hire 550 persons and receive $999,000; and Monarch was to hire 400 persons and receive $800,000. The hiring of these persons was to be completed by January 17, 1970.

Plaintiffs were allegedly members of a class of no more than 2,017 East Los Angeles residents who were certified as disadvantaged and were qualified for employment under the contracts. Although the Government paid $712,500 of the contractual consideration to Socoma, $299,700 to Lady Fair, and $240,000 to Monarch, all of these defendants failed to perform under their respective contracts, except that Socoma provided 186 jobs of which 139 were wrongfully terminated, and Lady Fair provided 90 jobs, of which all were wrongfully terminated.

The complaint contains 11 causes of action. The second, fourth, and sixth causes of action seek damages of $3,607,500 against Socoma, $3,052,500 against Lady Fair, and $2,220,000 against Monarch, calculated on the basis of 12 months' wages at minimum rates and $1,000 for loss of training for each of the jobs the defendant contracted to provide. The third and fifth causes of action seek similar damages for the 139 persons whose jobs were terminated by Socoma and the 90 persons whose jobs were terminated by Lady Fair. . . .

Each cause of action alleges that the "express purpose of the [Government] in entering into [each] contract was to benefit [the] certified disadvantaged hardcore unemployed residents of East Los Angeles [for whom defendants promised to provide training and jobs] and none other, and those residents are thus the express third party beneficiaries of [each] contract."

The general demurrers admitted the truth of all the material factual allegations of the complaint, regardless of any possible difficulty in proving them (Alcorn v. Anbro Engineering, Inc. (1970) 2 Cal.3d 493, 496, 86 Cal. Rptr. 88, 468 P.2d 216), but did not admit allegations which constitute conclusions of law (Faulkner v. Cal. Toll Bridge Authority (1953) 40 Cal.2d 317, 329, 253 P.2d 659) or which are contrary to matters of which we must take judicial notice (Chavez v. Times–Mirror Co. (1921) 185 Cal. 20, 23, 195 P. 666). (See Witkin, Cal. Procedure (2d ed. 1970) Pleading, §§ 328, 800.) When a complaint is based on a written contract which it sets out in full, a general demurrer to the complaint admits not only the contents of the instrument but also any pleaded meaning to which the instrument is reasonably susceptible. (Coast Bank v. Minderhout (1964) 61 Cal.2d 311, 315, 38 Cal.Rptr. 505, 392 P.2d 265.) Moreover, where, as here, the general demurrer is to an *original* complaint and is sustained without leave to amend, "the issues presented are whether the complaint states a cause of action, and if not, whether there is a reasonable possibility that it could be amended to do so." (MacLeod v. Tribune Publishing Co. (1959) 52 Cal.2d 536, 542, 343 P.2d 36, 38; see 3 Witkin, Cal.Procedure (2d ed. 1971) Pleading, § 845.) Thus, we must determine whether the pleaded written contracts support plaintiffs' claim either on their face or under any interpretation to which the contracts are reasonably susceptible and which is pleaded in the complaint or could be pleaded by proper amendment. This determination must be made in light of applicable federal statutes and other matters we must judicially notice. (Evid.Code, §§ 451, 459, subd. (a).)

Plaintiffs contend they are third party beneficiaries under Civil Code section 1559, which provides: "A contract, made expressly for the benefit of a third person, may be enforced by him at any time before the parties thereto rescind it." This section excludes enforcement of a contract by persons who are only incidentally or remotely benefited by it. (Lucas v. Hamm (1961) 56 Cal.2d 583, 590, 15 Cal.Rptr. 821, 824, 364 P.2d 685, 688.) American law generally classifies persons having enforceable rights under contracts to which they are not parties as either creditor beneficiaries or donee beneficiaries. (Restatement, Contracts, §§ 133, subds. (1), (2), 135, 136, 147; 2 Williston on Contracts (3d ed. 1959) § 356; 4 Corbin on Contracts (1951) § 774; see Restatement, Second, Contracts (Tentative Drafts 1973) § 133, coms. b, c.) California decisions follow this classification....

A person cannot be a creditor beneficiary unless the promisor's performance of the contract will discharge some form of legal duty owed to the beneficiary by the promisee. (Hartman Ranch Co. v. Associated Oil Co. (1937) 10 Cal.2d 232, 244, 73 P.2d 1163; Restatement, Contracts § 133, subd. (1)(b).) Clearly the Government (the promisee) at no time bore any legal duty toward plaintiffs to provide the benefits set forth in the contracts and plaintiffs do not claim to be creditor beneficiaries.

A person is a donee beneficiary only if the promisee's contractual intent is either to make a gift to him or to confer on him a right against the promisor. (Restatement, Contracts § 133, subd. (1)(a).) If the promisee intends to make a gift, the donee beneficiary can recover if such donative intent must have been understood by the promisor from the nature of the contract and the circumstances accompanying its execution. (Lucas v. Hamm, supra, 56 Cal.2d at pp. 590–591, 15 Cal.Rptr. 821, 364 P.2d 685.) This rule does not aid plaintiffs, however, because, as will be seen, no intention to make a gift can be imputed to the Government as promisee.

Unquestionably plaintiffs were among those whom the Government intended to benefit through defendants' performance of the contracts which recite that they are executed pursuant to a statute and a presidential directive calling for programs to furnish disadvantaged persons with training and employment opportunities. However, the fact that a Government program for social betterment confers benefits upon individuals who are not required to render contractual consideration in return does not necessarily imply that the benefits are intended as gifts. Congress' power to spend money in aid of the general welfare (U.S. Const., art. I, § 8) authorizes federal programs to alleviate national unemployment. (Helvering v. Davis (1937) 301 U.S. 619, 640–645, 57 S.Ct. 904, 81 L.Ed. 1307.) The benefits of such programs are provided not simply as gifts to the recipients but as a means of accomplishing a larger public purpose. The furtherance of the public purpose is in the nature of consideration to the Government, displacing any governmental intent to furnish the benefits as gifts. (See County of Alameda v. Janssen (1940) 16 Cal.2d 276, 281, 106 P.2d 11; Allied Architects v. Payne (1923) 192 Cal. 431, 438–439, 221 P. 209.)

Even though a person is not the intended recipient of a gift, he may nevertheless be "a donee beneficiary if it appears from the terms of the promise in view of the accompanying circumstances that the purpose of the promisee in obtaining the promise ... is ... to *confer upon him a right against the promisor* to some performance neither due nor supposed or asserted to be due from the promisee to the beneficiary." (Restatement, Contracts § 133, subd. (1)(a) (italics supplied); Gourmet Lane, Inc. v. Keller (1963) 222 Cal.App.2d 701, 705, 35 Cal.Rptr. 398.) The Government may, of course, deliberately implement a public purpose by including provisions in its contracts which expressly confer on a specified class of third persons a direct right to benefits, or damages in lieu of benefits, against the private contractor.

But a governmental intent to confer such a direct right cannot be inferred simply from the fact that the third persons were intended to enjoy the benefits. The Restatement, Contracts makes this clear in dealing specifically with contractual promises to the Government to render services to members of the public: "A promisor bound to the United States or to a State or municipality by contract to do an act or render a service to some or all of the members of the public, *is subject to no duty* under the contract to such members to give compensation for the injurious consequences of performing or attempting to perform it, or of failing to do so, unless, . . . *an intention is manifested in the contract,* as interpreted in the light of the circumstances surrounding its formation, *that the promisor shall compensate members of the public for such injurious consequences. . . .*" (Restatement, Contracts § 145 (italics supplied);[1] see City & County of San Francisco v. Western Air Lines, Inc. (1962) 204 Cal.App.2d 105, 121, 22 Cal.Rptr. 216.)

The present contracts manifest no intent that the defendants pay damages to compensate plaintiffs or other members of the public for their nonperformance. To the contrary, the contracts' provisions for retaining the Government's control over determination of contractual disputes and for limiting defendants' financial risks indicate a governmental purpose to exclude the direct rights against defendants claimed here.

Each contract provides that any dispute of fact arising thereunder is to be determined by written decision of the Government's contracting officer, subject to an appeal to the Secretary of Labor, whose decision shall be final unless determined by a competent court to have been fraudulent, capricious, arbitrary, in bad faith, or not supported by substantial evidence. These administrative decisions may include determinations of related questions of law although such determinations are not made final. The efficiency and uniformity of interpretation fostered by these administrative procedures would tend to be undermined if litigation such as the present action, to which the Government is a stranger, were permitted to proceed on the merits.

In addition to the provisions on resolving disputes each contract contains a "liquidated damages" provision obligating the contractor to refund all amounts received from the Government, with interest, in the event of failure to acquire and equip the specified manufacturing facility, and, for each employment opportunity it fails to provide, to refund a stated dollar amount equivalent to the total contract compensation divided by the number of jobs agreed to be provided. This liquidated damages provision limits liability for the breaches alleged by plaintiffs to the refunding of amounts received and indicates an absence of any contractual intent to impose liability directly in favor of plaintiffs, or, as claimed in the complaint, to impose liability for the value of the promised performance. To allow plaintiffs' claim would nullify the

---

1. The corresponding language in the Tentative Drafts of the Restatement, Second, Contracts (1973), section 145, is: "[A] promisor who contracts with a government or governmental agency to do an act for or render a service to the public *is not subject to contractual liability* to a member of the public for consequential damages resulting from performance or failure to perform unless . . . the terms of the promise provide for such liability. . . ."

The language omitted in this quotation and the quotation in the accompanying text relates to the creditor beneficiary situation in which the government itself would be liable for nonperformance of the contract. As noted earlier, plaintiffs do not claim to be creditor beneficiaries.

limited liability for which defendants bargained and which the Government may well have held out as an inducement in negotiating the contracts.

It is this absence of any manifestation of intent that defendants should pay compensation for breach to persons in the position of plaintiffs that distinguishes this case from Shell v. Schmidt (1954) 126 Cal.App.2d 279, 272 P.2d 82, relied on by plaintiffs. The defendant in *Shell* was a building contractor who had entered into an agreement with the federal government under which he received priorities for building materials and agreed in return to use the materials to build homes with required specifications for sale to war veterans at or below ceiling prices. Plaintiffs were 12 veterans, each of whom had purchased a home that failed to comply with the agreed specifications. They were held entitled to recover directly from the defendant contractor as third party beneficiaries of his agreement with the government. The legislation under which the agreement was made included a provision empowering the government to obtain payment of monetary compensation by the contractor to the veteran purchasers for deficiencies resulting from failure to comply with specifications. Thus, there was "an intention ... manifested in the contract ... that the promisor shall compensate members of the public for such injurious consequences [of nonperformance]."[2]

Plaintiffs contend that section 145 of the Restatement, Contracts, previously quoted, does not preclude their recovery because it applies only to promises made to a governmental entity "to do an act or render a service to ... the public," and, plaintiffs assert they and the class they represent are identified persons set apart from "the public." Even if this contention were correct it would not follow that plaintiffs have standing as third party beneficiaries under the Restatement. The quoted provision of section 145 "is a special application of the principles stated in §§ 133(1a), 135 [on donee beneficiaries]" (Restatement, Contracts § 145, com. a), delineating certain circumstances which preclude government contractors' liability to third parties. Section 145 itself does not purport to confer standing to sue on persons who do not otherwise qualify under basic third party beneficiary principles.[3] As pointed out above, plaintiffs are not donee beneficiaries under those basic principles because it does not appear from the terms and circumstances of the contract that the Government intended to make a gift to plaintiffs or to confer on them a legal right against the defendants.

Moreover, contrary to plaintiffs' contention, section 145 of the Restatement, Contracts does preclude their recovery because the services which the contracts required the defendants to perform *were* to be rendered to "members of the public" within the meaning of that section. Each contract recites it is made under the "Special Impact Programs" part of the Economic Opportu-

---

2. In contrast to *Shell,* supra, is City & County of San Francisco v. Western Air Lines, Inc., supra, 204 Cal.App.2d 105, 22 Cal.Rptr. 216. There, Western Air Lines claimed to be a third party beneficiary of agreements between the federal government and the City and County of San Francisco under which the city received federal funds for the development of its airport subject to a written condition that the airport "be available for public use on fair and reasonable terms and without unjust discrimination." Western Air Lines asserted that it had been charged for its use of the airport at a higher rate than some other air carriers in violation of the contractual condition, and therefore was entitled to recover the excess charges from the city. One of the reasons given by the court on appeal for rejecting this contention was the absence of any provision or indication of intent in the agreements between the government and the city to compensate third parties for noncompliance....

3. The same is true of the Tentative Draft of section 145 of the Restatement, Second, Contracts....

nity Act of 1964 and pursuant to a presidential directive for a test program of cooperation between the federal government and private industry in an effort to provide training and jobs for thousands of the hard-core unemployed or under-employed. The congressional declaration of purpose of the Economic Opportunity Act as a whole points up the public nature of its benefits on a national scale. Congress declared that the purpose of the act was to "strengthen, supplement, and coordinate efforts in furtherance of [the] policy" of "opening to everyone the opportunity for education and training, the opportunity to work, and the opportunity to live in decency and dignity" so that the "United States can achieve its full economic and social potential as a nation." (42 U.S.C.A. § 2701.)

In providing for special impact programs, Congress declared that such programs were directed to the solution of critical problems existing in particular neighborhoods having especially large concentration of low-income persons, and that the programs were intended to be of sufficient size and scope to have an appreciable impact in such neighborhoods in arresting tendencies toward dependency, chronic unemployment, and rising community tensions. (42 U.S.C.A. former § 2763.) Thus the contracts here were designed not to benefit individuals as such but to utilize the training and employment of disadvantaged persons as a means of improving the East Los Angeles neighborhood. Moreover, the means by which the contracts were intended to accomplish this community improvement were not confined to provision of the particular benefits on which plaintiffs base their claim to damages—one year's employment at minimum wages plus $1,000 worth of training to be provided to each of 650 persons by one defendant, 400 by another, and 550 by another. Rather the objective was to be achieved by establishing permanent industries in which local residents would be permanently employed and would have opportunities to become supervisors, managers and part owners. The required minimum capital investment of $5,000,000 by each defendant and the defendants' 22–year lease of the former Lincoln Heights jail building for conversion into an industrial facility also indicates the broad, long-range objective of the program. Presumably, as the planned enterprises prospered, the quantity and quality of employment and economic opportunity that they provided would increase and would benefit not only employees but also their families, other local enterprises and the government itself through reduction of law enforcement and welfare costs.

The fact that plaintiffs were in a position to benefit more directly than certain other members of the public from performance of the contract does not alter their status as incidental beneficiaries. (See Restatement, Contracts § 145, illus. 1: C, a member of the public cannot recover for injury from B's failure to perform a contract with the United States to carry mail over a certain route.)[4] For example, in City & County of San Francisco v. Western Air Lines, Inc., supra, 204 Cal.App.2d 105, 22 Cal.Rptr. 216, the agreement between the federal government and the city for improvement of the airport could be considered to be of greater benefit to air carriers using the airport than to many other members of the public. Nevertheless, Western, as an air carrier, was but an incidental, not an express, beneficiary of the agreement and therefore had no standing to enforce the contractual prohibition against

---

4. This illustration is repeated in Tentative Draft, Restatement, Second, Contracts, section 145, illustration 1.

discrimination in the airport's availability for public use. The court explains the distinction as follows: "None of the documents under consideration confers on Western the rights of a third-party beneficiary. The various contracts and assurances created benefits and detriments as between only two parties—the United States and the city. Nothing in them shows any intent of the contracting parties to confer any benefit directly and expressly upon air carriers such as the defendant. It is true that air carriers, including Western, may be *incidentally* benefited by City's assurances in respect to nondiscriminatory treatment at the airport. They may also be incidentally benefited by the fact that, through federal aid, a public airport is improved with longer runways, brighter beacons, or larger loading ramps, or by the fact a new public airport is provided for a community without one. The various documents and agreements were part of a federal aid program directed to the promoting of a national transportation system. Provisions in such agreements, including the nondiscrimination clauses, were intended to advance such federal aims and not for the benefit of those who might be affected by the sponsor's failure to perform." (204 Cal.App.2d at p. 120, 22 Cal.Rptr. at p. 225.)

For the reasons above stated we hold that plaintiffs and the class they represent have no standing as third party beneficiaries to recover the damages sought in the complaint under either California law or the general contract principles which federal law applies to government contracts.

The judgments of dismissal are affirmed.

McComb, Sullivan, and Clark, JJ., concur.

Burke, Justice (dissenting).

I dissent. The certified hard-core unemployed of East Los Angeles were the express, not incidental, beneficiaries of the contracts in question and, therefore, have standing to enforce those contracts. . . .

The majority err ... because the congressional purpose was to benefit *both* the communities in which the impact programs are established *and* the individual impoverished persons in such communities.[5] The benefits from the instant contracts were to accrue directly to the members of plaintiffs' class, as a reading of the contracts clearly demonstrates.[6] These direct benefits to members of plaintiffs' class were not merely the "*means* of executing the public purposes," as the majority contend ..., but were the *ends* in themselves and one of the public purposes to which the legislation and subsequent contracts were addressed. Accordingly, I cannot agree with the majority that "the contracts here were designed *not* to benefit individuals as such but to

5. Evidence of Congress' purpose to aid the *individual* impoverished persons in such communities can be gleaned from 42 U.S.C.A. § 2701, wherein Congress declared that if our country is to achieve its full potential, "every individual" must be given "the opportunity for education and training, the opportunity to work, and the opportunity to live in decency and dignity." Congress implemented this general policy of assisting our impoverished citizens in various ways, including the Special Impact Program involved in this case. Yet, contrary to the majority, nothing indicates that Congress' *exclusive* purpose in doing so was to assist the neighborhoods and communities in which these persons live. It seems clear that Congress intended *both* the communities and the individuals to be direct beneficiaries of the program. It is incorrect to label one as an intended *direct* beneficiary and the other as merely *incidental*.

6. In the contracts, the defendants agreed to provide training and jobs to a specified class of persons, whom plaintiffs represent. The government's express intent, therefore, was to confer a benefit, namely training and jobs, upon an ascertainable identifiable class and not simply the general public itself.

utilize the training and employment of disadvantaged persons as a *means* of improving the East Los Angeles neighborhood." (. . . italics added.)

The intent of the contracts themselves is expressed in their preambles. . . . By these provisions, the contracting parties clearly state as one of their purposes their intent to find jobs for the hard-core unemployed.

In accord with this expressed intent, the substantive provisions of the contracts confer a direct benefit upon the class seeking to enforce them. The contracts call for the hiring of stated numbers of hard-core unemployed from the East Los Angeles Special Impact Area for a period of at least one year at a starting minimum wage of $2.00 per hour for the first 90 days and a minimum wage of $2.25 per hour thereafter, or for the prevailing wage for the area, whichever is higher. In addition to requiring appropriate job training for such employees, the contracts also require "That the Contractor will arrange for the orderly promotion of persons so employed into available supervisory-managerial and other positions, and will arrange for all contract employees to obtain a total ownership interest not exceeding thirty (30) percent in the Contractor through an appropriate stock purchase plan. . . ." The scope of the stock purchase plans is detailed in each of the contracts. . . .

The language of section 133 [of the Restatement,[7]], standing alone, could reasonably suggest that members of the general public are "donee beneficiaries" under any contract whose purpose is to confer a "gift" upon them. Section 145 qualifies this broad language and treats the general public merely as incidental, not direct, beneficiaries under contracts made for the general public benefit, unless the contract manifests a clear intent to compensate such members of the public in the event of a breach. Section 145 does not, however, entirely preclude application of the "donee beneficiary" concept to every government contract. Whenever, as in the instant case, such a contract expresses an intent to benefit directly a particular person or ascertainable class of persons, section 145 is, by its terms, inapplicable and the contract may be enforced by the beneficiaries pursuant to the general provisions of section 133. Thus, I would conclude that section 145 is consistent with the holding of Shell v. Schmidt, supra, 126 Cal.App.2d 279, 272 P.2d 82, and the City and County of San Francisco v. Western Air Lines, Inc., supra, 204 Cal.App.2d 105, 22 Cal.Rptr. 216. . . .

The majority contend that the inclusion of liquidated damage clauses in each of the contracts limits defendants' financial risks and was intended to preclude the assertion of third party claims. . . . Yet, these clauses simply provide for various refunds of monies advanced by the government in the event of a default. These so-called "liquidated damages" clauses nowhere purport to limit damages to the specified refunds. Nothing in the contracts limits the right of the government or, more importantly, plaintiffs' class, to seek additional relief. . . .

The majority also rely on the fact that, "The present contracts manifest no intent that the defendants pay damages to compensate plaintiffs or other

---

7. Comment (c) to section 133 of the Restatement, Contracts states in part that "By gift is meant primarily some performance or right which is not paid for by the recipient and which is apparently designed to benefit him." Thus, section 133 states essentially the same rule as that enunciated in Shell v. Schmidt, supra, 126 Cal.App.2d 279, 290–291, 272 P.2d 82. Section 133 has been followed by the California courts. (Hartman Ranch Co. v. Associated Oil Co., supra, 10 Cal.2d 232, 244, 73 P.2d 1163; Southern Cal. Gas Co. v. ABC Construction Co., 204 Cal.App.2d 747, 752, 22 Cal.Rptr. 540.)

members of the public for their nonperformance." ... Therefore, it assertedly follows that giving plaintiffs the right to monetary benefits in lieu of performance would give to plaintiffs and the class they represent benefits never contemplated nor intended under the contracts. This argument disregards both the fact that the class was to receive a direct monetary benefit under the contracts in the form of wages, and that under well settled contract law, an aggrieved party is entitled to be compensated for all the detriment proximately caused by a breach of contract (Civ.Code, § 3300). ...

It is my conclusion, therefore, that the trial court erred in sustaining the demurrer without leave to amend. I would order the trial court to determine the propriety of plaintiffs' class action prior to proceeding upon the merits of the complaint.

TOBRINER and MOSK, JJ., concur.

———

ZIGAS v. SUPERIOR COURT, 120 Cal.App.3d 827, 174 Cal.Rptr. 806 (1981). The petitioners were tenants of an apartment building that was financed with a federally insured mortgage, pursuant to the National Housing Act. A provision of the financing agreement required the landlords to charge no more than the schedule of rents approved by the Department of Housing and Urban Development (HUD). Petitioners sought damages for the landlords' violation of that provision, by overcharges. Held, the tenants could sue the landlords as third–party beneficiaries.

"California law clearly allows third-party suits for breaches of contract where no government agency is a party to the contract.... Whether such suits are allowed when the government contracts with a private party depends upon analysis of the decisions in Shell v. Schmidt (1954) 126 Cal.App.2d 279 [272 P.2d 82] and Martinez v. Socoma Companies Inc., supra, 11 Cal.3d 394."

"[U]nder *Martinez,* standing to sue as a third-party beneficiary to a government contract depends on the intent of the parties as manifested by the contract and the circumstances surrounding its formation.... We therefore must determine, from the terms of the contract between HUD and real parties [landlords] and the attendant circumstances, whether there was manifested an intention that petitioners be compensated in the event of real parties' nonperformance.... [W]e are of the view that the case falls within *Shell;* that is to say, appellants [tenants] were direct beneficiaries of the contract and have standing, and not, as in *Martinez,* incidental beneficiaries without standing.

"We explicate:

"1. In *Martinez,* the contract between the government and Socoma provided that if Socoma breached the agreement, Socoma would refund to the government that which the government had paid Socoma pursuant to the contract between them. Thus, it is clear in *Martinez* that it was the government that was out of pocket as a consequence of the breach and should be reimbursed therefor, not the people to be trained and given jobs. In the case at bench, as in *Shell,* the government suffered no loss as a consequence of the breach, it was the renter here and the veteran purchaser in *Shell* that suffered the direct pecuniary loss.

"2. Unlike *Martinez,* too, in the case at bench, no governmental administrative procedure was provided for the resolution of disputes arising under the agreement. Thus, to permit this litigation would in no way affect the 'efficiency and uniformity of interpretation fostered by these administrative procedures.' (Martinez v. Socoma Companies, Inc., supra, 11 Cal.3d at p. 402.) On the contrary, as we earlier noted, lawsuits such as this promote the federal interest by inducing compliance with HUD agreements.

"3. In *Martinez,* the court held that 'To allow plaintiffs' claim would nullify the limited liability for which defendants bargained and which the Government may well have held out as an inducement in negotiating the contracts.' ... Here, there is no 'limited liability.' As we shall point out, real parties are liable under the agreement, *without limitation,* for breach of the agreement.

"4. Further, in *Martinez,* the contracts 'were designed not to benefit individuals as such but to utilize the training and employment of disadvantaged persons as a means of improving the East Los Angeles neighborhood.' ... Moreover, the training and employment programs were but one aspect of a 'broad, long-range objective' ... contemplated by the agreement and designed to benefit not only those to be trained and employed but also 'other local enterprises and the government itself through reduction of law enforcement and welfare costs.' ...

"Here, on the other hand, as in *Shell,* the purpose of the Legislature and of the contract between real parties and HUD is narrow and specific: to provide moderate rental housing for families with children; in *Shell,* to provide moderate priced homes for veterans.

"5. Finally, we believe the agreement itself manifests an intent to make tenants direct beneficiaries, not incidental beneficiaries, of [the landlords'] promise to charge no more than the HUD approved rent schedule.

"Section 4(a) and 4(c) of the agreement, providing that there can be no increase in rental fees, over the approved rent schedule, without the prior approval in writing of HUD, were obviously designed to protect the tenant against arbitrary increases in rents, precisely that which is alleged to have occurred here. Certainly, it was not intended to benefit the government as a guarantor of the mortgage....

"We are supported in our view by section 17 of the Agreement which specifically provides that [the landlords] are personally liable, '(a) for funds ... of the project coming into their hands which, by the provisions [of the Agreement] *they are not entitled to retain;* and (b) for their own acts and deeds or acts and deeds of other [sic] which they have authorized in violation of the provisions [of the Agreement].' ...

"By the allegations of the complaint, [the landlords] have 'retained' in excess of $2 million in violation of the Agreement. Therefore, they are liable for that sum. To whom should they be liable? To ask the question is to answer it. It is not the government from whom the money was exacted; it was taken from the tenants. Therefore, it should be returned to the tenants."

H.B. DEAL & CO. v. HEAD, 221 Ark. 47, 251 S.W.2d 1017 (1952). The Government made a contract with Deal calling for the construction by Deal of an ordnance plant. A provision in the contract required Deal to pay his laborers time–and–a–half for overtime. The Fair Labor Standards Act laid down a similar requirement for employees engaged in certain classes of work. Employees of Deal brought an action against him under the Act and, in the alternative, under the contract. Held, the Act was inapplicable to Deal's construction job, but the employees could sue under the contract, because the Government placed the time–and–a–half provision in the contract for their benefit.

––––––––

H.R. MOCH CO. v. RENSSELAER WATER CO., 247 N.Y. 160, 159 N.E. 896 (1928). A waterworks company entered into a contract with a city whereby the company: (1) agreed to furnish the city with water for sewer flushing, for street sprinkling, and for public buildings, and to provide service at fire hydrants at the rate of $42.50 a year for each hydrant; and (2) agreed to provide private and industrial takers with water at reasonable rates. The plaintiff was a property owner who alleged that his property was destroyed by fire in consequence of the failure of the waterworks company to comply with its contract with the city by providing a sufficient head of water at the fire hydrants. A demurrer to the complaint was sustained. The court said (through Cardozo, Ch. J.) that since the city did not owe its inhabitants a legal duty to provide them with water for the purpose of extinguishing fires, the contract between the city and the waterworks company could not be construed as an agreement to discharge a duty of the city to its inhabitants. That being so, the plaintiff had no rights as a third–party beneficiary unless "an intention appears that the promisor [the waterworks company] is to be answerable to individual members of the public as well as to the city for any loss ensuing from the failure to fulfil the promise. No such intention is discernible here."

The court conceded that "every city contract, not improvident or wasteful, is for the benefit of the public." But before the injured member of the public can have a right against the party contracting with the city, the benefit must not be merely "incidental and secondary," but rather "must be primary and immediate in such a sense and to such a degree as to bespeak the assumption of a duty to make reparation directly to the individual members of the public if the benefit is lost." Illustrating the principle the court said, "A promisor undertakes to supply fuel for heating a public building. He is not liable for breach of contract to a visitor who finds the building without fuel, and thus [catches] a cold.... The carrier of the mails under contract with the government is not answerable to the merchant who has lost the benefit of the bargain through negligent delay. The householder is without a remedy against manufacturers of hose and engines, though prompt performance of their contracts would have stayed the ravages of fire. 'The law does not spread its protection so far.'" If the defendant were liable to this plaintiff, the court said, the defendant would also be liable to all the property owners in the city if the whole city were laid low through a spreading of the fire. "A promisor will not be deemed to have had in mind the assumption of a risk so overwhelming for any trivial reward." (The court also held that the plaintiff had no cause of action for a common–law tort or for breach of a statutory duty.)

OGDEN v. EARL R. HOWARTH & SONS, INC., 58 Misc.2d 213, 294 N.Y.S.2d 430 (1968). " . . . The underlying rationale of *Moch* might well be a policy decision to promote the performance of essential governmental functions by municipalities by insulating parties to municipal contracts from liability for potentially catastrophic losses resulting from non–performance or a failure to properly perform such functions.

"Even at a time contemporaneous with its decision, however, the rationale upon which the *Moch* opinion turned was subjected to severe criticism. See, for example, Corbin, Liability of Water Companies for Losses by Fire, 19 Yale L.J. 425 (1910). Although *Moch* continues to be recognized as the majority rule, it is only grudgingly followed. . . . In fact with regard to third party beneficiary contractual rights the *Moch* rule is increasingly being strictly limited to its facts and subjected to exceptions. Thus, if a plaintiff can show a *special* benefit to himself generally, he may be able to bring an action as a third party beneficiary. . . . Also, it may be that courts are more willing to entertain a third party beneficiary claim where relatively minor property damage to a limited number of people is involved rather than potentially extensive personal injury liability to a large class of people. . . . Insurance protection against large scale catastrophes arising out of the non-performance or improper performance of municipal contracts may also be a factor weighing in favor of the mitigation of the *Moch* rule."

DOYLE v. SOUTH PITTSBURGH WATER CO., 414 Pa. 199, 199 A.2d 875 (1964). On facts comparable to *Moch Co. v. Rensselaer Water Co.* the court held that the plaintiffs had a valid complaint for negligence.

"[In *Moch*, Justice Cardozo concluded] that there was no liability on the part of the defendant company because:

> 'What we are dealing with at this time is a mere negligent omission, unaccompanied by malice or other aggravating elements. The failure in such circumstances to furnish an adequate supply of water is at most the denial of a benefit. It is not the commission of a wrong.'

"It must be stated, with some regret, that at this point Homer nodded. . . . A refusal to deny a benefit may in itself result in the refusal becoming an instrument of harm. Once Justice Cardozo recognized that the defendant was guilty of a 'negligent omission,' he admitted that the defendant had committed a breach of duty since negligence is defined in law as a breach of duty. If there was no breach of duty on the part of the defendant, its conduct could be not characterized as a negligent omission, but would be merely an omission that did not amount to negligence. . . .

"Commenting on Justice Cardozo's decision in the *Moch* case, Professor Seavey said in 52 Harvard Law Review, that here the distinguished jurist failed to pursue 'his accustomed method of facing realities.' "

LA MOUREA v. RHUDE, 209 Minn. 53, 295 N.W. 304 (1940). Defendants contracted to do certain sewer-construction work, involving blasting, for the city of Duluth. The contract provided that defendants should be "liable for any damages done to the work or other structure or public or private property and injuries sustained by persons" in the course of defendants' operations. Plaintiff sued for damage to his real estate caused by defendants' blasting. The court affirmed an order overruling a demurrer to the complaint, rejecting defendants' argument "that this promise was one to indemnify the city and nothing more."

COPELAND v. BEARD
Supreme Court of Alabama, 1928.
217 Ala. 216, 115 So. 389.

Suit by Mrs. B.V. Beard against Marvin Copeland. Judgment for plaintiff was affirmed by the Court of Appeals (22 Ala.App. 325, 115 So. 385), and defendant petitions for certiorari to review the judgment of the Court of Appeals. Writ granted. Judgment reversed, and case remanded.

BOULDIN, J. Taking the facts from the findings of the Court of Appeals, the essential question here for review on certiorari may be briefly stated thus: Where a debtor sells and conveys real and personal property, upon consideration in part that the purchaser shall assume and pay specified debts of the vendor, and, on the same day, before the creditors for whose benefit the promise is made have assented thereto, the purchaser resells and conveys the property upon consideration in part that the subpurchaser shall assume and pay the same indebtedness, and the original vendor debtor thereupon releases the original purchaser from his promise to pay, can such creditor thereafter maintain an action of assumpsit against the original purchaser?

In Clark v. Nelson, 216 Ala. 199, 112 So. 819, this court, after a review of the authorities, approved the general statement of the doctrine in cases of rescission by Mr. Williston:

"The creditor's right is purely derivative, and, if the debtor no longer has a right of action against the promisor, the creditor can have none." 1 Williston on Contracts, § 397.

After quoting from our own cases, it was said:

"We think, therefore, this court is definitely committed to the doctrine that the promisor may interpose any defense that was permissible as between himself and the original debtor, including, of course, mutual rescission of the contract so long as the creditor had not acted in good faith upon the promise so as to alter his position." Clark v. Nelson, 216 Ala. 199, 112 So. 821.

The Court of Appeals takes the view that the case at bar is to be differentiated from the *Nelson* case saying (22 Ala.App. 325, 115 So. 385):

"The recent case of Clark & Co. v. Nelson, 216 Ala. 199, 112 So. 819, is based upon the rescission of the contract, before acceptance by the debtor,[8] thereby placing the parties in statu quo. There is a vast differ-

---

8. So in copy. Presumably, the court meant to say, "acceptance by the creditor." (Footnote by ed.)

ence between a rescission, where the property transferred as the consideration for the agreement to pay a creditor is reconveyed to the contracting debtor[,] and a subsequent agreement to release a purchaser of the debtor's property who had agreed to pay a creditor in consideration of property transferred to him without a reconveyance of the property."

Is the distinction thus declared sound in principle?

The transaction between the debtor, his vendee, and the subvendee, whereby the latter purchased the property [and] assumed the obligation to pay creditors, and the debtor released the original promisor, was, as between them, a novation. It was supported by a valuable consideration, as in other cases of novation. All right of action in the promisee, the debtor, as against his promisor, the vendee, was released. Whether such release may be aptly called a rescission of the promise to pay creditors seems unimportant. As between the immediate parties to the transaction it had the same effect.

When a debtor contracts with another, for a valuable consideration, to assume and pay his debt, the creditor has an election to accept or reject the new party as his debtor. He may ignore the offer and proceed to enforce all his remedies against the original debtor. Henry v. Murphy, 54 Ala. 246.

An election requires knowledge of the facts. So a suit against the original debtor without notice that another has assumed to pay it does not constitute an election to reject the agreement. Young v. Hawkins, 74 Ala. 370. An action against the promisor assuming to pay the debt is a sufficient acceptance—an election to affirm the contract made for the creditor's benefit. Carver v. Eads, 65 Ala. 191.

There is difference of view as to the status of the parties after acceptance of the agreement by the creditor. Some authorities hold that upon election to accept the benefits of the contract, he releases the original debtor. These cases proceed on the idea that the contract made between the debtor and the assuming party, while binding between themselves, is, as to the creditor, an offer of novation. Several of our earlier cases quite clearly proceed on this view. The Nelson Case, in course of discussion, recognizes these decisions.

The other view is that by the contract wherein the debtor sells property in consideration that the purchaser assumes the payment of debt, the latter becomes, as between the immediate parties, the principal and the debtor a quasi surety, and the creditor, upon acceptance of the arrangement, may sue either or both. This latter view is distinctly held in People's Savings Bank v. Jordan, 200 Ala. 500, 76 So. 442; Tyson v. Austill, 168 Ala. 525, 53 So. 263; Moore v. First Nat. Bank of Florence, 139 Ala. 595, 606, 36 So. 777.

This is the prevailing doctrine in other jurisdictions. 1 Williston on Contracts, § 393. While our cases involved directly conveyances by a mortgagor, the purchaser assuming the mortgage debt, no sound distinction exists between them and the instant case.

The question is here involved only incidentally in defining when the right of the creditor to sue the promisor becomes fixed, and not subject to rescission or release. It is said the promisor and promisee may rescind at any time before the creditor alters his position. If bringing suit against the promisor releases the original debtor, this would clearly alter the creditor's position for the worse, if a right of rescission still exists. If such action does not release the original debtor, then the inquiry is, When is the creditor's position so altered that his rights become fixed and beyond the power of the original parties to rescind or release?

We now adopt the doctrine that by acceptance of the promise made for his benefit, and action thereon, the creditor does not release the original debtor, unless so stipulated in the contract and made known to the creditor.

Both parties invite the creditor to accept the contract. The debtor has the benefit of the promise for his protection in case he is still required to pay. The creditor being thus invited to avail himself of the contract, we think no fair intendment can be indulged that he shall thereby take the hazard of losing the debt, if the promise so recommended proves unavailing.

Coming then to the question of when the creditor's right of action against the promisor becomes fixed, we think it properly determinable on the basic law of contracts. So long as the contract to assume is between the debtor and his promisor only, the creditor is not a party thereto. He can become so only by his consent. At the same time, the contract, in the nature of it, is an open offer to the creditor. His assent while the offer is open is all that is required. When the minds of all parties consent to the same thing at the same time, and such consent is communicated between them, the contract is complete.

Consent in such case may be proven in the same manner as in other contracts. The consideration for the promise passing between promisor and promisee is also consideration for the completed contract between all parties. The tripartite contract being consummated, it cannot be rescinded without the consent of all. It follows that the creditor's assent to the contract, made known to the promisor, who is expected to pay, is the only change of position required. But the assent must be to a promise in force at the time. The right of contract is the right to rescind or modify. . . .

The Court of Appeals appears to hold the status quo as to ownership of the property must be restored. The ownership of the property is of no concern to the creditor except as it may affect his power to collect his debt. This turns upon an issue of fraud vel non in the transaction, as defined in the law of fraudulent conveyances. All participants in a fraud may be held to account in a proper form of action.

No such question is presented here. So far as appears, the original debtor and the subvendee, whose promise is still open to the plaintiff creditor, are solvent, able, and ready to pay the demand. It is a case of election to sue the vendee, who, before any acceptance of his promise, conveyed the property to another, who assumed the payment of plaintiff's demand, and after the promise [promisee?] had released defendant from the obligation.

Writ of certiorari granted; reversed and remanded.

All the Justices concur.

———

NOTE ON THE POWER OF THE CONTRACTING PARTIES TO VARY THE PROMISOR'S DUTY TO THE BENEFICIARY

Restatement First drew a sharp line between the power of the contracting practice to vary the promisor's duty to a creditor beneficiary, on the one hand, and to a donee beneficiary, on the other. Section 143 provided that:

> A discharge of the promisor by the promisee in a contract or a variation thereof by them is effective against a *creditor* beneficiary if, (a) the creditor beneficiary does not bring suit upon the promise or otherwise materially change his position in reliance thereon before he knows of the discharge or variation, and (b) the promisee's action is not a fraud on creditors.

However, Section 142 provided that:

> Unless the power to do so is reserved, the duty of the promisor to the *donee* beneficiary cannot be released by the promisee or affected by any agreement between the promisee and the promisor. . . .

(Emphasis added in both cases.)

The rule of Restatement First § 142 was dramatically exemplified by Illustration 2:

> A promises B to pay A's son, C, $1000 a year for five years, in consideration of which B promises A to pay B's daughter D, who is C's wife, the same amount. Before C or D learn of this contract A and B mutually agree to rescind it. C and D can treat the agreement of rescission as inoperative to destroy their respective rights to enforce the original contract.

Restatement Second § 311 drops the rule of Restatement First § 142, and gives unified treatment to all intended beneficiaries. However, Section 311 introduces new qualifications on the power of the contracting parties to vary the promisor's duty to the beneficiary.

RESTATEMENT, SECOND, CONTRACTS §§ 309, 311

[See Selected Source Materials Supplement]

ROUSE v. UNITED STATES

United States Court of Appeals, District of Columbia Circuit, 1954.
94 U.S.App.D.C. 386, 215 F.2d 872.

EDGERTON, CIRCUIT JUDGE. Bessie Winston gave Associated Contractors, Inc., her promissory note for $1,008.37, payable in monthly installments of $28.01, for a heating plant in her house. The Federal Housing Administration guaranteed the note and the payee endorsed it for value to the lending bank, the Union Trust Company.

Winston sold the house to Rouse. In the contract of sale Rouse agreed to assume debts secured by deeds of trust and also "to assume payment of $850 for heating plant payable $28 per Mo." Nothing was said about the note.

Winston defaulted on her note. The United States paid the bank, took an assignment of the note, demanded payment from Rouse, and sued him for $850 and interest.

Rouse alleged as defenses (1) that Winston fraudulently misrepresented the condition of the heating plant and (2) that Associated Contractors did not install it satisfactorily. The District Court struck these defenses and granted summary judgment for the plaintiff. The defendant Rouse appeals.

Since Rouse did not sign the note he is not liable on it. D.C.Code 1951, § 28–119; N.I.L. Sec. 18. He is not liable to the United States at all unless his contract with Winston makes him so. The contract says the parties to it are not "bound by any terms, conditions, statements, warranties or representations, oral or written" not contained in it. But this means only that the written contract contains the entire agreement. It does not mean that fraud cannot be set up as a defense to a suit on the contract. Rouse's promise to "assume payment of $850 for heating plant" made him liable to Associated Contractors, Inc., only if and so far as it made him liable to Winston; one who promises to make a payment to the promisee's creditor can assert against the creditor any defense that the promisor could assert against the promisee. Accordingly Rouse, if he had been sued by the corporation, would have been entitled to show fraud on the part of Winston. He is equally entitled to do so in this suit by an assignee of the corporation's claim. It follows that the court erred in striking the first defense. We do not consider whether Winston's alleged fraud, if shown, would be a complete or only a partial defense to this suit, since that question has not arisen and may not arise.

We think the court was right in striking the second defense. "If the promisor's agreement is to be interpreted as a promise to discharge whatever liability the promisee is under, the promisor must certainly be allowed to show that the promisee was under no enforceable liability. . . . On the other hand, if the promise means that the promisor agrees to pay a sum of money to A, to whom the promisee says he is indebted, it is immaterial whether the promisee is actually indebted to that amount or at all. . . . Where the promise is to pay a specific debt . . . this interpretation will generally be the true one."[9]

The judgment is reversed and the cause remanded with instructions to reinstate the first defense.

Reversed and remanded.

9. 2 [Williston, Contracts, rev. ed. 1936] § 399.

Chapter 21

ASSIGNMENT AND NEGOTIATION

The last Chapter concerned cases in which A and B made a contract that benefited a third party, who wants to enforce the contract. This Chapter concerns cases in which A and B have made a contract that did not benefit a third party at the outset, but in which A subsequently either (1) assigned (that is, transferred) or attempted to assign, to a third party, his rights under a contract, or (2) delegated or attempted to delegate, to a third party, his duties under a contract. A number of different issues can arise in this context, including what rights are assignable, what duties are delegable, and what formalities are required to make an effective assignment. Those issues are considered in Sections 1 and 2. Sections 3 and 4 concern the assignment of claims as security for loans. Section 5 considers assignments of negotiable instruments—that is, of financial instruments, such as checks, that satisfy certain legal criteria.

SECTION 1. INTRODUCTION

NOTE ON THE ECONOMIC SIGNIFICANCE OF THE ASSIGNMENT OF CLAIMS

A transfer of an intangible asset, such as a claim, by sale, gift, or as security, is called an *assignment*. A claim that is transferable is said to be *assignable*. Not all kinds of claims are transferable. Which kinds of claims are transferable, and which are not, depends on deeply held social norms. Under early English common law, the assignment of a claim (or "chose in action") was legally impossible. If Debtor B owed Creditor A $10, and A purported to transfer his claim against B to Third Party T, the courts early held that literally nothing happened to the claim by virtue of the attempted transfer. B still owed A, not T, and T gained no rights against B.

Most claims are held by creditors, and the rules concerning the assignability of claims eventually changed as the credit system matured. The economic institution of credit can exist in at least a limited way even if claims are not assignable. Money can be lent, and goods can be sold in return for promises of future payment, in a society that knows nothing of the transfer of claims.

However, the assignability of claims greatly increases the power of the credit system.

To discover what the assignability of creditors' claims adds to the credit system, it is necessary to analyze first what can be accomplished by that system even in the absence of a power in creditors to assign their claims. Without doubt, one of the principal advantages of the credit system lies in the flexibility it introduces into economic relations. Any existing distribution of economic power (that is, of control over the processes of production and distribution) runs the risk of becoming stagnated. Indeed, from the standpoint of world history the stagnant economy may be regarded as normal. Where economic power rests on private ownership, the institution of private property can easily degenerate into something equivalent to a caste system.

One of the elements that may prevent this from occurring is the device of credit. In a society in which it is possible to obtain present assets in return for a promise of future payment, those who are enterprising may find it possible to improve their economic condition. If A anticipates an increased demand for soy beans, and others have confidence in A's judgment, A can, by borrowing money and investing it in the lease of a farm, bring about an increased production of that commodity. If A has accurately predicted the demand, she will not only have increased her wealth by making a profit on her investment, but will also have given economic activity a desirable direction that it would not have taken had she been living in a society in which borrowing was unknown.

The flexibility of economic processes that results from the availability of credit is increased where it is possible to assign claims. Suppose A hold claims for $5,000 each against D, E, and F. If A is unable to assign these claims, although they represent wealth, they do not represent present control over the economy. For example, suppose A is reasonably sure that there will soon be a greatly increased demand for some commodity. If A has no liquid assets, and A's claims cannot be transferred to raise funds, A's ownership of the claims does not enable him to bring about an increase in the production of that commodity. On the other hand, if the claims are assignable, then by transferring the claims he owns to someone else, A can obtain funds whose investment may result in an expansion of some branch of the economy.

The assignability of claims therefore converts what would otherwise be merely an expectancy of future control over economic factors of production and distribution into present control. By dispersing control over a larger group, assignability widens the pool of human knowledge and increases the opportunity for a productive application of human energies.*

CLAPP v. ORIX CREDIT ALLIANCE, INC.

Court of Appeals of Oregon, 2004.
192 Or.App. 320, 84 P.3d 833.

Before LANDAU, Presiding Judge, and ARMSTRONG and BREWER, Judges.

BREWER, J.

This is an action for money had and received arising from the insured loss of a vehicle in a secured transaction. On appeal, plaintiff assigns error to the

---

* For a brief history of the law concerning the assignability of claims, see Appendix D.

trial court's denial of her motion for summary judgment and its grant of the cross-motion for summary judgment of defendant Orix Credit Alliance, Inc. (Orix). We review the summary judgment record to determine whether there are any genuine issues of material fact and whether either moving party is entitled to judgment as a matter of law. . . . We reverse and remand.

The material facts are undisputed. Plaintiff is an independent truck driver. Defendant Laser Express, Inc., (Laser) is an interstate common carrier with whom plaintiff contracted to provide truck driving services. Orix is a commercial finance company. In 1996, plaintiff decided to purchase a highway tractor. Laser agreed to act as an undisclosed agent for plaintiff [that is, Laser held itself out to the seller as if it were buying the truck on its own behalf, rather than as an agent acting on behalf of Clapp, the plaintiff.] Laser entered into a conditional sale contract note (the contract) that documented its installment purchase of the tractor. Orix is the vendor's assignee under the contract.

By the terms of the contract, Laser granted Orix a security interest in the tractor. The contract provided that "[b]uyer [Laser] shall not assign this contract note without the prior written consent of Holder [Orix]." Plaintiff made the down payment toward the purchase of the tractor, and she also made all payments received by Orix on the contract. In May 1998, Laser, as assignor, and plaintiff, as assignee, entered into an assignment of contract (the assignment) by the terms of which Laser transferred its interest in the contract to plaintiff. Orix did not give prior consent to the assignment.

The assignment provides, in part:

"1. [Laser], (as assignor, and vendee under contract) does hereby convey, assign, sell, transfer and set over unto [plaintiff], assignee, all of its right, title and interest in and to the written and attached contract of sale dated on or about December 26, 1996, together with any and all other documents relating to the sale by [Orix's assignor] and as assigned, conveyed to or otherwise delivered to [Orix]. . . .

"2. [Laser] does hereby direct [Orix], its successors or assigns, to deliver, upon completion of all payments provided in the aforementioned contract, the title to said vehicle to [plaintiff], to be hers absolutely, free and clear of any claims by [Laser].

"3. [Laser] also hereby conveys to [plaintiff] all of its right, title and interest in the property described in the contract and the legal title thereto, which is pledged to secure the performance of the vendee's obligations created thereby. . . .

"5. The parties hereto recognize that this assignment shall not relieve [Laser] from its obligations due on the contract between [Orix] and [Laser]. Therefore, [plaintiff] does hereby agree to indemnify, defend and hold harmless [Laser] from any and all obligations due under the contract and the payments due thereon for the purchase of the aforementioned vehicle."

In March 1999, the tractor was totally destroyed in a roll-over accident. Plaintiff notified Orix of the loss, and she advised Orix that she claimed the net insurance proceeds in excess of the balance due on the contract. Orix received $27,500 from the insurer for the loss of the tractor. Orix applied the insurance proceeds in full satisfaction of the contract balance, leaving a credit balance of $9,950.39. On May 10, 1999, plaintiff delivered a copy of the assignment to Orix, and she reasserted her demand for payment of the net insurance proceeds. On May 12, 1999, Orix nevertheless issued a check for the proceeds to Laser. Plaintiff then commenced this action against Laser and Orix for conversion and money had and received.

Plaintiff filed a motion for partial summary judgment against Orix on her claim for money had and received, in which she asserted that she was entitled, by virtue of the assignment, to the net insurance proceeds from the loss of the truck. Orix filed a cross-motion for summary judgment on both of plaintiff's claims, arguing that the prohibition of assignment contained in the contract invalidated the assignment and that, even if it did not, the assignment did not transfer the right to receive the insurance proceeds. The trial court denied plaintiff's motion for summary judgment, and it granted Orix's cross-motion. The court assumed that the prohibition was ineffective to prevent the assignment, but it agreed with Orix that "the assignment is a limited assignment and plaintiff is not entitled to net insurance proceeds under this agreement." On appeal, the parties renew their arguments made before the trial court.

[The court began by holding that the assignment included the right to receive the net insurance proceeds payable as a result of the loss of the truck.]

The issue remains whether the prohibition of assignment without [Orix's] prior consent restricted the assignment of *rights* in the contract or whether it applied only to the delegation of the contractual *obligations* thereby created. Because the contract encompassed both a sale of goods and a secured transaction, that issue is governed by the provisions of Articles 2 and 9 of the Uniform Commercial Code (UCC).

UCC § 2–210,* relating to assignments of contracts for the sale of goods, provides, in part:

> "(2) Except as otherwise provided in UCC § 9–406, unless otherwise agreed, all rights of either seller or buyer can be assigned except where the assignment would materially change the duty of the other party, or increase materially the burden or risk imposed on the other party by the contract, or impair materially the chance of the other party obtaining return performance. A right to damages for breach of the whole contract or a right arising out of the assignor's due performance of the entire obligation of the assignor can be assigned despite agreement otherwise. . . .

> "(4) Unless the circumstances indicate the contrary a prohibition of assignment of 'the contract' is to be construed as barring only the delegation to the assignee of the assignor's performance."

The contract prohibited Laser from assigning the "contract note without the prior written consent of Holder." By its terms, the prohibition focused on the vendee's *obligations* under the contract; it referred to the vendor as "[h]older," that is, the person toward whom contractual obligations are owed.

---

* For simplicity, the court's citations to sec-   to citations to the UCC itself. (Footnote by ed.)
tions of the Oregon UCC have been converted

See UCC § 1–201(20) (defining the "holder" of a negotiable instrument as "the person in possession of the negotiable instrument"). Nothing in the contract or the summary judgment record suggests that the prohibition was concerned with the assignment of the vendee's rights under the contract. Further, there was no evidence that such an assignment would materially change Orix's duty, or increase materially the burden or risk imposed on Orix by the contract, or materially impair its chance of obtaining return performance. *See* UCC § 2–210(2). Thus, the prohibition did not prevent the transfer to plaintiff of Laser's rights under the contract. *See* UCC § 2–210(4).

That conclusion is consistent with UCC § 9–401(2), which governs the alienability of a debtor's rights in collateral under Article 9. UCC § 9–401(2) provides that "[a]n agreement between the debtor and secured party which prohibits a transfer of the debtor's rights in collateral or makes the transfer a default does not prevent the transfer from taking effect." This case concerns the assignment of the right to receive the proceeds of collateral for the debt owed to Orix under the contract.[3] Those proceeds, in turn, constituted collateral. *See* UCC § 9–102(a)(12)(A)(stating that the term "collateral" includes "[p]roceeds to which a security interest attaches"). The prohibition therefore was ineffective to prevent the transfer of Laser's rights in the insurance proceeds to plaintiff from taking effect. *See* UCC § 9–401(2).

Because Orix had notice of the assignment when it paid the net insurance proceeds to Laser, it remained liable to plaintiff, the assignee of the right to receive the insurance proceeds. *See State Farm Ins. v. Pohl,* 255 Or. 46, 50, 464 P.2d 321 (1970) (stating that, "[w]hen a person obtains a right against a third person by subrogation or assignment, the law is that if the third person has notice of the subrogation or assignment and nevertheless pays the assignor or subrogor, rather than the assignee or subrogee, the third person continues to be liable to the assignee or subrogee"); *see also McCallums, Inc. v. Mountain Title Co.,* 60 Or.App. 693, 697, 654 P.2d 1157 (1982) (holding that "an obligor on a chose in action who has notice of the assignment of the beneficial interest in the chose in action is liable to the assignee if the obligation is paid other than by the terms of the assignment"). It follows that the trial court erred in denying plaintiff's motion for summary judgment and in granting Orix's cross-motion for summary judgment.

Reversed and remanded for entry of order granting plaintiff's motion for partial summary judgment.

UCC ARTICLE 9, § 9–406(a)

PRE–2000 UCC ARTICLE 9, § 9–318(3)*

[See Selected Source Materials Supplement]

---

3. UCC § 9–201 provides, in part:

"(a) As used in this chapter ...

"(64) 'Proceeds,' ... means the following property ...

"(E) To the extent of the value of collateral and to the extent payable to the debtor or the secured party, insurance payable by reason of the loss or nonconformity of, defects or infringement of rights in, or damage to, the collateral."

* Article 9 of the UCC was completely revised in the late 1990's. The revision became effective in 2000. Because the great bulk of

ERTEL v. RADIO CORPORATION OF AMERICA, 261 Ind. 573, 307 N.E.2d 471 (1974). "[UCC] § 9–318(3) clearly delineates the legal relationship between the account debtor ... and the assignee ... once the account debtor receives adequate notification of an assignment. The account debtor, upon receipt of said notification, is duty–bound to pay the assignee and not the assignor. Payment to an assignor, after notification of assignment, does not relieve the account debtor of his obligation to pay the assignee unless the assignee consents to such a collection process. (See Official Comment No. 3, 9–318.) The account debtor's failure to pay the assignee after receiving due notification gives rise to an assignee's claim for wrongful payment."

NOTE ON WHAT FORMALITIES ARE NECESSARY TO MAKE AN EFFECTIVE ASSIGNMENT

What formalities, if any, are required to make an assignment effective?

1. *Gratuitous assignments.* An assignment is a form of transfer. Just as the owner of a physical object may make a gift of the commodity by transferring it to a donee, so the owner of a claim against an obligor may make a gift of the claim by assigning it to a donee. Such assignments are usually referred to as gratuitous assignments. This leaves open the question of what formalities are required to make a gratuitous assignment.

In the case of a physical commodity, a gift is completed—and therefore irrevocable—if the donor either delivers the commodity to the donee or executes a writing in which he transfers ownership of the commodity to the donee. In contrast, claims cannot be physically delivered, because they are intangible. Accordingly, a gratuitous transfer of a claim can be made even by a donor-assignor's oral statement to the donee-assignee by which the donor makes a present assignment of the claim to the donee. Such an assignment is effective against the obligor—the person who owes money or some other performance that gives rise to the assigned claim—but without more, the claim is *revocable* by the donor-assignor. For example, suppose A, having lent $1,000 to B, orally assigns his $1,000 claim against B to T. T then sues B on the claim, asserting that he has become the assignee of the claim through A's oral gift. At the time of the suit, A is alive and has done nothing inconsistent with the assignment. B defends against T's suit on the ground that A's claim against her could not be validly transferred by an oral gift. According to Restatement Second, judgment should go for T on these facts. The oral gift of a claim is effective so long as the assignor remains alive, is not bankrupt, and has not repudiated the assignment.

Now suppose that a gratuitous assignor repudiates his gratuitous assignment by a revocation communicated to the assignee, or makes a later assignment of the same claim to another person, or dies or becomes incapacitated. Without more, the assignment will be revoked by the occurrence of any of these events. However, there are ways to make even a gratuitous assign-

cases decided prior to the time this Casebook was written were based on the pre–2000 version of Article 9—and also because many or most of the relevant rules in the prior and current version of Article 9 are highly comparable—both versions will be cross-referenced in this Chapter unless indicated otherwise.

ment irrevocable. Restatement Second § 332 sets out the following rules to govern when a gratuitous assignment is revocable or irrevocable:

(1) Unless a contrary intention is manifested, a gratuitous assignment is *irrevocable* if

(a) the assignment is in a writing either signed or under seal that is delivered by the assignor; or

(b) the assignment is accompanied by delivery of a writing of a type customarily accepted as a symbol or as evidence of the right assigned.

(2) Except as stated in this Section, a gratuitous assignment is *revocable* and the right of the assignee is terminated by the assignor's death or incapacity, by a subsequent assignment by the assignor, or by notification from the assignor received by the assignee or by the obligor.

(3) A gratuitous assignment ceases to be revocable to the extent that before the assignee's right is terminated he obtains

(a) payment or satisfaction of the obligation, or

(b) judgment against the obligor, or

(c) a new contract of the obligor by novation.

(4) A gratuitous assignment is irrevocable to the extent necessary to avoid injustice where the assignor should reasonably expect the assignment to induce action or forbearance by the assignee or a sub-assignee and the assignment does induce such action or forbearance. . . .

(Emphasis added.)

2. *Assignments for value.* Absent statute, an assignment made for value is fully effective and irrevocable, even though oral. Today, however, most although not all assignments are governed by the UCC—in particular, by Article 9 (see Section 3, infra)—and an assignment may need to be in writing to satisfy a relevant UCC Statute of Frauds provision. See Appendix A, Section 10, infra.

———

SPEELMAN v. PASCAL, 10 N.Y.2d 313, 222 N.Y.S.2d 324, 178 N.E.2d 723 (1961). The Estate of George Bernard Shaw licensed a corporation, which was almost wholly owned by Gabriel Pascal, to do a musical play and a musical motion picture based one of Shaw's plays, *Pygmalion.* The license was to terminate if within a certain period the corporation did not arrange with Lerner and Lowe, or similar well-known composers, to write the musical and arrange to produce it. While the license still had two years to run, Pascal signed and delivered to Kingman the following letter: "Dear Miss Kingman: This is to confirm to you our understanding that I give you from my shares of profits of the Pygmalion Musical stage version five per cent (5%) in England, and two per cent (2%) of my shares of profits in the United States. From the film version, five per cent (5%) from my profit shares all over the world. As soon as the contracts are signed, I will send a copy of this letter to my lawyer, Edwin Davies, in London, and he will confirm to you this arrangement in a legal form. This participation in my shares of profits is a present to you, in recognition for your loyal work for me as my Executive Secretary." Four and one–half months later, Pascal died. Held, delivery of the letter constituted a completed gift by way of assignment. Therefore, the gift was not revoked by Pascal's death.

SECTION 2. ASSIGNABILITY OF RIGHTS AND DELEGABILITY OF DUTIES

EVENING NEWS ASS'N v. PETERSON

United States District Court, District of Columbia, 1979.
477 F.Supp. 77.

BARRINGTON D. PARKER, DISTRICT JUDGE. The question presented in this litigation is whether a contract of employment between an employee and the owner and licensee of a television station, providing for the employee's services as a newscaster-anchorman, was assigned when the station was sold and acquired by a new owner and licensee.

Plaintiff Evening News Association (Evening News) a Michigan Corporation, acquired station WDVM–TV (Channel 9) a District of Columbia television station from Post–Newsweek Stations, Inc. (Post–Newsweek) in June of 1978. At that time, the defendant Gordon Peterson was and had been employed for several years as a newscaster-anchorman by Post–Newsweek. This defendant is a citizen of the State of Maryland. The plaintiff claims that Peterson's employment contract was assignable without the latter's consent, was indeed assigned, and thus otherwise enforceable. The defendant contends, however, that his Post–Newsweek contract required him to perform unique and unusual services and because of the personal relationship he had with Post–Newsweek the contract was not assignable.

Mr. Peterson was employed by the plaintiff for more than one year after the acquisition and received the compensation and all benefits provided by the Post–Newsweek contract. In early August, 1979, he tendered his resignation to the plaintiff. At that time the defendant had negotiated an employment contract with a third television station located in the District of Columbia, a competitor of the plaintiff. The Evening News then sued Peterson, seeking a declaration of the rights and legal relations of the parties under the contract and permanent injunctive relief against the defendant.

Following an accelerated briefing schedule and an expedited bench trial on the merits, the Court concludes that the contract was assignable and that Evening News is entitled to appropriate permanent injunctive relief against the defendant Gordon Peterson.

In accordance with Rule 52(a) Fed.R.Civ.P., the Court's findings of fact and conclusions of law in support of that determination are set forth.

FINDINGS OF FACT

The defendant was employed by Post–Newsweek Stations, Inc. from 1969 to 1978. During that period he negotiated several employment contracts. Post–Newsweek had a license to operate television station WTOP–TV (Channel 9) in the District of Columbia. In June of 1978, following approval by the Federal Communications Commission, Post–Newsweek sold its operating license to Evening News and Channel 9 was then designated WDVM–TV. A June 26, 1978, Bill of Sale and Assignment and Instrument of Assumption and Indemnity between the two provided in pertinent part:

> PNS has granted, bargained, sold, conveyed and assigned to ENA, ... all the property of PNS ... including, ... all right, title and interest, legal or equitable, of PNS in, to and under all agreements, contracts and commitments listed in Schedule A hereto....

When Evening News acquired the station, Peterson's Post–Newsweek employment contract, dated July 1, 1977, was included in the Bill of Sale and Assignment. The contract was for a three-year term ending June 30, 1980, and could be extended for two additional one-year terms, at the option of Post–Newsweek. The significant and relevant duties and obligations under that contract required Peterson:

> to render services as a news anchorman, and to perform such related services as news gathering, writing and reporting, and the organization and preparation of program material, to the extent required by the Stations, as are consistent with [his] primary responsibility as a news anchorman.... [To participate] personally as a newsman, announcer, on-the-air personality or other performer in any news, public affairs, documentary, news analysis, interview, special events or other program or segment of any program, designated by ... and to the extent required by the Stations ... as may reasonably be required by the Stations....

As compensation the defendant was to receive a designated salary which increased each year from 1977 through the fifth (option) year. Post–Newsweek was also obligated to provide additional benefits including term life insurance valued at his 1977 base salary, disability insurance, an annual clothing allowance and benefits to which he was entitled as provided in an underlying collective bargaining agreement with the American Federation of Television and Radio Artists.

There was no express provision in the 1977 contract concerning its assignability or nonassignability. However, it contained the following integration clause:

This agreement contains the entire understanding of the parties ... and this agreement cannot be altered or modified except in a writing signed by both parties.

A.

Aside from the various undisputed documents and exhibits admitted into evidence, there were sharp conflicts in testimony concerning various events and what was said and done by the parties and their representatives, both before and after the Evening News' acquisition. As trier of fact, having heard and seen the several witnesses testify and after assessing and determining their credibility, the Court makes the following additional findings.

The defendant's duties, obligations and performance under the 1977 contract did not change in any significant way after the Evening News' acquisition. In addition, the Evening News met all of its required contract obligations to the defendant and its performance after acquisition in June, 1978, was not materially different from that of Post–Newsweek.

Mr. Peterson testified that he had "almost a family relationship" with James Snyder, News Director, and John Baker, Executive Producer, for Post–Newsweek, which permitted and promoted a free exchange of ideas, frank expressions of dissent and criticism and open lines of communication. These men left Channel 9 when Post–Newsweek relinquished its license, and they have since been replaced by Evening News personnel. According to Mr. Peterson, the close relationship and rapport which existed between him and them was an important factor as he viewed the contract; these relationships made the contract in his view nonassignable and indeed their absence at the Evening News prevented defendant from contributing his full efforts. Even if Mr. Peterson's contentions are accepted, it should be noted that he contracted with the Post–Newsweek corporation and not with the News Director and Executive Producer of that corporation. Indeed, the 1977 contract makes no reference to either officer, except to provide that vacations should be scheduled and coordinated through the News Director. Had the defendant intended to condition his performance on his continued ability to work with Snyder and Baker, one would have expected the contract to reflect that condition.

The close, intimate and personal relationship which Mr. Peterson points to as characterizing his association with Post–Newsweek and its personnel, was highly subjective and was supported only by his testimony. The Court cannot find that Peterson contracted with Post–Newsweek in 1977 to work with particular individuals or because of a special policy-making role he had been selected to perform in the newsroom. For the fourteen-month period of Peterson's employment at the Evening News, there is no showing that he was in any way circumscribed, limited in his work or otherwise disadvantaged in his performance. Nor is there any credible evidence that the News Director or other top personnel of Evening News were rigid, inflexible, warded off any of Mr. Peterson's criticisms or even that at any time he gave suggestions and criticisms which were ignored or rejected. Finally, the Court does not find that Post–Newsweek contracted with Peterson because of any peculiarly unique qualities or because of a relationship of personal confidence with him.

B.

In his direct testimony, Mr. Peterson expressed a degree of disappointment because of Evening News' failure to keep apace with advances in technology and to seize opportunities for live in-depth coverage of current events. He characterized the plaintiff's news coverage as "less aggressive" than what he had experienced with Post–Newsweek.

On cross-examination, however, he was shown an exhibit comparing the broadcast of special assignments reported and produced by him for two one-year periods, one before and one after the June, 1978 acquisition. While he admitted to its accuracy with some reservation, the exhibit clearly showed that a comparable number of such assignments of similar quality, were broadcast within the two years. He also conceded that for the same period Evening News received two Peabody awards, an award for best editorials, and a number of Emmy awards for public affairs exceeding those received in prior years by Post–Newsweek. Finally, he acknowledged that Channel 9 still maintained the highest ratings for audience viewing among the television stations in the Washington, D.C. market area.

A great amount of testimony was generated as to when Peterson learned of the Evening News' acquisition and what then occurred relative to the assignment of the contract. The testimony on this issue was conflicting, largely cumulative and as now viewed, over-emphasized by the parties. The Court finds that the defendant gained first knowledge of a possible sale and transfer of the station in December, 1977. At that time, the president of Post–Newsweek publicly announced to the station's employees, including Peterson, that an agreement in principle had been reached, subject to approval by the Federal Communications Commission. At no time from December, 1977, until December, 1978, did the defendant or his attorney ever indicate or venture an opinion that the contract was not assignable. Indeed, through at least April, 1979, the defendant's attorney made representations that assignment of the contract presented no problem to his client.

In summary, the Court finds that the performance required of Mr. Peterson under the 1977 contract was (1) not based upon a personal relationship or one of special confidence between him and Post–Newsweek or its employees, and (2) was not changed in any material way by the assignment to the Evening News.

CONCLUSIONS OF LAW

There is diversity of citizenship; the amount in controversy exceeds $10,000; and the Court has jurisdiction over this proceeding by virtue of 28 U.S.C.A. § 1332.

A.

The distinction between the assignment of a right to receive services and the obligation to provide them is critical in this proceeding. This is so because duties under a personal services contract involving special skill or ability are generally not delegable by the one obligated to perform, absent the consent of the other party. The issue, however, is not whether the personal services Peterson is to perform are delegable but whether Post–Newsweek's right to receive them is assignable.

Contract rights as a general rule are assignable. Munchak Corp. v. Cunningham, 457 F.2d 721 (4th Cir.1972); Meyer v. Washington Times Co., 64 App.D.C. 218, 76 F.2d 988 (D.C.Cir.) cert. denied 295 U.S. 734, 55 S.Ct. 646, 79 L.Ed. 1682 (1935); 4 A. Corbin, Contracts § 865 (1951); Restatement, Contracts § 151 (1932). This rule, however, is subject to exception where the assignment would vary materially the duty of the obligor, increase materially the burden of risk imposed by the contract, or impair materially the obligor's chance of obtaining return performance. Corbin § 868; Restatement § 152. There has been no showing, however, that the services required of Peterson by the Post–Newsweek contract have changed in any material way since the Evening News entered the picture. Both before and after, he anchored the same news programs. Similarly he has had essentially the same number of special assignments since the transfer as before. Any additional policymaking role that he formerly enjoyed and is now denied was neither a condition of his contract nor factually supported by other than his own subjective testimony.

The general rule of assignability is also subject to exception where the contract calls for the rendition of personal services based on a relationship of confidence between the parties. *Munchak,* 457 F.2d at 725; *Meyer,* 64 App.

D.C. at 219, 76 F.2d at 989. As Corbin has explained this limitation on assignment:

> In almost all cases where a "contract" is said to be non-assignable because it is "personal," what is meant is not that the contractor's right is not assignable, but that the performance required by his duty is a personal performance and that an attempt to perform by a substituted person would not discharge the contractor's duty.

Corbin § 865. In *Munchak,* the Court concluded that a basketball player's personal services contract could be assigned by the owner of the club to a new owner, despite a contractual prohibition on assignment to another club, on the basis that the services were to the club. The Court found it "inconceivable" that the player's services "could be affected by the personalities of successive corporate owners." 457 F.2d at 725. The policy against the assignment of personal service contracts, as the Court noted, "is to prohibit an assignment of a contract in which the obligor undertakes to serve only the original obligee." 457 F.2d at 726.

Given the silence of the contract on assignability, its merger clause, and the usual rule that contract rights are assignable, the Court cannot but conclude on the facts of this case that defendant's contract was assignable. Mr. Peterson's contract with Post–Newsweek gives no hint that he was to perform as other than a newscaster-anchorman for their stations. Nor is there any hint that he was to work with particular Post–Newsweek employees or was assured a policy-making role in concert with any given employees. Defendant's employer was a corporation, and it was for Post–Newsweek Stations, Inc. that he contracted to perform. The corporation's duties under the contract did not involve the rendition of personal services to defendant; essentially they were to compensate him. Nor does the contract give any suggestion of a relation of special confidence between the two or that defendant was expected to serve the Post–Newsweek stations only so long as the latter had the license for them. . . .

C.

Plaintiff's argument that defendant has waived any objection to the assignment by accepting the contract benefits and continuing to perform for the Evening News for over a year has perhaps some merit. If defendant has doubts about assignability, he should have voiced them when he learned of the planned transfer or at least at the time of transfer. His continued performance without reservation followed by the unanticipated tender of his resignation did disadvantage Evening News in terms of finding a possible replacement for him and possibly in lost revenues. The Court, however, concludes that the contract was assignable in the first instance and thus it is not necessary to determine whether defendant's continued performance constitutes a waiver of objection to the assignment.

During the course of this trial Edwin W. Pfeiffer, an executive officer of WDVM–TV, testified that Mr. Peterson allegedly stated "if the Judge decides I should stay, I will stay." Assuming that he did not overstate Mr. Peterson's position and that Mr. Peterson was quoted in appropriate context, the television audience of the Washington, D.C. metropolitan area should anticipate his timely reappearance as news anchorman for station WDVM–TV. Of course, the avenue of appeal is always available.

An order consistent with this Memorandum Opinion will be entered. Counsel for the plaintiff shall submit immediately an appropriate order.

RESTATEMENT, SECOND, CONTRACTS § 317

[See Selected Source Materials Supplement]

UCC § 2–210(2), (4)

[See Selected Source Materials Supplement]

KENDALL v. ERNEST PESTANA, INC., 40 Cal.3d 488, 220 Cal.Rptr. 818, 709 P.2d 837 (1985). "This case concerns the effect of a provision in a commercial lease that the lessee may not assign the lease or sublet the premises without the lessor's prior written consent. The question we address is whether, in the absence of a provision that such consent will not be unreasonably withheld, a lessor may unreasonably and arbitrarily withhold his or her consent to an assignment. . . .

"[A] majority of jurisdictions have long adhered to the rule that where a lease contains an approval clause (a clause stating that the lease cannot be assigned without the prior consent of the lessor), the lessor may arbitrarily refuse to approve a proposed assignee no matter how suitable the assignee appears to be and no matter how unreasonable the lessor's objection. . . .

"The traditional majority rule has come under steady attack in recent years. A growing minority of jurisdictions now hold that where a lease provides for assignment only with the prior consent of the lessor, such consent may be withheld *only where the lessor has a commercially reasonable objection to the assignment,* even in the absence of a provision in the lease stating that consent to assignment will not be unreasonably withheld. . . .

"For the reasons discussed below, we conclude that the minority rule is the preferable position. . . .

"[One] impetus for change in the majority rule comes from the nature of a lease as a *contract.* . . . '[I]n every contract there is an implied covenant that neither party shall do anything which will have the effect of destroying or injuring the right of the other party to receive the fruits of the contract. . . .' '[W]here a contract confers on one party a discretionary power affecting the rights of the other, a duty is imposed to exercise that discretion in good faith and in accordance with fair dealing.' . . . Here the lessor retains the discretionary power to approve or disapprove an assignee proposed by the other party to the contract; this discretionary power should therefore be exercised in accordance with commercially reasonable standards. . . .

"In conclusion, both the policy against restraints on alienation and the implied contractual duty of good faith and fair dealing militate in favor of adoption of the rule that where a commercial lease provides for assignment only with the prior consent of the lessor, such consent may be withheld only where the lessor has a commercially reasonable objection to the assignee or the proposed use."

————

RESTATEMENT, SECOND, CONTRACTS § 322

[See Selected Source Materials Supplement]

————

RESTATEMENT, SECOND, CONTRACTS § 322, ILLUSTRATIONS 1, 2

1. A holds a policy of industrial insurance issued to him by the B Insurance Company. After lapse for failure to pay premiums, B refuses to pay the "cash surrender value" provided for in the policy. A and others similarly situated assign their claims to C for collection. The assignment is effective without regard to any contractual prohibition of assignment.

2. A and B contract for the sale of land by B to A. A fully performs the contract, becomes entitled to specific performance on B's refusal to convey the land, and then assigns his rights to C. C is entitled to specific performance against B without regard to any contractual prohibition of assignment. . . .

————

UCC ARTICLE 9, § 9–306(d)

PRE–2000 UCC ARTICLE 9, § 9–318(4)

[See Selected Source Materials Supplement]

————

MACKE CO. v. PIZZA OF GAITHERSBURG, INC.

Court of Appeals of Maryland, 1970.
259 Md. 479, 270 A.2d 645.

Argued before HAMMOND, C.J., and BARNES, FINAN, SINGLEY, SMITH and DIGGES, JJ.

SINGLEY, JUDGE. The appellees and defendants below, Pizza of Gaithersburg, Inc.; Pizzeria, Inc.; The Pizza Pie Corp., Inc. and Pizza Oven, Inc., four corporations under the common ownership of Sidney Ansell, Thomas S. Sherwood and Eugene Early and the same individuals as partners or proprietors (the Pizza Shops) operated at six locations in Montgomery and Prince George's Counties. The appellees had arranged to have installed in each of their locations cold drink vending machines owned by Virginia Coffee Service, Inc., and on 30 December 1966, this arrangement was formalized at five of the locations, by contracts for terms of one year, automatically renewable for a like term in the absence of 30 days' written notice. A similar contract for the sixth location, operated by Pizza of Gaithersburg, Inc., was entered into on 25 July 1967.

On 30 December 1967, Virginia's assets were purchased by The Macke Company (Macke) and the six contracts were assigned to Macke by Virginia. In January, 1968, the Pizza Shops attempted to terminate the five contracts having the December anniversary date, and in February, the contract which had the July anniversary date.

Macke brought suit in the Circuit Court for Montgomery County against each of the Pizza Shops for damages for breach of contract. From judgments for the defendants, Macke has appealed.

The lower court based the result which it reached on two grounds: first, that the Pizza Shops, when they contracted with Virginia, relied on its skill, judgment and reputation, which made impossible a delegation of Virginia's duties to Macke; and second, that the damages claimed could not be shown with reasonable certainty. These conclusions are challenged by Macke.

In the absence of a contrary provision—and there was none here—rights and duties under an executory bilateral contract may be assigned and delegated, subject to the exception that duties under a contract to provide personal services may never be delegated, nor rights be assigned under a contract where *delectus personae* was an ingredient of the bargain.[1] 4 Corbin on Contracts § 865 (1951) at 434; 6 Am.Jur.2d, Assignments § 11 (1963) at 196. Crane Ice Cream Co. v. Terminal Freezing & Heating Co., 147 Md. 588, 128 A. 280 (1925) held that the right of an individual to purchase ice under a contract which by its terms reflected a knowledge of the individual's needs and reliance on his credit and responsibility could not be assigned to the corporation which purchased his business. In Eastern Advertising Co. v. McGaw & Co., 89 Md. 72, 42 A. 923 (1899), our predecessors held that an advertising agency could not delegate its duties under a contract which had been entered into by an advertiser who had relied on the agency's skill, judgment and taste.

The six machines were placed on the appellees' premises under a printed "Agreement–Contract" which identified the "customer," gave its place of business, described the vending machine, and then provided:

"Terms

"1. The Company will install on the Customer's premises the above listed equipment and will maintain the equipment in good operating order and stocked with merchandise.

"2. The location of this equipment will be such as to permit accessibility to persons desiring use of same. This equipment shall remain the property of the Company and shall not be moved from the location at which installed, except by the Company.

"3. For equipment requiring electricity and water, the Customer is responsible for electrical receptacle and water outlet within ten (10) feet

---

1. Like all generalizations, this one is subject to an important exception. Uniform Commercial Code § 9–318 makes ineffective a term in any contract prohibiting the assignment of a contract right: i.e., a right to payment. Compare Restatement, Contracts § 151(c) (1932).

of the equipment location. The Customer is also responsible to supply the Electrical Power and Water needed.

"4. The Customer will exercise every effort to protect this equipment from abuse or damage.

"5. The Company will be responsible for all licenses and taxes on the equipment and sale of products.

"6. This Agreement–Contract is for a term of one (1) year from the date indicated herein and will be automatically renewed for a like period, unless thirty (30) day written notice is given by either party to terminate service.

"7. Commission on monthly sales will be paid by the Company to the Customer at the following rate:. . . ."

The rate provided in each of the agreements was "30% of Gross Receipts to $300.00 monthly[,] 35% over [$]300.00," except for the agreement with Pizza of Gaithersburg, Inc., which called for "40% of Gross Receipts."

We cannot regard the agreements as contracts for personal services. They were either a license or concession granted Virginia by the appellees, or a lease of a portion of the appellees' premises, with Virginia agreeing to pay a percentage of gross sales as a license or concession fee or as rent, see Charlotte Coca–Cola Bottling Co. v. Shaw, 232 N.C. 307, 59 S.E.2d 819 (1950) and Herbert's Laurel–Ventura, Inc. v. Laurel Ventura Holding Corp., 58 Cal.App.2d 684, 138 P.2d 43, 46–47 (1943), and were assignable by Virginia unless they imposed on Virginia duties of a personal or unique character which could not be delegated, S & L Vending Corp. v. 52 Thompkins Ave. Restaurant, Inc., 26 A.D.2d 935, 274 N.Y.S.2d 697 (1966).

The appellees earnestly argue that they had dealt with Macke before and had chosen Virginia because they preferred the way it conducted its business. Specifically, they say that service was more personalized, since the president of Virginia kept the machines in working order, that commissions were paid in cash, and that Virginia permitted them to keep keys to the machines so that minor adjustments could be made when needed. Even if we assume all this to be true, the agreements with Virginia were silent as to the details of the working arrangements and contained only a provision requiring Virginia to "install ... the above listed equipment and ... maintain the equipment in good operating order and stocked with merchandise." We think the Supreme Court of California put the problem of personal service in proper focus a century ago when it upheld the assignment of a contract to grade a San Francisco street:

"All painters do not paint portraits like Sir Joshua Reynolds, nor landscapes like Claude Lorraine, nor do all writers write dramas like Shakespeare or fiction like Dickens. Rare genius and extraordinary skill are not transferable, and contracts for their employment are therefore personal, and cannot be assigned. But rare genius and extraordinary skill are not indispensable to the workmanlike digging down of a sand hill or the filling up of a depression to a given level, or the construction of brick sewers with manholes and covers, and contracts for such work are not personal, and may be assigned." Taylor v. Palmer, 31 Cal. 240 at 247–248 (1866).

See also Devlin v. Mayor, Aldermen and Commonalty of the City of New York, 63 N.Y. 8, at 17 (1875). Moreover, the difference between the service the Pizza Shops happened to be getting from Virginia and what they expected to get from Macke did not mount up to such a material change in the performance of obligations under the agreements as would justify the appellees' refusal to recognize the assignment, Crane Ice Cream Co. v. Terminal Freezing & Heating Co., supra, 147 Md. 588, 128 A. 280. . . .

As we see it, the delegation of duty by Virginia to Macke was entirely permissible under the terms of the agreements. In so holding, we do not put ourselves at odds with Eastern Advertising Co. v. McGaw, supra, 89 Md. 72, 42 A. 923, for in that case, the agreement with the agency contained a provision that "the advertising cards were to be 'subject to the approval of Eastern Advertising Company as to style and contents'", at 82, 42 A. at 923, which the court found to import that reliance was being placed on the agency's skill, judgment and taste, at 88, 42 A. 923.

Having concluded that the Pizza Shops had no right to rescind the agreements, we turn to the question of damages.

[The court concluded that damages could be shown with reasonable certainty.]

Judgment reversed as to liability; judgment entered for appellant for costs, on appeal and below; case remanded for a new trial on the question of damages.

————

BRITISH WAGGON CO. v. LEA & CO., [1880] 5 Q.B.D. 149 "[W]e cannot suppose that in stipulating for the repair of these waggons by the company—a rough description of work which ordinary workmen conversant with the business would be perfectly able to execute—the defendants attached any importance to whether the repairs were done by the company, or by any one with whom the company might enter into a subsidiary contract to do the work. All that the hirers, the defendants, cared for in this stipulation was that the waggons should be kept in repair; it was indifferent to them by whom the repairs should be done. Thus if . . . the company had entered into a contract with any competent party to do the repairs, and so had procured them to be done, we cannot think that this would have been a departure from the terms of the contract to keep the waggons in repair. . . . [I]t is difficult to see how in repairing a carriage when necessary, or painting it once a year, preference would be given to one coachmaker over another. Much work is contracted for, which it is known can only be executed by means of subcontracts; much is contracted for as to which it is indifferent to the party for whom it is to be done, whether it is done by the immediate party to the contract, or by someone on his behalf. In all these cases the maxim qui facit per alium facit per se [he who acts through another acts himself] applies."

————

BASHIR v. MOAYEDI, 627 A.2d 997 (D.C.App.1993). This was a suit by an obligee under a contract against the obligor, Bashir. Bashir defended on the ground that it had delegated its obligations to Daou, who assumed the obligations. The court rejected this defense: "... [T]he general rule with respect to delegation is that a delegant cannot free herself from liability by delegating her duties of performance to another.... Were this not the case, 'every solvent person could obtain freedom from his debts by delegating them to an insolvent.' ... Thus, while [the assumption by Daou of the obligations of Bashir,] may have rendered [Daou] liable to appellant Bashir, that assumption did not discharge appellant Bashir's duty to [the obligee]. In arguing otherwise ... Bashir confuses delegation of performance of an obligation with delegation of responsibility for the performance of an obligation."

RESTATEMENT, SECOND, CONTRACTS § 318

[See Selected Source Materials Supplement]

RESTATEMENT, SECOND, CONTRACTS § 318, ILLUSTRATIONS 1–3, 5–7

1.   A owes B $100, and asks C to pay B. Payment or tender to B by C has the effect of payment or tender by A.

2.   A contracts to deliver to B coal of specified kind and quality. A delegates the performance of this duty to C, who tenders to B coal of the specified kind and quality. The tender has the effect of a tender by A.

3.   A contracts to build a building for B in accordance with specifications, and delegates the plumbing work to C. Performance by C has the effect of performance by A.

5.   A, a teacher employed in a public or private school, attempts to delegate the performance of his duties to B, a competent person. An offer by B to perform A's duties need not be accepted, and actual performance by B without the assent of the employer will create no right in either A or B to the salary stated in A's contract.

6.   A contracts with B, a corporation, to sing three songs over the radio as part of an advertisement of B's product. A's performance is not delegable unless B assents.

7.   A contracts with B that A will personally cut the grass on B's meadow. A cannot effectively delegate performance of the duty to C, however competent C may be.

CONTEMPORARY MISSION, INC. v. FAMOUS MUSIC CORP., 557 F.2d 918 (2d Cir.1977). "It is true, of course, as a general rule, that when rights are assigned, the assignor's interest in the rights assigned comes to an end. When duties are delegated, however, the delegant's obligation does not end.

[O]ne who owes money or is bound to any performance whatever, cannot by an act of his own, or by any act in agreement with any other person, except his creditor, divest himself of the duty and substitute the duty of another. 'No one can assign his liabilities under a contract without the consent of the party to whom he is liable.'

This is sufficiently obvious when attention is called to it, for otherwise obligors would find an easy practical way of escaping their obligations. . . .

3 Williston on Contracts § 411 (3d ed. 1960). . . . This is not to say that one may not delegate his obligations. In fact, most obligations can be delegated— as long as performance by the delegate will not vary materially from performance by the delegant. The act of delegation, however, does not relieve the delegant of the ultimate responsibility to see that the obligation is performed. If the delegate fails to perform, the delegant remains liable."

—————

UCC § 2–210(1)

[See Selected Source Materials Supplement]

—————

SALLY BEAUTY CO. v. NEXXUS PRODUCTS CO., 801 F.2d 1001 (7th Cir.1986). Nexxus Products Company entered into a contract with Best Barber & Beauty Supply Company, Inc., under which Best would be the exclusive distributor of Nexxus hair care products to barbers and hair stylists throughout most of Texas. Subsequently, Best was acquired by and merged into Sally Beauty Company, Inc. Nexxus then cancelled its contract with Best, because Sally Beauty was a wholly owned subsidiary of a major manufacturer of hair–care products, which was a competitor of Nexxus. Sally Beauty claimed that Nexxus breached the contract by cancelling; Nexxus asserted by way of defense that the contract was not assignable or, in the alternative, that the contract was not assignable to Sally Beauty. The district court granted Nexxus's motion for summary judgment. Affirmed.

"... The UCC recognizes that in many cases an obligor will find it convenient or even necessary to relieve himself of the duty of performance under a contract, *see* Official Comment 1, UCC § 2–210 ('[T]his section recognizes both delegation of performance and assignability as normal and permissible incidents of a contract for the sale of goods.'). The Code therefore sanctions delegation except where the delegated performance would be unsatisfactory to the obligee: 'A party may perform his duty through a delegate unless otherwise agreed to or unless the other party has a substantial interest in having his original promisor perform or control the acts required by the contract.' UCC § 2–210(1), Tex.Bus. & Com.Code Ann. § 2–210(a) (Vernon 1968). Consideration is given to balancing the policies of free alienability of commercial contracts and protecting the obligee from having to accept a bargain he did not contract for. . . .

"In the exclusive distribution agreement before us, Nexxus had contracted for Best's 'best efforts' in promoting the sale of Nexxus products in Texas.

UCC § 2–306(2), Tex.Bus. & Com.Code Ann. § 2–306(b) (Vernon 1968), states that '[a] lawful agreement by either buyer or seller for exclusive dealing in the kind of goods concerned imposes unless otherwise agreed an obligation by the seller to use best efforts to supply the goods and by the buyer to use best efforts to promote their sale.' This implied promise on Best's part was the consideration for Nexxus' promise to refrain from supplying any other distributors within Best's exclusive area. *See* Official Comment 5, UCC § 2–306. It was this contractual undertaking which Nexxus refused to see performed by Sally. . . .

" . . . We hold . . . that the duty of performance under an exclusive distributorship may not be delegated to a competitor in the market place—or the wholly-owned subsidiary of a competitor—without the obligee's consent. We believe that such a rule is consonant with the policies behind section 2–210, which is concerned with preserving the bargain the obligee has struck. Nexxus should not be required to accept the 'best efforts' of Sally Beauty when those efforts are subject to the control of Alberto–Culver. It is entirely reasonable that Nexxus should conclude that this performance would be a different thing than what it had bargained for."

BAXTER HEALTHCARE CORPORATION v. O.R. CONCEPTS, INC., 69 F.3d 785 (7th Cir.1995). Baxter Healthcare sold a wide range of products to health-care providers. Some of the products were manufactured by Baxter itself; others were purchased for resale from other distributors. O.R. Corporation also manufactured and sold health-care products, including Thermadrape, a heat-retention drape used to prevent hypothermia.

In January 1992, Baxter and O.R. signed a Distribution Agreement that obligated Baxter to purchase $3 million worth of Thermadrape from O.R. over a 27–month period. Paragraph 11(g) of the Agreement required Baxter's written consent for an assignment of O.R.'s interest in the Agreement. In November 1992, the owners of O.R. sold 95% of O.R.'s stock to Vital Signs Inc., and informed Baxter that Vital Signs' 120–person sales staff would begin selling Thermadrape. O.R. remained a separate corporation, and continued to produce and sell Thermadrape and a variety of other products. Baxter then claimed that O.R. was in breach of the Agreement, because the sale of O.R.'s stock constituted an assignment of O.R.'s interest in the Agreement to Vital Signs. Subsequently, Baxter notified O.R. that it was terminating the Agreement, and refused to purchase any further Thermadrape, although at that point it had only purchased $2 million worth of Thermadrape. Baxter then filed suit against O.R., alleging breach of contract and violation of UCC § 2–210. Held, for O.R.

" . . . Baxter alleged a breach of the Agreement on two independent bases. The first is that O.R. breached the Agreement because the sale of O.R. stock to Vital Signs was in violation of [the] non-assignability clause. . . .

"Baxter fails to demonstrate how the change of ownership of O.R. stock constitutes an assignment of O.R.'s interests in the Agreement. It is well settled that a change in corporate ownership does not constitute a variation of that corporation's contractual obligations.

"It is true that this Court held in *Sally Beauty* that a merger between a contracting corporation and another corporation could constitute an assignment of the contracting corporation's rights in a contract. However, *Sally Beauty* is distinguishable. First, *Sally Beauty* involved a distribution agreement which specifically provided that it was exclusive. The agreement between Baxter and O.R. had no such provision.... [and] most importantly, the *Sally Beauty* case involved a merger of two corporations, as opposed to a simple change of ownership. There, the contracting corporation lost its independent identity because of the merger. As we have already stated, O.R. has at all times remained an independent corporate entity whose ownership has merely changed. Therefore, *Sally Beauty* is inapplicable. Because the stockholders' sale of O.R. stock did not constitute an assignment by O.R. of its interests in the Agreement, the district court properly dismissed Baxter's claim that the sale violated paragraph 11(g) of the Agreement....

"Baxter's second claim is that the sale of O.R. stock to Vital Signs constituted an assignment of O.R.'s rights and delegation of O.R.'s performance in violation of Section 2–210 of the UCC.... [The] *Sally Beauty* case involved an agreement that provided Best with exclusive distribution rights and it was the distributor that was affected by a change in corporate form. These two facts placed Nexxus in a vulnerable position. Baxter is in no such position. Baxter is still the purchaser of a product which is still available to it, on the same terms that it bargained for, and from the same entity with which it bargained.

"This Court in *Sally Beauty* stated, '[w]e hold merely that the duty of performance under an exclusive distributorship may not be delegated to a competitor in the marketplace—or the wholly-owned subsidiary of a competitor—without the obligee's consent.' *Sally Beauty*, 801 F.2d at 1007–1008. We decline to extend that holding to a situation where there was no exclusive relationship and there has been no assignment of interests in the contract or delegation of duties. Thus, the district court properly dismissed Baxter's claim that the sale of O.R. stock violated Section 2–210 of the UCC."

———

RESTATEMENT, SECOND, CONTRACTS § 328

[See Selected Source Materials Supplement]

———

NOTE ON THE RIGHT OF THE OBLIGEE UNDER A CONTRACT TO DEMAND PERFORMANCE FROM AN ASSIGNEE OF THE CONTRACT

Assume that A and B have a contract, and that after the contract is made, one of two transaction types occurs between A and a third party, T.

In a *Type I Transaction*, A makes an agreement with T under which A assigns the contract to T, and T expressly promises A to perform the obligations that A owes to B under the contract. Because T has promised to discharge A's preexisting legal obligations to B, B is a creditor beneficiary of

T's promise. Therefore, it is well-established that in a Type I Transaction B can enforce T's promise. (Note that A will remain liable to B, even though T is also liable, because a party to a contract cannot get out of its obligations by delegating them. As between A and T, however, T will be ultimately liable.)

A *Type II Transaction* is identical to a Type I Transaction except that although A assigns the contract to T, T does not expressly agree to perform the obligations that A owes under the contract. In such a case, the agreement between A and T should normally be interpreted to mean that T has *impliedly* agreed to perform A's obligations. This interpretation of a Type II Transaction reflects both the usual way in which A and T probably would understand their transaction and the business economics of such transactions. Although there are transactions in which A would be willing to transfer all his benefits under a contract to T while remaining primarily liable for all the contract's burdens, such transactions are not typical. T should therefore be liable to B by virtue of his implied promise, just as he would be liable to B in a Type I Transaction by virtue of his express promise.

This interpretation of a Type II Transaction is adopted in both Restatement Second § 328 and UCC § 2–310(2). However, the majority rule in the case law is that T is not liable to B in a Type II Transaction, unless the transaction falls within UCC Article 2. Moreover, even the rule stated in Restatement Second § 328 is made subject to the caveat that "The American Law Institute expresses no opinion as to whether the rule ... applies to an assignment by a purchaser of his rights under a contract for the sale of land." This caveat was adopted in deference to Langel v. Betz, 250 N.Y. 159, 164 N.E. 890 (1928), a leading case that applied the majority rule to a contract for the sale of real estate.

SECTION 3. FINANCING THROUGH THE ASSIGNMENT OF CLAIMS

BACKGROUND NOTE ON FINANCING THROUGH THE ASSIGNMENT OF CLAIMS

It is common for commercial borrowers to obtain financing by using claims against third persons—in particular, accounts receivable, which represent amounts owed to the assignor by trade customers—either by assigning the claims outright or by assigning the claims as security for the commercial borrower's loans. In the United States, there are two major types of financing through the assignment of accounts receivable: *factoring* and *non-notification assignment*. Under the system of factoring, the assignor's accounts are assigned outright (in effect, sold) to a factor at a discount. The factor assumes the risk that the assignor's customers may default. The assignor's customers are notified of the assignment, and payments are made directly to the factor. In practice, this type of financing is largely confined to the textile field.

Non-notification assignment, on the other hand, involves an assignment of accounts as security for a loan to the assignor. The assignor retains the risk that his customers will default. Notice is not given to the customers, because giving notice would typically involve considerable practical difficulty. The assignor continues to collect payments from his customers, holding the payments as agent or trustee for the lender. It is asserted, by those connected with the business, that the absence of notice to the assignor's customers is of the essence in this type of financing, and that a requirement of notice, and a direct collection of accounts by the assignee, would be highly detrimental to the whole practice, because it would have a bad effect on the assignor's relationship with his customers.

Until recent times, the actual administration of non-notification financing involved a number of legal difficulties. Some of these difficulties concerned the validity of certain kinds of assignment, and are therefore of direct interest in the study of contract law. However, most of the difficulties related to the rights of competing creditors—for example, the rights of competing assignees of the same claim; or the rights of an assignee against a judgment creditor or a trustee in bankruptcy; or the rights of an assignee, as a secured creditor, against unsecured creditors. These issues have very little to do with contract law as such, and instead fall within the domain of courses in secured transactions and bankruptcy. Furthermore, much of the old law on the subject has gone by the boards with the adoption of UCC Article 9 and the Bankruptcy Reform Act of 1978. Accordingly, next two Notes will sketch just enough of the law to sensitize the student in a general way to some of the leading problems.

NOTE ON UCC ARTICLE 9 AND THE
LAW OF ASSIGNMENTS*

For purposes of assignments, the key Article of the UCC is Article 9 ("Secured Transactions"), which applies to contractual transactions that create a security interest in personal property or fixtures. Article 9 also extends to any "*sale* of accounts, chattel paper, payment intangibles, or promissory notes," subject to certain exclusions. (UCC § 9–109(a); emphasis added.)

Among the key terms in Article 9 are "account," "account debtor," "chattel paper," "general intangible," "payment intangible," and "promissory note." The definitions in Article 9 of each of these terms is complex, but at the core, and subject to various exceptions, the relevant definitions are as follows: An *account* is a right to payment of a monetary obligation. An *account debtor* is a person obligated on an account, chattel paper, or general intangible, other than a negotiable instrument. *Chattel paper* is a record, whether written or electronic, that evidences both a monetary obligation and a security interest in specific goods. A *general intangible* is personal property (normally, intangible personal property) other than an account, chattel paper, and certain other designated types of rights. A *payment intangible* is a general intangible under which the account debtor's principal obligation is a monetary obligation. A *promissory note* is an instrument that evidences a promise to pay a monetary obligation, but does not evidence an order to pay, such as a check.

---

* For simplicity of exposition, the balance of the Notes in this Chapter are based on the current version of Article 9, not on both that version and the pre–2000 version.

UCC § 9–109(d) enumerates transactions that are excluded from the coverage of Article 9. Among the major excluded categories are: (1) An assignment of a claim for wages, salary, or other compensation of an employee. (2) A sale of accounts, chattel paper, payment intangibles, or promissory notes as part of a sale of the business out of which they arose. (3) An assignment of accounts, chattel paper, payment intangibles, or promissory notes for the purpose of collection only. (4) An assignment of a right to payment under a contract where the assignment is made to an assignee who is also obliged to perform under the contract. (5) An assignment of a single account, payment intangible, or promissory note to an assignee in full or partial satisfaction of a preexisting indebtedness. In addition, Article 9 does not cover donative assignments, because they involve neither the creation of a security interest nor a sale. Assignments not covered by Article 9 are left to the common law or special statutes.

NOTE ON PRIORITY BETWEEN COMPETING ASSIGNEES OF THE SAME CLAIM

A major problem at common law was the extent to which a creditor-assignee had priority over competing creditors and a trustee in bankruptcy. The most troublesome issues of priority grew out of the problem that arose where the assignor had made two or more assignments of the same claim. As to this problem there was general agreement on two cases.

Case 1. Where the earlier assignment was either ineffective or revocable by the assignor (e.g., an oral gratuitous donative assignment), the rule was that the later assignee prevailed, on the ground that the later assignment worked a revocation of the earlier assignment.

Case 2. Where the assigned claim was embodied in a tangible token, such as a savings–account passbook, and the earlier assignee left the token in the assignor's possession, the rule was that the later assignee prevailed—at least if he gave value and took possession of the token—on the ground that the earlier assignee should be estopped because he left the token in the assignor's possession, which would mislead the later creditor into thinking that the assignor still held the claim.

Beyond these two cases, however, the treatment of the problem at common law was widely divergent. Basically, there were three different rules.

First was the so-called English rule. This rule was that the later assignee prevailed not only in *Case 1* and *Case 2*, but in every other case in which the later assignee paid value, took the assignment without notice of the prior assignment, and gave the obligor notice of the assignment before the earlier assignee gave such notice.

Second was the so-called New York Rule. This rule was that first in time was first in right—that is, except in *Case 1* and *Case 2*, the earlier assignee prevailed over the later assignee.

Third was the Massachusetts, or "four-horsemen" rule. This rule was that if the first assignment was not revocable at the time the later assignment was made, the earlier assignee prevailed, *unless* the later assignee acquired his assignment in good faith and for value and did one of four things: (1) Took a tangible token embodying the claim from the assignor. (2) Collected the claim from the obligor. (3) Obtained a judgment against the obligor. (4) Secured a novation from the obligor and assignor, whereby the claim in favor of the assignor was extinguished and superseded by a new claim in favor of the second assignee with the consent of the obligor and the assignor. The Massachusetts rule was adopted by Restatement First and is continued in Restatement Second.

Article 9 of the UCC largely supplants the common law in this area, and establishes a relatively clear statutory solution of the priority problem for those assignments to which that Article applies. It is impossible to fully describe the operation of Article 9 in this area in a brief Note, because almost every rule of Article 9 is subject to a number of exceptions. At the risk of oversimplification, the approach of Article 9 centers on six basic concepts: security interests, security agreements, attachment, financing statements, perfection, and filing.

Under Article 9, a *security agreement* is an agreement that creates or provides for a security interest. A *security interest* arises when a debtor or would-be debtor has property, such as accounts receivable, and gives his creditor or would-be creditor an interest in the property for the purpose of securing a debt or prospective debt owed or to be owed by the debtor to the creditor. Property used for this purpose is referred to as *collateral*. Unless and until a security interest attaches to the collateral, the creditor is unsecured, that is, he has no security interest in the collateral. In effect, "attachment" is a term of art for enforceability.

A security interest becomes enforceable—*attaches*—if and only if three conditions are satisfied: (1) the creditor has given value, (2) the debtor has rights in the collateral or the power to transfer rights in the collateral, and (3) the debtor has authenticated a security agreement describing the collateral, or some comparable event has occurred. A security interest that has attached is enforceable against the debtor and against third parties who do not claim an interest in the collateral. As to third parties who do claim an interest in the collateral, however, a security interest is unlikely to be effective, even though it has attached, unless it has also been *perfected*. In particular, it is unlikely to be effective against a creditor who obtains a judicial execution against the property, and unlikely to be effective in bankruptcy.

Accordingly, perfecting a security interest in collateral is usually a crucial step for a would-be secured creditor. Most kinds of security interests can be and are perfected by the filing of a *financing statement*—a written statement that includes the name of the debtor, the name and address of the secured party, and a statement describing the types or articles of collateral. If there are conflicting perfected security interests in the same collateral, the priority of the conflicting interests is normally determined by priority in time of perfection.

SECTION 4. DEFENSES OF THE OBLIGOR AGAINST THE ASSIGNEE IN A COMMERCIAL CONTEXT

UCC ARTICLE 9, §§ 9–404, 9–405

PRE–2000 UCC ARTICLE 9, § 318(1)

[See Selected Source Materials Supplement]

UNITED CALIFORNIA BANK v. EASTERN MOUNTAIN SPORTS, INC., 546 F.Supp. 945 (D.Mass.1982), affirmed mem., 705 F.2d 439 (1st Cir.1983). "[UCC] § 9–318(1) [the predecessor of current UCC § 9–404(a)] governs the rights of an account debtor [i.e., the obligor] against an assignee. Section 9–318(1) accommodates the competing interests of the assignee and the account debtor by separating claims and defenses of the latter against the former into two categories. The first category includes claims and defenses arising out of the terms of the contract from which the assigned account was created. Regardless of when they accrue, these claims and defenses may be asserted by the account debtor as offsets against the amount owed the assignee on the contract or assigned account. . . .

"Claims or defenses of the second type contemplated by § 9–318(1) are those that do not arise from the contract of sale that was the subject of assignment. An account debtor may assert these claims and defenses as offsets against the amount owed the assignee on the contract or assigned account only if the claims or defenses accrued before the account debtor received notice of the assignment. . . .

BANK OF KANSAS v. HUTCHINSON HEALTH SERVICES, INC., 13 Kan.App.2d 421, 773 P.2d 660 (1989), aff'd, 246 Kan. 83, 785 P.2d 1349 (1990). "The date of notification is critical when the claims arise independently of the contract creating the account because it determines what claims the assignee is subject to. [UCC] 9–318(1)(b) [the predecessor of current UCC § 9–404(a)(2)] provides: '[t]he rights of an assignee are subject to . . . any other defense or claim of the account debtor or against the assignor which accrues before the account debtor receives notification of the assignment.' . . .

"The UCC leaves the definition of when a claim 'accrues' to the law under which the claim arose. . . . In the absence of an express definition, two possibilities suggest themselves. A claim could 'accrue': (1) when the obligation to pay is incurred; or (2) when the obligation is actually due and payable. The first definition reflects a fiscal view, appropriate to accounting or tax law. The second definition reflects the more usual sense of accrue, that is, that 'a claim or setoff accrues when a cause of action exists.' Seattle First Nat'l Bk. v. Ore. Pac. Inc., 262 Or. 578, 583, 500 P.2d 1033 (1972).

"On balance, we believe that the policies of simplicity and commercial certainty underlying the UCC favor the second definition.... Under the first definition, the value of accounts assigned as security could never be accurately determined because the accounts would always be subject to an independent claim arising against the assignor after the assignment is made, but accruing beforehand. Under the second definition, the value of accounts can be determined with reasonable certainty at the time of the assignment. As the Oregon court noted, an assignment must have 'value and stability' to 'be used as an effective security device.' 262 Or. at 582, 500 P.2d 1033."

SECTION 5. NEGOTIATION; DEFENSES IN THE CONSUMER CONTEXT

NOTE ON THE DISTINCTION BETWEEN NEGOTIABLE AND NON–NEGOTIABLE CLAIMS

So far, this Chapter has dealt primarily with what are called *non–negotiable* "choses in action" or claims. It is advisable to say a few words at this point about *negotiable* claims. Such claims are evidenced by written documents called negotiable instruments. Negotiable instruments take two main forms: notes and bills. (Bills are also sometimes called bills of exchange, and very commonly in commercial parlance, drafts.) *Notes* are *two*-party instruments, with a *maker* (the person who makes or gives the note) and a *payee* (the person to whom the note is given and to whom it is payable). The typical example is the ordinary promissory note: "I promise to pay $100 thirty days from date to Jane Jones or order [that is, a person designated by Jane Jones]." *Bills* are *three*-party instruments, with a *drawer,* a *drawee,* and a *payee.* The most familiar example is a check on a commercial bank account, in which the customer of the bank (the *drawer*) directs the bank (the *drawee*) to pay a sum of money to the *payee* or the payee's order.

The law of negotiable instruments derives historically from the law merchant. The law of negotiable instruments is primarily codified in UCC Article 3, on Commercial Paper, Article 4, on Bank Deposits and Collections, Article 5, on Letters of Credit; and Article 8, on Investment Securities, also contain provisions relating to negotiable instruments.

What is the difference between a negotiable and non-negotiable claim? Whenever it is necessary to distinguish two kinds of legal transactions (say, a lease and a bailment, or a life estate and a fee simple) the whole story usually involves not simply a single distinction, but a complex relationship of similarities and differences. This is true of the distinction between negotiable and non-negotiable claims. For example, in a particular jurisdiction, the Statute of Limitations may grant a longer period within which to bring suit on a negotiable instrument than on other contract claims. In another jurisdiction, the same period may be prescribed for all written contracts. Various other comparisons may be drawn between the two kinds of claims with respect to particular legal qualities.

However, the principal difference between negotiable and non-negotiable claims lies in one key distinction, and it is this distinction lawyers have in mind when they speak of the quality of "negotiability." If a negotiable instrument is *negotiated* (that is, transferred in a prescribed form, such as an endorsement of a check) to a "holder in due course," the holder will take the instrument free of certain defenses that could have been asserted against a transferee of a non-negotiable instrument or a transferee who is not a holder in due course. (A "holder in due course" generally corresponds to a person who is called in other branches of the law is called "a bona fide purchaser for value without notice," which in this context means without notice of any defects in the assignor's claim.)

To illustrate: Suppose that Seller and Buyer enter into a contract which provides as follows: (1) Seller will deliver 1000 hairbrushes to Buyer for $5,000. (2) Immediately after the contract is signed, Buyer will deliver to Seller a negotiable promissory note for that amount, payable in two months. (3) Seller will deliver the hairbrushes to Buyer one month after the contract is signed. Buyer delivers the note to Seller, and Seller immediately transfers the note to Acme Bank as security for a loan of $4,600. The Bank has no reason to suppose there is anything wrong with the note, and in fact at the time of transfer there isn't. However, Seller fails to deliver the hairbrushes. If Seller had retained the note, and brought suit upon it, Buyer could defend on the ground that Seller had failed to perform. Similarly, if Seller transferred the note to the Bank, but the note was non–negotiable, the Bank would simply step into Seller's shoes. In that case, if the Bank brought suit on the note, Buyer could raise the same defense against the Bank that he could raise in a suit by Seller. However, if the note was negotiable, Seller's negotiation of the note to the Bank would "cut off" Buyer's right to use Seller's default as a defense against the Bank. (Even if Buyer cannot set up Seller's default as a defense in a suit against him by the Bank, he can sue Seller for damages under the contract between them. However, Seller may not be solvent. Indeed, if the Bank is suing Buyer rather than Seller, it is probably because Seller is insolvent. Typically, as in the illustration, Seller will have given Buyer's note as collateral for a loan from the Bank to Seller. If Seller was still solvent, normally the loan would have been repaid by Seller, and the collateral—the note—would have been returned to her.)

Economic treatises describe negotiable instruments as claims that "pass readily from hand to hand," "serve as a medium of exchange," or "are treated like money." This economic quality is, of course, the other side of the coin of the legal quality of negotiability. Negotiable promissory notes, or bank checks, pass freely from hand to hand partly because the purchaser of a negotiable instrument knows that he can generally count on not being confronted with an unexpected defense by the maker or drawer. On the other hand, viewing the matter historically, the courts have been moved to grant the legal quality of negotiability to those types of instruments which merchants and bankers employ as a medium of exchange.

As the following Report suggests, the principle of negotiability, which has by and large worked well in dealings between merchants, raises serious problems when applied to dealings between merchants and consumers.

NATIONAL COMMISSION ON CONSUMER FINANCE, REPORT—CONSUMER CREDIT IN THE UNITED STATES

34–38 (1972).

HOLDER IN DUE COURSE DOCTRINE—WAIVER OF DEFENSE—CLOSELY-CONNECTED LOANS

Of all creditors' remedies and collection devices used in consumer credit notes and contracts, perhaps none has received as much notoriety, commentary, and controversy as the holder in due course (HIDC) doctrine.

In 1758, in the case of Miller v. Race, the King's Bench of England held that a Bank of England promissory bearer note was "treated as money; as cash" by businessmen dealing "in the ordinary course and transaction of business." The court decided that when such a note was stolen and thereafter sold to a person who paid fair value and had no notice of the theft (a bona fide purchaser), that bona fide purchaser would prevail over all persons claiming the note, even the original owner. The rationale for this decision was based on the fear that the growth and soundness of commerce would have been impeded or destroyed if a contrary decision were reached. This fear was probably well-founded because promissory notes of the Bank of England were not "legal tender," but were nevertheless "passed from hand to hand, serving many of the purposes of paper money, which did not exist in England at the time." To allow persons other than bona fide purchasers to claim ownership to the note would indeed have had an adverse affect on commerce.

With the development of paper money, the emphasis on affording a good faith purchaser of notes and contracts freedom from claims to the instrument gradually shifted to permit the good faith purchaser to cut off defenses which the obligor may have against paying the note.

Today, under the [Uniform Commercial] Code an individual can qualify as HIDC if he takes [a negotiable] instrument for "value," "in good faith" and "without notice that it [the instrument] is overdue or has been dishonored or of any defense against or claim to it on the part of any person." The status of HIDC provides many advantages against the individual obligated on the instrument, and these advantages are brought into sharp focus where the instrument is used in a consumer credit transaction.

In a typical consumer credit purchase of durable goods, the purchaser signs an instalment note to the seller agreeing to repay the unpaid portion of the purchase price plus finance charges in accordance with a stipulated repayment schedule. The seller, in turn, "negotiates" the note to a financing institution (usually a sales finance company or bank). In most of these transactions the financing institution has the status of HIDC and can enforce the purchaser's obligation on the note irrespective of any defenses which the buyer may have against the seller regarding the underlying sale. For example, if a purchaser signs a note as payment or partial payment for a refrigerator, the financing institution holding the note as HIDC is entitled to receive payment even though the refrigerator was defective, was never delivered, or, if delivered was not as represented at the time of the sale.

Another legal device, the waiver of defense clause, provides financing institutions immunity from defenses to payment which the buyer may be able to assert against the seller. It operates in essentially the same way as the HIDC doctrine. A waiver of defense clause is part of an instalment sales contract (as distinguished from a note) and, in effect, provides to the assignee of the contract the benefits of negotiability and HIDC status through a contractual provision.

The following is an example of a typical waiver of defense clause:

"If the seller should assign the contract in good faith to a third party, the buyer shall be precluded as against such third party from attacking the validity of the contract on grounds of fraud, duress, mistake, want of consideration or. . . ."

The Code specifically permits such clauses, unless there is a "statute or decision which establishes a different rule for buyers or lessees of consumer goods. . . ."

Recently, both courts and legislatures have begun to reassess and scrutinize the validity and the impact of the HIDC doctrine and waiver of defense clauses in consumer credit transactions. A number of courts have denied HIDC status to lenders in "too close connection" with sellers of consumer goods. A number of state legislatures have prohibited use of negotiable instruments, and, therefore HIDC status, in retail installment sales of "service." Waiver of defense clauses in consumer sales contracts have also been held void as against public policy by a number of courts and prohibited by several legislatures.

Growing discontent with cut-off devices in consumer transactions, now apparent in legislatures, courts, and administrative agencies, has led many dealers and financing institutions to devise a new and effective method for the lender to cut off any defenses the buyer might have against the seller. The seller merely suggests that the buyer borrow money for the purchase by direct loan from a cash lender and directs the buyer to a financing institution willing to make the loan. Theoretically, at least, the loan is an independent transaction with no relation to the purchase of the goods. As a result, the obligation to repay the debt would not be subject to defenses arising out of the purchase transaction even in states limiting the HIDC doctrine and use of waiver of defense clauses. The Commission believes routine referral by a seller to a lender or group of lenders should not be permitted to subvert the policy behind a rule restricting or prohibiting use of negotiable promissory notes or waiver of defense clauses. However, drafting legislation barring routine referrals but not inhibiting direct lending for consumer purchases by institutions totally independent of sellers is a difficult task.

Whatever the methods, it is quite apparent that cut-off devices against defenses which a purchaser of consumer goods may have against the seller of such goods are in great disfavor in many courts and with many legislators. Many noted legal scholars also agree that cut-off devices are not necessary in consumer transactions. . . .

The [Commission's] cross-state econometric model indicates that in those states which have prohibited both HIDC and waiver of defense clauses there has been an observable reduction in the availability of other consumer goods credit* in two areas: consumer finance companies purchased less other

---

* "Other consumer goods credit" is consumer credit other than that incurred for the purchase of automobiles, for home repair or modernization, or as a result of personal loans. (Footnote by ed.)

consumer goods paper, and the total amount of other consumer goods credit made available in the retail market declined. Traditionally, finance companies have served the greatest proportion of retailers dealing with high risk credit customers, although banks, too, serve that market. The reductions in availability of other consumer goods credit from finance companies, in all likelihood, would have the greatest impact on consumers who are marginal credit risks and on those businesses which serve or may potentially serve such consumers. . . .

Of all the arguments for abolishing a financial institution's freedom from consumer defenses, Professor Homer Kripke of New York University, who describes himself "as a (former) finance company lawyer", provides perhaps the best rationale:

"Looking at the matter legislatively, we may ask who, as between the consumer and financer, ought to bear the risk of the merchant's breach of warranty or delivery of shoddy goods? The consumer sues the merchant only once or episodically. The financer, even though it does not control the merchant or participate in the breach of warranty, ordinarily has a continuing relationship with him and some experience of his performance of warranties. The financer is certainly better equipped with staff to check the merchant's reputation for reliability and fair dealing. It is submitted that the risk of cases of legitimate customer dissatisfaction should be thrown on the financer. The financer is best able to force redress by maintaining an action over against the merchant or by charging withheld amounts in the financer's hands, even where his basic purchase of the obligation from the merchant was without recourse. The financial institution always protects itself by warranties from the merchant as to freedom of the obligation from customer defenses. Moreover, such a rule would cut-off the sources of credit of a merchant with repeated bad warranty relations with his creditors.

"The clinching argument is the contrast between the legal relationships in consumer financing and the legal relationships in the financing of commercial accounts receivable. In that field the financing institutions, many of which are also engaged in the consumer field, have never sought to extend to the commercial field their assertion that they are entitled to freedom from customer defenses. There is one simple reason for this: the commercial buyers would not stand for it, for the purchase contracts in the commercial field are not contracts of adhesion. What then happens to the question of freedom from defenses in the commercial field? The financer as part of its credit determination studies the experience of the seller in respect to customer complaints and returned goods, and if the percentage is too high, refuses to do business with that merchant. The same type of credit thinking would provide the answer in the consumer field."

With abolition of cutoff devices it is only logical to assume that the financing institutions would probably protect themselves by increasing the dealer reserve (the percentage of each contract price retained by the financial institution as a fund against which to charge bad debts and other credit losses of that particular dealer) or by decreasing the dealer's participation (the dealer's share of the finance charge) in each consumer credit transaction. In either case, the ultimate burden of increased costs to dealers would likely be passed on to the consumer in the form of higher cash prices for the goods or services or in the form of higher finance charges, or both.

The Commission believes spreading the costs of abolishing third party cutoff devices to all consumers in the marketplace would be more than counter-balanced by the protections which the consuming public will receive in the form of better goods and services. Moreover, the repercussions will probably not be as significant as some have suggested. The Commission agrees with Professor Kripke, when he states:

> "In a reputable milieu—reputable merchants, reputable products, reputable financers—the freedom from defense rule is statistically unnecessary. . . . Its time has run out." . . .

Any attempt to deal with third party cutoff devices such as HIDC and waiver of defense clauses involves a question of balance. The needs of small businessmen to obtain capital to enter and remain in the market serving marginal risk consumers must be weighed against the protection of all consumers. The balance is sometimes a delicate one. In this case it is not. The Commission firmly believes that consumers have an absolute right to receive fair value in the purchase of goods and services. One way to help achieve this goal is to abolish the HIDC doctrine and waiver of defense clauses. The inevitable reduction in availability of consumer credit in some markets will be more than offset by increased consumer confidence in the market as a whole.

FEDERAL TRADE COMMISSION REGULATIONS— PRESERVATION OF CONSUMERS' CLAIMS AND DEFENSES

[See Selected Source Materials Supplement]

UCC §§ 1–201(19), 3–104, 3–106, 3–201, 3–302, 3–305;

UCC ARTICLE 9, §§ 9–403, 9–404;

PRE–2000 UCC ARTICLE 9, § 9–318

[See Selected Source Materials Supplement]

Part VII

PROBLEMS OF PERFORMANCE

Part VII of this book concerns problems of performance. These problems fall into a variety of categories.

Chapter 22 concerns the obligation to perform a contract in good faith. This obligation is important not only in itself, but because it directly or indirectly provides a foundation for many other doctrines concerning performance.

Chapter 23 concerns the doctrine of substantial performance. In cases to which this doctrine is applicable, a contracting party is entitled to bring suit on the contract if his performance is substantially what she promised to do, even though not exactly what she promised to do, subject to an offset to reflect the shortfall in her performance.

Chapter 24 concerns express conditions. An express condition differs from a promise in that it imposes no obligation, but instead provides that a contracting party either does not come under a duty to perform unless a certain state of affairs exists, or is released from a duty to perform if a certain state of affairs exists.

Chapter 25 concerns (1) the order in which performance under a contract must occur when the contract is not explicit on that issue, and (2) when a breach by one party makes it permissible for the other party to treat the contract as at an end.

Finally, Chapter 26 concerns the effect of a repudiation of a contract by one of the parties before that party's performance is due; the consequences that arise when it appears that one party will be unable to perform under the contract, although she has not yet either breached or repudiated the contract; and cases in which one party may justifiably insist that the other provide adequate assurance that performance will be forthcoming.

Chapter 22

THE OBLIGATION TO PERFORM
IN GOOD FAITH

PATTERSON v. MEYERHOFER

Court of Appeals of New York, 1912.
204 N.Y. 96, 97 N.E. 472.

Appeal from Supreme Court, Appellate Division, Second Department.

Action by Benjamin Patterson against Anna Meyerhofer. From a judgment of the Appellate Division (138 App.Div. 891, 122 N.Y.Supp. 1140) affirming a judgment for defendant, plaintiff appeals. Reversed, and new trial granted.

WILLARD BARTLETT, J. The parties to this action entered into a written contract whereby the plaintiff agreed to sell, and the defendant agreed to buy, four several parcels of land with the houses thereon for the sum of $23,000, to be partly in cash and partly by taking title subject to certain mortgages upon the property. When she executed this contract, the defendant knew that the plaintiff was not then the owner of the premises which he agreed to sell to her, but that he expected and intended to acquire title thereto by purchasing the same at a foreclosure sale. Before this foreclosure sale took place, the defendant stated to the plaintiff that she would not perform the contract on her part, but intended to buy the premises for her own account without in any way recognizing the said contract as binding upon her, and this she did, buying the four parcels for $5,595 each. The plaintiff attended the foreclosure sale, able, ready, and willing to purchase the premises, and he bid for the same, but in every instance of a bid made by him the defendant bid a higher sum. The result was that she acquired each lot for $155 less than she had obligated herself to pay the plaintiff therefor under the contract or $620 less in all.

In the foreclosure sale was included a fifth house, which the defendant also purchased. This was not mentioned in the written contract between the parties, but, according to the complaint, there was a prior parol agreement which provided that the plaintiff should buy all five houses at the foreclosure sale, and should convey only four of them to the defendant, retaining the fifth house for himself.

Upon these facts the plaintiff brought the present action, demanding judgment that the defendant convey to him the fifth house, and declaring that

886

he has a lien upon the premises purchased by her at the foreclosure sale, and that she holds the same in trust for the plaintiff subject to the contract. The complaint also prays that the plaintiff be awarded the sum of $620 damages, being the difference between the price which the defendant paid at the foreclosure sale for the four houses mentioned in the contract and the price which she would have had to pay the plaintiff thereunder. The learned judge who tried the case at Special Term rendered judgment in favor of the defendant, holding that, under the contract of sale, there was no relation of confidence between the vendor and vendee. "In the present case," he said, "each party was free to act for his own interest, restricted only by the stipulations of the contract." He was, therefore, of the opinion that "the defendant had a right to buy in at the auction, and that she is entitled to hold exactly as though she had been a stranger, and that the plaintiff is not entitled to recover the difference between the price paid at the auction and the contract price."

I am inclined to agree with the trial court that no relation of trust can be spelled out of the transactions between the parties. There is no finding of any parol agreement in respect to the fifth house which has been mentioned, and, even if there had been such an agreement resting merely in parol, I do not see that it would have been enforceable. As to the four parcels which constituted the subject-matter of the written contract, the defendant avowed her intention to ignore that contract before bidding for them, and cannot be regarded as having gone into possession under the plaintiff as vendor, but did so rather in defiance of any right of his. . . .

There is no need of judicially declaring any trust in the defendant, however, to secure to the plaintiff the profit which he would have made if the defendant had not intervened as purchaser at the foreclosure sale, and had fulfilled the written contract on her part. This is represented by his claim for $620 damages. That amount, under the facts as found, I think the plaintiff was entitled to recover. He has demanded it in his complaint, and he should not be thrown out of court because he has also prayed for too much equitable relief.

In the case of every contract there is an implied undertaking on the part of each party that he will not intentionally and purposely do anything to prevent the other party from carrying out the agreement on his part. This proposition necessarily follows from the general rule that a party who causes or sanctions the breach of an agreement is thereby precluded from recovering damages for its nonperformance or from interposing it as a defense to an action upon the contract. Young v. Hunter, 6 N.Y. 203; Barton v. Gray, 57 Mich. 622, 24 N.W. 638, and cases there cited. "Where a party stipulates that another shall do a certain thing, he thereby impliedly promises that he will himself do nothing which may hinder or obstruct that other in doing that thing." Gay v. Blanchard, 32 La.Ann. 497.

By entering into the contract to purchase from the plaintiff property which she knew he would have to buy at the foreclosure sale in order to convey it to her, the defendant impliedly agreed that she would do nothing to prevent him from acquiring the property at such sale. The defendant violated the agreement thus implied on her part by bidding for and buying the premises herself. Although the plaintiff bid therefor, she uniformly outbid him. Presumably, if she had not interfered, he could have bought the property for the same price which she paid for it. He would then have been able to sell it to her for the price specified in the contract (assuming that she fulfilled the contract), which was $620 more. This sum, therefore, represents the loss which he has suffered. It is the measure of the plaintiff's damages for the defendant's breach of contract.

I see no escape from this conclusion. It is true that the contract contemplated that the four houses should go to the defendant and they have gone to her; but that is not all. The contract contemplated that they should go to the plaintiff first. In that event the plaintiff would have received $620 which he has not got. This would have had to be paid by the defendant if she had fulfilled her contract; and she should be required to pay it now unless she can present some better defense than is presented in this record. This will place both parties in the position contemplated by the contract. The defendant will have paid no more than the contract obligated her to pay. The plaintiff will have received all to which the contract entitled him. I leave the fifth house out of consideration because as to that it seems to me there was no enforceable agreement.

For these reasons, the judgments of the Appellate Division and the Special Term should be reversed and a new trial granted, with costs to abide the event. . . .

CULLEN, C.J., and VANN and WERNER, JJ., concur with WILLARD BARTLETT, J.

[The dissenting opinion of Chase, J., concurred in by Hiscock and Collin, JJ., is omitted]

Judgment reversed, etc.

IRON TRADE PRODUCTS CO. v. WILKOFF CO.

Supreme Court of Pennsylvania, 1922.
272 Pa. 172, 116 A. 150.

WALLING, J. In July, 1919, plaintiff entered into a written contract with defendant for the purchase of 2,600 tons of section relaying rails, to be delivered in New York harbor at times therein specified for $41 a ton. Defendant failed to deliver any of the rails, and plaintiff brought this suit, averring by reason of such default, it had been compelled to purchase the rails elsewhere (2,000 tons thereof at $49.20 per ton and 600 tons at $49 per ton), also that the market or current price of the rails at the time and place of delivery was approximately $50 per ton, and claiming as damages the difference between what it had been compelled to pay and the contract price. Defendant filed an affidavit of defense and a supplement thereto, both of which the court below held insufficient and entered judgment for plaintiff, from which defendant brought this appeal.

In effect, the affidavit of defense avers the supply of such rails was very limited, there being only two places in the United States (one in Georgia and one in West Virginia) where they could be obtained in quantities to fill the contract, and that pending the time for delivery defendant was negotiating for the required rails when plaintiff announced to the trade its urgent desire to purchase a similar quantity of like rails, and in fact bought 887 tons and agreed to purchase a much larger quantity from the parties with whom defendant had been negotiating, further averring this conduct on behalf of plaintiff reduced the available supply of relaying rails and enhanced the price to an exorbitant sum, rendering performance by defendant impossible. The affidavit, however, fails to aver knowledge on part of plaintiff that the supply of rails was limited or any intent on its part to prevent, interfere with, or embarrass defendant in the performance of the contract; and there is no suggestion of any understanding, express or implied, that defendant was to secure the rails from any particular source, or that plaintiff was to refrain from purchasing other rails; hence it was not required to do so. The true rule is stated in Williston on Contracts, p. 1308, as quoted by the trial court, viz.:

> "If a party seeking to secure all the merchandise of a certain character which he could, entered into a contract for a quantity of the required goods, and subsequently made performance of the contract by the seller more difficult by making other purchases which increased the scarcity of the available supply, his conduct would furnish no excuse for refusal to perform the prior contract."

Mere difficulty of performance will not excuse a breach of contract. Corona C. & C. Co. v. Dickinson, 261 Pa. 589, 104 Atl. 741; Janes v. Scott, 59 Pa. 178, 98 Am.Dec. 328; 35 Cyc. 245. Defendant relies upon the rule stated in United States v. Peck, 102 U.S. 64, 26 L.Ed. 46, that—

> "The conduct of one party to a contract which prevents the other from performing his part is an excuse for nonperformance."

The cases are not parallel. Here plaintiff's conduct did not prevent performance by defendant, although it may have added to the difficulty and expense thereof. There is no averment that plaintiff's purchases exhausted the supply of rails, and the advance in price caused thereby is no excuse. The *Peck* case stands on different ground. There Peck contracted to sell the government a certain quantity of hay for the Tongue River station, and the trial court found it was mutually understood the hay was to be cut on government lands called "the Big Meadows," in the Yellowstone valley, which was the only available source of supply, also that thereafter the government caused all of that hay to be cut for it by other parties, in view of which Peck was relieved from his contract.

The affidavit "denies that there was any market or market price or current price for such relaying rails" at any time from the date of the contract to the beginning of this suit, but other statements therein amount to an admission of a market price. For example, it speaks of "the trade in Pittsburgh, New York, and other centers of such trade"; also of "the very small quantity of such rails in the market." . . .

The . . . admitted facts that plaintiff actually bought the 2,600 tons and had previously resold the same, indicate a market value, and the specific averment thereof in the statement of claim is not sufficiently denied in the affidavit. An affidavit of defense must be considered as a whole, and therein a general denial is of no avail against an admission of the same fact. An affidavit that is contradictory or equivocal is insufficient. See Noll v. Royal Exchange Assurance Corp., 76 Pa.Super.Ct. 510. . . .

The assignments of error are overruled, and the judgment is affirmed.

———

RESTATEMENT, SECOND, CONTRACTS § 237, ILLUSTRATIONS 6, 7: "6. A contracts to sell and B to buy on 30 days credit 3,000 tons of iron rails at a stated price. B purchases iron rails heavily from various sources for use in his business, and in consequence A has difficulty in securing 3,000 tons and the market price is substantially increased. A fails to deliver the rails. B has a claim against A for breach of contract. B's purchase of iron rails from other sources for use in his business is not a failure of performance because B is under no duty to refrain from purchasing for that purpose. A's failure to deliver the rails is therefore a breach.

"7. The facts being otherwise as stated in Illustration 6, B maliciously buys iron rails heavily from various sources in order to prevent A from performing his contract with B. B has no claim against A. B's malicious purchase of iron rails from other sources is a material breach of his duty of good faith and fair dealing ..., which operates as the non-occurrence of a condition of A's duty to deliver the rails, discharging it."

KIRKE LA SHELLE CO. v. PAUL ARMSTRONG CO., 263 N.Y. 79, 188 N.E. 163 (1933). "[I]n every contract there is an implied covenant that neither party shall do anything which will have the effect of destroying or injuring the rights of the other party to receive the fruits of the contract, which means that in every contract there exists an implied covenant of good faith and fair dealing."

RESTATEMENT, SECOND, CONTRACTS § 205

[See Selected Source Materials Supplement]

PRE–2001 UCC ARTICLE 1 (IN FORCE IN MOST STATES), §§ 1–201(19), 1–203

UCC § 2–103(1)(b)

2001 VERSION OF ARTICLE 1, § 1–201(20)

[See Selected Source Materials Supplement]

NOTE ON THE UCC DEFINITIONS OF GOOD FAITH

The UCC is promulgated by the National Conference of Commissioners on Uniform State Law (NCCUSL) and the American Law Institute (ALI). However, the UCC is only effective to the extent it is adopted by state legislatures. Prior to 2001, Section 1–201(19) of Article 1 (General Provisions) defined good faith narrowly, to mean "honesty in fact in the conduct or transaction concerned." In contrast, Section 2–201 of Article 2 (Sale of Goods) defined good faith broadly, to mean, in the case of a merchant, "honesty in fact and the observance of reasonable commercial standards of fair dealing in the trade."

In 2001, NCCUSL and the ALI promulgated a revised official version of UCC Article 1. Section 1–201(20) of the revised official version of Article 1 defined good faith broadly, for all Articles of the UCC except Article 5, to mean "honesty in fact and the observance of reasonable commercial standards of fair dealing." The adoption of this broad definition in the revised official version of Article 1 rendered superfluous the broad definition of good faith in the official version of Article 2. Accordingly, that definition was deleted from the official version of Article 2. However, as of early 2006 only sixteen states had adopted the revised official version of Article 1 and the counterpart revision of Article 2. Furthermore, about half of those states did not adopt the definition of good faith in revised Article 1 and retained the prior definition of good faith in Article 2. Accordingly, in most states the enacted definitions of good faith in Articles 1 and 2 continue as they were prior to 2001—that is, continue to be as set in the first paragraph of this Note.

———

CISG ART. 7(1)

[See Selected Source Materials Supplement]

———

UNIDROIT PRINCIPLES OF INTERNATIONAL COMMERCIAL CONTRACTS ART. 1.7

[See Selected Source Materials Supplement]

———

PRINCIPLES OF EUROPEAN CONTRACT LAW ART. 1.201

[See Selected Source Materials Supplement]

———

NOTE ON THE DUTY TO PERFORM IN GOOD FAITH UNDER THE UCC AND RESTATEMENT SECOND

UCC § 1–203 provides that "Every contract or duty within this Act imposes an obligation of good faith in its performance or enforcement." This concept permeates the entire UCC. Thus according to Summers, "Good Faith" in General Contract Law and the Sales Provisions of the Uniform Commercial Code, 54 Va.L.Rev. 195, 212, 219 n. 91 (1968), thirteen provisions in Article 2 explicitly use the term "good faith," and nineteen more have comments which use the term. For example, UCC § 2–311(1) provides that "An agreement for sale which is otherwise sufficiently definite ... to be a contract is not made invalid by the fact that it leaves particulars of performance to be specified by one of the parties. Any such specification must be made in good faith and within limits set by commercial reasonableness." Similarly, UCC § 2–305 provides that "a price to be fixed by the seller or by the buyer means a price for him to fix in good faith."

In accord with UCC § 1–203, Restatement Second has added a new provision, Section 205: "Every contract imposes upon each party a duty of good faith and fair dealing in its performance and its enforcement." The comments to § 205 state:

> a. *Meanings of "good faith"*. . . . The phrase "good faith" is used in a variety of contexts, and its meaning varies somewhat with the context. Good faith performance or enforcement of a contract emphasizes faithfulness to an agreed common purpose and consistency with the justified expectations of the other party; it excludes a variety of types of conduct characterized as involving "bad faith" because they violate community standards of decency, fairness or reasonableness. The appropriate remedy for a breach of the duty of good faith also varies with the circumstances. . . .

> d. *Good faith performance.* Subterfuges and evasions violate the obligation of good faith in performance even though the actor believes his conduct to be justified. But the obligation goes further: bad faith may be overt or may consist of inaction, and fair dealing may require more than honesty. A complete catalogue of types of bad faith is impossible, but the following types are among those which have been recognized in judicial decisions: evasion of the spirit of the bargain, lack of diligence and slacking off, willful rendering of imperfect performance, abuse of a power to specify terms, and interference with or failure to cooperate in the other party's performance. . . .

E. ALLAN FARNSWORTH, GOOD FAITH IN CONTRACT PERFORMANCE, IN GOOD FAITH AND FAULT IN CONTRACT LAW*

. . . What [is meant] by "good faith" in the context of performance of contracts?

The most restrictive answer is that the duty of good faith is "simply a rechristening of fundamental principles of contract law," as Justice Antonin Scalia put it in the days when he was a federal Court of Appeals judge. Three decades ago, in [an] article on good faith, I took much the same position, to which Scalia alluded in observing "correct . . . is the perception of Professor Farnsworth that the significance of the doctrine is 'in implying terms in the agreement.'" This restrictive answer has not satisfied . . . academics, however, and their search for the meaning of good faith has sparked a spirited debate.

In 1968, Professor Robert Summers published an influential article on good faith in which he sketched the contours of this mandate in terms of an

* J. Beatson & W. Friedman, eds., 1995. Reprinted by permission of Oxford University Press.

"excluder" analysis. He suggested "that in cases of doubt, a lawyer will determine more accurately what the judge means by using the phrase "good faith" if he does not ask what good faith itself means, but rather asks: "What . . . does the judge intend to rule out by his use of this phrase?" Summers argued that "good faith . . . is best understood as an 'excluder'—it is a phrase which has no general meaning or meanings of its own, but which serves to exclude many heterogeneous forms of bad faith." This excluder analysis . . . found its way into the commentary to the good faith provision in the Restatement 2d. . . .

In 1980, Professor Steven Burton, of the University of Iowa, in a major article on good faith, introduced "forgone opportunity analysis." Taking a swipe at Summers by lamenting that "neither courts or commentators have articulated an operational standard that distinguishes good faith performance from bad faith performance," he attempted to fashion a standard based on the expectations of the parties. "Good faith," he argued, "limits the exercise of discretion in performance conferred on one party by the contract," so it is bad faith to use discretion "to recapture opportunities forgone upon contracting" as determined by the other party's expectations—in other words, to refuse "to pay the expected cost of performance". . . .

Courts have looked to all three of these views—Burton's, Summers', and mine—for support, often without recognizing a conflict among them, which is scarcely surprising, because in the context of performance the meaning of good faith may turn on which of its several functions is in issue. Sometimes good faith is the basis of a limitation on the exercise of discretion conferred on a party, as under Burton's view. Sometimes good faith is the basis for proscribing behaviors which violate basic standards of decency, as under Summers' view. Sometimes it is merely the basis of an implied term to fill a gap or deal with an omitted case, as under [my] view. . . .

———

SOUTHWEST SAVINGS AND LOAN ASS'N v. SUNAMP SYSTEMS, 172 Ariz. 553, 838 P.2d 1314 (Ariz. Ct. App. 1992). "If contracting parties cannot profitably use their contractual powers without fear that a jury will second-guess them under a vague standard of good faith, the law will impair the predictability that an orderly commerce requires. Yet contracting parties, hard as they may try, cannot reduce every understanding to a stated term. Instances inevitably arise where one party exercises discretion retained or unforeclosed under a contract in such a way as to deny the other a reasonably expected benefit of the bargain. . . . The law of good faith, though inexact, attempts a remedy for such abuse. *See* Steven J. Burton, *Breach of Contract and the Common Law Duty to Perform in Good Faith*, 94 Harv. L.Rev. 369, 385–86 (1980):

> The good faith performance doctrine may be said to permit the exercise of discretion for any purpose—including ordinary business purposes—reasonably within the contemplation of the parties. A contract thus would be breached by a failure to perform in good faith if a party uses its discretion for a reason outside the contemplated range—a reason beyond the risks assumed by the party claiming a breach.

(Footnotes omitted.) *See also* Restatement (Second) of Contracts § 205 cmt. a (1981) ("Good faith performance or enforcement of a contract emphasizes faithfulness to an agreed common purpose and consistency with the justified expectations of the other party....").

"Consistently with [these formulations], our supreme court has decided in a variety of contexts that a contracting party may exercise a retained contractual power in bad faith. In insurance bad faith cases, for example, the supreme court has determined that an insurance company may act in bad faith by manipulating its power to evaluate and adjust claims in such a way as to defeat the reasonable expectations of its insured. *See, e.g., Rawlings,* 151 Ariz. at 153–57, 726 P.2d at 569–73; *cf. Farmers Ins. Exch. v. Henderson,* 82 Ariz. 335, 338–40, 313 P.2d 404, 407–09 (1957) (insurance company may act in bad faith by refusing to settle litigation against insured). In wrongful termination cases the supreme court has held that an employer-at-will may fire an employee for no cause, but may not exercise this power abusively for bad cause. *See, e.g., Wagenseller v. Scottsdale Memorial Hosp.,* 147 Ariz. 370, 385–86, 710 P.2d 1025, 1040–41 (1985).

"In this case, therefore, inquiry does not end with recognition that Southwest had contractual authority to freeze, and ultimately terminate, SunAmp's credit line. The question is whether the jury might reasonably have found that Southwest wrongfully exercised this power "for a reason beyond the risks" that SunAmp assumed in its loan agreement, Burton, *supra,* 147 Ariz. at 386, 710 P.2d at 1041, or for a reason inconsistent with SunAmp's 'justified expectations,' Restatement, *supra,* § 205 cmt. a."

BEST v. UNITED STATES NATIONAL BANK

Supreme Court of Oregon, 1987.
303 Or. 557, 739 P.2d 554.

Before PETERSON, C.J., and LENT, LINDE, CARSON, JONES and GILLETTE, JJ.

LENT, JUSTICE.

Defendant U.S. National Bank (the Bank) charges its checking account depositors a fee for processing nonsufficient fund (NSF) checks written on their accounts. Between 1973 and 1979, the Bank increased its NSF fee from $3 to $5 per check. Plaintiffs Lonnie and Teresa Best were among the Bank's depositors whose accounts were assessed NSF charges during this period. The Bests, individually and as representatives of a class of depositors, brought this action to recover the charges. They contend that the Bank's NSF fees were unlawful because the fees greatly exceeded the Bank's costs for processing NSF checks.

The Bests alleged six claims for relief, three of which were certified by the circuit court as class actions. Only the claims certified as class actions are at issue here. Those claims are (1) that the Bank breached its obligation to set NSF fees in good faith, (2) that its NSF fees were unconscionable and (3) that its NSF fees were an unlawful penalty for breach of contract. On the penalty and breach of good faith claims, the circuit court certified a plaintiff class comprising all natural persons who had nonbusiness checking accounts with the Bank and who paid NSF charges totaling $6 or more between May 31,

1973, and May 30, 1979. On the unconscionability claim, the court certified a plaintiff subclass comprising class members who opened checking accounts with the Bank on or after July 1, 1968.[1] (Hereinafter, we will refer to all plaintiffs as "the depositors.")

The circuit court granted the Bank's motion for summary judgment on the class claims and entered final judgment dismissing those claims. On appeal by the depositors, the Court of Appeals reversed and remanded with respect to the breach of good faith claim but otherwise affirmed the circuit court. *Best v. U.S. National Bank,* 78 Or.App. 1, 714 P.2d 1049 (1986). We allowed both the depositors' and the Bank's petitions for review and affirm the decision of the Court of Appeals.

I.

Before discussing the depositors' breach of good faith claim, we will briefly address their penalty and unconscionability claims.

The depositors claim that the Bank's NSF fees were unlawful penalties for breaches of the depositors' express or implied contractual agreements not to write NSF checks. We agree with the Court of Appeals that the depositors did not present any evidence from which a trier of fact could infer the existence of such an agreement. *See* 78 Or.App. at 4–10, 714 P.2d 1049. There being no agreement, there could be no unlawful penalty for breach of the agreement.

The depositors claim that the Bank's NSF fees were unconscionable because the fees were greatly in excess of the Bank's costs for processing NSF checks. The doctrine of unconscionability, however, is largely inapplicable to this case, and, to the extent that it may apply, we conclude that the fee set by the Bank was not unconscionable.

Unconscionability is a legal issue that must be assessed as of the time of contract formation. *W.L. May Co. v. Philco–Ford Corp.,* 273 Or. 701, 707, 543 P.2d 283 (1975). Thus the doctrine applies to contract terms rather than to contract performance. The only contract term relevant to NSF fees was a statement in the preprinted "account agreement" signed by the depositors when they opened their accounts: "This account is subject to Bank service charges existing at any time." The parties agree that "service charges" included NSF fees. The specific fee charged, then, was not part of the depositors' agreement with the Bank; rather, the fee was set by the Bank as part of its performance of the account agreement. The unconscionability doctrine is inapplicable to the amount of the fee.

If the depositors were or should have been aware of the fee amounts and tacitly agreed to the amounts through failing to close their accounts, see Part II, *infra,* they could challenge the agreements as unconscionable. Summary judgment on their unconscionability claim, however, would still be appropriate.

Although the depositors assert that the Bank's NSF fees were two or three times the Bank's NSF processing costs, the fees were relatively small and were similar to NSF fees charged by other banks. Moreover, apart from

---

1. July 1, 1968, appears to be the date on which the Bank instituted the $3 fee for NSF checks.

the adhesive nature of the account agreement, the record reflects few indicia of one-sided bargaining. The depositors could close their accounts at any time and for any reason. There is no evidence that the depositors were not of ordinary intelligence and experience. There is also no evidence that the Bank obtained any agreement from the depositors through deception or any other improper means. The circuit court's grant of summary judgment on the depositors' unconscionability claim was proper.

II.

The depositors claim that the Bank had an obligation to set its NSF fees in good faith and that it breached this obligation by setting its fees at amounts greatly in excess of the costs incurred by it in processing NSF checks.

Nothing in the depositors' account agreement with the Bank expressly limited the Bank's authority to set NSF fees. This court has long stated, however, that there is an obligation of good faith in the performance and enforcement of every contract. *See, e.g., Comini v. Union Oil Co.,* 277 Or. 753, 756, 562 P.2d 175 (1977); *Perkins v. Standard Oil Co.,* 235 Or. 7, 16, 383 P.2d 107 (1963); *see also* Restatement (Second) of Contracts § 205 (1979). This obligation limited the Bank's apparently unlimited authority to set NSF fees, and the depositors can recover for the breach of this obligation just as they could for the breach of any other contractual obligation.

The Bank and *amicus curiae* First Interstate Bank of Oregon argue that the doctrine of good faith is inapplicable because the depositors agreed to the NSF fees by maintaining their accounts, which they could close at any time.[2] Whether the depositors agreed to the specific fees charged, however, is a question of fact that cannot be decided on a motion for summary judgment. The argument of the Bank and *amicus* assumes that the depositors knew or should have known the amount of the fees when they wrote their NSF checks. This assumption does not necessarily follow from the evidence. The practice of Bank employees who opened accounts was not to inform depositors of the amount or even of the existence of NSF fees unless the depositor inquired. The Bank also did not notify depositors when it increased its NSF fees. In the absence of inquiry, a depositor would ordinarily know the amount of the fee only if the depositor had been charged a fee, in which case the amount would appear on the depositor's monthly statement of account. Moreover, even if the depositor discovered the current amount of the NSF fee, the depositor could never be certain of the fee that would be charged because the Bank could increase or decrease the fee at any time without notice. It would be improper under this evidence to conclude on a motion for summary judgment that the depositors agreed to the charges through failing to close their accounts.

Assuming that there was no agreement, the question before us is whether there is a genuine issue of material fact whether the Bank set its NSF fees in good faith.

The purpose of the good faith doctrine is to prohibit improper behavior in the performance and enforcement of contracts. Because the doctrine must be applied to the entire range of contracts, definitions of good faith tend to be

---

2. The Bank was also free to close the accounts. If it had not been free to do so, its argument would be much weaker because the depositors would have had a contractual entitlement to the continuation of account service fees that had been set in good faith.

either too abstract or applicable only to specific contexts. For this reason, Professor Summers has argued that good faith should be conceptualized as an "excluder," by which he means that good faith should be defined only by identifying various forms of bad faith. Summers, *The General Duty of Good Faith—Its Recognition and Conceptualization*, 67 Cornell L.Rev. 810 (1982); *see also* Summers, *"Good Faith" in General Contract Law and the Sales Provisions of the Uniform Commercial Code*, 54 Va.L.Rev. 195, 199–207 (1968). This is also the approach adopted by the Restatement (Second) of Contracts § 205 (1979):

> "The phrase 'good faith' is used in a variety of contexts, and its meaning varies somewhat with the context. Good faith performance or enforcement of a contract emphasizes faithfulness to an agreed common purpose and consistency with the justified expectations of the other party; it excludes a variety of types of conduct characterized as involving 'bad faith' because they violate community standards of decency, fairness or reasonableness."

Restatement (Second) of Contracts § 205, *comment a* (1979).

> "Subterfuges and evasions violate the obligation of good faith in performance even though the actor believes his conduct to be justified. But the obligation goes further; bad faith may be overt or may consist of inaction, and fair dealing may require more than honesty. A complete catalogue of types of bad faith is impossible, but the following types are among those which have been recognized in judicial decisions: evasion of the spirit of the bargain, lack of diligence and slacking off, willful rendering of imperfect performance, abuse of power to specify terms, and interference with or failure to cooperate in the other party's performance."

Restatement (Second) of Contracts § 205, *comment d* (1979).

This does not mean that decisions as to what constitutes bad faith must be *ad hoc* and standardless. Without attempting to give positive content to the phrase "good faith," it is possible to set forth operational standards by which good faith can be distinguished from bad faith within a particular context. Professors Summers and Burton, although in substantial disagreement with each other, have proposed such standards. *See* Summers, *supra*, 67 Cornell L.Rev. at 823–24; Burton, *Breach of Contract and the Common Law Duty to Perform in Good Faith*, 94 Harv.L.Rev. 369 (1980).

This court also has not attempted to set forth a comprehensive definition of good faith. But in line with the Restatement and traditional principles of contract law, the court has sought through the good faith doctrine to effectuate the reasonable contractual expectations of the parties. *See Comini*, 277 Or. at 756–57, 562 P.2d 175; *Perkins*, 235 Or. at 15–17, 383 P.2d 107. When one party to a contract is given discretion in the performance of some aspect of the contract, the parties ordinarily contemplate that that discretion will be exercised for particular purposes. If the discretion is exercised for purposes not contemplated by the parties, the party exercising discretion has performed in bad faith. *Id.; see also* Burton, *supra.*

To illustrate, in *Comini* the defendant oil company had a contractual right to disapprove the plaintiff distributor's transfer of the distributorship. This court concluded that the right was intended by the parties to protect the oil company's legitimate business interests in its distribution system. *Comini,* 277 Or. at 756, 562 P.2d 175. Thus the oil company could, consistent with its obligation to perform in good faith, reject a transfer to someone inexperienced in the oil business and even reject a transfer to an experienced distributor when it had decided to consolidate the distributorship with another distributorship. *Id.* at 756–57, 562 P.2d 175. But the oil company would have performed in bad faith if, for example, it had rejected a transfer in order to retaliate against the distributor for some reason. Similarly, the parties to an employment contract generally contemplate that an employer may use its discretion to fire an at-will employee if the employer is dissatisfied with the employee's performance or if the employee's services are no longer required. The parties do not ordinarily contemplate, however, that the employer may fire the employee in order to deprive the employee of benefits to which the employee would otherwise have become entitled if the employment had continued. An employer who does the latter breaches its obligation to perform in good faith. *State ex rel. Roberts v. Public Finance Co.,* 294 Or. 713, 719 n. 4, 662 P.2d 330 (1983); *cf. Swanson v. Van Duyn Choc. Shops,* 282 Or. 491, 494, 579 P.2d 239 (1978).

In this case, the Bank had the contractual discretion to set its NSF fees. Under *Comini* and *Perkins* that discretion had to be exercised within the confines of the reasonable expectations of the depositors. It is therefore not necessarily sufficient, as the Bank contends, that the Bank acted honestly in setting its NSF fees or that its fees were similar to those of other banks. Undoubtedly, parties to a contract always expect that the other party will perform the contract honestly and, where the performance of a commercial enterprise is at issue, ordinarily expect that it will do so in a commercially reasonable manner. But the reasonable expectations of the parties need not be so limited.

So far as we can discern from the record, the depositors did not explicitly argue before the circuit court that the Bank's setting of its NSF fees was not in accord with their contractual expectations. Their complaint alleged only that the Bank's NSF fees were greatly in excess of its reasonable costs. In their argument on the Bank's motion for summary judgment, they treated the good faith and unconscionability doctrines as substantively equivalent, arguing that the Bank's NSF fees were set in bad faith because they were set at amounts that were unconscionable. Before the Court of Appeals, however, the depositors argued that the fees were set in bad faith not only because the fees were unconscionable but because the depositors reasonably expected the Bank to exercise its discretion to set NSF fees for the purpose of permitting it to recover its costs of processing NSF checks. Although this argument was not explicitly made before the circuit court, we will address both arguments on review because the nature of the good faith obligation has been somewhat unclear.

When a party has the contractual right to specify a price term, the term specified may be so high or low that the party will be deemed to have acted in bad faith regardless of the reasonable expectations of the other party. In this respect the good faith and unconscionability doctrines tend to run together. In general, however, whether a specified price violates the obligation of good faith should be decided by the reasonable contractual expectations of the parties. In this instance we conclude that the Bank's NSF fees were not so high as to be evidence of bad faith for that reason alone.

Nevertheless, we believe that there is a genuine issue of material fact whether the Bank set its NSF fees in accordance with the reasonable expectations of the parties. The record shows that when the depositors opened their accounts, the only account fees that would ordinarily be discussed would be the Bank's monthly and per check charges, if any. The sole reference to NSF fees was contained in the account agreement signed by the depositors, which obligated them to pay the Bank's "service charges in effect at any time." Because NSF fees were incidental to the Bank's principal checking account fees and were denominated "service charges," a trier of fact could infer that the depositors reasonably expected that NSF fees would be special fees to cover the costs of extraordinary services. This inference could reasonably lead to the further inference that the depositors reasonably expected that the Bank's NSF fees would be priced similarly to those checking account fees of which the depositors were aware—the Bank's monthly checking account service fees and per check fees, if any. By "priced similarly," we mean priced to cover the Bank's NSF check processing costs plus an allowance for overhead costs plus the Bank's ordinary profit margin on checking account services.

Finally, assuming that the Bank's obligation of good faith required the Bank to set its NSF fees in accordance with its costs and ordinary profit margin, there was evidence that the Bank breached the obligation. The Bank's own cost studies show that its NSF fees were set at amounts greatly in excess of its costs and ordinary profit margin. Internal memoranda and depositions of Bank employees permit the inference that the Bank's NSF fees were set at these high levels in order to reap the large profits to be made from the apparently inelastic "demand" for the processing of NSF checks and in order to discourage its depositors from carelessly writing NSF checks. A trier of fact could find that both of these purposes were contrary to the reasonable expectations of the depositors when they agreed to pay whatever NSF fee was set by the Bank.

Because there are genuine issues of material fact with respect to the depositors' breach of good faith claim, the trial court erred in granting the Bank summary judgment on this claim. . . .

The decision of the Court of Appeals is affirmed. The circuit court's judgment with respect to the depositors' breach of good faith claim is reversed, and the case is remanded to the circuit court for further proceedings consistent with this opinion.

———

HILTON HOTELS v. BUTCH LEWIS PRODUCTIONS, INC., 107 Nev. 226, 808 P.2d 919 (1991). "When one party performs a contract in a manner that is unfaithful to the purpose of the contract and the justified expectations of the other party are thus denied, damages may be awarded against the party who does not act in good faith. Whether the controlling party's actions fall outside the reasonable expectations of the dependent party is determined by the various factors and special circumstances that shape these expectations."

———

BLOOR v. FALSTAFF BREWING CORP.

United States Court of Appeals, Second Circuit, 1979.
601 F.2d 609.

Before MOORE, FRIENDLY and MESKILL, CIRCUIT JUDGES.

FRIENDLY, CIRCUIT JUDGE. This action, wherein federal jurisdiction is predicated on diversity of citizenship, 28 U.S.C.A. § 1332, was brought in the District Court for the Southern District of New York, by James Bloor, Reorganization Trustee of Balco Properties Corporation, formerly named P. Ballantine & Sons (Ballantine), a venerable and once successful brewery based in Newark, N.J. He sought to recover from Falstaff Brewing Corporation (Falstaff) for breach of a contract dated March 31, 1972, wherein Falstaff bought the Ballantine brewing labels, trademarks, accounts receivable, distribution systems and other property except the brewery. The price was $4,000,000 plus a royalty of fifty cents on each barrel of the Ballantine brands sold between April 1, 1972 and March 31, 1978. Although other issues were tried, the appeals concern only two provisions of the contract. These are:

> 8. *Certain other covenants of buyer.* (a) After the Closing Date the [Buyer] will use its best efforts to promote and maintain a high volume of sales under the Proprietary Rights.

> 2(a)(v) [The Buyer will pay a royalty of $.50 per barrel for a period of 6 years], provided, however, that if during the Royalty Period the Buyer substantially discontinues the distribution of beer under the brand name "Ballantine" (except as the result of a restraining order in effect for 30 days issued by a court of competent jurisdiction at the request of a governmental authority), it will pay to the Seller a cash sum equal to the years and fraction thereof remaining in the Royalty Period times $1,100,000, payable in equal monthly installments on the first day of each month commencing with the first month following the month in which such discontinuation occurs. . . .

Bloor claimed that Falstaff had breached the best efforts clause, 8(a), and indeed that its default amounted to the substantial discontinuance that would trigger the liquidated damage clause, 2(a)(v). In an opinion that interestingly traces the history of beer back to Domesday Book and beyond, Judge Brieant upheld the first claim and awarded damages but dismissed the second. Falstaff appeals from the former ruling, Bloor from the latter. Both sides also dispute the court's measurement of damages for breach of the best efforts clause.

We shall assume familiarity with Judge Brieant's excellent opinion, 454 F.Supp. 258 (S.D.N.Y.1978), from which we have drawn heavily, and will state only the essentials. Ballantine had been a family owned business, producing low-priced beers primarily for the northeast market, particularly New York, New Jersey, Connecticut and Pennsylvania. Its sales began to decline in 1961, and it lost money from 1965 on. On June 1, 1969, Investors Funding Corporation (IFC), a real estate conglomerate with no experience in brewing, acquired substantially all the stock of Ballantine for $16,290,000. IFC increased advertising expenditures, levelling off in 1971 at $1 million a year. This and other promotional practices, some of dubious legality, led to steady growth in Ballantine's sales despite the increased activities in the northeast of the "nationals"[3] which have greatly augmented their market shares at the expense of smaller brewers. However, this was a profitless prosperity; there was no month in which Ballantine had earnings and the total loss was $15,500,000 for the 33 months of IFC ownership.

After its acquisition of Ballantine, Falstaff continued the $1 million a year advertising program, IFC's pricing policies, and also its policy of serving smaller accounts not solely through sales to independent distributors, the usual practice in the industry, but by use of its own warehouses and trucks— the only change being a shift of the retail distribution system from Newark to North Bergen, N.J., when brewing was concentrated at Falstaff's Rhode Island brewery. However, sales declined and Falstaff claims to have lost $22 million in its Ballantine brand operations from March 31, 1972 to June 1975. Its other activities were also performing indifferently, although with no such losses as were being incurred in the sale of Ballantine products, and it was facing inability to meet payrolls and other debts. In March and April 1975 control of Falstaff passed to Paul Kalmanovitz, a businessman with 40 years experience in the brewing industry. After having first advanced $3 million to enable Falstaff to meet its payrolls and other pressing debts, he later supplied an additional $10 million and made loan guarantees, in return for which he received convertible preferred shares in an amount that endowed him with 35% of the voting power and became the beneficiary of a voting trust that gave him control of the board of directors.

Mr. Kalmanovitz determined to concentrate on making beer and cutting sales costs. He decreased advertising, with the result that the Ballantine advertising budget shrank from $1 million to $115,000 a year. In late 1975 he closed four of Falstaff's six retail distribution centers, including the North Bergen, N.J. depot, which was ultimately replaced by two distributors servicing substantially fewer accounts. He also discontinued various illegal practices that had been used in selling Ballantine products. What happened in terms of sales volume is shown in plaintiff's exhibit 114 J, a chart which we reproduce in the margin. With 1974 as a base, Ballantine declined 29.72% in 1975 and 45.81% in 1976 as compared with a 1975 gain of 2.24% and a 1976 loss of 13.08% for all brewers excluding the top 15. Other comparisons are similarly devastating, at least for 1976. Despite the decline in the sale of its own labels as well as Ballantine's, Falstaff, however, made a substantial financial recovery. In 1976 it had net income of $8.7 million and its year-end working capital had increased from $8.6 million to $20.2 million and its cash and certificates of deposit from $2.2 million to $12.1 million.

---

3. Miller's, Schlitz, Anheuser–Busch, Coors and Pabst.

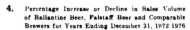

4. Percentage Increase or Decline in Sales Volume of Ballantine Beer, Falstaff Beer and Comparable Brewers for Years Ending December 31, 1972 1976

Seizing upon remarks made by the judge during the trial that Falstaff's financial standing in 1975 and thereafter "is probably not relevant" and a footnote in the opinion, 454 F.Supp. at 267 n. 7,[4] appellate counsel for Falstaff contend that the judge read the best efforts clause as requiring Falstaff to maintain Ballantine's volume by any sales methods having a good prospect of increasing or maintaining sales or, at least, to continue lawful methods in use at the time of purchase, no matter what losses they would cause. Starting from this premise, counsel reason that the judge's conclusion was at odds with New York law, stipulated by the contract to be controlling, as last expressed by the Court of Appeals in Feld v. Henry S. Levy & Sons, Inc., 37 N.Y.2d 466, 373 N.Y.S.2d 102, 335 N.E.2d 320 (1975).... [in which] the court said that, absent a cancellation on six months' notice for which the contract provided:

> defendant was expected to continue to perform in good faith and could cease production of the bread crumbs, a single facet of its operation, only in good faith. Obviously, a bankruptcy or genuine imperiling of the very existence of its entire business caused by the production of the crumbs would warrant cessation of production of that item; the yield of less profit from its sale than expected would not. Since bread crumbs were but a part of defendant's enterprise and since there was a contractual right of cancellation, good faith required continued production until cancellation, even if there be no profit. In circumstances such as these and without more, defendant would be justified, in good faith, in ceasing production of the single item prior to cancellation only if its losses from continuance would be more than trivial, which, overall, is a question of fact.

4. "Even if Falstaff's financial position had been worse in mid–1975 than it actually was, and even if Falstaff had continued in that state of impecuniosity during the term of the contract, performance of the contract is not excused where the difficulty of performance arises from financial difficulty or economic hardship. As the New York Court of Appeals stated in 407 E. 61st St. Garage, Inc. v. Savoy Corp., 23 N.Y.2d 275, 281, 296 N.Y.S.2d 338, 344, 244 N.E.2d 37, 41 (1968):

"'[W]here impossibility or difficulty of performance is occasioned only by financial difficulty or economic hardship, even to the extent of insolvency or bankruptcy, performance of a contract is not excused.' (Citations omitted.)"

37 N.Y.2d 471–72, 373 N.Y.S.2d 106, 335 N.E.2d 323.[5] Falstaff argues from this that it was not bound to do anything to market Ballantine products that would cause "more than trivial" losses.

We do not think the judge imposed on Falstaff a standard as demanding as its appellate counsel argues that he did. Despite his footnote 7, see note 6 supra, he did not in fact proceed on the basis that the best efforts clause required Falstaff to bankrupt itself in promoting Ballantine products or even to sell those products at a substantial loss. He relied rather on the fact that Falstaff's obligation to "use its best efforts to promote and maintain a high volume of sales" of Ballantine products was not fulfilled by a policy summarized by Mr. Kalmanovitz as being:

We sell beer and you pay for it. . . .

We sell beer, F.O.B. the brewery. You come and get it.

—however sensible such a policy may have been with respect to Falstaff's other products. Once the peril of insolvency had been averted, the drastic percentage reductions in Ballantine sales as related to any possible basis of comparison . . . required Falstaff at least to explore whether steps not involving substantial losses could have been taken to stop or at least lessen the rate of decline. The judge found that, instead of doing this, Falstaff had engaged in a number of misfeasances and nonfeasances which could have accounted in substantial measure for the catastrophic drop in Ballantine sales shown in the chart, see 454 F.Supp. at 267–72. These included the closing of the North Bergen depot which had serviced "Mom and Pop" stores and bars in the New York metropolitan area; Falstaff's choices of distributors for Ballantine products in the New Jersey and particularly the New York areas, where the chosen distributor was the owner of a competing brand; its failure to take advantage of a proffer from Guinness–Harp Corporation to distribute Ballantine products in New York City through its Metrobeer Division; Falstaff's incentive to put more effort into sales of its own brands which sold at higher prices despite identity of the ingredients and were free from the $.50 a barrel royalty burden; its failure to treat Ballantine products evenhandedly with Falstaff's; its discontinuing the practice of setting goals for salesmen; and the general Kalmanovitz policy of stressing profit at the expense of volume. In the court's judgment, these misfeasances and nonfeasances war-

5. The text of the *Feld* opinion did not refer to the case cited by Judge Brieant in the preceding footnote, 407 East 61st Garage, Inc. v. Savoy Fifth Avenue Corporation, 23 N.Y.2d 275, 296 N.Y.S.2d 338, 244 N.E.2d 37 (1968), which might suggest a more onerous obligation here. The Court of Appeals there reversed a summary judgment in favor of the defendant, which had discontinued operating the Savoy Hilton Hotel because of substantial financial losses, in alleged breach of a five-year contract with plaintiff wherein the defendant had agreed to use all reasonable efforts to provide the garage with exclusive opportunity for storage of the motor vehicles of hotel guests. Although the court did use the language quoted by Judge Brieant, the actual holding was simply that "an issue of fact is presented whether the agreement did import an implied promise by Savoy to fulfill its obligations for an entire five-year period." 23 N.Y.2d at 281, 296 N.Y.S.2d at 343, 244 N.E.2d at 41.

Other cases suggest that under New York law a "best efforts" clause imposes an obligation to act with good faith in light of one's own capabilities. In Van Valkenburgh v. Hayden Publishing Co., 30 N.Y.2d 34, 330 N.Y.S.2d 329, 281 N.E.2d 142 (1972), the court held a publisher liable to an author when, in clear bad faith after a contract dispute, he hired another to produce a book very similar to plaintiff's and then promoted it to those who had been buying the latter. On the other hand, a defendant having the exclusive right to sell the plaintiff's product may sell a similar product if necessary to meet outside competition, so long as he accounts for any resulting loses the plaintiff can show in the sales of the licensed product. Parev Products Co. v. I. Rokeach & Sons, 124 F.2d 147 (2 Cir.1941). . . .

ranted a conclusion that, even taking account of Falstaff's right to give reasonable consideration to its own interests, Falstaff had breached its duty to use best efforts as stated in the *Van Valkenburgh* decision, supra, 30 N.Y.2d at 46, 330 N.Y.S.2d at 334, 281 N.E.2d at 145.

Falstaff levels a barrage on these findings. The only attack which merits discussion is its criticism of the judge's conclusion that Falstaff did not treat its Ballantine brands evenhandedly with those under the Falstaff name. We agree that the subsidiary findings "that Falstaff but not Ballantine had been advertised extensively in Texas and Missouri" and that "[i]n these same areas Falstaff, although a 'premium' beer, was sold for extended periods below the price of Ballantine," while literally true, did not warrant the inference drawn from them. Texas was Falstaff territory and, with advertising on a cooperative basis, it was natural that advertising expenditures on Falstaff would exceed those on Ballantine. The lower price for Falstaff was a particular promotion of a bicentennial can in Texas, intended to meet a particular competitor.

However, we do not regard this error as undermining the judge's ultimate conclusion of breach of the best efforts clause. While that clause clearly required Falstaff to treat the Ballantine brands as well as its own, it does not follow that it required no more. With respect to its own brands, management was entirely free to exercise its business judgment as to how to maximize profit even if this meant serious loss in volume. Because of the obligation it had assumed under the sales contract, its situation with respect to the Ballantine brands was quite different. The royalty of $.50 a barrel on sales was an essential part of the purchase price. Even without the best efforts clause Falstaff would have been bound to make a good faith effort to see that substantial sales of Ballantine products were made, unless it discontinued under clause 2(a)(v) with consequent liability for liquidated damages. Cf. Wood v. Duff–Gordon, 222 N.Y. 88, 118 N.E. 214 (1917) (Cardozo, J.). Clause 8 imposed an added obligation to use "best efforts to promote and maintain a *high* volume of sales...." (emphasis supplied). Although we agree that even this did not require Falstaff to spend itself into bankruptcy to promote the sales of Ballantine products, it did prevent the application to them of Kalmanovitz' philosophy of emphasizing profit *über alles* without fair consideration of the effect on Ballantine volume. Plaintiff was not obliged to show just what steps Falstaff could reasonably have taken to maintain a high volume for Ballantine products. It was sufficient to show that Falstaff simply didn't care about Ballantine's volume and was content to allow this to plummet so long as that course was best for Falstaff's overall profit picture, an inference which the judge permissibly drew. The burden then shifted to Falstaff to prove there was nothing significant it could have done to promote Ballantine sales that would not have been financially disastrous.

Having correctly concluded that Falstaff had breached its best efforts covenant, the judge was faced with a difficult problem in computing what the royalties on the lost sales would have been. There is no need to rehearse the many decisions that, in a situation like this, certainty is not required; "[t]he plaintiff need only show a 'stable foundation for a reasonable estimate of royalties he would have earned had defendant not breached' ".... After carefully considering other possible bases, the court arrived at the seemingly sensible conclusion that the most nearly accurate comparison was with the combined sales of Rheingold and Schaefer beers, both, like Ballantine, being "price" beers sold primarily in the northeast, and computed what Ballantine sales would have been if its brands had suffered only the same decline as a composite of Rheingold and Schaefer. . . .

. . . It is true . . . that the award may overcompensate the plaintiff since Falstaff was not necessarily required to do whatever Rheingold and Shaefer did. But that is the kind of uncertainty which is permissible in favor of a plaintiff who has established liability in a case like this. . . .

We can dispose quite briefly of the portion of the plaintiff's cross-appeal which claims error in the rejection of his contention that Falstaff's actions triggered the liquidated damage clause. One branch of this puts heavy weight on the word "distribution"; the claim is that the closing of the North Bergen center and Mr. Kalmanovitz' general come-and-get-it philosophy was, without more, a substantial discontinuance of "distribution". On this basis plaintiff would be entitled to invoke the liquidated damage clause even if Falstaff's new methods had succeeded in checking the decline in Ballantine sales. Another fallacy is that, countrywide, Falstaff substantially increased the number of distributors carrying Ballantine labels. Moreover the term "distribution", as used in the brewing industry, does not require distribution by the brewer's own trucks and employees. The norm rather is distribution through independent wholesalers. Falstaff's default under the best efforts clause was not in returning to that method *simpliciter* but in its failure to see to it that wholesale distribution approached in effectiveness what retail distribution had done.

Plaintiff contends more generally that permitting a decline of 63.12% in Ballantine sales from 1974 to 1977 was the equivalent of quitting the game. However, as Judge Brieant correctly pointed out, a large part of this drop was attributable "to the general decline of the market share of the smaller brewers" as against the "nationals", 454 F.Supp. at 266, and even the 518,899 barrels sold in 1977 were not a negligible amount of beer.

The judgment is affirmed. Plaintiff may recover two-thirds of his costs.

WOOD v. LUCY, LADY DUFF–GORDON

[Chapter 2, supra]

UCC § 2–306

[See Selected Source Materials Supplement]

MARKET STREET ASSOCIATES v. FREY

United States Court of Appeals, Seventh Circuit, 1991.
941 F.2d 588.

POSNER, Circuit Judge.

Market Street Associates Limited Partnership and its general partner appeal from a judgment for the defendants, General Electric Pension Trust and its trustees, entered upon cross-motions for summary judgment in a diversity suit that pivots on the doctrine of "good faith" performance of a contract. Cf. Robert Summers, " 'Good Faith' in General Contract Law and the Sales Provisions of the Uniform Commercial Code," 54 Va.L.Rev. 195, 232–43 (1968). Wisconsin law applies—common law rather than Uniform Commercial Code, because the contract is for land rather than for goods, UCC § 2–102; Wis.Stat. § 402.102, and because it is a lease rather than a sale and Wisconsin has not adopted UCC art. 2A, which governs leases. . . .

. . . In 1968, J.C. Penney Company, the retail chain, entered into a sale and leaseback arrangement with General Electric Pension Trust in order to finance Penney's growth. Under the arrangement Penney sold properties to the pension trust which the trust then leased back to Penney for a term of 25 years. Paragraph 34 of the lease entitles the lessee to "request Lessor [the pension trust] to finance the costs and expenses of construction of additional Improvements upon the Premises," provided the amount of the costs and expenses is at least $250,000. Upon receiving the request, the pension trust "agrees to give reasonable consideration to providing the financing of such additional Improvements and Lessor and Lessee shall negotiate in good faith concerning the construction of such Improvements and the financing by Lessor of such costs and expenses." Paragraph 34 goes on to provide that, should the negotiations fail, the lessee shall be entitled to repurchase the property at a price roughly equal to the price at which Penney sold it to the pension trust in the first place, plus 6 percent a year for each year since the original purchase. So if the average annual appreciation in the property exceeded 6 percent, a breakdown in negotiations over the financing of improvements would entitle Penney to buy back the property for less than its market value (assuming it had sold the property to the pension trust in the first place at its then market value).

One of these leases was for a shopping center in Milwaukee. In 1987 Penney assigned this lease to Market Street Associates, which the following year received an inquiry from a drugstore chain that wanted to open a store in the shopping center, provided (as is customary) that Market Street Associates built the store for it. Whether Market Street Associates was pessimistic about obtaining financing from the pension trust, still the lessor of the shopping center, or for other reasons, it initially sought financing for the project from other sources. But they were unwilling to lend the necessary funds without a mortgage on the shopping center, which Market Street Associates could not give because it was not the owner but only the lessee. It decided therefore to try to buy the property back from the pension trust. Market Street Associates' general partner, Orenstein, tried to call David Erb of the pension trust, who was responsible for the property in question. Erb did not return his calls, so Orenstein wrote him, expressing an interest in buying the property and asking him to "review your file on this matter and call me so that we can discuss it further." At first, Erb did not reply. Eventually Orenstein did reach Erb, who promised to review the file and get back to him. A few days later an associate of Erb called Orenstein and indicated an interest in selling the property for $3 million, which Orenstein considered much too high.

That was in June of 1988. On July 28, Market Street Associates wrote a letter to the pension trust formally requesting funding for $2 million in improvements to the shopping center. The letter made no reference to paragraph 34 of the lease; indeed, it did not mention the lease. The letter asked Erb to call Orenstein to discuss the matter. Erb, in what was becoming a habit of unresponsiveness, did not call. On August 16, Orenstein sent a second letter—certified mail, return receipt requested—again requesting financing and this time referring to the lease, though not expressly to paragraph 34.

The heart of the letter is the following two sentences: "The purpose of this letter is to ask again that you advise us immediately if you are willing to provide the financing pursuant to the lease. If you are willing, we propose to enter into negotiation to amend the ground lease appropriately." The very next day, Market Street Associates received from Erb a letter, dated August 10, turning down the original request for financing on the ground that it did not "meet our current investment criteria": the pension trust was not interested in making loans for less than $7 million. On August 22, Orenstein replied to Erb by letter, noting that his letter of August 10 and Erb's letter of August 16 had evidently crossed in the mails, expressing disappointment at the turn-down, and stating that Market Street Associates would seek financing elsewhere. That was the last contact between the parties until September 27, when Orenstein sent Erb a letter stating that Market Street Associates was exercising the option granted it by paragraph 34 to purchase the property upon the terms specified in that paragraph in the event that negotiations over financing broke down.

The pension trust refused to sell, and this suit to compel specific performance followed. Apparently the price computed by the formula in paragraph 34 is only $1 million. The market value must be higher, or Market Street Associates wouldn't be trying to coerce conveyance at the paragraph 34 price; whether it is as high as $3 million, however, the record does not reveal.

The district judge granted summary judgment for the pension trust on two grounds that he believed to be separate although closely related. The first was that, by failing in its correspondence with the pension trust to mention paragraph 34 of the lease, Market Street Associates had prevented the negotiations over financing that are a condition precedent to the lessee's exercise of the purchase option from taking place. Second, this same failure violated the duty of good faith, which the common law of Wisconsin, as of other states, reads into every contract. In re Estate of Chayka, 47 Wis.2d 102, 107, 176 N.W.2d 561, 564 (1970); Super Valu Stores, Inc. v. D–Mart Food Stores, Inc., 146 Wis.2d 568, 577, 431 N.W.2d 721, 726 (App.1988); Ford Motor Co. v. Lyons, 137 Wis.2d 397, 442, 405 N.W.2d 354, 372 (App.1987); Sunds Defibrator AB v. Beloit Corp., 930 F.2d 564, 566 (7th Cir.1991); Restatement (Second) of Contracts § 205 (1981); 2 E. Allan Farnsworth, Farnsworth on Contracts § 7.17a (1990). In support of both grounds the judge emphasized a statement by Orenstein in his deposition that it had occurred to him that Erb mightn't know about paragraph 34, though this was unlikely (Orenstein testified) because Erb or someone else at the pension trust would probably check the file and discover the paragraph and realize that if the trust refused to negotiate over the request for financing, Market Street Associates, as Penney's assignee, would be entitled to walk off with the property for (perhaps) a song. The judge inferred that Market Street Associates didn't want financing from the pension trust—that it just wanted an opportunity to buy the property at a bargain price and hoped that the pension trust wouldn't realize the implications of turning down the request for financing. Market

Street Associates should, the judge opined, have advised the pension trust that it was requesting financing pursuant to paragraph 34, so that the trust would understand the penalty for refusing to negotiate.

We begin our analysis by setting to one side two extreme contentions by the parties. The pension trust argues that the option to purchase created by paragraph 34 cannot be exercised until negotiations over financing break down; there were no negotiations; therefore they did not break down; therefore Market Street Associates had no right to exercise the option. This argument misreads the contract. Although the option to purchase is indeed contingent, paragraph 34 requires the pension trust, upon demand by the lessee for the financing of improvements worth at least $250,000, "to give reasonable consideration to providing the financing." The lessor who fails to give reasonable consideration and thereby prevents the negotiations from taking place is breaking the contract; and a contracting party cannot be allowed to use his own breach to gain an advantage by impairing the rights that the contract confers on the other party. Variance, Inc. v. Losinske, 71 Wis.2d 31, 40, 237 N.W.2d 22, 26 (1976); Ethyl Corp. v. United Steelworkers of America, 768 F.2d 180, 185 (7th Cir.1985); Spanos v. Skouras Theatres Corp., 364 F.2d 161, 169 (2d Cir.1966) (en banc) (Friendly, J.); 3A Corbin on Contracts § 767, at p. 540 (1960). Often, it is true, if one party breaks the contract, the other can walk away from it without liability, can in other words exercise self-help. First National Bank v. Continental Illinois National Bank, 933 F.2d 466, 469 (7th Cir.1991). But he is not required to follow that course. He can stand on his contract rights.

But what exactly are those rights in this case? The contract entitles the lessee to reasonable consideration of its request for financing, and only if negotiations over the request fail is the lessee entitled to purchase the property at the price computed in accordance with paragraph 34. It might seem therefore that the proper legal remedy for a lessor's breach that consists of failure to give the lessee's request for financing reasonable consideration would not be an order that the lessor sell the property to the lessee at the paragraph 34 price, but an order that the lessor bargain with the lessee in good faith. But we do not understand the pension trust to be arguing that Market Street Associates is seeking the wrong remedy. We understand it to be arguing that Market Street Associates has no possible remedy. That is an untenable position.

Market Street Associates argues, with equal unreason as it seems to us, that it could not have broken the contract because paragraph 34 contains no express requirement that in requesting financing the lessee mention the lease or paragraph 34 or otherwise alert the lessor to the consequences of his failing to give reasonable consideration to granting the request. There is indeed no such requirement (all that the contract requires is a demand). But no one says there is. The pension trust's argument, which the district judge bought, is that either as a matter of simple contract interpretation or under the compulsion of the doctrine of good faith, a provision requiring Market Street Associates to remind the pension trust of paragraph 34 should be read into the lease.

It seems to us that these are one ground rather than two. A court has to have a reason to interpolate a clause into a contract. The only reason that has been suggested here is that it is necessary to prevent Market Street Associates from reaping a reward for what the pension trust believes to have been Market Street's bad faith. So we must consider the meaning of the contract duty of "good faith." The Wisconsin cases are cryptic as to its meaning though emphatic about its existence, so we must cast our net wider. We do so mindful of Learned Hand's warning, that "such words as 'fraud,' 'good faith,' 'whim,' 'caprice,' 'arbitrary action,' and 'legal fraud' ... obscure the issue." Thompson–Starrett Co. v. La Belle Iron Works, 17 F.2d 536, 541 (2d Cir. 1927). Indeed they do. Summers, supra, at 207–20; 2 Farnsworth on Contracts, supra, § 7.17a, at pp. 328–32. The particular confusion to which the vaguely moralistic overtones of "good faith" give rise is the belief that every contract establishes a fiduciary relationship. A fiduciary is required to treat his principal as if the principal were he, and therefore he may not take advantage of the principal's incapacity, ignorance, inexperience, or even naivete. Olympia Hotels Corp. v. Johnson Wax Development Corp., 908 F.2d 1363, 1373–74 (7th Cir.1990); United States v. Dial, 757 F.2d 163, 168 (7th Cir.1985); Faultersack v. Clintonville Sales Corp., 253 Wis. 432, 435–37, 34 N.W.2d 682, 683–84 (1948); Schweiger v. Loewi & Co., 65 Wis.2d 56, 64–65, 221 N.W.2d 882, 888 (1974); Meinhard v. Salmon, 249 N.Y. 458, 463–64, 164 N.E. 545, 546 (1928) (Cardozo, C.J.). If Market Street Associates were the fiduciary of General Electric Pension Trust, then (we may assume) it could not take advantage of Mr. Erb's apparent ignorance of paragraph 34, however exasperating Erb's failure to return Orenstein's phone calls was and however negligent Erb or his associates were in failing to read the lease before turning down Orenstein's request for financing.

But it is unlikely that Wisconsin wishes, in the name of good faith, to make every contract signatory his brother's keeper, especially when the brother is the immense and sophisticated General Electric Pension Trust, whose lofty indifference to small (= < $7 million) transactions is the signifier of its grandeur. In fact the law contemplates that people frequently will take advantage of the ignorance of those with whom they contract, without thereby incurring liability. Restatement, supra, § 161, comment d. The duty of honesty, of good faith even expansively conceived, is not a duty of candor. You can make a binding contract to purchase something you know your seller undervalues. Laidlaw v. Organ, 15 U.S. (2 Wheat.) 178, 181 n. 2, 4 L.Ed. 214 (1817); Teamsters Local 282 Pension Trust Fund v. Angelos, 762 F.2d 522, 528 (7th Cir.1985); United States v. Dial, supra, 757 F.2d at 168; 1 Farnsworth on Contracts, supra, § 4.11, at pp. 406–10; Anthony T. Kronman, "Mistake, Disclosure, Information, and the Law of Contracts," 7 J. Legal Stud. 1 (1978).

That of course is a question about formation, not performance, and the particular duty of good faith under examination here relates to the latter rather than to the former. But even after you have signed a contract, you are not obliged to become an altruist toward the other party and relax the terms if he gets into trouble in performing his side of the bargain. Kham & Nate's Shoes No. 2, Inc. v. First Bank, 908 F.2d 1351, 1357 (7th Cir.1990). Otherwise mere difficulty of performance would excuse a contracting party—which it does not. Northern Indiana Public Service Co. v. Carbon County Coal Co., 799 F.2d 265, 276–78 (7th Cir.1986); Jennie–O Foods, Inc. v. United States, 217 Ct.Cl. 314, 580 F.2d 400, 409 (1978) (per curiam); 2 Farnsworth on Contracts, supra, § 7.17a, at p. 330.

But it is one thing to say that you can exploit your superior knowledge of the market—for if you cannot, you will not be able to recoup the investment you made in obtaining that knowledge—or that you are not required to spend money bailing out a contract partner who has gotten into trouble. It is another thing to say that you can take deliberate advantage of an oversight by your contract partner concerning his rights under the contract. Such taking advantage is not the exploitation of superior knowledge or the avoidance of unbargained-for expense; it is sharp dealing. Like theft, it has no social product, and also like theft it induces costly defensive expenditures, in the form of overelaborate disclaimers or investigations into the trustworthiness of a prospective contract partner, just as the prospect of theft induces expenditures on locks. See generally Steven J. Burton, "Breach of Contract and the Common Law Duty to Perform in Good Faith," 94 Harv.L.Rev. 369, 393 (1980).

The form of sharp dealing that we are discussing might or might not be actionable as fraud or deceit. That is a question of tort law and there the rule is that if the information is readily available to both parties the failure of one to disclose it to the other, even if done in the knowledge that the other party is acting on mistaken premises, is not actionable. Kamuchey v. Trzesniewski, 8 Wis.2d 94, 98 N.W.2d 403 (1959); Southard v. Occidental Life Ins. Co., 36 Wis.2d 708, 154 N.W.2d 326 (1967); Lenzi v. Morkin, 103 Ill.2d 290, 82 Ill.Dec. 644, 469 N.E.2d 178 (1984); Guyer v. Cities Service Oil Co., 440 F.Supp. 630 (E.D.Wis.1977); W. Page Keeton et al., Prosser and Keeton on the Law of Torts § 106, at p. 737 (5th ed. 1984). All of these cases, however, with the debatable exception of *Guyer*, involve failure to disclose something in the negotiations leading up to the signing of the contract, rather than failure to disclose after the contract has been signed. (*Guyer* involved failure to disclose during the negotiations leading up to a renewal of the contract). The distinction is important, as we explained in Maksym v. Loesch, 937 F.2d 1237, 1242 (7th Cir.1991). Before the contract is signed, the parties confront each other with a natural wariness. Neither expects the other to be particularly forthcoming, and therefore there is no deception when one is not. Afterwards the situation is different. The parties are now in a cooperative relationship the costs of which will be considerably reduced by a measure of trust. So each lowers his guard a bit, and now silence is more apt to be deceptive. Cf. AMPAT/Midwest, Inc. v. Illinois Tool Works Inc., 896 F.2d 1035, 1040–41 (7th Cir.1990).

Moreover, this is a contract case rather than a tort case, and conduct that might not rise to the level of fraud may nonetheless violate the duty of good faith in dealing with one's contractual partners and thereby give rise to a remedy under contract law. Burton, supra, at 372 n. 17. This duty is, as it were, halfway between a fiduciary duty (the duty of *utmost* good faith) and the duty merely to refrain from active fraud. Despite its moralistic overtones it is no more the injection of moral principles into contract law than the fiduciary concept itself is. Tymshare, Inc. v. Covell, 727 F.2d 1145, 1152 (D.C.Cir.1984); Summers, supra, at 204–07, 265–66. It would be quixotic as well as presumptuous for judges to undertake through contract law to raise the ethical standards of the nation's business people. The concept of the duty of good faith like the concept of fiduciary duty is a stab at approximating the terms the parties would have negotiated had they foreseen the circumstances that have given rise to their dispute. The parties want to minimize the costs of performance. To the extent that a doctrine of good faith designed to do this by reducing defensive expenditures is a reasonable measure to this end, interpolating it into the contract advances the parties' joint goal.

It is true that an essential function of contracts is to allocate risk, and would be defeated if courts treated the materializing of a bargained-over, allocated risk as a misfortune the burden of which is required to be shared between the parties (as it might be within a family, for example) rather than borne entirely by the party to whom the risk had been allocated by mutual agreement. But contracts do not just allocate risk. They also (or some of them) set in motion a cooperative enterprise, which may to some extent place one party at the other's mercy. "The parties to a contract are embarked on a cooperative venture, and a minimum of cooperativeness in the event unforeseen problems arise at the performance stage is required even if not an explicit duty of the contract." AMPAT/Midwest, Inc. v. Illinois Tool Works, Inc., supra, 896 F.2d at 1041. The office of the doctrine of good faith is to forbid the kinds of opportunistic behavior that a mutually dependent, cooperative relationship might enable in the absence of rule. " 'Good faith' is a compact reference to an implied undertaking not to take opportunistic advantage in a way that could not have been contemplated at the time of drafting, and which therefore was not resolved explicitly by the parties." Kham & Nate's Shoes No. 2, Inc. v. First Bank, supra, 908 F.2d at 1357. The contractual duty of good faith is thus not some newfangled bit of welfare-state paternalism or (pace Duncan Kennedy, "Form and Substance in Private Law Adjudication," 89 Harv.L.Rev. 1685, 1721 (1976)) the sediment of an altruistic strain in contract law, and we are therefore not surprised to find the essentials of the modern doctrine well established in nineteenth-century cases, a few examples being Bush v. Marshall, 47 U.S. (6 How.) 284, 291, 12 L.Ed. 440 (1848); Chicago, Rock Island & Pac. R.R. v. Howard, 74 U.S. (7 Wall.) 392, 413, 19 L.Ed. 117 (1868); Marsh v. Masterson, 101 N.Y. 401, 410–11, 5 N.E. 59, 63 (1886), and Uhrig v. Williamsburg City Fire Ins. Co., 101 N.Y. 362, 4 N.E. 745 (1886).

The emphasis we are placing on postcontractual versus precontractual conduct helps explain the pattern that is observed when the duty of contractual good faith is considered in all its variety, encompassing not only good faith in the *performance* of a contract but also good faith in its *formation*, Summers, supra, at 220–32, and in its enforcement. Harbor Ins. Co. v. Continental Bank Corp., 922 F.2d 357, 363 (7th Cir.1990). The formation or negotiation stage is precontractual, and here the duty is minimized. It is greater not only at the performance but also at the enforcement stage, which is also postcontractual. "A party who hokes up a phony defense to the performance of his contractual duties and then when that defense fails (at some expense to the other party) tries on another defense for size can properly be said to be acting in bad faith." Id.; see also Larson v. Johnson, 1 Ill.App.2d 36, 46, 116 N.E.2d 187, 191–92 (1953). At the formation of the contract the parties are dealing in present realities; performance still lies in the future. As performance unfolds, circumstances change, often unforeseeably; the explicit terms of the contract become progressively less apt to the governance of the parties' relationship; and the role of implied conditions—and with it the scope and bite of the good-faith doctrine—grows.

We could of course do without the term "good faith," and maybe even without the doctrine. We could, as just suggested, speak instead of implied conditions necessitated by the unpredictability of the future at the time the contract was made. Farnsworth, "Good Faith Performance and Commercial Reasonableness under the Uniform Commercial Code," 30 U.Chi.L.Rev. 666, 670 (1963). Suppose a party has promised work to the promisee's "satisfaction." As Learned Hand explained, "he may refuse to look at the work, or to exercise any real judgment on it, in which case he has prevented performance and excused the condition." Thompson–Starrett Co. v. La Belle Iron Works, supra, 17 F.2d at 541. See also Morin Building Products Co. v. Baystone Construction, Inc., 717 F.2d 413, 415 (7th Cir.1983). That is, it was an implicit condition that the promisee examine the work to the extent necessary to determine whether it was satisfactory; otherwise the performing party would have been placing himself at the complete mercy of the promisee. The parties didn't write this condition into the contract either because they thought such behavior unlikely or failed to foresee it altogether. In just the same way—to switch to another familiar example of the operation of the duty of good faith—parties to a requirements contract surely do not intend that if the price of the product covered by the contract rises, the buyer shall be free to increase his "requirements" so that he can take advantage of the rise in the market price over the contract price to resell the product on the open market at a guaranteed profit. Empire Gas Corp. v. American Bakeries Co., 840 F.2d 1333 (7th Cir.1988). If they fail to insert an express condition to this effect, the court will read it in, confident that the parties would have inserted the condition if they had known what the future held. Of similar character is the implied condition that an exclusive dealer will use his best efforts to promote the supplier's goods, since otherwise the exclusive feature of the dealership contract would place the supplier at the dealer's mercy. Wood v. Duff–Gordon, 222 N.Y. 88, 118 N.E. 214 (1917) (Cardozo, J.).

But whether we say that a contract shall be deemed to contain such implied conditions as are necessary to make sense of the contract, or that a contract obligates the parties to cooperate in its performance in "good faith" to the extent necessary to carry out the purposes of the contract, comes to much the same thing. They are different ways of formulating the overriding purpose of contract law, which is to give the parties what they would have stipulated for expressly if at the time of making the contract they had had complete knowledge of the future and the costs of negotiating and adding provisions to the contract had been zero.

The two formulations would have different meanings only if "good faith" were thought limited to "honesty in fact," an interpretation perhaps permitted but certainly not compelled by the Uniform Commercial Code, see Summers, supra, at 207–20—and anyway this is not a case governed by the UCC. We need not pursue this issue. The dispositive question in the present case is simply whether Market Street Associates tried to trick the pension trust and succeeded in doing so. If it did, this would be the type of opportunistic behavior in an ongoing contractual relationship that would violate the duty of good faith performance however the duty is formulated. There is much common sense in Judge Reynolds' conclusion that Market Street Associates did just that. The situation as he saw it was as follows. Market Street Associates didn't want financing from the pension trust (initially it had looked elsewhere, remember), and when it learned it couldn't get the financing without owning the property, it decided to try to buy the property. But the pension trust set a stiff price, so Orenstein decided to trick the pension trust into selling at the bargain price fixed in paragraph 34 by requesting financing and hoping that the pension trust would turn the request down without noticing the paragraph. His preliminary dealings with the pension trust made this hope a realistic one by revealing a sluggish and hidebound bureaucracy unlikely to have retained in its brontosaurus's memory, or to be able at short notice to retrieve, the details of a small lease made twenty years earlier. So by requesting financing without mentioning the lease Market Street Associates might well precipitate a refusal before the pension trust woke up to paragraph 34. It is true that Orenstein's second letter requested financing "pursuant to the lease." But when the next day he received a reply to his first letter indicating that the pension trust was indeed oblivious to paragraph 34, his response was to send a lulling letter designed to convince the pension trust that the matter was closed and could be forgotten. The stage was set for his thunderbolt: the notification the next month that Market Street Associates was taking up the option in paragraph 34. Only then did the pension trust look up the lease and discover that it had been had.

The only problem with this recital is that it construes the facts as favorably to the pension trust as the record will permit, and that of course is not the right standard for summary judgment. The facts must be construed as favorably to the nonmoving party, to Market Street Associates, as the record permits (that Market Street Associates filed its own motion for summary judgment is irrelevant, as we have seen). When that is done, a different picture emerges. On Market Street Associates' construal of the record, $3 million was a grossly excessive price for the property, and while $1 million might be a bargain it would not confer so great a windfall as to warrant an inference that if the pension trust had known about paragraph 34 it never would have turned down Market Street Associates' request for financing cold. And in fact the pension trust may have known about paragraph 34, and either it didn't care or it believed that unless the request mentioned that paragraph the pension trust would incur no liability by turning it down. Market Street Associates may have assumed and have been entitled to assume that in reviewing a request for financing from one of its lessees the pension trust would take the time to read the lease to see whether it bore on the request. Market Street Associates did not desire financing from the pension trust initially—that is undeniable—yet when it discovered that it could not get financing elsewhere unless it had the title to the property it may have realized that it would have to negotiate with the pension trust over financing before it could hope to buy the property at the price specified in the lease.

On this interpretation of the facts there was no bad faith on the part of Market Street Associates. It acted honestly, reasonably, without ulterior motive, in the face of circumstances as they actually and reasonably appeared to it. The fault was the pension trust's incredible inattention, which misled Market Street Associates into believing that the pension trust had no interest in financing the improvements regardless of the purchase option. We do not usually excuse contracting parties from failing to read and understand the contents of their contract; and in the end what this case comes down to—or so at least it can be strongly argued—is that an immensely sophisticated enterprise simply failed to read the contract. On the other hand, such enterprises make mistakes just like the rest of us, and deliberately to take advantage of your contracting partner's mistake during the performance stage (for we are not talking about taking advantage of superior knowledge at the formation stage) is a breach of good faith. To be able to correct your contract partner's mistake at zero cost to yourself, and decide not to do so, is a species of opportunistic behavior that the parties would have expressly forbidden in the contract had they foreseen it. The immensely long term of the lease amplified the possibility of errors but did not license either party to take advantage of them.

The district judge jumped the gun in choosing between these alternative characterizations. The essential issue bearing on Market Street Associates' good faith was Orenstein's state of mind, a type of inquiry that ordinarily cannot be concluded on summary judgment, and could not be here. If Orenstein believed that Erb knew or would surely find out about paragraph 34, it was not dishonest or opportunistic to fail to flag that paragraph, or even to fail to mention the lease, in his correspondence and (rare) conversations with Erb, especially given the uninterest in dealing with Market Street Associates that Erb fairly radiated. To decide what Orenstein believed, a trial is necessary. As for the pension trust's intimation that a bench trial (for remember that this is an equity case, since the only relief sought by the plaintiff is specific performance) will add no illumination beyond what the summary judgment proceeding has done, this overlooks the fact that at trial the judge will for the first time have a chance to see the witnesses whose depositions he has read, to hear their testimony elaborated, and to assess their believability.

The judgment is reversed and the case is remanded for further proceedings consistent with this opinion.

REVERSED AND REMANDED.

———

WAGENSELLER v. SCOTTSDALE MEMORIAL HOSPITAL

[Chapter 13, supra]

———

Chapter 23

THE DOCTRINE OF SUBSTANTIAL PERFORMANCE

This Chapter concerns the following question: Suppose A and B have entered into a contract under which A is to render some designated performance and B is to pay a designated amount for the performance. A renders performance, but the performance is not perfect; that is, there is some difference between the performance that A promised and the performance that she rendered. Under what circumstances, if any, can A sue B on the contract for expectation damages (with an offset for the defects in A's performance), rather than being limited to suing B in restitution for the value of the benefit that A conferred on B?

It turns out that the answer to this question depends to at least some extent on the subject-matter of the contract. The general principle, considered in Section 1, is that A can sue B on the contract if she has rendered "substantial performance." However, special rules, considered in Section 2, are applicable to contracts for the sale of goods.

SECTION 1. THE GENERAL PRINCIPLE

JACOB & YOUNGS v. KENT

Court of Appeals of New York, 1921.
230 N.Y. 239, 129 N.E. 889, 23 A.L.R. 1429.

CARDOZO, J. The plaintiff built a country residence for the defendant at a cost of upwards of $77,000, and now sues to recover a balance of $3,483.46, remaining unpaid. The work of construction ceased in June, 1914, and the defendant then began to occupy the dwelling. There was no complaint of defective performance until March, 1915. One of the specifications for the plumbing work provides that "all wrought-iron pipe must be well galvanized, lap welded pipe of the grade known as 'standard pipe' of Reading manufacture."

The defendant learned in March, 1915, that some of the pipe, instead of being made in Reading, was the product of other factories. The plaintiff was accordingly directed by the architect to do the work anew. The plumbing was then encased within the walls except in a few places where it had to be exposed. Obedience to the order meant more than the substitution of other pipe. It meant the demolition at great expense of substantial parts of the completed structure. The plaintiff left the work untouched, and asked for a certificate that the final payment was due. Refusal of the certificate was followed by this suit.

The evidence sustains a finding that the omission of the prescribed brand of pipe was neither fraudulent nor wilful. It was the result of the oversight and inattention of the plaintiff's subcontractor. Reading pipe is distinguished from Cohoes pipe and other brands only by the name of the manufacturer stamped upon it at intervals of between six and seven feet. Even the defendant's architect, though he inspected the pipe upon arrival, failed to notice the discrepancy. The plaintiff tried to show that the brands installed, though made by other manufacturers, were the same in quality, in appearance, in market value, and in cost as the brand stated in the contract—that they were indeed, the same thing, though manufactured in another place. The evidence was excluded, and a verdict directed for the defendant. The Appellate Division reversed, and granted a new trial.

We think the evidence, if admitted would have supplied some basis for the inference that the defect was insignificant in its relation to the project. The courts never say that one who makes a contract fills the measure of his duty by less than full performance. They do say, however, that an omission, both trivial and innocent, will sometimes be atoned for by allowance of the resulting damage, and will not always be the breach of a condition to be followed by a forfeiture.... The distinction is akin to that between dependent and independent promises, or between promises and conditions. Anson on Contracts (Corbin's Ed.) § 367; 2 Williston on Contracts, § 842. Some promises are so plainly independent that they can never by fair construction be conditions of one another. Rosenthal Paper Co. v. Nat. Folding Box & Paper Co., 226 N.Y. 313, 123 N.E. 766; Bogardus v. N.Y. Life Ins. Co., 101 N.Y. 328, 4 N.E. 522. Others are so plainly dependent that they must always be conditions. Others, though dependent and thus conditions when there is departure in point of substance, will be viewed as independent and collateral when the departure is insignificant. 2 Williston on Contracts, §§ 841, 842; Eastern Forge Co. v. Corbin, 182 Mass. 590, 592, 66 N.E. 419; Robinson v. Mollett, L.R., 7 Eng. & Ir.App. 802, 814; Miller v. Benjamin, 142 N.Y. 613, 37 N.E. 631. Considerations partly of justice and partly of presumable intention are to tell us whether this or that promise shall be placed in one class or in another. The simple and the uniform will call for different remedies from the multifarious and the intricate. The margin of departure within the range of normal expectation upon a sale of common chattels will vary from the margin to be expected upon a contract for the construction of a mansion or a "skyscraper." There will be harshness sometimes and oppression in the implication of a condition when the thing upon which labor has been expended is incapable of surrender because united to the land, and equity and reason in the implication of a like condition when the subject-matter, if defective, is in shape to be returned. From the conclusion that promises may not be treated as dependent to the extent of their uttermost minutiae without sacrifice of justice, the progress is a short one to the conclusion that they may not be so treated without a perversion of intention. Intention not otherwise revealed may be presumed to hold in contemplation the reasonable and probable. If something else is in view, it must not be left to implication. There will be no assumption of a purpose to visit venial faults with oppressive retribution.

Those who think more of symmetry and logic in the development of legal rules than of practical adaptation to the attainment of a just result will be troubled by a classification where the lines of division are so wavering and blurred. Something doubtless, may be said on the score of consistency and certainty in favor of a stricter standard. The courts have balanced such considerations against those of equity and fairness, and found the latter to be the weightier. The decisions in this state commit us to the liberal view, which is making its way, nowadays, in jurisdictions slow to welcome it. Dakin & Co. v. Lee, 1916, 1 K.B. 566, 579. Where the line is to be drawn between the important and the trivial cannot be settled by a formula. "In the nature of the case precise boundaries are impossible." 2 Williston on Contracts, § 841. The same omission may take on one aspect or another according to its setting. Substitution of equivalents may not have the same significance in fields of art on the one side and in those of mere utility on the other. Nowhere will change be tolerated, however, if it is so dominant or pervasive as in any real or substantial measure to frustrate the purpose of the contract. Crouch v. Gutmann, 134 N.Y. 45, 51, 31 N.E. 271, 30 Am.St.Rep. 608. There is no general license to install whatever, in the builder's judgment, may be regarded as "just as good." Easthampton L. & C. Co., Ltd. v. Worthington, 186 N.Y. 407, 412, 79 N.E. 323. The question is one of degree, to be answered, if there is doubt, by the triers of the facts (Crouch v. Gutmann; Woodward v. Fuller, supra), and, if the inferences are certain, by the judges of the law (Easthampton L. & C. Co., Ltd. v. Worthington, supra). We must weigh the purpose to be served, the desire to be gratified, the excuse for deviation from the letter, the cruelty of enforced adherence. Then only can we tell whether literal fulfillment is to be implied by law as a condition. This is not to say that the parties are not free by apt and certain words to effectuate a purpose that performance of every term shall be a condition of recovery. That question is not here. This is merely to say that the law will be slow to impute the purpose, in the silence of the parties, where the significance of the default is grievously out of proportion to the oppression of the forfeiture. The wilful transgressor must accept the penalty of his transgression. Schultze v. Goodstein, 180 N.Y. 248, 251, 73 N.E. 21; Desmond–Dunne Co. v. Friedman–Doscher Co., 162 N.Y. 486, 490, 56 N.E. 995. For him there is no occasion to mitigate the rigor of implied conditions. The transgressor whose default is unintentional and trivial may hope for mercy if he will offer atonement for his wrong. Spence v. Ham [163 N.Y. 220, 57 N.E. 412].

In the circumstances of this case, we think the measure of the allowance is not the cost of replacement, which would be great, but the difference in value, which would be either nominal or nothing. . . . It is true that in most cases the cost of replacement is the measure. Spence v. Ham, supra. The owner is entitled to the money which will permit him to complete, unless the cost of completion is grossly and unfairly out of proportion to the good to be attained. When that is true, the measure is the difference in value. . . .

The order should be affirmed, and judgment absolute directed in favor of the plaintiff upon the stipulation, with costs in all courts....

[The dissenting opinion of McLaughlin, J. is omitted.]

R. DANZIG, THE CAPABILITY PROBLEM IN CONTRACT LAW 120–23 (1978). "The contract [in Jacob & Youngs v. Kent] specified a standard of pipe [wrought iron] which cost 30% more than steel pipe—then the most widely used (and now the almost universally used) pipe. The makers of wrought iron pipe, however, claimed that the savings due to durability and low maintenance more than made up for the added expense....

"The Reading Company was by its account the largest manufacturer of wrought iron pipe in the country....

"... According to a pipe wholesaler interviewed in New York City in 1975, genuine wrought iron pipe was manufactured in the pre-war period by four largely noncompeting companies: Reading, Cohoes, Byers and Southchester. According to this informant, all of these brands 'were of the same quality and price. The manufacturer's name would make absolutely no difference in pipe or in price.' ...

"Why then was Reading Pipe specified? Apparently because it was the normal trade practice to assure wrought iron pipe quality by naming a manufacturer. In contemporary trade bulletins put out by Byers and Reading, prospective buyers were cautioned that some steel pipe manufacturers used iron pipe and often sold under misleading names like 'wrought pipe.' To avoid such inferior products, Byers warned: 'When wrought iron pipe is desired, the specifications often read "genuine wrought iron pipe" but as this does not always exclude wrought iron containing steel scrap, it is safer to mention the name of a manufacturer known not to use scrap.' "

BRUNER v. HINES, 295 Ala. 111, 324 So.2d 265 (1975). "The doctrine of substantial performance is a necessary inroad on the pure concept of freedom of contracts. The doctrine recognizes countervailing interests of private individuals and society; and, to some extent, it sacrifices the preciseness of the individual's contractual expectations to society's need for facilitating economic exchange. This is not to say that the rule of substantial performance constitutes a moral or ethical compromise; rather, the wisdom of its application adds legal efficacy to promises by enforcing the essential purposes of contracts and by eliminating trivial excuses for nonperformance."

GOETZ & SCOTT, THE MITIGATION PRINCIPLE: TOWARD A GENERAL THEORY OF CONTRACTUAL OBLIGATION, 69 Va.L.Rev. 967, 1010 (1983). "The substantial performance doctrine reduces opportunistic claims by softening the breacher–nonbreacher distinction, thereby removing opportunities to exploit inadvertent breaches."

––––––––

JARDINE ESTATES, INC. v. DONNA BROOK CORP., 42 N.J.Super. 332, 126 A.2d 372 (1956). "Substantial performance is compliance in good faith with all important particulars of the contract.... [For the doctrine to apply,] a builder's default should not be willful, nor the defects so serious as to deprive the property of its value for the intended use, nor so pervade the whole work that a deduction in damages will not be fair compensation. 3 Williston on Contracts (Rev. ed.), § 805, p. 2256 et seq....

"Appellant stresses that since there was a verdict in its favor for incomplete and defective work in a sum equal to 31% of the contract price, it is conclusive that there was not substantial performance. We do not agree. The matter is not to be determined on a percentage basis, for the cost of remedying defects may sometimes even exceed the outlay for original construction."

––––––––

VINCENZI v. CERRO, 186 Conn. 612, 442 A.2d 1352 (1982). "The principal claim of the defendants is that the doctrine of substantial performance was inapplicable in this case because the plaintiffs were guilty of a wilful or intentional breach of contract by failing to complete all of the work required.... We have in several cases approved the common statement that a contractor who is guilty of a 'wilful' breach cannot maintain an action upon the contract.... The contemporary view, however, is that even a conscious and intentional departure from the contract specifications will not necessarily defeat recovery, but may be considered as one of the several factors involved in deciding whether there has been full performance. 3A Corbin, Contract § 707; 2 Restatement (Second), Contracts § 237, comment D. The pertinent inquiry is not simply whether the breach was 'wilful' but whether the behavior of the party in default 'comports with standard of good faith and fair dealing.' 2 Restatement (Second), Contracts § 241(e); see comment f. Even an adverse conclusion on this point is not decisive but is to be weighted with other factors, such as the extent to which the owner will be deprived of a reasonably expected benefit and the extent to which the builder may suffer forfeiture, in deciding whether there has been substantial performance. Id.; see § 237, comment d."

––––––––

KREYER v. DRISCOLL
Supreme Court of Wisconsin, 1968.
39 Wis.2d 540, 159 N.W.2d 680.

This is a suit to recover the contract price of an oral contract to construct a home for the defendants Winfred M. Driscoll and Ann Driscoll. The defense alleged a breach of contract and a failure to substantially perform. The case was tried to the court which found the plaintiff Robert J. Kreyer, doing business as R.J. Kreyer Construction Company and the defendants Driscolls entered into a contract about December 1, 1961, for the construction of a dwelling house according to drawings and specifications at a cost of $47,046.62, which was to be completed in the fall of 1962. Extras were found to amount to $2,787.83. There were difficulties in completing the house and a refusal by the Driscolls to pay the plaintiff because of alleged breaches on his part. However, the court found the plaintiff substantially performed the contract and deducted from the contract price $740 for imperfect workmanship; $1,233.32 damages for unreasonable delay in completion; $23,460 for payments made to the plaintiff; and $13,433.32 for payments made directly by the Driscolls to subcontractors either for lien satisfactions or on their accounts, $4,650 of which was work performed after difficulties arose between the plaintiff and the Driscolls. Judgment was entered in favor of the plaintiff for the balance, namely, $10,967.81, and the Driscolls appealed and the plaintiff cross appealed for interest.

HALLOWS, CHIEF JUSTICE. The plaintiff complains the findings of fact as to terms of the building contract are in error because they omit: (1) The plaintiff was to receive payment in four draws as the job progressed; (2) he was to use the draw money only for Driscolls' house; and (3) the plaintiff was to submit lien waivers to show for what he had used the draw money. The record is voluminous and contains much evidence relating to these three issues. The evidence is conflicting but it does appear the plaintiff was to receive payment in four draws on condition that he submit waivers of liens as a condition precedent to drawing on the mortgage money of the Driscolls after the first instalment payment. Some of the liens presented stated amounts in excess of that actually paid the subcontractors and some were for amounts in excess of material furnished. Apparently some of the money was used to pay bills other than for material used in Driscolls' house.

It is not material in the view we take of this case whether findings on this issue were made. We point out, however, that the Driscolls did not request the findings they now claim should have been made. The trial court found the plaintiff duly performed all the conditions of the contract with the exception of the defective work and the delay. The evidence does not sustain this finding in respect to the completion of the home.

The trial court thought the plaintiff substantially performed the contract because only $4,650 of uncompleted work remained at the time the plaintiff and the Driscolls reached an impasse. The trial court also concluded the Driscolls looked to the plaintiff to continue the contract and did not rescind it. We do not think that recission is a necessary condition precedent to a defense to substantial performance. The Driscolls were dissatisfied with the plaintiff's performance and notified him. They could accept so much of the work as the plaintiff performed without waiving full performance. Manthey v. Stock (1907), 133 Wis. 107, 113 N.W. 443. If the Driscolls had valid grounds to rescind the contract, that would have precluded substantial performance of the contract and required the plaintiff to sue in *quantum meruit.* However, failure to rescind does not make performance substantial which is unsubstantial.

The doctrine of substantial performance is an equitable doctrine and constitutes an exception in building contracts to the general rule requiring complete performance of the contract. To recover on an uncompleted construction contract on a claim of having substantially, but not fully, performed it, the contractor must make a good faith effort to perform and substantially perform his agreement. Nees v. Weaver (1936), 222 Wis. 492, 269 N.W. 266, 107 A.L.R. 1405. This doctrine of substantial performance was explained and the cases discussed in Manthey v. Stock, supra, and further explained and cases discussed in Plante v. Jacobs (1960)....

Most of the cases considering the doctrine of substantial performance involved defective work or work contrary to the terms of the contract which required substantial amounts of money to conform the work to the terms of the contract. In some cases, while the work was completed the performance of the subject of the contract did not meet the object and purpose of the contract. In the present case, we have on the findings of the court only an incompleteness in respect to the construction work and a cost of completing the dwelling to the owner which was readily ascertainable. Such a case by its nature presents a less difficult case of substantial performance than those involving defective work or inability of the subject matter to meet performance standards. But we should not consider as controlling the fact that the owner can obtain all he contracted for by self-help and by the expenditure of money.

Here, the defendant considered he had to take an active part in finishing the house because he could not trust the plaintiff to complete the house free of liens because of his prior conduct. We think the owner has a right to contract for the completed structure or work and in the building of a house the contract price pays for the relief from trouble and personal effort on the part of the owner in respect to building. Consequently, a dispensation in favor of the contractor on the theory of substantial performance should be granted in cases of incompleteness only when such details are inconsiderable and not the fault of the contractor. See Manthey v. Stock, supra.

The court made no finding on the good faith of the plaintiff and if we presume an affirmative finding on that question was impliedly made, we still do not consider it a saving grace because the plaintiff did not construct the house to the point of completeness which could be called substantial performance. In Plante v. Jacobs, supra, at 572, 103 N.W.2d at 298, we stated, "No mathematical rule relating to the percentage of the price, of cost of completion, or of completeness can be laid down to determine substantial performance of a building contract." At that time there remained to be done: Approximately one half of the plumbing at a cost of $800; one half of the electrical work at a cost of about $800; one half of the heating at a cost of about $800; one half of the tile work at a cost of about $1,500; and all the linoleum at a cost of $560; and about one fourth of the decorating.

We do not think a contractor who leaves this much work unfinished has substantially complied with his contract to completely build a home according to plans and specifications. It may be true that he should not be denied compensation, but neither should he be entitled to recover on the contract for substantially complete performance. We think the trial court was in error in granting recovery on the theory of substantial performance, but the plaintiff has a cause of action to be reimbursed for his services and material on the theory of *quantum meruit*. See Plante v. Jacobs, supra.

In Valentine v. Patrick Warren Construction Co. (1953), 263 Wis. 143, 56 N.W.2d 860, the rule was laid down in respect to restitution in favor of a plaintiff who is in default. In this case we adopted the rule found in Restatement, Second, Contracts, pp. 623–624, sec. 357(1), which provides that where a defendant justifiably refuses to perform his contract because of the plaintiff's breach but the plaintiff has rendered part performance which is of a net benefit to the defendant, the plaintiff can get judgment with some exceptions for the amount of such benefit in excess of the harm he has caused the defendant by his breach but in no case exceeding a ratable proportion of the agreed compensation. Under this rule, the defendant with knowledge of the plaintiff's breach must assent to the rendition of the part performance or accept the benefit of it. This is what the trial court found the Driscolls did by not rescinding the contract.

Illustration 3 to this rule is on all fours with the facts of this case and the computation made by the trial court is the computation which would be made under this section. The same rule as stated in 5 Williston, Contracts (rev.), pp. 41–44, secs. 1482–1483, is that the true measure of quasi-contractual recovery where the performance is incomplete but readily remedial is the unpaid contract price less the cost of completion and other additional harm to the defendant except that it must never exceed the benefit actually received by the defendant. This is the net benefit by which the defendant is enriched.

In this case the Driscolls have a house which now meets the conditions of the contract with adjustments made for delay in performance and for minor faulty work. It would be unjust to allow them to retain the $10,967.81. They should not receive a windfall because of the plaintiff's breach. It is immaterial to the Driscolls whether subcontractors are paid or not. There are no valid liens against their home and their agreement was not a third-party-beneficiary contract for subcontractors. The trial court found the dwelling was reasonably worth the purchase price and thus the amount found due the plaintiff by the court does not exceed the benefit actually received by [the] Driscolls. It would be useless to send this case back for a retrial which would reach the same result on the facts found. We therefore hold the amount of the judgment found by the lower court was not justified on the theory of substantial performance but is justified on the theory of *quantum meruit* or restitution.

On the cross appeal the plaintiff asks for interest on the amount of the judgment, but recovery is not now on the contract and this question is moot. In equity the plaintiff is not entitled to interest and, likewise, neither party should have costs on this appeal.

Judgment affirmed; costs denied to both parties.

———

O.W. GRUN ROOFING & CONSTR. CO. v. COPE, 529 S.W.2d 258 (Tex.Civ.App.1975). Grun agreed to install a new russet–colored shingle roof on Cope's home for $648. As actually installed, the roof had yellow streaks but was structurally sound. Cope refused to pay, and Grun filed a mechanic's lien. Cope then sued to set aside the lien and for damages equal to difference between (i) the $648 price under the contract with Grun and (ii) the cost of installing a new roof, which was 20% higher. The trial court set aside the lien and awarded Cope $123, based on the cost to install a new roof ($648 plus 20% for price increases). Affirmed:

> ... It should not come as a shock to anyone to adopt a rule to the effect that a person has, particularly with respect to his home, to choose for himself and to contract for something which exactly satisfies that

choice, and not to be compelled to accept something else. In the matter of homes and their decoration, as much as, if not more than, in many other fields, mere taste or preference, almost approaching whimsy, may be controlling with the homeowner, so that variations which might, under other circumstances, be considered trifling, may be inconsistent with that "substantial performance" on which liability to pay must be predicated. [M]ere incompleteness or deviations which may be easily supplied or remedied after the contractor has finished his work, and the cost of which to the owner is not excessive and readily ascertainable, present less cause for hesitation in concluding that the performance tendered constitutes substantial performance, since in such cases the owner can obtain complete satisfaction by merely spending some money and deducting the amount of such expenditure from the contract price.

In the case before us there is evidence to support the conclusion that plaintiff can secure a roof of uniform coloring only by installing a completely new roof. We cannot say, as a matter of law, that the evidence establishes that in this case that a roof which so lacks uniformity in color as to give the appearance of a patch job serves essentially the same purpose as a roof of uniform color which has the appearance of being a new roof. We are not prepared to hold that a contractor who tenders a performance so deficient that it can be remedied only by completely redoing the work for which the contract called has established, as a matter of law, that he has substantially performed his contractual obligation.

A recovery by Grun in quantum meruit for benefit conferred was denied:

... [T]he evidence does not conclusively establish that plaintiff has received any benefit from defendant's defective performance. As already pointed out, there is evidence that plaintiff will have to install a completely new roof.

SECTION 2. CONTRACTS FOR THE SALE OF GOODS

UCC §§ 2–508, 2–601, 2–608, 2–612

[See Selected Source Materials Supplement]

CISG ARTS. 35(1), 37, 45, 46, 48, 49

[See Selected Source Materials Supplement]

J. WHITE & R. SUMMERS, UNIFORM COMMERCIAL CODE § 8–2 (5th ed. 2000). "At the outset one should understand the significance of a self–help remedy which permits the buyer to return the goods to the seller (that is, rejection or revocation of acceptance). In these cases the buyer is freed from its obligation to pay the price, and the buyer has a right to recover that part of the price already paid. Moreover, except in unusual circumstances, the buyer need not resell the goods. One should understand the economic difference between the status of the buyer who has rejected and the status of the buyer who has accepted and sued for breach of warranty. The typical buyer who accepts and sues for breach of warranty under 2–714 will recover only for injury proximately resulting from defects in the goods at the time of sale. If, for example, the purchased automobile had a cracked piston that will cost $500 to repair (and the value of the car is so diminished by $500), buyer will recover that $500. On the other hand, if buyer rejects the goods, buyer is first recompensed for the losses resulting from the seller's failure to perform its end of the contract (for example, by a suit under 2–713 or 2–712); more important, buyer escapes the bargain, and throws any loss resulting from depreciation of the goods back upon the seller.

"The importance of goods oriented remedies can be illustrated by an example from a commodity market. Assume that the seller delivers 10,000 bushels of potatoes and that 100 of those bushels are rotten. If the buyer accepts the potatoes, it will have a cause of action under 2–714, and it will recover money approximately equivalent to the value of those 100 bushels. If, on the other hand, the buyer rejects the entire delivery, if the seller cannot cure, and if the price of the potatoes has fallen substantially, the buyer's rejection may save it thousands of dollars by allowing the purchase of conforming goods on the market at a much lower price than specified in the contract. Rejection avoids the economic injury of a bad bargain as well."

NOTE ON THE PERFECT–TENDER RULE AND THE UCC

Prior to the adoption of the Uniform Commercial Code, the doctrine of substantial performance was not applicable to contracts for the sale of goods. Instead, at least in theory and often in practice, a buyer could refuse to accept a delivery of goods that in any way failed to conform to the contract. This rule was known as the perfect-tender rule, because a buyer of goods could reject any tender of delivery that was not perfect. A leading case was Norrington v. Wright, 115 U.S. 188, 6 S.Ct. 12, 29 L.Ed. 366 (1885). UCC § 2–601 nominally preserves the perfect-tender rule for the sale of goods. However, other provisions of the UCC strip away much or most of the significance of this Section.

1. *Revocation of acceptance.* First, UCC § 2–601 applies only where a buyer rejects goods. It does not apply where the buyer accepts goods and then discovers a defect. Under UCC § 2–608, a buyer may revoke acceptance in such a case, but only if the nonconformity substantially impairs the value of the goods to her.

There are other limitations on the buyer's right to revoke acceptance under § 2–608, even if the nonconformity does substantially impair the value of the goods to him. If the buyer accepted the goods knowing that they were nonconforming, she can revoke her acceptance only if she accepted on the reasonable assumption that the nonconformity would be cured (for example, because the seller promised cure), and the nonconformity was not seasonally cured. If the buyer accepted the goods without knowing that they were nonconforming, she can revoke her acceptance only if her acceptance was reasonably induced either by the difficulty of discovering the defect before acceptance or by the seller's assurances.

2. *Installment contracts.* Section 2–601 is also inapplicable to installment contracts, that is, contracts that require or authorize the delivery of goods in separate lots, to be separately accepted. Such contracts are covered by Section 2–612. Under Section 2–612(2), a buyer normally can reject a nonconforming installment only if the nonconformity substantially impairs the value of the installment and cannot be cured. Furthermore, under Section 2–612(3) a buyer cannot treat the whole installment contract as breached on the ground of a nonconformity or default with respect to one or more installments, unless those nonconformities or defaults substantially impair the value of the whole contract.

3. *Cure.* The perfect-tender rule is also significantly ameliorated by Section 2–508, the "cure" provision. Under Section 2–508(1), in the case of a single-delivery (non-installment) contract, if a tender of goods is rejected because it is nonconforming, and the time for performance has not yet expired, the seller may cure the defect by making a conforming delivery within the contract time. Even more significantly, under Section 2–508(2) if a tender of goods is rejected because it is nonconforming, and the seller had reasonable grounds to believe that the tender would be acceptable with a money allowance or otherwise, the seller has a further reasonable time to substitute a conforming tender even if the time for performance has expired.

4. *Good Faith.* Under UCC § 1–203, "Every contract . . . within [the UCC] imposes an obligation of good faith in its performance or enforcement." Under UCC § 1–201(19), at a minimum good faith requires "honesty in fact in the conduct or transaction concerned." Under UCC § 2–103(1)(b), in the case of a merchant, in contracts for the sale of goods, good faith means not only honesty in fact but also "the observance of reasonable commercial standards of fair dealing in the trade."* A buyer who seized on a minor defect to justify a rejection that was really based on the fact that the contract is no longer favorable to her might not satisfy this minimum obligation. As stated in Printing Center of Texas, Inc. v. Supermind Publishing Co., 669 S.W.2d 779 (Tex.App.1984):

> Once the contract of the parties has been determined, the evidence must be reviewed to see if the right goods were tendered at the right time and place. If the evidence does establish nonconformity in some respect, the buyer is entitled to reject if he rejects in good faith. [UCC] § 1–203 provides that, "Every contract or duty within this Act imposes an obligation of good faith in its performance or enforcement." Since the rejection of goods is a matter of performance, the buyer is obligated to act in good faith when he rejects the goods. When the buyer is a merchant, his standard of good faith rejection requires honesty in fact and observance of reasonable commercial standards of fair dealing in the trade. [UCC § 2–103(2)]. . . . Evidence of circumstances which indicate that the

---

* The UCC sections quoted in this passage are those in force in most states. See Note on The Duty to Perform in Good Faith under the UCC and Restatement Second, Chapter 22, supra.

buyer's motivation in rejecting the goods was to escape the bargain, rather than to avoid acceptance of a tender which in some respect impairs the value of the bargain to him, would support a finding of rejection in bad faith. Neumiller Farms Inc. v. Cornett, 368 So.2d 272 (Ala.1979). Thus, evidence of rejection of the goods on account of a minor defect in a falling market would in some instances be sufficient to support a finding that the buyer acted in bad faith when he rejected the goods.

RAMIREZ v. AUTOSPORT, 88 N.J. 277, 440 A.2d 1345 (1982). "In the nineteenth century, sellers were required to deliver goods that complied exactly with the sales agreement. See Filley v. Pope, 115 U.S. 213, 220, 6 S.Ct. 19, 21, 29 L.Ed. 372, 373 (1885) (buyer not obliged to accept otherwise conforming scrap iron shipped to New Orleans from Leith, rather than Glasgow, Scotland, as required by contract); Columbia Iron Works & Dry-Dock Co. v. Douglas, 84 Md. 44, 47, 34 A. 1118, 1120–1121 (1896) (buyer who agreed to purchase steel scrap from United States cruisers not obliged to take any other kind of scrap). That rule, known as the 'perfect tender' rule, remained part of the law of sales well into the twentieth century. By the 1920's the doctrine was so entrenched in the law that Judge Learned Hand declared '[t]here is no room in commercial contracts for the doctrine of substantial performance.' Mitsubishi Goshi Kaisha v. J. Aaron & Co., Inc., 16 F.2d 185, 186 (2 Cir.1926).

"The harshness of the rule led courts to seek to ameliorate its effect and to bring the law of sales in closer harmony with the law of contracts, which allows rescission only for material breaches. LeRoy Dyal Co. v. Allen, 161 F.2d 152, 155 (4 Cir.1947). See 5 Corbin, Contracts § 1104 at 464 (1951); 12 Williston, Contracts § 1455 at 14 (3 ed. 1970). Nevertheless, a variation of the perfect tender rule appeared in the Uniform Sales Act. N.J.S.A. 46:30–75 (purchasers permitted to reject goods or rescind contracts for any breach of warranty).... The chief objection to the continuation of the perfect tender rule was that buyers in a declining market would reject goods for minor non-conformities and force the loss on surprised sellers....

"To the extent that a buyer can reject goods for any nonconformity, the UCC retains the perfect tender rule.... Section 2–601 authorizes a buyer to reject goods if they 'or the tender of delivery fail in any respect to conform to the contract.' ... The Code, however, mitigates the harshness of the perfect tender rule and balances the interests of buyer and seller."

COMMENTS OF GRANT GILMORE, IN ALI–ABA, ADVANCED ALI–ABA COURSE OF STUDY ON BANKING AND SECURED TRANSACTIONS UNDER THE UNIFORM COMMERCIAL CODE 145 (1968). "There was a considerable controversy in the early days of the Code as to why the Code had, apparently, although stating the strong substantial performance role in § 2–612 with respect to installment contracts, restated what many people considered [the] exploded theory of perfect tender in § 2–601. I think at that point few people realized how much substantial perform-ance there was buried in other, apparently unrelated, sections of the code to cut back § 2–601. There was considerable tendency in the academic discussions of the problem in law review articles to say that § 2–601 was all wrong and what the draftsman ought to have done was to have adopted a straight substantial performance rule all the way through.

"I remember hearing Professor Llewellyn discuss this problem once. He put it this way: He said that one of his advisers in the early years of drafting the sales article had been a Mr. Hiram Thomas of Boston, a Boston lawyer, for whom Llewellyn had great admiration, indeed reverence. Llewellyn said there was one meeting at which Hiram Thomas explained why it was that the perfect tender rule of § 2–601 was right with respect to ordinary contracts and the substantial performance rule of § 2–612 was right with respect to installment contracts. Anyone who heard Mr. Thomas that day, said Llewellyn, would be in no doubt that both sections were right. Unfortunately, said Llewellyn, he had since forgotten exactly what it was that Mr. Thomas said, and Mr. Thomas had since died, so that there was no way of reconstructing just why it was that § 2–601 was a good section of its type and § 2–612 was a good section of its type. But Professor Llewellyn was adamant that they were both right and that Mr. Thomas had once known the reason. (Laughter)"

T.W. OIL, INC. v. CONSOLIDATED EDISON CO.

Court of Appeals of New York, 1982.
57 N.Y.2d 574, 457 N.Y.S.2d 458, 443 N.E.2d 932.

FUCHSBERG, JUDGE.

In the first case to wend its way through our appellate courts on this question, we are asked, in the main, to decide whether a seller who, acting in good faith and without knowledge of any defect, tenders nonconforming goods to a buyer who properly rejects them, may avail itself of the cure provision of subdivision (2) of section 2–508 of the Uniform Commercial Code. We hold that, if seasonable notice be given, such a seller may offer to cure the defect within a reasonable period beyond the time when the contract was to be performed so long as it has acted in good faith and with a reasonable expectation that the original goods would be acceptable to the buyer.

The factual background against which we decide this appeal is based on either undisputed proof or express findings at Trial Term. In January, 1974, midst the fuel shortage produced by the oil embargo, the plaintiff (then known as Joc Oil USA, Inc.) purchased a cargo of fuel oil whose sulfur content was represented to it as no greater than 1%. While the oil was still at sea en route to the United States in the tanker *MT Khamsin,* plaintiff received a certificate from the foreign refinery at which it had been processed informing it that the sulfur content in fact was .52%. Thereafter, on January 24, the plaintiff entered into a written contract with the defendant (Con Ed) for the sale of this oil. The agreement was for delivery to take place between January 24 and January 30, payment being subject to a named independent testing agency's confirmation of quality and quantity. The contract, following a trade custom to round off specifications of sulfur content at, for instance, 1%, .5% or .3%, described that of the *Khamsin* oil as .5%. In the course of the negotiations, the plaintiff learned that Con Ed was then authorized to buy and burn oil with a sulfur content of up to 1% and would even mix oils containing more and less to maintain that figure.

When the vessel arrived, on January 25, its cargo was discharged into Con Ed storage tanks in Bayonne, New Jersey.[1] In due course, the independent testing people reported a sulfur content of .92%. On this basis, acting within a time frame whose reasonableness is not in question, on February 14 Con Ed rejected the shipment. Prompt negotiations to adjust the price failed; by February 20, plaintiff had offered a price reduction roughly responsive to the difference in sulfur reading, but Con Ed, though it could use the oil, rejected this proposition out of hand. It was insistent on paying no more than the latest prevailing price, which, in the volatile market that then existed, was some 25% below the level which prevailed when it agreed to buy the oil.

The very next day, February 21, plaintiff offered to cure the defect with a substitute shipment of conforming oil scheduled to arrive on the *S.S. Appollonian Victory* on February 28. Nevertheless, on February 22, the very day after the cure was proffered, Con Ed, adamant in its intention to avail itself of the intervening drop in prices, summarily rejected this proposal too. The two cargos were subsequently sold to third parties at the best price obtainable, first that of the *Appollonian* and, sometime later, after extraction from the tanks had been accomplished, that of the *Khamsin*.[2]

There ensued this action for breach of contract,[3] which, after a somewhat unconventional trial course, resulted in a nonjury decision for the plaintiff in the sum of $1,385,512.83, essentially the difference between the original contract price of $3,360,667.14 and the amount received by the plaintiff by way of resale of the *Khamsin* oil at what the court found as a matter of fact was a negotiated price which, under all the circumstances,[4] was reasonably procured in the open market. To arrive at this result, the Trial Judge, while ruling against other liability theories advanced by the plaintiff, which, in particular, included one charging the defendant with having failed to act in good faith in the negotiations for a price adjustment on the *Khamsin* oil (Uniform Commercial Code, § 1–203), decided as a matter of law that subdivision (2) of section 2–508 of the Uniform Commercial Code was available to the plaintiff even if it had no prior knowledge of the nonconformity. Finding that in fact plaintiff had no such belief at the time of the delivery, that what turned out to be a .92% sulfur content was "within the range of contemplation of reasonable acceptability" to Con. Ed., and that seasonable notice of an intention to cure was given, the court went on to hold that plaintiff's "reasonable and timely offer to cure" was improperly rejected (*sub nom. Joc Oil USA v. Consolidated Edison Co. of N.Y.*, 107 Misc.2d 376, 390, 434 N.Y.S.2d 623 [Shanley N. Egeth, J.]). The Appellate Division, 84 A.D.2d 970,

---

1. The tanks already contained some other oil, but Con Ed appears to have had no concern over the admixture of the differing sulfur contents. In any event, the efficacy of the independent testing required by the contract was not impaired by the commingling.

2. Most of the *Khamsin* oil was drained from the tanks and sold at $10.75 per barrel. The balance was retained by Con Ed in its mixed form at $10.45 per barrel. The original price in January had been $17.875 per barrel.

3. The plaintiff originally also sought an affirmative injunction to compel Con Ed to accept the *Khamsin* shipment or, alternatively, the *Appollonian* substitute. However, when a preliminary injunction was denied on the ground that the plaintiff had an adequate remedy at law, it amended its complaint to pursue the latter remedy alone.

4. These circumstances included the fact that the preliminary injunction was not denied until April so that, by the time the *Khamsin* oil was sold in May, almost three months had gone by since its rejection.

447 N.Y.S.2d 572, having unanimously affirmed the judgment entered on this decision, the case is now here by our leave (CPLR 5602, subd. [a], par. 1, cl. [i]).

In support of its quest for reversal, the defendant now asserts that the trial court erred ... in failing to interpret subdivision (2) of section 2–508 of the Uniform Commercial Code to limit the availability of the right to cure after date of performance to cases in which the seller knowingly made a nonconforming tender and ... in calculating damages on the basis of the resale of the nonconforming cargo rather than of the substitute offered to replace it. For the reasons which follow, we find [these assertions] unacceptable....

... Fairly interpreted, did subdivision (2) of section 2–508 of the Uniform Commercial Code require Con Ed to accept the substitute shipment plaintiff tendered? In approaching this question, we, of course, must remember that a seller's right to cure a defective tender, as allowed by both subdivisions of section 2–508, was intended to act as a meaningful limitation on the absolutism of the old perfect tender rule, under which, no leeway being allowed for any imperfections, there was, as one court put it, just "no room * * * for the doctrine of substantial performance" of commercial obligations (*Mitsubishi Goshi Kaisha v. Aron & Co.*, 16 F.2d 185, 186 [Learned Hand, J.]; see Note, Uniform Commercial Code, § 2–508; Seller's Right to Cure Non–Conforming Goods, 6 Rutgers—Camden L.J. 387–388).

In contrast, to meet the realities of the more impersonal business world of our day, the code, to avoid sharp dealing, expressly provides for the liberal construction of its remedial provisions (§ 1–102) so that "good faith" and the "observance of reasonable commercial standards of fair dealing" be the rule rather than the exception in trade (see § 2–103, subd. [1], par. [b]), "good faith" being defined as "honesty in fact in the conduct or transaction concerned" (Uniform Commercial Code, § 1–201, subd. [19]). As to section 2–508 in particular, the code's Official Comment advises that its mission is to safeguard the seller "against surprise as a result of sudden technicality on the buyer's part" (Uniform Commercial Code, § 2–106, Comment 2; see, also, Peters, Remedies for Breach of Contracts Relating to the Sale of Goods under the Uniform Commercial Code: A Roadmap for Article Two, 73 Yale L.J. 199, 210; 51 N.Y.Jur., Sales, § 101, p. 41).

Section 2–508 may be conveniently divided between provisions for cure offered when "the time for performance has not yet expired" (subd. [1]), a precode concept in this State (*Lowinson v. Newman*, 201 App.Div. 266, 194 N.Y.S. 253), and ones which, by newly introducing the possibility of a seller obtaining "a further reasonable time to substitute a conforming tender" (subd. [2]), also permit cure beyond the date set for performance. In its entirety the section reads as follows:

"(1) Where any tender or delivery by the seller is rejected because non-conforming and the time for performance has not yet expired, the seller may seasonably notify the buyer of his intention to cure and may then within the contract time make a conforming delivery.

"(2) Where the buyer rejects a non-conforming tender which the seller had reasonable grounds to believe would be acceptable with or without money allowance the seller may if he seasonably notifies the buyer have a further reasonable time to substitute a conforming tender."

Since we here confront circumstances in which the conforming tender came after the time of performance, we focus on subdivision (2). On its face, taking its conditions in the order in which they appear, for the statute to apply (1) a buyer must have rejected a nonconforming tender, (2) the seller must have had reasonable grounds to believe this tender would be acceptable (with or without money allowance), and (3) the seller must have "seasonably" notified the buyer of the intention to substitute a conforming tender within a reasonable time.[5]

In the present case, none of these presented a problem. The first one was easily met for it is unquestioned that, at .92%, the sulfur content of the *Khamsin* oil did not conform to the .5% specified in the contract and that it was rejected by Con Ed. The second, the reasonableness of the seller's belief that the original tender would be acceptable, was supported not only by unimpeached proof that the contract's .5% and the refinery certificate's .52% were trade equivalents, but by testimony that, by the time the contract was made, the plaintiff knew Con Ed burned fuel with a content of up to 1%, so that, with appropriate price adjustment, the *Khamsin* oil would have suited its needs even if, at delivery, it was, to the plaintiff's surprise, to test out at .92%. Further, the matter seems to have been put beyond dispute by the defendant's readiness to take the oil at the reduced market price on February 20. Surely, on such a record, the trial court cannot be faulted for having found as a fact that the second condition too had been established.

As to the third, the conforming state of the *Appollonian* oil is undisputed, the offer to tender it took place on February 21, only a day after Con Ed finally had rejected the *Khamsin* delivery and the *Appollonian* substitute then already was en route to the United States, where it was expected in a week and did arrive on March 4, only four days later than expected. Especially since Con Ed pleaded no prejudice (unless the drop in prices could be so regarded), it is almost impossible, given the flexibility of the Uniform Commercial Code definitions of "seasonable" and "reasonable" (n. 7, *supra*), to quarrel with the finding that the remaining requirements of the statute also had been met.

Thus lacking the support of the statute's literal language, the defendant nonetheless would have us limit its application to cases in which a seller *knowingly* makes a nonconforming tender which it has reason to believe the buyer will accept. For this proposition, it relies almost entirely on a critique in Nordstrom, Law of Sales (§ 105), which rationalizes that, since a seller who believes its tender is conforming would have no reason to think in terms of a reduction in the price of the goods, to allow such a seller to cure after the time for performance had passed would make the statutory reference to a money allowance redundant.[6] Nordstrom, interestingly enough, finds it useful to

---

5. Essentially a factual matter, "seasonable" is defined in subdivision (3) of section 1–204 of the Uniform Commercial Code as "at or within the time agreed or if no time is agreed at or within a reasonable time". At least equally factual in character, a "reasonable time" is left to depend on the "nature, purpose and circumstances" of any action which is to be taken (Uniform Commercial Code, § 1–204, subd. [2]).

6. The premise for such an argument, which ignores the policy of the code to prevent

buyers from using insubstantial remediable or price adjustable defects to free themselves from unprofitable bargains (Hawkland, Sales and Bulk Sales Under the Uniform Commercial Code, pp. 120–122), is that the words "with or without money allowance" apply only to sellers who believe their goods will be acceptable with such an allowance and not to sellers who believe their goods will be acceptable without such an allowance. But, since the words are part of a phrase which speaks of an otherwise unqualified belief that the goods will be acceptable, unless one strains for an opposite inter-buttress this position by the somewhat dire prediction, though backed by no empirical or other confirmation, that, unless the right to cure is confined to those whose nonconforming tenders are knowing ones, the incentive of sellers to timely deliver will be undermined. To this it also adds the somewhat moralistic note that a seller who is mistaken as to the quality of its goods does not merit additional time (Nordstrom, *loc. cit.*). Curiously, recognizing that the few decisions extant on this subject have adopted a position opposed to the one for which it contends, Con Ed seeks to treat these as exceptions rather than exemplars of the rule (e.g., *Wilson v. Scampoli,* 228 A.2d 848 (D.C.App.) [goods obtained by seller from their manufacturer in original carton resold unopened to purchaser; seller held within statute though it had no reason to believe the goods defective]; *Appleton State Bank v. Lee,* 33 Wis.2d 690, 148 N.W.2d 1 [seller mistakenly delivered sewing machine of wrong brand but otherwise identical to one sold; held that seller, though it did not know of its mistake, had a right to cure by substitution]).[7]

That the principle for which these cases stand goes far beyond their particular facts cannot be gainsaid. These holdings demonstrate that, in dealing with the application of subdivision (2) of section 2–508, courts have been concerned with the reasonableness of the seller's belief that the goods would be acceptable rather than with the seller's pretender knowledge or lack of knowledge of the defect (*Wilson v. Scampoli, supra;* compare *Zabriskie Chevrolet v. Smith,* 99 N.J.Super. 441, 240 A.2d 195).

It also is no surprise then that the aforementioned decisional history is a reflection of the mainstream of scholarly commentary on the subject. . . .

White and Summers, for instance, put it well, and bluntly. Stressing that the code intended cure to be "a remedy which should be carefully cultivated and developed by the courts" because it "offers the possibility of conforming the law to reasonable expectations and of thwarting the chiseler who seeks to escape from a bad bargain" . . ., the authors conclude, as do we, that a seller should have recourse to the relief afforded by subdivision (2) of section 2–508 of the Uniform Commercial Code as long as it can establish that it had reasonable grounds, tested objectively, for its belief that the goods would be accepted (*ibid.,* at p 321). It goes without saying that the test of reasonableness, in this context, must encompass the concepts of "good faith" and "commercial standards of fair dealing" which permeate the code (Uniform Commercial Code, § 1–201, subd. [19]; §§ 1–203, 2–103, subd. [1], par. [b]).

As to the damages issue raised by the defendant, we affirm without reaching the merits. At no stage of the proceedings before the trial court did the defendant object to the plaintiff's proposed method for their calculation. . . .

COOKE, C.J., and JASEN, GABRIELLI, JONES, WACHTLER and MEYER, JJ., concur.

Order affirmed.

---

pretation, we find insufficient reason to doubt that it intends to include both those who find a need to offer an allowance and those who do not.

7. The only New York case to deal with this section involved a seller who knowingly tendered a "newer and improved version of the model that was actually ordered" on the contract delivery date. The court held he had reasonable grounds to believe the buyer would accept the newer model (*Bartus v. Riccardi,* 55 Misc.2d 3, 284 N.Y.S.2d 222 [Utica City Ct., Hymes, J.]).

ZABRISKIE CHEVROLET v. SMITH, 99 N.J.Super. 441, 240 A.2d 195 (1968). Zabriskie Chevrolet, a new-car dealership, sold a new 1966 Chevrolet to Smith. As soon as Smith's wife drove off from the dealership, it became evident that the car had very serious problems. As a result, Smith stopped payment on his check and notified Zabriskie that the sale was canceled. Zabriskie then towed the car back, determined that the transmission was defective, replaced the transmission with a transmission it removed from a car on its showroom floor, and asked Smith to take delivery of the repaired car under the contract. When Smith refused to take delivery, Zabriskie brought suit. Held, Zabriskie did not have a right to cure the defective delivery:

"A 'cure' which endeavors by substitution to tender a chattel not within the agreement or contemplation of the parties is invalid.

"For a majority of people the purchase of a new car is a major investment, rationalized by the peace of mind that flows from its dependability and safety. Once their faith is shaken, the vehicle loses not only its real value in their eyes, but becomes an instrument whose integrity is substantially impaired and whose operation is fraught with apprehension. The attempted cure in the present case was ineffective."

MIDWEST MOBILE DIAGNOSTIC IMAGING, L.L.C. v. DYNAMICS CORPORATION OF AMERICA, 965 F.Supp. 1003 (W.D.Mich.1997). "[W]hich standard of conformity applies to cure under an installment contract, perfect tender or substantial impairment? Looking to the rationale behind § 2–612, the court notes that the very purpose of allowing the seller time to cure under this section is to permit it additional time to meet the obligations of the contract. The assumption is that, because the parties have an ongoing relationship, the seller should be given an opportunity to make up the deficiency. This section was not designed to allow the seller to have a never-ending series of chances to bring the item into conformity with the contract. Nor was it enacted to force the buyer to accept a nonconforming product as satisfaction of the contract. Consequently, it is logical that a tender of cure should be required to meet the higher "perfect tender" standard. On its face, however, § 2–612, which generally defines a buyer's right to reject goods under an installment contract, requires only substantial impairment in this context as well. Thus, there is some question as to which is the appropriate standard. The answer is not crucial [here] however, since the trailer in this case fails under *both* standards."

NOTE ON CURE

In 2003, the National Conference of Commissioners on State Laws and the American Law Institute promulgated an amended version of Article 2. Among other things, the amended version: (1) Excludes the application of section 2–508 to consumer contracts. (2) Deletes the requirement in section 2–508(2) that the seller must have had reasonable grounds to believe that the tender would be acceptable, and substitutes in its place a requirement that the seller performed in good faith. (3) Deletes the phrase "with or without a money allowance" from section 2–508(2).

Amended section 2–508 provides as follows:

§ 2–508. Cure by Seller of Improper Tender or Delivery; Replacement.

(1) If the buyer rejects goods or a tender of delivery under Section 2–601 or 2–612 or, except in a consumer contract, justifiably revokes acceptance under Section 2–608(1)(b) and the agreed time for performance has not expired, a seller that has performed in good faith, upon seasonable notice to the buyer and at the seller's own expense, may cure the breach of contract by making a conforming tender of delivery within the agreed time. The seller shall compensate the buyer for all of the buyer's reasonable expenses caused by the seller's breach of contract and subsequent cure.

(2) If the buyer rejects goods or a tender of delivery under Section 2–601 or 2–612 or, except in a consumer contract, justifiably revokes acceptance under Section 2–608(1)(b) and the agreed time for performance has expired, a seller that has performed in good faith, upon seasonable notice to the buyer and the seller's own expense, may cure the breach of contract, if the cure is appropriate and timely under the circumstances, by making a tender of conforming goods. The seller shall compensate the buyer for all of the buyer's reasonable expenses caused by the seller's breach of contract and subsequent cure.

Official Comment ...

3.   ... Original Section 2–508(2) was designed to prevent surprise rejections by requiring the seller to have "reasonable grounds to believe" the nonconforming tender was acceptable. Although this test has been abandoned, the requirement that the initial tender be made in good faith prevents a seller from deliberately tendering goods that the seller knows the buyer cannot use in order to save the contract and then, upon rejection, insisting on a second right to cure. The good faith standard applies under both subsection (1) and subsection (2).

4.   The seller's cure under both subsection (1) and subsection (2) must be of conforming goods. . . .

   ... The standard for quality on the second tender is governed by Section 2–601.

For variety of reasons as of early 2006, no state legislature has adopted the amended version of Article 2. At least for the moment, therefore, issues concerning cure will continue to be resolved under the pre–2003 version of section 2–508.

———

Chapter 24

EXPRESS CONDITIONS

SECTION 1. INTRODUCTION

NOTE ON THE DIFFERENCE BETWEEN PROMISES AND CONDITIONS

Up to now, the materials in this casebook have chiefly concerned promises. This Chapter concerns another basic set of contractual building blocks—express conditions. As previously discussed, the term "express condition" normally refers to an explicit contractual provision that either: (1) A party to the contract does not come under a duty to perform unless and until some designated state of affairs occurs or fails to occur; or (2) If some designated state of affairs occurs or fails to occur, a party's duty to perform is suspended or terminated. For example, Corporation A may agree to merge with Corporation B, but only on condition that the Commissioner of Internal Revenue rules that the transaction will be tax-free. Or, C may agree to purchase D's house, but only on condition that a termite-inspection report shows no infestation.

Why would parties use an express condition rather than a promise? In some cases, it is because neither party is willing to promise that the state of affairs in question will occur. In the merger hypothetical, for example, neither A nor B would normally be willing to promise that the Commissioner will issue a favorable ruling. In the sale-of-the-house hypothetical, D may not know whether the house is infested with termites, and therefore may not be willing to promise that there is no infestation.

Another possible reason for using express conditions, rather than promises, is to avoid—or at least attempt to avoid—the doctrine of substantial performance. Under that doctrine, if A promises to perform construction for B according to agreed-upon specifications, a slight deviation from the specifications will render A liable to a claim for damages by B, but may not prevent A from holding B to his promise to pay for the job, with an offset for the damages. On the other hand, if the contract expressly states that it is a condition to B's liability to A that A's performance meets the designated specifications, then B's chance of escaping liability for the contract price because of a departure from the specifications is improved.

As the next several cases illustrate, it is not always easy to determine whether a given contractual provision is a promise or a condition. The issue whether a given contractual provision is a promise or a condition is further confused by the fact that under modern contract terminology, where A and B have a contract, A's substantial performance of *his* promises may be an *implied condition* to B's obligation to perform *her* promises. This issue will be taken up in Chapter 25, infra.

The organization of this Chapter is as follows: Section 2 will explore the differences between the operation of promises and conditions. Section 3 will consider a distinction that is commonly drawn between two types of conditions—"conditions precedent" and "conditions subsequent." Section 4 concerns issues of interpretation in determining whether a contractual provision is a promise or a condition. Sections 5, 6, and 7 concern recurring kinds of conditions—conditions of cooperation, in which one party's cooperation is deemed to be a condition to the other party's duty to perform; conditions of payment, in which a duty to pay is conditioned on some event (usually, payment of the promisor by a third party); and conditions of satisfaction, in which a duty to pay for a performance is made conditional on satisfaction with the performance. Section 8 concerns excuses for the nonfulfillment of conditions.

SECTION 2. THE DISTINCTIONS BETWEEN THE OPERATION OF A PROMISE AND THE OPERATION OF A CONDITION

OPPENHEIMER & CO. v. OPPENHEIM, APPEL, DIXON & CO.

Court of Appeals of New York, 1995.
86 N.Y.2d 685, 660 N.E.2d 415, 636 N.Y.S.2d 734.

CIPARICK, Justice.

The parties entered into a letter agreement setting forth certain conditions precedent to the formation and existence of a sublease between them. The agreement provided that there would be no sublease between the parties "unless and until" plaintiff delivered to defendant the prime landlord's written consent to certain "tenant work" on or before a specified deadline. If this condition did not occur, the sublease was to be deemed "null and void." Plaintiff provided only oral notice on the specified date. The issue presented is whether the doctrine of substantial performance applies to the facts of this case. We conclude it does not for the reasons that follow.

I.

In 1986, plaintiff Oppenheimer & Co. moved to the World Financial Center in Manhattan, a building constructed by Olympia & York Company (O & Y). At the time of its move, plaintiff had three years remaining on its existing lease for the 33rd floor of the building known as One New York

Plaza. As an incentive to induce plaintiff's move, O & Y agreed to make the rental payments due under plaintiff's rental agreement in the event plaintiff was unable to sublease its prior space in One New York Plaza.

In December 1986, the parties to this action entered into a conditional letter agreement to sublease the 33rd floor. Defendant already leased space on the 29th floor of One New York Plaza and was seeking to expand its operations. The proposed sublease between the parties was attached to the letter agreement. The letter agreement provided that the proposed sublease would be executed only upon the satisfaction of certain conditions. Pursuant to paragraph 1(a) of the agreement, plaintiff was required to obtain "the Prime Landlord's written notice of confirmation, substantially to the effect that [defendant] is a subtenant of the Premises reasonably acceptable to Prime Landlord." If such written notice of confirmation were not obtained "on or before December 30, 1986, then this letter agreement and the Sublease shall be deemed null and void and of no further force and effect and neither party shall have any rights against nor obligations to the other."

Assuming satisfaction of the condition set forth in paragraph 1(a), defendant was required to submit to plaintiff, on or before January 2, 1987, its plans for "tenant work" involving construction of a telephone communication linkage system between the 29th and 33rd floors. Paragraph 4(c) of the letter agreement then obligated plaintiff to obtain the prime landlord's "written consent" to the proposed "tenant work" and deliver such consent to defendant on or before January 30, 1987. Furthermore, if defendant had not received the prime landlord's written consent by the agreed date, both the agreement and the sublease were to be deemed "null and void and of no further force and effect," and neither party was to have "any rights against nor obligations to the other." Paragraph 4(d) additionally provided that, notwithstanding satisfaction of the condition set forth in paragraph 1(a), the parties "agree not to execute and exchange the Sublease unless and until the conditions set forth in paragraph (c) above are timely satisfied."

The parties extended the letter agreement's deadlines in writing and plaintiff timely satisfied the first condition set forth in paragraph 1(a) pursuant to the modified deadline. However, plaintiff never delivered the prime landlord's written consent to the proposed tenant work on or before the modified final deadline of February 25, 1987. Rather, plaintiff's attorney telephoned defendant's attorney on February 25 and informed defendant that the prime landlord's consent had been secured. On February 26, defendant, through its attorney, informed plaintiff's attorney that the letter agreement and sublease were invalid for failure to timely deliver the prime landlord's written consent and that it would not agree to an extension of the deadline. The document embodying the prime landlord's written consent was eventually received by plaintiff on March 20, 1987, 23 days after expiration of paragraph 4(c)'s modified final deadline.

Plaintiff commenced this action for breach of contract, asserting that defendant waived and/or was estopped by virtue of its conduct[1] from insisting on physical delivery of the prime landlord's written consent by the February

---

1. Plaintiff argued that it could have met the deadline, but failed to do so only because defendant, acting in bad faith, induced plaintiff into delaying delivery of the landlord's consent. Plaintiff asserted that the parties had previously extended the agreement's deadlines as a matter of course.

25 deadline. Plaintiff further alleged in its complaint that it had substantially performed the conditions set forth in the letter agreement.

At the outset of trial, the court issued an order in *limine* barring any reference to substantial performance of the terms of the letter agreement. Nonetheless, during the course of trial, the court permitted the jury to consider the theory of substantial performance, and additionally charged the jury concerning substantial performance. Special interrogatories were submitted. The jury found that defendant had properly complied with the terms of the letter agreement, and answered in the negative the questions whether defendant failed to perform its obligations under the letter agreement concerning submission of plans for tenant work, whether defendant by its conduct waived the February 25 deadline for delivery by plaintiff of the landlord's written consent to tenant work, and whether defendant by its conduct was equitably estopped from requiring plaintiff's strict adherence to the February 25 deadline. Nonetheless, the jury answered in the affirmative the question, "Did plaintiff substantially perform the conditions set forth in the Letter Agreement?," and awarded plaintiff damages of $1.2 million.

Defendant moved for judgment notwithstanding the verdict. Supreme Court granted the motion, ruling as a matter of law that "the doctrine of substantial performance has no application to this dispute, where the Letter Agreement is free of all ambiguity in setting the deadline that plaintiff concededly did not honor." The Appellate Division reversed the judgment on the law and facts, and reinstated the jury verdict. The Court concluded that the question of substantial compliance was properly submitted to the jury and that the verdict should be reinstated because plaintiff's failure to deliver the prime landlord's written consent was inconsequential.

This Court granted defendant's motion for leave to appeal and we now reverse.

II.

Defendant argues that no sublease or contractual relationship ever arose here because plaintiff failed to satisfy the condition set forth in paragraph 4(c) of the letter agreement. Defendant contends that the doctrine of substantial performance is not applicable to excuse plaintiff's failure to deliver the prime landlord's written consent to defendant on or before the date specified in the letter agreement and that the Appellate Division erred in holding to the contrary. Before addressing defendant's arguments and the decision of the court below, an understanding of certain relevant principles is helpful.

A condition precedent is "an act or event, other than a lapse of time, which, unless the condition is excused, must occur before a duty to perform a promise in the agreement arises" (Calamari and Perillo, Contracts S 11–2, at 438 [3d ed.]; see, Restatement [Second] of Contracts S 224; see also, Merritt Hill Vineyards v. Windy Hgts. Vineyard, 61 N.Y.2d 106, 112–113, 472 N.Y.S.2d 592, 460 N.E.2d 1077). Most conditions precedent describe acts or events which must occur before a party is obliged to perform a promise made pursuant to an existing contract, a situation to be distinguished conceptually from a condition precedent to the formation or existence of the contract itself (see, M.K. Metals v. Container Recovery Corp., 645 F.2d 583). In the latter situation, no contract arises "unless and until the condition occurs" (Calamari and Perillo, Contracts § 11–5, at 440 [3d ed]).

Conditions can be express or implied. Express conditions are those agreed to and imposed by the parties themselves. Implied or constructive conditions are those "imposed by law to do justice" (Calamari and Perillo, Contracts § 11–8, at 444 [3d ed]). Express conditions must be literally performed, whereas constructive conditions, which ordinarily arise from language of promise, are subject to the precept that substantial compliance is sufficient. The importance of the distinction has been explained by Professor Williston:

> "Since an express condition depends for its validity on the manifested intention of the parties, it has the same sanctity as the promise itself. Though the court may regret the harshness of such a condition, as it may regret the harshness of a promise, it must, nevertheless, generally enforce the will of the parties unless to do so will violate public policy. Where, however, the law itself has imposed the condition, in absence of or irrespective of the manifested intention of the parties, it can deal with its creation as it pleases, shaping the boundaries of the constructive condition in such a way as to do justice and avoid hardship". (5 Williston, Contracts § 669, at 154 [3d ed].)

In determining whether a particular agreement makes an event a condition courts will interpret doubtful language as embodying a promise or constructive condition rather than an express condition. This interpretive preference is especially strong when a finding of express condition would increase the risk of forfeiture by the obligee (see, Restatement [Second] of Contracts § 227 [1]).

Interpretation as a means of reducing the risk of forfeiture cannot be employed if "the occurrence of the event as a condition is expressed in unmistakable language" (Restatement [Second] of Contracts § 229, comment a, at 185; see, § 227, comment b [where language is clear, "(t)he policy favoring freedom of contract requires that, within broad limits, the agreement of the parties should be honored even though forfeiture results"]). Nonetheless, the nonoccurrence of the condition may yet be excused by waiver, breach or forfeiture. The Restatement posits that "[t]o the extent that the non-occurrence of a condition would cause disproportionate forfeiture, a court may excuse the non-occurrence of that condition unless its occurrence was a material part of the agreed exchange" (Restatement [Second] of Contracts § 229).

Turning to the case at bar, it is undisputed that the critical language of paragraph 4(c) of the letter agreement unambiguously establishes an express condition precedent rather than a promise, as the parties employed the unmistakable language of condition ("if," "unless and until"). There is no doubt of the parties' intent and no occasion for interpreting the terms of the letter agreement other than as written.

Furthermore, plaintiff has never argued, and does not now contend, that the nonoccurrence of the condition set forth in paragraph 4(c) should be excused on the ground of forfeiture.[2] Rather, plaintiff's primary argument from the inception of this litigation has been that defendant waived or was equitably estopped from invoking paragraph 4(c). Plaintiff argued secondarily

---

2. The Restatement defines the term "forfeiture" as "the denial of compensation that results when the obligee loses [its] right to the agreed exchange after [it] has relied substan- tially, as by preparation or performance on the expectation of that exchange" (§ 229, comment b).

that it substantially complied with the express condition of delivery of written notice on or before February 25th in that it gave defendant oral notice of consent on the 25th.

Contrary to the decision of the Court below, we perceive no justifiable basis for applying the doctrine of substantial performance to the facts of this case. The flexible concept of substantial compliance "stands in sharp contrast to the requirement of strict compliance that protects a party that has taken the precaution of making its duty expressly conditional" (2 Farnsworth, Contracts § 8.12, at 415 [2d ed 1990]). If the parties "have made an event a condition of their agreement, there is no mitigating standard of materiality or substantiality applicable to the non-occurrence of that event" (Restatement [Second] of Contracts § 237, comment d, at 220). Substantial performance in this context is not sufficient, "and if relief is to be had under the contract, it must be through excuse of the non-occurrence of the condition to avoid forfeiture" (id.; see, Brown–Marx Assocs. v. Emigrant Sav. Bank, 703 F.2d 1361, 1367–1368 [11th Cir.]; see also, Childres, Conditions in the Law of Contracts, 45 NYU L.Rev. 33, 35).

Here, it is undisputed that plaintiff has not suffered a forfeiture or conferred a benefit upon defendant. Plaintiff alludes to a $1 million licensing fee it allegedly paid to the prime landlord for the purpose of securing the latter's consent to the subleasing of the premises. At no point, however, does plaintiff claim that this sum was forfeited or that it was expended for the purpose of accomplishing the sublease with defendant. It is further undisputed that O & Y, as an inducement to effect plaintiff's move to the World Financial Center, promised to indemnify plaintiff for damages resulting from failure to sublease the 33rd floor of One New York Plaza. Consequently, because the critical concern of forfeiture or unjust enrichment is simply not present in this case, we are not presented with an occasion to consider whether the doctrine of substantial performance is applicable, that is, whether the courts should intervene to excuse the nonoccurrence of a condition precedent to the formation of a contract.

The essence of the Appellate Division's holding is that the substantial performance doctrine is universally applicable to all categories of breach of contract, including the nonoccurrence of an express condition precedent. However, as discussed, substantial performance is ordinarily not applicable to excuse the nonoccurrence of an express condition precedent . . .

III.

In sum, the letter agreement provides in the clearest language that the parties did not intend to form a contract "unless and until" defendant received written notice of the prime landlord's consent on or before February 25, 1987. Defendant would lease the 33rd floor from plaintiff only on the condition that the landlord consent in writing to a telephone communication linkage system between the 29th and 33rd floors and to defendant's plans for construction effectuating that linkage. This matter was sufficiently important to defendant that it would not enter into the sublease "unless and until" the condition was satisfied. Inasmuch as we are not dealing here with a situation where plaintiff stands to suffer some forfeiture or undue hardship, we perceive no justification for engaging in a "materiality-of-the-nonoccurrence" analysis. To do so would simply frustrate the clearly expressed intention of the parties. Freedom of contract prevails in an arm's length transaction between sophisticated parties such as these, and in the absence of countervailing public policy concerns there is no reason to relieve them of the consequences of their bargain. If they are dissatisfied with the consequences of their agreement, "the time to say so [was] at the bargaining table" [Maxton Bldrs. v. Lo Galbo, 68 N.Y.2d 373, 509 N.Y.S.2d 507, 502 N.E.2d 184].

Finally, the issue of substantial performance was not for the jury to resolve in this case. A determination whether there has been substantial performance is to be answered, "if the inferences are certain, by the judges of the law" (Jacob & Youngs v. Kent, 230 N.Y. 239, 243, 129 N.E. 889 supra).

Accordingly, the order of the Appellate Division should be reversed, with costs, and the complaint dismissed.

Chief Judge KAYE, C.J., and Judges SIMONS, TITONE, BELLACOSA, SMITH and LEVINE, JJ., concur.

Order reversed, etc.

MERRITT HILL VINEYARDS, INC. v. WINDY HEIGHTS VINEYARD, INC.

Court of Appeals of New York, 1984.
61 N.Y.2d 106, 472 N.Y.S.2d 592, 460 N.E.2d 1077.

KAYE, JUDGE.

. . .

In September, 1981, plaintiff, Merritt Hill Vineyards, entered into a written agreement with defendants, Windy Heights Vineyard and its sole shareholder Leon Taylor, to purchase a majority stock interest in respondents' Yates County vineyard, and tendered a $15,000 deposit. The agreement provides that "[i]f the sale contemplated hereby does not close, Taylor shall retain the deposit as liquidated damages unless Taylor or Windy Heights failed to satisfy the conditions specified in Section 3 thereof." Section 3, in turn, lists several "conditions precedent" to which the obligation of purchaser to pay the purchase price and to complete the purchase is subject. Among the conditions are that, by the time of the closing, Windy Heights shall have obtained a title insurance policy in a form satisfactory to Merritt Hill, and Windy Heights and Merritt Hill shall have received confirmation from the Farmers Home Administration that certain mortgages on the vineyard are in effect and that the proposed sale does not constitute a default.

In April, 1982, at the closing, plaintiff discovered that neither the policy nor the confirmation had been issued. Plaintiff thereupon refused to close and demanded return of its deposit. When defendants did not return the deposit, plaintiff instituted this action, asserting two causes of action, one for return of the deposit, and one for approximately $26,000 in consequential damages allegedly suffered as a result of defendants' failure to perform.

Special Term denied plaintiff's motion for summary judgment on both causes of action. The Appellate Division unanimously reversed Special Term's order, granted plaintiff's motion for summary judgment as to the cause of action for return of the deposit, and . . . granted summary judgment in favor of defendants, dismissing plaintiff's second cause of action for consequential damages. Both plaintiff and defendants appealed from that decision. . . .

. . . [P]laintiff's right to return of its deposit or to consequential damages depends upon whether the undertaking to produce the policy and mortgage confirmation is a promise or a condition.

A promise is "a manifestation of intention to act or refrain from acting in a specified way, so made as to justify a promisee in understanding that a commitment has been made." (Restatement, Contracts 2d, § 2, subd. [1].) A *condition,* by comparison, is "an event, not certain to occur, which must occur, unless its non-occurrence is excused, before performance under a contract becomes due." (Restatement, Contracts 2d, § 224.) Here, the contract requirements of a title insurance policy and mortgage confirmation are expressed as conditions of plaintiff's performance rather than as promises by defendants. The requirements are contained in a section of the agreement entitled "Conditions Precedent to Purchaser's Obligation to Close," which provides that plaintiff's obligation to pay the purchase price and complete the purchase of the vineyard is "subject to" fulfillment of those requirements. No words of promise are employed.* Defendants' agreement to sell the stock of the vineyard, not those conditions, was the promise by defendants for which plaintiff's promise to pay the purchase price was exchanged.

Defendants' failure to fulfill the conditions of section 3 entitles plaintiff to a return of its deposit but not to consequential damages. While a contracting party's failure to fulfill a condition excuses performance by the other party whose performance is so conditioned, it is not, without an independent promise to perform the condition, a breach of contract subjecting the nonfulfilling party to liability for damages (Restatement, Contracts 2d, § 225, subds. [1], [3]; 3A Corbin, Contracts, § 663; 5 Williston, Contracts [Jaeger–3d ed.], § 665). This is in accord with the parties' expressed intent, for section 1 of their agreement provides that if defendants fail to satisfy the conditions of section 3 plaintiff's deposit will not be returned. It does not provide for payment of damages.

On the merits of this case the Appellate Division thus correctly determined that plaintiff was entitled to the return of its deposit but not to consequential damages.

Accordingly, the order of the Appellate Division should be affirmed.

COOKE, C.J., and JASEN, JONES, WACHTLER and MEYER, JJ., concur.

SIMONS, J., taking no part.

Order affirmed, without costs.

---

* Plaintiff contends that the failure to produce the policy and confirmation is also a breach of section 5, entitled "Representations, Warranties and Agreements." A provision may be both a condition and a promise, if the parties additionally promise to perform a condition as part of their bargain. Such a promise is not present here. The only provision of section 5 conceivably relevant is that "Windy Heights has good and marketable title to the Property and all other properties and assets * * * as of December 31, 1980". But this is quite different from the conditions of section 3 that a title insurance policy and mortgage confirmation be produced at the closing, which took place in April, 1982. Both the complaint and plaintiff's affidavits are premised on nonperformance of section 3 of the agreement, not section 5. [Footnote by the court.]

SECTION 3. CONDITIONS PRECEDENT AND CONDITIONS SUBSEQUENT

NOTE ON THE DISTINCTION BETWEEN CONDITIONS PRECEDENT AND CONDITIONS SUBSEQUENT

Conditions may be classified as *precedent, subsequent,* and *concurrent.* For the time being it will be well to set concurrent conditions to one side, and to examine the distinction between conditions precedent and conditions subsequent. (The former term is, incidentally, pronounced pre-CEE-dent, not PRESS-i-dent.)

In general, the distinction between these two kinds of conditions is conventionally stated in terms like the following: Where some designated state of affairs must occur or fail to occur *before* a party to a contract comes under a duty to perform, the condition is *precedent.* Where, on the other hand, the party has *already* come under a duty to perform, and will be *relieved* from that duty by the occurrence or nonoccurrence of some designated state of affairs, the condition is *subsequent.* A duty to perform *arises* when a condition precedent is satisfied; a duty to perform is *discharged* when a condition subsequent is triggered.

The standard illustrations of this distinction involve provisions commonly contained in insurance policies. One common provision in life-insurance policies is that the insurance company will not be liable under the policy unless proof of death is made within a designated period—say ninety days after death. This condition would ordinarily be described as *precedent,* since the company does not come under a duty to pay until the proof of death has been presented (or a legal excuse for failure to present the proof has been established). Another common provision in life-insurance policies is that suit must be brought against the company within a designated period—say, one year from the date of death. Since the running of the year operates to relieve the company from a duty that once existed, this condition would ordinarily be described as *subsequent.*

One may well ask, what actually hinges on the distinction between conditions precedent and conditions subsequent? After all, in practice a case will be decided according to the situation as it exists when suit is brought. In the case of a condition that proof of death be given, we ask, did the plaintiff give the required proof prior to the time suit is brought? Similarly, in the case where suit is required to be bought within a year, we ask, has the plaintiff in fact brought her suit within the year? In the former case, the plaintiff has to give proof of death before he can succeed in his suit. In the latter case, he has to file his complaint within the year in order to succeed. Where, then, is the practical significance distinction between conditions precedent and conditions subsequent?

Holmes answered this question by asserting that no such distinction exists. "When a man sues, the question is not whether he had a cause of action in the past, but whether he has one then." (The Common Law, 1881, p. 317.) Under this view, since a plaintiff's cause of action is judged by the situation existing when he brings his suit, not by what could have happened, all conditions are in reality conditions precedent.

Against this view of Holmes it has been argued that the distinction between conditions precedent and conditions subsequent becomes crucial for certain problems of procedure. For example, suppose a life-insurance policy requires notice of death within ninety days. At least two important sets of procedural questions can arise:

(1) Which party has the burden of *pleading* the facts with respect to this issue? Is the plaintiff's complaint subject to demurrer if he fails to allege that he gave the required notice within ninety days of death? Or is this a matter that must be raised in the defendant's pleadings?

(2) Which party has the burden of *proving* the facts bearing on this issue? Suppose the plaintiff asserts in his pleading that he gave the required notice, and the defendant insurance company denies this allegation, but sets up no other defense to the claim. At the trial, neither party introduces any evidence on this issue. Who gets judgment? Or again, suppose that both parties introduce evidence bearing on the issue, but the trier of fact cannot decide which side is right and considers the evidence evenly balanced? Here the outcome of the litigation will depend upon who has the burden of proof, or, in Wigmore's phrase, "the risk of non-persuasion."

Obviously these procedural issues are of considerable practical importance, and the actual outcome of the litigation may very well depend on them. Against Holmes's view it is therefore asserted that the distinction between conditions precedent and conditions subsequent must be retained because these procedural issues may turn on it. If the condition is precedent, then it is natural to put on the plaintiff the burden of pleading and proof. He has no case unless the condition has occurred; therefore, it is up to him to allege and prove that the condition has been fulfilled. On the other hand, if the condition is subsequent, then the burdens of pleading and proof should fall on the defendant. The defendant is attempting "to get out of something"; it is up to the defendant to show that the state of affairs that will excuse the defendant from liability has occurred.

This makes a persuasive case for retaining the distinction between conditions precedent and conditions subsequent until we ask with more particularity how conditions are actually phrased in a contract, and inquire in greater detail into the process by which courts actually distribute procedural burdens.

As to the actual phrasing of a condition, a provision relating to proof of death within ninety days could be expressed as follows: "In case proof of death is not made within ninety days, this policy shall become void and the company shall be released from all liability thereon." What have we now? The condition is *phrased* in condition-subsequent terms; it speaks of a *release* from liability. On the other hand, the case is not one where the company could once have been sued without the notice and then gains immunity to suit by the failure to give notice.

A common way out of this dilemma is to say that in such cases the condition is *precedent in fact* but *subsequent in form*. But this leaves unresolved the crucial question, what is the effect of such a provision on the burdens of pleading and proof? If the parties have seen fit to phrase the condition in terms of an excuse from liability, is this itself a sufficient reason for placing these burdens on the defendant? Does the form in which the clause is expressed show an intention or attitude that makes it appropriate to treat the defendant *as if* it were getting out of something?

The example just given shows that a provision normally regarded as a condition precedent can be put in the form of a condition subsequent. In the same way, a standard illustration of a condition subsequent can easily be put in precedent form: "It shall be a condition precedent to the liability of the company under this policy that suit thereon shall be brought within one year of the insured's death." Here again it is easy to say that this is a condition subsequent in fact although precedent in form. Once again, however, this leaves unresolved the only practical question involved, that is, the manner in which the burdens of pleading and proof are to be allocated in the case of such a condition.

Looking more closely at the considerations that have actually determined the distribution of these burdens, it is apparent that neither the form nor the substance of the distinction between conditions precedent and conditions subsequent is necessarily controlling. The problem is one of forensic fairness and convenience. In resolving that problem, factors in addition to those discussed above are frequently and properly given weight by courts and legislatures. For example, statutes or rules of court very commonly relieve the plaintiff from the burden of pleading the satisfaction of condition, without regard to whether the condition is described as precedent or subsequent. Thus Rule 3015(a) of the New York Civil Practice Law and Rules provides that, "The performance or occurrence of a condition precedent in a contract need not be pleaded. A denial of performance or occurrence shall be made specifically and with particularity. In case of such denial, the party relying on the performance or occurrence shall be required to prove on the trial only such performance or occurrence as shall have been so specified." The effect of this provision is to place the burden of pleading on the defendant. If the defendant wishes to raise the issue of the satisfaction of a particular condition precedent, it must allege that the condition was not satisfied.

Enactments like New York Rule 3015(a) owe their existence in part to the fact that contract suits are now often based on long, printed, standardized documents, the terms of which are not negotiated, but instead are imposed by one party on the other, the most familiar example being the insurance policy. Such contracts customarily contain a long list of conditions that limit the liability of the party who drafted the contract. To require the plaintiff to allege in detail satisfaction of all of these conditions would not only encumber the record needlessly, but would impose on the plaintiff's attorney the difficult task of seeing to it that every allegation in the complaint corresponds to the terms of the contract concerning each separate condition.

As to the burden of proof, as distinguished from the burden of pleading, reforms through statutes or rules of court are less common and the situation is more complicated. However, applying the principles that have generally been developed for the allocation of this burden, it is safe to say that the following factors would influence the determination of this question:

(1) Whether the condition is phrased in terms of an event relieving a party from a duty, or in terms of an event that must occur before a duty arises.

(2) Whether placing the burden on one party will require him to prove a negative fact (something did *not* happen). In such a case, the burden of proof may be placed on the other party, who will be asked to prove that the fact *did* happen. This conclusion is often grounded on the theory that an affirmative is easier to prove than a negative.

(3) Whether the fact is peculiarly within the knowledge of one party. In such a case, the burden of proof may for this reason be placed on that party.

(4) Whether the contract is a standardized form, not really negotiated, but dictated by one party to the other. This may itself furnish a reason for imposing procedural burdens on the party who drafted the agreement.

(5) There is also a consideration of symmetry, according to which the burden of proof ought to follow the burden of pleading unless there is some reason for allocating the two burdens differently.

(6) There is, finally, the question whether the condition was "in fact" precedent or subsequent, that is, whether the case is one where no suit could be brought until the event occurred, or a case where suit was once possible and the question is whether an event has occurred that extinguished a duty the defendant once had.

As Wigmore has stated, none of these factors is in any sense controlling; "There is not and cannot be any general solvent" for the problem of allocating the burdens of pleading and proof. When all of these factors are taken into account, the distinction between conditions precedent and conditions subsequent may not entirely disappear, but it is certainly greatly diminished in significance.

FEDERAL RULES OF CIVIL PROCEDURE, RULE 9(c): "Conditions precedent. In pleading the performance or occurrence of conditions precedent, it is sufficient to aver generally that all conditions precedent have been performed or have occurred. A denial of performance or occurrence shall be made specifically and with particularity."

SECTION 4. PROBLEMS OF INTERPRETATION IN DISTINGUISHING BETWEEN CONDITIONS AND PROMISES

HOWARD v. FEDERAL CROP INSURANCE CORP.

United States Court of Appeals, Fourth Circuit, 1976.
540 F.2d 695.

Before RUSSELL, FIELD and WIDENER, CIRCUIT JUDGES.

WIDENER, CIRCUIT JUDGE:

Plaintiff-appellants sued to recover for losses to their 1973 tobacco crop due to alleged rain damage. The crops were insured by defendant-appellee,

Federal Crop Insurance Corporation (FCIC). Suits were brought in a state court in North Carolina and removed to the United States District Court. The three suits are not distinguishable factually so far as we are concerned here and involve identical questions of law. They were combined for disposition in the district court and for appeal. The district court granted summary judgment for the defendant and dismissed all three actions. We remand for further proceedings. Since we find for the plaintiffs as to the construction of the policy, we express no opinion on the procedural questions.

Federal Crop Insurance Corporation, an agency of the United States, in 1973, issued three policies to the Howards, insuring their tobacco crops, to be grown on six farms, against weather damage and other hazards.

The Howards (plaintiffs) established production of tobacco on their acreage, and have alleged that their 1973 crop was extensively damaged by heavy rains, resulting in a gross loss to the three plaintiffs in excess of $35,000. The plaintiffs harvested and sold the depleted crop and timely filed notice and proof of loss with FCIC, but, prior to inspection by the adjuster for FCIC, the Howards had either plowed or disked under the tobacco fields in question to prepare the same for sowing a cover crop of rye to preserve the soil. When the FCIC adjuster later inspected the fields, he found the stalks had been largely obscured or obliterated by plowing or disking and denied the claims, apparently on the ground that the plaintiffs had violated a portion of the policy which provides that the stalks on any acreage with respect to which a loss is claimed shall not be destroyed until the corporation makes an inspection.

The holding of the district court is best capsuled in its own words:

"The inquiry here is whether compliance by the insureds with this provision of the policy was a condition precedent to the recovery. The court concludes that it was and that the failure of the insureds to comply worked a forfeiture of benefits for the alleged loss."

. . . Paragraph 5 of the tobacco endorsement is entitled *Claims*. Pertinent to this case are subparagraphs 5(b) and 5(f), which are as follows:

"5(b) *It shall be a condition precedent* to the payment of any loss that the insured establish the production of the insured crop on a unit and that such loss has been directly caused by one or more of the hazards insured against during the insurance period for the crop year for which the loss is claimed, and furnish any other information regarding the manner and extent of loss as may be required by the Corporation. (Emphasis added)"

"5(f) The tobacco stalks on any acreage of tobacco of types 11a, 11b, 12, 13, or 14 with respect to which a loss is claimed *shall not be destroyed until the Corporation makes an inspection.* (Emphasis added)"

The arguments of both parties are predicated upon the same two assumptions. First, if subparagraph 5(f) creates a condition precedent, its violation caused a forfeiture of plaintiffs' coverage. Second, if subparagraph 5(f) creates an obligation (variously called a promise or covenant) upon plaintiffs not to plow under the tobacco stalks, defendant may recover from plaintiffs (either in an original action, or, in this case, by a counterclaim, or as a matter of defense) for whatever damage it sustained because of the elimination of the stalks. However, a violation of subparagraph 5(f) would not, under the second premise, standing alone, cause a forfeiture of the policy.

Generally accepted law provides us with guidelines here. There is a general legal policy opposed to forfeitures. *United States v. One Ford Coach,* 307 U.S. 219, 226, 59 S.Ct. 861, 83 L.Ed. 1249 (1939); *Baca v. Commissioner of Internal Revenue,* 326 F.2d 189, 191 (5th Cir.1963). Insurance policies are generally construed most strongly against the insurer. *Henderson v. Hartford Accident & Indemnity Co.,* 268 N.C. 129, 150 S.E.2d 17, 19 (1966). When it is doubtful whether words create a promise or a condition precedent, they will be construed as creating a promise. *Harris and Harris Const. Co. v. Crain and Denbo, Inc.,* 256 N.C. 110, 123 S.E.2d 590, 595 (1962). The provisions of a contract will not be construed as conditions precedent in the absence of language plainly requiring such construction. *Harris,* 123 S.E.2d at 596. And *Harris,* at 123 S.E.2d 590, 595, cites *Jones v. Palace Realty Co.,* 226 N.C. 303, 37 S.E.2d 906 (1946), and *Restatement of the Law, Contracts,* § 261.

Plaintiffs rely most strongly upon the fact that the term "condition precedent" is included in subparagraph 5(b) but not in subparagraph 5(f). It is true that whether a contract provision is construed as a condition or an obligation does not depend entirely upon whether the word "condition" is expressly used. Appleman, *Insurance Law and Practice* (1972), vol. 6A, § 4144. However, the persuasive force of plaintiffs' argument in this case is found in the use of the term "condition precedent" in subparagraph 5(b) but not in subparagraph 5(f). Thus, it is argued that the ancient maxim to be applied is that the expression of one thing is the exclusion of another....

The *Restatement [First] of the Law of Contracts* states:

"§ 261. INTERPRETATION OF DOUBTFUL WORDS AS PROMISE OR CONDITION.

Where it is doubtful whether words create a promise or an express condition, they are interpreted as creating a promise; but the same words may sometimes mean that one party promises a performance and that the other party's promise is conditional on that performance."

Two illustrations (one involving a promise, the other a condition) are used in the *Restatement:*

"2. A, an insurance company, issues to B a policy of insurance containing promises by A that are in terms conditional on the happening of certain events. The policy contains this clause: 'provided, in case differences shall arise touching any loss, *the matter shall be submitted to impartial arbitrators,* whose award shall be binding on the parties.' This is a promise to arbitrate and does not make an award a condition precedent of the insurer's duty to pay.

3. A, an insurance company, issues to B an insurance policy in usual form containing this clause: 'In the event of disagreement as to the amount of loss it shall be ascertained by two appraisers and an umpire. The loss shall *not be payable until 60 days after the award of the appraisers when such an appraisal is required.*' This provision is not merely a promise to arbitrate differences but makes an award a condition of the insurer's duty to pay in case of disagreement." (Emphasis added)

We believe that subparagraph 5(f) in the policy here under consideration fits illustration 2 rather than illustration 3. Illustration 2 specifies something to be done, whereas subparagraph 5(f) specifies something not to be done.

Unlike illustration 3, subparagraph 5(f) does not state any conditions under which the insurance shall "not be payable," or use any words of like import. We hold that the district court erroneously held, on the motion for summary judgment, that subparagraph 5(f) established a condition precedent to plaintiffs' recovery which forfeited the coverage.

From our holding that defendant's motion for summary judgment was improperly allowed, it does not follow the plaintiffs' motion for summary judgment should have been granted, for if subparagraph 5(f) be not construed as a condition precedent, there are other questions of fact to be determined. At this point, we merely hold that the district court erred in holding, on the motion for summary judgment, that subparagraph 5(f) constituted a condition precedent with resulting forfeiture.

The explanation defendant makes for including subparagraph 5(f) in the tobacco endorsement is that it is necessary that the stalks remain standing in order for the Corporation to evaluate the extent of loss and to determine whether loss resulted from some cause not covered by the policy. However, was subparagraph 5(f) inserted because without it the Corporation's opportunities for proof would be more difficult, or because they would be impossible? Plaintiffs point out that the Tobacco Endorsement, with subparagraph 5(f), was adopted in 1970, and crop insurance goes back long before that date. Nothing is shown as to the Corporation's prior 1970 practice of evaluating losses. Such a showing might have a bearing upon establishing defendant's intention in including 5(f). Plaintiffs state, and defendant does not deny, that another division of the Department of Agriculture, or the North Carolina Department, urged that tobacco stalks be cut as soon as possible after harvesting as a means of pest control. Such an explanation might refute the idea that plaintiffs plowed under the stalks for any fraudulent purpose. Could these conflicting directives affect the reasonableness of plaintiffs' interpretation of defendant's prohibition upon plowing under the stalks prior to adjustment?

We express no opinion on these questions because they were not before the district court and are mentioned to us largely by way of argument rather than from the record. No question of ambiguity was raised in the court below or here and no question of the applicability of paragraph 5(c) to this case was alluded to other than in the defendant's pleadings, so we also do not reach those questions. Nothing we say here should preclude FCIC from asserting as a defense that the plowing or disking under of the stalks caused damage to FCIC if, for example, the amount of the loss was thereby made more difficult or impossible to ascertain whether the plowing or disking under was done with bad purpose or innocently. To repeat, our narrow holding is that merely plowing or disking under the stalks does not of itself operate to forfeit coverage under the policy.

The case is remanded for further proceedings not inconsistent with this opinion.

VACATED AND REMANDED.

HARMON CABLE COMMUNICATIONS v. SCOPE CABLE TELE-VISION, 237 Neb. 871, 468 N.W.2d 350 (1991). Under a purchase agreement for the sale of a cable–television system, sellers agreed to indemnify the purchaser if a minimum number of persons were not subscribers to the system at the time of the closing. The agreement also provided that "[purchaser] shall assert any claim or claims for indemnification ... by giving written notice of such claim or claims to seller within 30 days of discovery, but not later than 18 months from the date of closing." There was a subscriber shortfall, but the purchaser failed to comply with the notice provision, and the sellers contended that the purchaser could not recover damages resulting from the shortfall because the notice provision was a condition. The trial court granted summary judgment for the purchaser. Affirmed.

"Whether the sellers' contention ... has merit depends upon whether [the notice] provisions are conditional or promissory. Courts have struggled for centuries with differentiating between conditions and promises. See, e.g., Constable v. Cloberie, Palmer 397 (1626).... A condition has been defined as 'an operative fact, one on which the existence of some particular legal relation depends.' 3A A. Corbin, Corbin on Contracts § 627 at 11 (1960)....

"A promise, on the other hand, occurs when one 'expresses an intention that some future performance will be rendered and gives assurance of its rendition to the promisee.' 3A A. Corbin, supra, § 633 at 25.... In the event of nonfulfillment, the distinction between a promise and a condition becomes important. As a general rule, a condition must be exactly fulfilled before liability can arise on the contract....

"Nonfulfillment of a promise, however, gives rise to a different remedy. 'The nonfulfillment of a promise is called a breach of contract, and *creates in the other party a secondary right to damages*; it is the failure to perform that which was required by a legal duty.' ...

"Thus, if the notice requirements of the indemnification paragraphs are deemed to be a condition to the sellers' liability, the purchaser's noncompliance would discharge the sellers' liability. If the notice requirements are deemed to be a promise, then the remedy lies in an action for damages.

"Whether contractual language is deemed conditional or promissory generally depends upon the intention of the parties.... Where the intent of the parties is not clear, the disputed language is generally deemed to be promissory rather than conditional.... Howard v. Federal Crop Ins. Corp., 540 F.2d 695 (4th Cir.1976). Terms such as 'if,' 'provided that,' 'when,' 'after,' 'as soon as,' 'subject to,' 'on condition that,' or some similar phrase are evidence that performance of a contractual provision is a condition....

"... [U]nder the state of this record, the absence of any language indicative of a condition precludes a conclusion that the parties clearly intended the notice requirements to constitute a condition to the creation of the contract. They therefore are promises, the breach of which gives rise to an action for damages."

RESTATEMENT, SECOND, CONTRACTS § 227

[See Selected Source Materials Supplement]

SECTION 5. CONDITIONS OF COOPERATION; PREVENTION; THE IMPLICATION OF A PROMISE FROM AN EXPRESS CONDITION

VANADIUM CORP. v. FIDELITY & DEPOSIT CO.

Circuit Court of Appeals, Second Circuit, 1947.
159 F.2d 105.

CLARK, CIRCUIT JUDGE. This action against a surety on a bond securing performance of a contract of sale of mining leases was originally brought in the Supreme Court of the State of New York and came to the district court below through removal by defendant because of the diverse citizenship of the parties. The principal on the bond, Horace Ray Redington, then intervened as a party defendant. Since the contract of sale was not completed, plaintiff vendee by its terms became entitled to repayment of the consideration paid in advance of $13,000, unless its own acts justified defendants' refusal to make the refund. Accordingly the issues below concerned the defenses raised by defendants that plaintiff had refused that co-operation required by law in obtaining completion of the contract. These defenses, three in number, were upheld as legally sufficient by the District Court against attack by motions before and after verdict and by requests to charge. The jury having found for defendants, this appeal from the resulting judgment brings the issues of the validity of the defenses before us.

The two original mining leases were made in 1939 and 1940 to three lessees, John F. Wade, Thomas F. V. Curran, and Redington, and covered various lands belonging to the Navajo tribe of Indians in the Navajo Reservation in Arizona. The lands produced vanadium-bearing ore, vanadium being a critical war material. Since Indian lands were involved, all transfers required the approval of the Secretary of the Interior. 25 U.S.C.A. § 396a et seq.; 25 CFR § 186.26. The contract here in question was made by Redington with plaintiff on June 3, 1942. By it, in return for the payment of $13,000 which he acknowledged, Redington assigned to plaintiff his interest in the two leases, "subject only to approval by the Secretary of Interior." It also contained a provision that in the event the assignments were not approved, Redington would repay the purchase price and the agreement would be deemed cancelled. Redington further agreed to furnish a bond with appropriate surety for the return of the money in the event that his assignments "aforesaid shall not be approved by the Secretary of Interior of the United States within a period of six (6) months from the date hereof." At the same time Redington executed formal assignments of his interests in the leases, and he and the corporate defendant executed the bond in suit. By the latter the principal and surety bound themselves to return all amounts paid Redington "under protection of this bond." It also provided that plaintiff should be held harmless against all loss or damage arising "by reason of any invalidation of this purchase agreement."

From the beginning, however, it appears that the stumbling block was the unwillingness of the other two owners to go along with plaintiff's plans.

But plaintiff was not in the dark as to this situation; while it held only an option from, and before closing with, Redington, it had approached the other owners for a purchase of their interest, and had been refused. After taking the assignments from Redington, plaintiff tried to reopen negotiations with the others, either for purchase or for joint operations of the mines; but its proposals were again repulsed. Under date of June 7, 1942, Curran notified it that Wade, acting for all the owners, had made a contract with the Metals Reserve Corporation (a government corporation) for the entire output of ore from the properties for the duration of the war. Curran added that they would do all possible to get the largest possible tonnage from the leases, on their contract with the Metals Reserve Corporation, and "will welcome any aid you may give that will promote this end." It is defendants' contention that this information as to the prior right of the Metals Reserve Corporation to the output caused plaintiff's desire for the Redington interests to cool; and this disposal of the output obviously ran counter to plaintiff's program of securing a large flow of ore to a government-financed processing plant at Monticello, Utah, being built for operation by plaintiff on a fee basis. Plaintiff denies any lack of co-operation, calling attention to its general offers otherwise appearing as late as August 28, 1942, in a letter of that date to the Assistant Commissioner of Indian Affairs. But so far as an issue of fact was presented, that was resolved by the jury against the plaintiff.

Actually the proof adequately supported the allegations of fact of all the defenses. These were, first, that plaintiff refused reasonable assurances to the Department of an intent to co-operate with Curran and Wade in an amicable operation of the mines; second, that prior to November 18, 1942, it withdrew its request for approval of the assignments and caused the Department to withhold approval; and third, that after November 18, it prevented reconsideration of the disapproval already made. Thus when the Assistant Commissioner notified plaintiff by letter of September 4 of the official intent to disapprove the assignments because of plaintiff's failure to work out an operating agreement with Curran and Wade, plaintiff's immediate reaction was to perfect its rights against the surety by formal demand upon the latter and by request to the Department for final certification of the Secretary's disapproval. True, it acknowledged the communication from the Assistant Commissioner by letter of September 8; but this, like other acts of the plaintiff during the period, was subject to various interpretations, depending upon the background. For in this acknowledgment it expressed regret at the withholding of approval, since it had hoped to increase production of vanadium ore by "our co-operation" with the owners of the leases and that the maximum amount of ore would be removed from the claims, tendered "any assistance that we may properly offer to accomplish that end," and closed by stating that it was "immediately notifying" Redington and taking steps to secure the return of funds it had advanced. Further, there was evidence that in October it refused to give the assurances desired by the Department of its intent to co-operate with the other owners, but indeed went so far as to tell the General Superintendent of the Navajo Service in Arizona of its lack of further interest in the assignments. Accordingly the Assistant Secretary of the Interior, acting on a recommendation from the office of the Department Solicitor reciting that the officers of plaintiff had stated that they were no longer interested in obtaining the assignments, formally disapproved the assignments November 18, 1942.

The evidence is yet more direct on the issue that plaintiff prevented reconsideration of the disapproval after November 18, 1942. Here plaintiff's position is that its rights became fixed on that date and that later reconsideration could not affect them. It is not contested that the Assistant Secretary, on the appeal of Redington and his counsel, was prepared to reconsider the matter if the plaintiff would go along, and so wired plaintiff's president on November 28, saying that the disapproval was "being reconsidered with view to approving assignments. Wire your position," to which plaintiff's answer, November 30, was, "Our position therefore must be to respectfully request no reconsideration of your position." And so the Assistant Secretary on December 3 notified the parties that without "a joint request for reconsideration by both parties to the assignment," no further consideration could be given the matter. Plaintiff now argues that it understood the original assignments and contract to be dead, and hence was refusing merely to enter into an entirely new contract, not interfering with approval of those assignments or preventing fulfillment of the original conditions. But this seems only a different verbalization of its same argument that the time period granted for performance in the contract must be further restricted by an earlier disapproval by the Secretary. Of course it overlooks completely the Assistant Secretary's explicit statement that the action *disapproving* the Redington *assignments* was being reconsidered with a view to approval.

On the record, therefore, there seems to be no doubt of the plaintiff's complete disinterest in the Redington assignments at this time. But clearly it is in error in asserting that the rights of the parties became finally fixed on November 18, 1942. For the explicit provision of the contract, calling for the bond here in question, required only refund of the consideration if the Secretary did not approve within six months, i.e., by December 3, 1942. Nothing is said to suggest that the period is shortened by an earlier notice of disapproval. Particularly under the circumstances here where the Secretary was prepared to reconsider, it would be harsh to add to the contract such a provision which the parties themselves did not choose to incorporate in it. The District Court was correct in considering the third defense as on the same plane as the others.

The question therefore is reduced to that of the extent of plaintiff's legal duty in the premises. Professor Williston says that "wherever the cooperation of the promisee is necessary for the performance of the promise, there is a condition implied in fact that the cooperation will be given." 3 Williston on Contracts, Rev.Ed.1936, § 887A, p. 2495. See to the same effect, § 677, p. 1956; 2 Restatement, Contracts, 1932, § 395, comment c. Here an obligation to attempt in good faith to secure the prerequisite of the Secretary's approval would appear to rest upon both parties.... Indeed plaintiff may well have the heavier burden, for, as its counsel contended at the trial, it seems that the assignee must file the assignment for approval and apparently no one else can legally do so. It was surely not the intent of the parties when they made an apparently binding assignment that the plaintiff should have the power to invalidate the assignment by not filing it for approval. On the contrary, it must have been assumed that plaintiff would seasonably file it and in good faith seek its approval. Silverman v. Isaac Goldmann Realty Corp., 232 App.Div. 292, 249 N.Y.S. 505. And plainly plaintiff was obligated to refrain from positive actions to prevent approval by the Secretary. Patterson v. Meyerhofer, 204 N.Y. 96, 97 N.E. 472; Carns v. Bassick, 187 App.Div. 280, 175

N.Y.S. 670; Irving Trust Co. v. Park & Tilford Import Corp., 250 App.Div. 570, 294 N.Y.S. 822. Hence on the facts, as the jury could and did find them, the defendants' contractual duty herein was discharged by plaintiff's breach of a condition precedent. 2 Restatement, Contracts, 1932, § 395.

The court's denial of the plaintiff's various motions and requests to charge and its submission of the case to the jury with a brief, but adequate, charge were therefore without error. . . .

Affirmed.

———

WINSLOW v. MELL, 48 Wash.2d 581, 295 P.2d 319 (1956). Plaintiff alleged that defendant had broken a contract to finance plaintiff's logging operation on (1) 200 acres of timberland owned by defendant, and (2) an adjoining tract owned by Crown Zellerbach, provided that defendant obtained the timber rights on that tract. At the trial, plaintiff failed to show that defendant had obtained timber rights on the Crown Zellerbach tract. Held, the jury should not have been permitted to consider the claim based on that tract. "The appellant's promise that the respondent could also log the Crown Zellerbach tract was conditioned upon appellant's acquisition of the timber rights. There was no duty on the part of the appellant to acquire the Crown Zellerbach timber so that respondent might log it. Its acquisition was at appellant's option or pleasure."

———

LACH v. CAHILL, 138 Conn. 418, 85 A.2d 481 (1951). Lach signed an agreement with Cahill to purchase Cahill's house for $18,000, and paid a deposit of $1,000. The contract contained the following provision: "This agreement is contingent upon buyer being able to obtain mortgage in the sum of $12,000 on the premises. . . ." Lach then applied to six banks for a $12,000 mortgage, but was denied. thereafter, Lach wrote to Cahill that he was unable to secure a mortgage in the amount of $12,000, and requested the return of the deposit. Cahill offered to take back a purchase–money mortgage payable on demand, or to obtain a mortgage from another person, but he specified no terms. Lach had already made a deposit on another house, and declined Cahill's offer. Lach then sued for the return of his deposit. The trial court held for Lach. Affirmed.

" . . . The decisive issues in the case are whether the ability of the plaintiff to secure a $12,000 mortgage was a condition precedent to his duty to perform his promise to purchase and whether he made a reasonable effort to secure the mortgage.

"The . . . language used, read in the light of the situation of the parties, expressed an intention that the plaintiff should not be held to an agreement to purchase unless he could secure a mortgage for $12,000 on reasonable terms as to the amount and time of instalment payments.

"The condition in the contract implied a promise by the plaintiff that he would make reasonable efforts to secure a suitable mortgage. . . . The performance or nonperformance of this implied promise was a matter for the determination of the trial court. The conclusion reached upon the facts was proper."

NOTE ON IMPLIED CONDITIONS OF NOTICE

A landlord has agreed with his tenant that he will keep the leased premises in repair. The ceiling falls into disrepair, but the tenant does not notify the landlord of its condition. To put a strong case, it may be supposed that the landlord has reserved no right to enter and inspect the premises, so that his only source of information concerning their condition is through the tenant. Not knowing of the need for repairs, the landlord does nothing about the ceiling. The ceiling then falls on the tenant's piano, damaging it badly. The tenant sues the landlord for the loss. The landlord defends on the ground that he knew nothing of the need for repairing the ceiling. The tenant replies that the lease contains an absolute promise by the landlord to keep the premises in repair, and says nothing about the necessity for notice. Here, obviously, is an opportunity for the exercise of judicial common sense, which the courts have generally embraced. In cases like that supposed, it would ordinarily be held that there is an implied condition of notice—that is, the landlord will not be liable on his promise to keep the premises in good repair unless and until he has been notified of the need for repairs.

Naturally, this implication will be affected by many factors: whether the state of disrepair was observable from the outside, whether it was a readily foreseeable development when the premises were leased, the degree of control reserved by the landlord over the premises, and so forth. Similar implications of a condition of notice have been made in other situations. See, for example, Bishop v. Eaton, Chapter 12, supra.

SECTION 6. CONDITIONS OF SATISFACTION

INTRODUCTORY NOTE

Often a contract provides that one party, A, need not pay for the performance of the other party, B, unless A is satisfied with the performance. The question then arises whether A may escape liability even though his dissatisfaction, while honest, is unreasonable. In the determination of this question, the following factors would probably be influential:

(1) The language used. Did the contract say, for example, that A must be "personally satisfied," or merely that the performance must be "satisfactory"?

(2) The degree to which it is possible to apply an objective standard to the performance in question. For example, there is a decided difference in this respect between a contract to install a furnace and a contract to paint a

portrait. The inclination to interpret "satisfaction" as the actual personal satisfaction of A would obviously be stronger in the later case.

(3) The degree to which A will be enriched at B's expense if the contract is interpreted to require A's personal satisfaction. If A retains and uses in his house a furnace installed by B, and seeks to escape liability to pay anything for the furnace by declaring that he is not satisfied with its performance, the case would be a very strong one for B. Recovery in B's favor might be supported either on the basis of interpretation—the word "satisfaction" being interpreted to mean satisfaction of a reasonable person—or on the theory that one who has failed to comply with a condition may nevertheless recover the value of the benefit conferred on the other party. The case is less strong for B if he has, for example, painted a portrait under a contract whereby A is not to pay unless he is satisfied, and A refuses to accept the portrait. Here B has lost the value of his own performance, but A has not been enriched.

(4) The degree of forfeiture that will be imposed on B if A escapes liability to pay for B's performance.

The chief lesson that the draftsman should derive from the cases in this field is that even though the words used in the contract may seem clearly to imply that the actual, personal satisfaction of the defendant is a condition to his liability, in certain cases the courts may nevertheless construe the contract to require only such performance as would satisfy a reasonable person.

———

McCARTNEY v. BADOVINAC, 62 Colo. 76, 160 P. 190 (1916). A diamond had been stolen from Mrs. Ragsdale. Her husband, Dr. Ragsdale, accused Mrs. McCartney of the theft. Mr. McCartney then hired Badovinac, a private detective, to investigate the affair. Badovinac was to receive $500 for his services when he had "to the satisfaction of the said McCartney" determined whether the diamond was stolen, and if so, who had taken it. Badovinac's investigations led him to the uncomforting conclusion that Mrs. McCartney had in fact stolen the diamond, and he put his proofs before McCartney. On McCartney's refusal to pay, Badovinac brought suit. The case was tried without a jury. The trial judge found that Badovinac had clearly established that Mrs. McCartney had taken the jewel. McCartney, however, testified on the stand that he was not satisfied that his wife was the thief. Held, McCartney's statement that he is not satisfied is not conclusive of the issue. On these facts the trial judge properly found that McCartney's answers on the stand were "a mere subterfuge and pretext." A judgment for Badovinac was affirmed.

———

MORIN BUILDING PRODUCTS CO. v. BAYSTONE CONSTRUCTION, INC.

United States Court of Appeals, Seventh Circuit, 1983.
717 F.2d 413.

Before Posner and Coffey, Circuit Judges and Fairchild, Senior Circuit Judge.

Posner, Circuit Judge.

This appeal from a judgment for the plaintiff in a diversity suit requires us to interpret Indiana's common law of contracts. General Motors, which is not a party to this case, hired Baystone Construction, Inc., the defendant, to build an addition to a Chevrolet plant in Muncie, Indiana. Baystone hired Morin Building Products Company, the plaintiff, to supply and erect the aluminum walls for the addition. The contract required that the exterior siding of the walls be of "aluminum type 3003, not less than 18 B & S gauge, with a mill finish and stucco embossed surface texture to match finish and texture of existing metal siding." The contract also provided "that all work shall be done subject to the final approval of the Architect or Owner's [General Motors'] authorized agent, and his decision in matters relating to artistic effect shall be final, if within the terms of the Contract Documents"; and that "should any dispute arise as to the quality or fitness of materials or workmanship, the decision as to acceptability shall rest strictly with the Owner, based on the requirement that all work done or materials furnished shall be first class in every respect. What is usual or customary in erecting other buildings shall in no wise enter into any consideration or decision."

Morin put up the walls. But viewed in bright sunlight from an acute angle the exterior siding did not give the impression of having a uniform finish, and General Motors' representative rejected it. Baystone removed Morin's siding and hired another subcontractor to replace it. General Motors approved the replacement siding. Baystone refused to pay Morin the balance of the contract price ($23,000) and Morin brought this suit for the balance, and won.

The only issue on appeal is the correctness of a jury instruction which, after quoting the contractual provisions requiring that the owner (General Motors) be satisfied with the contractor's (Morin's) work, states: "Notwithstanding the apparent finality of the foregoing language, however, the general rule applying to satisfaction in the case of contracts for the construction of commercial buildings is that the satisfaction clause must be determined by objective criteria. Under this standard, the question is not whether the owner was satisfied in fact, but whether the owner, as a reasonable person, should have been satisfied with the materials and workmanship in question." There was much evidence that General Motors' rejection of Morin's exterior siding had been totally unreasonable. Not only was the lack of absolute uniformity in the finish of the walls a seemingly trivial defect given the strictly utilitarian purpose of the building that they enclosed, but it may have been inevitable; "mill finish sheet" is defined in the trade as "sheet having a nonuniform finish which may vary from sheet to sheet and within a sheet, and may not be entirely free from stains or oil." If the instruction was correct, so was the judgment. But if the instruction was incorrect—if the proper standard is not whether a reasonable man would have been satisfied with Morin's exterior siding but whether General Motors' authorized representative in fact was— then there must be a new trial to determine whether he really was dissatisfied, or whether he was not and the rejection therefore was in bad faith.

Some cases hold that if the contract provides that the seller's performance must be to the buyer's satisfaction, his rejection—however unreasonable—of the seller's performance is not a breach of the contract unless the rejection is in bad faith. See, e.g., *Stone Mountain Properties, Ltd. v. Helmer,*

139 Ga.App. 865, 869, 229 S.E.2d 779, 783 (1976). But most cases conform to the position stated in section 228 of the Restatement (Second) of Contracts (1979): if "it is practicable to determine whether a reasonable person in the position of the obligor would be satisfied, an interpretation is preferred under which the condition [that the obligor be satisfied with the obligee's performance] occurs if such a reasonable person in the position of the obligor would be satisfied." See Farnsworth, Contracts 556–59 (1982); Annot., 44 A.L.R.2d 1114, 1117, 1119–20 (1955). *Indiana Tri—City Plaza Bowl, Inc. v. Estate of Glueck,* 422 N.E.2d 670, 675 (Ind.App.1981), consistently with hints in earlier Indiana cases, see *Andis v. Personett,* 108 Ind. 202, 206, 9 N.E. 101, 103 (1886); *Semon, Bache & Co. v. Coppes, Zook & Mutschler Co.,* 35 Ind.App. 351, 355, 74 N.E. 41, 43 (1905), adopts the majority position as the law of Indiana.

We do not understand the majority position to be paternalistic; and paternalism would be out of place in a case such as this, where the subcontractor is a substantial multistate enterprise. The requirement of reasonableness is read into a contract not to protect the weaker party but to approximate what the parties would have expressly provided with respect to a contingency that they did not foresee, if they had foreseen it. Therefore the requirement is not read into every contract, because it is not always a reliable guide to the parties' intentions. In particular, the presumption that the performing party would not have wanted to put himself at the mercy of the paying party's whim is overcome when the nature of the performance contracted for is such that there are no objective standards to guide the court. It cannot be assumed in such a case that the parties would have wanted a court to second-guess the buyer's rejection. So "the reasonable person standard is employed when the contract involves commercial quality, operative fitness, or mechanical utility which other knowledgeable persons can judge.... The standard of good faith is employed when the contract involves personal aesthetics or fancy." *Indiana Tri–City Plaza Bowl, Inc. v. Estate of Glueck, supra,* 422 N.E.2d at 675; see also *Action Engineering v. Martin Marietta Aluminum,* 670 F.2d 456, 460–61 (3d Cir.1982).

We have to decide which category the contract between Baystone and Morin belongs in. The particular in which Morin's aluminum siding was found wanting was its appearance, which may seem quintessentially a matter of "personal aesthetics," or as the contract put it, "artistic effect." But it is easy to imagine situations where this would not be so. Suppose the manager of a steel plant rejected a shipment of pig iron because he did not think the pigs had a pretty shape. The reasonable-man standard would be applied even if the contract had an "acceptability shall rest strictly with the Owner" clause, for it would be fantastic to think that the iron supplier would have subjected his contract rights to the whimsy of the buyer's agent. At the other extreme would be a contract to paint a portrait, the buyer having reserved the right to reject the portrait if it did not satisfy him. Such a buyer wants a portrait that will please him rather than a jury, even a jury of connoisseurs, so the only question would be his good faith in rejecting the portrait. *Gibson v. Cranage,* 39 Mich. 49 (1878).

This case is closer to the first example than to the second. The building for which the aluminum siding was intended was a factory—not usually intended to be a thing of beauty. That aesthetic considerations were decidedly secondary to considerations of function and cost is suggested by the fact that the contract specified mill-finish aluminum, which is unpainted. There is much debate in the record over whether it is even possible to ensure a uniform finish within and among sheets, but it is at least clear that mill finish usually is not uniform. If General Motors and Baystone had wanted a uniform finish they would in all likelihood have ordered a painted siding. Whether Morin's siding achieved a reasonable uniformity amounting to satisfactory commercial quality was susceptible of objective judgment; in the language of the Restatement, a reasonableness standard was "practicable."

But this means only that a requirement of reasonableness would be read into this contract if it contained a standard owner's satisfaction clause, which it did not; and since the ultimate touchstone of decision must be the intent of the parties to the contract we must consider the actual language they used. The contract refers explicitly to "artistic effect," a choice of words that may seem deliberately designed to put the contract in the "personal aesthetics" category whatever an outside observer might think. But the reference appears as number 17 in a list of conditions in a general purpose form contract. And the words "artistic effect" are immediately followed by the qualifying phrase, "if within the terms of the Contract Documents," which suggests that the "artistic effect" clause is limited to contracts in which artistic effect is one of the things the buyer is aiming for; it is not clear that he was here. The other clause on which Baystone relies, relating to the quality or fitness of workmanship and materials, may seem all-encompassing, but it is qualified by the phrase, "based on the requirement that all work done or materials furnished shall be first class in every respect"—and it is not clear that Morin's were not. This clause also was not drafted for this contract; it was incorporated by reference to another form contract (the Chevrolet Division's "Contract General Conditions"), of which it is paragraph 35. We do not disparage form contracts, without which the commercial life of the nation would grind to a halt. But we are left with more than a suspicion that the artistic-effect and quality-fitness clauses in the form contract used here were not intended to cover the aesthetics of a mill-finish aluminum factory wall.

If we are right, Morin might prevail even under the minority position, which makes good faith the only standard but presupposes that the contract conditioned acceptance of performance on the buyer's satisfaction in the particular respect in which he was dissatisfied. Maybe this contract was not intended to allow General Motors to reject the aluminum siding on the basis of artistic effect. It would not follow that the contract put Morin under no obligations whatsoever with regard to uniformity of finish. The contract expressly required it to use aluminum having "a mill finish ... to match finish ... of existing metal siding." The jury was asked to decide whether a reasonable man would have found that Morin had used aluminum sufficiently uniform to satisfy the matching requirement. This was the right standard if, as we believe, the parties would have adopted it had they foreseen this dispute. It is unlikely that Morin intended to bind itself to a higher and perhaps unattainable standard of achieving whatever perfection of matching that General Motors' agent insisted on, or that General Motors would have required Baystone to submit to such a standard. Because it is difficult—maybe impossible—to achieve a uniform finish with mill-finish aluminum, Morin would have been running a considerable risk of rejection if it had agreed to such a condition, and it therefore could have been expected to demand a compensating increase in the contract price. This would have required General Motors to pay a premium to obtain a freedom of action that it could not have thought terribly important, since its objective was not aesthetic. If a uniform finish was important to it, it could have gotten such a finish by specifying painted siding.

All this is conjecture; we do not know how important the aesthetics were to General Motors when the contract was signed or how difficult it really would have been to obtain the uniformity of finish it desired. The fact that General Motors accepted the replacement siding proves little, for there is evidence that the replacement siding produced the same striped effect, when viewed from an acute angle in bright sunlight, that Morin's had. When in doubt on a difficult issue of state law it is only prudent to defer to the view of the district judge, *Murphy v. White Hen Pantry Co.*, 691 F.2d 350, 354 (7th Cir.1982), here an experienced Indiana lawyer who thought this the type of contract where the buyer cannot unreasonably withhold approval of the seller's performance.

Lest this conclusion be thought to strike at the foundations of freedom of contract, we repeat that if it appeared from the language or circumstances of the contract that the parties really intended General Motors to have the right to reject Morin's work for failure to satisfy the private aesthetic taste of General Motors' representative, the rejection would have been proper even if unreasonable. But the contract is ambiguous because of the qualifications with which the terms "artistic effect" and "decision as to acceptability" are hedged about, and the circumstances suggest that the parties probably did not intend to subject Morin's rights to aesthetic whim.

AFFIRMED.

MATTEI v. HOPPER

[Chapter 2, supra]

FORMAN v. BENSON, 112 Ill.App.3d 1070, 68 Ill.Dec. 629, 446 N.E.2d 535 (1983). Buyer made an offer to purchase certain real estate owned by seller, with the purchase price to be paid over a ten–year period. Before accepting the offer, seller expressed concern over buyer's creditworthiness. Seller's broker thereupon added the following provision to the offer: "subject to seller's approving buyer's credit report, oral on March 24, 1981, and written when ready." Seller accepted the offer, but thereafter refused to convey the property on the ground that he was not satisfied with buyer's credit. The court held that the subjective rather than the objective standard should be applied to interpret this provision, but nevertheless held for buyer:

"The personal judgment standard . . . does not allow the defendant to exercise unbridled discretion in rejecting plaintiff's credit, but rather is subject to the requirement of good faith. . . . In the instant case the trial court made no specific finding whether defendant Benson rejected plaintiff's credit in good faith. However, the trial court did find that between the time the contract was executed and the time the offer was rejected, defendant attempted to renegotiate the purchase price of the building as well as the interest rate.... [W]e hold that while defendant may have had a basis in his personal judgment for rejecting plaintiff's credit (i.e., outstanding debts and a $2,000 loss reflected in an income tax return), his attempted renegotiation demonstrates that his rejection was based on reasons other than plaintiff's credit rating and was, therefore, in bad faith."

———

FURSMIDT v. HOTEL ABBEY HOLDING CORP., 10 A.D.2d 447, 200 N.Y.S.2d 256 (1960). On February 1, 1958, Fursmidt entered into a contract with a hotel, which provided that Fursmidt would furnish valet and laundry services to guests at the hotel for a three–year period, and would pay the hotel $325 per month for the valet-and-laundry franchise. The agreement provided that "it is distinctly understood and agreed that the services to be rendered by [Fursmidt] shall meet with the approval of the [hotel], who shall be the sole judge of the sufficiency and propriety of the services."

In September 1958, the hotel informed Fursmidt that he was to discontinue his services as of October 1, 1958. Fursmidt then sued for breach of contract. The hotel counterclaimed for damages that it said it sustained by reason of Fursmidt's failure to render adequate and proper service. The trial court charged the jury that it had to decide not only whether the hotel was in fact dissatisfied but also whether the dissatisfaction was reasonable. Judgment was rendered for Fursmidt. Reversed.

"[A] literal construction of ... 'satisfaction' provisions is made where the agreements provide for performance involving 'fancy, taste, sensibility, or judgment' of the party for whose benefit it was made.... Such a result obtains in cases calling for performance to one's satisfaction in the making of a garment, the giving of a course of instruction, the services of an orchestra, the making of recordings by a singer and the painting of a portrait....

"The resolution of the issue here presented lies with the determination of whether the instant agreement is one relating to operative fitness, utility or marketability or one involving fancy, taste, sensibility or judgment. We find that it comes within the rules applicable to the latter class and thus conclude that the court erred in its charge....

"[I]t appears that the primary and overriding objective of the defendant in entering into this agreement was to ensure to its guests proper, efficient, courteous and reasonable valet and laundry facilities as an integral part of the overall personal services rendered by the hotel to the end that the good will of the guests be retained.... No objective standards of reasonableness can be set up by which the effectiveness of the plaintiff's performance in achieving the effect sought can be measured. It is for that reason that in cases of this nature the honest judgment of the party rather than that of a jury is all that is required and it was in order to make sure that that would be the measure of performance that the defendant inserted in the contract that it was to be the sole judge....

"It may very well be that the charge of the Court is correct for the purpose of determining whether the plaintiff breached the agreement so as to entitle the defendant to damages on its counterclaim as distinguished from its right to terminate the contract. Honest dissatisfaction on the part of the defendant, although entitling it to terminate will not, in and of itself, entitle it to recover damages on its counterclaim. Such determination will depend on the facts surrounding the manner of the plaintiff's performance in relation to what he was obliged to do under the agreement and accordingly we do not pass on that phase of the case at this time."

———

E. ALLAN FARNSWORTH, CONTRACTS § 8–4 (3d ed. 1999). "The risk to the contractor in conditioning the owner's duty to pay on even reasonable satisfaction can be avoided by making the condition the satisfaction of an independent third person. When this is done, courts have generally been willing to read 'satisfaction' to mean 'honest satisfaction.' In construction contracts, the owner's duty to pay as the work progresses is often conditioned on the satisfaction of the architect, evidenced by issuance of architects' certificates. If a certificate is refused, the fact that the architect's dissatisfaction may be unreasonable does not give the contractor a claim to payment as long as the dissatisfaction is honest. However, the requirement of a certificate will be dispensed with if the refusal can be characterized as 'not in good faith' or as 'dishonest' or 'fraudulent.' If the third party's dissatisfaction is unreasonable in the extreme, courts have sometimes dispensed with the requirement by using justifications that include characterizing the refusal as 'constructive fraud.' "

———

RESTATEMENT, SECOND, CONTRACTS § 227, ILLUSTRATIONS 5–8: "5. A contracts with B to repair B's building for $20,000, payment to be made 'on the satisfaction of C, B's architect, and the issuance of his certificate.' A makes the repairs, but C refuses to issue his certificate, and explains why he is not satisfied. Other experts in the field consider A's performance to be satisfactory and disagree with C's explanation. A has no claim against B.... If C is honestly not satisfied, B is under no duty to pay A, and it makes no difference if his dissatisfaction was not reasonable.

"6. The facts being otherwise as stated in Illustration 5, C refuses to issue his certificate although he admits that he is satisfied. A has a claim against B for $20,000. The quoted language will be interpreted so that the requirement of the certificate is merely evidentiary and the condition occurs when there is, as here, adequate evidence that C is honestly satisfied.

"7. The facts being otherwise as stated in Illustration 5, C does not make a proper inspection of the work and gives no reasons for his dissatisfaction. A has a claim against B for $20,000. In using the quoted language, A and B assumed that C would exercise an honest judgment and by failing to make a proper inspection, C did not exercise such a judgment....

"8. The facts being otherwise as stated in Illustration 5, C makes a gross mistake with reference to the facts on which his refusal to give a certificate is based. A has a claim against B for $20,000. In using the quoted language, A and B assumed that C would exercise his judgment without a gross mistake as to the facts...."

———

SECTION 7. CONDITIONS OF PAYMENT

KOCH v. CONSTRUCTION TECHNOLOGY, INC.

Supreme Court of Tennessee, 1996.
924 S.W.2d 68.

DROWOTA, Justice.

This case involves a contract dispute between Mark Koch (d/b/a Commercial Painting Company, Inc.) and Construction Technology, Inc., (CTI), the former a painting subcontractor and the latter the general contractor on a construction project owned by the Memphis Housing Authority (MHA). The issues for our determination [include] whether the Court of Appeals erred in construing the "pay when paid" clause in the subcontract as a condition precedent, thereby making Koch's right to payment dependent upon CTI's receipt of payment from MHA. . . . For the following reasons, we hold that the Court of Appeals erred . . . : therefore, we reverse the judgment of that court and remand the cause for further proceedings.

FACTS AND PROCEDURAL HISTORY

On March 17, 1988, CTI and the MHA entered into a contract in which CTI agreed to make improvements to the Dixie Homes Housing Development in Memphis. On March 30, 1988, CTI subcontracted the painting portion of the project to Koch . . . . The subcontract included a "payment" clause, which provides in pertinent part, that:

> Partial payments subject to all applicable provisions of the Contract shall be made when and as payments are received by the Contractor. The Subcontractor may be required as a condition precedent to any payment to furnish evidence satisfactory to the Contractor that all payrolls, material bills, and other indebtedness applicable to the work have been paid.

Koch completed all work required by the contract on July 31, 1989; and he was paid $148,110.96 for this work by CTI. However, because the amount of actual work performed exceeded this total, and because CTI refused to make any additional payments, Koch brought an action against it for breach of contract in the Shelby County Circuit Court. In its answer, CTI cited the payment clause as an affirmative defense, alleging that "CTI has not been paid in full by MHA and, therefore, is not obligated to pay plaintiff since payment to CTI by MHA is a condition precedent to CTI's obligation to pay plaintiff." . . .

Based on the sign-off sheets numbers and the actual observations and measurements of the project made by the plaintiff and/or his employees as it relates to the painting work, the Court finds that MHA has paid CTI $28,307.22 for work actually performed by plaintiff in addition to the $148,110.96 already paid to plaintiff by CTI. This amount . . . does not include any amounts for other work actually performed by plaintiff for which CTI has not been paid by MHA. . . .

. . . Koch filed a motion requesting that the trial court increase the judgment to $39,650.14, arguing that the uncontroverted evidence presented at trial in the instant case showed this to be the total amount due him under the subcontract. The trial court denied [the motion and also dismissed the claim against the surety, FDCM, on an unrelated ground], and Koch appealed to the Court of Appeals.

The Court of Appeals affirmed the judgment . . ., holding that the "pay when paid" clause was a condition precedent to CTI's promise to pay. . . .

I.

A. *Construction of the Payment Clause*

. . . Koch argues that the lower courts erred in [construing the payment clause in the subcontract to mean that MHA's payment to CTI was a condition precedent to CTI's obligation to pay Koch]. . . . [H]e argues that an overwhelming majority of jurisdictions reject that position, and instead hold that such language establishes an absolute promise to pay on the part of the general contractor, but simply affords it a reasonable amount of time to make the payments. This majority position is sound public policy, Koch contends, because it is inequitable to make the subcontractor's right to payment dependent upon the owner's performance, which might not be forthcoming for any number of reasons out of the subcontractor's control. . . .

. . . Although we have never specifically addressed the issue, there are a number of settled propositions of law to guide us. First, it is well-established that condition precedents are not favored in contract law, and will not be upheld unless there is clear language to support them. *Harlan v. Hardaway,* 796 S.W.2d 953, 958 (Tenn.App.1990). Furthermore, this general rule applies with particular force in the context of "pay when paid" clauses, for the plaintiff is correct that an overwhelming majority of jurisdictions do not construe such clauses so as to release the general contractor from all obligation to make payment to the subcontractor in case of nonperformance by the owner. Rather, these clauses are most often construed as simply affecting the timing of payments that the general contractor is required to make to the subcontractor, regardless of whether the owner performs or not. These courts refuse to shift the risk of the owner's nonperformance from the general contractor to the subcontractor unless the language clearly indicates that the parties intended to do so.

A good example of this reasoning is contained in the seminal case of *Thos. J. Dyer Co. v. Bishop International Engineering Co.,* 303 F.2d 655 (6th Cir.1962), wherein the Court was called upon to construe a clause which provided that "no part of [the subcontract price] shall be due until five days after Owner shall have paid Contractor therefor . . ." *Dyer,* 303 F.2d at 656. In holding that the clause was not a condition precedent, the *Dyer* court explained:

> It is, of course, basic in the construction business for the general contractor on a construction project of any magnitude to expect to be paid in full by the owner for the labor and material he puts into the project. He would not remain in business for long unless such was his intention and such intention was accomplished. That is a fundamental concept of

doing business with another. The solvency of the owner is a credit risk necessarily incurred by the general contractor, but various legal and contractual provisions, such as mechanic's liens and installment payments, are used to reduce this to a minimum. These evidence the intention of the parties that the contractor be paid even though the owner may ultimately become insolvent. This expectation and intention of being paid is even more pronounced in the case of a subcontractor whose contract is with the general contractor, not with the owner. In addition to his mechanic's lien, he is primarily interested in the solvency of the general contractor with whom he has contracted. He looks to him for payment. Normally and legally, the insolvency of the owner will not defeat the claim of the subcontractor against the general contractor. Accordingly, in order to transfer this normal credit risk incurred by the general contractor from the general contractor to the subcontractor, the contract between the general contractor and the subcontractor should contain an express condition clearly showing that to be the intention of the parties.

In the case before us we see no reason why the usual credit risk of the owner's insolvency assumed by the general contractor should be transferred from the general contractor to the subcontractor. It seems clear to us under the facts of this case that it was the intention of the parties that the subcontractor would be paid by the general contractor for the labor and materials put into the project. We believe that to be the normal relationship between the parties. If such was not the intention of the parties it could have been expressed in unequivocal terms dealing with the possible insolvency of the owner. . . .

Dyer, 303 F.2d at 660–61 (citations omitted).

With these rules in mind, we conclude that the language here does not evidence the parties' intention to shift the risk of the owner's nonperformance from the general contractor to the subcontractor with sufficient clarity to qualify as a condition precedent. The first sentence—"payments . . . shall be made when and as they are received by the contractor"—could be interpreted as a timing provision; it is not necessarily indicative of the parties' intent to make CTI's obligation to pay Koch dependent upon CTI's first being paid by MHA. This is particularly so in light of the following sentence in the clause, which provides: "[t]he subcontractor may be required as a condition precedent to any payment to furnish evidence satisfactory to the contractor that all payrolls, material bills, and other indebtedness applicable to the work have been paid." This sentence illustrates that the parties certainly knew how to create a condition precedent if they so desired. That they did not use such unambiguous language in the first sentence prevents us from construing that sentence as a condition precedent to Koch's right to payment. . . .

For the aforementioned reasons, the judgment of the Court of appeals is reversed and the case remanded for further proceedings consistent with this opinion.

ANDERSON, C.J., and REID, BIRCH and WHITE, JJ., concur.

———

NOTE ON PAY–WHEN–PAID PROVISIONS

"Pay-when-paid" (or "pay-if-paid") provisions are often found in contracts between contractors and subcontractors. Some courts effectively negate the impact of such provisions by means of interpretation, as in *Koch*. Other courts have struck down such provisions under mechanic's lien laws. These laws are complex, but essentially they provide that persons who contribute labor or material to the construction or repair of property have a lien (that is, a security interest) in the property for the value of their contribution. Lien laws often include anti-waiver provision, under which mechanic's lien rights cannot be waived except under narrow circumstances. Various courts have held that a pay-when-paid provision is in substance a waiver of such rights, and is therefore invalid under the statutory anti-waiver provisions. See, e.g., W.R. Clarke Corp. v. Safeco Ins. Co., 15 Cal.4th 882, 938 P.2d 372 (1997); West–Fair Elec. v. Aetna Cas. & Sur. Co. (1995) 87 N.Y.2d 148, 157, 638 N.Y.S.2d 394, 398, 661 N.E.2d 967, 971.

SECTION 8. EXCUSE

AETNA CASUALTY AND SURETY CO. v. MURPHY

Supreme Court of Connecticut, 1988.
206 Conn. 409, 538 A.2d 219.

PETERS, CHIEF JUSTICE.

The sole issue in this appeal is whether an insured who belatedly gives notice of an insurable claim can nonetheless recover on the insurance contract by rebutting the presumption that his delay has been prejudicial to the insurance carrier. The plaintiff, Aetna Casualty and Surety Company, brought an action against the defendant, George A. Murphy III, to recover for damage he allegedly caused to a building it had insured. The defendant then filed a third party complaint impleading his comprehensive liability insurer, Federal Insurance Company, Chubb Group of Insurance Companies (hereinafter Chubb), as third party defendant. Chubb successfully moved for summary judgment on the ground that Murphy, the defendant and third party plaintiff, had inexcusably and unreasonably delayed in complying with the notice provisions of the insurance contract. The defendant appeals from this judgment. We find no error.

The underlying facts are undisputed. The defendant, George A. Murphy III, a dentist, terminated a lease with Hopmeadow Professional Center Associates on or about November 30, 1982. The manner in which he had dismantled his office gave rise to a claim for damages to which the plaintiff, Aetna Casualty and Surety Company, became subrogated. Although served with the plaintiff's complaint on November 21, 1983, the defendant gave no notice of the existence of this claim to Chubb until January 10, 1986. The motion to implead Chubb as third party defendant was filed on May 14, 1986, and granted on June 2, 1986.

Chubb moved for summary judgment on its three special defenses,* alleging Murphy's noncompliance with the terms of his insurance policy. Its first claim was that it was entitled to judgment because Murphy had ignored two provisions in the Chubb policy imposing notice requirements on its policyholders. The first of these provisions states: "In the event of an occurrence, written notice ... shall be given by or for the insured to the company ... as soon as practicable." The other states: "If claim is made or suit is brought against the insured, the insured shall immediately forward to the company every demand, notice, summons, or other process received by him or his representative." In his answer to Chubb's special defenses, Murphy admitted his failure to comply with these provisions. Accordingly, his affidavit opposing summary judgment raised no question of fact but relied on his argument that, as a matter of law, an insurer may not deny coverage because of late notice without a showing, on its part, that it has been prejudiced by its insured's delay.

The trial court granted Chubb's motion for summary judgment on its first special defense. It found that Murphy's two year delay in giving notice to Chubb was inexcusable and unreasonable, and concluded that such a delay "voids coverage and insurer's duties under the contract [of insurance].... "

On appeal, Murphy challenges only the trial court's conclusion of law. Despite his inexcusable and unreasonable delay in giving notice, he maintains that he is entitled to insurance coverage because Chubb has failed to allege or to show prejudice because of his late notice.

As Murphy concedes, the trial court's decision accurately reflects numerous holdings of this court that, absent waiver, an unexcused, unreasonable delay in notification constitutes a failure of condition that entirely discharges an insurance carrier from any further liability on its insurance contract....

In our appraisal of the continued vitality of this line of cases, it is noteworthy that they do not reflect a searching analysis of what role prejudice, or its absence, should play in the enforcement of such standard clauses in insurance policies. That issue was put on the table, but not resolved, by a vigorous dissent in *Plasticrete Corporation v. American Policyholders Ins. Co.,* 184 Conn. 231, 240–44, 439 A.2d 968 (1981) (*Bogdanski, J.,* dissenting). The time has come for us to address it squarely.

We are confronted, in this case, by a conflict between two competing principles in the law of contracts. On the one hand, the law of contracts supports the principle that contracts should be enforced as written, and that contracting parties are bound by the contractual provisions to which they have given their assent. Among the provisions for which the parties may bargain are clauses that impose conditions upon contractual liability. "If the occurrence of a condition is required by the agreement of the parties, rather than as a matter of law, a rule of strict compliance traditionally applies." E. Farnsworth, Contracts (1982) § 8.3, p. 544; see *Grenier v. Compratt Construction Co.,* 189 Conn. 144, 148, 454 A.2d 1289 (1983); *Brauer v. Freccia,* 159

---

* Chubb, the third party defendant, had filed three special defenses, although the trial court ruled on only one. The first special defense relied on Murphy's admitted failure to give written notice of loss as soon as practicable and to forward notice of the claim against him immediately upon its filing by the plaintiff.

The second and third special defenses related to questions of coverage: whether the loss suffered by Murphy was excluded as having been "expected or intended from the standpoint of the insured" or as falling outside the policy definitions of "occurrence."

Conn. 289, 293–94, 268 A.2d 645 (1970); *Strimiska v. Yates,* 158 Conn. 179, 185–86, 257 A.2d 814 (1969). On the other hand, the rigor of this traditional principle of strict compliance has increasingly been tempered by the recognition that the occurrence of a condition may, in appropriate circumstances, be excused in order to avoid a 'disproportionate forfeiture.' See, e.g., 2 Restatement (Second), Contracts (1981) § 229;** *Johnson Controls, Inc. v. Bowes,* 381 Mass. 278, 280, 409 N.E.2d 185 (1980); 3A A. Corbin, Contracts (1960 & Sup.1984) § 754; E. Farnsworth, supra, § 8.7, pp. 570–71; 5 S. Williston, Contracts (3d Ed. Jaeger 1961) §§ 769 through 811.

In numerous cases, this court has held that, especially in the absence of conduct that is "wilful," a contracting party may, despite his own departure from the specifications of his contract, enforce the obligations of the other party with whom he has dealt in good faith. In construction contracts, a builder's deviation from contract specifications, even if such a departure is conscious and intentional, will not totally defeat the right to recover in an action against the owner on the contract. *Grenier v. Compratt Construction Co.,* supra, 148–49, 454 A.2d 1289; *Vincenzi v. Cerro,* 186 Conn. 612, 615, 442 A.2d 1352 (1982). In contracts for the sale of real property, the fact that a contract states a date for performance does not necessarily make time of the essence. *Kakalik v. Bernardo,* 184 Conn. 386, 392, 439 A.2d 1016 (1981); see *Ravitch v. Stollman Poultry Farms, Inc.,* 165 Conn. 135, 148, 328 A.2d 711 (1973). A purchaser of real property does not, despite his knowing default, forfeit the right to seek restitution of sums of money earlier paid under the contract of sale, even when such payments are therein characterized as liquidated damages. *Vines v. Orchard Hills, Inc.,* 181 Conn. 501, 509, 435 A.2d 1022 (1980); *Pierce v. Staub,* 78 Conn. 459, 466, 62 A. 760 (1906). Finally, despite a failure to deliver contract goods, a seller need not pay an amount contractually designated as liquidated damages to a buyer who has suffered no damages attributable to the seller's breach. *Norwalk Door Closer Co. v. Eagle Lock & Screw Co.,* 153 Conn. 681, 689, 220 A.2d 263 (1966).

This case law demonstrates that, in appropriate circumstances, a contracting party, despite his own default, may be entitled to relief from the rigorous enforcement of contract provisions that would otherwise amount to a forfeiture. On the question of what circumstances warrant such relief, no better guidelines have ever been proffered than those articulated by Judge Benjamin Cardozo in the celebrated case of *Jacob & Youngs, Inc. v. Kent,* 230 N.Y. 239, 129 N.E. 889 (1921). Discussing the interpretation of contracts to

---

** The Restatement (Second) of Contracts (1981) § 229, entitled "Excuse of a Condition to Avoid Forfeiture," provides: "To the extent that the non-occurrence of a condition would cause disproportionate forfeiture, a court may excuse the non-occurrence of that condition unless its occurrence was a material part of the agreed exchange."

Comment b elaborates on the concept of "disproportionate forfeiture" as follows: "The rule stated in the present Section is, of necessity, a flexible one, and its application is within the sound discretion of the court. Here, as in § 227(1), 'forfeiture' is used to refer to the denial of compensation that results when the obligee loses his right to the agreed exchange after he has relied substantially, as by prepara-

tion or performance on the expectation of that exchange. See Comment b to § 227. The extent of the forfeiture in any particular case will depend on the extent of that denial of compensation. In determining whether the forfeiture is 'disproportionate,' a court must weigh the extent of the forfeiture by the obligee against the importance to the obligor of the risk from which he sought to be protected and the degree to which that protection will be lost if the non-occurrence of the condition is excused to the extent required to prevent forfeiture. *The character of the agreement may, as in the case of insurance agreements, affect the rigor with which the requirement is applied.*" (Emphasis added.)

ascertain how the parties intended to govern their contractual relationship, Cardozo first notes that "[t]here will be no assumption of a [contractual] purpose to visit venial faults with oppressive retribution." Id., 242, 129 N.E. 889. The opinion then continues: "Those who think more of symmetry and logic in the development of legal rules than of practical adaptation to the attainment of a just result will be troubled by a classification where the lines of division are so wavering and blurred. Something, doubtless, may be said on the score of consistency and certainty in favor of a stricter standard. The courts have balanced such considerations against those of equity and fairness, and found the latter to be the weightier.... Where the line is to be drawn between the important and the trivial cannot be settled by a formula. 'In the nature of the case precise boundaries are impossible' (2 Williston on Contracts, sec. 841). The same omission may take on one aspect or another according to its setting.... The question is one of degree, to be answered, if there is doubt, by the triers of the facts ... and, if the inferences are certain, by the judges of the law.... We must weigh the purpose to be served, the desire to be gratified, the excuse for deviation from the letter, the cruelty of enforced adherence. Then only can we tell whether literal fulfilment is to be implied by law as a condition."*** Id., 242–43, 129 N.E. 889.

In the setting of this case, three considerations are central. First, the contractual provisions presently at issue are contained in an insurance policy that is a "contract of adhesion," the parties to this form contract having had no occasion to bargain about the consequences of delayed notice. Second, enforcement of these notice provisions will operate as a forfeiture because the insured will lose his insurance coverage without regard to his dutiful payment of insurance premiums. Third, the insurer's legitimate purpose of guaranteeing itself a fair opportunity to investigate accidents and claims can be protected without the forfeiture that results from presuming, irrebuttably, that late notice invariably prejudices the insurer.

There can be no question that the insurance policy in this case is a "contract of adhesion." That term was first introduced into American legal vocabulary by Professor Edwin Patterson, who noted that life insurance contracts are contracts of adhesion because "[t]he contract is drawn up by the insurer and the insured, who merely 'adheres' to it, has little choice as to its terms." E. Patterson, "The Delivery of a Life–Insurance Policy," 33 Harv. L.Rev. 198, 222 (1919). Standardized contracts of insurance continue to be prime examples of contracts of adhesion, whose most salient feature is that they are not subject to the normal bargaining processes of ordinary contracts. *Nationwide Ins. Co. v. Gode,* 187 Conn. 386, 404, 446 A.2d 1059 (1982) (*Shea, J.,* dissenting); *Weaver Bros., Inc. v. Chappel,* 684 P.2d 123, 125 (Alaska 1984); *Cooper v. Government Employees Ins. Co.,* 51 N.J. 86, 93, 237 A.2d 870 (1968); *Great American Ins. Co. v. C.G. Tate Construction Co.,* 303 N.C. 387, 392–93, 279 S.E.2d 769 (1981); *Brakeman v. Potomac Ins. Co.,* 472 Pa. 66, 72–73, 371 A.2d 193 (1977); F. Kessler, "Contracts of Adhesion—Some Thoughts about Freedom of Contract," 43 Colum.L.Rev. 629, 631–32 (1943). The fact that the

*** The court's opinion in *Jacob & Youngs, Inc. v. Kent,* 230 N.Y. 239, 243, 129 N.E. 889 (1921), suggests that the parties may, by express contractual language, "effectuate a purpose that performance of every term shall be a condition of recovery." That observation is not easy to reconcile with the fact that the record in the case discloses the existence of a clause specifically permitting rejection, whenever discovered, of any work of the contractor that failed "fully" to conform with contract specifications "in every respect." See J. Dawson, W. Harvey & S. Henderson, Contracts and Contract Remedies (4th Ed.1982) pp. 816–17.

notice provisions in the Chubb insurance policy were an inconspicuous part of a printed form; cf. General Statutes §§ 42a–1–201(10) and 42a–2–316(2); supports the characterization of these clauses as a "contract of adhesion." Nothing in the record suggests that they were brought to Murphy's attention or that, if they had been, their terms would have been subject to negotiation.

It is equally clear that literal enforcement of the notice provisions in this case will discharge Chubb from any further liability to Murphy with regard to the present claims for insurance coverage. That indeed is the necessary purport of Chubb's special defense and the consequence of the trial court's ruling on its motion for summary judgment. The operative effect of noncompliance with the notice provisions is a forfeiture of the interests of the insured that is, in all likelihood, disproportionate. *Johnson Controls, Inc. v. Bowes*, supra, 381 Mass. at 280–81, 409 N.E.2d 185.

In determining whether an insured is entitled to relief from such a disproportionate forfeiture, loss of coverage must be weighed against an insurer's legitimate interest in protection from stale claims. "The purpose of a policy provision requiring the insured to give the company prompt notice of an accident or claim is to give the insurer an opportunity to make a timely and adequate investigation of all the circumstances.... And further, if the insurer is thus given the opportunity for a timely investigation, reasonable compromises and settlements may be made, thereby avoiding prolonged and unnecessary litigation." 8 J. Appleman, Insurance Law and Practice (Rev.Ed. 1981) § 4731, pp. 2–5. If this legitimate purpose can be protected by something short of automatic enforcement of the notice provisions, then their strict enforcement is unwarranted.

In our judgment, a proper balance between the interests of the insurer and the insured requires a factual inquiry into whether, in the circumstances of a particular case, an insurer has been prejudiced by its insured's delay in giving notice of an event triggering insurance coverage. If it can be shown that the insurer suffered no material prejudice from the delay, the nonoccurrence of the condition of timely notice may be excused because it is not, in Restatement terms, "a material part of the agreed exchange." Literal enforcement of notice provisions when there is no prejudice is no more appropriate than literal enforcement of liquidated damages clauses when there are no damages. *Norwalk Door Closer Co. v. Eagle Lock & Screw Co.*, supra, 153 Conn. at 689, 220 A.2d 263.

A significant number of cases in other jurisdictions lend support to our conclusion that, absent a showing of material prejudice, an insured's failure to give timely notice does not discharge the insurer's continuing duty to provide insurance coverage. Most of these decisions place the burden of proof on the issue of prejudice on the insurer.... In a few jurisdictions, although prejudice from delay is presumed, that presumption is rebuttable if the insured can demonstrate an actual lack of material prejudice.... By contrast to these cases which afford some latitude for factual inquiry into prejudice, some jurisdictions continue to enforce delayed notice provisions literally....

In light of existing related precedents in this jurisdiction, although we are persuaded that the existence or nonexistence of prejudice from delayed notice should be determined on a factual basis, the burden of establishing lack of prejudice must be borne by the insured. It is the insured who is seeking to be excused from the consequences of a contract provision with which he has concededly failed to comply. His position is akin to that of the defaulting purchaser of real property in *Vines v. Orchard Hills, Inc.,* supra, 181 Conn. at 510, 435 A.2d 1022, where we held that, "[t]o prove unjust enrichment, in the ordinary case, the purchaser, because he is the party in breach, must prove that the damages suffered by his seller are less than the moneys received from the purchaser.... It may not be easy for the purchaser to prove the extent of the seller's damages, it may even be strategically advantageous for the seller to come forward with relevant evidence of the losses he has incurred and may expect to incur on account of the buyer's breach. Nonetheless, only if the breaching party satisfies his burden of proof that the innocent party has sustained a net gain may a claim for unjust enrichment be sustained." Principles of unjust enrichment and restitution bear a family resemblance to those involved in considerations of forfeiture. Under both sets of principles, the law has come to permit a complainant to seek a fair allocation of profit and loss despite the complainant's own failure to comply fully with his contract obligations. The determination of what is fair, as a factual matter, must however depend upon a proper showing by the complainant who seeks this extraordinary relief.

Applying these principles to the present case, we conclude that the trial court was correct in granting summary judgment, although not for the reason upon which it relied. *A & H Corporation v. Bridgeport,* 180 Conn. 435, 443, 430 A.2d 25 (1980); *Favorite v. Miller,* 176 Conn. 310, 317, 407 A.2d 974 (1978). Chubb, the third party defendant, was not automatically discharged because of the delay of Murphy, the third party plaintiff, in giving notice of an insured occurrence. Chubb was, however, entitled to summary judgment because Murphy's affidavit opposing summary judgment contained no factual basis for a claim that Chubb had not been materially prejudiced by Murphy's delay.

There is no error.

In this opinion ARTHUR H. HEALEY, CALLAHAN and GLASS, JJ., concurred.

COVELLO, J., concurred in the result.

RESTATEMENT, SECOND, CONTRACTS § 229

[See Selected Source Materials Supplement]

RESTATEMENT, SECOND, CONTRACTS
§ 229, ILLUSTRATIONS 1, 2

1. A contracts to build a house for B, using pipe of Reading manufacture. In return, B agrees to pay $75,000 in progress payments, each payment to be made "on condition that no pipe other than that of Reading manufacture has been used." Without A's knowledge, a subcontractor mistakenly uses pipe of Cohoes manufacture which is identical in quality and is distinguishable only by the name of the manufacturer which is stamped on it. The mistake is not discovered until the house is completed, when replacement of

the pipe will require destruction of substantial parts of the house. B refuses to pay the unpaid balance of $10,000. A court may conclude that the use of Reading rather than Cohoes pipe is so relatively unimportant to B that the forfeiture that would result from denying A the entire balance would be disproportionate, and may allow recovery by A subject to any claim for damages for A's breach of his duty to use Reading pipe.

2. A, an ocean carrier, carries B's goods under a contract providing that it is a condition of A's liability for damage to cargo that "written notice of claim for loss or damage must be given within 10 days after removal of goods." B's cargo is damaged during carriage and A knows of this. On removal of the goods, B notes in writing on the delivery record that the cargo is damaged, and five days later informs A over the telephone of a claim for that damage and invites A to participate in an inspection within the ten day period. A inspects the goods within the period, but B does not give written notice of its claim until 25 days after removal of the goods. Since the purpose of requiring the condition of written notice is to alert the carrier and enable it to make a prompt investigation, and since this purpose had been served by the written notice of damage and the oral notice of claim, the court may excuse the non-occurrence of the condition to the extent required to allow recovery by B.

BURNE v. FRANKLIN LIFE INS. CO., 451 Pa. 218, 301 A.2d 799 (1973). Franklin Life issued a life–insurance policy to Bartholemew Burne. The face amount of the policy was $15,000. The policy also contained a double–indemnity provision, under which the policy paid an additional $15,000 if the insured died from accidental means. However, the policy stated that accidental death benefits would be payable only if " ... such death occurred ... within ninety days from the date of the accident." While the policy was in effect, Burne was struck by a car. Immediate and extensive brain surgery was required. From the moment of the accident until his death, Mr. Burne's existence was that of a complete and hopeless invalid, unable to speak, subject to seizures and requiring constant nursing and medical care. Vast sums of money were expended by his wife, and the most sophisticated medical techniques utilized, merely to keep her husband medically alive, albeit in a vegetative state, for 4½ years. Franklin Life paid the face amount of the policy, but refused to pay the accidental-death benefits, on the ground that death had not occurred within 90 days of the accident. Held, the 90–day provision was unenforceable on the ground of public policy:

"There are strong public policy reasons which militate against the enforceability of the ninety day limitation. The provision has its origins at a much earlier stage of medicine. Accordingly, the leading case construing the provision predates three decades of progress in the field of curative medicine. Advancements made during that period have enabled the medical profession to become startlingly adept at delaying death for indeterminate periods. Physicians and surgeons now stand at the very citadel of death, possessing the awesome responsibility of sometimes deciding whether and what measure should be used to prolong, even though momentarily, an individual's life. The legal and ethical issues attending such deliberations are gravely complex.

"The result reached by the trial court presents a gruesome paradox indeed—it would permit double indemnity recovery for the death of an accident victim who dies instantly or within ninety days of an accident, but would deny such recovery for the death of an accident victim who endures the agony of prolonged illness, suffers longer, and necessitates greater expense by his family in hopes of sustaining life even momentarily beyond the ninety day period. To predicate liability under a life insurance policy upon death occurring only on or prior to a specific date, while denying policy recovery if death occurs after that fixed date, offends the basic concepts and fundamental objectives of life insurance and is contrary to public policy. Hence, the ninety day limitation is unenforceable."

GREAT AMERICAN INS. CO. v. C.G. TATE CONSTRUCTION CO., 303 N.C. 387, 279 S.E.2d 769 (1981). Great American issued a liability policy to C.G. Tate. Under the policy, Great American was obliged to defend and indemnify Tate in connection with an incident covered by a policy. It was a condition to this obligation that Tate notify Great American of such an incident "as soon as practicable." An automobile accident occurred which might have been covered by the policy. Tate believed its personnel had not been involved in causing the accident and therefore did not give notice to Great American as soon as practicable. Held, the provision should be construed according to the parties' reasonable expectations.

". . . [A]n unexcused delay by the insured in giving notice to the insurer of an accident does not relieve the insurer of its obligation to defend and indemnify unless the delay operates materially to prejudice the insurer's ability to investigate and defend. . . .

". . . . The terms of an insurance contract are not bargained for in the traditional sense. Insurance policies are offered on a take-it-or-leave-it basis and, frequently, the only term over which the insured has any say is the amount of coverage. Strict interpretation of the notice requirement leads to harsh results: failure to notify the insurer within a reasonable time, for whatever reason, relieves the insurer of its obligations to defend and indemnify, the essence of the contract, even though it may have suffered no prejudice whatsoever as a result of the delay. Rejection of the strict contractual approach means that the interpretation of the notice provision will be guided more by its purpose—the reason for its inclusion in the insurance contract—than by its seemingly conclusive terms. Additionally, adoption of the modern rule of reasonable expectations promotes the social function of insurance coverage: providing compensation for injuries sustained by innocent members of the public. The rule we adopt today has the advantages of promoting social policy and fulfilling the reasonable expectations of the purchaser while fully protecting the ability of the insurer to protect its own interests. . . .

"The rule we adopt today places the notice requirement in its proper context. No condition of timely notice will be given a greater scope than required to fulfill its purpose. Simply put, the scope of the condition precedent which will relieve an insurer of its obligations under an insurance contract, is only as broad as its purpose: to protect the ability of the insurer to defend by preserving its ability fully to investigate the accident, e.g., Peeler v. United States Casualty Co., 197 N.C. 286, 148 S.E. 261. If, under the circumstances of a particular case, the purpose behind the requirement has been met, the insurer will not be relieved of its obligations. If, on the other hand, the purpose of protecting the insurer's ability to defend has been frustrated, the insurer has no duty under the contract. This equitable approach to the interpretation of notice requirements in insurance contracts has the advantages of providing coverage whenever in the reasonable expectations of the parties it should exist and of protecting the insurer whenever failure strictly to comply with a condition has resulted in material prejudice."

RESTATEMENT, SECOND, CONTRACTS § 230

[See Selected Source Materials Supplement]

RESTATEMENT, SECOND, CONTRACTS § 230, ILLUSTRATIONS 1, 2

1. A, an insurance company, insures the property of B under a policy providing that no recovery can be had if suit is not brought on the policy within two years after a loss. A loss occurs and B lets two years pass before bringing suit. A's duty to pay B for the loss is discharged and B cannot maintain the action on the policy.

2. The facts being otherwise as stated in Illustration 1, B lives in a foreign country and is prevented by the outbreak of war from bringing suit against A for two years. A's duty to pay B for the loss is not discharged and B can maintain an action on the policy when the war is ended.

RESTATEMENT, SECOND, CONTRACTS § 271

[See Selected Source Materials Supplement]

RESTATEMENT, SECOND, CONTRACTS § 271, ILLUSTRATIONS 1, 2

1. A contracts with B to repair B's building for $20,000, payment to be made "on the satisfaction of C, B's architect, and the issuance of his certificate." A properly makes the repairs, but C dies before he is able to give a certificate. Since presentation of the architect's certificate is not a material part of the agreed exchange and forfeiture would otherwise result, the occurrence of the condition is excused, and A has a claim against B for $20,000....

2. A, an insurance company, issues to B a policy of accidental injury insurance which provides that notice within 14 days of an accident is a

condition of A's duty. B is injured as a result of an accident covered by the policy but is so mentally deranged that he is unable to give notice for 20 days. B gives notice as soon as he is able. Since the giving of notice within 14 days is not a material part of the agreed exchange, and forfeiture would otherwise result, the non-occurrence of the condition is excused and B has a claim against A under the policy.

_____

ROYAL–GLOBE INSURANCE CO. v. CRAVEN, 411 Mass. 629, 585 N.E.2d 315 (1992). "The uninsured motorist policy in effect at the time of the accident requires notice to both the police and the insurer '[w]ithin [twenty–four] hours ... if [the insured has] ... been involved in a hit and run accident.' The judge concluded, however, that Craven [the insured] 'was in the intensive care unit during the first twenty–four hours [after the accident]' and could not be expected to notify the police and her insurance company within twenty–four hours. The judge ruled that Craven therefore was excused from the twenty–four hour notice requirement.

"Royal–Globe maintains that the judge's ruling on excuse was error because someone hired an attorney to represent Craven the morning of the accident. If Craven or someone acting on her behalf was able within twenty-four hours to engage a lawyer to represent her, Royal–Globe argues, it was error for the judge to conclude that Craven was excused from the twenty-four hour notice requirement. It is undisputed that Craven remained in intensive care for several days after the accident. The judge determined that to expect Craven to give notice while she was in intensive care would be 'unreasonable.' There was no error in that determination."

_____

CLARK v. WEST

[Chapter 2, supra]

_____

RESTATEMENT, SECOND, CONTRACTS § 84

[See Selected Source Materials Supplement]

_____

VANADIUM CORP. v. FIDELITY & DEPOSIT CO.

[Section 5, supra]

_____

Chapter 25

BREACH AND RESPONSE

INTRODUCTORY NOTE ON THE MUTUAL DEPENDENCY OF PERFORMANCES AND THE ORDER OF PERFORMANCE

The previous Chapter considered the effect of an *express* contractual provision under which a party to a contract does not come under a duty to perform unless a certain state of events has occurred. Section 1 of this Chapter considers the question, when can it be fairly *implied* that one party to a contract does not come under a duty to perform unless the other party has either performed or tendered performance? The answer to this question turns to a significant extent on the order of performance that is explicitly or implicitly required under the contract. Thus suppose that Brenda Brown and Samuel Smith have entered a written agreement in the following form:

Plumbing Contract

I, Brenda Brown, hereby agree to fix Samuel Smith's sink for $200. I Samuel Smith, hereby agree to pay Brenda Brown $200. Signed this tenth day of May, 2001.

Samuel Smith
Brenda Brown

No conditions are expressly stated in this contract; both promises are by their terms unqualified and unconditional. Suppose, however, that Brown brings suit against Smith for $200 without having begun fixing the sink. Common sense, based on ordinary business practice, would tell us that Brown should not be allowed to recover from Smith until Brown has performed, and correspondingly that Smith should not be required to pay until Brown has performed. It was, however, some time before the courts felt free to embrace this common-sense view. The following quotation reveals the manner in which the early courts approached the problem: "If one covenant with me to serve me for a year and I covenant with him to give him £20, if I do not say 'for the said cause,' he shall have action for the £20 even though he has not served me. It is otherwise if I say that he shall have the £20 'for the said cause.'" (Fineux, C.J., in Y.B. 15 Hen. VII, Trinity Term, pl. 17, 1500.)

It is therefore apparent that in the year 1500 the word "for" was by way of being a £20 word. Even though it was clear that A's performance was in exchange for B's, and even though it was further clear that A's performance was intended to come before B's, A would nevertheless be permitted to hold B to his promise although A had defaulted on his own, unless the contract contained language that made B's performance conditional upon the prior performance of A. In the absence of such language, it was said that B's remedy was to bring suit against A for A's default. The curious expression was used that the promises were "mutual and independent," meaning that each party had a remedy against the other for breach, but that neither party's suit was affected by his own breach.

Though this treatment of contract obligations was said by a later English court to "outrage common sense" (Kenyon, J., in Goodisson v. Nunn, 1792, 4 Term R. 761), it persisted with only slight mitigation for a surprisingly long time. Such mitigation as was introduced took the form of a greater willingness to find that the parties had manifested a condition in their agreement.

The final break with the old view came in a decision by Mansfield in 1773, Kingston v. Preston, 2 Douglas 689. After that decision, it would be held in a case like the Smith–Brown plumbing hypothetical that the proper procedure for deciding the case would be as follows: It should first be determined which party's performance was to come first, Smith's or Brown's. On the basis of ordinary business understanding, Brown's performance (fixing the sink) is intended to come before Smiths's (paying the price). Accordingly, substantial performance by Brown of her promise is *an implied condition* to Smith's liability. In pleading terms, this means that to recover against Smith, Brown must allege substantial performance of her promise, or some excuse for her failure to perform.

Thus under modern contract law, the governing principle is that if A and B have a contract, and under the contract A's performance is to precede B's performance, then B is not obliged to perform until A has performed. This principle is sometimes known as the *mutual dependency of performances*. A common way to express this principle is to say that A's performance is an *implied condition* to B's duty to perform. (More accurately, in light of the doctrine of substantial performance, A's *substantial performance* is an implied condition to B's duty to perform.)

The result, that B owes nothing if A fails to perform without excuse, does not, of course, have to rest on the term "condition" or "implied condition." In fact, in cases of this sort the courts often do not employ the language of condition, but speak instead of B having "the defense of a failure of consideration." Nothing in the end hinges on mere nomenclature. The principal reason for preferring the implied-condition language is that it correctly suggests that the burden of proof is normally on A to prove his performance. To say that B has "the defense of a failure of consideration" is misleading, since it implies that the burden is on B to show that performance has not taken place.

Often a contract does not explicitly provide which performance is to come first. In such cases, contract law uses a set of rules to determine which performance must come first. Those rules are the subject of Section 1 of this Chapter.

Section 2 of this Chapter concerns an issue that is intermixed with Section 1: once the order of performance has been determined, what are implications of the fact that a party who brings suit for the other party's default would himself have been unable to perform?

Section 3 of this Chapter considers a related problem: Suppose that A is to perform first, and performs less than perfectly. That is, suppose that A both performs and breaches. Because A has breached, B can sue A for damages for the breach. Depending on the facts, B may also have a right to *terminate* the contract as a result of A's breach. Section 3 considers the question, when does A's breach give B a right to terminate the contract, and what are the consequences if B terminates when A's breach does not give B the right to terminate?

SECTION 1.   THE ORDER OF PERFORMANCE

Once it is accepted that contracted-for performances are mutually dependant, the question arises, in what order must the performances be rendered when the contract does not itself dictate the order of performance? This question arises in two closely related contexts:

(1) In the first context, A claims that B has not performed and is therefor in breach. B responds that she is not in breach because she was not obliged to perform until A had performed—or at least had tendered performance—and A had neither performed nor tendered. It must then be decided which party's performance was to come first, or alternatively whether the parties' performances were to be exchanged simultaneously.

(2) The second context is the flip side of the first: When must one party perform, or at least tender performance, to put the other party in breach?

The courts have developed somewhat elaborate rules to determine the order of performance for these purposes, which are reflected in Restatement Second §§ 233, 234.

RESTATEMENT, SECOND, CONTRACTS §§ 233, 234

[See Selected Source Materials Supplement]

RESTATEMENT, SECOND, CONTRACTS
§ 234, ILLUSTRATIONS 1–5, 9

1. A promises to sell land to B, delivery of the deed to be on July 1. B promises to pay A $50,000, payment to be made on July 1. Delivery of the deed and payment of the price are due simultaneously.

2. A promises to sell land to B, the deed to be delivered on July 1. B promises to pay A $50,000, no provision being made for the time of payment. Delivery of the deed and payment of the price are due simultaneously.

3. A promises to sell land to B and B promises to pay A $50,000, no provision being made for the time either of delivery of the deed or of payment. Delivery of the deed and payment of the price are due simultaneously.

4. A promises to sell land to B, delivery of the deed to be on or before July 1. B promises to pay A $50,000, payment to be on or before July 1. Delivery of the deed and payment of the price are due simultaneously.

5. A promises to sell land to B, delivery of the deed to be on or before July 1. B promises to pay A $50,000, payment to be on or before August 1. Delivery of the deed and payment of the [price] are not due simultaneously
. . . . .

9. A contracts to do the concrete work on a building being constructed by B for $10 a cubic yard. In the absence of language or circumstances indicating the contrary, payment by B is not due until A has finished the concrete work. . . .

UCC §§ 2–507, 2–511

[See Selected Source Materials Supplement]

CISG ART. 58

[See Selected Source Materials Supplement]

UNIDROIT PRINCIPLES OF INTERNATIONAL COMMERCIAL CONTRACTS ARTS. 6.1.4, 7.1.3

[See Selected Source Materials Supplement]

PRINCIPLES OF EUROPEAN CONTRACT LAW ARTS. 7.104, 9.201

[See Selected Source Materials Supplement]

NOTE ON CONCURRENT CONDITIONS

Seller and Buyer enter into a contract for the sale of Blackacre for $60,000 cash. May 2 is set for the delivery of the deed and the payment of the purchase price. Nothing is said about which performance is to come first. The natural implication is that the two performances will be simultaneous: the deed and the money will be passed across the table at the same time.

Suppose that in such a case one party brings suit for damages against the other, claiming that the other is in default? As part of his case, the party bringing suit must allege and show that it was the other party who was in default, not himself. If both parties stayed at home, and neither approached the other with a proposal for completing the sale, neither should be allowed to recover damages from the other. Accordingly, the rule is that where performances are to be simultaneous, neither party can recover damages unless he has done something to put the other party in default. This would usually mean making a definite offer to perform and having at the time the capacity to carry out the offer.

It is commonly said that such a case involves *concurrent conditions*, meaning that concurrent performance by each party is a condition to the other party's obligation to perform. The term "concurrent conditions" is something of a misnomer. What the term really means is that where the performances of the *promises* in a contract are to be concurrent, then it is normally a condition to a suit by either party for damages for breach of the contract that he must tender his own performance to put the other party in default.

Intermixed with problems concerning the order of performance are issues that are raised when one party lacks the ability to perform.

SECTION 2. ABILITY TO PERFORM

ILEMAR CORP. v. KROCHMAL, 44 N.Y.2d 702, 405 N.Y.S.2d 444, 376 N.E.2d 917 (1978). "In order to place the vendor of realty under a contract of sale in default for a claimed failure to provide clear title, the purchaser normally must first tender performance himself and demand good title (Cohen v. Kranz, 12 N.Y.2d 242, 238 N.Y.S.2d 928, 189 N.E.2d 473; Higgins v. Eagleton, 155 N.Y. 466, 50 N.E. 287). Tender of performance by the purchaser is excused only if the title defect is not curable, for in such a case it would serve no purpose to require the purchaser to go through the futile motions of tendering performance. In this case, the claimed defects were curable, and, in fact, were subsequently cured.... accordingly, the purchaser never placed the vendor in default...."

KANAVOS v. HANCOCK BANK & TRUST CO.

Supreme Judicial Court of Massachusetts, 1985.
395 Mass. 199, 479 N.E.2d 168.

Before WILKINS, LIACOS, ABRAMS, NOLAN and LYNCH, JJ.

Wilkins, Justice.

This appeal presents two basic questions. First, if, for valid consideration, the owner of stock in a corporation has agreed to give A the opportunity to purchase that stock at the price at which the owner intends to sell it to another in the future (a right of first refusal) but the owner instead sells the stock to a third party without giving A the opportunity to match the third party's offer and thus acquire the stock, does A's right to recover in an action for breach of contract in any way depend on whether A had the financial ability to purchase the stock during the relevant time? Second, if A's right does so depend, as we conclude it does, does A have the burden of proving his financial ability to perform or is the burden on the repudiating former stockholder to prove A's inability to perform?

The plaintiff Harold J. Kanavos (Kanavos) is A in the example given, an individual to whom the defendant Hancock Bank & Trust Company (bank) gave the right to acquire all the stock of 1025 Hancock, Inc., before the bank sold the stock to anyone else on the same terms. This corporation owned a fourteen-story apartment building, known as Executive House, on Hancock Street in Quincy. The corporation was a G.L. c. 121A limited dividend corporation, and the first mortgage was guaranteed by the Federal Housing Administration of the Department of Housing and Urban Development. On July 16, 1976, James M. Brown, then executive vice president of the bank, gave Kanavos a letter in which the bank agreed to pay him $40,000 for surrendering an option to purchase the stock and further gave Kanavos "the option to match the price of sale of said property to extend for a 60 day period from the time our offer is received." In November, 1976, the bank entered into a purchase and sale agreement to sell the stock for $760,000 to a third person and, early in December, the bank sold the stock accordingly without giving Kanavos notice and the opportunity to purchase the stock.

For the purpose of determining Kanavos's contract damages, apart from the $40,000 to be paid for the surrender of his option, the parties and the trial judge treated the value of the stock as equal to the value of the equity in the apartment building. The balance on the first mortgage was $2,500,000 at the relevant times. When the jury, in response to a special verdict question, concluded that the apartment complex was worth $4,000,000, contract damages were determined by subtracting from $4,000,000 the balance due on the mortgage ($2,500,000) and the sale price of the stock ($760,000). That damage figure ($740,000) equaled the amount by which the fair market value of the stock exceeded the price at which it was sold. The $40,000 option surrender payment was then added to arrive at a final judgment of $780,000.

The judge presented the case to the jury seeking a special verdict (see Mass.R.Civ.P. 49, 365 Mass. 812 [1974]) on (a) the authority of the bank's executive vice president to grant the plaintiff the right of first refusal,[1] (b) the market value of the apartment complex, and (c) the right of the plaintiff to recover the $40,000.[2] The bank's only challenge to the special verdict and resulting judgment is that the judge failed to instruct the jury (and give them an associated special verdict question) that the plaintiff had to be ready, willing, and able, pursuant to the letter creating the right of first refusal, to pay the bank $760,000 (i.e., within the sixty days, to match the offer the bank received and accepted).

The judge ruled, over objection, that Kanavos's ability to pay $760,000 was not material to this case. This is the first issue we stated above in the abstract. We conclude that Kanavos's financial ability was material because

---

1. The question whether the evidence warranted a finding that the executive vice president had authority to give the plaintiff a right of first refusal was decided favorably to the plaintiff in *Kanavos v. Hancock Bank & Trust Co.*, 14 Mass.App. 326, 439 N.E.2d 311 (1982)....

2. The bank does not challenge here the plaintiff's right to the $40,000.

he should not recover contract damages, even from a repudiating promisor, under an agreement to sell stock unless he could have complied with his concurrent obligation to pay for the stock (or, as is not the case here, unless the bank's conduct substantially prevented Kanavos from being able to meet his obligation).

When the bank received an offer for the stock that it was prepared to accept, the bank was obliged to give Kanavos the right to match that offer. At that point, Kanavos had an option to purchase the stock on the same terms, although, of course, in this case he was unaware that such an offer (and hence the option) existed. He could have exercised his option by tendering the purchase price, and the bank would have been obliged to deliver the shares of stock. In the circumstances of this case, Kanavos was not obliged to make a meaningless tender of the purchase price. The stock had already been sold. However, one party's repudiation of a bilateral contract containing simultaneous obligations does not normally make immaterial the question whether the other party could perform his obligation. "It is the general rule 'that when performance under a contract is concurrent, one party cannot put the other in default unless he is ready, able, and willing to perform and has manifested this by some offer of performance' although a tender of performance is not necessary 'if the other party has shown that he cannot or will not perform.' " *Mayer v. Boston Metropolitan Airport, Inc.,* 355 Mass. 344, 354, 244 N.E.2d 568 (1969), quoting *Leigh v. Rule,* 331 Mass. 664, 668, 121 N.E.2d 854 (1954).

The weight of authority in this country is that the financial ability of a prospective buyer of property is a material issue in his action for damages against a repudiating defendant for breach of an agreement to sell that property for an established price. See 5 S. Williston, Contracts § 699, at 352–353 (Jaeger ed. 1961), and 6 S. Williston, Contracts § 882, at 394 (Jaeger ed. 1962); 4 A. Corbin, Contracts § 978, at 924–925 (1951); Restatement (Second) of Contracts § 254, comment a (1981) (the duty of a repudiating party "to pay damages is discharged if it subsequently appears that there would have been a total failure of performance by the injured party").... We have taken the view that, even where promises were not concurrent, a plaintiff could only recover nominal or small damages against a defendant who repudiated a contract, where it would have been impossible for the plaintiff to perform a contractual obligation arising shortly after the defendant's breach. See *Randall v. Peerless Motor Car Co.,* 212 Mass. 352, 382, 99 N.E. 221 (1912).

Here, the bank's obligation to sell the shares and Kanavos's obligation to pay for them were concurrent obligations. If neither could perform, even if the bank repudiated the contract, neither could recover. 6 S. Williston, *supra* § 882, at 389–391. Kanavos did not have to show that he was ready, willing, and able to purchase the stock on the day the bank repudiated its agreement with him by selling the stock. *Thomas v. Christensen,* 12 Mass.App.Ct. 169, 177, 422 N.E.2d 472 (1981). That principle does not mean, however, that his ability to purchase the stock during the option period is irrelevant....

If, as we have concluded, Kanavos's ability to match the offer which the bank accepted is material to his right to recover, the question then is whether the burden of proof should be placed on Kanavos to show his ability or on the bank to show his lack of ability. The general rule is that the plaintiff must prove his ability to perform his obligations under a contract of the type involved here.... There is not, however, a unanimity of view in this country on the placing of the burden of proof in such a case....

The burden was on Kanavos to prove his ability to finance the purchase of the stock. The fact of his ability to do so was an essential part of establishing the defendant's liability. Circumstances concerning his ability to raise $760,000 for the stock were far better known to him than to the bank. It is, of course, true that the bank created the problem by selling the stock to another in violation of its contractual obligation, and one could argue that, therefore, it should take the risk of failing to establish Kanavos's inability to purchase the stock. Such an argument, however, has not been generally accepted, for to do so would in effect place on the defendant the burden of disproving a fact essential to the plaintiff's case.

There was evidence from which the jury would have been warranted in finding that Kanavos had the ability to finance the purchase of the stock. Although he admitted that he was in financial difficulty during the relevant times, he had connections with people who might have assisted him. He testified that he could have purchased the stock if the bank had given him timely notice of his rights. Moreover, the jury found that the apartment complex was worth $1,500,000 more than the principal balance of the first mortgage, and thus $780,000 more than Kanavos would have had to have paid the bank for the stock (the sale price of $760,000 less the $40,000 the bank owed him). This differential suggests that financing was not an impossibility for Kanavos. Considering Kanavos's admitted financial difficulties at that time, the question of his ability to purchase the stock (or to sell his rights to another) may depend on whether the earnings of the apartment complex were sufficient to support some arrangement to finance the acquisition within the various limitations applicable under the federally guaranteed first mortgage (assuming it were not to be discharged in the process).

The question of Kanavos's ability to purchase the stock should have been submitted to the jury. We see no reason, however, for a retrial of those issues already decided by the jury. We remand the case for a retrial on the question whether, if he had had proper notice of his right to purchase the stock, Kanavos would have been ready, willing, and able to do so during the option period.

So ordered.

SECTION 3. MATERIAL BREACH: FAILURE OF PERFORMANCE BY ONE PARTY AS AN EXCUSE FOR NONPERFORMANCE BY THE OTHER

RESTATEMENT, SECOND, CONTRACTS § 237

[See Selected Source Materials Supplement]

K & G CONSTR. CO. v. HARRIS

Court of Appeals of Maryland, 1960.
223 Md. 305, 164 A.2d 451.

Before Brune, C.J., and Henderson, Hammond, Prescott and Horney, JJ.

Prescott, Judge. Feeling aggrieved by the action of the trial judge of the Circuit Court for Prince George's County, sitting without a jury, in finding a judgment against it in favor of a subcontractor, the appellant, the general contractor on a construction project, appealed.[1]

The principal question presented is: Does a contractor, damaged by a subcontractor's failure to perform a portion of his work in a workmanlike manner, have a right, under the circumstances of this case, to withhold, in partial satisfaction of said damages, an installment payment, which, under the terms of the contract, was due the subcontractor, unless the negligent performance of his work excused its payment?

The appeal is presented on a case stated in accordance with Maryland Rule 826g.

The statement, in relevant part, is as follows:

"... K & G Construction Company, Inc. (hereinafter called Contractor), plaintiff and counter-defendant in the Circuit Court and appellant herein, was owner and general contractor of a housing subdivision project being constructed (herein called Project). Harris and Brooks (hereinafter called Subcontractor), defendants and counter-plaintiffs in the Circuit Court and appellees herein, entered into a contract with Contractor to do excavating and earth-moving work on the Project. Pertinent parts of the contract are set forth below:

"'Section 3. The Subcontractor agrees to complete the several portions and the whole of the work herein sublet by the time or times following:

"'(a) Without delay, as called for by the Contractor.

"'(b) It is expressly agreed that time is of the essence of this contract, and that the Contractor will have the right to terminate this contract and employ a substitute to perform the work in the event of delay on the part of Subcontractor, and Subcontractor agrees to indemnify the Contractor for any loss sustained thereby, provided, however, that nothing in this paragraph shall be construed to deprive Contractor of any rights or remedies it would otherwise have as to damage for delay.

"'Section 4. (b) Progress payments will be made each month during the performance of the work. Subcontractor will submit to Contractor, by the 25th of each month, a requisition for work performed during the preceding month. Contractor will pay these requisitions, less a retainer equal to ten per cent (10%), by the 10th of the months in which such requisitions are received.[2]

---

1. There are two appellees; the statement of the case refers to them as "subcontractor." We shall do likewise.

2. This section is not a model for clarity.

" "(c) No payments will be made under this contract until the insurance requirements of Sec. 9 hereof have been complied with. . . .

" 'Section 8. . . . All work shall be performed in a workmanlike manner, and in accordance with the best practices.

" 'Section 9. Subcontractor agrees to carry, during the progress of the work, . . . liability insurance against . . . property damage, in such amounts and with such companies as may be satisfactory to Contractor and shall provide Contractor with certificates showing the same to be in force.'

"While in the course of his employment by the Subcontractor on the Project, a bulldozer operator drove his machine too close to Contractor's house while grading the yard, causing the immediate collapse of a wall and other damage to the house. The resulting damage to contractor's house was $3,400.00. Subcontractor had complied with the insurance provision (Sec. 9) of the aforesaid contract. Subcontractor reported said damages to their liability insurance carrier. The Subcontractor and its insurance carrier refused to repair damage or compensate Contractor for damage to the house, claiming that there was no liability on the part of the Subcontractor.

"Contractor gave no written notice to Subcontractor for any services rendered or materials furnished by the Contractor to the Subcontractor . . .

"Contractor was generally satisfied with Subcontractor's work and progress as required under Sections 3 and 8 of the contract until September 12, 1958, with the exception of the bulldozer accident of August 9, 1958.

"Subcontractor performed work under the contract during July, 1958, for which it submitted a requisition by the 25th of July, as required by the contract, for work done prior to the 25th of July, payable under the terms of the contract by Contractor on or before August 10, 1958. Contractor was current as to payments due under all preceding monthly requisitions from Subcontractor. The aforesaid bulldozer accident damaging Contractor's house occurred on August 9, 1958. Contractor refused to pay Subcontractor's requisition due on August 10, 1958, because the bulldozer damage to Contractor's house had not been repaired or paid for. Subcontractor continued to work on the project until the 12th of September, 1958, at which time they discontinued working on the project because of Contractor's refusal to pay the said work requisition and notified Contractor by registered letters of their position and willingness to return to the job, but only upon payment. At that time, September 12, 1958, the value of the work completed by Subcontractor on the project for which they had not been paid was $1,484.50

"Contractor later requested Subcontractor to return and complete work on the Project which Subcontractor refused to do because of nonpayment of work requisitions of July 25 and thereafter. Contractor's house was not repaired by Subcontractor nor compensation paid for the damage.

"It was stipulated that Subcontractor had completed work on the Project under the contract for which they had not been paid in the amount of $1,484.50 and that if they had completed the remaining work to be done under the contract, they would have made a profit of $1,340.00 on the remaining uncompleted portion of the contract. It was further stipulated that it cost the Contractor $450.00 above the contract price to have another excavating contractor complete remaining work required under the contract. It was the opinion of the Court that if judgment were in favor of the Subcontractor, it should be for the total amount of $2,824.50.

". . . Contractor filed suit against the Subcontractor in two counts: (1), for the aforesaid bulldozer damage to Contractor's house, alleging negligence of the Subcontractor's bulldozer operator, and (2) for the $450.00 costs above the contract price in having another excavating subcontractor complete the uncompleted work in the contract. Subcontractor filed a counter-claim for recovery of work of the value of $1,484.50 for which they had not received payment and for loss of anticipated profits on uncompleted portion of work in the amount of $1,340.00. By agreement of the parties, the first count of Contractor's claim, i.e., for aforesaid bulldozer damage to Contractor's house, was submitted to jury who found in favor of Contractor in the amount of $3,400.00. Following the finding by the jury, the second count of the Contractor's claim and the counter-claims of the Subcontractor, by agreement of the parties, were submitted to the Court for determination, without jury. All of the facts recited herein above were stipulated to by the parties to the Court. Circuit Court Judge Fletcher found for counter-plaintiff Subcontractor in the amount of $2,824.50 from which Contractor has entered this appeal."

The $3,400 judgment has been paid.

It is immediately apparent that our decision turns upon the respective rights and liabilities of the parties under that portion of their contract whereby the subcontractor agreed to do the excavating and earth-moving work in "a workmanlike manner, and in accordance with the best practices," with time being of the essence of the contract, and the contractor agreed to make progress payments therefor on the 10th day of the months following the performance of the work by the subcontractor.[3] The subcontractor contends, of course, that when the contractor failed to make the payment due on August 10, 1958, he breached his contract and thereby released him (the subcontractor) from any further obligation to perform. The contractor, on the other hand, argues that the failure of the subcontractor to perform his work in a workmanlike manner constituted a material breach of the contract, which justified his refusal to make the August 10 payment; and, as there was no breach on his part, the subcontractor had no right to cease performance on September 12, and his refusal to continue work on the project constituted another breach, which rendered him liable to the contractor for damages. The vital question, more tersely stated, remains: Did the contractor have a right, under the circumstances, to refuse to make the progress payment due on August 10, 1958?

3. The statement of the case does not show the exact terms concerning the remuneration to be paid the subcontractor. It does not disclose whether he was to be paid a total lump sum, by the cubic yard, by the day, or in some other manner. It does state that the excavation finally cost the contractor $450 more than the "contract price."

. . . Promises are mutually dependent if the parties intend *performance* by one to be conditioned upon *performance* by the other, and, if they be mutually dependent, they may be (a) precedent, i.e., a promise that is to be performed before a corresponding promise on the part of the adversary party is to be performed, (b) subsequent, i.e., a corresponding promise that is not to be performed until the other party to the contract has performed a precedent covenant, or (c) concurrent, i.e., promises that are to be performed at the same time by each of the parties, who are respectively bound to perform each. . . .

. . . The modern rule, which seems to be of almost universal application, is that there is a presumption that mutual promises in a contract are dependent and are to be so regarded, whenever possible. . . .

Considering the presumption that promises and counter-promises are dependent and the statement of the case, we have no hesitation in holding that the promise and counter-promise under consideration here were mutually dependent, that is to say, the parties intended performance by one to be conditioned on performance by the other; and the subcontractor's promise was, by the explicit wording of the contract, precedent to the promise of payment, monthly, by the contractor. In Shapiro Engineering Corp. v. Francis O. Day Co., 215 Md. 373, 380, 137 A.2d 695, we stated that it is the general rule that where a total price for work is fixed by a contract, the work is not rendered divisible by progress payments. It would indeed present an unusual situation if we were to hold that a building contractor, who has obtained someone to do work for him and has agreed to pay each month for the work performed in the previous month, has to continue the monthly payments, irrespective of the degree of skill and care displayed in the performance of work, and his only recourse is by way of suit for ill-performance. If this were the law, it is conceivable, in fact, probable, that many contractors would become insolvent before they were able to complete their contracts. . . .

We hold that when the subcontractor's employee negligently damaged the contractor's wall, this constituted a breach of the subcontractor's promise to perform his work in a "workmanlike manner, and in accordance with the best practices." Gaybis v. Palm, 201 Md. 78, 85, 93 A.2d 269; Johnson v. Metcalfe, 209 Md. 537, 544, 121 A.2d 825; 17 C.J.S. Contracts § 515; Weiss v. Sheet Metal Fabricators, 206 Md. 195, 203, 110 A.2d 671. And there can be little doubt that the breach was material: the damage to the wall amounted to more than double the payment due on August 10. Speed v. Bailey, 153 Md. 655, 661, 662, 139 A. 534. 3A Corbin, Contracts, § 708, says: "The failure of a contractor's [in our case, the subcontractor's] performance to constitute 'substantial' performance may justify the owner [in our case, the contractor] in refusing to make a progress payment. . . . If the refusal to pay an install-ment is justified on the owner's [contractor's] part, the contractor [subcon-tractor] is not justified in abandoning work by reason of that refusal. His abandonment of the work will itself be a wrongful repudiation that goes to the essence, even if the defects in performance did not." See also Restatement, Contracts § 274; F.H. McGraw & Co. v. Sherman Plastering Co., D.C.Conn., 60 F.Supp. 504, 512, affirmed 2 Cir., 149 F.2d 301 . . . and compare Williston, op. cit., §§ 805, 841 and 842. Professor Corbin, in § 954, states further: "The unexcused failure of a contractor to render a promised performance when it is due is always a breach of contract ... Such failure may be of such great importance as to constitute what has been called herein a 'total' breach.... For a failure of performance constituting such a 'total' breach, an action for remedies that are appropriate thereto is at once maintainable. Yet the injured party is not required to bring such action. He has the option of treating the non-performance as a 'partial' breach only...." In permitting the subcontractor to proceed with work on the project after August 9, the contractor, obviously, treated the breach by the subcontractor as a partial one. As the promises were mutually dependent and the subcontractor had made a material breach in his performance, this justified the contractor in refusing to make the August 10 payment; hence, as the contractor was not in default, the subcontractor again breached the contract when he, on September 12, discontinued work on the project, which rendered him liable (by the express terms of the contract) to the contractor for his increased cost in having the excavating done—a stipulated amount of $450. Cf. Keystone Engineering Corp. v. Sutter, 196 Md. 620, 628, 78 A.2d 191....

Judgment against the appellant reversed; and judgment entered in favor of the appellant against the appellees for $450, the appellees to pay the costs.

E. ALLAN FARNSWORTH, CONTRACTS § 8.13 (4th ed. 2004). "A contract is said to be divisible if the performances to be exchanged can be divided into corresponding pairs of part performances in such a way that a court will treat the parts of each pair as if the parties had agreed that they were equivalents....

"Suppose, for example, that a builder has made a contract to build three houses at $100,000 each for a total price of $300,000. The builder breaks the contract by building only one of the houses and claims its price of $100,000. Will a court allow the builder to recover on the contract to build three houses, even though the builder has not substantially performed it? It will, if it regards the contract as divisible into three pairs of part performances, each pair consisting of the building of a house and the payment of $100,000. The builder is then entitled to recover $100,000 on the contract for the house that was built, less such damages as the owner can prove were suffered by the builder's breach in not building the other two. Indeed, if the contract is divisible, the builder is entitled to recover on the contract for building the first house even if performance of that part of the contract is only substantial. The builder's recovery will then be reduced by damages resulting from the defects in the first house as well as from the failure to build the other two houses.

"How does a court decide whether a contract is divisible? As the Supreme Court of Colorado warned that 'there is no set formula which furnishes a foolproof method for determining in a given case just which contracts are severable and which are entire.' The Restatement Second lays down two requirements: it must be possible to apportion the parties' performances into corresponding pairs of part performances; and it must be proper to regard the parts of each pair as agreed equivalents."

WALKER & CO. v. HARRISON

Supreme Court of Michigan, 1957.
347 Mich. 630, 81 N.W.2d 352.

Before the Entire Bench, except BOYLES, J.

SMITH, JUSTICE. This is a suit on a written contract. The defendants are in the dry-cleaning business. Walker & Company, plaintiff, sells, rents, and services advertising signs and billboards. These parties entered into an agreement pertaining to a sign. The agreement is in writing and is termed a "rental agreement." It specifies in part that:

"The lessor agrees to construct and install, at its own cost, one 18§ 9§ high § 8§ 8§ wide pylon type d.f. neon sign with electric clock and flashing lamps.... The lessor agrees to and does hereby lease or rent unto the said lessee the said SIGN for the term, use and rental and under the conditions, hereinafter set out, and the lessee agrees to pay said rental....

"(a) The term of this lease shall be 36 months....

"(b) The rental to be paid by lessee shall be $148.50 per month for each and every calendar month during the term of this lease;....

"(d) *Maintenance.* Lessor at its expense agrees to maintain and service the sign together with such equipment as supplied and installed by the lessor to operate in conjunction with said sign under the terms of this lease; this service is to include cleaning and repainting of sign in original color scheme as often as deemed necessary by lessor to keep sign in first class advertising condition and make all necessary repairs to sign and equipment installed by lessor...."

At the "expiration of this agreement," it was also provided, "title to this sign reverts to lessee." This clause is in addition to the printed form of agreement and was apparently added as a result of defendants' concern over title, they having expressed a desire "to buy for cash" and the salesman, at one time, having "quoted a cash price."

The sign was completed and installed in the latter part of July, 1953. The first billing of the monthly payment of $148.50 was made August 1, 1953, with payment thereof by defendants on September 3, 1953. This first payment was also the last. Shortly after the sign was installed, someone hit it with a tomato. Rust, also, was visible on the chrome, complained defendants, and in its corners were "little spider cobwebs." In addition, there were "some children's sayings written down in here." Defendant Herbert Harrison called Walker for the maintenance he believed himself entitled to under subparagraph (d) above. It was not forthcoming. He called again and again. "I was getting, you might say, sorer and sorer.... Occasionally, when I started calling up, I would walk around where the tomato was and get mad again. Then I would call up on the phone again." Finally, on October 8, 1953, plaintiff not having responded to his repeated calls, he telegraphed Walker that:

"You Have Continually Voided Our Rental Contract By Not Maintaining Signs As Agreed As We No Longer Have A Contract With You Do Not Expect Any Further Remuneration."

Walker's reply was in the form of a letter. After first pointing out that "your telegram does not make any specific allegations as to what the failure of maintenance comprises," and stating that "We certainly would appreciate your furnishing us with such information," the letter makes reference to a prior collateral controversy between the parties, "wondering if this refusal on our part prompted your attempt to void our rental contract," and concludes as follows:

> "We would like to call your attention to paragraph G in our rental contract, which covers procedures in the event of a Breach of Agreement. In the event that you carry out your threat to make no future monthly payments in accordance with the agreement, it is our intention to enforce the conditions outlined under paragraph G[1] through the proper legal channels. We call to your attention that your monthly rental payments are due in advance at our office not later than the 10th day of each current month. You are now approximately 30 days in arrears on your September payment. Unless we receive both the September and October payments by October 25th, this entire matter will be placed in the hands of our attorney for collection in accordance with paragraph G which stipulates that the entire amount is forthwith due and payable."

No additional payments were made and Walker sued in assumpsit for the entire balance due under the contract, $5,197.50, invoking paragraph (g) of the agreement. Defendants filed answer and claim of recoupment, asserting that plaintiff's failure to perform certain maintenance services constituted a prior material breach of the agreement, thus justifying their repudiation of the contract and grounding their claim for damages. The case was tried to the court without a jury and resulted in a judgment for the plaintiff. The case is before us on a general appeal.

Defendants urge upon us again and again, in various forms, the proposition that Walker's failure to service the sign, in response to repeated requests, constituted a material breach of the contract and justified repudiation by them. Their legal proposition is undoubtedly correct. Repudiation is one of the weapons available to an injured party in event the other contractor has committed a material breach. But the injured party's determination that there has been a material breach, justifying his own repudiation, is fraught with peril, for should such determination, as viewed by a later court in the calm of its contemplation, be unwarranted, the repudiator himself will have been guilty of material breach and himself have become the aggressor, not an innocent victim.

---

1. (g) *Breach of Agreement.* Lessee shall be deemed to have breached this agreement by default in payment of any installment of the rental herein provided for; abandonment of the sign or vacating premises where the sign is located; termination or transfer of lessee's interest in the premises by insolvency, appointment of a receiver for lessee's business; filing of a voluntary or involuntary petition in bankruptcy with respect to lessee or the violation of any of the other terms or conditions hereof. In the event of such default, the lessor may, upon notice to the lessee, which notice shall conclusively be deemed sufficient if mailed or delivered to the premises where the sign was or is located, take possession of the sign and declare the balance of the rental herein provided for to be forthwith due and payable, and lessee hereby agrees to pay such balance upon any such contingencies. Lessor may terminate this lease and without notice, remove and repossess said sign and recover from the lessee such amounts as may be unpaid for the remaining unexpired term of this agreement. Time is of the essence of this lease with respect to the payment of rentals herein provided for. Should lessee after lessor has declared the balance of rentals due and payable, pay the full amount of rental herein provided, he shall then be entitled to the use of the sign, under all the terms and provisions hereof, for the balance of the term of this lease . . . .

What is our criterion for determining whether or not a breach of contract is so fatal to the undertaking of the parties that it is to be classed as "material"? There is no single touchstone. Many factors are involved. They are well stated in section 275 of [the] Restatement, Law of Contracts in the following terms:

"In determining the materiality of a failure fully to perform a promise the following circumstances are influential:

"(a) The extent to which the injured party will obtain the substantial benefit which he could have reasonably anticipated;

"(b) The extent to which the injured party may be adequately compensated in damages for lack of complete performance;

"(c) The extent to which the party failing to perform has already partly performed or made preparations for performance;

"(d) The greater or less hardship on the party failing to perform in terminating the contract;

"(e) The wilful, negligent or innocent behavior of the party failing to perform;

"(f) The greater or less uncertainty that the party failing to perform will perform the remainder of the contract."*

We will not set forth in detail the testimony offered concerning the need for servicing. Granting that Walker's delay (about a week after defendant Herbert Harrison sent his telegram of repudiation Walker sent out a crew and took care of things) in rendering the service requested was irritating, we are constrained to agree with the trial court that it was not of such materiality as to justify repudiation of the contract, and we are particularly mindful of the lack of preponderant evidence contrary to his determination. Jones v. Eastern Michigan Motorbuses, 287 Mich. 619, 283 N.W. 710. The trial court, on this phase of the case, held as follows:

"Now Mr. Harrison phoned in, so he testified, a number of times. He isn't sure of the dates but he sets the first call at about the 7th of August and he complained then of the tomato and of some rust and some cobwebs. The tomato, according to the testimony, was up on the clock; that would be outside of his reach, without a stepladder or something. The cobwebs are within easy reach of Mr. Harrison and so would the rust be. I think that Mr. Bueche's argument that these were not materially a breach would clearly be true as to the cobwebs and I really can't believe in the face of all the testimony that there was a great deal of rust seven days after the installation of this sign. And that really brings it down to the tomato. And, of course, when a tomato has been splashed all over your clock, you don't like it. But he says he kept calling their attention to it, although the rain probably washed some of the tomato off. But the stain remained, and they didn't come. I really can't find that that was such a material breach of the contract as to justify rescission. I really don't think so."

Nor, we conclude, do we. There was no valid ground for defendants' repudiation and their failure thereafter to comply with the terms of the

* The citation is to Restatement First. (Footnote by ed.)

contract was itself a material breach, entitling Walker, upon this record, to judgment.

The question of damages remains. The parties, particularly appellants, have discussed at some length whether this contract is one of sale or of lease. Through much of its content it appears merely to be an ordinary lease, but when we come to its end we find that title, without more, is to pass to the "lessee" at the expiration of the agreement. Is the so-called rent merely the payment of a sale price in installments? We need not, in the light of the terms of the particular contract, and upon the record, vex this question, despite illustrious aid offered us by 2 Williston on Sales, § 336, extensive annotations in 17 A.L.R. 1435, 43 A.L.R. 1257, 92 A.L.R. 323, and 175 A.L.R. 1366, and the comprehensive analysis of Dalzell in 1 Oregon Law Review 9, "Lease–Contracts as a Means of Conveying Title to Chattels." For the parties before us have agreed, with particularity, as to remedies in event of breach, the remedy here sought, as provided, being acceleration of "rentals" due. The trial court cut down such sum by the amount that service would have cost Walker during the unexpired portion of the agreement (Restatement, Contracts, § 335) and as to such diminution Walker does not complain or cross-appeal. Judgment was, therefore, rendered for the cash price of the sign, for such services and maintenance as were extended and accepted, and interest upon the amount in default. There was no error.

Affirmed. Costs to appellee.

ZULLA STEEL, INC. v. A & M GREGOS, INC., 174 N.J.Super. 124, 415 A.2d 1183 (1980). Defendant was the prime contractor for the expansion of a post office. Plaintiff was a subcontractor. Plaintiff started performing under its contract in summer 1975. It continued working into 1976, when it left the job because it was not paid progress payments in accordance with its contract. On March 23, 1976, defendant telegraphed plaintiff to return to the job or its contract would be terminated. Plaintiff did not return. The trial court held that defendant had committed a material breach, and plaintiff was entitled to stop performing and sue for damages. Affirmed.

"The trial judge held that defendant, by reason of its delinquencies in payments, had breached the contract with plaintiff, and we agree.... Plaintiff presented substantial credible evidence that defendant's failure to pay plaintiff meant that plaintiff could not pay its [own] subcontractor and thus could not complete its contract with defendant. The trial judge accepted this testimony and so do we....

"Since defendant breached its contract we must determine whether the breach justified plaintiff in abandoning the project. It is true that it has been held that where a contract is entire so that the payment of the consideration in installments is not for a particular performance, nonpayment does not justify the contractor in failing to complete the work.... But there is contrary authority.... Certainly the current approach in contract construction is to honor the expressed or presumed intention of the parties.... We find it impossible to believe that in a major construction project the parties would expect that a subcontractor would be obliged to continue working even though there were material delays in payment to it. Ordinarily the parties would expect that the subcontractor would be using the installment payments to satisfy its own expenses. While we do not suggest that every delay in payment will justify a contractor in terminating performance under an installment contract, here there was a substantial underpayment for a prolonged period of time. In these circumstances we hold that plaintiff was justified in discontinuing performance."

RESTATEMENT, SECOND, CONTRACTS §§ 241, 242

[See Selected Source Materials Supplement]

CISG ARTS. 25, 49

[See Selected Source Materials Supplement]

UNIDROIT PRINCIPLES OF INTERNATIONAL COMMERCIAL CONTRACTS ARTS. 7.3.1, 7.3.5, 7.3.6

[See Selected Source Materials Supplement]

PRINCIPLES OF EUROPEAN CONTRACT LAW ARTS. 9.301, 9.302, 9.305, 9.307–309

[See Selected Source Materials Supplement]

NOTE ON THE DOCTRINES OF MATERIAL BREACH AND SUBSTANTIAL PERFORMANCE

The doctrine of material breach bears an obvious relationship to the doctrine of substantial performance. Both doctrines reflect the idea that although all breaches give rise to damages, some breaches may have other consequences as well. And both doctrines ordinarily distinguish between what could colloquially be called "major" or "very important" breaches, on the one hand, and "minor" or "less important" breaches, on the other. It has been said that the two doctrines are the opposite sides of the same coin: if a party has substantially performed, then any breach she may have committed is not material; if a party has committed a material breach, her performance cannot be substantial. This view is exemplified in Restatement Second § 237, Illustration 11:

A contracts to build a house for B, for which B promises to pay $50,000 in monthly progress payments equal to 85% of the value of the work with the balance to be paid on completion. When A completes construction, B refuses to pay the $7,500 balance claiming that there are defects that amount to an uncured material breach. If the breach is material, A's performance is not substantial and he has no claim under the contract against B, although he may have a claim in restitution (§ 374). If the breach is not material, A's performance is said to be substantial, he has a claim under the contract against B for $7,500, and B has a claim against A for damages because of the defects.

While this view of material breach and substantial performance as opposite sides of the coin may hold true in many cases, it is not true in all cases, and it masks an important difference between the two doctrines. This difference can be brought out with a simple illustration. Suppose A and B are parties to a contract that A has breached in some way. A would invoke the doctrine of *substantial performance* if he has *already* more or less completed his performance, and B refuses to pay the contract price on the ground that A has committed some breach. A's purpose in invoking that doctrine would be to enable him to sue B on the contract for the contract price (minus damages resulting from his breach), rather than being remitted to a suit based on benefit conferred.

In contrast, A would invoke the doctrine of *material breach*—or more accurately, the *lack* of material breach—if there is some disruption in his performance *before* he has more or less completed performance, and B then terminates the contract and sues A for *total breach* (as opposed to a suit for partial breach, based on the defects in A's performance). A then argues that while he may have breached the contract, and B can sue for damages based on the defects in A's performance, the breach was not sufficiently material to justify either termination by B or B's suit for total breach of the whole contract. And, as a corollary, A will claim that B has herself committed material breach in refusing to go forward with the contract.

To put this differently, the doctrine of substantial performance concerns the question, when can a party who has breached a contract nevertheless bring suit under the contract. The doctrine of material breach concerns the very different question, when can a party who has *not* breached a contract (i) invoke the sanction of terminating the contract for the other party's breach, and (ii) bring suit for damages for total breach.

As a consequence of the difference between the two doctrines, the doctrine of material breach may be relevant in cases where the doctrine of substantial performance would ordinarily not be. For example, suppose A commits a breach very early in his performance. In response, B terminates the contract and sues A for total breach. There is no question here of A invoking the doctrine of substantial performance. A may very well, however, invoke the doctrine of material breach, and claim that his breach was insufficiently material to justify B's response.

———

NOTE ON THE CONCEPT OF CURE UNDER
RESTATEMENT SECOND

Recall that one way in which the UCC limited the perfect-tender rule, in contracts for the sale of goods, was by introducing the concept of cure. Restatement Second § 237 introduces a version of cure into all contracts, not merely contracts for the sale of goods.

§ 237. Effect on Other Party's Duties of a Failure to Render Performance

... [I]t is a condition of each party's remaining duties to render performances to be exchanged under an exchange of promises that there be no *uncured* material failure by the other party to render any such performance due at an earlier time.*

The Comment adds:

... Under the rule stated in this Section, a material failure of performance, including defective performance as well as an absence of performance, operates as the non-occurrence of a condition. [T]he non-occurrence of a condition has two possible effects on the duty subject to that condition.... The first is that of preventing performance of the duty from becoming due, at least temporarily.... The second is that of discharging the duty when the condition can no longer occur.... A material failure of performance has, under this Section, these effects on the other party's remaining duties of performance with respect to the exchange. It prevents performance of those duties from becoming due, at least temporarily, and it discharges those duties *if it has not been cured* during the time in which performance can occur....

Illustrations:

1. A contracts to build a house for B for $50,000, progress payments to be made monthly in an amount equal to 85% of the price of the work performed during the preceding month, the balance to be paid on the architect's certificate of satisfactory completion of the house. Without justification B fails to make a $5,000 progress payment. A thereupon stops work on the house and a week goes by. A's failure to continue the work is not a breach and B has no claim against A. B's failure to make the progress payment is an uncured material failure of performance which operates as the non-occurrence of a condition of A's remaining duties of performance under the exchange. If B offers to make the delayed payment and in all the circumstances *it is not too late to cure* the material breach, A's duties to continue the work are not discharged. A has a claim against B for damages for partial breach because of the delay.

2. The factors being otherwise as stated in Illustration 1, B fails to make the progress payment or to give any explanation or assurances for one month. If, in all the circumstances, it is now *too late for B to cure* his material failure of performance by making the delayed payment, A's duties to continue the work are discharged. Because B's failure to make the progress payment was a breach, A also has a claim against B for total breach of contract....

Similarly, Restatement Second § 241 provides:

* Emphasis throughout this Note is added.

§ 241. Circumstances Significant in Determining
Whether a Failure Is Material

In determining whether a failure to render or to offer performance is material, the following circumstances are significant . . .

(d) the likelihood that the party failing to perform or to offer to perform *will cure his failure,* taking account of all the circumstances including any reasonable assurances. . . .

———

UNIDROIT PRINCIPLES OF INTERNATIONAL COMMERCIAL CONTRACTS ART. 7.1.4

[See Selected Source Materials Supplement]

———

PRINCIPLES OF EUROPEAN CONTRACT LAW ART. 8.104

[See Selected Source Materials Supplement]

———

STANLEY GUDYKA SALES, INC. v. LACY FOREST PRODUCTS CO., 915 F.2d 273 (7th Cir.1990). Gudyka and Lacy were each engaged in buying and selling lumber and related wood products. They agreed that Gudyka would work for Lacy as an independent contractor, and that Gudyka and Lacy would split the profits on sales made by Gudyka. In general, all customers were to pay Lacy, and Lacy was then to pay Gudyka his share of the commissions. However, one customer, P & E, was to pay Gudyka, who was to remit 50% of the commissions to Lacy. Gudyka failed to remit Lacy's share of the P & E Commissions (around $3,000), but during the relevant period Gudyka was entitled to about $46,000 from Lacy (which was eventually paid). Lacy terminated its contract with Gudyka on the ground that Gudyka had breached the contract by not remitting the P & E commissions. Gudyka then sued Lacy on the ground that the termination was improper. The trial court held for Gudyka. Affirmed:

". . . As the district court noted, [the termination] remedy is only available where termination is in proportion to the 'need' for accountability from the breaching party, and where the breach is material rather than 'insignificant.' . . . The district court determined that Lacy's use of the 'self-help remedy' of terminating Gudyka in this case was not proportional to its need and that the amount Gudyka owed to Lacy, as compared with the amounts Lacy owed Gudyka, was an 'insignificant' breach. In addition, the court found that because Lacy knew how much Gudyka owed it, Lacy was obligated to give Gudyka notice and an opportunity to cure its breach. In the event that Gudyka did not cure, Lacy still had the alternative self-help remedy of deducting (as it later did deduct) the amount owed on the P & E accounts from a commission check. Without having given notice and an opportunity to cure, the district court determined that Lacy terminated Gudyka without 'just cause.' . . .

"... [T]he district court found that Lacy had several options which it could have taken short of termination. Lacy takes exception to both options (notice and an opportunity to cure and taking an accounting) suggested by the district court. Although we have not discovered any Illinois case requiring a non-breaching party to provide notice and an opportunity to cure in circumstances similar to this case, this requirement comports with general contract theory and we agree with the district court's decision imposing this requirement on Lacy. . . ."

———

Chapter 26

ANTICIPATORY BREACH, PROSPECTIVE INABILITY TO PERFORM, AND ADEQUATE ASSURANCE OF PERFORMANCE

This Chapter concerns the following related topics: (1) The effect of a repudiation of a contract by a party before the party's performance is due. (2) The consequences that arise when it appears that one party to a contract will be unable to perform although she has not repudiated the contract. (3) Whether and when a party to a contract may justifiably insist that the other party provide adequate assurance that performance will be forthcoming.

SECTION 1. ANTICIPATORY BREACH

HOCHSTER v. DE LA TOUR

In the Queen's Bench, 1853.
2 Ellis & Bl. 678.

This was an action for breach of contract. On the trial, before Erle, J., at the London sittings in last Easter Term, it appeared that plaintiff was a courier, who, in April, 1852, was engaged by defendant to accompany him on a tour to commence on June 1st, 1852, on the terms mentioned in the declaration. On May 11th, 1852, defendant wrote to plaintiff that he had changed his mind, and declined his services. He refused to make him any compensation. The action was commenced on May 22d. The plaintiff, between the commencement of the action and June 1st, obtained an engagement with Lord Ashburton, on equally good terms, but not commencing till July 4th. The defendant's counsel objected that there could be no breach of the contract before the 1st of June. The learned judge was of a contrary opinion, but reserved leave to enter a nonsuit on this objection. The other questions were left to the jury, who found for plaintiff.

Hugh Hill, in the same term, obtained a rule nisi to enter a nonsuit or arrest the judgment. In last Trinity Term.

Hannon showed cause.... If one party to an executory contract gave the other notice that he refused to go on with the bargain, in order that the other side might act upon that refusal in such a manner as to incapacitate himself from fulfilling it, and he did so act, the refusal could never be retracted; and, accordingly, in Cort v. Ambergate & c. R. Co. (17 Q.B. 127) this court after considering the cases, decided that in such a case the plaintiff might recover, though he was no longer in a position to fulfil his contract. That was a contract under seal to manufacture and supply iron chairs. The purchasers discharged the vendors from manufacturing the goods; and it was held that an action might be maintained by the vendors. It is true, however, that in that case the writ was issued after the time when the chairs ought to have been received. In the present case, if the writ had been issued on the 2nd of June, Cort v. Ambergate & c. R. Co. would have been expressly in point. The question, therefore, comes to be: Does it make any difference that the writ was issued before the 1st of June? If the dicta of Parke, B., in Phillpotts v. Evans, 5 M. & W. 475, are to be taken as universally applicable it does make a difference; but they cannot be so taken. In a contract to marry at a future day, a marriage of the man before that day is a breach. Short v. Stone, 8 Q.B. 358. The reason of this is, that the marriage is a final refusal to go on with the contract. It is not on the ground that the defendant has rendered it impossible to fulfil the contract; for, as was argued in vain in Short v. Stone, the first wife might be dead before the day came. So also, on a contract to assign a term of years on a day future, a previous assignment to a stranger is a breach. Lovelock v. Franklyn, 8 Q.B. 371. [Lord Campbell, C.J. It probably will not be disputed that an act on the part of the defendant incapacitating himself from going on with the contract would be a breach. But how does the defendant's refusal in May incapacitate him from travelling in June? It was possible that he might do so.] It was; but the plaintiff, who, so long as the engagement subsisted, was bound to keep himself disengaged and make preparations so as to be ready and willing to travel with the defendant on the 1st of June, was informed by the defendant that he would not go on with the contract, in order that the plaintiff might act upon that information; and the plaintiff then was entitled to engage himself to another, as he did. In Planche v. Colburn (8 Bing. 14) the plaintiff had contracted with defendants to write a work for "The Juvenile Library"; and he was held to be entitled to recover on their discontinuing the publication; yet the time for the completion of the contract, that is for the work being published in "The Juvenile Library," had not arrived, for that would not be till a reasonable time after the author had completed the work. Now in that case the author never did complete the work. [Lord Campbell, C.J. It certainly would have been cruelly hard if the author had been obliged, as a condition precedent to redress, to compose a work which he knew could never be published. Crompton, J. When a party announces his intention not to fulfil the contract, the other side may take him at his word and rescind the contract. That word "rescind" implies that both parties have agreed that the contract shall be at an end as if it had never been. But I am inclined to think that the party may also say: "Since you have announced that you will not go on with the contract, I will consent that it shall be at an end from this time; but I will hold you liable for the damage I have sustained; and I will proceed to make that damage as little as possible by making the best use I can of my liberty." This is the principle of those cases in which there has been a discussion as to the measure of damages to which a servant is entitled on a wrongful dismissal. They were all considered in Elderton v. Emmens (6 C.B. 160). Lord Campbell, C.J. The counsel in support of the rule have to answer a very able argument.]

Hugh Hill and Deighton, contra. In Cort v. Ambergate & c. R. Co., the writ was taken out after the time for completing the contract. That case is consistent with the defendant's position, which is, that an act incapacitating the defendant, in law, from completing the contract is a breach, because it is implied that the parties to a contract shall keep themselves legally capable of performing it; but that an announcement of an intention to break the contract when the time comes is no more than an offer to rescind. It is evidence, till retracted, of a dispensation with the necessity of readiness and willingness on the other side; and, if not retracted, it is, when the time for performance comes, evidence of a continued refusal; but till then it may be retracted. Such is the doctrine in Phillpotts v. Evans (5 M. & W. 475) and Ripley v. McClure (4 Exch. 345). [Crompton, J. May not the plaintiff, on notice that the defendant will not employ him, look out for other employment, so as to diminish the loss?] If he adopts the defendant's notice, which is in legal effect an offer to rescind, he must adopt it altogether. [Lord Campbell, C.J. So that you say the plaintiff, to preserve any remedy at all, was bound to remain idle. Erle, J. Do you go one step further? Suppose the defendant, after the plaintiff's engagement with Lord Ashburton, had retracted his refusal and required the plaintiff to travel with him on the 1st of June, and the plaintiff had refused to do so, and gone with Lord Ashburton instead? Do you say that the now defendant could in that case have sued the now plaintiff for a breach of contract?] It would be, in such a case, a question of fact for a jury, whether there had not been an exoneration. In Phillpotts v. Evans, it was held that the measure of damages was the market price at the time when the contract ought to be completed. If a refusal before that time is a breach, how could these damages be ascertained? [Coleridge, J. No doubt it was possible, in this case, that, before the 1st of June, the plaintiff might die, in which case the plaintiff would have gained nothing had the contract gone on. Lord Campbell, C.J. All contingencies should be taken into account by the jury in assessing the damages. Crompton, J. That objection would equally apply to the action by a servant for dismissing him before the end of his term, and so disabling him from earning his wages; yet that action may be brought immediately on the dismissal; note to Cutter v. Powell (6 T.R. 320)]. It is quite possible that the plaintiff himself might have intended not to go on; no one can tell what intention is. [Lord Campbell, C.J. The intention of the defendant might be proved by showing that he entered in his diary a memorandum to that effect; and, certainly, no action would lie for entering such a memorandum. But the question is as to the effect of a communication to the other side, made that he might know that intention and act upon it.] . . .

Lord Campbell, C.J., now delivered the judgment of the Court.

On this motion in arrest of judgment, the question arises, whether if there be an agreement between A and B, whereby B engages to employ A on and from a future day for a given period of time, to travel with him into a foreign country as a courier, and to start with him in that capacity on that day, A being to receive a monthly salary during the continuance of such service, B may, before the day, refuse to perform the agreement and break and renounce it, so as to entitle A before the day to commence an action against B to recover damages for breach of the agreement; A having been ready and willing to perform it, till it was broken and renounced by B. The defendant's counsel very powerfully contended that, if the plaintiff was not contented to dissolve the contract and to abandon all remedy upon it, he was bound to remain ready and willing to perform it till the day when the actual employment as courier in the service of the defendant was to begin; and that there could be no breach of the agreement before that day to give a right of action.

But it cannot be laid down as a universal rule that, where by agreement an act is to be done on a future day, no action can be brought for a breach of the agreement till the day for doing the act has arrived. If a man promises to marry a woman on a future day, and before that day marries another woman, he is instantly liable to an action for breach of promise of marriage. Short v. Stone (8 Q.B. 358). If a man contracts to execute a lease on and from a future day for a certain term, and before that day executes a lease to another for the same term, he may be immediately sued for breaking the contract. Ford v. Tiley (6 B. & C. 325). So, if a man contracts to sell and deliver specific goods on a future day, and before the day he sells and delivers them to another, he is immediately liable to an action at the suit of the person with whom he first contracted to sell and deliver them. Bowdell v. Parsons (10 East. 359). One reason alleged in support of such an action is, that the defendant has, before the day, rendered it impossible for him to perform the contract at the day, but this does not necessarily follow; for prior to the day fixed for doing the act, the first wife may have died, a surrender of the lease executed might be obtained, and the defendant might have repurchased the goods so as to be in a situation to sell and deliver them to the plaintiff. Another reason may be that, where there is a contract to do an act on a future day, there is a relation constituted between the parties in the meantime by the contract, and that they impliedly promise that in the meantime neither will do anything to the prejudice of the other inconsistent with that relation. As an example, a man and woman engaged to marry are affianced to one another during the period between the time of the engagement and the celebration of the marriage.

In this very case of traveler and courier, from the day of the hiring till the day when the employment was to begin, they were engaged to each other; and it seems to be a breach of an implied contract if either of them renounces the engagement. This reasoning seems in accordance with the unanimous decision of the Exchequer Chamber in Elderton v. Emmens (6 C.B. 160), which we have followed in subsequent cases in this court. The declaration in the present case, in alleging a breach, states a great deal more than a passing intention on the part of the defendant which he may repent of, and could only be proved by evidence that he had utterly renounced the contract, or done some act which rendered it impossible for him to perform it.

If the plaintiff has no remedy for breach of the contract unless he treats the contract as in force, and acts upon it down to the 1st of June, 1852, it follows that, till then, he must enter into no employment which will interfere with his promise "to start with the defendant on such travels on the day and year," and that he must then be properly equipped in all respects as a courier for a three months' tour on the continent of Europe. But it is surely much more rational, and more for the benefit of both parties, that, after the renunciation of the agreement by the defendant, the plaintiff should be at liberty to consider himself absolved from any future performance of it, retaining his right to sue for any damage he has suffered from the breach of it. Thus, instead of remaining idle and laying out money in preparations which must be useless, he is at liberty to seek service under another employer, which would go in mitigation to the damages to which he would otherwise be entitled for a breach of the contract. It seems strange that the defendant, after renouncing the contract, and absolutely declaring that he will never act under it, should be permitted to object that faith is given to his assertion, and that an opportunity is not left to him of changing his mind. If the plaintiff is barred of any remedy by entering into an engagement inconsistent with starting as a courier with the defendant on the 1st of June, he is prejudiced by putting faith in the defendant's assertion: and it would be more consonant with principle, if the defendant were precluded from saying that he had not broken the contract when he declared that he entirely renounced it.

Suppose that the defendant, at the time of his renunciation, had embarked on a voyage for Australia, so as to render it physically impossible for him to employ the plaintiff as a courier on the continent of Europe in the months of June, July and August, 1852: according to decided cases, the action might have been brought before the 1st of June; but the renunciation may have been founded on other facts, to be given in evidence, which would equally have rendered the defendant's performance of the contract impossible. The man who wrongfully renounces a contract into which he has deliberately entered cannot justly complain if he is immediately sued for a compensation in damages by the man whom he has injured; and it seems reasonable to allow an option to the injured party, either to sue immediately, or to wait till the time when the act was to be done, still holding it as prospectively binding for the exercise of this option, which may be advantageous to the innocent party, and cannot be prejudicial to the wrongdoer.

An argument against the action before the 1st of June is urged from the difficulty of calculating the damages, but this argument is equally strong against an action before the 1st of September, when the three months would expire. In either case, the jury in assessing the damages would be justified in looking to all that had happened, or was likely to happen, to increase or mitigate the loss of the plaintiff down to the day of trial. We do not find any decision contrary to the view we are taking of this case....

Upon the whole, we think that the declaration in this case is sufficient. It gives us great satisfaction to reflect that, the question being on the record, our opinion may be reviewed in a court of error. In the meantime we must give judgment for the plaintiff.

Judgment for plaintiff.

––––––––

DANIELS v. NEWTON, 114 Mass. 530 (1874). In this case Wells, J., in criticizing the reasoning in Hochster v. De la Tour, said:

A renunciation of the agreement, by declarations or inconsistent conduct, before the time of performance, may give cause for treating it as rescinded, and excuse the other party from making ready for performance on his part, or relieve him from the necessity of offering performance in order to enforce his rights. It may destroy all capacity of the party, so disavowing its obligations to assert rights under it afterwards, if the other party has acted upon such disavowal. But we are unable to see how it can of itself constitute a present violation of any legal rights of the other party, or confer upon him a present right of action. An executory contract ordinarily confers no title or interest in the subject matter of the agreement. Until the time arrives when, by the terms of the agreement, he is or might be entitled to its performance, he can suffer no injury or deprivation which can form a ground of damages. There is neither violation of right, nor loss upon which to found an action . . . .

. . . Throughout the whole discussion . . . in Hochster v. De la Tour . . . the question as to what conduct of the defendant will relieve the plaintiff from the necessity of showing readiness and an offer to perform at the day, in order to make out a breach by the other, appears to us to be confounded with that of the plaintiff's cause of action; or rather, the question, in what consists the plaintiff's cause of action, is lost sight of; the court dealing only with the conduct of the defendant in repudiating the obligations of his contract.

WILLISTON, REPUDIATION OF CONTRACTS, Pt. 2, 14 Harv. L.Rev. 421, 428–29 (1901). "The . . . question remains, when may the injured party bring his action upon the contract [following an anticipatory repudiation]? from a technical point of view, it seems obvious that in an action on a contract the plaintiff must state that the defendant broke some promise which he had made. If he promised to employ the plaintiff upon June 1, the breach must be that he did not do that. A statement in may by the defendant that he was not going to employ the plaintiff upon june 1 can be a breach only of a contract not to make such statements. It is perhaps not wholly by chance that the doctrine of anticipatory breach has arisen as the exactness of common–law pleading has become largely a thing of the past; for the science of special pleading, in spite of the grave defects attending it, had the great merit of making clear the exact questions of law and fact to be decided.

"The matter is so plain on principle that theoretical discussion is hardly possible . . . ."

EQUITABLE TRUST CO. v. WESTERN PAC. RY., 244 Fed. 485, 501–502 (S.D.N.Y.1917), remanded for correction and affirmed, 250 Fed. 327 (2d Cir.), cert. denied 246 U.S. 672, 38 S.Ct. 423, 62 L.Ed. 932 (1918) (L. Hand, J.) "[The basis of the doctrine of anticipatory breach] is that a promise to perform in the future by implication includes an engagement not deliberately to compromise the probability of performance. A promise is a verbal act designed as a reliance to the promisee, and so as a means to the forecast of his own conduct. Abstention from any deliberate act before the time of performance which makes impossible that reliance and that forecast ought surely to be included by implication. Such intermediate uncertainties as arise from the vicissitudes of the promisor's affairs are, of course, a part of the risk, but it is hard to see how, except by mere verbalism, it can be supposed that the promisor may within the terms of his undertaking gratuitously add to those uncertainties by announcing his purpose to default."

BALLANTINE, ANTICIPATORY BREACH AND THE ENFORCE-MENT OF CONTRACTUAL DUTIES, 22 Mich.L.Rev. 329, 330–31 (1924). "Upon what theory, it is asked, can a person be held liable for a breach of contract before the time for its performance has arrived? Of what default can the repudiator be found guilty? Why should renunciation of a contract give an immediate right of action? There are two possible theories, (1) that repudiation is a present injury; and (2) that a threatened injury may furnish a ground of action. . . .

"Professor Williston assumes as obvious (but it is believed unadvisedly) the question-begging premise that in an action on a contract the plaintiff must state that the defendant broke some promise. . . .

" . . . It is believed, with all deference, that Professor Williston fails to distinguish between the promise and the duties arising from the promise. To be exact a breach of contract involves a failure to perform a contractual duty rather than a broken promise. And perhaps a mere threat to commit a breach should furnish a cause of action to enforce the contractual duty. The legal duties arising from a contractual engagement are not entirely measured by the literal terms of the promise. Professor Williston himself has well explained this in connection with the doctrine of implied conditions. If the promisee has a legitimate interest to be protected in the reasonable expectation of performance the law may well impose a duty on a promisor, on principles of good faith, not to destroy this interest and thereby impair the value of the contract. A repudiation may thus be a breach of duty and a cause of action to enforce the contract even if not literally a present breach of promise."

WHOLESALE SAND & GRAVEL, INC. v. DECKER

Supreme Judicial Court of Maine, 1993.
630 A.2d 710.

Before WATHEN, C.J., and ROBERTS, GLASSMAN, CLIFFORD, COLLINS, RUDMAN and DANA, JJ.

ROBERTS, JUSTICE.

Wholesale Sand & Gravel, Inc., appeals from a judgment entered in the Superior Court (Sagadahoc County, *Lipez, J.*) in favor of James Decker on its claim for the breach of their contract. On appeal, Wholesale contends that the court erred in holding that its conduct constituted an anticipatory repudiation of the contract and in deciding the case on a defense that had not been raised in the pleadings. Finding no error, we affirm the judgment.

On June 13, 1989, James Decker and Wholesale Sand & Gravel, Inc., entered into a contract whereby Wholesale agreed to perform earth work, including the installation of a gravel driveway, on Decker's property in Bowdoin. The contract contained no provision specifying a completion date for the work. Indeed, the only time reference made in the contract was that payment was to be made within 90 days. Although Carl Goodenow, Wholesale's president, believed the company had 90 days within which to complete the work, he told Decker that the driveway portion of the work would be completed within one week.

Wholesale began work on the driveway on the weekend after the contract was executed and immediately experienced difficulty because of the wetness of the ground. In fact, Wholesale's bulldozer became stuck in the mud and had to be removed with a backhoe. Wholesale returned to the site the following weekend, when it attempted to stabilize the driveway site by hauling out mud and hauling in gravel. Because the ground was too wet to allow Wholesale to perform the work without substantially exceeding the contract price, Goodenow decided to wait for the ground to dry out before proceeding further.

On July 12, 1989, Decker contacted Goodenow concerning the lack of activity at the site and his urgent need to have the driveway completed. Goodenow responded that he would "get right on it." On July 19, Decker telephoned Goodenow to inquire again about the lack of activity and gave him one week in which to finish the driveway. Again, Goodenow said that he would "get right on it." On July 28, Decker called Goodenow for the purpose of terminating the contract. When Goodenow stated that he would be at the site the next day, Decker decided to give him one more chance. Goodenow, however, did not appear at the site and Decker subsequently terminated the contract. At that point, Goodenow believed Wholesale still had 45 days to complete the job. Decker, however, hired another contractor to finish the driveway and complete the excavation work.

Wholesale commenced this action against Decker by a complaint seeking damages for a breach of their contract. After a jury-waived trial, the court entered a judgment in favor of Decker. Although it found that a reasonable time for the completion of performance was 60 days, the court concluded that Wholesale's conduct constituted an anticipatory repudiation of the contract, permitting Decker to terminate the contract during the 60–day period. This timely appeal followed.

An anticipatory repudiation of a contract is "a definite and unequivocal manifestation of intention on the part of the repudiator that he will not render the promised performance when the time fixed for it in the contract arrives." 4 Corbin, *Corbin on Contracts* § 973 (1951); *Restatement (Second) of Contracts* § 250 (1979). The manifestation of an intention to repudiate a contract may be made and communicated by either words or conduct. *See* 4 Corbin § 973; *Restatement* § 250(b). The words or conduct evidencing such refusal or inability to perform, however, must be definite, unequivocal, and absolute. *See Martell Bros., Inc. v. Donbury, Inc.,* 577 A.2d 334, 337 n. 1 (Me.1990). Wholesale contends that the court erred in concluding that its conduct constituted an anticipatory repudiation of the contract. We disagree. After its second weekend of work at the site, Wholesale removed its equipment and did not return. Moreover, on two occasions Goodenow, responding to Decker's inquiries about the progress of the job, promised to get right to work but did not do so. Indeed, when confronted by the fact that Wholesale would be fired if he did not appear at the job site the following day, Goodenow promised that he would be at the site but did not appear. On this record it was reasonable for Decker to conclude that Wholesale would never complete its performance under the contract. We conclude therefore that the court properly found that Wholesale, through its conduct, manifested an unequivo-cal and definite inability or unwillingness to perform within a reasonable time. . . .

The entry is:

Judgment affirmed.

GLASSMAN, COLLINS, RUDMAN and DANA, JJ., concur.

WATHEN, CHIEF JUSTICE, with whom CLIFFORD, J., joins, dissenting.

I must respectfully dissent. In my judgment both this Court and the Superior Court misapply the doctrine of anticipatory repudiation. The record is devoid of any words or conduct on the part of plaintiff that distinctly, unequivocally, and absolutely evidence a refusal or inability to perform. *See Martell Bros., Inc. v. Donbury, Inc.,* 577 A.2d 334, 337 n. 1 (Me.1990). There was a disagreement between the parties as to how much time was allowed for performance, but it is clear that plaintiff expected to perform the contract as soon as circumstances permitted. The Superior Court found a repudiation of the contract even though the 60 days it found available for performance had not passed.

I would vacate the judgment.

––––––

UNIQUE SYSTEMS, INC. v. ZOTOS INTERNATIONAL, INC., 622 F.2d 373 (8th Cir.1980). On January 30, 1974, Lilja contracted to manufacture and sell to Zotos, for resale by Zotos, 15,000 hair–spray systems that Lilja would develop. In an amendment to the contract, the parties agreed that Zotos's stocking and distribution of the systems would commence in "month one," defined as a "mutually agreed date in the year 1974." Later, Zotos began to fear a softening of the market, and indicated that it would not proceed unless Lilja would agree to a market test of completed systems. In light of Zotos's refusal to proceed without the market–test period, Lilja considered the contract repudiated, and brought suit. Held, for Lilja.

"If a party to a contract demands of the other party a performance to which he has no right under the contract and states definitely that, unless his demand is complied with, he will not render his promised performance, an anticipatory repudiation has been committed. 4 Corbin, Contracts § 973 (1951). When Zotos told Lilja in August of 1975 that it would not proceed until market tests were performed with results subject to Zotos's approval, Zotos repudiated the contract and was in total breach. No market tests were required by the contract, a fact that Zotos admits that it knew."

––––––

THERMO ELECTRON CORP. v. SCHIAVONE CONSTRUCTION CO., 958 F.2d 1158 (1st Cir.1992). " . . . Thermo repudiated only if it 'insist[ed] . . . upon terms' . . . to *the point where that insistence 'amounts to a statement of intention not to perform except on conditions which go beyond the contract.'* Restatement (Second) of Contracts § 250 cmt. b, at 273 (quoting U.C.C. § 2–610 cmt. 2) (emphasis added). Commentators have pointed out that there 'must be a definite and unequivocal manifestation of intention [not to render performance].... A mere request for a change in the terms or a request for cancellation of the contract is not in itself enough to constitute a repudiation.' 4 Arthur L. Corbin, Corbin on Contracts § 973, at 905–06 (1951) (footnotes omitted). A party's statements or actions 'must be sufficiently positive to be reasonably understood as meaning that the breach will actually occur. A party's expressions of doubt as to its willingness or ability to perform do not constitute a repudiation.' E. Allan Farnsworth, Contracts § 8.21, at 663 (2d ed. 1990); accord Restatement (Second) of Contracts § 250 cmt. b, at 273.''

RECORD CLUB OF AMERICA, INC. v. UNITED ARTISTS RECORDS, INC., 890 F.2d 1264 (2d cir.1989). "[T]hough a party need not continue to perform the contract after the other party has anticipatorily repudiated it, he must nonetheless demonstrate that he had the willingness and ability to perform before the repudiation and that the plaintiff would have rendered the agreed performance if the defendant had not repudiated.... Restatement (Second) of Contracts § 254, at 290 ('a party's duty to pay damages for total breach by repudiation is discharged if it appears after the breach that there would have been a total failure by the injured party to perform his return promise.'). This principle is merely an application of the general rule that the complaining party must demonstrate that the breach caused him injury; '[t]o do this he must prove that he intended to and was able to perform when his performance was due.' Scholle v. Cuban–Venezuelan Oil Voting Trust, 285 F.2d 318, 320 (2d Cir.1960).''

TAYLOR v. JOHNSTON, 15 Cal.3d 130, 123 Cal.Rptr. 641, 539 P.2d 425 (1975). "When a promisor repudiates a contract, the injured party faces an election of remedies: He can treat the repudiation as an anticipatory breach and immediately seek damages for breach of contract, thereby terminating the contractual relation between the parties, or he can treat the repudiation as an empty threat, wait until the time for performance arrives and exercise his remedies for actual breach if a breach does in fact occur at such time.... However, if the injured party disregards the repudiation and treats the contract as still in force, and the repudiation is retracted prior to the time of performance, then the repudiation is nullified and the injured party is left with his remedies, if any, invocable at the time of performance.''

UNITED STATES v. SEACOAST GAS CO., 204 F.2d 709 (5th Cir. 1953), cert. denied 346 U.S. 866, 74 S.Ct. 106, 98 L.Ed. 377 (1953). Seacoast had entered into a contract to supply gas to a federal housing project. While performance of the contract was in progress, Seacoast wrote to the Public Housing Authority that because of the Authority's alleged breach of the contract, Seacoast intended to cancel the contract as of November 15, 1947. It was admitted that this letter constituted an anticipatory breach. The Authority notified Seacoast that it did not recognize any right in Seacoast to stop performance, and proposed to advertise for bids to ensure a continued supply of gas if Seacoast's breach persisted. Thereafter, the Authority advertised for bids, and, having received the low bid from Trion Company on November 6, notified Seacoast that unless Seacoast retracted its repudiation of the contract within three days, Trion's bid would be accepted and Seacoast would be held liable for breach of contract.

Seacoast did not retract within the time fixed. On November 10, the Authority accepted Trion's bid and began preparations to execute a contract with Trion for a price above that provided in the Seacoast contract. On November 13 (two days before the November 15 termination date that Seacoast had fixed in its notice), Seacoast admitted that it had no right to cancel the contract and retracted its notice. On November 17, the Authority signed a contract with Trion. In a suit by the Authority, Seacoast defended on the ground that it had retracted its notice of repudiation, and given assurance of its intention to continue to perform, before the Authority had actually signed the new contract, and that since the Authority had not then substantially changed its position or suffered any damages the retraction was timely and healed the breach. Held, Seacoast's retraction was ineffective.

"All that is required to close the door to repentance is definite action indicating that the anticipatory breach has been accepted as final, and this requisite can be supplied either by the filing of a suit or a firm declaration, as here, that unless within a fixed time the breach is repudiated, it will be accepted."

NOTE ON REMEDIES FOR THE BREACH OF A CONTRACT IN WHICH ALL THE DUTIES ON ONE SIDE HAVE BEEN PERFORMED

There is a rule of contract law that (1) if A and B have a contract, all of A's duties have been performed, and the only duty remaining for B is to perform a series of separate acts in the future, then (2) in the case of breach by B, A can bring suit on the basis of the acts that are due and unperformed, but cannot bring suit based on the remaining future acts unless and until there is a breach of the duty to perform those acts. Contracts that fall within this rule are often characterized as having become "unilateral," because by the hypothesis only one party remains obliged to perform under the contract. Although this rule is conventionally dealt with under the category of anticipatory breach, it is applicable to a present breach as well. And although the issue addressed by this rule can arise regardless of the nature of the unperformed duty, as a practical matter the rule is usually invoked only when B's sole remaining unperformed duty is to make a series of payments in installments.

In Minor v. Minor, 184 Cal.App.2d 118, 7 Cal.Rptr. 455 (1960), the court stated the following rationale for the rule:

> ... [A] party who has fully performed need only await counterperformance; he is entitled to no more than such performance upon the future dates to which he has agreed. On the other hand, [a] party who has not yet performed must be ready to, or actually, undertake, further

performance. To call upon him to do so in the face of a repudiation of the other contracting party may cause him unmerited hardship. Hence his claim for immediate total performance is greater than that of his dormant counterpart who has fully performed.

This rationale strikes most commentators as thin. As the court in *Minor* went on to note: "[T]he dissenting critics point out that to gain a rather tenuous 'logical consistency,' we incongruously award judgment for future installments to the party who has not yet performed, and deny such judgment to the party who has fully performed." Perhaps the rule is simply an historical anachronism, or perhaps it represents a crude compromise between those who support the doctrine of anticipatory repudiation and those who oppose it. In some cases, the courts have circumvented the rule on the ground that the injured party party had some conceivable remaining obligation, no matter how minor. See, e.g., Long Island R.R. Co. v. Northville Industries Corp., 41 N.Y.2d 455, 393 N.Y.S.2d 925, 362 N.E.2d 558 (1977).

An obvious problem with the rule is that in theory it could force the injured party to bring one suit after another for each unpaid installment. In practice, however, in most cases the defendant will probably conform her conduct to the court's initial decision, and pay the remaining installments voluntarily. Furthermore, rule or no rule, if the defendant continues to withhold installments even after an initial judgement in the injured party's favor, the courts are unlikely to require the injured party to keep bringing one suit after another. Thus in Greguhn v. Mutual of Omaha Ins. Co., 23 Utah 2d 214, 461 P.2d 285 (1969), a disability-payment case, the court limited the plaintiff's judgment to installments already due, but added:

> The verdict and the decision of the trial court amounts to a determination that the plaintiff is entitled to the monthly payments as specified in the insurance policies so long as he is totally and permanently disabled. Defendants are not relieved of the obligation of making the payments unless the plaintiff should recover or die. Should the defendants fail in the future to make payment in accordance with the terms of the policies without just cause or excuse and the plaintiff is compelled to file another action for delinquent installments, the court at that time should be able to fashion such relief as will compel performance.

RESTATEMENT, SECOND, CONTRACTS §§ 250, 253, 256

[See Selected Source Materials Supplement]

UCC §§ 2–610, 2–611, 2–708(1), 2–713, 2–723

[See Selected Source Materials Supplement]

CISG ART. 72

[See Selected Source Materials Supplement]

UNIDROIT PRINCIPLES OF INTERNATIONAL COMMERCIAL CONTRACTS ART. 7.3.3

[See Selected Source Materials Supplement]

OLOFFSON v. COOMER

Appellate Court of Illinois, Third District, 1973.
11 Ill.App.3d 918, 296 N.E.2d 871.

ALLOY, PRESIDING JUSTICE. Richard Oloffson, d/b/a Rich's Ag Service appeals from a judgment of the circuit court of Bureau County in favor of appellant against Clarence Coomer in the amount of $1,500 plus costs. The case was tried by the court without a jury.

Oloffson was a grain dealer. Coomer was a farmer. Oloffson was in the business of merchandising grain. Consequently, he was a "merchant" within the meaning of section 2–104 of the Uniform Commercial Code. (Ill.Rev.Stat. 1969, ch. 26 § 2–104). Coomer, however, was simply in the business of growing rather than merchandising grain. He, therefore, was not a "merchant" with respect to the merchandising of grain.

On April 16, 1970, Coomer agreed to sell to Oloffson, for delivery in October and December of 1970, 40,000 bushels of corn. Oloffson testified at the trial that the entire agreement was embodied in two separate contracts, each covering 20,000 bushels and that the first 20,000 bushels were to be delivered on or before October 30 at a price of $1.12¾ per bushel and the second 20,000 bushels were to be delivered on or before December 15, at a price of $1.12¼ per bushel. Coomer, in his testimony, agreed that the 40,000 bushels were to be delivered but stated that he was to deliver all he could by October 30 and the balance by December 15.

On June 3, 1970, Coomer informed Oloffson that he was not going to plant corn because the season had been too wet. He told Oloffson to arrange elsewhere to obtain the corn if Oloffson had obligated himself to deliver to any third party. The price for a bushel of corn on June 3, 1970, for future delivery, was $1.16. In September of 1970, Oloffson asked Coomer about delivery of the corn and Coomer repeated that he would not be able to deliver. Oloffson, however, persisted. He mailed Coomer confirmations of the April 16 agreement. Coomer ignored these. Oloffson's attorney then requested that Coomer perform. Coomer ignored this request likewise. The scheduled delivery dates referred to passed with no corn delivered. Oloffson then covered his obligation to his own vendee by purchasing 20,000 bushels at $1.35 per bushel and 20,000 bushels at $1.49 per bushel. The judgment from which Oloffson appeals awarded Oloffson as damages, the difference between the contract and the market prices on June 3, 1970, the day upon which Coomer first advised Oloffson he would not deliver.

Oloffson argues on this appeal that the proper measure of his damages was the difference between the contract price and the market price on the dates the corn should have been delivered in accordance with the April 16 agreement. Plaintiff does not seek any other damages. The trial court prior to entry of judgment, in an opinion finding the facts and reviewing the law, found that plaintiff was entitled to recover judgment only for the sum of $1,500 plus costs as we have indicated which is equal to the amount of the difference between the minimum contract price and the price on June 3, 1970, of $1.16 per bushel (taking the greatest differential from $1.12¼ per bushel multiplied by 40,000 bushels). We believe the findings and the judgment of the trial court were proper and should be affirmed.

It is clear that on June 3, 1970, Coomer repudiated the contract "with respect to performance not yet due." Under the terms of the Uniform Commercial Code the loss would impair the value of the contract to the remaining party in the amount as indicated. (Ill.Rev.Stat.1969, ch. 26, § 2–610.) As a consequence, on June 3, 1970, Oloffson, as the "aggrieved party", could then:

> "(a) for a commercially reasonable time await performance by the repudiating party; or

> (b) resort to any remedy for breach (Section 2–703 or Section 2–711), even though he has notified the repudiating party that he would await the latter's performance and has urged retraction; ... "

If Oloffson chose to proceed under subparagraph (a) referred to, he could have awaited Coomer's performance for a "commercially reasonable time." As we indicate in the course of this opinion, that "commercially reasonable time" expired on June 3, 1970. The Uniform Commercial Code made a change in existing Illinois law in this respect, in that, prior to the adoption of the Code, a buyer in a position as Oloffson was privileged to await a seller's performance until the date that, according to the agreement, such performance was scheduled. To the extent that a "commercially reasonable time" is less than such date of performance, the Code now conditions the buyer's right to await performance. (See Ill.Rev.Stat.Ann.1969, ch. 26, § 2–610, Illinois Code Comment, Paragraph (a)).

If, alternatively, Oloffson had proceeded under subparagraph (b) by treating the repudiation as a breach, the remedies to which he would have been entitled were set forth in section 2–711 (Ill.Rev.Stat.1969, ch. 26, § 2–711), which is the only applicable section to which section 2–610(b) refers, according to the relevant portion of 2–711:

> "(1) Where the seller fails to make delivery or repudiates or the buyer rightfully rejects or justifiably revokes acceptance then with respect to any goods involved, and with respect to the whole if the breach goes to the whole contract (Section 2–612), the buyer may cancel and whether or not he has done so may in addition to recovering so much of the price as has been paid

> "(a) 'cover' and have damages under the next section as to all the goods affected whether or not they have been identified to the contract; or

"(b) recover damages for non-delivery as provided in this Article (Section 2–713). . . ."

Plaintiff, therefore, was privileged under Section 2–610 of the Uniform Commercial Code to proceed either under subparagraph (a) or under subparagraph (b). At the expiration of the "commercially reasonable time" specified in subparagraph (a), he in effect would have a duty to proceed under subparagraph (b) since subparagraph (b) directs reference to remedies generally available to a buyer upon a seller's breach.

Oloffson's right to await Coomer's performance under section 2–610(a) was conditioned upon his:

(i) waiting no longer than a "commercially reasonable time"; and

(ii) dealing with Coomer in good faith.

Since Coomer's statement to Oloffson on June 3, 1970, was unequivocal and since "cover" easily and immediately was available to Oloffson in the well-organized and easily accessible market for purchases of grain to be delivered in the future, it would be unreasonable for Oloffson on June 3, 1970, to have awaited Coomer's performance rather than to have proceeded under Section 2–610(b) and, thereunder, to elect then to treat the repudiation as a breach. Therefore, if Oloffson were relying on his right to effect cover under section 2–711(1)(a), June 3, 1970, might for the foregoing reason alone have been the day on which he acquired cover.

Additionally, however, the record and the finding of the trial court indicates that Oloffson adhered to a usage of trade that permitted his customers to cancel the contract for a future delivery of grain by making known to him a desire to cancel and paying to him the difference between the contract and market price on the day of cancellation. There is no indication whatever that Coomer was aware of this usage of trade. The trial court specifically found, as a fact, that, in the context in which Oloffson's failure to disclose this information occurred, Oloffson failed to act in good faith. According to Oloffson, he didn't ask for this information:

"I'm no information sender. If he had asked I would have told him exactly what to do. . . . I didn't feel my responsibility. I thought it his to ask, in which case I would tell him exactly what to do."

We feel that the words "for a commercially reasonable time" as set forth in Section 2–610(a) must be read relatively to the obligation of good faith that is defined in Section 2–103(1)(b) and imposed expressly in Section 1–203. (Ill.Rev.Stat.1969, ch. 26, § 2–103(1)(b) and § 1–203.)

The Uniform Commercial Code imposes upon the parties the obligation to deal with each other in good faith regardless of whether they are merchants. The Sales Article of the Code specifically defines good faith, "in the case of a merchant . . . [as] honesty in fact and the observance of reasonable commercial standards of fair dealing in the trade." For the foregoing reasons and likewise because Oloffson's failure to disclose in good faith might itself have been responsible for Coomer's failure to comply with the usage of trade which we must assume was known only to Oloffson, we conclude that a commercially reasonable time under the facts before us expired on June 3, 1970.

Imputing to Oloffson the consequences of Coomer's having acted upon the information that Oloffson in good faith should have transmitted to him,

Oloffson knew or should have known on June 3, 1970, the limit of damages he probably could recover. If he were obligated to deliver grain to a third party, he knew or should have known that unless he covered on June 3, 1970, his own capital would be at risk with respect to his obligation to his own vendee. Therefore, on June 3, 1970, Oloffson, in effect, had a duty to proceed under subparagraph (b) of Section 2–610 and under subparagraphs (a) and (b) of subparagraph 1 of Section 2–711. If Oloffson had so proceeded under subparagraph (a) of Section 2–711, he should have effected cover and would have been entitled to recover damages all as provided in section 2–712, which requires that he would have had to cover in good faith without unreasonable delay. Since he would have had to effect cover on June 3, 1970, according to section 2–712(2), he would have been entitled to exactly the damages which the trial court awarded him in this cause.

Assuming that Oloffson had proceeded under subparagraph (b) of Section 2–711, he would have been entitled to recover from Coomer under Section 2–713 and Section 2–723 of the Commercial Code, the difference between the contract price and the market price on June 3, 1970, which is the date upon which he learned of the breach. This would produce precisely the same amount of damages which the trial court awarded him. [See: Ill.Rev.Stat.1969, ch. 26 § 2–723(1)].

Since the trial court properly awarded the damages to which plaintiff was entitled in this cause, the judgment of the circuit court of Bureau County is, therefore, affirmed.

Affirmed.

STOUDER and SCOTT, JJ., concur.

TRINIDAD BEAN AND ELEVATOR CO. v. FROSH, 1 Neb.App. 281, 494 N.W.2d 347 (1992). Addressing the issue raised in Oloffson v. Coomer, the court said:

> The word "breach" as used in § 2–713(1) is ambiguous and must be interpreted within its statutory setting. There are essentially two views as to how the ambiguity is to be interpreted: (1) "learned of the breach" refers to time of repudiation or (2) "learned of the breach" refers to time of performance under the terms of the parties' contract.... Plausible arguments support both interpretations.

> ### Time of Repudiation

> The most common interpretation, accepted by a majority of courts, is that Code § 2–713(1) refers to time of repudiation. This interpretation was adopted in the leading case of *Oloffson v. Coomer,* 11 Ill.App.3d 918, 296 N.E.2d 871 (1973)....

> ### Time of Performance

> The performance date measurement is preferred by White and Summers. See 1 White & Summers, *supra*. The performance date measurement was adopted in *Cargill, Inc. v. Stafford,* 553 F.2d 1222 (10th Cir.1977), in which the court reasoned that before the adoption of the

Code, damages were measured from the time when performance was due and not from the time when the buyer learned of repudiation.

The court also noted that in Code § 2–723(1), providing for the measure of damages in a suit for anticipatory repudiation which comes to trial before the time for performance, the drafters stated, " '[A]ny damages based on market price ... shall be determined according to the price of such goods prevailing at the time when the aggrieved party learned of the repudiation.' " (Emphasis omitted.) *Cargill, Inc.,* 553 F.2d at 1226. The court reasoned that when the Code drafters intended to base damages on the date a party "learned of the repudiation," they did so by explicit language.

Analysis of the Alternatives

Since the Code's vocabulary is not consistent, both of these interpretations appear equally plausible. However, for the following reasons, we conclude that the repudiation date interpretation gives the provisions their best combined effect.

It must be conceded that the performance date interpretation has the advantage of achieving consistency between § 2–713 and Neb.U.C.C. § 2–708 (Reissue 1980), the section containing the seller's market-based remedy for a buyer's anticipatory repudiation. Section 2–708 establishes the performance date as the proper time for measuring a seller's damages. The performance date argument draws additional support from Neb.U.C.C. § 2–723 (Reissue 1980), which expressly refers to both § 2–708 and § 2–713.

The shortcoming of the performance date interpretation is that it fails to explain § 2–610(a), which appears to allow an aggrieved party to await performance only "for a commercially reasonable time." As one court has said: "If buyer is entitled to market-contract damages measured at the time of performance, it is difficult to explain why the anticipatory repudiation section limits him to a commercially reasonable time to await performance." *Cosden Oil v. Karl O. Helm Aktiengesellschaft,* 736 F.2d 1064, 1072 (5th Cir.1984)....

Moreover, the policy behind the commercial reasonableness of § 2–610(a) is to compensate a buyer based on the prevailing market. The goal in sales contract cases should be to compensate an aggrieved buyer in whole and this is accomplished by the Code's policy on cover. "[M]easuring buyer's damages at the time of performance will tend to dissuade the buyer from covering, in hopes that market price will continue upward until performance time." *Cosden Oil,* 736 F.2d at 1072. When a performance measure is applied, an aggrieved buyer in a rising market will speculate that prices will continue to rise. If the market falls after repudiation, the buyer will obtain the same goods at a price lower than under the contract. The effect is to over-compensate the buyer and penalize the seller. See Thomas H. Jackson, *"Anticipatory Repudiation" and the Temporal Element of Contract Law: An Economic Inquiry into Contract Damages in Cases of Prospective Nonperformance,* 31 Stanford L.Rev. 69 (1978).

Our interpretation is also influenced by § 2–712, under which a buyer may cover by making in good faith any reasonable purchase of substitute goods, so long as he does not delay unreasonably. See *Farmer's Union Co-op Company of Mead v. Flamme Brothers,* 196 Neb. 699, 245 N.W.2d 464 (1976). If the performance measure is correct, then "in a rising market, no reason would exist for requiring the buyer to act 'without unreasonable delay' when he seeks to cover following an anticipatory repudiation." *Cosden Oil,* 736 F.2d at 1072.

Holding

We conclude that best effect is given to the statutes if "learned of the breach," in § 2–713(1), refers to the time the buyer learned of the seller's repudiation. Therefore, we hold that the measure of damages for a buyer upon anticipatory repudiation by the seller is the difference between the contract price and the price of the goods on the date of repudiation, so long as it would be commercially reasonable for the buyer to cover on the date of repudiation. . . .

HESS ENERGY, INC. v. LIGHTNING OIL CO., 338 F.3d 357 (4th Cir. 2003). Lightning entered into a Master Agreement with Hess (more accurately, with Hess's assignor) which set various terms under which Lightning agreed to sell, and Hess agreed to buy, natural gas pursuant to specific purchase agreements or "confirmations" to be entered into later. The parties then agreed to a series of confirmations. Hess, in turn, made contracts to resell the gas to end users. Hess did not make a profit on any difference between the price it paid to its suppliers, such as Lightning, and the price it charged to its end-user customers. On the contrary, Hess's sole purpose in making advance purchases of gas was to lock in access to a supply of gas, which it could then promise to deliver to its customers. Rather than making a profit on price movements, Hess planned to make its profits by adding markups that reflected transportation and other services that Hess would provide to the end-users. Accordingly, each time Hess agreed to purchase natural gas from a supplier at a fixed price for delivery on a specific date, it also entered into a futures contract to sell to a counterparty the same quantity of natural gas for the same fixed price on the same date. Hess thereby made itself indifferent to fluctuations in the price of natural gas, because settlement of the futures contracts would offset any favorable or unfavorable swings in the market price of natural gas between the time Hess made a contract with a supplier and the date of delivery under that contract.

Subsequently, Lightning terminated the Master Agreement and repudiated the remaining confirmations. Hess brought suit. The trial court instructed the jury to measure Hess's damages by the difference between the prices under the Lightning confirmations and the market prices at the time that delivery of the gas by Lightning was due. Lightning appealed on the ground that the jury should have been instructed to measure damages by the difference between the contract prices and the market prices at the time of the repudiation. The Fourth Circuit held that the trial judge's instruction was correct. The court said:

> As one well-respected commentary explains:
>
>> When the seller of goods has promised delivery at a future time and prior thereto repudiates his contract, the buyer is not required to

go into the market at once and make another contract for future delivery merely because there is reason to expect a rise in the market price. If his forecast is incorrect and the price falls, his second contract on a high market increases the loss. If his forecast is correct and the price rises, his second contract avoids a loss and operates as a saving to the repudiator. But the risk of this rise or fall is exactly the risk that the repudiating seller contracted to carry. If at the time of repudiation he thinks that the price will rise, so that his performance will become more costly, he can make his own second contract transferring the risk to a third party and thus hedge against his first risky contract.

11 Arthur Linton Corbin, Corbin on Contracts § 1053, at 273 (Interim ed. 2002). Thus, if Lightning wished to avoid the risk that it undertook in entering into the contract and fix its damages on the date of repudiation, it could have done so by entering into hedge transactions in the futures market. But its repudiation of the contract cannot shift to Hess the very market risk that Hess had sought to avoid by entering into contracts for the future delivery of gas in the first place.

NOTE ON THE MEASURE OF DAMAGES
FOR ANTICIPATORY BREACH

In 2003, the National Conference of Commissioners on State Laws and the American Law Institute, which are jointly responsible for promulgating and amending the Uniform Commercial Code, adopted a number of amendments to the official version of Article 2. Amended section 2–713(1)(b) specifically addresses the issue, raised in *Oloffson*, *Trinidad Bean*, and *Hess*, when should a buyer's damages be measured for a seller's anticipatory repudiation:

> ... Subject to Section 2–723, if the seller wrongfully fails to deliver or repudiates or the buyer rightfully rejects or justifiably revokes acceptance ... the measure of damages for repudiation by the seller is the difference between the market price at the expiration of a commercially reasonable time after the buyer learned of the repudiation, but no later than [the time for tender under the contract], and the contract price together with any incidental or consequential damages ..., less expenses saved in consequence of the seller's breach.

Comment 4 to amended section 2–713 states:

> Under subsection (1)(b), in the case of an anticipatory repudiation by the seller the market price should be measured at the place where the buyer would have covered at a commercially reasonable time after the buyer learned of the repudiation, but no later than the time of tender under the agreement. This time approximates the market price at the time the buyer would have covered even though the buyer has not done so under Section 2–712. This subsection is designed to put the buyer in the position the buyer would have been in if the seller had performed by approximating the harm the buyer has suffered without allowing the

buyer an unreasonable time to speculate on the market at the seller's expense.

A corresponding amendment was made to section 2–708, for the seller's remedy on the buyer's anticipatory breach, by adding a new section, 2–708(1)(b):

> the measure of damages for repudiation by the buyer is the difference between the contract price and the market price at the place for tender at the expiration of the commercially reasonable time after the seller learned of the repudiation, but no later than the time [for tender under the contract], together with any incidental or consequential damages ... less expenses saved in consequence of the buyer's breach.

As of early 2006, the 2003 amendments to Article 2 have not been adopted by any state legislature. At least for the time being, therefore, the measure of damages for an anticipatory breach of a contract for the sale of goods is still governed by the pre–2003 version of Article 2.

SECTION 2. PROSPECTIVE INABILITY TO PERFORM AND ADEQUATE ASSURANCE OF PERFORMANCE

UCC §§ 2–609, 2–702(1), 2–705(1)

[See Selected Source Materials Supplement]

RESTATEMENT, SECOND, CONTRACTS § 251

[See Selected Source Materials Supplement]

CISG ART. 71

[See Selected Source Materials Supplement]

UNIDROIT PRINCIPLES OF INTERNATIONAL COMMERCIAL CONTRACTS ART. 7.3.4

[See Selected Source Materials Supplement]

PRINCIPLES OF EUROPEAN CONTRACT LAW ART. 8.105

[See Selected Source Materials Supplement]

PITTSBURGH–DES MOINES STEEL CO. v. BROOKHAVEN MANOR WATER CO.

United States Court of Appeals, Seventh Circuit, 1976.
532 F.2d 572.

Seller of one-million gallon water tank brought action against buyer for repudiation of the sales contract and buyer counterclaimed for breach of contract. The United States District Court for the Northern District of Illinois, Thomas R. McMillen, J., entered judgment notwithstanding the verdict in favor of the buyer and seller appealed. . . .

Before CLARK, ASSOCIATE JUSTICE (Retired),* and CUMMINGS and PELL, CIRCUIT JUDGES.

PELL, CIRCUIT JUDGE. This is an appeal by the Pittsburgh–Des Moines Steel Company (hereinafter PDM) from the district court's entry of a judgment notwithstanding the verdict against PDM on its complaint for repudiation of contract and for Brookhaven Manor Water Company (hereinafter Brookhaven) on its counterclaim for breach of contract and from the district court's subsequent adjudgment of damages. The questions raised on appeal are whether the district court erred in entering judgment notwithstanding the verdict in favor of Brookhaven on the liability issue and whether error was committed in the district court's subsequent assessment of damages against PDM.

The record discloses the following series of events. On July 24, 1968, PDM, a designer, fabricator, and engineer of steel products, submitted a proposal to Brookhaven for the construction of a one-million-gallon water tank for $175,000. The original proposal incorporated, as terms of payment, 60 percent upon receipt of materials in PDM's plant, 30 percent upon completion of erection, and 10 percent upon completion of testing, or within 30 days after the tank had been made ready for testing. The original terms were not satisfactory to Brookhaven's president, Irving Betke, and were subsequently changed. The altered payment term provided that 100% of the contract price was due and payable within 30 days after the tank had been tested and accepted. The altered proposal was signed and accepted by Brookhaven on November 26, 1968.

Sometime during the following month Norman Knuttel, PDM's district manager who had prepared and signed the original and revised proposals, talked to a representative of the Arbanas Construction Company which company had contracted with Brookhaven for the construction of the tank foundation. Knuttel was informed that Brookhaven had received a loan from Diversified Finance Corporation. Although this information as to the receipt

---

* Associate Justice Tom C. Clark, United States Supreme Court, Retired, is sitting by designation.

of the loan was incorrect, Brookhaven had negotiated with Diversified for a loan for the purpose of the construction which negotiations continued into the following year. Under date of January 3, 1969, PDM's credit manager wrote Diversified with a copy to Betke which letter in part was as follows:

> "[W]e hereby request a letter assuring that $175,000.00 for payment of the referenced project will be held in escrow and fully committed to payment to us upon completion of referenced elevated tank.
>
> "As a matter of good business we are holding this order in abeyance until receipt of such notification."

The contract contained no provision for escrow financing. Brookhaven, through Betke, took no action upon the receipt of the copy of the letter. Subsequently, after further correspondence and meetings, resulting primarily from Brookhaven's not having secured a planned loan of $275,000.00 from Diversified Finance, PDM's credit manager sent an air mail, special delivery letter to Betke, dated March 19, 1969, which suggested that Betke "mail us your personal guarantee of payment of $175,000.00 as per the contract, to protect us in the interim between now and the time your loan is completed."

While the contract specified the payment of the amount mentioned no later than 30 days after completion of the tank, it was silent as to any reference to a personal guarantee by Betke. The letter concluded as follows:

> "Upon receipt of such guarantee, we could immediately set in motion our shop fabrication which would result in earlier completion of your new tank.
>
> "When your loan is completed we will still require a letter of instructions to be forwarded from you to your bank, or other financial institution which extends this loan, that $175,000.00 is to be held in escrow for disbursement only to Pittsburgh–Des Moines Steel Company in accordance with our contract."

The construction of the water tower was scheduled to begin on April 15, 1969. A crew had been scheduled for the site three months previously, and a crew was ready to appear there on April 15, 1969. As matters transpired, however, the tank was never installed at Brookhaven's site. On March 31, 1969, Betke sent PDM Comptroller Harry Kelly his personal financial statement, but he did not send PDM his personal guarantee for the loan. After Betke failed to provide his personal guarantee of the $175,000.00 contract price, PDM took no further steps toward performance.[1] On April 22, 1969, Kelly, PDM Secretary–Treasurer Tom Morris, PDM Sales Manager Dwight Long, and Betke attended a meeting on the Brookhaven premises. Although the record reveals somewhat inconsistent versions of the details of that meeting, it appears that Morris told Betke that PDM would complete the fabrication of the tank and deliver it to the job site within a matter of weeks but that Betke replied that he had no need for the tank until the following year.

---

1. The record indicates that as of April 22, 1969, the foundation, the construction of which was the obligation of Brookhaven, had been completed and two-thirds of the required tankage parts, which were the obligation of PDM, had been fabricated. However, it is also noted that as late as March 19, 1969, PDM had written Betke that upon the receipt of the guarantee, the shop could immediately set in motion fabrication. It is not clear whether PDM did anything to dispel the clear inference to Betke that there would be no fabrication, or at least further fabrication, until the guarantee had been received.

Further efforts to implement the contract broke down completely after April 22, 1969. Brookhaven's installation of the reinforced concrete foundation for the tank had been accomplished at a cost to it of $18,895. Subsequent to the March meeting, Brookhaven purchased additional land and developed two wells which provided an adequate water supply. Brookhaven later sold all its assets, including both equipment and land, to the City of Darien. At the trial of the damages issue, an expert in demolition testified that the cost of removing the reinforced concrete foundation would be about $7,000. On the basis of this testimony, which was proffered upon the legal theory that Brookhaven had a right to recover the cost of the removal, the district court found that the total amount of damages sustained by Brookhaven was the sum of $25,895.00 and entered judgment in its favor for that amount. . . .

II.   CLAIMED BASES OF LIABILITY

Under the contract as executed, into which prior negotiations had been merged, Brookhaven's performance of its principal obligation to pay the purchase price was not due until after the completion of construction. Nevertheless within a period of time shortly more than one month after the contract became effective, PDM was requesting that a prospective lender of the funds to Brookhaven should hold the entire $175,000.00 in escrow. This was not a request that a lending institution give a letter of intent or otherwise confirm that it would make a particular loan when the payment became due after completion of construction. Instead the letter explicitly would, if honored, have required Brookhaven to complete all necessary loan papers and to arrange for the consummation of the loan, the proceeds of which would then be held by Diversified for some months until the work was completed. It is no answer to say that perhaps Brookhaven could have arranged for the escrowed fund to have been invested in some safe, readily liquidable form which might offset in part at least the loss to Brookhaven resulting from having to pay interest on money already borrowed. PDM having purported to agree not to ask for progress payments during the course of construction, more than half of which would have been due before the first act took place by PDM on the construction site, it now was substituting another requirement clearly beyond any requirement contemplated in the contract which would not have put the purchase price in hand but would nevertheless have it where it could be available for the picking at the appropriate time. The contract is silent as to any right of PDM to insist Brookhaven provide any such guarantee during the period before completion of construction. Further, PDM made it quite clear that it was "holding this order in abeyance until receipt of" notification that the money was being so held. We find no basis for an inference that at this time Brookhaven was not ready, willing and able to perform its obligations under the contract nor that it would not be able to pay when it owed. The fact that there had been negotiations for a loan of money that would not be needed for some months, which negotiations had not come to fruition, does not support such an inference. Two months after the letter to Diversified, PDM reaffirmed its lack of retreat from the position of requiring assurance that the money would be forthcoming.

PDM argues that its position was in accordance with Section 2–609 of the Uniform Commercial Code (UCC) enacted into law in Illinois as Ill.Rev.Stat. ch. 26, sec. 2–609. . . .

... The question ... is whether PDM's actions subsequent to the execution of the contract were within the protection provided by § 2–609. We hold that they were not.

The performance to which PDM was entitled was the full payment of the purchase price within a specified time after the completion of the tank. While we have a substantial question as to whether PDM made a written demand as required by the statute, in keeping with our concept that the UCC should be liberally construed, we do not desire to rest our decision on a formalistic approach. Letters were written which conveyed what PDM wanted done before they would pursue their obligations under the contract. The fundamental problem is that these letters, if they be deemed to be in the nature of a demand, demanded more than that to which PDM was entitled and the demand was not founded upon what in our opinion was an actuating basis for the statute's applicability.

We do not construe § 2–609 as being a vehicle without more for an implied term being inserted in a contract when a substantially equivalent term was expressly waived in the contract. The something more to trigger applicability of the statute is that the expectation of due performance on the part of the other party entertained at contracting time no longer exists because of "reasonable grounds for insecurity" arising. We find that PDM's actions in demanding either the escrowing of the purchase price or a personal guarantee lacked the necessary predicate of reasonable grounds for insecurity having arisen. The contract negates the existence of any basis for insecurity at the time of the contract when PDM was willing to wait 30 days beyond completion for payment. The fact that Brookhaven had not completed its loan negotiations does not constitute reasonable grounds for insecurity when the money in question was not to be needed for some months. Reasonable business men prefer in the absence of some compulsive reason not to commence paying interest on borrowed money until the time for the use for that money is at hand. The credit manager's January letter that the order was being held in abeyance until receipt of notification of escrowing was based upon a "matter of good business," but not upon any change of condition bearing upon Brookhaven's ability to discharge its payment obligation under the contract. With regard to the later request for a personal guarantee, it is not uncommon for an individual to decline assuming obligations of a corporation in which he is a shareholder. Indeed, the use of the corporate device frequently has as a principal purpose the limitation on individual exposure to liability. If an unfavorable risk in dealing with a corporation exists at contracting time, good business judgment may well indicate that an assurance be secured before contracting that there will be individual shareholder backup. None of this occurred and the record is silent as to any reasonable grounds for insecurity arising thereafter.

It is true that one officer of PDM testified that the company did not send a crew because we questioned whether we might be paid for the project "at that time." Some more objective factual basis than a subjective questioning, in our opinion, is needed to demonstrate reasonable grounds for insecurity. Likewise, another PDM officer testified that it was the company's normal and regular procedure not to erect a structure "until we have reason to believe that the funds to pay for the structure *are* available." The time of which he was speaking was a time at which there was no contractual requirement that the funds be available. The funds were only required to be available after completion of installation. He testified further that the normal procedure was not to erect until satisfactory arrangements were made. None of this subjectively normal procedure was imposed as a provision in the contract which in view of the withdrawn provision for progress payments showed reasonably to Brookhaven that not only payment, but arrangements for payment, would not be necessary until after completion.

We, of course, would not deprive PDM of resort to § 2–609 if there had been a demonstration that reasonable grounds for insecurity had arisen. The proof in that respect was lacking. The comptroller and supervisor of PDM's credit department testified that he had access to all of the credit information that the company had regarding Brookhaven, that he had reviewed that information, and that he was unaware of any change in the financial condition of Brookhaven between November of 1968 and the end of 1969. Finally, we note that despite the professed subjective questioning in April as to whether PDM might be paid, the credit manager as early as January had said that the job would be held in abeyance until arrangements had been made for escrowing and a month after the questioning, the questioning officer had offered to proceed with construction in exchange for an interest in Brookhaven, an unlikely course if Brookhaven were financially in a questionable condition. There was also testimony with the same inference that PDM was not fearful of Brookhaven's financial stability or ability to pay in connection with PDM lending to Brookhaven the amount involved at an interest rate of 9½% which rate was then unacceptable to Brookhaven. If the buyer was unable to pay for the performance of the contract, it is difficult to see that it was better able to pay a promissory note. We do not fault Brookhaven for its rejection of various proposals advanced by PDM each of which amounted to a rewriting of the contract in the absence of a proper § 2–609 basis. The fact, if it were a fact, that Brookhaven may not have had a large amount of cash lying in the bank in a checking account, not an unusual situation for a real estate developer, does not support the belief that it, as a company with substantial assets, would fail to meet its obligations as they fell due. Section 2–609 is a protective device when reasonable grounds for insecurity arise; it is not a pen for rewriting a contract in the absence of those reasonable grounds having arisen, particularly when the proposed rewriting involves the very factors which had been waived by the one now attempting to wield the pen. The situation is made no more persuasive for PDM when it is recalled that that company was the original scrivener.

Brookhaven's request to put off the contract for a year clearly came after PDM's repudiation of the contract and was indicative of nothing more than that Brookhaven was willing to undertake a new arrangement with PDM a year hence. Pursuant to § 2–610 of the UCC, Brookhaven was entitled to suspend its own performance by virtue of the anticipatory repudiation by PDM and to resort to available remedies, including damages pursuant to § 2–711 of the Code.[2] . . .

---

2. . . . [W]e find no merit in PDM's argument that even if its January action could be construed as an anticipatory repudiation under § 2–610, its subsequent actions demonstrated a retraction of the anticipatory repudiation pursuant to § 2–611. That section requires a clear indication to the aggrieved party "that the repudiating party intends to perform." PDM only made it clear throughout that it intended to perform if Brookhaven gave assurances not required of it legally or contractually.

For the reasons hereinbefore set out the judgment of the district court is affirmed.

CUMMINGS, CIRCUIT JUDGE (concurring).

Although I agree with the result reached in the majority opinion, I differ with the reasoning. Reasonable men could certainly conclude that PDM had legitimate grounds to question Brookhaven's ability to pay for the water tank. When the contract was signed, the parties understood that Brookhaven would obtain a loan to help pay for the project. When the loan failed to materialize, a prudent businessman would have "reasonable grounds for insecurity." I disagree that there must be a fundamental change in the financial position of the buyer before the seller can invoke the protection of UCC § 2–609. Rather, I believe that the Section was designed to cover instances where an underlying condition of the contract, even if not expressly incorporated into the written document, fails to occur. See Comment 3 to UCC § 2–609. Whether, in a specific case, the breach of the condition gives a party "reasonable grounds for insecurity" is a question of fact for the jury.

UCC § 2–609, however, does not give the alarmed party a right to redraft the contract. Whether the party invoking that provision is merely requesting an assurance that performance will be forthcoming or whether he is attempting to alter the contract is a mixed question of law and fact, depending in part upon the court's interpretation of the obligations imposed on the parties. In this case, PDM would have been assured only if significant changes in the contract were made, either by receiving Betke's personal guarantee, by attaining escrow financing or by purchasing an interest in Brookhaven. The district court could properly conclude as a matter of law that these requests by PDM demanded more than a commercially "adequate assurance of due performance."

J. WHITE & R. SUMMERS, UNIFORM COMMERCIAL CODE § 6–2 (5th ed. 2000). "All demands for adequate assurance call for more than was originally promised under the contract, and that is precisely what 2–609 authorizes. If, for example, it was appropriate to sell on open credit at the outset of a contract but subsequent events cause insecurity, 2–609 calls for modification of the contract to provide greater security to the seller than the seller could have demanded, absent such insecurity. Thus it is the very purpose of 2–609 to authorize one party to insist upon more than the contract gives. Of course there are limits. One can demand only 'adequate' assurances. If a party demands and receives specific assurances, then absent a further change of circumstances, the assurances demanded and received are adequate, and the party who has demanded the assurances is bound to proceed. Of course, the party receiving assurances is entitled to conforming performance. Read properly section 2–609 will mitigate the lawyer's dilemma about what to advise a client upon an apparent repudiation."

BAII BANKING CORP. v. UPG, INC., 985 F.2d 685, 703 (2d Cir.1993). The court here pointed out that a party to a losing contract, *A*, may opportunistically attempt to use UCC § 2–609 as a weapon to get out of an unprofitable contract by demanding adequate assurance of performance from the other party, B, in the hope that B's failure to provide such assurance will be treated as a breach that will justify A's failure to perform the contract. In this connection, the court quoted as follows from the report of the New York Law Revision Commission to the New York state legislature at the time that legislature was considering the adoption of the UCC:

> . . . In working out the application of this section, courts will face the necessity of resolving two sharply conflicting interests: (1) The danger to one party of future breach by the other; (2) The danger that parties who wish to escape from a contract obligation may make an unfounded claim that their 'expectation of receiving due performance' has been 'impaired', and use the powers conferred by this section to weaken the security of contractual undertakings. This possibility of such abuse might indicate that courts would be cautious in applying this section of the Code.

NORCON POWER PARTNERS v. NIAGARA MOHAWK POWER CORP.

Court of Appeals of New York, 1998.
92 N.Y.2d 458, 705 N.E.2d 656, 682 N.Y.S.2d 664.

BELLACOSA, J.

The doctrine, known as demand for adequate assurance of future performance, is at the heart of a Federal lawsuit that stems from a 1989 contract between Norcon Power Partners, L.P., an independent power producer, and Niagara Mohawk Power Corporation, a public utility provider. Niagara Mohawk undertook to purchase electricity generated at Norcon's Pennsylvania facility. The contract was for 25 years, but the differences emerged during the early years of the arrangement.

The case arrives on this Court's docket by certification of the substantive law question from the United States Court of Appeals for the Second Circuit. Our Court is presented with an open issue that should be settled within the framework of New York's common-law development. We accepted the responsibility to address this question involving New York contract law:

> "Does a party have the right to demand adequate assurance of future performance when reasonable grounds arise to believe that the other party will commit a breach by non-performance of a contract governed by New York law, where the other party is solvent and the contract is not governed by the U.C.C.?" (Norcon Power Partners v. Niagara Mohawk Power Corp., 110 F.3d 6, 9 (2d Cir.1997).)

As framed by the particular dispute, we answer the law question in the affirmative with an appreciation of this Court's traditional common-law developmental method, and as proportioned to the precedential sweep of our rulings.

I.

The Second Circuit Court of Appeals describes the three pricing periods, structure and details [of the contract between the parties] as follows:

"In the first period, Niagara Mohawk pays Norcon six cents per kilowatt-hour for electricity. In the second and third periods, the price paid by Niagara Mohawk is based on its 'avoided cost.' The avoided cost reflects the cost that Niagara Mohawk would incur to generate electricity itself or purchase it from other sources. In the second period, if the avoided cost falls below a certain floor price (calculated according to a formula), Niagara Mohawk is obligated to pay the floor price. By the same token, if the avoided cost rises above a certain amount (calculated according to a formula), Niagara Mohawk's payments are capped by a ceiling price. An 'adjustment account' tracks the difference between payments actually made by Niagara Mohawk in the second period and what those payments would have been if based solely on Niagara Mohawk's avoided cost.

"In the third period, the price paid by Niagara Mohawk is based on its avoided cost without any ceiling or floor price. Payments made by Niagara Mohawk in the third period are adjusted to account for any balance existing in the adjustment account that operated in the second period. If the adjustment account contains a balance in favor of Niagara Mohawk—that is, the payments actually made by Niagara Mohawk in the second period exceeded what those payments would have been if based solely on Niagara Mohawk's avoided cost—then the rate paid by Niagara Mohawk will be reduced to reflect the credit. If the adjustment account contains a balance in favor of Norcon, Niagara Mohawk must make increased payments to Norcon. If a balance exists in the adjustment account at the end of the third period, the party owing the balance must pay the balance in full within thirty days of the termination of the third period" (Norcon Power Partners v. Niagara Mohawk Power Corp., 110 F.3d 6, 7, supra).

In February 1994, Niagara Mohawk presented Norcon with a letter stating its belief, based on revised avoided cost estimates, that substantial credits in Niagara Mohawk's favor would accrue in the adjustment account during the second pricing period. "[A]nalysis shows that the Cumulative Avoided Cost Account will reach over $610 million by the end of the second period." Anticipating that Norcon would not be able to satisfy the daily escalating credits in the third period, Niagara Mohawk demanded that "Norcon provide adequate assurance to Niagara Mohawk that Norcon will duly perform all of its future repayment obligations."

Norcon promptly sued Niagara Mohawk in the United States District Court, Southern District of New York. It sought a declaration that Niagara Mohawk had no contractual right under New York State law to demand adequate assurance, beyond security provisions negotiated and expressed in the agreement. Norcon also sought a permanent injunction to stop Niagara Mohawk from anticipatorily terminating the contract based on the reasons described in the demand letter. Niagara Mohawk counterclaimed. It sought a counter declaration that it properly invoked a right to demand adequate assurance of Norcon's future payment performance of the contract.

The District Court granted Norcon's motion for summary judgment. It reasoned that New York common law recognizes the exceptional doctrine of demand for adequate assurance only when a promisor becomes insolvent, and also when the statutory sale of goods provision under UCC 2–609, is involved.

Thus, the District Court ruled in Norcon's favor because neither exception applied, in fact or by analogy to the particular dispute (decided sub nom. Encogen Four Partners v. Niagara Mohawk Power Corp., 914 F.Supp. 57 (S.D.N.Y.1996)).

The Second Circuit Court of Appeals preliminarily agrees (110 F.3d 6, supra) with the District Court that, except in the case of insolvency, no common-law or statutory right to demand adequate assurance exists under New York law which would affect non-UCC contracts, like the instant one. Because of the uncertainty concerning this substantive law question the Second Circuit certified the question to our Court as an aid to its correct application of New York law, and with an eye toward settlement of the important precedential impact on existing and future non-UCC commercial law matters and disputes.

II.

Our analysis should reference a brief review of the evolution of the doctrine of demands for adequate assurance. Its roots spring from the doctrine of anticipatory repudiation (see, Garvin, Adequate Assurance of Performance: Of Risk, Duress, and Cognition, 69 U. Colo. L. Rev. 71, 77 [1998]). Under that familiar precept, when a party repudiates contractual duties "prior to the time designated for performance and before" all of the consideration has been fulfilled, the "repudiation entitles the nonrepudiating party to claim damages for total breach" (Long Is. R.R. Co. v. Northville Indus. Corp., 41 N.Y.2d 455, 463, 393 N.Y.S.2d 925, 362 N.E.2d 558; see, II Farnsworth, Contracts § 8.20; Restatement [Second] of Contracts § 253; UCC 2–610). A repudiation can be either "a statement by the obligor to the obligee indicating that the obligor will commit a breach that would of itself give the obligee a claim for damages for total breach" or "a voluntary affirmative act which renders the obligor unable or apparently unable to perform without such a breach" (Restatement [Second] of Contracts § 250; see, II Farnsworth, Contracts § 8.21; UCC 2–610, Comment 1).

That switch in performance expectation and burden is readily available, applied and justified when a breaching party's words or deeds are unequivocal. Such a discernible line in the sand clears the way for the nonbreaching party to broach some responsive action. When, however, the apparently breaching party's actions are equivocal or less certain, then the nonbreaching party who senses an approaching storm cloud, affecting the contractual performance, is presented with a dilemma, and must weigh hard choices and serious consequences. One commentator has described the forecast options in this way:

> "If the promisee regards the apparent repudiation as an anticipatory repudiation, terminates his or her own performance and sues for breach, the promisee is placed in jeopardy of being found to have breached if the court determines that the apparent repudiation was not sufficiently clear and unequivocal to constitute an anticipatory repudiation justifying non-performance. If, on the other hand, the promisee continues to perform after perceiving an apparent repudiation, and it is subsequently determined that an anticipatory repudiation took place, the promisee may be denied recovery for post-repudiation expenditures because of his or her failure to avoid those expenses as part of a reasonable effort to mitigate damages after the repudiation" (Crespi, The Adequate Assurances Doc-

trine after U.C.C. § 2–609: A Test of the Efficiency of the Common Law, 38 Vill. L. Rev. 179, 183 [1993])....

III.

The Uniform Commercial Code settled on a mechanism for relieving some of this uncertainty. It allows a party to a contract for the sale of goods to demand assurance of future performance from the other party when reasonable grounds for insecurity exist (see, UCC 2–609; II Farnsworth, Contracts § 8.23). When adequate assurance is not forthcoming, repudiation is deemed confirmed, and the nonbreaching party is allowed to take reasonable actions as though a repudiation had occurred (see, 4 Anderson, Uniform Commercial Code § 2–609:3 [3d ed. 1997 rev.]).

UCC 2–609 provides, in relevant part:

"(1) A contract for sale imposes an obligation on each party that the other's expectation of receiving due performance will not be impaired. When reasonable grounds for insecurity arise with respect to the performance of either party the other may in writing demand adequate assurance of due performance and until he receives such assurance may if commercially reasonable suspend any performance for which he has not already received the agreed return.

"(4) After receipt of a justified demand failure to provide within a reasonable time not exceeding thirty days such assurance of due performance as is adequate under the circumstances of the particular case is a repudiation of the contract."

In theory, this UCC relief valve recognizes that "the essential purpose of a contract between commercial [parties] is actual performance and that a continuing sense of reliance and security that the promised performance will be forthcoming when due, is an important feature of the bargain" (UCC 2–609, Comment 1). In application, section 2–609 successfully implements the laudatory objectives of quieting the doubt a party fearing repudiation may have, mitigating the dilemma flowing from that doubt, and offering the nonbreaching party the opportunity to interpose timely action to deal with the unusual development (see, II Farnsworth, Contracts § 8.23a ...).

Indeed, UCC 2–609 has been considered so effective in bridging the doctrinal, exceptional and operational gap related to the doctrine of anticipatory breach that some States have imported the complementary regimen of demand for adequate assurance to common-law categories of contract law, using UCC 2–609 as the synapse (see, e.g., Lo Re v. Tel–Air Communications, 200 N.J.Super. 59, 490 A.2d 344 [finding support in UCC 2–609 and Restatement (Second) of Contracts § 251 for applying doctrine of adequate assurance to contract to purchase radio station]; Conference Ctr. v. TRC—The Research Corp. of New England, 189 Conn. 212, 455 A.2d 857 [analogizing to UCC 2–609, as supported by Restatement (Second) of Contracts § 251, in context of constructive eviction]).

Commentators have helped nudge this development along. They have noted that the problems redressed by UCC 2–609 are not unique to contracts for sale of goods, regulated under a purely statutory regime. Thus, they have cogently identified the need for the doctrine to be available in exceptional and qualifying common-law contractual settings and disputes because of similar practical, theoretical and salutary objectives (e.g., predictability, definiteness, and stability in commercial dealings and expectations) (see, e.g., Campbell, op. cit., at 1299–1304; see generally, White, Eight Cases and Section 251, 67 Cornell L. Rev. 841 [1982]; Dowling, op. cit.).

The American Law Institute through its Restatement (Second) of Contracts has also recognized and collected the authorities supporting this modern development. Its process and work settled upon this black letter language:

"(1) Where reasonable grounds arise to believe that the obligor will commit a breach by non-performance that would of itself give the obligee a claim for damages for total breach under § 243, the obligee may demand adequate assurance of due performance and may, if reasonable, suspend any performance for which he has not already received the agreed exchange until he receives such assurance.

"(2) The obligee may treat as a repudiation the obligor's failure to provide within a reasonable time such assurance of due performance as is adequate in the circumstances of the particular case" (Restatement [Second] of Contracts § 251).

Modeled on UCC 2–609, § 251 tracks "the principle that the parties to a contract look to actual performance 'and that a continuing sense of reliance and security that the promised performance will be forthcoming when due, is an important feature of the bargain' "(Restatement [Second] of Contracts § 251, comment a, quoting UCC 2–609, Comment 1). The duty of good faith and fair dealing in the performance of the contract is also reflected in section 251 (see, Restatement [Second] of Contracts § 251, comment a).

Some States have adopted Restatement § 251 as their common law of contracts, in varying degrees and classifications (see, e.g., Carfield & Sons v. Cowling, 616 P.2d 1008 [Colo] [construction contract]; L.E. Spitzer Co. v. Barron, 581 P.2d 213 [Alaska] [construction contract]; Drinkwater v. Patten Realty Corp., 563 A.2d 772 [Me] [sale of real estate]; Jonnet Dev. Corp. v. Dietrich Indus., 316 Pa.Super. 533, 463 A.2d 1026 [real estate lease]; but see, Mollohan v. Black Rock Contr., 160 W.Va. 446, 235 S.E.2d 813 [declining to adopt section 251, except to the extent that failure to give adequate assurance on demand may be some evidence of repudiation]).

IV.

New York, up to now, has refrained from expanding the right to demand adequate assurance of performance beyond the Uniform Commercial Code (see, Sterling Power Partners v. Niagara Mohawk Power Corp., 239 A.D.2d 191, 657 N.Y.S.2d 407, appeal dismissed 92 N.Y.2d 877, 677 N.Y.S.2d 783, 700 N.E.2d 322; Schenectady Steel Co. v. Trimpoli Gen. Constr. Co., 43 A.D.2d 234, 350 N.Y.S.2d 920, affd. on other grounds 34 N.Y.2d 939, 359 N.Y.S.2d 560, 316 N.E.2d 875). The only other recognized exception is the insolvency setting (see, Hanna v. Florence Iron Co...., 222 N.Y. 290, 118 N.E. 629; Pardee v. Kanady, 100 N.Y. 121, 2 N.E. 885; Updike v. Oakland Motor Car Co., 229 App.Div. 632, 242 N.Y.S. 329). Hence, the need for this certified question emerged so this Court could provide guidance towards a correct resolution of the Federal lawsuit by settling New York law with a modern pronouncement governing this kind of contract and dispute.

Niagara Mohawk, before our Court through the certified question from the Federal court, urges a comprehensive adaptation of the exceptional demand tool. This wholesale approach has also been advocated by the commentators (see generally, Dowling, op. cit.; Campbell, op. cit.). Indeed, it is even reflected in the breadth of the wording of the certified question.

This Court's jurisprudence, however, usually evolves by deciding cases and settling the law more modestly (Rooney v. Tyson, 91 N.Y.2d 685, 694, 674 N.Y.S.2d 616, 697 N.E.2d 571, citing Cardozo, Nature of the Judicial Process, in Selected Writings of Benjamin Nathan Cardozo, at 115, 134 [Margaret E. Hall ed. 1947] [observing that Judges proceed interstitially]). The twin purposes and functions of this Court's work require significant professional discipline and judicious circumspection.

We conclude, therefore, that it is unnecessary, while fulfilling the important and useful certification role, to promulgate so sweeping a change and proposition in contract law, as has been sought, in one dramatic promulgation. That approach might clash with our customary incremental common-law developmental process, rooted in particular fact patterns and keener wisdom acquired through observations of empirical application of a proportioned, less than absolute, rule in future cases.

It is well to note the axiom that deciding a specific case, even with the precedential comet's tail its rationale illuminates, is very different from enacting a statute of general and universal application (see, Breitel, The Lawmakers, 2 Benjamin N. Cardozo Memorial Lectures 761, 788 [1965] ["(P)rocedurally, courts are limited to viewing the problem as presented in a litigated case within the four corners of its record. A multiplication of cases will broaden the view because of the multiplication of records, but the limitation still persists because the records are confined by the rules of procedure, legal relevance, and evidence."]).

Experience and patience thus offer a more secure and realistic path to a better and fairer rule, in theory and in practical application. Therefore, this Court chooses to take the traditionally subtler approach, consistent with the proven benefits of the maturation process of the common law, including in the very area of anticipatory repudiation which spawns this relatively newer demand for assurance corollary (see, Garvin, op. cit., at 77–80; Robertson, op. cit., at 307–310; Dowling, op. cit., at 1359–1362; see also, Breitel, op. cit., at 781–782 [1965] ["The commonplace, for which the Holmeses and the Cardozos had to blaze a trail in the judicial realm, assumes the rightness of courts in making interstitial law, filling gaps in the statutory and decisional rules, and at a snail-like pace giving some forward movement to the developing law. Any law creation more drastic than this is often said and thought to be an invalid encroachment on the legislative branch."]).

This Court is now persuaded that the policies underlying the UCC 2–609 counterpart should apply with similar cogency for the resolution of this kind of controversy. A useful analogy can be drawn between the contract at issue and a contract for the sale of goods. If the contract here was in all respects the same, except that it was for the sale of oil or some other tangible commodity instead of the sale of electricity, the parties would unquestionably be governed by the demand for adequate assurance of performance factors in UCC 2–609. We are convinced to take this prudent step because it puts commercial parties in these kinds of disputes at relatively arm's length equilibrium in terms of reliability and uniformity of governing legal rubrics. The availability of the doctrine may even provide an incentive and tool for parties to resolve their own differences, perhaps without the necessity of judicial intervention. Open, serious renegotiation of dramatic developments and changes in unusual contractual expectations and qualifying circumstances would occur because of and with an eye to the doctrine's application.

The various authorities, factors and concerns, in sum, prompt the prudence and awareness of the usefulness of recognizing the extension of the doctrine of demand for adequate assurance, as a common-law analogue. It should apply to the type of long-term commercial contract between corporate entities entered into by Norcon and Niagara Mohawk here, which is complex and not reasonably susceptible of all security features being anticipated, bargained for and incorporated in the original contract. Norcon's performance, in terms of reimbursing Niagara Mohawk for credits, is still years away. In the meantime, potential quantifiable damages are accumulating and Niagara Mohawk must weigh the hard choices and serious consequences that the doctrine of demand for adequate assurance is designed to mitigate. This Court needs to go no further in its promulgation of the legal standard as this suffices to declare a dispositive and proportioned answer to the certified question.

Accordingly, the certified question should be answered in the affirmative.

Chief Judge KAYE and Judges SMITH, LEVINE, CIPARICK and WESLEY concur.

Following certification of a question by the United States Court of Appeals for the Second Circuit and acceptance of the question by this Court pursuant to section 500.17 of the Rules of the Court of Appeals (22 NYCRR 500.17), and after hearing argument by counsel for the parties and consideration of the briefs and the record submitted, certified question answered in the affirmative.

NOTE ON AFFIRMATIVE RECOVERY UNDER
UCC § 2–609

Although UCC § 2–609 is normally used as a defense by a buyer or seller who has stopped performing on the ground of insecurity, Subsection (4) provides that "[a]fter receipt of a justified demand [for assurance,] failure to provide within a reasonable time not exceeding thirty days such assurance of due performance as is adequate under the circumstances of the particular case is a repudiation of the contract." A repudiation is itself a breach, and therefore gives rise to a right of action by a party who rightfully but unsuccessfully demanded assurance. See Creusot–Loire International, Inc. v. Coppus Engineering Corp., 585 F.Supp. 45 (S.D.N.Y.1983); Universal Builders Corp. v. United Methodist Convalescent Homes, Inc., 7 Conn.App. 318, 508 A.2d 819 (1986).

*

Appendix A

THE STATUTE OF FRAUDS

Analysis

Sec.

1. Introduction.

2. The Text of the Original Statute.

3. The Purpose of the Statute.

4. How it was Decided What Kinds of Contracts Should be Required to be in Writing.

5. American Variations on the English Theme.

6. Judicial Interpretations of the Various Subsections of the Statute of Frauds—Introduction.

7. Contracts for the Sale of an Interest in Land (Section 4(4)).

8. Contracts for the Sale of Goods.

9. Some Other Formal Requirements in the Uniform Commercial Code.

10. Agreements not to be Performed Within One Year From the Making Thereof (Section 4(5)).

11. The Suretyship (Section 4(2))—Generally.

12. The Suretyship Section Continued—"The Main Purpose Rule".

13. The Suretyship Section Continued—Miscellaneous Problems.

14. Promises Made by Executors and Administrators (Section 4(1)).

15. Contracts Upon Consideration of Marriage (Section 4(3)).

16. What Kind of Writing Will Satisfy the Statute.

17. Electronic Contracting and the Statute of Frauds.

18. The Effect of Part Performance of, or Reliance Upon, An Oral Contract Within the Statute—Introduction.

19. The Restitution of Benefits Conferred Under the Oral Agreement.

20. Reimbursement for Reliance on the Oral Contract.

21. The Right to the "Value of The Bargain" Where There Has Been Part Performance of, or Reliance Upon, the Oral Contract.

22. The Effect of Non–Compliance—Legal Consequences of the Unenforceable Agreement.

23. Oral Rescission.

Sec.
24.   Oral Modifications.

25.   The Interaction of the Statute of Frauds With the Parol Evidence Rule.

26.   The Interaction of the Statute of Frauds With the Remedy of Reformation.

27.   Pleading and Procedural Problems in Connection With the Statute.

28.   A Glance Backward and Ahead.

SECTION 1. INTRODUCTION

Under the Statute of Frauds, certain types of contracts are unenforceable against a party unless the contract is in writing, or evidenced by a writing (or, to use the terminology of the Statute, by a "memorandum") signed by the party to be charged, that is, the party sought to be held liable under the contract. (For ease of exposition, in the balance of this Appendix this requirement, where applicable, will be referred to simply as a requirement that a contract be in writing.) The purpose of this Appendix is to provide an introduction to problems that can arise under the Statute.

This Appendix is organized as follows: Sections 2–6 provide a general introduction to the Statute of Frauds. Sections 7–15 concern judicial interpretations of the provisions of the Statute that are most important in contract law (for example, provisions concerning contracts for the sale of an interest in land or for the sale of goods). The balance of this Appendix concerns exceptions to the Statute (that is, instances in which contracts of a type that are covered by the Statute are nevertheless enforceable in whole or in part even though not in writing) and miscellaneous problems, such as the interaction of the Statute of Frauds with certain other rules of other contract law.

This Appendix includes a number of Examples, in the form of hypothetical cases and their resolutions. The resolutions offered in the Examples are those that would normally be rendered in a typical American jurisdiction, although not necessarily in every jurisdiction.

A note on terminology: When a contract is of a type that is covered by the Statute, and is not in writing, the contract is said to be "within the Statute." However, when an exception to the Statute applies, the contract is said to be "taken out of the Statute" by virtue of the exception. Thus a contract that is within the Statute and is not in writing is unenforceable unless it is taken out of the Statute by an exception. If it is taken out of the Statute, the contract is enforceable although not in writing.

SECTION 2. THE TEXT OF THE ORIGINAL STATUTE

The original English Statute of Frauds was passed in 1677. Its title was "An Act for Prevention of Frauds and Perjuries." It contained twenty-five sections, and attempted to prevent fraud in the proof of many different kinds of legal transactions—not only in the area of contracts, but also in the areas of assignments, deeds to land, trusts, and wills. To insure a trustworthy memorial of what occurred, and thereby to prevent perjury, many sections of the Statute required a signed writing to make particular kinds of acts or transactions enforceable. In some cases an additional formality, such as attestation by witnesses, was required. In others, an alternative formality was permitted, such as providing that a will may be effectively revoked if it is canceled, torn, or obliterated by the testator or under his immediate direction. Certain sections of the Statute related to matters of procedure and land law that had only an indirect relation to the general object of the Statute.

The provisions of the original Statute that are chiefly relevant to contract law are Sections 4 and 17, reproduced below. In the balance of this Appendix, references to "the Statute of Frauds" or "the Statute" refer to those two sections and their modern counterparts. Spelling and punctuation have been modernized, and some liberties have been taken with the original in the paragraphing and numbering of subsections.

Section 4

And be it further enacted ... that ... no action shall be brought

    (1) whereby to charge any executor or administrator upon any special promise to answer damages out of his own estate; or

    (2) whereby to charge the defendant upon any special promise to answer for the debt, default or miscarriages of another person; or

    (3) to charge any person upon any agreement made upon consideration of marriage; or

    (4) upon any contract or sale of lands, tenements or hereditaments, or any interest in or concerning them; or

    (5) upon any agreement that is not to be performed within the space of one year from the making thereof;

unless the agreement upon which such action shall be brought, or some memorandum or note thereof, shall be in writing, and signed by the party to be charged therewith, or some other person thereunto by him lawfully authorized.

Section 17

[The "sale-of-goods" section]

And be it further enacted ... that ... no contract for the sale of any goods, wares or merchandises for the price of ten pounds sterling or upwards shall be allowed to be good, except

    (a) the buyer shall accept part of the goods so sold and actually receive the same; or

    (b) give something in earnest to bind the bargain or in part payment; or

    (c) that some note or memorandum in writing of the said bargain be made and signed by the parties to be charged by such contract or their agents thereunto lawfully authorized.

(Note that the Statute uses the terms "agreement" and "contract" interchangeably. The same usage will be followed in this Appendix.)

SECTION 3. THE PURPOSE OF THE STATUTE

Legislation that makes the enforceability of an act or transaction depend upon the observance of certain formalities may be adopted for a variety of reasons. In contract law, Austin discerned two principal reasons for requiring formalities: (1) "to provide evidence of the existence and purport of the contract, in case of controversy," and (2) "to prevent inconsiderate [not well-thought-through] engagements." J. Austin, Fragments—On Contracts, 2 Lectures on Jurisprudence 940 (4th ed., 1879).

Certainly the Statute of Frauds was intended to serve the first purpose. It was an act to prevent "frauds and perjuries," and stated in its preamble that it was aimed at "many fraudulent practices which are commonly endeavored to be upheld by perjury, and subornation of perjury." To handicap the plaintiff who might seek to establish a contract by perjured testimony, the Statute required him to base his case on a writing signed by the defendant. In this respect the purpose of the Statute was evidentiary. It sought a trustworthy memorial of the transaction and its terms.

On the other hand, it is clear that the Statute could also have had another purpose, that which Austin described as preventing "inconsiderate engagements." When a person is not bound unless and until she has signed a writing, a procedure has been established that will tend to prevent persons from slipping into legal undertakings without a full appreciation of what they are doing, because the writing may serve as a warning or deterrent against hasty action.

If the drafters of the Statute of Frauds had this second object in mind, they left no trace of it in the historical records of the time or in the language of the act they drew up. On the other hand, the judges who have interpreted the Statute have occasionally assumed that ensuring deliberation in the making of contracts was a collateral and secondary purpose of the Statute. Thus in Warden v. Jones, 1857, 2 De.Gex & J. 76, 83–84, the court said, "The law has ... wisely forbidden [oral proof of contracts in consideration of marriage]. Persons are so likely to be led into such promises inconsiderately, that the law has wisely required them to be manifested by writing." Expressions tending toward the same thought will be found in cases involving some other sections of the Statute, particularly the "suretyship" provision, section 4(2).

However, there are holdings that can only be justified on the view that the sole purpose of the Statute is to ensure reliable evidence of the contract. If the purpose of the Statute was to protect persons against hasty engagements, it would seem that the Statute could not be satisfied simply by a writing that repudiates the contract. Indeed, Restatement Second provides that in the case of a contract in consideration of marriage, "a subsequent writing does not satisfy the Statute unless made as a memorandum of the agreement," because "[t]he marriage provision ... performs a cautionary function" as well as an evidentiary one. Restatement Second § 133, comment a. See also Restatement

Second § 124, comment d. However, the general rule is that a writing that sets forth an earlier oral contract but repudiates the contract serves as a memorandum that satisfies the Statute. Restatement Second § 133.

Example No. 1:

As part of a land-development scheme, Susan Slide wanted to buy Blackacre, owned by Oliver Oakapple. Slide enters an agreement for the purchase of Blackacre for $40,000. This agreement is incorporated in an elaborate written contract, which Oakapple signs but Slide does not. When the development scheme collapses, Slide wishes to escape her obligation. Oakapple writes a letter to Slide reminding her of the contract, which he encloses, demanding performance. Slide returns the contract, with a letter that reads: "It is true that I entered an oral contract with you on the terms of the enclosed written document. However, the law requires that the contract or a memorandum of it be signed by the party to be charged therewith. You will note that I did not sign this contract, and therefore I am not bound by it. Hoping this incident will teach you some law, Yours truly, Susan Slide."

The decision will go for Oakapple. Slide has provided Oakapple with a signed memorandum of the contract, which will take the contract out of the Statute and permit a successful suit against her.

The conclusions in this Section may be summarized as follows: Everyone agrees that the primary purpose of the Statute of Frauds is to ensure reliable evidence of certain types of contracts on which suit is brought. Cases like *Example No. 1* indicate that the courts usually view the "memorandum" that is required by the Statute, in the absence of a written contract, not as a writing designed to warn a party against "inconsiderate engagements," but as a means of ensuring the existence of a contract and its terms. On the other hand, some cases discern, as a secondary purpose of the Statute, ensuring against hasty action, and this conception of the Statute may influence the interpretation of some of its provisions.

SECTION 4. HOW IT WAS DECIDED WHAT KINDS OF CONTRACTS SHOULD BE REQUIRED TO BE IN WRITING

The question addressed in this Section is, How did the drafters of the Statute of Frauds decide which contracts to include in their requirement of a writing and which to exclude? This question is closely related to that raised in the last Section, because we cannot know why the drafters included some contracts and left out others unless we know in general what objectives the drafters were trying to achieve.

Offhand, it might be thought that important and complex kinds of contracts would be covered by the Statute, and simple and unimportant kinds of contracts would not be. As applied to the modern business world, however, the Statute leaves out some very important and often complex kinds of contracts.

Example No. 2:

Bertram Builder and Teresa Turf enter an oral contract under which Builder promises to construct a commercial building according to certain plans and specifications, commencing work on January 1 and finishing by December 1, and Turf agrees to pay Builder $15 million for the job.

The enforceability of this oral agreement is unaffected by the Statute of Frauds, because it does not come within any of the Statute's sections. (If this seems hard to believe, read Sections 4 and 17 over again, which is a good idea at this point anyway.)

Example No. 3:

In the case supposed in *Example No. 2,* after the completion of the building, Turf enters into an agreement with the Rock of Ages Insurance Company, under which Rock of Ages insures the building for one year against fire in the amount of $15 million, and Turf agrees to pay a premium of $200,000.

This contract is also enforceable, although oral, because it too does not come within any of the Statute's sections.

If we were to attempt to retrace the actual mental processes of the drafters of the original Statute when they drew up their list, we would have to know much about the commercial and feudal practices of the time. We would also have to study closely the rules of procedure then prevailing, since the need for evidentiary safeguards in the proof of a particular type of transaction would depend in part on the procedural rules applied to suits founded on that transaction-type. Pursuing the same principle of inquiry, we would also have to ask similar questions about each American state when it adopted its Statute of Frauds, and decided either to accept the English original or to take the English Statute with certain changes or omissions. No one seriously contends that a scholarly inquiry of that sort would contribute much to a solution of the problem how the Statute ought to be construed today. A general analysis of the possible reasons for including the types of contracts that were enumerated in the original Statute may, however, be helpful.

Of contracts to sell land or any interests therein (section 4(4)), and of contracts "upon consideration of marriage" (section 4(3)), we can say that their inclusion is readily explained on the grounds that they are fairly important agreements, often rather complex in their terms. Contracts not to be performed within a year also look like important contracts, proof of which may require witnesses to stretch their memories over an uncomfortably long period if there is no written evidence of the contract. Similarly, Section 17, the sales-of-goods provision, explicitly made the importance of the contract, as measured in monetary terms, the test of whether a writing was required.

It is harder to explain why sections 4(1) and 4(2) were included. In general, these two sections mean that where a person is to be held as a surety or guarantor for another, she can only be charged on a writing that she has signed. (Section 4(1) covers the special case of an executor or administrator who undertakes to be surety on a debt of the deceased for which the estate is liable. See Section 14 of this Appendix.) A contract of suretyship is usually not a complicated contract; it generally amounts in effect to saying, "If he doesn't pay or perform, I will." On the other hand, the very simplicity of the agreement, and its vital importance to the surety, who often acts without compensation, may be a reason for taking steps to guard against perjury. In civil-law countries, provisions requiring the undertaking of a surety to be in writing are generally interpreted to have a cautionary purpose, on the theory that people are often drawn into becoming sureties without a full appreciation of what they are doing. There are occasional intimations of a similar view in discussions of the English Statute of Frauds or its American counterparts. Whatever intention the draftsmen of the original Statute may have harbored, it is certainly true that some of the judicial interpretations of the suretyship section would be easier to understand if we were free to assume that it had a cautionary or deterrent purpose. (See Section 12 of this Appendix.)

SECTION 5. AMERICAN VARIATIONS ON THE ENGLISH THEME

Ambit. All the American states except Louisiana, Maryland, and New Mexico copied Section 4 of the English Statute of Frauds, and in Maryland and New Mexico the Statute of Frauds is in force by judicial decision. See Restatement Second, ch. 5, Statutory Note. Some states originally omitted Section 17 from their Statutes of Frauds, but the substance of Section 17 was later incorporated in the Uniform Commercial Code. Other states have in a very few instances left out particular provisions of Section 4 of the original Statute, or more commonly have extended the requirement of a writing to transactions not included in the English Statute. One common extension requires a suit to recover a real estate broker's commission to be founded on a written agreement. A contract to make a will is sometimes required to be in writing. Many statutes require a promise to pay certain types of barred or discharged debts to be in writing.

Phraseology. Sometimes American enactments of the original statute introduce minor changes in phraseology. For example, instead of saying "no action shall be brought" on a specified type of oral contract (section 4 of the English Statute), or that the oral contract shall not "be allowed to be good" (section 17 of the English Statute), a Statute of Frauds may simply say that oral contracts of certain types shall be "void." Though the word "void" is probably not to be taken in a literal sense, its use may have some influence in the application of a Statute of Frauds. (See Section 22 of this Appendix.)

Another change sometimes introduced in American Statutes of Frauds is to say that "the contract" must be in writing, instead of following the language of the English Statute, which requires only that "the agreement" or "some memorandum or note thereof" be in writing. This change may be significant as destroying the efficacy of a memorandum executed for some purpose other than that of serving as a statement of the agreement. (See *Example No. 1.* Slide's letter is perhaps a memorandum of the agreement; it is certainly not "the contract.")

SECTION 6. JUDICIAL INTERPRETATIONS OF THE VARIOUS SUBSECTIONS OF THE STATUTE OF FRAUDS—INTRODUCTION

The best general guide to the judicial interpretation of the Statute of Frauds is to remember this simple truth: The courts have not favored the Statute of Frauds. Generally—although certainly not invariably—whenever the words of the Statute leave any leeway (and often when they do not), the courts have restricted its meaning and found ways of making an oral agreement enforceable.

Example No. 4:

Sally Smooth and Plastic Age, Inc., enter a written contract whereby Smooth is to work for Plastic Age for five years as Personnel Manager, at a salary of $30,000 a year. After Smooth has been on the job for one month, the parties orally rescind the contract and release each other from it. The next day Smooth repents of her decision and insists on her rights under the written contract. Her attorney argues as follows: This contract of employment fell within Section 4(5) of the Statute of Frauds, because it was not to be performed within one year from the time it was made. The Statute requires that the creation of such a contract be evidenced by a writing, and it is only logical that the same formality should be required for its rescission.

The decision would go for Plastic Age. The Statute of Frauds does not explicitly address the question of rescission, and as a general proposition rescission does not fall within the Statute, on the theory that a rescission does not call for the performance of any duties. (For exceptions to this proposition, see Section 23 of this Appendix.)

SECTION 7. CONTRACTS FOR THE SALE OF AN INTEREST IN LAND (SECTION 4(4))

Section 4(4) covers broadly and somewhat verbosely contracts for the sale of any kind of interest in land. The price, value, or extent of the interest is immaterial.

Example No. 5:

Jim Joad orally agrees with Jane Jukes that he will sell her his eroded tract, Redacre, for ten cents. The contract is within section 4(4) of the Statute of Frauds.

Test. In determining what constitutes an interest in land for purposes of the Statute of Frauds, the test applied is generally that furnished by the law of property. Restatement Second § 127.

Example No. 6:

To obtain a shortcut from his farm to the highway, Paul Pass wants the right to drive through Bilbo Block's land. The parties orally agree that in consideration of the payment of $1000, Pass shall have that right during his life. This contract falls within Section 4(4), because it is a contract for the sale of an interest in land. If the parties had called in a lawyer to draw up the papers for their transaction, the lawyer would have treated this right as an "easement," a familiar heading in books dealing with interests in land.

Example No. 7:

Richard Rocksie, a theatre proprietor, who owns his theatre and the land on which it rests, orally agrees with Julia Roberts that if she will attend the theater's opening night, he will give her a pass, good for life, to sit in seat F11, sixth-row center, for all future performances.

This contract is not within section 4(4). The right to sit in a certain seat during a theatrical performance would not be viewed generally as an interest in the land. No lawyer with a sense of linguistic proprieties would call this right an "easement."

Conveyances. The language of section 4(4) speaks of "any contract *or* sale" of lands. One might assume that this covers either a contract *to* convey, or a *present* conveyance by way of sale. Actually, however, present conveyances are covered by the first three sections of the Statute of Frauds, which have not been reproduced in this Appendix. Accordingly, it is safe to assume that despite its language, section 4(4) really means any contract for the sale of an interest in land, with the qualification that the term "contract or sale of lands ... or any interest concerning them" is used here in a broad sense that includes contracts to devise land by will or to exchange land for something other than money, as well as the more common contract to convey land by deed in return for an agreed money price. (Restatement Second § 125, comments a, c, and Illustrations.)

Leases. In very general terms, the first three Sections of the original Statute state that a writing is necessary to create or transfer an interest in land, except that a tenancy at will and, under certain conditions, a lease not to exceed three years, may be created orally. The substance of these provisions is very generally carried over into American Statutes of Frauds, but the exception for oral short-term leases is usually reduced to either one year or two years.

SECTION 8. CONTRACTS FOR THE SALE OF GOODS

The basic provision. In this country, Section 17 of the Statute of Frauds (the sale-of-goods section) was eventually succeeded by UCC § 2–201:

§ 2–201. Formal Requirements; Statute of Frauds

(1) Except as otherwise provided in this section a contract for the sale of goods for the price of $500 or more is not enforceable by way of action or defense unless there is some writing sufficient to indicate that a contract for sale has been made between the parties and signed by the party against whom enforcement is sought or by his authorized agent or

broker. A writing is not insufficient because it omits or incorrectly states a term agreed upon but the contract is not enforceable under this paragraph beyond the quantity of goods shown in such writing.

(2) Between merchants if within a reasonable time a writing in confirmation of the contract and sufficient against the sender is received and the party receiving it has reason to know its contents, it satisfies the requirements of subsection (1) against such party unless written notice of objection to its contents is given within 10 days after it is received.

(3) A contract which does not satisfy the requirements of subsection (1) but which is valid in other respects is enforceable

(a) if the goods are to be specially manufactured for the buyer and are not suitable for sale to others in the ordinary course of the seller's business and the seller, before notice of repudiation is received and under circumstances which reasonably indicate that the goods are for the buyer, has made either a substantial beginning of their manufacture or commitments for their procurement; or

(b) if the party against whom enforcement is sought admits in his pleading, testimony or otherwise in court that a contract for sale was made, but the contract is not enforceable under this provision beyond the quantity of goods admitted; or

(c) with respect to goods for which payment has been made and accepted or which have been received and accepted. . . .

Three points are worth noting at the outset.

First, UCC § 2–201(1) relates only to the sale of "goods"—that is, physical property other than realty, or what the comment to the UCC calls "movables." It does not include sales of "choses in action" or other intangibles.

Second, the writing required by UCC § 2–201(1) need only be "sufficient to indicate that a contract for sale has been made between the parties." There is no requirement that the writing either specify the kind of goods involved or state the price. Curiously, there is not even a requirement that the quantity of goods sold be stated, but this apparent looseness is illusory, because subsection (1) provides that "the contract is not enforceable ... beyond the quantity of goods shown in such writing." Accordingly, if no quantity is shown the extent of enforcement is zero; if the oral agreement was for 1000 units, while the writing says 500 units, the contract is enforceable only to the extent of 500 units. (The UCC does not itself deal with the possibility of reforming the writing to correct a mistake. Presumably, if both parties intended the writing to state 1000 units, a court might in a proper case reform the memorandum, which then would become enforceable to the extent of 1000 units. See Section 25 of this Appendix.)

Third, UCC § 2–201 applies only if the price is $500 or more. However, if the price is $500 or more, and § 2–201 is not satisfied, the entire contract (not merely that portion of the contract in excess of $500) is unenforceable.

Exceptions. As indicated by introductory clause to UCC § 2–201, the basic requirement of section 2–201(1) is subject to several exceptions.

Part performance. Subsection (3)(c) provides that "A contract which does not satisfy the requirements of [section 2–201(1)] but which is valid in other respects is enforceable ... with respect to goods for which payment has been made and accepted or which have been received and accepted...." Even in the absence of subsection (3)(c), if a buyer has accepted goods she would be liable for the value of the goods under the law of unjust enrichment. See Section 19 of this Appendix. The significance of subsection (3)(c) is that if seller sues under the law of unjust enrichment, he would be entitled to recover only the value of the goods at the time they were accepted by the buyer. In contrast, under subsection (3)(c) the seller can recover the contract price of the accepted goods.

Goods made specially to order. Suppose a patient orders a dental bridge from his dentist and orally agrees to pay a price of $2000. The dentist faithfully prepares the bridge to fit the patient's teeth, but when the time comes for installation of the bridge, the patient refuses to pay for it or to receive and accept it. If this contract was held to be a contract for the sale of goods, and unenforceable unless in writing, a serious injustice would be done to the dentist, who will obviously have some difficulty finding a market for the bridge that the patient rejected. Subsection (3)(a) deals with this problem by providing that "A contract which does not satisfy the requirements of [§ 2–201(1)] but which is valid in other respects is enforceable ... if [i] the goods are to be specially manufactured for the buyer and [ii] are not suitable for sale to others in the ordinary course of the seller's business and [iii] the seller, before notice of repudiation is received and under circumstances which reasonably indicate that the goods are for the buyer, has made either a substantial beginning of their manufacture or commitments for their procurement...." (Subdivisions inserted by ed.)

Receipt of confirmation. Subsection (2) adds another exception to the requirement of a writing for a contract for the sale of goods, based upon modern methods of contracting. That subsection provides, "Between merchants if within a reasonable time a writing in confirmation of the contract and sufficient against the sender is received and the party receiving it has reason to know its contents, it satisfies the requirements of [§ 2–201(1)] against such party unless written notice of objection to its contents is given within 10 days after it is received." Note that subsection (2) is confined to transactions between merchants. (For the UCC definition of "merchant," see UCC § 2–104(1).)

Admissions. Subsection (3)(b) provides that "A contract which does not satisfy the requirements of [§ 2–201(1)] but which is valid in other respects is enforceable ... if the party against whom enforcement is sought admits in his pleading, testimony or otherwise in court that a contract for sale was made, but the contract is not enforceable under this provision beyond the quantity of goods admitted...." The weight of authority is that the admission may be involuntary as well as voluntary. Accordingly, under subsection 3(b) a plaintiff can bring suit on an oral contract and then try to make the defendant admit, in discovery proceedings or on cross-examination, that the oral contract was in fact made. Indeed, there is much authority that where a complaint is based on an oral contract for the sale of goods it should ordinarily not be dismissed on motion before the plaintiff has had the chance to depose the defendant, because the plaintiff should have an opportunity to elicit such an admission. See, e.g., ALA, Inc. v. CCAIR, Inc., 29 F.3d 855 (3d Cir. 1994) (decided under an analogous statute); Theta Products, Inc. v. Zippo Mfg. Co., 81 F. Supp. 2d 346 (D.R.I. 1999). This is as it should be. The Statute of Frauds is designed to protect against the danger that a plaintiff may, by perjury, establish a contract to the jury's satisfaction where there was no contract in fact. If the defendant *admits* the contract existed, the purpose of the Statute is satisfied. As stated in the *ALA* case:

> In order for [the admissions exception] to function, the plaintiff must have some opportunity to obtain an admission from the defendant. A Rule 12(b)(6) motion [for failure to state a claim on which relief can be granted], however, would derail the plaintiff's case pre-pleading and allow the defendant to defeat a cause of action on an oral contract before the plaintiff has any opportunity to seek an admission that a contract existed. Allowing a defendant to dispose of a case on a Rule 12(b)(6) motion would eviscerate [the admissions exception] and potentially allow a defendant to avoid the obligations of an oral contract into which he or she actually entered.*

The following two Examples illustrate some of the problems of interpretation raised by UCC § 2–201:

Example No. 8:

Seller and Buyer enter an oral contract whereby Seller is to deliver 12,000 widgets over a twelve months' period, in twelve shipments of 1000 each. The agreed price is $1 per widget. The first ten shipments are accepted and paid for. After the eleventh shipment has been accepted, but before it has been paid for, Buyer repudiates the contract, refusing to pay for the eleventh shipment, and stating that he will not accept the final shipment for the twelfth month. Seller sues to recover $1000 due for the eleventh shipment and damages of $400 for Buyer's refusal to accept the final shipment. Buyer pleads UCC § 2–201 as a defense.

The cases would be resolved as follows: The contract involves the sale of goods, and therefore comes within § 2–201. The successive deliveries and payments made before Buyer repudiated the agreement do not take the entire contract out of the Statute, but only those deliveries and payments. Since Buyer has already paid for the first ten shipments, Seller is entitled to the price of the eleventh shipment–$1000. Seller cannot recover $400 as damages for Buyer's refusal to take the final delivery. Although the $400 in damages that Seller seeks is less than the $500 figure in § 2–201, that figure relates not to the amount of damages but to the total price set in the contract, which in this case was $12,000.

* However, in DF Activities Corp. v. Brown, 851 F.2d 920 (7th Cir.1988), the court held that suit on an oral contact could be dismissed on summary judgement where the defendant by sworn affidavit denied that she ever agreed to sell the goods in question (a Frank Lloyd Wright chair) to the plaintiff:

"... When there is a bare motion to dismiss, or an answer, with no evidentiary materials, the possibility remains a live one that, if asked under oath whether a contract had been made, the defendant would admit it had been. The only way to test the proposition is for the plaintiff to take the defendant's deposition, or, if there is no discovery, to call the defendant as an adverse witness at trial. But where as in this case the defendant swears in an affidavit that there was no contract, we see no point in keeping the lawsuit alive. Of course the defendant may blurt out an admission in a deposition, but this is hardly likely, especially since by doing so he may be admitting to having perjured himself in his affidavit. Stranger things have happened, but remote possibilities do not warrant subjecting the parties and the judiciary to proceedings almost certain to be futile." (Footnote by ed.)

Example No. 9:

Seller and Buyer orally agree that Seller will deliver her used Camry to Buyer next Monday for an agreed price of $5000. Buyer pays Seller $500 with a promise to pay the remaining $4500 when the car is delivered. When Monday comes, Seller refuses to go through with the oral bargain. Buyer sues for damages.

Because a sale of goods is involved, the applicable provision is UCC § 2–201. According to subsection (3)(c), Buyer's rights are limited to the "goods for which payment has been made." This seems to suggest that Buyer is entitled to $500 worth of automobile. The cases are not unanimous, but under the weight of authority a down payment on an indivisible unit makes the entire contract enforceable, on the ground that the payment evidences the contract and identifies the party to be charged, and that in such cases there is no room for a dispute over quantity. White & Summers state: "Some courts have had to consider whether a down payment on a single nondivisible unit . . . indicates a contract and permits the party making the payment to prove and recover in full on his oral contract. A court might say that 2–201(3)(c) is not satisfied, because payment must be made in full with respect to the single unit. Williamson v. Martz, [11 Pa.D. & C.2d 33 (1958)], a Pennsylvania lower court case, so held. Other courts (correctly, in our opinion) have gone the other way. Lockwood v. Smigel [18 Cal.App.3d 800, 96 Cal.Rptr. 289 (1971)] is illustrative. There the court held that a $100 down payment on an $11,000 Rolls Royce brought 2–201(3)(c) into play and permitted the seller to try to prove his oral contract for the whole." J. White & R. Summers, Uniform Commercial Code § 2–5 (5th ed. 2000).

The CISG. So far, we have been dealing only with the provisions of the UCC that concern when a contract for the sale of goods must be in writing. Many international contracts for the sale of goods are governed by the CISG (Convention for the International Sale of Goods) rather than the UCC. Article 11 of the CISG provides that "A contract of sale need not be concluded in or evidenced by writing and is not subject to any other requirement as to form." See Dodge, Teaching the CISG in Contracts, 50 J. Leg. Ed. 72 (2000).

Amendments to the official version of UCC section 2–201. In 2003, the National Conference of Commissioners on State Laws and the American Law Institute, who are jointly responsible for promulgating and amending the Uniform Commercial Code, adopted a number of amendments to the official version of Article 2 of the Code. One of the amended sections is 2–201. Some of the amendments to this section are technical, but two are substantive. First, the threshold amount under section 2–201(1) is increased from $500 to $5,000. Second, a new subsection (4) provides, "A contract that is enforceable under this section is not unenforceable merely because it is not capable of being performed within one year or any other period after its making." As of early 2006, however, no state legislature has adopted the amended version of Article 2. Accordingly, the pre–2003 version of section 2–201 remains the governing law.

SECTION 9. SOME OTHER FORMAL REQUIREMENTS IN THE UNIFORM COMMERCIAL CODE

The UCC has several other provisions that bear on the requirement of a writing. In particular:

1. UCC § 9–203 provides that security interests in most types of collateral that are already not in the creditor's possession are enforceable only if described in a security agreement that is authenticated by the debtor.

2. UCC § 8–113 provides that "A contract or modification of a contract for the sale or purchase of a security is enforceable whether or not there is a writing signed or record authenticated by a party against whom enforcement is sought, even if the contract or modification is not capable of performance within one year of its making."

3. UCC § 1–206 ("Statute of Frauds for Kinds of Personal Property Not Otherwise Covered") provides:

> (1) Except in the cases described in subsection (2) of this section a contract for the sale of personal property is not enforceable by way of action or defense beyond five thousand dollars in amount or value of remedy unless there is some writing which indicates that a contract for sale has been made between the parties at a defined or stated price, reasonably identifies the subject matter, and is signed by the party against whom enforcement is sought or by his authorized agent.

> (2) Subsection (1) of this section does not apply to contracts for the sale of goods (Section 2–201) nor of securities (Section 8–113) nor of security agreements (Section 9–203).

Note that no matter how great is the price, UCC § 1–206 is only applicable if the value of the *remedy* is $5,000 or more.

In 2005, the National Conference of Commissioners on Uniform State Laws and the American Law Institute promulgated a revised version of Article 1 ("Revised Article 1"). Revised Article 1 drops section 1–206. A Legislative Note to Revised Article 1 explains the reasons for dropping section 1–206 as follows:

> Former Section 1–206, a Statute of Frauds for sales of "kinds of personal property not otherwise covered," has been deleted. The other articles of the Uniform Commercial Code make individual determinations as to requirements for memorializing transactions within their scope, so that the primary effect of former Section 1–206 was to impose a writing requirement on sales transactions not otherwise governed by the UCC. Deletion of former Section 1–206 does not constitute a recommendation to legislatures as to whether such sales transactions should be covered by a Statute of Frauds; rather, it reflects a determination that there is no need for uniform commercial law to resolve that issue.

As of early 2006, only sixteen states have adopted the revised version of Article 1, so that in most states section 1–206 remains the law.

SECTION 10. AGREEMENTS NOT TO BE PER-
FORMED WITHIN ONE YEAR FROM THE
MAKING THEREOF (SECTION 4(5))

Section 4(5) of the Statute of Frauds concerns actions "upon any agreement that is not to be performed within the space of one year from the making thereof."

To the casual reader, the language of section 4(5) contains no warning of the interpretation the courts have put on this section. It will be easier to understand this interpretation if one considers first the problem that faced courts that had to apply the section.

There was no mystery about the reason for requiring a signed writing in the case of a contract not to be performed within one year; in Holt's words, "the design of the statute was, not to trust to the memory of witnesses for a longer time than one year." Smith v. Westall, 1697, 1 Lord Raymond 317. The trouble lay, not in any obscurity of purpose, but in a failure to provide an apt means for effectuating that purpose.

In the first place, there is no direct relation between the time when a witness may be called to testify and the time that is required to perform the contract; a contract might be scheduled for completion within one month and yet first come into proof in court two years later. Furthermore, the drafters failed to ask themselves what should be done in the case of a contract as to which it is impossible to say in advance how much time its performance will require. For example, the performance of a contract to support A for life might be completed within a month if A died so soon, or might on the other hand stretch over decades if A were sufficiently long-lived. In a case coming up for decision shortly after the Statute was enacted, it was suggested that the validity of the contract should depend on the actual course of events. (Smith v. Westall, supra.) But this solution was never accepted, and could not be. Parties need to know from the outset, or at least as soon as trouble develops, whether they have a contract. To make the existence of a binding contract depend upon later events would invite all kinds of jockeying for position and produce an intolerable confusion.

The courts were, then, confronted with a statute that simply could not be applied in a way to carry out the likely conceived intention of its drafters. One stab at a solution that easily comes to mind is to measure expected duration for performance according to the expectation of the parties when they entered the contract. There are, in fact, a few cases that speak as if this were the governing principle, but this way out is scarcely acceptable. Where the time that will be required for performance is uncertain, there is usually no reason to suppose that the parties have made some calculation of probabilities and have in their minds some expected duration, such as six months or five years. Where a contract requires that A be supported for the rest of his life, the parties do not know how long A will live, and know that they do not know.

Accordingly, most courts have said that the applicability of Section 4(5) depends not on what actually happens, or on what the parties thought would happen, but on what *could have* happened. When the contract was entered, was there any *possibility* that it could have been performed within a year? If so, it is not within the Statute and is therefore enforceable although oral.

Restatement Second § 130. As stated by Chief Justice Peters in C.R. Klewin, Inc. v. Flagship Properties, Inc., 220 Conn. 569, 600 A.2d 772 (1991):

> ... [The] issue can be framed as follows: in the exclusion from the statute of frauds of all contracts except those "whose performance cannot possibly be completed within a year" ... what meaning should be attributed to the word "possibly"? One construction of "possibly" would encompass only contracts whose completion within a year would be inconsistent with the express terms of the contract. An alternate construction would include as well contracts ... in which, while no time period is expressly specified, it is ... realistically impossible for performance to be completed within a year. We now hold that the former and not the latter is the correct interpretation. "The critical test ... is whether 'by its terms' the agreement is not to be performed within a year, so that the statute will not apply where "the alleged agreement contain[s] [no] provision which directly or indirectly regulated the time for performance." Freedman v. Chemical Construction Corporation, 43 N.Y.2d 260, 265, 372 N.E.2d 12, 401 N.Y.S.2d 176 (1977). "It is the law of this state, as it is elsewhere, that a contract is not within this clause of the statute unless its terms are so drawn that it cannot by any possibility be performed fully within one year." (Emphasis added.) Burkle v. Superflow Mfg. Co., ... 137 Conn. at 492, 78 A.2d 698....

We therefore hold that an oral contract that does not say, in express terms, that performance is to have a specific duration beyond one year is, as a matter of law.... enforceable because it is outside the prescriptive force of the statute regardless of how long completion of performance will actually take.

Under this rule, an oral agreement to hire A for life is not within the Statute of Frauds, because there is a possibility that the agreement can be performed within a year through the death of A within that time. It is immaterial that in fact A lives and works on the job for twenty years. If A is then discharged, he can base a suit against the employer on proof of the oral agreement made years before, when he accepted employment. (*Warning.* In some states it is specifically provided that a contract that is not to be completed before the end of a lifetime *is* within the Statute. A few cases reach the same result. See, e.g., McInerney v. Charter Golf, Inc., 176 Ill.2d 482, 680 N.E.2d 1347 (1997), where the court so held over a vigorous dissent.)

What shall be said of a contract to employ A for ten years? Shall we say that such a contract is not within the Statute of Frauds because it would have been dissolved by the death of either party, and therefore might have been ended within the first year? The difficulty is that if this line of reasoning was accepted, it would be hard to find any contract to which the one-year provision would apply. In the case of almost any contract it is possible to imagine some cataclysmic event that might occur during the first year, preventing performance and excusing the parties from their obligations. Accordingly, the courts have generally distinguished between the time in which performance can possibly occur, on the one hand, and discharge or excuse from performance, on the other. Restatement Second § 130. On this basis, an agreement to hire an octogenarian for thirteen months is within the Statute of Frauds, and therefore unenforceable unless in writing, while an agreement to hire a healthy young person of twenty-one for life is not within the Statute, and therefore enforceable although oral. (Suppose the stated term of a contract is more than a year, but one or both parties are explicitly given the right to terminate the contract on three months' notice. Is the contract within the Statute? The cases are divided.)

The one-year provision has been heavily criticized in recent years. A good example is the decision of Judge Peters in *C.R. Klewin, supra*:

> Modern scholarly commentary has found much to criticize about the continued viability of the statute of frauds. The statute has been found wanting because it serves none of its purported functions very well; ... and because it permits or compels economically wasteful behavior.... It is, however, the one-year provision ... that has caused the greatest puzzlement among commentators. As Professor Farnsworth observes, "of all the provisions of the statute, it is the most difficult to rationalize.
>
> > "If the one-year provision is based on the tendency of memory to fail and of evidence to go stale with the passage of time, it is ill-contrived because the one-year period does not run from the making of the contract to the proof of the making, but from the making of the contract to the completion of performance. If an oral contract that cannot be performed within a year is broken the day after its making, the provision applies though the terms of the contract are fresh in the minds of the parties. But if an oral contract that can be performed within a year is broken and suit is not brought until nearly six years (the usual statute of limitations for contract actions) after the breach, the provision does not apply, even though the terms of the contract are no longer fresh in the minds of the parties.
> >
> > "If the one-year provision is an attempt to separate significant contracts of long duration, for which writings should be required, from less significant contracts of short duration, for which writings are unnecessary, it is equally ill-contrived because the one-year period does not run from the commencement of performance to the completion of performance, but from the making of the contract to the completion of performance. If an oral contract to work for one day, 13 months from now, is broken, the provision applies, even though the duration of performance is only one day. But if an oral contract to work for a year beginning today is broken, the provision does not apply, even though the duration of performance is a full year." 2 E. Farnsworth, Contracts (2d Ed.1990) § 6.4, pp. 110–11 (footnotes omitted)....
>
> Historians have had difficulty accounting for the original inclusion of the one-year provision. Some years after its enactment, one English judge stated that "the design of the statute was, not to trust to the memory of witnesses for a longer time than one year." Smith v. Westall, 1 Ld.Raym. 316, 317, 91 Eng.Rep. 1106, 1107 (1697). That explanation is, however, unpersuasive, since, as Farnsworth notes, the language of the statute is ill suited to this purpose. One eminent historian suggested that because such contracts are continuing contracts, it might be very difficult to give evidence of their formation, inasmuch as the rules of evidence of that time prohibited testimony by the parties to an action or any person who had an interest in the litigation. 6 W. Holdsworth, [A History of English Law, p.] 392. That argument, however, proves too much, since it would apply equally to all oral contracts regardless of the duration of their

performance. The most extensive recent study of the history of English contract law offers plausible explanations for all of the other provisions, but acknowledges that this one is "curious." A. Simpson, A History of the Common Law of Contract (1975) p. 612. . . .

In any case, the one-year provision no longer seems to serve any purpose very well, and today its only remaining effect is arbitrarily to forestall the adjudication of possibly meritorious claims. For this reason, the courts have for many years looked on the provision with disfavor, and have sought constructions that limited its application. . . .

———

SECTION 11. THE SURETYSHIP SECTION (SECTION 4(2))—GENERALLY

Section 4(2) of the Statute of Frauds concerns actions "whereby to charge the defendant upon any special promise to answer for the debt, default or miscarriages of another person."

It is not easy to know just what the scope of section 4(2) was originally intended to be. There are many situations in which a person may, in varying degrees and under varying conditions, be bound to "answer for" another. The courts have construed this section so that a person does not "answer for" another within the meaning of the section unless his oral promise places him in the position of a surety or guarantor of the obligation of another person. Restatement Second § 112. A *surety* is a person who is liable for a debt or other obligation that a second person, the *principal,* owes to a third person, the *creditor,* in cases where the principal is primarily liable for the debt or obligation. In such cases, both the principal and the surety owe the same debt, or have the duty to perform the same obligation, and the creditor can sue either the principal or the surety if the principal defaults. However, the principal's obligation is primary, so that if the surety is forced to pay the debt or perform the obligation, she can sue the principal for indemnification.

Suretyship is often used to afford security to a creditor. For example, suppose Peter Prince wishes to borrow from Marvin Moneypenny, but Prince's credit is weak. Prince may then not only promise to repay the loan herself, but may also get Angela Answer, whose credit is stronger, to promise Moneypenny that she will repay the loan if Prince does not. Answer is then a surety for Prince's debt.

If a promisor is a surety or guarantor, then under section 4(2) the nature of the guaranteed obligation is not material. Thus an oral promise to answer for another's obligation that is based on a tort comes within the broad language that speaks of "the debt, default or miscarriages of another." Restatement Second § 112. But for the suretyship provision to be applicable, the other person must be under some obligation to the creditor, although even an imperfect obligation may suffice. See Section 13 of this Appendix.

Example No. 10:

Richard Rash buys a $100 suit from a tailor. Though he has no real or apparent authority from his uncle to charge the suit to him, Rash says to the tailor, "Charge the suit to my uncle, Milton Means. I will answer for him if he doesn't pay." Rash's promise is not within the Statute of Frauds, and is therefore enforceable although oral, because Means is under no obligation to the tailor, so that Rash is not the surety of another.

SECTION 12. THE SURETYSHIP SECTION CONTINUED—"THE MAIN PURPOSE RULE"

It will be convenient to start this Section with a hypothetical case.

Example No. 11:

Manley Minus owes Charley Claim $1,000. Minus gives Claim a mortgage on Blackacre to secure his debt. Thereafter, Minus conveys Blackacre to Paula Owne, subject to the mortgage. Owne does not assume Minus's obligation to pay off the mortgage. However, Minus promises Owne that he will pay off the mortgage and thereby release the mortgage lien on Blackacre. Minus fails to do so, and Claim brings a suit to foreclose the mortgage. To save her land, Owne orally promises Claim that if Claim will discontinue the suit, she, Owne, will stand in back of Minus's debt. Claim discontinues the suit but Owne refuses to honor her promise. When Claim sues Owne on the oral agreement, Owne pleads the Statute of Frauds, asserting that her promise to Claim was a promise to answer for the debt of another, namely, Minus.

A well-established line of authorities would hold that Owne's promise is not within the Statute, so that it is enforceable although oral. Although it is possible to predict with considerable assurance that *Example No. 11* would generally be decided as indicated, it is difficult to find any justification for the result in the language of the Statute.

If the Statute concerns an oral promise that makes the promisor a surety, Pawn is clearly becoming a surety for Minus. The only difference between Pawn's case and the usual case is that in making the promise Pawn was advancing her own interest by freeing her land from the threat of foreclosure.

If it were not for certain embarrassments that will be discussed in a minute, it might be possible to construct a rationale for the decision reached in cases like *Example No. 11* along the following lines: The suretyship provision of the Statute of Frauds is intended to perform a cautionary or deterrent function. The legislators were thinking of the typical victim of family or sentimental pressures, who says to the creditor, "Advance $1000 to my niece and I will see that it is paid," and who receives no financial advantage from the transaction. It was the legislators' intention to erect a legal safeguard on generous impulses. This section of the Statute is therefore inapplicable when the promisor undertakes to be surety to advance some business advantage of her own.

This simple explanation runs into two inconvenient facts: (1) It is generally assumed that the formalities prescribed by the Statute of Frauds normally serve an *evidentiary* rather than a *cautionary* purpose. (2) Although there is little case law on the subject, and that divided, it is generally asserted that the receipt of a monetary premium by a surety for undertaking the risk does not take the surety's oral promise out of the Statute, although a surety who receives such a premium is obviously making the promise to advance its own interests. See Restatement Second § 116.

The result is that in cases like *Example No. 11* we have a judicially established exception to the suretyship section whose rationale is doubtful. Since the underlying basis for the exception is obscure, it is difficult to know just what its scope is. It has often been called "the main purpose rule," meaning that exception applies when the main purpose of the surety is to serve a pecuniary interest of her own. According to Restatement Second § 116, the question is whether the consideration given for the promise of the surety "is in fact or apparently desired by the promisor mainly for his own economic advantage, rather than in order to benefit the third person." However, the Restatement excepts from the exception—and thereby renders unenforceable—an oral promise (typically made by a guaranty company) to answer for the obligation of another where the consideration given the surety consists simply of a premium.

The "main purpose rule" is applied chiefly to two types of cases: (1) Those like *Example No. 11*, where the promisor is willing to become surety in order to save her own property from the assertion of a lien that secures the debtor's obligation. (2) Those in which the promisor, who steps forward as surety, has a pecuniary interest in the debtor's affairs and wishes to procure a breathing spell for him. The promisor may have a pecuniary interest in the debtor's affairs, and a corresponding interest in staving off suit by the creditor against the debtor, because she is herself a creditor; or because she is a shareholder in a debtor-corporation; or because the debtor is under contract to construct a building for her, the completion of which she does not want impeded; or for a great variety of other reasons. See Restatement Second § 116, illustrations.

SECTION 13. THE SURETYSHIP SECTION CONTINUED—MISCELLANEOUS PROBLEMS

The account just concluded covers the major surprises to be encountered in the judicial interpretation of Section 4(2). It omits several disputed issues that are mentioned briefly below.

1. A promise is within section 4(2) only if it is made *to the creditor*. If Prince is indebted to Moneypenny, and Answer promises *Prince* that she will pay off Prince's debt, the promise is not within the Statute, and is therefore enforceable although oral.

2. Often, a creditor deals with two or more persons without knowing what their internal relationship is. For example, Moneypenny may negotiate primarily with Prince, but at some stage of the negotiations, either at the outset or later, Answer come in alongside Prince as a person obligated on the agreement. Moneypenny may not know whether the funds that he is furnishing are to be used by Prince and Answer in some common venture, or whether one of the parties is merely lending his or her name and credit to the other. If

the relationship of Prince and Answer to one another is such that Answer is surety and Prince is principal debtor, then the oral promise of Answer is within section 4(2) if, but only if, Moneypenny knew or had reason to know of Answer's true position. Restatement Second §§ 112–113.

3.   Even though Moneypenny knows in such a case that Answer is a surety, there is one situation where Answer may be held on her oral promise. This situation is illustrated by the case where Moneypenny renders services to Prince, and charges the services, with Answer's consent, to Answer and Prince as if they were jointly purchasing the services. Here, even though Moneypenny knows that Answer is lending her credit to Prince, it has been held that since Answer and Prince become joint debtors, Section 4(2) does not apply, and Answer is liable on her oral promise. Restatement Second § 113. (Since this rule is applicable only where the debt is joint, rather than either several or joint and several, the possibility of holding Answer on her oral promise may be affected by statutes, adopted in many states, that convert joint obligations into joint and several obligations.)

4.   The principle that section 4(2) applies to the promise of a surety or guarantor gives rise to another kind of difficulty, illustrated in the following case. Moneypenny lends money to Prince on the oral promise of Answer to be surety. It is known to all concerned that Prince is under age, and therefore has the defense of infancy to any suit on the debt. Moneypenny argues that Answer's promise is not within Section 4(2), on the ground that since Prince legally owed nothing, Answer's obligation is not that of a surety. This argument has been accepted in some cases. Others have held that Answer is not liable on her oral promise, on the following line of reasoning: The debt of a minor may be affirmed, without new consideration, after the minor comes of age. The minor's obligation is therefore not "void" but "voidable." It is not a legal zero, but a legal something, although the minor has a defense unless when he comes of age he affirms the agreement. Since there is an imperfect (although unenforceable) obligation running from the minor to the creditor, a promisor who agrees to stand in back of the minor's undertaking is really a surety, and her promise is therefore within section 4(2).

SECTION 14. PROMISES MADE BY EXECUTORS AND ADMINISTRATORS (SECTION 4(1))

Section 4(1) of the Statute of Frauds concerns actions "to charge any executor or administrator upon any special promise to answer damages out of his own estate."

The case aimed at by section 4(1) is that where an executor or administrator of an estate promises a creditor of the decedent that if the decedent's estate proves insufficient to discharge the debt owed by the decedent, the executor or administrator will personally answer for it. Although the Statute speaks in terms of "any ... promise" by an executor or administrator, in fact it covers only a promise by an executor or administrator to pay an *existing* debt of the estate—that is, in effect, a debt contracted by the decedent. A promise by an executor or administrator to personally pay a *fresh* debt contracted by her on the estate's behalf is not deemed within the Statute, on the theory that under principles of estate law the administrator or executor is primarily liable on such an obligation, rather than being liable merely as a surety. Restatement Second § 111.

Section 4 (1) is quite unimportant. Few cases arise under it. In effect, it is a special case of suretyship, since the promise of the executor or administrator contemplated by Section 4(1) is a promise to answer for the debt of another, the "other" in this case being the decedent. The distinctions applied to such cases are similar to those developed under the suretyship provision. Restatement Second § 111.

SECTION 15. CONTRACTS UPON CONSIDERATION OF MARRIAGE (SECTION 4(3))

Section 4(3) of the Statute of Frauds concerns actions "to charge any person upon any agreement made upon consideration of marriage." The chief thing to know about the marriage section is that it does not apply to the case one would most expect it to be applied to, namely, a simple engagement by which two persons promise to marry each other. Such an agreement is a contract "to marry," not a contract "made upon consideration of marriage." At least, that is the way the courts interpret the Statute. Restatement Second § 124.

Conversely, even a promise running between the parents of the prospective spouses may not be "made upon consideration of marriage" within the meaning of the Statute, as the following Example shows.

Example No. 12:

Pater Primus, father of one prospective spouse, and Joan Secundus, mother of the other, exchange oral promises that if the marriage takes place they will each give $10,000 to the couple.

This agreement is not within section 4(3) of the Statute, because the consideration for the promise of each party is the promise of the other party, not the marriage. The occurrence of the marriage is merely the occasion for the parties' contributions to the couple, and a condition of their liability. Restatement Second § 124, Illus. 5.

The typical situation to which section 4(3) *does* apply is that of a "marriage settlement," in which a parent of a prospective spouse promises the prospective spouse to settle money or property on the couple upon their marriage. Similarly, if the prospective spouses make an oral contract with each other concerning their anticipated marriage, and the contract involves pecuniary features, such as a promise by one prospective spouse to convey certain sculptures to the other upon their marriage, the Statute of Frauds will apply, and all of the terms of the contract being intertwined, the contract as a whole becomes unenforceable.

As a by-point, it should be noted that there is considerable doubt whether a later writing, not intended as a statement of the contract itself, will satisfy section 4(3). See Section 3 of this Appendix.

SECTION 16. WHAT KIND OF WRITING WILL SATISFY THE STATUTE

The issue, what type of writing is required to satisfy the Statute of Frauds, has become recast in recent years, because the broader concept of a *record* has for many purposes, including the Statute, replaced the narrower concept of a *writing*. That complication will be put aside for the moment, and discussed in the next Section of this Appendix. Much of the discussion in this Section will use the term "writing," because that is the traditional term used in Statute and in most of the cases. The discussion of the term "record" in the next Section will build on the discussion of the term "writing" in this Section, because most of the points made in this Section apply to a record as well.

The principal points to note are the following:

First. Unless the relevant Statute requires "the contract" to be in writing, the Statute is satisfied by almost any kind of signed document (using the term *document* extremely broadly, for present purposes only, to include both writings and records) that evidences the terms of the parties' agreement. This result follows from the language of section 4, which states, in effect, that there must either be a written contract *or* some memorandum or note *of* the contract.

Second. The requirement of a "signed" document does not mean that a document must be signed by the party in her own hand and with her full name. Any symbol used with an intent to authenticate a document will suffice. For instance, an "O.K." with initials is sufficient. Even a photocopied or computer-printed name will count as a signature if it reflects an intent to authenticate a document.

The UCC defines the term "signed" to include "any symbol executed or adopted by a party with present intention to authenticate a writing." UCC § 1–201(39) (as in force in most states). The Comment states: "The inclusion of authentication in the definition of 'signed' is to make clear that as the term is used in [the Code] a complete signature is not necessary. Authentication may be printed, stamped, or written; it may be by initials or by thumbprint. It may be on any part of the document and in appropriate cases may be found in a billhead or letterhead. No catalog of possible authentications can be complete and the court must use common sense and commercial experience in passing upon these matters. The question always is whether the symbol was executed or adopted by the party with present intention to authenticate the writing."

Restatement Second is somewhat broader, in that it allows either actual or apparent intent to suffice. Restatement Second § 134. Farnsworth wrote similarly that the "modern test is whether the other party reasonably believes that the asserted signer's intention is to authenticate the writing as the asserted signer's own." E. Allan Farnsworth, Contracts, § 6.8 (4th ed. 2004). In Donovan v. RRL Corp., 26 Cal.4th 261, 27 P.3d 702 (Cal. 2001), the court held that "[w]hen an advertisement constitutes an offer, the printed name of the merchant is intended to authenticate the advertisement as that of the merchant.... In other words, where the advertisement reasonably justifies the recipient's understanding that the communication was intended as an offer, the offeror's intent to authenticate his or her name as a signature can be established from the face of the advertisement."

Third. If an agreement or memorandum is to satisfy the Statute, it must state the terms of the contract with reasonable adequacy. A document that failed to identify the parties, the subject-matter, and the essential terms would normally not be sufficient. On the other hand, the courts do not demand perfection, and some degree of ambiguity or ellipsis is not fatal.

Fourth. An adequate statement of the terms of the contract would normally reveal the consideration that made the promise or promises binding. However, it is not uncommon for a surety to guarantee a debt in writing without stating the consideration for her own undertaking as surety—which may be, for example, an advance made by the creditor to the debtor or an extension of time granted by the creditor to the debtor. An early English case construing section 4(2) of the Statute of Frauds declared such a memorandum to be fatally defective. Some American courts have followed this English decision; more have refused to. In 1856 the English law was changed by a statute that dispensed with the need for stating the consideration in a written guaranty.

In the United States there are a variety of statutes concerning whether the consideration must be stated to make a document effective. Some statutes say the consideration *must* be stated; some say the consideration need not be stated in a guaranty; some say the consideration need not be stated in any case. It is the last form of statute that gives the most difficulty. Does it mean, for example, that a written contract to sell land is effective although it makes no mention of the price, or states the price incorrectly? The cases are divided, but some have gone so far as to accept this conclusion. And note that the UCC Statute of Frauds, § 2–201, does not require the price to be stated in the writing. See *Ninth,* infra.

Fifth. Generally the document need not be signed by both parties, but only by the "party to be charged." This may result in a contract that can be enforced in one direction only.

Sixth. Even where no single document exists that is sufficient to satisfy the Statute, a memorandum that satisfies the statute may sometimes be obtained by piecing together several documents. If the documents are physically attached, or contain internal references to one another, there is no difficulty. More doubtful is the question whether piecing together is permissible where doing so rests entirely on oral evidence or general appearances. In Crabtree v. Elizabeth Arden Sales Corp., 305 N.Y. 48, 110 N.E.2d 551 (1953), the court stated:

> The statute of frauds does not require the "memorandum to be in one document. It may be pieced together out of separate writings, connected with one another either expressly or by the internal evidence of subject-matter and occasion." Marks v. Cowdin, supra, 226 N.Y. 138, 145, 128 N.E. 139, 141, see, also, 2 Williston, op. ct., p. 1671; Restatement, Contracts, § 208. subd. [a]. Where each of the separate writings has been subscribed by the party to be charged, little if any difficulty is encountered. See, e.g., Marks v. Cowdin, supra, 226 N.Y. 138, 144–145, 123 N.E. 139, 141. Where, however, some writings have been signed, and others have not—as in the case before us—there is basic disagreement as to what constitutes a sufficient connection permitting the unsigned papers to be considered as part or the statutory memorandum. The courts of some jurisdictions insist that there be a reference, of varying degrees of specificity, in the signed writing to that unsigned, and, if there is no such reference, they refuse to permit consideration of the latter in determining whether the memorandum satisfies the statute. See, e.g., Osborn v.

Phelps, 19 Conn. 63; Hewett Grain & Provision Co. v. Spear, 222 Mich. 608, 193 N.W. 291. That conclusion is based upon a construction of the statute which requires that the connection between the writings and defendant's acknowledgment of the one not subscribed, appear from examination of the papers alone, without the aid of parol evidence. The other position—which has gained increasing support over the years—is that a sufficient connection between the papers is established simply by a reference in them to the same subject matter or transaction. See, e.g., Frost v. Alward, 176 Cal. 691, 169 P. 379; Lerned v. Wannemacher, 9 Allen, 412, 91 Mass. 412. The statute is not pressed "to the extreme of a literal and rigid logic", Marks v. Cowdin, supra, 226 N.Y. 138, 144, 123 N.E. 139, 141, and oral testimony is admitted to show the connection between the documents and to establish the acquiescence, of the party to be charged, to the contents of the one unsigned. . . .

The view last expressed impresses us as the more sound, and, indeed—although several of our cases appear to have gone the other way, see, e.g., Newbery v. Wall, 65 N.Y. 484; Wilson v. Lewiston Mill Co., 150 N.Y. 314, 44 N.E. 959—this court has on a number of occasions approved the rule, and we now definitively adopt it, permitting the signed and unsigned writings to be read together, provided that they clearly refer to the same subject matter or transaction. . . .

Seventh. A memorandum may fail to satisfy the Statute of Frauds because it does not *correctly* state the agreement. Restatement Second § 131, comment g. (But note that UCC § 2–201(1) specifically provides otherwise in the case of a sale of goods. See *Ninth*, below.)

Example No. 13:

On May 1, Frederick Firm and Quincy Qualm enter an oral agreement whereby Firm is to convey Dreamacre to Qualm on June 1, and on that date Qualm is to pay $50,000 cash as the full price of the land. On May 5 Qualm writes to Firm: "This is about the contract we entered on May 1, whereby you are to convey Dreamacre to me on June 1 and I am to pay $49,000. I heard a rumor that you had offered this land to someone else, and I want to know whether you are going through with our contract. Yours truly, Quincy Qualm." Before Firm can answer this letter, Qualm repudiates the contract. Firm sues Qualm for damages, asserting that Qualm's letter satisfies the Statute.

The letter might be held to be an insufficient memorandum, since it does not correctly state the terms of the oral agreement.

Lovers of paradox will observe: The Statute of Frauds finds its rationale in the untrustworthiness of oral agreements. Yet the document that the Statute requires may itself be impugned, and its effect destroyed, by showing that it does not correctly state the oral agreement.

Eighth. A principal will normally be bound by the signature of an authorized agent on the principal's behalf, even if the agent's authority is not in writing. In some states, however, a statute provides that if a contract signed by an agent is required to be in writing, the agent's authority must also be evidenced in a writing signed by the principal. The doctrine that such statutes embody is sometimes called the "equal-dignity rule"—meaning that the authority of an agent to enter into a contract on behalf of a principal must be evidenced by a formality equal to that required for the contract itself. Note that the equal-dignity rule is normally applicable only in states where it has been specifically adopted by statute.

Ninth. As regards contracts for the sale of goods, UCC § 2–201(1) changes this whole corner of Statute of Frauds law in a fairly substantial way. It will be recalled that under § 2–201(1):

> Except as otherwise provided in this section a contract for the sale of goods for the price of $500 or more is not enforceable by way of action or defense unless there is some writing sufficient to indicate that a contract for sale has been made between the parties and signed by the party against whom enforcement is sought or by his authorized agent or broker. A writing is not insufficient because it omits or incorrectly states a term agreed upon but the contract is not enforceable under this paragraph beyond the quantity of goods shown in such writing.

According to the Official Comment to this Section:

> ... The required writing need not contain all the material terms of the contract and such material terms as are stated need not be precisely stated. All that is required is that the writing afford a basis for believing that the offered oral evidence rests on a real transaction. It may be written in lead pencil on a scratch pad. It need not indicate which party is the buyer and which the seller. The only term which must appear is the quantity term which need not be accurately stated but recovery is limited to the amount stated. The price, time and place of payment or delivery, the general quality of the goods, or any particular warranties may all be omitted.

> Special emphasis must be placed on the permissibility of omitting the price term in view of the insistence of some courts on the express inclusion of this term even where the parties have contracted on the basis of a published price list. In many valid contracts for sale the parties do not mention the price in express terms, the buyer being bound to pay and the seller to accept a reasonable price which the trier of the fact may well be trusted to determine. Again, frequently the price is not mentioned since the parties have based their agreement on a price list or catalogue known to both of them and this list serves as an efficient safeguard against perjury. Finally, "market" prices and valuations that are current in the vicinity constitute a similar check. Thus if the price is not stated in the memorandum it can normally be supplied without danger of fraud. Of course if the "price" consists of goods rather than money the quantity of goods must be stated.

> Only three definite and invariable requirements as to the memorandum are made by this subsection. First, it must evidence a contract for the sale of goods; second, it must be "signed," a word which includes any authentication which identifies the party to be charged; and third, it must specify a quantity.

In Howard Construction Co. v. Jeff–Coles Quarries, Inc., 669 S.W.2d 221 (Mo.App.1983), the court pointed out that UCC § 2–201(1) requires only "some writing sufficient to indicate that a contract for sale has been made," and. ... one writer has suggested that the spirit of the comments seems to be that 'sufficient to indicate' is roughly equivalent to 'more probable than not.'

... In other words, if it is more probable than not that the writing evidences a deal between the parties, then the writing should be found sufficient."

There is some division of authority concerning whether a purchase order or a sales order will by itself satisfy UCC § 2–201. A naked purchase order or sales order signed by one party is unlikely to meet the test of that section, because it does not provide evidence that a contract had been concluded. See Bazak International Corp. v. Mast Industries, 73 N.Y.2d 113, 538 N.Y.S.2d 503, 535 N.E.2d 633 (1989); Trilco Terminal v. Prebilt Corp., 167 N.J.Super. 449, 400 A.2d 1237 (Law Div.1979), aff'd, 174 N.J.Super. 24, 415 A.2d 356 (App.Div.1980). However, a purchase order or sales order that has more to it may satisfy § 2–201. For example, in *Bazak,* supra, the New York Court held that § 2–201 was satisfied by the purchase orders in that case, partly on the ground that the purchase orders had been sent by the seller from the premises of the buyer's parent company to the buyer's subsidiary. That fact, the court concluded, suggested that the purchase orders were not unsolicited, but instead reflected that an agreement had already been reached. Other courts have held that a purchase order suffices if it is signed by both parties, or can be matched with a document sent by the other party, or indicates that a down payment has been made. See Lonnie Hayes & Sons Staves, Inc. v. Bourbon Cooperage Co., 777 S.W.2d 940 (Ky.App.1989); Koenen v. Royal Buick Co., 162 Ariz. 376, 783 P.2d 822 (App.1989). Furthermore, UCC § 2–201(2) provides that "Between merchants if within a reasonable time a writing"—which could include a purchase order or sales order–"in confirmation of the contract and sufficient against the sender is received and the party receiving it has reason to know its contents, it satisfies the requirements of [section 2–201] against such party unless written notice of objection to its contents is given within 10 days after it is received."

Tenth. As shown in the next Section of the Appendix, two new statutes provide that for Statute of Frauds and many other purposes the requirement of a writing can normally be satisfied by a "record"—a term that includes both information that is inscribed on a tangible medium, such as a traditional writing on paper, and information that is stored in an electronic or other medium and is retrievable in perceivable form. Most of the issues considered in this Section of the Appendix, concerning the standards that a traditional writing must meet to satisfy the Statute of Frauds, also apply to the standards that a record other than a traditional writing must meet to satisfy the Statute.

SECTION 17. ELECTRONIC CONTRACTING AND THE STATUTE OF FRAUDS

Within the last few years, the concept and term record has come into use in place of the concept and term *writing*. A *record* is defined slightly differently in different statutes, but at its core the term has the meaning given by section 2(13) of the Uniform Electronic Transactions Act, discussed below: "information that is inscribed on a tangible medium or that is stored in an electronic or other medium and is retrievable in perceivable form." In connection with the shift from *writing* to *record*, two important legislative developments have affected the issue of what kinds of records and signatures satisfy the Statute of Frauds.

UETA. First, the Uniform Electronics Transactions Act (UETA) was promulgated in 1999 by the National Conference of Commissioners on Uniform State Laws, and has been adopted by almost all the states. UETA § 7 provides as follows:

> (a) A record or signature may not be denied legal effect or enforceability solely because it is in electronic form.

> (b) A contract may not be denied legal effect or enforceability solely because an electronic record was used in its formation.

> (c) If a law requires a record to be in writing, an electronic record satisfies the law.

> (d) If a law requires a signature, an electronic signature satisfies the law.

The terms used in section 7 are defined in section 2. Section 2(13) provides that the term "record" means "information that is inscribed on a tangible medium or that is stored in an electronic or other medium and is retrievable in perceivable form." The Comment to section 2(13) states:

> This is a standard definition designed to embrace all means of communicating or storing information except human memory. It includes any method for storing or communicating information, including "writings." A record need not be indestructible or permanent, but the term does not include oral or other communications which are not stored or preserved by some means. Information that has not been retained other than through human memory does not qualify as a record. As in the case of the terms "writing" or "written," the term "record" does not establish the purposes, permitted uses or legal effect which a record may have under any particular provision of substantive law.

Section 2(8) provides that the term "electronic signature" means "an electronic sound, symbol, or process attached to or logically associated with a record and executed or adopted by a person with the intent to sign the record." The Comment to section 2(8) states:

> The idea of a signature is broad and not specifically defined. Whether any particular record is "signed" is a question of fact. Proof of that fact must be made under other applicable law. This Act simply assures that the signature may be accomplished through electronic means. No specific technology need be used in order to create a valid signature. One's voice on an answering machine may suffice if the requisite intention is present. Similarly, including one's name as part of an electronic mail communication also may suffice, as may the firm name on a facsimile.... In any case the critical element is the intention to execute or adopt the sound or symbol or process for the purpose of signing the related record.... It is that intention that is understood in the law as a part of the word "sign", without the need for a definition.

This Act establishes, to the greatest extent possible, the equivalency of electronic signatures and manual signatures. Therefore the term "signature" has been used to connote and convey that equivalency. . . .

This definition includes as an electronic signature the standard webpage click through process. For example, when a person orders goods or services through a vendor's website, the person will be required to provide information as part of a process which will result in receipt of the goods or services. When the customer ultimately gets to the last step and clicks "I agree," the person has adopted the process and has done so with the intent to associate the person with the record of that process. The actual effect of the electronic signature will be determined from all the surrounding circumstances[;] however, the person adopted a process which the circumstances indicate s/he intended to have the effect of getting the goods/services and being bound to pay for them. The adoption of the process carried the intent to do a legally significant act, the hallmark of a signature.

Another important aspect of this definition lies in the necessity that the electronic signature be linked or logically associated with the record. In the paper world, it is assumed that the symbol adopted by a party is attached to or located somewhere in the same paper that is intended to be authenticated, e.g., an allonge firmly attached to a promissory note, or the classic signature at the end of a long contract. These tangible manifestations do not exist in the electronic environment, and accordingly, this definition expressly provides that the symbol must in some way be linked to, or connected with, the electronic record being signed. . . .

The Illustrations to UETA § 7 exemplify how this section operates:

Illustration 1: A sends the following e-mail to B: "I hereby offer to buy widgets from you, delivery next Tuesday. /s/ A." B responds with the following e-mail: "I accept your offer to buy widgets for delivery next Tuesday. /s/ B." The e-mails may not be denied effect solely because they are electronic. In addition, the e-mails . . . qualify as records under the Statute of Frauds. However, because there is no quantity stated in either record, the parties' agreement would be unenforceable under existing UCC Section 2–201(1).

Illustration 2: A sends the following e-mail to B: "I hereby offer to buy 100 widgets for $1000, delivery next Tuesday. /s/ A." B responds with the following e-mail: "I accept your offer to purchase 100 widgets for $1000, delivery next Tuesday. /s/ B." In this case the analysis is the same as in Illustration 1 except that here the records otherwise satisfy the requirements of UCC Section 2–201(1). The transaction may not be denied legal effect solely because there is not a pen and ink "writing" or "signature".

E-Sign. The second major legislative development affecting records and signatures is the Electronic Signatures in Global and National Commerce Act ("E–Sign"). E–Sign is a federal statute which is generally comparable to UETA as regards the effect of electronic records and electronic signatures. Because E–Sign is a federal statute, it would normally preempt UETA. However, E–Sign specifically recognizes and avoids preempting UETA, and on the contrary, provides that with limited exceptions, states may preempt E–

sign by adopting UETA. Because all but four states have adopted UETA, UETA generally takes precedence over E–Sign.

SECTION 18. THE EFFECT OF PART PERFORMANCE OF, OR RELIANCE UPON, AN ORAL CONTRACT WITHIN THE STATUTE—INTRODUCTION

This Section will consider the following question: A has entered an oral contract with B, and A has broken the contract after B acted upon it. Should B be given any recovery? This question is best approached if it is first put in general terms, without reference to specific provisions the Statute of Frauds. The basic opposing considerations that must be weighed in answering this question are: (1) the dangers involved in founding a legal liability on mere spoken words; and (2) the possible hardship to A resulting from a denial of relief on the oral agreement.

To balance these opposing considerations, it is necessary to know the particular hardship of which A complains and the specific measure of relief that he demands. Three situations may be distinguished: (1) B seeks restitutionary damages for a benefit that he conferred on A under the oral contract. (2) B seeks reliance damages for losses he incurred in reliance on the oral contract, but A received no benefit as the result of B's reliance. (3) B seeks expectation damages for the value of the performance promised by A.

The next three Sections of this Appendix take up these three classes of claims.

————

SECTION 19. THE RESTITUTION OF BENEFITS CONFERRED UNDER THE ORAL AGREEMENT

It is well settled that normally B may recover the value of any benefits he conferred on A under an oral contract that falls within the Statute of Frauds.

Example No. 14:

Under an oral contract with Marian Means, Steven Smock, an artist, agrees to paint a mural in Means's home in exchange for a conveyance of Passacre. After full performance by Smock, Means refuses to give him a deed to Passacre.

Although this transaction is a contract for the sale of land within Section 4(4) of the Statute of Frauds, Smock can recover the value of the mural.

There are two explanations for reconciling this result with the Statute of Frauds. One explanation is normative; the other is doctrinal.

The normative explanation is that to allow a party to retain benefits that she has received under a contract that is unenforceable only because not in writing would be a result too unjust for the law to countenance.

The doctrinal explanation is that the Statute of Frauds only bars actions to enforce a contract, and doctrinally a suit for restitution is not an action to enforce the contract. Such an action is based not on contract law, but on an entirely separate body of law, the law of unjust enrichment and restitution. Correspondingly, the measure of recovery in a suit in restitution is basically different from the measure of recovery in a suit on the contract. In a suit on the contract, the plaintiff's recovery is measured by the value of the performance promised by the defendant. In *Example No. 14*, this would be the value of Passacre. In contrast, in a suit in restitution the plaintiff's recovery is measured by the value of his own performance as received by the defendant. In *Example No. 14*, this would be the value of the mural. A suit in contract is based on redressing a breach of contract; a suit in restitution is based on preventing unjust enrichment.

Concerning the amount recovered by Smock, the following practical point should also be observed. According to some authorities, in proving the value of the mural, Smock would be permitted to introduce evidence of the market value of Passacre. This evidence would be admitted on the theory that Means by her oral contract conceded that the mural, if properly done, would be equal in value to Passacre. Although in theory this concession or admission by Means is not conclusive, and is only relevant as tending to show how much the mural itself was worth, the practical result may be that Smock will recover the value of Passacre, just as if his suit was for breach of the oral agreement. This result could especially be anticipated if there was no satisfactory way of measuring the value of the mural or of Smock's services, while Passacre had a fairly definite market value, as by being a lot in a subdivision in which all lots were selling for $5,000 each.)

Caution: In one special case, a plaintiff who has conferred a benefit under an oral contract is not permitted the restitutionary recovery described in this Section. This is the case where the contract falls within one of the statutes, mentioned in Section 5 of this Appendix, that require a contract with a real-estate broker, involving a potential commission for the sale of real estate, to be in writing. A seller's engagement of a real-estate broker is usually in legal effect an offer for a unilateral contract (for example, a promise that the seller will pay a commission to the broker if the broker causes a sale to occur), and involves no explicit promise by the broker. Accordingly, the broker normally has no right to a commission unless and until he has performed his services in connection with the sale. Therefore, a statute that provides that real-estate commission contracts must be in writing is normally directed precisely against a suit by a broker to recover for services that the broker has performed. To allow restitutionary recovery for the value of such services would deprive such a statute of any real effect.

SECTION 20. REIMBURSEMENT FOR RELIANCE ON THE ORAL CONTRACT

Suppose a plaintiff seeks, not restitution for a benefit conferred under a contract that is unenforceable under the Statute of Frauds, but damages based on losses that he incurred in acting under the contract, which losses did not result in a benefit to the defendant. The issue here is not as clear-cut as it is in the case of a benefit conferred under a contract that is unenforceable under the Statute of Frauds.

Normatively, a rule that allowed a defendant to retain a benefit that has been conferred upon her under a contract that is unenforceable only because it is not in writing would be more shocking to the sense of justice than a rule that a defendant need not reimburse the plaintiff for his losses under such contract, where those losses did not result in a benefit to the defendant. (This is not to say that a rule of the second kind would be just; only that the injustice is less intense in the reliance case than in the restitution case.)

Doctrinally, unlike an action to recover the value of a benefit conferred, which is brought under the law of unjust enrichment and restitution, an action to recover reliance damages is a suit under contract law. Such an action therefore runs more squarely into the Statute of Frauds than an action to recover the value of a benefit conferred.

At least until recently, the prevailing view has been that it would be contrary to the Statute of Frauds to allow a recovery for losses from reliance on a contract that is unenforceable under the Statute when those losses did not benefit the defendant. Today, that view is gradually changing. Two of the leading cases are Monarco v. Lo Greco, 35 Cal.2d 621, 220 P.2d 737 (1950) and Alaska Airlines v. Stephenson, 217 F.2d 295 (9th Cir.1954).

In Monarco v. Lo Greco, Christie Lo Greco's mother and stepfather orally promised Christie that if he would stay on the family farm and help in its management, they would leave him the bulk of their property. Christie did as they asked, and the family farm prospered. However, Christie's stepfather left the property to his grandson. The court held for Christie, despite Section 4(4) of the Statute of Frauds (the land section) on the basis of Christie's reliance. The opinion qualified the reliance exception to the Statute of Frauds by stating that reliance was a ground for overcoming the Statute only "where either an unconscionable injury or unjust enrichment would result from refusal to enforce the contract."

In Alaska Airlines v. Stephenson, Alaska Airlines orally promised to give an airline pilot a two-year written contract as soon as the airline obtained a required certificate to fly between Seattle and Alaska. In reliance on this promise, the pilot let his right to return to his previous employer expire. The airline broke its promise. Here too the court held that the pilot's reliance overcame the Statute. See also, e.g., Alaska Democratic Party v. Rice, 934 P.2d 1313 (Alaska 1997).

Going one step further, Restatement Second § 139 gives full recognition to the reliance principle in the Statute of Frauds area. Furthermore, under the principle embodied in this section, a relying promisee may be entitled to expectation damages:

§ 139. Enforcement by Virtue of Action in Reliance

(1) A promise which the promisor should reasonably expect to induce action or forbearance on the part of the promisee or a third person and which does induce the action or forbearance is enforceable notwithstanding the Statute of Frauds if injustice can be avoided only by enforcement of the promise. The remedy granted for breach is to be limited as justice requires.

(2) In determining whether injustice can be avoided only by enforcement of the promise, the following circumstances are significant:

(a) the availability and adequacy of other remedies, particularly cancellation and restitution;

(b) the definite and substantial character of the action or forbearance in relation to the remedy sought;

(c) the extent to which the action or forbearance corroborates evidence of the making and terms of the promise, or the making and terms are otherwise established by clear and convincing evidence;

(d) the reasonableness of the action or forbearance;

(e) the extent to which the action or forbearance was foreseeable by the promisor. . . .

Comment . . .

d. *Partial enforcement; particular remedies.* The same factors which bear on whether any relief should be granted also bear on the character and extent of the remedy. In particular, the remedy of restitution is not ordinarily affected by the Statute of Frauds . . . ; where restitution is an adequate remedy, other remedies are not made available by the rule stated in this Section. Again, when specific enforcement is available . . . an ordinary action for damages is commonly less satisfactory, and justice then does not require enforcement in such an action. . . . In some cases it may be appropriate to measure relief by the extent of the promisee's reliance rather than by the terms of the promise. See § 90. . . .

Restatement Second § 139 has undoubtedly reinforced the tendency of the courts to adopt a reliance exception to the Statute of Frauds. However, not all courts adopt the reliance exception. See, e.g., Stearns v. Emery–Waterhouse Co., 596 A.2d 72 (Maine 1991) ("We affirm that equitable estoppel, based upon a promisor's fraudulent conduct, can avoid application of the statute of frauds and that this principle applies to a fraudulent promise of employment. But we decline [the plaintiff's] invitation to accept *promissory* estoppel as permitting avoidance of the statute in employment contracts that require longer than one year to perform"). Furthermore, some courts that adopt the reliance exception continue to qualify the exception in the same manner as *Monarco.*

The cases are divided on whether the reliance exception applies to UCC § 2–201. Some cases take the position that the exceptions in § 2–201 should be deemed to be exclusive of any others, partly to promote uniformity in the application of the Code. See, e.g., Renfroe v. Ladd, 701 S.W.2d 148 (Ky.App. 1985); Lige Dickson Co. v. Union Oil Co., 96 Wash.2d 291, 635 P.2d 103 (1981). Other cases take the position that the reliance exception applies to cases that fall within § 2–201 because UCC § 1–103 provides that "Unless displaced by the particular provisions of this Act, the principles of law and equity, including . . . the law relative to . . . estoppel . . . or other validating or invalidating cause shall supplement its provisions." See, e.g., Allen M. Campbell Co. v. Virginia Metal Industries, 708 F.2d 930 (4th Cir.1983); Ralston Purina Co. v. McCollum, 271 Ark. 840, 611 S.W.2d 201 (1981).

SECTION 21. THE RIGHT TO THE "VALUE OF THE BARGAIN" WHERE THERE HAS BEEN PART PERFORMANCE OF, OR RELIANCE UPON, THE ORAL CONTRACT

From the standpoint of a plaintiff who has acted under an oral contract falling within the Statute of Frauds, the state of the law summarized in the last two Sections of this Appendix is unsatisfactory in two respects: (1) Despite some straining in that direction, the law does not in all cases reimburse the plaintiff's losses in acting under the contract. (2) Where the plaintiff has performed his side of the contract, it would often be to his advantage if his measure of recovery was the value of the performance promised by the defendant, rather than the value of his own performance. If the plaintiff seeks the former measure simply to realize the advantage of a profitable bargain, we may say that this objective is contrary to the Statute of Frauds. But a plaintiff's right to restitution is clearly recognized by the cases, and the plaintiff has legitimate grounds for complaint if this right is impaired in practice by the imposition of an uncertain measure of recovery. He may point out that the uncertainty in the amount of his claim not only jeopardizes his recovery in case of actual litigation, but (and this is more important in practice) impairs his bargaining power in any negotiations looking toward a settlement without litigation.

This objection has particular application where the benefit conferred on the defendant by the plaintiff's performance does not have a definite market value, and the defendant has promised to pay a flat sum of money for the performance. As an original question, it would seem sensible to avoid the hazards and doubts involved in measuring the value of the plaintiff's performance in such cases by taking, as the value of that performance, the amount the defendant promised to pay for it. By way of reinforcing this argument, the plaintiff may point out that his having acted under the contract is a voucher of his good faith and corroborative evidence that a contract did in fact exist; it thus serves in some measure as a substitute for a writing.

Against this reasoning stands, of course, the plain language of the Statute of Frauds itself. One section of the original Statute of Frauds—section 17, the sale-of-goods section (now supplanted by the UCC)—expressly recognized and gave legal effect to the kind of considerations advanced above, by providing that the plaintiff could sue for the contract price if certain kinds of part performance had occurred. The omission of part-performance exceptions in section 4 of the Statute might seem to indicate that there could be no recovery of the contract price in cases falling within that section, even if the contract had been partly performed or had otherwise given rise to a serious change of position.

In spite of the force of the last argument, the courts, by a process extending over the centuries, have read into certain provisions of the Statute of Frauds exceptions under which the Statute becomes inapplicable, and the plaintiff can bring suit under the contract for expectation damages, where the contract has been fully or even partly performed on one side. The exact nature of the part-performance exceptions vary from provision to provision of the Statute. A summary of the law on this question follows.

The Suretyship Section

Generally no exception to the Statute of Frauds is read into the suretyship section of the Statute in favor of a party who performs on the basis of an oral guaranty. For example, if Seller delivers goods to Buyer in reliance on Surety's oral promise to answer for Buyer's obligation to pay the price, Surety does not thereby become bound.

The Marriage Section

It is generally assumed that an oral contract upon consideration of marriage is not taken out of the Statute of Frauds simply because the marriage has taken place in reliance on the promise. (There are, however, cases enforcing the oral agreement where a serious change of position, involving acts in addition to marriage, has occurred.)

The Land Section

In the case of contracts for the sale of an interest in land ("land contracts"), a part-performance exception—perhaps more accurately, a part-performance-and-reliance exception—has become institutionalized and has been built into an imposing body of case law.

The traditional rules. Traditionally, the cases in this area make explicit two different considerations: (1) The equity in favor of a party who has acted under the oral contract and who will suffer hardship if the contract is not enforced. (2) The evidentiary value of acts of reliance or part performance in pointing to the existence of a contract. Because these considerations may appear in varying degrees, there are strict and liberal applications of the part-performance exception in this context. Furthermore, some decisions place greater weight on the evidentiary significance of acts of performance or reliance, while others place greater weight on the element of hardship.

In discussing the case law on the part-performance exception for land contracts, it is necessary to distinguish between acts under the contract by the *vendor* and acts under the contract by the *purchaser*.

A *vendor* is entitled to recover the price under an oral contract for the sale of land as soon as the vendor has actually conveyed the land to the purchaser. Restatement Second § 125(3). Thus the vendor can obtain the price promised by the purchaser, and with it the benefit of the vendor's oral bargain, instead of being thrown back upon either an action in restitution for the reasonable value of the land or a suit in equity to compel a reconveyance of the land (specific restitution).

Where it is the *purchaser* who acts under the oral contract, the law is more complicated. A good summary of the traditional rule in this area was set out in Restatement First § 197. That Section provided that an oral agreement for the sale of an interest in land becomes *specifically enforceable* if "the purchaser with the assent of the vendor (a) makes valuable improvements on the land, or (b) takes possession thereof or retains a possession thereof existing at the time of the bargain, and also pays a portion or all of the purchase price."

As indicated by Restatement First § 197, under the traditional rule payment of all or part of the purchase price does not alone make the contract enforceable, although there are some cases to the contrary. The theory is that such a payment does not identify the land sold. (However, the payment can be recovered in a suit for restitution.) Similarly, under the traditional rule the purchaser's act of taking possession does not alone make the contract enforceable by the plaintiff. The theory is that although taking possession may have evidentiary value as indicating some kind of agreement and identifying its object, taking possession is as consistent with a lease as with a sale, and may not always involve a serious change of position by the purchaser.

These limitations are by no means universally respected by the courts. In addition to some cases indicating that taking possession is sufficient, even without payment of the purchase price, there are many cases holding that the rendition of services over a long period will suffice to take the contract out of the Statute. This type of holding is found typically in "care-for-me-for-the-rest-of-my-life-and-you-can-have-the-farm-when-I-am-gone" contracts.

Concerning the traditional rule that certain acts by the purchaser under a land contract may make the contract specifically enforceable, the following points should be noted.

(1) This rule was developed by courts of equity, and therefore it is generally assumed to affect only the purchaser's right to specific performance, and not to give the purchaser a right to recover damages measured by the value of the land. Restatement Second § 129, Comment c. In contrast, the *vendor's* right to the price after conveying land under an oral contract is a right to sue at law.

(2) Generally it is the purchaser who, having made improvements or otherwise acted under the contract, brings suit for specific performance against the vendor. There are cases, however, holding that the same acts under the contract by the purchaser that will create in him a right to specific performance will also create a right to specific performance in the vendor. Here it is not the hardship to the plaintiff-vendor that makes the oral contract enforceable, but either (1) the evidentiary value of the purchaser's acts, or (2) a notion that if it is fair for the purchaser to enforce the contract, equality of treatment should allow the vendor to sue on the same set of facts.

(3) In a few jurisdictions, the courts have stated that they do not recognize the principle that part performance of an oral contract for the sale of an interest in land will make the contract specifically enforceable.

(4) There is a general tendency to very liberally enforce an oral contract that settles a disputed boundary. Where parties are in dispute or doubt about the boundary between their lands, and orally agree to settle the issue by running a fence or other marker along a designated line, generally the agreement becomes enforceable as soon as any action is taken under it. Restatement Second § 128(1).

The rule in Restatement Second. Restatement Second § 129 completely reconceptualizes and reformulates the part-performance exception for land contracts, by making the exception center on reliance. That section provides:

> A contract for the transfer of an interest in land may be specifically enforced notwithstanding failure to comply with the Statute of Frauds if it is established that the party seeking enforcement, in reasonable reli-

ance on the contract and on the continuing assent of the party against whom enforcement is sought, has so changed his position that injustice can be avoided only by specific enforcement.

Whether the law in this area will shift to the rule stated in Restatement Second § 129 remains to be seen.

The One–Year Provision

Taking as a guide Restatement Second § 130 and many cases, the part-performance rule concerning the one-year provision—section 4(5)—is as follows: As soon as one side of the contract has been fully performed the promise of the other party becomes binding, whether or not that promise can be performed within one year. (The rationale of this rule is seldom discussed. Perhaps the explanation lies in the fact that difficulties intrinsic to section 4(5) had already compelled so much departure from the literal meaning of the section (see Section 10 of this Appendix) that the courts have felt free to take further liberties with its language in order to make its operation more equitable.) Piecing this principle together with the basic interpretation of section 4(5), it may be said that an oral contract is either not within or is taken out of the one-year provision if (1) the whole contract *could* have been performed within one year, although neither party has as yet fully performed or (2) one party has fully performed, no matter how long it took for performance to take place.

Caution: The case law is more ambiguous than the rule laid down by Restatement Second, and the general tendency of the law is less favorable to removing the oral contract from the Statute's one-year provision as a result of part performance. According to some cases, if the defendant's performance will require more than a year, the fact that the plaintiff has fully performed is immaterial. Under this view, the plaintiff's only relief is in restitution. Still other cases say that full performance on one side will take the contract out of the Statute only if that performance itself takes place within one year after the contract is made.

SECTION 22. THE EFFECT OF NON–COMPLIANCE—LEGAL CONSEQUENCES OF THE UNENFORCEABLE AGREEMENT

It is a safe guess that the problem, what are the legal consequences of an agreement that is unenforceable under the Statute of Frauds, is one that never occurred to the drafters of the original Act. When they said in Section 4 that "no action shall be brought" on the oral contract, or in Section 17 that the oral contract shall not "be allowed to be good," they probably meant in both cases something roughly equivalent to: "the oral contract is not good." It is equally doubtful that those occasional American legislatures who changed the wording of the Statute to make the oral contract "void" had any clearer idea of what they were doing.

A contractual transaction between two persons may give rise to a multitude of legal consequences. It may, for example, make the participants guilty of a crime, transfer or affect rights, create duties, rebut the implication that property was transferred as a gift, furnish the substratum of moral obligation that will make a later promise enforceable, or create a relationship with which others cannot interfere without liability. Terms like "unenforceable," "void," and "voidable" are blind verbal jabs into a complex molecule of relationships. When they are used in legislation, it is the unhappy task of the courts to decide what changes in the structure of the molecule the words were intended to bring about and what changes are in keeping with the general purpose of the legislation.

Sometimes this task is easy, as in the next *Example*.

Example No. 15:

Gilbert Gore orally agrees with Catherine Cabal that he will murder Delbert Doom in return for a conveyance of Bloodacre. The agreement is discovered before it is carried out, and Gore is indicted for criminal conspiracy. The local Statute of Frauds makes any contract for the sale of an interest in land "void." Gore's attorney relies on dictionary definition of "void" as meaning "of no legal force or effect." He argues that since this contract was "void" it cannot have the legal effect of making his client guilty of a crime.

This argument would be rejected. Criminal liability is a matter that is beyond the purpose of the Statute of Frauds. Although in Gore's jurisdiction the Statute uses the word "void," that doesn't not mean that entering the oral contract has no legal consequences, but only that the oral contract will be deprived of those legal consequences that would be inconsistent with the purpose of the Statute.

Simple and obvious as is *Example No. 15*, it illustrates the basic difficulty the courts have faced in determining the legal effect of the unenforceable oral contract. What legal effects *are* inconsistent with the purpose of the Statute?

One generalization that holds fairly firm is that the Statute of Frauds affects only the legal relations of the contracting parties. Accordingly, that a contract is oral and therefore unenforceable between the parties makes it no less a binding contract so far as third persons are concerned. Restatement Second § 144. Accordingly, persuading a party to break an oral contract may constitute the tort of inducing breach of contract even though the contract is within the Statute.

The most knotty problem the courts have faced in this area has arisen in connection with suits for restitution.

Example No. 16:

Recall *Example No. 14:* Steven Smock orally agrees to paint a mural in Marian Means's home in return for Passacre. Smock paints the mural; Means conveys Passacre to him. Smock then sues Means for $10,000, based on the principle of unjust enrichment, alleging that the reasonable value of the mural is $15,000 and that he has so far only received a piece of land worth $5,000. Means pleads performance of the oral agreement. Smock replies by asserting that the oral agreement was within the Statute of Frauds and therefore without legal effect. He argues that when Means seeks to restrict Smock to the orally agreed price for her work, Means is in effect holding Smock to the agreement. If the contract cannot be enforced by the plaintiff, it ought to be unenforceable on behalf of the defendant.

Judgment would go for Means. Since she has paid the price orally agreed upon, there is no basis for a suit founded on a theory of unjust enrichment. Her use of the oral contract to show that she had paid the agreed price is not "enforcing" that contract. If Smock had presented the mural to her as a gift, Smock could not later change her mind and recover its value from Means. In such a case, Means could show an oral statement by Smock that his mural was to be given gratuitously. The fact that such a statement words would impose no liability on Smock to carry out the gift would be immaterial. In the same way here, the fact that suit could not have been brought on the oral contract is immaterial to Means's use of the contract to rebut the claim of unjust enrichment.

The result reached in *Example No. 16* is one that can be predicted with some assurance. Generally, a person may not undo an executed transaction simply because the contract under which he acts would not have been enforceable if it were an executory agreement. This would probably be true even if the Statute says that the oral contract is "void." Restatement Second § 145. The following case is more troublesome:

Example No. 17:

Quigley Quail orally agrees to serve Fiona Fast as secretary for six months, and Fast agrees to pay for Quail's services by conveying Penacre to him at the end of the six months' period. When Quail has served two months, he learns that his contract is unenforceable under section 4(4) of the Statute of Frauds (the land section). Quail brings suit for the reasonable value of two months' services. Fast asserts that she is willing to abide by the agreement, and that she stands ready to convey Penacre when Quail's work is finished. She argues that Quail's discontinuance of performance is a breach of the oral agreement that should disentitle him to relief. Quail argues that he should not be asked to complete his work under the contract when he has no assurance that Fast will in fact pay him. Restatement Second § 141(2) proposes, as a solution for this problem, that "[where] a party to a contract which is unenforceable against him refuses either to perform the contract or to sign a sufficient memorandum, the other party is justified in suspending any performance for which he has not already received the agreed return, and such a suspension is not a defense in an action for the value of performance rendered before the suspension."

SECTION 23. ORAL RESCISSION

The problem of the validity of an oral rescission arises chiefly in connection with the following situation: The original contract was in writing, and its terms were such as to bring it within the Statute of Frauds. In short, the contract had to be in writing—as it was—to be enforceable. The contract is then orally rescinded by the parties' mutual agreement. As a general proposition, in such cases the rescission is effective, on the theory that the rescission does not call for the performance of any duties, and therefore does not fall within any of the classes covered by the Statute. See *Example No. 4* in Section 6 of this Appendix; Restatement Second § 148 and comment a.

This general proposition requires two qualifications:

1. *Sale of land.* Where the rescinded contract is for the sale of land, and the original transaction was fully executed, the rescission itself effectively calls for a conveyance—albeit a reconveyance—and therefore falls within the Statute. Suppose the original contract was executory at the time the contract of rescission was entered into? Even here, there are cases saying that the rescission is ineffective unless in writing. The theory of these cases is that an executory contract to sell land creates a present property interest in the purchaser, so that a rescission of such a contract also involves the reconveyance of an interest in land. However, according to Restatement Second § 148, comment c, "[t]he prevailing rule"—which is adopted by Restatement Second—"is that an executory land contract may be rescinded orally like other contracts within the Statute. . . ."

2. *Sale of goods.* If the original contract was for the sale of goods, and title had already passed to the buyer, "rescission" is really a resale of the goods, and comes within UCC § 2–201 if the amount involved is sufficient. Restatement Second § 148, comment b and Illustration 2.

SECTION 24. ORAL MODIFICATIONS

Generally speaking, a modification of a contract falls within the Statute of Frauds if, but only if, the new agreement that results from putting together the original agreement and the modification is within the Statute. However, a special rule applies to modifications of contracts for the sale of goods, which are governed by UCC § 2–209(3). That section provides:

> The requirements of the statute of frauds section of this Article (Section 2–201) must be satisfied if [a contract for the sale of goods] as modified is within its provisions.

Comment 3 adds:

> The Statute of Frauds provisions of this Article are expressly applied to modifications by subsection (3). Under those provisions the "delivery and acceptance" test is limited to the goods which have been accepted, that is, to the past. "Modification" for the future cannot therefore be conjured up by oral testimony if the price involved is $500.00 or more since such modification must be shown at least by an authenticated memo. And since a memo is limited in its effect to the quantity of goods set forth in it there is safeguard against oral evidence.

The Comment suggests that *any* modification of a contract for the sale of goods must be in writing. This position was taken in Zemco Mfg., Inc. v. Navistar Int'l Transp. Corp., 186 F.3d 815 (7th Cir. 1999), decided by the Seventh Circuit under Indiana law. In 1983, the parties entered into a written contract for the sale of parts. Originally, the contract was to last one year, but it was extended to 1987 by successive written agreements. After 1987, the parties orally agreed to extend the contract. Navistar argued that the oral contract extensions were unenforceable under the Statute of Frauds. The Seventh Circuit agreed:

We begin our analysis of this question with [UCC] § 2–209(3), which generally applies to contract modifications. It states that "[t]he requirements of the statute of frauds ... must be satisfied if the contract as modified is within its provisions." ... The interpretation of this provision ... has generated controversy among courts and commentators. One view is that all contract modifications must be in writing; another view is that only modifications of terms that are required to be in writing under [UCC] § 2–201 must be in writing. Under the second view, the time extension would not need to be in writing because the length of a contract is not a type of term that needs to be in writing.

Indiana courts have not interpreted the meaning of [UCC § 2–209(3).] A substantial number of the courts in other jurisdictions that have considered identical UCC provisions have held that every contract modification must be in writing.... Although these courts have provided little analysis, they essentially interpret § 2–209(3) to mean that, if the post-modification contract fits within the terms of § 2–201 (i.e., it is a sale of goods for more than $500), then any modification of it must be in writing....

At least one court has held that the writing requirement for modifications applies only to either a change in consideration, or a change in a term that the UCC statute of frauds requires to be in writing. *See Costco Wholesale Corp. v. World Wide Licensing Corp.*, 78 Wash.App. 637, 898 P.2d 347, 351 & n. 5 (1995). This view also appears to be favored among commentators. The general theory behind this approach is that it would be anomalous, if not inconsistent, to require that a modification be in writing if the same term in the original contract could be proven by parol evidence. Moreover, proponents of this view argue, § 2–209(3) explicitly invokes only the writing requirements contained in § 2–201—nothing less and nothing more....

We need not decide in the abstract the correct interpretation of § 2–209(3). Because the jurisdiction of the district court was based on the diversity of citizenship of the parties, it was obligated to apply the law of Indiana.... Although the Indiana courts have not spoken directly on the matter, we believe ... that Indiana would follow the majority of jurisdictions and hold that the extension of the contract needed to be in writing.... [because there] is no suggestion in this record that Indiana would not follow the majority rule or that its courts would not consider important the goal of uniformity in the interpretation of the Commercial Code. ... [T]he influential [Official Comment] suggests strongly that Indiana would require compliance with the statute of frauds in this case.

In contrast, White & Summers comment, "Assuming that a party can establish a modifying agreement, must one show that it was reduced to writing? Section 2–209(3) states that '[t]he requirements of the statute of frauds section of this Article (2–201) must be satisfied if the contract as modified is within its provisions.' The impact of this provision is not clear. We see at least the following possible interpretations: (1) that if the original contract was within 2–201, any modification thereof must also be in writing; (2) that a modification must be in writing if the term it adds brings the entire deal within 2–201 for the first time, as where the price is modified from $400 to $500; (3) that a modification must be in writing if it falls in 2–201 on its own; (4) that the modification must be in writing if it changes the quantity term of an original agreement that fell within 2–201; and (5) some combination of the foregoing. Given the purposes of the basic statute of frauds section 2–201, we believe interpretations (2), (3), and (4) are each justified, subject, of course, to the exceptions in 2–201 itself and to any general supplemental principles of estoppel." J. White & R. Summers, Uniform Commercial Code § 1–6 (5th ed. 2000).

Finally there is emergent in this area another doctrine of part performance or reliance, according to which an oral modification becomes effective if action has been taken under it. Restatement Second § 150. In this connection, UCC § 2–209(4) provides that an attempt at modification that does not satisfy § 2–209(3) can operate as a waiver, and § 2–209(5) provides that such a waiver cannot be retracted if retraction would be unjust in view of a material change of position in reliance on the waiver.

SECTION 25. THE INTERACTION OF THE STATUTE OF FRAUDS WITH THE PAROL EVIDENCE RULE

There is obvious similarity between the Statute of Frauds and the parol evidence rule, since both are concerned with oral evidence. However, the two rules have different functions, which give rise to differences in operation. The following points should be noted.

First. The parol evidence rule does not invalidate a later oral modification of a written agreement. The Statute of Frauds may. See Section 24 of this Appendix.

Second. The Statute of Frauds requires a writing and, where applicable, prevents the use of an oral agreement as the basis for suit. The parol evidence rule may exclude *written* as well as oral proof of an agreement.

Third. Unless the Statute of Frauds requires "the contract" to be in writing, it may be satisfied by writings that do not call into operation the parol evidence rule. Thus the Statute may often be satisfied by piecing together a series of informal letters. Such a series of letters would not ordinarily be construed as an "integration" of the contract, and therefore would not prevent the introduction of parol evidence.

Fourth. In litigation involving a written contract, one party may object that the contract is incomplete. The other party may then offer parol evidence to supply the apparent gap in the written contract. The admission of such evidence may raise two questions: (1) Is the testimony offered admissible under the parol evidence rule? (2) Is the gap in the written contract so serious that the writing fails to satisfy the Statute of Frauds, thus making the offered testimony legally irrelevant? These are different questions, the answers to which depend on distinct considerations.

Example No. 18:

Seller and Buyer sign a written contract covering the sale of certain land for $10,000. The contract is complete in every respect except that it does not identify or describe the land in any way, but merely says, "This contract covers the land that we have this day orally agreed shall be conveyed." Seller sues Buyer for breach of the contract. Buyer pleads the Statute of Frauds. Seller relies on the written contract as satisfying the Statute, while Buyer contends that the writing is insufficient because it does not describe the land sold. Seller answers by saying, "The parol evidence rule does not prevent introducing oral evidence showing what the land is. Therefore, I can supplement the written contract by parol evidence identifying the land intended to be conveyed. Hence the writing satisfies the Statute." Seller is right about the parol evidence rule, but wrong about the Statute of Frauds.

SECTION 26. THE INTERACTION OF THE STATUTE OF FRAUDS WITH THE REMEDY OF REFORMATION

The interaction of the Statute of Frauds and the remedy of reformation can also raise problems. In considering this interaction, it would be well to start with a case where the Statute of Frauds is plainly not involved. C contracts to build a house for O in nine months. A written contract is drawn up and signed, which contains all the requisite terms except that through a typist's error the price is stated as $10,000 instead of the agreed figure of $100,000. Here, on clear proof that both parties understood the price to be $100,000, the court would order reformation. Would it make any difference if the contract had been one that was required by the Statute to be in writing? There is something disturbing about the idea of a court's rewriting a contract to make it conform to an oral agreement of a type that the Statute of Frauds declares to be legally unenforceable. Yet is there any real reason for disquietude here? After all, the basic purpose of the Statute is to obtain for certain transactions the security of a written document. In the case of the building contract the parties sought that security for themselves in a formal written contract signed by both of them. A court would not hesitate to rewrite that contract to make it conform to an intention plainly shared by both parties. Why should it make any difference if the contract were such that had it been wholly unwritten it would have been unenforceable? If the Statute is thought, as it often is, to be grounded in large measure on a distrust of juries, no jury is involved in the remedy of reformation, which in any event is granted only on clear and convincing proof.

Today it is generally accepted that the circumstance that a contract falls within the Statute of Frauds does not of itself bar the possibility of reformation. There are, however, substantial traces of discomfort in some cases concerning reformation of contracts that fall within the Statute:

(1) There is authority for restricting reformation of such contracts to situations where the party seeking reformation has seriously relied on the contract; reformation of the wholly executory agreement may be refused.

(2) Reformation may be denied where it concerns the central term of a contract that falls within the Statute of Frauds—for example, where a written contract for the sale of land inadvertently omits any hint of what land is to be conveyed.

(3) Some cases say that the obligation expressed in a writing that failed within the Statute of Frauds can be "contracted" by reformation, but not "expanded."

SECTION 27. PLEADING AND PROCEDURAL PROBLEMS IN CONNECTION WITH THE STATUTE

What procedure must be followed to utilize the Statute of Frauds as a defense? A defendant who took the words "no action shall be brought" literally might decide to say nothing of the Statute in her pleading, wait until the plaintiff attempted to introduce evidence to prove the oral agreement, and then ask for a ruling that the offered proof was incompetent under the Statute. In most jurisdictions, however, such a course of action would forfeit a defense under the Statute, because a defendant's failure to plead the Statute will usually be treated as waiving it. Correspondingly, in many or most jurisdictions a defendant who wants to invoke the Statute must raise the Statute as a specially pleaded affirmative defense, and cannot simply rely on pleading a general denial or the like. A companion rule in most jurisdictions is that the Statute of Frauds cannot be raised for the first time on appeal.

SECTION 28. A GLANCE BACKWARD AND AHEAD

Little is known about the legislative deliberations by which the Statute of Frauds was reduced to the form in which it was finally enacted in 1677. We do know, however, the precise language of its original draft. In the bill as it was first introduced in the House of Lords in 1673, the provision relating to contracts read as follows:

> And be it further enacted by Authority aforesaid that in all actions upon the case, actions of debt, or other personal actions which from and after the [blank] day of [blank] shall be commenced upon any assumpsit, promise, contract or agreement made, or supposed to be made, by parol and whereof no memorandum, note or memorial in writing shall be taken by the direction of the parties thereunto no greater damages shall at any time be recovered than the sum of [blank], any law or usage to the contrary notwithstanding.

> Provided that this Act shall not extend to such actions or suits which shall or may be grounded upon contracts or agreements for wares sold or money lent or upon any *quantum meruit* or any other assumpsits or promises which are created by the construction or operation of law; but that all and every such actions shall and may be sued and prosecuted in such manner as the same might have been before the making of this Act, anything hereinbefore to the contrary notwithstanding.

In contrast with the legislation that was actually enacted, it should be noted that the original draft: (1) Required a written memorandum, note, or memorial "taken by direction of the parties" rather than a written agreement, or a memorandum or note thereof, signed by the party to be charged. (2) Did not attempt to separate off certain defined kinds of contracts as requiring a writing, but instead contemplated imposing (subject to the qualifications in the second paragraph) a limitation on the recovery that could be had on *any* kind of oral contract. (3) Provided generally in its last paragraph that even in the absence of a memorandum, an appropriate recovery might be had, without limit of amount, where the plaintiff had actually conferred a benefit on the defendant under the agreement, and brought suit for the value of the benefit. It is remarkable that except as to the sales-of-goods section this last qualification should have disappeared in the final legislation, so that the concept of recovery for benefit conferred had to be supplied, in a somewhat irregular way, by a judicial gloss on the Statute.

The question may well be raised whether the Lords would have done better by subsequent generations if they had stood by their original draft. It should be noted that UCC § 1–206, in the form adopted in most states, is similarly based on a limit on recovery for contracts to which it applies.

The question may also be raised whether the Statute of Frauds has not long since outlived its usefulness. The Statute was, from the beginning, badly drafted. Its authors plainly did not clearly think through the relation between the disease they sought to cure and the remedy they prescribed, most notably so with respect to contracts not to be performed within one year. Furthermore, the principles by which the authors of the Statute decided the question, what contracts deserved the protection of a writing, were based on the needs of the seventeenth century, not those of modern commerce. And the tangled web of judicial interpretation that has gathered about the words of the Statute through the centuries surely deserves to be called, as it was by a British writer, "filthily technical." To the laudatory comment that every line of the Statute is worth a subsidy, the apt rejoinder has been made that every line of it has cost a subsidy.

In 1954 the British Parliament repealed the provisions of the English Statute of Frauds concerning (1) special promises of executors or administrators, (2) agreements in consideration of marriage, (3) agreements not to be performed within one year, and (4) contracts for the sale of goods. This leaves in effect, from the original Statute, only a promise to be a surety for another and a contract for the sale of an interest in land. (As in this country, however, since the adoption of the original Statute of Frauds, England has enacted statutes requiring a signed writing for certain other special kinds of contracts.)

The Permanent Editorial Board for the UCC ["PEB"] Study Group on the Revision of Article 2 of the Uniform Commercial Code concluded that "Despite its ancient lineage, there is no persuasive evidence either that the statute of frauds has prevented fraud in the proof of the making of a contract or that its presence has channeled behavior toward more reliable forms of record keeping.... England repealed the statute of frauds for sales in 1953. Since [then] there has been little discussion and no reports about the impact, if any. In short, the statute of frauds has apparently sunk in England without an adverse trace." PEB Study Group Report on Article 2 at 50–51 (1990). Furthermore, Article 11 of the CISG provides: "A contract of sale need not be concluded in or evidenced by writing and is not subject to any other requirements as to form." Similarly, Unidroit Art. 1.2 provides that "Nothing in these Principles requires that a contract be concluded in or evidenced by writing. It may be proven by any means, including witnesses.''

The PEB Study Group suggested that even if the Statute of Frauds requirement for the sale of goods was not repealed, the quantity requirement ought to be deleted and certain other changes ought to be made, including possibly the addition of a reliance exception. An ABA Task Force on the revision of Article 2 was divided on whether the Statute of Frauds in Article 2 should be repealed, but suggested that one alternative would be to require that an oral contract be proven by clear and convincing evidence, rather than merely a preponderance of the evidence. ABA Task Force Report on Article 2, 16 Del.J.Corp.Law 981, 1039 (1991). Through the late 1990s, the National Conference of Commissioners on Uniform State Law and the American Law Institute worked to produce a thoroughly revised version of Article 2. At one point in the drafting process, the proposed revision entirely dropped a Statute of Frauds provision for contracts for the sale of goods. At that point, Section 2–201 was entitled "No Formal Requirements." Section 2–201(a) then provided that "A contract or modification is enforceable, whether or not there is a record signed by the party against whom enforcement is sought, even if the contract or modification is not capable of performance within one year after its making." Later, however, a Statute of Frauds provision was reinstated in the proposed revision.

In the end, the attempt to produce a thorough revision of Article 2 was abandoned. Instead, in 2003 NCCUSL and the ALI promulgated limited amendments to Article 2. Among these amendments was a revision to section 2–201 that raised the price for which a writing is required, in the case of a contract for the sale of goods, from $500 to $5,000. As of early 2006, however, no state has adopted the amended version of Article 2.

Appendix B

A NOTE ON THE HISTORY OF CONTRACT IN THE COMMON LAW

The role of contract in early law. In his chapter on the early history of contract, Maine wrote, "The point which before all others has to be apprehended in the constitution of early societies is that the individual creates for himself few or no rights, and few or no duties. The rules which he obeys are derived first from the station into which he is born, and next from the imperative commands addressed to him by the chief of the household of which he forms a part. Such a system leaves the very smallest room for Contract."

If Maine's remark is taken to describe the role which agreement, as a social institution, plays in early society, it may contain some element of exaggeration. Since Maine's time, anthropologists have come increasingly to see that there is more give and take in early society than appears on the surface, and that a lively interplay of personalities often takes place behind the screen of social forms which seem rigid and unyielding. If, however, Maine meant by "contract" an agreement enforced by formally organized social pressures (in other words, by "law"), his statement would probably still be generally accepted as conveying an accurate picture of early society.

Compared with the law of property, crimes, and torts, the law of contracts presents a comparatively late development in English law. Even Blackstone, writing shortly before the American Revolution, disposes of the subject in a few pages forming a kind of appendix to his treatment of the law of property. The earlier writers, of course, have even less to say about contract, and in general the scope of the subject narrows as we go back in legal history.

The English law of contracts that is important for an understanding of modern law is chiefly that which was developed in the royal courts, and does not antedate the Norman Conquest. Before and after the Conquest, the local courts exercised some jurisdiction over the enforcement of agreements. It is not clear on what principles this local folk-law of contracts proceeded. Whatever these principles were, their influence on later law was, at the most, indirect, and due to such recognition as the royal courts may, consciously or unconsciously, have accorded to them.

The English law of contracts prior to the development of assumpsit. The early English common law provided only two limited forms of action to

1077

enforce liability of the kind which we would classify as contractual—*covenant* and *debt*. The principles of liability involved in these two actions were, respectively, that (1) one ought to pay for what one has bargained for and received, and (2) a formally made promise should be binding.

Half-completed bargains—the action of debt. At common law, a defendant who had promised to pay for goods or services became liable to pay the agreed price (which might be in terms of money or goods) after having received the plaintiff's performance. The appropriate action to enforce this liability was the action of debt or detinue.[1] This action reflected the principle that one ought to pay for what one has bargained for and received. Probably the situation in which the action of debt was originally granted was that where the plaintiff had transferred property to the defendant, which the defendant had agreed to pay for. In such cases, a tangible benefit was conferred directly on the defendant. This was termed in the later cases a "quid pro quo," and there is evidence in the early cases of a struggle to liberate the notion of quid pro quo from the physical conception that originally dominated it. Probably the first development in this direction was that of allowing services rendered to the defendant, instead of only a transfer of property to the defendant, to stand as the quid pro quo. Still later, after considerable wavering, it was held that a benefit conferred on a third person at the request of the defendant, and on the defendant's promise to pay for it, could serve as a quid pro quo to bind the defendant. But traces of the origin of the quid pro quo conception in a physical transfer of value to the defendant remained with the action of debt to the end, although the resulting limitations lost most of their importance after the later-developed action of assumpsit had in practice largely superseded the action of debt. For example, it was stated in 1695 that debt could not be maintained for a sum won on a wager. Walker v. Walker, 5 Mod. 13. Here there was a "sum certain" and an element of bargain, but the quid pro quo— a mere chance that the defendant might have won—bore so remote an analogy to the physical transfer originally involved in the action of debt that the court considered that action inappropriate in this context. (It should be observed that at the time of the case cited, the view now generally prevailing, that wagers are unenforceable as a matter of public policy, had not yet been adopted. In fact, the court indicated that an action in the form known as assumpsit might have been brought for the sum won.)

Formal promises—the action of covenant. Mature systems of law often provide some blanket formality, that is, a device that suffices to make any kind of promise enforceable, except, of course, one that would be denied legal sanction because it promotes an illegal or otherwise improper purpose. In ancient Rome we find the *stipulation*, and in the modern civil law, the

---

1. Debt and detinue were originally two forms of the same action, debt being allowed where the defendant had promised a sum of money, or a fixed quantity of fungible goods, while detinue was the appropriate form where the defendant had promised to deliver a specific and identified chattel. Detinue was also used against a bailee who wrongfully refused to return the bailed article. By a gradual process of extension, detinue came to be available as a remedy for the wrongful detention of a chattel regardless of the manner in which the defendant came into possession of it. Thus, though in its original form detinue savored of contract, being connected with sales and bailments, it later came to be regarded as a tort action, since it was available against anyone wrongfully detaining a chattel belonging to the plaintiff. As a means of enforcing an obligation by the seller to deliver to the buyer a chattel for which the buyer had paid, detinue did not preserve its contractual quality, since the cases where the action was permitted were cases in which, in terms of later analysis, title had passed to the buyer, so that his suit to secure possession was conceived to rest on property rather than contract.

notarial contract. At common law, the *seal* became in time a blanket formality. A defendant who had made a promise under seal was liable in an action of covenant.[2] Just as the action of debt reflected the principle that one ought to pay for what he has bargained for and received, the action of covenant reflected the principle of form.

Because of the pervading formality of early law, it has been supposed that the notion involved in these devices (that form may bind without reference to content) is a notion of great antiquity. The available facts do not bear out this assumption. In early society, formalities and ceremonies were identified only with particular transactions of restricted purposes. The notion of a blanket formality seems historically to have been arrived at by the process of broadening the purposes for which a particular ceremony could be used. The formal contract of the Middle Ages in Germanic Europe apparently descended from a transaction originally used only for the purpose of giving hostages in settlement of a blood feud. This transaction came gradually to be used for other purposes, and, by curious development, it became possible for the debtor to offer himself as a hostage or surety for his own obligation. This notion of self-pledge was on the Continent the source of a formality which became in time a general means of making promises binding.

It is not known when the seal first became a blanket formality in England, although it was certainly by the latter part of the thirteenth century. The actual practice of using seals was introduced by the Norman invaders, so that the binding effect of the seal was not a "product of ancient folk-law." On the other hand, it seems likely that the seal did not originally have an obligatory effect that was independent of the transaction in which it was used. Originally, its significance seems to have been primarily evidentiary, and when a greater effect was first attributed to the seal, it was apparently on the theory that a seal might make conclusive the acknowledgment of an obligation to pay for something already received. In time, however, by a process that cannot be traced in detail, the seal came to have the effect which the later common law took for granted, that is, making a promise—generally speaking, *any* promise—enforceable.

The limits of debt and covenant. If we compare the early English law of contracts with modern law, we will notice that the most important difference lies in the fact that there was no relief for breach of an informal executory bargain. A and B agree on the sale of a horse for £10. When the time comes for delivery, A, the seller, tenders the horse, and B refuses to accept it. Unless B's promise was under seal, early law granted no remedy to A in this situation. Suit could be brought in debt for the price of goods *delivered,* or services *rendered;* and at least by the middle of the fifteenth century, A could sue in debt for the *price* of the undelivered horse (although it is thought by many of the commentators that the theory justifying recovery by A in such a case was that the property was in B by force of the bargain). But for another hundred years there was no action for "damages" for the other party's refusal to carry out an unsealed executory agreement.

The early English law of contracts was, by modern standards at least, deficient in other important, but less obvious ways. The suit for the price of a

---

2. Originally *debt* would lie on promises under seal in which the promise was to pay a "sum certain"—that is, a definite sum of money—while *covenant* would lie in other cases.   Later covenant became an alternative remedy to debt—for a promise under seal, even where the promise was to pay a sum certain.

performance rendered was itself subject to certain limitations, understandable only in the light of the conceptions of legal procedure that prevailed in early English law.

The business of deciding other persons' disputes has never been a comfortable one; those charged with judicial functions have in all ages sought means of minimizing their personal responsibility for the decision rendered. The modern judge may depict himself as an inert conduit through which the force of statutes and precedents is communicated. During periods when a general belief in witchcraft and magic exists, another means is open to the judge for obscuring or eliminating personal responsibility for the decision rendered. This consists of converting the trial into a ritualistic appeal to the supernatural, in which the judge acts as a mere umpire to see that the proper forms are observed, and to announce the decision when it has been determined. The modes of trial in early English law that illustrate this conception are trial by battle, by ordeal, and by oath of compurgation. It is disputed whether the conception of procedure, and of the judge's function, embodied in these modes of trial is a general characteristic of early justice, or arises only during periods when, for one reason or another, the judge's position has become insecure, either toward those below him or toward the king above him. Apparently in some cases "supernatural" modes of trial, originally used only in cases where actual evidence was lacking, were later extended to all cases. Another point of obscurity is the extent to which these modes of trial were manipulated by the judge to produce the result he considered proper "on the merits." In any event, these methods of trial were in wide use at the time when the law of contracts took its beginnings in England, and we may infer from the prominence given to them that the judge's role was at that time conceived as being not so much that of "deciding" the case as that of supervising a ritualistic and supposedly objective test of the truth of the parties' claims.

This early conception of legal procedure inevitably had its repercussions on the substantive law of contracts. It is one thing to have a claim for £10 that can be established by rational proof and which the sheriff will collect out of the debtor's goods. It is another to have a claim for £10 that must be vindicated in a judicially supervised duel or by submission to an ordeal. With a gradual change in the conception of legal procedure and the role of the judge, the plaintiff's claim in debt developed in the direction of the conception which we recognize today. Trial by battle, for example, ceased to be possible in the action of debt at a comparatively early time.

On the other hand, where the defendant's promise was not under seal, and the plaintiff had to rely on an action in debt, two consequences of the early conception of procedure persisted for several centuries. These were as follows: (1) The promise of payment was enforceable only if it was for a "sum certain," a specified chattel, or some fixed quantity. (2) The defendant might at his option "wage his law."

When the defendant "waged his law," he brought into court a number of witnesses (finally set at twelve) who repeated an oath affirming that the defendant's oath was "clean." The theory of this mode of trial seems to have rested partly on rational grounds (if twelve persons were willing to swear that the defendant was telling the truth, he probably was), and partly on supernatural grounds (God would intervene to cause the witnesses to trip in repeating the oath if in fact the defendant and his oath-helpers were swearing falsely). Though wager of law gradually fell into disuse, it was theoretically possible in England until 1833, when it was abolished by statute.

The plaintiff in debt had to demand a "sum certain" or its equivalent because in the absence of a sum certain it would be necessary to determine damages. (Such a determination could not have been made by wager of law, because wager of law was suitable only for yes-or-no questions. It could not have been made by the judge, because determination of damages by the judge would have taken him out of his passive role.) Therefore, unless the parties by their agreement had set a definite price that the plaintiff was to receive for his performance, the action of debt would not lie. (An important consequence of this requirement of sum certain was that implied contracts, for "reasonable compensation," could not be enforced.) This requirement of the action of debt remained until the abolition of the distinction between forms of action; in England until 1852.

The development of the action of assumpsit. Due to the substantive and procedural limitations of covenant and debt, there developed a third form of contract action, which eventually came to occupy almost the entire field. This action was known as assumpsit ("he undertook"), since the key allegation in the complaint was that defendant had undertaken—in modern parlance, had promised—to render a certain performance. The action required neither a writing under seal nor a sum certain, did not involve wager of law, and, in its maturity, could be brought even on an executory contract.

In its origin, assumpsit was a tort action. At common law, if the defendant had carelessly left a log lying in a darkened road, which injured the plaintiff's horse, the plaintiff's remedy would be in trespass on the case, or "case" as it was later called. In this suit there would be no need to include any allegation of an undertaking or promise by the defendant; the defendant was liable for his carelessness—not as a promise-breaker. The notion of assumpsit was first introduced in cases like the Humber Ferryman case, decided in 1348, Lib.Ass. 22 Edw. III, pl. 41, where the defendant injured a chattel that had been entrusted to him by the plaintiff. A ferryman receives the plaintiff's horse for transportation across a river, and negligently causes his boat to overturn, so that the horse is lost. Here the plaintiff would allege that the defendant received the horse (later, undertook, *assumpsit*) to carry safely.

Notwithstanding this allegation, the theory of the suit was not that the defendant had broken a promise, but that he had wronged the plaintiff by causing the loss of the horse. Why, then, was the allegation of an undertaking included in the plaintiff's declaration? Apparently it was through a fear that without this allegation the court might consider that the plaintiff was as much to blame for the loss as the defendant, since he voluntarily turned his horse over to the defendant. An analogous case in modern law would be that of a plaintiff who was injured by some remedy suggested during an illness by a lay friend. Unless the friend claimed some special competence, or expressed some definite assurance, probably no liability would be imposed on him. We would say that the plaintiff was injured through his own folly in acting on the medical advice of a layman. At the time when assumpsit was developed, this notion of "plaintiff's folly" was given a broader extension than it is today, and apparently the undertaking of the defendant was first alleged merely to rebut this notion of an assumption of risk by the plaintiff.

So long as the "gist" of the plaintiff's action was not the defendant's breach of promise, the action of "case in assumpsit" was not a contractual remedy in the modern sense. It became such a remedy by a gradual development which involved: (1) a shift of emphasis from the wrongful act of the defendant to the undertaking or promise; and (2) the introduction of the notion that the defendant could be liable not only for doing something improperly, but for neglecting to do what he had promised to do. In its original form, assumpsit was allowed only where the defendant had acted unskillfully, not where he had failed to act altogether. Thus it was said that if a carpenter should undertake to build a house, he would be liable for misbuilding it, but not for failing altogether to build it. When assumpsit had developed so as to permit recovery against a defendant who had failed to do anything toward the performance of his promise, it had become a contractual action in the modern sense. This development occurred during the fifteenth century.

It may be said that the action of assumpsit eventually introduced the following reforms into the English law of contracts:

(1) It removed the last traces of early formalism from the law of contracts, by finally supplanting debt, with its attendant attributes of sum certain and wager of law.

(2) It made possible for the first time a development in the direction of a general theory of promissory liability, which could include both executory and informal contracts. In assumpsit as finally developed, it was not the fact that the defendant had made a promise in a particular *form* that led to her being bound, nor that the promise involved a particular type of *subject-matter* (quid pro quo and sum certain), but simply that defendant had *made a promise*.

(3) The action of debt had been tied to the notion of exchange or barter. The origin of assumpsit was such as to free it somewhat from the limitations of this conception. Accordingly, it was held that a defendant might be liable in assumpsit on a promise to pay for a performance received in the past, although there was no definite agreement for payment at the time the performance was received. It was also held in certain cases that the plaintiff's reliance on a promise might make the promise enforceable even though the reliance was not bargained for as the price of the defendant's promise.

(4) Finally, it was through the action of assumpsit that the executory exchange (an exchange that is incomplete on both sides) became enforceable. Toward the end of the sixteenth century it was finally held in England that a "promise against a promise will maintain an action." If two parties had agreed on the sale of a horse, and the buyer refused to accept the horse or to pay for it, the seller could now sue for "damages" measured by the profit which he expected to obtain from the bargain. He was no longer restricted to a suit for the price.

The history of exchange. The development last mentioned suggests that a portion of the history just reviewed can be recapitulated in terms of a history of the economic and legal institution of exchange. Three stages in the development of this institution may be distinguished.

The first stage is that of the instantaneous exchange, or barter, as, for example, where a skin is traded for a measure of oats and both articles are immediately handed over to their new owners. The evidence of contemporary early societies indicates that even this first stage is arrived at only with difficulty. The notion of trading one thing against another, obvious as it seems to us, is apparently an idea for which society has had to struggle. When exchange or barter first makes its appearance in early societies it is often in the guise of reciprocal gifts. A makes a present to B in the hope or expectation that B will see fit then or later to make some return gift. As this practice grows, the feeling of obligation on the part of the recipient may be increasingly fortified by social pressures until it amounts to a practical compulsion, even though no machinery of courts and officers is as yet available to "enforce" it. That the notion of exchanging one thing for another is even in the Middle Ages not yet a normal part of most men's lives is shown by the peculiar significance of fairs and markets. In the words of Lipson, "They represent in fact a phase of commerce which can best be described as periodic; where distribution and exchange take place at periodical gatherings and not in permanent centers."

As long as exchange remains instantaneous, it involves nothing corresponding to "contract" in the Anglo–American sense of the term. Each party becomes the owner of a new thing, and his rights rest not on a promise, but on property. Exchange first assumes a contractual aspect when it is left half-completed, so that an obligation on one side remains. A delivers a skin to B in return for B's promise to deliver a measure of oats at the next harvest. So soon as the law enforces B's promise, a second stage in the development of exchange as a legal institution has been reached, and the economic institution of credit has begun. It is not known when this development occurred in England, though it was certainly as early as the twelfth century, when the action of debt became available. The half-completed exchange, or what Henry has called the "delivery-promise," seems to have played a prominent role in the law of contracts of most early societies. It appears in Rome as the "real contract," and was perhaps the most ancient of the various forms of contract enforced by the Roman law.

The third and final stage in the development occurs when an executory exchange becomes enforceable. It should be noted that this development marks a corresponding development in the economic institution of credit. It was certainly no accident that it coincided in England with a period of commercial expansion, when economic activity generally had become increasingly intense. It is, in fact, not difficult to see why the development of open markets for the purchase and sale of goods should lead to a recognition of the binding effect of the executory exchange. Where trade is infrequent, and opportunities for the exchange of goods are rare, breach of an executory bargain will be resented only as the destruction of a hope or expectation, unless the disappointed party has in some way changed his position, as by preparing to perform his side of the agreement. But when the channels of trade become more numerous, the mere entry into an executory bargain involves itself a change of position in the sense that the contracting party forgoes the opportunity of covering his needs elsewhere. Suppose A needs a hundred pounds of spices, and B contracts to deliver them to him next month. If in consequence of a rise in the market, B breaks his promise, A may very well feel that he was misled by B, in the sense that but for B's promise, A would have supplied his needs from another source before the advance in prices. This particular kind of resentment against the promise-breaker can only arise where other sources of supply exist. Accordingly, there is probably a causal connection between the economic development of open markets and the legal development of the enforceable executory exchange.

The formulation of the doctrine of consideration. If the question of consideration is viewed as that of determining what promises ought to be enforced, it is apparent that the courts have been answering that question from the time they first enforced contracts. As the historical sketch just presented shows, the courts gave an increasingly broad answer to this question as time went on. There was, however, no occasion to formulate "a doctrine of consideration" until, with the development of assumpsit, a general theory of promissory liability began to emerge in English law. Prior to that time the question of consideration was answered by that body of substantive law which, as Maine says, was "concealed in the interstices of procedure." However, so soon as assumpsit began to expand in scope as an action for breach of a promise, it became apparent that the courts would sooner or later have to decide how far the development should be allowed to continue. In a case in 1424, Y.B. 3 Hen. VI, 36, pl. 33, one of the judges, in denying the suit of the plaintiff, remarked, "Truly if this action is maintained, one shall have trespass on the case for breach of any agreement in the world."

When the word "consideration" first came to be employed, there was no fixed usage concerning the word. Sometimes it was used in a very general sense as meaning, apparently, a sufficient reason or occasion for enforcing a promise. Sometimes it was used as the equivalent of the quid pro quo. When a definite requirement of consideration finally emerged as a general limitation on the enforcement of promises not under seal, its definition had become, in verbal form at least, relatively fixed. This definition treated consideration as either a detriment incurred by the promisee or a benefit received by the promisor. Still later, "consideration" came to mean bargain. Today, with the recognition that elements other than bargain, such as reliance, may make a promise enforceable, the word "consideration" has become ambiguous. Sometimes it is still used to mean bargain. Other times it is used to mean any element that makes a promise enforceable, including but not limited to the element of bargain.

———

Appendix C

INCIDENTS OF THE SEAL

Placing a promise under seal had a number of legal consequences at common law, in addition to making the promise legally enforceable. In general, it might fairly be said that at common law a sealed contract was to be taken "at face value," and its effect could not be varied by matter outside the four corners of the instrument. The object of the seal, and of the writing to which it was attached, was to provide a safe and certain memorial of the obligation, and it was thought that this object would be defeated if the terms or effect of the obligation could be varied by proof that was itself not under seal. This general attitude toward the sealed promise had the following specific consequences:

1. *Payment.* Apparently, it was originally held that even payment would not discharge a sealed contract, unless the sealed instrument was destroyed or cancelled. This rule has without question disappeared today.

2. *Fraud.* After the courts of common law had come to permit fraud to be pleaded as a defense in an action on a simple contract, fraud was still disallowed as a defense to an action on a sealed contract. This stringency of the common law was relieved by equity, which would enjoin an action at law on a sealed instrument where it was obtained by fraud. Later the common law rule was changed to permit the pleading of fraud as a defense at law even on a sealed contract, thus obviating the necessity for resort to a separate court to prevent enforcement of a sealed promise obtained by fraud.

3. *Subsequent modification by agreement not under seal.* The early view was that an unsealed modification of a sealed contract was ineffective to change the terms of the sealed contract even if the modification was an otherwise-enforceable bargain. The first relaxation of this rule occurred in the case where one would naturally expect it, that is, where after one party had changed his position in reliance on the modification, the other party attempted to hold him to the terms of the original sealed obligation. It would probably be generally held today that a sealed contract may be effectively altered by a modification not under seal and is in this respect no different from an unsealed writing. This does not mean that no problems are presented by the subsequent modification of a written contract (sealed or unsealed). The Statute of Frauds may be an issue, and the question is also complicated by the legal-duty rule and possible lingering traces of the old rules concerning executory accords.

4. *Rights and duties of a principal not designated as such in the contract.* Agent A, acting on behalf of Principal P, enters a written contract with T. A signs the contract in his own name, as if he was acting on his own behalf, rather than on P's behalf, and there is no mention in the contract of P's connection with the affair. If the contract is not under seal, P is treated as a party to the contract, and may sue or be sued on it. This is true even though T did not know that A was acting on behalf of P, that is, even though P was an "undisclosed principal."

If, on the other hand, the contract was under seal, and P was not named in the contract as a party to it, suit by or against him was excluded. Here P can only be connected with the transaction by evidence outside the sealed instrument, and the admission of such evidence was viewed as a threat to the internal integrity and self-sufficiency of the sealed instrument. As late as 1925, the New York Court of Appeals applied this rule to disallow a suit against an undisclosed principal where the contract was under seal. Crowley v. Lewis, 239 N.Y. 264, 146 N.E. 374. Although the court recognized that many of the old incidents of the seal had disappeared, it did not feel free to dispense with this one, particularly in view of the fact that "thousands of sealed instruments" had been executed in reliance on the rule, and "many times the seal must have been used for the express purpose of relieving the undisclosed principal from personal liability." The New York rule has now been changed by statute. McKinney's N.Y.Gen.Constr.Law § 44–a, which provides that except as otherwise expressly provided by statute, the presence of a seal on a written instrument shall have no legal effect. However, the status of the rule concerning a principal who is not described as such in a sealed instrument may remain in doubt in some other jurisdictions.

———

Appendix D

HISTORY OF THE ASSIGNABILITY
OF CHOSES IN ACTION

---

(1) *The original common-law rule.* The rule with which the English legal history of assignments starts is a simple one: the assignment of a claim or "chose in action" is legally impossible. If D owed C £10, and C executed a grant of this claim to A, the courts early held that literally nothing happened to the claim by virtue of the attempted assignment. D still owed C, not A, and A gained no rights against D by the assignment. The subsequent history of the matter—which is traced briefly below—is primarily a story of the devious manner in which the common-law courts themselves first undermined and finally abandoned this rule.

Various reasons have been assigned for the early refusal of the courts to recognize a transaction that today seems so innocent and useful. In a precommercial society it was natural that a dubious attitude should be taken toward the assignment of contract claims. Where contract claims are themselves rarities, an assignment would be a double rarity—an unusual and deviational kind of transaction, immediately subject to suspicion. Perhaps too it was thought that an assignment cast doubt on the assigned claim: if the claim was legitimate, why did not the assignor bring suit on the claim? And perhaps the courts suspected the assignee of stirring up litigation ("maintenance") and purchasing a lawsuit on speculation. However we may attempt to explain and justify the courts' early attitude toward assignment, clearly this attitude stemmed from a feeling that the transaction was unusual and out of the ordinary course of human dealings.

(2) *The development of the concept that an assignment creates a power of attorney.* With the gradual expansion of commerce and credit, the need for some means of transferring contract claims increased. In its first response to this need, English law paralleled in a striking manner a development that had previously taken place in Roman law. Where C attempted to assign a claim to A, the courts came in time to hold that the transaction, though invalid as an assignment, had the effect of creating in A a power of attorney to sue *in C's name.* Indeed, in the older standard forms for assignments the language used was that of appointing the intended assignee as an agent or attorney, rather than that of transferring a right. However, even if the assignment took the form of a transfer of the claim, the courts held that it only created a power of attorney in the intended assignee.

Apparently, the conception of the assignment as creating a power of attorney was well established by the seventeenth century. The objection of maintenance persisted for a longer period, however, and resulted in a curious distinction. It was held that an assignment creating a power of attorney could be made for the payment of an *existing debt* to the assignee, but that a claim could not be sold "for a consideration then given by way of contract." Harvey v. Bateman, Noy, 52 c. 1600. Where the assignor was assigning a claim as a way of paying his own debt to the assignee, there was an understandable motive for the transaction, which dissipated the suspicions it might otherwise have aroused. The sale of a claim, however, remained objectionable, and was not finally permitted, even under the guise of creating a power of attorney, until the latter part of the seventeenth century.

In many situations, an intended assignee of a claim who secured a power of attorney to sue in the name of his assignor was quite content with the treatment he received at the hands of the common law. If he got what he wanted—a right to sue and collect from the debtor—he was not particularly interested in the words his lawyer needed to use to achieve that result. In three situations, however, the protection given by the common-law courts to the intended assignee was radically defective. When the assignee was considered only an agent, with a power of attorney to collect the assigned claim as an agent on behalf of the assignor/principal, then the rules of agency and bankruptcy law applied to assignments, with highly undesirable results. In particular: (1) Under a rule of agency law, the death of the principal terminates the agent's power to act on the principal's behalf. Applying this rule in the assignment context, if the assignor died before the assignee collected the assigned claim, the assignee's power of attorney—and therefore his right to the assignment—automatically terminated. (2) Under another rule of agency law, a principal can terminate an agent's authority at any time. Applying this rule in the assignment context, if the assignor, being still alive, repudiated the assignment, this would operate as a revocation of the assignee's agency, and would therefore destroy his right to recover against the debtor in the name of the assignor. (3) If the assignee was merely considered an agent, then ownership or "property" in the assigned claim remained in the assignor/principal even after the assignment. Under the law of bankruptcy, therefore, if the assignor became bankrupt before the assignee collected on the assigned claim, the assignor's creditors could treat the assigned debt as an asset of the assignor's estate.

These limitations on the rights of the assignee made it clear that the courts took seriously their own statements that an assignment created only a power of attorney. They applied to the assignment the rules which would be appropriate to a real relationship of principal and agent. This attitude persisted in the common-law courts through most of the eighteenth century.

Meanwhile the pressure on the common-law courts for a more adequate protection of the assignee's interest was mounting from three directions. First, the continued expansion of trade and credit created an increasingly urgent economic demand for such protection. Second, the courts of chancery (the equity courts) began granting assignees the protection they needed—for example, protection against "after-bankruptcy" attacks on the assignment by the assignor's creditors. This introduced an element of intercurial competition, forcing the common-law courts to overcome their technical scruples or lose judicial business if they did not. Third, the common-law rule of nonassignability was made to seem increasingly anachronistic by the fact that the common-law courts took over the law of negotiable instruments from the law merchant. That law recognized the free transferability of claims in the form of "credit paper."

The last two points require expansion, and are discussed in the next two sections.

(3) *Protection of the assignee's rights in equity.* The relief that the assignee could obtain in the common-law courts was, as we have seen, subject to defeat if the assignor died, revoked, or became bankrupt. Because of this defect in the legal remedy, it became common during the seventeenth century for assignees to make application to equity where their rights at law were insufficient. The courts of chancery granted the assignee a broad protection, treating him as owner of the claim, not as a mere agent to act in the name of the assignor. In equity, accordingly, the assignee was secure against the death, revocation, or bankruptcy of the assignor. There is reason to think that the volume of these applications to the equity courts was considerable. Suits by assignees of claims became a regular and significant heading of equity jurisdiction, and so remained until the common-law courts, responding to the pressures described above, finally came to rule that it was legally possible to transfer a claim from one person to another.

(4) *The reception into the common law of the law merchant concerning credit paper.* During the feudal period, the status of merchant placed one in a special legal position, involving a particular relationship to one's king and to one's fellows. Generally speaking, controversies between merchants were not submitted to the ordinary courts, but to special courts which resembled in many ways the arbitration boards set up today by trade associations. Some of these courts were permanently located in large commercial centers; others were temporary and attached to seasonal fairs. They had jurisdiction over such matters as insurance, contracts of sale, bills of exchange, and the like. The law they applied was largely international in character, and represented the customs and interests of the international community of merchants and traders.

These courts early recognized the free transferability of "credit paper"—instruments corresponding to modern notes and bills of exchange. Although common-law courts at first resisted the adoption of these merchants' rules, by 1704 the essentials of the modern law of negotiable instruments (including the free transferability of both bills and notes) had gone over into the law administered by the ordinary courts. Once this development occurred, it became increasingly difficult to maintain that there was something legally impossible and inconceivable about the transfer of other money claims. Accordingly, the time was ripe for a final abandonment of the common-law rule, though the final plunge was not taken for about eighty years.

(5) *The common law takes over the equity rule.* In 1787 the assignee of a non-negotiable chose brought a suit in the King's Bench in the name of this assignor, who had become bankrupt after the assignment, and before the suit. Winch v. Keeley, 1 Term R. 619. The debtor contended that he was liable to the assignor's trustees in bankruptcy, and argued "that this debt, being a chose in action could not be assigned.... Bills of exchange are assignable by the law of merchants; but promissory notes can only be assigned under the [statute] 3 & 4 Ann. c. 9, which shows that at common law they could not."

As a matter of precedent this argument was unimpeachable. However, the court held for the assignee. The manner in which the court supported its conclusion deserves attention, as illustrating the lawyer's skill in pouring new wine into old bottles. The court declared that it had "been found productive of great expense to send the parties to the other side of the Hall," that is, to the equity courts. Thus, new wine was needed. At the same time, the court had to concede that it is "certainly true that a chose in action cannot strictly be assigned." The wine must, in other words, go into old bottles. The problem then was to find a way of permitting the assignment of a claim without infringing the rule that such an assignment is impossible. This was done by saying that the common-law courts can "take notice of an equity," that is, can take notice of, and give effect to, the rights that the assignee would have in equity, and thus avoid sending him "to the other side of the Hall." The assignee still *sued* at law as attorney or agent for the assignor, but the law now gave the assignee the same rights that he would have in equity, and equity treated an assignee as the owner of the claim, not as merely an agent of the assignor. It was as if a court were to say, "X is not the owner of Blackacre, but we will give him all the rights an owner has."

When this view was established, the reality of the view that the assignee obtained only a "power of attorney" had disappeared, and in its place only a form or legal fiction remained. The assignee was now secure against the revocation, death, or bankruptcy of the assignor. Although suit was still brought in the name of the assignor, the assignor had become a purely nominal party to the action, without any power to control or direct it.

(6) *The real-party-in-interest statutes.* The English learning concerning the assignment of claims was imported into the United States as a part of the common law. Accordingly, the early American courts generally applied the rule that the assignment of a claim created only a power of attorney. However, they also followed the English development (marked by *Winch v. Keeley,* discussed in the last section) by which the assignee's "power of attorney" had become a mere form, without any real influence on the determination of his rights.

There was left, fossilized in the law of procedure, the now meaningless requirement that the assignee must sue in the name of the assignor. This final vestige of the old rule was eliminated by statutes, which in most states took the form of a legislative declaration that henceforth all suits must be brought "in the name of the real party in interest."

(7) *The aftermath of this history.* A general acquaintance with the history traced above is essential to an understanding of the older cases and of modern statutes. A more debatable question is whether it has any further relevance to the decision of cases arising today. One view is that we should put this history behind us, and say that today the assignee of a claim becomes its owner, just as a person becomes the owner of a bicycle when it is transferred to him. By calling the assignee the new owner of the claim, we would not imply that his ownership was absolute and indefeasible under all circumstances. Ownership is never that. Nor would we mean that the legal incidents or qualities of ownership of an assigned claim are precisely like those of the owner of a bicycle, a piece of land, or a negotiable instrument. The qualifications on the ownership of an assigned claim would be matters to be worked out in the light of the needs of commerce and credit and the demands of this particular kind

of human relationship. Under this view, it would neither be necessary or helpful to begin the inquiry with a definition of the "nature" of an assignee's ownership.

Opposed to this view is that sponsored by Professor Williston, who believed that it is convenient and advisable to say that the assignee's rights, although now fully protected in courts of law, remain essentially "equitable" in nature. By this is meant that these rights more nearly resemble those which courts of equity have historically protected than those which were protected by courts of law. For example, if a debtor, in ignorance of an assignment of a claim against her, and without reason to be put on his guard, pays the original creditor, the debtor is discharged from liability to the assignee. Restatement Second § 170(1). Accordingly, an assignee's "ownership" of a claim is subject to being cut off by the debtor's payment in good faith to the assignor. In this respect, ownership of an assigned claim resembles an equitable interest in property, which can be cut off where the legal title is sold to a bona fide purchaser. Generally speaking, an "equitable interest" is a more destructible kind of property than a "legal interest."

For those thoroughly familiar with the history of the matter, there may be a certain utility in the comparison implied in saying that the assignee's rights are "equitable in nature." Against this utility must be weighed a danger: this method of speaking about the matter may imply that the assignee's rights are to be deduced from the "essential nature" of the legal relation between the assignor and the assignee, instead of being worked out to correspond to the practical needs of the situation. Furthermore, the distinction between interests that are "equitable" in nature and those that are "legal" in nature becomes every day more difficult to maintain. For example, today in most states law and equity are administered by the same courts. Similarly, where property interests are subject to a recording statute, a recorded equitable interest is secure against a bona fide purchaser, while an unrecorded legal interest is subject to being cut off in favor of such a purchaser. Generally the lines of division which formerly separated one body of law (the common law) from another (equity) are becoming increasingly blurred, so that the wisdom of preserving a sharp distinction between "legal" and "equitable" interests is doubtful, particularly since, in this case, the "equitable" interest in question has been protected by courts of law for more than a century and a half.

So far as the modern case law is concerned, courts have not generally considered that deciding problems concerning assignment necessitates a preliminary inquiry as to the "essential nature" of the assignee's rights. Nor does the Restatement of Contracts take any position with respect to this question, but contents itself with a specific enumeration and definition of the rights of the parties in recurring situations of conflict in this area.

———

*

Index

References are to Pages

ACCEPTANCE
Generally, 461–503
Act, acceptance by, 462–471
Automated transactions, 502
Conduct, acceptance by, 475–478, 642
Crossed revocation and acceptance, 456–457
Death of offeror before acceptance, 436–438
Delay or failure of transmission, 457
Electronic agent, acceptance by, 501–503
Electronic commerce, 459–460
Incapacity of offeror before acceptance, 436–438
Late acceptance, effect of failing to notify offeree, 488–490
Modes of acceptance, 461–503
    Act, acceptance by, 462–471
    Conduct, acceptance by, 475–478
    Electronic agent, acceptance by, 501–503
    Late acceptance, effect of failing to notify offeree, 488–490
    Silence as acceptance, 490–501
    Subcontractor's bid, effect of using, 478–488
    Subjective acceptance, 471–747
    Wrong mode, consequences of utilizing, 461–462
Negative option plans, 500
Offer and Revocation, this index
Revocation of acceptance, 924–925
Silence as acceptance, 490–501
Subcontractor's bid, effect of using, 478–488
Subjective acceptance, 471–747
UCC, what constitutes acceptance under, 643–644
Unjust enrichment, 500
Variance between offer and acceptance, 435–436
When effective, 456–457
Written acceptance, what constitutes receipt, 441–442
Wrong mode of acceptance, consequences of utilizing, 461–462

ACCOUNTS RECEIVABLE
Assignment of, 874–877

ADMINISTRATORS
Promises made by, statute of frauds, 1051–1052

AGENTS
Principal bound by signature of agent, 1055–1056

ANTICIPATORY BREACH
Generally, 997–1016
Breach and Response, this index

APPORTIONMENT
Equitable apportionment of losses following impossibility, 785–786

ASSENT
Generally, 367–637
Acceptance, this index
Good faith, duty to bargain in, 536–583
Implied-in-Law and Implied-in-Fact Contracts, this index
Indefiniteness, 536–583
Interpretation of Contracts, this index
Parol Evidence Rule, this index
Preliminary negotiations, 536–583

ASSIGNMENT AND NEGOTIATION
Generally, 853–884
Choses in action, history of assignability, 1087–1091
Closely-connected loans, 881–884
Commercial context, defenses of obligor against assignee, 878–879
Consumer context, defenses, 879–884
Defenses
    Commercial context, 878–879
    Consumer context, 879–884
Duties, delegability, 860–874
Economic significance of assignment of claims, 853–854
Equity, protection of assignee's rights in, 1089
Factoring, 874
Financing through assignment of claims, 874–877
Formalities necessary to make effective assignment, 858–859
Gratuitous assignments, 858–859
Holder in due course doctrine, 881–884
Loans, closely-connected, 881–884
Negotiable and non-negotiable claims, distinction between, 879–884
Non-notification assignment, 874–875
Performance from assignee, obligee's right to demand, 873–874
Power of attorney, creation by assignment, 1087–1091
Priority between competing assignees of same claim, 876–877
Real party in interest statutes, 1090
Restatement, 866, 870
Rights, assignability, 860–874

ASSIGNMENT AND NEGOTIATION—Cont'd
Uniform Commercial Code, 875–877
Value, assignments for, 859

ASSUMPSIT
Historical background, 508–509, 1077 et seq.

AT–WILL EMPLOYMENT
Generally, 530–531

AUCTIONS
Note on, 423–424

AUTOMATED TRANSACTIONS
Generally, 502

BARGAIN
Consideration, bargain theory, 9
Executory accord, legal effect, 135–138
Good faith, duty to bargain in, 536–583
Half-completed bargains, 1078
Legal duty, performance of, 107–150
Modification of contractual duties, 107–150
Mutuality, this index
Offer and Revocation, this index
Price gouging, 60–62
Principle of bargain
    Generally, 47–63
    Limits of principle, 58–60
Reliance damages in bargain context, 341–348
Statute of frauds and right to value of bargain,
    1064–1067
Substituted contract, 136–137
Theory, 9
Transacting at a distance, 456–460
Unconscionability, this index
Value of bargain and statute of frauds,
    1064–1067
Waiver of contractual duties, 107–150

BILATERAL CONTRACTS
Mutuality, 87–88

BINARY/MULTIFACETED SPECTRUM
Contract law rules, 85–86

BREACH AND RESPONSE
Generally, 975–996
Ability to perform
    Generally, 979–982
Anticipatory breach
    Generally, 997–1016
    Measure of damages, 1015–1016
    Remedies for breach in which all duties on
        one side have been performed,
        1007–1008
    Repudiation of contracts, 1002
Divisible contracts, 987
Failure of performance by once party as excuse
    for nonperformance by the other,
    982–996
Material breach
    Generally, 982–996
    Cure, concept of, 994–995
    Substantial performance doctrine, relation-
        ship to, 992–993
Mutual dependency of performances
    Introductory note, 975–977
Order of performance
    Generally, 977–979

BREACH AND RESPONSE—Cont'd
Order of performance—Cont'd
    Concurrent conditions, 978–979
    Introductory note, 975–977
    Restatement, 977–978
Remedies for Breach of Contract, this index
Repudiation of contracts, 1002

CAUSATION
Damages and causation, 290–291

CERTAINTY
Damages, 292–302

CHANNELING FUNCTION
Contract law rules, 14

CHILD SUPPORT
Who is a parent, 182–185

CHOSES IN ACTION
History of assignability, 1087–1091

CIRCUMSTANCES
Unexpected Circumstances, this index

CLASSICAL CONTRACT LAW
Mirror image rule, 435–436, 642
Note on, 83–86
Offer and acceptance, 536
Unilateral contract, offer for, 446

COMMERCIAL CONTRACTS
Reliance, 46
Uniform Commercial Code, this index

COMMODITIES
Requirements and output contracts, 103–104

COMMON LAW
History of contract, 1077–1084

COMPENSATION
Expectation and reliance conceptions, 36,
    200–203

CONDITIONS
    Generally, 89–90, 934–974
Concurrent conditions, 978–979
Conditions precedent and conditions subse-
    quent, distinction between, 942–945
Cooperation conditions, 950–954
Donative promises, conditional, 12–13
Excuse, 965–974
Form contracts, expressly made conditional
    clause, 655–656
Implication of promise from express condition,
    950–951
Implied conditions of notice, 954
Interpretation problems in distinguishing be-
    tween conditions and promises, 945–949
Notice, implied conditions, 954
Operation of promise and operation of condi-
    tion, difference between, 935–941
Payment, conditions of, 962–965
Prevention, 950–954
Promises and conditions, difference between
    Generally, 934–935
    Implication of promise from express condi-
        tion, 950–951
    Interpretation problems in distinguishing
        between, 945–949

CONDITIONS—Cont'd
Satisfaction, conditions of, 954–961

CONDUCT
Acceptance by, 475–478, 642

CONSIDERATION
    Generally, 5–187
Bargain, this index
Beneficial reliance, 11
Channeling function of contract law rules, 14
Civil law analogues, 589–590
Commercial contracts, reliance, 46
Compensation, expectation and reliance con-
    ceptions, 36
Concept of, 8–9
Conditional donative promises, 12–13
Donative promises, simple, 6–13
Estoppel in pais, 25–28
Exceptions to general principle, 88
Expectation interest, injury to, 35–36
Form, element of
    Generally, 13–23
    Seals, below
Formulation of doctrine, 1084
Gifts, 9–10
Illusory promises, 95–98
Injury to reliance and expectation interests,
    35–36
Lack of consideration
    Sealed instruments, 19–20
Limits of contract, 163–187
Nominal consideration, 17–18, 22
Options, effect on consideration, 95
Past consideration, 151–162
Performance of legal duty, 107–150
Presumption of consideration
    Seal, 19
    Written instrument, 21
Promissory estoppel, 26–28
Reliance
    Generally, 23–46
    Beneficial reliance, 11
    Commercial contracts, 46
    Damages, 36
    Estoppel in pais, 25–28
    Injury to reliance interest, 35–36
    Opportunity costs, 37
    Out-of-pocket costs, 37
    Promissory estoppel, 26–28
Remedies and consideration, 35–39
Seals, this index
Unenforceable obligation, when promise to dis-
    charge is binding, 151–152
Written instrument, statutory provisions,
    21–22

COOPERATION
Conditions of cooperation, 950–954

COSTS
Opportunity costs, reimbursement, 37
Out-of-pocket costs, reimbursement, 37

COURSE OF DEALING
Role of, interpretation of contracts, 405–412

COVENANT
Action of covenant, 1078–1081

CROPS
Contracts to sell, 801

CURE
Material breach, 994–995
Substantial Performance, this index

DAMAGES
Anticipatory breach, measure of damages,
    1015–1016
Causation, note on, 290–291
Certainty, 292–302
Donative promise, breach of, 37–39
Employment contracts, 266–279
Expectation Measure, this index
Foreseeability, 279–292
Introduction to contract damages, 190–216
Limitations on contract damages, 290
Liquidated damages, 308–323
Mental distress, 302–306
Mitigation, 266–279
Profession, damages for loss of opportunity to
    practice, 277–279
Punitive damages, 215–216
Reliance damages
    Generally, 200–203
    Bargain context, 341–348
    Expectation as cap on reliance damages,
      354–355
    Note on, 354
Remedies, this index
Restitution Measure of Damages, this index
Sale of Goods, this index
Services Contracts, this index

DEALING
Course of dealing, interpretation of contracts,
    405–412, 626–637

DEATH
Offeror, death before acceptance, 436–438

DEBT
Action of debt, 1078–1081

DELEGATION OF DUTIES
Generally, 860–874

DISCLAIMERS
Employee handbooks, 533–534

DISCLOSURE
Requirement of, 733–764

DIVISIBLE CONTRACTS
Generally, 987

DONATIVE PROMISES
    Generally, 6–13
Consideration, this index

DUTIES
Delegability, 860–874

EFFICIENT BREACH
Theory of, 209–214

ELECTRONIC AGENT
Acceptance by, 501–503

ELECTRONIC COMMERCE
Offer and acceptance, 459–460

ELECTRONIC CONTRACTING
Statute of frauds, 1057–1060

ELECTRONIC DATA INTERCHARGE (EDI)
Generally, 501

EMPLOYEE HANDBOOKS
Disclaimers, effect of, 533–534
Modification, 531–533

EMPLOYMENT CONTRACTS
Generally, 266–279
At-will employment, 530–531
Opportunity to practice profession, loss of, 277–279
Reputation damages, 276–277
Specific performance, 338–340

E–SIGN
Generally, 1059–1060

ESTOPPEL IN PAIS
Generally, 25–28
Promissory Estoppel, this index

EUROPEAN CONTRACT LAW, PRINCIPLES OF
Generally, 56

EVIDENCE
Parol Evidence Rule, this index

EXCUSE
Express conditions, 965–974
Failure of performance by once party as excuse for nonperformance by the other, 982–996
Restatement of Contracts, 970 et seq.

EXECUTORS AND ADMINISTRATORS
Promises made by, statute of frauds, 1051–1052

EXECUTORY ACCORD
Legal effect, 135–138

EXPECTATION INTEREST
Injury to, 35–36

EXPECTATION MEASURE OF DAMAGES
Generally, 217–324
Certainty, 292–302
Employment contracts, 266–279
Foreseeability, 279–292
Liquidated damages, 308–323
Mental distress, 302–306
Mitigation, 266–279
New business rule, 296–297
Reliance damages, expectation as cap on, 354–355
Sale of Goods, this index
Services Contracts, this index

EXPRESS CONDITIONS
Conditions, this index

FACTORING
Generally, 874

FINANCING
Assignment of claims, financing through, 874–877

FORESEEABILITY
Expectation measure of damages, 279–292

FORM CONTRACTS
Generally, 639–712
Acceptance under UCC, what constitutes, 643–644
Battle of the forms, 641–664
Conditional assent provision, 655–656
Confirmation with additional terms, effect of, 656–657
Expressly made conditional clause, 655–656
Formation in form contract setting
Generally, 641–691
Basic issues, 641–664
Rolling contracts, 664–691
Interpretation, 692–712
Knockout rule, 653
Materially alter, meaning of, 653–655
Mirror image rule, 642
Parol evidence rule, 594–595
Purchase order, 641
Rolling contracts, 664–691
Sales order, 641
Unconscionability, 692–712
Uniform Commercial Code
Acceptance, what constitutes, 643–644
Confirmation with additional terms, effect of, 656–657
Expressly made conditional clause, 655–656
Materially alter, meaning of, 653–655

FORMALITIES
Effective assignment, necessary formalities, 858–859
Statute of frauds, 1044

FORMATION
Acceptance, this index
Form Contracts, this index
Offer and Revocation, this index

FRAUD
Parol evidence rule, fraud exception, 604–606
Seal, incidents of, 1085

GAP FILLERS
Sale of goods, 545

GIFTS
Manner of making gift, 9–10
Promise to make gift, 9

GOOD FAITH
Bargaining in good faith, duty, 536–583
Forgone opportunity analysis, 893
Perfect tender rule, 925
Performing in good faith, obligation
Generally, 886–914
Forgone opportunity analysis, 893
Restatement, 891–892
UCC, 890–892

GOODS
Sale of Goods, this index

GRATUITIES
Unlawful, giving or receiving, 109–110

HERMENEUTICS
Legal and political hermeneutics, 405

HISTORICAL BACKGROUND
Assumpsit, 508–509, 1081
Classical and modern contract law, note on, 83–86
Common law, history of contract, 1077–1084
Consideration, formulation of doctrine, 1084
Exchange, history of, 1082–1084
Law merchant and credit paper, 1089
Specific performance, 324–325

HOLDER IN DUE COURSE DOCTRINE
Generally, 881–884

HOTEL RESERVATION
Offer and acceptance, 424

HUSBAND AND WIFE
Contracts upon consideration of marriage, statute of frauds, 1052, 1065

ILLUSORY PROMISES
Generally, 95–98

IMPLIED–IN–LAW AND IMPLIED–IN–FACT CONTRACTS
Generally, 504–535
Distinction between, 508–510
Terminology, 508

IMPOSSIBILITY
Unexpected Circumstances, this index

INALIENABILITY
Market inalienability, 186–187

INCAPACITY
Offeror, incapacity before acceptance, 436–438

INDEFINITENESS
Generally, 536–583

INJURY
What constitutes, 35–36

INSTALLMENT CONTRACTS
Substantial performance, 925
Unconscionability, protection of buyer of goods, 68–69

INTEGRATION CLAUSES
Parol evidence rule, 602

INTENTION
Test of legal consequences, 396

INTERPRETATION OF CONTRACTS
Generally, 368–412
Dealing, course of, 405–412, 626–637
Form contracts, 692–712
Hermeneutics, legal and political, 405
Intention as test of legal consequences, 396
Language and the law, 397–398
Offer, interpretation of, 457
Parol evidence rule
Generally, 584–637
Parol Evidence Rule, this index
Performance, course of, 405–412, 626–637
Plain meaning rule and parol evidence, 637
Promises and conditions, interpretation problems in distinguishing between, 945–949
Purposive language, problems of interpreting, 397–405

INTERPRETATION OF CONTRACTS—Cont'd
Restatement, 369–370, 409–410
Subjective and objective elements
Generally, 368–396
Intention as test of legal consequences, 396
Introductory note, 368–369
Trade usage, role of
Generally, 405–412
Written contract, as part of, 626–637
Written contracts, interpretation of, 608–626

JUSTICE
Theory of justice, 1–2

KNOCKOUT RULE
Conflicting terms in form contracts, 653

LAND SALES
Statute of Frauds, this index

LANDLORD AND TENANT
Implied conditions of notice, 954

LEGAL DUTY
Note on legal duty rule, 116–117, 123–125
Performance as consideration, 107–150

LIMITS OF CONTRACT
Generally, 163–187

LIQUIDATED DAMAGES
Generally, 308–323
Provisions limiting damages, note on, 322–323
Special judicial scrutiny, 318

LOANS
Closely-connected loans, 881–884

LOW–INCOME MARKET RETAILERS
Unconscionable practices, 69–70

MAILBOX RULE
When acceptance effective, 456–460

MARRIAGE
Contracts upon consideration of, statute of frauds, 1052, 1065

MATERIAL ALTERATION
Meaning of, 653–655

MEASURE OF DAMAGES
Expectation Measure of Damages, this index
Restitution Measure of Damages, this index

MENTAL DISTRESS
Damages, 302–306

MERGER CLAUSES
Parol evidence rule, 602
Promissory fraud, 605

MINING LANDS RECLAMATION ACT
Generally, 228

MIRROR IMAGE RULE
Generally, 435–436
Form contracts, 642

MISTAKE
Generally, 714–764
Factual assumption, mistaken, 732
Mechanical errors, 715–728
Mutual mistakes, 732–749

MISTAKE—Cont'd
Nondisclosure, 733–764
Reformation, 728–732
Restatement, 762–763
Shared mistaken assumptions, 732–749
Tacit assumptions, 733, 768–769
Transcription, mistakes in, 728–732
Unilateral mistakes, 715–728

MITIGATION OF DAMAGES
Generally, 266–279
Substantial performance, 918–919

MODERN CONTRACT LAW
Note on, 83–86

MODIFICATION
Contractual duties, 107–150
Oral modification
Generally, 1070–1072
No oral modification clauses, 607–608
Subsequent modification by agreement not under seal, 1085

MUTUAL MISTAKES
Generally, 732–749

MUTUALITY
Generally, 86–106
Exceptions, 87–88
Illusory promises, 95–98
Output contracts, 103–104
Requirements contracts, 103–104
Specific performance, 88

NEGATIVE OPTION PLANS
Acceptance, 500

NEGOTIATION
Assignment and Negotiation, this index
Preliminary negotiations, 536–583

NEW BUSINESS RULE
Certainty of damages, 296–297

NONDISCLOSURE
Generally, 733–764

NON–NOTIFICATION ASSIGNMENT
Generally, 874–875

NORMATIVELY BEST RULE
Generally, 84

NOTICE
Implied conditions of notice, 954

OBJECTIVITY/SUBJECTIVITY SPECTRUM
Contract law rules, 85

OFFER AND REVOCATION
Generally, 413–455
Acceptance, this index
Auctions, note on, 423–424
Counter-offers, 424–438
Crossed revocation and acceptance, 456–457
Date on which contractual liability arises, 457
Death of offeror before acceptance, 436–438
Delay or failure of transmission, 457
Electronic commerce, 459–460
Hotel reservation, 424

OFFER AND REVOCATION—Cont'd
Incapacity of offeror before acceptance, 436–438
Interpretation of offer, 457
Lapse of offer, 424–438
Mailbox rule, 456–460
Mirror image rule, 435–436
Offer, what constitutes
Generally, 413–424
Auctions, note on, 423–424
Record, note on concept of, 460
Rejection of offer
Generally, 424–438
Expressions by offeree, effect of, 429
Restatement of contracts, 434
Revocation
Generally, 438–455
Crossed revocation and acceptance, 456–457
Unilateral contract, offer for, 446–448
Transacting at a distance, 456–460
Unilateral contracts, offers for, 446–448
Variance between offer and acceptance, 435–436
Written acceptance, what constitutes receipt, 441–442

OPPORTUNITY COSTS
Reimbursement, 37

OPTIONS
Effect on consideration, 95
Negative option plans, 500

ORAL CONTRACTS
Part performance of, or reliance on, oral contract within statute of frauds, 1060

ORAL MODIFICATIONS
Generally, 1070–1072

ORAL RESCISSION
Generally, 1069–1070

ORGAN PURCHASES
Statutory prohibition, 185

OUT–OF–POCKET COSTS
Reimbursement, 37

OUTPUT CONTRACTS
Generally, 103–104

PARENT AND CHILD
Who is a parent, 182–185

PAROL EVIDENCE RULE
Generally, 584–608
Condition-to-legal effectiveness exception, 606–607
Course of performance and course of dealing as part of written contract, 626–637
Fraud exception, 604–606
Merger or integration clauses, 602
Plain meaning rule, 637
Restatement, 592–594
Standardized agreements, 594–595
Statute of frauds, interaction with, 1072–1073
Trade usage as part of written contract, 626–637
Written contracts, interpretation of, 608–626

PAYMENT
Conditions of payment, 962–965
Pay-when-paid provisions, 965
Seal, incidents of, 1085

PERFECT TENDER RULE
Generally, 924–926

PERFORMANCE
Ability to perform, 979–982
    Generally, 979–982
  Prospective inability, 1016–1029
Adequate assurance of performance, 1016–1029
Affirmative recovery under UCC § 2–609, 1029
Breach and Response, this index
Course of performance, interpretation of contracts, 405–412, 626–637
Divisible contracts, 987
Express Conditions, this index
Failure of performance by once party as excuse for nonperformance by the other, 982–996
Good Faith, this index
Legal duty, performance as consideration, 107–150
Order of performance
    Generally, 977–979
  Breach and Response, this index
Part performance of oral contract within statute of frauds, 1060, 1064–1067
Prospective inability to perform, 1016–1029
Substantial Performance, this index

PLAIN MEANING RULE
Parol evidence, 637

PLEADING
Statute of frauds, 1074

POWER OF ATTORNEY
Creation by assignment, 1087–1089

PRELIMINARY NEGOTIATIONS
Generally, 536–583

PRESUMPTIONS
Consideration, this index

PREVENTION
Express conditions, 950–954

PRICE GOUGING
Statutory provisions, 60–62

PRINCIPALS
Signature of agent, binding effect, 1055–1056
Undisclosed principal, 1086

PRIORITIES
Competing assignees of same claim, priority between, 876–877

PROFESSION
Damages for loss of opportunity to practice, 277–279

PROMISSORY ESTOPPEL
    Generally, 26–28
Traditional contract doctrine and, 580–581

PROMISSORY FRAUD
Parol evidence rule, 604–606

PUNITIVE DAMAGES
Generally, 215–216

PURCHASE ORDERS
Form contracts, 641
Statute of frauds, 1057

QUASI–CONTRACT
Defined, 507

REAL PROPERTY
Specific performance, contracts for sale of land, 338–340
Statute of Frauds, this index

REASONING
Nature of contract law reasoning, 83–84

RECORDS
Electronic records, 460

REFORMATION
Mistakes in transcription, 728–732
Statute of frauds, interaction with, 1073–1074

REIMBURSEMENT
Opportunity costs, 37
Reliance on oral contract, 1061–1063

RELIANCE
Consideration, this index
Damages, this index
Statute of Frauds, this index

REMEDIES FOR BREACH OF CONTRACT
    Generally, 189–365
Consideration, contract remedies and, 35–39, 54–55
Damages, this index
Efficient breach, theory of, 209–214
Specific Performance, this index
When all duties on one side have been performed, 1007–1008

REPUDIATION OF CONTRACTS
Generally, 1002

REPUTATION
Injury to, 276–277

REQUIREMENTS CONTRACTS
Generally, 103–104

RESCISSION
Oral rescission, 1069–1070

RESERVE RULES
Auctions, 423–424

RESTATEMENT OF CONTRACTS
Assignment and negotiation, 866, 870
Background and history, 7–8
Conditions of satisfaction, 961
Excuse, 970 et seq.
Good faith performance, 891–892
Illusory promises, 96–98
Interpretation of contracts
    Generally, 369–370, 409–410
Legal duty rule, note on, 116–117, 123–125

RESTATEMENT OF CONTRACTS—Cont'd

Measure of damages, breach of donative promise, 38–39

Mistake, 762–763

No oral modification clauses, 607–608

Nominal consideration, 18

Offer and revocation, 434

Order of performance, 977–978

Parol evidence rule, 592–594, 606–607

Punitive damages, 215–216

Reimbursement for reliance on oral contract, 1062–1063

Services contract, breach by person who contracted to have services performed, 239–240

Signed writing, what constitutes, 1053

Third person, contractual duty to, 127

Third-party beneficiaries, 814, 823

Unexpected circumstances, 779

Unilateral contracts, 447–448, 455

RESTATEMENT OF DAMAGES

Restitutionary damages for breach of contract, 350

RESTITUTION MEASURE OF DAMAGES

Generally, 348–365

Benefits conferred under oral agreement, 1060–1061

Breach of contract, 348–355

Defined, 507

Note on restitutionary damages, 354

Plaintiff in default, restitution in favor of, 355–365

REVOCATION

Offer and Revocation, this index

ROLLING CONTRACTS

Generally, 664–691

SALE OF GOODS

Damages for breach of contract
    Generally, 241–266
    Buyer, breach by, 253–266
    Market price damages, availability to buyer who has covered, 247
    Seller, breach by, 241–253

Form Contracts, this index

Gap fillers, 545

Installment contracts, 925

Market price damages, availability to buyer who has covered, 247

Modification of contract, 608

Perfect tender rule and UCC, 924–926

Revocation of acceptance, 924–925

Specific performance, traditional rule, 334–335

Statute of frauds
    Generally, 1039–1043
    Oral rescission, 1069–1070
    Value of bargain, right to, 1056–1057

Substantial performance, 923–933

UCC
    Damages for breach of contract, 241–242
    Statute of frauds, 1056–1057
    Substantial performance, 924–926

SATISFACTION

Conditions of satisfaction, 954–961

SEALS

Generally, 18–22

Abolishing distinction between sealed and unsealed instruments, 20–21

Historical background, 19

Incidents of, 1085–1086

Presumption of consideration, 19

Statutory provisions, 19–20

SECURED TRANSACTIONS

Assignments and UCC Article 9, 875–877

Perfection of security interest, 877

SERVICES CONTRACTS

Damages for breach
    Generally, 217–241
    Breach by person who contracted to have services performed, 236–241
    Breach by person who contracted to perform services, 217–236

SIGNATURES

Agent's signature, 1055–1056

E-Sign, 1059–1060

SILENCE

As acceptance, 490–501

SPECIFIC PERFORMANCE

Generally, 324–340

Employment contracts, 338–340

Goods, contracts for sale of, 334–335

Historical background, 324–325

Land, contracts for sale of, 338–340

Law and equity, relation of, 325

Mutuality, 88

STANDARDIZATION/INDIVIDUALIZATION SPECTRUM

Contract law rules, 85

STANDARDIZED AGREEMENTS

Form Contracts, this index

STATIC/DYNAMIC SPECTRUM

Contract law rules, 85, 124–125

STATUTE OF FRAUDS

Generally, 1031–1076

Agent's signature, 1055–1056

American variations, 1037

Bargain principle and, 49

Correct statement of agreement, 1055

Electronic contracting, 1057–1060

Executors and administrators, promises made by, 1051–1052

Formal requirements under UCC, 1044

Judicial interpretation, 1038

Kinds of contracts subject to statute, 1035–1037

Kinds of writings that will satisfy statute, 1053–1057

Land, sale of interest in
    Generally, 1038–1039
    Oral rescission, 1070
    Value of bargain, right to, 1065–1067

Marriage, contracts upon consideration of, 1052, 1065

Modifications, oral, 1070–1072

Non-compliance, effect of, 1067–1069

One year provision, 1045–1048, 1067

STATUTE OF FRAUDS—Cont'd
Oral contracts
 Part performance, below
 Reliance, below
Oral modifications, 1070–1072
Original statute, 1032–1033
Parol evidence rule, interaction with, 1072–1073
Part performance of oral contract within statute
 Generally, 1060
 Value of bargain, right to, 1064–1067
Piecing together several writings, 1054–1055
Pleading and procedural problems, 1074
Purpose, 1034–1035
Real estate. Land, sale of interest in, above
Reformation remedy, interaction with, 1073–1074
Reliance on oral contract within statute
 Generally, 1060
 Reimbursement for reliance, 1061–1063
 Value of bargain, right to, 1064–1067
Rescission, oral, 1069–1070
Restitution of benefits conferred under oral agreement, 1060–1061
Sale of Goods, this index
Signed writing, what constitutes, 1053
Single writing, 1054
Suretyship, 1048–1051, 1065
Terms of contract, adequate statement, 1053–1054
Unenforceable agreement, legal consequences, 1067–1069
Value of bargain, right to, 1064–1067

SUBCONTRACTORS
Acceptance, effect of using subcontractor's bid, 478–488

SUBSTANTIAL PERFORMANCE
Generally, 915–933
Capability problem in contract law, 918
Cure
 Generally, 932–933
 Perfect tender rule, 925
General principle, 915–923
Installment contracts, 925
Material breach doctrine, relationship to, 992–993
Mitigation principle, 918–919
Perfect tender rule, 924–926
Revocation of acceptance, 924–925
Sale of goods, contracts for, 923–933
UCC provisions, 924–926, 933

SUBSTITUTED CONTRACT
Accord distinguished, 136–137

SURETYSHIP
Statute of frauds, 1048–1051, 1065

SURROGATE PARENTING
Legislation, 185

TENDER
Cure of improper tender, 933
Perfect tender rule, 924–926

THIRD–PARTY BENEFICIARIES
Generally, 812–852

THIRD–PARTY BENEFICIARIES—Cont'd
Definitions, 823
Nomenclature, 813
Power of contracting parties to vary promisor's duty to beneficiary, 851
Restatement, 814, 823

TRADE USAGE
Generally, 405–412
Written contract, trade usage as part of, 626–637

UNCONSCIONABILITY
Generally, 63–86
Form contracts, 692–712
Installment buyer of goods under UCC, protection of, 68–69
Low-income market retailers, 69–70
Statutory protections, 67–68
UCC
 Installment buyer of goods, protection of, 68–69
 Note on, 72–74

UNENFORCEABLE OBLIGATION
When promise to discharge is binding, 151–152

UNEXPECTED CIRCUMSTANCES
Generally, 765–809
Commercial impossibility, 779–780
Costs, significantly increased, effect of, 794–795
Crops, contracts to sell, 801
Equitable apportionment of losses following impossibility, 785–786
Impossibility
 Commercial impossibility, 779–780
 Development of doctrine, 805–806
 Equitable apportionment of losses, 785–786
Restatement, 779
Tacit assumptions, 768–769

UNIDROIT PRINCIPLES
Generally, 55–56

UNIFORM COMMERCIAL CODE
Affirmative recovery under UCC § 2–609, 1029
Assignments and Article 9, 875–877
Comments to UCC, note on, 75
Costs, significantly increased, effect of, 794–795
Cure of improper tender, 933
Damages for seller's breach of contract for sale of goods, 241–242
Form Contracts, this index
Formal requirements, 1044
Gap fillers, 545
Good faith performance, 890–892
Offer and acceptance, variance between, 435–436
Oral modifications, 608
Reimbursement for reliance on oral contract, 1063
Sale of Goods, this index
Signed writing, what constitutes, 1053
Unconscionability, this index
Usage, course of dealing and course of performance, 412

UNIFORM ELECTRONIC TRANSACTIONS ACT
Generally, 1057–1060

UNIFORM PARENTAGE ACT
Who is a parent, 182–185

UNILATERAL CONTRACTS
Implied-in-law and implied-in-fact, 504–535
Mutuality, 87–88
Offers for, 446–448
Restatement of Contracts, 447–448, 455

UNJUST ENRICHMENT
Defined, 507

UNJUST ENRICHMENT—Cont'd
Silence treated as acceptance, 500

USAGE
Trade Usage, this index

WAIVER
Contractual duties, 107–150

WRITING
Consideration, presumption of, 21–22
Statute of Frauds, this index

†